Chilton
Automotive Multi-Guide

Spring 1931

A Facsimile Reproduction of
One of Chilton's
Rare, Early Automotive Guides

Produced by the
Automotive Book Department

John Milton, *Managing Editor*

Chilton Book Company
Philadelphia   New York   London

Copyright © 1970 by Chilton Book Company
Reissue of First Edition   *All Rights Reserved*
Published in Philadelphia by Chilton Book Company,
and simultaneously in Ontario, Canada,
by Thomas Nelson & Sons, Ltd.
SBN: 8019 5564 5
Library of Congress Catalog Card Number 74-107631
Manufactured in the United States of America

In 1931, the *Chilton Automotive Multi-Guide* was looked to by everybody in the automotive business who needed information about cars and trucks and their parts in production since 1925. More than 500 car and truck models were covered —from Auburn to Windsor. One of the big things people wanted to know then was what part of one car could be interchanged with that of another car—very useful information when one needed it. Today, thirty-nine years later, the same information is sought by many. The auto buff or restorer— the classic car enthusiast or historian—would gladly give his eye teeth for facts that elude him. Thousands of such hard-to-come-by facts are in this Multi-Guide, *reprinted exactly as it was* all those years ago. Some of the categories of information are Interchangeable Data Section for Parts, Dimensions, Specifications for Tune-Up and Service, Serial Numbers, Prices, Capacities, Production Records (1913-1930), New Car Registrations by Makes (1926-1931), Manufacturers of Auto Products, Speed Records, Birth Dates of Autos, Firsts in Auto Events, Buyer's Guide, Clearance Standards and much more. Not the least interesting or useful feature is the advertisements current in 1931 which describe and illustrate hundreds of automotive parts and products.

The following 392 pages are reproduced without change of any kind from the original 1931 edition.

CHILTON AUTOMOTIVE MULTI-GUIDE

SPRING   1931

Basic Units Vital to the Control of Gasoline Power

BENDIX MECHANICAL BRAKES
Bendix Brake Company, South Bend, Indiana

LOCKHEED HYDRAULIC BRAKES
Hydraulic Brake Company, Detroit, Michigan

B-K VACUUM BRAKE BOOSTER
Bragg-Kliesrath Corporation, South Bend, Indiana

BENDIX STARTER DRIVE
Eclipse Machine Company, Elmira, New York

STROMBERG CARBURETOR
Bendix Stromberg Carburetor Company, South Bend, Indiana

SCINTILLA MAGNETO
Scintilla Magneto Co., Inc., Sidney, New York

BENDIX-WESTINGHOUSE AUTOMOTIVE AIR BRAKE
Bendix-Westinghouse Automotive Air Brake Company, Pittsburgh, Pa.
(Owned jointly with Westinghouse Air Brake Company)

COWDREY BRAKE TESTER
Bendix-Cowdrey Brake Tester, Inc., South Bend, Indiana

BENDIX AVIATION CORPORATION · CHICAGO · NEW YORK

BENDIX PRODUCTS

AUTOMOBILE · AVIATION · MARINE

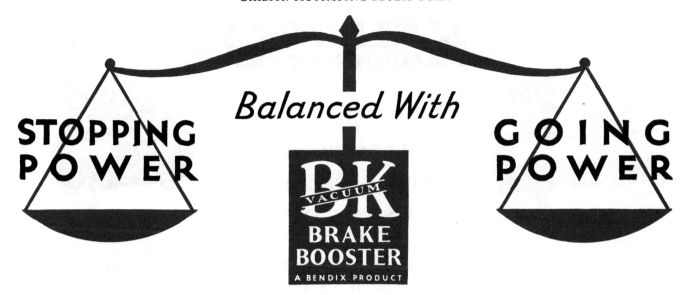

STOPPING POWER *Balanced With* **GOING POWER**

BK VACUUM **BRAKE BOOSTER** A BENDIX PRODUCT

DISTRIBUTORS

Alabama—Birmingham: Alabama Truck Equipment Co., 1730 Vanderbilt Ave.
California—Los Angeles: Electric Equipment Co., 1240 S. Hope St ; San Francisco: The Lathan Co., 1454 Pine St.
Colorado—Denver: Quinn & McGill Motor Supply Co., 437 Broadway.
Connecticut—Bridgeport: The Egan Tire & Rubber Co., 31 Cortland St.; Hartford: The Auto Tire Co., Inc., 168 High St.; New Haven: Connecticut Wheel & Rim Co., 669 Chapel St.
District of Columbia—Washington: L. S. Jullien, Inc., 1439 P Street, N. W.
Florida—Jacksonville: Scott Sales, Inc., 200 Park Street.
Georgia—Atlanta: Harris Rim & Wheel Co., 376 Spring St., N. W.
Illinois—Chicago: Bendix Stromberg Carburetor Co., 2459 S. Wabash Ave.; Chicago Wheel & Spring Co., 414 East 34th St.
Indiana—Evansville: Fausch-Enders Co., 424 Sycamore St.; Indianapolis: Madden-Copple Co., Inc., 733 N. Capital Ave.; South Bend: National Brake Service, 223 West Jefferson Blvd.
Iowa—Des Moines: Des Moines Wheel & Rim Co., 1427 Walnut St.
Kentucky—Louisville: Broadway Center Auto Service, 301 Broadway East.
Louisiana—New Orleans: John M. Walton, 762 St. Charles St.; Shreveport: Kayser-Waller-Helm, Inc., 222-24 N. Market St.
Maryland—Baltimore: Parks & Hull, Inc., 1031 Cathedral St.
Massachusetts—Boston: H. G. Davis, Inc., 96 Cumington St.; Harvey Sales & Service Co., 1375 Boylston St.; Springfield: The Newhouse Service Co., 64-66 Howard St.
Michigan—Detroit: B-K Brake Appliance Co., 3961 Cass Ave; Grand Rapids: Aupperlee & Veltman, 316 Bond Ave., N.W.; Kalamazoo: Niels Automotive Service, 167 E. Kalamazoo St.
Minnesota—Minneapolis: Wheels Service Co., 139 South 11th St.; Bendix Stromberg Carburetor Co., 20 North 16th St.
Missouri—Kansas City: Luthy Equipment Co., 2400 Grand Ave.; St. Louis: Borbein-Young & Co., 3301 Washington Blvd.
Nebraska—Omaha: Yousem Battery & Tire Co., 2124 St. Marys Ave.
New Hampshire—Manchester: Williams Motor Co., 48 W. Bridge St.
New Jersey—Newark: Essex Sales Company, 234 Central Ave.
New York—Albany: J. Becker & Sons, 1268 Broadway; Brooklyn: Gunderman & Son, Inc., 370 Fourth Ave; Buffalo: Truck Equipment Co., 1791 Fillmore Ave.; Long Island City: Bragg-Kliesrath Corp., 3711 Queens Blvd.; Mount Vernon: Oakwood Motor Co., 32 South 6th St.; New York City: Smith & Gregory Co., 426 W. 55th St.; Rochester: Gordon Motor Parts, Inc., 30-36 Joseph Ave.; Syracuse: Syracuse Auto Parts, Inc., 1115 W. Genesee St.; Utica: Broadway Brake Service, 411 Broadway.
North Carolina—Charlotte: Power Brake Company, 432 South Tryon St.
Ohio—Cincinnati: F & N Motor Company, 2130 Spring Grove Ave.; Cleveland: Raybestos Brake Service Co., 1721 Superior Ave.; Raybestos Brake Service Co., Carnegie and 55th St.; Columbus: Hughes-Scott-Stillinger Co., 165-7 North 4th St.; Toledo: The Turner Brake Service Co., 1927 Spielbusch Ave.
Oklahoma—Oklahoma City: J. C. Hamilton Co., 123 West 3rd St.; Tulsa: Williamson Motors, Inc., 425 East 3rd St.
Oregon—Portland: Trombley Truck Equipment Co., East 2nd and Irving Streets.
Pennsylvania—Allentown: Allentown Brake & Wheel Service, 201 South 11th Street; Erie: Richard B. Wolfe, 32 East 18th St.; Harrisburg: Shaffer's Super Service Sta., 50-68 S. Cameron St.; Philadelphia: J. H. McCullough & Son, 1248 N. Broad St.; Pittsburgh: The Schnabel Company, South 10th Street; Bendix-Westinghouse Automotive Air Brake Co., 5001 Center Ave.

BETTER roads + higher powered engines = higher speeds. A good brake system + the B-K Vacuum Brake Booster = Power Brakes; the safe and sane answer, easy and inexpensive.

This simple effective device uses the vacuum of the intake manifold and supplies it as braking power; putting to useful work a supply of power otherwise wasted.

For truck, bus, trailer, limousine or roadster—there's a model of B-K Brake Booster for every need; for every type and make of vehicle.

So popular have B-K Vacuum Power Brakes become that B-K distributors are reaping rich harvests of profits. Better check into this opportunity; a few territories are still open. Write us about it.

BRAGG-KLIESRATH CORPORATION
401 Bendix Drive, South Bend, Indiana
(SUBSIDIARY OF BENDIX AVIATION CORPORATION)

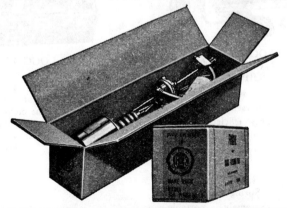

Pennsylvania (Contd.)—Reading: David Sternbergh, Inc., 228 North 5th Street; Wilkes-Barre: Hughes Brake Specialist, 12 Butler Lane.
Rhode Island—Providence: Palmer Spring Co., 1 Althea Street.
Tennessee—Memphis: Borbein-Young & Co., 658 Union Street.
Texas—Dallas: The J. J. Gibson Co., 2016 Canton St.; Fort Worth: The J. J. Gibson Co., 317 West 13th St.; Houston: Houston Trailmobile Equipment Co., 1304 Nance St.; San Antonio: Emig Service Stores, 408 Bowie Street.
Utah—Salt Lake City: Intermountain Electric Co., 43 East 4th Street S.
Virginia—Richmond: Dixie Wheel Co., Inc., 1012 North Blvd.
Washington—Seattle: Earl B. Staley Co., 911-15

Eleventh Ave.; Spokane: Bearing & Rim Supply Co., 1125 First Ave.
West Virginia—Charleston: National Brake Service, 617 Washington Street.
Wisconsin—Milwaukee: Johnson & Weborg, Inc., 2206 North 32nd Street.

FOREIGN DISTRIBUTORS

Australia—Sydney: J. B. Clarkson & Co., Ltd., Sirius House, 11 Macquarie Pl.
British Isles—Birmingham: Bendix-Perrot Brakes, Ltd., Kings Road, Tyseley, England.
Canada—British Columbia: Boultbee, Ltd., 999 Seymour St., Vancouver; Toronto: Toronto Brake Service, 137 Richmond St., W.; Walkerville: Eclipse Machine Company.
South America—Argentina: LaGrange & Hasfeld, Ltd., Supacha No. 26, Buenos Aires.

CHILTON AUTOMOTIVE MULTI-GUIDE

Registered in U. S. Patent Office

- The Original Guide to Interchangeable Parts for Motor Vehicles, Including also Replacement Parts Sizes, Directory of Supplies, Lists of Companies and Other Reference Information

Compiled and Edited Especially for wholesalers of parts, accessories, tools, shop equipment; distributors and retailers of passenger cars, motor trucks and buses; repair shops, service managers, accessory stores, truck and bus fleet operators, sales executives.

Copyright, 1931, by Chilton Class Journal Company

Published in Spring and Autumn by

CHILTON CLASS JOURNAL COMPANY

Chestnut and Fifty-sixth Sts. Philadelphia, Pa.

NEW YORK **CHICAGO** **CLEVELAND**
239 W. 39th St. 367 W. Adams St. 1140 Guardian Bldg.

DETROIT
710 Stephenson Bldg.

C. A. MUSSELMAN, *President and General Manager* G. C. BUZBY, *Vice-President*
J. S. HILDRETH, *Vice-President and Director of Sales* A. H. VAUX, *Secy. and Treas.*
J. A. CLEMENTS, *Ass't Treas.*
T. L. KANE, *Business Manager*
W. I. RALPH, *Vice-President* G. D. ROBERTS, *Advertising Mgr.*

Publishers of

Automobile Trade Journal Automotive Industries
Commercial Car Journal Automotive Industrial Red Book
Chilton Aero Directory and Catalog Chilton Automotive Multi-Guide
Motor World Wholesale

Controlled by

UNITED BUSINESS PUBLISHERS, INC.
239 W. 39th St. New York City

A. C. PEARSON, *Board Chairman* C. A. MUSSELMAN, *Vice-Pres.*
F. J. FRANK, *President* F. S. STEVENS, *Treasurer*

SPRING 1931

Contents

For Detailed Alphabetical Index to Contents See Pages 7, 9

For Detailed Alphabetical Index to Contents See Pages 7, 9

Purpose and Use of This Book

¶ You have essential information here, condensed, easily found, and all in one place.

¶ You have a record of Interchangeability of nearly 100 different parts in all cars back five years. This is the only place where such data appear as complete and accurate. You can use it in many ways. See Pages 161 to 266.

¶ You have a complete buying guide—a list of leading manufacturers selling the trade (Page 364), a directory classified by products (Page 309), a list of trade names of products (Page 384) and the advertisements of 205 manufacturers (indexed on Pages 12-13).

¶ Gathered on Pages 131 to 160 are facts and figures on Marketing, Production, History, Registration, Speed Records, Shop Equipment, Truck Fleet Operation, and other subjects.

¶ From Pages 267 to 308 are important Replacement Parts Sizes, Car Serial Numbers, Service Specifications, Anti-freeze Data, Orphan Parts Sources, and Engine-Make Lists.

AMONG NEW FEATURES THIS ISSUE:

¶ Actual Specifications for Each CHILTON Parts Number for Pistons, Piston Pins, Timing Chains, Valves. (Pages 196, 198, 209, 210.)

¶ Separate Record Showing Number of Times Each CHILTON Number Appears, Indicating Number of Car Models in Tables That Use That Part. (Pages 194, 195, 207, 208, 218, 225, 226, 235, 243, 244, 250, 257, 259.)

Clearance Standards for Checking Parts—Illustrated. (Pages 268-271.)

Tune-Up and Service Specifications. (Pages 272-275.)

Hose Connection Sizes. (Pages 277-278.)

Speed Records. (Page 135.)

Equipment Needs and Buying Seasons for Truck Fleets by Types of Business. (Page 154.)

The Detailed Table of Contents, Pages 7 (opposite) and 9, will show you what a collection of helpful information you have all in one place.

CONTENTS

Detailed Alphabetical Index

For Detailed Index to Individual Items in Various
Tables of Interchangeability See Pages 161-162

CONTENTS, Detailed Alphabetical Index—Continued

A WORD ABOUT
the advertisements

In a guide of this nature, sales information by different companies is very necessary, therefore should be placed in positions easily found by the user.

Outside of Special Positions and in the Interchangeable Tables themselves, advertisements appear on the pages immediately following. For convenience in use they are arranged, as far as practical after the color forms, so that those featuring the same or closely related products are together.

Essential buying information, such as branches, distributors, specifications, prices, etc., when furnished in the advertisement, is indicated in detail under the advertiser's name in the Buyer's Guide starting page 305. Some advertisers, in order to save the time of those using the Interchangeable Tables, have arranged to place their sales information in the Interchangeable Tables on pages 165, 167, 169, 171, 173, 175, 185, 187, 189, 201, 203, 221, 237, 253, 255, 279.

ADVERTISERS' INDEX

★ *Five years or more advertising without missing an issue.*
★★ *Ten years or more advertising without missing an issue.*
★★★ *Fifteen years or more advertising without missing an issue.*
★★★★ *Twenty years or more advertising without missing an issue.*

ADVERTISERS' INDEX

BUICK MANAGEMENT PLAN FOR DEALERS ASSURES SUCCESSFUL BUSINESS OPERATION

WITH

the 8 as Buick builds it

Complete information regarding the Buick franchise in your community may be had by writing the Buick Zone Office in any of the following cities, or the factory at Flint, Michigan.

Atlanta, Ga.
Boston, Mass.
Buffalo, N.Y.
Charlotte, N.C.
Chicago, Ill.
Cincinnati, O.
Cleveland, O.
Dallas, Texas
Denver, Colo.
Detroit, Mich.
El Paso, Texas
Flint, Mich.
Grand Rapids, Mich.
Indianapolis, Ind.
Jacksonville, Fla.
Kansas City, Mo.
Lincoln, Nebr.
Los Angeles, Cali
Memphis, Tenn.
Milwaukee, Wisc.
Minneapolis, Minn
New York N.Y.
Oklahoma City, Okla.
Philadelphia, Pa.
Pittsburgh, Pa.
Portland, Oregon
Rochester, N. Y.
Saginaw, Mich.
Salt Lake City, U.
San Antonio, Texas
San Francisco, Calif.
St. Louis, Mo.
Washington, D.C.

Buick dealers now have an Eight for everybody . . . 4 series—all Valve-in-Head Straight Eights, with Silent-shift Syncro-Mesh Transmissions and Insulated Bodies by Fisher—priced from $1025 to $2035, f. o. b. Flint.

And because of the additional series of Buick Eight models listing as low as $1025 to $1095, Buick dealers are now assured thousands of additional sales from those who heretofore bought below Buick's price range.

Further, Buick's 1,500,000 owners—nearly 750,000 more than the second car in Buick's field—assure Buick dealers twice the volume of sales and service of any other fine car.

Then, too, Buick dealers are given unlimited factory assistance with which to turn this greater volume into greater profit. The Buick Management Plan—embracing the closest possible factory co-operation and counsel in merchandising and selling procedure—has been designed to help Buick dealers to become successful merchants on a *permanent, profitable basis.*

If you are in the automobile business—or are considering going into it—it will pay you to investigate promptly the exceptional opportunity now available to those who hold a Buick franchise. Write or wire today.

BUICK MOTOR COMPANY, FLINT, MICHIGAN
A GENERAL MOTORS VALUE
WHEN BETTER AUTOMOBILES ARE BUILT . . . BUICK WILL BUILD THEM

You Want What Reo Offers

Responsible business men, qualified by character and experience, can build a permanently profitable business with the Reo franchise.

They are the kind of dealers Reo wants—and the kind who will be attracted by what Reo offers.

Reo's line penetrates the choicest markets. The Reo-Royales are definitely established in the fine car field. The new Reo Flying Clouds at $1295 and $1395 are certain to command good volume. Reo trucks, now augmented by a remarkable new 1½-Ton Speedwagon at $625, never looked better as a source of year-round profit.

Back of these fine products is a basic managerial policy that has proved itself sound over a period of more than 26 years.

Inquiries are invited from established dealers and others who share Reo's confidence in Reo's future.

REO MOTOR CAR COMPANY
LANSING – TORONTO

18

Supplying World Markets

The Continental 17 E Six Cylinder Engine is used all over the world by progressive automobile and truck manufacturers. Rated at 49 h. p. at 2000 r. p. m.—the 17 E engine carries an abundant surplus of power.

This engine, built with the strongest and finest material available, precision machined — with aluminum pistons, 7-bearing crankshaft and gear-driven pressure feed lubrication system, will outperform and outlive any engine in its power class. ¶ Continental builds to the manufacturer's needs—for the consumer's satisfaction.

CONTINENTAL MOTORS CORPORATION
Offices: Detroit, Michigan, U. S. A.
Factories: Detroit and Muskegon

Continental Engines

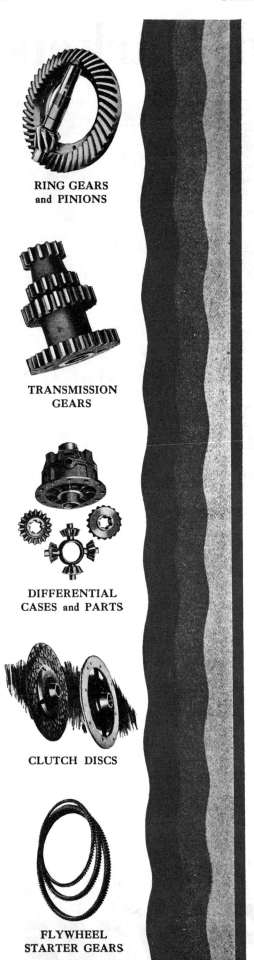

1 GAL ?

What does the gallon mark mean?

ALL that the gallon mark means on *any* lacquer container is that you have slightly more than 231 cubic inches of *that kind* of lacquer. But coverage, quality, cost of application are not indicated by quantity. It is strange, then that even men who know lacquers sometimes think in terms of "cost per gallon" when the *real* standard should be cost-on-the-job!

With the enormous purchasing, manufacturing and distributing power of the world's largest makers of protective coatings, Sherwin-Williams has produced in OPEX a lacquer which makes

important savings when *all* factors of finishing costs are considered. Consistent with *quality*, OPEX has been found by thousands of users to be the most economical "on the job" lacquer.

This is not an idle claim. You can prove it to your own satisfaction and to your own profit by making an actual over-all cost test. Your request will bring more complete information and the name of the nearest OPEX distributor serving your city. The Sherwin-Williams Co., Dept. 733, Cleveland, Ohio.

S-W Aero Finishes

A complete line of fabric and metal finishes of great flexibility and durability, perfected by extensive research and experiment. Write for complete information.

SHERWIN-WILLIAMS

PAINTS - VARNISHES - LACQUERS - ENAMELS
World's Largest Manufacturers of Protective Coatings

THESE DISTRIBUTORS CARRY
GENUINE WILLYS·OVERLAND PARTS

TOWN	FIRM NAME	STREET ADDRESS
Albany N. Y.	Albany Garage Co.	28 Howard St.
Atlanta, Ga.	W. A. Christ & Co.	17-25 North Ave. N. E.
Baltimore, Md.	Mid-City Sales Co.	Mt. Royal and McMechen Sts.
Bangor, Me.	Wentworth Motor Corp.	40 Post Office Square
Beatrice, Nebr.	Spiegel Automobile Co.	620-22 Court St.
Billings, Mont.	Mulvaney Motor Co.	2605 First Ave. N.
Binghamton, N. Y.	Overland Binghamton Co.	
Birmingham, Ala.	Pryor Motor Company	500 S. 21st St.
Boise, Idaho	Boise Overland Co.	309 N. Tenth St.
Boston, Mass.	J. C. Harvey	971 Commonwealth Ave.
Buffalo, N. Y.	Overland Knight Co., Inc.	368 Massachusetts Ave.
Cedar Rapids, Ia.	Schierbrock-Kelly, Inc.	605 Second Ave.
Charlotte, N. C.	Dorris-Greene Motor Co., Inc.	211-213 N. College St.
Chattanooga, Tenn.	Smith-Bond Motor Co.	4704 Rossville Blvd.
Chicago, Ill.	Thomas J. Hay, Inc.	19 W. 26th St.
Cincinnati, Ohio	The Pfaff Motor Car Co.	1002 Gilbert Ave.
Cleveland, Ohio	The North Ohio Motor Co.	5005 Euclid Ave.
Dallas, Tex.	Gough Motor Co.	826 S. Ervay St.
Davenport, Ia.	Lytle Motor Co.	218-22 Ripley St.
Decatur, Ill.	W. C. Starr, Inc.	232-240 S. Main St.
Denver, Colo.	E. J. Johnson, Inc.	945 Broadway
Des Moines, Ia.	Duffield-Hinton, Inc.	11th and Walnut St.
Detroit, Mich.	A. D. Geissler Co.	2965 Woodward Ave.
Dodge City, Kan.	Carl Fay Motor Co.	100 E. Military Ave.
Duluth, Minn.	Kent Motors, Inc.	210 E. Superior St.
Easton, Pa.	Clyde F. Sandt	30 South 10th St.
Eau Claire, Wisc.	Drake Auto Co.	1131 W. Grand Ave.
Elmira, N. Y.	Southern Tier Motor Co., Inc.	Church and State Sts.
El Paso, Tex.	Hinton Motors, Inc.	601 Montana St.
Evansville, Ind.	Bennighof-Nolan Co.	212 N. W. Fourth St.
Fort Worth, Tex.	Knight Motors, Inc.	5th and Taylor
Grand Island, Nebr.	Brandes Motor Co.	102 E. 2nd St.
Green Bay, Wisc.	Cliff Wall Motor Sales	1285 Main St.
Harrisburg, Pa.	Clyde F. Sandt Co.	90-92 S. Cameron St.
Hartford, Conn.	Elmer Automobile Co.	348 Trumbull St.
Hastings, Nebr.	Hunt Motor Co.	508 W. 3rd St.
Honolulu, Hawaii	Graystone Corp., Ltd.	505 S. Beretania St.
Houghton, Mich.	Hansen Motor Sales	63-67 Sheldon St.
Huntington, W. Va.	Bruce Perry Motor Co.	608-10 Fourth Ave.
Hutchinson, Kans.	Carl Fay Motor Co.	100-106 Sherman W.
Indianapolis, Ind.	The I. Boyd Huffman Motor Co.	833 N. Meridian St.
Jackson, Miss.	Robinson Brothers	Cor. Amite and McQuade
Jacksonville, Fla.	Wm. A. Estaver Co.	Julia and Monroe Sts.
Kansas City, Mo.	Hemphill Motor Co.	2501 Grand Ave.
LaCrosse, Wisc.	Tri-State Motors, Inc.	505 South 4th St.
Lidgerwood, N. D.	Lidgerwood Auto & Machine Co.	
Lincoln, Nebr.	King Motors, Inc.	1608 "O" St.
Los Angeles, Calif.	Willys Distributors, Inc.	11th and Hope

TOWN	FIRM NAME	STREET ADDRESS
Louisville, Ky.	Bacon-Pence, Inc.	909 E. Broadway
Macon, Ga.	Yates Motor Co.	707 Third St.
Madison, Wisc.	Whippet Knight Sales Co.	437 W. Gilman St.
Manchester, N. H.	Knight Motor Co.	313 Chestnut St.
Mankato, Minn.	Brandes-Wing Motor Co.	633-635 S. Front St.
Mason City, Ia.	Hathorn Auto Co.	109-11 First St. S. E.
Memphis, Tenn.	Whippet & Willys Knight Repair & Parts Co.	180 S. Dudley
Miami, Fla.	Biscayne Motor Corp.	1214 N. E. Second Ave.
Milwaukee, Wisc.	Arndorfer & Kuhl, Inc.	3719 Wisconsin Ave.
Minneapolis, Minn.	Halverson Motors, Inc.	600 9th Street S.
New Orleans, La.	Knight Motors Co., Inc.	719-21 Baronne St.
New York, N. Y.	Willys-Overland, Inc.	1631 Broadway
Norfolk, Va.	Arthur W. Depue, Inc.	700-2 West 21st St.
North Platte, Nebr.	Schierbrock Motor Co.	
Oklahoma City, Okla.	King-Godfrey, Inc.	Broadway at 5th St.
Omaha, Nebr.	Brandes-Campbell Motor Co.	2523-25 Farnum St.
Peoria, Ill.	Kaemmerling Motor Co.	427 Franklin St.
Philadelphia, Pa.	Herbert Brothers	Broad and Masters Sts.
Pittsburgh, Pa.	Rea-Seagert Co.	5800 Baum Blvd.
Portland, Me.	Elliott S. Peterson Co.	327-29 Forest Ave.
Portland, Ore.	Tarola Motor Car Co.	11th and Burnside Sts.
Rapid City, S. D.	Cordes Motor, Inc.	707-9 Main St.
Reading, Pa.	O. W. Lindgren, Inc.	525 Franklin St.
Rockford, Ill.	Midway Motor Sales, Inc.	125 S. Third St.
St. Joseph, Mo.	Calkins Motor Co.	9th and Frederick
St. Louis, Mo.	E. J. Johnson, Inc.	Locust and 23rd St.
Sacramento, Calif.	W. J. Mannix & Son	1422 K. St.
Salina, Kans.	Marshall Motor Co.	125-131 N. 7th St.
Salt Lake City, Utah.	Brown Motors, Inc.	216 East South Temple St.
San Angelo, Tex.	Allen Motor Sales Co.	20 E. Twohig Ave.
San Antonio, Tex.	Murray-Winerich Motor Co.	Broadway at 9th
San Diego, Calif.	Davies Motors, Inc.	1437-53 Broadway
San Francisco, Calif.	Bell & Boyd	1414 Van Ness
Savannah, Ga.	Stephen N. Harris	230 Drayton Ave.
Seattle, Wash.	Transport Corporation	1519-31 Twelfth Ave.
Shreveport, La.	Henry Wheeler	1605 Marshall St.
Sioux City, Ia.	J. V. Thorndike Co.	100 W. 7th St.
Sioux Falls, S. D.	Kehrer Motor Co.	10th St. and Dakota Ave.
Spokane, Wash.	Transport Corporation	Sprague and Madison
Springfield, Tenn.	Glover Auto Co.	502 S. Main St.
Stevens Point, Wisc.	G. A. Gullikson Co.	301-3 Strongs Ave.
Syracuse, N. Y.	Rusterholtz-Rossell, Inc.	917 W. Genesee St.
Texarkana, Ark.	Overland Texarkana Co.	8th and State Line Ave.
Toledo, Ohio	Willys-Overland, Inc.	14th and Adams
Tulsa, Okla.	Charles R. Eckes, Inc.	1014 S. Boston Ave.
Waterloo, Ia.	Schierbrock-Waterloo Co.	Franklin and Sixth
Wheeling, W. Va.	Auto Sales Co., Inc.	23 14th St.
Wichita, Kans.	R. D. McKay Motor Co.	235 S. Lawrence St.
Youngstown, Ohio	The Henderson Overland Co.	Boardman and Walnut Sts.
Zanesville, Ohio	The F. Wilking Sons Co.	40-42 N. 5th St.

WILLYS·OVERLAND, INC.
TOLEDO, OHIO

WILLYS·OVERLAND, LTD., TORONTO. CANADA

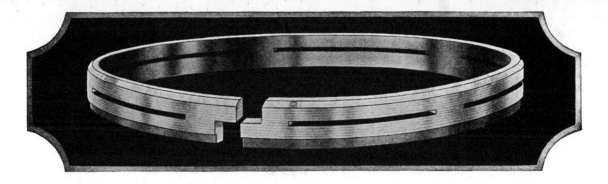
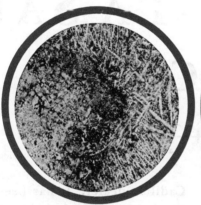
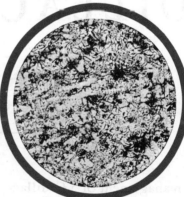

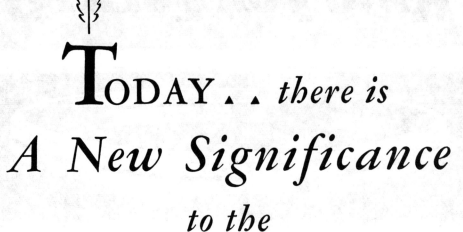

TODAY .. *there is*
A New Significance
to the
CADILLAC·LA SALLE
FRANCHISE

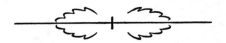

For years, successful management of a Cadillac-La Salle dealership has been generously rewarded —not only from the standpoint of dollars and cents, but in the satisfaction that comes from commercial recognition in one's community.

During the past twelve months, a change in Cadillac's manufacturing policy has served still further to heighten the desirability of the Cadillac-La Salle franchise—for Cadillac now offers complete coverage of the fine-car field.

The result is a two-fold advantage for the Cadillac dealer. It has been possible to lower the base price of the celebrated La Salle by several hundred dollars—thus increasing its potential market by 40,000 cars. And the new V-8, V-12 and V-16 have brought to the higher-priced markets the added attraction of ultra-luxurious motoring.

Such complete and detailed coverage of a market so broad and so responsive is a new accomplishment for the automotive industry. It means an exceptional opportunity for holders of the Cadillac-La Salle franchise.

CADILLAC   MOTOR   CAR   COMPANY
Division of General Motors
Detroit, Michigan   Oshawa, Canada

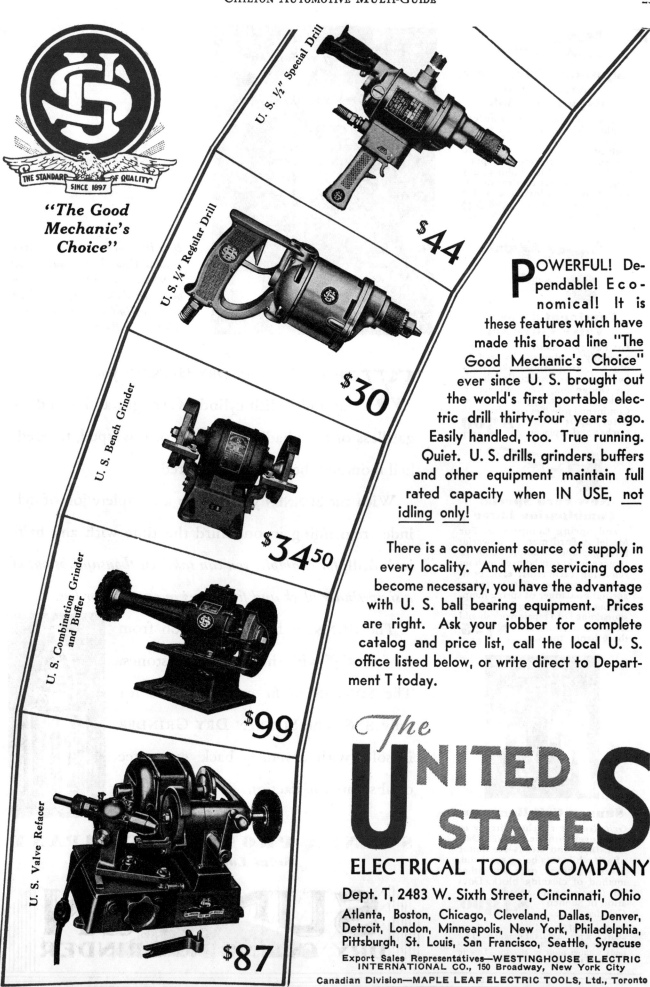

Adjustable Valve Lifter with 3-Step Expansion Link

Can be set for three different heights without changing leverage —low lift 1¾, medium lift 2″ and high lift 2⅜″. Jaws adjustable to any size spring; jaws raise practically parallel; lock holds at any height; no ratchet to wear out or slip. Sunnen Adjustable Valve Lifters are known and used the world over... **$2⁵⁰** LIST

Continental Special Valve Lifter Set

For new type motors where valve assembly is almost obscured by block casting—and makes these hard jobs easy. Especially valuable on Dodge Six, Reo, Wolverine, Erskine, Durant, Jordan and other Continental jobs. Set complete with lifter, split lock catcher and replacer... **$5⁰⁰** LIST

New Ford Special Combination Lifter

—and Spring Compressor. For Model A Ford motors. Powerful leverage; allows ample room to remove lock; can be used without removing carburetor; easy, positive action; makes it easy to replace spring; no danger of spring jumping out when being replaced. Every shop doing Ford repair work should have one or more of these handy tools... **$1²⁵** LIST

Sunnen Grit Remover

Grit Remover attaches directly to and moves with the SUNNEN DRY GRINDER—and cleans the motor of grit while it is being reground. Saves 1½ hours over any other method of cleaning block. Does not interfere with speed or operation of Sunnen Grinder... **$48⁰⁰** LIST

The Universal Stand also shown in picture above is a practical light weight stand for portable grinders. Can be set up in 30 seconds without tools of any sort. Low in cost. Will last a lifetime. $10.00 List.

In a little over three years over 26,000 shops have bought the SUNNEN DRY GRINDER. *Seven out of ten of these shops discarded other cylinder reconditioning tools to use the* SUNNEN.

WITH THE SUNNEN DRY GRINDER you can rough out and polish cylinders straight and round regardless of how badly they are worn, warped, tapered, bell mouthed, bellied or pin scored.

With the SUNNEN you can do a complete job of cylinder regrinding in one-third the time with any half-inch drill; *for example, you can take ten-thousandths out of a six-cylinder block and fit pistons in one hour or less.*

The SUNNEN handles any job from 2 11/16″ to 4¼″ with the same set of stones. The SUNNEN outfit complete sells for only $56. The SUNNEN DRY GRINDER is sold with a money-back guarantee of absolute satisfaction.

SUNNEN PRODUCTS COMPANY
Saint Louis, Missouri

SUNNEN DRY CYLINDER GRINDER

THE SENSATION OF THE TRUCK INDUSTRY

THE NEW Stewart 8

50 to 60 miles per hour with load

3½ Tonner $3990 chassis

Wheelbases
150″, 160″, 170″, 180″, 196″, 226″ and 241″

Still another Stewart triumph! This time an "8" developing 130 horsepower, capable of 50 to 60 miles an hour. A marvel of power and speed for long, fast hauls. The new Stewart "8" is rugged, powerful, yet smooth and vibrationless. Its heavy duty motor is designed for gruelling work. No road is too rough, no job too tough for this "8".

From radiator to tail light, it's an honestly rated truck built by exclusive truck makers. The new Stewart 3½-tonner, like all Stewart models, is built to give years of constant service.

If your demands include long, fast hauls at low operating cost, get the "World's Greatest Truck Value" on the job. Let Stewart performance prove Stewart claims. A ride behind the wheel of this new Stewart "8" will amaze you.

Free catalog sent upon request.

MODELS

Bevel Axle

1	ton,	4 Cylinder	$695
1	ton,	6 Cylinder	$795
1½	ton,	4 Cylinder	$895
1½	ton,	6 Cylinder	$995
1½	ton,	6 Cylinder	$1195
2	ton,	6 Cylinder	$1495
2	ton,	6 Cylinder	$1695
2½	ton,	6 Cylinder	$1990
3	ton,	6 Cylinder	$2590

Worm Axle

2½	ton,	6 Cylinder	$2690
3	ton,	6 Cylinder	$2990
3½	ton,	6 Cylinder	$3690
3½	ton,	6 Cylinder	$3990
3½	ton,	8 Cylinder	$3990
5	ton,	6 Cylinder	$4990
7	ton,	6 Cylinder	$5700

Double Gear Reduction Axle

2½	ton,	6 Cylinder	$2690
3	ton,	6 Cylinder	$2990
3½	ton,	6 Cylinder	$3690
3½	ton,	6 Cylinder	$3990
3½	ton,	8 Cylinder	$3990
5	ton,	6 Cylinder	$4990
7	ton,	6 Cylinder	$5700

Fire Apparatus

The Stewart liberal dealer franchise offers both car and truck dealers an unusual money-making opportunity

Stewart MOTOR TRUCKS

STEWART MOTOR CORPORATION

Depatrment 16

BUFFALO, N. Y.

Cables: Stewartruk Buffalo.
Codes: Acme, Bentley.

SPECIFICATIONS

MOTOR—8 cylinder truck type bore 3¾″, stroke 4¾″. Horse power 130. Built-in oil cleaner.

CARBURETOR—Latest Stromberg with accelerator pump, fuel economizer and air cleaner. Swan manifold.

IGNITION—Delco-Remy — direct gear driven. Also Delco-Remy starter with Bendix gear shift.

TRANSMISSION—12 speeds forward, 3 reverse and overdrive. The overdrive permits slow motor speeds on long, fast runs.

STEERING GEAR — Latest Ross roller gear type.

FRAME—Side rails unusual depth of 9″.

SPRINGS—Front 40″ x 3″. Rear 56″ x 3″, equipped with helper type standard.

REAR AXLE—Timken double reduction type—full floating. Worm optional.

BRAKES — Bendix 4 wheel mechanical, equipped with vacuum booster.

TIRES—9.00-20 all around. Duals rear.

WHEELBASE—170″ Standard. At extra cost 150″, 160″, 180″, 196″, 226″ and 241″.

WEIGHT—7600 lbs.

Stewart Trucks have won—By costing less to run

20 out of every 25 motor car buyers are now Hudson or Essex prospects

With a base price of only $595, Essex now competes with the lowest-priced cars. It challenges the finest in quality and *any* four or six at *any* price in performance. It is the Value Sensation in a year of sensational values—a big, roomy, full-sized car with a 60 horsepower motor, 70 miles an hour speed, and *Rare Riding and Driving Comfort.*

The Greater Hudson Eight is the finest car Hudson ever built. It is the smoothest of Eights at the price of a six—only $875 f. o. b. Detroit for the Business Coupe, $895 for the Coach. Its 87-horsepower motor gives sensational performance in speed, get-away and hill-climbing. It is individual and smart in design—interior appointments are tastefully done.

There are 18 body styles priced from $595 to $1445 in the combined lines —a range that includes 20 out of every 25 motor car buyers. Think what it means to sell a line like this—world-famous cars, that give lasting satisfaction to their owners, now offered at the lowest prices in their history. The average service cost since the cars were introduced in November, has been less than two cents per car!

Write today! Your inquiry will be held in strict confidence.

ESSEX
The Finest Performing SIX
Hudson Ever Built
$595
COACH or BUSINESS COUPE

HUDSON
The Finest Car
Hudson Ever Built
$875
BUSINESS COUPE • COACH $895

All prices F. O. B. Detroit

HUDSON MOTOR CAR COMPANY
Detroit, Michigan

Weatherproof
TRANSPORTATION

Write for descriptive literature on the new Weatherproof Sleeper Truck Cab. A new development for long distance hauling. Seating capacity for three men. Air-bound cushions of graduated cone type. Lazyback and Seat covered with Fobafimi Pads and highest quality artificial leather obtainable.

Sleeping berth is long enough to accommodate the average man full length. Spring constructed cushion, well padded 20" wide, 80" long. Pillow constructed in cushion. Cab can be supplied with two sleeping bunks, one located above the other. Two-piece, full ventilating steel frame Windshield. Plate glass rear window.

Weatherproof's New Ultra Cab

Weatherproof Truck Cabs are of heavy wood construction, entirely covered with 20 gauge Autobody sheet steel. Our latest type, ball cornered design—optional 1 or 2-piece windshield, clear vision. Doors are held in place with air-tight continuous hinge, running full length—also equipped with heavy duty spring door catch.

Write for details and folders describing the new Weatherproof Ultra Cab—*the last word in cab construction and design.*

THE WEATHERPROOF BODY CORPORATION
CORUNNA   MICHIGAN

Williams
AUTOMOTIVE PRODUCTS
FAST MOVING ACCESSORIES
REPLACEMENT CAPS & PARTS

REPLACEMENT RADIATOR AND GAS TANK CAPS STAINLESS STEEL

Gas tank caps to fit practically all cars—attractively priced.

ROLLER AND SLIP-IN AWNINGS FOR ALL CARS

UNI-CAPS FIT 96% OF ALL CARS

Radiator caps for many cars.

A most complete line of roller and Slip-in door and window awnings for all cars.

UNIVERSAL RUMBLE SEAT CANOPIES

REPLACEMENT GAS TANK CAPS

Universal Rumble Seat Canopies for all popular cars.

AUTO TRUNKS SKELETON FRAME AIRPLANE STYLE

ADJUSTABLE HOSE CLAMPS

Complete trunk and luggage carrying equipment of every type—low prices.

UNIVERSAL TRUNK RACKS WITH GUARD RAILINGS

STARTER SCREWS AND MISCELLANEOUS REPLACEMENT PARTS

Miscellaneous replacement parts principally for Chevrolets and Fords.

UNIVERSAL PLATFORM TRUNK RACKS

WINDSHIELD DEFROSTERS

Tire Covers, both of polished metal and fabric.

FOLDAWAY RUNNING BOARD LUGGAGE CARRIERS

UNIVERSAL SEAT COVERS

Universal seat covers.

Lock and Thrust Washers, Starter Screws, Straps, Trunk and Luggage Racks, Splash Guards, Breathers and Caps, Bushings, Fender Braces, Anti-Rattlers.

METAL TIRE COVERS FABRIC TIRE COVERS

WRITE FOR CATALOG & QUOTATIONS

Williams Products
H.E.Williams Products Co.
CARTHAGE, MO.

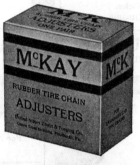

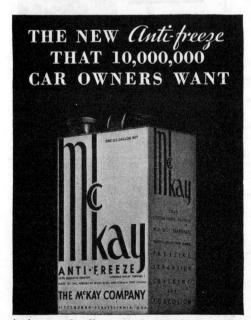

THE AUTO-VEHICLE PARTS COMPANY

"Foldown" ALUMINUM MOULDINGS

REG. U. S. PATENT OFFICE   *EXTRUDED ALUMINUM*   PATENT APPLIED FOR

NO FILLERS—NO ATTACHMENTS—NO FILING—Punched with Nail Holes—Convenient Lengths in Tubes

"FOLDOWN" DRIP MOULDING

No. 403 — 7' lengths, ¾" wide, 6 lengths to tube.

No. 406—8½' lengths, ¾" wide, 6 lengths to tube.

"FOLDOWN" CROWN ROOF MOULDING

No. 506 — ⅝" wide, 8½' lengths, 12 lengths to tube.

No. 536 — ¾" wide, 8½' lengths, 12 lengths to tube.

STANDARD EQUIPMENT—Chevrolet, Pontiac, Oakland, Oldsmobile, Buick, Nash, La Salle, Hupmobile, Cadillac, Viking, Packard

TRIM CLIPS
Pat. July 31, 1928

A—For top and side of Ford Door Panels.

B—For across bottom of Ford Door Panels.

Packed 100 in a carton.

TOP PROP NUTS

No. 324—1½"
No. 424—1¾"

Black Japan
Nickel
Chrome

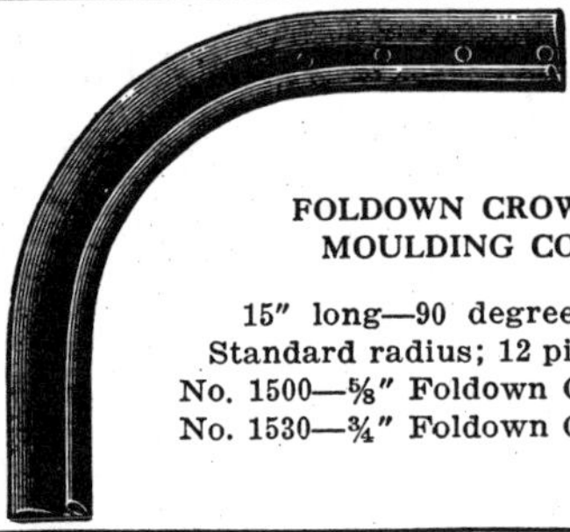

FOLDOWN CROWN ROOF MOULDING CORNERS

Curved to fit the roof

15" long—90 degrees angle. Standard radius; 12 pieces to carton
No. 1500—⅝" Foldown Crown Moulding
No. 1530—¾" Foldown Crown Moulding

ROOF AND DECK MOULDING

Punched with nail holes.
No. 656—⅝" wide, 8½' lengths, 12 lengths to tube.

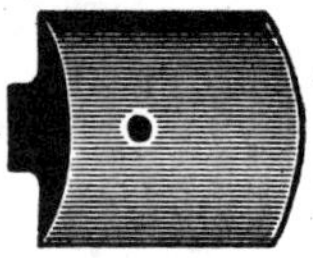

AU-VE-CO-LITE MOULDING
FOR RUNNING BOARDS
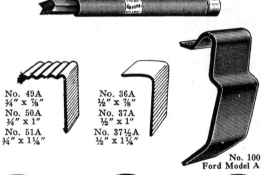
No. 49A ¾" x ⅞"
No. 50A ¾" x 1"
No. 51A ¾" x 1¼"

No. 36A ½" x ⅞"
No. 37A ½" x 1"
No. 37½A ½" x 1¼"

No. 100 Ford Model A

DRIVE SCREWS
Nickel Plated
No. 6— ¾"
No. 8— 1"

No. 100 NAILS
Nickel Rust-Proof Heads for Wood Running Boards

No. 150 RIVETS for Metal Running Boards Nickel on Brass

COUNTERSUNK WASHERS

For No. 4 to No. 20 Screws.

SCREW WASHERS FLUSH TYPE

for No. 4 to No. 12 Screws

FOOTMAN LOOPS

Sizes ⅞", 1", 1⅛", 1¼", 1½". Black Japanned or Nickel on Steel.

No. 995—"NAIL-ON" Panel Metal Edging
Used on door panel (concealed) on all Fisher closed car bodies.

12 pieces 6 ft. long to tube.

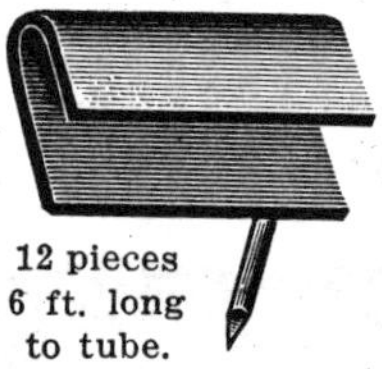

Double Pointed Tacks

7/16" LONG—BLUED

Especially for tacking on wire mesh on closed car tops. 1 pound.

No. 90

GROMMETS WITH WASHERS

BRASS

OPENINGS
7/32 inch
5/16 inch
11/32 inch
7/16 inch
15/32 inch
⅝ inch

PERFECTRIM HID'EM WELT

For seats, tops, door panels, 15-foot rolls in display cartons with 90 Trimmer's Tacks, 6 Finishing tips and tip nails; also in 50 yd. rolls.

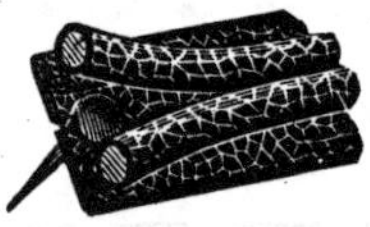

WINDOW CHANNEL CLIPS
For attaching window glass channel to steel doors. 
No. 51 UNIVERSAL   No. 152 FORD   No. 153 FORD   No. 154 FORD   No. 155 FORD

DOOR CHECK STRAPS

1¼ inch firm harness leather. Pressed steel hardware.

PIN FASTENERS

Double and Single with Locking Device

THE AUTO-VEHICLE PARTS CO., *Manufacturers*, 1040 Saratoga St., NEWPORT, KY.

THE AUTO-VEHICLE PARTS COMPANY

AU-VE-CO
INTERIOR BODY
SPECIAL SCREWS   SLEEVE NUTS
WASHERS   HEXAGON NUTS
LOCK SPRINGS

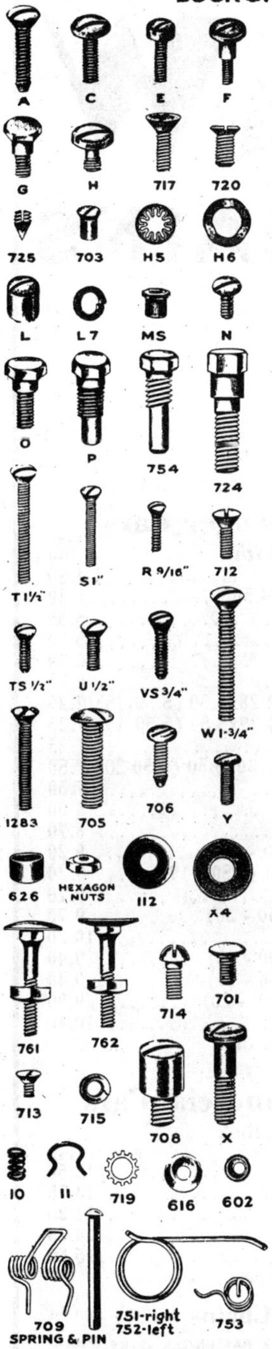

A   C   E   F

G   H   717   720

725   703   H5   H6

L   L7   MS   N

O   P   754   724

T 1½   S1   R 9/16   712

T5 ½   U ½   VS ¾   W 1-¾

1283   705   706   Y

626   HEXAGON NUTS   112   X4

761   762   714   701

713   715   708   X

10   11   719   616   602

709 SPRING & PIN   751-right 752-left   753

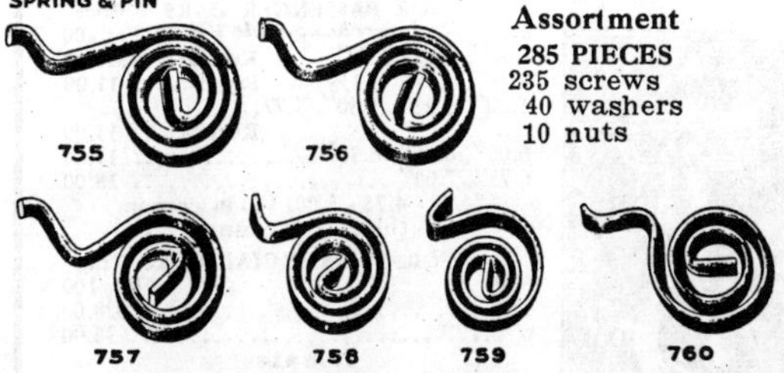

755   756

757   758   759   760

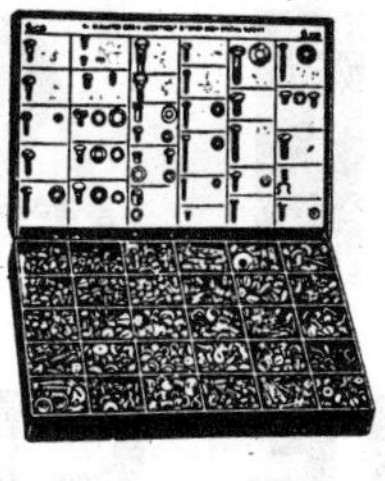

IN ASSORTMENTS AND PACKED INDIVIDUALLY

No. 36
"The Master" Screw Assortment

"All-In-One"—an attractive steel cabinet divided into convenient compartments.

750 PIECES
460 Screws
190 Washers
60 Nuts
20 Spacers
10 Coil Springs
10 Wire Clips

No. 27
Chevrolet Assortment

342 PIECES
171 special screws
101 washers
40 nuts
10 coil springs
10 spring wire clips
10 spacers

No. 18
Ford Model "A" Assortment

172 PIECES
117 screws
30 washers
25 nuts

No. 9
Fisher and Other Bodies Assortment

285 PIECES
235 screws
40 washers
10 nuts

AU·VE·CO
QUALITY PRODUCTS

AU-VE-CO Body Screw Assortments
Bolts, Running Board
Buckles, Web Strap
Buttons, Clinch
Buttons, Drive
Buttons, Tufting
Clips, Cushion Spring
Clips, Spring Wire
Clips, Trim
Clips, Window Channel
Clips, Windshield Channel, Glass "Snugger"
Corners, FOLDOWN
Cushion Spring Stay Assembly
Edging, "Nail-on" Panel
Escutcheon Pins
Eyelets, Fastener
Eyelets and Washers, Seat Cover
Eyelets and Washers, Tire Cover
Fasteners, Curtain
FOLDOWN Moulding Grommets
Hooks and Rings
Hooks, Side Curtain
Knobs and Knob Eyelets
Loops, Footman
Moulding Running Board
Moulding, Drip
Moulding, Ledge
Moulding, Corners
Moulding, Crown Roof
Moulding, Deck
Nails, Concealed Head
Nails, Countersunk Body
Nails, Interior Body Trim
Nails, Upholstery, "Hit 'em"
Nails, Saddle
Nails, Wire Shank, Upholsterers'
Nut Locks
Nuts, Hexagon
Nuts, Sleeve
Pin Fasteners for Seat Covers
Running Board Moulding
Running Board Moulding, Nails
Running Board Moulding, Rivets
Running Board Moulding, Screws
Springs, Lock
Straps, Curtain Commercial Car
Straps, Curtain Truck
Straps, Ford Door Check
Tacks
Tacks, Double Pointed
Tips, Web Strap
Tips, Welt
Top Prop Nuts
Trimclips
Wagon Patches
Washers, Countersunk Finishing
Washers, Screw Flush Type
Washers, Compression
Washers, Floor Board
Washers, Lock
Washers, Shakeproof

NUT LOCKS

Black Japan
Norus White Metal

"HIT'EM" Upholstery Nails
Reinforced heads, sharp tack point;—superior for all upholstery purposes. Black, any solid color or Spanish effects.

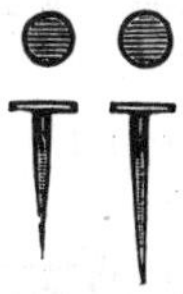

AU-VE-CO SANITARY TACKS
Trimmers
Upholsterers
Gimp
Lace

WAGON CURTAIN PATCHES

Sizes
No. 1
No. 2
No. 3

BEST HARNESS LEATHER

"SNUGGER" SPRING TENSION

GLASS CHANNEL

STOP THOSE RATTLING WINDOWS

NO. 8 CUSHION SPRING CLIPS

Black Japanned

FINISHING TIPS
A complete line

No. 1   No. 12   No. 23   No. 52
Hid'em   "Wire-on"   Her-Zim   Ford
    Coppertite

Concealed Head Finishing Nails

For attaching Body and Drip Mouldings where a concealed head finish is necessary.

No. 91—Size No. 16...... 1"
No. 92—Size No. 14...... 1"
No. 93—Size No. 14...... 1¼"
No. 94—Size No. 14...... 1½"
No. 82—Size No. 12...... 1"
No. 83—Size No. 12...... 1¼"
No. 84—Size No. 12...... 1½"
No. 85—Size No. 12...... 1¾"

For Auto Body Mouldings
Barbed Shank, japanned
In one pound papers

Cement Coated Countersunk Body Nails

No. 95—Size No. 15.... ½"
No. 96—Size No. 15.... ¾"
No. 98—Size No. 15.... 1"
No. 99—Size No. 14.... ¾"
No. 101—Size No. 14.... 1"
No. 102—Size No. 14.... 1¼"
No. 104—Size No. 14.... 1½"

For attaching body panels also for slat tops and Foldown Drip and Crown Roof Mouldings and corners.
In one pound papers

Interior Body Trim Nails

Japanned—Neutral Gray
Flat Head—For Inside Trimming—Slats and Panels

No. 125—Size No. 18. ⅝"
No. 126—Size No. 18. ¾"
No. 127—Size No. 18. ⅞"
No. 128—Size No. 18. 1"
No. 129—Size No. 16. ¾"
No. 130—Size No. 16. ⅞"
No. 131—Size No. 16. 1"
No. 132—Size No. 16. 1¼"

Packed in 1 lb. papers

Countersunk Small and Long Tapered Head Perfect for Blind Nail Trimming

No. 133—Size No. 18. ⅝"
No. 134—Size No. 18. ¾"
No. 135—Size No. 18. ⅞"
No. 136—Size No. 18. 1"
No. 137—Size No. 16. ¾"
No. 138—Size No. 16. ⅞"
No. 139—Size No. 16. 1"
No. 140—Size No. 16. 1¼"

Packed in 1 lb. papers

Escutcheon Pins

Japan and Nickel on Steel

No. 15—⅞"
No. 14—1"
No. 14—1¼"
No. 12—1"
No. 12—1¼"
No. 12—1½"

For attaching Finishing Tips and other purposes.

THE AUTO-VEHICLE PARTS CO., *Manufacturers,* **1040 Saratoga St., NEWPORT, KY.**

AXLE STRAIGHTENING PRESS AND WHEEL ALIGNING GAGES

Straightening axles cold—without removing axle from car is accepted practice. Manley Axle Straightening Press and Wheel Aligning Table make the job quick and easy. Duby-Manley Gages check in a few minutes, Caster, Camber, Toe-in and King Pin outward slant—so that you can guarantee a perfect job to factory specifications. A Manley Text Book on Wheel Aligning explains all axle and steering ailments and how to cure them.

IMPROVED TIRE CHANGER

The last word in speedy tire changing. Fewer turns are needed to open and close. Handles all size rims. Solid rim tire remover is applied in a few seconds. Service men who appreciate the value of a fast, efficient tire changer say this is the sweetest operating tire changer at any price.

NEW MANLEY TIRE SPREADER

Operates entirely by air with a six inch cylinder and compound action controlled by a foot operated valve. The platen pushes up as the arms pull the tire beads outward. Tire rests on rollers, making it easy to position tire. Note self adjusting inspection light.

MANLEY PRODUCTS ARE QUALITY PRODUCTS

Manley Manufacturing Company is one of the oldest manufacturers of auto servicing equipment. Manley engineers recognize the importance of sturdy construction—and equipment that enables service men to do a better job faster. The Manley Manufacturing Company is an Associate Company of the American Chain Company, *Inc.*, located at Bridgeport, Connecticut.

ELEVATORS

JACKS

WRECKING CRANES

PRESSES

AIR COMPRESSORS

PORTABLE WORK BENCH

VISES

CAR WASHER

PAINT SPRAYING EQUIPMENT

MANLEY SERVICING EQUIPMENT

The new WEED AMERICAN TIRE CHAIN

•

70% more mileage

Endorsed by over a million satisfied users

3 exclusive features:

1. Reinforcing bars electrically welded across contact links of the cross chains. Doubles the wear-resisting steel surface.

2. Better electrically-welded, non-kinking side chains.

3. Quick-acting positive locking connecting hooks.

•

The most profitable and most necessary automobile accessory

A product of
AMERICAN CHAIN COMPANY, Inc.
Bridgeport, Connecticut

New *Sterling Electric*
AUTOMOBILE CLOCK

NEW RETAIL PRICE $9⁷⁵

OVERHEAD MODEL

Artistic, thin design, silvered dial, polished steel hands, tarnish-proof satin finish case. Furnished complete ready for installation above windshield. Price $9⁷⁵, with luminous dial, $10⁷⁵.

Cars are judged from the driver's seat!

Today's cars...ultra-modern in design... advanced in every phase of engineering, are judged by factors of convenience at the driver's seat!

The Sterling Electric Clock...accurate and dependable...standard equipment on some of the finest cars ... nationally advertised . . . demanded by individual car owners everywhere, is an essential convenience.

STERLING CLOCK CO., INC., La Salle, Ill.

Detroit Office: 2-244 General Motors Building

DIVISION OF WESTERN CLOCK COMPANY

FEATURES
Sterling Electric Clock

Jeweled and precision built, run by automobile battery, current consumption negligible.

Compensated hairspring provides for accuracy under changing temperatures.

Not affected by road shocks or vibration.

Requires no winding or attention.

Fully guaranteed.

FRONT VIEW

DASH MODEL RETAIL PRICE $8⁷⁵

Requires only ½" hole in dash to mount. Trim design, silvered dial; tarnish-proof case. Very simple to install. Furnished complete. With luminous dial, $9⁷⁵.

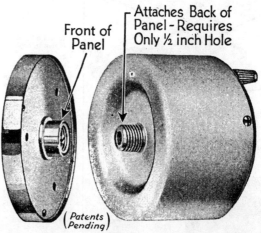

Front of Panel

Attaches Back of Panel - Requires Only ½ inch Hole

(Patents Pending)

DASH MODEL—SIDE VIEW

C & H FUEL PUMP REPAIR KIT

Over seven million cars now equipped with Fuel Pumps. This handy inexpensive kit contains necessary repair parts. A complete set of directions is furnished with each kit. These pumps have wearing parts that must be replaced. Get a kit today and cash in on this work that is now going to your competitor. Good profits in this kind of work. Each set of Super Diaphragms neatly packed in a separate glassine envelope. 10 complete sets in a package. 90% of Fuel Pump trouble is worn out or defective diaphragms. A half hour's work and a few cents material give you a liberal profit job and a satisfied customer. Price Complete $2.50.

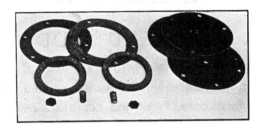

C & H FUEL PUMP REPAIR KIT consists of 10 complete sets of Super Diaphragms, 4 valve springs, 4 valves, 2 Diaphragm gaskets, 2 Strainer bowl gaskets.

C & H SYNCHRONIZING GAUGE

Endorsed by Leading Car and Truck Manufacturers. Most efficient synchronizer for modern motors.

LIST
$12.50

The C & H Gauge will handle any distributor on any car. Its dial segment is equal to a distributor nine inches in diameter permitting extremely accurate readings.

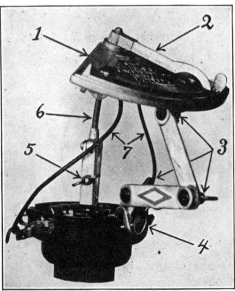

1. Dial, Calibrated in degrees.

2. Indicating arm.

3. Wing nuts to hold adjustable arm.

4. Adj. arm clamp.

5. Distributor cam clamp.

6. Flexible shaft.

7. Signal Lamp leads.

YOU NEED this instrument to do the job right. Order one today. Write for Ignition Synchronizing booklet.

BRUNSWICK ENGINEERING COMPANY
New Brunswick, N. J.

Dole PRODUCTS

DOLE DRAFT DEFLECTORS

Frequently ventilation in closed cars is sacrificed for immediate comfort; windows are closed. Result—headaches, danger from poor vision and not hearing and giving signals.

Dole Draft Deflectors act like louvers in the hood. The vacuum they create sucks the stale air out of the car—yet lets in fresh air—without drafts and cross-currents.

Dole Draft Deflectors are permanent and add a touch of distinction to a car. They can be installed in 5 minutes without marring the body finish. Chromium plated. Best quality shatter proof glass (standard) and plate glass (on request). Prices $12.50 to $25.00 per pair.

THE DOLE LEAK PROOF PRIMER

For instant starting of gasoline engines in any weather. Introduces highly vaporized gas directly into the cylinders. Saves the engine by definite reduction of dilution of crank case oil.

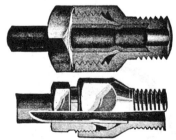

DOLE DOUBLE COMPRESSION COUPLINGS

Only two parts, yet two distinct compressions. "Reconnectable," a truly leak proof union each time. No collars, sleeves, flaring, brazing or soldering. Underwriters' approval.

DOLE BALL-ROLL COUPLINGS

A perfected joint, quickly connected, easily reconnected. Withstands vibration. Economical in purchase and service. Underwriters' approval.

Write manufacturer direct for full particulars.

THE DOLE VALVE COMPANY
1913-1933 Carroll Avenue
Chicago, Illinois, U. S. A.

Makes friends for you and profits, too

THE DILL COMPLETE MODERN LINE

Athletic Ball Valves

Air Chucks and Fittings

Dust Caps

Deflating Caps

Extensions

Instant-On Valves

Instant-On Dust Caps

Swimming Tube Valves

Super Pressure Testers

Super Service Display Board

Tire Valves—all types

Tools and Accessories

Valve Caps

Valve Insides

In this day of highly developed service for the automobile, Dill plays an important part.

For no car can satisfactorily serve its owner without adequate tire maintenance.

Dill specializes on those vital accessories which put air in tires and keep it there.

Every Dill product is designed and built to deliver the utmost in dependability— in protecting that feeling of confidence in tires which is so necessary a part of present day motoring.

This complete modern line of tire valves, and accessories, used by over 90% of all tire manufacturers, and handled by leading jobbers everywhere, has made friends for Dill and for those who serve the motorist. And profits, too.

THE DILL MANUFACTURING COMPANY
Cleveland, Ohio

Manufactured in Canada by The Dill Manufacturing Company of Canada, Ltd., Toronto, Ontario

DILL
THE MODERN LINE OF TIRE VALVES

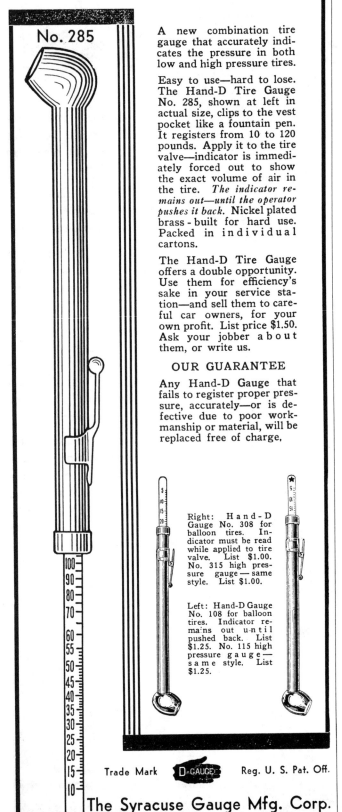

SERVICE INSTRUCTIONS FOR THE K-S GASOLINE TELEGAGE

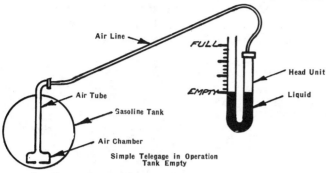

Simple Telegage in Operation
Tank Empty

1. Remove tank filler cap. On cars where a hole in filler cap is necessary see that it is free from dirt and open. Do not replace filler cap, or drain gas tank.

2. Try Tank Unit connection to be sure it is tight. Use a second wrench to prevent tube from twisting.

3. Disconnect Air Line at front end only. Red liquid must now read even with bottom line of Dial. Add or remove liquid as required at top of Brass Tube where Air Line was disconnected. Use a medicine dropper to add liquid; use a toothpick to absorb some. NEVER loosen lock nuts to move Brass Tube up or down. If Dial or Paper Reflector back of Glass Tube is stained at the bottom, install a new complete Gauge Head. Use only K-S Telegage Liquid—no other will do.

4. Dry Air Line. Follow exactly—
   a. Use a good Hand Tire Pump. (Never use compressed air.)
   b. Cut metal tip from Tire Pump Hose.
   c. Push hose securely over front end of Line.
   d. Give 50 good full strokes continuously.

5. Reconnect Air Line, making tight joint.

6. Replace tank filler cap.

TEST

1. If gas outlet is in Tank Unit, disconnect the fuel feed line from the top of the vacuum tank or fuel pump and blow with the mouth through this line into the main tank.

2. If gas outlet is not in Tank Unit, drive the car until the red liquid no longer comes up. A correction cannot be made if the tank is more than three-fourths full.

   Now if the reading stays set with the car standing, then the Telegage is O. K. and the job is completed. But if you cannot get a reading by driving or blowing back through the feed line; or you can get a reading, but it will not hold for an hour with the motor dead; then there is a defective unit to be located by following these Repair Instructions.

1. Disconnect the Air Line front and rear.

2. Inspect cones and seats for dirt or flaws.

3. Blow out Air Line (see Check 4) and test for a leak. Hold finger over one end and suck on the other end. If the suction created will hold the tongue *for one minute* the Line is O. K.

4. If the Air Line shows a leak, or is plugged, change it.

5. If the Air Line and connections check O. K., the defect is in the Tank Unit, which should be changed.

KING-SEELEY CORP.
General Offices and Factory
ANN ARBOR, MICH.

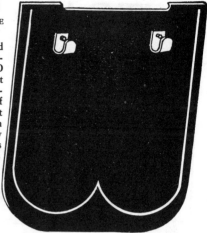

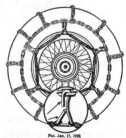

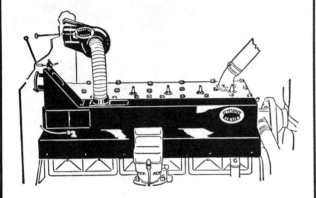

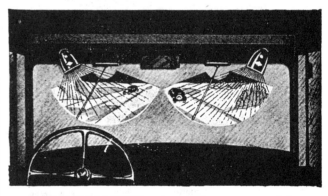

TWIN HORNS *have* **TRIPLED** *horn profits—* **GET YOURS . .**

Horn sales have been completely revolutionized with the coming of Twin Mountings. They are selling twice as fast and the sales are twice as large. Horn business this year promises to become one of the really major accessory lines, and Sparton is prepared for it with four distinct twin models of rare beauty and unforgettable tone. Get your share of this multiplying business. Consult your Sparton distributor.

THE SPARKS-WITHINGTON COMPANY
JACKSON, MICH., U.S.A.

Also makers of Sparton Radio Receivers

(621)

Sparton horns

MOTOR CARS HAVE BEEN IMPROVED FROM YEAR TO YEAR

But it remained for

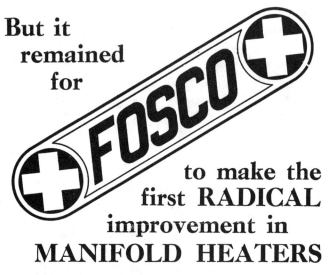

FOSCO

to make the first RADICAL improvement in **MANIFOLD HEATERS**

NO MERCHANDISING CAMPAIGN IS COMPLETE

without the

FOSCO

MANIFOLD HEATER LINE

Do not fail to secure our 1931 prices and discounts before placing any orders.

The FOSCO LINE also includes Forced Circulation Heaters for most cars and Muffler Types for Fords. Write today.

F. O. SCHOEDINGER

MANUFACTURER

322-358 MT. VERNON AVE., COLUMBUS, OHIO, U.S.A.

Monarch of All Jacks
One and a Half to Thirty Tons
$6.⁵⁰ to $75.⁰⁰

Silver King Hydraulic Jacks are stronger, faster and easier to operate, more convenient and less expensive to service, and due to the simplicity of their design, are unusually low priced.

Strength
Power
Speed
Simplicity

Just the qualities you want in a Jack. One-piece certified malleable body insures maximum strength with minimum weight. Full lift can be reached in less than one minute. Any average mechanic can service Silver King Hydraulic Jacks. Before you buy another Jack get all the facts on the Silver King—Monarch of all Jacks.

Guarantee—Silver King Jacks are guaranteed to be free from defects of workmanship and materials and to operate with ease under all weather conditions and temperatures ranging from that of the hottest climate to 25° below zero.

Model	Capacity		Weight		Low Height	Lift	Total Height
B2	2	Ton	15	lbs.	6½″	6½″	13 ″
B2S	2	Ton	15	lbs.	6½″	6½″	16 ″
J1½	1½	Ton	8	lbs.	7¾″	5½″	13¼″
T2	2	Ton	10	lbs.	7¾″	4¼″	13⅝″
T3	3	Ton	13½	lbs.	9½″	5½″	17 ″
T7	7	Ton	17	lbs.	10 ″	5¼″	17¼″
T12	12	Ton	27½	lbs.	11½″	6½″	20 ″
T20	20	Ton	60	lbs.	12 ″	6¾″	18¾″
T30	30	Ton	60	lbs.	12 ″	6¾″	18¾″

THE SILVER KING HYDRAULIC JACK CO.
5604 Cedar Ave., Cleveland, Ohio

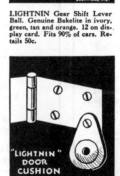

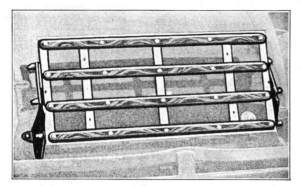

GLOBE
AUTOMOTIVE PRODUCTS

HERE ARE THREE ACCESSORIES that are sales successes—that give volume sales and big profits. They are priced to sell quickly so that you can do a large volume and make greater profits.

GLOBE
Radiator Grilles

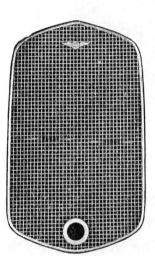

Not all your profits today need be hard earned. The demand for smartness in the radiator assembly makes Globe Grilles easy to sell. Concealing the dull lines of the radiator core, Globe Grilles give new cars, floor stock, and many models of used cars, the extra eye appeal that often makes the sale.

Globe Grilles are made of Chrome Plated brass *Metalace* or steel in 104 sizes, shapes and patterns. The entire Grille is buffed to a highly polished finish.

Liberal discounts bring you a real profit on each Grille. Thousands of car owners are installing them on their cars, resulting in a very large volume of business.

GLOBE
Wheel
Rings

Wire wheels make a neat, snappy appearance when equipped with Globe Wheel Rings. They dress-up the car with their smartness and beauty.

Well made, designed to harmonize with wire wheels. Finished in durable Chrome Plate. Easily installed, they will not rattle or jar loose.

Only one size is required for cars having 19" drop center wheels. Furnished in sets of five and six rings.

GLOBE
Radiator
Shutters

The outstanding radiator shutter, featured to sell at popular prices. Built for service, better motor performance, driving comfort, smarter car appearance.

The shutter your customers demand—the shutter that gives you more profit.

Your sales will gain sharply by offering these three accessories to your customers. There is a liberal profit for you. The prices are within the reach of everyone. The discounts are right—so scheduled that you are sure to make liberal profits.

Write us for complete data on them.

THE GLOBE
MACHINE & STAMPING CO.

1212 WEST 76TH ST., CLEVELAND, OHIO

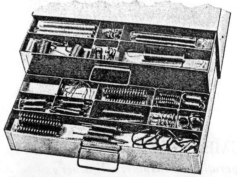

Check This Point Carefully When Buying

Every *genuine* Timken Bearing has the name Timken stamped on both the cup and cone.

It is your protection to insist on getting the genuine article.

A nation-wide chain of Authorized Distributors is ready to serve you. The Timken Roller Bearing Service and Sales Company, Canton, Ohio.

TIMKEN *Tapered Roller* BEARINGS

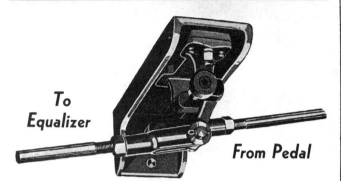
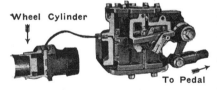

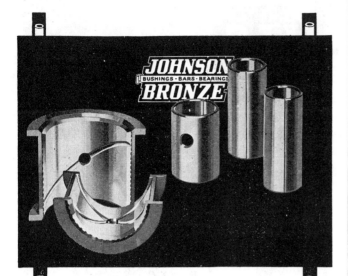

USED THROUGHOUT
THE AUTOMOTIVE INDUSTRY
R B & W EMPIRE BOLTS & NUTS

BOURKE-WHITE PHOTO

—And the proof of satisfaction may be seen in the fact that, year in, year out, leading automotive manufacturers are large consumers of R B & W products. In an industry where high standards of quality and workmanship are demanded, R B & W is an important supplier because of "constant quality rigidly maintained." That is your assurance that in specifying R B & W EMPIRE Bolts and Nuts on your order to your jobber you will receive the self-same quality and accuracy that are being furnished to the builders of the nation's leading cars.

RIM BOLTS   HUB BOLTS
RIM NUTS SHACKLE BOLTS
BATTERY BOLTS

Specify to your jobber:
R B & W Bolts & Nuts

RUSSELL, BURDSALL & WARD BOLT & NUT CO.

PORT CHESTER, N. Y. ROCK FALLS, ILL.
CORAOPOLIS, PA.

Sales Offices at Philadelphia, Detroit, Chicago, San Francisco, Los Angeles, Seattle, Portland, Ore.

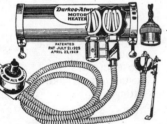

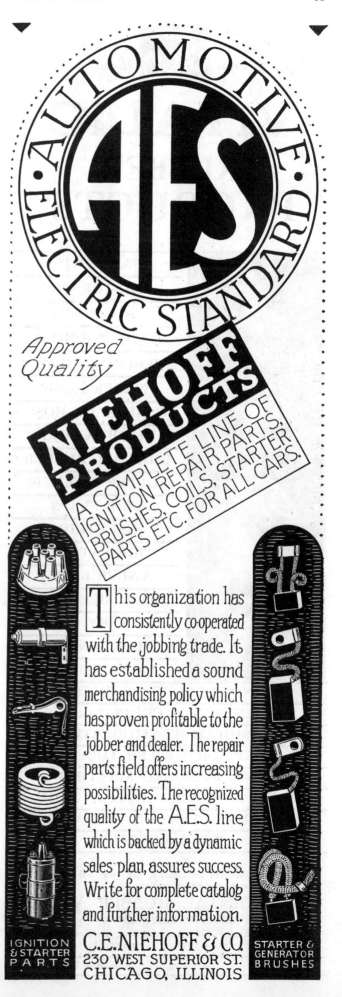

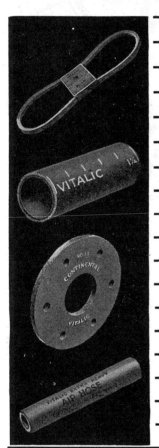

MANHATTAN *Supercable*

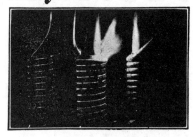

YOU can offer Manhattan Supercable to your trade with the assurance that it will give long and satisfactory service. Its superiority over other makes of cable has been repeatedly demonstrated in scientific laboratory tests for determining resistance to corona, voltage, heat, oil, gasoline and water. All Manhattan Supercable is made in strict accordance with S. A. E. standards.

IGNITION CABLE SETS

Each set complete, including Rajah Distributor Terminals and attached spark plug terminals and hoods; cable cut to right lengths. All cable Standard Manhattan 26 BS Coronaproof Supercable, 12 coats of Insulac. Wide variety of standard and special sets for all cars in use today. Also Special Dealer Assortment No. 4 in 3-color all-metal merchandiser as shown, containing 12 assorted sets for servicing practically all cars.

CABLE DISPLAYS

Furnished in three Special Assortments to meet all renewal requirements. Types include: Primary, Heavy Primary, Double Braided Primary, Single and Duplex Armored, 7 m/m High Tension, braided and plain rubber.

Dealers' Assortment No. 1—1000 feet.
10 Spools, 100 ft. each.
Includes one spool rubber drop light cable.

Dealers' Assortment No. 2—1000 feet.
10 Spools, 100 ft. each.
For the dealer or service station requiring a good general service stock.

Dealers' Assortment No. 3—500 feet.
5 Spools, 100 ft. each.
Adapted to the needs of smaller garages.

BATTERY CABLE MERCHANDISERS

Two types of Battery Cable Merchandisers are furnished Free with all Special Assortments of Manhattan Replacement Battery Cables.
ALL-METAL MERCHANDISER—The attractive 3-color Cabinet, as illustrated, height 28 in., is a convenient container for either one of two Special Assortments comprising 36 and 22 cables in individual cartons. These sets are offered at a low dealer price, enabling the garage to service 95% of all cars in use today, on a conservative outlay.
WALL RACK MERCHANDISER—Three Special Assortments comprising 57, 41 and 22 cables for complete replacement service. Specification chart and price list included with each Assortment.
All Standard Manhattan Battery Cables are No. 2 gauge, rubber insulated, with heavy braided waterproof covering.

Write for new Catalogs and Price Lists covering every automotive wiring assembly and type of terminal for replacement service.

MANHATTAN INSULATED WIRE CO.
17-23 West 60th Street, New York, N. Y.
Export Representative: CHAS. F. LYNGAAS CO.
Bush Terminal Bldg. No. 19, Brooklyn, N. Y.
Continental Europe: CORNELIUSSEN & STAKGOLD, A./S.
Brussels, Belgium

HOLFAST

An unusually profitable line of rubber replacement items, sold through jobbers.

Merchandising helps include Belt Cabinets, Belt Hooks, Radiator Hose Display Racks, etc., with well chosen assortments.

Write for full information.

FAN BELTS
RADIATOR HOSE
AIR HOSE
TUBE PATCHES
UNIVERSAL DISCS
MAGNETO DISCS
FRICTION TAPE
GENERATOR COUPLINGS
WATER PUMP COUPLINGS
DROP CENTER RIM PROTECTORS
TOP DRESSINGS
TOP REPAIR
TOP PUTTY
RADIATOR CEMENT

MADE BY

HOLFAST RUBBER CO.
ATLANTA, GA., U. S. A.

"Ask Your Jobber's Salesman!"

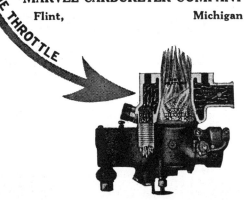

←THIS

useful wall chart is sent you, Free! It lists the Fostoria Fender Line giving complete data from which to order. A POSTCARD will bring you this chart together with the name of the nearest Fostoria Distributor.

FOSTORIA FENDERS

FOSTORIA PRESTEEL CARRIER

TWO-TONED FINISH

OPEN

FOSTORIA FENDER TOOLS

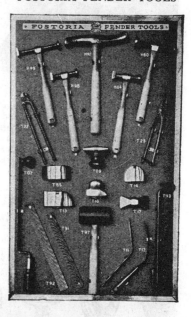

There's plenty of fender business—and there's a dependable source of supply for all the makes and models of fenders you have to replace. You can get them right away from your local Fostoria Distributor. Each Fostoria Fender matches exactly the one it replaces. It is jigged for fit at the factory. The weight of metal, shape and finish duplicate the original.

All you need to take advantage of Fostoria fender service is a Wall Chart from which to order, and the address of the Fostoria Distributor. You get these from us direct. Write today.

FOSTORIA FENDER TOOLS

Every repair shop needs a set of fender repair tools—Fostoria Fender tools recommended by the builders of Fostoria Fenders are the ideal tools. Can be purchased individually or in sets. Complete set No. T 300, in metal tote tray, containing 9 tools, costs $15.50. Set No. T 200, in Steel Tool Box, containing 15 tools, costs $29.00.

NEW!—THE FOSTORIA PRESTEEL CARRIER

The FOSTORIA PRESTEEL is a profitable handsome luggage carrier that combines all advantages known up to now with a number of completely new and exclusive features. Sells for $27.50 up. Write today for complete information about this line.

THE FOSTORIA PRESSED STEEL CORP., Dept. CM-1, FOSTORIA, OHIO

FOSTORIA FENDER DISTRIBUTORS AND WAREHOUSES THROUGHOUT THE COUNTRY

The Complete Fastener Service

Satisfactory fastener results depend upon the perfection of design, construction, and finish of the fasteners you use. Genuine "Dot" fasteners are made with the care and precision necessary to insure the satisfactory results you should have. Make sure the letters "U.C.F. Corp." are stamped on your fastener parts—your guarantee of "Dot" quality fasteners.

The "Dot" Line of Fasteners

- LIFT THE DOT
- PUSH THE DOT
- DURABLE DOT
- BABY DURABLE
- VELTEX DOT
- ANZO DOT
- SEGMA DOT
- COMMON SENSE TURN-BUTTON
- BURCO TURN-BUTTON
- TRIMOUNT
- DOT PLUG BUTTONS
- DOT TEENUTS
- PIN FASTENERS

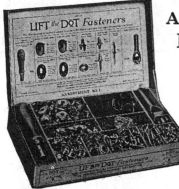

ASSORTMENT #1 LIFT the DOT Fasteners

Convenient assortment for the auto body trimmer. List price, $17.75.

Ask your Jobber for a catalog, listing the complete line of "Dot" Fasteners and Attaching Machines. Leading Jobbers of Automobile Top and Trimming materials located at strategic points throughout the country are equipped to supply promptly your need for fasteners and current literature.

UNITED · CARR FASTENER CORP.
Cambridge   *Mass.*

MONMOUTH PRODUCTS

MONMOUTH CLUTCH PLATES

Monmouth Replacement Clutch Plates are made to factory specification assuring 100% quality and accuracy. We have replacement clutch plates to fit more than 100 different types of passenger cars and trucks, including replacement parts for Borg and Beck, Long and Rockford Clutches.

With prompt service from our 50 warehouses, the jobber needs only a small stock of clutch plates to service all popular makes of cars and trucks. A handsome profit from this large, steady turnover.

STEELCLAD BUSHINGS

Steelclad Bushings are made of an outer jacket of steel, for extra strength, and a bronze lining or bearing surface. A special Monmouth process permanently bonds the two metals.

Steelclads are accurately burnished to specified size, eliminating necessity for reaming in most cases. Reaming only necessary when part to be rebushed is out of alignment. Saves many hours of labor.

MONMOUTH REPLACEMENT BOLTS

Our Warehouses carry in stock a full line of Monmouth Steering Knuckle, Tie Rod and Spring Shackle Bolts, with Bushings.

MONMOUTH GRAPHITE BRONZE BUSHINGS FOR ELECTRIC STARTERS AND GENERATORS

50 numbers fitting all cars, trucks and buses. Boxed assortments for jobbers and electrical service stations. The investment is small and the turnover rapid.

Quick Selling Monmouth Assortments should be in every shop servicing electrical repairs.

MONMOUTH PRODUCTS COMPANY
882 East 72nd St.   Cleveland, O.

GAS AND OIL LINE — Compression and Flared Tube Couplings

LINCOLN

Fig. No.	Tube Diam.	I.P.T.
701	1/8"	1/8
701a	3/16"	1/8
701b	1/4"	1/8
701b4	1/4"	1/4
701c	5/16"	1/8
701d	5/16"	1/4
701e	3/8"	1/8
701f	3/8"	1/4
701g	1/2"	3/8
701h	5/8"	1/2
7011	3/4"	1/2

Fig. No.	Tube Diam.	I.P.T.
741	1/8"	1/8
741a	3/16"	1/8
741b	1/4"	1/8
741b4	1/4"	1/4
741c	5/16"	1/8
741c4	5/16"	1/4
741d	3/8"	1/8
741e	3/8"	1/4
741f	1/2"	3/8
741g	5/8"	1/2
741h	3/4"	1/2

Fig. No.	Tube Diam.	I.P.T.
801	1/8"	1/4
801a	3/16"	1/8
801b	1/4"	1/8
801b4	1/4"	1/4
801c	5/16"	1/8
801d	5/16"	1/4
801e	3/8"	1/4
801f	3/8"	1/4
801g	1/2"	3/8
801h	5/8"	1/2
801i	3/4"	1/2

Fig. No.	Tube Diam.	I.P.T.
554	1/8"	1/8
554a	3/16"	1/8
554b	1/4"	1/8
554b4	1/4"	1/4
554c	5/16"	1/8
554c4	5/16"	1/4
554d	3/8"	1/8
554e	3/8"	1/4
554f	1/2"	3/8
554g	5/8"	1/2
554h	3/4"	1/2

Fig. No.	Tube Diam.	I.P.T.
552	1/8"	1/8
552a	3/16"	1/8
552b	1/4"	1/8
552b4	1/4"	1/4
552c	5/16"	1/8
552c4	5/16"	1/4
552d	3/8"	1/8
552e	3/8"	1/4
552f	1/2"	3/8
552g	5/8"	1/2
552h	3/4"	1/2

Fig. No.	Tube Diam.	I.P.T.
901	1/8"	1/8
901a	3/16"	1/8
901b	1/4"	1/8
901c	5/16"	1/8
901d	3/8"	1/4
901e	1/2"	3/8
901f	5/8"	1/2
901g	3/4"	1/2

Fig. No.	Tube Diam.
760	1/8"
760a	3/16"
760b	1/4"
760c	5/16"
760d	3/8"
760e	1/2"
760f	5/8"
760g	3/4"

Fig. No.	Tube Diam.
802	1/8"
802a	3/16"
802b	1/4"
802c	5/16"
802d	3/8"
802e	1/2"
802f	5/8"
802g	3/4"

Fig. No.	Tube Diam.	I.P.T.
557	1/8"	1/8
557a	3/16"	1/8
557b	1/4"	1/8
557c	5/16"	1/8
557d	3/8"	1/4
557e	3/8"	1/4
557f	1/2"	3/8
557g	5/8"	1/2
557h	3/4"	1/2

Fig. No.	Tube Diam.
556	1/8"
556a	3/16"
556b	1/4"
556c	5/16"
556d	3/8"
556e	3/8"
556f	1/2"
556g	5/8"
556h	3/4"

Fig. No.	Tube Diam.
750	1/8"
750a	3/16"
750b	1/4"
750c	5/16"
750d	3/8"
750e	1/2"
750f	5/8"
750g	3/4"

Fig. No.	Tube Diam.
702	1/8"
702a	3/16"
702b	1/4"
702c	5/16"
702d	3/8"
702e	1/2"
702f	5/8"
702g	3/4"

Fig. No.	Tube Diam.	I.P.T.
811	1/8"	1/8
811a	3/16"	1/8
811b	1/4"	1/8
811c	5/16"	1/8
811d	3/8"	1/4
811e	3/8"	1/4
811f	1/2"	3/8

Fig. No.	Tube Diam.	I.P.T.
565	1/8"	1/8
565a	3/16"	1/8
565b	1/4"	1/8
565c	5/16"	1/8

Fig. No.	Tube Diam.	I.P.T.
564	1/8"	1/8
564a	3/16"	1/8
564b	1/4"	1/8
564c	5/16"	1/8
564d	3/8"	1/4
564e	3/8"	1/4
564f	1/2"	3/8
564g	5/8"	1/2

Fig. No.	Tube Diam.	I.P.T.
903	1/8"	1/8
903a	3/16"	1/8
903b	1/4"	1/8
903c	5/16"	1/8
903d	3/8"	1/4
903e	1/2"	3/8
903f	5/8"	1/2
903g	3/4"	1/2

Fig. No.	Tube Diam.
902	1/8"
902a	3/16"
902b	1/4"
902c	5/16"
902d	3/8"
902e	1/2"
902f	5/8"
902g	3/4"

Fig. No.	Tube Diam.
558	1/8"
558a	3/16"
558b	1/4"
558c	5/16"
558d	3/8"
558e	1/2"
558f	1/2"
558g	5/8"
558h	3/4"

Fig. No.	Tube Diam.	I.P.T.
559	1/8"	1/8
559a	3/16"	1/8
559b	1/4"	1/8
559c	5/16"	1/8
559d	3/8"	1/4
559e	3/8"	1/4
559f	1/2"	3/8
559g	5/8"	1/2
559h	3/4"	1/2

Fig. No.	Tube Diam.
553	1/8"
553a	3/16"
553b	1/4"
553c	5/16"
553d	3/8"
553e	3/8"
553f	1/2"
553g	5/8"
553h	3/4"

Fig. No.	Tube Diam.	I.P.T.
904	1/8"	1/8
904a	3/16"	1/8
904b	1/4"	1/8
904c	5/16"	1/8
904f	5/8"	1/2

Fig. No.	Tube Diam.
551	1/8"
551a	1/4"
551b	1/4"
551c	5/16"
551d	3/8"
551e	1/2"
551f	1/2"
551g	5/8"
551h	3/4"

Also Manufacture

Priming Cups, Pet Cocks, Needle Valves, Two-way Tank Valves and Tube Fittings Cases.

Sold Through Reliable Jobbers Everywhere

Fig. No.	Tube Diam.
550	1/8"
550a	3/16"
550b	1/4"
550c	5/16"
550d	3/8"
550e	1/2"
550f	1/2"
550g	5/8"
550h	3/4"

Fig. No.	Tube Diam.	I.P.T.
555	1/8"	1/8
555a	3/16"	1/8
555b	1/4"	1/8
555c	5/16"	1/8
555c4	5/16"	1/4
555d	3/8"	1/4
555e	3/8"	1/4
555f	1/2"	3/8
555g	5/8"	1/2
555h	3/4"	1/2

LINCOLN

LINCOLN BRASS WORKS, DETROIT, MICH.

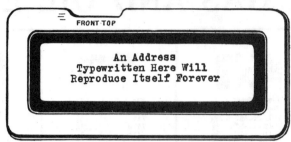

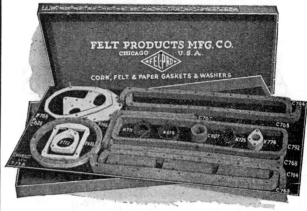

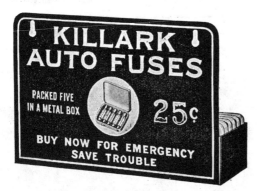

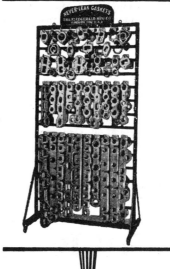

FOR THAT OVERHAULING JOB

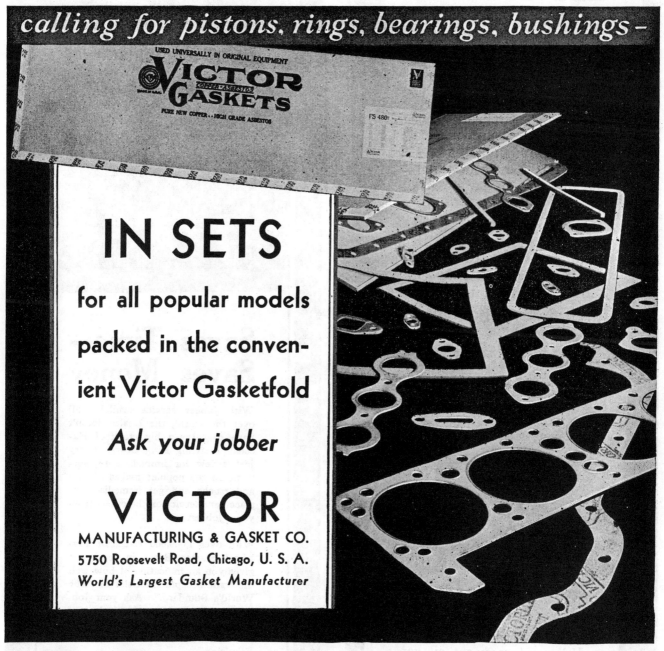

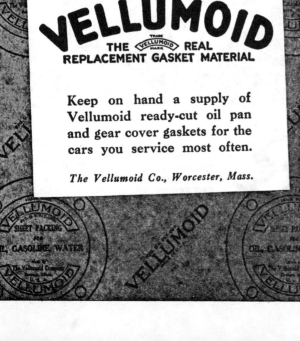

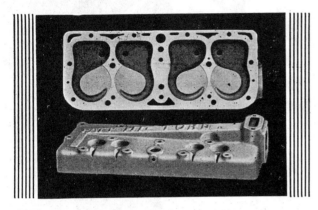

The FERODO Line

FERODO BONDED ASBESTOS BRAKE LINING—Recognized the world over as a lining of high quality, capable of extraordinary performance. Used on passenger cars, trucks and buses, generally applicable on all types of external and internal brakes. Supplied in roll form.

FERODO BONDED ASBESTOS PATENT DIE PRESSED BRAKE SHOE LINERS—Recommended for heavy duty vehicles where the greatest possible length of service is desired from one lining installation. Supplied in segments formed to the required radius for rigid shoe brakes.

FERODO M-R BRAKE LINING—A Molded type of Lining in roll form, supplied in sizes up to 2½″ x ¼″. For use on all types of internal brakes.

FERODO M-R BRAKE BLOCKS, rivet-on-type—A Molded type of Lining in formed segments for use on rigid shoe brakes in the heavier sizes for trucks and buses.

FERODO M-R BRAKE BLOCKS, bolted-on-type—Full coverage blocks, designed to accommodate both the Keeper type of brake shoe and those installations using thick blocks.

FERODO MOLDED BRAKE LINING—For all passenger cars equipped with internal brakes. Supplied by the set in formed segments.

SAFE-T-GRIP BRAKE LINING—A woven type of Lining applicable on all types of external and internal brakes. Competitively priced for use when first cost is of primary consideration. Supplied in roll form.

FERODO AND ASBESTOS
Incorporated

Factory and General Offices: New Brunswick, New Jersey

CM-4

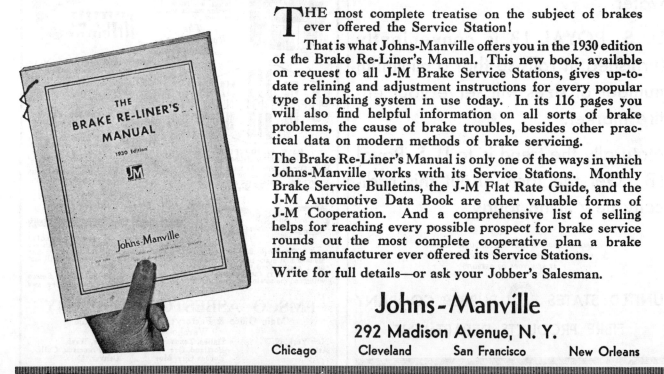

U. S. ROYAL

{LATEX BONDED} **LB** {LATEX BONDED}

BRAKE LINING

The use of natural Latex, the fluid of the rubber tree, in patented processes permits maximum asbestos content and minimum bonding material.

The result is a flexible moulded asbestos lining that offers extreme resistance to abrasion, heat, oil, and water.

U. S. ROYAL LB is conveniently furnished in rolls so that a minimum number of sizes will serve your entire market.

Naturally the trend is to U. S. Royal LB. Get the facts about this radically new lining today.

(PLEASE ADDRESS THE FIBRE PRODUCTS DEPARTMENT OF THE UNITED STATES RUBBER COMPANY AT NEW YORK OR DETROIT)

UNITED STATES RUBBER COMPANY

FIBRE PRODUCTS DEPARTMENT

Automotive Products
are
DEPENDABLE

A Brake Lining for Every Type of Brake

EMSCO HYDRAULIC BRAKE LINING
EMSCO MOLDED BRAKE LINING
EMSCO WOVEN BRAKE LINING
EMSCO ROYAL (Heavy Duty Woven)

EMSCO HYDRAULIC BRAKE LINING (Above) For quick stopping and heavy loads. Embodies a higher coefficient of friction, requires little foot pressure, yet effects a smooth, sure braking action.

EMSCO MOLDED BRAKE LINING (Right) Made from woven asbestos tape. Eliminates internal brake shoe troubles. Put up in rolls of 50 feet, and in sets.

For Internal or External Brakes

EMSCO WOVEN CLUTCH FACINGS Made from highest quality asbestos, woven into a firm tape. Packed in cartons of 25 facings, standard sizes, drilled and countersunk.

EMSCO MOLDED CLUTCH FACINGS

EMSCO SUREFLO RADIATOR HOSE Will not harden, crack or become brittle. Three-ply heavy fabric prevents swelling and blow-outs.

EMSCO MOLDED PUMP PACKING RINGS Designed for quick insertion in inaccessible places. Packed in metal containers of assorted rings. Two sizes — Handy Size and Super Service Size.

JADSON-EMSCO ALLOY PISTONS The best pistons on the market and up to Emsco quality in every way. Made in our own plant—fully equipped with the latest appliances for testing metals and all products.
The Race Driver's Choice

EMSCO AUTOMOTIVE RIVETS We make all types and sizes for brake linings, instrument panels, hood lacing, running board strips, clutch facings, and other requirements.

EMSCO PISTON PINS— Plain and Self-Locking We make all types to meet the most exacting requirements for motor cars, motorcycles, motor trucks, airplane motors, tractors and engines.

EMSCO VALVE STEM PACKING For automobile water pumps, compressors, grease guns, etc. Especially suited for use where there is possible contact with oils and chemicals.

JADSON VALVES *Used in Racing Cars*

EMSCO FAN BELTS Made of first grade rubber and finest quality Cord Tire Fabric. They carry the load and withstand the strain.

Forged from one piece of special analysis alloy steel — heat resistant and so tough it can be twisted into a knot without breaking. Will not warp, pit, or scale.
Write for complete list of Emsco Automotive Products, prices and full particulars.

EMSCO ASBESTOS COMPANY
Main Office & Factory: Downey, California
Warehouses:

New York, N. Y.	Dallas, Texas	Seattle, Wash.
Atlanta, Ga.	Portland, Ore.	San Francisco, Calif.
	Kansas City, Mo.	Denver, Colo.

For better repairs...
Thermoid products

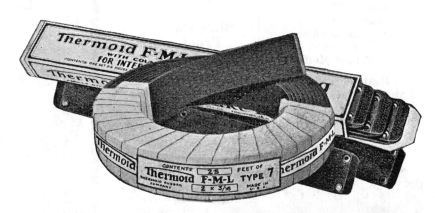

A Brake Lining for every make of car and brake

Thermoid F-M-L (Flexible Moulded Lining) is designed with the right frictional qualities for every type of internal brake. It is impregnated with a compound that reduces grabbing to an absolute minimum and the finely powdered lead distributed evenly throughout the compound deadens noise and actually prevents drum scoring.

Thermoid engineers have prepared a chart which recommends the right F-M-L or other Thermoid Brake Lining for each job and entirely eliminates guesswork. It is free upon request.

RADIATOR HOSE
Strong plies of heavy fabric, exceptionally durable tube and extra quality outer cover make Thermoid the Better Radiator Hose.

CLUTCH RINGS
Thermoid V-G Clutch Rings are constructed of spiral woven asbestos tape. They are scientifically treated to meet the most exacting requirements of automotive engineers.

THERMOID RUBBER COMPANY, *Factories and Main Offices,* TRENTON, N. J.

Thermoid AUTOMOTIVE PRODUCTS

POWELL PRODUCTS

Due to their high quality, their superiority, Powell Products make customers—keep customers. Every Powell product carries a guarantee of satisfaction. Every Powell Muffler is guaranteed Blow-Out Proof.

THE POWELL LINE — THE COMPLETE LINE

Cup Muffler
Shell Muffler
By-Pass Muffler
(Hill Climber)
Multi-Fit Muffler

} **Blow-Out Proof**

Car Heaters
Exhaust Pipes
Multi-Fit Tail Pipe
Standard Tail Pipes

Muffler Nipple Bushing
Rubber Spring Bushing
Rubber Spring Shackles
Rubber Motor Mounting

CUP MUFFLER

The Cup Muffler —standard of quality — largest selling replacement muffler on the market.

SHELL MUFFLER

The Shell Muffler gives lasting satisfaction. Interior construction is similar to the cup type muffler.

BY-PASS MUFFLER HILL CLIMBER

The Hill Climber is a quiet by-pass valve built into the Powell Muffler. It relieves the motor of the power reducing pent up exhaust gases.

RUBBER SPRING BUSHING

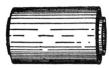

Chassis Spring Expanded Rubber Bushing. A replacement item in large demand. Made to fit various models of Chrysler, Dodge, De-Soto, Hupmobile, Pontiac, and Oakland.

MULTI-FIT TAIL PIPE

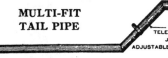

The Multi-Fit Tail Pipe solves tail pipe problems. Ten different size pipes will service practically all motor cars.

The MULTI-FIT MUFFLER is similar in construction to the Type A Muffler. Where the Powell Cup or the Type A Mufflers are not available it is possible with a stock of nine different sizes to satisfactorily take care of the motorist's requirements.

The PURE AIR HEATER—Blower and Funnel Type.

MUFFLER NIPPLE BUSHING reduces Muffler Stock requirements. Supplied in many size combinations.

RUBBER SHACKLE—the eliminator of shackle troubles.

POWELL MUFFLER CO., Utica, N. Y., U. S. A.

Hygrade Line AUTOMOTIVE PRODUCTS

NEW BUSINESS
SMALL INVESTMENT
LARGE PROFITS with
HYGRADE'S REPLACEMENT PARTS

AC Fuel Pump replacement parts now made available by HYGRADE. Not only bowls and gaskets but every single part used in AC Fuel Pumps is now supplied by HYGRADE. These parts long sought by repairmen open up new fields for both jobber and dealer.

Glass bowls and gaskets for all types of pumps and filters including AC, Stewart Warner, and Ford now put up in economical, attractive merchandising kits to give complete service on all cars at low cost. Dealer and jobber assortments.

The Rapid Transit Kit is HYGRADE'S solution for quick high tension cable service. Cable, terminals, and cutting and stripping tool, all compactly arranged, easy to handle and low in cost.

The Master Cable Kit for primary circuits contains cable, terminals, terminal tool, and cutter and stripper in the same type of kit. Complete cable sets and cable in bulk also available by HYGRADE.

Speedometer Shafts as put up by HYGRADE mean small stock and complete service. Condensed to 4 small units that will service all cars. Also assortments containing shafts, tips and tool in metal cabinets to make your own shafts. New combination squaring and cramping tool solves all installation problems.

Carburetor floats and screens and other carburetor parts put up in small assortments with complete replacement data.

A new source of income is open to dealers and jobbers with HYGRADE'S new and much wanted replacement parts. Attractive and convenient merchandising cabinets make them easily saleable. Write for Catalog for full information on these parts and on HYGRADE'S Ignition Wrench Kits, Thickness Gauges, Throttle Ball Joints, Carbon Bearings, Brake Parts.

HYGRADE PRODUCTS CO.
333 W. 52d St., New York

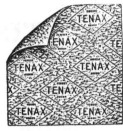

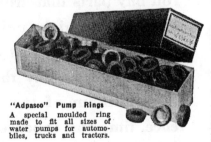

OHIO HAMMERED PISTON RINGS

CAST INDIVIDUALLY

MADE WITH MODERN MACHINERY

CAREFULLY INSPECTED

PACKED NEATLY

OHIO HAMMERED
MADE BY
OHIO HAMMERED
PISTON RING COMPANY
CLEVELAND, OHIO

SIZE___ PLUS___

THE OHIO HAMMERED PISTON RING CO.
Cleveland, Ohio

HOW ABOUT IT?

If you saw two one-dollar bills on the street, you wouldn't pick up one and leave the other.

Getting down to facts, isn't that what you're doing if you patch up worn-out parts where you *could* sell the car-owner a first-class replacement job?

Business won't worry you if you'll take the trouble to do a little selling of new parts.

And you'll build up new customer confidence if you give your patrons the benefit of Thompson Products when you replace.

THOMPSON PRODUCTS, INC.
General Offices: Cleveland, Ohio, U. S. A.
Factories: Cleveland and Detroit

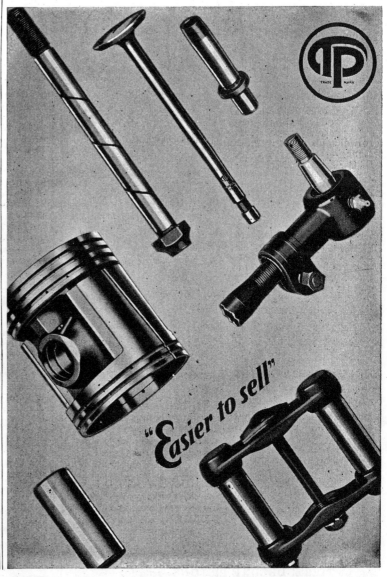

"Easier to sell"

Thompson Products

INCLUDING THE ONLY *COMPLETE* CHASSIS PARTS SERVICE ON THE MARKET

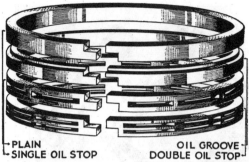

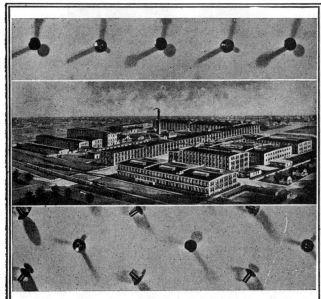

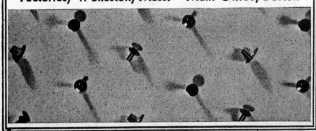
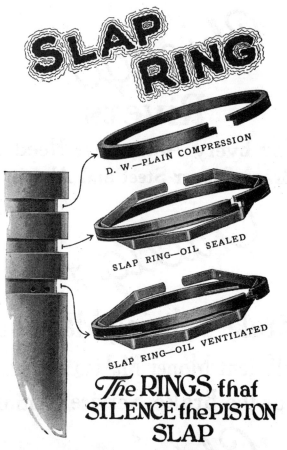

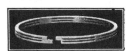

Duo Elastic
Oil Regulating Rings

THEY'RE GOOD!

The DUO ELASTIC OIL REGU-LATING Ring is built in two sections —stepped to keep sections in proper relative positions; it has a positive locking joint. Duo Elastics maintain at least two edges against the cylinder wall at all speeds—regardless of piston rock.

The Duo Elastic Oil Regulating Ring forces surplus oil through its vents by maintaining a center edge against the cylinder wall. DUO ELASTICS are high-grade concentric rings, made of the finest materials—packed conveniently and priced to allow you a good profit. Ask your jobber for them or write us.

ELASTIC COMPRES-SION RINGS

ELASTIC OIL WIPER RINGS

ELASTIC VENTED RINGS

ELASTIC DOUBLE-VENTED RINGS

CONTINENTAL
PISTON RING COMPANY
Memphis, Tennessee

L-X
BRAKE BAND AND CLUTCH FACING
RIVETS

Better rivets—lower cost — immediate shipments in desired lots. L-X rivets are designed to meet every requirement: approved and designated by automotive engineers, brake lining manufacturers; made by an organization of rivet experts whose concentrated experience, tremendous output and intensified methods enable us to produce rivets of superior design and quality at a price equal, and on some sizes cheaper than the lowest competition.

You can greatly increase your sales and profit by carrying this foremost and universally recognized line.

Prices and details on request.

See Editorial Pages 262 and 263 for Rivet Numbers.

L-X Riveting Machines and Equipment

L-X PRODUCTS

No. 12 — BRASS SEMI-TUBULAR For Brake Bands — No. 38

No. 2 — BRASS FULL TUBULAR For Clutch Facing — No. 33

No. A — ALUMINUM SEMI-TUBULAR For Brake Bands — No. B

No. 9 — BRASS BIFURCATED For Brake Bands — No. 11

No. 4 — BRASS COUNTERSUNK HEAD For Brake Bands — No. 45

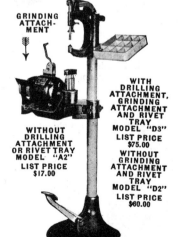

GRINDING ATTACH-MENT

WITHOUT DRILLING ATTACHMENT OR RIVET TRAY MODEL "A2" LIST PRICE $17.00

WITH DRILLING ATTACHMENT, GRINDING ATTACHMENT AND RIVET TRAY MODEL "D3" LIST PRICE $75.00

WITHOUT GRINDING ATTACHMENT AND RIVET TRAY MODEL "D2" LIST PRICE $60.00

MANUFACTURER'S BELT HOOK COMPANY
1315-21 W. CONGRESS ST.
CHICAGO, ILL.

       CHILTON AUTOMOTIVE MULTI-GUIDE

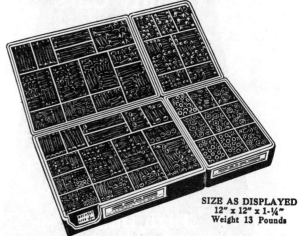

INTERLOX

METAL HOSE

For Carburetors, Exhaust Heaters, Wiring Conduit
Also used for Air Cleaners, Blowers, Exhaust and Dust Conveying Systems
When ordering be sure and mention type of tubing
The leading Motor Car, Truck, Tractor, Carburetor and Heater Manufacturers use our
Interlox Tubing as their standard Equipment

SPECIFICATIONS

Brass Nickeled—Plated Conduit for Spotlight or Headlight Wires

Type "AA"

9/32" In. Dia. x 3/8" Out. Dia.
3/8" " " x 15/32" " "
7/16" " " x 17/32" " "

Single Groove Conduit or Wire Casing — Cord Packed

Type "AE"

1/4" In. Dia. x 11/32" Out. Dia.
9/32" " " x 3/8" " "
5/16" " " x 13/32" " "
3/8" " " x 15/32" " "
7/16" " " x 17/32" " "
1/2" " " x 5/8" " "
5/8" " " x 3/4" " "

Exhaust Tubing for Trucks, Tractors, Interlocking. Heavy Four-Wall Type

Type "BB"

1 3/4" In. Dia. x 2" Out. Dia.
2" " " x 2 3/8" " "
2 1/8" " " x 2 1/4" " "
2 5/8" " " x 2 1/2" " "
2 1/2" " " x 2 3/4" " "
2 3/4" " " x 3" " "
3" " " x 3 1/4" " "

Tubing Sizes Used by These Leading Manufacturers Carried in Stock

CARBURETORS
STROMBERG
SWAN
WINFIELD
ZENITH
SCHEBLER
CARTER
MARVEL

HEATERS
CHANSON
LINDENDOLL
FRANCISCO
BOVEY
GLADIATOR
TEMME
KUNKEL
STEWART-WARNER
PERFECTION
ARVIN, WEATHER-KING
KELCH, WOLVERINE, IRVING
COOPER
RED-CAT
KYSOR
N-L

Interlocking Carburetor Tubing. No Unravelling or Loose Ends when Cutting.

Type "B"

27/32" In. Dia. x 1" Out. Dia.
7/8" " " x 1 1/16" " "
29/32" " " x 1 1/8" " "
31/32" " " x 1 1/8" " "
1 1/16" " " x 1 1/4" " "
1 1/8" " " x 1 5/16" " "
1 3/16" " " x 1 3/8" " "
1 1/4" " " x 1 7/16" " "
1 5/16" " " x 1 1/2" " "
1 3/8" " " x 1 9/16" " "
1 7/16" " " x 1 5/8" " "
1 1/2" " " x 1 11/16" " "
1 9/16" " " x 1 3/4" " "
1 11/16" " " x 1 7/8" " "
1 3/4" " " x 1 15/16" " "
1 13/16" " " x 2" " "
2" " " x 2 3/16" " "
2 1/16" " " x 2 1/4" " "
2 1/8" " " x 2 5/16" " "
2 1/4" " " x 2 7/16" " "
2 5/16" " " x 2 1/2" " "
2 1/2" " " x 2 11/16" " "
2 5/8" " " x 2 13/16" " "
2 3/4" " " x 2 15/16" " "
2 13/16" " " x 3" " "
3" " " x 3 3/16" " "
3 1/16" " " x 3 1/4" " "
3 1/4" " " x 3 7/16" " "
3 5/8" " " x 3 1/2" " "
3 1/2" " " x 3 11/16" " "
3 13/16" " " x 4" " "
4" " " x 4 1/4" " "

*All sizes in stock
From 3/16" to 6"*

JOBBERS
SEND FOR NEW
LIST AND NEW
DISCOUNT SHEET

CAUTION
When ordering be sure and mention type and employment of tubing with inside and outside diameters.

Manufacturers of Interlocking Flexible Metal Tubing, Gasoline Hose (Metal Lined, Rubber and Fabric), Flexible Metallic Hose, Flexible Car Wiring Conduit, Hose Couplings.

International Metal Hose Co., Inc.

Factory: 10709-15 Quincy Ave.   *Cleveland, Ohio*

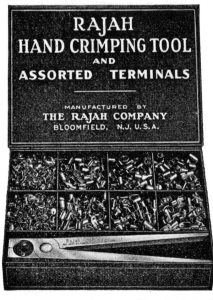

RICH

in Quality as well as in Name

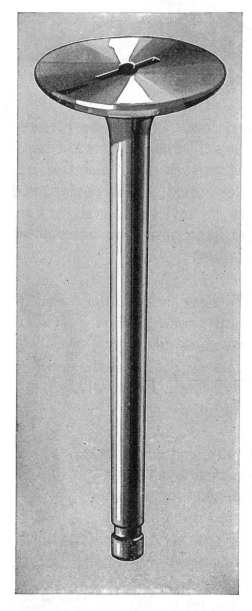

Rich Valves vary in size, shape and the grade of steel used—depending on the engineering specifications of the different motor car manufacturers. But all Rich Valves of one certain type are as alike as two peas, because uniform quality and precise workmanship are inflexible laws in every Wilcox-Rich plant!

Consequently, each Rich Valve is as perfect as man and machine can make it. Thus, sheer merit has lifted Rich Valves to first place. They are original factory equipment on more makes of cars than any other valve.

This explains why more and more repairmen every day are changing to Rich Valves for replacements. Experience has taught them to depend on Rich Valves for uniform quality and customer satisfaction.

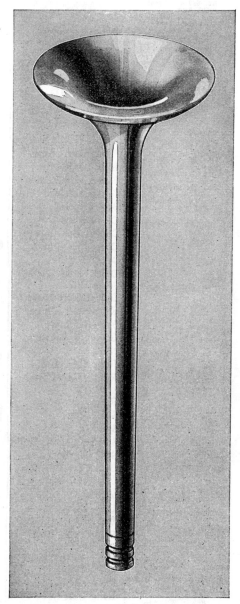

manufactured by

WILCOX-RICH CORPORATION, *Detroit*
World's Largest Manufacturer of Automotive Valves

Sold for Replacement Purposes Exclusively Through
McQUAY-NORRIS MFG. CO. - - - ST. LOUIS *and*
KING QUALITY PRODUCTS CO. - - - ST. LOUIS

Changing Styles and Wheels

People are becoming more and more conscious of wheel-style. This means money for the dealer who is in a position to make change-overs. There is very little shop work required as all wheels by Motor Wheel are interchangeable. Repainting, enameling and wheel-aligning are other branches of the business bringing in extra profits.

Note the list below and write your nearest distributor for full particulars.

 MOTOR WHEEL MASTER DISTRIBUTORS:

ALABAMA
Birmingham, Cruse-Crawford Wheel & Rim Co., 2921 Second Ave. S.
CALIFORNIA
Los Angeles, Pacific Wheel & Rim Service, 324 West Venice Blvd.
Oakland, Pacific Wheel and Rim Service, 443 25th St.
San Francisco, Claude H. Shayer, 1690 Pine St.
CANADA
Edmonton, Alberta, Loveseth Service Station, Ltd., Jasper at 106th St.
Montreal, Que., General Automobile Equipment Co., Ltd., 4010 St. Catherine St. West.
Toronto, 5, Ont., Wheel & Rim Co. of Canada, Ltd., 27 Yorkville Ave.
Vancouver, B. C., Standard Equipment Co., Ltd., 1255 Seymour St.
Winnipeg, Manitoba, Ronald J. J. Muir, Ltd., Colony St. and Ellice Ave.
COLORADO
Denver, Quinn & McGill Motor Supply Co., 437 Broadway.
DISTRICT OF COLUMBIA
Washington, Washington Automotive Service, Inc., 2011 M St., N.W.
FLORIDA
Jacksonville, Southeast Wheel & Rim Co., 927 W. Forsyth St.
GEORGIA
Atlanta, Harris Rim & Wheel Co., 376 Spring St., N. W.
ILLINOIS
Chicago, Stone Wheel & Rim Co., 2540 S. Wabash Ave.
INDIANA
Indianapolis, Indiana Wheel & Rim Co., 40 W. North St.
IOWA
Des Moines, Des Moines Wheel & Rim Co., 1427 Walnut St.
KANSAS
Wichita, Wheel & Rim Service, Inc., 220 S. Emporia St.
LOUISIANA
New Orleans, Shuler Supply Co., 1700-20 Poydras St.
MARYLAND
Baltimore, R. W. Norris & Sons, Gay & High Sts.

MASSACHUSETTS
Boston, Bearings & Motor Equipment Co., 784 Commonwealth Ave.
Springfield, United Wheel & Rim, Inc., 136 Dwight St.
MICHIGAN
Detroit, Rim & Wheel Service Co., 5132 Third Ave.
Grand Rapids, Rim & Wheel Service Co., 147 Weston St. S. W.
Lansing, Rule & Roberts, Inc., Grand & Kalamazoo Streets.
MINNESOTA
Minneapolis, Pioneer Rim & Wheel Co., 24 S. 10th St.
St. Paul, Pioneer Rim & Wheel Co., 344 N. Exchange St.
MISSOURI
Kansas City, Wheel & Rim Service, Inc., 2110 Grand Ave.
St. Louis, Borbein, Young & Co., 3301 Washington Blvd.
NEBRASKA
Omaha, Morgan Wheel & Rim Co., 2216-18 Farnam St.
NEW JERSEY
Newark, Wheels, Incorporated, 262 Central Ave.
NEW YORK
Buffalo, Frey the Wheelman, Inc., 520 Ellicott St.
New York, Wheels, Incorporated, 630 W. 52nd St.
Rochester, Frey the Wheelman, Inc., 50 Scio St.
NORTH CAROLINA
Charlotte, Carolina Rim & Wheel Co., 308 N. Graham St.
Raleigh, Carolina Rim & Wheel Co., 114 E. Davie St.

Motor Wheel

OHIO
Akron, Motor Rim Manufacturers Co., 153 Wooster Ave.
Cincinnati, Rim & Wheel Service, Inc., 804 Sycamore St.
Cleveland, Motor Rim Manufacturers Co., 1835 E. 24th St.
Columbus, Hayes Wheel & Spring Service, 203 E. Town St.
Toledo, Motor Rim Manufacturers Co., 1101-09 Monroe St.
OKLAHOMA
Tulsa, Southwest Wheel & Rim Co., 919 S. Elgin St.
OREGON
Portland, Wheel & Rim Service, Inc., 14th and Everett Sts.
PENNSYLVANIA
Harrisburg, United Wheel & Rim Service, Inc., Evergreen & Thompson Sts.
Philadelphia, United Wheel & Rim Service, Inc., 3617-23 Lancaster Ave.
Pittsburgh, Joseph Woodwell Company, 4917 Liberty Ave.
TENNESSEE
Memphis, Borbein, Young & Co., 660 Union Ave.
TEXAS
Dallas, Southwest Wheel & Rim Co., 2500 Commerce St.
Houston, Southwest Wheel & Rim Co., Travis and Bell Sts.
San Antonio, Southwest Wheel & Rim Co., 606-8 N. Alamo St.
UTAH
Salt Lake City, Henderson Rim and Wheel Service, 992 S. Main St.
VIRGINIA
Richmond, Dixie Wheel Company, 1012-14 North Blvd.
WASHINGTON
Seattle, McAlpin-Schreiner Co., Inc., 12th Ave. at East Pine St.
Spokane, Bearing & Rim Supply Co., 1202 Second Ave.
Tacoma, McAlpin-Schreiner Co., Inc., 218-220 St. Helens Ave.
WISCONSIN
Milwaukee, Stone Wheel & Rim Co., 928 N. Milwaukee St.
EXPORT DEPARTMENT
New York, N. Y., 30 Water St.

MOTOR WHEEL CORPORATION, LANSING, MICHIGAN

BERLOY BINS AND COUNTERS

*f*or the storage of parts and the display of accessories ~

BERLOY Steel Automotive Bins and Display Equipment combine strength, durability and efficiency at the lowest cost consistent with quality.

The exclusive BERLOY Bin features include: (1) One-Piece, Quickly Movable Boltless Divider, (2) Boltless Subdivider, (3) 1½″ Shelf Front, (4) 1½″ Full Length Card Holder, (5) 1½″ Vertical Adjustment, (6) 1½″ and 2″ Horizontal Adjustment, (7) 3″ Sanitary Base, (8) Reinforced Shelf and (9) Sturdy 6-point Suspension.

The adaptability of BERLOY units enable them to fit into any type and size of building and conform to the storage requirements with maximum efficiency.

Bring your storage and display problems to your local BERLOY Jobber. If you do not know the jobber handling the line in your territory, this information may be obtained by writing

There is a *factory-approved* BERLOY installation for every make of motor car. Catalog No. 169 contains all data on BERLOY Automotive Storage and Display Equipment. A copy will gladly be mailed upon request to your local jobber, your Berger Branch or the home office at Canton, Ohio.

Ⓑ BERLOY

THE BERGER MANUFACTURING CO. *Division of* Republic Steel Corporation, CANTON, O.

BRANCHES AND DEALERS
IN PRINCIPAL CITIES

SHOEMAKER
Bearing and Line Boring Machines

♦

Automotive Service Equipment

SHOEMAKER
Model "E" Con-Rod Boring Machine

The SHOEMAKER MODEL "E" Con-Rod Boring Machine is the latest development in semi or regular production equipment (depending on incidental tool equipment used.) It is easily operated within a very high degree of efficiency, and is recommended either as a supplement to large rod stocks or to those who wish to use it in connection with our H.A. Casting Jig, in independently "maintaining their own" rod stocks. Price upon request.

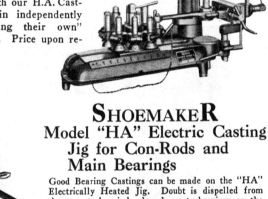

SHOEMAKER
Model "HA" Electric Casting Jig for Con-Rods and Main Bearings

Good Bearing Castings can be made on the "HA" Electrically Heated Jig. Doubt is dispelled from the operator's mind when he casts bearings on the SHOEMAKER H.A. JIG. Bearings with a fine texture, well bonded to the rod is the result. Cuts rod costs. Saves metal and labor. Mandrel changes are easily made in a minute's time. Parts are accurately made to insure ease of interchangeability. Different thickness of filler plates are provided for shim and no shim bearings. Plates are held in place by the mandrel.

SHOEMAKER
Model "KA" Line Boring Machine

The Model KA Line Boring Tool has been developed after long years of experience in motor rebuilding. We do not hesitate in saying that it is the finest Line Boring Tool manufactured in America today. Its design and construction has been approved by many of the leading users of this type of equipment. The Model KA Machine is very easily set-up on the job and after being set-up with ordinary care will be properly aligned with the crankcase for boring of the bearings. The illustration clearly outlines method of using the centering bushings, etc. Price upon request.

Prices ... specifications on request. Ask for catalog on complete line of
Connecting Rod Aligning Jigs.
Main Bearing & Connecting Rod Babbitting Jigs.
Main Bearing & Connecting Rod Boring Machines.
Main Bearing & Connecting Rod Babbitting Machines.

SHOEMAKER
AUTOMOTIVE EQUIPMENT CO.
Henney Bldg., Freeport, Illinois, U. S. A.

·LYON STEEL·
Storage, Display and Shop
·EQUIPMENT·

There is a piece of Lyon Steel Equipment for every storage or display need of the Automobile Dealer, Service Station or Garage.

If you need storage, display, or shop equipment that is neither illustrated nor listed here, write direct to the factory for specifications and descriptive literature.

Lyon engineers have designed practicable storage systems for the parts of all current automobiles. Being completely adjustable, these are quickly brought up-to-date after every change in model. Lyon Jobbers, located in all principal cities, are equipped to give you immediate service.

Accessory Display Racks

Automobile Parts Storage Systems

Storage Shelving

Tire Racks

Tool Cribs

Wash Rack Equipment Cabinet

Display Cases and Counters

Tool Cabinets

STORAGE

Parts Storage Systems for each make of car.

Racks: Fender, Tire, Spring, Curtain, Dust Shield, Long Parts, Glass, Gasket, Radiator, Tool, Wheel, Rim.

Cabinets: Mechanic's tool, Wash rack equipment, Spray booth equipment, Office, Wardrobe.

Stock Shelving, Shelving box inserts, Universal storage units, Small parts cases.

DISPLAY

Display cases, Display counters, Merchandising tables, Accessory display racks, Store fixtures, Wall display shelving, Display stands, Tire display racks.

SHOP

Tool stands, Tool cabinets, Work benches, Tool cribs, Service desks, Bench drawers, Tool boxes, Shop desks, Tote pans, Lockers, Spray booth equipment cabinets, Wash rack equipment cabinets, Bins, Shelving.

Shop Lockers

Steel Work Benches

LYON METAL PRODUCTS, INCORPORATED
2931 Montgomery Street
AURORA, ILLINOIS
Assembly Plants: Jersey City, N. J.; Los Angeles, Calif.
JOBBERS IN ALL PRINCIPAL CITIES

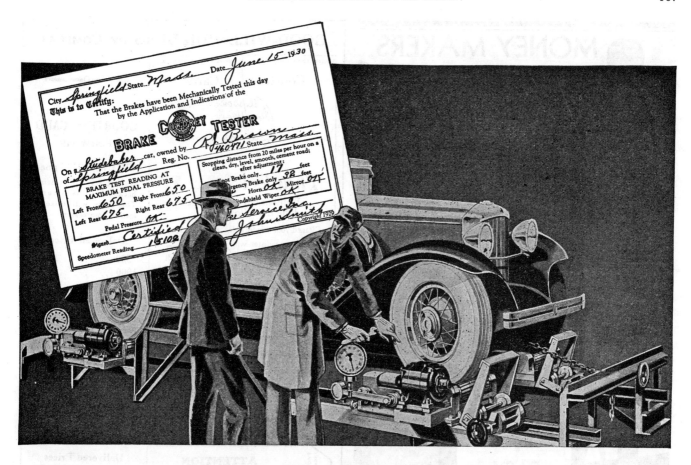

The COWDREY Brake Tester

COWDREY certified stopping is the most vital contribution to motoring safety since the adoption of 4-wheel brakes. Car owners appreciate Cowdrey certificates.

The Cowdrey machine attracts business—not only for brake service but for other trade as well. It substitutes *knowing* for *guessing*.

The Cowdrey machine saves money. With it, one man can do as much brake adjustment work in a day—and do much better work—than two men can do without the machine.

The Cowdrey machine eliminates road testing for brakes—thereby saving time, rubber, gasoline and accident hazard. It is made in many sizes and styles to meet every requirement as to location, and character of brake work.

Write for full particulars, including details of our liberal time payment plan.

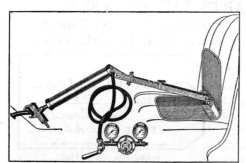

The "Human Leg" Pedal Pusher—a new Cowdrey product—cuts your brake service overhead. Set the dial for any pressure you want—you get it exactly; no guessing, no mistakes. Works better than a man, and cuts an average of five minutes off each job. Quickly pays for itself.
Drop us a line for information

BENDIX-COWDREY BRAKE TESTER, Inc.
SOUTH BEND, INDIANA
(SUBSIDIARY OF BENDIX AVIATION CORPORATION)

NATIONAL DISTRIBUTORS: Multibestos Company—The Raybestos Division of Raybestos Manhattan, Inc.—The Russell Manufacturing Company—United States Rubber Company—Wagner Electric Corporation.

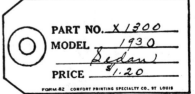

Everybody knows —
GENERAL ELECTRIC

The best-known name in the electrical world guarantees you quality and dependability in these electrical

 AUTOMOTIVE PRODUCTS

Tungar Battery Charger

Reliable, efficient. In five sizes—1, 6, 12, 15, 30 battery—to fit all needs. $18, $45, $75, $84, $135.*

Tungar Bulbs

The standard of quality the world over.

G-E Tungar Battery Tester

Rugged as a wrench, accurate as a watch. Makes every battery test. Spots trouble in generator, starter or car wiring. Wins customer confidence for you. Helps you sell new batteries and equipment. $39.*

G-E Lacquered Ignition Cable

In sets to fit any car. List prices $1.50 to $5.00. Adds power, smoothness, mileage. *Only* G-E sets are equipped with Textolite Caps to protect connections.

G-E Portable Hand Lamps

Three sizes. Husky, stand the gaff. Kinkless rubber cords endure water, oil, acid and abrasion. Plugs are unbreakable. $2.70 and $4.50.*

G-E Hand Cleaner

Quickly cleans and freshens a car's interior. A new service to your customers at little cost to you. $14.50 List price.

G-E Rubber Cord Set

G-E Flex all-rubber cord with non-breakable moulded rubber plug. Doesn't kink or crack. Resists water, oil, acids and abuse. Keeps equipment working. $.90 to $2.70. *

*(Prices are net East of the Rockies)

See your nearest G-E Automotive Distributor or write us.

MERCHANDISE DEPARTMENT   -   GENERAL ELECTRIC COMPANY   -   BRIDGEPORT, CONNECTICUT

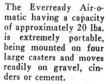

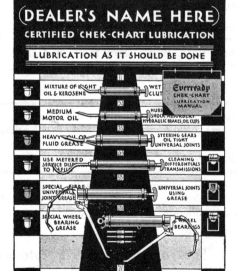

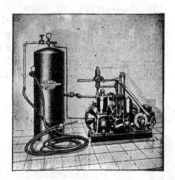

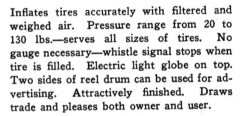

BRUNNER
MANUFACTURING COMPANY

ESTABLISHED 1906

KANSAS CITY, MO. UTICA, N. Y. TORONTO, ONT.

Specialists in Air Compressors . . . Spray Paint Outfits . . . Hydraulic Car Washers . . . .

BRUNNER AIR COMPRESSORS

Brunner Air Compressors are designed and built to measure up to the strenuous needs of the modern garage and service station. Nearly every profitable service job depends upon compressed air—and Brunner equipment responds with reliable, uninterrupted operation.

Greasing, spring oiling, tire inflation and changing, lift operation, motor cleaning—these are only a few of the services made attractively profitable by Brunner Air.

Model 854 General Duty

Brunner Air Compressors are distinguished by substantial pressed-steel construction, simplicity of assembly and accessibility of parts. They are rugged, vibrationless, furnishing a smooth uninterrupted supply of air power. Every mechanical part is tested; every machine carefully assembled, thoroughly "run-in," and finally inspected by competent engineers.

The models listed below will supply an adequate amount of air for a wide variety of equipment, in addition to tire inflation service.

SPECIFICATIONS

MODEL No.	Bore and Stroke	Compr. R.P.M.	Compr. Cu. Ft. Displ.	Motor Size H.P.	Tank Size Gals.	Max. Pressure Lbs.	Shipping Weight Lbs.	DIMENSIONS			Boxed for Export Cu. Ft.
								Length	Width	Height	
833	3x4	280	4.7	1	30	150	580	52″	23″	37″	30
853	3x4	450	7.3	1½	53	150	710	65″	25″	39″	38
*854	3x3	355	8.7	2	53	150	745	65½″	25″	38″	35
855	4x4	300	8.7	2	53	150	770	65″	25″	39″	38
*1054	3x3	495	12.2	3	53	150	810	65½″	25″	38″	39

* Two cylinders, other models are one-cylinder design.

BRUNNER CAR WASHERS

Heavy Duty Model

There's real profits in car washing, but it takes up-to-date equipment to do the job. Brunner Washers are designed just for this kind of service: dependable, efficient, speedy.

The Brunner Washer has 3 large cylinders operating smoothly at slow speed, delivering abundant water at 300 lbs. pressure. Large cushioning chambers eliminate surging, hammering and vibration. Operation is trouble-free: bearings and valves are easily accessible; glands repacked and adjusted in 5 minutes' time.

Three popular models for all types of duty.

SPECIFICATIONS

	Junior One Gun Model	Standard Two Gun Model	Heavy Duty Three Gun Model
Horsepower motor	1	2	3
Bore and Stroke pump	1½x3 in.	1½x3 in.	2x4 in.
Speed	87 R.P.M.	106 R.P.M.	77 R.P.M.
Gals. water per minute	4	7	11
Guaranteed pressure	300	300	300
Floor space	53x22 in.	53x22 in.	62x28 in.
Height	45 in.	45 in.	54 in.
Net Weight	535 lbs.	585 lbs.	895 lbs.
Shipping Weight	800 lbs.	830 lbs.	1,095 lbs.
Boxed for Export	34 cu. ft.	34 cu. ft.	52 cu. ft.

BRUNNER AIR SCALES, AIR TANKS, AIR VALVES

Brunner Air Scales are attractive trade-winners. Convenient to operate. Furnished in 4 popular models for inside or outside use. Model EL shown to the right.

Brunner Air Tanks are absolutely safe and free from leaks. The Seamless Drawn Steel Tanks, guaranteed for 175 lbs. pressure, are highly recommended for general usage.

Brunner Air Valves are supplied in three models: Needle Valve, Safety Valve, Check Valve. All are ruggedly built and guaranteed.

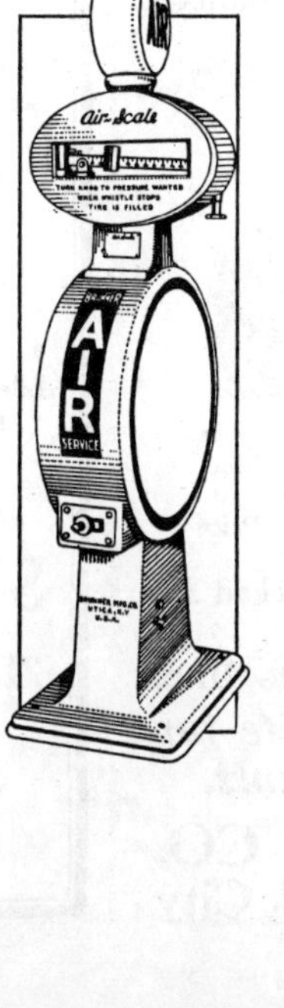

SPRAY PAINT EQUIPMENT

Painting with Brunner equipment has come to be known as the "speed method." It is the modern and efficient way to apply paint, lacquer, varnish and special finishes.

Brunner Spray Paint equipment includes everything from compressor to gun. Brunner Compressors insure a constant dependable supply of air, free of both oil and moisture. Brunner Spray Guns are three to six times faster than the hand brush and afford a uniform finish, complete coverage, even on inaccessible areas.

Model 734

SPECIFICATIONS

Outfit No.	Compr. Model No.	Bore and Stroke (In.)	Compr. R.P.M.	Compr. Cu. Ft. Displ.	Motor Size H.P.	Ship. Weight (Lbs.)
704P	204	3 x3	390	9.5	1½	488
*700P	200	1 13/16x2½	545	2.	⅓	120
734	204	3 x3	390	9.5	1½	550

*One cylinder. Others are two-cylinder design.

SPRAY AND BLOW GUNS

Brunner Spray Guns are unrivalled for high speed work or careful touch-up jobs. Atomize perfectly, lay materials evenly. Simple to adjust.

No. 300 Spray Gun produces fan or round spray with twist of cap. Spun aluminum cup holds quart. Comfortable grip. No. 400 Gun is for light duty.

No. 78 Engine Cleaner. Can be used for blowing out clogged lines, for lubricating springs or for cleaning purposes. No. 79 Liquid Sprayer has similar uses. Cup holds one quart. No. 35 Blow Gun useful for cleaning away scraped carbon, motors, upholstery, etc.

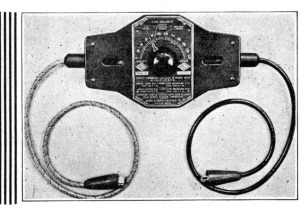

PROOF SELLS THE CAR OWNER

ABOVE: The New "M-A-E-C-O" Engine Gauge.
List $42.50
UPPER RIGHT: The New "M-A-E-C-O" Ignition Meter.
List $27.50

Muther Pedal Depressor

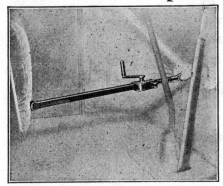

Super Service Tool

The Muther Pedal Depressor saves the time of one man in the driver's seat during brake, clutch and stop-light adjustment. It never gets tired. It holds the pedal with unvarying pressure. Double latch permits adjustments to tenths of an inch as marked on rack. $3.75 (Canada $3.95).

Visual proof, where the car owner can see and understand for himself, sells merchandise and it sells service. That is why you will find the "M-A-E-C-O" Ignition Meter and the "M-A-E-C-O" Engine Gauge exceedingly valuable in selling ignition and engine jobs and replacement parts. Write for detailed specifications showing operation and range of service.

"M-A-E-C-O" ENGINE GAUGE

With engine running will quickly and accurately show your customer the need of grinding or replacing Valves, Rings, Pistons and Gaskets. These are shown by synchronized measurement of engine vacuum and compression. Saves time in locating trouble and saves argument with the owner.

"M-A-E-C-O" IGNITION METER

Shows ignition troubles with your customer present. Demonstrates the need of replacing Coils, Spark Plugs and Wires. Shows defective distributor. Tests made in a few minutes with engine running. Capacity of ignition units measured against engine compression resistance.

Manufactured by
MAXWELL AUTOMOTIVE ENGINEERING CO.
Subsidiary to Muther Mfg. Co., Boston, Mass.

THE NEW MUTHER
Self-Indicating Stopmeter

The New Muther Self-Indicating Stopmeter is an accurate, full-jeweled, non-corrosive, dust proof instrument of scientific accuracy. It indicates *automatically* the number of feet in which a car can be stopped from a speed of 20 miles an hour. Used by highway and police officials of Mass., Penna., N. Y., Conn., Calif., and a number of other states. $40.00.

MUTHER MFG. CO.
44 Binford Street, Boston, Massachusetts

Warehouses

PACIFIC SALES CORPORATION
426 Larkin St., San Francisco, Calif.

COLONIAL TRADERS, LTD.
78 William St., Chatham, Ont., Canada

BUY WISELY

Advertisers in this book are not trying to high-pressure you.

They are trying to help you exercise your best judgment in buying.

They give you this help by furnishing essential information about their company and product.

It will pay you to study these advertisements frequently.

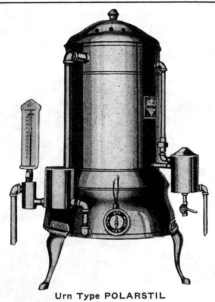

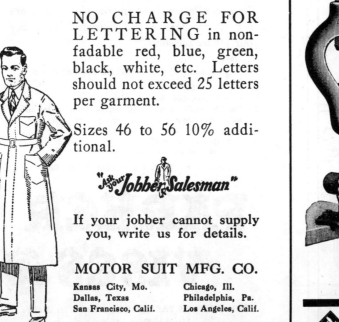

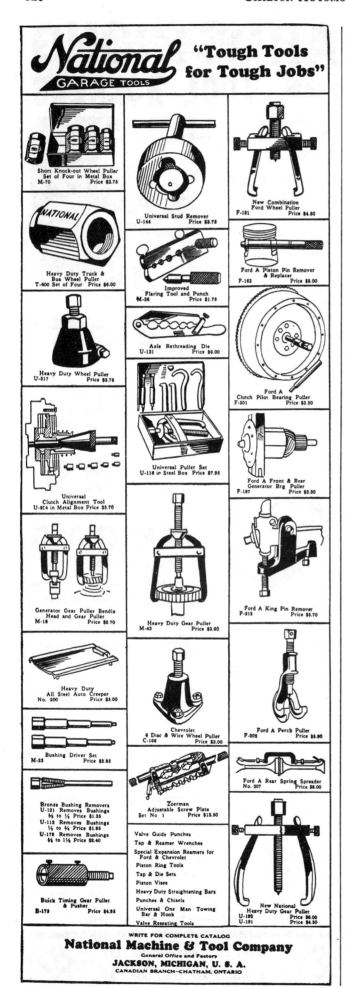

National GARAGE TOOLS — "Tough Tools for Tough Jobs"

Short Knock-out Wheel Puller Set of Four in Metal Box
M-70   Price $3.75

Universal Stud Remover
U-144   Price $3.75

New Combination Ford Wheel Puller
F-181   Price $4.50

Heavy Duty Truck & Bus Wheel Puller
T-600 Set of Four   Price $6.00

Improved Flaring Tool and Punch
M-36   Price $1.75

Ford A Piston Pin Remover & Replacer
F-163   Price $2.00

Heavy Duty Wheel Puller
U-317   Price $2.75

Axle Rethreading Die
U-131   Price $6.00

Ford A Clutch Pilot Bearing Puller
F-201   Price $3.30

Universal Clutch Alignment Tool
U-2C4 in Metal Box Price $5.70

Universal Puller Set
U-116 in Steel Box Price $7.95

Ford A Front & Rear Generator Brg Puller
F-197   Price $3.30

Generator Gear Puller Bendix Head and Gear Puller
M-18   Price $2.70

Heavy Duty Gear Puller
M-43   Price $3.60

Ford A King Pin Remover
F-212   Price $5.70

Heavy Duty All Steel Auto Creeper
No. 200   Price $5.00

Chevrolet 6 Disc & Wire Wheel Puller
C-166   Price $3.00

Ford A Perch Puller
F-202   Price $5.90

Bushing Driver Set
M-23   Price $2.85

Ford A Rear Spring Spreader
No. 307   Price $8.00

Bronze Bushing Removers
U-121 Removes Bushings ⅜ to ½ Price $1.35
U-113 Removes Bushings ½ to ¾ Price $1.85
U-178 Removes Bushings ¾ to 1½ Price $2.40

Zoerman Adjustable Screw Plate
Set No. 1   Price $13.50

Valve Guide Punches
Tap & Reamer Wrenches
Special Expansion Reamers for Ford & Chevrolet
Piston Ring Tools
Tap & Die Sets
Piston Vises
Heavy Duty Straightening Bars
Punches & Chisels
Universal One Man Towing Bar & Hook
Valve Reseating Tools

Buick Timing Gear Puller & Pusher
B-175   Price $4.95

New National Heavy Duty Gear Puller
U-192   Price $6.00
U-191   Price $4.50

WRITE FOR COMPLETE CATALOG

National Machine & Tool Company

General Office and Factory

JACKSON, MICHIGAN, U. S. A.

CANADIAN BRANCH—CHATHAM, ONTARIO

Here's the Vise

The Parker Big Bear Swivel Base Vise is best for all around service.

that Stands the Gaff of Service Station Work

The Parker Vise stands the gaff of hard work because it has the weight and strength where it is most needed. It is from 15 to 30 lbs. OVER WEIGHT and the anvil is in proportion to the size of the vise.

The Parker Vise is made particularly to meet your working requirements and our long experience assures you of years of satisfactory service.

Use more Parker Vises in your shop—they are real Service Station and Garage Vises. See your jobber salesman.

7 REASONS FOR PARKER PREFERENCE

1. Renewable Steel Jaws.
2. Swivel base, 360 degrees gripping power.
3. Outside saddle permits easy removal of screw for oiling.
4. Solid underportion gives added strength.
5. Set Screw in handle.
6. Castings of Parkco Metal.
7. Full sized screw and nut.

Send for the Booklet describing Parker Vises

PARKER VISES

GRIP LIKE A GRIZZLY

THE CHARLES PARKER CO., *Master Vise Makers*

Meriden, Conn., U. S. A.

N. Y. Salesroom, 25 Murray St., N. Y. C.

MAKERS OF THE FAMOUS PARKER GUN

ECO Service Equipment has Stood the Test of Time···

Model 40

Model 46

Model 48

Model 35

TIREFLATOR—*The Only Automatic Air Measuring Unit With an Eight-Year Record of Trouble-Free Service*

MODEL 40—The most popular of all TIREFLATOR models. Restyled for greater eye appeal with improved lighting; larger, more legible dials; the correct pressure range; and hose lock. Equipped complete with 25 ft. highest quality air hose, 10″ top air globe; automatic shut-off valve and centrifugal air cleaner (sediment trap) with convenient blow-off. Water connections or color other than ECO standard red at slight additional cost.

MODEL 39—Identical with Model 40 except that it does not have air globe and standard.

MODEL 46—Column type. Embodies same features as Model 40, except that it is hose-hook operated with semi-automatic shut-off valve and centrifugal air cleaner (sediment trap) with convenient blow-off.

MODEL 47—Same as Model 46, except that cast column extends above case and light globe is mounted on top.

MODEL 61—Tower type. Head has rotary packing chamber, permitting full revolving of arm without twisting or kinking the hose.

MODEL 49—A combination of Model 48 for wall installation and Model 35 steel covered Ceiling Reel. Reel is adjustable to four different mounting positions.

Model TS-601

Model TS-762

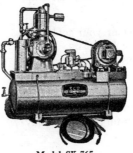

Model SK-765

ECO COMPRESSORS
with the Patented
ECO-MATIC
TANK DRAINER

A Compressor for Every Purpose Single and Double Stage 1.8 to 23.5 cu. ft.

MODEL TS-601 Two-stage outfit. Displacement 4.5 cu. ft. 1 H.P. Motor. Two cylinder sizes, 3 x 3, 1⅝ x 3, air cooled. Maximum tank pressure 200 lbs. Complete with V-belt Drive, Automatic Switch and ECO-MATIC Tank Drainer.

MODEL TS-762 Two-stage outfit complete. Displacement 9.25. 425 R.P.M. Two V-type cylinders, sizes 4 x 3, 2¼ x 3 air cooled. Maximum pressure 200 pounds. Motor 2 H.P. General Electric. Tank 76 gallon capacity; size 20 x 60. Unit furnished complete with V-belt Drive, Automatic Switch, ECO-MATIC Tank Drainer and 25 ft. Air Hose complete with fittings. Shipping weight, 750 lbs.

MODEL SK-765 Single stage, water cooled, heavy duty outfit. Displacement 23½ cu. ft. 430 R.P.M. Two cylinders, sizes 3⅞ x 4. Maximum pressure 150 pounds. Motor 5 H.P. General Electric. Tank 77 gallon capacity, size 20 x 60. Furnished complete with V-belt Drive, Automatic Switch and ECO-MATIC Tank Drainer.

ECO CAR WASHERS

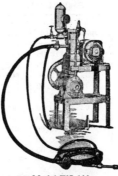

Model WS-110

···Standard and Heavy Duty 1-2-4 Gun Piston Type, Self-Oiling Units

Model WS-110—One Gun Standard 1¾ x 1½ Duplex Pump. 133 R.P.M. 4.12 gal. displacement per minute. 1 H.P. General Electric Motor. Complete with V-belt Drive, Automatic Regulator maintaining constant pressure of 300 lbs. 1 gun and hose, 6 ft. suction hose and strainer and 4 ft. intake hose for connection to water supply line.

Write for BULLETINS

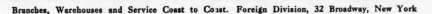

SERVICE STATION EQUIPMENT COMPANY
Main Office: Conshohocken, Pa. (Suburb of Philadelphia)

Precision Made
ECO
Automotive
Servicing Equipment

Branches, Warehouses and Service Coast to Coast. Foreign Division, 32 Broadway, New York

BEAR ALIGNMENT
makes the BIG profit!
WHEEL ALIGNMENT *stops*
Shimmy, Hard-steering, Tire Wear

Many garages making over $500 a month from alignment alone—some over $1,000! Half the cars on the road need this service. The Bear System is complete. Bear gauges—simple, accurate, easy to operate—check *every alignment angle*, show your customer what is wrong, make it easy to sell the job.

Bear Tools lick every job where others fall down—make *every car* steer and handle like new and return them to factory specifications.

The Bear Axle Press straightens bent and *twisted* axles cold, *in the car;* a one man job that takes two hours or less! Average job only 30 minutes.

Illustration shows Bear Axle Press No. 83 mounted on new Bear Florack which eliminates use of pit and requires no floor space when in use. Weight approximately 300 lbs.

SET UP FOR CORRECTING CAMBER

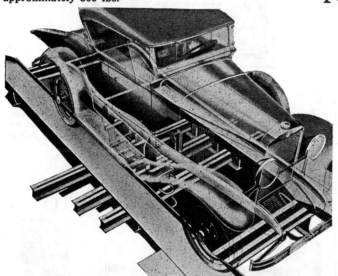

NEW FRAME STRAIGHTENER

This new addition to the Bear Line straightens swayed, diamond shaped, bent and buckled frames *in the car*. The Bear Frame Straightener is of heavy, durable construction, weighing 3,200 pounds. Two parallel 14-inch runways, each 17 feet long, are 24 inches from the floor, giving elevation sufficient for easy access to all under-chassis parts. Large enough for all cars and ordinary trucks.

Three pairs of sliding brackets holding transverse I-beams hang from the runways. On these vertical abutments are mounted. All are easily adjustable, yet an ingenious "kink-lock" arrangement holds brackets and beams immovable when pressure is applied. The actual bending pressure is applied to the frame with powerful hydraulic jacks.

Two transverse channel irons are built into the front end of the Bear Frame Straightener on which the Bear Axle Press may be mounted.

THESE ARE THE TOOLS YOU NEED!!

With the Bear Frame Straightener and Bear Axle Press No. 83, any required straightening operation on either frame or axle is done cold without any dismounting or dis-assembly work whatever.

Straightening Equipment
Bear Frame Straightener
Bear Axle Press No. 83
Bear Bending Tools

Supplies
Special Garage Assortment of Bear Shims, 16 dozen.
Bear Wheel Balancing Lugs, 2 dozen
No. 4 for wood wheels, and 2 dozen
No. 4-A for wire wheels. 2 dozen
No. 4-B for wood and wire wheels.

Gauges
Bear Wheel Aligner No. 10 with Templet
Bear Axle Gauge No. 40
Bear Tracking Gauge No. 50
Bear Axle Straightening Gauge No. 70
Rod and Cone Attachments for Ford A
Bear Spindle Gauge No. 2
Bear Wheel Balancer No. 3
Bear Spindle Arm Gauge No. 5
Bear Pedal Depressor
Bear Measuring Rods No. 5-A

This represents complete equipment for the average garage and general repair shop. For heavy duty, wide gauge trucks and large buses some extra heavy Bear equipment must be added.

We also make the Bear Teete-rack—an all purpose rack equipped for Alignment, Brake Adjusting, Washing, Greasing and all Under-Chassis work.

Ask Your Jobber Salesman

BEAR MANUFACTURING COMPANY
Rock Island, Illinois

New Model
South Bend Back-Geared Screw Cutting Precision Lathes

96 Sizes and Types

South Bend Lathes are made in sizes 9″ to 24″ swing with 3′ to 12′ bed lengths and may be had with countershaft or motor drive, in tool room, production and gap bed types. Below are listed a few popular models

9″ x 3′ Junior Back-Geared, Screw Cutting, Precision Lathe, made in 2½′, 3′, 3½′, 4′ and 4½′ bed lengths with bench or floor legs in both countershaft and motor drive types. Lathe will cut screw threads, true commutators, reface valves, make bushings, finish pistons, and do hundreds of other jobs. *Weight 375 lbs.*

Complete with Countershaft and Equipment, Price . . **\$169**
Payments: \$33.80 Down, Balance \$11.83 a Month for 12 Mos.

16″ x 6′ Quick Change Back-Geared, Screw Cutting, Precision Lathe made in 6′, 7′, 8′, 10′ and 12′ bed lengths, with countershaft or motor drive, in standard change, tool room and gap bed types. Used by thousands of plants and shops all over the world.

Complete with Countershaft and Equipment, Weight 1,875 lbs., Price **\$598**

Easy Payments: \$119.60 Down, Balance \$41.86 a Month for 12 Mos.

18″ x 8′ Motor Driven Quick Change, Back-Geared, Screw Cutting, Precision Lathe, furnished in 6′, 7′, 8′, 10′, 12′ and 14′ bed lengths; also furnished in countershaft drive and in standard change, tool room, production and gap bed types. Handles large and small work equally well — the practical size for flywheel and ring gear replacement work.

Complete with Reversing Motor, Reversing Switch and Regular Lathe Equipment, Weight 3,240 lbs., Price . . . **\$997**
Payments: \$199.40 Down and \$69.79 a Month for 12 Mos.

Brake Drum Lathe, Motor Drive — A standard change, back-geared, screw cutting lathe; handles all wheel and brake drum work for passenger cars, buses and trucks without removing tires; also does flywheel and ring gear replacement work as well as hundreds of other regular lathe jobs; cuts screw threads 4 to 40 per inch. Can be had fitted with quick change gear box and with either countershaft or motor drive. *Easy Payments if desired.*

36″ x 6′ Size Handles Wheels 36″ in Diameter, Price . . . **\$867**

WRITE FOR THESE BOOKS

"How to Run a Lathe," 25c
Latest Edition, contains 160 pages, with more than 300 illustrations. Most complete and practical book on lathe operation. Shows how to handle 400 different types of lathe jobs as practiced in the modern machine shop. Furnished in either English or Spanish language. Sent postpaid for only 25 cents; coin or stamps of any country accepted.

Auto Mechanics' Service Book No. 66—25c postpaid
This 96 page book, with 200 illustrations, describes the correct and most practical way to do 60 automobile service jobs that come to the shop. A valuable book for any mechanic.

Catalog No. 91-A—Free
This 104 page book illustrates and describes the 96 different sizes and types of New Model South Bend Lathes. Also printed in Spanish language. Sent free postpaid upon request.

South Bend Lathe Works

373 East Madison Street, South Bend, Indiana, U. S. A.
Lathe Builders for 24 Years — Over 50,000 South Bend Lathes in Use

---

PEXTO
BODY AND FENDER TOOLS

SPECIALLY DESIGNED FOR THE MODERN ALL-STEEL BODIES

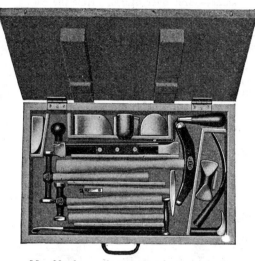

No. 22, the perfect Assortment, packed in the popular PEXTO Wood Case.

To profitably realize in full upon the requirements for auto body and fender repairs the mechanic must be equipped with modern tools adequate for this type of work. Set No. 22 serves this purpose and affords both a modern and practical assortment of body and fender tools.

Size of case, 23½″x14½″x3¾″. Weight complete, 37 lbs.
List per assortment, including case, \$27.35
Other PEXTO Sets and Assortments priced from \$8.80 to \$25.00

Original Designs by PEXTO

No. 9990MP
Multi-Purpose Block
List each \$2.50

No. 9300
Corner Dolly Block
List each \$1.80

These Dolly Blocks are forged steel, hardened, ground and polished. With these two blocks nearly all body and fender dent removing work can be accomplished.

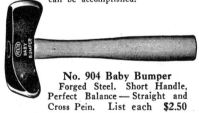

No. 904 Baby Bumper
Forged Steel. Short Handle, Perfect Balance — Straight and Cross Pein. List each \$2.50

In addition to a large variety of Body and Fender Tools, featuring the latest improved designs of the industry, the Pexto line includes pliers, screw drivers, braces, squares, hammers, wrenches and many other Mechanics' Hand Tools.   *Write for Booklet No. 28*

THE PECK, STOW & WILCOX CO.
SOUTHINGTON, CONN., U. S. A.

PREST-O-WELD
Welding Equipment and Supplies

The Prest-O-Weld Type W-105-A Auto Repair Outfit will efficiently fill the many needs of the service station for oxy-acetylene welding and heating equipment. The cost is so reasonable that a few jobs will pay for it. Any good mechanic can readily learn to use it effectively for the wide range of profitable jobs that can be done by welding in the repair and maintenance of automobiles.

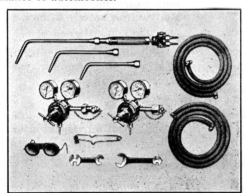

Type W-105-A Auto Repair Outfit

This outfit consists of:

1 Type W-105 Welding Blowpipe with Nos. 6, 8 and 10 Tips, Friction Lighter, and Wrench.
1 R-106 Oxygen Regulator with 50-lb. and 3000-lb. gauges and Wrench.
1 R-107 Acetylene Regulator with 30-lb. and 350-lb. gauges.
12½ feet ¼ in. red Acetylene Hose.
12½ feet ¼ in. green oxygen Hose.
4 ¼ in. Hose Clamps.
1 Pair No. 8 Spectacles.
1 Instruction Manual.
Price $55.00

The Prest-O-Weld Type W-105 Welding Blowpipe which is featured in this outfit represents an entirely new idea in blowpipe design. It has a detachable valve body to which the handle is attached by an ingenious but simple locking device. This design enables the operator to change easily and quickly to a smaller welding blowpipe handle, to a cutting attachment or to a full size cutting blowpipe without detaching the hose or hose connections and without the use of a wrench.

Useful additions available for the outfit include the W-105 to W-107 Stem Tip Adaptor, which offers an economical means of increasing the range of the Prest-O-Weld Type W-105 Welding Blowpipe in the lighter welding field, and the

Two-Wheel Truck which makes the outfit, including oxygen and acetylene cylinders, easy to move about the shop. The prices of these are:

W-105 to W-107 Stem Tip Adaptor

Type W-105 Blowpipe Stem Adaptor for
W-107 Aircraft Blowpipe Tips....$ 1.50
Prest-O-Weld Two-Wheel Truck with
14-inch wheels 18.00
With 24-inch wheels............. 21.00

The Service Station doing the average type of repair and maintenance welding will find it useful to keep on hand moderate stocks of the following supplies:

Two-Wheel Truck

Oxweld No. 7 Drawn Iron Welding Rod
Oxweld No. 13 Drawn Brass Welding Rod
Oxweld No. 21 H. S. Bronze Welding Rod
Oxweld No. 9 Cast Iron Alloy Welding Rod
Oxweld No. 23 Aluminum Welding Rod
Oxweld Ferro Flux (for cast iron)
Oxweld Brazo Flux (for bronze welding)

Prest-O-Weld Equipment and Supplies

Prest-O-Weld apparatus and supplies are made by the largest manufacturers of welding and cutting equipment in the world. The quarter-century of manufacturing experience behind Prest-O-Weld equipment is a guarantee of economy and absolute dependability.

Your Prest-O-Weld jobber can supply you with Prest-O-Weld regulators and blowpipes for every range of welding and cutting operations. He also carries a full stock of Prest-O-Weld accessories and supplies, including goggles, gloves, oxygen and acetylene hose, and hose connections, as well as Prest-O-Weld blowpipe stems and tips, cutting nozzles, regulator gauges and spark lighters.

Inspect the Prest-O-Weld line at your jobbers— or write us for complete information and prices.

Sold by Prest-O-Weld Jobbers Everywhere

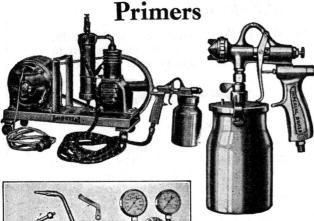
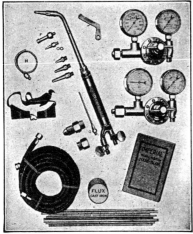

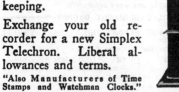

MORE SALES INFORMATION
by other companies

given on the following pages—

MANUFACTURER'S REPRESENTATIVES

OR

WAREHOUSE ACCOUNTS

We Solicit Additional Non-competitive Accounts

Parts manufacturers will find it profitable to use our sales and distributing warehouse facilities in the Metropolitan territory. We are district representatives and carry a warehouse stock for these manufacturers:

Whitney Manufacturing Co.
(Timing Chains)
Hartford, Conn.

U. S. Axle Co.
(Axle Shafts)
Pottstown, Penna.

Roller Bearing Co. of America
Trenton, N. J.

Multibestos Company
Cambridge, Mass.

Bearings Company of America
Lancaster, Pa.

Timing Gears Corporation
Cy-lent Gears
Chicago, Ill.

We offer to a limited number of parts manufacturers a service equal to that rendered our present accounts, consisting of factory sales representation and the carrying of warehouse stocks; coverage of the Metropolitan territory, part of Connecticut, and New Jersey; and several hundred Jobber accounts who regularly purchase through us.

We shall be pleased to hear from any interested manufacturer.

Est. 1921

L. C. Biglow & Company, Inc.
250 West 54th St.
NEW YORK CITY

AVBVRN

Powered by Lycoming

1931's Greatest Dealer Opportunity

Auburn dealers have the unique advantage of offering five new models on a new chassis; with more than sixty new features, improvements, and advantages, many of which are not obtainable on any other car; at new and lower prices creating Greater Value than has even been known in the history of the industry. Such extraordinary sales features and advantages offer alert dealers their greatest opportunity to build a profitable business. Complete line Auburn cars $945 to $1345. Prices f.o.b. Connersville, Ind.

CORD

FRONT-DRIVE

Out of approximately 44 different makes of American automobiles, the Cord offers the exclusive advantages of Front-Drive. In a time of less than two years, the Cord has assumed the position of fine car leadership. Now that a Cord is available at the extremely low new price of $2395, the market for the Cord is greatly widened, and the dealer opportunity markedly increased. Prices f.o.b. Auburn, Ind.

AUBURN AUTOMOBILE COMPANY
Auburn, Indiana

Armored Car Bodies

Descriptive bulletins and prices are already waiting for your inquiry.

NATIONAL
steel
Dumping Bodies

Are available in every model and type to fit correctly every size of chassis you sell.

Your customer receives an unconditional guarantee for one year. Should any part of a National body or hoist prove defective it will be replaced without question.

The same guarantee goes with all the automotive equipment that we manufacture.

National Steel Products Co.
1611 Crystal Ave.   Kansas City, Mo.

GENERAL
Automotive
REFERENCE SECTION

Including

Data on Markets and Merchandising—Registration and Sales—Trade
Outlets—Production—Design—Historical Data—Shop Equipment—
Tires—Fleet Operation—Aviation—Export and Foreign Markets.

(See Detailed Index to Contents, pages 7, 9)

6,962 Used Car Sales Are Analyzed*

Only Cars Sold Within Thirty Days Turn a Profit

Per Cent of Cars	Carried in Stock	Percentage of Total Loss
71	Less than 30 days	Profit
15	30 to 60 days	14
6	60 to 90 days	18
8	Over 90 days	68

Quick Sales Assure a Minimum of Expense

Carried in Stock	No. of Times in Shop	Reconditioning Expense
Under 30 days	1	$11.03
30-60 days	1½	29.11
60-90 days	2	36.48
Over 90 days	3	44.16

*Based on accumulated data from Standard Accounting System established among its dealers by Chevrolet Motor Car Co.

Prompt Reconditioning Helps Move Used Cars

Time Interval Before End of First Reconditioning	Days Carried in Stock
4 days	30 days or less
12 days	30-60 days
24 days	60-90 days
32 days	Over 90 days

Delayed Attention Creates Sure Losses

Days in Stock	Days Before Reconditioning	No. of Times in Shop	Gross Loss
321	233	7	102.16
141	41	9	38.29
361	50	7	141.02
286	55	4	91.16
180	29	7	96.37
179	66	5	69.67
130	87	3	89.13

Data From National Retail Credit Survey—1930

	CASH SALES Per Cent of Total	OPEN-CREDIT SALES Per Cent of Total	Per Cent with Credit Losses Less than 1%	INSTALLMENT SALES Per Cent of Total	Per Cent with Credit Losses Less than 1%
569 Automobile Dealers	37.1	16.0	46.4[1]	46.9	82.1
678 Accessory Dealers	53.8	44.5	42.9[2]	1.7	54.4

[1]Only 489 automobile dealers reported open-credit sales losses.
[2]Only 494 accessory dealers reported open-credit sales losses.

Sales Data by States for

COMPILED BY RESEARCH DEPARTMENT OF CHILTON CLASS

	State	Total Population Government Estimate (1930)	Income Tax Paid Millions of Dollars (1930)	No. of Towns with Wholesalers	DISTRIBUTION OF POPULATION BY SIZE OF COMMUNITY										
					Rural and Up to 2,500		2,500—10,000		10,000—100,000		100,000-500,000		Over 500,000		
					No. of Places	Per Cent of State	No. of Places	Per Cent of State	No. of Places	Per Cent of State	No. of Places	Per Cent of State	No. of Places	Per Cent of State	
1	Alabama..................	2,646,248	5,464	15	243	71.9	39	6.2	13	12.1	1	9.8	......	......	1
2	Arizona.................	435,573	3,033	.7	20	65.6	12	15.9	2	18.5	....	....	......	......	2
3	Arkansas................	1,854,482	2,748	10	340	79.4	40	8.7	9	11.9	....	....	......	......	3
4	California...............	5,677,251	110,646	87	125	27.6	106	9.5	42	19.8	3	10.1	2	33.0	4
5	Colorado................	1,035,791	14,721	18	214	49.8	19	8.9	7	13.5	1	27.8	......	......	5
6	Connecticut.............	1,606,903	46,830	19	12	35.0	9	3.1	17	32.5	3	29.4	......	......	6
7	Delaware................	238,380	46,084	2	47	48.3	4	7.0	....	....	1	44.6	......	......	7
8	Dist. of Columbia........	486,869	*	1	....	....	....	....	....	....	1	100.0	......	......	8
9	Florida.................	1,468,211	9,707	23	231	48.3	44	13.7	11	14.8	3	23.2	......	......	9
10	Georgia.................	2,908,506	9,060	17	529	69.2	49	7.9	14	13.6	1	9.3	......	......	10
11	Idaho...................	445,032	794	8	129	70.9	19	20.6	2	8.5	....	....	......	......	11
12	Illinois.................	7,630,654	214,640	61	937	26.1	134	8.8	56	19.5	1	1.4	1	44.2	12
13	Indiana.................	3,238,503	22,150	42	428	44.5	61	9.2	29	22.0	5	24.3	......	......	13
14	Iowa...................	2,470,939	11,348	30	836	60.4	60	10.6	20	23.2	1	5.8	......	......	14
15	Kansas..................	1,880,999	17,753	37	518	61.2	42	10.0	18	16.4	2	12.4	......	......	15
16	Kentucky...............	2,614,589	14,373	17	316	69.4	40	7.6	12	11.2	1	11.8	......	......	16
17	Louisiana...............	2,101,593	9,141	14	162	60.3	40	8.3	7	9.6	1	21.8	......	......	17
18	Maine..................	797,423	7,925	11	22	59.7	17	11.7	9	28.6	....	....	......	......	18
19	Maryland..............	1,631,526	48,768*	8	116	40.2	15	3.9	5	6.5	....	....	1	49.4	19
20	Massachusetts...........	4,249,614	106,848	37	177	4.7	105	12.8	64	40.7	8	23.4	1	18.4	20
21	Michigan................	4,842,325	127,332	48	361	31.8	74	7.6	37	21.5	2	6.7	1	32.4	21
22	Minnesota...............	2,563,953	26,069	14	654	51.0	59	10.2	11	6.2	3	32.6	......	......	22
23	Mississippi..............	2,009,821	2,043	15	273	83.0	27	5.2	13	11.8	....	....	......	......	23
24	Missouri................	3,629,367	49,550	29	701	48.8	56	7.6	14	10.0	1	11.0	1	22.6	24
25	Montana................	537,606	2,193	9	98	66.3	12	10.6	6	23.1	....	....	......	......	25
26	Nebraska...............	1,377,963	5,106	22	494	64.7	27	8.6	7	11.2	1	15.5	......	......	26
27	Nevada.................	91,058	1,371	1	11	62.2	4	17.5	1	20.3	....	....	......	......	27
28	New Hampshire..........	465,293	3,255	8	214	33.7	20	16.8	10	49.5	....	....	......	......	28
29	New Jersey..............	4,041,334	93,523	38	171	22.6	103	13.3	49	33.0	6	31.1	......	......	29
30	New Mexico.............	423,317	736	5	40	74.8	13	13.7	3	11.5	....	....	......	......	30
31	New York...............	12,588,066	791,277	83	400	16.6	126	4.7	62	12.0	5	7.1	2	59.6	31
32	North Carolina..........	3,170,276	15,566	26	430	74.5	47	6.8	21	18.7	....	....	......	......	32
33	North Dakota............	680,845	433	7	314	83.4	8	5.9	4	10.7	....	....	......	......	33
34	Ohio....................	6,646,697	124,386	74	689	32.3	114	8.8	51	18.8	7	26.6	1	13.5	34
35	Oklahoma...............	2,396,040	17,333	31	444	65.7	52	11.2	14	9.5	2	13.6	......	......	35
36	Oregon..................	953,786	4,988	18	176	48.7	22	11.0	5	8.7	1	31.6	......	......	36
37	Pennsylvania............	9,631,350	215,330	87	641	34.4	252	13.2	87	21.4	3	3.8	2	27.2	37
38	Rhode Island............	687,497	14,036	6	12	2.5	13	10.0	13	50.7	1	36.8	......	......	38
39	South Carolina...........	1,738,765	2,509	12	225	78.7	31	7.8	9	13.5	....	....	......	......	39
40	South Dakota............	692,849	902	7	283	81.1	10	5.6	6	13.3	....	....	......	......	40
41	Tennessee...............	2,616,556	11,051	12	185	65.7	40	7.4	4	2.7	4	24.2	......	......	41
42	Texas...................	5,824,715	36,890	48	421	59.0	123	10.1	31	12.8	5	18.1	......	......	42
43	Utah...................	507,847	2,892	5	122	47.6	18	14.0	2	10.8	1	27.6	......	......	43
44	Vermont................	359,611	2,127	9	61	67.0	11	18.2	3	14.8	....	....	......	......	44
45	Virginia.................	2,421,851	18,259	18	170	67.6	31	6.1	12	13.4	2	12.9	......	......	45
46	Washington..............	1,563,396	14,147	19	183	43.4	23	5.9	12	13.1	3	37.6	......	......	46
47	West Virginia............	1,729,205	9,441	16	169	71.6	29	8.5	10	19.9	....	....	......	......	47
48	Wisconsin...............	2,939,006	32,718	26	419	47.1	56	9.2	26	24.0	....	....	1	19.7	48
49	Wyoming................	225,565	642	5	76	68.9	6	16.0	2	15.1	....	....	......	......	49
	U. S.................	122,775,046	2,332,968	1,162	13,731	44.1	2,262	8.9	862	17.4	80	12.6	13	17.0	

* Maryland includes income for Dist. of Columbia.

The data here in tabular form are ready for many uses. The 12 subjects on which figures are given will help you measure your markets, analyze your position with respect to the average in your state and indicate the direction of changes to make in your business to put you in line to meet the conditions in the current market and make plans for the future.

The data here, by themselves and combined with other related data elsewhere in this book, will enable you to compare your operations with the average for stores of your kind and size and you can thus see where you

Analyzing Markets and Planning Sales

JOURNAL COMPANY FOR CHILTON AUTOMOTIVE GUIDE

	Total Miles of Surface Highways (Excluding City Streets) (1930)	Registration of Motor Vehicles (1930)		Approximate Sales of Motor Vehicles (1930)		No. of Passenger Car Dealers*	No. of Whole-salers*	No. of Repair Shops*	No. of Motor Vehicles per Repair Shop.	No. of Retail Accessory Stores*	1930 Gasoline Consumption in Gallons† (Add 000)	Gasoline Tax per Gallon (Cents)	
		Passenger Cars	Trucks Including Buses	Passenger Cars	Trucks								
1	18,369	238,105	39,022	26,400	6,200	458	44	899	308	843	172,537	4	1
2	3,597	98,147	13,476	9,300	1,900	205	26	392	284	403	76,044	4	2
3	7,958	191,033	26,986	20,000	3,500	425	24	691	335	832	138,632	5	3
4	25,381	1,974,429	99,387(d)	190,900	26,900	2,107	371	6,741	307	5,812	1,335,556	3	4
5	7,157	276,847	31,662	27,700	5,800	618	59	1,316	235	996	170,855	4	5
6	3,572	297,781	49,709	42,800	5,900	619	90	1,281	271	1,100	223,297	2	6
7	1,180	45,533	10,523	7,500	1,200	74	7	152	368	111	35,997	3	7
8	....	154,238	19,196	20,700	1,800	62	22	214	808	116	80,538	2	8
0	15,123	277,210	52,596	32,800	6,100	461	81	1,103	299	1,091	227,037	6	9
10	14,831	294,461	46,716	28,600	5,000	575	58	1,169	292	755	224,188	6	10
11	8,884	102,706	15,563	10,600	2,400	314	28	516	233	490	61,262	5	11
12	21,375	1,429,146	209,114	169,000	20,100	2,907	268	5,948	276	4,290	973,208	3	12
13	51,314	746,354	129,097	72,300	10,500	1,494	153	3,198	274	3,004	445,016	4	13
14	18,021	709,985	72,190	79,700	10,000	1,904	108	3,267	240	2,475	390,826	3	14
15	5,685	511,384	83,139	46,300	9,300	1,482	91	2,573	231	1,943	386,755	3	15
16	17,030	294,178	36,486	35,900	5,400	771	56	1,566	212	1,218	168,278	5	16
17	11,152	229,086	44,697	27,100	4,700	394	54	842	335	744	184,774	5	17
18	5,777	147,791	33,557	18,600	4,500	443	31	916	198	327	108,679	4	18
19	5,704	283,120	38,060	38,100	6,000	516	54	958	335	688	182,348	4	19
20	9,324	745,064	107,058	108,100	13,700	1,247	188	2,743	311	1,471	536,083	2	20
21	25,143	1,161,051	167,158	143,400	15,800	2,128	164	4,140	321	3,853	792,776	3	21
22	35,501	618,661	108,361	69,100	10,300	1,835	87	3,050	238	2,899	401,440	3	22
23	16,112	203,312	33,782	21,300	5,500	481	29	847	303	841	135,239	5	23
24	13,074	671,920	91,455	89,400	14,800	1,372	148	3,150	242	1,824	445,227	2	24
25	3,437	111,089	25,807	12,000	2,600	455	33	784	175	686	77,476	5	25
26	5,364	367,410	58,819	42,800	7,000	1,232	64	1,922	222	1,457	228,898	4	26
27	2,237	23,388	6,257	3,600	600	118	4	174	170	166	18,615	4	27
28	2,784	93,155	18,398	11,200	2,300	275	15	597	187	354	64,743	4	28
29	9,077	711,527	138,888	101,600	14,800	1,396	136	3,527	241	2,471	547,977	3	29
30	2,539	74,900	15,800	7,400	2,000	196	8	387	234	387	54,661	5	30
31	32,713	1,920,255	396,569	275,600	38,700	3,590	499	8,472	273	4,982	1,511,997	2	31
32	29,649	412,042	62,259	35,000	6,500	716	68	1,617	294	1,292	250,669	5	32
33	3,592	155,383	27,636	13,300	2,400	770	15	1,046	175	1,021	120,034	3	33
34	48,503	1,549,077	204,058	163,900	20,100	2,855	329	6,383	282	5,064	975,582	4	34
35	4,774	490,947	59,384	55,000	8,100	893	74	1,769	311	1,436	323,112	4	35
36	12,123	233,787(e)	24,360(e)	22,900	4,200	507	70	1,429	181	1,166	170,169	4	36
37	26,145	1,528,721	244,497	206,200	30,100	3,617	343	7,037	251	5,651	928,842	3	37
38	1,025	115,176	20,691	16,300	2,100	217	33	529	257	409	88,832	2	38
39	17,576	195,210	26,456	19,300	3,700	344	35	807	274	586	119,213	6	39
40	6,147	180,000	24,306	19,000	3,100	710	22	1,174	174	964	140,580	4	40
41	15,184	332,417	40,126	39,000	5,100	574	55	1,333	306	1,088	215,244	5	41
42	26,012	1,152,904	206,639	124,100	22,200	2,079	201	5,293	257	3,685	806,505	4	42
43	4,237	93,628	17,369	10,600	2,200	227	27	517	215	472	60,137	3½	43
44	4,983	78,260	8,364	9,100	1,700	244	18	625	139	211	46,998	4	44
45	12,327	319,061	62,872	46,200	8,900	830	61	1,947	195	1,525	228,453	5	45
46	16,718	388,719	63,792	39,200	6,700	822	134	2,291	197	1,970	271,167	3	46
47	4,450	225,101	41,031	29,400	4,600	690	62	1,545	172	1,322	140,411	4	47
48	27,815	677,963	110,539	74,700	12,100	2,161	113	3,306	239	3,117	437,878	2	48
49	1,760	51,579	9,922	5,000	1,200	248	8	373	165	372	36,615	4	49
	662,435	23,183,241	3,473,831	2,718,000	410,300	48,625	4,668	102,556	260	79,980	15,761,400		

d—Includes only trucks weighing over 3,000 lb.
e—Change in fiscal year from Jan. 1 to July 1.

*—From 1931 Chilton Trade List.
†—Figures from American Petroleum Institute.

are weak or strong and readjust yourself on the basis of such data.

Here you can compare sales per capita in passenger cars in your state with similar sales per capita in other states to see if your state is behind or ahead in consumption.

You can see also the number of potential customers upon whom you can draw for business and you can estimate their probable annual purchase of your merchandise or service and thus see if you are getting all the business that ought properly to come to a store like yours in your territory.

BIRTH DATES of Automobiles

To Find Any Name, Look Down All Names Under That Letter of the Alphabet, as Names Beginning With A, are Arranged by Year, Etc. Also, See Footnote

99 AUTOCAR	01 CRESTMOBILE	20 DUPONT	06 HEWITT	03 MOHAWK	08 PALMER-SINGER	09 SELLERS
01 AJAX	01 CONRAD	21 DRIGGS	07 HALLADAY	02 MOYEA	08 PATERSON	09 SEBRING
01 AMERICAN	01 COTTA	21 DURANT	07 HATFIELD	04 MAHONING	08 PONTIAC	09 SPOERER
01 APPERSON	01 COVERT	25 DIANA	08 HEINE VELOX	04 MAXWELL	09 PAIGE	09 STERLING
01 AUTOMOTOR	02 CADILLAC	28 DESOTO	08 HUPP	04 MERCURY	09 PETREL	10 S. G. V.
03 AUBURN	02 CENTAUR	31 DE VAUX	09 HERRESHOFF	05 MARION	11 PATHFINDER	11 STAFFORD
03 AUTO VEHICLE	02 CLARKMOBILE		09 HOUPT	05 MARSH	11 PENN	11 STEARNS-KNIGHT
04 ACME	02 CLEVELAND	01 ELMORE	09 HUDSON	05 MOLINE	11 PICKARD	11 STODDARD KNIGHT
04 ADAMS FARWELL	03 CAMERON	01 ESSEX	11 HAVERS	06 MARVEL	11 PILOT	11 STUYVESANT
04 AMERICAN MERCEDES	03 CHELSEA	02 ECLIPSE	12 HENDERSON	06 METEOR	11 PRATT	12 STUTZ
04 AUSTIN	03 CHURCH	03 ELDRIDGE	14 HERFF-BROOKS	06 MONARCH	12 PERFEX	14 SAXON
05 ARDSLEY	03 CLOUGHLEY	05 EAGLE	15 HACKETT	06 MOON	13 PARTIN-PALMER	14 SCRIPPS-BOOTH
06 AEROCAR	03 CORBIN	08 E-M-F	15 HARVARD	06 MOORE	16 PILGRIM	14 SPHYNX
06 AMERICAN MORS	04 COMPOUND	08 EARL	16 H. A. L.	06 MUNCIE	17 PAN AMERICAN	15 SUN
07 ALBANY	04 COURIER	09 ENGER	16 HARROUN	07 MORA	19 PIEDMONT	16 STEPHENS
07 ATLAS	05 CHADWICK	09 EVERITT	16 HOLLIER	08 MARYLAND	19 PORTER	17 SAYERS
08 ALLEN KINGSTON	05 CRAWFORD	12 EDWARDS-KNIGHT	16 HOMER LAUGHLIN	08 McCUE	26 PONTIAC	17 SENECA
08 AMERICAN SIMPLEX	05 CULVER	14 EMPIRE	18 HOLMES	08 MIDLAND	28 PLYMOUTH	17 STANDARD EIGHT
09 ABBOTT DETROIT	06 CRAIG TOLEDO	16 ELCAR	20 H. C. S.	08 MIER	05 QUEEN	18 STATES
09 ALCO	07 COLBURN	16 ELGIN	20 HANSON	09 MARATHON	00 RAMBLER	19 SPACKE
09 ANCHOR	07 CONTINENTAL	17 ESSEX	21 HANDLEY-KNIGHT	09 MASON	03 REBER	20 SKELTON
10 AMPLEX	07 COSMOPOLITAN	21 EARL	22 HUFFMAN	09 McINTYRE	03 REGAS	20 STANWOOD
11 ALPENA	07 CROWN HIGH WHEEL	26 ERSKINE	00 IMPERIAL	09 MERCER	03 RUSSELL	21 SHERIDAN
11 ATLAS KNIGHT	08 CHALMERS	01 FOSTER	01 INTERNATIONAL	09 METZ	04 RELIANCE	22 STAR
14 ALLEN	08 COATES GOSHEN	02 FANNING	03 IROQUOIS	10 McFARLAND	04 REO	23 STERLING KNIGHT
16 ANDERSON	08 CORREJA	02 FLINT	08 INTER-STATE	11 MARQUETTE	04 ROYAL TOURIST	00 THOMSON
20 ACE	09 COLE	02 FRANKLIN	99 JACKSON	11 MOTORETTE	05 RAINIER	01 TAUNTON
21 AMBASSADOR	09 COURIER	02 FREDONIA	00 JEFFERY	12 B. & F. MOYER	08 REEVES	02 THOMAS
25 AJAX	09 CROXTON KEETON	02 FRIEDMAN	03 JAXON	13 MOLINE KNIGHT	08 REGAL	02 TWYFORD
30 AUSTIN	09 CUTTING	03 FORD	06 JEWELL	15 MADISON	08 RICHMOND	03 TINCHER
00 BOLTE	10 CASE	04 FRAYER-MILLER	08 JENKINS	15 MECCA	08 RIDER-LEWIS	11 TRIUMPH
01 BACHELLES	11 CARHARTT	06 FEDERAL	11 JONZ	15 MONITOR	11 R. C. H.	12 TOURAINE
01 BALDNER	11 COEY	07 FIRESTONE-COLUMBUS	16 JONES	15 MONROE	11 RAYFIELD	13 TRIBUNE
01 BUCKEYE	11 COLBY	08 FARMOBILE	16 JORDAN	16 MAIBOHM	11 REPUBLIC	14 TRUMBULL
01 BUFFALO	11 CORBITT	08 FULLER	22 JEWETT	16 MARION HANDLEY	11 ROADER	14 TWOMBLY
02 BERG	11 CROW-ELKHART	09 F-A-L CAR	00 KNOX	16 MURRAY	11 ROGERS	17 TULSA
02 BRECHT	11 CUNNINGHAM	10 FLANDERS	03 KENSINGTON	20 MERIT	13 READ	18 TEMPLAR
02 BUFFUM	12 CRANE	11 FIAT	03 KONIGSLOW	29 MARQUETTE	15 ROSS	22 TARKINGTON
03 BARTHOLOMEW	12 CHEVROLET	11 FOUR WHEEL DRIVE	06 KISSEL	02 NORTHERN	16 ROAMER	02 UNION
03 BLACKHAWK	13 CHANDLER	14 F.R.P.	09 KENMORE	03 NATIONAL	18 REVERE	02 UPTON
03 BLOOD	17 COMET	15 FARMACK	09 KLINE	03 NIAGARA	20 R & V KNIGHT	08 VIKING
03 BRAMWELL	17 COMMONWEALTH	17 FAGEOL	09 K-R-I-T	12 NORWALK	20 RALEIGH	09 VELIE
03 BRAZIER	19 CLEVELAND	17 FERGUS	10 KING	12 NYBERG	20 ROCK FALLS	11 VIRGINIAN
03 BRISTOL	20 CLIMBER	20 FERRIS	14 KERNS	17 NASH	21 ROLLS-ROYCE	13 VULCAN
03 BUCKMOBILE	22 COURIER	20 FRIEND	16 KENT	17 NELSON	22 RICKENBACKER	14 VIXEN
04 BATES	24 CHRYSLER	21 FOX	20 KENWORTHY	19 NOMA	22 RUBAY	21 VOGUE
04 BREW & HATCHER	29 CORD	23 FLINT	21 KURTZ	97 OLDSMOBILE	23 ROLLIN	29 VIKING
04 BUICK	95 DURYEA	26 FALCON-KNIGHT	22 KELSEY	98 OAKMAN	29 ROOSEVELT	97 WINTON
05 BERKSHIRE	00 DETROIT	99 GROUT	00 LOOMIS	00 ORIENT	30 RUXTON	01 WARWICK
05 BLOMSTROM	00 DYKE	00 GASMOBILE	02 LAW	03 OVERLAND	99 ST. LOUIS	01 WOODS
05 BREEZE & LAWRENCE	01 DESBERON	00 GURLEY	02 LOCOMOBILE	07 OAKLAND	00 SPAULDING	02 WICK
06 BLISS	02 DAVENPORT	02 GAETHMOBILE	02 LONG DISTANCE	07 OKEY	00 STEARNS	03 WARD LEONARD
07 BAY STATE	03 DARROW	03 GENERAL	02 LOZIER	08 OWEN THOMAS	01 SEARCHMONT	03 WELCH
07 BELDEN	03 DECKER	03 GLIDE	04 LAMBERT	09 OHIO	01 SMITH & MABLEY	03 WHITNEY
07 BRUSH	04 DOLSON	03 GRAHAM-FOX	04 LOGAN	09 OTTO	02 SANDUSKY	04 WAYNE
08 BENDIX	06 DEERE	03 GREELEY	04 LYMAN	12 OMAHA	02 STEVENS-DURYEA	04 WOLVERINE
08 BENNER	06 DE SHAW	04 GALE	05 LA PETITE	14 OWEN	03 SHAIN	07 WOLF
08 BLACK	06 DORRIS	07 GARFORD	06 LUVERNE	16 OGREN	03 SHELBY	09 WARREN-DETROIT
08 BOSTON HIGH WHEEL	07 DELUXE	07 GEARLESS	08 LORRAINE	17 OLYMPIAN	04 SCHACHT	09 WASHINGTON
09 BERGDOLL	07 DRAGON	07 GRISWOLD	09 LEXINGTON	97 POPE HARTFORD	04 SPEEDWAY	09 WHITE
12 BURG	07 DUER	08 GREAT WESTERN	09 LYON	98 PITTSBURGH	04 SPRINGER	09 WILCOX
14 BRISCOE	07 DUROCAR	11 GAYLORD	11 LEADER	99 PACKARD	04 STUDEBAKER	10 WESTCOTT
15 BELL	09 DE TAMBLE	11 GREAT EAGLE	11 LENOX	00 PEERLESS	04 STURTEVANT	11 WARREN
15 BIDDLE	09 DETROIT DEARBORN	11 GREAT SOUTHERN	12 LITTLE	01 PEOPLES	05 STODDARD-DAYTON	13 WILLYS-KNIGHT
15 BOUR DAVIS	10 DAVIS	13 GRANT	13 LEWIS	01 POPE TOLEDO	06 SHAWMUT	18 WOODS
16 BREWSTER KNIGHT	11 DALTON	17 GHENT	14 LAUREL	02 PIERCE-ARROW	06 SMITH	20 WASP
20 BEGGS	11 DISPATCH	19 GARDNER	16 LIBERTY	02 POMEROY	06 SUCCESS	22 WILLS-ST. CLAIRE
22 BARLEY	12 DETROITER	22 GRAY	20 LAFAYETTE	02 POPE ROBINSON	06 SUNSET	26 WHIPPET
29 BLACK HAWK	12 DUQUESNE	27 GRAHAM-PAIGE	20 LEACH BILTWELL	02 PHELPS	07 SHOEMAKER	29 WINDSOR-WHITE PRINCE
00 COLUMBIA	13 DESOTO	95 HAYNES-APPERSON	21 LONE STAR	03 PAN AMERICAN	07 SIMPLICITY	31 WILLYS
01 CENTURY	14 DILE	01 HAYNES	27 LASALLE	03 PREMIER	07 SINGLE CENTER	03 YALE
	14 DODGE	01 HOLLEY	03 MACKLE THOMPSON	04 POPE TRIBUNE	07 SPRINGFIELD	05 YORK
	15 DANIELS	03 HOFFMAN	03 MARMON	05 PUNGS-FINCH	08 SELDEN	03 ZENTMOBILE
	15 DORT	03 HOWARD	03 MARR	05 PRINCESS	08 SPEEDWELL	09 ZIMMERMAN
	16 DIXIE FLYER	05 HAMMER	03 MATHESON	06 PALMER	08 STAVER	
	16 DRUMMOND	05 HOLSMAN	03 MICHIGAN	06 PAGE	08 STILSON	
	17 DISBROW		03 MITCHELL	06 PARAGON	08 SULTAN	
	20 DUESENBERG		03 MODEL	07 PAYNE-MODERN	09 SALTER	
			03 PULLMAN	07 PENNSYLVANIA		
				07 PULLMAN		

Automobile Trade Journal, Horseless Age, Motor Age, The Automobile, Motor World—all Chilton Class Journal publications—were searched in the preparation of these birth records of over five hundred gasoline passenger cars.

As first mention in these different Chilton Class Journal publications in some cases was car description before production, while in others it was at the time of first produc-tion, these dates do not necessarily indicate exactly the same state of development for each automobile at time shown.

The dates, however, are an interesting guide to the time when the trade first heard of these cars through their trade journals from the beginning of the industry.

In case the same name is used by different companies at different times each date is given.

What the Records Say of
SPEED

History of Land Speed

Year	Driver	Car	Speed M.P.H.
1898	Chasseloup-Laubat	Jeantaud	39.24
1899	Jenatzy	Jenatzy	65.79
1902	Augiers	Mors	77.13
1903	Henry Ford	Ford	91.37
1904	Baras	Darracq	104.53
1905	Bowden	Mercedes	109.75
1906	Marriott	Stanley Steamer	127.66
1910	Oldfield	Benz	131.72
1911	Burman	Benz	141.73
1919	De Palma	Packard	149.88
1920	Milton	Duesenberg	156.05
1926	Parry-Thomas	Thomas Sp.	170.62
1927	Segrave	Sunbeam	203.79
1928	Keech	White Triplex	207.55
1929	Segrave	Irving Napier	231.36
1931	Campbell	Bluebird	245.73

91½-122 CU. IN. PISTON DISPLACEMENT

Distance or Time	Date	Place	Driver	Car	Speed M.P.H.
1 mile	1926	Arpajon	Eldridge	Miller	136.26
10 miles	1926	Montlhery	Eldridge	Miller	131.75
100 miles	1930	Montlhery	Dunfee	Sunbeam	117.31
500 miles	1930	Brooklands	Team	Alfa-Romeo	95.23

67-91½ CU. IN. PISTON DISPLACEMENT

1 mile	1927	Muroc Lake	Lockhart	Miller	164.01
10 miles	1929	Montlhery	Duray	Packard Cable Sp.	135.33
100 miles	1930	Montlhery	Stewart	Derby-Miller	118.13

46-67 CU. IN. PISTON DISPLACEMENT

1 mile	1928	Arpajon	Morel	Amilcar	128.02
10 miles	1928	Montlhery	Morel	Amilcar	126.89
100 miles	1928	Montlhery	Ghika	Cozette	103.43

30.6-46 CU. IN. PISTON DISPLACEMENT

1 mile	1931	Daytona	Campbell	Austin	94.03
10 miles	1927	Montlhery	Vinatier	Grazide	96.22
100 miles	1930	Brooklands	Team	Austin	84.96

World's Records

Distance or Time	Date	Place	Driver	Car	Speed M.P.H.
1 mile	1931	Daytona	Campbell	Bluebird	245.73
5 miles	1929	Verneuk Pan	Campbell	Napier	211.49
10 miles	1930	Montlhery	Mrs. Stewart	Derby-Miller	137.21
50 miles	1926	Montlhery	Breton	Panhard	129.66
100 miles	1927	Montlhery	Marchand	Voisin	128.55
500 miles	1927	Montlhery	Team	Voisin	117.72
1,000 miles	1927	Montlhery	Team	Voisin	112.34
5,000 miles	1929	Montlhery	Team	Voisin	91.17
10,000 miles	1929	Montlhery	Team	Voisin	85.25
20,000 miles	1929	Montlhery	Team	Voisin	82.73
30,000 miles	1930	Montlhery	Team	Voisin	74.44
1 hour	1927	Montlhery	Marchand	Voisin	128.35
12 hours	1927	Montlhery	Team	Voisin	112.82
24 hours	1927	Montlhery	Team	Voisin	113.50

305-488 CU. IN. PISTON DISPLACEMENT

1 mile	1930	Arpajon	Duray	Panhard	137.61
10 miles	1926	Brooklands	Thomas	Leyland	126.03
100 miles	1926	Montlhery	Ortsmans	Panhard	123.69
200 miles	1930	Montlhery	Marendaz	Graham	101.86
500 miles	1926	Brooklands	Thomas	Leyland	110.04
1,000 miles	1924	Brooklands	Team	Lanchester	95.27
5,000 miles	1928	Atlantic City	Team	Studebaker	68.80
10,000 miles	1928	Atlantic City	Team	Studebaker	68.81
25,000 miles	1928	Atlantic City	Team	Studebaker	68.47
30,000 miles	1928	Atlantic City	Team	Studebaker	68.36
24 hours	1929	Montlhery	Team	Graham	86.35

122-305 CU. IN. PISTON DISPLACEMENT

1 mile	1930	Tat	Hartmann	Bugatti	122.80
10 miles	1930	Montlhery	Dunfee	Sunbeam	126.48
100 miles	1930	Montlhery	Dunfee	Sunbeam	117.02
500 miles	1930	Brooklands	Team	Talbot	105.17

American Racing Records

122 CU. IN PISTON DISPLACEMENT

Distance	Place	Driver	Car	Speed M.P.H.
5 miles	Los Angeles	Hill	Miller	137.93
10 miles	Los Angeles	Duray	Miller	136.05
25 miles	Atlantic City	McDonough	Miller	137.43
50 miles	Atlantic City	McDonough	Miller	135.89
100 miles	Los Angeles	Lewis	Miller	133.71
500 miles	Indianapolis	De Paolo	Duesenberg	101.13*

*Indianapolis record.

91½ CU. IN. PISTON DISPLACEMENT

5 miles	Atlantic City	Lockhart	Miller	133.56
10 miles	Atlantic City	Lockhart	Miller	135.66
25 miles	Charlotte	Lockhart	Miller	132.41
50 miles	Atlantic City	Lewis	Miller	131.08
100 miles	Atlantic City	Keech	Simplex Sp.	131.81
500 miles	Indianapolis	Meyer	Miller	99.48

MILE DIRT TRACK RECORDS

1 mile	Cleveland	Lockhart	Miller	85.82
2 miles	Cleveland	Lockhart	Miller	86.20
3 miles	Syracuse	Arnold	Duesenberg	86.57
4 miles	Syracuse	Arnold	Duesenberg	86.98
5 miles	Syracuse	Arnold	Duesenberg	87.07
10 miles	Syracuse	Arnold	Duesenberg	86.91
25 miles	Syracuse	Arnold	Duesenberg	85.47
50 miles	Syracuse	Arnold	Duesenberg	83.89
75 miles	Syracuse	Cummings	Duesenberg	83.64
100 miles	Langhorne, Pa.	Farmer	Miller	85.84

SPEEDWAY QUALIFYING RECORD

1½ miles	Atlantic City	Lockhart		147.73

SPEEDWAY SPEED RECORD

2½ miles	Detroit	Duray		148.17

MILE DIRT TRACK QUALIFYING RECORD

1 mile	Cleveland	Lockhart		92.45

FIRST RECORDS of
Significant Automotive Events

Milestones in Nearly Forty Years of Automotive History
Design—Engineering—Materials—Production—Marketing

Gathered here in one place for convenient reference are dates of the most important happenings in the development of the automotive vehicle in the United States, and of the introduction of the more important features in design, construction and equipment.

The information in this form is ready for many uses—preparing speeches, writing advertising literature, settling controversies about events, getting a general perspective of the growth of this industry quickly.

Of course, the origin of different practices in automobile design in many cases is somewhat indefinite as regards time. Any new device or practice is first conceived by the engineer or inventor; it is then embodied in the form of a model, and finally it is incorporated in vehicles in regular production. These different stages naturally are reached at different times. In preparing the information here, the effort has been—unless otherwise stated—to give the year during which any given feature was first incorporated in cars that were *sold* to the public. Of course, no record of this kind can ever be complete, but it is believed that most of the major events of lasting interest and most of the important features of present-day car construction are included.

1892
First gasoline automobile built in the U. S. (Duryea).

1895
First public automobile contest in the U. S. (Times-Herald race, Chicago).

1896
First automobile track races in U. S. (Narragansett, R. I.).

1898
Aluminum alloy first used for automobiles (Haynes).

First gasoline car delivered to purchaser (Winton).

Nickel steel used for axles and other parts (Haynes).

Electric cabs placed in service in New York.

1899
First public garage and repair shop opened in New York.

First automobile supply business. A. L. Dyke, St. Louis.

1900
Automatic spark advance used (Mercedes, Packard, Olds).

Automobile speedometer placed on market by Joseph W. Jones.

First front-mounted powerplant in U. S. (Columbia).

First four-cylinder air-cooled engine (Franklin).

First New York automobile show (old Madison Square Garden).

Wheel steering introduced in American practice (superseding tiller steering.)

1901
Shaft drive introduced.

First automobile endurance contest (New York-Buffalo).

Rear-entrance tonneau type of body introduced.

First law regulating automobile traffic (Connecticut).

1902
Chrome nickel steel in automobile construction.

High-speed tool steel (tungsten steel) in automobile manufacture.

Divided front seats or bucket seats for runabouts made their appearance.

First four-cylinder engines (of water-cooled, longitudinal-front-mounted type) in regular production cars in America (Locomobile).

Three-point support for powerplant introduced (Marmon).

1903
First pressed-steel automobile frame made in America (by A. O. Smith Co. for Peerless racer).

Radiators were first placed at front of engine space in American practice.

Glass windshields (glass fronts) made their appearance.

Canopy tops came into use.

Anti-skid chains introduced (Parsons).

1904
Side-entrance tonneau body superseded rear-entrance type.

Shock absorbers were brought to America from France by E. V. Hartford.

Automatic carburetors first fitted in American practice.

First straight eight vertical, longitudinal-mounted engine used in racing car (Peerless).

Blower cooling introduced (Frayer-Miller).

Engine lubrication under pressure (Pierce-Arrow).

1905
First magnetos for automobile ignition made in this country by Remy Brothers.

Beginning of the era of the high-wheeled motor-buggy type of car which lasted for several years.

Folding tops, then generally known as cape-cart tops, became regular equipment.

Annular ball bearings placed on American market (Hess-Bright).

Universal rim taking either clincher or straight side tire introduced (Goodyear).

Sleeve-valve engine (Knight) invented.

Six-cylinder engines introduced for stock cars (National).

Ignition locks first fitted.

1906
Integral cylinder and crankcase construction (Northern).

Air brakes and air clutch control (now used on large buses) first used on four-cylinder Northern passenger car.

Direct high-tension magnetos introduced on American market (Bosch).

Drop frame (single drop at rear) introduced (Peerless).

A spring bumper, the forerunner of the present-day bumper, was developed by Ray Harroun.

Vibrator-type horn introduced.

Woven asbestos brake linings (Raybestos).

Valance (piece which connects mudguard proper with body or frame) used in unit with mud guard. Basic patents owned by Frank Miller of Frayer-Miller.

1907
Taximeter cabs or taxicabs made their appearance in New York.

Vanadium steel was introduced in automobile construction (Ford).

Demountable rims (Firestone).

Magnetic-drag-type speedometer (Warner).

1908
Motor-driven horns introduced (Klaxon).

Cars with sleeve-valve engines put into production (Daimler-Knight).

Silent (toothed) chains were first used for front drives of production cars (Knight).

Left-hand steering (Ford).

1909

Bakelite placed on market.

1910

Torpedo-type (four-door) open bodies became the style.

1911

Electric starter introduced (Delco, on Cadillac).

Transversely split detachable rims introduced.

Phenol-condensation-product gears for front-end drives.

Worm-gear final drive for trucks (Pierce-Arrow).

1912

Engine temperature indicator (Boyce Motometer) placed on market.

Spiral bevel final drive adopted by Packard.

1913

Wire wheels of the triple-laced type first placed on American stock cars.

Bendix drive developed.

Beginning of the cyclecar era, which lasted only a few years.

Worm-gear drive for passenger cars (Edwards-Knight).

1914

Eight-cylinder V engine introduced by Cadillac.

Vacuum fuel feed was developed by Stewart-Warner Speedometer Corp.

Thermostatic water circulation control (Cadillac).

1915

Aluminum alloy pistons for stock cars.

Self-locking differential (M. & S.).

First twelve-cylinder car (Packard).

Lanchester torsional vibration damper first used in American practice (Packard).

1917

Wood wheels with steel felloes.

Steel disk wheels (Budd).

1919

Electric vaporizer in carburetor (Franklin).

1921

Hydraulic brakes (Duesenberg).

Cobalt-chrome steel and high-tungsten steel used for automobile exhaust valves (Rich Tool Co.).

Molybdenum steel in automobile construction (Wills-Ste. Claire).

First straight eight stock car on American market (Duesenberg).

First use of four-wheel brakes on American stock cars (Duesenberg).

First overhead camshaft engine for stock cars (Duesenberg and Wills-Ste. Claire).

1922

Silicon-chromium steel for exhaust valves (Thompson Products, Inc.).

Nickel plating of radiator shells, lamp covers, etc., became very popular.

1923

Balloon tires made their first appearance in this country.

High-pressure chassis lubrication was introduced (Alemite).

Lacquer finish for automobiles (Duco).

Ethyl fluid, the gasoline dope, was placed on the market.

Air cleaners on automobiles.

1924

Oil filters for the crankcase oil first fitted to stock cars (Purolator on Chrysler).

Vibration damper in clutch introduced (Franklin).

1925

Electric transmissions for buses came into use in this country.

1926

Hypoid gear drive (Packard).

Safety glass (wired-glass) in automobile body construction (Stutz).

Centralized chassis lubrication system (Bowen on Chandler).

1927

Chromium plating for automobile parts introduced.

Transmission with silent intermediate gears (Warner Hiflex on Paige).

1928

Fuel feed by mechanical pump (AC).

Change-gear synchronizing device introduced by Cadillac.

1929

Front-wheel drive cars (Cord, Ruxton).

1930

Sixteen-cylinder cars (Cadillac).

First use of stainless steel for radiator shells in quantity production car (Ford).

Oil cooling adopted for first time as standard equipment on American production car (Hupmobile).

Free-wheeling device first used on American stock car (Studebaker).

Dealers and Repair Shops—How Many and Where

U. S.

	1930	1931	Per Cent Change
Repair shops and service stations	101,189	102,556	+ 1
Number of car and truck dealers	54,354	50,990	— 6
Number of car dealers	51,560	47,144	— 9
Number of car dealers handling *only* one make	41,368	37,172	—10
Number of car dealers handling more than one make	21,686	21,432	— 1

Number of car dealer franchises by population groups:

	1930	1931	Per Cent Change
1,000 and under population	18,278	15,722	—14
1,001 to 2,500	12,624	11,039	—13
2,501 to 5,000	8,675	7,516	—13
5,001 to 10,000	7,001	6,833	— 2
10,001 to 25,000	5,737	6,986	+22
25,001 to 50,000	3,124	3,098	— 1
50,001 to 100,000	2,113	2,017	— 4
100,001 and up	5,502	5,393	— 2
Total number of car dealer franchises*	63,054	58,604	— 7

*Number of car dealer franchises in excess of number of dealers because some dealers handle more than one line of cars and hence hold more than one franchise.

Number of Car Dealer Franchises by Makes

(According to Count of Chilton Trade List made in January, 1931)

Auburn	581	Marmon	663
Buick	3,003	Nash	1,884
Cadillac	700	Oakland-Pontiac	3,435
Chevrolet	9,558	Oldsmobile	1,592
Chrysler	3,007	Packard	721
De Soto	1,369	Peerless	250
Dodge	2,842	Pierce-Arrow	312
Durant	1,664	Plymouth	3,081
Ford	8,833	Reo	772
Franklin	315	Studebaker	1,971
Graham	1,469	Willys-Overland	3,783
Hudson-Essex	2,863	Miscellaneous	819
Hupmobile	1,084		
Lincoln	2,033	Total	58,604

REGISTRATION RECORDS—

New and Total Passenger Car and Motor Truck Registrations

STATE	NEW CAR REGISTRATIONS			TOTAL CAR REGISTRATIONS		NEW TRUCK REGISTRATIONS			TOTAL TRUCK REGISTRATIONS (Includes Trucks and Buses)	
	1928	1929	1930	1929	1930	1928	1929	1930	1929	1930
Alabama	36,300	55,900	26,400	246,640	238,105	6,500	10,400	6,200	39,751	39,022
Arizona	12,400	18,600	9,300	110,743	98,147	2,100	3,100	1,900	12,583	13,476
Arkansas	25,900	36,200	190,900	193,500	191,033	3,300	8,300	3,500	39,533	26,986
California	200,800	263,900	190,900	1,745,308	1,974,429	17,600	32,000	26,900	229,033	99,387*
Colorado	33,100	40,400	27,700	273,960	276,847	3,700	6,200	5,800	29,529	31,662
Connecticut	47,600	57,900	42,800	281,800	297,781	6,600	8,300	5,900	51,080	49,709
Delaware	7,200	9,300	7,500	44,728	45,533	1,000	1,400	1,200	9,775	10,523
District of Columbia	18,600	23,800	20,700	157,639	154,238	1,600	2,400	1,800	17,702	19,196
Florida	37,300	39,300	32,800	284,383	277,210	3,500	5,500	6,100	57,975	52,596
Georgia	35,200	12,400	28,600	310,362	294,461	4,100	7,200	5,000	48,166	46,716
Idaho	13,500	16,600	10,600	103,838	102,706	2,100	2,700	2,400	13,688	15,563
Illinois	192,500	244,300	169,000	1,410,913	1,429,146	18,600	27,000	20,100	204,175	209,114
Indiana	96,300	125,200	72,300	755,161	746,354	10,400	14,500	10,500	128,703	129,099
Iowa	91,100	111,800	79,700	715,466	709,985	9,300	11,400	10,000	68,402	72,190
Kansas	55,900	76,600	46,300	507,529	511,384	5,200	13,500	9,300	73,694	83,139
Kentucky	42,400	54,900	35,900	294,706	294,178	5,200	6,200	5,400	34,132	36,486
Louisiana	34,200	44,500	27,100	234,565	229,086	3,500	7,200	4,700	46,303	44,697
Maine	19,700	23,800	18,600	148,870	147,791	3,100	5,100	4,500	31,646	33,557
Maryland	38,300	48,600	38,100	276,140	283,120	5,200	7,200	6,000	9,303	38,060
Massachusetts	114,900	138,700	108,100	786,000	745,064	12,400	18,600	13,700	100,230	107,058
Michigan	209,100	262,900	143,400	1,220,848	1,161,051	17,600	26,900	15,800	176,824	167,158
Minnesota	71,400	92,100	69,100	620,342	618,661	7,700	11,400	10,300	100,057	108,361
Mississippi	30,000	38,300	21,300	224,000	203,312	3,100	7,200	5,500	31,000	33,782
Missouri	98,300	118,000	89,400	669,320	671,920	10,400	16,600	14,800	84,756	91,455
Montana	18,600	22,800	12,000	115,260	111,089	4,200	4,600	2,600	25,092	25,807
Nebraska	55,900	67,300	42,800	373,086	367,410	5,500	8,300	7,000	41,513	58,819
Nevada	3,100	4,700	3,600	25,219	23,388	334	967	600	6,604	6,257
New Hampshire	12,400	14,500	11,200	89,975	93,155	2,070	2,600	2,300	19,025	18,398
New Jersey	114,900	126,300	101,600	638,334	711,527	14,500	18,500	14,800	139,116	138,888
New Mexico	9,300	12,400	7,400	75,000	74,900	1,400	2,200	2,000	2,750	15,800
New York	302,000	343,600	275,600	1,878,300	1,920,255	35,200	48,600	38,700	399,900	396,569
North Carolina	60,000	66,200	35,000	447,055	412,042	7,200	10,400	6,500	56,535	62,259
North Dakota	21,700	24,800	13,300	162,092	155,383	4,500	4,200	2,400	25,954	27,636
Ohio	223,600	275,300	163,900	1,538,000	1,549,077	19,700	27,900	20,100	200,000	204,058
Oklahoma	78,700	96,300	55,000	514,729	490,947	8,600	13,500	8,100	60,646	59,384
Oregon	26,900	36,200	22,900	247,577	233,787	3,100	6,200	4,200	25,693	24,360
Pennsylvania	226,700	278,400	206,200	1,524,799	1,528,721	25,900	38,300	30,100	250,124	244,497
Rhode Island	17,600	21,700	16,300	112,496	115,176	2,100	3,100	2,100	22,350	20,691
South Carolina	24,800	32,000	19,300	205,683	195,210	3,100	5,200	3,700	25,591	26,456
South Dakota	27,900	31,000	19,000	181,419	180,000	4,100	4,300	3,100	22,780	24,306
Tennessee	44,500	56,900	39,000	324,000	332,417	4,100	6,200	5,100	34,400	40,126
Texas	170,800	215,300	124,100	1,160,869	1,152,904	20,700	34,200	22,200	186,719	206,639
Utah	13,500	18,300	10,600	97,200	93,628	1,300	3,100	2,200	17,500	17,369
Vermont	10,400	12,400	9,100	84,321	78,260	1,400	2,100	1,700	8,709	8,364
Virginia	50,700	62,100	46,200	328,947	319,061	6,300	10,400	8,900	61,711	62,872
Washington	40,400	56,900	39,200	385,033	388,719	4,600	8,300	6,700	63,247	63,792
West Virginia	33,100	40,400	29,400	229,011	225,101	3,600	5,100	4,600	39,332	41,031
Wisconsin	91,100	107,600	74,700	689,133	677,963	10,400	14,500	12,100	105,810	110,539
Wyoming	8,300	9,300	5,000	51,980	51,579	1,100	1,600	1,200	8,800	9,922
U. S. Total	3,248,900	4,016,700	2,718,000	23,146,279	23,183,241	358,804	544,667	410,300	3,487,931	3,473,831

* Includes only trucks over 3000 lb.

Motor Boat Registration

By U. S. Customs Districts to Dec. 31, 1930

Showing the growing market possibilities in these territories for sale of replacement engine parts and service work in this branch of automotive field.

PORT	Symbol Letter	1926	1927	1928	1929	1930
Baltimore, Md.	N-P	12,566	13,219	13,913	14,461	15,123
Boston, Mass.	C-D-E	11,425	11,762	12,201	12,648	13,119
Bridgeport, Conn.	H-J	5,981	5,757	5,867	6,057	5,921
Buffalo, N. Y.	Z	1,652	1,563	1,377	1,398	1,251
Charleston, S. C.	U Preceding	997	1,042	1,093	1,155	1,190
Chicago, Ill.	S-T	5,708	6,032	6,302	6,614	6,957
Cleveland, Ohio	N	4,003	4,287	4,289	4,569	5,006
Des Moines, Iowa	H	2,679	2,746	2,849	2,920	2,978
Detroit, Mich.	P-R-A	9,059	10,424	11,188	12,012	10,083
Duluth, Minn.	U	1,056	1,056	1,056	1,055	1,055
Galveston, Tex.	E	1,519	1,702	1,935	2,147	2,371
Great Falls, Mont.	G	12	14	14	15	17
Honolulu, T. H.	X-Y	656	712	764	841	894
Indianapolis, Ind.	K	1,018	1,103	1,240	1,377	1,459
Juneau, Alaska	T-U	3,782	3,729	4,201	3,891	3,676
Los Angeles, Calif.	A	2,776	2,974	3,215	3,425	3,584
Louisville, Ky.	L	1,898	2,039	2,187	2,287	2,299
Memphis, Tenn.	M	3,147	3,348	3,673	3,990	4,164
Milwaukee, Wis.	W	1,878	1,997	2,069	2,093	2,179
Minneapolis, Minn.	Z	650	657	672	693	614
Mobile, Ala.	A	2,813	2,998	3,231	3,367	3,518
New Orleans, La.	B-C	10,956	11,540	12,014	12,430	12,862
New York, N. Y.	K	27,439	28,962	30,717	32,247	33,971
Norfolk, Va.	R-S	11,905	12,626	13,318	13,772	14,251
Ogdensburg, N. Y.	Y	3,329	3,414	3,418	3,422	3,527
Omaha, Nebraska	Y	236	252	340	396	341
Pembina, N. Dakota.	J	14	15	16	20	23
Philadelphia, Pa.	L-M	12,251	12,840	13,480	14,162	14,975
Pittsburgh, Pa.	V	472	546	664	739	477
Port Arthur, Tex.	D	1,171	1,228	1,298	1,340	1,392
Portland, Me.	A-B	11,800	12,233	12,563	12,840	13,187
Portland, Ore.	G-H-J	6,204	6,694	6,537	6,864	7,163
Providence, R. I.	F-G	2,778	2,800	2,861	2,956	3,128
Rochester, N. Y.	Q	2,695	2,885	3,123	3,230	3,448
St. Albans, Vt.	X	665	543	556	580	573
St. Louis, Mo.	X	5,179	5,666	6,029	6,499	6,870
San Antonio, Tex.	F	356	409	457	527	674
San Francisco, Calif.	B-C-D-E-F	4,325	4,628	4,982	5,264	5,572
San Juan, P. R.	F-G	150	161	174	187	216
Savannah, Ga.	U after	1,191	1,247	1,310	1,340	1,368
Seattle, Wash.	K-L-M	6,579	6,841	7,079	7,504	7,867
Tampa, Fla.	V-W	16,792	18,155	19,217	20,180	21,204
Wilmington, N. C.	T	6,176	6,729	7,093	7,530	7,901

Total................Dec. 31, 1930	248,448
Total................Dec. 31, 1929	241,040
Total................Dec. 31, 1928	230,582
Total................Dec. 31, 1927	219,575
Total................Dec. 31, 1926	208,037
Total................Dec. 31, 1925	198,636
Total................Dec. 31, 1924	186,441
Total................Dec. 31, 1923	173,307
Total................Dec. 31, 1922	159,701
Total................Dec. 31, 1921	148,482
Total................Dec. 31, 1920	130,826
Total................Dec. 31, 1919	111,791
Total................June 30, 1919	91,779

CURRENT AND HISTORICAL

Motor Vehicle Registrations, 1919 to 1930

	1919	1920	1921	1922	1923	1924	1925	1926	1927	1928	1929	1930
Alabama	58,898	74,637	82,343	90,052	126,642	157,262	194,580	225,651	243,539	255,850	286,391	277,127
Arizona	28,979	34,559	35,049	38,034	48,741	57,828	68,029	73,574	74,527	91,800	123,326	111,623
Arkansas	49,450	59,082	67,446	86,425	111,946	141,983	183,764	209,419	206,568	214,960	233,442	218,019
California	477,450	568,892	673,830	861,805	1,100,283	1,321,480	1,439,463	1,600,475	1,699,955	1,727,024	1,988,347	2,073,816
Colorado	104,865	127,549	145,739	162,328	189,356	213,247	240,097	252,787	268,026	245,260	303,479	308,509
Connecticut	109,651	119,134	137,526	154,675	177,931	214,318	248,474	260,911	282,892	315,234	332,880	347,490
Delaware	16,152	18,300	21,413	24,560	29,977	35,136	40,681	44,418	46,707	51,210	54,503	56,056
Dist. of Col.	35,400	39,712	61,745	85,425	103,171	80,720	93,612	129,792	126,136	150,915	175,341	173,434
Florida	55,400	73,914	97,837	115,891	160,000	194,196	260,720	416,930	391,168	358,063	342,358	329,806
Georgia	127,326	144,422	131,942	145,584	173,794	209,300	244,871	274,037	296,567	318,180	358,528	341,177
Idaho	42,220	50,873	51,264	53,874	62,379	69,225	81,484	95,861	103,000	108,931	118,411	118,269
Illinois	478,438	568,759	670,434	786,190	969,331	1,123,724	1,263,177	1,370,503	1,438,985	1,504,359	1,615,088	1,638,260
Indiana	277,255	332,707	400,342	469,939	353,342	650,219	725,410	772,215	813,496	843,092	883,864	875,453
Iowa	363,857	437,300	460,528	500,148	576,398	620,906	657,567	689,036	706,829	736,666	783,868	782,175
Kansas	227,752	265,396	291,309	327,194	375,594	410,891	457,033	491,276	501,901	536,262	581,223	594,523
Kentucky	90,641	112,685	126,371	154,021	198,347	231,784	260,754	278,337	285,099	305,291	330,242	330,664
Louisiana	51,000	66,000	80,500	102,284	138,500	178,000	207,000	239,500	255,000	277,000	280,868	273,783
Maine	53,425	62,907	77,527	92,539	108,609	127,178	140,134	150,916	164,250	166,621	180,516	181,348
Maryland	95,634	116,341	140,572	165,624	209,938	195,581	230,684	249,056	284,267	234,849	315,579	321,180
Massachusetts	247,183	304,631	360,732	385,231	566,150	572,315	654,338	689,593	696,107	757,720	829,147	852,122
Michigan	325,813	412,717	477,037	578,980	730,658	868,587	990,709	1,118,785	1,156,344	1,248,080	1,397,672	1,328,209
Minnesota	259,743	309,569	328,700	380,557	448,187	502,987	569,694	624,478	640,102	668,155	720,399	727,022
Mississippi	45,030	63,484	65,139	77,001	104,400	134,547	177,262	210,500	227,103	235,826	255,000	237,094
Missouri	244,363	296,919	346,437	392,969	476,373	544,635	602,900	651,350	678,564	714,437	754,076	763,375
Montana	59,325	60,646	58,785	62,649	73,828	79,695	94,656	103,946	112,756	127,442	140,352	136,896
Nebraska	192,000	223,000	238,704	256,654	286,053	308,713	338,718	367,838	373,912	375,972	414,599	426,220
Nevada	9,305	10,464	10,819	12,647	15,700	18,387	21,185	24,014	25,851	27,134	31,823	29,645
New Hampshire	31,625	34,680	42,039	48,293	59,571	71,929	81,250	89,001	96,000	102,750	109,000	111,553
New Jersey	190,873	227,737	272,994	341,626	430,958	504,190	579,886	650,891	712,402	754,841	827,450	850,415
New Mexico	18,077	22,109	24,703	25,473	31,737	41,750	49,101	54,341	60,000	67,643	77,750	90,700
New York	571,662	669,290	812,031	1,002,293	1,214,642	1,412,879	1,613,141	1,815,437	1,900,866	2,093,792	2,278,200	2,316,824
North Carolina	109,017	140,860	148,684	182,550	247,612	305,756	351,767	385,763	422,544	486,000	503,590	474,301
North Dakota	82,885	90,840	92,644	99,052	109,244	117,061	144,956	157,822	160,696	173,944	188,046	183,019
Ohio	511,031	615,397	720,632	859,504	1,068,700	1,244,000	1,305,000	1,510,000	1,570,418	1,662,000	1,738,000	1,753,135
Oklahoma	144,500	204,300	221,300	249,659	307,000	342,982	438,000	510,000	644,450	585,346	575,375	550,331
Oregon	83,332	103,790	118,325	134,299	166,412	192,629	216,324	234,134	246,623	254,415	273,270	258,147
Pennsylvania	482,117	570,164	689,589	829,737	1,064,624	1,228,586	1,317,053	1,463,261	1,568,617	1,642,866	1,774,923	1,773,218
Rhode Island	44,833	50,375	54,957	66,466	85,480	90,652	102,476	109,145	119,335	126,918	134,846	135,867
South Carolina	70,143	93,843	90,546	95,978	128,656	163,382	170,658	180,967	199,794	216,964	231,274	221,666
South Dakota	104,628	120,395	119,274	125,238	131,720	142,280	168,118	168,230	170,592	191,900	204,199	204,306
Tennessee	80,422	101,852	117,025	135,716	173,365	204,680	248,021	279,639	295,530	325,406	358,400	372,543
Texas	331,310	427,693	467,616	526,238	688,899	834,040	968,406	1,047,202	1,110,986	1,213,224	1,347,588	1,359,543
Utah	35,236	42,578	47,523	49,156	66,025	69,227	72,490	81,633	78,976	98,541	114,700	110,997
Vermont	26,807	31,625	36,965	43,881	52,776	61,179	69,576	73,871	79,510	86,231	93,000	86,624
Virginia	94,120	134,000	141,000	169,000	219,092	261,643	281,100	320,367	335,275	358,633	390,658	381,933
Washington	148,775	173,920	185,359	220,957	261,224	294,812	332,442	367,093	389,409	408,156	448,280	452,511
West Virginia	50,203	78,862	93,894	112,763	162,191	190,134	217,069	221,001	241,042	251,419	268,333	266,132
Wisconsin	236,981	293,298	341,841	388,044	457,271	525,221	596,373	662,328	698,944	743,815	794,943	788,502
Wyoming	21,371	23,926	26,619	30,637	39,831	43,639	47,712	49,633	52,222	56,867	60,680	61,501
Totals	7,596,503	9,206,141	10,505,630	12,299,770	15,312,658	17,605,495	19,857,915	22,046,957	23,253,882	24,501,004	26,623,857	26,657,072

New Motor Truck Sales by Makes

Make	1930	1929	1928	1927	Per Cent of Total				Rank			
					1930	1929	1928	1927	1930	1929	1928	1927
Atterbury	....	100	....	....	..	.03	..	..	..	24	..	..
Autocar	2,000	2,900	2,300	3,200	.49	.56	.66	.97	15	13	13	11
Brockway-Indiana	3,800	4,500	3,600	1,900	.92	.86	1.07	.57	11	11	10	12
Chevrolet	118,300	160,900	133,800	104,700	28.79	30.50	39.20	31.94	2	2	1	1
Diamond T	2,900	3,600	2,300	1,900	.71	.68	.67	.57	12	12	12	13
Dodge	15,600	28,600	36,600	42,300	3.80	5.41	10.70	12.94	4	4	3	3
Federal	2,100	2,800	3,100	3,900	.51	.54	.91	1.18	14	14	11	10
Ford	197,100	223,400	65,300	99,400	48.00	42.40	19.10	30.30	1	1	2	2
G.M.C.	9,100	14,200	17,500	6,600	2.22	2.71	5.13	2.02	5	5	5	8
International	24,000	31,400	26,200	16,400	5.86	5.98	7.64	4.98	3	3	4	5
La France-Republic	600	800	700	1,100	.15	.16	.20	.34	19	19	18	15
Mack	4,900	6,800	6,900	6,300	1.19	1.30	2.09	1.92	8	8	8	9
Moreland	400	700	....	....	.10	.14	..	..	21	20	..	..
Pierce-Arrow	....	500	500	....	..	.09	.13	..	..	22	20	..
Relay	500	700	600	....	.12	.14	.18	..	20	21	19	..
Reo	6,400	12,900	16,300	10,300	1.56	2.45	4.77	3.15	7	6	6	6
Rugby	700	1,200	200	....	.17	.23	.04	..	18	18	21	..
Schacht	400	300	....	....	.10	.05	..	..	22	23	..	..
Sterling	1,200	1,600	1,000	700	.29	.30	.33	.22	17	17	16	16
Stewart	2,300	2,200	2,000	1,500	.56	.41	.58	.47	13	15	15	14
Studebaker	1,600	1,700	1,000	....	.39	.32	.29	..	16	16	17	..
White	4,400	6,100	6,300	7,100	1.07	1.17	1.84	2.17	9	10	9	7
Willys-Overland	4,300	6,500	2,200	....	1.05	1.24	.66	..	10	9	14	..
Miscellaneous	7,700	12,200	13,000	20,600	1.95	2.33	3.81	6.26	6	7	7	4
Total	410,300	526,600	341,400	327,900	100%	100%	100%	100%	..	..	..	..

FIVE-YEAR RECORD OF NEW CAR REGISTRA

New Car Registrations

	1926	1927	1928	1929	1930	5 Yrs. (1926-1930)
Auburn Automobile Co.	7,117	9,835	11,153	18,652	13,149	59,906
Auburn	7,117	9,835	11,153	17,853	11,270	57,228
Cord	......	......	......	799	1,879	2,678
Austin	......	......	......	......	4,354	4,354
Chrysler Motors	353,343	278,152	334,190	344,877	224,581	1,535,143
Chrysler	129,966	154,234	141,800	84,520	60,908	571,428
De Soto	......	......	14,528	59,614	35,267	109,409
Dodge	223,377	123,918	148,541	115,774	64,105	675,715
Plymouth	......	......	29,321	84,969	64,301	178,591
Durant	91,794*	56,781*	71,263	47,716	21,440	288,994
Ford Motor Co.	1,196,674	399,884	487,371	1,316,298	1,059,453	4,459,680
Ford	1,189,004	393,424	481,344	1,310,147	1,055,097	4,429,016
Lincoln	7,670	6,460	6,027	6,151	4,356	30,664
Franklin	7,173	7,526	7,423	10,704	7,482	40,308
General Motors	896,110	1,115,579	1,295,046	1,271,134	905,427	5,483,296
Buick	229,597	232,428	195,691	172,307*	122,656	952,679
Cadillac	24,735	18,748	18,133	14,936	12,078	88,630
LaSalle	......	10,971	18,755	20,290	11,262	61,278
Chevrolet	493,852	647,810	767,867	780,014	618,884	3,308,427
Oakland	49,539	41,843	37,168	31,831	21,648	182,029
Pontiac	49,875	115,206	183,825	158,273	68,389	575,568
Oldsmobile	48,512	48,573	73,607	93,483*	50,510*	314,685
Graham	30,401*	18,588*	58,415	60,487	30,140	198,031
Hudson Motors	199,509	225,468	225,463	254,029	93,804	998,273
Essex	130,812	167,810	177,152	191,337	63,338	730,449
Hudson	68,697	57,658	48,311	62,692	30,466	267,824
Hupmobile	37,874	33,809	55,441	44,337	24,307	195,768
Marmon	3,546	10,095	14,759	22,323*	12,369	63,092
Nash	118,256	109,979	115,019	105,146	51,086	499,486
Packard	28,727	31,355	42,890	44,634	28,318	175,924
Peerless	10,164	9,872	7,748	8,318	4,021	40,123
Reo	10,435	22,144	21,367	17,319	11,450	82,715
Studebaker Corp.	99,605	100,675	112,769	91,225	63,321	467,595
Pierce-Arrow	5,526	5,836	5,736	8,386	6,795	32,279
Studebaker	94,079	94,839*	107,033*	82,839*	56,526	435,316
Stutz	3,532	2,906	2,412	2,949*	814	12,613
Willys-Overland	142,510	139,406	230,962	199,709	65,766	778,353
Willys-Whippet-Overland ..	96,848	100,206	191,301	162,366	51,687	602,408
Willys-Knight	45,662	39,200	39,661	37,343	14,079	175,945
Miscellaneous	62,163*	51,484*	39,708*	20,390*	4,697*	178,442
Total	3,298,933	2,623,538	3,133,399	3,880,247	2,625,979	15,562,096

*Durant Includes Star and Flint.
*Graham Includes Paige and Jewett.
*Miscellaneous in 1926 includes Chandler, Cleveland, Jordan, Locomobile, Moon, Gardner, Rickenbacker, Velie, Wills-Ste. Claire and others.
*Studebaker includes Erskine.
*Miscellaneous in 1927 includes Falcon, Stearns, Chandler, Jordan, Locomobile, Moon, Gardner, Velie and others.
*Buick includes Marquette.

The Share Each Car Had
in the 15,562,096 Total

TIONS BY MAKES

	Per Cent of Total						Rank				
	1926	1927	1928	1929	1930	5 Yrs. (1926-1930)	1926	1927	1928	1929	1930
Auburn Automobile Co.	.22	.37	.35	.49	.50	**.39**	..	..	..	..	..
Auburn	.22	.37	.35	.47	.43	**.37**	24	24	25	23	**24**
Cord	....	....	....	.02	.07	**.02**	..	..	..	31	**31**
Austin	....	....	....	....	.17	**.03**	..	..	..	..	**29**
Chrysler Motors	10.71	10.60	10.65	8.87	8.53	**9.86**	..	..	..	..	..
Chrysler	3.94	5.88	4.51	2.18	2.32	**3.67**	6	5	8	11	**8**
De Soto	....	....	.46	1.54	1.34	**.70**	..	..	24	15	**13**
Dodge	6.77	4.72	4.74	2.96	2.43	**4.34**	4	6	7	7	**6**
Plymouth	....	....	.94	2.19	2.44	**1.15**	..	..	19	10	**5**
Durant	2.79	2.17	2.29	1.23	.82	**1.86**	10	12	12	16	**19**
Ford Motor Co.	36.27	15.25	15.54	33.92	40.34	**28.64**	..	..	..	..	..
Ford	36.04	15.00	15.35	33.76	40.17	**28.44**	1	2	2	1	**1**
Lincoln	.23	.25	.19	.16	.17	**.20**	22	26	28	29	**28**
Franklin	.22	.29	.25	.29	.28	**.26**	23	25	27	26	**26**
General Motors	27.13	42.53	41.34	32.79	34.48	**35.24**	..	..	..	..	..
Buick	6.95	8.86	6.25	4.45	4.67	**6.12**	3	3	3	4	**3**
Cadillac	.75	.71	.58	.38	.46	**.57**	19	19	22	25	**22**
LaSalle	....	.42	.60	.52	.43	**.39**	..	21	21	22	**25**
Chevrolet	14.95	24.70	24.51	20.12	23.56	**21.27**	2	1	1	2	**2**
Oakland	1.50	1.60	1.19	.82	.82	**1.17**	12	14	18	20	**18**
Pontiac	1.51	4.39	5.86	4.07	2.61	**3.70**	13	7	5	6	**4**
Oldsmobile	1.47	1.85	2.35	2.42	1.93	**2.02**	14	13	11	9	**12**
Graham	.92	.71	1.86	1.57	1.15	**1.27**	17	20	13	14	**15**
Hudson Motors	6.02	8.60	7.20	6.52	3.57	**6.41**	..	..	..	..	..
Essex	3.94	6.40	5.66	4.91	2.41	**4.69**	5	4	6	3	**7**
Hudson	2.08	2.20	1.54	1.61	1.16	**1.72**	11	11	15	13	**14**
Hupmobile	1.15	1.29	1.77	1.14	.93	**1.26**	16	16	14	18	**17**
Marmon	.12	.38	.47	.58	.47	**.41**	26	22	23	21	**21**
Nash	3.58	4.19	3.67	2.72	1.95	**3.21**	7	8	9	8	**11**
Packard	.87	1.19	1.37	1.15	1.08	**1.13**	18	17	16	17	**16**
Peerless	.32	.37	.26	.21	.15	**.26**	21	23	26	28	**30**
Reo	.31	.84	.68	.44	.44	**.53**	20	18	20	24	**23**
Studebaker Corp.	3.03	3.83	3.59	2.35	2.41	**3.01**	..	..	..	..	..
Pierce-Arrow	.17	.22	.18	.21	.26	**.21**	25	27	29	27	**27**
Studebaker	2.86	3.61	3.41	2.14	2.15	**2.80**	9	10	10	12	**9**
Stutz	.12	.11	.08	.07	.03	**.08**	27	28	30	30	**32**
Willys-Overland	4.32	5.32	7.37	5.14	2.52	**5.00**	..	..	..	..	..
Willys-Whippet-Overland	2.94	3.82	6.10	4.18	1.98	**3.87**	8	9	4	5	**10**
Willys-Knight	1.38	1.50	1.27	.96	.54	**1.13**	15	15	17	19	**20**
Miscellaneous	1.90	1.96	1.26	.52	.18	**1.15**	..	..	..	..	..
Total	100.00	100.00	100.00	100.00	100.00	**100.00**	..	..	..	..	..

*Miscellaneous in 1928 Includes Falcon, Stearns-Knight, Chandler, J o r d a n, Moon, Gardner and others.
*Oldsmobile includes Viking.

*Stutz includes Blackhawk.
*Miscellaneous in 1929 includes Stearns, Chandler, Jordan, Locomobile, Moon, Gardner and others.

*Miscellaneous in 1930 includes Gardner, Jordan, Windsor and others.
*Marmon includes Roosevelt.

PRODUCTION RECORDS

Giving Here for Permanent Reference the Current and
Historical Production Records of the Industry. Trends
are Indicated by Some of the Special Tabulations

18 Years Motor Vehicle Production

United States and Canada

	PASSENGER CARS		MOTOR TRUCKS	
Year	Number	Value, Wholesale	Number	Value, Wholesale
1913	461,500	$399,902,000	23,500	$44,000,000
1914	543,679	413,859,379	25,375	45,098,464
1915	895,930	565,978,950	74,000	125,800,000
1916	1,525,578	921,378,000	92,130	161,000,000
1917	1,745,792	1,053,505,781	128,157	220,982,668
1918	943,436	801,937,925	227,250	434,168,992
1919	1,657,652	1,461,785,925	275,943	423,326,621
1920	1,905,560	1,809,170,963	321,789	423,249,410
1921	1,518,061	1,091,752,452	164,304	169,914,098
1922	2,369,089	1,561,740,645	277,140	231,282,063
1923	3,753,945	2,274,554,488	426,505	317,478,940
1924	3,303,646	2,040,706,519	434,140	326,706,496
1925	3,870,744	2,544,528,799	557,056	470,634,763
1926	3,948,843	2,746,064,722	556,818	468,752,769
1927	3,083,360	2,265,633,102	497,020	435,072,641
1928	4,012,158	2,703,753,500	588,983	459,045,380
1929	4,794,898	2,981,141,842	826,811	595,504,039
1930	2,939,791	1,768,000,000	569,271	389,000,000

U. S. Dept. of Commerce Figures.

Car and Truck Production by Months

United States and Canada

	CARS			TRUCKS		
	1929	1930	1931	1929	1930	1931
Jan.....	364,773	245,049	142,869	57,765	38,557	35,478
Feb.....	431,755	294,868	187,948	65,950	51,087	41,862
March..	546,489	350,559	241,728	79,587	66,555	47,606
April....	571,956	397,043	....	91,855	71,238	......
May....	541,310	386,203	....	94,940	58,496	......
June....	469,260	301,138	....	98,164	48,458	......
July....	439,598	233,622	....	78,703	42,099	......
August..	452,857	192,951	....	59,985	41,209	......
Sept.....	375,046	184,305	....	54,683	44,301	......
Oct......	328,305	119,264	....	66,235	39,678	......
Nov.....	176,629	106,494	....	50,368	34,667	......
Dec.....	96,920	128,398	....	28,582	32,930	......
Total..	4,794,898	2,939,894	....	826,817	569,275	......

Approximate Percentage of 1930
Car Production Unequipped

Trunks 98%		Radiator Shutters 84%	
Clocks 96%		Spring Covers 40%	
Wind Deflectors 91%		Engine Thermometers ..51%	
Cigar Lighters 85%		Tire Locks 20%	

A smaller percentage of 1930 cars than 1929 cars are originally
equipped with clocks and engine thermometers so the market for
these is proportionately greater for wholesalers and retailers.

Car Production by List Price Classes*

	$650 and under	$651-$1,000	$1,001-$1,400	$1,401-$2,150	$2,150 and up	Total
1924	2,020,900	419,800	332,300	369,900	160,700	3,303,600
1925	2,036,100	660,700	540,900	452,900	180,100	3,870,700
1926	1,640,900	1,149,300	500,400	473,700	184,500	3,948,800
1927	1,040,400	958,000	446,900	466,700	171,400	3,083,400
1928	1,701,600	1,219,300	462,500	456,100	172,700	4,012,200
1929	2,585,500	1,317,100	387,800	347,300	157,200	4,794,900
1930	1,785,000	680,400	203,700	179,200	91,500	2,939,800

*The price class limits are approximate.

Motor Truck Production by Capacities
United States and Canada

	1930	1929	1928	1927	1926	1925	1924	1923	1922	1921
¾ ton or less	130,562	141,853	95,232	88,046	99,286	81,567	64,988	70,611	90,932	44,913
1 ton and less than 1½	29,844	78,786	313,270	319,637	347,167	391,165	310,930	288,896	146,288	86,962
1½ ton and less than 2............	359,300	523,691	112,171	29,107	47,000	29,401	20,465	24,031	4,388	5,608
2 ton and less than 2½............	15,788	28,416	30,456	27,313	19,993	12,456	8,225	14,998	13,830	11,206
2½ ton and less than 3½...........	21,563	33,530	21,813	16,584	18,231	16,691	14,294	12,516	11,235	3,958
3½ ton and less than 5............	5,581	8,643	4,746	4,471	5,514	6,191	3,643	6,761	3,319	3,343
5 ton	1,040	2,384	2,219	4,128	9,030	7,990	6,635	4,611	5,718	4,714
Over 5 ton and special types*........	5,593	9,508	9,076	7,734	10,597	11,595	4,960	4,081	1,430	3,600
Totals	569,271	826,811	588,983	497,020	556,818	557,056	434,140	426,505	277,140	164,304

*Special types include ambulances, hearses, fire apparatus, buses, etc.

Car and Truck Sales In United States by Months

	CARS			TRUCKS	
	1928	1929	1930	1929	1930
January........	135,843	227,383	186,397	29,857	30,241
February.......	165,256	243,429	219,052	32,565	31,882
March.........	254,723	391,416	309,283	46,348	42,182
April..........	332,056	498,559	369,561	56,278	47,032
May...........	351,332	469,870	357,107	52,875	43,245
June..........	317,032	399,966	266,991	45,075	33,512
July..........	324,021	447,771	262,991	57,946	39,888
August........	329,827	390,040	210,867	52,540	33,758
September......	271,777	315,011	181,421	46,561	33,933
October........	284,656	298,858	155,477	49,885	34,237
November......	212,062	190,043	96,323	33,634	22,012
December......	154,601	143,587	99,416	23,271	18,665
Total........	3,133,186	4,015,933	2,717,886	526,835	410,587

Analysis of 1930 Truck Sales and Production

Domestic Truck Sales 410,587
Foreign Truck Sales(1) 186,702

Total Truck Sales 597,289
Dept. of Commerce Truck Production 569,271

(1) Includes exports, foreign assemblies and Canadian production.

Note: While the difference between production and sales might generally be attributed to reduction in dealer stocks, it must be borne in mind that many passenger car chassis, recorded as such in Dept. of Commerce Production figures, find their way into use as trucks and are recorded as truck sales on sales figures.

8,000,000 Junkers to Be Replaced

	Sales of Cars and Trucks	In Service at End of 1930	Junked in 1930
1930	3,100,000	3,092,000	8,000
1929	4,800,000	4,690,000	99,000
1928	3,783,000	3,520,000	178,000
1927	2,998,000	2,600,000	189,000
1926	3,986,000	3,100,000	351,000
1925	3,380,000	*2,570,000*	410,000
1924	3,717,000	*2,060,000*	430,000
1923	3,793,000	*1,640,000*	458,000
1922	2,446,000	*782,000*	278,000
1921	1,556,000	*342,000*	155,000
1920	2,057,000	*286,000*	166,000
1919	1,851,000	*148,000*	110,000
1918	1,044,000	*44,000*	40,000
1917	1,789,000	*34,000*	41,000
1916	1,504,000	*12,000*	17,000
1915	829,000	*2,000*	4,000
1914	548,000	....	1,000
Total	43,181,000	24,922,000	2,935,000
Total Junkers....		*7,920,000*	

Figures in italics represent cars which the Blue Book shows are junk from a commercial standpoint. From the transportation standpoint they may not be, as their owners would not continue to register them if they were.

The table represents the totals normally due for junking in 1930. Probably higher than actual because of depression last year.

1930-31 Possibilities on Parts and Service for 30 Major Jobs

Based on *Motor World Wholesale* survey of thousands of actual repair orders in several thousand service stations. Covers cars and light trucks, such as Chevrolet, Ford and Dodge. Helpful as a yardstick, as these figures show average.

Jobs Done and Parts Installed Per Month and Per Year for Every 100,000 Registrations

Rear axle assembly jobs..............	1,145	3,690,000
Axle shafts installed	562	1,775,000
Roller bearings	445	1,435,000
Ball bearings	826	2,660,000
Gears	1,300	4,180,000
Gaskets	877	2,820,000
Rear wheel bearing jobs	185	2,594,000
Roller bearings	195	628,000
Front end jobs	1,730	5,570,000
Ball bearings	249	803,000
Roller bearings	746	2,405,000
Spindle bolts	1,505	4,850,000
Bushings, knuckle	2,630	8,470,000
Tie rod bolts	616	1,990,000
Bushings, tie rod	616	1,990,000
Reline brakes	3,440	11,100,000
Engine jobs	9,450	30,400,000
Valves	4,670	15,050,000
Valve springs	4,430	14,300,000
Head gaskets	9,530	30,700,000
Pistons	4,730	15,600,000
Piston pins	6,720	21,700,000
Piston rings	29,500	93,500,000
Piston pin bushings	1,380	4,400,000
Manifold gaskets	12,300	39,600,000
Miscellaneous gaskets	15,050	48,500,000
Clutch jobs	1,870	6,110,000
Throwout bearings	1,130	3,640,000
Bushings	185	594,000
Gaskets	98	314,000
Facings	3,980	12,850,000
Transmission jobs	249	802,000
Ball bearings	152	488,000
Roller bearings	54	174,000
Gaskets	195	628,000
Gears	660	2,130,000
Spring jobs	985	3,180,000
Springs	1,080	3,480,000
Bolts	432	1,390,000
Bushings	162	523,000
Timing jobs	1,020	3,280,000
Chains	270	871,000
Gears	1,030	3,310,000
Gaskets	876	2,820,000

Repair Shop Men Buy More Small Tools from Wholesalers

A sampling investigation by the publishers of the MULTI-GUIDE, covering all repair shops along 30 miles of a main highway, going through communities of all sizes, showed the average repair shop proprietor owns $626 worth of small tools, bought $164 worth in 1930 and is buying 25 per cent of all his small tools from tool peddlers, hardware stores and chain stores, as compared with 40 per cent purchased from these sources two years ago. This represents a gain of 15 per cent for the wholesaler.

The mechanic, on the other hand, owns $72 worth of small tools, bought $23.50 worth in 1930, and appears to buy about 57 per cent of his tools from peddlers and sources other than automotive wholesalers, as compared with 71 per cent bought from these sources two years ago. This represents a gain for the wholesaler or jobber of about 14 per cent.

On specific items the buying practice of repair shop owners is:

	Jobbers	Peddlers	Other Sources	Unknown Sources
Valve lifters	74%	3%	8%	15%
Reamers	41%	..	*52%	7%
Open-end wrenches	45%	38%	5%	12%
Screw drivers	34%	35%	8%	23%

*Includes special reamers bought from car manufacturers.

Design Trends That Affect Business Opportunities

Greater performance and higher acceleration because of higher engine speed increase demand for pistons, pins, rings, valves for replacement.

Larger number of eight-cylinder engines expands market for piston, pin, ring, valve, spring and other similar reciprocating engine parts.

Rebabbitted rods are in greater demand because of use by several builders of non-adjustable type connecting-rod bearings. The need for reaming the bearing is causing jobbers to stock suitable reamers.

85 per cent of makers use chains to drive the camshaft, but 69 per cent of all cars use gears.

Chain drives tend toward two-point type and accessory drives here are by fan belt or separate belt. Jobbers are restocking with belt sizes to take care of this market.

Growing tendency is to check valve spring tension and discard those not up to standard, or replace all with matched sets. Valves with 30 deg. seats are steadily increasing.

With an average compression ratio of 5.23 : 1, spark plugs have been redesigned for better cooling and reduced detonation. These newer types of plugs are supposed to fit more engines and reduce the number of types the jobber and repair shop need stock.

Downdraft carburetors are becoming more popular and with redesigned manifolds are said to be giving more fuel mileage and smoother operation.

The number of cars using front fender parking lights is increasing.

Chromium-plated tire covers introduced in 1930 have been widely favored. Jobber sales on this item should be good.

Reduction in size of some wheel diameters to 17 in. means stocking rims and rim parts to cover this.

1930 Sales by Wholesalers by Zones

	Total Wholesale Sales	Per Cent of U. S.
Zone 1	$39,067,500	7.9
Zone 2	114,672,900	22.4
Zone 3	48,277,200	9.8
Zone 4	104,826,550	21.2
Zone 5	68,605,700	13.9
Zone 6	18,033,300	3.6
Zone 7	42,702,500	8.6
Zone 8	18,626,500	3.8
Zone 9	53,304,300	10.8
Total U. S.	$508,116,450	

STATES IN EACH ZONE

Zone 1—Maine, New Hampshire, Vermont, Massachusetts, Rhode Island and Connecticut.

Zone 2—New York, Pennsylvania, and New Jersey.

Zone 3—Delaware, Maryland, District of Columbia, Virginia, North Carolina, South Carolina, Georgia, Florida, and West Virginia.

Zone 4—Ohio, Indiana, Illinois, Michigan, and Wisconsin.

Zone 5—Minnesota, Missouri, Iowa, North Dakota, South Dakota, Nebraska, and Kansas.

Zone 6—Kentucky, Tennessee, Alabama, and Mississippi.

Zone 7—Arkansas, Louisiana, Oklahoma, and Texas.

Zone 8—Montana, Idaho, Wyoming, Colorado, New Mexico, Arizona, Utah, and Nevada.

Zone 9—Washington, Oregon, and California.

Major Automotive Sales Through Independent Retailers

In its market survey in the nine cities of Atlanta, Baltimore, Chicago, Denver, Seattle, Syracuse, Kansas City, Providence and San Francisco, the U. S. Bureau of Foreign and Domestic Commerce secured comparative data on the business of group-operated or chain automotive stores and independent or unit operated.

COMPARATIVE TRADE OF AUTOMOTIVE RETAIL STORES

AUTOMOBILE DEALERS

	Number of Establishments	Sales	Inventory	Number Employees	Salaries and Wages
Totals (Actual Figures)	1,003	291,309,600	28,186,100	12,389	23,755,300
Unit Operated...	74.1%	67.6%	70.8%	70.1%	69.3%
Group Operated.	25.9%	32.4%	29.2%	29.9%	30.7%

AUTOMOBILE ACCESSORIES

	Number of Establishments	Sales	Inventory	Number Employees	Salaries and Wages
Unit Operated...	92.0%	81.2%	81.8%	81.4%	80.2%
Group Operated.	8.0%	18.8%	18.2%	18.6%	19.8%
Totals (Actual Figures)	2,069	$62,217,000	$9,481,300	4,632	$7,418,300

Sources of New Automobile Dealerships in United States

45.0% organized by automobile salesmen, sales managers, etc., who were employed by other dealers.

19.9% organized by proprietors of garages or repair shops.

5.3% organized by former employees of automobile, parts and accessory manufacturers.

2.9% organized by men formerly employed in garages as mechanics or bookkeepers.

2.3% organized by accessory store proprietors.

1.6% organized by men formerly employed by automotive wholesale houses as salesmen or executives.

77.0% of new dealers were formerly in automotive environment, as shown above.

The remaining 23% of new car dealers were recruited from other fields. Of these—

18% Bankers

13% Mercantile Dealers

10% Finance

5% Flour and Feed

5% Salesmen

49% were Lumber Mill, Taxi Business, Hardware, Mining Engineer, Forestry Service, Radio Store, Accountant, Bookkeeper, Farmer, Contractor, Resort Operator, Sheriff, Public Utility, Commissary Manager, Insurance, Sheet Metal Business, Wholesale Gas and Oil, Filling Station Operator.

Cities Having 100,000 or More Motor Vehicles, 1930

Baltimore, Md.
Boston, Mass.
Buffalo, N. Y.
Chicago, Ill.
Cincinnati, Ohio
Cleveland, Ohio
Detroit, Mich.

Indianapolis, Ind.
Kansas City, Mo.
Los Angeles, Cal.
Milwaukee, Wis.
Minneapolis, Minn.
Newark, N. J.
New York, N. Y.

Philadelphia, Pa.
Pittsburgh, Pa.
San Francisco, Cal.
St. Louis, Mo.
Toledo, Ohio
Washington, D. C.

TOOLS and SHOP EQUIPMENT Needed

To Be Well Equipped as Small, Medium or Large Repair Shop—Also for Specialized Service

BASED ON DATA COMPILED BY *Automobile Trade Journal and Motor Age—1930*

GUIDE TO TYPE OF SERVICE SHOP

1. **Small General Repair Shop**
2. **Medium General Repair Shop**
3. **Large General Repair Shop**
4. **Electrical and Battery Dept.**
5. **Brake Service Dept.**
6. **Axle and Wheel Aligning Dept.**
7. **Lubricating Dept.**
8. **Washing and Polishing Dept.**

Tools Needed	1	2	3	4	5	6	7	8
Air Compressor	x	x	x	x	x	x	x	x
Air Dispenser	x	x	x	x	x	x	x	x
Garage Jack	x	x	x	x	x	x	x	x
Floor Brushes	x	x	x	x	x	x	x	x
Waste Cans	x	x	x	x	x	x	x	x
Repair Card Holder	x	x	x	x	x	x	x	x
Seat Covers	x	x	x	x	x	x	x	x
Fire Extinguishers	x	x	x	x	x	x	x	x
Adjustable Wrenches	x	x	x	x	x	x	x	x
Socket Wrench Set	x	x	x	x	x	x	x	x
Open End Wrenches	x	x	x	x	x	x	x	x
Tire Pressure Gages	x	x	x	x	x	x	x	x
Hammers	x	x	x	x	x	x	x	x
Screw Drivers	x	x	x	x	x	x	x	x
Pliers	x	x	x	x	x	x	x	x
Putty Knives	x	x	x	x	x	x	x	x
Creepers	x	x	x	x	x	x	x	
Fender Covers	x	x	x	x	x	x	x	
Door Covers	x	x	x	x	x	x	x	
Work Bench	x	x	x	x	x	x	x	
Thread Pitch Gage	x	x	x	x	x	x	x	
Thread Chaser	x	x	x	x	x	x	x	
Screw Extractor	x	x	x	x	x	x	x	
Pipe Taps	x	x	x	x	x	x	x	
Vises	x	x	x	x	x	x	x	
Drifts	x	x	x	x	x	x	x	
Cold Chisels	x	x	x	x	x	x		
Soft Hammer	x	x	x	x	x	x		
Pipe Wrench	x	x	x	x	x	x		
Tool Boxes	x	x	x	x	x	x		
Cotter Key Pullers	x	x	x	x	x	x		
Hand Oil Cans	x	x	x	x	x	x		
Rack, Lift or Pit	x				x	x	x	x
Portable Light		x	x	x	x	x	x	x
Stud Bolt Wrench	x	x	x	x	x	x		
Bolt Cutters	x	x	x	x	x			
Taper Reamers	x	x	x	x	x			
Expanding Reamers	x	x	x	x	x			
Adjustable Reamers	x	x	x	x	x			
Tap and Die Sets	x	x	x	x	x			
Wire Gage	x	x	x	x	x			
Calipers, Inside and Outside	x	x	x	x	x	x		
Dividers	x	x	x	x	x	x		
Dial Gage Outfit	x	x	x	x	x	x		
Bushing Puller	x	x	x	x	x			
Bearing Puller	x	x	x	x	x			
Gasket Cutter	x	x	x	x	x			
C Clamps	x	x	x	x	x			
Jacks	x	x	x	x	x			
Breast Drill	x	x	x	x	x			
Bench Grinder	x	x	x	x	x			
Emery Wheel Dresser	x	x	x	x	x			
Bench Arbor Press	x	x	x	x	x			
Center Punches	x	x	x	x	x			
Hack Saws	x	x	x	x	x			
Files	x	x	x	x	x			
Metal Shears	x	x	x	x	x			
Drill Sets	x	x	x	x	x			
Steel Rule	x	x	x	x	x			
Feelers Gages	x	x	x	x	x			

Tools Needed	1	2	3	4	5	6	7	8
Scissors	x	x	x	x	x	x		
Hand Drill	x	x	x	x	x	x		
File Cleaner	x	x	x	x	x	x		
Hub Cap Wrenches	x	x	x		x	x	x	
Display Cases	x	x	x	x		x	x	x
Pedal Depressor	x	x	x	x	x			x
Spray Guns for Penetrating Oil	x	x	x		x	x	x	
Micrometers, Inside and Outside	x	x	x	x	x			
Spring Scale	x	x	x	x	x			
Blow Torch	x	x	x	x	x			
Steel Bins	x	x	x	x	x			
Cleaning Tank	x	x	x	x	x			
Sledge Hammer	x	x	x	x	x			
Steel Tape	x	x	x		x	x		
Bushing Pusher	x	x	x		x	x		
Wheel Puller	x	x	x		x	x		
Engine Cleaner	x	x	x	x				x
Tubing Flaring Tools	x	x	x		x		x	
Tire Changing Equip	x	x	x		x			
Radiator Filling Cans	x	x	x		x		x	x
Car Horses	x	x	x		x	x		
Electric Drill, Medium	x		x	x	x	x		
Funnels	x	x	x	x	x			
Surface Plate	x	x	x	x				
Vee Blocks	x	x	x	x				
Speed Indicators	x	x	x	x				
Head Light Testing Equipment	x	x	x	x				
Gear Puller	x	x	x	x				
Wire Terminal Tools	x	x	x	x				
Soldering Iron	x	x	x	x				
Hole Saw	x	x	x	x				
Glass Cutters	x	x	x	x				
Engine Testing Equip	x	x	x	x				
Spark Plug Cleaners	x	x	x	x				
Electrical Test Light	x	x	x	x				
Spark Plug Tester	x	x	x	x				
Battery Discharge Set	x	x	x	x				
Battery Carriers	x	x	x	x				
Battery Fillers	x	x	x	x				
Steel Stamps	x	x	x	x				
Hydrometers	x	x	x	x				
Bearing Scrapers	x	x	x	x				
Breaker Point Synchronizing Tools	x	x	x	x				
Point File or Stone	x	x	x	x				
Protractor	x	x	x			x		
Steel Square	x	x	x			x		
Spirit Level	x	x	x			x		
Surface Gage	x	x	x			x		
Decelerometer	x	x	x		x			
Spring Bushing Jack	x	x	x			x		
Step Ladder	x	x	x					x
Toe-in Gages	x	x	x			x		
Oil Measures	x	x	x					
Pry Bars	x	x	x				x	
Upholstery Brushes	x	x	x				x	
Whisk Brooms	x	x	x				x	

Tools Needed	1	2	3	4	5	6	7	8
Buckets	x	x	x				x	
Body and Fender Tools	x	x	x				x	
Straight Reamers	x	x	x					
Weighing Scale	x	x	x					
Cylinder Head Lifting Hook	x	x	x					
Tire Tube Testing Equip	x	x	x					
Tire Tube Repair Equip	x	x	x					
Wood Saws	x	x	x					
Wood Planes	x	x	x					
Wood Chisels	x	x	x					
Brace and Wood Bits	x	x	x					
Chain Hoists	x	x	x					
Towing and Wrecking Equipment	x	x	x					
Radiator Flushers	x	x	x					
Connecting Rod Aligner	x	x	x					
Crank Pin Reconditioner	x	x	x					
Bearing Testing Equip	x	x	x					
Piston Pin Inserter	x	x	x					
Piston Vise	x	x	x					
Piston Ring Compressor	x	x	x					
Piston Ring Groove Cleaner	x	x	x					
Piston Ring Remover	x	x	x					
Piston Pin Hole Reconditioner	x	x	x					
Valve Seat Tester	x	x	x					
Carbon Brushes	x	x	x					
Valve Spring Compressor	x	x	x					
Valve Seat Reconditioner	x	x	x					
Valve Refacer	x	x	x					
Anti-Freeze Hydrometer	x	x	x					
Skid Chain Tools	x	x	x					
Valve Lifter	x	x	x					
Spanner Wrench	x	x	x					
Box End Wrenches	x	x	x					
Carbon Scrapers	x	x	x					
Valve Keeper Tool	x	x	x					
Valve Lapper	x	x	x					
Paint Spray Gun		x	x					x
Electric Drill, Small		x	x	x				
Floor Arbor Press		x	x			x		
Electric Drill, Large		x	x					
Drill Press		x	x					
Portable Grinder and Buffer		x	x					
Floor Grinder		x	x					
Welding Outfit		x	x					
Transmission Dolly		x	x					
Rear Axle Stand		x	x					
Engine Stand		x	x					
Connecting Rod Bearing Reconditioner		x	x					
Cylinder Reconditioner		x	x					
Valve Seat Renewer		x	x					
Portable Sander and Polisher		x						x
Lathe and Equipment		x	x					
Rubber Aprons		x	x					

Additional Tools—Each Needed by Only One of the Eight Service Shop Classifications Given Here

3. Large General Repair Shop: Anvil, Forge, Blacksmith Tools, Trimmers' Kit, Trolleys, Power Saw.

4. Electrical and Battery Department: Volt-Ammeter with Shunt, Remagnetizer, Growler, Generator Vise, Mica Undercutter, Distributor and Magneto Tester, Electric Test Stand, Battery Charger, Acid Funnels, Battery Post Drills, Battery Terminal Pullers, Acid Syringe, Rubber Gloves, Fire Pot, Hand Reamer, Correction Thermometer, Battery Compound Pot, Lead Pot, Lead Ladle, Lead Scraper, Battery-Plate Burning Racks, Battery-Plate Separator Trimmer, Battery-Plate Press, Plate Press Separators, Battery-Post Builder Set, Battery-Post Reducer Set, Lead Molds, Battery Compound Remover, Battery-Plate Group Puller, Lead Burning Equipment, Battery Brushes, Battery Connectors, Battery Pliers.

5. Brake Service Department: Brake-Shoe Clearance Gages, Brake Lining Drill, Brake Lining Riveter, Brake Lining Cutter, Brake Lining Clamps, Brake Band Rounding Tool, Hydraulic Brake Bleeder, Hydraulic Brake Cylinder Reconditioner, Brake Wrench Sets, Brake Testing Equipment, Brake Drum Reconditioner.

6. Axle and Wheel Aligning Department: Wheel Aligning Instruments, Axle Bending Equipment, Wheel Service Equipment.

7. Lubricating Department: Spring Leaf Spreader, Hand Oil Guns, Gear Case Flushers, Lubricating Outfit for Transmissions and Differentials, Hand Lubricating Gun for Pressure Fittings, Lubricating Outfit for Pressure Fittings, Drain Plug Wrenches.

8. Washing and Polishing Department: Power Car Washer, Soap Mixer, Chamois, Sponges, Vacuum Cleaners, Rubber Boots, Wringer, Rubber Hose, Fender-Brushes, Wheel Brushes, Barrels.

Analysis of Tire Outlets

Based on figures compiled by Rubber Division, U. S. Department of Commerce, from returns from upwards of 25,000 dealers, as of October 1, 1929.

Other Functions Performed by Tire Dealers Reporting

Function	Number Reporting	Per Cent	Number of These Outlets in Chilton Trade List
Sell Automobiles.........	10,203	39.2	58,870
Repair Vehicles..........	12,642	48.5	104,834
Sell Batteries...........	15,550	59.7	56,391
Sell Gasoline............	19,318	74.1	....
Do Vulcanizing..........	3,589	13.8	....

Relation of Tire-and-Tube Sales to Total Volume

	Under 25 Per Cent	25 to 50 Per Cent	50 to 75 Per Cent	Over 75 Per Cent
Number Reporting........	21,667	2,874	704	812
Per Cent of Total........	83.13	11.03	2.70	3.12

Obviously, from the above, the tire merchants who are selling by far the major volume of casings and tubes are those handling other automobile lines also, and what is more significant, those actually *majoring* in other lines. 83.13 per cent of all the outlets get less than 25 per cent of their total volume from tires and tubes.

The average stock of automobile tires held by the average tire dealer in the U. S. on Oct. 1, 1929, was 68.4, and the average number of tubes was 103.4.

Special Analysis of Types of Dealers in Tires

This analysis is representative of all sections of the country, although covering only 7,295 of the 26,057 returns.

	Number of Dealers	Total No. of Casings	Average Casings per Dealer	Per Cent of Total Dealers	Per Cent of Total Casings
Total Dealers Considered...	7,295	529,275	72.55	100.00	100.00
All Dealers Selling Autos...	2,800	171,955	61.41	38.38	32.48
All Dealers Selling Batteries.	4,234	313,263	73.98	58.04	59.18
All Dealers Vulcanizers.....	990	151,145	152.67	13.57	28.55
Selling Both Auto and Batteries..............	2,151	143,097	66.52	29.48	27.04
Selling Autos and Vulcanizing.................	209	30,193	144.46	2.86	5.70
Selling Batteries and Vulcanizing............	565	106,444	188.39	7.74	20.11
Total Selling Autos, or Batteries, or with Vulcanizing Equipment.............	5,409	432,668	79.99	74.14	81.75

This table shows that of 7,295 dealers with average stocks of 72.55 tires each, 2,800 were automobile dealers with average stocks of 61.41 tires each, representing 32.48 per cent of the total tire business. Further, 4,234 were battery dealers (and 75 per cent of the automobile dealers are duplicated here) with average tire stocks of 73.98 each, representing 59.18 per cent of the total.

Radio and the Automotive Dealer

17 per cent of radio outlets are among automotive establishments, being the second most important type of outlet for radio in point of numbers.

8 per cent of total radio sales flow through these automotive concerns—tied for fourth place with department stores.

The average radio sales volume of the automotive dealers is $7,420, fifth in size among 13 types of outlets.

These data are from reports to the Electrical Equipment Division of the U. S. Bureau of Foreign and Domestic Commerce.

Car Cost 6.43 Cents Per Mile

(Figures from Bulletin No. 91 by T. R. Agg and H. S. Carter, Iowa State College)

NOTE: The figure 6.43 cents is comparable with the 10 cents per mile compiled by the same authority in 1924. Greater mileage of cars and improved highways account for the lower operating cost per mile.

Average Cost of Automobile Operation

Based on detailed cost records covering about 800 automobiles operated in various parts of the United States and an average of 11,000 miles per year.

Type of Car	Light 4	Medium 4	Heavy 4	Light 6	Medium 6	Heavy 6
	Average Cents Per Mile	Average Cents Per Mile	Average Cents Per Mile	Average Cents Per Mile	Average Cents Per Mile	Average Cents Per Mile
1. Gasoline at 20 cents per gal.	1.34	1.14	1.31	1.36	1.52	1.42
2. Oil	.25	.17	.16	.18	.20	.17
3. Tires and tubes	.60	.65	.70	.75	.80	.90
4. Maintenance ..	1.55	1.90	2.06	1.95	2.14	2.53
5. Depreciation ..	1.25	1.40	1.57	1.74	2.09	2.57
6. License	.11	.14	.20	.20	.24	.27
7. Garage at $4 per month	.44	.44	.44	.44	.44	.44
8. Interest at 6%.	.27	.38	.55	.55	.71	.81
9. Insurance (fire, theft, tornado, liability)	.21	.20	.21	.21	.26	.28
Total	6.02	6.42	7.20	7.38	8.40	9.45
Annual mileage	11,000	11,000	11,000	11,000	11,000	11,000
Average miles per gallon gas..	14.95	17.53	15.29	14.68	13.19	14.02

Cost of Operation of an Imaginary "Average" Automobile

(Annual Mileage of 11,000)

Item of Cost	Cents Per Mile
Gasoline	1.31
Oil	0.22
Tires and tubes	0.64
Maintenance	1.72
Depreciation	1.39
License	0.14
Garage at $4 per month	0.44
Interest at 6 per cent	0.36
Insurance (fire, theft, tornado)	0.21
Total cents per mile	6.43

Government Revenue from Each Motor Vehicle Steadily Increasing*

	Total Registration	Registration Fees	Gas Tax		Average Receipts Per Vehicle
1909	294,000	$942,675		....	$3.20
1914	1,711,339	12,382,031		....	7.20
1919	7,566,446	64,697,255	(4)	1,022,514	8.68
1923	15,092,177	188,970,992	(35)	38,566,338	15.07
1925	19,937,274	260,619,621	(44)	148,358,087	20.50
1928	24,493,124	322,630,025	(46)	304,871,766	25.63
1929	26,623,857	346,988,958		428,970,854	29.14
1930	26,657,072	328,316,058		476,666,189	31.97

*Highway Education Board.
Figures in parentheses show number of states collecting gasoline tax.

TOOLS and SHOP EQUIPMENT Needed

To Handle 21 Most-Frequently-Performed Flat-Rate Repair and Service Operations

You Can Check the Tools Required for Each Operation and Also the Number of Different Operations for Which Each Tool Can Be Used

BASED ON DATA COMPILED BY *Automobile Trade Journal and Motor Age—1930*

LIST OF FLAT-RATE OPERATIONS TAKEN FROM *Chilton Flat-Rate Book*

GUIDE TO FLAT RATE OPERATIONS

1. Adjust service brakes
2. Grind valves, clean carbon, tune engine
3. Complete lubrication
4. Tune engine
5. Reline brakes
6. Adjust steering gear
7. Repack water pump
8. Install fan belt
9. Install pins, rings, adjust rod bearings
10. Renew front axle bushings and pins
11. Install timing chain or gear
12. Check and correct steering geometry
13. Adjust shackle bolts
14. Overhaul clutch
15. Overhaul generator
16. Repair fender
17. Tighten body bolts
18. Overhaul differential
19. Renew all spring bolts
20. Test battery and recharge
21. Wash and polish car

FLAT RATE OPERATIONS (For Guide to Numerals See Above)

Tools Needed	1	2	3	4	5	6	7	8	9	10	11	12	13	14	15	16	17	18	19	20	21
Socket Wrench Sets	x	x	x	x	x	x	x	x	x	x	x	x	x	x	x	x	x	x	x	x	
Open End Wrench Sets	x	x	x	x	x	x	x	x	x	x	x	x	x	x	x	x	x	x	x	x	
Adjustable Wrenches	x	x	x	x	x	x	x	x	x	x	x	x	x	x	x	x	x	x	x	x	
Stillson Wrenches	x	x	x	x	x			x	x	x	x	x	x	x	x	x	x	x			
Hammers	x	x	x		x			x	x	x	x	x	x	x	x	x	x	x	x	x	
Screw Drivers	x	x	x	x	x	x	x	x	x	x	x	x	x	x	x	x	x	x	x	x	
Pliers	x	x	x	x	x	x	x	x	x	x	x	x	x	x	x	x	x	x	x	x	
Chisels	x	x	x		x		x	x	x	x	x	x	x	x	x	x	x				
Center Punches		x		x	x		x	x	x		x	x	x		x	x		x			
Drifts	x	x		x	x	x		x	x	x	x	x	x	x	x	x	x				
Files	x	x		x	x	x	x		x	x	x	x	x	x	x	x	x	x	x		
Abrasive Paper and Cloth	x	x		x	x	x	x		x	x	x	x		x	x	x		x	x		
Screw Extractor Set	x	x	x	x	x	x	x	x		x		x	x	x	x	x	x				
Cotter Pin Puller	x	x		x	x	x		x	x	x	x	x	x	x	x	x					
Thread Chasers	x		x		x				x					x	x						
Hub Cap Wrenches	x		x			x		x	x		x	x	x		x	x					
Electric Drill	x	x		x	x		x	x	x	x	x	x	x	x	x	x	x	x			
Putty Knife	x	x		x	x	x		x	x	x	x	x	x	x	x	x	x	x	x		
Drill Set	x	x		x	x	x	x	x	x	x	x	x	x	x	x	x	x	x	x		
Tap and Die Set	x	x		x	x	x	x	x	x	x	x	x	x	x	x	x	x	x	x		
Reamer Sets		x			x		x	x	x	x	x	x		x	x		x				
Dial Gage				x			x		x	x	x		x		x						
Feeler Gages	x	x		x	x			x	x		x	x		x	x		x				
Micrometer Calipers					x	x		x	x		x		x		x		x				
Surface Plate					x	x		x	x			x		x		x					
Bushing Pullers		x				x		x	x	x	x	x		x		x	x				x
Gear Pullers						x			x	x			x		x		x				
Wheel Pullers	x		x		x			x		x		x	x		x		x				
Hack Saw	x	x		x		x		x	x	x	x	x	x	x	x	x	x	x			
Bench Arbor Press						x	x	x	x		x		x	x	x		x				
Vise	x	x			x		x	x	x	x	x	x	x	x	x		x				
Work Bench	x	x		x		x	x	x	x	x	x	x	x	x	x		x				
Creepers	x		x	x		x	x	x	x	x	x	x	x	x	x	x	x	x	x		
Drop Lights	x	x	x	x	x	x	x	x	x	x	x	x	x	x	x	x	x	x	x	x	x
Fender Covers	x	x	x	x	x	x	x	x	x	x	x	x	x	x	x	x	x	x	x	x	x
Seat Covers	x	x	x	x	x	x	x	x	x	x	x	x	x	x	x	x	x	x	x	x	x
Repair Card Holders	x	x	x	x	x	x	x	x	x	x	x	x	x	x	x	x	x	x	x	x	x
Waste Cans	x	x	x	x	x	x	x	x	x	x	x	x	x	x	x	x	x	x	x	x	x
Chain Hoists									x	x			x	x				x			
Radiator Filling Cans	x		x			x	x	x	x				x								
Jacks	x		x		x	x	x	x	x	x	x	x	x	x	x	x	x	x			
Garage Jacks	x	x	x	x	x	x	x	x	x	x	x	x	x	x	x	x	x	x	x		
Horses	x		x	x		x	x	x	x	x	x	x	x	x							
Rack, Lift or Pit	x		x		x	x		x	x	x	x	x	x	x	x	x					

FLAT RATE OPERATIONS (For Guide to Numerals See Above)

Tools Needed	1	2	3	4	5	6	7	8	9	10	11	12	13	14	15	16	17	18	19	20	21
Bench Grinder	x	x		x	x	x			x	x	x	x		x	x	x	x	x	x	x	
Air Compressor		x	x		x				x		x			x	x			x			x
Engine Testing Instruments		x							x		x				x						
Carbon Cleaning Brushes		x							x												
Breaker Point Synchronizing Tools		x													x						
Cylinder Head Lifting Hooks		x							x												
Spark Plug Cleaning Brushes		x	x																		
Breaker Point File or Stone		x		x											x						
Rod and Piston Aligner									x		x										
Bearing Scrapers									x		x						x		x	x	
Brake Testing Machine	x				x									x							
Brake Lining Driller					x									x							
Brake Lining Riveter					x									x							
Cut-out Brake Drums or Gages	x				x							x			x			x			
Brake Lining Cutter					x																x
Pedal Depressor	x				x							x		x							x
Hydraulic Pressure Bleeders	x				x																
Brake Band Rounding Tool	x				x													x			
Pressure Lubricators			x																	x	
Gear Oil Lubricator			x															x			
Hand Lubricating Guns	x	x	x	x	x	x									x			x	x		
Oil Measures	x	x		x			x		x		x							x		x	
Hand Oil and Grease Guns		x		x		x											x	x	x		
Oil Cans	x	x	x	x	x	x	x	x	x	x	x	x	x	x	x	x	x	x	x	x	
Gear Case Flushers			x											x				x			
Spray Gun for Penetrating Oil	x			x		x										x	x	x			x
Funnels	x	x	x	x	x	x	x	x				x		x	x			x	x		
Pry Bars	x	x	x	x	x	x	x	x			x	x	x	x	x	x	x	x	x	x	
Caster, Camber and Toe-in Gages						x						x									
Lathe		x			x									x	x			x			
Soldering Irons		x		x											x	x				x	
Welding Outfit															x	x					
Blow Torch	x				x	x			x	x			x	x	x	x		x	x		
Anti-freeze Hydrometer		x					x		x	x	x	x									
Electric Test Stand															x					x	
Volt and Ammeter with Shunt															x					x	
Bushing Pusher						x			x	x					x			x			
Bearing Puller									x					x	x			x			
Buckets	x	x	x		x	x	x	x		x	x		x	x		x		x			x

NOTES:

Operation No. 2 requires also Valve Refacer, Valve Seat Reconditioner, Valve Lifters, Valve Spring Compressor, Valve Spring Tester, Valve Lapper, Valve Seat Renewing Tool and Carbon Scrapers.

Operation No. 4 requires also Hydraulic Cylinder Hones and Gages.

Operation No. 5 requires also Brake Testing Machine, Brake Lining Clamps.

Operation No. 9 requires also Piston Ring Compressors, Piston Ring Removers, Piston Ring Groove Cleaners, Crankpin Reconditioner, Conrod Bearing Reconditioning Tools, Engine Bearing Testing Equipment.

Operation No. 12 requires also Axle and Wheel Straightening Equipment.

Operation No. 15 requires also Growler.

Operation No. 16 requires also Fender Tools.

Operation No. 18 requires also Rear Axle Stand.

Operation No. 19 requires also Spring Bushing Jack.

Operation No. 20 requires also Storage Battery Cell Tester, Battery Hydrometers, Battery Filler, Battery Charger.

Operation No. 21 requires also Car Washer, Chamois Sponges, Vacuum Cleaner, Fender Brush, Rubber Boots, Rubber Aprons, Wringer.

Extent Repair Shops Are Actually Equipped With 20 Items—and What is Recommended

Compiled from a survey of over 3000 service stations by *Motor World Wholesale*. Should be helpful to service station operators in determining proper equipment, and to wholesalers in recommending equipment to service stations.

Of the 3000 Service Stations:

3% do 1000	jobs and	16% of work
4% do 700-1000	jobs and	11% of work
9% do 500-700	jobs and	16% of work
21% do 300-500	jobs and	26% of work
47% do 100-300	jobs and	28% of work
16% do under 100	jobs and	3% of work

	ACTUAL			RECOMMENDED			Total Number of Tools in All Shops	Recommended	Present State of Under-Equipment
	Jobs per Tool per Month	Tools per Shop	Tools per 100,000 Registrations	Jobs per Tool per Month	Tools per Shop	Tools per 100,000 Registrations			
PORTABLE ELECTRIC DRILLS 1/4"	354	.8	300	130	2.2	820	80,500	219,000	138,500
1/2"	394	.7	270	143	2.0	740	72,300	199,000	126,700
5/8"	827	.3	128	220	1.3	480	34,400	129,000	94,600
3/4"	1,500	.2	71	168	1.7	630	18,950	169,000	150,050
JACKS Garage on wheels	251	1.1	420	95	3.0	1,110	113,000	298,500	185,500
Other types	102	2.8	1,004	82,	3.5	1,300	278,000	348,000	70,000
ARBOR PRESSES	392	.7	271	300	1.0	370	72,700	99,500	26,800
CHASSIS LUBRICATING DEVICES Electric	1,580	.2	67	240	1.2*	440*	18,000	119,000*	52,100*
Air	580	.5	183				48,900		
WHEEL PULLERS (Sets)	109	2.6	970	95	3.0	1,110	261,000	298,500	37,500
BRAKE BAND RIVETING MACHINES Power driven	1,000	.3	106	300	1.0*	370*	28,500	99,500*	14,300*
Foot operated	502	.6	212				56,700		
BRAKE BAND COUNTERSINK AND DRILL Power driven	537	.5	197	300	1.0*	370*	53,000	99,500*	27,550*
Foot operated	1,500	.2	71				18,950		
CONNECTING ROD ALIGNERS	350	.8	304	220	1.3	480	81,300	129,000	47,700
CYLINDER RECONDITIONING DEVICES Hone type	344	.8	309	191	1.5	570	82,800	149,000	66,200
Boring and grinding and reaming	810	.4	131	220	1.3	480	35,200	129,000	93,800
HORSES (Pairs)	102	2.8	1,040	57	5.0	1,860	279,000	497,500	218,500
VALVE REFACERS Hand operated	955	.3	111	—	—	—	29,800	—	
Power operated	369	.8	288	191	1.5	570	77,200	149,000	71,800
CAR WASHING MACHINES	1,100	.3	97	300	1.0	370	25,900	99,500	73,600
BATTERY CHARGING EQUIPMENT Rectifier or bulb	438	.7	242	300	1.0	370	64,900	99,500	34,600
Motor generator	1,260	.2	84	300	1.0	370	22,600	99,500	76,900
SPRAY PAINTING EQUIPMENT	477	.6	224	300	1.0	370	59,900	99,500	39,600
WRECKING CRANES	550	.5	193	168	1.7	630	51,700	169,000	117,300
BENCH AND FLOOR GRINDING WHEELS Foot	5,725	.05	19				4,970		
Power	262	1.1	407	240	1.2*	440*	109,000	119,000*	5,030
SHOP HOISTS AND CRANES	197	1.5	541	114	2.5	930	145,000	249,000	104,000
WELDING EQUIPMENT	382	.7	278	300	1.0	370	74,400	99,500	25,100
MICA UNDERCUTTERS Hand	1,290	.2	83		—	—	22,100		
Power	1,800	.2	59	950	.3	112	15,900	29,900	14,900
GROWLERS	556	.5	191		—		51,100	—	—
METERS Volt	480	.6	221		—		59,200	—	
Ampere	523	.5	202		—		54,300	—	

* Either type.   — No recommendations received.

AVERAGE NUMBER OF TOOLS PER SHOP, PER JOB, PER MONTH

A-Actual. R-Recommended.	Over 1000 A	R	700-1000 A	R	500-700 A	R	300-500 A	R	100-300 A	R	Under 100 A	R	Total A	R
PORTABLE ELECTRIC DRILLS 1/4"	1.4	4	1.	3	1.2	2	.9	2	.7	1	.5	1	.8	2.2
1/2"	.9	3	.6	3	.8	2	.8	2	.7	1	.7	1	.7	2.0
5/8"	.5	2	.5	2	.5	1	.4	1	.3	1	.3	1	.3	1.3
3/4"	.3	3	.3	2	.3	2	.3	1	.1	1	.09	1	.2	1.7
JACKS Garage on wheels	1.8	6	1.7	4	2.	3	1.3	2	.9	2	.7	1	1.1	3.0
Other types	5.7	6	3.5	4	2.8	4	2.8	3	2.7	2	2.4	2	2.8	3.5
ARBOR PRESSES	1.2	1	1.2	1	1.1	1	.9	1	.6	1	.5	1	.7	1.0
CHASSIS LUBRICATING DEVICES Electric	.4	2	.4	1	.3	1	.2	1	.1	1	.1	1	.2	1.2*
Air	1.3				.6			.5		.5		.3		.5	
WHEEL PULLERS (Sets)	3.8	5	3.7	4	2.9	3	3.	3	2.5	2	2.	1	2.6	3.0
BRAKE BAND RIVETING MACHINES Power driven	.4	1	.3	1	.4	1	.4	1	.3	1	.2	1	.3	1.0*
Foot operated	.8		.8		.7		.6		.6		.4		.6	
BRAKE BAND COUNTERSINK AND DRILL Power driven	.8	1	.5	1	.6	1	.6	1	.5	1	.4	1	.5	1.0*
Foot operated	.3		.3		.3		.1		.2		.2		.2	
CONNECTING ROD ALIGNERS	1.1	2	1.3	2	1.1	1	.8	1	.8	1	.6	1	.8	1.3
CYLINDER RECONDITIONING DEVICES Hone type	1.4	2	.9	2	1.2	2	.9	1	.8	1	.7	1	.8	1.5
Boring and grinding and reaming	.6	2	.6	2	.6	1	.5	1	.3	1	.2	1	.4	1.3
HORSES (Pairs)	6.2	9	5.	7	3.7	5	3.2	4	2.5	3	1.7	2	2.8	5.0
VALVE REFACERS Hand operated	.1		.5	—	.1		.4		.3		.4		.3	
Power operated	1.	2	1.	2	.9	2	.8	1	.7	1	.7	1	.8	1.5
CAR WASHING MACHINES	.8	1	.6	1	.4	1	.3	1	.2	1	.1	1	.3	1.0
BATTERY CHARGING EQUIPMENT Rectifier or bulb	1.2	1	.6	1	.8	1	.7	1	.6	1	.6	1	.7	1.0
Motor generator	.4	1	.3	1	.3	1	.3	1	.2	1	.2	1	.2	1.0
SPRAY PAINTING EQUIPMENT	.9	1	.9	1	1.1	1	.6	1	.5	1	.4	1	.6	1.0
WRECKING CRANES	.8	3	1.	2	.5	2	.6	1	.5	1	.4	1	.5	1.7
BENCH AND FLOOR GRINDING WHEELS Foot	—		—		.02		.07		.05		.05		.05	
Power	1.7	2	1.1	1	1.4	1	1.2	1	1.	1	.9	1	1.1	1.2*
SHOP HOISTS AND CRANES	1.9	4	2.1	3	2.3	3	1.8	2	1.2	2	1.	1	1.5	2.5
WELDING EQUIPMENT	1.3	1	1.	1	1.	1	.8	1	.7	1	.5	1	.7	1.0
MICA UNDERCUTTERS Hand	.1		.3		.2		.2		.2		.2		.2	
Power	.8	1	.4	1	.2		.1		.1		.07		.2	.3
GROWLERS	.9		.8		.7		.6		.5		.3		.5	
METERS Volt	.9		.5		.7		.6		.7		.4		.6	
Ampere	1.		.9		.7		.5		.6		.3		.5	

* Either type.   — No recommendations received.

REAMER SIZES That Are Most Needed In Important Service Jobs

Here Are the Sizes of Expansion Reamers that the Well-Equipped Shop Needs to Perform Service Work on the Items Listed Below for Passenger Car Models from 1925-1929.

SIZES SHOWN IN DECIMALS. FOR CORRESPONDING FRACTIONS, SEE TABLE BELOW

Wristpin

.734	.843	.875	.984	1.093	1.186
.740	.850	.917	.990	1.108	1.218
.750	.856	.927	1.000	1.109	1.225
.796	.859	.937	1.047	1.125	1.235
.812	.865	.968	1.062	1.156	1.250

Valve Guide

.312	.328	.343	.375

Push Rod Guide

.375	.625	.750	.828	.875	1.000
.500	.640	.797	.859	.990	1.062
.609	.687				

Connecting Rod

1.250	1.685	1.875	2.109	2.250	2.562
1.375	1.750	1.984	2.125	2.312	2.625
1.500	1.812	2.000	2.187	2.375	2.687
1.625	1.859	2.093	2.234	2.500	2.750

Water Pump Bushing

.613	.730	.8437	.9375	1.0937	1.225
.618	.7343	.850	.9687	1.105	1.2343
.625	.740	.8593	.9843	1.125	1.250
.6562	.750	.865	1.000	1.1562	1.2968
.668	.7812	.875	1.0312	1.1875	1.3125
.6875	.7968	.9062	1.0468	1.2187	1.375
.7187	.8125	.917	1.0625		

King Bolt Bushing

.421	.625	750	.843	.875	1.000
.500	.687	.812	.859	.937	1.937
.562	.734				

Tie Rod Bushing

.437	.562	.625	.687	.750
.500	.565			

Spring Bolt Bushing

.500	.565	.687	.812	.875	1.000
.562	.625	.750			

Generator Bushing

.500	.6562	.750	.865	1.000	1.1562
.5312	668	.7812	.875	1.0312	1.1875
.5625	.6875	.7968	.9062	1 0468	1.2187
.5937	.7187	.8125	.917	1.0625	1.225
.609	.730	.8437	.9375	1.0937	1.2343
.618	.7343	.850	.9687	1.105	1.250
.625	.740	.8593	.9843	1.125	

Starter Bushing

.500	6562	.750	.865	1.000	1.1562
.5312	668	.7812	.875	1.0312	1.1875
5625	.6875	.7968	.9062	1.0468	1.2187
.5937	.7187	.8125	.917	1.0625	1.225
.609	.730	.8437	.9375	1.0937	1.2343
.618	.7343	.850	.9687	1.105	1.250
.625	.740	.8593	.9843	1.125	

DECIMAL TO FRACTION CONVERSION TABLE

	015625	9/64	.140625	17/64	.265625	25/64	.390625	33/64	.515625	41/64	.640625	49/64	.765625	57/64	.890625
	.03125	5/32	.15625	9/32	.28125	13/32	.40625	17/32	.53125	21/32	.65625	25/32	.78125	29/32	.90625
	.046875	11/64	.171875	19/64	.296875	27/64	.421875	35/64	.546875	43/64	.671875	51/64	.796875	59/64	.921875
	.0625	3/16	.1875	5/16	.3125	7/16	.4375	9/16	.5625	11/16	.6875	13/16	.8125	15/16	.9375
	.078125	13/64	.203125	21/64	.328125	29/64	.453125	37/64	.57812	45/64	.703125	53/64	.828125	61/64	.953125
	.09375	7/32	.21875	11/32	.3475	15/32	.46875	19/32	.593755	23/32	.71875	27/32	.84375	31/32	.96875
	.109375	15/64	.234375	23/64	.359375	31/64	.484375	39/64	.609375	47/64	.734375	55/64	.859375	63/64	.904375
	.1250	1/4	.2500	3/8	.3750	1/2	.50000	5/8	.625	3/4	.7500	7/8	.875	In.	1.000000

Analysis of Truck Operating Experience from 5,584 Concerns

46,017 Vehicles Owned by Concerns Grouped Here by Type of Business for Easy Comparison.
Information Came from All Types of Concerns All Over the United States and is Quite Representative.

TYPE OF BUSINESS (Vocation)	Number of Firms	Number of Vehicles by Capacity*: Light, ½ to 1½ Tons	Number of Vehicles by Capacity*: Medium, 1½ to 3 Tons	Number of Vehicles by Capacity*: Heavy, 3 Tons Up	Bodies Used†: % Using Special Bodies	Bodies Used†: % Using Standard Bodies	Bodies Used†: % Using both Special and Standard Bodies	Method of Paying Drivers: % Paying Drivers Straight Salary	Method of Paying Drivers: % Paying Drivers Salary and Bonus	Method of Paying Drivers: % Paying Drivers Straight Commission	Hauling by Own or Hired Trucks: % Do all Hauling Delivering in Own Trucks	Hauling by Own or Hired Trucks: % Hiring Trucks for One or More Purposes
					%	%	%	%	%	%	%	%
Auto Supplies and Accessories	177	381	163	27	28	57	15	87	8	5	55	45
Bakeries	121	2,755	365	113	38	49	13	28	36	36	53	47
Bottlers	97	460	798	84	71	19	10	45	38	17	83	17
Building Material and Supplies	295	644	809	617	52	41	7	91	6	3	63	37
Department Stores	132	744	275	28	48	41	11	85	13	2	56	44
Coal, Coke and Ice	101	597	364	114	66	22	12	78	20	2	82	18
Coal and Fuel Exclusively	146	379	320	152	68	26	6	80	7	13	62	38
Confectioners	34	99	26	0	41	47	12	73	18	9	50	50
Creameries, Dairies and Ice Cream Mfrs.	184	1,259	514	74	46	44	10	67	24	9.	71	29
Drugs, Chemicals and Drug Sundries	23	161	46	9	48	43	9	96	4	..	57	43
Electrical Contractors	51	136	36	1	32	62	6	98	2	..	57	43
Flour and Feed Mills and Grain Elevators	94	124	118	16	50	48	2	97	3	..	79	21
Florists	59	142	15	2	19	78	3	97	3	..	59	41
Furniture and House Furnishings	179	509	184	16	73	19	8	95	5	..	71	29
General Merchandise	219	656	105	7	36	59	5	86	10	4	68	32
Groceries and Other Food Products	341	2,554	683	303	39	54	17	92	6	2	67	33
Hardware	100	200	56	12	36	60	4	97	2	1	73	27
Hay, Grain and Feed	48	142	70	8	46	50	4	91	9	..	78	22
Lumber, Logging and Mill Work	317	598	525	141	74	21	5	94	6	..	75	25
Machinery and Tools	62	93	71	25	40	53	7	93	5	2	45	55
Meats and Other Packing House Products	74	1,099	921	224	51	38	11	82	16	2	68	32
Metals and Metal Products	107	150	101	80	33	54	3	93	6	1	58	42
Oils and Gasoline	322	1,532	1,940	291	71	21	8	72	22	6	86	14
Plumbing and Heating	87	232	80	27	40	56	4	96	3	1	46	54
Produce and Com. Merchants	120	346	297	16	55	38	7	85	13	2	82	18
Publishers	59	724	123	8	25	61	14	89	11	..	37	63
General Contractors	165	475	317	201	49	43	8	95	4	1	50	50
Road Contractors	83	490	946	665	42	49	9	88	9	3	58	42
General Trucking	339	993	1,007	534	61	31	8	78	17	5	79	21
Laundries and Cleaners	131	2,836	86	1	30	62	8	22	56	22	78	22
Warehouses	87	248	353	143	67	22	11	77	17	6	86	14
Municipal, County and State	57	433	366	415	33	49	18	96	4	..	64	36
Gas, Electric and Water Utilities	130	2,163	1,281	231	39	34	27	91	8	1	55	45
Unclassified	339	585	354	127	52	44	4	91	8	1	51	49
Miscellaneous Industries	432	1,051	518	61	46	48	6	88	7	5	74	26

OPERATING EXPERIENCE

TYPE OF BUSINESS (Vocation)	Average Miles Per Gallon of Gas: Light Duty	Average Miles Per Gallon of Gas: Medium Duty	Average Miles Per Gallon of Gas: Heavy Duty	Average Miles Per Quart of Oil: Light Duty	Average Miles Per Quart of Oil: Medium Duty	Average Miles Per Quart of Oil: Heavy Duty	Average Payload: Light Duty	Average Payload: Medium Duty	Average Payload: Heavy Duty	Average Length of Haul of Route: Light Duty	Average Length of Haul of Route: Medium Duty	Average Length of Haul of Route: Heavy Duty	Average Number of Stops Per Day: Light Duty	Average Number of Stops Per Day: Medium Duty	Average Number of Stops Per Day: Heavy Duty	Total Operating Costs Per Mile Including Maintenance and Depreciation: Light Duty	Total Operating Costs Per Mile Including Maintenance and Depreciation: Medium Duty	Total Operating Costs Per Mile Including Maintenance and Depreciation: Heavy Duty
	Miles	Miles	Miles	Miles	Miles	Miles	Lbs.	Lbs.	Lbs.	Miles	Miles	Miles	Stops	Stops	Stops	Cents	Cents	Cents
Auto Supplies and Accessories	13.1	9.5	6.1	128.7	116.7	95.2	2004.	4924.	11091.	33.7	71.0	53.6	22.6	14.3	12.8	15.2	18.8	51.7
Bakeries	12.9	9.8	5.5	124.4	86.0	55.2	1215.	2981.	9500.	60.5	123.9	52.	93.2	54.9	8.0	7.9	13.4	40.0
Bottlers	13.4	9.8	6.6	109.2	90.3	97.0	3459.	4741.	9583.	40.0	56.3	57.5	49.4	45.6	52.3	7.8	11.9	..
Building Material and Supplies	12.1	9.7	5.0	104.3	90.8	59.2	2894.	6160.	12712.	11.6	17.1	11.8	21.0	17.3	12.8	16.0	20.7	29.2
Department Stores	12.3	9.9	4.7	106.6	95.1	88.0	1848.	4902.	12857.	40.4	45.5	44.9	81.6	29.6	12.3	12.1	15.9	31.5
Coal, Coke and Ice	12.9	9.7	4.7	81.9	80.8	43.0	3006.	4574.	9500.	19.7	25.9	45.4	85.2	83.2	17.4	11.2	17.2	22.8
Coal and Fuel Exclusively	11.8	8.6	4.9	110.5	92.8	60.2	3323.	5470.	10069.	5.1	15.2	9.2	25.0	24.1	16.9	18.7	24.7	42.8
Confectioners	13.2	11.4	..	119.5	125.6	..	1482.	3417.	..	57.4	72.6	..	39.3	43.3	..	9.4	18.1	..
Creameries, Dairies and Ice Cream Mfrs.	12.3	9.4	6.0	105.4	91.2	78.4	2202.	5222	10742.	42.0	59.4	65.2	129.0	63.3	35.9	10.3	13.9	18.1
Drugs, Chemicals and Drug Sundries	13.0	7.4	5.5	82.5	85.2	42.7	1687.	4500.	11750.	41.2	22.4	15.0	30.5	25.7	4.0	33.4	39.6	56.5
Electrical Contractors	14.6	11.4	..	128.0	100.4	..	1055.	3187.	..	14.7	25.7	..	19.3	22.9	..	9.2	10.5	..
Flour and Feed Mills and Grain Elevators	13.2	11.4	6.0	113.3	91.6	75.0	3207.	5330.	8800	18.5	36.5	8.2	29.3	18.9	11.5	9.9	11.6	..
Florists	14.2	12.3	11.0	114.4	127.1	85.0	1082.	2860.	..	17.2	31.2	33.0	32.0	18.2	8.0	8.6	15.2	..
Furniture and House Furnishings	13.2	10.5	6.7	104.4	110.5	96.2	1584.	3573.	8000.	27.6	82.3	120.0	24.7	18.4	6.7	10.9	17.0	27.0
General Merchandise	14.0	10.6	6.3	111.9	101.3	80.5	1946.	4462.	8571.	26.8	46.3	39.7	48.7	24.7	7.6	11.9	13.5	28.6
Groceries and Other Food Products	13.0	10.6	6.9	108.3	109.2	65.1	1836.	5239.	10717.	21.9	45.2	37.9	56.9	29.9	11.9	9.5	16.8	39.4
Hardware	14.1	11.2	5.0	108.2	107.2	85.0	1512.	3841.	6500.	12.0	18.0	15.0	27.1	17.8	12.5	10.9	13.5	..
Hay, Grain and Feed	13.8	9.5	6.7	112.5	89.4	59.6	2707.	6542.	16400.	21.2	29.9	46.4	19.5	10.5	5.7	8.8	14.7	..
Lumber, Logging and Mill Work	12.5	9.4	5.9	86.8	80.0	71.7	2645.	5307.	9612.	11.5	16.8	30.8	19.6	14.9	8.2	15.0	20.6	29.0
Machinery and Tools	13.4	9.9	5.4	96.0	114.1	55.6	1358.	4278.	12167.	23.2	32.7	33.5	20.1	15.7	10.5	14.7	24.5	38.5
Meats and Other Packing House Products	12.7	9.9	4.8	122.0	84.2	60.4	1758.	4058.	10000.	34.3	56.3	43.5	49.4	39.1	30.8	9.0	12.0	36.1
Metals and Metal Products	12.4	9.1	4.9	94.1	85.7	53.7	2821.	5162.	9618.	33.2	40.2	16.6	22.5	17.3	10.5	15.2	30.2	44.3
Oils and Gasoline	13.5	10.8	6.7	113.3	96.3	84.6	2883.	4459.	8893.	23.5	25.7	49.8	15.4	13.5	13.7	9.2	12.5	18.3
Plumbing and Heating	15.1	10.3	3.7	94.8	89.3	42.5	1198.	3641.	7500.	12.6	26.4	30.0	30.0	18.1	17.4	13.3	17.7	..
Produce and Com. Merchants	14.3	11.4	8.0	115.8	108.0	78.5	2597.	5468.	11000.	78.7	122.4	121.8	27.7	26.1	11.4	11.1	13.3	..
Publishers	13.5	9.6	4.7	105.0	94.1	48.0	2053.	3437.	18000.	63.2	27.9	15.5	67.9	51.0	20.0	10.3	20.9	55.0
General Contractors	13.1	9.2	6.8	101.6	101.8	60.5	2538.	6528.	10583	14.3	16.7	17.6	21.2	21.1	29.7	10.9	18.4	37.0
Road Contractors	11.9	7.8	5.8	106.0	86.6	79.7	5311.	7068.	10955.	9.4	17.5	11.2	34.3	38.2	32.4	9.6	16.3	18.0
General Trucking	12.7	9.3	5.7	109.2	105.1	80.3	3313.	6935.	14442.	44.0	63.4	74.4	34.0	19.0	22.0	13.2	17.1	23.6
Laundries and Cleaners	13.6	12.4	..	105.2	102.3	..	1025.	1691.	..	47.8	62.0	..	90.4	78.6	..	7.8	8.2	..
Warehouses	12.0	9.9	6.3	100.1	99.9	98.6	2844.	5802.	11976.	57.5	86.7	91.7	35.1	22.1	10.1	15.6	19.5	28.4
Municipal, County and State	12.0	7.6	4.6	98.3	83.8	41.7	2429.	5662.	9429.	26.1	36.5	18.6	26.6	..	..	8.9	15.8	20.4
Gas, Electric and Water Utilities	12.9	8.3	4.5	121.6	88.4	54.2	1590.	3897.	10938	27.1	23.4	28.2	36.5	23.0	20.8	8.9	17.4	29.0
Unclassified	12.4	9.0	4.9	105.3	95.3	55.0	2737.	4503.	11030.	20.3	24.1	22.2	23.4	14.6	8.7	14.1	20.4	23.7
Miscellaneous Industries	13.6	10.5	6.1	113.9	85.1	54.5	2410.	4856.	11625.	30.4	38.9	35.1	30.4	26.6	15.1	11.6	16.3	37.5

* Total number of vehicles represented in this analysis: 46,017. Light-duty, 26,656; medium-duty, 14,504; heavy-duty, 4857.

† Summarizing bodies used: 2709 firms or 50% used special bodies (made and adapted to their requirements by body builders; 2249 firms or 42% used standard bodies (furnished by the truck manufacturers); 430 firms or 8% used both types of bodies.

Data from National Survey made by General Motors Truck Co. between September, 1929, and April, 1930.

THIS MUCH Will Make a LOAD for Your Truck

If the Product You Plan to Haul is Listed Here, You Will Find the Quantity Required to Make Various Tonnages in Terms of the Unit of Weight or Measurement Shown.

EXAMPLE: Suppose you have a 2-ton truck. You are estimating on hauling a large beet crop to market. Here you can determine that a barrel of beets weighs 120 lb. and that 33 barrels will give you a 2-ton load.

MATERIAL TO BE HAULED — UNIT OF MEASUREMENT	WEIGHT PER UNIT (Lbs.)	QUANTITY OF UNITS REQUIRED TO MAKE THESE LOADS								
		One Ton	1½ Tons	2 Tons	2½ Tons	3 Tons	3½ Tons	5 Tons	7½ Tons	10 Tons
Aluminum (cu. yd.)	4500	⅜	⅔	⅞	1⅛	1⅓	1½	2¼	3⅓	4½
Apples (bu.)										
Apples (bbl.)	150	14	20	27	34	40	47	67	100	134
Asbestos (cu. yd.)	5180	⅜	⅝	¾	1	1¼	1⅓	2	3	3¾
Ashes (cu. yd.)	1080	1⅞	2¾	3¾	4⅝	5½	6½	9¼	14	18½
Asphalt (cu. yd.)	2700	¾	1⅛	1½	1⅞	2¼	2½	3¾	5½	7⅓
Bananas (bbl.)	105	19	29	38	48	57	67	95	143	191
Barley (bu.)	48	42	63	84	105	125	146	209	313	417
Beans (bu.)	60	34	50	67	82	100	117	167	250	335
Beef (bbl.)	200	10	15	20	25	30	35	50	75	100
Beer (case, 24 pt.)	59	34	51	68	85	102	119	169	255	339
Beer (case, 36 pt.)	91	22	33	44	55	66	77	108	165	220
Beer (case, 24 qt.	94	21	32	43	54	64	75	107	160	213
Beer (bbl. 31½ gal.)	355	6	9	12	14	17	20	29	43	57
Beer (half bbl. 15¾ gal.)	195	10	15	20	26	31	36	52	77	103
Beer (hogshd, 63 gal.)	650	3	5	6	8	9	11	16	23	31
Beeswax (cu. yd.)	1633	1¼	1⅞	2½	3⅛	3¾	4⅜	6⅛	9¼	12¼
Beets (bu.)	55	36	55	73	91	109	127	182	273	364
Beets (bbl.)	120	17	25	33	42	50	58	84	125	167
Beverages (5 gal.)	60	34	50	67	84	100	117	167	250	334
Beverages (case, 24 ½ gal.)	180	11	17	22	28	34	39	56	83	112
Beverages (case, 24 ½ pt.)	40	50	75	100	125	150	175	250	375	500
Beverages (case, 50 qt.)	187	11	16	21	27	32	38	54	67	108
Blocks, Paving (cu. yd.)	3700	⅝	⅞	1	1¼	1⅝	1⅞	2¾	4	5½
Bran (bu.)	20	100	150	200	250	300	350	500	750	1000
Brass (cu. ft.)	523	4	6	8	10	12	14	19	29	38
Bronze (cu. ft.)	552	4	6	7	9	11	13	18	27	35
Brick, Clay (cu. yd.)	2720	¾	1⅛	1½	1⅞	2¼	2½	3¾	5½	7⅓
Brick, Common Hard (cu. yd.)	3400	⅝	⅞	1⅛	1½	1¾	2	3	4½	6
Brick, Paving (cu. yd.)	4250	½	¾	1	1¼	1⅓	1⅔	2⅓	3½	4¾
Brick, Fire (cu. yd.)	3915	½	¾	1	¼	1½	1¼	2½	3¾	5
Brick, Pressed (cu. yd.)	3800	½	¾	1	1⅓	1⅝	1⅞	2⅔	4	5¼
Brick, Soft, Interior (cu. yd.)	2700	¾	1⅛	1½	1⅞	2¼	2½	3¾	5½	7⅓
Buckwheat (bu.)	48	42	63	84	104	125	146	209	313	418
Cabbage (bu.)	50	40	60	80	100	120	140	200	300	400
Carrots (bu.)	50	40	60	80	100	120	140	200	300	400
Carrots (bbl.)	100	20	30	40	50	60	70	100	150	200
Celery (bbl.)	120	17	25	33	42	50	58	84	125	167
Cement, Natural (cu. yd.)	1510	1⅓	2	2⅔	3⅓	4	4⅔	6⅔	10	13⅓
Cement, Porland (cu. yd.)	2430	⅔	1¼	1⅔	2	2½	2⅞	4	6⅓	8
Cement, Portland, (bbl.)	380	5	8	11	13	16	19	27	40	53
Cement, Western (cu. yd.)	1750	1⅛	1¾	2¼	2⅞	3⅜	4	5¾	8½	11½
Cinders (cu. yd.)	1080	1⅞	2¾	3¾	4⅝	5½	6½	9¼	14	18½
Clay, dry (cu. yd.)	1700	1⅛	1¾	2⅓	3	3½	4	5⅞	8⅞	11¾
Clay, wet (cu. yd.)	2970	¾	1	1⅓	1⅔	2	2⅓	3⅓	5	6¾
Clay and Gravel, wet (cu. yd.)	2700	¾	1⅛	1½	1⅞	2¼	2½	3¾	5½	7⅓
Clover (bu.)	25	80	120	160	200	240	280	400	600	800
Coal, Anthracite (cu. yd.)	1520	1⅓	2	2⅔	3⅓	4	4⅔	6⅔	10	13⅓
Coal, Bituminous (cu. yd.)	1275	1½	2⅜	3⅛	3⅞	4¾	5½	7¾	11¾	15½
Coal, Channel (cu. yd.)	1325	1½	2¼	3	3¾	4½	5⅓	7½	11⅓	15
Coal, Indiana (cu. yd.)	1160	1¾	2⅔	3½	4⅓	5¼	6	8½	13	17
Coal, Pocahontas (cu. yd.)	1410	1½	2⅛	2⅞	3½	4¼	5	7	10½	14
Coke (cu. yd.)	1000	2	3	4	5	6	7	10	13	15
Concrete Cinder (cu. yd.)	2970	¾	1	1⅓	1⅔	2	2⅓	3⅓	5	6¾
Concrete Gravel (cu. yd.)	4100	½	¾	1	1¼	1½	1¾	2½	3⅔	5
Concrete Stone (cu. yd.)	4200	½	¾	1	1¼	1⅓	1⅔	2⅜	3⅝	4¾
Copper (cu. yd.)	7075	⅜	½	⅝	¾	⅞	1	1½	2⅛	3
Cork (cu. yd.)	405	5	7½	10	12½	15	17½	25	37½	50
Corn, Green (bbl.)	98	20	31	41	51	62	72	102	153	204
Corn Shelled (bu.)	56	36	55	73	91	109	127	182	273	364
Corn Meal bolted (bu.)	44	45	68	91	114	137	159	227	342	255
Cotton (bale)	515	4	6	8	10	12	14	20	29	39
Cotton Compressed (bale)	515	4	6	8	10	12	14	20	29	39
Crushed Stone (cu. yd.)	2700	¾	1⅛	1½	1⅞	2¼	2⅔	3¾	5½	7½

(continued on next page)

This Much Will Make a Load for Your Truck—Continued

MATERIAL TO BE HAULED — UNIT OF MEASUREMENT	WEIGHT PER UNIT (Lbs.)	QUANTITY OF UNITS REQUIRED TO MAKE THESE LOADS								
		One Ton	1½ Tons	2 Tons	2½ Tons	3 Tons	3½ Tons	5 Tons	7½ Tons	10 Tons
Cucumbers (bu.)	48	42	63	84	104	125	146	209	313	418
Cucumbers (bbl.)	120	17	25	33	42	50	58	84	125	167
Earth, dry, loose (cu. yd.)	1890	1	1 5/8	2 1/8	2 2/3	3 1/8	3 3/4	5 1/4	8	10 3/4
Earth, moist (cu. yd.)	2214	7/8	1 3/8	1 3/4	2 1/4	2 3/4	3 1/8	4 1/2	6 3/4	9
Eggs (crate, 30 doz.)	52	39	58	77	96	115	134	192	289	385
Fats (cu. yd.)	1566	1 1/4	1 7/8	2 1/2	3 1/4	3 7/8	4 1/2	6 1/2	9 2/3	13
Feed (bu.)	40	50	75	100	125	150	175	250	375	500
Flour, loose (cu. yd.)	756	3	4	5 1/3	6 1/2	8	9 1/3	13 1/3	20	26.6
Flour, pressed (cu. yd.)	1269	1 1/2	2 3/8	3 1/8	3 7/8	4 3/4	5 1/2	7 3/4	11 3/4	13 1/3
Fuel Oil (bbl. 55 gal.)	400	5	8	10	13	15	18	25	38	50
Garbage (cu. yd.)	1150	1 3/4	2 2/3	3 1/2	4 1/3	5 1/4	6	8 1/2	13	17
Granite (cu. yd.)	4540	3/8	5/8	7/8	1 1/8	1 1/3	1 1/2	2 1/4	3 1/3	4 1/2
Gravel, dry (cu. yd.)	2970	3/4	1	1 1/3	1 3/4	2	2 1/3	3 1/3	5	6 3/4
Greens (bbl.)	60	34	50	67	84	100	117	167	250	334
Hay (std. bale)	210	10	14	19	24	29	33	47	71	94
Hay (small bale)	120	17	25	33	42	50	58	84	125	167
Hominy (bu.)	60	34	50	67	84	100	117	167	250	334
Horseradish (bu.)	50	40	60	80	100	120	140	200	300	400
Indian Wheat (bu.)	46	42	63	84	104	125	146	209	313	418
Iron, Brown (cu. yd.)	6400	1/4	1/2	5/8	3/4	7/8	1 1/8	1 1/2	2 1/4	3
Iron, Hematite (cu. yd.)	8780	1/4	1/3	1/2	5/8	2/3	3/4	1 1/8	1 3/4	2 1/4
Iron, Magnetite (cu. yd.)	8400	1/4	1/4	1/2	5/8	2/3	7/8	1 1/4	1 3/4	2 1/4
Iron, Ordinary (cu. yd.)	7590	1/4	3/8	1/2	2/3	3/4	1	1 1/4	2	2 2/3
Lard (cu. yd.)	1593	1 1/4	1 7/8	2 1/2	3 1/4	3 7/8	4 1/2	6 1/2	9 2/3	13
Lead (cu. yd.)	12,250	1/8	1/4	1/3	1/2	1/2	5/8	3/4	1 1/4	1 3/4
Leather (cu. yd.)	1593	1 1/4	1 7/8	2 1/2	3 1/4	3 7/8	4 1/2	6 1/2	9 2/3	13
Lettuce (bbl.)	60	34	50	67	82	100	117	167	250	335
Lime (cu. yd.)	1450	1 3/8	2	2 3/4	3 1/2	3 7/8	4 7/8	7	10 3/8	14
Lime (bbl.)	320	6	10	18	16	19	22	32	47	63
Limestone, solid (cu. yd.)	4540	3/8	2/3	7/8	1 1/8	1 1/3	1 1/2	2 1/4	3 1/3	4 1/2
Limestone, loose (cu. yd.)	2600	3/4	1 1/8	1 1/2	2	2 1/3	2 3/8	3 7/8	5 3/4	7 3/4
Linseed Oil (bbl. 50 gal.)	400	5	8	10	13	15	18	25	38	50
Malt (bu.)	35	57	86	114	143	171	200	286	429	572
Manganese (cu. yd.)	6990	3/4	1/2	5/8	3/4	7/8	1	1 1/8	2 1/8	3
Marble, solid (cu. yd.)	4450	3/8	1	7/8	1 1/8	1 1/4	1 1/2	2 1/4	3 1/3	4 1/2
Marble, loose (cu. yd.)	2600	3/4	1 1/8	1 1/2	2	2 1/3	2 3/8	3 7/8	5 3/4	7 3/4
Meal (bu.)	50	40	60	80	100	120	140	200	300	400
Milk (case, 20 pt.)	54	36	55	73	91	109	127	182	273	364
Milk (case, 12 qt.)	63	32	48	64	80	95	111	159	238	318
Milk (can)	113	18	27	36	45	53	62	89	133	178
Molasses (bbl. 50 gal.)	650	3	5	6	8	9	11	16	23	31
Nickel (cu. ft.)	549	3 2/3	5 1/2	7 1/3	9	11	13	18 1/3	27 1/3	36 1/2
Oats (bu.)	32	63	94	125	157	188	219	313	469	626
Onions (bu.)	55	36	55	73	91	109	127	182	273	364
Onions (bbl.)	160	13	19	25	32	38	44	63	94	125
Paper (cu. yd.) / Paper, Newsprint (cu. yd.)	1570	1 1/3	2	2 2/3	3	4	4 1/2	6 1/2	9 1/2	12 1/2
Parsley (bu.)	8	250	375	500	....	....	....	....	....	....
Peanuts (bu.)	20	100	150	200	250	300	350	500	750	1,000
Peas (bu.)	60	34	50	67	82	100	117	167	250	335
Pears (bbl.)	150	14	20	27	34	40	47	67	100	134
Peppers (bbl.)	60	34	50	67	82	100	117	167	250	335
Pie Plant (bu.)	50	40	60	80	100	120	140	200	300	400
Pitch (cu. yd.)	1860	1	1 5/8	2 1/8	2 2/3	3 1/4	3 3/4	5 3/8	8	10 3/4
Plaster Paris (cu. yd.)	2650	3/4	1 1/8	1 1/2	1 7/8	2 1/4	2 3/4	3 3/4	5 2/3	7 1/2
Pork (bbl.)	200	10	15	20	25	30	35	50	75	100
Potatoes (bu.)	60	34	50	67	84	100	117	167	250	334
Potatoes (bbl.)	175	12	17	23	29	34	40	57	85	115
Powder (cu. yd.)	1682	1 1/4	1 7/8	2 1/2	3	3 5/8	4 1/8	6	9	12
Quartz (cu. yd.)	4375	3/8	2/3	7/8	1 1/8	1 3/8	1 2/3	2 1/4	3 1/2	4 1/2
Resin (cu. yd.)	1215	1 5/8	2 1/2	3 1/3	4 1/8	4 7/8	5 3/4	8 1/4	12 1/3	16 1/2
Rhubarb (bu.)	50	40	60	80	100	120	140	200	300	400
Rice (bu.)	43	47	70	93	117	140	163	233	349	465
Rubbish (cu. yd.)	200	10	15	20	25	30	35	50	75	100
Rye (bu.)	55	36	55	73	91	109	127	182	273	364
Salt (bbl.)	280	7	11	14	18	22	25	36	54	72
Sand, wet (cu. yd.)	3190	5/8	7/8	1 1/4	1 1/2	1 7/8	2 1/4	3 1/8	4 3/4	6 1/4
Sand, dry, loose (cu. yd.)	2620	3/4	7 1/8	1 1/2	2	2 1/4	2 2/3	3 3/4	5 5/8	7 1/2
Sandstone (cu. yd.)	4025	1/2	3/4	1	1 1/4	1 1/2	1 3/4	2 1/2	3 3/4	5
Shale (cu. yd.)	4375	3/8	2/3	7/8	1 1/8	1 3/8	1 2/3	2 1/4	3 3/4	4 1/2
Shorts (bu.)	20	100	150	200	250	300	350	500	750	1,000
Slag Bank (cu. yd.)	1900	1	1 5/8	2 1/8	2 2/3	3 1/8	3 3/4	5 1/4	8	10 3/4
Slag Sand (cu. yd.)	1490	1 1/3	2	2 2/3	3 3/8	4	4 3/4	6 3/4	10	13 1/2
Slate (cu. yd.)	4725	1/2	2/3	7/8	1 1/8	1 1/4	1 1/2	2 1/8	3 1/8	4 1/4
Spinach (bu.)	20	100	150	200	250	300	350	500	750	1,000
Spinach (bbl.)	60	34	50	67	84	100	117	167	250	334
Steel (cu. ft.)	490	4	6	8	10	12	14	21	31	41
Straw (bale)	180	11	17	22	28	34	39	56	84	112
Street Sweepings (cu. yd.)	850	2 1/2	3 1/2	5	6	7	8 1/2	12	18	24
Sugar (bbl.)	300	7	10	13	17	20	23	33	50	70
Sugar Cane (bu.)	57	36	55	73	91	109	127	182	273	364
Sulphur (cu. yd.)	3380	5/8	7/8	1 1/8	1 1/2	1 3/4	2	3	4 1/2	6
Tar (cu. yd.)	1674	1 1/4	1 7/8	2 1/2	3	3 5/8	4 1/8	6	9	12
Tile (cu. yd.)	2970	3/4	1	1 1/3	1 3/4	2	2 1/3	3 1/3	5	6 3/4
Tin (cu. yd.)	11,290	1/8	1/4	1/3	1/2	1/2	5/8	3/4	1 1/4	1 3/4
Tomatoes (bu.)	55	36	55	73	91	109	127	182	273	364
Trap Stone (cu. yd.)	5050	1/3	5/8	3/4	1	1 1/8	1 3/8	2	3	4
Turnips (bbl.)	120	17	25	33	42	50	58	84	125	167
Turnips (bu.)	55	36	55	73	91	109	127	182	273	364
Turpentine (bbl. 51 gal.)	432	5	7	9	12	14	16	23	35	46
Vinegar (bbl. 48 gal.)	400	5	8	10	13	15	18	25	38	50
Wheat (bu.)	60	34	50	67	82	100	117	167	250	335
Wool, pressed (cu. yd.)	2214	7/8	1 1/3	1 7/8	2 1/4	2 3/4	3 1/4	4 5/8	6 3/4	9 1/3
Zinc (cu. yd.)	7830	1/4	3/8	1/2	5/8	3/4	7/8	1 1/4	2	2 1/2

TOOLS and EQUIPMENT
in Motor Truck Trade Shops†

$26,000,000 worth of shop equipment is needed by the various trade sales and service outlets in the truck industry to enable them to handle with normal efficiency their present volume of repair business. This includes an item of $3,316,800 worth of equipment which shops already normally efficient will require for expansion purposes and which new shops entering the field will require.

$6,115,350 worth of shop equipment is needed for purely replacement purposes.

$32,115,350 is therefore the potential shop equipment market for 1931 among trade outlets in the truck industry, comprising 1700 exclusive truck dealers, 450 branches, 1250 independent grinders and engine rebuilders, 2750 independent repair shops, and 27,000 combination truck and passenger car dealers.

Type of Shop Equipment	Number of Shops Sold	Estimated Value of Market Sold	Estimated Value of Replacement Market	Number of Unsold Shops	Estimated Value of Unsold Market	Potential Market Replacement Plus Unsold Market
Air Compressors	28,637	$3,228,018	$538,001	4,513	$625,128	$1,163,129
Anvils	18,596	74,672	5,000	14,554	55,800	60,800
Bearing, Boring, Aligning Fixtures	768	208,347	21,134	4,211	603,959	625,093
Bins or Shelves	33,150	7,896,562	526,007	*	789,656	1,315,663
Car Washing Equipment	7,042	713,685	118,948	11,358	1,604,565	1,723,513
Chargers and Other Electrical	12,748	917,569	122,469	20,402	1,985,331	2,107,800
Connecting Rods & Piston Aligners	11,050	154,564	30,912	20,400	260,903	291,815
Drills—Portable Electric	32,650	1,581,606	316,322	500	48,797	365,119
" —Pedestal	8,390	1,095,988	99,666	6,760	1,282,127	1,381,793
Fire Extinguishers	8,266	46,084	5,760	24,884	167,907	173,667
Forges	3,928	83,401	4,170	4,597	115,105	119,275
Grinders—Bench	30,958	414,873	69,146	2,192	136,630	205,776
" —Portable Hand Electric	7,850	325,424	65,085	10,800	498,188	563,273
" —Crankshaft, Cylinder, etc.	1,250	5,001,750	500,175	*	500,175	1,000,350
" —Pedestal	5,562	398,088	66,348	8,131	509,312	575,660
Hacksaws (Power)	3,681	118,225	29,531	4,055	145,587	175,118
Hammers, Air, Electric	3,511	176,810	44,202	3,627	194,310	238,512
Hoist—Block & Fall	24,663	1,294,311	215,731	8,487	478,709	694,440
" —Floor Cranes	20,289	773,217	77,320	12,444	640,748	718,068
" —Monorails & Hoists	16,125	460,349	76,559	7,077	648,389	724,948
Jacks—Hydraulic	13,105	267,555	74,180	20,000	475,425	549,605
" —Mechanical	21,457	1,222,177	271,635	11,693	473,067	744,702
Lathes	8,448	3,556,047	237,702	24,702	5,876,302	6,114,004
Lubricators—Grease Guns	28,382	758,081	151,615	4,768	133,126	284,741
Millers—Shapers-Planers	368	207,040	13,803	1,011	680,160	693,963
Motors	8,334	380,122	38,011	11,316	538,752	576,763
Presses—Bench Type	4,409	134,336	8,956	28,741	345,493	354,449
" —Floor Type	27,920	955,445	63,703	5,230	364,618	428,321
Relining and Riveting	21,414	476,833	79,471	11,736	238,721	318,192
Running-in Stands	3,056	232,800	15,520	3,611	366,540	382,060
Spray Painters	9,857	190,256	47,564	22,043	524,880	572,444
Stands—Engine	14,752	424,651	42,465	7,568	231,264	273,729
" —Drill	8,727	123,966	12,395	24,423	273,939	286,334
" —Transmission	12,113	83,300	51,553	6,331	42,044	93,597
Tanks—Cleaning	4,012	59,639	3,976	5,054	152,884	156,860
Tire Changing Equipment	3,056	31,040	6,208	19,070	295,628	301,836
Valve Grinders	3,798	53,184	10,637	29,352	386,909	397,546
Valve Seat Refacers	23,978	1,129,454	188,243	9,172	634,724	822,967
Vises	33,150	1,256,817	253,365	*	125,681	379,046
Welding-Cutting Torches	20,356	956,111	239,027	12,794	435,845	674,872
Wheel Aligners	3,056	23,280	3,880	28,844	305,745	309,625
Work Benches	33,150	1,001,197	100,119	*	471,200	571,319
Total for Above Items	...	$38,486,874	$4,846,514	...	$24,664,273	$29,510,787
Miscellaneous Items		2,973,126	1,268,836	...	1,335,727	2,604,563
Grand Total	....	$41,460,000	$6,115,350		$26,000,000	$32,115,350

*Expansion market estimated at 10 per cent of existing inventory.
NOTE: This tabulation does not include estimates for hand tools, which is a considerable item in itself.
†From data compiled by Commercial Car Journal.

Equipment Needs and Buying Time for Businesses Using Motor Trucks

NAME OF VOCATION OR BUSINESS	Number of Trucks Registered as of Jan. 1, 1930	Spec. Vocational	Concrete	Dump	Express	Insulated	Refrigerator	Panel	Platform	Rack	Sleeper Cabs	Stake	Van	Compressors	Derricks	Earth Borers	Extra Axles	Hoists	House to House Vehicles	Pumps	Tanks	Trailers	Trench Diggers	Winches	Start Canvass	Get Busy	Peak Month
		BODIES												SPECIAL EQUIPMENT											BUYING TIME		
Automotive Service and Access..	182,000	⊗			⊗			⊗						⊗	⊗		⊗							⊗	Mar./June	Apl./July	May/Aug.
Bakers, Retail and Wholesale....	88,500	⊗				⊗		⊗									⊗		⊗			⊗			Jan.	Feb.	Mar.
Bottlers............	41,150	⊗			⊗				⊗								⊗	⊗	⊗	⊗	⊗	⊗			Aug.	Sept.	Oct.
Building Material & Supplies....	48,920	⊗	⊗	⊗	⊗			⊗	⊗				⊗		⊗	⊗	⊗	⊗		⊗	⊗	⊗	⊗	⊗	Dec.	Jan.	Feb.
Contractors, General..........	194,500	⊗	⊗	⊗				⊗				⊗		⊗	⊗		⊗	⊗				⊗		⊗	Nov.	Dec.	Jan.
Creameries and Dairies........	88,405	⊗			⊗	⊗	⊗										⊗		⊗		⊗	⊗			Dec.	Jan.	Feb.
Department Stores and Retail...	53,710	⊗			⊗	⊗		⊗					⊗				⊗		⊗						Mar./Aug.	Apl./Sept.	May/Oct.
Farms......................	767,200			⊗						⊗							⊗	⊗				⊗		⊗	June	July	Aug.
Fuel, Coal, Coke, Wood......	77,750	⊗		⊗						⊗							⊗	⊗				⊗			....	....	....
Furniture, Retail, Wholesale and Moving..	88,050				⊗			⊗					⊗				⊗					⊗		⊗	May	June	July
Gasoline and Oil.............	129,000	⊗										⊗					⊗			⊗	⊗	⊗			Mar.	Apl.	May
Grocers and Food Products....	343,950				⊗	⊗	⊗	⊗									⊗					⊗			Nov.	Dec.	Jan.
Hardware, Retail and Wholesale..	83,750	⊗			⊗			⊗	⊗								⊗					⊗			Jan./July	Feb./Aug.	Mar./Sep.
Ice Cream, Delivery..........	(C)	⊗					⊗	⊗																	Jan.	Feb.	Mar.
Laundries, Cleaners and Dyers...	84,700	⊗				⊗		⊗									⊗		⊗			⊗			Feb.	Mar.	Apl.
Lumber, Logging, Millwork....	118,800	⊗		⊗				⊗		⊗		⊗					⊗					⊗		⊗	Feb.	Mar.	Apl.
Meat and Meat Products......	93,450				⊗	⊗	⊗																		Feb.	Mar.	Apl.
Municipalities................	81,300	(A)	⊗	⊗								⊗	⊗	⊗	⊗		⊗	⊗			⊗	⊗		⊗	July/Sept.	Aug./Oct.	Sept./Nov.
Plumbing and Heating........	75,100	⊗			⊗	⊗		⊗	⊗								⊗					⊗			Oct./Apl.	Nov./May	Dec./June
Produce, Retail and Wholesale...	50,350	⊗			⊗		⊗	⊗	⊗			⊗					⊗					⊗			Oct.	Nov.	Dec.
Public Utilities..............	53,200	⊗		⊗	⊗			⊗						⊗	⊗	⊗	⊗	⊗		⊗		⊗	⊗	⊗	Sept.	Oct.	Nov.
Road Work.................	12,550	(B)	⊗	⊗											⊗		⊗					⊗	⊗	⊗	Dec.	Jan.	Feb.
Trucking and Warehousing.....	177,400	⊗			⊗			⊗			⊗	⊗	⊗	⊗	⊗		⊗	⊗	⊗	⊗	⊗	⊗		⊗	Jan./Aug.	Feb./Sept.	Mar./Oct.

REFERENCE NOTES:

(A) Additional equipment used by municipalities not listed in columns includes: Gully cleaners, gate closers, garbage and refuse collectors, police patrols, fire apparatus and ambulance bodies.

(B) Additional equipment includes: Scrapers, snowplows, flushers, sweepers, sand and chip spreaders, road magnets, bulldozers, bituminous and oil spreaders.

(C) Trucks for this service are included in creameries and dairies.

*Obviously no buying chart is of universal application. Seasons throughout the country and abroad change peak buying periods. The table will, however, serve as a guide for selling and for buying.

Registration of Motor Trucks
by Vocations and Capacities

This tabulation, based on 1929 registrations, shows the approximate number of motor trucks and their capacity in use by the different industries and businesses in the United States. The Major Group of Vehicles in Use by Most Vocations is in the one-ton class. The standing of each vocation as a buyer of trucks is shown in the last column.

Industry or Business	Total Trucks in Use Over 1 Ton	Total Trucks in Use 2½ Tons and Over	Total of All Trucks in Use	Ranking	Industry or Business	Total Trucks in Use Over 1 Ton	Total Trucks in Use 2½ Tons and Over	Total of All Trucks in Use	Ranking
Agricultural Machinery and Implements	2,347	1,123	14,700	42	Metals and Metal Products	14,680	8,490	49.150	21
Autos, Accessories and Supplies	25,750	11.150	182,000	4	Mines and Quarries	6,220	4,298	18,390	37
Bakeries	15,470	3,690	88,500	10	Novelties and Toys	2,221	771	12,200	47
Bottlers	13,650	5,210	41,150	25	Office and Store Equipment	2,024	1,025	8,535	52
Building Material and Supplies	15,230	8,725	48,920	23	Oil and Gasoline	50,450	26,990	129,000	6
Cigars and Tobacco	1,995	814	15,850	40	Paper and Paper Products	5,790	3,110	14,420	44
Clothing, Men's and Women's	2,155	833	12,710	46	Plumbing and Heating	7,040	2,850	75,100	18
Dry Goods	5,825	2,042	23,390	34	Printers	1,595	651	9,300	51½
Department Stores	6,040	2,255	17,610	38	Produce and Commission Merchants	10,720	3,899	50,350	20
Coal, Coke and Ice	11,510	5,145	42,450	24	Publishers	1,613	616	8,615	50
Coal and Fuels Exclusively	31,040	17,590	77,750	17	Rubber Products	1,412	779	3,120	62
Confectioners	6,135	2,519	36,300	26	Shoes	1,070	444	5,650	55
Creameries, Dairies and Ice Cream	21.550	11,620	88,405	13	Textiles	4,520	1,925	16,450	39
Drugs, Chemicals and Drug Sundries	7,051	3,805	26,450	31	Banks	535	197	3,150	60
Electrical Contractors	733	274	10,810	49	General Contractors	35,100	19,420	194,500	3
Electrical Machinery and Contractors' Supply	2.100	750	18,885	36	Road Contractors	4,250	3,070	12,550	48
Flour, Feed Mills and Grain Elevators	6.749	2,699	27,855	29	General Trucking	77,700	49,400	164,700	5
Florists	2,322	619	25,190	33	Hospitals and Public Institutions	616	160	3,985	57
Furniture and Home Furnishing	15,092	5,095	88,050	12	Hotels, Clubs and Restaurants	3,350	1,160	25,750	32
General Merchandise	8.450	2,498	115,250	8	Laundries and Cleaners	5,825	1,535	84,100	14
Groceries and Food Products	49,209	19,000	343,950	2	Schools	1,375	274	9,850	51
Hardware	12,055	4,570	83,750	15	Undertakers	4,505	319	36,890	30
Hay, Grain and Feed	3,139	1,380	15,100	41	Warehouses	6,320	3,995	12,700	45
Household Appliances	479	213	3,375	61	R. F. D. Owners	43,650	1,345	579,000	1
Jewelry	597	220	3,640	57	Real Estate	1,840	829	14,300	43
Leather Goods and Luggage	1.380	614	5,780	53	Municipal County and State	3,180	16,000	81,300	16
Lumber, Logging and Mill Work	40,100	20,720	118,800	7	U. S. Post Office	1,085	579	5,690	54
Machinery and Tools	7,099	3,640	28,850	27	U. S. Army, Etc.	526	342	47,900	22
Meats and Packing House Products	16.990	7,045	93,450	9	Electric Railways	1,340	709	3,640	58
					Gas, Electric and Water Utilities	13,720	6,210	53,200	19
					Railroads and Steamships	9,350	5,610	21,200	35
					Telephone and Telegraph	4,110	1,705	45,010	28

Number of Motor Truck FLEETS by States by Size of Fleet

This Count, Limited to Fleets of Five or More Vehicles Each, is From the Verified Records of the List Department of Chilton Class Journal Company, as of April, 1930.

STATE	SIZE OF FLEETS 5-9	10-24	25-49	50 Up	TOTAL	Operate Own Service Shop*	STATE	SIZE OF FLEET 5-9	10-24	25-49	50 Up	TOTAL	Operate Own Service Shop*
Alabama	108	63	8	6	185	103	Nebraska	126	74	10	5	215	111
Arizona	45	34	5	1	85	32	Nevada	10	5	...	...	15	8
Arkansas	101	44	5	1	151	70	New Hampshire	38	13	...	1	52	35
California	899	608	179	123	1,809	1,088	New Jersey	724	296	72	41	1,133	537
Colorado	116	84	17	5	222	107	New Mexico	5	5	...	...	10	7
Connecticut	244	105	30	13	392	242	New York	2,288	890	213	208	3,599	991
Delaware	28	10	4	2	44	29	North Carolina	132	88	18	8	246	105
Dist. Columbia	92	54	39	21	206	101	North Dakota	10	8	2	1	21	10
Florida	170	131	32	8	341	162	Ohio	937	432	142	86	1,597	1,000
Georgia	177	74	11	7	269	104	Oklahoma	145	92	22	16	275	134
Idaho	16	10	...	2	28	16	Oregon	108	63	18	5	194	102
Illinois	943	450	148	111	1,652	882	Pennsylvania	1,132	491	127	110	1,860	1,023
Indiana	459	189	47	27	722	412	Rhode Island	124	61	16	11	212	137
Iowa	212	76	17	7	312	160	South Carolina	98	36	5	6	145	67
Kansas	158	59	10	9	236	141	South Dakota	12	3	...	1	16	9
Kentucky	137	62	26	6	231	122	Tennessee	155	86	18	9	268	131
Louisiana	144	78	18	10	250	124	Texas	318	221	51	19	609	275
Maine	54	28	2	4	88	31	Utah	64	44	13	3	124	61
Maryland	179	91	31	17	318	151	Vermont	25	6	...	1	32	15
Massachusetts	611	296	90	51	1,048	675	Virginia	167	90	19	5	281	129
Michigan	579	322	117	66	1,084	922	Washington	235	117	30	13	395	166
Minnesota	227	115	33	17	392	228	West Virginia	163	79	9	8	259	148
Mississippi	61	17	1	1	80	31	Wisconsin	296	127	26	19	468	243
Missouri	369	157	43	40	609	353	Wyoming	19	9	1	1	30	15
Montana	56	21	3	3	83	39							
							TOTAL	13,516	6,514	1,728	1,135	22,893	11,704

1503 of these fleets operate all Ford vehicles; 8,492 have no Fords; 12,749 have various makes.
*This count of fleet owners who operate their own service shop is based on returns from 17,748 concerns. On 5,143 this information is not yet available. If the same ratio carried through on the remainder, 3,850 service shops would be added.

DISCOUNT, NET PROFIT AND MARK-UP TABLES

Discount Tables

Showing net of $1.00 after discounts in top row and first column have been taken off.

Rate %	5	7½	10	12½	15	20	25	30	33 1/3	35
2½	.92625	.90188	.8775	.85313	.82875	.78	.73125	.6825	.65	.63375
5	.9025	.87875	.855	.83125	.8075	.76	.7125	.665	.63333	.6175
5 2½	.87994	.85678	.83363	.81047	.78731	.741	.69469	.64838	.6175	.60206
5 5	.85738	.83481	.81225	.78969	.76713	.722	.67688	.63175	.60167	.58663
5 5 2½	.83594	.81394	.79194	.76995	.74795	.70395	.65995	.61596	.58663	.57196
7½		.85563	.8325	.80938	.78625	.74	.69375	.6475	.61667	.60125
7½ 2½		.83423	.81169	.78914	.76659	.7215	.67641	.63131	.60125	.58622
7½		.81284	.79088	.76891	.74694	.703	.65906	.61513	.58583	.57119
10			.81	.78750	.765	.72	.675	.63	.6	.585
10 2½			.78975	.76781	.74588	.702	.65813	.61425	.585	.57038
10 5			.7695	.74813	.72675	.684	.64125	.5985	.57	.55575
10 5 2½			.75026	.72942	.70858	.6669	.62522	.58354	.55575	.54186
10 7½			.74925	.72844	.70763	.666	.62438	.58275	.555	.54113
10 10			.729	.70875	.6885	.648	.6075	.567	.54	.5265
10 10 5			.69256	.67331	.65408	.6156	.57713	.53865	.513	.50018
10 10 5 2½			.67524	.65648	.63772	.60021	.5627	.52518	.50018	.48767

Rate %	40	45	50	55	60	65	66 2/3	70	75	80	85	87½	90
2½	.585	.53625	.4875	.43875	.39	.34125	.325	.2925	.24375	.195	.14625	.12188	.0975
5	.57	.5225	.475	.4275	.38	.3225	.31667	.285	.2375	.19	.1425	.11875	.095
5 2½	.55575	.50944	.46313	.41681	.3705	.32419	.30875	.27788	.23156	.18525	.13894	.11578	.09263
5 5	.5415	.49638	.45125	.40613	.361	.31588	.30083	.27075	.22563	.1805	.13583	.11281	.09025
5 5 2½	.52796	.48397	.43997	.39597	.35198	.30789	.29331	.26398	.21998	.17599	.13199	.10999	.08799
7½	.555	.50875	.4625	.41625	.37	.32375	.30833	.2775	.23125	.185	.13875	.11563	.0925
7½ 2½	.54113	.49603	.45094	.40584	.36075	.31566	.30063	.27056	.22547	.18038	.13528	.11273	.09019
7½	.52725	.48331	.43938	.39544	.3515	.30756	.29292	.26363	.21969	.17575	.13181	.10984	.08788
10	.54	.495	.45	.405	.36	.315	.3	.27	.225	.18	.135	.1125	.09
10 2½	.5265	.48263	.43875	.39488	.351	.30713	.2925	.26325	.21938	.1755	.13163	.10969	.08775
10 5	.513	.47025	.4275	.38475	.342	.29925	.285	.2565	.21375	.171	.12825	.10688	.0855
10 5 2½	.50018	.45849	.41681	.37513	.33345	.29177	.27788	.25009	.20841	.16673	.12504	.1042	.08336
10 7½	.4995	.45788	.41625	.37463	.333	.29138	.2775	.24975	.20813	.1665	.12488	.10406	.08325
10 10	.486	.4455	.405	.3645	.324	.2835	.27	.243	.2025	.162	.1215	.10125	.081
10 10 5	.4617	.42323	.38475	.34628	.3078	.26933	.2565	.23085	.19238	.1539	.11543	.09619	.07695
10 10 5 2½	.45016	.41264	.37513	.33762	.3001	.26259	.25009	.22508	.18757	.15005	.11254	.09378	.07503

Example: To find the decimal equivalent of a chain discount of, for instance, 50, 10 and 5 per cent, find the column headed 50 and at the junction of this column with the row marked 10-5 the decimal equivalent of .4275 is found. By the same procedure the decimal equivalent of 30-5 and 2½ per cent is found to be .64838.

Net Profit Table

Giving the net profit when the overhead and the percentage of increase of selling price over cost arc known.

Per Cent	25	33⅓	40	50	60	75	100
10	10	15	18 4/7	23⅓	27½	32 6/7	40
11	9	14	17 4/7	22⅓	26½	31 6/7	39
12	8	13	16 4/7	21⅓	25½	30 6/7	38
13	7	12	15 4/7	20⅓	24½	29 6/7	37
14	6	11	14 4/7	19⅓	23½	28 6/7	36
15	5	10	13 4/7	18⅓	22½	27 6/7	35
16	4	9	12 4/7	17⅓	21½	26 6/7	34
17	3	8	11 4/7	16⅓	20½	25 6/7	33
18	2	7	10 4/7	15⅓	19½	24 6/7	32
19	1	6	9 4/7	14⅓	18½	23 6/7	31
20	0	5	8 4/7	13⅓	17½	22 6/7	30
21	—1	4	7 4/7	12⅓	16½	21 6/7	29
22	—2	3	6 4/7	11⅓	15½	20 6/7	28
23	—3	2	5 4/7	10⅓	14½	19 6/7	27
24	—4	1	4 4/7	9⅓	13½	18 6/7	26
25	—5	0	3 4/7	8⅓	12½	17 6/7	25

Explanation and Example

The overhead is given in per cent in the left hand column of the Net Profit table and the percentage of increase of selling price over cost is given in the top line. The net profit is then found at the intersection of the two lines.

Example: If your overhead is 20 per cent and you add 50 per cent to the cost of a certain article then the net profit is found to be 13⅓ per cent. On the other hand if the overhead is 25 per cent and a 12½ per cent net profit is desired 60 per cent must be added to the cost price.

Locate in the columns headed A in the Mark-Up tables the per cent of gross profit desired and in the adjacent B column is given the per cent necessary to add to the cost to obtain the desired profit.

Example: To obtain a gross profit of 33⅓ per cent it is necessary to mark up the cost price 50 per cent.

Mark-Up Table

Giving the amount in per cent it is necessary to add to the cost of an article to obtain a certain gross profit.

A Per Cent Gross Profit	B Per Cent Add to Cost	A Per Cent Gross Profit	B Per Cent Add to Cost	A Per Cent Gross Profit	B Per Cent Add to Cost
4¾	5	19	23.46	35	53.85
5	5.26	20	25.00	35½	55.00
7½	8.10	21	26.58	37½	60.00
9	10.0	22	28.21	39½	65.00
10	11.11	23	29.88	40	66.66
11⅛	12.5	24	31.58	41	70.00
12½	14.28	25	33.33	42¾	75.00
14¼	16.66	26	35.00	44½	80.00
15	17.65	28½	40.00	46	85.00
16⅔	20.00	30	42.86	47½	90.00
17	20.49	31	45.00	50	100.00
18	21.96	33⅓	50.00	..	....

Tire CHANGE-OVER Data

Dealers and fleet operators need information like the following in making a change-over from high pressure to balloon tires, or in determining just what wheel and rim equipment or what size tires can be used under given circumstances or must be used to secure certain results.

Often it is possible to accomplish what you want at much less cost if you can find out in advance how much of your present equipment can be used. The data here will show you. It was arranged by *Commercial Car Journal and Operation & Maintenance* from Tire and Rim Association standards and from original sources.

High-Pressure and Balloon Tire Interchangeability

Light figures = High Pressure Tire Data.   Heavy Figures = Corresponding Balloon Tire Data

Tire Size	Wheel Size	Rated Rim Size	Maximum Load (Lb.)	Pressure (Lb.)
30 x 5 (6-ply)	20	5	1575	75
6.00/20	20	5	1400	45
30 x 5	20	5	1700	80
6.50/20	20	5	1650	50
32 x 6 (8-ply)	20	5	1950	80
7.00/20	20	5	1900	55
32 x 6	20	6	2200	90
7.50/20	20	6	2100	55
34 x 7	20	7	2800	100
8.25/20	20	7	2550	60
9.00/20	20	7	3250	65
36 x 8	20	8	3600	110
9.75/20	20	8	3900	70
38 x 9	20	8 or 9-10	4500	120
10.50/20	20	9-10	4700	75
40 x 10	20	9-10	5500	130
11.25/20	20	9-10	5450	75
36 x 6	24	6	2500	90
8.25/24	24	7	2950	60
38 x 7	24	7	3200	100
9.00/24	24	7	3650	65
40 x 8	24	8	4000	110
9.75/24	24	8	4400	70
42 x 9	24	9-10	5000	120
10.50/24	24	9-10	5200	75
44 x 10	24	9-10	6000	130
11.25/24	24	9-10	6050	80

TABLE 1

Table 1: This is a table of interchangeability between high-pressure and balloon tires. If you want to know what size balloon tires you can put on your present wheel and rim equipment these data will help. Suppose you have 34 x 7 high-pressure tires. The data above show they are on 20-in. wheel with 7-in. rim. The heavy type directly under indicates you can change-over to 8.25/20

balloons or 9.00/20 balloons without changing wheel or rim. The maximum-load column shows the 8.25/20's will carry a load of 2550 lb., while the 9.00/20's will carry 3250 lb. The data here can be worked from different angles. It will help you determine what to install as new equipment in tires or wheels and rims to get a desired carrying capacity, etc.

Guide to Determining Rated Rim Size from Dimensions

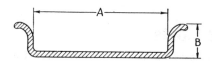

Rated Rim Size	Inches at "A"	Inches at "B"
5	3.75″	1.00″
6	4.33″	1.25″
7	5.00″	1.312″
8	6.00″	1.50″
9-10	7.33″	1.75″
11	8.37″	1.75″

TABLE 2

Table 2: Most information on rims and tires is given in terms of rated rim size which doesn't correspond with inch dimensions. With this table you can tell what the rated size of your rim is by measuring your rim at the points shown in the illustration and getting the corresponding rated size here.

Guide to Whether or Not Oversize Dual Tires Can Be Installed

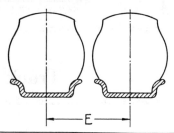

Present Tire Size	Dual Spacing (Dimension E)	Rated Rim Size	Oversizes Permitted
5	7¼	5	None
5.50			6.00
5	7¾	5	6*; 6.00; 6.50
6.00			6.50
6	9	6	†; 7.00
7.00			7.50
7	10	7	†; 7.50
7.50			8.25
8.25	10½	7	9.00
8	11½	8	†; 9.00
9.00			9.75
9.75	12	8	10.50
9.00	12¾	9-10	10.00; 10.50

* 8-ply only.
† Oversize high-pressure permitted, but no standard listed.

TABLE 3

Table 3: This table tells you if you can mount oversize tires on your dual rims and the oversize permitted. For instance, suppose your present tires are 5-in. high-pressure duals. The rated rim size is 5. Measure the dual spacing at "E." If it is 7¼ in. the last column shows oversize tires are not recommended. If it is 7¾ in., table shows you can use 8-ply 6-in. high-pressure duals 5.50 or 6.00 balloon duals (checking, however, to make sure the larger tires would not interfere with brake rigging, fenders or other parts of the vehicle). To determine your rated rim size from measurements see table 2.

How Your Ford Model T Market Will Go

Estimates of Ford Model "T" cars registered in the United States each year from 1931 to 1936 inclusive.

Year	Number Registered
1931	4,329,100
1932	3,411,700
1933	2,548,700
1934	1,842,300
1935	1,247,100
1936	792,500

These are the approximate numbers of Fords (both A and T) actually in operation on Jan. 1, 1931.

Year Sold	Number Registered
1930	*1,090,000
1929	*1,325,000
1928	*464,000
1927	†353,000
1926	†955,000
1925	†884,000
1924	†788,000
1923	†662,000
1922	†319,000
1921	†170,000
1920	†112,000
1919	†51,000
1918	†13,000
1917	†14,000
1916	†4,000
1915	†800
1914	†160
1913	†30

*Model A.
†Model T.
Research Department—Chilton Class Journal Co.

Who Sells Batteries, Tires, Accessories?

	Batteries	Tires	Accessories
Car Dealers	31,835	36,007	38,128
Independent Repair Shops and Accessory Stores	26,906	30,110	36,375
Exclusive Accessory Stores	...	...	5,879
	58,741	66,117	80,382

*From count of names in Chilton Trade List.

2,896,400 Cars Retire from Service in Year

Auburn	4,400
Buick (Marquette)	141,000
Cadillac (LaSalle)	23,000
Chevrolet	317,000
Chrysler (Maxwell-Plymouth)	59,000
Dodge	157,000
Durant (Star-Flint)	83,000
Essex	85,000
Ford	1,375,000
Franklin	10,000
Graham (Paige-Jewett)	31,000
Hudson	50,000
Hupmobile	29,000
Lincoln	3,000
Nash (Ajax)	52,000
Oakland	30,000
Oldsmobile (Viking)	29,000
Packard	11,000
Peerless	5,200
Pierce-Arrow	2,900
Pontiac	6,900
Reo	14,000
Studebaker (Erskine)	101,000
Stutz	2,000
Willys (Overland-Whippet)	122,000
Willys-Knight	15,000
Misc. (all others)	138,000
Total	2,896,400

The number of passenger cars retired from active service during the period from July 1, 1929, to July 1, 1930, is estimated by *Automobile Trade Journal* at 2,896,400. The basis of calculation was as follows: Total registrations of each make on July 1, 1929, plus registrations of new cars of that make between July 1, 1929, and June 30, 1930, less total registrations on July 1, 1930.

Truck Fleet Operating Costs

The average operating experience of 5584 fleet owners having a total of 46,017 vehicles was found to be as follows:

	Average for 26,656 Light Duty Trucks	Average for 14,504 Medium Duty Trucks	Average for 4857 Heavy Duty Trucks
How many miles per gallon of gas?	13.0 miles	9.8 miles	5.7 miles
How many miles per quart of oil?	109.2 miles	95.2 miles	56.7 miles
What is average payload?	2396.0 lbs.	5230.0 lbs.	11,256.0 lbs.
Average length of haul or route?	29.8 miles	41.4 miles	38.9 miles
Average number of stops per day?	43.5 stops	26.5 stops	17.3 stops
What is your total truck operating cost including maintenance and depreciation per mile?	11.6 cents	17.1 cents	28.8 cents

From a survey made between September, 1929, and April, 1930, by General Motors Truck Co.

15-Year Record of Total Foreign Consumption of Motor Vehicles of U.S. Design

	1914	1915	1916	1917	1918	1919	1920	1921	1922	1923	1924	1925	1926	1927	1928	1929	1930
U. S. Exports (including foreign assembly)	27,574	67,373	85,364	85,092	51,260	56,389	177,297	60,739	125,880	240,091	293,115	428,564	393,600	462,880	582,764	734,211	405,716
Canadian Production				93,810	82,408	87,835	94,144	66,246	102,053	146,438	135,246	161,389	204,727	178,427	242,382	263,295	154,192
TOTAL Foreign Consumption	27,574	67,373	85,364	178,902	133,668	144,224	271,441	126,933	227,980	386,529	428,361	589,953	598,327	641,307	825,146	997,506	559,909

AVIATION Facts by States for Automotive Dealers and Service Shops

Many wholesalers of automobile and truck equipment, repair and maintenance tools, dealers in antomobiles and trucks, service-shop operators already are including aviation in their plans and work. For them, as well as for others in the trade who are interested in studying the growth and possibilities here, the following fundamental facts are presented to give a quick picture of this branch of the automotive industry.

BASED ON DATA FROM 1931 ISSUE OF *Chilton Aero Directory and Catalog*

STATE	AIRCRAFT REGISTRATION	LICENSED PILOTS	LICENSED MECHANICS	AIRPORTS [1]	OPERATING COMPANIES [2]	AIRCRAFT FACTORIES	AIR LAW STATUS [3]	TOTAL POPULATION	TOTAL INCOME (000,000 omitted)	MOTOR VEHICLE REGISTRATION	AIRPORT EXPENDITURES MUNICIPAL Anticipated expenditures last half 1930, all of 1931, on established airports only.	AIRPORT EXPENDITURES COMMERCIAL Anticipated expenditures last half 1930, all of 1931, on established airports only.
Alabama.............	45	64	49	19	1	1	N	2,646,248	720	277,127	$ 199,000	$ 200,500
Arizona.............	38	83	37	34	1	......	FA	435,573	234	111,623	51,500	76,500
Arkansas............	72	122	57	16	2	1	SA	1,854,482	563	231,300	212,000	217,000
California..........	1,175	2,852	1,665	165	18	32	FA	5,677,251	4,635	2,073,816	796,000	1,589,000
Colorado...........	74	147	76	31	4	2	FC	1,035,791	760	308,509	17,500	29,000
Connecticut........	147	174	129	13	14	7	SA	1,606,903	1,259	347,490	174,500	179,000
Delaware..........	49	25	16	2	0	1	FA	238,380	198	56,056	....	5,000
Dist. of Col........	73	270	144	4	1	1	FA	486,869	683	173,434	....	110,000
Florida............	135	196	280	44	3	......	SA	1,468,211	568	329,806	313,000	355,000
Georgia............	74	71	44	31	1	2	N	2,908,506	910	341,177	161,500	162,500
Idaho..............	26	36	20	21	6	......	FA	445,032	282	120,446	13,000	13,000
Illinois.............	667	931	553	75	21	10	FC	7,630,654	6,673	1,638,260	207,000	421,000
Indiana............	245	325	144	48	22	2	FA	3,238,503	1,792	875,453	359,000	410,000
Iowa...............	176	265	139	47	6	6	FA	2,470,939	1,181	782,175	319,000	378,000
Kansas.............	312	273	190	53	4	19	SA	1,880,999	1,185	594,523	112,000	643,000
Kentucky...........	65	91	42	15	1	......	FA	2,614,589	934	330,664	....	6,000
Louisiana..........	101	91	63	15	3	2	N	2,101,593	710	282,000	64,000	104,500
Maine.............	46	67	21	10	3	......	FSA	797,423	562	181,348	12,000	17,000
Maryland..........	96	158	112	17	2	5	FSA	1,631,526	1,119	321,180	....	30,000
Massachusetts.......	240	456	206	29	7	1	SA	4,249,614	4,080	852,122	653,000	722,000
Michigan...........	475	732	447	53	29	19	FA	4,842,325	3,016	1,328,209	1,417,000	1,527,000
Minnesota..........	117	267	132	21	8	2	FSA	2,563,953	1,521	727,022	313,000	317,500
Mississippi.........	41	56	16	11	2	......	FA	2,009,821	472	257,000	73,000	73,000
Missouri...........	365	490	272	31	5	7	FA	3,629,367	2,038	763,375	1,210,000	1,240,000
Montana...........	70	75	51	32	2	......	FA	537,606	338	136,896	25,500	27,500
Nebraska...........	246	215	120	29	3	3	FC	1,377,963	894	426,229	456,000	467,000
Nevada............	11	13	18	25	1	......	FC	91,058	81	29,645	8,000	23,000
New Hampshire.....	28	54	19	7	0	......	FSA	465,293	330	111,553	20,500	22,500
New Jersey.........	301	404	301	30	3	8	FC	4,041,334	3,247	850,415	1,854,000	2,001,000
New Mexico........	24	47	14	27	0	......	FA	423,317	157	90,700	12,000	35,000
New York..........	1,193	1,641	879	82	32	31	FC	12,588,066	14,681	2,316,824	138,000	1,581,000
North Carolina.....	93	86	45	24	2	......	FC	3,170,276	968	474,301	76,000	90,000
North Dakota.......	73	64	26	13	10	1	FA	680,845	347	183,019	19,500	21,000
Ohio...............	582	802	511	85	10	10	FC	6,646,697	4,486	1,798,666	752,000	811,000
Oklahoma..........	326	390	156	52	3	4	N	2,396,040	1,110	550,331	733,500	774,500
Oregon............	119	180	106	45	10	4	FSA	953,786	679	258,147	205,000	235,000
Pennsylvania.......	498	810	401	94	17	6	SA	9,631,350	8,225	1,773,218	3,552,000	3,838,000
Rhode Island.......	40	52	20	8	3	2	FA	687,497	668	135,867	....	8,000
South Carolina.....	39	46	18	18	5	......	FA	1,738,765	572	221,666	77,500	80,500
South Dakota.......	69	112	46	22	10	......	FA	692,849	490	204,306	8,000	35,000
Tennessee..........	117	143	70	15	2	......	N	2,616,556	942	372,543	122,000	138,000
Texas..............	436	732	402	119	12	3	FA	5,824,715	3,046	1,359,543	609,000	685,000
Utah..............	40	76	62	25	4	......	N	507,847	290	110,997	6,000	6,000
Vermont...........	19	28	10	7	3	......	FA	359,611	306	86,624	10,000	12,000
Virginia...........	68	195	270	34	11	......	FSA	2,421,851	976	381,933	31,000	44,000
Washington.........	190	295	184	32	12	2	FA	1,563,396	1,221	452,511	51,000	62,000
West Virginia.......	43	69	25	10	4	2	FC	1,729,205	817	266,132	15,000	23,500
Wisconsin..........	249	285	99	52	8	2	FA	2,939,006	1,708	788,502	308,000	366,000
Wyoming...........	57	36	63	26	4	......	FA	225,565	178	61,501	13,000	13,000
Totals.............	9,785	15,092	8,770	1,718	336	198	......	124,835,046	82,852	26,746,184	$15,779,500	$20,225,000

[1] All types—Municipal, Commercial, Army, Navy, Intermediate, Etc.

[2] Scheduled and Non-Scheduled operators of planes; headquarters only.

[3] FA—Federal license required for ALL aircraft and airmen; FSA—Federal or State license required for ALL aircraft and airmen; FC—Federal license required for all aircraft and airmen engaged in commercial flight but not pleasure; SA—State license required for all aircraft and airmen engaged in commercial flight but not pleasure; N—No license required.

Sale of Airplane and Engine Spare Parts—1930

	Commercial	Military	Miscellaneous	Total
Airplane	$3,442,573	$4,108,167	$475,002	$8,025,742
Engine	2,487,576	2,231,368	469,935	5,188,879
Total	$5,930,149	$6,339,535	$944,937	$13,214,621

Data on Selected Foreign Automotive Markets

Including Number of Trade Outlets, Chief Distributing Centers, Registration, Chief Ports of Entry, Peak Sales Seasons, etc.

Country	Registration Motor Vehicles – Total	Passenger Cars	Buses	Trucks	Per Cent American Vehicles in Service	Relative Standing – Service Equipment	Passenger Cars	Motor Trucks	Accessories	Replacements	Peak Sales Season for Automobiles	Chief Distributing Centers	Count – Car Dealers and Distributors	Truck Dealers and Distributors	Service Stations	Accessory and Equip. Dealers and Distributors	Total Trade Without Duplication	Chief Ports of Entry	Commercial Language Used	Total Highway Mileage
Argentina	387,864	306,331	3,150	78,383	97.5	4	2	1	2	5	Oct. to March	Buenos Aires	1,767	940	809	1,481	4,216	Bahia Blanca, Buenos Aires, Rosario	Spanish	131,697
Australia	593,510	469,000	2,110	122,400	84	5	16	4	5	9	Oct. to Dec.	Sydney, Melbourne, Adelaide, Brisbane, Perth	1,372	503	986	1,899	3,136	Adelaide, Brisbane, Freemantle, Melbourne, Sydney	English	329,662
Belgium	158,000	103,000	1,500	53,500	60	21	3	3	17	7	May to Oct.	Antwerp, Brussels	98	30	77	123	281	Antwerp, Ghent	French, Flemish	18,894
Brazil	159,986	107,095		52,891	98	13	31	27	13	18	Sept. to Jan.	Rio de Janeiro	632	420	164	499	1,275	Rio de Janeiro, Santos	Portuguese, English	75,497
Canada	1,215,071	1,053,632	1,625	159,814		3	1	2	1	1	March to Oct.	Montreal, Toronto, Halifax, Winnipeg, Vancouver	178	118	99	285	530	Halifax, Montreal, Quebec, Vancouver	French (Que.)	390,060
Chile	40,500	26,500	2,000	12,000	98	10	22	17	14	20	Sept. to Feb.	Santiago	145	189	89	213	322	Antofagasta, Iquique, Valparaiso	Spanish	24,414
China, inc Hong Kong	37,950	24,783		12,993	90	31	32	26	26	27	April to Nov.	Shanghai, Hong Kong, Canton, Hankow	138	113	42	283	392	Shanghai, Hong Kong	English	34,810
Dutch East Indies	88,178	67,238	6,538	14,402	91		39	47	8	17	Sept. to April							Balik Marassar	Dutch, English	36,175
Germany	658,686	488,838	12,416	157,432	22	8	8	24	12	10	March to Oct.	Berlin, Frankfort, Hamburg, Munich						Bremen, Hamburg	German	217,479
India	171,000	9,500		41,500	82	18	11	6	16	13	Nov. to March	Calcutta, Bombay, Karachi, Rangoon	312	235	143	653	863	Bombay, Calcutta, Karachi, Madras	English	225,280
Italy	269,500	200,000	8,500	61,000	8	13	33	65	20	4	Sept. to March	Milan, Turin, Rome, Naples, Genoa						Genoa, Naples, Trieste, Venice	Italian	114,129
Japan	98,500	60,500		38,000	95	19	10	10	18	11	May to Oct.	Yokohama, Nagaya, Osaka, Kobe	104	45	34	286	460	Kobe, Nagasaki, Osaka, Yokohama	English	659,215
Malaya	38,409	31,595		6,814	83	32	41	62	31	28	Oct. to May		54	21	26	127	164	Penang, Port Swettenham, Singapore	English	7,146
Mexico	80,800	59,500	4,800	16,500	99	9	4	7	6	16	April to Oct.	Mexico City, Monterey	329	181	254	453	1,112	Guayamas, Tampico, Vera Cruz, Progreso, Ciudad Juarez, Laredo (Texas)	Spanish	62,137
Netherlands	98,428	61,928		36,500	74	12	21	18	24	24	May to Oct.	Rotterdam, Amsterdam	381	184	58	590	1,133	Amsterdam, Rotterdam	Dutch, English	15,534
New Zealand	189,777	154,674	1,309	33,794	86	14	19	20	3	21	Sept. to April	Auckland, Christchurch, Wellington						Auckland, Dunedin, Lyttelton, Wellington	English	48,433
Philippine Islands	33,800	23,200		10,600	100	24	15	13	22	22	Sept. to March	Manila	35	25	17	122	145	Cavite, Ceba, Iloilo, Manila	English	7,854
Poland	38,700	27,500	4,200	7,000	60	47	45	57	33	29	July to Sep.	Warsaw, Poznan, Katowice	54	30	23	68	108	Danzig, Gdynia	Polish, English	141,040
South Africa, Union of	159,689	142,094	1,200	17,595	86	7	6	16	7	15		Capetown, Johannesburg, Durban, Port Elizabeth	300	178	318	385	918	Capetown, Durban, East London, Port Elizabeth	English	85,598
Spain	189,650	133,305		56,345	68	53	13	5	8	19	March to Sept.	Barcelona, Cadiz, Madrid, Malaga, Seville	452	280	328	828	1,424	Barcelona, Bilboa, Valencia	Spanish	54,114
Sweden	151,150	108,650	3,000	39,500	90	17	5	8	11	17	March to Aug.	Stockholm, Guteborg, Malmo	273	238	56	134	435	Guteborg, Malmo, Stockholm	Swedish, English	81,026
Switzerland	79,100	63,000	300	15,800	38	28	21	38	34	30	March to Sept.	Berne, Geneva, Lausanne	83	11	70	125	186		German, French, Italian	9,233
United Kingdom	1,558,032	1,110,930	100,865	346,237	15	2	9	11	4	6	March to Sept.	London, Liverpool, Glasgow, Belfast						Liverpool, London, Belfast, Glasgow, Hull	English	179,286
Uruguay	45,597	37,017	1,071	7,500	97.5	15	20	22	21	3	Aug. to Jan.	Montevideo	254	148	142	252	641	Montevideo	Spanish	22,487
Venezuela	15,000				98	26	17	15	9	26	Sept. to Jan.	Caracas, Maracaibo	104	75	48	154	279	La Guaira, Maracaibo	Spanish	2,211

Count of Trade Outlets: From records of Business Publishers International Corp.

INTERCHANGEABLE DATA SECTION

Showing Exclusive Chilton Compilation of Interchangeability Between Nearly 100 Different Parts in the Following Tables

ADDED FEATURES

Separate Record After Each Table Showing Number of Times Each CHILTON Number Appears.

Separate Record Giving Actual Specifications for Each CHILTON Number for Pistons, Pins, Valves, Timing Chains.

For detailed index to individual parts included here see next page

USES YOU CAN MAKE OF THE DATA HERE

To find what other car models use a part that is interchangeable with the one you seek for the car you are servicing.

To order a particular part of a particular model from a manufacturer when that manufacturer gives you his own parts numbers alongside the corresponding Chilton numbers in his adv., as pages 187, 201, 203.

To check your inventory of parts by comparing it with the need revealed by interchangeability of parts on various models.

To make up parts catalogs of all items carried in stock, by checking interchangeability here against manufacturers numbers.

To compare one vehicle model using a certain part with other vehicle models using the same part.

To determine stock of any part to carry from count of car models using it and data on registration—local, sectional, national.

To check duplication of parts you may be stocking or manufacturing.

On bearings and rivets, to find actual manufacturers numbers of the part desired.

To make it more possible to get original parts from other dealers as well as interchangeable parts of other makes, as the data here indicates the sources.

To determine immediately how many other car models use the same part as in the car you have in mind.

The jobber, with an order from a repair shop for a part he does not stock, can determine here if he has another part which he does stock and which is interchangeable.

For Serial Numbers of Cars See Pages 304-307

For Sizes of Replacement Parts See Index in Detail on Next Page and Page 267

DETAILED INDEX
TO PARTS INCLUDED IN
TABLES OF INTERCHANGEABILITY

For Detailed Index to All Contents, See Pages 7, 9

INDEX TO TABLES OF PARTS SIZES

(For Detailed Index to Other Replacement Service Dtat, See Page 267)

B E A R I N G S
Ball and Roller

Showing Interchangeability of Bearings According to Passenger Car Make and Model—Including 22 Different Locations

---

NOTE: On Ball and Roller Bearings There is Included Another Table Showing Interchangeability According to Make of Bearing. See Pages 179-184, Where You Can Find Any One or All of Nearly Twenty Different Manufacturers' Numbers for Any Bearing Corresponding to the Chilton Number.

A different series of CHILTON NUMBERS has been given to each of 7 classes of Bearings. You can always tell the type of bearing anywhere in these tables, therefore, by noting the series in which its CHILTON NUMBER is included. Here is the Guide:

TYPE OF BEARING	SERIES OF CHILTON NUMBERS
Magneto-Type Bearings	100 Series
Wheel Bearings	500 Series
Single-Row Radial Ball Bearings (Standard and Shielded Types	2200, 2300, 2400 Series
Single-Row Radial Thrust Bearings	3200, 3300, 3400 Series
Double-Row Ball Bearings	4200, 4300, 4400 Series
Tapered Roller Bearings	6000 Series
Straight Roller Bearings	8000 Series

Chilton Automotive Multi-Guide Believes These Bearing Tables Alone Represent the Most Colossal Compilation Task Ever Attempted by a Publisher for Printing and Distribution to the Trade. And Yet They Are Only a Small Part of the Vast Amount of Information Here

BEARINGS—Ball and Roller

HOW TO USE THIS TABLE

1. Locate in the first column the car and model for which the bearing is needed.
2. Follow this line across to the column pertaining to that bearing.
3. In this column opposite your car model you will find the CHILTON NUMBER for the bearing you want.
4. Look up and down this column—or any other bearing column—for the same

CHILTON NUMBER. Wherever you find this same number anywhere in this table you have an interchangeable bearing. The car make opposite tells you what car uses it.

Example: Suppose a Rear Pinion-Shaft Bearing is needed for a Chevrolet Superior AA (1927). Locate this car in the first column. Follow across to the column on Rear Pinion or Worm Shaft, which is the fourth column. Here you see the CHILTON NUMBER for this bearing is 2307. Checking through the CHILTON NUMBERS in all the columns, you will find the number 2307 many times; for instance, opposite the Buick 128 (1927), the Chandler Royal 8 (1928) and several models of the Packard. In each case, no matter where this 2307 bearing is used in the Buick, Chandler, Packard and other cars, it is interchangeable with the Rear Pinion-Shaft Bearing on the Chevrolet Superior AA (1927).

Straight Roller Bearings Not Always Used As Complete Assemblies immediately following the CHILTON NUMBERS at that particular installation. In many installations only the roller assembly or the roller assembly with one A means roller assembly only. B means roller assembly and outer race combination. C means roller assembly and inner race combination. race is used. Where this occurs here it is indicated by letters A, B and C

An Equivalent Table of Chilton Numbers and Manufacturers' Numbers is Given on Pages 179-184

Interchangeable Bearings have the same CHILTON NUMBER in Any Column

Passenger Car Make, Model and Year	King Pin	Pinion or Worm Shaft, Front	Pinion or Worm Shaft, Rear	Differential, Right	Differential, Left	Flywheel Pilot	Release	Generator, Commutator End	Generator, Drive End	Distributor Shaft	Fan	Column, Upper	Column, Lower	Drive Gear Shaft, Rear or Single	Main Shaft, Rear	Main Shaft, Pilot	Countershaft, Front	Countershaft, Rear	Front, Inner	Front, Outer	Rear, Inner	Rear, Outer or Single
Ajax (1925-26)		7057	7063	7074	7074			2201	2203					2306	2306	8129B			6460	6381	6515	
Apperson Str. 8 (1925)		6455	6084	6088	6088	2205		2303	2303		2303			6099	6513		6482	6482	6084	6432	6595	6609
Apperson 6 (1926)		6457	6607	6088	6088	2205		2201	2203		2303			2207	2306				6084	6432	6609	6609
Apperson Str. 8 (1926)		6457	6607	6088	6088	2205		2303	2303		2303								6084	6432	6609	6609
Auburn 4 (1925)				6079	6079	2205								2209	2306	8660A			7058	6336	6629	7013
Auburn 6-43 (1925)		6455	6084	6089	6089	2205		2201	2203					2209	1306	8660A			6055	6432	6595	7013
Auburn 8-88 (1925)		6455	6084	6079	6088	2205								2209	1306	8660A			7058	6386		7013
Auburn 4-44 (1926-27)		4307	2305	6088	6079	2205		2201	2203					2209	2306	8660A			6055	6432		7013
Auburn 8-88 (1926-27)		6457	6084	6088	6088	2205		2201	2203					2209	2306	8660A			6084	6432	6608	7013
Auburn 6-66 (1926)		6457	6084	6079	6088	2205		2201	2203					2209	2306	8660A			6084	6432	7013	7013
Auburn 8-88 (1926)		6457	6084	6088	6088	2205		2201	2203					2209	2306	8660A			7009	6986	7013	7013
Auburn 6-66A (1927)		6457	6514	6088	6079	2205		2201	2203					2209	2306				6084	6432	6608	7013
Auburn 8-88 (1927-28)		6457	6084	6079	6088	2205		2203	2203					2209	2306	8660A			7009	6986	7013	7013
Auburn 8-77 (1927-28)		6457	6514	6088	6088	2205		2203	2203					2207	2206	8660A			7009	6986	7013	7013
Auburn 76 (1928-29)		6457	6059	6095	6095	2205		2203	2203					2207	2306				7009	6986	7013	7013
Auburn 88 (1928-29)	7206	6457	6059	6090	6090	2205		2203	2203					2207	2306	8660A			6064	6432	6608	7013
Auburn 115 (1928-29)		6457	6064	6061	6061	2204		2203	2203					2209	2305	8660A			7009	6986	7013	7013
Auburn 6-80 (1929)		6457	6518	6061	6061	2205		2203	2203					2208	2306		8010A	8010A	7009	6986	7013	7013
Auburn 8-90 (1929)		6457	6064	6097	6097	2205		2203	2203					2207	2306				6064	6432	6517	6517
Auburn 120 (1929)		6457	6064	6061	6061	2204		2203	2203					2209	2305	8010A	8010A	8010A	7009	6986	7013	7013
Auburn 6-85 (1930)		6457	6059	6098	6098	2205		2203	2203					2207	2306	8010A	8010A	8010A	7009	6986	7013	7013
Auburn 8-95 (1930)		6457	6059	6098	6098	2205		2203	2203					2209	2306	8010A			7009	6986	7013	7013

BEARINGS—Ball and Roller—Continued

Interchangeable Bearings have the same CHILTON NUMBER in Any Column

Passenger Car Make, Model and Year	King Pin	Rear Axle – Pinion or Worm Shaft, Front	Rear Axle – Pinion or Worm Shaft, Rear	Differential, Right	Differential, Left	Clutch – Flywheel Pilot	Clutch – Release	Generator, Commutator End	Generator, Drive End	Distributor Shaft	Fan	Steering – Column, Upper	Steering – Column, Lower	Trans. – Drive Gear Shaft, Rear or Single	Trans. – Main Shaft, Rear	Trans. – Main Shaft, Pilot	Trans. – Countershaft, Front	Trans. – Countershaft, Rear	Wheels Front, Inner	Wheels Front, Outer	Wheels Rear, Inner	Wheels Rear, Outer
Auburn 125 (1930)		6457	6064	6097	6097	2205		2203	2203	2200				2208	2306				6064	6432	6517	6517
Blackhawk L6 (1929)			7081	6124	6124	2205		2203	2203		2203			2210	2307				6462	6381	6079	6079
Blackhawk L8 (1929)			7081	6124	6124	2205				2200				2210	2307				6462	6381	6079	6079
Blackhawk L6 (1930)			7081	6124	6124	2205		2203	2203		2203			2210	2307				6462	6381	6079	6079
Blackhawk L8 (1930)			7081	6124	6124	2205		2203		2200				2210	2307				6462	6381	6079	6079
Buick Master (1925)		4307	2309	3210	3210	2204		2203						2209	4307				508	507	4310	4310
Buick Std (1925)		4306	2308	3210	3210	2203		2203						2210	4307				504	507	8075	8075
Buick Master (1926)		4307	2309	3210	3210	2203		2203						2209	2306				508	507	4311	4311
Buick Std (1926)		4306	2309	3210	3210	2203		2203				3206		2209	2306				504	503	8075	8075
Buick Std (1927)		4307	2309	3210	3210	2203		2203				3206		2210	2307				508	503	8075	8077
Buick 115 (1927)		4307	2310	3210	3210	2204		2203				3206		2209	2306				508	507	8075	8077
Buick 120 (1927)		4206	2309	3211	3211	2203		2203				3206		2210	2306				504	503	2311	2310
Buick 115 (1928)		4307	2309	3211	3211	2204		2203				3206		2209	2307				508	507	2311	2311
Buick 120 (1928)		4307	2310	3211	3211	2203		2203				3206		2210	2306				508	503	8075	8077
Buick 128 (1928)		4306	2309	3211	3211	2204		2203				3206		2209	2307				504	507	2310	2310
Buick 116 (1929)		4307	2310	3211	3211	2203		2203				3206		2210	2306				508	503	8075	8077
Buick 121, 129 (1929)		4307	2309	3211	3211	2203		2203				3206		2209	2306				524	523	8080	8080
Buick 40 (1930)		4307	2309	3211	3211	2204		2203				3206		2209	2307				528	527	8080	8080
Buick 50, 60 (1930)		4307	2310	3211	3211	2204		2203						2210	2306				528	527	8080	8080
Cadillac V63 (1925)		2309	2310	6213	6213	2204		2203	2204			3206		2209	2307				528	527	6110	6110
Cadillac 314 (1926)	6675	4309	2409	6213	6213	8622A		2203	2204	2200		7209	7209	2309	2407	8272A	8216A	8216A	6146	6038	6110	6110
Cadillac 314 (1927)	6675	4309	2409	6213	6213	8622A		2203	2204	2200		7209	7209	2309	2407	8272A	8216A	8216A	6146	6038	6110	6110
Cadillac 341A (1928)	6675	4309	2409	6213	6213	2204		2203	2204	2200				2309	2407	8272A	8216A	8216A	6146	6038	6110	6110
Cadillac 341B (1929)	6675	4309	2409	6213	6213	2204		2203	2204	2200				2210	2407	8028A	8216A	8216A	6146	6038	6110	6110
Cadillac 353 (1930)	6675	4309	2409	6213	6213	2204		2203	2204	2200				2209	2307	8018A	8216A	8216A	530	529	6110	6110
Cadillac V16 (1930)		4309	2409	6213	6213	2204		2203	2204	2200	(2303F / 2204R)			8132B	8131	8018A	8216A	8216A	530	529	8132B	
Case JIC (1925)		6059	6185	6088	6088			2203	2203					8132B	4307	8208A			6002	6064	6155	
Case X (1925)		6059	6185	6110	6110			2203	2203		7182	7209		6997	7023	7029	7021	7050	6007	6154	6110	6110
Case Y (1925)				6110	6110			2203	2203			7209		8072B	4307	8208A			6007	6154	6110	6110
Case Y (1926-27)		6059	6167	6110	6110			2203	2203					8072B	4307	8208A						
Case JIC (1926-27)		6059	6167	6110	6110			2203	2203					2308	2307		2306	2307	6064	6432	2310	2310
Chandler 33 (1925)		6059	6167	6110	6110		2209	2203	2203	2200				2308	2307		2306	2307	6064	6432	2310	2310
Chandler 35 (1926)		6059	6167	6110	6110		2209	2203	2203	2200				2308	2306		2306	2307	6064	6432	2310	2310
Chandler Big 6 (1927)		6561	6632	6096	6096		2209	2203	2204	2200				2207	2306		2306	2306	6513	6380	6135	
Chandler Royal 8 (1927)		6552	6167	6096	6096		2209	2203	2204	2200				2308	2306		2306	2306	7009	6986	6564	2310
Chandler Std. 6 (1927)		6059	6167	6110	6110			2203	2203	2200				2308	2306		2306	2306	6064	6432	2310	2310
Chandler Royal 8 (1928)		6059	6185	6096	6096			2203	2204	2200				2308	2306		2306	2306	6064	6432	6564	
Chandler Big 6 (1928)		6632	2307	6110	6110			2201	2203					2207	2306		2306	2306	7009	6986	6564	2310
Chandler Spec. 6 (1928)		6632	2307	6096	6096			2203	2203					2308	2306		2306	2306	7009	6986	6564	2310
Chandler Spec. Invincible 6 (1928)		6632	2307	6096	6096			2203	2203					2308	2306		2306	2306	6064	6432	2307	
Chevrolet V (1925)		4305	4305	3208	3208	2205		2203	2203					2207	2306				502	501	2307	2307
Chevrolet Superior AA (1926)		4305	4305	3208	3208			2203	2203					2207	2306				502	501	2307	2307
Chevrolet AB (1927)		4305	4305	3208	3208			2203	2203					2207	2306				502	501	2307	2307
Chevrolet AC (1928)		4206	4206	3208	3208			2203	2203					2207	2306				502	501	2307	2307
Chevrolet AD (1930)		7057	7091	7074	7074	2205		2201	2203					2207	2306				7058	6381	2307	2307
Chrysler 6B (1925)		6483	6521	7074	7074			2203	2203					2209	2306	8660A	8018A	8018A		6381	2308	2308
Chrysler 58 (1926)		6483	6521	6105	6105	2204		2203	2203	2302				2209	2306	8660A	8018A	8018A	6603	6381	2308	2308
Chrysler 60 (1926)		6561	6632	7070	7070			2201	2203	4302				2209	2305	8660A			7011	6481	6636	
Chrysler 70 (1926)		6483	6521	7074	7074			2203	2203	4302				8072B	2307	8018A			7010	6986	6159	
Chrysler 80 (1927)		6552	6632	7074	7074	2204		2203	2203					2206	2305				6603	6370	6526	
Chrysler 50 (1927)		7093	7093	6105	6105			2201	2203	2302				2209	2305	8018A	8018A	8018A	7010	6481	6525	
Chrysler 70 (1927)		6483	6521	7070	7070	2204		2201	2203	4302				2209	2307	8060A	8060A	8018A	7011	6986	6159	
Chrysler 52 (1928)		6552	6632	7074	7074			2201	2203					2206	2307	8060A	8060A	8018A	7010	6370	6526	
Chrysler 62 (1928)		6552	6521	6109	6109	2204		2201	2203	2302				2209	2305				6603	6481	6525	
Chrysler 72 (1928)		4307	2310	6109	6109			2201	2203	2302				2210	2307	8018A	8018A	8018A	7010	6370	6525	2308
Chrysler Imp. 80 (1928)		6552	6632	6109	6109	2204		2201	2203	2302				2206	2307	8060A	8060A	8018A	6603	6481	6525	2308
Chrysler 65 (1929)		6552	6632	6109	6109			2203	2203	2302				2209	2307	8062A	8018A	8018A	7010	6370	2310	2310

FAFNIR
BALL BEARINGS
...for every replacement job!

... carried in stock by these jobbers

Jasper Auto Parts Co., 241 N. Crawford Rd.
Motor Car Supply Co., 1451-55 Michigan Ave.
L. C. Smith Bearings Co., 2120 S. Michigan Ave.
Southside Unit Parts Co., 6515 Cottage Grove Ave.
Triangle Machine Works, 3650 N. Ashland Ave.
Unxld Motor Supply Co., 7710 S. Halsted St.
West Side Unit Parts Co., 3941 W. Washington Blvd.
Cicero—Slager & Son
Elgin—Phillips Auto Supply Co., 191 Division St.
Highland Park—Haak's Auto Supply Co.
Kankakee—Automotive Supply Co.
Maywood—Schroeder & Son, 11 N. Second Ave.
Quincy—Clough-Racine Co.

ALABAMA
Birmingham—Southern Bearing & Parts Co., 305 S. 20th St.
Lawson Auto Parts Co., 208 S. 21st St.
Montgomery—Auto Parts & Tool Co., Bibb & Katoma Sts.

ARIZONA
Phoenix Pacific Ball Bearing Co.

ARKANSAS
Little Rock—J. B. Cook Auto Machine Co., 622 W. 7th St.

CALIFORNIA
Los Angeles—Pacific Ball Bearing Co., 415 W. Pico St.
Bakersfield—Automotive Sales Co., Inc., 900 18th St.
El Centro—Auto Gear & Supply Co.
Hollywood—Automotive Sales Co., Inc., 6501 Sunset Blvd.
Huntington Park—Hasse Auto Parts Co., 6016 Pacific Blvd.
Long Beach—Automotive Sales Co., Inc., 1345 Locust Ave.
Los Angeles—Automotive Sales Co., Inc., 1337 S. Flower St.
Redlands—Automotive Sales Co., Inc., 348 Orange St.
San Diego—Auto Gear & Supply Co., 136 B St.
San Pedro—Automotive Sales Co., Inc., 1136 S. Pacific St.
Santa Ana—Automotive Sales Co., Inc., 3rd & French Sts.
SUBS
Calusa—Calusa Implement Co.
Marysville—Hurst Bros.
Oakland—Motor Parts Co.
Petaluma—Inwood & Flohr
Salinas—Lacy Automotive Parts Co.
San Jose—Penniman & Richards
Stockton—Stockton Bearing & Parts Co.
Colyear Motor Sales Co., San Francisco
Henderson Bros., Sacramento
Stanislaus Auto Supply Co., Merced
Lindley & Harrison, Fresno
Stanislaus Auto Supply Co., Modesto
Kramer Auto Supply Co., Eureka

COLORADO
Colorado Springs—Glen Shultz, 208-212 E. Colorado Ave.
Denver—M. L. Foss, Corner 19th & Arapahoe St.
Buda Engine Parts Co., 1023 Broadway

CONNECTICUT
Bridgeport—Standard Motor Parts Co., 553 Fairfield Ave.
Hartford—Kenyon Bearings & Auto Parts Co., Inc., 191 Church St.
Grinold Auto Parts, Inc., 65 Elm St.
Middletown—Standard Auto Parts Co., 614 Main St.
New Haven—Connecticut Bearings Co., 294 York St.

DISTRICT OF COLUMBIA
Washington—Phelps Roberts Corp., 1818 14th St., N.W.

FLORIDA
Daytona Beach—Consolidated Automotive Co., 114 E. Fairview Ave.
Gainesville—Baird Hardware Co., 802 1st Ave., S.
Consolidated Automotive Co., 737 W. University Ave.
Jacksonville—Consolidated Automotive Co., 1131-9 W. Forsyth St.
Miami—Frank T. Budge, 5 E. Flagler St.
Miami Auto Repair Shop
Orlando—Consolidated Automotive Co., 55 W. Pine St.
Pensacola—Girdlestone Auto Supply Co., 106-8 N. Tarragona St.
St. Petersburg—Marine Ways Machine Co., 236 7th Ave., S.
Tampa—Moody & Wetherell, Inc., 920 Twigg St.
General Automobile Supply Co., 1100-04 Florida Ave.
West Palm Beach—Consolidated Automotive Co., 527 Datura St.

GEORGIA
Albany—Keenan Auto Parts Co., 112 Front St.
Atlanta—Southern Bearings & Parts Co., 449 Peachtree St.
Macon—Bearings Supply Co.
Savannah—Allen Parts Co., 207 W. Liberty St.

IDAHO
Boise—Idaho Electric Supply Co., 911 Main St.

ILLINOIS
Chicago—Auto Parts & Gear Co., 2451 Milwaukee Ave.
Fafnir Bearing Co., 806 W. Washington Blvd.
General Auto Parts, 4547 Northwestern Ave.
Guaranteed Gear Service Co., 1714 S. Michigan Ave.
H & E Standard Auto Parts Co., 3925 Irving Park Blvd.
Ideal Auto Supply Co., 4750 W. Washington Blvd.

INDIANA
Anderson—John Garrett & Co., 17 W. Ninth St.
Ft. Wayne—Piston Service, Inc., 227 W. Main St.
Gary—Triple H. Auto Parts Co., 632 Washington St.
Hammond—United Motor Parts Co., 620 Sohl St.

IOWA
Cedar Rapids—Cedar Rapids Auto Supply Co., 613 Second Ave., E.
Davenport—Sieg Co., 500-516 Iowa St.
Des Moines—Carl Youngstrom Co., 1312 Grand Ave.
Standard Bearings Co.
Fort Dodge—Fort Dodge Machine & Sup. Co., 612 First Ave., S.
Mason City—J. B. Snyder Co., 119 E. State St.
Waterloo—Repass Automobile Co., 170 Park Ave., W.
Sioux City—Wm. Warnock Co., Inc.

KANSAS
Topeka—Southwick Automotive Sup. Co.

KENTUCKY
Owensboro—Wright Machine Co.

MARYLAND
Baltimore—Mitchell & Dale, 24 W. Biddle St.
Hagerstown—Maryland Motor Co., 56-62 W. Franklin St.

MASSACHUSETTS
Boston—Bearings Specialty Co., 711 Beacon St.
Northampton—Rubber Store, Cor. Court & Gothic Sts.
Springfield—Parmenter Co., 812 Main St.

MICHIGAN
Detroit—Detroit Ball Bearing Co., 110 W. Alexandrine Ave.

MINNESOTA
Mankato—National Bushings & Parts Co., 609 S. Front St.
Minneapolis—National Bushings & Parts Co.
Rochester—National Bushings & Parts Co., 12 S. W. 4th St.
St. Paul—National Bushings & Parts Co., 141-5 West 7th Street.

MISSISSIPPI
Clarksdale—Johnston Auto Parts Co.

MISSOURI
Kansas City—Dayton Auto Parts Co., 1625 McGee St.
Springfield—Herman-Brownlow Co.
St. Louis—Auto Parts Co., 3225 Locust St.

MONTANA
Butte—Crawley Motor Supply Co., 220 E. Broadway
Great Falls—Starter & Battery Co., 320 First Ave.

NEVADA
Reno—Motor Parts Co.

NEW JERSEY
Camden—General Auto Supply Co., 1176 Kaighn Ave.
Newark—The Fafnir Bearing Co., 270 Central Ave.
Trenton—Ufert Auto Parts Service, 25 Barnes St.
Vineland—Automotive Replacement Parts Co.

NEW MEXICO
Albuquerque—R. L. Harrison Co., 123 N. Fourth St.

NEW YORK
Albany—Albany Spring Service, 425 Central Ave.
Brooklyn—E. Krieger & Son, Inc., 420-424 Tompkins Ave.
Buffalo—Vulcan Supply Co., 1067 Main St.
L. I. City—E. Krieger & Son, Inc.
Shapse Auto Radiator Co., 65-67 Prospect St.
New York City—G. & B. Motor Parts Co., 941 8th Ave.
Niagara Falls—Gebell Auto Parts Co., 1416 Pine St.
Port Richmond—New York Motor Supply Co., 112-114 Richmond Ave.
Rochester—Gordon Motor Parts, Inc., 30-36 Joseph Ave.
Saranac Lake—Glen J. Harvey & Co.
Syracuse—Group Parts, Inc., 222 Harrison St.
Utica—Genuine Auto Parts Co.
Watertown—Thomas Hardman Corp., 166 Arsenal St.

NORTH CAROLINA
Charlotte—Southern Bearing & Parts Co., 12 S. Poplar St.
Durham—Motor Bearings & Parts Co., 407 E. Chapel Hill
Goldsboro—Standard Automotive Parts Co., E. Center St., N.
Greensboro—Motor Bearings & Parts Co.
Hickory—Hickory Auto Parts, Inc.

High Point—Southern Bearings & Parts Co., 139 S. Wrenn St.
Raleigh—Motor Bearings & Parts Co., Dixie Bldg., S. Salisbury St.
Winston-Salem—Southern Bearings & Parts Co.

OHIO
Cincinnati—Automotive Bearings & Equip. Co., 205-7 E. Eighth St.
Ohio Ball Bearing Co., 330 E. Eighth St.
Cleveland—Cleveland Ball Bearing Co., 1369 W. 9th St.
Ohio Ball Bearing Co.
Columbus—G. W. Holmes Co., 196-198 E. Gay St.
Dayton—M. D. Larkin Supply Co., E. Third St.
Youngstown—Ohio Ball Bearing Co.

OKLAHOMA
Oklahoma City—Sharp Auto Supply Co., 121-123 W. Eighth St.

OREGON
Portland—Smith Auto Parts Co., 15th & Burnside Ave.
Salem—B & W Parts Store, 445 Chemeketa St.

PENNSYLVANIA
Allentown—F. Hersh Hardware Co., Hamilton St.
Altoona—Motor Parts Sales & Service Co., 712 19th St.
Hazleton—Automobile Supply Co.
Johnstown—Johnstown Bearing & Supply Co., 77-79 Baumer St.
Lancaster—Reilly Bros. & Raub, 44-46 N. Queen St.
Rosey's Auto Parts Co., 1521 N. Prince St.
Lebanon—Whittle's Machine & Spring Works
Philadelphia—Auto Gear & Parts Co., 1728-30 Fairmount Ave.
E. P. Rotzell Co., 1633 Fairmount Ave.
Pittsburgh—Condon Bearing & Supply Co., 4642 Baum Blvd.
Motive Parts Co. of Pa., 6314 Penn. Ave.
Pottsville—Rewall Auto Supply Co., 109-15 Nichols St.
Wilkes-Barre—Kitsee Auto Store, 60 N. Main St.
Williamsport—Jakes Auto Parts Co.

SOUTH CAROLINA
Anderson—Cox-Stubbs, Inc., 206 W. Whitner St.
Columbia—Jenkins Automotive Parts Co., Inc.
Charlestown—H. Steenken Co., 450 Meeting St.
Florence—H. Steenken Co., 146 S. Dargan St.

TENNESSEE
Chattanooga—Harts Automotive Parts Co., 1250 Market St.
Knoxville—Service Auto Parts Co., Emory Park
Memphis—Memphis Piston Service Co., 286 Union Ave.
Nashville—Automotive Parts Co., Inc., 1601 Church St.

TEXAS
Beaumont—C. H. Mountjoy Parts Co., Maine & Pine Sts.
Simmonds Motor Supply Company, 345 Pine St.
Houston—C. H. Mountjoy Parts Co., 1420 Dallas Ave.
Corpus Christi—C. H. Mountjoy Parts Co.
Lubbock—Lubbock Parts Company.
Dallas—Herbert Sierk & Co.
Fort Worth—Gabert Auto Works
San Antonio—C. H. Mountjoy Parts Co., 514 5th St.
McAllen—C. H. Mountjoy Parts Co., Highway at Canal
El Paso—Smith Machine Co., 211 S. Kansas St.
Waco—Ward-Dossett-Floyd Co.

UTAH
Salt Lake City—Felt Auto Parts Co., 643-45 S. State St.

VERMONT
Brattleboro—Brattleboro Battery & Ignition Co., Inc., 29 Flat St.

VIRGINIA
Lynchburg—Southern Parts & Bearing Co., 617 Main St.
Richmond—Standard Parts Corp., 1806 W. Broad St.
Roanoke—Shepard's Auto Supply Co.

WASHINGTON
Aberdeen—Piston Service, Inc., 204 W. Market St.
Bellingham—Piston Service, Inc.
Everett—Piston Service, Inc., 2807 Wetmore St.
Mount Vernon—Piston Service, Inc.
Seattle—Piston Service, Inc., 801 E. Pike St.
Hoge Piston & Ring, Inc., 520 E. Pike St.
Piston Service Co., 307 Westlake Ave., N.
Spokane—Auto Gear & Axle Co., 1103 W. First Ave.
Tacoma—Hoge Piston & Ring, Inc., 714 St. Helena St.
Piston Service, Inc., 737 Broadway
Wenatchee—Piston Service, Inc.
Yakima—Piston Service, Inc., 122 S. Second St.

WEST VIRGINIA
Moundsville—O. H. Miller, 401 Sixth St.
Williamson—Williamson Supply Co.

WISCONSIN
Madison—Madison Auto Parts & Mach. Co., 1475 Butter St.
Manitowoc—Auto Parts Co., 1018 S. Tenth St.
Milwaukee—Motive Parts Co. of America, 1409 W. Mitchell St.
Racine—Racine Supply Co., 337 Main St.

WYOMING
Casper—Wyoming Automotive Co., 500 E. Yellowstone

THE FAFNIR BEARING CO.   NEW BRITAIN, CONN.

BEARINGS—Ball and Roller—Continued

Interchangeable Bearings have the same CHILTON NUMBER in Any Column

Passenger Car Make, Model and Year	King Pin	Rear Axle Pinion or Worm Shaft, Front	Rear Axle Pinion or Worm Shaft, Rear	Rear Axle Differential, Right	Rear Axle Differential, Left	Clutch Flywheel Pilot	Clutch Release	Generator, Commutator End	Generator, Drive End	Distributor Shaft	Fan	Steering Gear Column, Upper	Steering Gear Column, Lower	Transmission Drive Gear Shaft, Rear or Single	Transmission Main Shaft, Rear	Transmission Main Shaft Pilot	Transmission Countershaft, Front	Transmission Countershaft, Rear	Wheels Front, Inner	Wheels Front, Outer	Wheels Rear, Inner	Wheels Rear, Outer or Single
Chrysler 66........(1929)		6566	6553	7070	7070				2203		2302			2209	2307	8062A			7011	6986	7014	7014
Chrysler 75........(1929)		6552	6632	6109	6109				2203		2302			2209	2307	8018A	8018A	8018A	7010	6370	7017	2310
Chrysler Imp. 80...(1929)		4307	2310	6109	6109				2203					2210	2307	8010A			6603	6481	2310	7014
Chrysler 6.........(1930)		6553	6553	6097	6100	8010A			2203					2207	2305	8010A			7011	6986	7014	7014
Chrysler 66........(1930)		6553	6553	6109	6097				2203					2308	2307	8010A			7016	6370	6074	6074
Chrysler 70........(1930)		6632	6632	6109	6109	2204			2203					2308	2307	8010A			7011	6370	6074	6074
Chrysler 77........(1930)		6553	6553	6100	6100				2203					2208	2306	8010A			7011	7011	7014	7014
Chrysler 8.........(1930)		6553	6553	6996	6996			115	2203					2208	2306				7009	6986	6564	
Cleveland 31.......(1925)		7042	7059	6996	6996									2207	2306				6513	6380	6135	
Cleveland 43.......(1925)		6553	7050	7074	7074									2207	2306				7009	6380	6564	7015
Cleveland 31.......(1926)		6451	6561	6079	6079									2208	2306				6513	6380	6135	
Cleveland 43.......(1926)		6561	6632	6096	6096									2207	2306				6097	6120	6145	6381
Cord..............(1930)	7204	4309	4309	2210	2210	2205		2201	2203		2204			2209	4309				7058	6381	6605	6381
Davis 90.........(1925-26)		6455	7065	2210	2210									2209	2306	8660A	8587A	8587A	7058	6381	6605	
Davis 91.........(1925-26)		6455	7065	6088	6088									2207	2306	8660A	8587A	8587A	7058	6381	6605	
Davis 92...........(1926)		6457	6064	6088	6088	2205			2203		2302			2207	2306	8660A	8587A	8587A	7009	6986	6605	7013
Davis 93...........(1926)		6457	6064	6088	6088				2203		2302			2209	2306	8660A	8587A	8587A	7009	6986	7013	
Davis 92...........(1927)		6456	6513	6088	6088				2204					2207	2306	8660A	8587A	8587A	7058	6381	6605	7013
Davis 98...........(1927)		6456	6513	6079	6088	2205			2204		2302			2209	2306				7058	6381	6605	
Davis 94...........(1927)		6456	6513	6088	6088				2204					2207	2306				7058	6381	7013	
Davis 93...........(1928)		6457	6064	6088	6088				2203					2209	2305				7058	6381	6605	
Davis 98...........(1928)		6457	6064	6088	7070				2203					2209	2306	8010A			7011	6986	7014	7014
Davis 99...........(1928)		6457	6064	6088	7074				2203					2209	2306	8010A			7011	6986	7014	7014
Davis 98...........(1928)		6457	6064	6088	6097	2205			2203					2207	2306				7058	6381	6605	6605
De Soto...........(1929)		6566	6553	7070	7070				2203					2208	2308	8010A			7058	6381	6605	6605
De Soto 6.........(1930)		6553	6553	6097	6097				2203					2209	2308	8010A			7058	6381	6605	
De Soto 8.........(1930)		6553	6553	6088	6088				2203					2209	2308	8010A			7058	6381	6605	
Diana Str. 8.......(1926)		6457	6084	6088	6088					2200				4207	2308	8018A	8587A	8587A	6518	6380	6153	6153
Diana Str. 8.......(1927)		6455	6084	6088	6088					2200				2207	2308	8018A	8018A	8018A	6518	6380	6153	
Diana Str. 8.......(1928)		6457	6084	6088	6088	2205					2303			2209	2308	8018A	8018A	8018A	6518	6380	6153	
Dodge Brothers 4...(1925)		7057	7090	6105	6105	2304			2203		7182			4207	2308		8587A	8587A	6518	6380	6153	
Dodge Brothers 4...(1926)		7057	7090	6105	6105	8007A			2203		7182			2209	2308	8018A	8018A	8018A	6518	6380	6153	
Dodge Senior 6.....(1927)		7057	7090	6105	6105	2304			2203					2207	2308		8018A	8018A	6518	6380	6153	
Dodge Bros. 4, before March(1927)		7057	7090	6100	6100	2304			2203					2209	2308	8018A	8018A	8018A	6518	6380	6153	
Dodge Bros. 4, after March(1927)		7057	7090	6100	6100	8007A			2203		7182			2209	2308	8018A	8018A	8018A	6518	6380	6153	
Dodge Brothers Senior 6(1928)		7063	7063	6100	6100				2203					2209	2308	8018A	8587A	8587A	6518	6380	6153	
Dodge 4-128.......(1928)		7063	8166B	6100	6100	8007A			2203					2209	2308	8018A	8018A	8018A	7012	6985	6636	
Dodge Std. 6.......(1928)		7063	7063	6100	6100	8007A			2203					2209	2308	8018A	8018A	8018A	7012	6985	6636	
Dodge Brothers Victory 6(1928)		7063	8166B	6100	6100	8007A			2203					2209	2308	8018A	8018A	8018A	6518	6380	6636	
Dodge Brothers Senior.(1929)		4307	4205	6100	6100	8007A			2203					(8068B) 2209	2308	8018A	8018A	8018A	6518	6380	6153	
Dodge Brothers DA-6.(1929)		4307	8166B	6100	6100	8007A		2203	2203		2303			2209	2307	8018A	8018A	8018A	7011	6986	7017	7017
Dodge DC-8........(1930)		6553	6553	6097	6097			2203	2203					2208	2306	8010A			7011	6986	7014	7014
Dodge DD-6........(1930)		6553	6555	6097	6097			2203	2203					2207	2306	8010A			7011	6986	7014	7014
Durant D55........(1928)		6483	6555	2208	2208				2203					2207	2206				7011	6986	7187	
Durant 65........(1928-29)		6555	6633	7074	7074			2203	2203					4207	2204	4204			6458	6378	6634	
Durant 75........(1928-29)		6483	7189	2208	2208				2203					2204	2204				7187	6986	7187	
Durant 4-40.......(1929)		6483	6555	2208	2208									2209	2206	4204			7011	6986	7187	
Durant 6-60.......(1929)		6555	6555	7074	7074			2203	2203					2207	2306				6458	6378	6634	
Durant 66.........(1929)		6551	6633	7074	7074	8002A		2203	2203					2306	2305	8660A			7011	6378	7015	7015
Durant 614........(1930)		7046	6551	6080	6080	8063A								2207	2206	4204			6458	6381	6564	6564
Durant 617........(1930)		4307	2305	6096	6096			2203				6000	6000	2207	2206	8660A			6517	6004	6602	
Elcar 4-40.........(1925)		4207	2305	6096	6096							6000	6000	2207	2306	4204			6517	6004	6602	6602
Elcar 6-50.........(1925)		7090	7033	6032	6099			2203	2203					2209	2306	8660A			6062	6004	6602	
Elcar 6-60.........(1925)		4307	2407	6105	6100			2203	2203					2207	2206	8660A			6146	6038	6156	
Elcar 8-80.........(1925)				6096	6096			2203	2203						2306	8660A			6517	6433	6602	6602
Elcar 4-55.......(1926-27)		4306	2304	6079	6079			2203	2203					2207	2306	8660A			7058	6381	6605	6605
Elcar 6-65.........(1926)		4307	2305	6105	6105			2203	2203					2209	2306	8660A			6601	6480	6156	6156
Elcar 8-81.........(1926)								2203	2203	2200				2207	2306	8660A			7011	6986	6156	4310
Elcar 6-70.........(1927)		4306	2304	6079	6079			2203	2203					2207	2306	8660A			6601	6986	6156	6156
Elcar 8-82.........(1927)		4307	2305	6105	6105			2203	2203					2209	2306	8660A			6517	6381	6156	6156

PRECISION

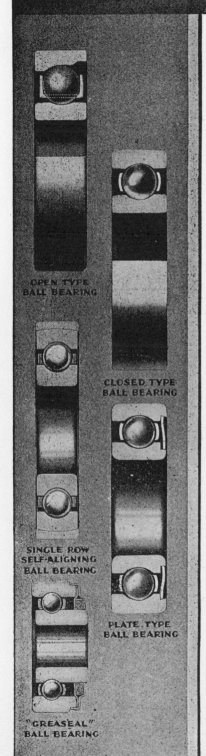

FOR BETTER PERFORMANCE

In comparing values, performance should be the determining factor. It is the only true test of worth—gauged not by first cost, but by ultimate cost over a useful life. It is the standard by which true economy must be measured.

In every field of engineering and industry, over a period of twenty years, NORMA-HOFFMANN Precision Bearings have made a distinguished record for dependable stand-up-ability. For greater economy, longer sustained, they stand pre-eminent.

There is a PRECISION Bearing for every load, speed and duty. Let our engineers help you select the type best adapted to your special conditions. And write for the Catalogs.

NORMA-HOFFMANN BEARINGS
CORPORATION
STAMFORD   CONN., U.S.A.

"NORMA-HOFFMANN"
PRECISION BEARINGS

BEARINGS

BEARINGS—Ball and Roller—Continued

Interchangeable Bearings have the same CHILTON NUMBER in Any Column

Passenger Car Make, Model and Year	King Pin	Rear Axle — Pinion/Worm Shaft Front	Rear Axle — Pinion/Worm Shaft Rear	Rear Axle — Differential Right	Rear Axle — Differential Left	Clutch — Flywheel Pilot	Clutch — Release	Electrical — Generator Commutator End	Electrical — Generator Drive End	Electrical — Distributor Shaft	Fan	Steering Gear — Column Upper	Steering Gear — Column Lower	Transmission — Drive Gear, Rear or Single	Transmission — Main Shaft, Rear	Transmission — Main Shaft, Pilot	Transmission — Countershaft, Front	Transmission — Countershaft, Rear	Wheels — Front Inner	Wheels — Front Outer	Wheels — Rear Inner	Wheels — Rear, Outer or Single
Elcar 8-90 (1927)		4308	2306	6105	6105	2205		2203	2203					2209	2306	8660A			6517	6381	6156	
Elcar 6-78 (1928-29)		4306	2304	6079	6079	2205		2203	2203					2207	2306				7011	6986	6652	
Elcar 8-78 (1928-29)		4307	2305	6096	6096	2205		2203	2203					2207	2306				7009	6986	6605	
Elcar 8-82 (1928-29)		4307	2306	6105	6105	2205		2203	2203					2209	2306				6517	6381	6156	
Elcar 8-91 (1928)		4308	2306	6105	6105	2205		2203	2203					2209	2306				6517	6478	6156	
Elcar 8-92 (1928)		4308	2306	6105	6105	2204		2203	2203					2207	2305				7011	6986	6516	
Elcar 75, 96 (1929)		6566	6553	7071	7071	2204		2203	2203		6986			2209	2306				7011	6986	6080	6080
Elcar 95, 96 (1929)		4307	2305	6096	6096	2205		2203	2203		6986			2207	2305				6517	6381	6156	
Elcar 120 (1929)		4308	2306	6105	6105	2204		2203	2203					2209	2306				7011	6986	6080	6080
Elcar 6-75 (1930)		6566	6553	7071	7071	2204		2203	2203					2207	2305				6517	6381	6156	
Elcar 95, 96 (1930)		4307	2305	6105	6105	2205		2203	2203					2209	2306				7011	6986	6156	
Elcar 130 (1930)		4308	2306	6080	6080	2205		2203	2203					2206	2305				6517	6986	6522	
Erskine 50 (1927)	7198	7050	7021	7026	7026	8007A								(2206)	2305				7002	6986	6156	6523
Erskine 6-51 (1928)	7198	7050	7050	6080	6080	8007A								2207	2305				6998	6986	6522	6523
Erskine 52 (1929)	7198	7050	6556	6062	6062	9316A	3207	115	2203		2302			2207	8128				7008	6986	6515	6515
Erskine 53 (1930)	7193	6550	6549	6062	6062	2202	3207	115	2203		2302			8129B	8128				6441	6433	6137	6137
Essex 6 (1925)		6484	6083	6062	6061	2202		115	2203					2207	8128				6441	6433	6137	6137
Essex 6 (1926)		6486	6083	6062	6062	2202		115	2203					8129B	8128				6441	6433	6137	
Essex Super 6 (1927)		6486	6552	6062	6062	2202	3207	115	2203		2202			2207	8128				6441	6986	6137	
Essex Super 6 (1928)		6486	6552	6062	6061	2202	3207	2203	2203		2202			2207	8128				6441	6380	6137	
Essex Challenger (1929)		7046	6553	6096	6096	2202	3207	2202	2203					2208	2307				7011	6479	6599	
Essex Challenger (1930)		4306	2307	6105	6105	2202		2201	2203					2208	2307				6513	6382	2308	2308
Falcon Knight 10 (1927-28)	7195	4307	2307	7074	7074	2202		2201	2204					2210	2306	8010A	2305	2305	6598	6479	7013	
Falcon Knight 12 (1928-29)	6369	4306	2407	2208	2208	2202		2203	2204					2207	2406	8010A	2305	2305	6998	6382	6564	2308
Flint E55 (1925-26)		4307	2308	6105	6105	2202		2203	2203					2210	2406	8010A			6598	6479	6139	6139
Flint 60 (1926)		7189	2407	7074	7074	2202	2207	2203	2203					2207	2307	8010A	8010A	8010A	6998	6382	7187	6139
Flint 80 (1926)		4306	2308	2208	2208	2203		2201	2203					2210	2307				6598	6479	6564	6564
Flint Jr. (1926-27)		4307	2407	6105	6105	2203	2207	2202	2203		2302			2207	2306				6998	6382	6139	6139
Flint 80 (1927-28)		4306	2308	2208	2208	2203		2202	2203		2302			2206	2306				6598	6479	6564	6564
Flint Jr. (1927-28)		4307		6105	6105	2203		2202	2203					2206	2306				6999	6386	6139	6139
Flint T (1927)		6483	7189	2208	2208	2203	2207	115	2203					2206	2306				6999	6386	7187	7187
Ford T (1925)	7177	7191	7191	7181	7181	2203		2202	2203			7177	7177	2208	2306				6999	6987	6150	
Ford T (1926)	7177	7191	7191	7181	7181	2203		2203	2203			7177	7177	2208	2306				6999	6987	6137	
Ford T (1927)	7178	7191	7191	7181	7181	2203		2203	2204			7178	7178	2208	2306				6999	7020	6137	
Ford A (1928)		3407	3407	3210	3210	2203		2201	2204			6100	6100	2208	2406				7063	7020	6137	
Ford A (1929)		6633	6633	6117	6117	2203		2203	2204			6967	6967	2208	2406				7063	7020	6137	
Ford A (1930)		6633	6633	6117	6117	2203		2202	2203			6405	6405	2208	2407				7063	7020	6137	
Franklin 11 (1926)		6633	6633	6117	6117	2203		2203	2203			6405	6405	2209	2307				7063	7020	6137	
Franklin 11-B (1927)	7177	6633	6633	6117	6117	2203		2203	2203			6405	6405	8063B	2307				7184	7185	6564	
Franklin 11-B (1928)	7177	6633	6633	6117	6117	2203		2203	2203			6405	6405	2209	2307				7184	7185	6139	
Franklin Series 12 (1928)	7178	6633	6633	6117	6117	2203		2203	2203					8063B	2306				7063	7020	7187	
Franklin 130 (1929)			2407	2208	2208	2203		2203	2203					2207	2307	8080B	8062B	8125B	6458	6388	6564	
Franklin 135, 137 (1929)				6105	6105	2203		2203	2203					2209	2307				6458	6388	6139	
Franklin 145, 147 (1930)				2208	2208	2203		2201	2203					2209	2307				6458	6388	6082	6082
Gardner 6-A (1925)		7050	7050	6088	6088	2203		2203	2203					2209	2306	8660A	2305	2305	6084	6602	6608	6082
Gardner 8-A (1925)		6457	7086	8582B	8582B	8635A		2203	2203					2209	2306	8660A	2305	2305	6511	6380	8900	8900
Gardner Series 5 (1925)		6457	6514	6088	6088	2203		2201	2203					2207	2305	8660A	8010A	8010A	6084	6002	6608	
Gardner 6-B (1926-27)		6064	6457	6079	6079	2203		2203	2203					2209	2306	8660A			6084	6432	6596	
Gardner 6-B (1926-27)		6457	6514	6088	6088	2203		2203	2203					2209	2306	8660A			7009	6986	7013	7013
Gardner 8-B (1927)		6457	6514	6088	6088	2203		2203	2203			6405	6405	2209	2306	8660A			7009	6986	7013	7013
Gardner 90 (1927)		6457	6059	6079	6079	2203		2203	2203					2209	2306	8660A			6064	6432	6608	
Gardner 75 (1928)		6457	6064	6098	6098	2204		2203	2203					2209	2306	8660A			7009	6986	7013	7013
Gardner 85 (1928)		6457	6059	6088	6088	2204		2203	2204					2209	2306	8660A			7009	6986	7013	7013
Gardner 95 (1929)		6457	6059	6095	6095	2204		2203	2204					2209	2306	8660A			6064	6432	6608	
Gardner 120 (1929)		6457	6059	6090	6090	2204		2203	2203					2209	2305	8660A			7009	6986	7013	7013
Gardner 125 (1929)		6457	6059	6090	6090	2204		2203	2203					2209	2306	8660A			7009	6986	7013	7013
Gardner 130 (1930)		6457	6059	6098	6098	2204		2203	2203					2209	2306	8660A			6064	6432	6608	
Gardner 136 (1930)		6457	6059	6090	6090	2204		2203	2203					8063B	2306	8660A			7009	6986	7013	7013
Gardner 140 (1930)		6457	6064	6090	6090	2204		2203	2203					2209	2306	8660A			7009	6986	7013	7013
Gardner 150 (1930)		6457	6064	6090	6090	2204		2203	2203					2209	2306	8660A			6064	6432	6608	
Graham Paige 610 (1928-29)		7047	6561	7070	7070	9320A		2203	2203					(2207)	2305				7011	6986	6516	

BEARINGS—Ball and Roller—Continued

Interchangeable Bearings have the same CHILTON NUMBER in Any Column

Passenger Car Make, Model and Year	King Pin	Rear Axle Pinion or Worm Shaft, Front	Rear Axle Pinion or Worm Shaft, Rear	Rear Axle Differential, Right	Rear Axle Differential, Left	Clutch Flywheel Pilot	Clutch Release	Gen. Commutator End	Gen. Drive End	Distributor Shaft	Fan	Steering Column, Upper	Steering Column, Lower	Drive Gear, Rear Shaft or Single	Main Shaft, Rear	Main Shaft, Pilot	Countershaft, Front	Countershaft, Rear	Wheels Front, Inner	Wheels Front, Outer	Wheels Rear, Inner	Wheels Rear, Outer or Single
Graham Paige 614 (1928-29)	7192	4307	2305	6096	6096	9320A								8063B	2305				7011	6986	6652	6091
Graham Paige 619 (1928-29)	7192		2306	6117	6117	9320A								8132B	2307				6518	6381	6091	6091
Graham Paige 629 (1928-29)	7192		2306	6117	6117	9320A								8132B	2307				6518	6381	6091	6091
Graham Paige 835 (1928-29)	7193	6567	6552	6117	7071	9320A								8132B	2307				7011	6986	6516	6080
Graham Paige 612 (1929)	7192	4307	2305	6096	6096	9320A								8063B	2305				7011	6986	6080	6080
Graham Paige 615 (1929)	7192		2306	6117	6117	9320A								8132B	2307				6518	6381	6091	6091
Graham Paige 621 (1929)	7192	6567	2306	6117	6117	9320A								8132B	2307				6518	6381	6091	6091
Graham Paige 827 (1929)	7192	4307	2306	6117	6117	9320A								8132B	2307				6518	6381	6091	6091
Graham Paige 837 (1929)	7193	4307	6553	7071	7071	9320A								8063B	2305				7011	6986	6516	6516
Graham Std. 6 (1930)	7192	4307	2305	6096	6096	9320A		2203						8132B	2307				6518	6381	6080	6080
Graham Spec. 6 (1930)	7192	4307	2306	6117	6117	9320A		2203						8132B	2307				6518	6381	6091	6091
Graham Custom 8 (1930)	7192	6563	6163	6117	6117	9320A	3211	2203	2203		120			8959B	8940	9322A	8284B	8284B	6138	6037	6204	6091
Graham Special 8 (1930)	7192	6565	6163	6117	6117	9320A	3211	2203	2203		120			8959B	8940	8077	8284B	8284B	6138	6037	6204	6091
Graham Standard 8 (1930)		6565	6163	6114	6114	2205	3210	2203	2203					2308	8940	9322A	8284B	8284B	6138	6037	6204	6091
Hudson Super 6 (1925)		6565	6163	6117	6117	2204	3210	115	2203	2200	120			2308	8940	9322A	8284B	8284B	6138	6037	6204	6599
Hudson Super 6 (1926)		6565	6163	6117	6117	2204	3207	2203	2203					2308	8940				6138	6037	6204	6597
Hudson Super 6 (1927)		7048	6553	6061	6061	2202		2203	2204	2200				2207	8128				7011	6386	6597	6597
Hudson Super 6 (1928)	7194	4307	2305	7074	7074	2204	2209	2203	2204		8487B			2306	2306	8060A	8587A	8587A	6601	6485	6604	6597
Hudson Greater 6 (1929)	7194	4307	2305	7074	7074	9320A		2203	2202	2200				2209	2306	8018A	8010A	8018A	6068	6006	6597	6597
Hudson Great 8 (1930)		4556	6633	6105	6105	2204	2210	2202	2204		8487B			2209	2207	8018A	8010A	8018A	7009	6382	6152	6152
Hupmobile E1 (1925-26)	7194	4307	2310	6100	6100	9320A		2203	2202					2209	2207	8018A	8010A	8010A	6601	6485	6597	6597
Hupmobile Series R (1925)		6556	6633	6105	6105	2205		2202	2202					8128B	2306	8018A	8010A	8010A	7009	6382	6152	6152
Hupmobile A1 (1926-27)	7194	4307	2310	6100	6100	9320A	2210	2203	2204	2200				2209	2306	8018A	8010A	8010A	6601	6485	6597	6597
Hupmobile E2 (1926-27)		6551	6633	7074	7074	2205		2202	2202					8128B	2206	8018A	8010A	8010A	6511	6382	6152	6152
Hupmobile A2 (1927)	7194	6553	2310	6100	6100	9320A		2202	2202	2200				2209	2306	8018A	8010A	8010A	7009	6382	6597	6597
Hupmobile E3 (1927-28)		6632	6633	7074	7074	9320A		2203	2204					8128B	2206	8018A	8010A	8010A	6601	6382	6152	6152
Hupmobile Century 6 (1928)	7205	6632	6716	6100	6100	9320A		2202	2202					2209	2206	8018A	8010A	8010A	7009	6382	6597	6597
Hupmobile Century 8 (1928)	7193	6551	6633	7074	7074	9320A		2202	2202	2200				8128B	2206	9347A	9347A	9347A	7011	6382	7007	7007
Hupmobile Century 125 (1929)	7193	6553	6553	6100	6100	9320A		2202	2203					8062B	2307	8018A	8018A	8018A	6517	6382	6074	6074
Hupmobile Big 8, 7 Pass. (1929)		6632	6717	7071	7071	9320A		2201	2203	2200	120			2209	2307	9347A	9347A	9347A	7009	6382	6610	6610
Hupmobile Century 6 (1929)		6633	6654	6100	6100	9320A		2203	2203		4302			8128B	2206	8018A	8018A	8018A	7011	6382	6605	6605
Hupmobile M8 (1929)		4306	2304	6079	6079	9320A		2203	2203		120			2207	2206	9323A	9324A	9324A	6455	6380	6074	6074
Hupmobile Big 8 (1930)		7090	7093	6105	6105	2205	2210	115	2204		7182			2209	2207	9323A	9324A	9324A	6601	6479	7074	7074
Hupmobile S6 (1930)		7093	7093	6105	6105	2205	2210	115	2204		7182			2209	2207	8010A	8018A	8018A	6601	6479	6091	6091
Hupmobile H, U8 (1930)	7195	7086	7086	6101	6101	9320A	2210	115	2204		7182			2209	2307	9323A	9324A	9324A	6601	6479	7065	7065
Hupmobile C8 (1930)	7195	7090	2306	6105	6105	9320A		2202	2204					2209	2307	8010A	8018A	8018A	6601	6381	6091	6091
Jewett 6-50 (1925)	7195	7081	8167B	6100	6100	8007A		115	2204					2207	2305	8010A			7058	6386	7065	7065
Jewett New Day 6-40 (1926)	7195	7090	8167B	6100	6118	8007A		2203	2203					2207	2307				7058	6381	7065	7065
Jordan K, L (1925)		7090	6518	6100	6100	8007A		2203	2203		2303			2207	2306	8010A	8018A	8018A	7009	6986	7013	7013
Jordan A (1925)		6457	6064	6061	6061	2205		2201	2203					2209	2207				6517	6388	7065	6517
Jordan A (1926)		6457	6517	6097	6097	2205		2201	2203		2203			2209	2306				6517	6388	7013	7013
Jordan J (1926)	7195	6457	6064	6061	6061	2205		2201	2203					2207	2307				6458	6388	6517	6517
Jordan AA (1927)		6457	6064	6105	6105	2205		2201	2203					2209	2307				6517	6479	7013	7013
Jordan J (1927)		7093	7093	6105	6105	2205		2203	2203					2209	2306				6601	6479	6091	6091
Jordan R (1927-28)		7093	7093	6105	6105	2205		2203	2203					2209	2306				6601	6479	6091	6091
Jordan JJ (1927-28)	7195	7093	7086	6105	6105	2205		2201	2203					2207	2306				6601	6479	6091	6091
Jordan JE (1928-29)		7093	7093	6118	6118	2205		2201	2203					2209	2306				6601	6479	6091	6091
Jordan E (1929)		7093	7093	6105	6105	2205		2203	2203					2209	2306				6601	6479	6091	6091
Jordan G (1929)		7093	7093	6105	6105	2205		2203	2203					2207	2305				6601	6479	6517	6517
Jordan G (1930)		7093	7093	6105	6105	2205		2203	2203					2209	2307	8010A	8018A	8018A	6601	6479	7013	7013
Kissel 6-55 (1925)		7093	7093	6105	6105	2205		2203	2203		2203			2209	2206				6601	6381	6091	6091
Kissel 8-75 (1925)	7195	7093	7093	6105	6105	2205		2203	2203					2209	2306	8010A	8018A	8018A	6601	6479	6091	6091
Kissel 6-55 (1926)		7093	7093	6105	6105	2205		2203	2203					2209	2206				6601	6479	6091	6091
Kissel 8-75 (1926)		7093	7093	6105	6105	2205		2203	2203					2207	2306	8010A	8018A	8018A	6601	6479	6517	6517
Kissel 6-65 (1927)		7093	7093	6105	6105	2205		2203	2203					2209	2306				6601	6479	7013	7013
Kissel 8-65 (1927)														2209	2306							
Kissel 8-75 (1927)	7195	7093	7093	6105	6105	2205		2203	2203					2207	2306	8010A	8018A	8018A	6601	6479	6091	6091
Kissel 6-70 (1928)		7093	7093	6105	6105	2205		2203	2203					2209	2306							
Kissel 6-55 (1928)		7093	7093	6105	6105	2205		2203	2203					2209	2306				6146	6038	6091	6091
Kissel 8-80 (1928)		7093	7093	6105	6105	2205		2203	2203					2209	2306	8010A	8018A	8018A	6146	6038	6091	6091
Kissel 8-80S (1928)		7093	7093	6105	6105	2205		2203	2203					2209	2306				6146	6038	6091	6091
Kissel 8-90 (1928)		7093	7093	6105	6105	2205		2201	2203					2209	2306				6146	6038	6091	6091

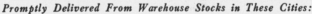

BEARINGS—Ball and Roller—Continued

Interchangeable Bearings have the same CHILTON NUMBER in Any Column

Passenger Car Make, Model and Year	King Pin	Rear Axle Pinion/Worm Shaft, Front	Rear Axle Pinion/Worm Shaft, Rear	Differential, Right	Differential, Left	Clutch Flywheel Pilot	Clutch Release	Generator, Commutator End	Generator, Drive End	Distributor Shaft	Fan	Steering Column, Upper	Steering Column, Lower	Trans. Drive Gear Shaft, Rear or Single	Trans. Main Shaft, Rear	Trans. Main Shaft Pilot	Trans. Countershaft, Front	Trans. Countershaft, Rear	Wheels Front, Inner	Wheels Front, Outer	Wheels Rear, Inner	Wheels Rear, Outer or Single
Kissel 6-73 (1929)	6457	6457	6517	6061	6061	2205		2203	2203	2200				2209	2306				7009	6986	7013	7013
Kissel 8-95 (1929)	7093	7093	6059	6105	6105	2205		2203	2203	2200				2209	2306				6146	6038	6091	6091
Kissel 8-126 (1929)	7093	7093	6064	6098	6098	2205		2201	2203	2200				2209	2307				6146	6038	6091	6091
Kissel 6-73 (1930)	6457	6457		6098	6098	2205		2203	2203	2200				2209	2306				6517	6986	7013	7013
Kissel 8-95 (1930)	6457	6457		6105	6105	2205		2203	2203	2200				2209	2307				6146	6388	6517	6517
Kissel 8-126 (1930)	7093	7093		6120	6120	2204		2203	2203	2200				2209	2307				6146	6038	6091	6091
La Salle 303 (1927)		4308	2408	6120	6120	2204		2203	2204	2200 U				2209	2307	8018A	8028A	8028A	508	507	2311	2311
La Salle 303 (1928)		4308	2408	6120	6120	2204		2203	2204	2200 U				2209	2308	8018A	8028A	8028A	508	507	2311	2311
La Salle 328 (1929)		4308	2408	6120	6120	2204		2203	2204	2200 U				2209	8132	8018A	8216A	8216A	530	529	2311	2311
La Salle 340 (1930)		6162	6263	6279	6279	2204		2203	2204	2200 U	4303F 2303R	7210	7210	8132B / 2309	8131B / 2407	9348A	9318A	9318A	6146	6038	6110	6110
Lincoln 8 (1925)	6669	6162	6263	6213	6213	2204		2203	2204	2200 U	4303F 2303R	7210	7210	2309	2407	9348A	9318A	9318A	6146	6038	6110	6110
Lincoln (1926)	6669	6162	6263	6213	6213	2204		2203	2204	2200 U	120	7210	7210	2309	2407	9348A	9318A	9318A	6146	6038	6110	6110
Lincoln (1927)	7196	7102	7102	6278	6278	2204		2203	2204	2200 U	4303F 2303R	7210	7210	2309	2407	9348A	9318A	9318A	6146	6038	6110	6110
Lincoln 8 (1929)	7196	7102	7102	6278	6278	2204			2204	2200 U		7210	7210	2309	2407	9322A	9318A	9318A	6146	6038	6110	6110
Lincoln 8 (1930)	7196	7102	7102			2204				2204 U		7210	7210	2309	2407	9322A	9318A	9318A	6146	6038	6110	6110
Locomobile 48 (1925)		4311	2412	2312	2312	4307	2210			2201 2203 2200 (2)	4303F 2303R	6062	6008	2211	2308	2206	2307	2307	6441	6585	2311	2211
Locomobile 48 (1926)		4311	2412	2312	2211	4307	2210	2203	2303	2200	4303F 2303R	6062	6008	2211	4307 / 2306	2207	2307	2307	6441	6658	2311	2211
Locomobile 90 (1926)		4309	2307	4211	4211		2201	2303	2208	2200 (2)	120			4210 / 2307			2306	2306	6147	6556	2310	2310
Locomobile Jr. 8 (1926)		4306	2308	2211				2202														
Locomobile 48 (1927)		4311	2412	2312	2312	4307	2210	2203	2204	2201 2203 2200 (2)	4303F 2303R	6062	6008	2211	2308	2206	2307	2307	6441	6558	2311	2311
Locomobile 8-66 (1927)		4306	2308			2305		2203	2204	2200	120			2307	2306	2206	2306	2306	6147	6556	2310	2310
Locomobile 8-80 (1927)		4308	2306		2211			2203	2203		2303			2209	2307	2207	2307	2307	6648	6585	2311	2211
Locomobile 90 (1927)		4309	2307		4211		3209	2203	2204					4210	4307		2306		6380	6380	6600	
Locomobile 48 (1928)		4311	2412	2211		2205	3209	2201	2204					2211	2306	2206	2306	2306	7188	6480	6156	2310
Locomobile 8-70 (1928)		4306	2308	7074	7074	2305		2203	2204		120			2206	2307		2306	2306	6601	6556	6156	
Locomobile 8-80 (1928)		4308	2306	6105	6105			2203	2204					2209	2306	2207			6147	6480	6600	2310
Locomobile 90 (1928)		4309	2307	6105	6105	2305	3209	2203	2303					2210	4307		2306	2306	7188	6380	2310	
Locomobile 8-80 (1928)		4308	2306	8533B	4212	2305	3209	2203	2303	2200	120	6062	6008	2209	2307	8208	2306	2306	6147	6556	2310	2310
Locomobile 86, 88 (1929)		4309	2307	8533B	4212	4206	2209B	2203	2303	2200	120	2206R	2207L	2210	9209B	8208			6136	6479	2311	2311
Locomobile 90 (1929)		2209	4310	4208*	4212	4206	2211	2203	2303		116 120	2206R	2207L	2209	9209B	8208A			6136	6479	2311	2311
Marmon 74 (1925)		2209	4310	8533B	4208*	9320A	2211	2203	2303		116 120	2206R	2207L	2207	2306	8208A	2306	7013A	6986	7009	7013	7013
Marmon 74 (1926)		4306	2308	8533B	8533B	4212	2211	2203	2303	2200	116 120	2206R	2207L	2209	9209B	8208A	2306	2307	6136	6479	2311	2311
Marmon Little 8 (1927)																						
Marmon E-75 (1927)		2209	4310	4212	4212	9320A	2211	2203	2203	2200	116 120	2206R	2207L	2209	2306	820SA	2307	2307	6136	6479	2311	2311
Marmon 68 (1928)		2209	2304	6080	6080	9320A	2211	2203	2203	2200	116 120	2206R	2207L	2207	9209B	820SA			7011	6986	2307	2307
Marmon E-75 (1928)		2209	4310	8533B	8533B	4212		2203	2203		120			2209	9209B				136	6479	2311	2311
Marmon 78 (1928)		4306	2308	6080	6080	9320A		2203	2203		2303			2208	2306	8010A	2306		524	523	7013	7013
Marmon 68 (1929)		4306	2304	6080	6080	9320A		2203	2203	2200	116 120			2207	2306	8010A	2306		7009	6986	2307	2307
Marmon 78 (1929)		4306	2308	6105	6105	9320A		2203	2203		120			2208	2306		2306		524	523	7013	7013
Marmon Roosevelt (1929)		6566	6553	7071	7071	9320A		2203	2203					2206	2305		2305		7071	6986	6516	
Marmon 8-69 (1930)		4306	2304	6079	6079	9320A		2203	2203					2207	2305	8010A	2305	8010A	7011	6986	2307	2307
Marmon 8-79 (1930)		4307	2305	6096	6096	9320A		2203	2203					8128B	2306	8010A	2306		6517	6381	6652	
Marmon H Big 8 (1930)		4306	2306	6105	6105	9320A		2203	2203					2209††	2306	8010A	2306		6517	6381	6156	8131B
Marquette (1930)		4306	2307	3208	3208	9320A		2203	2203		116 120			2208	2306	8660A	2306		524	523	6156	8131B
Maxwell 25 (1925)		4307	2305	6096	6096			2203	2203					2209	2306				2308		2308	2308

HELIFLEX

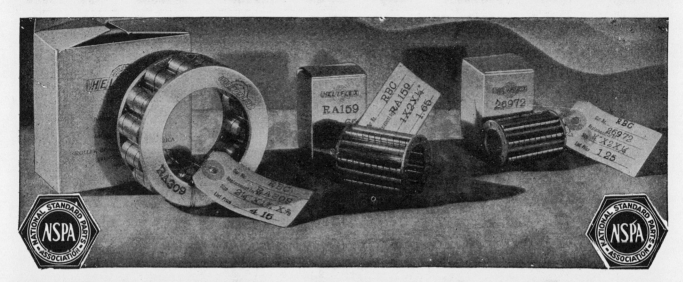

ROLLER BEARINGS ARE GUARANTEED FOR QUALITY, INTER-CHANGEABILITY AND PERFORMANCE

HELIFLEX stocks just can't go wrong...if the package is broken, there is a Heliflex number and price tag on each piece.

HELIFLEX service stocks are conveniently located throughout the country. Your Parts Jobber can serve your every requirement.

HELIFLEX Bearings are available for every car, truck, bus or tractor, regardless of make, year or model.

For Heliflex complete bearing numbers see Roller Bearing Table in this section of Chilton Multi-Guide.

HELIFLEX New Complete Catalogs are now ready. Write for your copy...complete service specifications, interchangeability table, prices, etc.

Service Parts Wholesalers who have found it impossible to get an adequate roller bearing line, are invited to join the Heliflex organization.

ROLLER BEARING CO. OF AMERICA

Replacement Division—Whitehead Road, Trenton, New Jersey

Export Replacement Department—55 West 42nd St., New York City

Dallas Warehouse	New York City Warehouse	Kansas City Warehouse	Chicago Warehouse	Atlanta Warehouse	Los Angeles Warehouse
2705 Williams Street	250 W. 54th St.	14th & Oak	2073 S. Wabash Ave.	580 Spring St., N. W.	Pacific Ball Bearing Co.
Dallas, Texas	New York City	Kansas City, Missouri	Chicago, Ill.	Atlanta, Ga.	415 West Pico Street
					Los Angeles, California

We also ship direct from our warehouse stocks at San Francisco and Seattle

BEARINGS—Ball and Roller—Continued

Interchangeable Bearings have the same CHILTON NUMBER in Any Column

Passenger Car Make, Model and Year	King Pin	Rear Axle — Pinion or Worm Shaft, Front	Pinion or Worm Shaft, Rear	Differential, Right	Differential, Left	Clutch — Flywheel Pilot	Release	Electrical — Generator, Commutator End	Generator, Drive End	Distributor Shaft	Fan	Steering — Column, Upper	Column, Lower	Transmission — Drive Gear Shaft, Rear or Single	Main Shaft, Rear	Main Shaft Pilot	Countershaft, Front	Countershaft, Rear	Wheels — Front, Inner	Front, Outer	Rear, Inner	Rear, Outer or Single
Moon Series A (1925)		6007	6064	6088	6088			2203	2204					2207	2306				7058	6381	6605	6605
Moon Series A (1926)		6007	6064	6088	6088			2203	2204					2207	2306				7058	6381	6605	6605
Moon 6-60 (1926)		6457	6479	6079	6079				2204					2207	2306				7009	6986	7013	7013
Moon Series A (1927)		6454	6513	6088	6088				2204					2207	2306				7058	6986	7013	7013
Moon 6-60 (1928)		6456	6064	6088	6088				2204		2303			2207	2306				7009	6986	7013	7013
Moon 6-60 (1928)		6457	6454	6079	6079	2205	2210	2201	2203		2302			2207	2306				7009	6986	7013	
Moon 6-72 (1928)		6457	6064	6088	6088			2203	2203					2209	2306				7009	6381	7013	7013
Moon 8-80 (1928)		6457	6064	6088	6088			2201	2203					2207	2307				7058	6381	6605	7013
Moon 6-72 (1929)		4308	6514	6079	6079			2203	2203					2207	2306				7009	6986	7013	7013
Nash Special 6 (1925)						2210			2203												2309	2309
Nash Adv. 6 (1926)		4308		6088	6088	2205	2210	2203	2203						2306							
Nash Light 6 (1926)				6079	6079			2201	2203					8128B							2309	2309
Nash Spec. 10L-6 (1926)		4308	7063	7074	7074	2205	2210	2203	2203					8128B	2307				6461	6381	2309	2309
Nash Adv. 6 (1927)		4308	7057	7074	7074			2202	2203						2306						6515	
Nash Spec. 10L-6 (1927)		7057	7063	7074	7074	2205	2210	2203	2203					8128B	2307				6460	6381	6515	2309
Nash Light 6 (1927)		6553	6553	6095	6095			2202	2203					8128B	2306				7008	6986	7014	
Nash Adv. 6 (1928)		4308																	7008	6986		
Nash Spec. 6, 431 (1928)		7057	7063	3208	3208				2203						2306							
Nash Std. 6, 400 (1928)		7057	7063	3208	3208				2203						2306							
Nash Adv. 6 (1929)		6553	6553	3208	3208				2203													
Nash Single 6 (1930)	7175	4306	2307	3208	3208				2203		8062A	7175	7175	2207	2306	8010A			504	503		8131
Nash Twin Ign. 6 (1930)		4306	2307	3208	3208				2203		8007A			2207	2306	8010A			6958	6959		8131
Nash Twin Ign. 8 (1930)		4306	2307	3208	3208				2203					2208	2306				504	503		8131
Oakland 6-54 (1925)		4306	2307	3208	3208				2203			3206		2208	2306				504	503	8131	8131
Oakland O6 (1926)		4306	2304	3208	3208				2203			3206		2207	2306	9325A			524	523	8131	8131
Oakland GO-6 (1927)		4306	2304	3208	3208				2203			3206		2208	2307				502	501	8131	8131
Oakland AA-6 (1928)		4406	2304	3208	3208				2203					2208	2307				502	501	2207	2307
Oakland AA-6 (1929)		4406	2308	3208	3208				2203					2208	2307				502	501	2207	2307
Oakland 8 (1930)		4306	2307	3208	3208				2203					2208	2307				524	523	2207	2307
Oldsmobile 30C (1925)		4308	2304	6110	6110	2205	2210		2203	2200	8353B	7208	7208	2208	2306	9326A	8272A	8272A	524	523	2307	2307
Oldsmobile 30D (1926)		4308	4305	6193	6193	2205	2210		2203	2200	8353B	7208	7208	2208	2306	9326A	8272A	8272A	524	523	2307	2307
Oldsmobile E (1927)		4308	4305	6110	6110	2205	2210		2203	2200	8353B	7208	7208	2208	2306	9326A	8272A	8272A	7009	6986	2308	2308
Oldsmobile F-28 (1928)		4308	2304	6110	6110	2205	2210		2203	2200	8353B			2208	2306	9326A	8272A	8272A	6008	6380	2308	2308
Oldsmobile F-29 (1929)		4309	2305	6193	6193	2205	2210		2203		8357			2208	2306	9326A	8272A	8272A	7009	6986	2308	2308
Oldsmobile F-30 (1930)		4308	2306	6117	6117	2205	2210		2203		8353B			2208	2306	9326A	8272A	8272A	7009	6986	2308	2308
Overland 91 (1925)		4309	7093	6117	6117									2211	2307				6008	6380	2308	2308
Overland 93 (1925)		7090	7033	6032	6099			2202			2303	7208	7019	2211	2307	9326A	8216A	8216A	6008	6380	2309	2309
Overland 91 (1926)		4306	2304	6079	6079			2202			2303	7019	7019	2210	2307	8032A	8216A	8216A	6606	6479	2309	2309
Overland 93 (1926)		4307	2305	6096	6096				2203		2302	7019	7019	2209	2307	8032A	8216A	8216A	6606	6479	2310	2310
Packard 6 cyl., 236, 243 (1925)		4308	2306	6105	6105	2205	2210	2201	2203	2200				2210	2206				6606	6479	2309	2309
Packard 8 cyl., 236, 333 (1925)		4308	6084	6105	6105	2205	2210	2201	2203	2200				2209	2307				6606	6479	2309	2309
Packard 6 cyl., 326, 243 (1926)		7093	6084	6088	6088	2205		2201	2203		7182								7058	6381	6074	6074
Packard 8 cyl., 236, 243 (1926)		6455	6306	6105	6105	2205		2201	2203					2309	2307		2306	2306	6601	6381	6005	2310
Packard 6 cyl., 426, 433 (1927)		4309	2306			2205		2203	2203					2309	2307		2306	2306	6517	6381	6156	6156
Paige 6-70 (1925-26)																					6156	6156
Paige 6-72 (1926)																					6091	6091
Peerless 72 (1926)						2205								2309	2308				7074	6479	7074	6605

Peerless 67	(1926)
Peerless 69	(1926)
Peerless 60	(1927)
Peerless 69	(1927)
Peerless 73	(1927)
Peerless 72	(1927)
Peerless 80	(1927-28)
Peerless 90	(1928)
Peerless 60	(1928)
Peerless 72	(1928)
Peerless 69	(1928)
Peerless 80	(1928-29)
Peerless 61	(1929)
Peerless 125, first 500 cars	(1929)
Peerless 125, after 500 cars	(1929)
Peerless 81	(1929)
Peerless A	(1930)
Peerless B	(1930)
Peerless C	(1930)
Peerless 72	(1930)
Pierce Arrow 80	(1926)
Pierce Arrow 33	(1926)
Pierce Arrow 80	(1927)
Pierce Arrow 36	(1927)
Pierce Arrow 80	(1927)
Pierce Arrow 36	(1928)
Pierce Arrow 81	(1928)
Pierce Arrow, 133, 143	(1929)
Pierce Arrow A, B, C	(1930)
Plymouth 4 cyl	(1929)
Plymouth	(1930)
Pontiac 6	(1926)
Pontiac 6	(1927)
Pontiac 6	(1928)
Pontiac Big 6	(1929)
Pontiac 6-30	(1930)
Reo T6	(1925)
Reo T6	(1926-27)
Reo Flying Cloud	(1927)
Reo Wolverine	(1927)
Reo Flying Cloud	(1928)
Reo Wolverine	(1928)
Reo Flying Cloud Master	(1929)
Reo Flying Cloud Mate	(1929)
Reo 15	(1930)
Reo Flying Cloud 20-25	(1930)
Riekenbacker A-8	(1925)
Riekenbacker D-6	(1925)
Riekenbacker 8-B	(1925)
Riekenbacker E-6	(1926)
Riekenbacker 6-70	(1926)
Riekenbacker 8-80	(1927)
Riekenbacker 8-90	(1927)
Riekenbacker 8-90	(1927-28)
Star F	(1926)
Star M	(1926)
Star R	(1926)
Star M	(1927-28)
Star R	(1927-28)
Stearns Knight B (4 cyl.)	(1925)
Stearns Knight C (6 cyl.)	(1925)
Stearns Knight S (6 cyl.)	(1925)
Stearns Knight B (4 cyl.)	(1926)
Stearns Knight C-75	(1926)
Stearns Knight S-95	(1926)
Stearns Knight F6-85	(1927)
Stearns Knight F6-85	(1927-28)
Stearns Knight 8-85	(1928)
Stearns Knight H & J 8-90	(1928)
Stearns Knight H & J 8-90	(1929)
Stearns Knight M & N 6-80	(1928-29)
Studebaker Big 6	(1925)
Studebaker Spec. 6	(1925)
Studebaker Std. 6	(1925)
Studebaker Big 6	(1926)
Studebaker Light 6	(1926)
Studebaker Spec. 6	(1926)
Studebaker Big 6 120	(1927)

BEARINGS—Ball and Roller—Continued

Interchangeable Bearings have the same CHILTON NUMBER in Any Column

Passenger Car Make, Model and Year	King Pin	Rear Axle — Pinion or Worm Shaft, Front	Rear Axle — Pinion or Worm Shaft, Rear	Rear Axle — Differential, Right	Rear Axle — Differential, Left	Clutch — Flywheel Pilot	Clutch — Release	Electrical — Generator, Commutator End	Electrical — Generator, Drive End	Electrical — Distributor Shaft	Fan	Steering Gear — Column, Upper	Steering Gear — Column, Lower	Drive Gear Shaft, Rear or Single	Transmission — Main Shaft, Rear	Transmission — Main Shaft, Pilot	Transmission — Countershaft, Front	Transmission — Countershaft, Rear	Wheels — Front, Inner	Wheels — Front, Outer	Wheels — Rear, Inner	Wheels — Rear, Outer or Single
Studebaker Big 6 EP .... (1927)		7092	7093	6105	6105	2205		2201	2203					2308	4308				6603	6481	6156	6156
Studebaker Spec. 6 .... (1927)		6631	6654	6105	6105	2205		2201	2203					2308	4308				6510	6388	6149	6149
Studebaker Std. 6 .... (1927)		6631	6654	6105	6105	2205		2201	2203					2307	4207				6510	6388	6639	6639
Studebaker Commander 6 ..... (1928)	7197	6631	6654	6105	6105	2205		2201	2203					2307	4207				6510	6388	6639	
Studebaker Dictator 6 ...... (1928)	7197	6631	6654	6105	6105	2204			2203		2303			2209	4207	8018A			6518	6388	6149	
Studebaker President 8 ..... (1928)	7194	6631	6633	6075	6075	2204		2201	2203					2207	2305	8018A			6459	6370	6149	7014
Studebaker Commander 6 ..... (1929)	7193	6557	6633	6105	6075	2204		2201	2203					2307	2305				6459	6370	7014	7014
Studebaker Commander 8 ..... (1929)	7193	6557	6633	6075	6075	2204		2203	2203					2307	2305				6459	6370	7014	7014
Studebaker Dictator 6 ...... (1929)	7193	6557	6633	6105	6075			2201	2203		116F 120R			2207	2207	8018A			6459	6370	7014	7014
Studebaker President 8 ..... (1929)	7197	6637	6715	6105	6105	2204		2203	2203		116F 120R			2209	4207				6518	6388	6074	6074
Studebaker President 8 ..... (1930)	7197	6637	6715	6105							116F 120R			2209	4307	9349A			6518	6388	6074	6074
Studebaker Dictator 8 ...... (1930)	7193	6630	6656	6075	6075	9316A	2209	2203	2203		116F 120R			2207	2305				7008	6986	6515	6515
Studebaker Commander 8 ..... (1930)	7193	6630	6657	6075	6075	9316A	2209	2203	2203					2207	2305				6459	6370	6515	7014
Studebaker Dictator 6 ...... (1930)	7193	6550	6551	6075	6075	9316A		2203	2203					2207	2305				7008	6986	6515	6515
Studebaker 6-53 .... (1930)	7193	6550	6549	6075	6075	9316A		2203	2203					2207	2305				7008	6986	6515	7014
Studebaker Com. 6 .... (1925)		6630	6657	6117	6117	2205		2201						2209	2210				6459	6370	6089	6089
Stutz 695 .... (1926)		6162	6566	6750	6750	2205				2200				2209	2307				6601	6479	6089	6089
Stutz AA .... (1927)			7093	6750	6750			2203	2204	2200				2209	2307				6601	6479	6102	6102
Stutz AA .... (1928)			7093	6750	6750			2203	2204	2200				2209	2307				6601	6038	6102	6102
Stutz BB, 131" WB .... (1928)	7196	6455	7093	6750	6750	2205		2203	2204					2209	2307	8080B	8062B	8062B	6146	6038	6102	6102
Stutz BB, 145" WB .... (1929)	7196	6457	7093	6088	6088	2205		2201	2204					2210	2307	8080B	8062B	8125B	6146	6038	6102	6102
Stutz Series M .... (1930)	7195	6457	6084	6088	6088	2204		2201	2203					2208	2306				6055	6432	6629	6596
Velie 60 .... (1925)	7195	6481	6084	6088	6088	2204		2201	2203		2202			2207	2306				7009	6986	7013	7013
Velie 60 .... (1926)	7206	6457	6059	6079	6079	2204		2201	2203		2202			2208	2306				6513	6388	7013	7013
Velie Std. 50 .... (1927-28)	7206	6457	6084	6088	6088	2204		2201	2203		2202			2207	2306				6458	6381	7013	7013
Velie Spec. 60 .... (1927-28)	7206	6457	6084	6088	6088	2204		2201	2203					2208	2306				6458	6381	6517	6517
Velie 6-66 .... (1928)			7081	6123	6123	2205		2202	2203					2208	2307				6055	6432	6629	8077
Velie 6-77 .... (1928)		4307	4307	3210	2309	3210		2201	2203					2208	2306				524	523	8077	8077
Velie 88 .... (1929)	7195	6481	6449	6079	6079			2203	2203					2207	2307	8010A			7011	6986	2308	2308
Viking .... (1930)	7195	4306	2307	6079	6079	2204			2204	2200	2202			2209	2307				7011	6986	2308	2308
Whippet 96, 4 cyl .... (1927)	7195	6481	2406	6088	6088	2204		2203	2204	2200	2202			2208	2305				7011	6986	6522	
Whippet 93-A, 6 cyl .... (1928)	7195	7046	2407	6088	6088	2204		2201	2204	2200	2202			2210	2305				7011	6986	6522	
Whippet 96, 4 cyl .... (1928)	7195	7046	2406	6088	6088	2204		2201	2203	2200				2208	2306				7011	6986	6522	
Whippet 98, 6 cyl .... (1929)	7195	6481	2407	6079	6079	2204		2201	2203	2200				2208	6406				7011	6986	6523	
Whippet 96-A .... (1929)	7195	6481	2407	6079	6079	2205		2202	2203					2208	6407				7011	6986	6091	
Whippet 96-A .... (1930)	7195	7093	2633	6079	6079	3210		2203	2203		2303			7023	2307			2404	6601	6479	6091	6091
Whippet 98-A .... (1925)		7093	6633	6079	6079	2206	2209	2201	2204		2206	3207	3206	2308	7023	2304	2305	2404	6601	6479	2308	2308
Wills St. Claire 8 ...... (1925-26)		7093	6655	6105	6105	2206		2203	2203		2303	3207	3206	2211	2308		2305	2404	6601	6479	6091	
Wills St. Claire 6 .... (1926)		7093	6561	6105	6105	2206		2201	2204		2206	3207	3207	2308	2309	2304	2305		6601	6479	6091	6091
Wills St. Claire 8 .... (1930)	7195	7046	6561	6079	6079			2203	2203		2202			2207	2308				7011	6986	6522	6522
Willys 6 .... (1925)	7032	4307	2407	6105	6105			2201	2203		2202			2210	2306				6601	6481	2310	2310
Willys 8 .... (1925)	6369	4307	2407	6105	6105			2203	2203		8272B			2210	4307				6517	6380	2310	2310
Willys Knight 66 .... (1925)	6369	4306	2406	6105	6105			2201	2203		2202			2210	4207				6601	6481	2310	2310
Willys Knight 65 .... (1926)	7032	4307	2407	6105	6105			2203	2203		8272B			2211	4307				6601	6481	2310	2310
Willys Knight 4-65 .... (1926)	6369	6551	2407	6105	6100			2201	2203		2202			2210	4308				6513	6378	2310	2310
Willys Knight 66-66 ...... (1927)	7032	4307	2633	6105	6100			2203	2203		2302			2210	4308				6513	6378	2308	2308
Willys Knight 66-A .... (1927)	6369	6551	6633	6100	6100			2202	2203		2302			2211	4308				6513	6378	2308	2308
Willys Knight 70-A ..... (1928-29)	6369	7046	6561	6096	6096			2202	2203		2302			2208	2307				6513	6380	2308	2308
Willys Knight 66-A ..... (1928-29)	7194	6633	6561	6096	6096			2202	2203		2302			2211	2307				6513	6378	7013	7018
Willys Knight 6-70A ...... (1929)	7194	7046	6561	6122	6122			2202	2203					2208	2307				7013	6380	7018	7013
Willys Knight Std 6-56 ... (1929)	7194	7046	6655	6096	6096			115	2203		2302			2210	2307				7011	6370	7013	7018
Willys Knight 66-B .... (1929)	7194	6633	6561	6097	6097			2202	2203					2208	2307				6517	6378	7013	7013
Willys Knight 66-B .... (1930)	7193	7046	6561	6096	6096			115	2203		2302			2208	2307				7011	6370	7013	7013
Willys Knight 70-B .... (1930)	7193	7046	6565	6096	6096				2203					2208	2307				7011	6370	7013	7013

*4209 also used.   †2307 with special chamfer also used.   †† Three-speed, use 2210 in 4-speed cars.

U.—Upper.   L.—Left or Lower.   R.—Right.

BEARINGS—Ball and Roller

Equivalent Table

Bearing Table Starts on Page 164. Read Directions There Carefully.

BALL BEARINGS—Single Row Radial (CHILTON NUMBERS, Series 2200, 2300, 2400)

Chilton No.	S.A.E. No.	Bearings Co. of America	CJB—Ahlberg	F&S—C&C Sales (Imp.)	FAFNIR Std.	FAFNIR Shield	FEDERAL Std.	FEDERAL Shield	GURNEY Std.	GURNEY Shield	Hoover	N.D. Max. Cap.	N.D. Non-Load.	N.D. Shield	Norma-Hoffman	RBF	RHL (Imp.)	RIV (Imp.)	Schubert	SKF Hess-Bright	SKF Self-Align.	SRB Std.	SRB Shield	STROM Std.	STROM Shield	Torrington
2200	200	200	6200	A-10	200	200-D	1200	1200-CP	200-C	200-F	200	1200	3200	7200	200	6200	7200	04-A	200	6200	1200	200	200-F	200	200-F	T-200
2201	201	201	6201	A-12	201	201-D	1201	1201-CP	201-C	201-F	201	1201	3201	7201	201	6201	7201	03-A	201	6201	1201	201	201-F	201	201-F	T-201
2202	202	202	6202	A-15	202	202-D	1202	1202-CP	202-C	202-F	202	1202	3202	7202	202	6202	7202	02-A	202	6202	1202	202	202-F	202	202-F	T-202
2203	203	203	6203	A-17	203	203-D	1203	1203-CP	203-C	203-F	203	1203	3203	7203	203	6203	7203	01-A	203	6203	1203	203	203-F	203	203-F	T-203
2204	204	204	6204	A-20	204	204-D	1204	1204-CP	204-C	204-F	204	1204	3204	7204	204	6204	7204	1-A	204	6204	1204	204	204-F	204	204-F	T-204
2205	205	205	6205	A-25	205	205-D	1205	1205-CP	205-C	205-F	205	1205	3205	7205	205	6205	7205	2-A	205	6205	1205	205	205-F	205	205-F	T-205
2206	206	206	6206	A-30	206	206-D	1206		206-C	206-F	206	1206	3206	7206	206	6206	7206	3-A	206	6206	1206	206	206-F	206	206-F	
2207	207	207	6207	A-35	207	207-D	1207		207-C	207-F	207	1207	3207	7207	207	6207	7207	4-A	207	6207	1207	207	207-F	207	207-F	
2208	208	208	6208	A-40	208	208-D	1208		208-C	208-F	208	1208	3208	7208	208	6208	7208	5-A	208	6208	1208	208	208-F	208	208-F	
2209	209	209	6209	A-45	209	209-D	1209		209-C	209-F	209	1209	3209	7209	209	6209	7209	6-A	209	6209	1209	209	209-F	209	209-F	
2210	210	210	6210	A-50	210	210-D	1210		210-C	210-F	210	1210	3210	7210	210	6210	7210	7-A	210	6210	1210	210	210-F	210	210-F	
2211	211	211	6211	A-55	211		1211				211	1211	3211		155	6211	7211	8-A	211	6211	1211	211		211		
2212	212	212	6212	A-60	212	212-D	1212		212-C	212-F	212	1212	3212	7212	160	6212	7212	9-A	212	6212	1212	212	212-F	212	212-F	
2213	213	213	6213	A-65	213	213-D	1213		213-C		213	1213	3213		165	6213	7213	10-A	213	6213	1213	213		213		
2214	214	214	6214	A-75	214		1214				214	1214	3214		170	6214	7214	11-A	214	6214	1214	214		214		
2215	215	215	6215	A-80	215	215	1215		215-C	215-F	215	1215	3215		175	6215	7215	12-A	215	6215	1215	215	215-F	215	215-F	
2216	216	216	6216	A-85	216		1216		216-C		216	1216	3216		180	6216	7216	13-A	216	6216	1216	216		216		
2217	217	217	6217	A-90	217		1217		217-C	217-F	217	1217	3217		185	6217	7217	14-A	217	6217	1217	217	217-F	217	217-F	
2218	218	218	6218	A-95	218		1218		218-C		218	1218	3218		190	6218	7218	15-A	218	6218	1218	218		218		
2219	219	219	6219	A-100	219		1219		219-C		219	1219	3219		195	6219	7219	16-A	219	6219	1219	219		219		
2220	220	220	6220	A-105	220		1220		220-C	220-F	220	1220	3220		200 H	6220	7220	17-A	220	6220	1220	220	220-F	220	220-F	
2221	221	221	6221	A-110	221		1221		221-C		221	1221	3221		205 H	6221	7221	18-A	221	6221	1221	221		221		
2222	222	222	6222		222		1222		222-C		222	1222	3222		210 H	6222	7222	19-A	222	6222	1222	222		222		
2224	224										224				220 H											
2300	300	300	6300	B-10	300		1300		300-C	300-F	300	1300	3300	7300	300	6300	7300	1-B	300	6300	1300	300	300-F	300	300-F	T-300
2301	301	301	6301	B-12	301		1301		301-C	301-F	301	1301	3301	7301	301	6301	7301	2-B	301	6301	1301	301	301-F	301	301-F	T-301
2302	302	302	6302	B-15	302		1302		302-C	302-F	302	1302	3302	7302	302	6302	7302	3-B	302	6302	1302	302	302-F	302	302-F	T-302
2303	303	303	6303	B-17	303	303	1303		303-C	303-F	303	1303	3303	7303	303	6303	7303	4-B	303	6303	1303	303	303-F	303	303-F	T-303
2304	304	304	6304	B-19	304	304	1304		304-C	304-F	304	1304	3304	7304	304	6304	7304	5-B	304	6304	1304	304	304-F	304	304-F	T-304
2305	305	305	6305	B-25	305	305	1305		305-C	305-F	305	1305	3305	7305	305	6305	7305	6-B	305	6305	1305	305	305-F	305	305-F	
2306	306	306	6306	B-30	306	306	1306		306-C	306-F	306	1306	3306	7306	306	6306	7306	7-B	306	6306	1306	306	306-F	306	306-F	
2307	307	307	6307	B-35	307	307	1307		307-C	307-F	307	1307	3307	7307	307	6307	7307	8-B	307	6307	1307	307	307-F	307	307-F	
2308	308	308	6308	B-40	308	308	1308		308-C	308-F	308	1308	3308	7308	308	6308	7308	9-B	308	6308	1308	308	308-F	308	308-F	
2309	309	309	6309	B-45	309	309	1309		309-C	309-F	309	1309	3309	7309	309	6309	7309	10-B	309	6309	1309	309	309-F	309	309-F	
2310	310	310	6310	B-50	310	310	1310		310-C	310-F	310	1310	3310	7310	310	6310	7310	11-B	310	6310	1310	310	310-F	310	310-F	
2311	311	311	6311	B-55	311	311	1311		311-C	311-F	311	1311	3311		350	6311	7311	12-B	311	6311	1311	311	311-F	311	311-F	
2312	312	312	6312	B-60	312	312	1312		312-C	312-F	312	1312	3312		355	6312	7312	13-B	312	6312	1312	312	312-F	312	312-F	
2313	313	313	6313	B-65	313	313	1313		313-C	313-F	313	1313	3313		360	6313	7313	14-B	313	6313	1313	313	313-F	313	313-F	
2314	314	314	6314	B-70	314		1314		314-C		314	1314	3314		365	6314	7314	15-B	314	6314	1314	314		314		
2315	315	315	6315	B-75	315		1315		315-C	315-F	315	1315	3315		370	6315	7315	16-B	315	6315	1315	315	315-F	315	315-F	
2316	316	316	6316	B-80	316		1316		316-C		316	1316	3316		375	6316	7316	17-B	316	6316	1316	316		316		
2317	317	317	6317	B-85	317		1317		317-C	317-F	317	1317	3317		380	6317	7317	18-B	317	6317	1317	317	317-F	317	317-F	
2318	318	318	6318	B-90	318		1318		318-C		318	1318	3318		385	6318	7318	19-B	318	6318	1318	318		318		
2319	319	319	6319	B-95	319		1319		319-C		319	1319	3319		390	6319	7319	20-B	319	6319	1319	319		319		
2403	403	403	6403	C-17	403		1403		403-C		403				517	6403	7403		403			403		403		
2404	404	404	6404	C-20	404		1404		404-C		404	1404	3404		520	6404	7404	1-C	404			404		404		
2405	405	405	6405	C-25	405		1405		405-C	405-F	405	1405	3405		525	6405	7405	2-C	405	6405	405	405	405-F	405	405-F	
2406	406	406	6406	C-30	406		1406		406-C	406-F	406	1406	3406		530	6406	7406	3-C	406	6406	406	406	406-F	406	406-F	
2407	407	407	6407	C-35	407		1407		407-C	407-C	407	1407	3407		535	6407	7407	4-C	407	6407	407	407	407-F	407	407-F	
2408	408	408	6408	C-40	408		1408		408-C		408	1408	3408		540	6408	7408	5-C	408	6408	408	408		408		
2409	409	409	6409	C-45	409		1409		409-C		409	1409	3409		545	6409	7409	6-C	409	6409	409	409		409		
2410	410	410	6410	C-50	410		1410		410-C	410-F	410	1410	3410		550	6410	7410	7-C	410	6410	410	410	410-F	410	410-F	
2411	411	411	6411	C-55	411		1411		411-C	411-F	411	1411	3411		555	6411	7411	8-C	411	6411	411	411	411-F	411	411-F	
2412	412	412	6412	C-60	412		1412		412-C		412	1412	3412		560	6412	7412	9-C	412	6412	412	412		412		
2413	413	413	6413	C-65	413		1413		413-C	413-F	413	1413	3413		565	6413	7413	10-C	413	6413	413	413	413-F	413	413-F	
2414	414	414	6414	C-70	414		1414		414-C		414	1414	3414		570	6414	7414	11-C	414	6414	414	414		414		
2415	415	415	6415	C-75	415		1415		415-C	415-F	415	1415	3415		575	6415	7415	12-C	415	6415	415	415	415-F	415	415-F	

BEARINGS—Continued

BALL BEARINGS—Single-Row Radial Thrust   (CHILTON NUMBERS, *Series* 3200, 3300, 3400)

CHILTON NUMBER	S.A.E. Number	BCA—Bearings Co. of America	CJB—Ahlberg Bearing Co.	F&S—C & C Sales Corp. (Imported)	Fafnir	Federal	Gurney 100% Thrust	Gurney 200% Thrust	Hoover	New Departure Radax Type 0	New Departure Radax 20,000 Series	Norma-Hoffmann	RBF (Imported)	Schubert	SKF	Strom
3200	7200	7200	......	AS-10	7200	7200	....	7200	0200	0200	....	110-AC	200-Z	7200	....	7200
3201	7201	7201	......	AS-12	7201	7201	....	7201	0201	0201	....	112-AC	201-Z	7201	....	7201
3202	7202	7202	......	AS-15	7202	7202	202-R	7202	0202	0202	....	115-AC	202-Z	7202	....	7202
3203	7203	7203	......	AS-17	7203	7203	203-R	7203	0203	0203	....	117-AC	203-Z	7203	....	7203
3204	7204	7204	4204	AS-20	7204	7204	204-R	7204	0204	0204	20204	120-AC	204-Z	7204	....	7204
3205	7205	7205	4205	AS-25	7205	7205	205-R	7205	0205	0205	20205	125-AC	205-Z	7205	7205	7205
3206	7206	7206	4206	AS-30	7206	7206	206-R	7206	0206	0206	20206	130-AC	206-Z	7206	7206	7206
3207	7207	7207	4207	AS-35	7207	7207	207-R	7207	0207	0207	20207	135-AC	207-Z	7207	7207	7207
3208	7208	7208	4208	AS-40	7208	7208	208-R	7208	0208	0208	20208	140-AC	208-Z	7208	7208	7208
3209	7209	7209	4209	AS-45	7209	7209	209-R	7209	0209	0209	20209	145-AC	209-Z	7209	7209	7209
3210	7210	7210	4210	AS-50	7210	7210	210-R	7210	0210	0210	20210	150-AC	210-Z	7210	7210	7210
3211	7211	7211	4211	AS-55	7211	7211	211-R	7211	0211	0211	20211	155-AC	211-Z	7211	7211	7211
3212	7212	7212	4212	AS-60	7212	7212	212-R	7212	0212	0212	20212	160-AC	212-Z	7212	7212	7212
3213	7213	7213	4213	AS-65	7213	7213	213-R	7213	0213	0213	20213	165-AC	213-Z	7213	7213	7213
3214	7214	7214	4214	AS-70	7214	7214	214-R	7214	0214	0214	20214	170-AC	214-Z	7214	7214	7214
3215	7215	7215	4215	AS-75	7215	7215	215-R	7215	0215	0215	20215	175-AC	215-Z	7215	7215	7215
3216	7216	7216	4216	AS-80	7216	7216	216-R	7216	0216	0216	20216	180-AC	216-Z	7216	7216	7216
3217	7217	7217	4217	AS-85	7217	7217	217-R	7217	0217	0217	20217	185-AC	217-Z	7217	7217	7217
3218	7218	7218	4218	AS-90	7218	7218	218-R	7218	0218	0218	20218	190-AC	218-Z	7218	7218	7218
3219	7219	7219	4219	AS-95	7219	7219	219-R	7219	0219	0219	20219	195-AC	219-Z	7219	7219	7219
3220	7220	7220	4220	AS-100	7220	7220	220-R	7220	0220	0220	20220	200-AC	220-Z	7220	7220	7220
3221	7221	7221	4221	AS-105	7221	7221	221-R	7221	....	....	20221	205-AC	221-Z	7221	7221	7221
3222	7222	7222	4222	AS-110	7222	7222	222-R	7222	....	....	20222	210-AC	222-Z	7222	7222	7222
3300	7300	7300	......	BS-10	7300	7300	....	7300	....	....	....	310-AC	300-Z	7300	....	7300
3301	7301	7301	......	BS-12	7301	7301	....	7301	....	....	....	312-AC	301-Z	7301	....	7301
3302	7302	7302	......	BS-15	7302	7302	302-R	7302	....	....	....	315-AC	302-Z	7302	....	7302
3303	7303	7303	......	BS-17	7303	7303	303-R	7303	0303	0303	....	317-AC	303-Z	7303	....	7303
3304	7304	7304	4304	BS-20	7304	7304	304-R	7304	0304	0304	20304	320-AC	304-Z	7304	....	7304
3305	7305	7305	4305	BS-25	7305	7305	305-R	7305	0305	0305	20305	325-AC	305-Z	7305	7305	7305
3306	7306	7306	4306	BS-30	7306	7306	306-R	7306	0306	0306	20306	330-AC	306-Z	7306	7306	7306
3307	7307	7307	4307	BS-35	7307	7307	307-R	7307	0307	0307	20307	335-AC	307-Z	7307	7307	7307
3308	7308	7308	4308	BS-40	7308	7308	308-R	7308	0308	0308	20308	340-AC	308-Z	7308	7308	7308
3309	7309	7309	4309	BS-45	7309	7309	309-R	7309	0309	0309	20309	345-AC	309-Z	7309	7309	7309
3310	7310	7310	4310	BS-50	7310	7310	310-R	7310	0310	0310	20310	350-AC	310-Z	7310	7310	7310
3311	7311	7311	4311	BS-55	7311	7311	311-R	7311	0311	0311	20311	355-AC	311-Z	7311	7311	7311
3312	7312	7312	4312	BS-60	7312	7312	312-R	7312	0312	0312	20312	360-AC	312-Z	7312	7312	7312
3313	7313	7313	4313	BS-65	7313	7313	313-R	7313	0313	0313	20313	365-AC	313-Z	7313	7313	7313
3314	7314	7314	4314	BS-70	7314	7314	314-R	7314	0314	0314	20314	370-AC	314-Z	7314	7314	7314
3315	7315	7315	4315	BS-75	7315	7315	315-R	7315	0315	0315	20315	375-AC	315-Z	7315	7315	7315
3316	7316	7316	4316	BS-80	7316	7316	316-R	7316	....	....	20316	380-AC	316-Z	7316	7316	7316
3317	7317	7317	4317	BS-85	7317	7317	317-R	7317	....	....	20317	385-AC	317-Z	7317	7317	7317
3318	7318	7318	4318	BS-90	7318	7318	318-R	7318	....	....	20318	390-AC	318-Z	7318	7318	7318
3319	7319	7319	4319	BS-95	7319	7319	319-R	7319	....	....	20319	395-AC	319-Z	7319	7319	7319
3320	7320	7320	4320	BS-100	7320	7320	320-R	7320	....	----	20320	400-AC	320-Z	7320	7320	7320
3321	7321	7321	4321	BS-105	7321	7321	321-R	7321	....	....	20321	405-AC	321-Z	7321	7321	7321
3322	7322	7322	4322	BS-110	7322	7322	322-R	7322	....	....	20322	410-AC	322-Z	7322	7322	7322
3403	7403	7403	4403	CS-17	7403	7403	403-R	7403	....	....	....	517-AC	403-Z	7403	....	7403
3404	7404	7404	4404	CS-20	7404	7404	404-R	7404	0404	0404	20404	520-AC	404-Z	7404	7404	7404
3405	7405	7405	4405	CS-25	7405	7405	405-R	7405	0405	0405	20405	525-AC	405-Z	7405	7405	7405
3406	7406	7406	4406	CS-30	7406	7406	406-R	7406	0406	0406	20406	530-AC	406-Z	7406	7406	7406
3407	7407	7407	4407	CS-35	7407	7407	407-R	7407	0407	0407	20407	535-AC	407-Z	7407	7407	7407
3408	7408	7408	4408	CS-40	7408	7408	408-R	7408	0408	0408	20408	540-AC	408-Z	7408	7408	7408
3409	7409	7409	4409	CS-45	7409	7409	409-R	7409	0409	0409	20409	545-AC	409-Z	7409	7409	7409
3410	7410	7410	4410	CS-50	7410	7410	410-R	7410	....	....	20410	550-AC	410-Z	7410	7410	7410
3411	7411	7411	4411	CS-55	7411	7411	411-R	7411	....	....	20411	555-AC	411-Z	7411	7411	7411
3412	7412	7412	4412	CS-60	7412	7412	412-R	7412	....	....	20412	560-AC	412-Z	7412	7412	7412
3413	7413	7413	4413	CS-65	7413	7413	413-R	7413	....	....	20413	565-AC	413-Z	7413	7413	7413
3414	7414	7414	4414	CS-70	7414	7414	414-R	7414	....	....	20414	570-AC	414-Z	7414	7414	7414
3415	7415	7415	4415	CS-75	7415	7415	415-R	7415	....	....	20415	575-AC	....	7415	7415	7415
3416	7416	7416	4416	CS-80	7416	7416	416-R	7416	....	....	20416	580-AC	416-Z	7416	7416	7416
3417	7417	7417	4417	CS-85	7417	7417	417-R	7417	....	....	20417	585-AC	....	7417	7417	7417
3418	7418	7418	4418	CS-90	7418	7418	418-R	7418	....	....	20418	590-AC	418-Z	7418	7418	7418
3419	....	7419	4419	CS-95	7419	7419	419-R	7419	....	....	....	595-AC	....	7419	7419	7419
3420	....	7420	4420	CS-100	7420	7420	420-R	7420	....	....	....	600-AC	420-Z	7420	7420	7420
3421	....	....	....	....	....	7421	421-R	7421	....	....	....	....	....	....	....	7421
3422	....	....	....	....	....	7422	422-R	7422	....	....	....	....	....	....	....	7422

BEARINGS—Continued

BALL BEARINGS—Double Row   (CHILTON NUMBERS, Series 4200, 4300, 4400)

CHILTON NUMBER	S.A.E. Number	CJB—Ahlberg Bearing Co.	F&S—C & C Sales Corp. (Imported)	Fafnir	Federal	Gurney	SKF & Hess-Bright	MRC	New Departure	RBF	RHL (Imported)	R.I.V. (Imported)	Schubert	S.R.B.	Strom
4200	5200	....	AA-10	200-DR	5200	5200	5200	5200	5200	....	....	1490	5202	5200	5200-A
4201	5201	....	AA-12	201-DR	5201	5201	5201	5201	5201	....	....	1491	5203	5201	5201-A
4202	5202	....	AA-15	202-DR	5202	5202	5202	5202	5202	....	....	1492	5204	5202	5202-A
4203	5203	....	AA-17	203-DR	5203	5203	5203	5203	5203	....	....	1493	5205	5203	5203-A
4204	5204	5204	AA-20	204-DR	5204	5204	5204	5204	5204	204-NC	6204-NA	1494	5206	5204	5204-A
4205	5205	5205	AA-25	205-DR	5205	5205	5205	5205	5205	205-NC	6205-NA	1495	5207	5205	5205-A
4206	5206	5206	AA-30	206-DR	5206	5206	5206	5206	5206	206-NC	6206-NA	1496	5208	5206	5206-A
4207	5207	5207	AA-35	207-DR	5207	5207	5207	5207	5207	207-NC	6207-NA	1497	5209	5207	5207-A
4208	5208	5208	AA-40	208-DR	5208	5208	5208	5208	5208	208-NC	6208-NA	1498	5210	5208	5208-A
4209	5209	5209	AA-45	209-DR	5209	5209	5209	5209	5209	209-NC	6209-NA	1499	5211	5209	5209-A
4210	5210	5210	AA-50	210-DR	5210	5210	5210	5210	5210	210-NC	6210-NA	1500	5212	5210	5210-A
4211	5211	5211	AA-55	211-DR	5211	5211	5211	5211	5211	211-NC	6211-NA	1501	5213	5211	5211-A
4212	5212	5212	AA-60	212-DR	5212	5212	5212	5212	5212	212-NC	6212-NA	1502	5214	5212	5212-A
4213	5213	5213	AA-65	213-DR	5213	5213	5213	5213	5213	213-NC	6213-NA	1503	5215	5213	5213-A
4214	5214	5214	AA-70	214-DR	5214	5214	5214	5214	5214	214-NC	6214-NA	1504	5216	5214	5214-A
4215	5215	5215	AA-75	215-DR	5215	5215	5215	5215	5215	215-NC	6215-NA	1505	5217	5215	5215-A
4216	5216	5216	AA-80	216-DR	5216	5216	5216	5216	5216	216-NC	6216-NA	1506	5218	5216	5216-A
4217	5217	5217	AA-85	217-DR	5217	5217	5217	5217	5217	217-NC	6217-NA	1507	5219	5217	5217-A
4218	5218	5218	AA-90	218-DR	5218	5218	5218	5218	5218	218-NC	6218-NA	1508	5220	5218	5218-A
4219	5219	5219	AA-95	219-DR	5219	5219	5219	5219	5219	219-NC	6219-NA	....	....	5219	5219-A
4220	5220	5220	AA-100	220-DR	5220	5220	5220	5220	5220	220-NC	6220-NA	....	....	5220	5220-A
4221	5221	5221	AA-105	221-DR	5221	5221	5221	5221	....	....	6221-NA	....	5221	5221	5221-A
4222	5222	5222	AA-110	222-DR	5222	5222	5222	5222	....	....	6222-NA	....	5222	5222	5222-A
4300	5300	....	BB-10	300-DR	5300	5300	....	5300	5300	....	....	....	....	5300	5300-A
4301	5301	....	BB-12	301-DR	5301	5301	5301	5301	5301	....	....	....	....	5301	5301-A
4302	5302	....	BB-15	302-DR	5302	5302	5302	5302	5302	302-NC	6302-NA	3-BBN	5302	5302	5302-A
4303	5303	5303	BB-17	303-DR	5303	5303	5303	5303	5303	303-NC	6303-NA	1509	5303	5303	5303-A
4304	5304	5304	BB-20	304-DR	5304	5304	5304	5304	5304	304-NC	6304-NA	1510	5304	5304	5304-A
4305	5305	5305	BB-25	305-DR	5305	5305	5305	5305	5305	305-NC	6305-NA	1087	5305	5305	5305-A
4306	5306	5306	BB-30	306-DR	5306	5306	5306	5306	5306	306-NC	6306-NA	1201	5306	5306	5306-A
4307	5307	5307	BB-35	307-DR	5307	5307	5307	5307	5307	307-NC	6307-NA	1511	5307	5307	5307-A
4308	5308	5308	BB-40	308-DR	5308	5308	5308	5308	5308	308-NC	6308-NA	1512	5308	5308	5308-A
4309	5309	5309	BB-45	309-DR	5309	5309	5309	5309	5309	309-NC	6309-NA	1513	5309	5309	5309-A
4310	5310	5310	BB-50	310-DR	5310	5310	5310	5310	5310	310-NC	6310-NA	1514	5310	5310	5310-A
4311	5311	5311	BB-55	311-DR	5311	5311	5311	5311	5311	311-NC	6311-NA	1515	5311	5311	5311-A
4312	5312	5312	BB-60	312-DR	5312	5312	5312	5312	5312	312-NC	6312-NA	1516	5312	5312	5312-A
4313	5313	5313	BB-65	313-DR	5313	5313	5313	5313	5313	313-NC	6313-NA	1517	5313	5313	5313-A
4314	5314	5314	BB-70	314-DR	5314	5314	5314	5314	314	314-NC	6314-NA	1518	5314	5314	5314-A
4315	5315	5315	BB-75	315-DR	5315	5315	5315	5315	315	315-NC	6315-NA	1519	5315	5315	5315-A
4316	5316	5316	BB-80	316-DR	5316	5316	5316	5316	316	316-NC	6316-NA	17-BB	5316	5316	5316-A
4317	5317	5317	BB-85	317-DR	5317	5317	5317	5317	317	317-NC	6317-NA	1520	5317	5317	5317-A
4318	5318	5318	BB-90	318-DR	5318	5318	5318	5318	318	318-NC	6318-NA	19-BB	5318	5318	5318-A
4319	5319	5319	BB-95	319-DR	5319	5319	5319	5319	319	319-NC	6319-NA	1611	5319	5319	5319-A
4320	5320	5320	BB-100	320-DR	5320	5320	5320	5320	320	320 NC	6320 NA	21-BB	5320	5320	5320-A
4321	5321	5321	BB-105	321-DR	5321	5321	5321	5321	321	....	6321-NA	22-BB	5321	5321	5321-A
4322	5322	5322	BB-110	322-DR	5322	5322	5322	5322	322	....	6322-NA	23-BB	5322	5322	5322-A
4403	5403	5403	CC-17	403-DR	5403	5403	....	5403	....	....	....	....	....	5403	5403-A
4404	5404	5404	CC-20	404-DR	5404	5404	....	5404	404	....	....	....	....	5404	5404-A
4405	5405	5405	CC-25	405-DR	5405	5405	5405	5405	405	405-NC	....	1521	5405	5405	5405-A
4406	5406	5406	CC-30	406-DR	5406	5406	5406	5406	406	406-NC	....	1522	5406	5406	5406-A
4407	5407	5407	CC-35	407-DR	5407	5407	5407	5407	407	407-NC	....	1523	5407	5407	5407-A
4408	5408	5408	CC-40	408-DR	5408	5408	5408	5408	5408	408-NC	....	1524	5408	5408	5408-A
4409	5409	5409	CC-45	409-DR	5409	5409	5409	5409	5409	409-NC	....	1525	5409	5409	5409-A
4410	5410	5410	CC-50	410-DR	5410	5410	5410	5410	410	410-NC	....	1526	5410	5410	5410-A
4411	5411	5411	CC-55	411-DR	5411	5411	5411	5411	411	411-NC	....	1527	5411	5411	5411-A
4412	5412	5412	CC-60	412-DR	5412	5412	5412	5412	412	412-NC	....	1528	5412	5412	5412-A
4413	5413	5413	CC-65	413-DR	5413	5413	5413	5413	413	413-NC	....	11-CC	5413	5413	5413-A
4414	5414	5414	CC-70	414-DR	5414	5414	5414	5414	414	....	....	12-CC	5414	5414	5414-A
4415	5415	5415	CC-75	415-DR	5415	5415	5415	5415	....	....	....	....	5415	5415	5415-A
4416	5416	5416	CC-80	416-DR	5416	5416	5416	5416	....	....	....	13-CC	5416	5416	5416-A
4417	5417	5417	CC-85	417-DR	5417	5417	5417	5417	....	....	....	....	5417	5417	5417-A
4418	5418	5418	CC-90	418-DR	5418	5418	5418	5418	....	....	....	14-CC	5418	5418	5418-A
4419	5419	5419	CC-95	419-DR	5419	5419	....	5419	....	....	....	....	5419	5419	5419-A
4420	5420	5420	CC-100	420-DR	5420	5420	....	5420	....	....	....	15-CC	5420	5420	5420-A
4421	....	....	....	....	....	5421	....	....	....	....	....	....	....	....	....
4422	....	....	....	....	....	5422	....	....	....	....	....	....	....	....	....

BEARINGS—Continued

ROLLER BEARINGS—Tapered   (CHILTON NUMBERS, *Series* 6000, 7000)

CHILTON NUMBER	S.A.E.	Pratt	Timken	CHILTON NUMBER	S.A.E.	Pratt	Timken	CHILTON NUMBER	S.A.E.	Pratt	Timken
6000			11-13	6145	418-414	418-414	418-414	6335	782-772	782-772	782-772
6001			235	6146		419-412	419-412	6369		1351-1330	1351-1330
6002		235-2320	235-2320	6147		419-414	419-414	6370		1380-1329	1380-1329
6003			235-2330	6148		419-412A	419-412A				
6004		236-2320	236-2320	6149		419T-414	419T-414	6378		1751-1729	1751-1729
				6150		421-412A	421-412A	6380		1751-1730	1751-1730
6006		237-233	237-233	6151		420-414	420-414	6381	1755-1729	1755-1729	1755-1729
6007		255-2520	255-2520	6152	422-414	422-414	422-414	6382			1755-1730
6008		256-2520	256-2520	6153	422T-414	422T-414	422T-414	6386	1775-1729	1775-1729	1775-1729
6010		257	257	6154		435-4320	435-4320				
6011		257-2520	257-2520	6155	435T-4320	435T-4320	435T-4320	6388		1779-1729	1779-1729
				6156		435T-432	435T-432	6403			1985
6020		277-273	277-273	6157			435-432	6405	1985-1931		1985-1931
6021		277-274	277-274	6158			436-4320	6406		1986-1930	1986-1930
6032		290-284	290-284					6407	1986-1931		1986-1931
6033		306	306	6159	438-432	438-432	438-432				
6036			360-21212	6160			438-4320	6431		2381-2330	2381-2330
				6161		439-4320	439-4320	6432		2381-2320	2381-2320
6037		315-312	315-312	6162		439-432	439-432	6433		2382-2320	2382-2320
6038		316-312	316-312	6163	439T-432	439T-432	439T-432	6434			2382-2330
6039			316-313	6164	439-432A	439-432A	439-432A	6441		2554-2520	2554-2520
6041		317-312	317-312	6165		436-453	436-453				
6046		319-312	319-312	6167		444-4320	444-4320	6448		2558-2520	2558-2520
6047		319-313	319-313	6173	444-432	444-432	444-432	6449	2558-2523		2558-2523
6055		325-312	325-312	6174		443-4320	443-4320	6450	2558		2558
6056			325W-312					6451		2559-2530	2559-2530
6057			335	6176	440-4320	440-4320	440-4320	6454	2580-2523	2580-2523	2580-2523
6058	334-333	334-333	334-333	6181		447-432A	447-432A				
				6182		447-432	447-432	6455		2580-2520	2580-2520
6059	335-3320	335-3320	335-3320	6184	449-432	449-432	449-432	6456		2580W-2523	2580W-2523
6060			335W-3320	6185			449-4320	6457			2580W-2520
6061			336-332					6458	2581-2523	2581-2523	2581-2523
6062	336-3320	336-3320	336-3320	6188		455-452	455-452	6459		2582-2523	2582-2523
6064	337-3320	337-3320	337-3320	6189			455-4520				
				6190	455-453A	455-453A	455-453A	6460		2582-2530	2582-2530
6065			337W-3320	6191		455-453	455-453	6461	2582-2520		2582-2520
6068	339-333	339-333	339-333	6193		456-452	456-452	6462			2585-2523
6071		341-3320	341-3320					6478			2684-2631
6072			341W-3320	6194	456-4520		456-4520	6479		2687-2620	2687-2620
6074		242-332	342-332	6195		456-453	456-453				
				6196		456-453A	456-453A	6480			2684-2620
6075			342S-332	6198		457-453	457-453	6481	2687-2631		2687-2631
6078			344-3320	6201		458-452	458-452	6482		2689-2620	2689-2620
6079	344-333	344-333	344-333					6483	2689-2631		2689-2631
6080			344-332	6202		458T-452	458T-452	6484		2690-2620	2690-2620
6082		347-332	347-332	6204		458T-454	458T-454	6485	2687-2630		2687-2630
6083	346-3320	346-3320	346-3320	6213		462-454	462-454	6486		2691-2620	2691-2620
6084		347-3320	347-3320	6214		462-452	462-452	6510		2785-2729	2785-2729
6085		349-3320	349-3320	6215			462-453	6511		2785-2720	2785-2720
6086		349W-3320	349W-3320					6512	2787T-2729	2787T-2729	2787T-2729
6087	350-352	350-352	350-352	6216	462-455		462-455				
				6217	462-453A		462-453A	6513		2786-2720	2786-2720
6088		355-3520	355-3520	6219		463-452	463-452	6514	2786-2729		2786-2720
6089	355-353		355-353	6225			465-454	6515	2787-2720	2787-2720	2787-2720
6090			355-354A	6228		467T-452	467T-452	6516		2787-2729	2787-2729
6091			355-354					6517	2788-2720	2788-2720	2788-2720
6092			357-3520	6230			468T-453A	6518			2788-2729
6093		357-354	357-354	6235	478-472A		478-472A	6521		2790-2729	2790-2729
6094		357-353	357-353	6236		477-473	477-473	6522			2790T-2729
6095		358-354A	358-354A	6237	478-472		478-472	6523		2790T-2720	2790T-2720
6096	358-354	358-354	358-354	6238		478-473	478-473	6525		2794-2732	2794-2732
6097			359S-354A								
6098		358-3520	358-3520	6239	480-472		480-472	6526		2796-2729	2796-2729
6099		359S-3520	359S-3520	6240		480-473	480-473	6545		3159-3120	3159-3120
6100	359S-354		359S-354	6241	482-472	482-472	482-472	6546		3160-3120	3160-3120
6101	359-354	359-354	359-354	6247	526-522		526-522	6547		3161-3120	3161-3120
6102		359S-353	359S-353	6248	527-522		527-522	6549			3187-3120
								6550		3187-3124	3187-3124
6104		366-362	366-362	6251	529-522		529-522	6551			3187-3130
6105	366-363	366-363	366-363	6253	535-534C	535-534C	535-534C	6552	3188-3120		3188-3120
6109		370-362	370-362	6254		535-532	535-532	6553			3188A-3120A
6110	375-3720	375-3720	375-3720	6256	536T-532A		536T-532A	6554	3189-3120	3189-3120	3189-3120
6111			375-373	6257		536T-532	536T-532				
								6555		3190-3120	3190-3120
6113	377-372		377-372	6258	537-532A		537-532A	6556	3191-3120	3191-3120	3191-3120
6114			377-373	6259		537-532	537-532	6557			3191-3128
6115		376-373	376-373	6261		537T-532A	537T-532A	6558		3188-3130	3188-3130
6116		376-3720	376-3720	6263		539-532	539-532	6561	3193-3120	3193-3120	3193-3120
6117	377-3720	377-3720	377-3720	6264	539-532A		539-532A				
6118	385-383	385-383	385-383	6265		539T-532	539T-532	6563		3196-3120	3196-3120
6120		387-383	387-383	6275		557-552	557-552	6564		3196T-3120	3196T-3120
6122			395S-394A	6278	559-552A		559-552A	6565		3197-3120	3197-3120
6123			395-394A	6279		559-552	559-552	6566		3198-3120A	3198-3120A
6124	395-3920	395-3920	395-3920	6283	560-552A		560-552A	6567			3198-3129
								6583		3360-3320	3360-3320
6131		397-394	397-394	6284		560-552	560-552	6593		3366-3320	3366-3320
6132		397-3920	397-3920	6286			565-563	6595			3367-3320
6134		414-412	414-412	6287	566-563	566-563	566-563	6596		3377T-3320	3377T-3320
6135		415-412	415-412	6289	567-563	567-563	567-563	6597		3378-3331	3378-3331
6136		415T-412	415T-412	6293	575-572		575-572				
								6598		3379-3320	3379-3320
6137		415T-412A	415T-412A	6296	580-572		580-572	6599		3381T-3329	3381T-3329
6138		415-412A	415-412A	6304		596-592	596-592	6600		3380T-3320	3380T-3320
6139	415T-414	415T-414	415T-414	6306		598-592	598-592	6601		3381-3320	3381-3320
6141			415-414	6319	749-742	749-742	749-742	6602		3381T-3320	3381T-3320
6143	416-414	416-414	416-414	6320			750-742				
								6603			3381-3331
6144		418-412	418-412	6326	759-752	759-752	759-752	6604		3382-3320	3382-3320
				6331	780-772	780-772	780-772	6605		3382T-3320	3382T-3320

BEARINGS—Continued

ROLLER BEARINGS—Tapered—Continued (CHILTON NUMBERS, Series 6000, 7000)

CHILTON NUMBER	S.A.E.	Pratt	Timken
6606		3383-3320	3383-3320
6607			3385-3327
6608		3385T-3320	3385T-3320
6609			3385-3320
6610		3383-3331	3383-3331
6629		3463-3422	3463-3422
6630			3474-3420
6631		3476-3420	3476-3420
6632	3477-3420	3477-3420	3477-3420
6633	3478-3420	3478-3420	3478-3420
6634	3478T-3420	3478T-3420	3478T-3420
6635		3477-3425	3477-3425
6636	3479T-3420	3479T-3420	3479T-3420
6637			3480-3420
6639		3490T-3420	3490T-3420
6648		3554-3520	3554-3520
6652		3575T-3525	3575T-3525
6653			3577-3520
6654	3577-3525	3577-3525	3577-3525
6655	3576-3525		3576-3525
6656			3581-3521
6657			3581-3525
6669		3656-3620	3656-3620
6672			3659
6674	3659-3620	3659-3620	3659-3620
6675			3659D-3621D
6676			3659K-3620
6677			3659K
6681		3750-3720	3750-3720
6704		3762-3720	3762-3720
6715			3776-3731
6716	3778-3720		3778-3720
6717	3780-3720		3780-3720
6748			3979-3920
6750	3982-3920	3982-3920	3982-3920
6755		4351-4320	4351-4320
6773		4361-4320	4361-4320
6778		4364-4320	4364-4320
6782		4367-4320	4367-4320
6783		4368-4320	4368-4320
6784			4370-4320
6785		4550-4520	4550-4520
6791		4553-4520	4553-4520
6792		4554-4520	4554-4520
6798		4558-4520	4558-4520
6800		4559-4520	4559-4520
6809		4580-4520	4580-4520
6810			4580-4524
6813		5351-5320	5351-5320
6818		5354-5320	5354-5320
6820		5355-5320	5355-5320
6821		5356-5320	5356-5320
6823		5358-5320	5358-5320
6830		5550-5520	5550-5520
6833		5553-5520	5553-5520
6834		5554-5520	5554-5520
6839		5557-5520	5557-5520
6840		5558-5520	5558-5520
6856		5578-5521	5578-5521
6857		5578-5520	5578-5520
6858			5582-5521
6864		5752-5720	5752-5720
6867		5755-5720	5755-5720
6868		5756-5720	5756-5720
6869		5757-5720	5757-5720

CHILTON NUMBER	S.A.E.	Hoover	Pratt	Timken
6872			5760-5720	5760-5720
6873			5784-5720	5784-5720
6875	6277-6220			6277-6220
6888			6553-6521	6553-6521
6893			6358-6320	6358-6320
6894			6358-6321	6358-6321
6897	6375-6323		6375-6323	6375-6323
6898			6375-6322	6375-6322
6899			6375-6320	6375-6320
6900			6375-6321	6375-6321
6901			6377-6321	6377-6321
6902			6378-6320	6378-6320
6903	6379-6320		6379-6320	6379-6320
6914			6455-6422	6455-6422
6915			6456-6422	6456-6422
6925			6552-6520	6552-6520
6926			6552-6521	6552-6521
6958				01755-01729
6959			02582-02523	02582-02523
6967	05079-05185		05079-05185	05079-05185
6972		07098-07204	07098-07204	07098-07024
6982	09070-09194	09070-09194	09070-09194	09070-09194
6985			09074-09193	09074-09193
6986	09074-09194	09074-09194	09074-09194	09074-09194
6987		09075-09174		09075-09174
6993			10062-10159	10062-10159
6996			11157-11315	11157-11315
6997			11158-11315	11158-11315
6998		14117-14274	14117-14274	14117-14274
6999		14120-14273	14120-14273	14120-14273
7001	14118-14283	14118-14283	14118-14283	14118-14283
7002				14118-14274
7007				14138-14274
7008	14125-14274	14125-14274	14125-14274	14125-14274
7009	14131-14274	14131-14274	14131-14274	14131-14274
7010			14132-14282	14132-14282
7011	14132-14274	14132-14274	14132-14274	14132-14274
7012				14131-14276
7013	14137-14274	14137-14274	14137-14274	14137-14274
7014		14138-14276	14138-14276	14138-14276
7015				14132-14276
7016				16143-16282
7017			16143-16284	16143-16284
7018			16150-16284	16150-16284
7019				15010-15250
7020	17098-17244		17098-17244	17098-17244
7021	17118-17244		17118-17244	17118-17244
7023	19138-19283		19138-19283	19138-19283
7026			19150T-19283	19150T-19283
7028			20074-20181	20074-20181
7029			20074-20187	20074-20187
7030			20074	20074
7031				20074-20188
7032	21075-21212		21075-21212	21075-21212
7033			21087-21212	21087-21212
7034			21088-21212	21088-21212
7035			23092-23256	23092-23256
7036			23093	23093
7042				24112-24261
7046			26112-26274	26112-26274
7047				26112-26300
7048	26112-26283		26112-26283	26112-26283
7049			26117T-26283	26117T-26283
7050	26118-26283		26118-26283	26118-26283
7053			26124T-26283	26124T-26283

CHILTON NUMBER	S.A.E.	Pratt	Timken
7056			26131-26274
7057	26126-26283	26126-26283	26126-26283
7058	26131-26283	26131-26283	26131-26283
7059	28118-28315	28118-28315	28118-28315
7062			28138
7063	28138-28315	28138-28315	28138-28315
7065		28150-28316	28150-28316
7066			28158-28313
7070		28157-28315	28157-28315
7071			28158-28315
7074		29177-29334	29177-29334
7075		29178-29334	29178-29334
7076			32100
7079			39236-39433
7080	41100-41286	41100-41286	41100-41286
7081	41106-41286		41106-41286
7084		43112-43325	43112-43325
7085			43112-43315
7089		43125-43349	43125-43349
7090	43125-43312	43125-43312	43125-43312
7091	43131-43312	43131-43312	43131-43312
7092	44117-43312	44117-43312	44117-43312
7093	44150-44348	44150-44348	44150-44348
7094	44143-44348	44143-44348	44143-44348
7097			44162-44150
7098	44162-44348	44162-44348	44162-44348
7101			53162-53386
7102	53162-53387	53162-53387	53162-53387
7105	53176-53387	53176-53387	53176-53387
7108			71450-71750
7111			72187-72487
7112	72200-72487	72200-72487	72200-72487
7113			72212-72487
7122	78216-78551	78216-78551	78216-78551
7125		78250-78551	78250-78551
7175			A-3044 A-3045
7177			A-3123
7178			3123B
7181			A-4221 A-4222
7182			A-6067-6157
7184			A-1201 A-1202
7185			A-1216 A-1217
7187		RO-261T	RO-261T
7188		RO-2527	RO-2527
7189			R-317 R-312
			R-319 R-312
7191			A-4221 A-4616
7192			T-95
7193			T-82
7194			T-88
7195			T-76
7196			T-102
7197			T-101
7199			T-63
7199			T-113
7200			T-176
7201			T-127
7202			T-151
7203			T-144
7204			T-107
7205			T-83
7206			T-94
7208			21-23
7209			31-32
7210			35-36

BEARINGS—Continued

ROLLER BEARINGS—STRAIGHT (CHILTON NUMBERS, Series 8000, 9000)

CHILTON NUMBER	Heliflex Flexible Type	Hyatt Flexible Type	Rollway Solid Type
ROLLER ASSEMBLIES			
8002-A	RBC-RA-121	RA-121	WS-1416
8007-A	RBC-RA-133	RA-133	WS-1716
8010-A	RBC-RA-135	RA-135	WS-1724
8011-A	RBC-RA-136	RA-136	WS-1728
8018-A	RBC-RA-145	RA-145	WS-8128
8021-A	RBC-RA-148	RA-148	WS-2026
8023-A	RBC-RA-149	RA-149	WS-2032
8028-A	RBC-RA-155	RA-155	....
8032-A	RBC-RA-159	RA-159	WS-2132
COMPLETE BEARINGS			
8062	RBC-206	206	....
8063	RBC-207	207	D-207-15
8065		208	....
8072	RBC-SC-209	SC-209	....
8074	RBC-TXW-209	TXW-209	....
8077	RBC-SW-210	SW-210	....
8080	RBC-W-211	W-211	D-211-29
8125	RBC-305	305	D-305-18
8128	RBC-N-306	N-306	D-306-15
8129	RBC-NC-306	NC-306	B-306-15
8131	RBC-307	307	D-307
8132	RBC-NC-307	NC-307	B-307-16
8135	RBC-308	308	D-308
8140	RBC-NC-309	NC-309	HXB-309-21
8149	RBC-312	312	D-312-17
8165	RBC-324	324	....
8166	RBC-SC-403	SC-403	B-304
8167	RBC-SC-404	SC-404	....
8168	RBC-S-405	S-405	....
8169	RBC-S-406	S-406	SD-406
8170	RBC-407	407	....
8171	RBC-408	408	....
8172	RBC-409	409	....
8199	RBC-16079	16079	....
8200	RBC-16080	16080	....
8208	RBC-16124	16124	....
8216	RBC-16148	16148	....
8269	RBC-16415	16415	....
8270	RBC-16421	16421	....
8272	RBC-16455	16455	....
8274	RBC-16465	16465	B-10039
8277	RBC-16476	16476	....
8284	RBC-16506	16506	....
8353	RBC-17093	17093	B-10024
8357	RBC-17103	17103	....
8385	RBC-18127	18127	....
8487	RBC-19081	19081	....
8518	RBC-19200	19200	....
8533	RBC-26056	26056	....
8541	RBC-26069	26069	A-8632
8569	RBC-26329	26329	....
8577	RBC-26401	26401	....
8582	RBC-26469	26469	....
8586	RBC-26480	26480	....
8587	RBC-26482	26482	....
8605	RBC-26668	26668	....
8622	RBC-27056	27056	....
8633	RBC-27095	27095	....
8634	RBC-27096	27096	....
8635	RBC-27097	27097	....
8660	RBC-27787	27787	....
8738	RBC-29097	29097	A-1940
8900	RBC-46394	46394	....
8925	RBC-46618	46618	....
8959	RBC-47026	47026	....
9047	RBC-49275	49275	....
9202	RBC-56777	56777	....
9209	RBC-57026	57026	....
9310	RBC-600203	600203	....

CHILTON NUMBER	Heliflex Flexible Type	Hyatt Flexible Type	Rollway Solid Type
ROLLER ASSEMBLIES			
9316-A	....	10133-RA	....
9317-A	....	16945-RA	WS-2330
9318-A	....	17980-RA	WS-2336
9320-A	....	26954-RA	WS-1818
9321-A	....	16953-RA	WS-8126
9322-A	....	16820-RA	WS-2030
9323-A	....	26922-RA	WS-1828
9324-A	....	26972-RA	WS-1832
9325-A	....	00523-RA	....
9326-A	....	16949-RA	WS-2132
9327-A	....	16961-RA	....
9328-A	....	57996-RA	....
9329-A	....	26825-RA	....
9330-A	....	26996-RA	....
9331-A	....	26839-RA	....
9332-A	....	16935-RA	....
9333-A	....	16931-RA	....
9334-A	....	16930-RA	....
9335-A	....	17966-RA	....
9336-A	....	16936-RA	....
9337-A	....	15935-RA	....
9338-A	....	16933-RA	....
9339-A	....	17987-RA	WS-2536
9340-A	....	00524-RA	....
9341-A	....	27977-RA	WS-2522
9342-A	....	16948-RA	WS-2028
9343-A	....	16944-RA	WS-2128
9344-A	....	27988-RA	WS-7632
9345	....	C-1207	....
9346	....	C-1308	....
9347-A	....	10135-RA	....
9348-A	....	16942-RA	....
9349-A	....	10145-RA	....

BALL BEARINGS—Magneto (CHILTON NUMBERS, Series 100)

CHILTON	S.A.E. Number	F&S C&C Sales (Imported)	Fafnir	Federal	New Departure	Norma-Hoffmann	RBF	RHL (Imported)	R.I.V. (Imported)	Torrington
105	5	E-5	....	....	....	E-5	....	....	....	T-5
106	6	....	....	....	....	....	8106	....	....	....
107	7	....	7	....	....	....	8107	....	....	....
108	8	E-8	8	FB-8	8	E-8	8108	E-8	....	T-8
109	9	E-9	9	FB-9	....	E-9	8109	....	....	T-9
110	10	E-10	10	FB-10	10	E-10	8110	E-10	2-M	T-10
111	11	E-11	11	FB-11	....	E-11	8111	....	7-M	T-11
112	12	E-12	12	FB-12	12	E-12	8112	E-12	....	T-12
113	13	E-13	13	FB-13	13	E-13	8113	E-13	3-M	T-13
114	14	E-14	14	FB-14	....	E-14	8114	....	....	T-14
115	15	E-15	15	FB-15	15	E-15	8115	E-15	8-M	T-15
116	16	E-16	16	FB-16	16	E-16	8116	E-16	1696	T-16
117	17	E-17	17	FB-17	17	E-17	8117	E-17	12-M	T-17
118	18	E-18	18	FB-18	....	....	....	....	....	....
119	19	E-19	19	FB-19	....	E-19	....	....	....	T-19
120	....	L-20	L-20	FB-20	20	L-20	8120	....	13-M	TL-20
125	....	L-25	L-25	FB-25	25	L-25	....	....	1252	TL-25

BEARINGS—Front Wheel (CHILTON NUMBERS, Series 500)

CHILTON NUMBER	CJB	Fafnir	Federal	Hoover	MRC	New Departure	Shafer (Roller Bearing)	CHILTON NUMBER	CJB	Fafnir	Federal	Hoover	MRC	New Departure	Shafer (Roller Bearing)
501	1	10001	F-001	909001	1	909001	S-1	510	....	....	F-010	....	....	909010	C-155DP
502	2	10002	F-002	909002	2	909002	S-2	523	....	....	F-023	....	23	909023	....
503	....	10003	F-003	....	3	909003	C-70	524	....	....	F-024	....	24	909024	....
504	....	10004	F-004	....	4	909004	C-152DP								
505	....	....	....	....	5	....	C-68	527	....	....	F-027	....	27	909027	....
506	....	....	....	....	6	....	C-151DP								
507	....	10007	F-007	....	7	909007	C-72	528	....	....	F-028	....	28	909028	....
508	....	10008	F-008	....	8	909008	C-154DP	529	....	....	F-029	....	29	909029	....
509	....	....	F-009	....	....	909009	C-93	530	....	....	F-030	....	30	909030	....

Engine Assembly

IN TWO SECTIONS—SECTION 1

HOW TO USE THIS TABLE

1. Locate in the first column the car and model for which the part is needed.
2. Follow this line across to the column pertaining to that part.
3. In this part column opposite your car model you will find the CHILTON NUMBER for the part you want.
4. Look up and down the part column for the same CHILTON NUMBER. Wherever you find this same number you have an interchangeable part. The car make opposite tells you where to get the part—probably from a local dealer or a nearby jobber.
Example: Suppose a Piston Pin is needed for a Durant 55 (1928) car. Locate this car in the first column. Follow across to the column on Piston Pins. Here you see the CHILTON NUMBER for this part is GM-42. Checking through the CHILTON NUMBERS in this same column you will find the number GM-42 opposite the Davis 93 (1928), the Flint Jr. (1926-7), the Jewett New Day (1926), and the Star R (1926-7). The Piston Pin used in all of these cars is interchangeable with the one used in your Durant 55 car.
5. At the end of this table, pages 194, 195, you will find a count showing how many times any CHILTON NUMBER appears in the table.
Example: GP-12 under Oil Pump Gears opposite the Cadillac 314 (1926) in this table will appear again in the count at the end of the table followed by the figure 9 under the heading Oil Pump Gears. This indicates part number GP-12 appears opposite nine car models in this table.
6. Immediately following this count is a table giving the actual specifications for each CHILTON NUMBER for Pistons and Pins. Piston Ring specifications are also given.

Interchangeable Parts have the same CHILTON NUMBER in Any Column

Car Make and Model	CRANKSHAFT MAIN BEARINGS				PISTON AND CONNECTING ROD ASSEMBLY				Oil Pump Gears	Flywheel Starter Gears (Ring Gear)
	Front Main Bearing	†Center Main Bearing	Rear Main Bearing	‡Intermediate Main Bearing	Piston (See Footnote)	Piston Pin (See Footnote)	Piston Pin Bushing	Connecting Rod		
Ajax (Nash L6)........(1925-26)	GKA-1	GKB-1	GKC-1	GKD-1	GL-1	GM-1	GN-1	GO-1	GP-1	GW-1
Apperson 6, Velie 50.......(1925)	GKA-4	GKB-4	GKC-4	None	GL-186	GM-154	GN-155	GO-6	GP-4	GW-2
Apperson Str. 8, Lyc. 2H..(1925)	GKA-5	GKB-5	GKC-5	{GKD-4, GKD-5}	GL-5	GM-5	None	GO-5	GP-6	GW-5
Auburn 4, Lyc. CF........(1925)	GKA-6	GKB-6	GKA-6	GKD-6	GL-6	GM-6	GN-5	GO-7	GP-6	GW-5
Auburn 6-43, Cont. 7U....(1925)	*GKA-2	*GKB-2	*GKC-2	*GKB-2	GL-2	GM-2	GN-2	GO-2	GP-2	GW-2
Auburn 8-88, Lyc. 2H.....(1925)	GKA-5	GKB-5	GKC-5	{GKD-4, GKD-5}	GL-5	GM-5	None	GO-5	GP-6	GW-5
Auburn 6-66, Lyc. 4 SM...(1926)	GKA-7	GKB-7	GKC-7	GKB-5	GL-4	GM-4	GN-4	GO-5	GP-6	GW-5
Auburn 4-44, Lyc. CF..(1926-27)	GKA-6	GKB-6	GKA-6	GKD-6	GL-6	GM-6	GN-5	GO-7	GP-6	GW-5
Auburn 8-88, Lyc. 4HM...(1926)	GKA-5	GKB-5	GKC-5	{GKD-4, GKD-5}	GL-4	GM-4	GN-4	GO-41	GP-6	GW-5
Auburn 6-66, Lyc. 4 SM...(1927)	GKA-7	GKB-7	GKC-7	GKB-5	GL-4	GM-4	GN-4	GO-41	GP-6	GW-5
Auburn 6-66A, Cont. 28L.(1927)	GKA-140	GKB-8	GKC-8	GKB-8	GL-7	GM-8	GN-7	GO-8	GP-2	GW-6
Auburn 8-88, Lyc. 4HM(1927-28)	GKA-5	GKB-5	GKC-5	{GKD-4, GKD-5}	GL-4	GM-4	None	GO-81	GP-76	GW-5
Auburn 8-77, Lyc. GT..(1927-28)	GKA-8	GKB-9	GKC-9	GKB-165	GL-8	GM-9	GN-4	GO-9	GP-76	GW-27
Auburn 76, Lyc. WS...(1928-29)	GKA-8	GKB-165	GKC-9	GKB-9	GL-9	GM-10	None	GO-150	GP-76	GW-27
Auburn 88, Lyc. GS....(1928-29)	GKA-8	GKB-9	GKC-9	GKB-165	GL-9	GM-10	None	GO-150	GP-76	GW-27
Auburn 115, Lyc. 4MD. (1928-29)	GKA-5	GKB-5	GKC-5	{GKD-4, GKD-5}	GL-10	GM-7	None	GO-10	GP-76	GW-5
Auburn 6-80, Lyc. WR Early (1929)	GKA-8	GKB-165	GKC-9	GKB-9	GL-208	GM-10	None	GO-150	GP-76	GW-27
Auburn 6-80, Lyc. WR Late (1929)	GKA-139	GKB-166	GKC-161	GKB-167	GL-39	GM-10	None	GO-11	GP-76	GW-27
Auburn 8-90, Lyc. GR Early (1929)	GKA-8	GKB-9	GKC-9	GKB-165	GL-208	GM-10	None	GO-150	GP-76	GW-27
Auburn 120, Lyc. MDA Early (1929)	GKA-5	GKB-5	GKC-5	{GKD-4, GKD-5}	GL-10	GM-7	None	GO-10	GP-76	GW-5
Auburn 120, Lyc. MDA Late (1929)	GKA-5	GKB-5	GKC-5	{GKD-4, GKD-5}	GL-10	GM-7	None	GO-182	GP-76	GW-5
Auburn 8-90, Lyc. GR Late (1929)	GKA-139	GKB-167	GKC-161	GKB-166	GL-39	GM-10	None	GO-11	GP-76	GW-27
Auburn 6-85, Lyc. WR.....(1930)	GKA-139	GKB-166	GKC-161	GKB-167	GL-39	GM-10	None	GO-11	GP-76	GW-27
Auburn 8-95, Lyc. GR.....(1930)	GKA-139	GKB-9	GKC-161	GKB-166	GL-39	GM-10	None	GO-11	GP-76	GW-27
Auburn 125, Lyc. MDA...(1930)	GKA-5	GKB-5	GKC-5	{GKD-4, GKD-5}	GL-10	GM-7	None	GO-182	GP-76	GW-5
Blackhawk, L6...........(1929)	GKA-9	GKB-11	GKC-10	GKD-9	GL-11	GM-11	GN-12	GO-12	GP-89	GW-9
Blackhawk, L8...........(1929)	GKA-10	GKB-12	GKC-11	GKB-12	GL-12	GM-12	GN-13	GO-39	GP-8	GW-21
Blackhawk, L6...........(1930)	GKA-9	GKB-11	GKC-10	GKD-9	GL-11	GM-11	GN-12	GO-12	GP-89	GW-9
Blackhawk, L8...........(1930)	GKA-10	GKB-12	GKC-11	GKB-12	GL-12	GM-12	GN-13	GO-39	GP-8	GW-10
Buick Master...........(1925)	*GKA-11	*GKB-13	*GKC-12	*GKD-12	GL-13	GM-13	GN-14	GO-14	GP-9	GW-11
Buick Std.............(1925)	*GKA-12	*GKB-14	*GKC-13	*GKD-12	GL-14	GM-14	GN-15	GO-15	GP-9	GW-12
Buick Master...........(1926)	*GKA-11	*GKB-13	*GKC-12	*GKD-11	GL-15	GM-167	GN-16	GO-14	GP-9	GW-12
Buick Std.............(1926)	*GKA-12	*GKB-13	*GKC-13	*GKD-12	GL-16	GM-16	GN-15	GO-16	GP-9	GW-11
Buick 115.............(1927)	*GKA-30	*GKB-34	*GKC-33	*GKD-2	GL-17	GM-16	GN-16	GO-16	GP-9	GW-11
Buick 120, 128.........(1927)	*GKA-11	*GKB-13	*GKC-12	GKD-11	GL-18	GM-167	GN-16	GO-17	GP-9	GW-12
Buick 115.............(1928)	*GKA-30	*GKB-34	*GKC-33	GKD-2	GL-17	GM-16	GN-16	GO-16	GP-9	GW-11
Buick 120, 128.........(1928)	*GKA-11	*GKB-13	*GKC-12	GKD-11	GL-18	GM-167	GN-16	GO-17	GP-9	GW-12
Buick 116.............(1929)	GKA-13	GKB-15	GKC-14	GKD-13	GL-19	GM-17	GN-17	GO-18	GP-9	GW-14
Buick 121, 129.........(1929)	GKA-14	GKB-16	GKC-15	GKD-14	GL-20	GM-18	GN-11	GO-19	GP-10	GW-14
Buick 40..............(1930)	GKA-13	GKB-15	GKC-14	GKD-13	GL-29	GM-13	GN-16	GO-54	GP-10	GW-14
Buick 50..............(1930)	GKA-14	GKB-16	GKC-15	GKD-14	GL-41	GM-38	GN-11	GO-19	GP-10	GW-14
Buick 60..............(1930)	GKA-14	GKB-16	GKC-15	GKD-14	GL-41	GM-38	GN-11	GO-19	GP-10	GW-14
Cadillac V-63..........(1925)	GKA-15	GKA-16	GKC-16	None	GL-21	GM-19	GN-18	{GO-20, GO-97}	GP-11	GW-16
Cadillac 314..........(1926)	GKA-16	GKA-16	GKC-17	None	GL-22	GM-19	GN-18	{GO-21, GO-101}	GP-12	GW-17
Cadillac 314..........(1927)	GKA-16	GKA-16	GKC-17	None	GL-22	GM-19	GN-18	{GO-21, GO-101}	GP-12	GW-17
Cadillac 341-A.........(1928)	GKA-17	GKB-19	GKC-18	None	GL-23	GM-20	GN-19	GO-22	GP-12	°GW-7
Cadillac 341-B.........(1929)	GKA-17	GKB-19	GKC-18	None	GL-23	GM-20	GN-19	GO-23	GP-12	GW-7
Cadillac 353...........(1930)	GKA-17	GKB-19	GKC-18	None	GL-44	GM-20	GN-19	GO-23	GP-12	GW-8
Case JIC, Cont. 8R.....(1925)	GKA-3	GKB-3	GKC-3	GKB-3	GL-3	GM-3	GN-3	GO-3	GP-3	GW-3
Case X, Cont. 8R.......(1925)	GKA-3	GKB-3	GKC-3	GKB-3	GL-3	GM-3	GN-3	GO-3	GP-3	GW-3
Case Y, Cont. 6T.......(1925)	GKA-3	GKB-20	GKC-19	GKB-20	GL-224	GM-201	GN-20	GO-24	GP-3	GW-3
Case JIC, Cont. 8R.....(1926-27)	GKA-3	GKB-3	GKC-3	GKB-3	GL-3	GM-3	GN-3	GO-3	GP-3	GW-3
Case Y, Cont. 6J.......(1926-27)	*GKA-10	*GKB-10	*GKC-31	*GKB-10	GL-24	GM-21	GN-20	GO-24	GP-2	GW-3
Chandler 33............(1925)	GKA-19	GKB-21	GKC-20	GKD-19	GL-25	GM-22	GN-21	GO-25	GP-14	GW-18
Chandler 35............(1926)	GKA-20	GKB-22	GKC-21	GKD-20	GL-25	GM-22	GN-21	GO-26	GP-14	GW-18
Chandler Big 6.........(1927)	GKA-20	GKB-22	GKC-21	GKD-20	GL-25	GM-22	GN-21	GO-26	GP-14	GW-18
Chandler Royal 8.......(1927)	GKA-21	GKB-23	GKC-22	GKB-23	GL-26	GM-25	GN-22	GO-27	GP-14	GW-15

Footnote: For corresponding piston and pin numbers advertised, see page

Order by B-N or Dall number—not Chilton number.

CONVERSION TABLE

Piston Pin Fits Piston shown in same line.

Chilton Piston No.	Dall Piston No.	Chilton Pin No.	B-N Pin No.
GL-1	D-231	GM-1	P-189
GL-2	D-141	GM-2	P-507 X
	DL-1141		P-507 X
GL-3	D-119	GM-3	P-509
GL-4	D-258	GM-4	P-588
GL-5	D-214	GM-5	P-559
GL-7	D-272	GM-8	P-599
GL-8	D-283	GM-9	P-605
GL-9	DL-1623	GM-10	P-631
	DU-1729		P-631
GL-10	DL-1622	GM-7	P-610
GL-12	....	GM-43	P-624
GL-13	D-154	GM-13	P-108
GL-14	D-194	GM-14	P-553
GL-15	D-226	GM-167	P-584
GL-16	D-225	GM-16	P-583
	D-225A		P-583
GL-17	D-263	GM-16	P-583
	D-263A		P-583
GL-18	D-264	GM-167	P-584
GL-19	D-328	GM-17	P-640
GL-20	D-329	GM-18	P-641
GL-21	D-50	GM-19	P-133
GL-22	D-259	GM-19	P-133
GL-23	D-331	GM-20	P-643
GL-24	D-142	GM-21	P-540
GL-25	D-213	GM-22	P-561
GL-26	D-378	GM-25	P-611
GL-27	D-228	GM-26	P-581
GL-28	D-274	GM-15	P-580
GL-29	D-393	GM-13	P-108
GL-30	D-270	GM-27	P-592
	DL-1608		P-592
GL-31	D-372 B	GM-28	P-644
	DL-1524		P-645
	DL-1618		P-645
	DU-1702		P-645
GL-32	DL-1500	GM-29	P-551
	DL-1600		P-551
GL-33	D-236	GM-30	P-518
	DL-1502		P-518
GL-34	D-201	GM-88	P-215
GL-35	DL-1508	GM-32	P-596
GL-36	DL-1610	GM-33	P-617
GL-37	DL-1625	GM-34	....
GL-38	D-267	GM-45	P-554
GL-39	D-396	GM-10	P-631
	DU-1725		P-631
GL-41	D-394	GM-38	P-657
	DL-1561		P-657
GL-42	D-266	GM-40	P-591
	DL-1624		P-526
GL-43	D-243	GM-42	P-589
	DL-1243		P-589
	DL-1602		P-609
GL-44	D-408	GM-20	P-643
GL-45	D-262	GM-45	P-554
GL-46	D-424	GM-48	P-638
	DL-1609		P-638
	DU-1705		P-638
GL-47	D-261	GM-41	P-586
GL-48	D-63	GM-46	P-111
	DL-1063		P-111
	DL-1603		P-111
GL-49	D-284	GM-47	P-613
	DL-1604		P-613
	DU-1718		P-613
GL-51	DL-1501	GM-31	P-579
	DL-1601		P-579
GL-52	DL-1633	GM-35	P-601
GL-53	DL-1629	GM-48	P-638
GL-54	D-411	GM-33	P-617
GL-55	D-155	GM-54	P-244

Chilton Piston No.	Dall Piston No.	Chilton Pin No.	B-N Pin No.
GL-56	DL-1631	GM-49	P-666
GL-57	D-246	GM-44	P-563
	DL-1246		P-563
	DL-1606		P-563
GL-58	....	GM-50	P-625
GL-59	DU-1715	GM-51	P-664
GL-61	DU-1716	GM-90	P-148
GL-63	DL-1649	GM-70	P-665
GL-64	DL-1628	GM-98	P-637
GL-65	DL-1635	GM-72	P-662
GL-66	D-384	GM-52	P-652
GL-67	D-406	GM-78	P-661
GL-68	DL-1639	GM-81	P-639
GL-71	D-412	GM-91	P-663
GL-72	....	GM-92	P-674
GL-74	D-282	GM-57	P-606
GL-75	D-327	GM-58	P-623
GL-76	D-211	GM-59	P-560
	DL-1211		P-560
GL-77	DL-1536	GM-59	P-560
	DU-1721		P-560
GL-78	DL-1507	GM-60	P-597
GL-79	D-42 X	GM-61	F-3022
	DL-1042		F-3022
GL-80	D-380	GM-62	F-6135
	DL-1516		F-6135
	DU-1703		F-6135
GL-81	....	GM-63	P-149
GL-83	DL-1643	GM-49	P-666
GL-84	DL-1634	GM-116	P-600
GL-86	DL-1637	GM-67	P-627
GL-89	DL-1620	GM-168	P-633
GL-90	DL-1627	GM-223	P-658
GL-91	DL-1615	GM-95	P-636
GL-96	D-185	GM-71	P-501
	D-185 A		P-501
	DL-1185		P-501
	DL-1605		P-501
GL-97	D-208	GM-56	P-565
GL-98	D-179	GM-73	P-158
	D-179A		P-158
	DL-1179		P-158
GL-99	D-254	GM-56	P-565
GL-100	D-251	GM-74	P-587
GL-101	D-330	GM-75	P-622
GL-102	D-339	GM-76	P-625
GL-105	DL-1616	GM-98	P-637
GL-106	DL-1617	GM-96	P-635
GL-107	D-290	GM-97	P-614
GL-109	....	GM-55	P-603
GL-111	....	GM-79	P-260
GL-112	D-410	GM-148	P-647
	DL-1626		P-647
	DU-1720		P-647
GL-113	D-239	GM-231	P-578
GL-114	D-232	GM-114	P-139
GL-115	D-391	GM-20	P-643
GL-117	DL-1512	GM-77	P-609
	DL-1607		P-609
GL-118	DL-1504	GM-82	P-516
GL-120	D-273	GM-86	P-582
GL-121	....	GM-84	P-549
GL-123	D-287	GM-53	P-615
GL-124	DL-1520	GM-89	P-620
GL-125	DL-1519	GM-8	P-599
GL-126	D-230	GM-93	P-595
GL-129	D-195	GM-94	P-556
GL-130	D-210	GM-99	P-570
GL-131	D-229	GM-100	P-590
GL-132	D-286	GM-101	P-594
GL-133	DL-1527	GM-102	P-642
GL-134	D-219	GM-103	P-577
	D-219 X		P-577

Chilton Piston No.	Dall Piston No.	Chilton Pin No.	B-N Pin No.
GL-135	D-271	....	P-607
GL-136	D-392	GM-104	P-649
	DL-1326		P-649
	D-326		P-619
GL-137	D-158	GM-105	P-536
GL-138	D-220	GM-106	P-566
	DL-1220		P-566
	DL-1646		P-566
GL-139	D-260	GM-107	P-598
	DL-1260		P-598
GL-140	D-249	GM-109	P-573
	D-249 A		P-573
	DL 1651		P-573
GL-141	....	GM-110	P-573
GL-142	DL-1531	GM-109	P-573
GL-145	D-279	GM-113	P-602
GL-146	D-235	GM-112	P-585
GL-147	....	GM-115	P-275
GL-149	D-341	GM-118	P-558
GL-150	D-340	GM-119	P-513
GL-151	....	GM-120	P-655
GL-154	D-381	GM-122	P-648
GL-155	D-178	GM-123	P-195
	D-1178		P-195
GL-156	D-285	GM-124	P-608
	DL-1517		P-608
	DL-1549		P-608
GL-157	DL-1532	GM-232	P-646
	DL-1551		P-646
GL-162	D-255	GM-132	P-526
GL-170	D-163	GM-137	P-569
GL-174	D-57	GM-144	P-517
	DL-1638		P-517
GL-175	D-88	GM-145	P-118
GL-176	D-193	GM-146	P-557
GL-178	D-415	GM-147	P-654
	DL-1619		P-654
	DU-1722		P-654
GL-179	DL-1530	GM-90	P-148
	DU-1717		P-148
GL-184	D-181 X	GM-154	P-535
GL-185	D-298	GM-154	P-535
GL-186	D-299	GM-154	P-535
GL-187	D-397	GM-157	P-656
GL-188	D-233	GM-166	P-220
	DL-1506		P-220
	DL-1506B		P-220
GL-189	D-234	GM-158	P-567
GL-190	....	GM-160	P-612
GL-191	DL-1612	GM-159	P-628
GL-192	DL-1613	GM-161	P-630
GL-194	DL-1534	GM-164	P-653
GL-195	DU-1707	GM-35	P-605
GL-196	DL-1614	GM-65	P-634
GL-208	D-396	GM-10	P-631
	DU-1725		P-631
GL-209	D-370	GM-23	P-604
GL-213	D-276	GM-69	P-604
GL-215	D-212	GM-111	P-564
GL-217	D-379	GM-78	P-651
GL-218	D-353		
	D-427	GM-146	P-557
GL-220	D-325	GM-108	P-629
	DL-1611		P-629
GL-222	D-333	GM-80	P-621
GL-224	....	GM-201	P-528
GL-225	D-140	GM-202	P-525
GL-227	....	GM-230	P-521
GL-233	D-238	GM-101	P-594
	DL-1238		P-594

D—Semi-Steel Piston. DL—1000-1599 incl. Aluminum Alloy Pistons DL—1600-1699 Steel Strut Pistons DU—1700-1799 Unitype Pistons P—Piston Pins

ENGINE ASSEMBLY, Section I—Continued

Interchangeable Parts have the same CHILTON NUMBER in Any Column

Car Make and Model	CRANKSHAFT MAIN BEARINGS				PISTON AND CONNECTING ROD ASSEMBLY				Oil Pump Gears	Flywheel Starter Gears (Ring Gear)
	Front Main Bearing	†Center Main Bearing	Rear Main Bearing	‡Intermediate Main Bearing	Piston (See Footnote)	Piston Pin (See Footnote)	Piston Pin Bushing	Connecting Rod		
Chandler Spec. 6..........(1927)	GKA-22	GKB-24	GKC-23	None	GL-27	GM-26	GN-23	GO-28	GP-15	GW-19
Chandler Std. 6...........(1927)	GKA-23	GKB-25	GKC-24	None	GL-28	GM-15	GN-24	GO-29	GP-16	GW-20
Chandler Big 6...........(1928)	GKA-20	GKB-22	GKC-21	GKD-20	GL-209	GM-23	GN-21	GO-26	GP-14	GW-18
Chandler Royal 8.........(1928)	GKA-21	GKB-23	GKC-22	GKB-23	GL-26	GM-25	GN-22	GO-27	GP-14	GW-15
Chandler Spec. 6.........(1928)	GKA-22	GKB-24	GKC-23	None	GL-28	GM-26	GN-24	GO-29	GP-15	GW-19
Chandler Spec. Inv. 6...(1928)	GKA-22	GKB-24	GKC-23	None	GL-27	GM-26	GN-24	GO-29	GP-15	GW-19
Chevrolet K............(1925)	GKA-24	GKB-26	GKC-25	None	GL-30	GM-27	None	GO-30	GP-17	GW-21
Chevrolet V............(1926)	GKA-24	GKB-26	GKC-25	None	GL-30	GM-27	None	GO-30	GP-18	GW-21
Chevrolet AA...........(1927)	GKA-24	GKB-26	GKC-25	None	GL-30	GM-27	None	GO-31	None	GW-21
Chevrolet AB...........(1928)	GKA-24	GKB-26	GKC-25	None	GL-30	GM-27	None	GO-30	None	GW-21
Chevrolet AC...........(1929)	GKA-25	GKB-27	GKC-26	None	GL-31	GM-28	GN-26	GO-31	None	GW-22
Chevrolet AD...........(1930)	GKA-25	GKB-27	GKC-26	None	GL-31	GM-28	GN-26	GO-31	None	GW-22
Chrysler 6-B...........(1925)	GKA-26	GKB-28	GKC-27	GKD-27	GL-32	GM-29	None	GO-32	GP-19	GW-23
Chrysler 58............(1926)	GKA-27	GKB-29	GKC-28	None	GL-33	GM-30	None	GO-33	GP-20	GW-24
Chrysler 70............(1926)	GKA-23	GKB-30	GKC-29	GKD-28	GL-51	GM-31	None	GO-34	GP-22	GW-23
Chrysler Imp. 80........(1926)	GKA-29	GKA-29	GKC-30	GKD-29	GL-35	GM-32	None	GO-35	GP-21	GW-25
Chrysler 50............(1927)	GKA-27	GKB-29	GKC-28	None	GL-33	GM-30	None	GO-33	GP-20	GW-24
Chrysler 60............(1927)	GKA-26	GKB-28	GKC-27	GKD-3	GL-32	GM-29	None	GO-36	GP-19	GW-26
Chrysler 70............(1927)	GKA-28	GKB-30	GKC-29	GKD-28	GL-51	GM-31	None	GO-34	GP-22	GW-23
Chrysler 80............(1927)	GKA-29	GKA-29	GKC-30	GKD-29	GL-35	GM-32	None	GO-35	GP-21	GW-25
Chrysler 52............(1928)	GKA-27	GKB-29	GKC-28	None	GL-33	GM-30	None	GO-33	GP-20	GW-24
Chrysler 62............(1928)	GKA-26	GKB-28	GKC-27	GKD-3	GL-32	GM-29	None	GO-36	GP-29	GW-26
Chrysler 72............(1928)	GKA-28	GKB-30	GKC-29	GKD-28	GL-36	GM-33	None	GO-37	GP-29	GW-23
Chrysler Imp. 80........(1928)	GKA-29	GKA-29	GKC-30	GKD-29	GL-37	GM-34	None	GO-38	GP-21	GW-25
Chrysler 65............(1929)	GKA-32	GKB-35	GKC-34	GKD-15	GL-51	GM-31	None	GO-152	GP-61	GW-26
Chrysler 75............(1929)	GKA-28	GKB-30	GKC-29	GKD-28	GL-36	GM-33	None	GO-37	GP-61	GW-23
Chrysler Imp. 80.......(1929-30)	GKA-29	GKA-29	GKC-30	GKD-29	GL-37	GM-34	None	GO-38	GP-21	GW-25
Chrysler 6.............(1930)	GKA-37	GKB-40	GKC-38	GKB-40	GL-51	GM-31	None	GO-183	GP-61	GW-26
Chrysler 66............(1930)	GKA-28	GKB-30	GKC-29	GKD-28	GL-51	GM-31	None	GO-184	GP-61	GW-23
Chrysler 70............(1930)	GKA-28	GKB-30	GKC-29	GKD-28	GL-51	GM-31	None	GO-185	GP-61	GW-23
Chrysler 77............(1930)	GKA-33	GKB-35	GKC-28	GKD-28	GL-53	GM-48	GN-42	GO-186	GP-61	GW-23
Cleveland 31...........(1925)	GKA-23	GKB-25	GKC-24	None	GL-28	GM-15	GN-24	GO-29	GP-16	GW-19
Cleveland 43...........(1925)	GKA-22	GKB-24	GKC-23	None	GL-27	GM-26	GN-23	GO-28	GP-15	GW-19
Cleveland 31...........(1926)	GKA-23	GKB-25	GKC-24	None	GL-28	GM-15	GN-24	GO-29	GP-16	GW-19
Cleveland 43...........(1926)	GKA-22	GKB-24	GKC-23	None	GL-27	GM-26	GN-23	GO-28	GP-15	GW-20
Cord, Lyc. FDA.........(1930)	GKA-144	GKB-5	GKC-162	{GKB-4 GKB-5	GL-10	GM-7	None	GO-182	GP-6	GW-5
Davis 90, Cont. 7U.....(1925-26)	*GKA-2	*GKB-2	GKC-2	GKB-2	GL-2	GM-2	GN-2	GO-2	GP-2	GW-2
Davis 91, Cont. 8R.....(1925-26)	GKA-3	GKB-3	GKC-3	GKB-3	GL-3	GM-3	GN-3	GO-3	GP-3	GW-3
Davis 92, Cont. 11U....(1926)	GKA-35	GKB-37	GKC-36	GKD-35	GL-42	GM-40	GN-38	GO-44	GP-2	GW-6
Davis 93, Cont. 20L....(1926)	GKA-34	GKB-45	GKC-45	GKB-45	GL-43	GM-42	GN-7	GO-8	GP-2	GW-6
Davis 92, Cont. 11U....(1927)	GKA-35	GKB-37	GKC-36	GKD-35	GL-42	GM-40	GN-38	GO-44	GP-2	GW-2
Davis 94, Cont. 28L....(1927)	GKA-140	GKB-8	GKC-8	GKB-8	GL-7	GM-8	GN-7	GO-8	GP-2	GW-6
Davis 98, Cont. 8S.....(1927)	*GKA-36	*GKB-39	*GKC-37	GKB-39	GL-47	GM-41	GN-40	GO-39	GP-8	GW-21
Davis 99, Cont. 14S....(1928)	GKA-36	GKB-39	GKC-37	GKB-39	GL-12	GM-43	GN-40	GO-39	GP-8	GW-21
De Soto 6..............(1929)	GKA-37	GKB-40	GKC-38	GKB-40	GL-32	GM-29	None	GO-46	GP-61	GW-26
De Soto Finer 6..........(1930)	GKA-37	GKB-40	GKC-38	GKB-40	GL-51	GM-31	None	GO-187	GP-61	GW-26
De Soto 8..............(1930)	GKA-43	GKB-112	GKC-43	GKD-16	GL-52	GM-35	GN-31	GO-188	GP-98	GW-23
Diana Str. 8, Cont. 12Z..(1926)	*GKA-38	*GKB-41	*GKC-39	*GKB-41	GL-38	GM-45	GN-6	GO-47	GP-2	GW-2
Diana Str. 8, Cont. 12Z..(1927)	*GKA-38	*GKB-41	*GKC-39	*GKB-41	GL-38	GM-45	None	GO-47	GP-2	GW-2
Diana Str. 8, Cont. 12Z..(1928)	*GKA-38	*GKB-41	*GKC-39	*GKB-41	GL-38	GM-45	None	GO-47	GP-2	GW-2
Dodge Brothers 4........(1925)	GKA-39	GKB-42	GKC-40	GKB-42	GL-48	GM-46	GN-41	GO-48	None	GW-11
Dodge Brothers 4........(1926)	GKA-39	GKB-42	GKC-40	GKB-42	GL-48	GM-46	GN-41	GO-48	None	GW-11
Dodge Brothers 4........(1927)	GKA-39	GKB-42	GKC-40	GKB-42	GL-48	GM-46	GN-41	GO-48	GP-27	GW-11
Dodge Brothers Senior....(1928)	GKA-40	GKB-43	GKC-41	GKD-40	GL-49	GM-47	GN-42	GO-49	GP-28	GW-23
Dodge Brothers Std. 6..(1928-29)	GKA-41	GKB-44	GKC-42	{GKD-10 GKD-41	GL-46	GM-48	GN-42	GO-189	GP-28	GW-30
Dodge Brothers Vic. 6..(1928-29)	GKA-41	GKB-44	GKC-42	{GKD-10 GKD-41	GL-46	GM-48	GN-42	GO-189	GP-28	GW-30
Dodge Brothers Senior....(1929)	GKA-40	GKB-43	GKC-41	GKD-40	GL-46	GM-48	GN-42	GO-49	GP-23	GW-23
Dodge Brothers DA-6.....(1929)	GKA-41	GKB-44	GKC-42	{GKD-10 GKD-41	GL-46	GM-48	GN-42	GO-50	GP-28	GW-30
Dodge Brothers DC8......(1930)	GKA-43	GKB-112	GKC-43	GKD-16	GL-52	GM-35	GN-31	GO-190	GP-98	GW-23
Dodge Brothers DD6......(1930)	GKA-37	GKB-40	GKC-38	GKB-40	GL-51	GM-31	None	GO-187	GP-61	GW-26
Durant A-22, Cont.......(1925)	GKA-47	GKB-50	GKC-48	None	GL-55	GM-54	GN-48	GO-56	GP-33	GW-32
Durant 55, Cont. 14L....(1928)	GKA-140	GKB-8	GKC-8	GKB-8	GL-43	GM-42	GN-7	GO-8	GP-2	GW-6
Durant D65, Cont. 15L...(1928)	GKA-140	GKB-8	GKC-8	GKB-8	GL-195	GM-8	GN-7	GO-8	GP-2	GW-6
Durant M2, Cont. W5...(1928-29)	*GKA-48	*GKB-52	*GKC-50	None	GL-57	GM-44	GN-49	GO-57	GP-2	GW-15
Durant 75, Cont. 15U...(1928-29)	GKA-35	GKB-37	GKC-36	GKD-35	GL-46	GM-48	GN-42	GO-58	GP-28	GW-15
Durant 4-40, Cont. W5...(1929)	*GKA-48	*GKB-52	*GKC-50	None	GL-57	GM-44	GN-49	GO-57	GP-2	GW-15
Durant 6-60, Cont. 14L...(1929)	GKA-140	GKB-8	GKC-8	GKB-8	GL-43	GM-42	GN-7	GO-8	GP-2	GW-33
Durant 66, Cont. 15L....(1929)	GKA-140	GKB-8	GKC-8	GKB-8	GL-195	GM-8	GN-7	GO-8	GP-2	GW-33
Durant 70, Cont. 20E....(1930)	GKA-35	GKB-37	GKC-36	GKD-35	GL-46	GM-48	GN-42	GO-58	GP-2	GW-15
Durant 614, Cont. 22A...(1930)	GKA-42	GKA-48	GKC-65	GKD-147	GL-49	GM-47	GN-42	GO-191	GP-28	GW-33
Durant 617, Cont. 15U...(1930)	GKA-35	GKB-37	GKC-36	GKD-35	GL-46	GM-36	GN-42	GO-58	GP-28	GW-15
Elcar 4-40, Lyc. CF......(1925)	GKA-6	GKB-6	GKA-6	GKD-6	GL-6	GM-6	GN-5	GO-7	GP-6	GW-5
Elcar 6-50, Cont. 7U....(1925)	*GKA-2	*GKB-2	*GKC-2	*GKB-2	GL-2	GM-2	GN-2	GO-2	GP-2	GW-2
Elcar 6-60, Cont. 8R....(1925)	GKA-3	GKB-3	GKC-3	GKB-3	GL-3	GM-3	GN-3	GO-3	GP-3	GW-3
Elcar 8-80, Lyc. H........(1925)	GKA-5	GKB-5	GKC-5	{GKD-4 GKD-5	GL-5	GM-5	None	GO-5	GP-6	GW-5
Elcar 4-55, Lyc. CF.....(1926-27)	GKA-6	GKB-6	GKA-6	GKD-6	GL-6	GM-6	GN-5	GO-7	GP-6	GW-5
Elcar 6-65, Lyc. 4SM......(1926)	GKA-7	GKB-7	GKC-7	GKB-5	GL-4	GM-4	GN-4	GO-5	GP-6	GW-5
Elcar 8-81, Lyc. 4H......(1926)	GKA-5	GKB-5	GKC-5	{GKD-4 GKD-5	GL-4	GM-4	GN-4	GO-5	GP-6	GW-5
Elcar 6-70, Lyc. WS.......(1927)	GKA-8	GKB-165	GKC-9	GKB-9	GL-9	GM-10	None	GO-150	GP-76	GW-27
Elcar 8-82, Lyc. GT......(1927)	GKA-8	GKB-9	GKC-9	GKB-165	GL-8	GM-9	GN-4	GO-9	GP-76	GW-27
Elcar 8-90, Lyc. 4HM.....(1927)	GKA-5	GKB-5	GKC-5	{GKD-4 GKD-5	GL-4	GM-4	None	GO-41	GP-76	GW-5
Elcar 8-91, Lyc. 4HM.....(1928)	GKA-5	GKB-5	GKC-5	{GKD-4 GKD-5	GL-4	GM-4	None	GO-81	GP-76	GW-5
Elcar 8-120, Lyc. MD.....(1928)	GKA-5	GKB-5	GKC-5	{GKD-4 GKD-5	GL-10	GM-7	None	GO-10	GP-76	GW-5
Elcar 6-70, Lyc. WS....(1928-29)	GKA-8	GKB-165	GKC-9	GKB-9	GL-9	GM-10	None	GO-150	GP-76	GW-27
Elcar 8-78, Lyc. GT....(1928-29)	GKA-8	GKB-9	GKC-9	GKB-165	GL-8	GM-9	GN-4	GO-9	GP-76	GW-27
Elcar 8-82, Lyc. GS....(1928-29)	GKA-8	GKB-9	GKC-9	GKB-165	GL-9	GM-10	None	GO-150	GP-76	GW-27
Elcar 75, Lyc. WS.....(1929-30)	GKA-8	GKB-165	GKC-9	GKB-9	GL-9	GM-10	None	GO-150	GP-76	GW-27
Elcar 95-96, Lyc. GS...(1929-30)	GKA-8	GKB-9	GKC-9	GKB-165	GL-9	GM-10	None	GO-150	GP-76	GW-27
Elcar 120, Lyc. MD....(1929-30)	GKA-5	GKB-5	GKC-5	{GKD-4 GKD-5	GL-10	GM-7	None	GO-10	GP-76	GW-5

Footnote: For corresponding piston and pin numbers advertised, see page **187**

USE THIS 100% COMPLETE BEARING SERVICE

ONE STANDARD
OF QUALITY . . .

ONE SOURCE
OF SUPPLY . . .

for every Bearing Requirement

FEDERAL-MOGUL Bearing Service, combined with Watkins Connecting Rod Babbitting Service, presents to the automotive trade the one and only 100% complete bearing service . . . service on every part used in the bearing assembly.

This service is more than a mere source of supply for parts. It is a service on bearings, bushings, bronze bars and babbitt metals backed by an engineering, technical, and metallurgical staff that has made history in its field by satisfying leading automotive manufacturers since 1899. The replacement trade likewise has been served by these same dependable facilities.

This background of experience and skill now stands back of every Watkins Babbitted Connecting Rod. Watkins Rods are babbitted with genuine Federal-Mogul babbitt, and completely rebuilt with new nuts, bolts, bushings and Laminum shims. A nation-wide group of manufacturing plants, and a widespread jobbing organization bring this prompt, efficient service as near you as your telephone.

The Complete Federal-Mogul Replacement Line

Bronze-Back, Babbitt-Lined and Die-Cast Connecting Rod and Main Bearings
(Standard and Undersize)

Piston Pin Bushings

Connecting Rod Bolts and Nuts

Bearing Anchor Screws

Laminum Shims

Bronze Bars and Babbitt Metals

Babbitting Service

Connecting Rod Exchange Service

•

FEDERAL-MOGUL WAREHOUSES

LOS ANGELES, CALIF.	BOSTON, MASS.
236 W. 15th Street	61 Kilnarnock St.
SAN FRANCISCO, CALIF.	DETROIT, MICHIGAN
1710 Howard St.	4809 John R Street
TORONTO, CANADA	KANSAS CITY, MO.
40 Lombard St.	502 E. 18th Street
ATLANTA, GEORGIA	NEW YORK, N. Y.
279 Ivy Street	117 W. 63rd St.
CHICAGO, ILLINOIS	PHILADELPHIA, PA.
2346 So. Dearborn St.	2323 No. 11th St.
INDIANAPOLIS, IND.	DALLAS, TEXAS
19-29 W. South St.	2230 San Jacinto St.

•

WATKINS BABBITTING PLANTS OWNED AND OPERATED BY FEDERAL-MOGUL AT:

SAN FRANCISCO, CALIF.	WICHITA, KANSAS
1710 Howard St.	200 No. Wace Ave.
TORONTO, CANADA	DETROIT, MICHIGAN
40 Lombard St.	4809 John R Street
E. HARTFORD, CONN.	SYRACUSE, N. Y.
251 Connecticut Blvd.	310 W. Taylor Street
ATLANTA, GEORGIA	PHILADELPHIA, PA.
29 Harris St., N.W.	2323 No. 11th St.
CHICAGO, ILLINOIS	PITTSBURGH, PA.
2346 So. Dearborn St.	5706 Harvard St., E.E.
INDIANAPOLIS, IND.	DALLAS, TEXAS
19-29 W. South St.	2230 San Jacinto St.

Licensed Plants: St. Louis, Mo., 4216-18 W. Easton Ave.
Portland, Ore., 14th & Everett Streets

FEDERAL-MOGUL CORPORATION
═══ Operating Watkins Babbitting Service ═══
DETROIT, MICHIGAN

ENGINE ASSEMBLY, Section I—Continued

Interchangeable Parts have the same CHILTON NUMBER in Any Column

Car Make and Model	CRANKSHAFT MAIN BEARINGS				PISTON AND CONNECTING ROD ASSEMBLY				Oil Pump Gears	Flywheel Starter Gears (Ring Gear)
	Front Main Bearing	†Center Main Bearing	Rear Main Bearing	‡Intermediate Main Bearing	Piston (See Footnote)	Piston Pin (See Footnote)	Piston Pin Bushing	Connecting Rod		
Elcar 130-140............(1930)	GKA-46	GKB-49	GKC-47	GKD-46	GL-46	GM-48	GN-42	GO-55	GP-23	GW-13
Erskine 50, Cont. 8F......(1927)	GKA-49	GKB-53	GKC-51	GKB-53	GL-74	GM-57	GN-47	GO-60	GP-2	GW-34
Erskine 51, Cont. 9F......(1928)	GKA-49	GKB-53	GKC-51	GKB-53	GL-75	GM-58	GN-7	GO-60	GP-2	GW-34
Erskine 52, Cont. 9F......(1929)	GKA-49	GKB-53	GKC-51	GKB-53	GL-75	GM-58	GN-7	GO-60	GP-2	GW-34
Erskine 53.............(1930)	GKA-45	GKB-120	GKC-123	GKD-17	GL-54	GM-33	GN-8	GO-193	GP-86	GW-36
Essex 6.................(1925)	GKA-51	GKB-54	GKC-52	None	GL-76	GM-59	GN-50	GO-62 / GO-66	None	GW-35
Essex 6.................(1926)	GKA-51	GKB-54	GKC-52	None	GL-76	GM-59	GN-50	GO-62 / GO-66	None	GW-35
Essex Super 6..........(1927)	GKA-52	GKB-55	GKC-53	None	GL-76	GM-59	GN-50	GO-4 / GO-61	None	GW-35
Essex Super 6..........(1928)	GKA-52	GKB-55	GKC-53	None	GL-76	GM-59	GN-50	GO-63 / GO-64	None	GW-35
Essex Challenger.........(1929)	GKA-53	GKB-56	GKC-54	None	GL-77	GM-59	GN-50	GO-63 / GO-64	None	GW-35
Essex.................(1930)	GKA-44	GKB-66	GKC-65	None	GL-77	GM-59	GN-50	GO-197 / GO-198	None	GW-31
Falcon Knight 10......(1927-28)	GKA-54	GKB-57	GKC-55	GKD-18 / GKD-54	GL-78	GM-60	None	GO-65	GP-66	GW-37
Falcon Knight 12......(1928-29)	GKA-54	GKB-57	GKC-55	GKD-18 / GKD-54	GL-192	GM-161	GN-51	GO-59	GP-66	GW-37
Flint B40, Cont. 7U.....(1925-26)	*GKA-2	*GKB-2	*GKC-2	*GKB-2	GL-2	GM-2	GN-2	GO-2	GP-2	GW-2
Flint E55, Cont. 6E...(1925-26)	*GKA-55	*GKB-58	*GKC-56	*GKD-55	GL-3	GM-3	GN-3	GO-67	GP-2	GW-32
Flint 60, Cont. 14U.......(1926)	*GKA-75	*GKB-38	*GKC-32	*GKD-53	GL-42	GM-40	GN-38	GO-58	GP-2	GW-2
Flint 80, Cont. 6E........(1926)	*GKA-55	*GKB-58	*GKC-56	*GKD-55	GL-3	GM-3	GN-3	GO-67	GP-2	GW-32
Flint Jr., Cont. 9L......(1926)	*GKA-34	*GKB-45	*GKC-45	*GKB-45	GL-43	GM-42	GN-7	GO-192	GP-2	GW-6
Flint 60, Cont. 14U.....(1927-28)	*GKA-75	*GKB-38	*GKC-32	*GKD-53	GL-42	GM-40	GN-38	GO-58	GP-2	GW-2
Flint 80, Cont. 6E.....(1927-28)	*GKA-55	*GKB-58	*GKC-56	*GKD-55	GL-3	GM-3	GN-3	GO-67	GP-2	GW-32
Flint Jr., Cont. 9L......(1927)	*GKA-34	*GKB-45	*GKC-45	*GKB-45	GL-43	GM-42	GN-7	GO-192	GP-2	GW-6
Ford T.................(1925)	GKA-56	GKB-59	GKC-57	None	GL-79	GM-61	GN-53	GO-68	None	GW-32
Ford T.................(1926)	GKA-56	GKB-59	GKC-57	None	GL-79	GM-61	GN-53	GO-68	None	GW-32
Ford T.................(1927)	GKA-56	GKB-59	GKC-57	None	GL-79	GM-61	GN-53	GO-68	None	GW-32
Ford A.................(1928)	GKA-57	GKB-60	GKC-58	None	GL-80	GM-62	GN-54	GO-69	GP-36	GW-15
Ford A.................(1929)	GKA-57	GKB-60	GKC-58	None	GL-80	GM-62	GN-25	GO-194	GP-36	GW-15
Ford A.................(1930)	GKA-57	GKB-60	GKC-58	None	GL-80	GM-62	GN-25	GO-194	GP-36	GW-39
Franklin Series 11........(1925)	GKA-58	GKB-61	GKC-59	GKD-58	GL-81	GM-63	None	GO-70	GP-37	GW-40
Franklin Series 11........(1926)	GKA-58	GKB-61	GKC-59	GKD-58	GL-81	GM-63	None	GO-70	GP-37	GW-40
Franklin Series 11-B......(1927)	GKA-58	GKB-61	GKC-59	GKD-58	GL-81	GM-63	None	GO-71	GP-37	GW-40
Franklin Series 12......(1927-28)	GKA-62	GKB-126	GKC-78	GKD-21	GL-81	GM-63	None	GO-72	GP-38	GW-40
Franklin 130............(1929)	GKA-59	GKB-62	GKC-117	GKD-59	GL-82	GM-64	None	GO-72	GP-38	GW-40
Franklin 135, 137.........(1929)	GKA-59	GKB-62	GKC-60	GKD-59	GL-83	GM-49	None	GO-74	GP-38	GW-40
Franklin 145, 147.........(1930)	GKA-59	GKB-62	GKC-60	GKD-59	GL-56	GM-49	None	GO-74	GP-38	GW-40
Gardner 6-A, Lyc. 4S......(1925)	GKA-7	GKB-7	GKC-7	GKD-7	GL-5	GM-5	GN-4	GO-5	GP-6	GW-5
Gardner 8-A, Lyc. 2H......(1925)	GKA-5	GKB-5	GKC-5	GKD-4 / GKD-5	GL-5	GM-5	None	GO-5	GP-6	GW-5
Gardner Series 5, Lyc. CE.(1925)	GKA-6	GKB-6	GKA-6	GKD-6	GL-40	GM-6	GN-5	GO-7	GP-6	GW-5
Gardner 6B, Lyc. 4SM..(1926-27)	GKA-7	GKB-7	GKC-7	GKB-5	GL-4	GM-4	GN-4	GO-41	GP-6	GW-5
Gardner 8B, Lyc. 4HM.(1926-27)	GKA-5	GKB-5	GKC-5	GKD-4 / GKD-5	GL-4	GM-4	GN-4	GO-41	GP-6	GW-5
Gardner 80, Lyc. GT......(1927)	GKA-8	GKB-9	GKC-9	GKB-165	GL-8	GM-9	GN-4	GO-9	GP-76	GW-2
Gardner 90, Lyc. 4HM......(1927)	GKA-5	GKB-5	GKC-5	GKD-4 / GKD-5	GL-4	GM-4	None	GO-81	GP-76	GW-5
Gardner 75, Lyc. GT......(1928)	GKA-8	GKB-9	GKC-9	GKB-165	GL-8	GM-9	GN-4	GO-9	GP-76	GW-27
Gardner 85, Lyc. GS......(1928)	GKA-8	GKB-9	GKC-9	GKB-165	GL-9	GM-10	None	GO-150	GP-76	GW-27
Gardner 95, Lyc. MD.....(1928)	GKA-5	GKB-5	GKC-5	GKD-4 / GKD-5	GL-10	GM-7	None	GO-10	GP-76	GW-5
Gardner 120, Lyc. GT.....(1929)	GKA-8	GKB-9	GKC-9	GKB-165	GL-8	GM-9	GN-4	GO-9	GP-76	GW-5
Gardner 125, Lyc. GS.....(1929)	GKA-8	GKB-9	GKC-9	GKB-165	GL-9	GM-10	None	GO-150	GP-76	GW-27
Gardner 130, Lyc. MD.....(1929)	GKA-5	GKB-5	GKC-5	GKD-4 / GKD-5	GL-10	GM-7	None	GO-10	GP-76	GW-5
Graham Paige 610......(1928-29)	GKA-60	GKB-63	GKC-61	GKD-61	GL-196	GM-65	None	GO-76	GP-39	GW-6
Graham Paige 614......(1928-29)	GKA-60	GKB-63	GKC-61	GKD-61	GL-69	GM-66	None	GO-76	GP-39	GW-6
Graham Paige 619......(1928-29)	GKA-61	GKB-64	GKC-62	GKD-62	GL-86	GM-67	None	GO-77	GP-39	GW-13
Graham Paige 629......(1928-29)	GKA-61	GKB-64	GKC-63	GKD-62	GL-86	GM-67	None	GO-77	GP-39	GW-13
Gra'm Paige 835, Cont. 12K (1928)	GKA-46	GKB-49	GKC-47	GKD-46	GL-46	GM-48	GN-47	GO-55	GP-23	GW-13
Graham Paige 612...(Early 1929)	GKA-60	GKB-63	GKC-61	GKD-61	GL-89	GM-168	None	GO-79	GP-23	GW-6
Graham Paige 612.....(Late 1929)	GKA-60	GKB-63	GKC-61	GKD-61	GL-69	GM-66	None	GO-79	GP-23	GW-6
Graham Paige 615........(1929)	GKA-60	GKB-63	GKC-61	GKD-61	GL-90	GM-223	None	GO-79	GP-23	GW-26
Graham Paige 621.........(1929)	GKA-61	GKB-64	GKC-62	GKD-62	GL-86	GM-67	None	GO-77	GP-23	GW-13
Gra'm Paige 827, Cnt. 12K (1929)	GKA-46	GKB-49	GKC-47	GKD-46	GL-46	GM-48	GN-47	GO-55	GP-23	GW-13
Gra'm Paige 837, Cnt. 12K (1929)	GKA-46	GKB-49	GKC-47	GKD-46	GL-46	GM-48	GN-47	GO-55	GP-23	GW-13
Graham Std. 6...........(1930)	GKA-60	GKB-63	GKC-61	GKD-61	GL-69	GM-66	None	GO-196	GP-23	GW-26
Graham Spec. 6..........(1930)	GKA-60	GKB-63	GKC-61	GKD-61	GL-90	GM-223	None	GO-79	GP-23	GW-26
Graham Std. and Spec. 8..(1930)	GKA-63	GKB-157	GKC-131	GKD-22	GL-90	GM-223	None	GO-195	GP-23	GW-59
Graham Cust. 8..........(1930)	GKA-46	GKB-49	GKC-47	GKD-46	GL-46	GM-48	GN-47	GO-55	GP-23	GW-13
Hudson Super 6..........(1925)	GKA-65	GKB-68	GKC-66	GKD-65	GL-96	GM-71	GN-64	GO-82	None	GW-12
Hudson Super 6..........(1926)	GKA-65	GKB-68	GKC-66	GKD-65	GL-96	GM-71	GN-64	GO-82	None	GW-12
Hudson Super 6..........(1927)	GKA-65	GKB-68	GKC-66	GKD-65	GL-96	GM-71	GN-27	GO-82	None	GW-12
Hudson Super 6..........(1928)	GKA-66	GKB-69	GKC-67	GKD-66	GL-96	GM-71	GN-27	GO-73 / GO-83	None	GW-12
Hudson Greater 6.........(1929)	GKA-66	GKB-69	GKC-67	GKD-66	GL-96	GM-71	GN-27	GO-73 / GO-83	None	GW-12
Hudson 8..............(1930)	GKA-64	GKB-47	GKC-156	GKD-23	GL-77	GM-59	GN-50	GO-197 / GO-198	None	GW-31
Hupmobile E1.........(1925-26)	GKA-67	GKB-70	GKC-68	GKD-67	GL-97	GM-56	None	GO-84	GP-43	GW-42
Hupmobile R...........(1925)	GKA-68	GKB-71	GKC-69	None	GL-98	GM-73	None	GO-85	GP-44	GW-32
Hupmobile A1...........(1926)	GKA-69	GKB-72	GKC-70	GKD-69	GL-100	GM-74	GN-67	GO-86	GP-45	GW-2
Hupmobile E2.........(1926-27)	GKA-67	GKB-70	GKC-68	GKD-67	GL-99	GM-56	None	GO-84	GP-43	GW-42
Hupmobile A2...........(1927)	GKA-69	GKB-72	GKC-70	GKD-69	GL-100	GM-74	GN-67	GO-86	GP-45	GW-2
Hupmobile E3.........(1927-28)	GKA-67	GKB-70	GKC-68	GKD-67	GL-99	GM-56	None	GO-75	GP-43	GW-42
Hupmobile Century 6.....(1928)	GKA-69	GKB-72	GKC-70	GKD-69	GL-101	GM-75	GN-67	GO-87	GP-45	GW-2
Hupmobile Century 8.....(1928)	GKA-67	GKB-70	GKC-68	GKD-67	GL-102	GM-76	GN-70	GO-88	GP-43	GW-42
Hupmobile Century 125...(1928)	GKA-67	GKB-70	GKC-68	GKD-67	GL-102	GM-76	GN-70	GO-88	GP-43	GW-42
Hupmobile Century 6.....(1929)	GKA-69	GKB-72	GKC-70	GKD-69	GL-101	GM-75	GN-67	GO-87	GP-31	GW-2
Hupmobile M8.........(1928-29)	GKA-71	GKB-163	GKC-159	GKD-24 / GKD-25	GL-102	GM-76	GN-70	GO-88	GP-32	GW-42
Hupmobile S............(1930)	GKA-69	GKB-72	GKC-70	GKD-69	GL-101	GM-75	GN-67	GO-201	GP-31	GW-2
Hupmobile C............(1930)	GKA-73	GKB-158	GKC-157	GKD-30	GL-58	GM-50	GN-70	GO-199 / GO-200	GP-30	GW-57

Footnote: For corresponding piston and pin numbers advertised, see page **187**

ENGINE ASSEMBLY, Section I—Continued

Interchangeable Parts have the same CHILTON NUMBER in Any Column

Car Make and Model	CRANKSHAFT MAIN BEARINGS				PISTON AND CONNECTING ROD ASSEMBLY				Oil Pump Gears	Flywheel Starter Gears (Ring Gear)
	Front Main Bearing	†Center Main Bearing	Rear Main Bearing	‡Intermediate Main Bearing	Piston (See Footnote)	Piston Pin (See Footnote)	Piston Pin Bushing	Connecting Rod		
Hupmobile H, U..........(1930)	GKA-77	GKB-159	GKC-158	GKD-31	GL-59	GM-51	GN-28	GO-202	GP-30	GW-57
Jewett 6-50...............(1925)	GKA-70	GKB-73	GKC-71	None	GL-197	GM-8	None	GO-89	GP-39	GW-43
Jewett New Day, Cont. 18L (1926)	GKA-34	GKB-45	GKC-45	GKB-45	GL-43	GM-42	GN-7	GO-8	GP-2	GW-6
Jordan K, L, Cont. 6S.....(1925)	*GKA-3	*GKB-75	*GKC-72	*GKB-75	GL-225	GM-202	GN-3	GO-3	GP-3	GW-3
Jordan A, Cont. 9K.......(1925)	*GKA-72	*GKB-76	*GKC-73	*GKB-76	GL-45	GM-45	GN-6	GO-90	GP-8	GW-48
Jordan A, Cont. 9K.......(1926)	*GKA-72	*GKB-76	*GKC-73	*GKB-76	GL-45	GM-45	GN-6	GO-90	GP-8	GW-48
Jordan J, Cont. 8S........(1926)	*GKA-36	*GKB-39	*GKC-37	*GKB-39	GL-47	GM-41	GN-40	GO-39	GP-8	GW-21
Jordan AA, Cont. 9K...(1927-28)	*GKA-72	*GKB-76	*GKC-73	*GKB-76	GL-45	GM-45	GN-6	GO-90	GP-8	GW-48
Jordan J, Cont. 8S........(1927)	*GKA-36	*GKB-39	*GKC-37	*GKB-39	GL-47	GM-41	GN-40	GO-39	GP-8	GW-21
Jordan R, Cont. 12E...(1927-28)	*GKA-86	GKB-51	GKC-49	GKD-45	GL-49	GM-47	GN-42	GO-91	GP-28	GW-44
Jordan JJ, Cont. 14S......(1928)	*GKA-36	GKB-39	GKC-37	GKB-39	GL-12	GM-43	GN-40	GO-39	GP-8	GW-21
Jordan JE, Cont. 14S...(1928-29)	*GKA-36	*GKB-39	*GKC-37	*GKB-39	GL-12	GM-43	GN-40	GO-39	GP-8	GW-21
Jordan E, Cont. 16C......(1929)	GKA-35	GKB-37	GKC-36	GKD-35	GL-46	GM-48	GN-42	GO-44	GP-28	GW-21
Jordan G, Cont. 15S......(1929)	GKA-10	GKB-12	GKC-11	GKB-12	GL-12	GM-43	GN-40	GO-39	GP-8	GW-21
Kissel 6-55...............(1925)	GKA-74	GKB-78	GKC-75	GKD-74	GL-111	GM-79	GN-74	GO-92	GP-40	GW-5
Kissel 8-75, Lyc. 3H.......(1925)	GKA-5	GKB-5	GKC-5	{GKD-4 {GKD-5	GL-109	GM-55	GN-4	GO-5	GP-6	GW-5
Kissel 6-55...............(1926)	GKA-74	GKB-78	GKC-75	GKD-74	GL-111	GM-79	GN-74	GO-92	GP-40	GW-5
Kissel 8-75, Lyc. 3H.......(1926)	GKA-5	GKB-5	GKC-5	{GKD-4 {GKD-5	GL-109	GM-55	GN-4	GO-5	GP-6	GW-5
Kissel 6-55...............(1927)	GKA-74	GKB-78	GKC-75	GKD-74	GL-111	GM-79	GN-74	GO-92	GP-40	GW-5
Kissel 8-65, Lyc. GS......(1927)	GKA-8	GKB-9	GKC-9	GKB-165	GL-9	GM-10	None	GO-150	GP-76	GW-27
Kissel 8-75, Lyc. 3H.......(1927)	GKA-5	GKB-5	GKC-5	{GKD-4 {GKD-5	GL-109	GM-55	GN-4	GO-5	GP-76	GW-27
Kissel 6-70, Lyc. WS......(1928)	GKA-8	GKB-165	GKC-9	GKB-9	GL-9	GM-10	None	GO-150	GP-76	GW-27
Kissel 8-80, Lyc. GS......(1928)	GKA-8	GKB-9	GKC-9	GKB-165	GL-9	GM-10	None	GO-150	GP-76	GW-27
Kissel 8-80-S, Lyc. GS....(1928)	GKA-8	GKB-9	GKC-9	GKB-165	GL-9	GM-10	None	GO-150	GP-76	GW-27
Kissel 8-90, Lyc. HM......(1928)	GKA-5	GKB-5	GKC-5	{GKD-4 {GKD-5	GL-4	GM-4	None	GO-5	GP-76	GW-5
Kissel 6-73, Lyc. WR......(1929)	GKA-8	GKB-9	GKC-9	GKB-9	GL-208	GM-10	None	GO 150	GP-76	GW-27
Kissel 8-95, Lyc. GS......(1929)	GKA-8	GKB-9	GKC-9	GKB-165	GL-9	GM-10	None	GO-150	GP-76	GW-27
Kissel 8-126, Lyc. MD.....(1929)	GKA-5	GKB-5	GKC-5	{GKD-4 {GKD-5	GL-10	GM-7	None	GO-10	GP-76	GW-5
La Salle 303...............(1927)	GKA-17	GKB-19	GKC-18	None	GL-22	GM-19	GN-18	GO-22	GP-12	GW-17
La Salle 303...............(1928)	GKA-17	GKB-19	GKC-18	None	GL-222	GM-80	GN-79	GO-22	GP-12	*GW-7
La Salle 328...............(1929)	GKA-17	GKB-19	GKC-18	None	GL-115	GM-20	GN-19	GO-23	GP-12	*GW-7
La Salle 340...............(1930)	GKA-17	GKB-19	GKC-18	None	GL-23	GM-20	GN-19	GO-23	GP-12	GW-8
Lincoln 8.................(1925)	GKA-78	GKB-82	GKC-79	GKD-78	GL-118	GM-82	GN-83	GO-100	GP-49	GW-45
Lincoln 8.................(1926)	GKA-78	GKB-82	GKC-79	GKD-78	GL-118	GM-82	GN-83	GO-100	GP-49	GW-45
Lincoln 8.................(1927)	GKA-78	GKB-82	GKC-79	GKD-78	GL-118	GM-82	GN-83	GO-100	GP-49	GW-45
Lincoln 8.................(1928)	GKA-78	GKB-82	GKC-79	GKD-78	GL-194	GM-164	GN-83	GO-180	GP-49	GW-45
Lincoln 8.................(1929)	GKA-78	GKB-82	GKC-79	GKD-78	GL-194	GM-164	GN-83	GO-180	GP-49	GW-45
Lincoln 8.................(1930)	GKA-78	GKB-82	GKC-79	GKD-78	GL-194	GM-164	GN-83	GO-180	GP-49	GW-45
Locomobile Jr., 8.........(1925)	GKA-80	GKB-84	GKC-81	GKD-80	GL-120	GM-86	GN-84	GO-102	GP-50	GW-48
Locomobile 48............(1925)	GKA-81	GKB-85	GKC-82	GKD-81	GL-121	GM-84	GN-85	GO-103	GP-51	GW-46
Locomobile 48............(1926)	GKA-81	GKB-85	GKC-82	GKD-81	GL-227	GM-230	GN-85	GO-103	GP-51	GW-46
Locomobile 90............(1926)	GKA-82	GKB-86	GKC-83	GKD-82	GL-122	GM-85	GN-86	GO-104	GP-52	GW-48
Locomobile Jr. 8.........(1926)	GKA-80	GKB-84	GKC-81	GKD-80	GL-120	GM-86	GN-84	GO-102	GP-50	GW-48
Locomobile 48............(1927)	GKA-81	GKB-85	GKC-82	GKD-81	GL-227	GM-230	GN-85	GO-103	GP-51	GW-46
Locomobile 8-66...........(1927)	GKA-80	GKB-84	GKC-81	GKD-80	GL-120	GM-86	GN-84	GO-102	GP-50	GW-48
Locomobile 8-80, Lyc. HD.(1927)	GKA-5	GKB-5	GKC-5	{GKD-4 {GKD-5	GL-4	GM-4	None	GO-10	GP-76	GW-5
Locomobile 90............(1928)	GKA-82	GKB-86	GKC-83	GKD-82	GL-122	GM-85	GN-86	GO-104	GP-52	GW-48
Locomobile 48............(1928)	GKA-81	GKB-85	GKC-82	GKD-81	GL-227	GM-230	GN-85	GO-103	GP-51	GW-46
Locomobile 8-80, Lyc. HD.(1928)	GKB-5	GKB-5	GKC-5	{GKD-4 {GKD-5	GL-10	GM-7	None	GO-10	GP-76	GW-5
Locomobile 90............(1928)	GKA-82	GKB-86	GKC-83	GKD-82	GL-122	GM-85	GN-86	GO-104	GP-52	GW-48
Locomo. 8-70, Cont. 8S.(1928-29)	*GKA-36	*GKB-39	*GKC-37	GKB-39	GL-47	GM-41	GN-40	GO-39	GP-8	GW-21
Locomobile 8-80, Lyc. HD.(1929)	GKA-5	GKB-5	GKC-5	{GKD-4 {GKD-5	GL-10	GM-7	None	GO-10	GP-76	GW-5
Locomo. 86, 88, Lyc. HDL.(1929)	GKA-5	GKB-5	GKC-5	{GKD-4 {GKD-5	GL-10	GM-7	None	GO-10	GP-76	GW-5
Locomobile 90............(1929)	GKA-82	GKB-86	GKC-83	GKD-82	GL-122	GM-85	GN-86	GO-104	GP-52	GW-48
Marmon 74................(1925)	GKA-83	GKB-87	GKC-84	GKD-83	GL-34	GM-88	GN-91	GO-105	GP-54	GW-47
Marmon 74................(1926)	GKA-83	GKB-87	GKC-84	GKD-83	GL-34	GM-88	GN-91	GO-105	GP-54	GW-47
Marmon, Little...........(1927)	GKA-84	GKB-88	GKC-85	GKD-84	GL-117	GM-77	GN-92	GO-106	GP-55	GW-44
Marmon E75...............(1927)	GKA-83	GKB-87	GKC-84	GKD-83	GL-123	GM-53	GN-91	GO-107	GP-53	GW-47
Marmon 68................(1928)	GKA-85	GKB-89	GKC-86	GKD-85	GL-60	GM-89	None	GO-108	GP-56	GW-44
Marmon E75...............(1928)	GKA-83	GKB-87	GKC-84	GKD-83	GL-123	GM-53	GN-91	GO-107	GP-53	GW-47
Marmon 78................(1928)	GKA-84	GKB-88	GKC-85	GKD-84	GL-125	GM-8	GN-92	{GO-109 {GO-203	GP-55	GW-44
Marmon 68................(1929)	GKA-85	GKB-89	GKC-86	GKD-85	GL-124	GM-89	None	GO-108	GP-56	GW-66
Marmon 78................(1929)	GKA-84	GKB-88	GKC-85	GKD-84	GL-125	GM-8	GN-92	{GO-109 {GO-203	GP-55	GW-44
Marmon-Roosevelt.....(1929-30)	GKA-85	GKB-89	GKC-86	GKD-85	GL-60	GM-89	None	GO-108	GP-56	GW-66
Marmon 69................(1930)	GKA-85	GKB-89	GKC-86	GKD-85	GL-124	GM-89	None	GO-108	GP-56	GW-66
Marmon 79................(1930)	GKA-110	GKB-164	GKC-152	GKD-32	GL-61	GM-90	GN-29	{GO-204 {GO-205	GP-55	GW-44
Marmon Big 8............(1930)	GKA-110	GKB-164	GKC-152	GKD-32	GL-62	GM-36	GN-29	{GO-204 {GO-205	GP-55	GW-44
Marquette.................(1930)	GKA-79	GKB-83	GKC-153	GKD-33	GL-66	GM-52	GN-30	GO-209	GP-56	GW-26
Maxwell 25................(1925)	GKA-27	GKB-29	GKC-28	None	GL-33	GM-30	None	GO-33	GP-20	GW-24
Moon Series A, Cont. 7Z...(1925)	*GKA-2	*GKB-2	*GKC-2	*GKB-2	GL-113	GM-231	GN-2	GO-2	GP-2	GW-27
Moon Series A, Cont. 7Z...(1926)	*GKA-2	*GKB-2	*GKC-2	*GKB-2	GL-113	GM-231	GN-2	GO-2	GP-2	GW-27
Moon Series A, Cont. 7Z...(1927)	*GKA-2	*GKB-2	*GKC-2	*GKB-2	GL-113	GM-231	GN-2	GO-2	GP-2	GW-27
Moon 6-60, Cont. 26L....(1927)	GKA-140	GKB-8	GKC-8	GKB-8	GL-7	GM-8	GN-7	GO-8	GP-2	GW-27
Moon Series A, Cont. 7Z...(1928)	*GKA-2	*GKB-2	*GKC-2	*GKB-2	GL-113	GM-231	GN-2	GO-2	GP-2	GW-27
Moon 6-60, Cont. 26L....(1928)	GKA-140	GKB-8	GKC-8	GKB-8	GL-7	GM-8	GN-7	GO-8	GP-2	GW-27
Moon 6-72, Cont. 11E....(1928)	GKA-86	GKB-51	GKC-49	GKD-45	GL-46	GM-48	GN-42	GO-91	GP-28	GW-21
Moon, 8-80, Cont. 15S....(1928)	GKA-10	GKB-12	GKC-11	GKB-12	GL-12	GM-43	GN-40	GO-39	GP-8	GW-21
Moon 6-72, Cont. 11E....(1929)	GKA-86	GKB-51	GKC-49	GKD-45	GL-46	GM-48	GN-42	GO-91	GP-28	GW-21
Nash Spec. 6.............(1925)	GKA-89	GKB-92	GKC-89	None	GL-129	GM-94	GN-101	GO-113	GP-58	GW-25
Nash Adv. 6............(1925-26)	GKA-88	GKB-91	GKC-88	None	GL-152	GM-68	GN-100	GO-111	GP-59	GW-25
Nash Adv. 6..............(1926)	GKA-90	GKB-93	GKC-90	GKD-89	GL-128	GM-93	GN-32	GO-111	GP-59	GW-25
Nash Spec. 6.............(1926)	GKA-89	GKB-92	GKC-89	GKD-88	GL-129	GM-94	GN-101	GO-113	GP-58	GW-49
Nash Adv. 6..............(1927)	GKA-90	GKB-93	GKC-90	GKD-89	GL-128	GM-93	GN-32	GO-112	GP-59	GW-49
Nash Spec. 6.............(1927)	GKA-89	GKB-94	GKC-91	GKD-88	GL-213	GM-69	GN-101	GO-114	GP-58	GW-49
Nash Light 6.............(1927)	GKA-1	GKB-1	GKC-1	GKD-1	GL-1	GM-1	GN-1	GO-1	GP-1	GW-1

Footnote: For corresponding piston and pin numbers advertised, see page

ENGINE ASSEMBLY, Section I—Continued

Interchangeable Parts have the same CHILTON NUMBER in Any Column

Car Make and Model	CRANKSHAFT MAIN BEARINGS				PISTON AND CONNECTING ROD ASSEMBLY				Oil Pump Gears	Flywheel Starter Gears (Ring Gear)
	Front Main Bearing	†Center Main Bearing	Rear Main Bearing	‡Intermediate Main Bearing	Piston (See Footnote)	Piston Pin (See Footnote)	Piston Pin Bushing	Connecting Rod		
Nash Adv. 6...............(1928)	GKA-90	GKB-93	GKC-90	GKD-89	GL-128	GM-93	GN-32	GO-112	GP-59	GW-26
Nash Spec. 6..............(1928)	GKA-91	GKB-94	GKC-91	GKD-89	GL-213	GM-69	GN-101	GO-114	GP-58	GW-26
Nash Std. 6...............(1928)	GKA-92	GKB-95	GKC-92	GKD-91	GL-107	GM-97	GN-102	GO-115	GP-1	GW-1
Nash Adv. 6...............(1929)	GKA-90	GKB-93	GKC-90	GKD-89	GL-106	GM-96	GN-33	GO-206	GP-59	GW-26
Nash Spec. 6..............(1929)	GKA-91	GKB-94	GKC-91	GKD-88	GL-105	GM-98	GN-101	GO-207	GP-58	GW-26
Nash Std. 6...............(1929)	GKA-92	GKB-95	GKC-92	GKD-91	GL-91	GM-95	GN-34	GO-208	GP-1	GW-1
Nash Single Ignition 6.....(1930)	GKA-92	GKB-95	GKC-92	GKD-91	GL-63	GM-70	GN-34	GO-210	GP-1	GW-1
Nash Twin Ignition 6......(1930)	GKA-91	GKB-94	GKC-91	GKD-89	GL-64	GM-98	GN-101	GO-211	GP-59	GW-67
Nash Twin Ignition 8......(1930)	GKA-76	GKB-81	GKC-154	GKD-34	GL-65	GM-72	None	GO-212	GP-59	GW-67
Oakland 6-54.............(1925)	GKA-93	GKB-96	GKC-93	None	GL-130	GM-99	GN-103	GO-116	GP-60	GW-32
Oakland 6................(1926)	GKA-93	GKB-96	GKC-93	None	GL-131	GM-100	GN-103	GO-117	GP-60	GW-32
Oakland 6................(1927)	GKA-94	GKB-97	GKC-93	None	GL-131	GM-100	GN-97	GO-117	GP-60	GW-32
Oakland AA-6.............(1928)	GKA-95	GKB-98	GKC-95	GKD-94	GL-132	GM-101	GN-105	GO-118	GP-62	GW-51
Oakland AA-6 (Early).....(1929)	GKA-95	GKB-98	GKC-95	GKD-94	GL-133	GM-102	GN-106	GO-118	GP-62	GW-51
Oakland AA-6 (Late)......(1929)	GKA-95	GKB-98	GKC-95	GKD-94	GL-217	GM-78	GN-106	GO-118	GP-48	GW-51
Oakland 8................(1930)	GKA-87	GKB-134	GKC-155	GKD-36	GL-67	GM-78	GN-35	GO-213	GP-24	GW-68
Oldsmobile C.............(1925)	GKA-96	GKB-99	GKC-96	None	GL-134	GM-103	GN-107	GO-119	GP-63	GW-32
Oldsmobile D.............(1926)	GKA-97	GKB-100	GKC-97	None	GL-134	GM-103	GN-107	GO-110	GP-63	GW-32
Oldsmobile E.............(1927)	GKA-97	GKB-100	GKC-97	None	GL-135	GM-103	GN-107	GO-110	GP-63	GW-32
Oldsmobile F-28..........(1928)	GKA-98	GKB-101	GKC-98	GKD-97	GL-136	GM-104	GN-108	GO-120	GP-64	GW-26
Oldsmobile F-29..........(1929)	GKA-98	GKB-101	GKC-98	GKD-97	GL-136	GM-104	GN-108	GO-120	GP-64	GW-26
Oldsmobile F-30..........(1930)	GKA-98	GKB-101	GKC-98	GKD-97	GL-136	GM-104	GN-108	GO-120	GP-64	GW-26
Overland 91..............(1925)	GKA-99	GKA-99	GKC-99	None	GL-137	GM-105	None	GO-121	None	GW-1
Overland 93..............(1925)	GKA-100	GKB-103	GKC-100	None	GL-138	GM-106	None	GO-122	GP-65	GW-37
Overland 91..............(1926)	GKA-99	GKA-99	GKC-99	None	GL-137	GM-105	None	GO-121	None	GW-1
Overland 93..............(1926)	GKA-100	GKB-103	GKC-100	None	GL-138	GM-106	None	GO-122	GP-65	GW-37
Packard 6 Cyl. 326-333....(1925)	GKA-104	GKB-107	GKC-104	GKD-37 GKD-103	GL-140	GM-109	GN-112	GO-125	GP-67	GW-12
Packard 8 Cyl. 236-243....(1925)	GKA-104	GKB-107	GKC-104	GKD-37 GKD-103	GL-141	GM-110	GN-112	GO-125	GP-67	GW-12
Packard 6 Cyl. 326-333....(1926)	GKA-149	GKB-151	GKC-80	GKD-38 GKD-39	GL-140	GM-109	GN-112	GO-126	GP-67	GW-12
Packard 8 Cyl. 236-243....(1926)	GKA-149	GKB-151	GKC-80	GKD-39 GKD-42	GL-141	GM-110	GN-112	GO-126	GP-67	GW-12
Packard 6 Cyl. 426-433....(1927)	GKA-149	GKB-151	GKC-148	GKD-38 GKD-39	GL-140	GM-109	GN-112	GO-127	GP-67	GW-12
Packard 8 Cyl. 336-343....(1927)	GKA-149	GKB-151	GKC-148	GKD-39 GKD-42	GL-140	GM-109	GN-112	GO-127	GP-67	GW-12
Packard 526, 533.........(1928)	GKA-103	GKB-154	GKC-148	GKD-38 GKD-43	GL-142	GM-109	GN-112	GO-127	GP-25	GW-12
Packard Std. 8 Cyl. 443....(1928)	GKA-103	GKB-154	GKC-148	GKD-42 GKD-47	GL-142	GM-109	GN-112	GO-127	GP-25	GW-12
Packard 626, 633.........(1929)	GKA-150	GKB-152	GKC-149	GKD-48 GKD-49	GL-179	GM-90	GN-112	GO-128	GP-25	GW-12
Packard 640, 645.........(1929)	GKA-151	GKB-153	GKC-150	GKD-50 GKD-51	GL-142	GM-109	GN-112	GO-130	GP-25	GW-12
Packard 726, 733.........(1930)	GKA-105	GKB-155	GKC-151	GKD-56 GKD-57	GL-179	GM-90	GN-112	GO-214	GP-25	GW-12
Packard 740, 745.........(1930)	GKA-117	GKB-156	GKC-160	GKD-70 GKD-71	GL-142	GM-109	GN-112	GO-215	GP-25	GW-12
Paige 6-70, Cont. 10A...(1925-26)	*GKA-31	*GKB-10	*GKC-31	*GKB-10	GL-24	GM-21	GN-20	GO-24	GP-3	GW-24
Paige 6-72...............(1926)	GKA-70	GKB-73	GKC-71	GKD-105	GL-215	GM-111	GN-114	GO-132	GP-39	GW-43
Paige 6-45, Cont. 19L'..(1927-28)	GKA-140	GKB-8	GKC-8	GKB-8	GL-7	GM-8	GN-7	GO-8	GP-2	GW-17
Paige 6-65..............(1927-28)	GKA-70	GKB-73	GKC-71	GKD-105	GL-215	GM-111	GN-20	GO-89	GP-39	GW-43
Paige 6-75..............(1927-28)	GKA-70	GKB-73	GKC-71	GKD-105	GL-145	GM-113	GN-20	GO-89	GP-39	GW-43
Paige 8-85, Lyc. MD...(1927-28)	GKA-5	GKB-5	GKC-5	GKD-4 GKD-5	GL-10	GM-7	None	GO-10	GP-76	GW-5
Peerless 70..............(1925)	GKA-107	GKB-110	GKC-107	GKD-106	GL-114	GM-114	GN-117	GO-133	GP-26	GW-12
Peerless 80, Cont. 8U....(1926)	*GKA-35	*GKB-37	*GKC-36	*GKD-35	GL-42	GM-40	GN-38	GO-44	GP-2	GW-2
Peerless 69..............(1926)	GKA-108	GKB-111	GKC-108	None	GL-147	GM-115	GN-118	GO-134	GP-68	GW-43
Peerless 6-60............(1927)	GKA-86	GKB-51	GKC-49	GKD-45	GL-49	GM-47	GN-42	GO-91	GP-28	GW-44
Peerless 69..............(1927)	GKA-108	GKB-111	GKC-108	None	GL-147	GM-115	GN-118	GO-134	GP-68	GW-43
Peerless 80, 8U..........(1927)	GKA-35	GKB-37	GKC-36	GKD-35	GL-42	GM-40	GN-38	GO-44	GP-28	GW-2
Peerless 90............(1927-28)	GKA-107	GKB-110	GKC-107	GKD-106	GL-84	GM-116	GN-36	GO-135	GP-26	GW-12
Peerless 72..............(1928)	GKA-107	GKB-110	GKC-107	GKD-106	GL-146	GM-112	GN-36	GO-135	GP-26	GW-12
Peerless 60, Cont. 10E.....(1928)	GKA-86	GKB-51	GKC-49	GKD-45	GL-49	GM-47	GN-42	GO-91	GP-28	GW-44
Peerless 69..............(1928)	GKA-108	GKB-111	GKC-108	None	GL-147	GM-115	GN-118	GO-134	GP-68	GW-43
Peerless 80, Cont. 8U.....(1928)	GKA-35	GKB-37	GKC-36	GKD-35	GL-42	GM-40	GN-38	GO-44	GP-2	GW-2
Peerless 91..............(1928)	GKA-107	GKB-110	GKC-107	GKD-106	GL-84	GM-116	GN-36	GO-135	GP-26	GW-12
Peerless 61, Cont. 11E.....(1929)	GKA-86	GKB-51	GKC-49	GKD-45	GL-46	GM-48	GN-42	GO-91	GP-28	GW-44
Peerless 81, Cont. 18C.....(1929)	GKA-35	GKB-37	GKC-36	GKD-35	GL-46	GM-48	GN-42	GO-44	GP-13	GW-2
Peerless 91..............(1929)	GKA-107	GKB-110	GKC-107	GKD-106	GL-84	GM-116	GN-36	GO-135	GP-26	GW-12
Peerless 125, Cont. 12K....(1929)	GKA-46	GKB-49	GKC-47	GKD-46	GL-46	GM-48	GN-42	GO-55	GP-23	GW-13
Peerless A, Cont. 17S.....(1930)	GKA-106	GKB-160	GKC-110	GKD-72	GL-50	GM-43	GN-37	GO-216	GP-5	GW-70
Peerless B, C............(1930)	GKA-46	GKB-49	GKC-47	GKD-47	GL-46	GM-48	GN-42	GO-55	GP-23	GW-13
Pierce Arrow 80..........(1925)	GKA-111	GKB-114	GKC-111	GKD-110	GL-149	GM-118	GN-121	GO-138	GP-69	GW-3
Pierce Arrow 33..........(1926)	GKA-112	GKB-115	GKC-112	GKD-111	GL-150	GM-119	GN-122	GO-139	GP-70	GW-58
Pierce Arrow 80..........(1926)	GKA-111	GKB-114	GKC-111	GKD-110	GL-149	GM-118	GN-121	GO-124	GP-69	GW-3
Pierce Arrow 36..........(1927)	GKA-112	GKB-115	GKC-112	GKD-111	GL-150	GM-119	GN-122	GO-139	GP-70	GW-58
Pierce Arrow 80..........(1927)	GKA-111	GKB-114	GKC-111	GKD-110	GL-149	GM-118	GN-121	GO-124	GP-69	GW-3
Pierce Arrow 36..........(1928)	GKA-112	GKB-115	GKC-112	GKD-111	GL-150	GM-119	GN-122	GO-139	GP-70	GW-58
Pierce Arrow 81..........(1928)	GKA-118	GKB-109	GKC-109	GKD-75	GL-151	GM-120	GN-124	GO-140	GP-69	GW-3
Pierce Arrow 133, 143....(1929)	GKA-113	GKB-116	GKC-113	GKD-112	GL-178	GM-147	None	GO-141	GP-57	GW-60
Pierce Arrow A & B......(1930)	GKA-113	GKB-116	GKC-113	GKD-112	GL-178	GM-147	None	GO-141	GP-82	GW-60
Pierce Arrow C..........(1930)	GKA-113	GKB-116	GKC-113	GKD-112	GL-68	GM-81	None	GO-141	GP-82	GW-60
Plymouth 4 Cyl...........(1929)	GKA-27	GKB-29	GKC-28	None	GL-33	GM-30	None	GO-33	GP-20	GW-24
Plymouth................(1930)	GKA-27	GKB-29	GKC-28	None	GL-33	GM-30	None	GO-217	GP-20	GW-23
Pontiac 6................(1926)	GKA-114	GKB-117	GKC-114	None	GL-233	GM-101	GN-105	GO-142	GP-71	GW-21
Pontiac 6................(1927)	GKA-114	GKB-117	GKC-114	None	GL-233	GM-101	GN-105	GO-143	GP-71	GW-21
Pontiac 6................(1928)	GKA-114	GKB-117	GKC-114	None	GL-233	GM-101	GN-105	GO-143	GP-34	GW-21
Pontiac Big 6............(1929)	GKA-114	GKB-117	GKC-114	None	GL-154	GM-122	GN-106	GO-143	GP-34	GW-21
Pontiac.................(1930)	GKA-114	GKB-117	GKC-114	None	GL-70	GM-122	GN-106	GO-143	GP-34	GW-21
Reo T6..................(1925)	GKA-115	GKB-118	GKC-115	GKB-118	GL-155	GM-123	GN-127	GO-144	None	None
Reo T6................(1926-27)	GKA-115	GKB-118	GKC-115	GKB-118	GL-155	GM-123	GN-127	GO-144	None	None
Reo Flying Cloud........(1927)	GKA-116	GKB-119	GKC-116	GKD-115	GL-156	GM-124	None	GO-145	GP-72	GW-24
Reo Wolverine, Cont. 15E. (1927)	GKA-86	GKB-51	GKC-49	GKD-45	GL-49	GM-47	GN-42	GO-91	GP-28	GW-44
Reo Flying Cloud........(1928)	GKA-116	GKB-119	GKC-116	GKD-115	GL-156	GM-124	None	GO-145	GP-72	GW-24
Reo Wolverine, Cont. 15E. (1928)	GKA-86	GKB-51	GKC-49	GKD-45	GL-49	GM-47	GN-42	GO-91	GP-28	GW-44

Footnote: For corresponding piston and pin numbers advertised, see page

187

ENGINE ASSEMBLY, Section I—Continued

Interchangeable Parts have the same CHILTON NUMBER in Any Column

Car Make and Model	CRANKSHAFT MAIN BEARINGS				PISTON AND CONNECTING ROD ASSEMBLY				Oil Pump Gears	Flywheel Starter Gears (Ring Gear)
	Front Main Bearing	†Center Main Bearing	Rear Main Bearing	‡Intermediate Main Bearing	Piston (See Footnote)	Piston Pin (See Footnote)	Piston Pin Bushing	Connecting Rod		
Reo Flying Cloud Master..(1929)	GKA-116	GKB-119	GKC-116	GKD-115	GL-157	GM-232	None	GO-218	GP-35	GW-24
Reo F. C. Mate, Cnt. 16E (1929)	GKA-86	GKB-51	GKC-49	GKD-45	GL-46	GM-48	GN-42	GO-91	GP-28	GW-44
Reo 15 Cont. 19E.........(1930)	GKA-86	GKB-51	GKC-49	GKD-45	GL-46	GM-48	GN-42	GO-91	GP-28	GW-44
Reo 20 and 25.........(1930)	GKA-116	GKB-119	GKC-116	GKD-115	GL-157	GM-232	None	GO-218	GP-35	GW-24
Rickenbacker D6.........(1925)	GKA-120	GKB-122	GKC-120	GKD-119	GL-160	GM-126	GN-131	GO-148	GP-74	GW-2
Rickenbacker 8-B......(1925-26)	GKA-120	GKB-122	GKC-120	GKD-119	GL-160	GM-127	GN-131	GO-149	GP-74	GW-2
Rickenbacker 6-E.........(1926)	GKA-120	GKB-122	GKC-120	GKD-119	GL-160	GM-126	GN-132	GO-149	GP-74	GW-2
Rickenbacker 6-70.........(1927)	GKA-120	GKB-122	GKC-120	GKD-119	GL-160	GM-126	GN-132	GO-149	GP-74	GW-2
Rickenbacker 8-80.........(1927)	GKA-120	GKB-122	GKC-120	GKD-119	GL-160	GM-129	GN-132	GO-149	GP-74	GW-2
Rickenbacker 8-90.........(1927)	GKA-120	GKB-122	GKC-120	GKD-119	GL-160	GM-127	GN-132	GO-149	GP-74	GW-2
Roamer 6-54-E...........(1925)	GKA-122	GKB-125	GKC-122	GKD-121	GL-162	GM-132	GN-135	GO-151	GP-3	GW-61
Roamer 8-88, Lyc. 3H.....(1925)	GKA-5	GKB-5	GKC-5	GKD-4 GKD-5	GL-109	GM-55	None	GO-5	GP-76	GW-5
Roamer 6-50, Cont. 7U..(1925-26)	*GKA-2	*GKB-2	*GKC-2	*GKB-2	GL-2	GM-2	GN-2	GO-2	GP-2	GW-2
Roamer 8-88, Lyc. 3H.....(1926)	GKA-5	GKB-5	GKC-5	GKD-4 GKD-5	GL-4	GM-4	GN-4	GO-5	GP-76	GW-5
Roamer 8-78, Lyc. GT....(1927)	GKA-8	GKB-9	GKC-9	GKB-165	GL-8	GM-9	GN-4	GO-9	GP-76	GW-27
Roamer 8-80, Lyc. 4HM(1926-27)	GKA-5	GKB-5	GKC-5	GKD-4 GKD-5	GL-4	GM-4	GN-4	GO-41	GP-76	GW-5
Roamer 8-88, Lyc. 4H.....(1927)	GKA-5	GKB-5	GKC-5	GKD-4 GKD-5	GL-4	GM-4	GN-4	GO-5	GP-76	GW-5
Roamer 8-78, Lyc. GT.....(1928)	GKA-8	GKB-9	GKC-9	GKB-165	GL-8	GM-9	GN-4	GO-9	GP-76	GW-27
Roamer 8-80, Lyc. 4HM...(1928)	GKA-5	GKB-5	GKC-5	GKD-4 GKD-5	GL-4	GM-4	None	GO-81	GP-76	GW-5
Roamer 8-88, Lyc. 4H.....(1928)	GKA-5	GKB-5	GKC-5	GKD-4 GKD-5	GL-4	GM-4	None	GO-81	GP-76	GW-5
Roamer 8-78, Lyc. GT.....(1929)	GKA-8	GKB-9	GKC-9	GKB-165	GL-8	GM-9	GN-4	GO-9	GP-76	GW-27
Roamer 8-80, Lyc. 4HM...(1929)	GKA-5	GKB-5	GKC-5	GKD-4 GKD-5	GL-4	GM-4	None	GO-81	GP-76	GW-5
Roamer 8-88, Lyc. 4H.....(1929)	GKA-5	GKB-5	GKC-5	GKD-4 GKD-5	GL-4	GM-4	None	GO-81	GP-76	GW-5
Star F, Cont. W5.........(1925)	*GKA-48	*GKB-52	*GKC-50	None	GL-57	GM-44	GN-49	GO-57	GP-2	GW-15
Star M, Cont. W5........(1926)	*GKA-48	*GKB-52	*GKC-50	None	GL-57	GM-44	GN-49	GO-57	GP-2	GW-15
Star R, Cont. 14L.........(1926)	GKA-140	GKB-8	GKC-8	GKB-8	GL-43	GM-42	GN-7	GO-8	GP-2	GW-15
Star M, Cont. W5......(1927-28)	*GKA-48	*GKB-52	*GKC-50	None	GL-57	GM-44	GN-49	GO-57	GP-2	GW-15
Star R, Cont. 14L......(1927-28)	GKA-140	GKB-8	GKC-8	GKB-8	GL-43	GM-42	GN-7	GO-8	GP-2	GW-15
Stearns Knight B, 4 Cyl....(1925)	GKA-125	GKB-128	GKC-125	GKD-124	GL-169	GM-135	GN-139	GO-155	GP-77	GW-64
Stearns Knight C, 6 Cyl....(1925)	GKA-126	GKB-129	GKC-126	GKD-125	GL-170	GM-137	GN-140	GO-156	GP-78	GW-65
Stearns Knight S, 6 Cyl....(1925)	GKA-124	GKB-127	GKC-124	GKD-123	GL-168	GM-134	GN-141	GO-154	GP-92	GW-71
Stearns Knight B, 4 Cyl....(1926)	GKA-125	GKB-128	GKC-125	GKD-124	GL-169	GM-135	GN-139	GO-155	GP-77	GW-64
Stearns Knight C-75.......(1926)	GKA-126	GKB-129	GKC-126	GKD-125	GL-170	GM-137	GN-140	GO-156	GP-78	GW-65
Stearns Knight S-95.......(1926)	GKA-124	GKB-127	GKC-124	GKD-123	GL-171	GM-134	GN-141	GO-154	GP-92	GW-71
Stearns Knight F-6-85.....(1927)	GKA-129	GKB-132	GKC-129	GKD-128	GL-171	GM-134	GN-144	GO-99	GP-79	GW-65
Stearns Knight G-8-85..(1927-28)	GKA-127	GKB-130	GKC-127	GKD-126	GL-171	GM-134	GN-144	GO-157	GP-80	GW-60
Stearns Knight F-6-85.....(1928)	GKA-129	GKB-132	GKC-129	GKD-128	GL-171	GM-134	GN-144	GO-99	GP-79	GW-65
Stearns Knight H, J 8-90..(1928)	GKA-127	GKB-130	GKC-127	GKD-126	GL-171	GM-134	GN-144	GO-157	GP-80	GW-65
Stearns Kni. M, N 6-80.(1928-29)	GKA-130	GKB-133	GKC-130	GKD-129	GL-172	GM-142	GN-145	GO-159	GP-81	GW-32
Stearns Knight H, J, 8-90..(1929)	GKA-127	GKB-130	GKC-127	GKD-126	GL-171	GM-134	GN-144	GO-157	GP-80	GW-65
Studebaker Spec. 6........(1925)	GKA-132	GKB-135	GKC-132	GKD-131	GL-175	GM-145	GN-148	GO-161	GP-83	None
Studebaker Std. 6.........(1925)	GKA-133	GKB-136	GKC-133	GKD-132	GL-176	GM-146	GN-149	GO-162	GP-84	GW-12
Studebaker Big 6.......(1925-26)	GKA-132	GKB-135	GKC-132	GKD-131	GL-174	GM-144	GN-147	GO-161	GP-83	None
Studebaker Std. 6.........(1926)	GKA-133	GKB-136	GKC-133	GKD-132	GL-176	GM-146	GN-149	GO-162	GP-84	GW-12
Studebaker Spec. 6........(1926)	GKA-132	GKB-135	GKC-132	GKD-131	GL-175	GM-145	GN-148	GO-161	GP-83	None
Studebaker Big 6.........(1927)	GKA-132	GKB-135	GKC-132	GKD-131	GL-174	GM-144	GN-147	GO-161	GP-83	None
Studebaker Spec. 6........(1927)	GKA-132	GKB-135	GKC-132	GKD-131	GL-175	GM-145	GN-148	GO-161	GP-83	None
Studebaker Std. 6.........(1927)	GKA-133	GKB-136	GKC-133	GKD-132	GL-176	GM-146	GN-149	GO-162	GP-84	GW-12
Studebaker Com. 6........(1928)	GKA-134	GKB-137	GKC-134	GKD-133	GL-174	GM-144	GN-147	GO-161	GP-85	None
Studebaker Dict. 6........(1928)	GKA-135	GKB-138	GKC-135	GKD-134	GL-218	GM-146	GN-145	GO-93 GO-94	GP-86	GW-12
Studebaker Pres. 8........(1928)	GKA-136	GKB-139	GKC-136	GKD-135	GL-68	GM-81	None	GO-95 GO-163	GP-87	GW-15
Studebaker Com. 6........(1929)	GKA-134	GKB-137	GKC-134	GKD-133	GL-218	GM-146	GN-149	GO-96	GP-86	GW-30
Studebaker Com. 8........(1929)	GKA-137	GKB-140	GKC-137	GKD-136	GL-112	GM-148	GN-24	GO-165	GP-93	GW-30
Studebaker Dict. 6........(1929)	GKA-135	GKB-138	GKC-135	GKD-134	GL-218	GM-146	GN-145	GO-98	GP-86	GW-30
Studebaker Pres. 8........(1929)	GKA-136	GKB-139	GKC-136	GKD-135	GL-178	GM-147	None	GO-163	GP-87	GW-15
Studebaker Dict. 6........(1930)	GKA-135	GKB-138	GKC-135	GKD-134	GL-218	GM-146	GN-145	GO-129	GP-86	GW-30
Studebaker Dict. 8........(1930)	GKA-137	GKB-140	GKC-137	GKD-136	GL-112	GM-148	GN-24	GO-136	GP-93	GW-30
Studebaker Com. 6........(1930)	GKA-135	GKB-138	GKC-135	GKD-134	GL-218	GM-146	GN-149	GO-96	GP-86	GW-30
Studebaker Com. 8........(1930)	GKA-137	GKB-140	GKC-137	GKD-136	GL-112	GM-148	GN-24	GO-165	GP-93	GW-30
Studebaker Pres. 8........(1930)	GKA-136	GKB-139	GKC-136	GKD-135	GL-178	GM-147	None	GO-163	GP-87	GW-15
Studebaker 6...........(1930)	GKA-45	GKB-120	GKC-122	GKD-17	GL-54	GM-33	GN-8	GO-193	GP-86	GW-36
Stutz 695..............(1925)	GKA-138	GKB-141	GKC-138	None	GL-180	GM-150	GN-137	GO-166	GP-88	GW-3
Stutz AA.............(1926)	GKA-9	GKB-11	GKC-10	GKD-9	GL-181	GM-151	GN-12	GO-167	GP-89	GW-9
Stutz AA.............(1927)	GKA-9	GKB-11	GKC-10	GKD-9	GL-182	GM-151	GN-12	GO-167	GP-89	GW-9
Stutz BB.............(1928)	GKA-9	GKB-11	GKC-10	GKD-9	GL-182	GM-151	GN-12	GO-168	GP-89	GW-9
Stutz Series M...........(1929)	GKA-9	GKB-11	GKC-10	GKD-9	GL-11	GM-11	GN-12	GO-12	GP-89	GW-12
Stutz M..............(1930)	GKA-9	GKB-11	GKC-10	GKD-9	GL-11	GM-11	GN-12	GO-12	GP-89	GW-12
Velie 60...............(1925)	GKA-141	GKB-143	GKC-140	GKB-143	GL-184	GM-154	GN-155	GO-164	GP-90	GW-3
Velie 60...............(1926)	GKA-141	GKB-143	GKC-140	GKB-143	GL-184	GM-154	GN-155	GO-164	GP-90	GW-3
Velie Spec. 60..........(1927-28)	GKA-141	GKB-143	GKC-140	GKB-143	GL-185	GM-154	GN-155	GO-163	GP-90	GW-3
Velie Std. 50...........(1927-28)	GKA-4	GKB-4	GKC-4	None	GL-186	GM-154	GN-155	GO-6	GP-4	GW-2
Velie 6-66............(1928)	GKA-141	GKB-143	GKC-140	GKB-143	GL-184	GM-154	GN-155	GO-137	GP-90	GW-3
Velie 6-77............(1928)	GKA-141	GKB-143	GKC-140	GKB-143	GL-185	GM-154	GN-155	GO-51	GP-90	GW-3
Velie 88, Lyc. 4HM......(1928)	GKA-5	GKB-5	GKC-5	GKD-4 GKD-5	GL-4	GM-4	None	GO-10	GP-76	GW-5
Viking...............(1929-30)	GKA-142	GKB-144	GKC-141	None	GL-187	GM-157	GN-156	GO-170	GP-64	GW-19
Westcott 44, Cont. 8 R....(1925)	GKA-3	GKB-3	GKC-3	GKB-3	GL-3	GM-3	GN-3	GO-3	GP-3	GW-3
Westcott 60, Cont. 8 R....(1925)	GKA-3	GKB-3	GKC-3	GKB-3	GL-3	GM-3	GN-3	GO-3	GP-3	GW-3
Whippet 96, 4 Cyl........(1927)	GKA-101	GKB-104	GKC-101	None	GL-139	GM-107	None	GO-123	GP-66	GW-35
Whippet 93-A.....(1927)	GKA-100	GKB-103	GKC-100	None	GL-138	GM-106	None	GO-122	GP-65	GW-37
Whippet 96, 4 Cyl........(1928)	GKA-101	GKB-104	GKC-101	None	GL-220	GM-108	None	GO-123	GP-66	GW-35
Whippet 98, 6 Cyl........(1928)	GKA-102	GKB-105	GKC-102	GKB-105 GKC-102	GL-220	GM-108	GN-111	GO-176	GP-65	GW-55
Whippet 96-A.........(1929-30)	GKA-121	GKB-106	GKC-102	None	GL-220	GM-108	GN-111	GO-42	GP-66	GW-35
Whippet 98-A.........(1929-30)	GKA-102	GKB-105	GKC-102	GKB-105 GKC-102	GL-220	GM-108	GN-111	GO-176	GP-65	GW-55
Wills Ste. Claire 8.........(1925)	GKA-148	GKB-150	GKC-147	None	GL-193	GM-163	GN-163	GO-179	GP-94	GW-32

Footnote: For corresponding piston and pin numbers advertised, see page **187**

ENGINE ASSEMBLY, Section 1—Continued

Interchangeable Parts have the same CHILTON NUMBER in Any Column

Car Make and Model	CRANKSHAFT MAIN BEARINGS				PISTON AND CONNECTING ROD ASSEMBLY				Oil Pump Gears	Flywheel Starter Gears (Ring Gear)
	Front Main Bearing	†Center Main Bearing	Rear Main Bearing	‡Intermediate Main Bearing	Piston (See Foot-note)	Piston Pin (See Foot-note)	Piston Pin Bushing	Connecting Rod		
Wills Ste. Claire 6......(1925-26)	GKA-147	GKB-149	GKC-146	GKD-145	GL-193	GM-162	GN-163	GO-178	GP-95	GW-38
Wills Ste. Claire 8........(1926)	GKA-148	GKB-150	GKC-147	None	GL-193	GM-163	GN-163	GO-179	GP-94	GW-32
Willys 6.................(1930)	GKA-131	GKB-161	GKC-105	GKD-60	GL-71	GM-91	GN-111	GO-53	GP-97	GW-56
Willys 8.................(1930)	GKA-123	GKB-162	GKC-106	GKD-52	GL-72	GM-92	GN-44	GO-36	GP-98	GW-56
Willys Knight 66..........(1925)	GKA-143	GKB-146	GKC-143	GKD-63 GKD-64	GL-189	GM-158	None	GO-171	GP-91	GW-38
Willys Knight 65..........(1925)	GKA-128	GKB-145	GKC-142	None	GL-188	GM-166	GN-157	GO-43	GP-96	GW-38
Willys Knight 66..........(1926)	GKA-143	GKB-146	GKC-143	GKD-63 GKD-64	GL-189	GM-158	None	GO-171	GP-91	GW-38
Willys Knight 70........(1926)	GKA-102	GKB-105	GKC-102	GKB-105 GKC-102	GL-78	GM-60	GN-111	GO-173	GP-96	GW-37
Willys Knight 66-A.......(1927)	GKA-143	GKB-146	GKC-143	GKD-63 GKD-64	GL-189	GM-158	None	GO-174	GP-97	GW-38
Willys Knight 70-A.......(1927)	GKA-102	GKB-105	GKC-102	GKB-105 GKC-102	GL-190	GM-160	GN-111	GO-175	GP-66	GW-37
Willys Knight Std. 6-56.(1928-29)	GKA-102	GKB-105	GKC-102	GKB-105 GKC-102	GL-192	GM-161	GN-111	GO-176	GP-66	GW-37
Willys Kni. Sp. 6-70A...(1928-29)	GKA-102	GKB-105	GKC-102	GKB-105 GKC-102	GL-192	GM-161	GN-111	GO-175	GP-66	GW-37
Willys Knight 66-A.....(1928-29)	GKA-143	GKB-146	GKC-143	GKD-63 GKD-64	GL-191	GM-159	None	GO-52	GP-97	GW-38
Willys Knight 70-B.......(1929)	GKA-102	GKB-105	GKC-102	GKB-105 GKC-102	GL-192	GM-161	GN-111	GO-175	GP-66	GW-37
Willys Knight 66D........(1930)	GKA-143	GKB-146	GKC-143	GKD-63 GKD-64	GL-191	GM-159	GN-43	GO-52	GP-97	GW-38
Willys Knight 70-B.......(1930)	GKA-102	GKB-105	GKC-102	GKB-105 GKC-102	GL-192	GM-161	GN-111	GO-175	GP 66	GW-37

  ° GW-7, Starter gear on clutch.
  * Block bearing only, cap is babbitted.
  † When no crankshaft center main bearing is used, as in engines with four main bearings, the Chilton number in the third column refers to number two main bearing, or the second one from the front.
  ‡ When no crankshaft center main bearing is used, as in engines with four main bearings, the Chilton number in the fifth column refers to number three bearing, or the third one from the front

Key of Engine Abbreviations
Ans.—Ansted.   Cont., Ct.—Continental.   Lyc.—Lycoming.   Wisc.—Wisconsin.

INTERCHANGEABLE COUNT

Showing the exact number of times each Chilton Number occurs in the Engine Table, Section 1, beginning Page 186.

Front Main Bearing	GKA 52-2	GKA 105-1	GKB 8-22	GKB 71-1	GKB 136-3	GKB 137-2	GKC 22-2	GKC 83-4	GKC 143-5

Front Main Bearing
GKA 52-2
GKA 53-1
GKA 54-2

GKA 1-2
GKA 2-9
GKA 3-8
GKA 4-2
GKA 5-37
GKA 6-5
GKA 7-5
GKA 8-26
GKA 9-7
GKA 10-4
GKA 11-4
GKA 12-2
GKA 13-2
GKA 14-3
GKA 15-1
GKA 16-5
GKA 17-7
GKA 18-1
GKA 19-1
GKA 20-3
GKA 21-2
GKA 22-5
GKA 23-4
GKA 24-4
GKA 25-2
GKA 26-3
GKA 27-6
GKA 28-5
GKA 29-8
GKA 30-2
GKA 31-2
GKA 32-1
GKA 33-1
GKA 34-4
GKA 35-10
GKA 36-7
GKA 37-4
GKA 38-3
GKA 39-3
GKA 40-2
GKA 41-3
GKA 42-1
GKA 43-2
GKA 44-1
GKA 45-2
GKA 46-7
GKA 47-1
GKA 48-6
GKA 49-3
GKA 51-2

GKA 55-3
GKA 56-3
GKA 57-3
GKA 58-3
GKA 59-3
GKA 60-7
GKA 61-3
GKA 62-1
GKA 63-1
GKA 64-1
GKA 65-3
GKA 66-2
GKA 67-5
GKA 68-1
GKA 69-5
GKA 70-4
GKA 71-1
GKA 72-3
GKA 73-1
GKA 74-3
GKA 75-2
GKA 76-1
GKA 77-1
GKA 78-6
GKA 79-1
GKA 80-3
GKA 81-4
GKA 82-4
GKA 83-4
GKA 84-4
GKA 85-4
GKA 86-1
GKA 87-1
GKA 88-1
GKA 89-2
GKA 90-4
GKA 91-4
GKA 92-3
GKA 93-2
GKA 94-1
GKA 95-3
GKA 96-1
GKA 97-2
GKA 98-3
GKA 99-4
GKA 100-3
GKA 101-2
GKA 102-8
GKA 103-2
GKA 104-2

GKA 106-1
GKA 107-5
GKA 108-3
GKA 110-2
GKA 111-3
GKA 112-3
GKA 113-3
GKA 114-5
GKA 115-2
GKA 116-4
GKA 117-1
GKA 118-1
GKA 120-6
GKA 121-1
GKA 122-1
GKA 123-1
GKA 124-2
GKA 125-2
GKA 126-2
GKA 127-3
GKA 128-1
GKA 129-2
GKA 130-1
GKA 131-1
GKA 132-5
GKA 133-3
GKA 134-2
GKA 135-4
GKA 136-3
GKA 137-3
GKA 138-1
GKA 139-4
GKA 140-11
GKA 141-5
GKA 142-1
GKA 143-5
GKA 144-1
GKA 147-1
GKA 148-2
GKA 149-4
GKA 150-1
GKA 151-1

Center Main Bearing
GKB 1-2
GKB 2-18
GKB 3-14
GKB 4-3
GKB 5-45
GKB 6-5
GKB 7-5

GKB 9-28
GKB 10-4
GKB 11-7
GKB 12-8
GKB 13-4
GKB 14-2
GKB 15-2
GKB 16-3
GKB 17-8
GKB 19-7
GKB 20-2
GKB 21-1
GKB 22-3
GKB 23-4
GKB 24-5
GKB 25-3
GKB 26-4
GKB 27-2
GKB 28-3
GKB 29-6
GKB 30-7
GKB 34-2
GKB 35-1
GKB 37-10
GKB 38-2
GKB 39-14
GKB 40-8
GKB 41-6
GKB 42-6
GKB 43-2
GKB 44-3
GKB 45-7
GKB 47-1
GKB 49-7
GKB 50-1
GKB 51-10
GKB 52-5
GKB 53-6
GKB 54-2
GKB 55-2
GKB 56-1
GKB 57-2
GKB 58-3
GKB 59-3
GKB 60-3
GKB 61-3
GKB 63-7
GKB 64-3
GKB 66-1
GKB 68-3
GKB 69-2
GKB 70-5

GKB 72-5
GKB 73-4
GKB 75-2
GKB 76-6
GKB 78-3
GKB 81-1
GKB 82-6
GKB 83-1
GKB 84-3
GKB 85-4
GKB 87-4
GKB 88-3
GKB 89-4
GKB 91-1
GKB 92-2
GKB 93-4
GKB 94-1
GKB 95-3
GKB 96-2
GKB 97-1
GKB 98-3
GKB 99-1
GKB 100-2
GKB 101-3
GKB 103-3
GKB 104-2
GKB 105-16
GKB 106-1
GKB 107-2
GKB 109-1
GKB 110-5
GKB 111-3
GKB 112-2
GKB 114-3
GKB 115-3
GKB 116-3
GKB 117-5
GKB 118-3
GKB 119-4
GKB 120-2
GKB 122-6
GKB 126-1
GKB 127-2
GKB 128-2
GKB 129-2
GKB 130-3
GKB 132-2
GKB 133-1
GKB 134-1
GKB 135-5

GKB 137-2
GKB 138-4
GKB 139-3
GKB 140-3
GKB 141-1
GKB 143-10
GKB 144-1
GKB 145-1
GKB 146-5
GKB 149-1
GKB 150-2
GKB 151-4
GKB 152-1
GKB 153-1
GKB 154-2
GKB 155-1
GKB 156-1
GKB 157-1
GKB 158-1
GKB 159-1
GKB 160-1
GKB 161-1
GKB 162-1
GKB 163-1
GKB 164-1
GKB 165-25
GKB 166-4
GKB 167-3

Rear Main Bearing
GKC 1-2
GKC 2-9
GKC 3-7
GKC 4-2
GKC 5-38
GKC 6-3
GKC 7-5
GKC 8-11
GKC 9-26
GKC 10-7
GKC 11-4
GKC 12-4
GKC 13-2
GKC 14-2
GKC 15-3
GKC 16-1
GKC 17-2
GKC 18-7
GKC 19-1
GKC 20-1
GKC 21-3

GKC 22-2
GKC 23-5
GKC 24-3
GKC 25-4
GKC 26-2
GKC 27-3
GKC 28-6
GKC 29-7
GKC 30-4
GKC 31-6
GKC 32-2
GKC 33-2
GKC 34-1
GKC 36-10
GKC 37-7
GKC 38-4
GKC 39-3
GKC 40-3
GKC 41-2
GKC 42-3
GKC 43-2
GKC 45-4
GKC 47-7
GKC 49-10
GKC 50-5
GKC 51-3
GKC 52-2
GKC 53-2
GKC 54-1
GKC 55-2
GKC 56-3
GKC 57-3
GKC 58-3
GKC 59-3
GKC 60-2
GKC 61-7
GKC 62-3
GKC 65-2
GKC 66-3
GKC 67-2
GKC 68-5
GKC 69-1
GKC 70-5
GKC 71-4
GKC 72-1
GKC 73-3
GKC 75-3
GKC 78-1
GKC 79-6
GKC 80-2
GKC 81-3
GKC 82-4

GKC 83-4
GKC 84-4
GKC 85-3
GKC 86-4
GKC 88-1
GKC 89-2
GKC 90-4
GKC 91-4
GKC 92-3
GKC 93-3
GKC 95-3
GKC 96-1
GKC 97-2
GKC 98-3
GKC 99-2
GKC 100-3
GKC 101-4
GKC 102-16
GKC 103-1
GKC 104-2
GKC 105-1
GKC 106-1
GKC 107-5
GKC 108-3
GKC 109-1
GKC 110-1
GKC 111-3
GKC 112-3
GKC 113-3
GKC 114-5
GKC 115-2
GKC 116-4
GKC 117-1
GKC 120-6
GKC 122-1
GKC 123-2
GKC 124-2
GKC 125-2
GKC 126-2
GKC 127-3
GKC 129-2
GKC 130-1
GKC 131-1
GKC 132-5
GKC 133-3
GKC 134-2
GKC 135-4
GKC 136-3
GKC 137-3
GKC 138-1
GKC 140-5
GKC 141-1
GKC 142-1

GKC 143-5
GKC 146-1
GKC 147-2
GKC 148-4
GKC 149-1
GKC 150-1
GKC 151-1
GKC 152-2
GKC 153-1
GKC 154-1
GKC 155-1
GKC 156-1
GKC 157-1
GKC 158-1
GKC 159-1
GKC 160-1
GKC 161-4
GKC 162-1

Intermediate Main Bearing
GKD 1-2
GKD 2-2
GKD 3-2
GKD 4-37
GKD 5-38
GKD 6-5
GKD 7-1
GKD 9-7
GKD 10-2
GKD 11-4
GKD 12-2
GKD 13-2
GKD 14-3
GKD 15-1
GKD 16-2
GKD 17-2
GKD 18-2
GKD 19-1
GKD 20-3
GKD 21-1
GKD 22-1
GKD 23-1
GKD 24-1
GKD 25-1
GKD 27-1
GKD 28-7
GKD 29-4
GKD 30-1
GKD 31-1
GKD 32-2
GKD 33-1
GKD 34-1

ENGINE ASSEMBLY, Section I—Continued

INTERCHANGEABLE COUNT—Continued

Showing the exact number of times each Chilton Number occurs in the Engine Table, Section 1, beginning Page 186.

Intermediate Main Bearing Continued

GKD 35-10
GKD 36-1
GKD 37-2
GKD 38-3
GKD 39-4
GKD 40-2
GKD 41-3
GKD 42-3
GKD 43-1
GKD 45-10
GKD 46-6
GKD 47-2
GKD 48-1
GKD 49-1
GKD 50-1
GKD 51-1
GKD 52-1
GKD 53-2
GKD 54-2
GKD 55-3
GKD 56-1
GKD 57-1
GKD 58-3
GKD 59-3
GKD 60-1
GKD 61-7
GKD 62-3
GKD 63-5
GKD 64-5
GKD 65-3
GKD 66-2
GKD 67-5
GKD 69-5
GKD 70-1
GKD 71-1
GKD 72-1
GKD 74-3
GKD 75-1
GKD 78-6
GKD 80-3
GKD 81-4
GKD 82-4
GKD 83-4
GKD 84-3
GKD 85-4
GKD 88-3
GKD 89-6
GKD 91-3
GKD 94-3
GKD 97-3
GKD103-2
GKD105-3
GKD106-5
GKD110-3
GKD111-3
GKD112-3
GKD115-4
GKD119-6
GKD121-1
GKD123-2
GKD124-2
GKD125-2
GKD126-3
GKD128-2
GKD129-1
GKD131-5
GKD132-3
GKD133-2
GKD134-4
GKD135-3
GKD136-3
GKD145-1
GKD147-1

Piston

GL 1-2
GL 2-5
GL 3-10
GL 4-21
GL 5-5
GL 6-4
GL 7-5
GL 8-9
GL 9-14
GL 10-14
GL 11-4
GL 12-7
GL 13-1
GL 14-1
GL 15-1
GL 16-1
GL 17-2
GL 18-2
GL 19-1
GL 20-1
GL 22-3
GL 23-3
GL 24-2
GL 25-3
GL 26-2
GL 27-4
GL 28-4
GL 29-1
GL 30-4
GL 31-2
GL 32-4
GL 33-6
GL 34-2
GL 35-2
GL 36-2
GL 37-2
GL 38-3
GL 39-4
GL 40-1
GL 41-2
GL 42-7
GL 43-8
GL 44-1
GL 45-3
GL 46-21
GL 47-4
GL 48-3
GL 49-6
GL 50-1
GL 51-8
GL 52-2
GL 53-1
GL 54-2
GL 55-1
GL 56-1
GL 57-5
GL 58-1
GL 59-1
GL 60-2
GL 61-1
GL 62-1
GL 63-1
GL 64-1
GL 65-1
GL 66-1
GL 67-1
GL 68-2
GL 69-3
GL 70-1
GL 71-1
GL 72-1
GL 74-1
GL 75-2
GL 76-4
GL 77-3
GL 78-2
GL 79-3
GL 80-3
GL 81-4
GL 82-1
GL 83-1
GL 84-1
GL 86-3
GL 89-1
GL 90-3
GL 91-1
GL 96-5
GL 97-1
GL 98-1
GL 99-2
GL100-2
GL101-3
GL102-3
GL105-1
GL106-1
GL107-1
GL109-4
GL111-3
GL112-3
GL113-4
GL114-1
GL115-1
GL117-1
GL118-3
GL120-3
GL121-1
GL122-4
GL123-4
GL124-2
GL125-2
GL128-3
GL129-2
GL130-1
GL131-2
GL132-1
GL133-1
GL134-2
GL135-1
GL136-3
GL137-2
GL138-3
GL139-1
GL140-4
GL141-2
GL142-4
GL145-1
GL146-1
GL147-3
GL149-3
GL150-3
GL151-1
GL152-1
GL154-1
GL155-2
GL156-2
GL157-2
GL160-6
GL162-1
GL168-1
GL169-2
GL170-2
GL171-6
GL172-1
GL174-3
GL175-3
GL176-3
GL178-4
GL179-2
GL180-1
GL181-1
GL182-2
GL184-3
GL185-2
GL186-2
GL187-1
GL188-1
GL189-3
GL190-1
GL191-2
GL192-5
GL193-3
GL194-3
GL195-2
GL196-1
GL197-1
GL208-3
GL209-1
GL213-2
GL215-2
GL217-1
GL218-5
GL220-4
GL222-1
GL224-1
GL225-1
GL227-3
GL233-3

Piston Pin

GM 1-2
GM 2-5
GM 3-10
GM 4-21
GM 5-5
GM 6-5
GM 7-14
GM 8-10
GM 9-9
GM 10-21
GM 11-4
GM 12-2
GM 13-2
GM 14-1
GM 15-3
GM 16-3
GM 17-1
GM 18-1
GM 19-4
GM 20-5
GM 21-2
GM 22-3
GM 23-1
GM 25-2
GM 26-5
GM 27-4
GM 28-2
GM 29-2
GM 30-6
GM 31-8
GM 32-2
GM 33-4
GM 34-2
GM 35-2
GM 36-2
GM 38-2
GM 40-7
GM 41-4
GM 42-8
GM 43-6
GM 44-5
GM 45-6
GM 46-3
GM 47-7
GM 48-21
GM 49-2
GM 50-1
GM 51-1
GM 52-1
GM 53-2
GM 54-1
GM 55-4
GM 56-3
GM 57-1
GM 58-2
GM 59-7
GM 60-2
GM 61-3
GM 62-3
GM 63-4
GM 64-1
GM 65-1
GM 66-3
GM 67-3
GM 68-1
GM 69-2
GM 70-1
GM 71-5
GM 72-1
GM 73-1
GM 74-2
GM 75-3
GM 76-3
GM 77-1
GM 78-2
GM 79-3
GM 80-1
GM 81-2
GM 82-3
GM 84-1
GM 85-4
GM 86-3
GM 88-2
GM 89-4
GM 90-3
GM 91-1
GM 92-1
GM 93-3
GM 94-2
GM 95-1
GM 96-1
GM 97-1
GM 98-2
GM 99-1
GM 100-4
GM 101-4
GM 102-1
GM 103-3
GM 104-3
GM 105-2
GM 106-3
GM 107-1
GM 108-4
GM 109-8
GM 110-2
GM 111-2
GM 112-1
GM 113-1
GM 114-1
GM 115-3
GM 116-3
GM 118-3
GM 119-3
GM 120-1
GM 122-2
GM 123-2
GM 124-2
GM 126-3
GM 127-2
GM 129-1
GM 132-1
GM 134-7
GM 135-2
GM 137-2
GM 142-1
GM 144-3
GM 145-3
GM 146-8
GM 147-4
GM 148-3
GM 150-1
GM 151-3
GM 154-7
GM 157-1
GM 158-3
GM 159-2
GM 160-1
GM 161-5
GM 162-1
GM 163-2
GM 164-3
GM 166-1
GM 167-3
GM 168-1
GM 201-1
GM 202-1
GM 223-3
GM 230-3
GM 231-4
GM 232-2

Piston Pin Bushing

GN 1-2
GN 2-9
GN 3-11
GN 4-23
GN 5-5
GN 6-4
GN 7-17
GN 8-2
GN 11-3
GN 12-7
GN 13-2
GN 14-1
GN 15-3
GN 16-5
GN 17-1
GN 18-4
GN 19-5
GN 20-5
GN 21-4
GN 22-2
GN 23-3
GN 24-8
GN 25-2
GN 26-2
GN 27-3
GN 28-1
GN 29-2
GN 30-1
GN 31-2
GN 32-3
GN 33-1
GN 34-2
GN 35-1
GN 36-4
GN 37-1
GN 38-7
GN 40-9
GN 41-3
GN 42-25
GN 43-1
GN 44-1
GN 47-5
GN 48-1
GN 49-5
GN 50-7
GN 51-1
GN 53-3
GN 54-1
GN 64-2
GN 67-5
GN 70-4
GN 74-3
GN 79-1
GN 83-6
GN 84-3
GN 85-4
GN 86-4
GN 91-4
GN 92-3
GN 97-1
GN 100-1
GN 101-6
GN 102-1
GN 103-2
GN 105-4
GN 106-4
GN 107-3
GN 108-3
GN 111-10
GN 112-12
GN 114-1
GN 117-1
GN 118-3
GN 121-3
GN 122-3
GN 124-1
GN 127-2
GN 131-2
GN 132-4
GN 135-1
GN 137-1
GN 139-2
GN 140-2
GN 141-2
GN 144-5
GN 145-4
GN 147-3
GN 148-3
GN 149-5
GN 155-7
GN 156-1
GN 157-1
GN 163-3

Connecting Rod

GO 1-2
GO 2-9
GO 3-8
GO 4-1
GO 5-15
GO 6-2
GO 7-5
GO 8-13
GO 9-9
GO 10-13
GO 11-4
GO 12-4
GO 14-2
GO 15-1
GO 16-3
GO 17-2
GO 18-1
GO 19-3
GO 20-1
GO 21-2
GO 22-3
GO 23-4
GO 24-3
GO 25-1
GO 26-3
GO 27-2
GO 28-3
GO 29-5
GO 30-3
GO 31-3
GO 32-1
GO 33-5
GO 34-2
GO 35-2
GO 36-3
GO 37-2
GO 38-2
GO 39-11
GO 41-6
GO 42-1
GO 43-1
GO 44-7
GO 46-1
GO 47-3
GO 48-3
GO 49-2
GO 50-1
GO 51-1
GO 52-2
GO 53-1
GO 54-1
GO 55-7
GO 56-1
GO 57-5
GO 58-5
GO 59-1
GO 60-3
GO 61-1
GO 62-2
GO 63-2
GO 64-2
GO 65-1
GO 66-2
GO 67-3
GO 68-3
GO 69-1
GO 70-2
GO 71-1
GO 72-2
GO 73-2
GO 74-2
GO 75-2
GO 76-2
GO 77-3
GO 79-4
GO 81-7
GO 82-3
GO 83-2
GO 84-2
GO 85-1
GO 86-2
GO 87-2
GO 88-3
GO 89-3
GO 90-3
GO 91-10
GO 92-3
GO 93-1
GO 94-1
GO 95-1
GO 96-2
GO 97-1
GO 98-1
GO 99-2
GO100-3
GO101-2
GO102-3
GO103-4
GO104-4
GO105-2
GO106-1
GO107-2
GO108-4
GO109-2
GO110-2
GO111-2
GO112-2
GO113-2
GO114-2
GO115-1
GO116-1
GO117-2
GO118-3
GO119-1
GO120-3
GO121-2
GO122-3
GO123-2
GO124-2
GO125-2
GO126-2
GO127-4
GO128-1
GO129-1
GO130-1
GO132-1
GO133-1
GO134-3
GO135-4
GO136-1
GO137-1
GO138-1
GO139-3
GO140-1
GO141-3
GO142-1
GO143-4
GO144-2
GO145-2
GO148-1
GO149-5
GO150-17
GO151-1
GO152-1
GO154-2
GO155-2
GO156-2
GO157-3
GO159-1
GO161-6
GO162-3
GO163-4
GO164-2
GO165-2
GO166-1
GO167-2
GO168-1
GO170-1
GO171-2
GO173-1
GO174-1
GO175-4
GO176-3
GO178-1
GO179-2
GO180-3
GO182-3
GO183-1
GO184-1
GO185-1
GO186-1
GO187-2
GO188-1
GO189-2
GO190-1
GO191-1
GO192-2
GO193-2
GO194-2
GO195-1
GO196-1
GO197-2
GO198-2
GO199-1
GO200-1
GO201-1
GO202-1
GO203-2
GO204-2
GO205-2
GO206-1
GO207-1
GO208-1
GO209-1
GO210-1
GO211-1
GO212-1
GO213-1
GO214-1
GO215-1
GO216-1
GO217-1
GO218-2

Oil Pump Gears

GP 1-5
GP 2-46
GP 3-11
GP 4-2
GP 5-1
GP 6-20
GP 8-14
GP 9-9
GP 10-4
GP 11-1
GP 12-9
GP 13-1
GP 14-6
GP 15-5
GP 16-3
GP 17-1
GP 18-1
GP 19-2
GP 20-6
GP 21-4
GP 22-2
GP 23-15
GP 24-1
GP 25-6
GP 26-5
GP 27-1
GP 28-19
GP 29-2
GP 30-2
GP 31-2
GP 32-1
GP 33-1
GP 34-3
GP 35-2
GP 36-3
GP 37-3
GP 38-4
GP 39-8
GP 40-3
GP 43-5
GP 44-1
GP 45-3
GP 48-1
GP 49-6
GP 50-3
GP 51-3
GP 52-4
GP 53-2
GP 54-2
GP 55-5
GP 56-5
GP 57-1
GP 58-6
GP 59-6
GP 60-3
GP 61-9
GP 62-2
GP 63-3
GP 64-4
GP 65-5
GP 66-10
GP 67-6
GP 68-3
GP 69-4
GP 70-3
GP 71-2
GP 72-2
GP 74-6
GP 76-59
GP 77-2
GP 78-2
GP 79-2
GP 80-3
GP 81-1
GP 82-2
GP 83-5
GP 84-3
GP 85-1
GP 86-7
GP 87-3
GP 88-1
GP 89-7
GP 90-5
GP 91-2
GP 92-2
GP 93-3
GP 94-2
GP 95-1
GP 96-2
GP 97-4
GP 98-3

Flywheel Starter Gears (Ring Gear)

GW 1-7
GW 2-30
GW 3-20
GW 5-52
GW 6-12
GW 7-4
GW 8-2
GW 9-6
GW 10-1
GW 11-7
GW 12-31
GW 13-10
GW 14-5
GW 15-17
GW 16-1
GW 17-4
GW 18-4
GW 19-6
GW 20-3
GW 21-22
GW 22-2
GW 23-13
GW 24-10
GW 25-8
GW 26-18
GW 27-35
GW 30-10
GW 31-2
GW 32-17
GW 33-3
GW 34-3
GW 35-8
GW 36-2
GW 37-11
GW 38-7
GW 39-1
GW 40-7
GW 42-6
GW 43-7
GW 44-14
GW 45-6
GW 46-4
GW 47-4
GW 48-10
GW 49-2
GW 51-3
GW 55-2
GW 56-2
GW 57-2
GW 58-3
GW 59-1
GW 60-4
GW 61-1
GW 64-2
GW 65-3
GW 66-3
GW 67-2
GW 68-11
GW 70-1
GW 71-2

Dimensions of Pistons

Listed Here by Chilton Numbers are Pistons as They Appear in the Preceding Engine Table by Car Models.

To Find the Cars in Which Any of the Following Size Pistons Are Used, Consult the Piston Column, Pages 186-194.

To Find How *Many* Car Models Use Any Size Here, Locate the Same Chilton Number in the Interchangeable Count, Page 195.

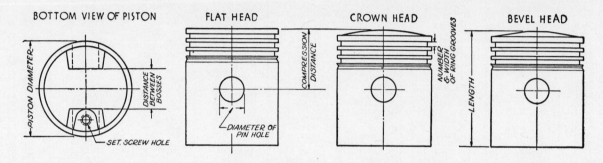

BOTTOM VIEW OF PISTON — FLAT HEAD — CROWN HEAD — BEVEL HEAD

CHILTON PISTON NUMBER	Diameter of Bore	RING GROOVES Number	RING GROOVES Width	Length of Piston	Distance, Pin Center to Top of Piston	Distance Between Bores	Set-Screw Hole Dimensions	Diameter of Piston Pin
GL-1	3	3	1/8	3 1/4	1 3/16	1 1/2	5/16-24	.750
GL-2	3 1/8	3	3/16	1 15/16	1	None		.750
GL-3	3 3/8	3	3/16	4 5/32	2 7/16	1 9/16	3/8-16	.859
GL-4	3 1/4	4	1/8	3 1/2	1 15/16	1 5/8	5/16-24	.875
GL-5	3 1/4	4	1/8	3 1/2	1 15/16	1 5/8	5/16-24	.875
GL-6	3 5/8	4	1/8	4 1/8	2 1/8	1 9/16	None	1.125
GL-7	2 7/8	2, 1	3/16	3 9/32	1 27/32	1 1/8	None	.734
GL-8	2 3/4	4	1/8	3 1/2	1 15/16	1 1/2	None	.875
GL-9	2 7/8	4, 2, 1	1/8	3 1/2	1 15/16	1 1/4	None	.875
GL-10	3 1/4	3, 1	1/8, 3/16	4	2 7/16	1 5/32	None	.875
GL-11	3 3/8	3, 1	1/8, 3/16	4 17/64	2 27/64	1 7/16	None	.875
GL-12	3	4, 3	1/8, 3/16	3 5/8	2 1/8	1 3/16	None	.859
GL-13	3 3/8	3	3/16	4 1/4	2 7/16	1 1/8	None	.875
GL-14	3	3	1/8	3 15/16	2 1/4	1 1/16	None	.750
GL-15	3 1/2	3	1/8	4 1/4	2 1/4	1 1/4	None	.875
GL-16	3 1/8	3	1/8	3 15/16	2 1/4	1 3/16	None	.750
GL-17	3 1/8	3	1/8	3 49/64	2 13/16	1 3/16	None	.750
GL-18	3 1/2	2, 1	1/8	3 15/16	2 5/16	1 1/4	None	.875
GL-19	3 5/16	2, 1	1/8, 3/16	3 31/32	1 1/32	1 3/16	None	.875
GL-20	3 5/8	2, 1	1/8, 3/16	4 5/64	2 11/64	1 1/4	None	.937
GL-21	3 1/8	3	5/16	3 5/16	1 3/4	1 1/2	5/16-24	.750
GL-22	3 1/8	3	5/16	3 3/8	1 63/64	1 17/32	5/16-24	.750
GL-23	3 5/16	3	5/16	3 23/64	2	1	5/16-24	.875
GL-24	3 3/4	3	1/8	4 1/2	2 5/8	1 15/16	3/8-16	1.125
GL-25	3 1/2	2, 1	1/8	4 1/2	2 1/2	1 1/16	None	1.093
GL-26	3 1/4	2, 1	1/8	4	2 3/8	1 1/16	None	.968
GL-27	3 1/8	2, 1	1/8	4 1/4	2 3/8	1 1/16	None	.968
GL-28	3	2, 1	1/8	3 23/32	2 7/32	1 1/16	None	.875
GL-29	3 7/16	2, 1	1/8	4	2 5/16	1 3/16	None	.875
GL-30	3 11/16	3	1/8	3 5/8	1 7/8	1 1/8	None	.850
GL-31	3 5/16	3	5/32	3 11/16	1 7/8	1 1/16	None	.990
GL-32	3	3	1/8	3 7/16	2	1 1/16	None	.750
GL-33	3 5/8	3	1/8	4 1/4	2	1 1/8	None	.750
GL-34	3 3/4	3	5/32	4 11/16	2 1/8	1 5/8	None	1.187
GL-35	3 1/2	3	1/8	4	2 1/8	1 17/32	None	1.00
GL-36	3 1/4	4	1/8	4 1/8	2 5/16	1 1/2	None	.875
GL-37	3 5/8	4	5/32	4 5/16	2 5/16	1 3/16	None	1.00
GL-38	3	3	3/16	3 1/2	2	1 11/16	3/8-16	.859
GL-39	2 7/8	3	3/16	3 3/4	2 5/16	1 3/8	None	.875
GL-40	3 11/16	4	1/8	4 1/8	2 1/8	1 3/16	None	1.125
GL-41	3 3/4	3	1/8	4 1/16	2 1/4	1 1/4	None	.937
GL-42	3 1/4	2, 1	1/8	3 3/4	2 5/16	1 1/8	3/8-16	1.00
GL-43	2 3/4	2	1/8	3 3/8	1 15/16	1 1/8	None	.734
GL-44	3 3/8	2, 2	1/8, 3/16	3 11/32	1 31/64	1 5/8	5/16-24	.875
GL-45	3	3	3/16	3 3/4	2 1/4	1 3/8	3/8-16	.859
GL-46	3 3/8	3, 1	1/8	3 15/16	2 5/16	1 17/32	None	.859
GL-47	2 7/8	3	3/16	3 5/8	2 1/8	1 3/16	3/8-16	.859
GL-48	3 7/8	3	3/16	4 3/8	2 5/16	2	3/8-24	.812
GL-49	3 1/4	3, 1	1/8	3 15/16	2 5/16	1 5/8	None	.859
GL-50	2 7/8	3, 1	1/8	3 5/8	2 1/8	1 3/16	None	.859
GL-51	3 1/8	2, 1	1 1/4, 1/8	3 11/16	2	1 1/16	None	.812
GL-52	2 7/8	3, 1	1/8	3 11/16	2	1 3/16	None	.734
GL-53	3 3/8	4, 1	9/64	4 1/8	2 5/16	1 1/2	None	.859
GL-54	3 1/4	3, 1	1/8	3 7/8	2 11/32	1 1/16	None	.875
GL-55	3 7/8	3	1/8	4 1/8	1 7/8	1 1/4	None	.850
GL-56	3 1/2	3	1/8	4 1/8	2 1/4	1 1/2	None	.937
GL-57	3 3/8	2, 1	3/16	4	1 15/16	1 3/8	None	.859
GL-58	3	2, 1	1/8	3 11/16	2 3/16	1 1/2	1/4-20	.874
GL-59	3 1/2	4, 1	1/8	4 1/4	2 13/32	1 3/8	None	.937
GL-60	2 3/4	2, 1	1/8	3 9/64	1 31/32	1 3/16	None	.750
GL-61	3 3/16	3	1/8	3 7/32	2 11/32	1 3/16	None	.875
GL-62	3 1/4	3	1/8	3 13/16	2 5/16	1 3/16	None	.875
GL-63	3 1/8	3, 1	1/8	3 13/16	2 1/4	1 5/16	None	.812
GL-64	3 3/8	3	1/8	3 7/8	2 3/8	1 7/16	None	.875
GL-65	3 1/4	3	1/8	3 7/8	2 5/16	1 3/16	None	.875
GL-66	3 1/8	2, 1	1/8	3 13/16	2 1/4	1 3/16	None	.812
GL-67	3 1/16	3	1/8	3 3/4	2 1/4	1 1/2	None	1.062
GL-68	3 3/8	3	1/8	4 1/4	2 13/32	1 3/16	None	.937
GL-69	3 1/8	3, 1	1/8	3 9/32	2 5/16	1 1/16	None	.812
GL-70	3 5/16	3	1/8	3 29/32	2 1/8	1 5/8	None	1.062
GL-71	3 1/4	2, 1	1/8	3 13/16	2 1/4	1 3/16	5/16-24	.797
GL-72	3 1/8	3	1/8	3 5/8	2	1 3/16	5/16-24	.797
GL-74	2 5/8	3	1/8	3	1 3/4	1 1/8	None	.734
GL-75	2 3/4	3	1/8	3	1 3/4	1 1/8	None	.734
GL-76	2 11/16	3	1/8	3 1/16	1 11/16	1 1/8	None	.750
GL-77	2 3/4	3	1/8	3 1/16	1 11/16	1 1/8	None	.750
GL-78	2 15/16	3	1/8	3 5/8	2	1 5/32	None	.735
GL-79	3 3/4	3	1/8	3 13/16	1 15/16	1 1/8	None	.740
GL-80	3 1/8	2, 1	1/8	3 27/32	1 29/32	1 3/4	None	1.00
GL-81	3 1/4	4, 1	1/8	3 27/32	2 1/4	1 1/4	None	.875
GL-82	3 1/4	4	1/8	3 27/32				.875

DIMENSIONS OF PISTONS—Continued

CHILTON PISTON NUMBER	Diameter of Bore	RING GROOVES Number	RING GROOVES Width	Length of Piston	Distance, Pin Center to Top of Piston	Distance Between Bores	Set-Screw Hole Dimensions	Diameter of Piston Pin
GL-83	3 1/2	4	1/8	4 3/16	2 11/32	1 1/16	None	.937
GL-84	3 1/2	2 1	1/8 3/16	3 3/4	1 7/8	1 1/2	None	1.125
GL-86	3 1/2	2 1	1/8 3/16	4 9/32	2 15/32	1 3/16	None	1.00
GL-89	3	2 1	1/8 3/16	3 19/32	2 3/32	1 1/16	None	.812
GL-90	3 1/4	2 1	1/8 3/16	3 23/32	2 3/32	1 1/16	None	.812
GL-91	3 1/8	3 1	1/8 3/16	3 13/16	2 1/4	1 5/16	5/16–24	.812
GL-96	3 1/2	3	1/8	4 1/16	2 1/4	1 3/8	None	1.093
GL-97	2 7/8	2 1	1/8 3/16	3 1/8	1 25/32	1 1/16	None	.750
GL-98	3 1/4	2 1	1/8 3/16	4	2 13/32	1 3/16	None	.865
GL-99	3	2 1	1/8 3/16	3 1/8	1 25/32	1 1/16	None	.750
GL-100	3 1/8	2 1	1/8 3/16	3 1/8	1 45/64	1 1/32	None	.865
GL-101	3 1/4	2 1	1/8 3/16	3 1/4	1 25/32	1 5/8	5/16–18	.985
GL-102	3	2 1	1/8 3/16	3 1/4	1 49/64	1 1/2	5/16–18	.875
GL-105	3 1/4	3 1	1/8 3/16	3 7/8	2 3/8	1 7/16	None	.875
GL-106	3 7/16	3 1	1/8 3/16	4 1/32	2 13/32	1 1/2	None	.937
GL-107	3 1/8	3 1	1/8 3/16	3 7/16	1 7/8	1 1/2	5/16–24	.937
GL-109	3 3/16	4	1/8	3 1/2	1 15/16	1 5/8	5/16–24	.875
GL-111	3 5/16	4	1/8	3 13/16	1 15/16	1 5/32	None	.875
GL-112	3 1/16	3 1	1/8 3/16	3 3/4	2 7/32	1 1/16	None	.875
GL-113	3 1/8	3	3/16	3 1/4	1 15/16	1 3/16	3/8–16	.860
GL-114	3 1/2	4	1/8	3 1/2	1 7/8	1 3/4	5/16–18	1.125
GL-115	3 1/4	3	3/16	3 23/64	1 31/64	1 9/16	5/16–24	.875
GL-117	2 3/4	2 1	1/8 3/16	3 1/4	1 15/16	1 1/8	None	.735
GL-118	3 3/8	3	1/8	3 3/4	2	1 3/4	5/16–24	.875
GL-120	2 13/16	3 1	1/8 3/16	3	1 19/32	1 3/16	None	.750
GL-121	4 1/2	3	1/4	5 13/16	2 13/16	2 1/2	None	1.125
GL-122	3 7/8	3	3/16	4 17/32	2 5/8	2 1/16	5/16–18	1.125
GL-123	3 3/4	3	3/16	4 11/16	2 9/16	1 15/16	None	1.187
GL-124	2 13/16	2 1	1/8 3/16	3 1/4	1 15/16	1 3/16	None	.750
GL-125	2 15/16	2 1	1/8 3/16	3 3/16	1 15/16	1 3/16	None	.735
GL-128	3 7/16	4	3/16	4	1 5/8	1 11/16	3/8–16	.937
GL-129	3 1/8	4	1/8	3 11/16	1 1/2	1 9/16	3/8–16	.875
GL-130	2 7/8	3	1/8	3 5/16	1 25/32	1 7/32	5/16–24	.730
GL-131	2 7/8	3	1/8	3 5/16	1 25/32	1 15/32	5/16–24	.918
GL-132	3 1/4	3	3/16	4	2 3/16	1 3/4	5/16–24	1.062
GL-133	3 3/8	3	3/16	3 15/16	2 3/16	1 5/8	5/16–24	1.062
GL-134	2 3/4	2 1	1/8 3/16	3 3/8	1 7/8	1 3/8	5/16–24	.856
GL-135	2 7/8	2 1	1/8 3/16	3 3/8	1 7/8	1 5/16	5/16–24	.856
GL-136	3 3/16	2 1	1/8 3/16	3 7/8	2 3/16	1 11/16	5/16–24	.856
GL-137	3 1/2	3	3/16	3 1/2	1 7/8	15/16	None	.735
GL-138	3	3	1/8	3 1/2	2	1 1/16	None	.735
GL-139	3 1/8	3	3/8	3 3/4	2	1	None	.735
GL-140	3 1/2	3	1/8	3 3/8	1 7/8	1 1/2	None	.875
GL-141	3 3/8	3	1/8	3 3/8	1 7/8	1 7/16	None	.875
GL-142	3 1/2	4	1/8	4 1/4	2 1/2	1 1/2	None	.875
GL-145	3 3/8	3 1	1/8 3/16	3 13/16	2 3/16	1 1/16	None	1.00
GL-146	3 1/2	4	1/8	3 3/4	1 7/8	1 3/4	5/16–18	1.125
GL-147	3 1/4	3	1/8	3 1/4	1 19/32	1 5/8	5/16–18	.875
GL-149	3 1/2	3	3/16	3 7/8	2 17/64	1 11/16	None	.875
GL-150	4	3	3/16	5 1/2	3 1/4	1 15/16	None	1.062
GL-151	3 1/2	2 1	1/8 3/16	4	2 17/64	1 11/16	None	1.00
GL-152	3 1/4	3	1/8	4	1 5/8	1 11/16	3/8–16	.937
GL-154	3 5/16	3	3/16	3 29/32	2 1/8	1 5/8	5/16–24	1.062
GL-155	3 3/16	3	3/16	4	2 1/4	1 9/16	1/4–20	.985
GL-156	3 1/4	3	3/16	4 1/16	2 5/16	1 1/8	None	.984
GL-157	3 3/8	3 1	1/8 3/16	4	2 15/64	1 1/8	None	.985
GL-160	3 1/4	4	1/8	4 1/16	1 13/16	1	None	1.00
GL-162	3 1/2	3	1/8	4 1/2	2 1/16	1 11/16	None	1.00
GL-164	3 1/4	4	1/8	4 1/4	2 9/16	1 15/16	None	.859
GL-168	3 1/2	4	1/8	4 5/16	2 1/2	......	None	.984
GL-169	3 3/4	4	3/16	4 15/32	2 19/32	......	......	.984
GL-170	3 1/4	4	1/8	4 1/32	2 1/8	1 1/4	None	.984
GL-171	3 1/2	4	1/8	4 5/16	2 1/2	......	None	.984
GL-172	3 3/8	4	1/8	4 1/4	2 7/16	1/2	5/16–24	.875
GL-174	3 7/8	4	3/16	4 11/16	2 17/32	1 1/4	None	1.00
GL-175	3 1/2	4	3/16	4 11/16	2 9/16	1 1/4	None	1.00
GL-176	3 3/8	4	3/16	3 7/8	1 15/16	15/16	None	.875
GL-178	3 1/2	3 1	1/8 3/16	4 1/4	2 13/32	1 3/16	None	.936
GL-179	3 3/16	4	1/8	4 1/4	2 1/2	1 5/16	None	.875
GL-180	3 1/2	3 1	1/8 3/16	4 1/8	2	1 11/16	None	.875
GL-181	3 3/16	3	1/8	4 3/16	2 7/16	1 5/8	None	.875
GL-182	3 1/4	3	1/8	4 3/16	2 7/16	1 9/16	None	.875
GL-184	3 3/16	3 1	1/8 3/16	3 1/2	1 7/8	1 5/8	5/16–18	.874
GL-185	3 3/16	3 1	1/8 3/16	3 7/8	2 1/8	1 5/8	5/16–18	.874
GL-186	3 1/8	3 1	1/8 3/16	3 1/2	1 7/8	1 5/8	5/16–18	.874
GL-187	3 3/8	2 1	5/32 3/16	3 7/8	2 3/16	1 3/4	5/16–24	.855
GL-188	3 5/8	4	3/16	4 3/4	2 3/8	1 1/4	None	.937
GL-189	3 1/4	4	1/8	4 3/8	1 15/16	1 1/4	None	.875
GL-190	2 15/16	3	1/8	3 5/8	2	1 1/16	None	.796
GL-191	3 3/8	3 1	1/8 3/16	4 1/4	2 7/16	1 1/2	5/16–24	.874
GL-192	2 15/16	4	1/8	3 5/8	2	1 1/16	5/16–24	.796
GL-193	3 1/4	3	5/32	3 43/64	1 27/32	1 5/8	5/16–18	.750
GL-194	3 1/2	3	1/8	3 3/4	2	1 3/4	5/16–24	.875
GL-195	2 7/8	2 1	1/8 3/16	3 7/16	1 15/16	1 7/32	None	.734
GL-196	2 7/8	2 1	1/8 3/16	3 19/32	2 3/32	1 1/16	None	.812
GL-197	3 1/4	3	3/16	3 15/16	2 5/16	1 1/16	None	.100
GL-206	3	3	1/8	3 11/16	2 3/16	1 1/2	1/4–20	.875
GL-208	2 7/8	2 1	1/8 3/16	3 1/2	1 15/16	1 5/16	None	.875
GL-209	3 3/4	2 1	1/8 3/16	4 1/2	2 3/4	1 3/16	None	1.093
GL-213	3 1/4	4	1/8	3 11/16	1 9/16	1 9/16	3/8–16	.875
GL-215	3 1/4	3	3/16	3 15/16	2 5/16	1 23/32	5/16–18	1.00
GL-217	3 3/8	3	3/16	3 15/16	2 3/16	1 5/8	None	1.062
GL-218	3 3/8	4 1	1/8 3/16	3 7/8	2 11/32	15/16	None	.875
GL-220	3 1/8	3	1/8	3 3/4	2	1 11/32	5/16–24	.796
GL-222	3 1/8	3	3/16	3 23/64	1 31/64	1 1/2	5/16–24	.876
GL-224	3 5/8	3	3/16	4 3/8	2 1/2	1 15/16	3/8–16	1.125
GL-225	3 5/16	3	3/16	3 15/16	2 5/16	1 5/8	3/8–16	.869
GL-227	4 1/2	4	1/4	5 1/2	2 13/16	2 1/2	5/16–20	1.125
GL-233	3 1/4	3	3/16	4 1/32	2 3/16	1 3/4	5/16–24	1.062

Dimensions of Piston Pins

Listed Here by Chilton Numbers are Pins as They Appear in the Preceding Engine Table by Car Models.

To Find the Cars in Which Any of the Following Size Piston Pins Are Used, Consult the Piston Pin Column, Pages 186-194.

To Find How *Many* Car Models Use Any Size Here, Locate the Same Chilton Number in the Interchangeable Count, Page 195.

TYPE A   TYPE B   TYPE C   TYPE D   TYPE E   TYPE F

CHILTON PIN NUMBER	Diameter of Pin	Length of Pin	Type of Pin	CHILTON PIN NUMBER	Diameter of Pin	Length of Pin	Type of Pin	CHILTON PIN NUMBER	Diameter of Pin	Length of Pin	Type of Pin	CHILTON PIN NUMBER	Diameter of Pin	Length of Pin	Type of Pin
GM-1	.750	2 13/16	A	GM-42	.734	2 21/64	C	GM-80	.876	2 29/32	E	GM-120	1.00	3 1/16	C
GM-2	.750	2 3/4	D	GM-43	.859	2 15/32	C	GM-81	.937	2 7/8	B	GM-122	1.062	3 1/16	C
GM-3	.859	3	E	GM-44	.859	2 13/16	C	GM-82	.875	3 1/8	E	GM-123	.985	2 7/8	E
GM-4	.875	2 7/8	A	GM-45	.859	3 1/2	E	GM-84	1.125	4 1/4	E	GM-124	.985	2 15/16	B
GM-5	.875	2 3/4	A	GM-46	.812	2 5/8	A	GM-85	1.125	3 5/8	A	GM-126	1.00	2 13/16	B
GM-6	1.125	2 29/32	C	GM-47	.860	2 3/4	C	GM-86	.750	2 5/8	C	GM-127	1.00	2 13/16	B
GM-7	.875	2 13/16	B	GM-48	.860	2 7/8	B	GM-87	.735	2 1/2	C	GM-129	1.00	2 1/4	B
GM-8	734	2 1/2	C	GM-49	.937	2 1/8	B	GM-88	1.187	3 1/4	C	GM-132	1.156	3 1/4	A
GM-9	.875	2 17/64	B	GM-50	.874	2 3/4	B	GM-89	.750	2 7/16	B	GM-134	.968	3 1/8	B
GM-10	.875	2 25/64	B	GM-51	.941	2 13/16	E	GM-90	.875	2 47/64	C	GM-135	.968	3 3/8	B
GM-11	.875	2 25/64	C	GM-52	.812	2 11/16	B	GM-91	.797	3 1/16	E	GM-137	.984	2 7/8	B
GM-12	.859	2 1/2	C	GM-53	1.187	3 7/16	A	GM-92	.797	2 15/16	E	GM-142	.875	3 5/16	B
GM-13	.875	2 15/16	B	GM-54	.850	3 7/16	D	GM-93	.937	3 5/32	E	GM-144	1.00	3 1/16	B
GM-14	.750	2 9/16	B	GM-55	.750	2 3/4	B	GM-94	.875	2 7/8	E	GM-145	1.00	3 1/16	B
GM-15	.875	2 5/8	B	GM-56	.750	2 5/8	B	GM-95	.812	2 7/8	E	GM-146	.875	3	B
GM-16	.750	2 11/16	B	GM-57	.735	2 5/8	C	GM-96	.937	2 7/8	C	GM-147	.937	2 1/8	B
GM-17	.875	2 27/32	B	GM-58	.735	2 9/32	C	GM-97	.937	2 13/16	C	GM-148	.875	2 5/8	C
GM-18	.937	3 5/32	B	GM-59	.750	2 25/32	C	GM-98	.875	2 47/64	C	GM-150	.875	3 1/4	C
GM-19	.750	2 15/16	E	GM-60	.735	2 5/16	B	GM-99	.730	2 27/64	B	GM-151	.875	2 25/32	A
GM-20	.875	3 5/32	E	GM-61	.740	3 1/2	B	GM-100	.730	2 27/64	A	GM-154	.874	2 7/8	A
GM-21	1.125	3 1/16	E	GM-62	1.00	3 9/16	F	GM-101	1.062	2 15/16	A	GM-157	.855	3 1/16	B
GM-22	1.093	3 1/16	B	GM-63	.875	2 7/8	B	GM-102	1.062	3 1/8	A	GM-158	.875	2 7/8	B
GM-23	1.093	3 5/16	B	GM-64	.937	2 7/8	B	GM-103	.856	2 1/2	A	GM-160	.796	2 5/8	E
GM-25	.968	2 25/32	B	GM-65	.812	2 13/32	B	GM-104	.856	2 7/8	A	GM-161	.796	2 3/4	E
GM-26	.968	2 11/16	B	GM-66	.812	2 5/8	B	GM-105	.735	3 1/8	B	GM-162	.750	3 1/16	A
GM-27	.850	3 5/16	B	GM-67	1.00	2 15/16	B	GM-106	.735	2 3/4	B	GM-163	.687	3 1/16	A
GM-28	.990	2 7/8	A	GM-68	.937	3	E	GM-107	.734	2 13/16	B	GM-164	.875	3 1/4	E
GM-29	.750	2 15/16	B	GM-69	.875	3	C	GM-108	.797	2 7/8	B	GM-166	.937	3 5/32	B
GM-30	.750	3	B	GM-70	.812	2 1/2	C	GM-109	.875	3 3/4	C	GM-167	.875	2 7/8	B
GM-31	.812	2 13/16	B	GM-71	1.093	2 11/16	C	GM-110	.875	2 29/32	C	GM-168	.875	2 9/16	E
GM-32	1.00	3 1/8	B	GM-72	.875	2 3/4	B	GM-111	1.00	2 13/16	A	GM-201	1.125	3 3/16	E
GM-33	.875	2 7/8	B	GM-73	.865	2 13/16	B	GM-112	1.125	3 5/16	C	GM-202	.860	2 1/8	E
GM-34	1.00	3 1/4	B	GM-74	.865	2 11/16	B	GM-113	1.00	2 13/16	B	GM-223	.812	2 13/16	A
GM-35	.734	2 5/16	C	GM-75	.985	2 31/32	A	GM-114	1.125	3 5/16	E	GM-230	1.125	4 1/4	E
GM-36	.875	2 15/16	C	GM-76	.875	2 3/4	A	GM-115	.875	3	E	GM-231	.860	2 21/32	B
GM-38	.937	3 5/32	B	GM-77	.735	2 3/8	C	GM-116	1.125	2 25/32	E	GM-232	.984	3 1/16	
GM-40	1.00	2 13/16	E	GM-78	1.062	3 1/4	C	GM-118	.875	3 1/2	C				
GM-41	.860	2 3/8	E	GM-79	.875	3	B	GM-119	1.062	3 1/2	C				

Engine Assembly—Section 2

ENGINE ASSEMBLY STARTS ON PAGE 186.   READ DIRECTIONS THERE CAREFULLY.

Interchangeable Parts have the same CHILTON NUMBER in Any Column

Car Make and Model	VALVE ASSEMBLY						TIMING DRIVE			
	Inlet Valve	Exhaust Valve	Valve Stem Guide	Valve Springs	Valve Lifters (Tappets)	Valve Lifter Adjusting Screws	Cam-shaft Gear or Sprocket	Crank-shaft Gear or Sprocket	Generator Gear or Sprocket	Timing Chain (See Footnote)
Ajax........................(1925-26)	GR-1	GR-1	GS-1	GT-1	GU-1	GV-2	GF-1	GH-1	None	None
Apperson 6, Velie 50..........(1925)	GR-4	GR-4	GS-4	GT-4	GU-4	GV-11	GF-35	GH-4	KE-3	None
Apperson Str. 8, Lyc. 2-H......(1925)	GQ-1	GR-5	GS-5	GT-5	GU-5	GV-2	GF-4	GH-9	KE-4	GJ-2
Apperson 6, Velie 50..........(1926)	GR-4	GR-4	GS-4	GT-4	GU-4	GV-11	GF-35	GH-4	KE-3	None
Apperson Str. 8, Lyc. 2-H......(1926)	GQ-1	GR-5	GS-5	GT-5	GU-5	GV-2	GF-4	GH-9	KE-4	GJ-2
Auburn 4, Lyc. CF.............(1925)	GR-6	GR-6	GS-6	GT-9	GU-6	GV-2	GF-6	GH-6	KE-5	None
Auburn 6-43, Cont. 7-U........(1925)	GR-2	GR-2	GS-2	GT-2	GU-2	GV-2	GF-2	GH-2	KE-1	None
Auburn 8-88, Lyc. 2-H.........(1925)	GQ-1	GR-5	GS-5	GT-5	GU-5	GV-2	GF-5	GH-5	KE-36	GJ-2
Auburn 4-44, Lyc. CF.........(1926)	GR-6	GR-6	GS-6	GT-9	GU-0	GV-2	GF-6	GH-6	KE-5	None
Auburn 6-66, Lyc. 4-SM.......(1926)	GQ-1	GR-5	GS-5	GT-5	GU-5	GV-2	GF-7	GH-7	KE-7	GJ-3
Auburn 8-88, Lyc. 4-HM.......(1926)	GQ-1	GR-5	GS-5	GT-5	GU-5	GV-2	GF-8	GH-5	KE-6	GJ-3
Auburn 6-66 A, Cont. 28-L.....(1927)	GQ-2	GR-7	GS-2	GT-6	GU-2	GV-2	GF-9	GH-8	KE-8	GJ-4
Auburn 8-88, Lyc. 4-HM.......(1927)	GQ-1	GR-5	GS-5	GT-5	GU-5	GV-2	GF-8	GH-5	KE-6	GJ-6
Auburn 8-77, Lyc. GT.........(1927)	GQ-3	GR-8	GS-5	GT-7	GU-5	GV-2	GF-10	GH-10	KE-9	GJ-5
Auburn 76, Lyc. WS...........(1928)	GQ-3	GR-8	GS-5	GT-7	GU-5	GV-2	GF-10	GH-9	None	GJ-5
Auburn 88, Lyc. GS...........(1928)	GQ-3	GR-8	GS-5	GT-7	GU-5	GV-2	GF-10	GH-9	None	GJ-5
Auburn 115, Lyc. 4-MD.......(1928)	GQ-1	GR-5	GS-5	GT-7	GU-14	GV-2	GF-8	GH-5	KE-6	GJ-6
Auburn 6-80, Lyc. WR........(1929)	GQ-3	GR-8	GS-5	GT-7	{GU5Early / GU13Late}	GV-2	GF-10	GH-9	None	GJ-5
Auburn 8-90, Lyc. GR.........(1929)	GQ-3	GR-8	GS-5	GT-7	{GU5Early / GU13Late}	GV-2	GF-10	GH-9	None	GJ-5
Auburn 120, Lyc. MDA........(1929)	GQ-1	GR-5	GS-5	GT-7	GU-14	GV-2	GF-8	GH-5	KE-6	GJ-6
Auburn 6-85, Lyc. WR........(1930)	GQ-3	GR-8	GS-5	GT-7	GU-13	GV-2	GF-10	GH-9	None	GJ-5
Auburn 8-95, Lyc. GR.........(1930)	GQ-3	GR-8	GS-5	GT-7	GU-13	GV-2	GF-10	GH-9	None	GJ-5
Auburn 125, Lyc. MDA........(1930)	GQ-1	GR-5	GS-5	GT-7	GU-14	GV-2	GF-8	GH-5	KE-6	GJ-6
Blackhawk L6................(1929)	GR-99	GR-99	{GS-7 Ex. / GS-8 In.}	GT-12	GU-15	GV-4	GF-11	GH-12	KE-10	*GJ-7
Blackhawk L8, Cont. 16-S.....(1929)	GQ-5	GR-10	GS-41	GT-29	GU-3	GV-3	GF-12	GH-13	KE-11	GJ-9
Blackhawk L6................(1930)	GR-99	GR-99	{GS-7 Ex. / GS-8 In.}	GT-12	GU-15	GV-4	GF-11	GH-12	KE-10	*GJ-7
Blackhawk L8, Cont. 16S......(1930)	GQ-5	GR-10	GS-41	GT-29	GU-3	GV-3	GF-12	GH-13	KE-11	GJ-9
Buick Master.................(1925)	GQ-6	GR-11	GS-9	{GT-11 In. / GT-14 Out.}	GU-17	GV-6	GF-13	GH-14	KE-12	None
Buick Std....................(1925)	GR-12	GR-12	GS-10	{GT-11 In. / GT-14 Out.}	GU-17	GV-6	GF-14	GH-15	KE-13	None
Buick Master.................(1926)	GQ-6	GR-11	GS-9	{GT-11 In. / GT-14 Out.}	GU-18	GV-6	GF-13	GH-14	KE-12	None
Buick Std....................(1926)	GR-12	GR-12	{GS-132 In. / GS-12 Ex.}	{GT-11 In. / GT-14 Out.}	GU-18	GV-6	GF-14	GH-15	KE-13	None
Buick 115....................(1927)	GR-12	GR-12	{GS-132 In. / GS-12 Ex.}	{GT-11 In. / GT-14 Out.}	GU-18	GV-6	GF-14	GH-15	KE-13	None
Buick 120, 128...............(1927)	GQ-6	GR-11	GS-9	{GT-11 In. / GT-14 Out.}	GU-18	GV-6	GF-13	GH-14	KE-12	None
Buick 115....................(1928)	GR-13	GR-13	{GS-132 In. / GS-12 Ex.}	{GT-8 In. / GT-15 Out.}	GU-19	GV-6	GF-14	GH-15	KE-13	None
Buick 120, 128...............(1928)	GQ-7	GR-14	GS-9	{GT-8 In. / GT-15 Out.}	GU-19	GV-6	GF-13	GH-14	KE-12	None
Buick 116....................(1929)	GR-15	GR-15	{GS-133 In. / GS-13 Ex.}	{GT-8 In. / GT-15 Out.}	GU-19	GV-6	GF-15	GH-16	KE-14	None
Buick 121, 129...............(1929)	GQ-8	GR-16	{GS-134 In. / GS-14 Ex.}	{GT-8 In. / GT-15 Out.}	GU-19	GV-6	GF-16	GH-17	KR-15	None
Buick 40.....................(1930)	GR-15	GR-15	{GS-133 In. / GS-13 Ex.}	{GT-8 In. / GT-15 Out.}	GU-19	GV-6	GF-15	GH-16	KE-14	None
Buick 50.....................(1930)	GQ-8	GR-16	{GS-134 In. / GS-14 Ex.}	{GT-8 In. / GT-15 Out.}	GU-19	GV-6	GF-16	GH-17	KE-15	None
Buick 60.....................(1930)	GQ-8	GR-16	{GS-134 In. / GS-14 Ex.}	{GT-8 In. / GT-15 Out.}	GU-19	GV-6	GF-16	GH-17	KE-15	None
Cadillac V63.................(1925)	GR-17	GR-17	GS-15	GT-16	GU-20	GV-7	GF-17	GH-18	KE-16	*GJ-10
Cadillac 314.................(1926)	GR-17	GR-18	GS-16	GT-17	GU-21	GV-8	GF-18	GH-19	KE-17	GJ-12
Cadillac 314.................(1927)	GR-17	GR-18	GS-16	GT-17	GU-21	GV-8	GF-18	GH-19	KE-17	*GJ-10
Cadillac 341-A...............(1928)	GQ-9	GR-19	GS-17	GT-18	GU-21	GV-8	GF-19	GH-20	KE-18	*GJ-13
Cadillac 341-B...............(1929)	GQ-9	GR-19	GS-17	GT-18	GU-21	GV-8	GF-19	GH-20	KE-19	*GJ-13
Cadillac 353.................(1930)	GQ-35	GR-127	GS-17	GT-18	GU-21	GV-8	GF-19	GH-20	KE-19	*GJ-13
Case JIC, Cont. 8-R..........(1925)	GR-3	GR-3	GS-3	GT-3	GU-3	GV-3	GF-3	GH-3	KE-2	None
Case X, Cont. 8-R............(1925)	GR-3	GR-3	GS-3	GT-3	GU-3	GV-3	GF-3	GH-3	KE-2	None
Case Y, Cont. 6-T............(1925)	GR-20	GR-20	GS-18	GT-3	GU-3	GV-3	GF-20	GH-21	KE-2	GJ-15
Case JIC, Cont. 8-R..........(1926)	GR-3	GR-3	GS-3	GT-3	GU-3	GV-3	GF-3	GH-3	KE-2	None
Case Y, Cont. 6-J............(1926)	GR-20	GR-20	GS-18	GT-3	GU-3	GV-3	GF-3	GH-3	KE-2	GJ-15
Chandler 33..................(1925)	GR-21	GR-21	GS-19	GT-21	GU-23	GV-9	GF-21	GH-22	KE-16	GJ-16
Chandler 35..................(1926)	GR-21	GR-21	GS-19	GT-21	GU-23	GV-9	GF-21	GH-23	KE-17	GJ-16
Chandler Big 6...............(1927)	GR-21	GR-21	GS-19	GT-21	GU-23	GV-9	GF-21	GH-23	KE-17	GJ-16
Chandler Royal 8.............(1927)	GQ-10	GR-22	GS-20	GT-21	GU-24	GV-2	GF-22	GH-24	KE-18	GJ-17
Chandler Spec. 6.............(1927)	GR-23	GR-23	GS-21	{GT-19 In. / GT-20 Out.}	GU-25	GV-9	GF-23	GH-25	KE-16	GJ-18
Chandler Std. 6..............(1927)	GR-24	GR-24	GS-22	GT-22	GU-26	GV-2	GF-24	GH-26	KE-16	GJ-16
Chandler Big 6...............(1928)	GR-21	GR-21	GS-19	GT-21	GU-23	GV-9	GF-21	GH-23	KE-17	GJ-16
Chandler Royal 8.............(1928)	GQ-4	GR-60	GS-20	GT-21	GU-24	GV-2	GF-22	GH-24	KE-18	GJ-17
Chandler Spec. 6.............(1928)	GR-61	GR-61	GS-22	GT-22	GU-26	GV-2	GF-24	GH-26	KE-19	GJ-18
Chandler Spec. Inv. 6........(1928)	GR-61	GR-61	GS-22	GT-22	GU-26	GV-2	GF-24	GH-26	KE-19	GJ-18
Chevrolet K..................(1925)	GR-25	GR-25	None	GT-23	GU-27	GV-11	GF-25	GH-28	KE-20	None
Chevrolet V..................(1926)	GR-25	GR-25	None	GT-23	GU-27	GV-11	GF-25	GH-28	KE-20	None
Chevrolet AA.................(1927)	GR-25	GR-25	None	GT-23	GU-27	GV-11	GF-26	GH-28	None	None
Chevrolet AB.................(1928)	GR-26	GR-26	None	GT-23	GU-29	GV-11	GF-27	GH-27	None	None

Footnote: For corresponding timing chain numbers advertised, see pages 201, 203.

ENGINE ASSEMBLY, Section 2—Continued

Interchangeable Parts have the same CHILTON NUMBER in Any Column

Car Make and Model	VALVE ASSEMBLY						TIMING DRIVE			
	Inlet Valve	Exhaust Valve	Valve Stem Guide	Valve Springs	Valve Lifters (Tappets)	Valve Lifter Adjusting Screws	Cam-shaft Gear or Sprocket	Crank-shaft Gear or Sprocket	Generator Gear or Sprocket	Timing Chain (See Footnote)
Chevrolet AC...............(1929)	GR-27	GR-27	GS-135	GT-24	GU-30	GV-11	GF-28	GH-37	None	None
Chevrolet AD...............(1930)	GQ-11	GR-149	GS-135	GT-24	GU-30	GV-11	GF-28	GH-37	None	None
Chrysler 6-B...............(1925)	GR-28	GR-28	GS-23	GT-25	GU-31	GV-2	GF-31	GH-32	KE-22	GJ-19
Chrysler 58................(1926)	GR-29	GR-29	GS-24	GT-26	GU-32	GV-2	GF-30	GH-31	None	None
Chrysler 70................(1926)	GR-28	GR-28	GS-23	GT-25	GU-31	GV-2	GF-31	GH-32	KE-22	GJ-19
Chrysler 80................(1926)	GR-30	GR-30	GS-25	GT-28	GU-33	GV-2	GF-32	GH-33	KE-24	GJ-20
Chrysler 50................(1927)	GR-29	GR-29	GS-24	GT-26	GU-32	GV-2	GF-30	GH-34	None	None
Chrysler 60................(1927)	GR-31	GR-31	GS-23	GT-27	GU-31	GV-2	GF-33	GH-30	KE-21	GJ-21
Chrysler 70................(1927)	GR-28	GR-28	GS-23	GT-25	GU-31	GV-2	GF-31	GH-32	KE-22	GJ-19
Chrysler 80................(1927)	GR-30	GR-30	GS-25	GT-28	GU-33	GV-2	GF-32	GH-33	KE-24	GJ-20
Chrysler 52................(1928)	GR-29	GR-29	GS-24	{GT-26 Early GT-117 Late	GU-32	GV-2	GF-30	GH-34	None	None
Chrysler 62................(1928)	GR-31	GR-31	GS-23	GT-27	GU-31	GV-2	GF-33	GH-30	KE-21	GJ-21
Chrysler 72................(1928)	GQ-13	GR-32	GS-26	GT-25	GU-31	GV-2	GF-31	GH-32	KE-23	GJ-19
Chrysler Imp. 80...........(1928)	GQ-14	GR-30	GS-25	GT-28	GU-33	GV-2	GF-32	GH-33	KE-24	GJ-20
Chrysler 65................(1929)	GQ-12	GR-31	GS-23	GT-27	GU-31	GV-2	GF-34	GH-36	None	GJ-5
Chrysler 75................(1929)	GQ-13	GR-32	GS-26	GT-25	GU-31	GV-2	GF-31	GH-32	KE-23	GJ-19
Chrysler Imp. 80...........(1929)	GQ-14	GR-30	GS-25	GT-28	GU-33	GV-2	GF-32	GH-33	KE-24	GJ-20
Chrysler 6.................(1930)	GR-38	GR-38	GS-34	GT-40	GU-31	GV-2	GF-188	GH191	None	None
Chrysler 66................(1930)	GQ-75	GR-46	GS-23	GT-27	GU-31	GV-2	GF-34	GH-36	None	GJ-5
Chrysler 70................(1930)	GQ-75	GR-46	GS-23	GT-27	GU-31	GV-2	GF-34	GH-36	None	GJ-5
Chrysler 77................(1930)	GQ-76	GR-62	GS-26	GT-25	GU-31	GV-2	GF-78	GH-150	None	GJ-95
Cleveland 31..............(1925)	GR-24	GR-24	GS-22	{GT-19 In. GT-20 Out.	GU-26	GV-2	GF-24	GH-26	KE-19	GJ-19
Cleveland 43..............(1925)	GR-23	GR-23	GS-21	{GT-19 In. GT-20 Out.	GU-25	GV-9	GF-23	GH-25	KE-16	GJ-18
Cleveland 31..............(1926)	GR-24	GR-24	GS-22	{GT-19 In. GT-20 Out.	GU-26	GV-2	GF-24	GH-26	KE-19	GJ-19
Cleveland 43..............(1926)	GR-23	GR-23	GS-21	{GT-19 In. GT-20 Out.	GU-25	GV-9	GF-23	GH-25	KE-16	GJ-18
Cord Lyc. FDA.............(1930)	GQ-1	GR-5	GS-5	GT-7	GU-14	GV-2	GF-174	GH-184	KE-6	GJ-2
Davis 90, Cont. 7-U........(1925)	GR-2	GR-2	GS-2	GT-2	GU-2	GV-2	GF-2	GH-2	KE-1	GJ-1
Davis 91, Cont. 8-R........(1925)	GR-3	GR-3	GS-3	GT-3	GU-3	GV-3	GF-3	GH-3	KE-2	None
Davis 92, Cont. 11-U.......(1926)	GR-34	GR-34	GS-11	GT-32	GU-37	GV-2	GF-38	GH-40	KE-27	GJ-23
Davis 93, Cont. 20-L.......(1926)	GQ-2	GR-7	GS-2	GT-6	GU-2	GV-2	GF-39	GH-41	KE-28	GJ-4
Davis 92, Cont. 11-U.......(1927)	GR-34	GR-34	GS-11	GT-32	GU-37	GV-2	GF-38	GH-40	KE-27	GJ-23
Davis 94, Cont. 28-L.......(1927)	GQ-2	GR-7	GS-2	GT-6	GU-2	GV-2	GF-9	GH-8	KE-8	GJ-4
Davis 98, Cont. 8-S........(1927)	GQ-5	GR-10	GS-32	{GT-10 In. GT-33 Out.	GU-3	GV-3	GF-40	GH-43	KE-29	GJ-24
Davis 99, Cont. 14-S.......(1928)	GQ-5	GR-10	GS-41	{GT-10 In. GT-33 Out.	GU-3	GV-3	GF-40	GH-44	KE-30	GJ-24
De Soto 6..................(1929)	GR-38	GR-38	GS-34	GT-34	GU-31	GV-2	GF-41	GH-36	None	GJ-25
De Soto Finer 6............(1930)	GR-38	GR-38	GS-34	GT-40	GU-31	GV-2	GF-41	GH-36	None	GJ-25
De Soto 8..................(1930)	GR-126	GR-126	GS-34	GT-40	GU-31	GV-2	GF-41	GH-36	None	GJ-25
Diana Str. 8, Cont. 12-Z...(1926)	GQ-17	GR-39	GS-2	GT-6	GU-34	GV-2	GF-42	GH-46	KE-31	GJ-26
Diana Str. 8, Cont. 12-Z...(1927)	GQ-17	GR-39	GS-2	GT-6	GU-34	GV-2	GF-42	GH-46	KE-31	GJ-26
Diana Str. 8, Cont. 12-Z...(1928)	GQ-17	GR-39	GS-2	GT-6	GU-34	GV-2	GF-42	GH-46	KE-31	GJ-26
Dodge Brothers 4...........(1925)	GR-40	GR-40	GS-35	GT-35	GU-39	GV-2	GF-43	GH-47	KE-32	None
Dodge Brothers 4...........(1926)	GR-40	GR-40	GS-35	GT-35	GU-39	GV-2	GF-43	GH-48	KE-32	None
Dodge Brothers 4........(1927-28)	GR-40	GR-40	GS-35	GT-35	GU-39	GV-2	GF-43	GH-48	KE-33	GJ-14
Dodge Brothers Senior......(1928)	GQ-18	GR-41	GS-36	GT-37	GU-40	GV-2	GF-44	GH-49	KE-34	GJ-27
Dodge Std. 6...............(1928)	GQ-19	GR-42	GS-37	GT-36	GU-41	GV-2	GF-45	GH-50	KE-35	GJ-14
Dodge Brothers Vic. 6...(1928-29)	GQ-19	GR-42	GS-37	GT-36	GU-41	GV-2	GF-45	GH-50	KE-35	GJ-14
Dodge Brothers Senior......(1929)	GQ-18	GR-41	GS-36	GT-37	GU-40	GV-2	GF-44	GH-49	KE-34	GJ-27
Dodge Brothers DA 6........(1929)	GQ-19	GR-42	GS-37	GT-36	GU-22	GV-2	GF-46	GH-51	None	GJ-25
Dodge DC 8.................(1930)	GR-126	GR-126	GS-34	GT-53	GU-31	GV-2	GF-41	GH-36	None	GJ-25
Dodge DD6..................(1930)	GR-38	GR-38	GS-34	GT-40	GU-31	GV-2	GF-41	GH-36	None	GJ-25
Durant A22, Cont. Spec.....(1925)	GR-48	GR-48	{GS-27 In. GS-43 Ex.	GT-13	GU-46	GV-11	GF-52	GH-55	KE-38	None
Durant D55, Cont. 14-L.....(1928)	GQ-2	GR-7	GS-2	GT-41	GU-2	GV-2	GF-53	GH-56	KE-39	GJ-4
Durant 65, Cont. 15-L......(1928)	GQ-2	GR-7	GS-2	GT-41	GU-2	GV-2	GF-53	GH-56	KE-41	GJ-4
Durant M2, Cont. W5........(1928)	GR-2	GR-2	GS-11	GT-2	GU-2	GV-2	GF-54	GH-57	KE-40	GJ-24
Durant 75, Cont. 15-U......(1928)	GR-49	GR-49	GS-11	GT-32	GU-37	GV-2	GF-55	GH-59	KE-42	GJ-23
Durant 4-40, Cont. W5......(1929)	GR-2	GR-2	GS-11	GT-2	GU-2	GV-2	GF-54	GH-57	KE-40	GJ-24
Durant 6-60, Cont. 14-L....(1929)	GQ-2	GR-7	GS-2	GT-41	GU-2	GV-2	GF-53	GH-56	KE-39	GJ-31
Durant 66, Cont. 15-L......(1929)	GQ-2	GR-7	GS-2	GT-41	GU-2	GV-2	GF-53	GH-56	KE-41	GJ-31
Durant 70, Cont. 20-E......(1929)	GR-49	GR-49	GS-11	GT-32	GU-37	GV-2	GF-55	GH-59	KE-43	GJ-23
Durant 63, Cont. 14-L......(1930)	GQ-2	GR-7	GS-2	GT-41	GU-2	GV-2	GF-53	GH-56	KE-39	GJ-31
Durant 614, Cont. 22A......(1930)	GQ-16	GR-35	GS-45	GT-30	GU-37	GV-2	GF-189	GH-192	None	GJ-89
Durant 617, Cont. 15-U.....(1930)	GR-49	GR-49	GS-11	GT-32	GU-37	GV-2	GF-55	GH-59	KE-42	GJ-23
Elcar 4-40, Lyc. CF........(1925)	GR-6	GR-6	GS-6	GT-6	GU-6	GV-2	GF-6	GH-6	KE-5	None
Elcar 6-50, Cont. 7-U......(1925)	GR-2	GR-2	GS-2	GT-2	GU-2	GV-2	GF-2	GH-2	KE-1	GJ-1
Elcar 6-60, Cont. 8-R......(1925)	GR-3	GR-3	GS-3	GT-3	GU-3	GV-3	GF-3	GH-3	KE-2	None
Elcar 8-80, Lyc. H.........(1925)	GQ-1	GR-5	GS-5	GT-5	GU-5	GV-2	GF-56	GH-5	KE-44	GJ-2
Elcar 6-65, Lyc. 4-SM......(1926)	GQ-1	GR-5	GS-5	GT-5	GU-5	GV-2	GF-7	GH-7	KE-7	GJ-3
Elcar 8-81, Lyc. 4-H.......(1926)	GQ-1	GR-5	GS-5	GT-5	GU-5	GV-2	GF-57	GH-5	KE-45	GJ-3
Elcar 4-55, Lyc. CF, CE....(1926)	GR-6	GR-6	GS-6	GT-9	GU-6	GV-2	GF-6	GH-6	KE-5	None
Elcar 6-70, Lyc. WT........(1927)	GQ-3	GR-8	GS-5	GT-7	GU-5	GV-2	GF-10	GH-10	None	GJ-5
Elcar 8-82, Lyc. GT........(1927)	GQ-3	GR-8	GS-5	GT-7	GU-5	GV-2	GF-10	GH-9	None	GJ-5
Elcar 8-90, Lyc. 4-HM......(1927)	GQ-1	GR-5	GS-5	GT-5	GU-5	GV-2	GF-8	GH-5	KE-6	GJ-6
Elcar 6-70, Lyc. WS........(1928)	GQ-3	GR-8	GS-5	GT-7	GU-5	GV-2	GF-10	GH-9	None	GJ-5
Elcar 8-78, Lyc. GT........(1928)	GQ-3	GR-8	GS-5	GT-7	GU-5	GV-2	GF-10	GH-10	KE-9	GJ-5
Elcar 8-91, Lyc. 4-HM......(1928)	GQ-1	GR-5	GS-5	GT-5	GU-5	GV-2	GF-8	GH-5	KE-6	GJ-6
Elcar 8-120, Lyc. MD.......(1928)	GQ-1	GR-5	GS-5	GT-7	GU-14	GV-2	GF-8	GH-5	KE-6	GJ-6
Elcar 8-82, Lyc. GS......(1928-29)	GQ-3	GR-8	GS-5	GT-7	GU-5	GV-2	GF-10	GH-9	None	GJ-5
Elcar 75, Lyc. WS..........(1929)	GQ-3	GR-8	GS-5	GT-7	GU-5	GV-2	GF-10	GH-9	None	GJ-5
Elcar 95, 96, Lyc. GS......(1929)	GQ-3	GR-8	GS-5	GT-7	GU-5	GV-2	GF-10	GH-9	None	GJ-5
Elcar 8-120, Lyc. MD.......(1929)	GQ-1	GR-5	GS-5	GT-7	GU-14	GV-2	GF-8	GH-5	KE-6	GJ-6
Elcar 130, Lyc. 12-K.......(1930)	GQ-22	GR-47	GS-42	GT-30	GU-40	GV-2	GF-51	GH-35	KE-37	GJ-30
Erskine 50, Cont. 8-F......(1927)	GQ-24	GR-50	GS-124	GT-31	GU-50	GV-8	GF-58	GH-63	KE-46	GJ-31
Erskine 6, 51, Cont. 9-F...(1928)	GQ-24	GR-50	GS-124	GT-31	GU-50	GV-8	GF-58	GH-62	KE-46	GJ-31
Erskine 52, Cont. 9-F......(1929)	GQ-24	GR-50	GS-124	GT-31	GU-50	GV-8	GF-58	GH-62	KE-46	GJ-31
Erskine 53.................(1930)	GQ-66	GR-130	GS-73	GT-106	GU-117	GV-2	GF-156	GH-160	KE-121	GJ-76
Essex 6....................(1925)	GR-53	GR-53	GS-46	GT-44	GU-52	GV-8	GF-59	GH-64	KE-47	GJ-14
Essex 6....................(1926)	GR-53	GR-53	GS-46	GT-44	GU-52	GV-8	GF-59	GH-64	KE-47	GJ-14
Essex Super 6..............(1927)	GR-53	GR-53	GS-46	GT-44	GU-53	GV-8	GF-59	GH-64	KE-47	GJ-14
Essex Super 6..............(1928)	GR-53	GR-53	GS-46	GT-44	GU-53	GV-8	GF-59	GH-64	KE-47	GJ-14
Essex Challenger...........(1929)	GR-53	GR-53	GS-46	GT-39	GU-53	GV-8	GF-59	GH-65	KE-47	GJ-14
Essex Super................(1930)	GR-53	GR-53	GS-46	GT-39	GU-53	GV-8	GF-59	GH-78	KE-47	GJ-14
Falcon Knight 10...........(1927)	None	None	None	None	None	None	GF-60	GH-66	KE-48	GJ-34

WHITNEY
SILENT TIMING CHAINS

are satisfactorily quiet and smooth in operation, and dependable in performance, with large bearing area in the joint construction

which insures long life. There is a WHITNEY Chain for every American car originally chain equipped.

CONVERSION TABLE

Giving Whitney Number corresponding to each Chilton Multi-Guide Number in the TIMING CHAIN column of the accompanying Interchangeable Table.

Order by WHITNEY Number　　　　　　　　　Accurately Made to Correct Specifications.

Chilton Multi-Guide Number	WHITNEY Number	Chilton Multi-Guide Number	WHITNEY Number	Chilton Multi-Guide Number	WHITNEY Number	Chilton Multi-Guide Number	WHITNEY Number	Chilton Multi-Guide Number	WHITNEY Number
GJ-1	M205-67	GJ-18	M205-61	GJ-37	T105-91	GJ-55	BC105-66	GJ-72	CM204-54
GJ-2	BL106-100	GJ-19*	SM205-59*	GJ-38*	BU106-110*	GJ-56	CM206-50	GJ-73	CM205-55
GJ-3	T106-89	GJ-20	M006-78	GJ-40	BU106-108	GJ-57	C104-85	GJ-75	CM206-51
GJ-4*	M005-81*	GJ-21	M005-74	GJ-41	M206-72	GJ-58	C105-85	GJ-76	M206-71
GJ-5*	V205-49*	GJ-23	M005-82	GJ-42	M205-75	GJ-59	BU106-106	GJ-77	BT-105-90
GJ-6	M006-85	GJ-24	M205-63	GJ-43	C106-96	GJ-60	C106-84	GJ-78	BL-106-110
GJ-7	BF105-90	GJ-25	CM205-48	GJ-44	C105-82	GJ-61*	BL106-96*	GJ-79	N105-84
GJ-8	BH106-128	GJ-26	C105-76	GJ-45	T105-89	GJ-62	CM206-50	GJ-82	BH106-112
GJ-9	M005-76	GJ-27*	SM206-63*	GJ-46	M206-67	GJ-63	BH106-102	GJ-83	BL106-128
GJ-10	CM207-56	GJ-28	E-105-91	GJ-47	M005-70	GJ-64	CM-205-44	GJ-85	SM206-65
GJ-11	CM206-57	GJ-29	BL106-112	GJ-48	M005-75	GJ-65	M005-71	GJ-86	N104-85
GJ-12	C107-88	GJ-30	BK106-107	GJ-49	BU106-84	GJ-66	M206-70	GJ-87	BC103-66
GJ-13	CM207-54	GJ-31*	M005-80*	GJ-50	BU106-102	GJ-67	T106-94	GJ-88	R104-2-85
GJ-14*	CM205-57*	GJ-33	N104-2-64	GJ-51	BE107-112	GJ-68	C106-95	GJ-89	CM205-46
GJ-15	M206-66	GJ-34	BT105-98	GJ-52	BC103-62	GJ-69	CM206-52	GJ-90	K205-48
GJ-16	SM206-77	GJ-35	BF105-98	GJ-53	BC103-64	GJ-70	CM204-56	GJ-91	N103-21
GJ-17	M206-64	GJ-36	M206-73	GJ-54	CM205-52	GJ-71	CM205-54	GJ-95	CM206-48

*GJ-4 For DURANT 65, 66, 1928-29 order WHITNEY M005-80.
GJ-5 For CHRYSLER 65, 66, 70, 1928-30 and for AUBURN 8 (Late 1929-30) and AUBURN 6 (Late 1929-30) order WHITNEY CM205-49.
GJ-14 For DODGE 4, 1927-8, Standard 1928, Victory 1928-29; ESSEX 1925-30 and HUDSON 8, 1930 order WHITNEY No. SM205-57.
　　For FRANKLIN 1925-6-7 and OLDSMOBILE 1928-9F order WHITNEY No. M205-57.
GJ-19 For CLEVELAND 31, 1925-6; FRANKLIN 12B, 1928; FRANKLIN 130, 135, 137, 1929; FRANKLIN 140, 145, 147, 1930 order WHITNEY No. M205-59.
GJ-27 For PACKARD 6 & 8, 1925-6-7 and PEERLESS 70, 1925 order WHITNEY No. M206-63.
GJ-31 For DURANT 60, 1929 and 63, 1930 order WHITNEY No. M005-81.
GJ-38 For GRAHAM-PAIGE 615 (Late) order WHITNEY No. E105-91, for 619, 621, 629 late order WHITNEY BK106-110.
GJ-61 For PIERCE-ARROW, engines with M order WHITNEY BH106-96.

THE WHITNEY MFG. CO.
Hartford, Conn.

JOBBERS IN ALL PRINCIPAL DISTRIBUTING CENTERS

Warehouse Stocks in

Atlanta, Ga.　　Chicago, Ill.　　Dallas, Texas　　Los Angeles, Cal.　　New York City　　Seattle, Wash.　　San Francisco, Cal.

ENGINE ASSEMBLY, Section 2—Continued

Interchangeable Parts have the same CHILTON NUMBER in Any Column

Car Make and Model	VALVE ASSEMBLY						TIMING DRIVE			
	Inlet Valve	Exhaust Valve	Valve Stem Guide	Valve Springs	Valve Lifters (Tappets)	Valve Lifter Adjusting Screws	Camshaft Gear or Sprocket	Crankshaft Gear or Sprocket	Generator Gear or Sprocket	Timing Chain (See Footnote)
Falcon Knight 12............(1928)	None	None	None	None	None	None	GF-61	GH-66	KE-48	GJ-34
Flint B40, Cont. 7-U....(1925-26)	GR-2	GR-2	GS-2	GT-2	GU-2	GV-2	GF-2	GH-2	KE-49	GJ-24
Flint E55, Cont. 6-E......(1925-26)	GR-54	GR-54	GS-47	GT-3	GU-3	GV-3	GF-63	GH-67	KE-50	GJ-36
Flint B60, Cont. 14-U.........(1926)	GR-49	GR-49	GS-11	GT-6	GU-54	GV-3	GF-62	GH-68	KE-49	GJ-23
Flint E80, Cont. 6-E.........(1926)	GR-54	GR-54	GS-47	GT-3	GU-3	GV-3	GF-63	GH-67	KE-50	GJ-36
Flint, Jr., Cont. 9-L.........(1926)	GQ-2	GR-7	GS-2	GT-6	GU-2	GV-2	GF-64	GH-41	KE-51	GJ-4
Flint 60, Cont. 14-U.........(1927)	GR-49	GR-49	GS-11	GT-6	GU-54	GV-5	GF-62	GH-68	KE-49	GJ-23
Flint 80, Cont. 6-E.........(1927)	GR-54	GR-54	GS-47	GT-3	GU-3	GV-3	GF-63	GH-67	KE-50	GJ-36
Flint Jr., Cont. 9-L.........(1927)	GQ-2	GR-7	GS-2	GT-6	GU-2	GV-2	GF-64	GH-41	KE-51	GJ-4
Ford T.................(1925)	GR-55	GR-55	None	GT-45	GU-55	None	GF-65	GH-69	KE-52	None
Ford T.................(1926)	GR-55	GR-55	None	GT-45	GU-55	None	GF-65	GH-69	KE-52	None
Ford T.................(1927)	GR-55	GR-55	None	GT-45	GU-55	None	GF-65	GH-69	KE-52	None
Ford A.................(1928)	GR-56	GR-56	GS-50	GT-46	GU-56	None	GF-66	GH-70	None	None
Ford A.................(1929)	GR-56	GR-56	GS-50	GT-46	GU-56	None	GF-66	GH-70	None	None
Ford A.................(1930)	GR-56	GR-56	GS-50	GT-46	GU-56	None	GF-66	GH-70	None	None
Franklin 11.............(1925)	GR-57	GR-57	GS-51	GT-47	GU-57	GV-24	GF-67	GH-71	KE-53	GJ-14
Franklin 11.............(1926)	GR-57	GR-57	GS-51	GT-47	GU-57	GV-24	GF-67	GH-71	KE-53	GJ-14
Franklin 11-B.............(1927)	GR-57	GR-57	GS-51	GT-47	GU-57	GV-24	GF-67	GH-71	KE-53	GJ-14
Franklin Ser. 12.............(1928)	GQ-27	GR-58	GS-51 In. / GS-52 Ex.	GT-42 In. / GT-48 Out.	GU-57	GV-24	GF-67	GH-71	KE-53	GJ-19
Franklin 130.............(1929)	GQ-27	GR-58	GS-51 In. / GS-52 Ex.	GT-42 In. / GT-48 Out.	GU-57	GV-24	GF-67	GH-71	KE-53	GJ-19
Franklin 135, 137.............(1929)	GR-36	GR-36	GS-51 In. / GS-52 Ex.	GT-43 In. / GT-66 Out.	GU-57	GV-24	GF-67	GH-71	KE-53	GJ-19
Franklin 145, 147.............(1930)	GQ-44	GR-147	GS-72 In. / GS-77 Ex.	GT-50 In. / GT-52 Out.	GU-48	GV-24	GF-67	GH-71	KE-53	GJ-19
Gardner 6-A, Lyc. 4-S.........(1925)	GQ-1	GR-5	GS-5	GT-5	GU-5	GV-2	GF-7	GH-7	KE-7	GJ-34
Gardner 8-A, Lyc. 2-H.........(1925)	GQ-1	GR-5	GS-5	GT-5	GU-5	GV-2	GF-5	GH-5	KE-4	GJ-2
Gardner Series 5, Lyc. CE.......(1925)	GR-6	GR-6	GS-6	GT-9	GU-6	GV-2	GF-6	GH-6	KE-5	None
Gardner 6-B, Lyc. 4-S......(1926-27)	GQ-1	GR-5	GS-5	GT-5	GU-5	GV-2	GF-7	GH-7	KE-7	GJ-3
Gardner 8-B, Lyc. 2-H......(1926-27)	GQ-1	GR-5	GS-5	GT-5	GU-5	GV-2	GF-8	GH-5	KE-6	GJ-3
Gardner 80, Lyc. GT.........(1927)	GQ-3	GR-8	GS-5	GT-7	GU-5	GV-2	GF-10	GH-10	KE-9	GJ-5
Gardner 90, Lyc. 4-HM.........(1927)	GQ-1	GR-5	GS-5	GT-5	GU-5	GV-2	GF-8	GH-5	KE-6	GJ-6
Gardner 75, Lyc. GT.........(1928)	GQ-3	GR-8	GS-5	GT-7	GU-5	GV-2	GF-10	GH-10	KE-9	GJ-5
Gardner 85, Lyc. GS.........(1928)	GQ-3	GR-8	GS-5	GT-7	GU-5	GV-2	GF-10	GH-9	None	GJ-5
Gardner 95, Lyc. MD.........(1928)	GQ-1	GR-5	GS-5	GT-7	GU-14	GV-2	GF-8	GH-5	KE-6	GJ-6
Gardner 120, Lyc. GT.........(1929)	GQ-3	GR-8	GS-5	GT-7	GU-5	GV-2	GF-10	GH-10	None	GJ-5
Gardner 125, Lyc. GS.........(1929)	GQ-3	GR-8	GS-5	GT-7	GU-5	GV-2	GF-10	GH-9	None	GJ-5
Gardner 130, Lyc. MD.........(1929)	GQ-1	GR-5	GS-5	GT-7	GU-14	GV-2	GF-8	GH-5	KE-6	GJ-6
Gardner 136, Lyc. WR.........(1930)	GQ-3	GR-8	GS-5	GT-7	GU-13	GV-2	GF-10	GH-190	None	GJ-5
Gardner 140, Lyc. GS.........(1930)	GQ-3	GR-8	GS-5	GT-7	GU-5	GV-2	GF-10	GH-9	None	GJ-5
Gardner 150, Lyc. MDG.......(1930)	GQ-3	GR-8	GS-5	GT-7	GU-13	GV-2	GF-8	GH-191	KE-6	GJ-6
Graham Paige 835, Cont.12K.(1928-29)	GQ-22	GR-47	GS-42	GT-36	GU-40	GV-22	GF-51	GH-35	KE-37	GJ-30
Graham Paige 610.........(1928-29)	GQ-28	GR-33	GS-53	GT-49	GU-5	GV-2	GF-68	GH-74	KE-54	GJ-37
Graham Paige 614.........(1928-29)	GQ-28	GR-33	GS-53	GT-49	GU-5	GV-2	GF-68	GH-74	KE-54	GJ-37
Graham Paige 619.........(1928-29)	GQ-29	GR-59	GS-54	GT-51	GU-14	GV-2	GF-69	GH-75	KE-55	GJ-38
Graham Paige 629.........(1928-29)	GQ-29	GR-59	GS-54	GT-51	GU-14	GV-2	GF-69	GH-75	KE-55	GJ-38
Graham Paige 612 (Early).....(1929)	GQ-28	GR-33	GS-53	GT-49	GU-5	GV-2	GF-68	GH-74	KE-54	GJ-37
Graham Paige 612 (Late)......(1929)	GQ-28	GR-33	GS-53	GT-49	GU-5	GV-2	GF-190	GH-193	KE-140	GJ-28
Graham Paige 615.............(1929)	GQ-28	GR-33	GS-53	GT-49	GU-5	GV-2	GF-68	GH-74	KE-54	GJ-37
Graham Paige 621.............(1929)	GQ-72	GR-59	GS-54	GT-51	GU-14	GV-2	GF-70	GH-77	KE-56	GJ-38
Grah'm P. 827, Cnt.12K, Early.(1929)	GQ-22	GR-47	GS-42	GT-36	GU-40	GV-2	GF-51	GH-35	KE-37	GJ-30
Grah'm P. 827, Cnt. 12K, Late.(1929)	GQ-22	GR-47	GS-139	GT-61	GU-40	GV-2	GF-51	GH-35	KE-37	GJ-30
Grah'm P. 837, Cnt. 12K, Early (1929)	GQ-22	GR-47	GS-42	GT-36	GU-40	GV-2	GF-51	GH-35	KE-37	GJ-30
Grah'm P. 837, Cnt. 12K, Late(1929)	GQ-22	GR-47	GS-139	GT-61	GU-40	GV-2	GF-51	GH-35	KE-37	GJ-30
Graham Std. 6.............(1930)	GQ-28	GR-33	GS-53	GT-49	GU-5	GV-2	GF-190	GH-193	KE-140	GJ-28
Graham Spec. 6.............(1930)	GQ-28	GR-33	GS-53	GT-49	GU-5	GV-2	GF-190	GH-193	KE-140	GJ-28
Graham Std. and Spec. 8.......(1930)	GQ-28	GR-33	GS-53	GT-49	GU-5	GV-2	GF-190	GH-193	KE-140	GJ-28
Graham Custom 8.............(1930)	GQ-22	GR-47	GS-139	GT-61	GU-40	GV-2	GF-51	GH-35	KE-37	GJ-30
Hudson Super 6.............(1925)	GR-63	GR-63	GS-58	GT-54	GU-64	GV-2	GF-73	GH-79	KE-59	GJ-27
Hudson Super 6 ·· ....(1926)	GR-63	GR-63	GS-58	GT-54	GU-64	GV-2	GF-73	GH-79	KE-59	GJ-27
Hudson Super 6.............(1927)	GR-63	GR-63	GS-58	GT-54	GU-64	GV-2	GF-73	GH-80	KE-59	GJ-27
Hudson Super 6 ···.........(1928)	GQ-32	GR-65	GS-28 In. / GS-59 Ex.	GT55-63Int. / GT-54 Ex.	GU-65	GV-2	GF-73	GH-80	KE-59	GJ-27
Hudson Greater 6.............(1929)	GQ-32	GR-65	GS-28 In. / GS-60 Ex.	GT55-63Int. / GT-54 Ex.	GU-65	GV-2	GF-73	GH-80	KE-59	GJ-27
Hudson 8.................(1930)	GQ-20	GR-53	GS-46	GT-39	GU-53	GV-8	GF-180	GH-78	KE-47	GJ-14
Hupmobile R.............(1925)	GR-67	GR-67	GS-62	GT-58	GU-14	GV-2	GF-75	GH-82	KE-62	GJ-42
Hupmobile E1.............(1925-26)	GQ-31	GR-66	GS-61	GT-57	None	None	GF-74	GH-81	KE-60	GJ-41
Hupmobile A1.............(1926)	GR-68	GR-68	GS-63	GT-59	GU-68	GV-3	GF-76	GH-84	KE-61	GJ-44
Hupmobile E2.............(1926-27)	GQ-33	GR-66	GS-61	GT-57	None	None	GF-74	GH-83	KE-60	GJ-41
Hupmobile A2.............(1927)	GR-68	GR-68	GS-63	GT-59	GU-63	GV-27	GF-76	GH-84	KE-61	GJ-44
Hupmobile E3.............(1927-28)	GQ-33	GR-66	GS-61	GT-57	None	None	GF-74	GH-83	KE-60	GJ-43
Hupmobile Cent. 6.............(1928)	GR-68	GR-68	GS-63	GT-59	GU-63	GV-27	GF-76	GH-84	KE-61	GJ-44
Hupmobile Cent. 8.............(1928)	GQ-33	GR-66	GS-61	GT-57	None	None	GF-74	GH-83	KE-60	GJ-43
Hupmobile Cent. 125.............(1928)	GQ-33	GR-66	GS-61	GT-57	None	None	GF-74	GH-83	KE-60	GJ-43
Hupmobile M8.........(1928-29)	GQ-33	GR-66	GS-61	GT-57	None	None	GF-74	GH-83	KE-60	GJ-43
Hupmobile Cent.............(1929)	GR-68	GR-68	GS-63	GT-59	GU-63	GV-27	GF-76	GH-84	KE-61	GJ-44
Hupmobile C8.............(1930)	GQ-73	GR-146	GS-140	GT-38 In. / GT-64 Out.	None	None	GF-182	GH-194	KE-132	GJ-85
Hupmobile H, U.............(1930)	GQ-77	GR-150	GS-140	GT-38 In. / GT-64 Out.	None	None	GF-182	GH-194	KE-132	GJ-85
Hupmobile S6.............(1930)	GR-68	GR-68	GS-63	GT-59	GU-63	GV-27	GF-181	GH-193	KE-131	GJ-18
Jewett 6-50.............(1925)	GR-69	GR-69	GS-64	GT-60	GU-3	GV-3	GF-77	GH-85	KE-62	GJ-59
Jewett ND, Ct. 18-L.............(1926)	GQ-36	GR-73	GS-2	GT-6	GU-2	GV-2	GF-78	GH-41	KE-63	GJ-45
Jordan K, L, Cont. 6-S.........(1925)	GR-43	GR-43	GS-3	GT-3	GU-3	GV-3	GF-79	GH-86	KE-139	GJ-17
Jordan A, Cont. 9-K.........(1925)	GQ-37	GR-72	GS-11	GT-62 In. / GT-69 Out.	GU-3	GV-3	GF-80	GH-87	KE-64	GJ-46
Jordan A, Cont. 9-K.........(1926)	GQ-37	GR-72	GS-11	GT-62 In. / GT-69 Out.	GU-3	GV-3	GF-80	GH-87	KE-64	GJ-46
Jordan J, Cont. 8-S.........(1926)	GQ-5	GR-10	GS-32	GT-10 In. / GT-33 Out.	GU-3	GV-3	GF-40	GH-43	KE-29	GJ-24
Jordan AA, Cont. 9-K.........(1927)	GQ-37	GR-72	GS-11	GT-62 In. / GT-69 Out.	GU-3	GV-3	GF-80	GH-87	KE-64	GJ-46
Jordan J1, Cont. 8-S.........(1927)	GQ-5	GR-10	GS-32	GT-10 In. / GT-33 Out.	GU-3	GV-3	GF-40	GH-43	KE-29	GJ-24
Jordan R, Cont. 12E........(1927-28)	GQ-21	GR-44	GS-45	GT-32	GU-37	GV-2	GF-81	GH-88	KE-65	GJ-47
Jordan JJ, Cont. 14-S.........(1928)	GQ-5	GR-10	GS-41	GT-10 In. / GT-33 Out.	GU-3	GV-3	GF-40	GH-43	KE-29	GJ-24

Footnote: For corresponding timing chain numbers advertised, see pages 201, 203.

ENGINE ASSEMBLY, Section 2—Continued

Interchangeable Parts have the same CHILTON NUMBER in Any Column

Car Make and Model	VALVE ASSEMBLY						TIMING DRIVE			
	Inlet Valve	Exhaust Valve	Valve Stem Guide	Valve Springs	Valve Lifters (Tappets)	Valve Lifter Adjusting Screws	Cam-shaft Gear or Sprocket	Crank-shaft Gear or Sprocket	Generator Gear or Sprocket	Timing Chain (See Footnote)
Jordan JE, Cont. 15-S.........(1928)	GQ-5	GR-10	GS-41	{GT-10 In. {GT-33 Out.	GU-3	GV-3	GF-40	GH-43	KE-30	GJ-48
Jordan E, Cont. 16-C.........(1929)	GQ-38	GR-37	GS-45	GT-32	GU-37	GV-2	GF-83	GH-88	KE-66	GJ-23
Jordan G, Cont. 15-S.........(1929)	GQ-5	GR-10	GS-41	{GT-10 In. {GT-33 Out.	GU-3	GV-3	GF-40	GH-43	KE-66	GJ-48
Jordan G90, Cont. 15-S.......(1930)	GQ-5	GR-10	GS-41	{GT-10 In. {GT-33 Out.	GU-3	GV-3	GF-40	GH-43	KE-84	GJ-48
Jordan T80, Cont. 17-S........(1930)	GQ-5	GR-10	GS-49	{GT-10 In. {GT-33 Out.	GU-3	GV-2	GF-82	GH-195	KE-84	GJ-48
Kissel 6-55.................(1925)	GR-75	GR-75	GS-29	GT-122	GU-72	GV-2	GF-84	GH-89	KE-67	GJ-49
Kissel 8-75, Lyc. 3-H.........(1925)	GQ-1	GR-5	GS-5	GT-5	GU-5	GV-2	GF-8	GH-5	KE-68	GJ-2
Kissel 6-55.................(1926)	GR-75	GR-75	GS-29	GT-122	GU-72	GV-2	GF-84	GH-89	KE-67	GJ-49
Kissel 8-75, Lyc. 3-H.........(1926)	GQ-1	GR-5	GS-5	GT-5	GU-5	GV-2	GF-8	GH-5	KE-68	GJ-2
Kissel 6-55.................(1927)	GR-75	GR-75	GS-29	GT-122	GU-72	GV-2	GF-84	GH-89	KE-67	GJ-49
Kissel 8-65, Lyc. WS.........(1927)	GQ-3	GR-8	GS-5	GT-7	GU-5	GV-2	GF-10	GH-9	None	GJ-5
Kissel 8-75, Lyc. 3H.........(1927)	GQ-1	GR-5	GS-5	GT-5	GU-5	GV-2	GF-8	GH-5	KE-68	GJ-2
Kissel 6-70, Lyc. WS.........(1928)	GQ-3	GR-8	GS-5	GT-7	GU-5	GV-2	GF-10	GH-9	None	GJ-5
Kissel 8-80, Lyc. GS.........(1928)	GQ-3	GR-8	GS-5	GT-7	GU-5	GV-2	GF-10	GH-9	None	GJ-5
Kissel 8-80 S, Lyc. GS.........(1928)	GQ-3	GR-8	GS-5	GT-7	GU-5	GV-2	GF-10	GH-9	None	GJ-5
Kissel 8-90, Lyc. HM.........(1928)	GQ-1	GR-5	GS-5	GT-5	GU-5	GV-2	GF-85	GH-5	KE-6	GJ-6
Kissel 6-73, Lyc. WR.........(1929)	GQ-3	GR-8	GS-5	GT-7	GU-5	GV-2	GF-10	GH-9	None	GJ-5
Kissel 8-95, Lyc. GS.........(1929)	GQ-3	GR-8	GS-5	3T-7	GU-5	GV-2	GF-10	GH-9	None	GJ-5
Kissel 8-126, Lyc. MD.......(1929)	GQ-1	GR-5	GS-5	GT-5	GU-14	GV-2	GF-85	GH-9	KE-6	GJ-6
La Salle 303.................(1927)	GQ-9	GR-19	GS-17	GT-18	GU-21	GV-8	GF-19	GH-93	KE-18	*GJ-13
La Salle 303.................(1928)	GQ-9	GR-19	GS-17	GT-18	GU-21	GV-8	GF-19	GH-20	KE-18	*GJ-13
La Salle 328.................(1929)	GQ-9	GR-19	GS-17	GT-18	GU-21	GV-8	GF-19	GH-20	KE-19	*GJ-13
La Salle 340.................(1930)	GQ-35	GR-127	GS-17	GT-18	GU-21	GV-8	GF-19	GH-20	KE-19	*GJ-13
Lincoln 8...................(1925)	GR-80	GR-80	GS-74	GT-65	GU-82	GV-14	GF-88	GH-95	KE-71	GJ-16
Lincoln 8...................(1926)	GR-80	GR-80	GS-74	GT-65	GU-82	GV-14	GF-88	GH-95	KE-71	GJ-16
Lincoln 8...................(1927)	GQ-43	GR-81	GS-74	GT-65	GU-82	GV-14	GF-88	GH-95	KE-71	GJ-16
Lincoln 8...................(1928)	GQ-43	GR-81	GS-74	GT-65	GU-82	GV-14	GF-88	GH-95	KE-71	GJ-16
Lincoln 8...................(1929)	GQ-43	GR-81	GS-74	GT-65	GU-82	GV-14	GF-88	GH-95	KE-71	GJ-16
Lincoln....................(1930)	GQ-43	GR-81	GS-74	GT-65	GU-82	GV-14	GF-88	GH-95	KE-71	GJ-16
Locomobile Jr. 8.............(1925)	GR-83	GR-83	GS-75	{GT-67 In. {GT-83 Out.	GU-84	GV-30	GF-90	GH-97	KE-73	GJ-50
Locomobile 48...............(1925)	GR-84	GR-84	GS-76	GT-68	GU-85	GV-27	GF-91	GH-98	KE-74	None
Locomobile 48...............(1926)	GR-84	GR-84	GS-76	GT-68	GU-85	GV-27	GF-91	GH-98	KE-74	None
Locomobile 90...............(1926)	GR-85	GR-85	GS-30	GT-68	GU-86	GV-31	GF-92	GH-99	KE-75	GJ-51
Locomobile Jr. 8.............(1926)	GR-83	GR-83	GS-75	{GT-67 In. {GT-83 Out.	GU-84	GV-30	GF-90	GH-97	KE-73	GJ-50
Locomobile 48...............(1927)	GR-84	GR-84	GS-76	GT-68	GU-85	GV-27	GF-91	GH-98	KE-74	None
Locomobile 8-66.............(1927)	GR-83	GR-83	GS-75	{GT-67 In. {GT-83 Out.	GU-84	GV-30	GF-93	GH-100	KE-76	GJ-50
Locomobile 8-80, Lyc. HD.....(1927)	GQ-1	GR-5	GS-5	GT-7	GU-14	GV-2	GF-94	GH-5	KE-77	GJ-2
Locomobile 90...............(1927)	GR-85	GR-85	GS-30	GT-68	GU-86	GV-31	GF-92	GH-99	KE-75	GJ-51
Locomobile 48...............(1928)	GR-84	GR-84	GS-76	GT-68	GU-85	GV-27	GF-91	GH-98	KE-74	None
Locomobile 8-70, Con. 8-S....(1928)	GQ-5	GR-10	GS-32	{GT-10 In. {GT-33 Out.	GU-3	GV-2	GF-40	GH-43	KE-29	GJ-24
Locomobile 8-80, Lyc. HD.....(1928)	GQ-1	GR-5	GS-5	GT-7	GU-14	GV-2	GF-94	GH-5	KE-77	GJ-6
Locomobile 90...............(1928)	GR-85	GR-85	GS-30	GT-68	GU-86	GV-31	GF-92	GH-99	KE-75	GJ-51
Locomobile 8-80, Lyc. HD....(1929)	GQ-1	GR-5	GS-5	GT-7	GU-14	GV-2	GF-94	GH-5	KE-77	GJ-6
Locomobile 86, 88, Lyc. HDL..(1929)	GQ-1	GR-5	GS-5	GT-7	GU-14	GV-2	GF-94	GH-5	KE-77	GJ-6
Locomobile 90...............(1929)	GR-85	GR-85	GS-30	GT-68	GU-86	GV-31	GF-92	GH-99	KE-75	GJ-51
Marmon 74..................(1925)	GR-86	GR-86	GS-78	{GR-70 In. {GT-72 Out.	GU-90	GV-6	GF-95	GH-102	KE-78	None
Marmon 74..................(1926)	GR-86	GR-86	GS-78	{GT-70 In. {GT-72 Out.	GU-90	GV-6	GF-95	GH-102	KE-78	None
Marmon, Little...............(1927)	GQ-46	GR-87	GS-79	GT-73	GU-91	GV-11	GF-96	GH-103	None	GJ-33
Marmon E75.................(1927)	GR-86	GR-86	GS-78	{GT-70 In. {GT-72 Out.	GU-90	GV-6	GF-97	GH-104	KE-79	None
Marmon 68..................(1928)	GQ-47	GR-88	GS-80	GT-74	GU-92	GV-2	GF-99	GH-105	None	GJ-52
Marmon E75.................(1928)	GR-86	GR-86	GS-78	{GT-70 In. {GT-72 Out.	GU-90	GV-6	GF-97	GH-104	KE-79	None
Marmon 78..................(1928)	GQ-48	GR-89	GS-79	GT-73	GU-91	GV-11	GF-98	GH-106	None	GJ-53
Marmon 68..................(1929)	GQ-47	GR-88	GS-80	GT-74	GU-42	GV-2	GF-99	GH-105	None	GJ-52
Marmon, Roosevelt..........(1929)	GQ-47	GR-88	GS-80	GT-74	GU-42	GV-2	GF-99	GH-105	None	GJ-52
Marmon 78..................(1929)	GQ-48	GR-89	GS-80	GT-73	GU-91	GV-11	GF-98	GH-106	None	GJ-53
Marmon 69..................(1930)	GQ-47	GR-88	GS-80	GT-88	GU-42	GV-2	GF-99	GH-105	None	GJ-52
Marmon 79..................(1930)	GQ-79	GR-145	GS-31	GT-98	GU-40	GV-2	GF-184	GH-198	None	GJ-87
Marmon Big 8...............(1930)	GQ-79	GR-145	GS-31	GT-98	GU-40	GV-2	GF-184	GH-198	None	GJ-87
Marquette..................(1930)	GQ-25	GR-45	GS-33	GT-102	GU-38	GV-2	GF-100	GH-200	None	GJ-54
Maxwell....................(1925)	GR-29	GR-29	GS-24	GT-26	GU-32	GV-2	GF-30	GH-31	None	None
Moon Series A, Cont. 7-Z....(1925)	GR-2	GR-2	GS-2	GT-2	GU-2	GV-2	GF-101	GH-2	KE-81	GJ-24
Moon Series A Cont. 7-Z......(1926)	GR-2	GR-2	GS-2	GT-2	GU-2	GV-2	GF-101	GH-2	KE-81	GJ-24
Moon Series A, Cont. 7-Z......(1927)	GR-2	GR-2	GS-2	GT-2	GU-2	GV-2	GF-101	GH-2	KE-81	GJ-24
Moon 6-60, Cont. 26-L....(1927)	GQ-2	GR-7	GS-2	GT-6	GU-2	GV-2	GF-102	GH-8	KE-82	GJ-4
Moon Series A, Cont. 7-Z......(1928)	GR-2	GR-2	GS-2	GT-2	GU-2	GV-2	GF-101	GH-2	KE-81	GJ-24
Moon 6-60, Cont. 26-L....(1928)	GQ-2	GR-7	GS-2	GT-6	GU-2	GV-2	GF-102	GH-8	KE-82	GJ-4
Moon 6-72, Cont. 11-E....(1928)	GQ-21	GR-44	GS-45	GT-75	GU-37	GV-2	GF-103	GH-109	KE-83	GJ-47
Moon 8-80, Cont. 15-S.....(1928-29)	GQ-5	GR-10	GS-41	{GT-10 In. {GT-33 Out	GU-3	GV-3	GF-40	GH-101	KE-84	GJ-48
Moon 6-72, Cont. 11-E........(1929)	GQ-21	GR-44	GS-45	GT-75	GU-37	GV-2	GF-103	GH-109	KE-83	GJ-47
Nash Adv. 6.................(1925)	GR-91	GR-91	GS-86	{GT-76 In. {GT-77 Out.	GU-94	GV-6	GF-104	GH-110	None	None
Nash Spec. 6................(1925)	GR-92	GR-92	GS-87	{GT-76 In. {GT-77 Out.	GU-94	GV-6	GF-105	GH-111	None	None
Nash Adv. 6.................(1926)	GR-93	GR-93	GS-86	{GT-76 In. {GT-77Out.	GU-94	GV-6	GF-104	GH-110	None	None
Nash Spec. 6................(1926)	GR-92	GR-92	GS-87	{GT-76 In. {GT-77 Out.	GU-94	GV-6	GF-105	GH-111	None	None
Nash Adv. 6.................(1927)	GR-93	GR-93	GS-86	{GT-76 In. {GT-77 Out.	GU-94	GV-6	GF-106	GH-112	None	None
Nash Spec. 6................(1927)	GR-94	GR-94	GS-87	{GT-76 In. {GT-77 Out.	GU-94	GV-6	GF-107	GH-113	None	None
Nash Light 6................(1927)	GR-1	GR-1	GS-1	GT-1	GU-1	GV-2	GF-1	GH-1	None	None
Nash Adv. 6.................(1928)	GR-93	GR-93	GS-86	{GT-76 In. {GT-77 Out.	GU-94	GV-6	GF-106	GH-112	None	None
Nash Spec. 6................(1928)	GR-94	GR-94	GS-87	{GT-76 In. {GT-77Out.	GU-94	GV-6	GF-107	GH-113	None	None
Nash Std. 6.................(1928)	GR-95	GR-95	GS-1	GT-1	GU-1	GV-2	GF-1	GH-114	None	None

Footnote: For corresponding timing chain numbers advertised, see pages 201, 203.

ENGINE ASSEMBLY, Section 2—Continued

Interchangeable Parts have the same CHILTON NUMBER in Any Column

Car Make and Model	VALVE ASSEMBLY						TIMING DRIVE			
	Inlet Valve	Exhaust Valve	Valve Stem Guide	Valve Springs	Valve Lifters (Tappets)	Valve Lifter Adjusting Screws	Cam-shaft Gear or Sprocket	Crank-shaft Gear or Sprocket	Generator Gear or Sprocket	Timing Chain (See Footnote)
Nash Adv. 6..............(1929)	GR-93	GR-93	GS-89	{GT-76 In. {GT-78 Out.	GU-94	GV-6	GF-106	GH-112	None	None
Nash Spec. 6..............(1929)	GR-94	GR-94	GS-88	{GT-76 In. {GT-78 Out.	GU-94	GV-6	GF-107	GH-113	None	None
Nash Std. 6..............(1929)	GR-95	GR-95	GS-90	GT-103	GU-1	GV-2	GF-1	GH-114	None	None
Nash Single Ignition 6........(1930)	GQ-26	GR-51	GS-38	GT-103	GU-1	GV-2	{GF-1 {GF-191	{GH-114 {GH-195	None	None
Nash Twin Ignition 6..........(1930)	GR-143	GR-143	GS-39	{GT-76 In. {GT-78 Out.	GU-94	GV-6	GF-192	GF-196	None	None
Nash Twin Ignition 8..........(1930)	GQ-30	GR-144	GS-89	{GT-111 In. {GT-71 Out.	GU-94	GV-6	GF-191	GH-194	None	GJ-55
Oakland 6-54..............(1925)	GR-96	GR-96	GS-92	GT-136	GU-97	GV-2	GF-108	GH-115	KE-86	GJ-19
Oakland O6..............(1926)	GR-96	GR-96	GS-92	GT-137	GU-98	GV-2	GF-108	GH-115	KE-86	GJ-19
Oakland GO6..............(1927)	GR-96	GR-96	GS-92	GT-137	GU-98	GV-2	GF-108	GH-115	KE-86	GJ-19
Oakland AA-6..............(1928)	GQ-49	GR-98	GS-94	GT-79	GU-98	GV-2	GF-109	GH-116	None	GJ-56
Oakland AA-6..............(1929)	GQ-49	GR-98	GS-94	GT-79	GU-98	GV-2	GF-109	GH-116	None	GJ-56
Oakland 8..............(1930)	GQ-34	GR-148	GS-40	GT-140	GU-16	GV-10	GF-186	GH-201	None	GJ-89
Oldsmobile C..............(1925)	GR-99	GR-99	GS-95	GT-130	GU-100	GV-2	GF-110	GH-117	KE-87	GJ-19
Oldsmobile D..............(1926)	GR-99	GR-99	GS-95	GT-130	GU-100	GV-2	GF-111	GH-118	KE-88	GJ-19
Oldsmobile E..............(1927)	GR-100	GR-100	GS-93	{GT-131 In. {GT-138 Out.	GU-101	GV-2	GF-111	GH-118	KE-88	GJ-19
Oldsmobile F28..............(1928)	GQ-51	GR-101	GS-96	GT-80	GU-38	GV-2	GF-112	GH-119	KE-88	GJ-14
Oldsmobile F29..............(1929)	GQ-50	GR-52	{GS-96 In. {GS-44 Ex.	GT-139	GU-38	GV-2	GF-112	GH-119	KE-88	GJ-14
Oldsmobile F30..............(1930)	GQ-50	GR-52	{GS-96 In. {GS-44 Ex.	GT-139	GU-38	GV-2	GF-112	GH-119	KE-88	GJ-14
Overland 91..............(1925)	GR-102	GR-102	GS-97	GT-81	GU-103	GV-2	GF-113	GH-120	KE-89	None
Overland 93..............(1925)	GR-103	GR-103	GS-98	GT-82	GU-104	GV-2	GF-114	GH-121	KE-90	None
Overland 91..............(1926)	GR-102	GR-102	GS-97	GT-81	GU-103	GV-2	GF-113	GH-120	KE-89	None
Overland 93..............(1926)	GR-103	GR-103	GS-98	GT-82	GU-104	GV-2	GT-114	GH-121	KE-90	None
Packard 6 cyl., 326, 333........(1925)	GQ-52	GR-106	{GS-48 In. {GS-100 Ex.	GT-84	GU-107	GV-2	GF-117	GH-125	KE-93	GJ-27
Packard 8 cyl., 236, 243........(1925)	GQ-52	GR-106	{GS-48 In. {GS-100 Ex.	GT-84	GU-107	GV-2	GF-117	GH-126	KE-93	GJ-27
Packard 6 cyl., 326, 333........(1926)	GQ-52	GR-106	{GS-48 In. {GS-100 Ex.	GT-84	GU-107	GV-2	GF-117	GH-125	KE-93	GJ-27
Packard 8 cyl., 236, 243........(1926)	GQ-52	GR-106	{GS-48 In. {GS-100 Ex.	GT-84	GU-107	GV-2	GF-117	GH-126	KE-93	GJ-27
Packard 6 cyl., 426, 433........(1927)	GQ-52	GR-106	{GS-48 In. {GS-100 Ex.	GT-85	GU-107	GV-2	GF-117	GH-125	KE-93	GJ-27
Packard 8 cyl., 336, 343........(1927)	GQ-52	GR-106	{GS-48 In. {GS-100 Ex.	GT-85	GU-107	GV-2	GF-118	GH-126	KE-93	GJ-27
Packard 6 cyl., 526, 533........(1928)	GQ-53	GR-107	{GS-85 In. {GS-101 Ex.	GT-85	GU-107	GV-2	GF-119	GH-125	KE-93	GJ-17
Packard Std. 8, 443..........(1928)	GQ-53	GR-107	{GS-85 In. {GS-101 Ex.	GT-85	GU-107	GV-2	GF-119	GH-125	KE-93	GJ-17
Packard 626, 633..............(1929)	GQ-54	GR-108	{GS-85 In. {GS-101 Ex.	GT-85	GU-107	GV-2	GF-119	GH-125	KE-93	GJ-17
Packard 640, 645..............(1929)	GQ-53	GR-107	{GS-85 In. {GS-101 Ex.	GT-85	GU-107	GV-2	GF-119	GH-125	KE-93	GJ-17
Packard 726, 733..............(1930)	GQ-54	GR-108	{GS-85 In. {GS-101 Ex.	GT-85	GU-107	GV-2	GF-119	GH-202	KE-93	GJ-17
Packard 740, 745..............(1930)	GQ-53	GR-107	{GS-85 In. {GS-101 Ex.	GT-85	GU-107	GV-2	GF-119	GH-203	KE-93	GJ-17
Paige 70, Cont. 10-A........(1925-26)	GR-20	GR-20	GS-18	GT-86	GU-3	GV-3	GF-120	GH-127	KE-94	GJ-40
Paige 72..............(1926)	GR-69	GR-69	GS-102	GT-60	GU-3	GV-3	GF-121	GH-128	KE-94	GJ-59
Paige 6-45, Cont. 19-L......(1927-28)	GQ-36	GR-73	GS-2	GT-6	GU-2	GV-2	GF-78	GH-8	KE-63	GJ-45
Paige 6-65..............(1927-28)	GR-69	GR-69	GS-102	GT-60	GU-3	GV-3	GF-122	GH-129	KE-94	GJ-59
Paige 6-75..............(1927-28)	GR-69	GR-69	GS-102	GT-60	GU-3	GV-3	GF-123	GH-129	KE-94	GJ-59
Paige 8-85, Lyc. MD..........(1927)	GQ-1	GR-5	GS-5	GT-7	GU-14	GV-2	GF-8	GH-5	KE-6	GJ-2
Paige 8-85, Lyc. MD..........(1928)	GQ-1	GR-5	GS-5	GT-7	GU-14	GV-2	GF-8	GH-5	KE-6	GJ-2
Peerless 70..............(1925)	GR-110	GR-110	GS-104	GT-89	GU-111	GV-1	GF-124	GH-130	KE-95	GJ-27
Peerless 69..............(1925)	GR-111	GR-111	GS-105	GT-90	GU-112	GV-12	GF-126	GH-131	None	None
Peerless 80, Cont. 8-U........(1926)	GR-49	GR-49	GS-11	GT-32	GU-37	GV-2	GF-127	GH-68	KE-96	GJ-23
Peerless 69..............(1926)	GR-111	GR-111	GS-105	GT-90	GU-112	GV-12	GF-126	GH-131	None	None
Peerless 60, Cont. 10-E........(1927)	GQ-21	GR-44	GS-45	GT-32	GU-37	GV-2	GF-127	GH-109	KE-98	GJ-47
Peerless 69..............(1927)	GR-111	GR-111	GS-105	GT-90	GU-112	GV-12	GF-126	GH-131	None	None
Peerless 80, Cont. 8-U........(1927)	GR-49	GR-49	GS-11	GT-32	GU-37	GV-2	GF-127	GH-68	KE-96	GJ-23
Peerless 90..............(1927)	GR-110	GR-110	GS-104	GT-89	GU-111	GV-1	GF-128	GH-133	KE-99	GJ-60
Peerless 72..............(1927-28)	GR-110	GR-110	GS-104	GT-89	GU-111	GV-1	GF-128	GH-130	KE-99	GJ-60
Peerless 60, Cont. 10-E........(1928)	GQ-21	GR-44	GS-45	GT-32	GU-37	GV-2	GF-129	GH-109	KE-98	GJ-47
Peerless 69..............(1928)	GR-111	GR-111	GS-105	GT-90	GU-112	GV-12	GF-126	GH-131	None	None
Peerless 80, Cont. 8-U........(1928)	GR-49	GR-49	GS-11	GT-32	GU-37	GV-2	GF-127	GH-68	KE-96	GJ-23
Peerless 91..............(1928)	GR-110	GR-110	GS-104	GT-89	GU-111	GV-1	GF-128	GH-133	KE-100	GJ-60
Peerless 61, Cont. 11-E......(1929)	GQ-21	GR-44	GS-45	GT-75	GU-37	GV-2	GF-81	GH-109	KE-98	GJ-47
Peerless 81, Cont. 18-C......(1929)	GR-49	GR-49	GS-11	GT-32	GU-37	GV-2	GF-130	GH-68	KE-96	GJ-23
Peerless 91..............(1929)	GR-110	GR-110	GS-104	GT-89	GU-111	GV-1	GF-128	GH-133	KE-101	GJ-60
Peerless 125, Cont. 12-K....(1929)	GQ-22	GR-47	GS-42	GT-36	GU-40	GV-2	GF-51	GH-35	KE-37	GJ-30
Peerless A, Cont. 17S..........(1930)	GQ-5	GR-10	GS-49	{GT-10 In. {GT-33 Out.	GU-3	GV-2	GF-86	GH-94	KE-98	GJ-48
Peerless B&C, Cont. 13K......(1930)	GQ-22	GR-47	GS-42	GT-36	GU-40	GV-2	GF-51	GH-35	None	GJ-75
Pierce Arrow 80..............(1925)	GQ-56	GR-113	GS-107	GT-91	GU-114	GV-9	GF-131	GH-135	KE-102	GJ-61
Pierce Arrow 33..............(1926)	GR-114	GR-114	GS-108	GT-92	GU-115	GV-9	GF-134	GH-136	KE-103	None
Pierce Arrow 80..............(1926)	GQ-56	GR-113	GS-107	GT-91	GU-114	GV-9	GF-131	GH-135	KE-102	GJ-61
Pierce Arrow 36..............(1927)	GQ-57	GR-115	GS-108	GT-92	GU-115	GV-9	GF-135	GH-137	KE-104	None
Pierce Arrow 80..............(1927)	GQ-56	GR-113	GS-107	GT-91	GU-114	GV-9	GF-131	GH-135	KE-102	GJ-61
Pierce Arrow 36..............(1928)	GQ-57	GR-115	GS-108	GT-92	GU-115	GV-9	GF-135	GH-137	KE-104	None
Pierce Arrow 81..............(1928)	GQ-56	GR-13	GS-107	GT-91	GU-114	GV-9	GF-132	GH-138	KE-105	GJ-61
Pierce Arrow 133, 143........(1929)	GQ-58	GR-116	GS-109	GT-93	GU-31	GV-2	GF-133	GH-139	KE-106	GJ-63
Pierce Arrow A..............(1930)	GQ-58	GR-116	GS-55	GT-93	GU-31	GV-2	GF-87	GH-150	None	GJ-62
Pierce Arrow B..............(1930)	GQ-58	GR-116	GS-109	GT-93	GU-31	GV-2	GF-87	GH-150	None	GJ-62
Pierce Arrow C..............(1930)	GQ-58	GR-116	GS-109	GT-93	GU-31	GV-2	GF-146	GH-37	None	GJ-62
Plymouth..............(1929)	GQ-23	GR-29	GS-24	GT-117	GU-32	GV-2	GF-30	GH-34	None	None
Plymouth..............(1930)	GQ-23	GR-29	GS-24	GT-117	GU-31	GV-2	GF-30	GH-34	None	None
Pontiac 6..............(1926)	GR-117	GR-117	GS-110	GT-94	GU-117	GV-2	GF-136	GH-140	None	GJ-64
Pontiac 6..............(1927)	GR-117	GR-117	GS-110	GT-94	GU-117	GV-2	GF-136	GH-140	None	GJ-64
Pontiac 6..............(1928)	GR-117	GR-117	GS-110	GT-94	GU-117	GV-2	GF-136	GH-140	None	GJ-64
Pontiac Big 6..............(1929)	GQ-39	GR-117	GS-110	GT-94	GU-117	GV-2	GF-136	GH-140	None	GJ-64
Pontiac..............(1930)	GQ-39	GR-117	GS-90	GT-94	GU-117	GV-2	GF-136	GH-140	None	GJ-64
Reo T6..............(1925)	GQ-60	GR-118	{GS-82 In. {GS-112 Ex.	{GT-95 In. {GT-135 Ex.	GU-118	{GV-6 In. {GV-5 Ex.	GF-137	GH-141	KE-107	None

Footnote: For corresponding timing chain numbers advertised, see pages 201, 203.

ENGINE ASSEMBLY, Section 2—Continued

Interchangeable Parts have the same CHILTON NUMBER in Any Column

Car Make and Model	VALVE ASSEMBLY						TIMING DRIVE			
	Inlet Valve	Exhaust Valve	Valve Stem Guide	Valve Springs	Valve Lifters (Tappets)	Valve Lifter Adjusting Screws	Cam-shaft Gear or Sprocket	Crank-shaft Gear or Sprocket	Generator Gear or Sprocket	Timing Chain (See Footnote)
Reo T6....................(1926)	GQ-60	GR-118	GS-82 In. / GS-112 Ex.	GT-95 In. / GT-135 Ex.	GU-118	GV-6 In. / GV-5 Ex.	GF-137	GH-141	KE-107	None
Reo Flying Cloud............(1927)	GR-119	GR-119	GS-113	GT-96	GU-120	GV-2	GF-138	GH-142	KE-108	GJ-27
Reo Wolverine Cont. 15-E.....(1927)	GR-44	GR-44	GS-45	GT-32	GU-37	GV-2	GF-139	GH-132	KE-109	GJ-65
Reo Flying Cloud............(1928)	GR-119	GR-119	GS-113	GT-96	GU-120	GV-2	GF-138	GH-142	KE-108	GJ-27
Reo Wolverine Cont. 15-E.....(1928)	GR-44	GR-44	GS-45	GT-32	GU-37	GV-2	GF-139	GH-132	KE-109	GJ-65
Reo Flying Cloud Master......(1929)	GR-119	GR-119	GS-113	GT-96	GU-120	GV-2	GF-138	GH-142	KE-108	GJ-27
Reo Flying Cloud Mate 16E....(1929)	GR-44	GR-44	GS-45	GT-32	GU-37	GV-2	GF-139	GH-132	KE-109	GJ-65
Reo 15, Cont. 19E...........(1930)	GQ-87	GR-142	GS-45	GT-32	GU-37	GV-2	GF-139	GH-132	KE-109	GJ-65
Reo 20, 25.................(1930)	GR-119	GR-119	GS-113	GT-96	GU-120	GV-2	GF-138	GH-142	KE-108	GJ-27
Rickenbacker A8.............(1925)	GR-122	GR-122	GS-116 In. / GS-70 Ex.	GT-99	GU-123	GV-2	GF-141	GH-145	KE-110	GJ-66
Rickenbacker D6.............(1925)	GR-122	GR-122	GS-116 In. / GS-70 Ex.	GT-99	GU-123	GV-2	GF-142	GH-144	KE-111	GJ-67
Rickenbacker 8-B............(1926)	GR-122	GR-122	GS-116 In. / GS-70 Ex.	GT-99	GU-123	GV-2	GF-141	GH-145	KE-110	GJ-67
Rickenbacker E..............(1926)	GR-122	GR-122	GS-116 In. / GS-70 Ex.	GT-99	GU-123	GV-2	GF-142	GH-144	KE-111	GJ-68
Rickenbacker 6-70...........(1927)	GR-123	GR-123	GS-116 In. / GS-70 Ex.	GT-99	GU-123	GV-2	GF-142	GH-146	KE-111	GJ-68
Rickenbacker 8-80...........(1927)	GR-123	GR-123	GS-116 In. / GS-70 Ex.	GT-99	GU-123	GV-2	GF-143	GH-145	KE-110	GJ-67
Rickenbacker 8-90...........(1927)	GR-123	GR-123	GS-116 In. / GS-70 Ex.	GT-99	GU-123	GV-2	GF-143	GH-145	KE-110	GJ-68
Roamer 6-54 E...............(1925)	GR-125	GR-125	GS-118	GT-101	GU-127	GV-7	GF-145	GH-147	KE-113	GJ-1
Roamer 6-50, Cont. 7-U.......(1926)	GR-2	GR-2	GS-2	GT-2	GU-2	GV-2	GF-2	GH-2	KE-1	GJ-1
Roamer 6-54 E...............(1926)	GR-125	GR-125	GS-118	GT-101	GU-127	GV-7	GF-145	GH-147	KE-113	GJ-1
Roamer 8-80, Lyc. 4-HM.......(1926)	GQ-1	GR-5	GS-5	GT-5	GU-5	GV-2	GF-8	GH-5	KE-6	GJ-3
Roamer 8-78 Lyc. G.T.........(1927)	GQ-3	GR-8	GS-5	GT-7	GU-5	GV-2	GF-10	GH-10	KE-9	GJ-5
Roamer 8-80, Lyc. 4-HM.......(1927)	GQ-1	GR-5	GS-5	GT-5	GU-5	GV-2	GF-8	GH-5	KE-6	GJ-6
Roamer 8-88, Lyc. 4-H........(1927)	GQ-1	GR-5	GS-5	GT-5	GU-5	GV-2	GF-8	GH-5	KE-45	GJ-2
Roamer 8-78, Lyc. GT.........(1928)	GQ-3	GR-8	GS-5	GT-7	GU-5	GV-2	GF-10	GH-10	KE-9	GJ-5
Roamer 8-80, Lyc. 4-HM.......(1928)	GQ-1	GR-5	GS-5	GT-5	GU-5	GV-2	GF-8	GH-5	KE-6	GJ-6
Roamer 8-88, Lyc. 4-H........(1928)	GQ-1	GR-5	GS-5	GT-5	GU-5	GV-2	GF-8	GH-5	KE-45	GJ-2
Roamer 8-78, Lyc. GT.........(1929)	GQ-3	GR-8	GS-5	GT-7	GU-5	GV-2	GF-10	GH-10	KE-9	GJ-5
Roamer 8-80, Lyc. 4-HM.......(1929)	GQ-1	GR-5	GS-5	GT-5	GU-5	GV-2	GF-8	GH-5	KE-6	GJ-6
Roamer 8-88, Lyc. 4-H........(1929)	GQ-1	GR-5	GS-5	GT-5	GU-5	GV-2	GF-8	GH-5	KE-45	GJ-2
Star F. Cont. W5............(1925)	GR-2	GR-2	GS-11	GT-2	GU-2	GV-2	GF-54	GH-57	KE-40	GJ-24
Star M, Cont. W5............(1926)	GR-2	GR-2	GS-11	GT-2	GU-2	GV-2	GF-54	GH-57	KE-40	GJ-24
Star Std. R, Cont. 14-L......(1926)	GQ-2	GR-7	GS-2	GT-41	GU-2	GV-2	GF-53	GH-56	KE-39	GJ-4
Star M, Cont. W5............(1927)	GR-2	GR-2	GS-11	GT-2	GU-2	GV-2	GF-54	GH-57	KE-40	GJ-24
Star R, Cont. 14-L..........(1927)	GQ-2	GR-7	GS-2	GT-41	GU-2	GV-2	GF-53	GH-56	KE-39	GJ-4
Stearns Knight B, 4 cyl......(1925)	None	None	None	None	None	None	GF-147	GH-152	KE-114	*GJ-71
Stearns Knight C, 6 cyl......(1925)	None	None	None	None	None	None	GF-148	GH-153	KE-115	*GJ-69
Stearns Knight S, 6 cyl......(1925)	None	None	None	None	None	None	GF-149	GH-151	KE-115	*GJ-69
Stearns Knight B, 4 cyl......(1926)	None	None	None	None	None	None	GF-147	GH-152	KE-114	*GJ-71
Stearns Knight C, 75.........(1926)	None	None	None	None	None	None	GF-148	GH-155	KE-114	*GJ-69
Stearns Knight S, 95.........(1926)	None	None	None	None	None	None	GF-149	GH-154	KE-115	*GJ-69
Stearns Knight F, 6-85.......(1927)	None	None	None	None	None	None	GF-150	GH-156	KE-116	*GJ-69
Stearns Knight G, 8-85.....(1927-28)	None	None	None	None	None	None	GF-151	GH-154	KE-117	*GJ-73
Stearns Knight F, 6-85.......(1928)	None	None	None	None	None	None	GF-150	GH-156	KE-117	*GJ-69
Stearns Knight H & J, 8-90...(1928)	None	None	None	None	None	None	GF-152	GH-154	KE-118	*GJ-73
Stearns Knight H & J, 8-90...(1929)	None	None	None	None	None	None	GF-152	GH-154	KE-118	*GJ-73
Stearns Knight M & N, 6-80...(1929)	None	None	None	None	None	None	GF-153	GH-158	KE-117	GJ-82
Studebaker Big 6............(1925)	GR-128	GR-128	GS-56	GT-104	GU-130	GV-27	GF-155	GH-160	KE-120	None
Studebaker Spec. 6..........(1925)	GR-128	GR-128	GS-56	GT-104	GU-130	GV-27	GF-155	GH-160	KE-120	None
Studebaker Std. 6...........(1925)	GR-129	GR-129	GS-123	GT-100	GU-131	GV-8	GF-156	GH-161	KE-121	GJ-76
Studebaker Big 6............(1926)	GR-128	GR-128	GS-56	GT-104	GU-130	GV-27	GF-155	GH-160	KE-120	None
Studebaker Std. 6...........(1926)	GR-129	GR-129	GS-123	GT-100	GU-131	GV-8	GF-156	GH-161	KE-121	GJ-76
Studebaker Spec. 6..........(1926)	GR-128	GR-128	GS-56	GT-104	GU-130	GV-27	GF-155	GH-160	KE-120	None
Studebaker Big 6............(1927)	GR-128	GR-128	GS-84	GT-104	GU-116	GV-27	GF-155	GH-160	KE-120	None
Studebaker Spec. 6..........(1927)	GR-128	GR-128	GS-84	GT-104	GU-116	GV-27	GF-155	GH-160	KE-120	None
Studebaker Std. 6...........(1927)	GR-129	GR-129	GS-124	GT-100	GU-131	GV-8	GF-156	GH-161	KE-121	GJ-76
Studebaker Com. 6...........(1928)	GR-131	GR-131	GS-84	GT-104	GU-116	GV-2	GF-155	GH-160	KE-120	GJ-76
Studebaker Dict. 6..........(1928)	GQ-64	GR-130	GS-124	GT-97	GU-117	GV-2	GF-156	GH-163	KE-121	GJ-76
Studebaker Pres. 8..........(1928)	GQ-58	GR-116	GS-109	GT-108	GU-31	GV-2	GF-157	GH-162	None	None
Studebaker Com. 6...........(1929)	GR-68	GR-130	GS-84	GT-106	GU-117	GV-2	GF-156	GH-160	KE-120	GJ-76
Studebaker Com. 8...........(1929)	GQ-65	GR-132	GS-73	GT-106	GU-117	GV-2	GF-158	GH-164	None	None
Studebaker Dict. 6..........(1929)	GQ-68	GR-130	GS-73	GT-106	GU-117	GV-2	GF-156	GH-160	KE-121	GJ-76
Studebaker Pres. 8..........(1929)	GQ-58	GR-132	GS-55	GT-108	GU-31	GV-2	GF-157	GH-162	None	None
Studebaker Com. 6...........(1930)	GR-68	GR-130	GS-84	GT-106	GU-117	GV-2	GF-156	GH-160	KE-121	GJ-76
Studebaker Com. 8...........(1930)	GQ-65	GR-132	GS-73	GT-106	GU-117	GV-2	GF-158	GH-164	None	None
Studebaker Dict. 6..........(1930)	GQ-68	GR-130	GS-73	GT-106	GU-117	GV-2	GF-156	GH-160	KE-121	GJ-76
Studebaker Pres. 8..........(1930)	GQ-58	GR-132	GS-55	GT-108	GU-31	GV-2	GF-157	GH-162	None	None
Studebaker 6-53............(1930)	GQ-66	GR-130	GS-73	GT-106	GU-117	GV-2	GF-156	GH-160	KE-121	GJ-76
Studebaker Dict. 8..........(1930)	GQ-65	GR-132	GS-73	GT-106	GU-117	GV-2	GF-158	GH-164	None	None
Stutz 6-95.................(1925)	GR-134	GR-134	GS-125	GT-109	GU-134	GV-13	GF-159	GH-165	KE-122	GJ-29
Stutz AA...................(1926)	GR-9	GR-9	GS-8 In. / GS-7 Ex.	GT-110	GU-15	GV-4	GF-160	GH-166	KE-123	*GJ-77
Stutz AA...................(1927)	GR-9	GR-9	GS-8 In. / GS-7 Ex.	GT-110	GU-15	GV-4	GF-160	GH-166	KE-123	*GJ-77
Stutz BB...................(1928)	GR-9	GR-9	GS-8 In. / GS-7 Ex.	GT-12	GU-15	GV-4	GF-160	GH-166	KE-123	*GJ-77
Stutz M....................(1929)	GR-9	GR-9	GS-8 In. / GS-7 Ex.	GT-12	GU-15	GT-4	GF-161	GH-167	KE-123	*GJ-7
Stutz M....................(1930)	GR-9	GR-9	GS-8 In. / GS-7 Ex.	GT-12	GU-137	GV-4	GF-161	GH-167	KE-123	*GJ-7
Velie 60...................(1925)	GQ-45	GR-137	GS-130	GT-112	GU-4	GV-11	GF-35	GH-168	KE-3	None
Velie 60...................(1926)	GQ-45	GR-137	GS-130	GT-112	GU-4	GV-11	GF-35	GH-168	KE-3	None
Velie Std. 50..............(1927)	GR-4	GR-4	GS-4	GT-4	GU-4	GV-11	GF-35	GH-4	KE-3	None
Velie Spec. 60...........(1927-28)	GQ-45	GR-137	GS-30	GT-112	GU-4	GV-11	GF-35	GH-168	KE-124	None
Velie Std. 50..............(1928)	GR-4	GR-4	GS-4	GT-4	GU-4	GV-11	GF-35	GH-4	KE-3	None
Velie 6-66.................(1928)	GQ-45	GR-137	GS-130	GT-112	GU-4	GV-11	GF-35	GH-168	KE-125	None
Velie 6-77.................(1928)	GQ-45	GR-137	GS-130	GT-112	GU-4	GV-11	GF-35	GH-168	KE-126	None
Velie 8-88, Lyc. 4-HM.......(1928)	GQ-1	GR-5	GS-5	GT-7	GU-5	GV-2	GF-8	GH-5	KE-6	GJ-6
Viking.................(1928-29)	GQ-70	GR-138	GS-65 Ex. / GS-57 In.	GT-115	GU-43	GV-2	GF-162	GH-170	None	GJ-69
Westcott 44, Cont. 8-R......(1925)	GR-3	GR-3	GS-3	GT-3	GU-3	GV-2	GF-3	GH-3	KE-2	None
Westcott 60, Cont. 8-R......(1925)	GR-3	GR-3	GS-3	GT-3	GU-3	GV-2	GF-3	GH-3	KE-2	None
Whippet 96, 4 cyl..........(1927)	GR-104	GR-104	GS-99	GT-105	GU-105	GV-2	GF-115	GH-122	KE-91	GJ-57-86

Footnote: For corresponding timing chain numbers advertised, see pages 201, 203.

ENGINE ASSEMBLY, Section 2—Continued

Interchangeable Parts have the same CHILTON NUMBER in Any Column

Car Make and Model	VALVE ASSEMBLY						TIMING DRIVE			
	Inlet Valve	Exhaust Valve	Valve Stem Guide	Valve Springs	Valve Lifters (Tappets)	Valve Lifter Adjusting Screws	Cam-shaft Gear or Sprocket	Crank-shaft Gear or Sprocket	Generator Gear or Sprocket	Timing Chain (See Footnote)
Whippet 93-A, 6 cyl.......... (1927)	GR-105	GR-105	GS-99	GT-132	GU-104	GV-2	GF-114	GH-121	KE-91	None
Whippet 96, 4 cyl............ (1928)	GR-104	GR-104	GS-99	GT-105	GU-28	GV-2	GF-115	GH-122	KE-91	GJ-57-86
Whippet 98, 6 cyl............ (1928)	GR-64	GR-64	GS-99	GT-129	GU-104	GV-2	GF-116	GH-123	KE-91 / KE-92	GJ-57-86
Whippet 96-A............... (1929)	GR-142	GR-71	GS-99	GT-133	GU-104	GV-2	GF-115	GH-122	KE-91	GJ-58-88
Whippet 98-A............... (1929)	GR-105	GR-71	GS-99	GT-133	GU-104	GV-2	GF-116	GH-124	KE-91	GJ-58-88
Wills Ste. Claire 8........... (1925)	GQ-71	GR-139	GS-67 In. / GS-66 Ex.	GT-116	GU-35	GV-15	GF-169	GH-176	None	None
Wills Ste. Claire 6......... (1925-26)	GQ-40	GR-140	GS-69 In. / GS-68 Ex.	GT-134	GU-36	GV-16	GF-170	GH-175	None	None
Wills Ste. Claire 8........... (1926)	GQ-71	GR-139	GS-67 In. / GS-66 Ex.	GT-134	GU-35	GV-15	GF-169	GH-176	None	None
Willys 6.................... (1930)	GQ-41	GR-141	GS-71	GT-107	GU-7	GV-17	GF-187	GH-204	None	GJ-90
Willys 8-80................. (1930)	GQ-42	GR-141	GS-71	GT-113	GU-44	GV-18	GF-50	GH-54	None	GJ-90
Willys Knight 66............. (1925)	None	None	None	None	None	None	GF-163	GH-172	KE-127	GJ-78
Willys Knight 65............. (1925)	None	None	None	None	None	None	GF-164	GH-171	KE-127	*GJ-79
Willys Knight 66............. (1926)	None	None	None	None	None	None	GF-163	GH-172	KE-128	GJ-29
Willys Knight 70............. (1926)	None	None	None	None	None	None	GF-165	GH-173	KE-129	GJ-34
Willys Knight 66-A........... (1927)	None	None	None	None	None	None	GF-166	GH-172	KE-128	GJ-29
Willys Knight 70-A........... (1927)	None	None	None	None	None	None	GF-165	GH-173	KE-129	GJ-34
Willys Knight Std. 6-56..... (1928-29)	None	None	None	None	None	None	GF-165	GH-173	KE-129	GJ-35
Willys Knight Sp. 6, 70-A... (1928-29)	None	None	None	None	None	None	GF-165	GH-173	KE-129	GJ-35
Willys Knight 66-A......... (1928-29)	None	None	None	None	None	None	GF-166	GH-172	KE-128	GJ-29-82
Willys Knight 70-B........... (1929)	None	None	None	None	None	None	GF-168	GH-174	KE-130	GJ-35
Willys Knight 70-B........... (1930)	None	None	None	None	None	None	GF-168	GH-174	KE-130	GJ-35
Willys Knight 87............. (1930)	None	None	None	None	None	None	GF-168	GH-174	KE-128	GJ-35

*Blackhawk L6 (1929-30). Use accessory chain GJ-8.
Cadillac V63 (1925). Use generator chain GJ-11.
Cadillac 314, 341 A&B, 353 (1927-30). Use generator chain GJ-14.
La Salle, All (1927-30). Use generator chain GJ-14.
Stearns Knight B, S, F6-85 (1925-28). Use accessory chain GJ-70.
Stearns Knight C (1925-26). Use accessory chain GJ-72.
Stearns Knight 8-85, H&J 8-90 (1927-29). Use accessory chain GJ-82.
Stutz AA, BB (1926-28). Use accessory chain GJ-83.
Stutz M (1929-30). Use accessory chain GJ-8.
Willys Knight 65 (1925). Use accessory chain GJ-91.

KEY TO ENGINE ABBREVIATIONS:
Ans.—Ansted.   Cont.—Continental.   Lyc.—Lycoming.   In.—Intake.
Ex.—Exhaust.   In.—Inner.   Out.—Outer.

Footnote: For corresponding timing chain numbers advertised, see pages 201, 203.

INTERCHANGEABLE COUNT

Showing exact number of times each CHILTON NUMBER occurs in Engine Table, Section 2, beginning Page 199.

Inlet Valves

	GQ-48-2	GR-21-8	GR-69-8	GR-131-2	GS-28-2	GS-76-4	GT-2-14	GT-50-1
	GQ-49-2	GR-22-1	GR-71-2	GR-132-5	GS-29-3	GS-77-1	GT-3-13	GT-51-3
GQ-1-43	GQ-50-2	GR-23-6	GR-72-3	GR-134-2	GS-30-5	GS-78-4	GT-4-4	GT-52-1
GQ-2-13	GQ-51-1	GR-24-6	GR-73-2	GR-137-5	GS-31-2	GS-79-2	GT-5-28	GT-53-1
GQ-3-31	GQ-52-6	GR-25-6	GR-75-6	GR-138-1	GS-32-4	GS-80-5	GT-6-14	GT-54-5
GQ-4-1	GQ-53-4	GR-26-2	GR-80-4	GR-139-2	GS-33-1	GS-82-2	GT-7-46	GT-55-2
GQ-5-14	GQ-54-2	GR-27-2	GR-81-4	GR-140-1	GS-34-6	GS-84-5	GT-8-7	GT-57-6
GQ-6-3	GQ-56-4	GR-28-6	GR-83-6	GR-141-2	GS-35-3	GS-85-6	GT-9-5	GT-58-1
GQ-7-1	GQ-57-2	GR-29-10	GR-84-8	GR-142-2	GS-36-2	GS-86-4	GT-10-12	GT-59-5
GQ-8-3	GQ-58-7	GR-30-6	GR-85-8	GR-143-2	GS-37-3	GS-87-4	GT-11-6	GT-60-4
GQ-9-5	GQ-60-2	GR-31-5	GR-86-8	GR-144-1	GS-38-1	GS-88-1	GT-12-5	GT-61-3
GQ-10-1	GQ-64-1	GR-32-2	GR-87-1	GR-145-2	GS-39-1	GS-89-2	GT-13-1	GT-62-3
GQ-11-1	GQ-65-3	GR-33-8	GR-88-4	GR-146-1	GS-40-1	GS-90-2	GT-14-6	GT-63-2
GQ-12-1	GQ-66-2	GR-34-4	GR-89-2	GR-147-1	GS-41-8	GS-92-3	GT-15-7	GT-64-2
GQ-13-2	GQ-68-2	GR-35-1	GR-91-2	GR-148-1	GS-42-6	GS-93-1	GT-16-1	GT-65-6
GQ-14-2	GQ-70-1	GR-36-2	GR-92-4	GR-149-1	GS-43-1	GS-94-2	GT-17-2	GT-66-1
GQ-16-1	GQ-71-2	GR-37-1	GR-93-8	GR-150-1	GS-44-2	GS-95-2	GT-18-7	GT-67-3
GQ-17-3	GQ-72-1	GR-38-8	GR-94-6		GS-45-11	GS-96-3	GT-19-5	GT-68-8
GQ-18-2	GQ-73-1	GR-39-3	GR-95-4	**Valve Stem Guides**	GS-46-7	GS-97-2	GT-20-5	GT-69-3
GQ-19-3	GQ-75-2	GR-40-6	GR-96-6		GS-47-3	GS-98-2	GT-21-6	GT-70-4
GQ-20-1	GQ-76-1	GR-41-2	GR-98-2	GS-1-3	GS-48-6	GS-99-6	GT-22-3	GT-71-1
GQ-21-6	GQ-77-1	GR-42-3	GR-99-8	GS-2-28	GS-49-2	GS-100-6	GT-23-4	GT-72-4
GQ-22-9	GQ-79-2	GR-43-2	GR-100-2	GS-3-8	GS-50-3	GS-101-6	GT-24-2	GT-73-3
GQ-23-2	GQ-87-1	GR-44-12	GR-101-1	GS-4-4	GS-51-6	GS-102-3	GT-25-6	GT-74-3
GQ-24-3		GR-45-1	GR-102-4	GS-5-74	GS-52-3	GS-104-5	GT-26-4	GT-75-3
GQ-25-1	**Exhaust Valves**	GR-46-2	GR-103-4	GS-6-5	GS-53-8	GS-105-4	GT-27-5	GT-76-11
GQ-26-1		GR-47-9	GR-104-4	GS-7-7	GS-54-3	GS-107-4	GT-28-4	GT-77-8
GQ-27-2		GR-48-2	GR-105-3	GS-8-7	GS-55-3	GS-108-3	GT-29-2	GT-78-3
GQ-28-8	GR-1-4	GR-49-18	GR-106-6	GS-8-7	GS-56-4	GS-109-4	GT-30-1	GT-79-2
GQ-29-2	GR-2-29	GR-50-3	GR-107-4	GS-9-4	GS-57-1	GS-110-4	GT-31-3	GT-80-1
GQ-30-1	GR-3-14	GR-51-1	GR-108-2	GS-10-1	GS-58-3	GS-112-3	GT-32-17	GT-81-2
GQ-31-1	GR-4-8	GR-52-2	GR-110-10	GS-11-19	GS-59-1	GS-113-4	GT-33-12	GT-82-2
GQ-32-2	GR-5-43	GR-53-13	GR-111-8	GS-12-3	GS-60-1	GS-116-7	GT-34-1	GT-83-3
GQ-33-5	GR-6-10	GR-54-6	GR-113-3	GS-13-2	GS-61-6	GS-118-2	GT-35-3	GT-84-4
GQ-34-1	GR-7-14	GR-55-6	GR-114-2	GS-14-3	GS-62-1	GS-123-2	GT-36-9	GT-85-8
GQ-35-2	GR-8-31	GR-56-6	GR-115-2	GS-15-1	GS-63-5	GS-124-5	GT-37-2	GT-86-1
GQ-36-2	GR-9-10	GR-57-6	GR-116-5	GS-16-2	GS-64-1	GS-125-1	GT-38-2	GT-88-1
GQ-37-3	GR-10-14	GR-58-2	GR-117-8	GS-17-7	GS-65-1	GS-130-4	GT-39-3	GT-89-5
GQ-38-1	GR-11-13	GR-59-3	GR-118-2	GS-18-3	GS-66-2	GS-132-3	GT-40-4	GT-90-4
GQ-39-2	GR-12-6	GR-60-1	GR-119-8	GS-19-4	GS-67-2	GS-133-2	GT-41-7	GT-91-4
GQ-40-1	GR-13-3	GR-61-4	GR-122-8	GS-20-2	GS-68-1	GS-134-3	GT-42-2	GT-92-3
GQ-41-1	GR-14-1	GR-62-1	GR-123-6	GS-21-3	GS-69-1	GS-135-2	GT-43-1	GT-93-4
GQ-42-1	GR-15-4	GR-63-6	GR-125-4	GS-22-5	GS-70-7	GS-139-3	GT-44-4	GT-94-5
GQ-43-4	GR-16-3	GR-64-2	GR-126-4	GS-23-8	GS-71-2	GS-140-2	GT-45-3	GT-95-2
GQ-44-1	GR-17-4	GR-65-2	GR-127-2	GS-24-6	GS-72-1		GT-46-3	GT-96-4
GQ-45-5	GR-18-2	GR-66-6	GR-128-12	GS-25-4	GS-73-7	**Valve Springs**	GT-47-3	GT-97-1
GQ-46-1	GR-19-5	GR-67-2	GR-129-6	GS-26-3	GS-74-6		GT-48-2	GT-98-2
GQ-47-4	GR-20-6	GR-68-12	GR-130-7	GS-27-1	GS-75-3	GT-1-3	GT-49-8	GT-99-7

ENGINE ASSEMBLY, Section 2—Continued

INTERCHANGEABLE COUNT—Continued

Showing exact number of times each CHILTON NUMBER occurs in Engine Table, Section 2, beginning Page 199.

GT-100-3	GU-55-3	GF-8-27	GF-94-4	GF-186-1	GH-81-1	GH-171-1	KE-54-4	GJ-3-7
GT-101-2	GU-56-3	GF-9-1	GF-95-2	GF-187-1	GH-82-1	GH-172-4	KE-55-2	GJ-4-11
GT-102-2	GU-57-6	GF-10-30	GF-96-1	GF-188-1	GH-83-5	GH-173-4	KE-56-1	GJ-5-31
GT-103-2	GU-63-4	GF-11-2	GF-97-2	GF-189-1	GH-84-4	GH-174-3	KE-59-5	GJ-6-21
GT-104-7	GU-64-3	GF-12-2	GF-98-2	GF-190-4	GH-85-1	GH-175-1	KE-60-6	GJ-7-4
GT-105-2	GU-65-2	GF-13-3	GF-99-4	GF-191-2	GH-86-1	GH-176-2	KE-61-4	GJ-9-2
GT-106-9	GU-68-1	GF-14-5	GF-100-1	GF-192-1	GH-87-3	GH-184-1	KE-62-2	GJ-10-2
GT-107-1	GU-72-3	GF-15-2	GF-101-4		GH-88-2	GH-190-1	KE-63-2	GJ-12-1
GT-108-3	GU-82-6	GF-16-3	GF-102-2	**Crankshaft**	GH-89-3	GH-191-2	KE-64-3	GJ-13-7
GT-109-1	GU-84-3	GF-17-1	GF-103-2	**Gear or Sprocket**	GH-93-1	GH-192-1	KE-65-1	GJ-14-16
GT-110-2	GU-85-4	GF-18-2	GF-104-2		GH-94-1	GH-193-5	KE-66-2	GJ-15-2
GT-111-1	GU-86-4	GF-19-7	GF-105-2	GH-1-2	GH-95-6	GH-194-3	KE-67-3	GJ-16-10
GT-112-5	GU-90-4	GF-20-1	GF-106-3	GH-2-9	GH-97-2	GH-195-2	KE-68-3	GJ-17-9
GT-113-1	GU-91-3	GF-21-4	GF-107-3	GH-3-8	GH-98-4	GH-196-1	KE-71-6	GJ-18-6
GT-115-1	GU-92-1	GF-22-2	GF-108-3	GH-4-4	GH-99-4	GH-198-2	KE-73-2	GJ-19-18
GT-116-1	GU-94-12	GF-23-3	GF-109-2	GH-5-34	GH-100-1	GH-200-1	KE-74-4	GJ-20-4
GT-117-3	GU-97-1	GF-24-5	GF-110-1	GH-6-5	GH-101-1	GH-201-1	KE-75-4	GJ-21-2
GT-122-3	GU-98-4	GF-25-2	GF-111-2	GH-7-4	GH-102-2	GH-202-1	KE-76-1	GJ-23-12
GT-129-1	GU-100-2	GF-26-1	GF-112-3	GH-8-5	GH-103-1	GH-203-1	KE-77-4	GJ-24-16
GT-130-2	GU-101-1	GF-27-1	GF-113-2	GH-9-23	GH-104-2	GH-204-1	KE-78-2	GJ-25-6
GT-131-1	GU-103-2	GF-28-2	GF-114-3	GH-10-9	GH-105-4		KE-79-2	GJ-26-3
GT-132-1	GU-104-6	GF-30-6	GF-115-3	GH-12-2	GH-106-2		KE-81-4	GJ-27-18
GT-133-2	GU-105-1	GF-31-5	GF-116-2	GH-13-2	GH-109-5	**Generator**	KE-82-2	GJ-28-4
GT-134-2	GU-107-12	GF-32-4	GF-117-5	GH-14-4	GH-110-2	**Gear or**	KE-83-2	GJ-29-4
GT-135-1	GU-111-5	GF-33-2	GF-118-1	GH-15-4	GH-111-2	**Sprocket**	KE-84-3	GJ-30-8
GT-136-1	GU-112-4	GF-34-3	GF-119-6	GH-16-2	GH-112-3		KE-86-3	GJ-31-6
GT-137-2	GU-114-4	GF-35-9	GF-120-1	GH-17-3	GH-113-3	KE-1-4	KE-87-1	GJ-33-1
GT-138-1	GU-115-3	GF-38-2	GF-121-1	GH-18-1	GH-114-4	KE-2-9	KE-88-5	GJ-34-5
GT-139-2	GU-116-3	GF-39-1	GF-122-1	GH-19-2	GH-115-3	KE-3-6	KE-89-2	GJ-35-5
GT-140-1	GU-117-15	GF-40-10	GF-123-1	GH-20-6	GH-116-2	KE-4-3	KE-90-2	GJ-36-3
	GU-118-2	GF-41-5	GF-124-1	GH-21-1	GH-117-1	KE-5-5	KE-91-6	GJ-37-4
Valve Lifters	GU-120-4	GF-42-3	GF-126-4	GH-22-1	GH-118-2	KE-6-24	KE-92-1	GJ-38-3
(Tappets)	GU-123-7	GF-43-3	GF-127-4	GH-23-3	GH-119-3	KE-7-4	KE-93-12	GJ-41-1
	GU-127-2	GF-44-2	GF-128-4	GH-24-2	GH-120-2	KE-8-2	KE-94-4	GJ-41-2
GU-1-1	GU-130-4	GF-45-2	GF-129-1	GH-25-3	GH-121-3	KE-9-7	KE-95-1	GJ-42-1
GU-2-19	GU-131-3	GF-46-1	GF-130-1	GH-26-5	GH-122-3	KE-10-2	KE-96-4	GJ-43-4
GU-3-35	GU-134-1	GF-50-1	GF-131-3	GH-27-1	GH-123-1	KE-11-2	KE-98-4	GJ-44-4
GU-4-9	GU-137-1	GF-51-9	GF-132-1	GH-28-3	GH-124-1	KE-12-4	KE-99-2	GJ-45-2
GU-5-63		GF-52-1	GF-133-1	GH-30-2	GH-125-7	KE-13-4	KE-100-1	GJ-46-3
GU-6-5		GF-53-7	GF-134-1	GH-31-2	GH-126-3	KE-14-2	KE-101-1	GJ-47-6
GU-7-1	**Valve Lifter**	GF-54-5	GF-135-2	GH-32-5	GH-127-1	KE-15-3	KE-102-3	GJ-48-6
GU-13-6	**Adjusting Screws**	GF-55-3	GF-136-5	GH-33-4	GH-128-1	KE-16-6	KE-103-1	GJ-49-3
GU-14-19		GF-56-1	GF-137-2	GH-34-4	GH-129-2	KE-17-5	KE-104-2	GJ-50-3
GU-15-6	GV-1-5	GF-57-1	GF-138-4	GH-35-9	GH-130-2	KE-18-5	KE-105-1	GJ-51-4
GU-16-1	GV-2-288	GF-58-3	GF-139-4	GH-36-8	GH-131-4	KE-19-8	KE-106-1	GJ-52-4
GU-19-11	GV-3-32	GF-59-6	GF-141-2	GH-37-3	GH-132-4	KE-20-2	KE-107-2	GJ-53-2
GU-20-1	GV-4-7	GF-60-1	GF-142-3	GH-40-2	GH-133-3	KE-21-2	KE-108-4	GJ-54-1
GU-21-9	GV-5-3	GF-61-1	GF-143-2	GH-41-4	GH-135-3	KE-22-3	KE-109-4	GJ-55-1
GU-22-1	GV-6-31	GF-62-2	GF-145-2	GH-43-8	GH-136-1	KE-23-2	KE-110-4	GJ-56-2
GU-23-4	GV-7-3	GF-63-3	GF-146-1	GH-44-1	GH-137-1	KE-24-4	KE-111-3	GJ-57-3
GU-24-2	GV-8-22	GF-64-2	GF-147-2	GH-46-3	GH-138-1	KE-27-2	KE-113-2	GJ-58-2
GU-25-3	GV-9-14	GF-65-3	GF-148-2	GH-47-1	GH-139-1	KE-28-1	KE-114-3	GJ-59-4
GU-26-5	GV-10-1	GF-66-3	GF-149-2	GH-48-2	GH-140-5	KE-29-5	KE-115-3	GJ-60-4
GU-27-3	GV-11-19	GF-67-7	GF-150-2	GH-49-2	GH-141-2	KE-30-2	KE-116-1	GJ-61-4
GU-28-1	GV-12-4	GF-68-2	GF-151-1	GH-50-2	GH-142-4	KE-31-3	KE-117-3	GJ-62-3
GU-29-1	GV-13-1	GF-69-2	GF-152-2	GH-51-1	GH-144-2	KE-32-2	KE-118-2	GJ-63-1
GU-30-2	GV-14-6	GF-70-1	GF-153-1	GH-54-1	GH-145-4	KE-33-1	KE-120-8	GJ-64-5
GU-31-25	GV-15-2	GF-73-5	GF-155-7	GH-55-1	GH-146-1	KE-34-2	KE-121-9	GJ-65-5
GU-32-5	GV-16-1	GF-74-6	GF-156-10	GH-56-7	GH-147-2	KE-35-2	KE-122-1	GJ-66-1
GU-33-4	GV-17-1	GF-75-1	GF-157-3	GH-57-5	GH-150-2	KE-36-1	KE-123-5	GJ-67-3
GU-34-3	GV-18-1	GF-76-4	GF-158-3	GH-59-3	GH-151-2	KE-37-8	KE-124-1	GJ-68-3
GU-35-2	GV-22-1	GF-77-1	GF-159-1	GH-62-2	GH-152-2	KE-38-1	KE-125-1	GJ-69-7
GU-36-1	GV-24-7	GF-78-3	GF-160-3	GH-63-1	GH-153-1	KE-39-5	KE-126-1	GJ-71-2
GU-37-21	GV-27-14	GF-79-1	GF-161-2	GH-64-4	GH-154-4	KE-40-5	KE-127-2	GJ-73-3
GU-38-4	GV-30-3	GF-80-3	GF-162-1	GH-65-1	GH-155-1	KE-41-2	KE-128-4	GJ-75-1
GU-39-3	GV-31-3	GF-81-2	GF-163-2	GH-66-2	GH-156-2	KE-42-2	KE-129-4	GJ-76-11
GU-40-13		GF-82-1	GF-164-1	GH-67-3	GH-158-1	KE-43-1	KE-130-2	GJ-77-3
GU-41-2		GF-83-1	GF-165-4	GH-68-6	GH-160-13	KE-44-1	KE-131-1	GJ-78-1
GU-42-3	**Camshaft**	GF-84-3	GF-166-2	GH-69-3	GH-161-3	KE-45-4	KE-132-2	GJ-79-1
GU-43-1	**Gear or Sprocket**	GF-85-2	GF-168-3	GH-70-3	GH-162-3	KE-46-3	KE-139-1	GJ-82-2
GU-44-1		GF-86-1	GF-169-2	GH-71-7	GH-163-1	KE-47-7	KE-140-4	GJ-85-2
GU-46-1	GF-1-5	GF-87-2	GF-170-1	GH-74-4	GH-164-3	KE-48-2		GJ-86-3
GU-48-1	GF-2-5	GF-88-6	GF-174-1	GH-75-2	GH-165-1	KE-49-3	**Timing**	GJ-87-2
GU-50-1	GF-3-8	GF-90-2	GF-180-1	GH-77-1	GH-166-3	KE-50-3	**Chains**	GJ-88-2
GU-52-2	GF-4-2	GF-91-4	GF-181-1	GH-78-2	GH-167-2	KE-51-2		GJ-89-2
GU-53-5	GF-5-2	GF-92-4	GF-182-2	GH-79-2	GH-168-5	KE-52-3	GJ-1-6	GJ-99-2
GU-54-2	GF-6-9	GF-93-1	GF-184-2	GH-80-3	GH-170-1	KE-53-7	GJ-2-15	GJ-95-1
	GF-7-4							

Footnote: For corresponding timing chain numbers advertised, see pages 201 203.

Dimensions of Timing Chains

Listed here by **CHILTON NUMBERS** are Timing Chains as they appear in the preceding Engine **Table** by car models.

To find the cars in which any of the following size Timing Chains are used, consult the Timing Chain column, pages 199-207.

To find how many car models use any size here, locate the same CHILTON NUMBER in the Interchangeable Count, Page 208.

ILLUSTRATIONS OF GUIDE TYPES ON DIFFERENT CHAINS

CG

SG

R

BT

TIMING CHAINS					
CHILTON TIMING CHAIN NUMBER	Guide Type	Pitch	Width	Length: Links	Length: Inches
GJ 1	CG	½	1¼	67	33½
GJ 2	BT	⅜	1½	100	37½
GJ 3	CG	⅜	1½	89	33⅜
GJ 4	CG	4/10	1¼	81	32.4
GJ 5	GG	½	1¼	49	24½
GJ 6	CG	4/10	1½	85	34
GJ 7	BT	⅜	1¼	90	33¾
GJ 8	BT	⅜	1½	128	48
GJ 9	CG	.4	1¼	76	30.4
GJ 10	CG	½	1¾	56	28
GJ 11	CG	½	1½	57	28½
GJ 12	CG	⅜	1¾	88	33
GJ 13	CG	½	1¾	54	27
GJ 14	GG	½	1¼	57	28½
GJ 15	CG	½	1½	66	33
GJ 16	CG	½	1½	77	38½
GJ 17	CG	½	1½	64	32
GJ 18	CG	½	1¼	61	30½
GJ 19	CG	½	1¼	59	29½
GJ 20	GG	.4	1½	78	31.2
GJ 21	GG	.4	1¼	74	29.6
GJ 23	CG	.4	1¼	82	32.8
GJ 24	CG	½	1¼	63	31½
GJ 25	CG	½	1¼	48	24
GJ 26	CG	⅜	1¼	76	28½
GJ 27	CG	½	1½	63	31½
GJ 28	CG	½	1¼	91	45½
GJ 29	BT	⅜	1½	112	42
GJ 30	BT	⅜	1½	107	40⅛

TIMING CHAINS					
CHILTON TIMING CHAIN NUMBER	Guide Type	Pitch	Width	Length: Links	Length: Inches
GJ 31	CG	4/10	1¼	80	32
GJ 33	SG	⅜	1⅛	64	24
GJ 34	BT	⅜	1¼	98	36¾
GJ 35	BT	⅜	1¼	98	36¾
GJ 36	CG	½	1½	73	36½
GJ 37	CG	⅜	1¼	91	34⅛
GJ 38	BT	⅜	1½	110	41¼
GJ 40	BT	⅜	1½	108	40½
GJ 41	CG	⅜	1½	72	27
GJ 42	CG	½	1¼	75	37½
GJ 43	CG	⅜	1½	96	36
GJ 44	CG	⅜	1¼	82	30¾
GJ 45	CG	⅜	1¼	89	33⅜
GJ 46	CG	½	1½	67	33½
GJ 47	CG	4/10	1¼	70	28
GJ 48	CG	4/10	1¼	75	30
GJ 49	BT	⅜	1½	84	31½
GJ 50	BT	⅜	1½	102	38¼
GJ 51	BT	⅜	1 11/16	112	42
GJ 52	R	⅜	⅞	62	23½
GJ 53	R	⅜	⅞	64	24
GJ 54	CG	½	1¼	52	26
GJ 55	R	⅜	1¼	66	24¾
GJ 56	CG	½	1½	50	25
GJ 57	CG	⅜	1	85	31⅞
GJ 58	CG	⅜	1¼	85	31⅞
GJ 59	BT	⅜	1½	106	39¾
GJ 60	CG	⅜	1½	84	31½
GJ 61	BT	⅜	1½	96	36

TIMING CHAINS					
CHILTON TIMING CHAIN NUMBER	Guide Type	Pitch	Width	Length: Links	Length: Inches
GJ 62	CG	½	1½	50	25
GJ 63	BT	⅜	1½	102	38¼
GJ 64	CG	½	1¼	44	22
GJ 65	CG	4/10	1¼	71	28 4/10
GJ 66	CG	½	1½	70	35
GJ 67	CG	⅜	1½	94	35¼
GJ 68	CG	⅜	1½	95	35⅝
GJ 69	CG	½	1½	52	26
GJ 70	CG	½	1	56	28
GJ 71	CG	½	1¼	54	27
GJ 72	CG	½	1	54	27
GJ 73	CG	½	1¼	55	27½
GJ 75	CG	½	1½	51	25½
GJ 76	CG	½	1½	71	35½
GJ 77	BT	⅜	1¼	90	33¾
GJ 78	BT	⅜	1½	110	41¼
GJ 79	SG	⅜	1¼	84	31½
GJ 82	BT	⅜	1½	112	42
GJ 83	BT	⅜	1½	128	48
GJ 85	CG	½	1½	65	32½
GJ 86	SG	⅜	1	85	31⅞
GJ 87	R	⅜	⅞	66	24¾
GJ 88	SG	⅜	1⅛	85	25⅞
GJ 89	CG	½	1¼	46	23
GJ 90	SG	½	1¼	48	24
GJ 91	SC	⅜	¾	21	7⅞
GJ 95	CG	½	1½	48	24

Dimensions of Valves

Listed here by CHILTON NUMBERS are inlet and exhaust valves as they appear in the preceding engine table by car models. If any intake valve is interchangeable with any exhaust valve it is given the exhaust valve CHILTON NUMBER and is listed in the exhaust valve columns.

To find the cars in which any of the following size valves are used, consult the valve columns, Pages 199-207.

To find how many car models use any size here, locate the same CHILTON NUMBER in the interchangeable count, Page 207.

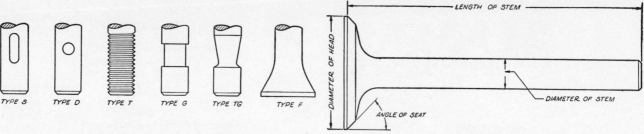

CHILTON EXHAUST VALVE NUMBER	Head Diameter	Stem Diameter	Top of Seat to End of Stem	Style of Stem End
GR 1	1 13/32	.310	4 13/16	G
GR 2	1 5/8	.371	5 3/16	D
GR 3	1 5/8	.372	5 11/16	G
GR 4	1 9/16	.373	5 9/32	G
GR 5	1 15/32	.341	5 1/2	G
GR 6	1 25/32	.373	7 9/32	G
GR 7	1 5/16	.372	5 17/32	D
GR 8	1 13/32	.341	5 1/8	D
GR 9	1 21/32	.371	6 11/32	T
GR 10	1 3/8	.308	5 61/64	TG
GR 11	1 25/32	.372	6 1/4	G
GR 12	1 19/32	.372	5 3/4	GD
GR 13	1 19/32	.370	5 9/16	G
GR 14	1 25/32	.370	5 5/8	G
GR 15	1 25/32	.370	5 7/32	G
GR 16	1 25/32	.370	5 1/2	G
GR 17	1 27/32	.372	7 1/32	G
GR 18	1 43/64	.370	7 3/64	G
GR 19	1 41/64	.371	6 13/64	G
GR 20	1 15/16	.372	6 9/16	G
GR 21	1 23/32	.372	6 9/16	D
GR 22	1 17/32	.371	6 13/32	D
GR 23	1 17/32	.340	6 9/16	D
GR 24	1 13/32	.310	5 7/64	S
GR 25	1 1/2	.310	4 5/8	S
GR 26	1 31/32	.310	4 19/32	S
GR 27	1 13/32	.310	4 5/8	S
GR 28	1 19/32	.340	6 3/16	G
GR 29	1 15/32	.372	5 1/16	G
GR 30	1 13/16	.371	6 13/16	G
GR 31	1 15/32	.340	5 9/16	G
GR 32	1 19/32	.340	7 1/16	G
GR 33	1 15/32	.340	5 1/2	G
GR 34	1 5/8	.370	5 5/8	D
GR 35	1 7/16	.347	5 9/32	D
GR 36	1 5/8	.372	5 1/16	TG
GR 37	1 11/16	.370	5 5/8	D
GR 38	1 15/32	.340	5 1/2	D
GR 39	1 7/16	.371	5 1/2	D
GR 40	1 23/32	.372	6 15/32	G
GR 41	1 19/32	.371	5 11/32	TG
GR 42	1 3/8	.370	5 5/16	TG
GR 43	1 5/8	.370	5 11/16	D
GR 44	1 7/16	.340	5 3/8	G
GR 45	1 17/32	.370	5 23/64	G
GR 46	1 17/32	.340	5 51/64	G
GR 47	1 9/16	.371	5 7/16	TG
GR 48	1 9/16	.310	5 9/16	S
GR 49	1 5/8	.371	5 5/8	D
GR 50	1 11/16	.308	4 31/32	D
GR 51	1 13/32	.310	5 3/8	G
GR 52	1 13/32	.371	5 5/16	G
GR 53	1 3/8	.310	5 3/32	G
GR 54	1 13/32	.371	6 13/32	G
GR 55	1 15/32	.310	5 3/32	D
GR 56	1 35/64	.311	5 5/8	F
GR 57	1 3/8	.340	4 7/8	D, TG
GR 58	1 1/2	.338	4 63/64	D, TG
GR 59	1 3/4	.340	6 41/64	D
GR 60	1 19/32	.372	6 1/4	G
GR 61	1 29/32	.309	6 13/32	G
GR 62	1 21/32	.340	7 1/16	G
GR 63	1 31/32	.372	6 7/8	G
GR 64	1 31/32	.340	6 1/2	G
GR 65	1 27/32	.372	6 7/8	G
GR 66	1 11/32	.325	7 11/32	T

CHILTON EXHAUST VALVE NUMBER	Head Diameter	Stem Diameter	Top of Seat to End of Stem	Style of Stem End
GR 67	1 49/64	.366	6 15/64	G
GR 68	1 17/32	.367	4 53/64	G
GR 69	1 11/16	.372	6 3/8	G
GR 71	1 7/16	.339	6 3/64	G
GR 72	1 1/2	.371	6 1/2	G
GR 73	1 3/8	.370	5 29/32	D
GR 75	1 13/16	.375	5 3/4	G
GR 80	1 7/8	.368	7 1/4	G
GR 81	1 3/4	.368	7 1/4	G
GR 83	1 13/32	.309	4 15/16	G
GR 84	2 5/16	.437	8 15/32	S
GR 85	1 15/16	.375	7 11/16	G
GR 86	2	.375	5 15/16	3G
GR 87	1 11/64	.309	5 23/32	3G
GR 88	1 11/32	.309	4 57/64	G
GR 89	1 17/64	.309	5 23/32	3G
GR 91	1 19/32	.372	5 17/32	G
GR 92	1 7/16	.372	5 9/32	G
GR 93	1 25/32	.372	5 17/64	G
GR 94	1 1/2	.372	5 17/64	DG
GR 95	1 13/32	.310	5 5/32	G
GR 96	1 13/32	.310	5 21/64	G
GR 98	1 1/2	.310	5 53/64	G
GR 99	1 1/2	.310	5 1/2	G
GR100	1 7/16	.310	5 9/32	G
GR101	1 11/32	.341	5 5/16	D
GR102	1 11/16	.372	4 1/2	D
GR103	1 5/16	.310	4 3/4	D
GR104	1 13/16	.340	6 1/16	D
GR105	1 9/16	.307	4 3/4	S
GR106	1 11/16	.341	7 1/2	S
GR107	1 11/16	.340	7 11/32	S
GR108	1 11/16	.340	7 11/32	S
GR110	1 13/16	.371	6 7/8	S
GR111	1 3/4	.371	6 17/64	S
GR113	1 5/8	.371	7	G
GR114	1 5/8	.406	8 7/16	S
GR115	1 15/32	.406	8 7/16	S
GR116	1 9/16	.371	5 19/32	2G
GR117	1 11/32	.310	4 47/64	G
GR118	1 13/32	.375	6	D
GR119	1 13/16	.342	6 13/32	D
GR122	1 5/8	.372	5 17/64	D
GR123	1 11/16	.372	5 23/64	D
GR125	1 11/16	.373	6 13/64	G
GR126	1 13/32	.341	5 1/4	G
GR127	1 43/64	.371	6 13/64	G
GR128	1 7/8	.372	6 1/2	G
GR129	1 5/8	.310	5 13/32	G
GR130	1 1/2	.310	5 3/8	G
GR131	1 7/8	.372	6 1/2	G
GR132	1 9/32	.310	5 1/2	G
GR134	1 23/32	.371	6	G
GR137	1 13/16	.371	5 17/32	G
GR138	1 11/32	.371	6 49/64	TG
GR139	1 3/8	.312	5 1/8	TG
GR140	1 13/32	.312	5 1/8	TG
GR141	1 15/32	.371	5 7/16	G
GR143	1 13/32	.372	5 29/64	G
GR144	1 17/32	.372	5 17/32	G
GR145	1 13/32	.340	5 13/16	G
GR146	1 13/32	.341	7 5/16	T
GR147*	1 13/32	.375	5 7/16	G
GR148	1 3/8	.341	6 27/64	G
GR149	1 11/32	.311	4 41/64	S
GR150	1 19/32	.341	...	...

CHILTON INLET VALVE NUMBER	Head Diameter	Stem Diameter	Top of Seat to End of Stem	Style of Stem End
GQ 1*	1 5/8	.341	5 1/2	G
GQ 2	1 7/16	.370	5 17/32	D
GQ 3	1 17/32	.341	5 7/8	G
GQ 4	1 23/32	.372	6 1/4	D
GQ 5	1 1/2	.308	5 61/64	TG
GQ 6	2 1/32	.372	6 1/4	G
GQ 7	2 1/32	.372	5 5/8	G
GQ 8	2 1/32	.372	5 1/2	G
GQ 9	1 21/32	.371	6 13/64	G
GQ 10	1 21/32	.371	6 13/64	D
GQ 11	1 29/64	.311	4 41/64	S
GQ 12	1 19/32	.340	5 9/16	G
GQ 13	1 23/32	.340	7 1/16	G
GQ 14	1 15/16	.371	6 15/16	G
GQ 15	1 11/16	.340	5 15/16	G
GQ 16	1 9/16	.347	5 9/32	D
GQ 17	1 1/2	.371	5 1/2	TG
GQ 18	1 21/32	.371	5 41/64	TG
GQ 19	1 21/32	.370	5 9/16	TG
GQ 20	1 1/2	.310	5 9/32	G
GQ 21	1 9/16	.340	5 3/8	D
GQ 22	1 5/8	.371	5 7/16	TG
GQ 23	1 45/64	.372	5 7/16	D
GQ 24	1 27/32	.308	4 31/64	D
GQ 25	1 21/32	.370	5 23/64	G
GQ 26	1 13/32	.310	5 3/8	G
GQ 27	1 5/8	.337	4 63/64	DTG
GQ 28	1 9/16	.340	5 1/2	G
GQ 29	1 27/32	.340	6 1/16	G
GQ 30	1 11/16	.372	5 17/32	G
GQ 31	1 13/32	.325	7 11/32	T
GQ 32	2 1/32	.372	6 3/8	T
GQ 33	1 15/32	.325	7 11/32	G
GQ 34	1 1/2	.341	6 27/64	G
GQ 35	1 23/32	.371	6 13/64	G
GQ 36	1 1/2	.370	5 29/32	D
GQ 37	1 5/8	.371	6 1/2	D
GQ 38	1 5/8	.370	5 5/8	D
GQ 39	1 13/32	.310	4 47/64	G
GQ 40	1 5/8	.312	5 1/8	TG
GQ 41	1 5/8	.371	5 7/16	G
GQ 42	1 17/32	.371	5 7/16	G
GQ 43	2	.368	7 1/4	G
GQ 44*	1 27/32	.375	6 13/64	G
GQ 45	1 11/16	.371	5 17/32	G
GQ 46	1 23/64	.309	5 23/32	3G
GQ 47	1 15/32	.309	4 57/64	G
GQ 48	1 29/64	.309	5 23/32	3G
GQ 49	1 5/8	.310	5 13/64	G
GQ 50	1 17/32	.371	5 5/16	G
GQ 51	1 15/32	.341	5 5/16	G
GQ 52	1 13/16	.341	7 1/32	S
GQ 53	1 13/16	.340	7 11/32	S
GQ 54	1 21/32	.340	7 11/32	S
GQ 56	1 7/8	.371	7	G
GQ 57	1 23/32	.406	8 7/16	2G
GQ 58	1 21/32	.371	5 19/32	S
GQ 60	2 1/4	.437	4 1/8	S
GQ 64	1 5/8	.310	5 3/8	G
GQ 65	1 13/32	.310	5 3/8	G
GQ 68	1 5/8	.310	5 3/8	G
GQ 70	1 15/32	.343	6 49/64	G
GQ 71	1 1/2	.312	5 1/2	G
GQ 72	1 27/32	.340	6 5/8	G
GQ 73	1 17/32	.341	7 5/16	G
GQ 75	1 19/32	.340	5 51/64	G
GQ 76	1 23/32	.340	7 1/16	G
GQ 77	1 3/4	.341	...	...

*GR 147—30° Angle.   *GQ 1—60° Angle.   *GQ 44—30° Angle.

COOLING SYSTEM and MUFFLER

HOW TO USE THIS TABLE

1. Locate in the first column the car and model for which the part is needed.
2. Follow this line across to the column pertaining to that part.
3. In this part column opposite your car model you will find the CHILTON NUMBER for the part you want.
4. Look up and down the part column for the same CHILTON NUMBER. Wherever you find this same number you have an interchangeable part. The car make opposite tells you where to get the part—probably from a local dealer or a nearby jobber.

EXAMPLE: Suppose a Water Pump Body is needed for an Auburn 76 (1928) car. Locate this car in the first column. Follow across to the column on Water Pump Bodies. Here you see the CHILTON NUMBER for this part is FA-7. Checking through the

CHILTON NUMBERS in this same column you will find the number FA-7 opposite the Auburn 6-80 (1929), the Auburn 6-85 (1930), the Elcar 6-70 (1928), the Elcar 75 (1929), the Gardner 136 (1930), the Kissel 6-73 (1929). The Water Pump Body Assembly used in all these cars is interchangeable with the one used in your Auburn 76 (1928) car.

5. At the end of this table, Pages 217, 218, you will find a count showing the number of times any part number appears in this table.

EXAMPLE: FG-7 under Radiator Filler Caps opposite Buick Master (1925) in this table will appear again in the count at the end of the table followed by the figure 7 under the heading Radiator Filler Caps. This indicates part number FG-7 appears 7 times in this table.

Interchangeable Parts have the same CHILTON NUMBER in Any Column

| Car Make and Model | WATER PUMP | | | | | Radiator Filler Cap | Fan Belt | Muffler |
	Body Assembly	Shaft	Impeller	Bushings	Packing Nut or Gland			
Ajax, Nash L6 (1925–26)	FA-1	FB-1	FC-1	FD-1 / FD-6	FE-1	FG-1	FH-1	HA-1
Apperson 6, Velie 50 (1925)	FA-4	FB-4	FC-4	FD-4	FE-4	FG-3	FH-4	HA-4
Apperson Str. 8, Lyc. 2-H (1925)	FA-5	FB-5	FC-5	FD-23	FE-6 / FE-10	FG-3	FH-5	HA-5
Auburn 4, Lyc. CF (1925)	None	None	None	None	None	FG-4	FH-2	HA-6
Auburn 6-43, Cont. 7-U (1925)	FA-2	FB-2	FC-2	FD-2	FE-2	FG-4	FH-6	HA-7
Auburn 8-88, Lyc. 2-H (1925)	FA-5	FB-5	FC-5	FD-23	FE-6 / FE-10	FG-4	FH-1	HA-8
Auburn 8-88, Lyc. 4-HM (1926)	FA-9	FB-8	FC-8	FD-5	FE-10	FG-4	FH-8	HA-8
Auburn 4-44, Lyc. CF (1926)	None	None	None	None	None	FG-4	FH-2	HA-6
Auburn 6-66, Lyc. 4-SM (1926)	FA-8	FB-8	FC-6	FD-5	FE-10	FG-4	FH-8	HA-6
Auburn 6-66 A, Cont. 28L (1927)	FA-10	FB-10	FC-10	FD-7	FE-11	FG-4	FH-9	HA-10
Auburn 6-66, Lyc. 4 GM (1927)	FA-9	FB-8	FC-8	FD-5	FE-10	FG-4	FH-8	HA-6
Auburn 8-88, Lyc. 4HM (1927)	FA-9	FB-8	FC-8	FD-5	FE-10	FG-4	FH-8	HA-8
Auburn 8-77, Lyc. GT (1927)	FA-9	FB-8	FC-8	FD-5	FE-10	FG-4	FH-10	HA-8
Auburn 76, Lyc. WS (1928)	FA-7	FB-8	FC-8	FD-5	FE-10	FG-5	FH-8	HA-11
Auburn 88, Lyc. GS (1928)	FA-9	FB-8	FC-8	FD-5	FE-10	FG-5	FH-8	HA-12
Auburn 115, Lyc. 4-MD (1928)	FA-9	FB-8	FC-8	FD-5	FE-10	FG-5	FH-11	HA-13
Auburn 6-80, Lyc. WR (1929)	FA-7	FB-8	FC-8	FD-5	FE-10	FG-5	FH-10	HA-11
Auburn 8-90, Lyc. GR (1929)	FA-9	FB-8	FC-8	FD-5	FE-10	FG-5	FH-10	HA-12
Auburn 120, Lyc. MDA (1929)	FA-9	FB-8	FC-8 / FC-28	FD-5	FE-10	FG-5	FH-11	HA-13
Auburn 6-85, Lyc. WR (1930)	FA-7	FB-8	FC-8	FD-5	FE-10	FG-5	FH-10	HA-11
Auburn 8-95, Lyc. GR (1930)	FA-9	FB-8	FC-8	FD-5	FE-10	FG-5	FH-10	HA-12
Auburn 125, Lyc. MDA (1930)	FA-9	FB-8	FC-28	FD-5	FE-10	FG-5	FH-11	HA-13
Blackhawk L6 (1929)	FA-11	FB-11	FC-11	FD-10	FE-15	FG-5	FH-12	HA-17
Blackhawk L8, Cont. 16S (1929)	FA-12	FB-12	FC-12	FD-8	FE-16	FG-5	FH-19	HA-17
Blackhawk L6 (1930)	FA-11	FB-11	FC-11	FD-10	FE-15	FG-5	FH-12	HA-17
Blackhawk L8 (1930)	FA-12	FB-12	FC-12	FD-8	FE-16	FG-5	FH-19	HA-17
Buick Master (1925)	FA-13	FB-13	FC-13	FD-9	FE-17	FG-7	FH-13	HA-18
Buick Std (1925)	FA-14	FB-14	FC-14	FD-9	FE-17	FG-1	FH-14	HA-19
Buick Master (Early 1926)	FA-32	FB-15	FC-15	FD-12 / FD-113	FE-18	FG-7	FH-13	HA-18
Buick Master (Late 1926)	FA-59	FB-16	FC-16	FD-12 / FD-113	FE-18	FG-36	FH-13	HA-18
Buick Std (Early 1926)	FA-15	FB-16	FC-16	FD-12 / FD-113	FE-18	FG-7	FH-14	HA-20
Buick Std (Late 1926)	FA-16	FB-16	FC-16	FD-12 / FD-113	FE-18	FG-36	FH-14	HA-20
Buick 115 (1927)	FA-16	FB-16	FC-16	FD-12 / FD-113	FE-18	FG-7	FH-14	HA-21
Buick 120, 128 (1927)	FA-59	FB-16	FC-16	FD-12 / FD-113	FE-18	FG-7	FH-13	HA-22
Buick 115 (1928)	FA-16	FB-16	FC-16	FD-12 / FD-113	FE-18	FG-7	FH-14	HA-2
Buick 120, 128 (1928)	FA-59	FB-16	FC-16	FD-12 / FD-113	FE-18	FG-7	FH-7	HA-54
Buick 116 (1929)	FA-16	FB-16	FC-16	FD-12 / FD-113	FE-18	FG-8	FH-15	HA-23
Buick 121, 129 (1929)	FA-59	FB-16	FC-16	FD-12 / FD-113	FE-18	FG-8	FH-15	HA-25
Buick 40 (1930)	FA-16	FB-16	FC-16	FD-12 / FD-113	FE-18	FG-8	FH-15	HA-25
Buick 50, 60 (1930)	FA-59	FB-16	FC-16	FD-12 / FD-113	FE-18	FG-8	FH-15	HA-25
Cadillac, V63 (1925)	FA-17	FB-17	FC-17	FD-13 / FD-114	FE-7 / FE-8	FG-9	None	HA-27
Cadillac 314 (1926)	FA-18	FB-18	FC-18	FD-11 / FD-120	FE-20	FG-9	FH-16	HA-26
Cadillac 314 (1927)	FA-18	FB-18	FC-18	FD-33 / FD-85	FE-20	FG-38	FH-16	HA-26
Cadillac 314 (Late 1927); 341-A (1928)	FA-19	FB-6	FC-38	FD-14 / FD-115	FE-14	FG-21	FH-17	HA-28
Cadillac 341-B (1929)	FA-19	FB-6	FC-38	FD-14 / FD-115	FE-14	FG-45	FH-17	HA-24
Cadillac 353 (1930)	FA-19	FB-6	FC-38	FD-14 / FD-115	FE-14	FG-61	FH-51	HA-29
Case JIC, Cont. 8-R (1925)	FA-3	FB-3	FC-3	FD-3	FE-3 / FE-9	FG-10	FH-3	HA-30
Case X, Cont. 8-R (1925)	FA-3	FB-3	FC-3	FD-3	FE-3 / FE-9	FG-10	FH-3	HA-31
Case Y, Cont. 6-T (1925)	FA-20	FB-7	FC-7	FD-45 / FD-106	FE-3 / FE-9	FG-10	FH-8	HA-32

COOLING SYSTEM and MUFFLER—Continued

Interchangeable Parts have the same CHILTON NUMBER in Any Column

Car Make and Model	WATER PUMP					Radiator Filler Cap	Fan Belt	Muffler
	Body Assembly	Shaft	Impeller	Bushings	Packing Nut or Gland			
Case JIC, Cont. 8-R............(1926)	FA-3	FB-3	FC-3	FD-3	FE-3 / FE-9	FG-10	FH-3	HA-30
Case Y, Cont. 6-J............(1926)	FA-3	FB-9	FC-3	FD-3	FE-30 / FE-21	FG-10	FH-8	HA-32
Chandler 33............(1925)	FA-21	FB-19	FC-20	FD-15 / FD-116	FE-13 / FE-22	FG-11	FH-18	HA-70
Chandler 35............(1926)	FA-21	FB-19	FC-20	FD-15 / FD-116	FE-13 / FE-22	FG-11	FH-18	HA-70
Chandler Big 6............(1927)	FA-21	FB-19	FC-20	FD-15 / FD-116	FE-13 / FE-22	FG-11	FH-18	HA-70
Chandler Royal 8............(1927)	FA-22	FB-20	FC-21	FD-16	FE-23	FG-13	FH-19	HA-117
Chandler Spec. 6............(1927)	FA-23	FB-21	FC-22	FD-17 / FD-117	FE-24	FG-11	FH-9	HA-36
Chandler Std. 6............(1927)	FA-23	FB-22	FC-9	FD-17 / FD-117	FE-24	FG-11	FH-9	HA-36
Chandler Big 6............(1928)	FA-21	FB-19	FC-20	FD-15 / FD-116	FE-13 / FE-22	FG-11	FH-18	HA-70
Chandler Royal 8............(1928)	FA-22	FB-20	FC-21	FD-16	FE-23	FG-13	FH-20	HA-117
Chandler Spec. 6............(1928)	FA-23	FB-22	FC-9	FD-17 / FD-117	FE-24	FG-12	FH-21	HA-36
Chandler Spec. Inv. 6............(1928)	FA-23	FB-22	FC-9	FD-17 / FD-117	FE-24	FG-12	FH-21	HA-36
Chevrolet K............(1925)	FA-24	FB-23	FC-23	FD-18 / FD-88	FE-25	FG-14	FH-23	HA-37
Chevrolet V............(1926)	FA-24	FB-23	FC-23	FD-18 / FD-88	FE-25	FG-14	FH-23	HA-37
Chevrolet AA............(1927)	FA-24	FB-23	FC-23	FD-18 / FD-88	FE-25	FG-14	FH-23	HA-37
Chevrolet AB............(1928)	FA-24	FB-24	FC-24	FD-18 / FD-88	FE-25	FG-15	FH-23	HA-37
Chevrolet AC............(1929)	FA-27	FB-25	FC-25	FD-19 / FD-126	FE-27	FG-15	FH-24	HA-39
Chevrolet AD............(1930)	FA-27	FB-25	FC-25	FD-19 / FD-126	FE-27	FG-15	FH-24	HA-39
Chrysler 6-B............(1925)	FA-28	FB-26	FC-26	FD-20	FE-28	FG-12	FH-26	HA-40
Chrysler 58............(1926)	None	None	None	None	None	FG-12	FH-26	HA-41
Chrysler 70............(1926)	FA-28	FB-26	FC-26	FD-20	FE-28	FG-12	FH-25	HA-42
Chrysler 80............(1926)	FA-29	FB-27	FC-27	FD-20	FE-28	FG-9	FH-27	HA-43
Chrysler 50............(1927)	None	None	None	None	None	FG-12	FH-26	HA-44
Chrysler 60............(1927)	FA-28	FB-26	FC-26	FD-20	FE-28	FG-12	FH-26	HA-45
Chrysler 70............(1927)	FA-28	FB-26	FC-26	FD-20	FE-28	FG-12	FH-25	HA-42
Chrysler 80............(1927)	FA-29	FB-27	FC-27	FD-20	FE-28	FG-9	FH-27	HA-46
Chrysler 52............(1928)	None	None	None	None	None	FG-12	FH-26	HA-44
Chrysler 62............(1928)	FA-28	FB-26	FC-26	FD-20	FE-28	FG-12	FH-26	HA-45
Chrysler 72............(1928)	FA-28	FB-26	FC-26	FD-20	FE-28	FG-12	FH-9	HA-48
Chrysler Imp. 80............(1928)	FA-30	FB-27	FC-27	FD-20	FE-28	FG-9	FH-9	HA-49
Chrysler 65............(1929)	FA-31	FB-29	FC-29	FD-21 / FD-127	FE-31	FG-17	FH-19	HA-50
Chrysler 75............(1929)	FA-28	FB-26	FC-26	FD-128	FE-28	FG-18	FH-9	HA-48
Chrysler Imp. 80............(1929)	FA-30	FB-27	FC-27	FD-128	FE-28	FG-18	FH-9	HA-49
Chrysler 6............(1930)	FA-25	FB-39	FC-30	FD-129 / FD-130	FE-19	FG-17	FH-54	HA-47
Chrysler 66............(1930)	FA-31	FB-29	FC-29	FD-21 / FD-127	FE-31	FG-17	FH-19	HA-50
Chrysler 70............(1930)	FA-31	FB-29	FC-29	FD-21 / FD-127	FE-31	FG-18	FH-19	HA-52
Chrysler 77............(1930)	FA-28	FA-56	FC-57	FD-129 / FD-131	FE-19	FG-18	FH-22	HA-136
Cleveland 31............(1925)	FA-23	FB-22	FC-22	FD-17 / FD-117	FE-24	FG-12	FH-9	HA-36
Cleveland 43............(1925)	FA-23	FB-21	FC-22	FD-17 / FD-117	FE-24	FG-12	FH-9	HA-36
Cleveland 31............(1926)	FA-23	FB-22	FC-22	FD-17 / FD-117	FE-24	FG-12	FH-9	HA-36
Cleveland 43............(1926)	FA-23	FB-21	FC-22	FD-17 / FD-117	FE-24	FG-12	FH-9	HA-36
Cord............(1930)	FA-6	FB-5	FC-41	FD-23	FE-6 / FE-10	FG-61	FH-1	HA-55
Davis 90, Cont. 7-U............(1925-26)	FA-2	FB-2	FC-2	FD-2	FE-2	FG-4	FH-6	HA-60
Davis 91, Cont. 8-R............(1925-26)	FA-3	FB-3	FC-8	FD-3	FE-3 / FE-9	FG-4	FH-3	HA-60
Davis 92, Cont. 11-U............(1926)	FA-35	FB-28	FC-31	FD-26	FE-35	FG-4	FH-9	HA-61
Davis 93, Cont. 20-L............(1926)	FA-10	FB-10	FC-10	FD-7	FE-11	FG-4	FH-9	HA-61
Davis 92, Cont. 11-U............(1927)	FA-35	FB-28	FC-31	FD-26	FE-35	FG-4	FH-9	HA-61
Davis 94, Cont. 28-L............(1927)	FA-10	FB-10	FC-10	FD-7	FE-11	FG-4	FH-9	HA-61
Davis 98, Cont. 8-S............(1927)	FA-36	FB-33	FC-10	FD-108	FE-36	FG-4	FH-30	HA-62
Davis 99, Cont. 14-S............(1928)	FA-36	FB-33	FC-10	FD-108	FE-36	FG-39	FH-30	HA-62
De Soto............(1929)	FA-31	FB-29	FC-29	FD-21 / FD-127	FE-31	FG-40	FH-29	HA-44
De Soto Finer 6............(1930)	FA-25	FB-39	FC-30	FD-129 / FD-130	FE-19	FG-17	FH-54	HA-47
De Soto 8............(1930)	FA-25	FB-66	FC-30	FD-129 / FD-130	FE-19	FG-62	FH-48	HA-11
Diana Str. 8, Cont. 12-Z............(1926)	FA-37	FB-34	FC-33	FD-28	FE-37	FG-20	FH-31	HA-8
Diana Str. 8, Cont. 12-Z............(1927)	FA-37	FB-34	FC-33	FD-28	FE-37	FG-20	FH-28	HA-8
Diana Str. 8, Cont. 12-Z............(1928)	FA-37	FB-34	FC-33	FD-28	FE-37	FG-20	FH-28	HA-8
Dodge Brothers 4............(1925)	FA-26	FB-35	FC-34	FD-29 / FD-118	FE-29 / FE-38	FG-12	FH-4	HA-66
Dodge Brothers 4............(1926)	FA-38	FB-35	FC-34	FD-29 / FD-118	FE-29 / FE-38	FG-12	FH-4	HA-66
Dodge Brothers 4............(1927-28)	FA-39	FB-36	FC-35	FD-29 / FD-118	FE-12	FG-12	FH-4	HA-67
Dodge Brothers Senior............(1928)	FA-40	FB-37	FC-36	FD-30	FE-40	FG-12	FH-9	HA-7
Dodge Std. 6............(1928)	FA-41	FB-38	FC-37	FD-22	FE-12	FG-12	FH-33	HA-7
Dodge Bros. Vic. 6............(1928-29)	FA-41	FB-38	FC-37	FD-22	FE-12	FG-41	FH-33	HA-7
Dodge Bros. Senior............(1929)	FA-43	FB-31	FC-19	FD-24	FE-26	FG-42	FH-9	HA-7
Dodge Brothers DA 6............(1929)	FA-44	FB-132	FC-32	FD-132 / FD-133	FE-19	FG-43	FH-54	HA-7
Dodge DD 6............(1930)	FA-25	FB-39	FC-30	FD-129 / FD-130	FE-19	FG-17	FH-54	HA-47
Dodge DD 8............(1930)	FA-25	FB-39	FC-30	FD-129 / FD-130	FE-19	FG-62	FH-48	HA-11
Durant A-22, Cont. Spec............(1925)	FA-46	FB-43	FC-40	FD-70	FE-45	FG-1	FH-9	HA-71
Durant D-55, Cont. 14-L............(1928)	FA-47	FB-45	FC-43	FD-34	FE-11	FG-1	FH-35	HA-72

COOLING SYSTEM and MUFFLER—Continued

Interchangeable Parts have the same CHILTON NUMBER in Any Column

Car Make and Model	WATER PUMP					Radiator Filler Cap	Fan Belt	Muffler
	Body Assembly	Shaft	Impeller	Bushings	Packing Nut or Gland			
Durant D-65, Cont. 15-L.........(1928)	FA-47	FB-45	FC-43	FD-34	FE-11	FG-1	FH-6	HA-73
Durant M2, Cont. W-5.........(1928)	FA-48	FB-44	FC-44	FD-34	FE-11	FG-1	FH-35	HA-72
Durant 75, Cont. 15-U.........(1928)	FA-47	FB-45	FC-43	FD-34	FE-11	FG-1	FH-36	HA-74
Durant 4-40, Cont. W-5.........(1929)	FA-48	FB-44	FC-44	FD-34	FE-11	FG-46	FH-35	HA-72
Durant 6-60, Cont. 14-L.........(1929)	FA-47	FB-45	FC-43	FD-34	FE-11	FG-1	FH-3	HA-73
Durant 66, Cont. 15-L.........(1929)	FA-47	FB-45	FC-43	FD-34	FE-11	FG-47	FH-3	HA-75
Durant 70, Cont. 20-E.........(1929)	FA-47	FB-45	FC-43	FD-34	FE-11	FG-47	FH-3	HA-74
Durant 63, Cont. 14-L.........(1930)	FA-47	FB-45	FC-43	FD-34	FE-11	FG-47	FH-3	HA-75
Durant 614, Cont. 22-A.........(1930)	FA-71	FB-42	FC-39	FD-134	FE-32	FG-47	FH-63	HA-14
Durant 617, Cont. 15-U.........(1930)	FA-47	FB-45	FC-43	FD-34	FE-11	FG-47	FH-36	HA-15
Elcar 440, Lyc. CF.........(1925)	None	None	None	None	None	FG-4	FH-2	HA-76
Elcar 6-50, Cont. 7-U.........(1925)	FA-2	FB-2	FC-2	FD-2	FE-2	FG-4	FH-6	HA-77
Elcar 6-60, Cont. 8-R.........(1925)	FA-3	FB-3	FC-3	FD-3	FE-9 FE-9	FG-4	FH-3	HA-77
Elcar 8-80, Lyc. H.............(1925)	FA-5	FB-5	FC-5	FD-5	FE-6 FE-10	FG-4	FH-5	HA-9
Elcar 6-65, Lyc. 4-SM.........(1926)	FA-8	FB-8	FC-8	FD-5	FE-10	FG-4	FH-8	HA-77
Elcar 8-81, Lyc. 4-H.........(1926)	FA-9	FB-8	FC-5	FD-5	FE-10	FG-4	FH-10	HA-9
Elcar 4-55, Lyc. CE.........(1926–27)	None	None	None	None	None	FG-4	FH-6	HA-76
Elcar 6-70, Lyc. WT.........(1927)	FA-7	FB-8	FC-8	FD-5	FE-10	FG-4	FH-26	HA-80
Elcar 8-82, Lyc. GT.........(1927)	FA-9	FB-8	FC-8	FD-5	FE-10	FG-4	FH-10	HA-81
Elcar 8-90, Lyc. 4-HM.........(1927)	FA-9	FB-8	FC-8	FD-5	FE-10	FG-4	FH-10	HA-82
Elcar 8-91, Lyc. 4-HM.........(1928)	FA-9	FB-8	FC-8	FD-5	FE-10	FG-4	FH-20	HA-82
Elcar 120, Lyc. MD.........(1928)	FA-9	FB-8	FC-8	FD-5	FE-10	FG-4	FH-20	HA-84
Elcar 6-70, Lyc. WS.........(1928–29)	FA-7	FB-8	FC-8	FD-5	FE-10	FG-4	FH-37	HA-80
Elcar 8-78, Lyc. GT.........(1928–29)	FA-9	FB-8	FC-8	FD-5	FE-10	FG-4	FH-20	HA-77
Elcar 8-82, Lyc. GS.........(1928–29)	FA-9	FB-8	FC-8	FD-5	FE-10	FG-4	FH-20	HA-81
Elcar 75, Lyc. WS.........(1929)	FA-7	FB-8	FC-8	FD-5	FE-10	FG-22	FH-20	HA-33
Elcar 95, 96, Lyc. GS.........(1929–30)	FA-9	FB-8	FC-8	FD-5	FE-10	FG-22	FH-20	HA-85
Elcar 120, Lyc. MD.........(1929–30)	FA-9	FB-8	FC-8	FD-5	FE-10	FG-22	FH-20	HA-84
Elcar 130, 140, Cont. 12-K.......(1930)	FA-45	FB-55	FC-42	FD-39 FD-109	FE-35	FG-61	FH-34	HA-34
Erskine 6-50, Cont. 8F...........(1927)	FA-49	FB-46	FC-47	FD-107	FE-35	FG-12	FH-33	HA-86
Erskine 6-51, Cont. 9-F.........(1928)	FA-49	FB-46	FC-47	FD-107	FE-35	FG-48	FH-33	HA-86
Erskine 6-52, Cont. 9-F.........(1929)	FA-49	FB-46	FC-47	FD-107	FE-35	FG-48	FH-33	HA-86
Erskine 6-53.........(1930)	FA-128	FB-41	FC-45	FD-25	FE-104*	FG-48	FH-52	HA-16
Essex 6...........(1925)	None	None	None	None	None	FG-14	FH-4	HA-87
Essex 6...........(1926)	None	None	None	None	None	FG-14	FH-4	HA-87
Essex Super 6...........(1927)	None	None	None	None	None	FG-9	FH-25	HA-87
Essex Super 6...........(1928)	None	None	None	None	None	FG-9	FH-25	HA-87
Essex Challenger.........(1929)	None	None	None	None	None	FG-9	FH-25	HA-88
Essex...........(1930)	None	None	None	None	None	FG-9	FH-67	HA-35
Falcon Knight 10.........(1927)	FA-51	FB-47	FC-49	FD-35	FE-47	FG-16	FH-9	HA-41
Falcon Knight 12.........(1928)	FA-51	FB-47	FC-49	FD-35	FE-47	FG-16	FH-9	HA-90
Flint E-55, Cont. 6-E.........(1925)	FA-53	FB-49	FC-51	FD-106 FD-110	FE-21 FE-30	FG-1	FH-31	HA-92
Flint B-40, Cont. 7-U........(1925–26)	FA-2	FB-2	FC-2	FD-2	FE-2	FG-1	FH-37	HA-91
Flint 60, Cont. 14-U.........(1926)	FA-52	FB-34	FC-10	FD-28	FE-37	FG-1	FH-9	HA-56
Flint 80, Cont. 6-E.........(1926)	FA-53	FB-49	FC-51	FD-106 FD-110	FE-21 FE-30	FG-1	FH-31	HA-92
Flint Jr., Cont. 9-L.........(1926)	FA-10	FB-10	FC-10	FD-7	FE-11	FG-16	FH-28	HA-94
Flint Jr., Cont. 9-L.........(1927)	FA-10	FB-10	FC-10	FD-7	FE-11	FG-16	FH-28	HA-94
Flint 60, Cont. 14-U.........(1927)	FA-52	FB-34	FC-10	FD-28	FE-37	FG-1	FH-9	HA-56
Flint 80, Cont. 6-E.........(1927)	FA-53	FB-49	FC-51	FD-106 FD-110	FE-21 FE-30	FG-1	FH-31	HA-92
Ford T.........(1925)	None	None	None	None	None	FG-49	FH-44	HA-95
Ford T.........(1926)	None	None	None	None	None	FG-49	FH-45	HA-95
Ford T.........(1927)	None	None	None	None	None	FG-49	FH-45	HA-95
Ford A.........(1928)	FA-55	FB-48	FC-53	FD-36	FE-50	FG-23	FH-20	HA-96
Ford A.........(1929)	FA-55	FB-48	FC-53	FD-36	FE-50	FG-23	FH-20	HA-96
Ford A.........(1930)	FA-55	FB-48	FC-53	FD-36	FE-50	FG-23	FH-20	HA-96
Gardner 6-A, Lyc. 4-S.........(1925)	FA-8	FB-8	FC-8	FD-5	FE-10	FG-9	FH-27	HA-102
Gardner 8-A, Lyc. 2-H.........(1925)	FA-5	FB-5	FC-5	FD-5	FE-6 FE-10	FG-9	FH-5	HA-103
Gardner Ser. 5, Lyc. CE.........(1925)	None	None	None	None	None	FG-9	FH-2	HA-104
Gardner 6-B, Lyc. 4-SM.........(1926)	FA-9	FB-8	FC-8	FD-5	FE-10	FG-9	FH-37	HA-102
Gardner 8-A, Lyc. 4-HM.........(1926)	FA-9	FB-8	FC-8	FD-5	FE-10	FG-9	FH-8	HA-103
Gardner 80, Lyc. GT.........(1927)	FA-9	FB-8	FC-8	FD-5	FE-10	FG-9	FH-26	HA-102
Gardner 90, Lyc. 4-HM.........(1927)	FA-9	FB-8	FC-8	FD-5	FE-10	FG-9	FH-8	HA-104
Gardner 75, Lyc. GT.........(1928)	FA-9	FB-8	FC-8	FD-5	FE-10	FG-9	FH-37	HA-102
Gardner 85, Lyc. GS.........(1928)	FA-9	FB-8	FC-8	FD-5	FE-10	FG-9	FH-37	HA-101
Gardner 95, Lyc. MD.........(1928)	FA-9	FB-8	FC-8	FD-5	FE-10	FG-9	FH-11	HA-101
Gardner 120, Lyc. GT.........(1929)	FA-9	FB-8	FC-8	FD-5	FE-10	FG-24	FH-10	HA-101
Gardner 125, Lyc. GS.........(1929)	FA-9	FB-8	FC-8	FD-5	FE-10	FG-24	FH-10	HA-101
Gardner 130, Lyc. MD.........(1929)	FA-9	FB-8	FC-8	FD-5	FE-10	FG-24	FH-11	HA-104
Gardner 136, Lyc. WR.........(1930)	FA-7	FB-8	FC-8	FD-8	FE-10	FG-24	FH-36	HA-99
Gardner 140, Lyc. GR.........(1930)	FA-9	FB-8	FC-8	FD-5	FE-10	FG-24	FH-10	HA-101
Gardner 150, Lyc. MD.........(1930)	FA-9	FB-8	FC-8	FD-5	FE-10	FG-24	FH-11	HA-103
Graham Paige 610...........(1928–29)	FA-56	FB-53	FC-54	FD-27 FD-37	FE-53 FE-54	FG-50	FH-39	HA-113
Graham Paige 614...........(1928–29)	FA-56	FB-53	FC-54	FD-27 FD-37	FE-53 FE-54	FG-51	FH-39	HA-114
Graham Paige 619...........(1928–29)	FA-57	FB-54	FC-55	FD-31 FD-38	FE-53 FE-54	FG-51	FH-40	HA-115
Graham Paige 629...........(1928–29)	FA-57	FB-54	FC-55	FD-31 FD-38	FE-53 FE-54	FG-51	FH-40	HA-115
Graham Paige 835, Cont. 12-K.(1928–29)	FA-45	FB-55	FC-42	FD-39 FD-109	FE-35	FG-51	FH-41	HA-115
Graham Paige 612...............(1929)	FA-56	FB-53	FC-54	FD-27 FD-37	FE-53 FE-54	FG-17	FH-42	HA-113
Graham Paige 615...............(1929)	FA-56	FB-53	FC-54	FD-27 FD-37	FE-53 FE-54	FG-18	FH-42	HA-114
Graham Paige 621...............(1929)	FA-57	FB-54	FC-55	FD-31 FD-38	FE-53 FE-54	FG-18	FH-40	HA-115
Graham Paige 827, Cont. 12K.....(1929)	FA-45	FB-55	FC-42	FD-39 FD-109	FE-35	FG-18	FH-75	HA-115
Graham Paige 837, Cont. 12K.....(1929)	FA-45	FB-55	FC-42	FD-39 FD-109	FE-35	FG-18	FH-75	HA-115
Graham Std. 6.................(1930)	FA-73	FB-53	FC-54	FD-27 FD-32	FE-53 FE-54	FG-17	FH-39	HA-57
Graham Spec. 6.................(1930)	FA-73	FB-53	FC-54	FD-27 FD-32	FE-53 FE-54	FG-18	FH-39	HA-114
Graham Std. and Spec. 8.........(1930)	FA-123	FB-53	FC-46	FD-32 FD-27	FE-53 FE-54	FG-18	FH-10	HA-115

COOLING SYSTEM and MUFFLER—Continued

Interchangeable Parts have the same CHILTON NUMBER in Any Column

Car Make and Model	WATER PUMP					Radiator Filler Cap	Fan Belt	Muffler
	Body Assembly	Shaft	Impeller	Bushings	Packing Nut or Gland			
Graham Custom 8...............(1930)	FA-45	FB-55	FC-42	FD-39 FD-109	FE-35	FG-18	FH-75	HA-115
Hudson Super 6.,.................(1925)	FA-60	FB-57	FC-58	FD-40 FD-119	FE-39 FE-57	FG-9	FH-4	HA-118
Hudson Super 6..................(1926)	FA-60	FB-57	FC-58	FD-40 FD-119	FE-39 FE-57	FG-9	FH-4	HA-118
Hudson Super 6...........(Early 1927)	FA-60	FB-57	FC-58	FD-40 FD-119	FE-39 FE-57	FG-9	FH-4	HA-118
Hudson Super 6............(Late 1927)	FA-61	FB-58	FC-59	FD-41 FD-121	FE-39 FE-57	FG-9	FH-20	HA-118
Hudson Super 6..................(1928)	FA-61	FB-58	FC-59	FD-41 FD-121	FE-39 FE-57	FG-9	FH-20	HA-118
Hudson Greater 6................(1929)	FA-61	FB-58	FC-59	FD-41 FD-141	FE-39 FE-57	FG-9	FH-20	HA-15
Hudson 8.......................(1930)	FA-50	FB-40	FC-48	FD-135 FD-136	FD-34	FG-9	FH-10	HA-110
Hupmobile R....................(1925)	None	None	None	None	None	FG-25	FH-43	HA-10
Hupmobile E1 ....(1925-26)	FA-62	FB-59	FC-60	FD-42	FE-58	FG-25	FH-11	HA-120
Hupmobile A1...................(1926)	FA-63	FB-60	FC-61	FD-43	FE-59	FG-25	FH-15	HA-111
Hupmobile E2..............(1926-27)	FA-62	FB-59	FC-60	FD-42	FE-58	FG-25	FH-11	HA-120
Hupmobile A2 ....(1927)	FA-63	FB-60	FC-61	FD-43	FE-59	FG-25	FH-15	HA-111
Hupmobile E3.............(1927-28)	FA-62	FB-59	FC-60	FD-42	FE-58	FG-25	FH-36	HA-120
Hupmobile Cent. 6.............(1928)	FA-58	FB-52	FC-56	FD-43	FE-60	FG-25	FH-15	HA-122
Hupmobile Cent. 8.............(1928)	FA-62	FB-59	FC-60	FD-42	FE-58	FG-52	FH-36	HA-123
Hupmobile Cent. 125...........(1928)	FA-62	FB-59	FC-60	FD-42	FE-58	FG-52	FH-36	HA-123
Hupmobile M8.............(1928–29)	FA-62	FB-59	FC-60	FD-42	FE-58	FG-52	FH-36	HA-123
Hupmobile Cent. 6.............(1929)	FA-58	FB-52	FC-56	FD-43	FE-60	FG-52	FH-15	HA-122
Hupmobile S..................(1930)	FA-54	FB-30	FC-50	FD-137	FE-60	FG-52	FH-15	HA-122
Hupmobile C..................(1930)	FA-42	FB-32	FC-66	FD-138	FE-41	FG-52	FH-22	HA-127
Hupmobile H & U..............(1930)	FA-42	FB-32	FC-66	FD-138	FE-41	FG-52	FH-22	HA-125
Jewett 6-50...................(1925)	FA-64	FB-51	FC-52	FD-44	FE-52	FG-53	FH-46	HA-57
Jewett New Day, 6-40, Cont. 18L..(1926)	FA-10	FB-10	FC-10	FD-7	FE-11	FG-53	FH-28	HA-128
Jordan KL, Cont. 6-S..........(1925)	FA-66	FB-61	FC-7	FD-106 FD-111	FE-3 FE-9	FG-26	FH-10	HA-130
Jordan A, Cont. 9-K...........(1925)	FA-67	FB-34	FC-10	FD-28	FE-37	FG-26	FH-11	HA-130
Jordan A, Cont. 9-K...........(1926)	FA-67	FB-34	FC-10	FD-28	FE-37	FG-26	FH-11	HA-130
Jordan J, Cont. 8-S...........(1926)	FA-36	FB-33	FC-10	FD-108	FE-36	FG-26	FH-19	HA-131
Jordan AA, Cont. 9-K..........(1927)	FA-67	FB-34	FC-10	FD-28	FE-37	FG-27	FH-11	HA-129
Jordan J, Cont. 8-S...........(1927)	FA-36	FB-33	FC-10	FD-108	FE-36	FG-27	FH-19	HA-131
Jordan R Cont. 12-E.........(1927–28)	FA-69	FB-46	FC-69	FD-107	FE-35	FG-27	FH-49	HA-21
Jordan JJ, Cont. 14-S........(1928)	FA-36	FB-33	FC-10	FD-108	FE-36	FG-27	FH-19	HA-131
Jordan JE, Cont. 14-S.....(1928–29)	FA-36	FB-33	FC-10	FD-108	FE-36	FG-27	FH-19	HA-131
Jordan E, Cont. 16-C.........(1929)	FA-47	FB-45	FC-43	FD-34	FE-11	FG-28	FH-19	HA-134
Jordan G, Cont. 15-S.........(1929)	FA-68	FB-65	FC-64	FD-47	FE-35	FG-28	FH-33	HA-136
Jordan 90, Cont. 15-S.........(1930)	FA-68	FB-65	FC-64	FD-47	FE-35	FG-28	FH-33	HA-136
Kissel 6-55...................(1925)	FA-65	FB-64	FC-62	FD-48	FE-51	FG-3	FH-4	HA-137
Kissel 8-75, Lyc. 3-H..........(1925)	FA-5	FB-5	FC-5	FD-5	FE-6 FE-10	FG-3	FH-5	HA-101
Kissel 6-55...................(1926)	FA-65	FB-64	FC-62	FD-48	FE-51	FG-3	FH-4	HA-137
Kissel 8-75, Lyc. 3-H..........(1926)	FA-5	FB-5	FC-5	FD-5	FE-10	FG-3	FH-5	HA-101
Kissel 6-55...................(1927)	FA-65	FB-64	FC-62	FD-48	FE-51	FG-3	FH-4	HA-196
Kissel 8-65, Lyc. GS..........(1927)	FA-9	FB-8	FC-8	FD-5	FE-10	FG-3	FH-8	HA-140
Kissel 8-75, Lyc. 3-H..........(1927)	FA-5	FB-5	FC-5	FD-5	FE-10	FG-3	FH-5	HA-101
Kissel 6-70, Lyc. WS..........(1928)	FA-7	FB-8	FC-8	FD-5	FE-10	FG-3	FH-20	HA-141
Kissel 8-80, Lyc. GS..........(1928)	FA-9	FB-8	FC-8	FD-5	FE-10	FG-3	FH-20	HA-142
Kissel 8-80 S, Lyc. GS........(1928)	FA-9	FB-8	FC-8	FD-5	FE-10	FG-3	FH-20	HA-142
Kissel 8-90, Lyc. HM..........(1928)	FA-9	FB-8	FC-8	FD-5	FE-10	FG-3	FH-5	HA-142
Kissel 6-73, Lyc. WR..........(1929)	FA-7	FB-8	FC-8	FD-8	FE-10	FG-30	FH-36	HA-143
Kissel 8-95, Lyc. GS..........(1929)	FA-9	FB-8	FC-8	FD-5	FE-10	FG-30	FH-36	HA-142
Kissel 8-126, Lyc. MD.........(1929)	FB-9	FB-8	FC-8	FD-5	FE-10	FG-30	FH-52	HA-144
La Salle 303..................(1927)	FA-19	FB-6	FC-19	FD-14 FD-115	FE-14	FG-5	FH-53	HA-145
La Salle 303..................(1928)	FA-19	FB-6	FC-19	FD-14 FD-115	FE-14	FG-5	FH-53	HA-28
La Salle 328..................(1929)	FA-19	FB-6	FC-19	FD-14 FD-115	FE-14	FG-5	FH-53	HA-24
La Salle 340..................(1930)	FA-19	FB-6	FC-38	FD-14 FD-115	FE-14	FG-5	FH-51	HA-29
Lincoln 8.....................(1925)	FA-72	FB-67	FC-68	FD-53	FE-62	FG-9	FH-50	HA-149
Lincoln 8.....................(1926)	FA-72	FB-67	FC-68	FD-53	FE-62	FG-9	FH-50	HA-149
Lincoln 8.....................(1927)	FA-72	FB-67	FC-68	FD-53	FE-62	FG-9	FH-50	HA-149
Lincoln 8.....................(1928)	FA-72	FB-67	FC-68	FD-53	FE-62	FG-9	FH-50	HA-149
Lincoln 8.....................(1929)	FA-72	FB-67	FC-68	FD-53	FE-62	FG-9	FH-50	HA-149
Lincoln 8.....................(1930)	FA-72	FB-67	FC-68	FD-53	FE-62	FG-9	FH-50	HA-150
Locomobile Jr. 8..............(1925)	FA-74	FB-69	FC-70	FD-55	FE-64	FG-16	FH-15	HA-132
Locomobile 48.................(1925)	FA-75	FB-70	FC-71	FD-56	FE-65	FG-32	FH-31	HA-152
Locomobile 48.................(1926)	FA-75	FB-70	FC-71	FD-56	FE-65	FG-32	FH-31	HA-152
Locomobile 90.................(1926)	FA-76	FB-71	FC-72	FD-57	FE-66	FG-54	FH-11	HA-153
Locomobile Jr. 8..............(1926)	FA-74	FB-69	FC-70	FD-55	FE-64	FG-16	FH-15	HA-132
Locomobile 48.................(1927)	FA-75	FB-70	FC-71	FD-56	FE-65	FG-32	FH-31	HA-152
Locomobile 8-66...............(1927)	FA-74	FB-69	FC-70	FD-55	FE-64	FG-54	FH-15	HA-154
Locomobile 8-80, Lyc. HD.......(1927)	FA-9	FB-8	FC-8	FD-5	FE-10	FG-54	FH-5	HA-133
Locomobile 90.................(1927)	FA-76	FB-71	FC-72	FD-57	FE-66	FG-54	FH-11	HA-153
Locomobile 48.................(1928)	FA-75	FB-70	FC-71	FD-56	FE-65	FG-32	FH-31	HA-152
Locomobile 8-70, Cont. 8S.....(1928)	FA-36	FB-33	FC-10	FD-108	FE-36	FG-54	FH-19	HA-156
Locomobile 8-80, Lyc. HD......(1928)	FA-9	FB-8	FC-8	FD-5	FE-10	FG-54	FH-5	HA-133
Locomobile 90.................(1928)	FA-76	FB-71	FC-72	FD-57	FE-66	FG-54	FH-11	HA-153
Locomobile 8-80, Lyc. HD......(1929)	FA-9	FB-8	FC-8	FD-5	FE-10	FG-9	FH-5	HA-133
Locomobile 86, 88, Lyc. HDL....(1929)	FA-9	FB-8	FC-8	FD-5	FE-10	FG-9	FH-5	HA-133
Locomobile 90.................(1929)	FA-76	FB-71	FC-72	FD-57	FE-66	FG-9	FH-11	HA-153
Marmon 74....................(1925)	FA-78	FB-72	FC-73	FD-60	FE-55	FG-29	FH-31	HA-149
Marmon 74....................(1926)	FA-78	FB-72	FC-73	FD-60	FE-55	FG-29	FH-31	HA-149
Marmon, Little...............(1927)	FA-79	FB-73	FC-74	FD-61	FE-67	FG-31	FH-56	HA-21
Marmon E-75..................(1927)	FA-78	FB-72	FC-113	FD-60	FE-55	FG-29	FH-31	HA-149
Marmon E-75..................(1928)	FA-78	FB-72	FC-113	FD-60	FE-55	FG-29	FH-31	HA-149
Marmon 68....................(1928)	FA-80	FB-74	FC-75	FD-54	FE-68	FG-14	FH-19	HA-157
Marmon 78....................(1928)	FA-81	FB-75	FC-76	FD-61	FE-69	FG-31	FH-56	HA-157
Marmon 68....................(1929)	FA-80	FB-74	FC-75	FD-54	FE-68	FG-14	FH-19	HA-157
Marmon 78....................(1929)	FA-81	FB-75	FC-76	FD-61	FE-69	FG-31	FH-56	HA-157
Marmon Roosevelt.............(1929)	FA-80	FB-74	FC-75	FD-54	FE-68	FG-14	FH-19	HA-146
Marmon 69....................(1930)	FA-70	FB-50	FC-63	FD-46	FE-42	FG-14	FH-3	HA-157
Marmon 79....................(1930)	FA-77	FB-62	FC-65	FD-49	FE-43	FG-31	FH-31	HA-136
Marmon Big 8.................(1930)	FA-77	FB-62	FC-65	FD-49	FE-43	FG-31	FH-31	HA-158
Marquette....................(1930)	FA-144	FB-131	FC-88	FD-50 FD-51	FE-77	FG-8	FH-15	HA-77

COOLING SYSTEM and MUFFLER—Continued

Interchangeable Parts have the same CHILTON NUMBER in Any Column

Car Make and Model	WATER PUMP					Radiator Filler Cap	Fan Belt	Muffler
	Body Assembly	Shaft	Impeller	Bushings	Packing Nut or Gland			
Maxwell.................(1925)	None	None	None	None	None	FG-4	FH-26	HA-41
Moon Series A, Cont. 7-Z........(1925)	FA-86	FB-63	FC-43	FD-34	FE-11	FG-20	FH-30	HA-8
Moon Series A, Cont. 7-Z........(1926)	FA-86	FB-63	FC-43	FD-34	FE-11	FG-20	FH-30	HA-8
Moon Series A, Cont. 7-Z........(1927)	FA-86	FB-63	FC-43	FD-34	FE-11	FG-20	FH-30	HA-8
Moon 6-60, Cont. 26-L.........(1927)	FA-10	FB-10	FC-10	FD-7	FE-11	FG-20	FH-28	HA-159
Moon Series A, Cont. 7-Z........(1928)	FA-86	FB-63	FC-43	FD-34	FE-11	Special	FH-30	HA-8
Moon 6-60, Cont. 26-L.........(1928)	FA-10	FB-10	FC-10	FD-7	FE-11	Special	FH-28	HA-159
Moon 6-72, Cont. 11-E.........(1928)	FA-85	FB-77	FC-78	FD-107	FE-35	Special	FH-49	HA-160
Moon 8-80, Cont. 15-S.......(1928–29)	FA-68	FB-65	FC-64	FD-47	FE-35	Special	FH-34	HA-161
Moon 6-72, Cont. 11-E.........(1929)	FA-85	FB-77	FC-78	FD-107	FE-35	Special	FH-49	HA-160
Nash Adv. 6...............(1925)	FA-88	FB-78	FC-80	FD-63	FE-70	FG-1	FH-59	HA-162
Nash Spec. 6..............(1925)	FA-89	FB-79	FC-81	FD-64	FE-71	FG-1	FH-47	HA-163
Nash Adv. 6...............(1926)	FA-88	FB-78	FC-80	FD-63	FE-70	FG-1	FH-59	HA-162
Nash Spec. 6..............(1926)	FA-89	FB-79	FC-81	FD-64	FE-71	FG-1	FH-5	HA-163
Nash Adv. 6...............(1927)	FA-88	FB-78	FC-80	FD-63	FE-70	FG-1	FH-59	HA-162
Nash Spec. 6..............(1927)	FA-87	FB-82	FC-82	FD-65	FE-72	FG-1	FH-52	HA-163
Nash Light 6..............(1927)	FA-1	FB-1	FC-1	FD-1 / FD-6	FE-1	FG-1	FH-5	HA-1
Nash Adv. 6...............(1928)	FA-88	FB-78	FC-80	FD-63	FE-70	FG-55	FH-59	HA-162
Nash Spec. 6..............(1928)	FA-87	FB-82	FC-82	FD-65	FE-72	FG-55	FH-52	HA-163
Nash Std. 6...............(1928)	FA-1	FB-1	FC-1	FD-1 / FD-6	FE-1	FG-17	FH-5	HA-1
Nash Adv. 6...............(1929)	FA-88	FB-78	FC-80	FD-63	FE-70	FG-55	FH-59	HA-162
Nash Spec. 6..............(1929)	FA-87	FB-82	FC-82	FD-65	FE-72	FG-55	FH-53	HA-163
Nash Std. 6...............(1929)	FA-91	FB-133	FC-79	FD-66 / FD-122	FE-73	FG-17	FH-60	HA-59
Nash Single Ignition 6..........(1930)	FA 84	FB-80	FC-67	FD-52 / FD-58	FE-73	FG-17	FH-22	HA-59
Nash Twin Ignition 6...........(1930)	FA-90	FB-81	FC-77	FD-59	FE-44	FG-55	FH-56	HA-68
Nash Twin Ignition 8...........(1930)	FA-105	FB-76	FC-115	FD-139 / FD-140	FE-46	FG-55	FH-72	HA-69
Oakland 6-54...............(1925)	FA-93	FB-83	FC-85	FD-62 / FD-68	FE-74	FG-1	FH-5	HA-165
Oakland O-6...............(1926)	FA-93	FB-83	FC-85	FD-62 / FD-68	FE-74	FG-1	FH-5	HA-165
Oakland GO-6..............(1927)	FA-93	FB-83	FC-85	FD-62 / FD-68	FE-74	FG-1	FH-5	HA-166
Oakland AA-6..............(1928)	FA-94	FB-84	FC-86	FD-69 / FD-123	FE-75	FG-34	FH-36	HA-167
Oakland AA-6..............(1929)	FA-94	FB-84	FC-86	FD-69 / FD-123	FE-75	FG-34	FH-36	HA-168
Oakland 8.................(1930)	FA-8	FB-68	FC-120	FD-69 / FD-141	FE-48	FG-35	FH-72	HA-162
Oldsmobile C-30............(1925)	FA-95	FB-85	FC-87	FD-142 / FD-143	FE-76	FG-14	FH-52	HA-169
Oldsmobile D-30............(1926)	FA-95	FB-85	FC-87	FD-142 / FD-143	FE-76	FG-14	FH-52	HA-164
Oldsmobile 30-E............(1927)	FA-95	FB-85	FC-87	FD-142 / FD-143	FE-76	FG-14	FH-52	HA-170
Oldsmobile F-28............(1928)	FA-96	FB-86	FC-88	FD-50 / FD-71	FE-77	FG-35	FH-52	HA-171
Oldsmobile F-29............(1929)	FA-96	FB-86	FC-88	FD-50 / FD-71	FE-77	FG-35	FH-52	HA-171
Oldsmobile F-30............(1930)	FA-96	FB-86	FC-88	FD-50 / FD-71	FE-77	FG-35	FH-52	HA-171
Overland 91...............(1925)	None	None	None	None	None	FG-16	FH-55	HA-172
Overland 93...............(1925)	FA-97	FB-87	FC-89	FD-72	FE-78	FG-16	FH-57	HA-41
Overland 91...............(1926)	None	None	None	None	None	FG-16	FH-55	HA-172
Overland 93...............(1926)	FA-97	FB-87	FC-89	FD-72	FE-78	FG-16	FH-57	HA-41
Packard 6 Cyl. 326, 333..........(1925)	FA-100	FB-89	FC-91	FD-75	FE-79	Special	FH-15	HA-174
Packard 8 Cyl., 236, 243........(1925)	FA-100	FB-89	FC-91	FD-75	FE-79	Special	FH-33	HA-175
Packard 6 Cyl. 326, 333..........(1926)	FA-100	FB-89	FC-91	FD-75	FE-79	Special	FH-15	HA-174
Packard 8 Cyl., 236, 243........(1926)	FA-100	FB-89	FC-91	FD-75	FE-79	Special	FH-33	HA-175
Packard 6 Cyl., 426, 433........(1927)	FA-100	FB-89	FC-91	FD-75	FE-79	Special	FH-15	HA-176
Packard 8 Cyl., 336, 343........(1927)	FA-101	FB-89	FC-91	FD-75	FE-79	Special	FH-33	HA-175
Packard 526, 533............(1928)	FA-100	FB-89	FC-91	FD-75	FE-79	Special	FH-28	HA-176
Packard Std. 8, 443..........(1928)	FA-101	FB-89	FC-91	FD-75	FE-79	Special	FH-28	HA-177
Packard 626, 633............(1929)	FA-102	FB-91	FC-91	FD-67	FE-80	Special	FH-34	HA-178
Packard 640, 645............(1929)	FA-92	FB-89	FC-91	FD-75	FE-80	Special	FH-34	HA-179
Packard 726, 733............(1930)	FA-115	FB-90	FC-90	FD-76	FE-49	Special	FH-73	HA-178
Packard 740, 745............(1930)	FA-125	FB-110	FC-90	FD-76	FE-49	Special	FH-73	HA-179
Paige 6-70, Cont. 10-A........(1925–26)	FA-103	FB-110	FC-92	FD-3	FE-81	FG-53	FH-3	HA-180
Paige 6-72................(1926)	FA-104	FB-92	FC-93	FD-31 / FD-38	FE-53 / FE-54	FG-9	FH-35	HA-77
Paige 6-45, Cont. 19L.......(1927–28)	FA-10	FB-10	FC-10	FD-7	FE-11	FG-53	FH-28	HA-86
Paige 6-65................(1927–28)	FA-104	FB-92	FC-93	FD-31 / FD-38	FE-53 / FE-54	FG-53	FH-35	HA-21
Paige 6-75................(1927–28)	FA-104	FB-92	FC-93	FD-31 / FD-38	FE-53 / FE-54	FG-9	FH-58	HA-157
Paige 8-85, Lyc. MD.........(1927–28)	FA-9	FB-8	FC-8	FD-5	FE-10	FG-53	FH-50	HA-183
Peerless 70................(1925)	FA-83	FB-94	FC-97	FD-77	FE-83	FG-16	FH-7	HA-184
Peerless 67................(1925)	FA-107	FB-95	FC-98	FD-78	FE-84	FG-9	FH-62	HA-185
Peerless 80, Cont. 8-U........(1926)	FA-106	FB-93	FC-10	FD-148	FE-37	FG-16	FH-61	HA-77
Peerless 69................(1926)	FA-107	FB-95	FC-98	FD-78	FE-84	FG-9	FH-62	HA-185
Peerless 60, Cont. 10-E.......(1927)	FA-85	FB-46	FC-47	FD-107	FE-35	FG-16	FH-33	HA-77
Peerless 69................(1927)	FA-107	FB-95	FC-98	FD-78	FE-84	FG-9	FH-62	HA-185
Peerless 72..............(1927–28)	FA-83	FB-94	FC-97	FD-77	FE-83	FG-16	FH-61	HA-184
Peerless 80, Cont. 8-U........(1927)	FA-106	FB-93	FC-10	FD-148	FE-37	FG-16	FH-61	HA-77
Peerless 90..............(1927–28)	FA-83	FB-98	FC-100	FD-77	FE-83	FG-16	FH-19	HA-184
Peerless 60, Cont., 10E.......(1928)	FA-85	FB-46	FC-47	FD-107	FE-35	FG-16	FH-33	HA-77
Peerless 69................(1928)	FA-107	FB-95	FC-98	FD-78	FE-84	FG-9	FH-62	HA-185
Peerless 80, Cont. 8-U........(1928)	FA-106	FB-93	FC-10	FD-148	FE-37	FG-16	FH-61	HA-77
Peerless 91................(1928)	FA-83	FB-98	FC-100	FD-77	FE-83	FG-16	FH-19	HA-184
Peerless 61, Cont. 11E........(1929)	FA-85	FB-77	FC-78	FD-107	FE-35	FG-56	FH-33	HA-77
Peerless 81, Cont. 18-C.......(1929)	FA-47	FB-45	FC-43	FD-34	FE-11	FG-51	FH-20	HA-77
Peerless 91................(1929)	FA-83	FB-98	FC-100	FD-77	FE-83	FG-51	FH-19	HA-184
Peerless 125, Cont. 12-K.......(1929)	FA-45	FB-55	FC-42	FD-39 / FD-109	FE-35	FG-57	FH-64	HA-28
Peerless A, Cont. 17-S.........(1930)	FA-12	FB-12	FC-12	FD-8	FE-16	FG-51	FH-9	HA-77
Peerless B & C.............(1930)	FA-145	FB-96	FC-99	FD-143 / FD-144	FE-50	FG-57	FH-74	HA-136
Pierce Arrow 80............(1925)	FA-112	FB-99	FC-102	FD-79	FE-87	FG-20	FH-15	HA-101
Pierce Arrow 33............(1926)	FA-113	FB-100	FC-103	FD-80	FE-88	FG-20	FH-10	HA-187
Pierce Arrow 80............(1926)	FA-112	FB-99	FC-102	FD-79	FE-87	FG-20	FH-15	HA-101

COOLING SYSTEM and MUFFLER—Continued

Interchangeable Parts have the same CHILTON NUMBER in Any Column

Car Make and Model	WATER PUMP					Radiator Filler Cap	Fan Belt	Muffler
	Body Assembly	Shaft	Impeller	Bushings	Packing Nut or Gland			
Pierce Arrow 36..................(1927)	FA-113	FB-100	FC-103	FD-80	FE-88	FG-20	FH-10	HA-143
Pierce Arrow 80..................(1927)	FA-112	FB-99	FC-102	FD-79	FE-87	FG-20	FH-15	HA-101
Pierce Arrow 36..................(1928)	FA-113	FB-100	FC-103	FD-80	FE-88	FG-20	FH-37	HA-143
Pierce Arrow 81..................(1928)	FA-112	FB-99	FC-102	FD-79	FE-87	FG-20	FH-26	HA-101
Pierce Arrow 133, 143............(1929)	FA-114	FB-101	FC-104	FD-81	FE-89	FG-5	FH-10	HA-189
Pierce Arrow A...................(1930)	FA-108	FB-97	FC-101	FD-74	FE-52	FG-5	FH-65	HA-189
Pierce Arrow B...................(1930)	FA-108	FB-97	FC-101	FD-74	FE-52	FG-5	FH-65	HA-189
Pierce Arrow C...................(1930)	FA-110	FB-97	FC-101	FD-74	FE-52	FG-5	FH-66	HA-189
Plymouth 4 Cyl...................(1929)	None	None	None	None	None	FG-17	FH-26	HA-44
Plymouth.........................(1930)	FA-120	FB-39	FC-30	FD-129 FD-130	FE-19	FG-17	FH-33	HA-44
Pontiac 6........................(1926)	FA-116	FB-102	FC-105	FD-145 FD-146	FE-75	FG-1	FH-26	HA-132
Pontiac 6........................(1927)	FA-116	FB-102	FC-105	FD-145 FD-146	FE-75	FG-1	FH-26	HA-132
Pontiac 6........................(1928)	FA-116	FB-103	FC-107	FD-145 FD-146	FE-75	FG-1	FH-26	HA-190
Pontiac Big 6....................(1929)	FA-111	FB-103	FC-107	FD-69 FD-146	FE-75	FG-34	FH-29	HA-167
Pontiac 6........................(1930)	FA-111	FB-103	FC-132	FD-145 FD-146	FE-48	FG-34	FH-29	HA-167
Reo T6...........................(1925)	FA-117	FB-104	FC-108	FD-82	FE-56 FE-90	FG-36	FH-33	HA-63
Reo T6........................(1926–27)	FA-117	FB-104	FC-108	FD-82	FE-56 FE-90	FG-36	FH-33	HA-63
Reo Flying Cloud.................(1927)	FA-118	FB-105	FC-109	FD-83	FE-91	FG-48	FH-28	HA-9
Reo Wolverine, Cont. 15-E........(1927)	FA-85	FB-46	FC-69	FD-107	FE-35	FG-58	FH-33	HA-8
Reo Flying Cloud.................(1928)	FA-118	FB-105	FC-109	FD-83	FE-91	FG-48	FH-28	HA-9
Reo Wolverine, Cont. 15-E........(1928)	FA-85	FB-46	FC-69	FD-107	FE-35	FG-58	FH-33	HA-8
Reo Flying Cloud Master..........(1929)	FA-118	FB-105	FC-109	FD-83	FE-91	FG-58	FH-28	HA-8
Reo Flying Cloud Mate, Cont. 16-E.(1929)	FA-85	FB-46	FC-7	FD-34	FE-11	FG-58	FH-33	HA-135
Reo 15, Cont. 19-E...............(1930)	FA-85	FB-46	FC-7	FD-34	FE-11	FG-58	FH-33	HA-135
Reo 20, 25.......................(1930)	FA-118	FB-105	FC-109	FD-83	FE-91	FG-58	FH-28	HA-8
Rickenbacker A-8.................(1925)	FA-121	FB-108	FC-111	FD-86	FE-93	FG-16	FH-37	HA-194
Rickenbacker D-6.................(1925)	FA-122	FB-109	FC-112	FD-87	FE-94	FG-16	FH-37	HA-8
Rickenbacker 8-B.................(1926)	FA-121	FB-108	FC-112	FD-86	FE-93	FG-16	FH-37	HA-196
Rickenbacker 6-E.................(1926)	FA-122	FB-109	FC-112	FD-87	FE-94	FG-16	FH-37	HA-197
Rickenbacker 6-70................(1927)	FA-122	FB-109	FC-112	FD-87	FE-94	FG-16	FH-37	HA-198
Rickenbacker 8-80................(1927)	FA-122	FB-109	FC-112	FD-87	FE-94	FG-16	FH-37	HA-196
Rickenbacker 8-90................(1927)	FA-122	FB-109	FC-112	FD-87	FE-94	FG-16	FH-37	HA-196
Roamer 6-54 E, Cont. 9-N.........(1925)	FA-124	FB-111	FC-114	FD-89	FE-93	FG-9	FH-25	HA-137
Roamer 6-50, Cont. 7-U.......(1925–26)	FA-2	FB-2	FC-2	FD-2	FE-2	FG-9	FH-2	HA-147
Roamer 6-54-E, Cont. 9-N.........(1926)	FA-124	FB-111	FC-114	FD-89	FE-96	FG-9	FH-25	HA-137
Roamer 8-80, Lyc. 4-HM.......(1926–27)	FA-9	FB-8	FC-8	FD-5	FE-10	FG-9	FH-18	HA-148
Roamer 8-78, Lyc. GT.............(1927)	FA-9	FB-8	FC-8	FD-5	FE-10	FG-9	FH-18	HA-151
Roamer 8-80, Lyc. 4-HM...........(1927)	FA-9	FB-8	FC-8	FD-5	FE-10	FG-9	FH-18	HA-148
Roamer 8-88, Lyc. 4-H............(1927)	FA-5	FB-5	FC-8	FD-5	FE-10	FG-9	FH-26	HA-148
Roamer 8-78, Lyc. GT.............(1928)	FA-9	FB-8	FC-8	FD-5	FE-10	FG-9	FH-18	HA-151
Roamer 8-80, Lyc. 4-HM...........(1928)	FA-9	FB-8	FC-8	FD-5	FE-10	FG-9	FH-18	HA-148
Roamer 8-88, Lyc. 4-H............(1928)	FA-5	FB-5	FC-8	FD-5	FE-10	FG-9	FH-26	HA-148
Roamer 8-78, Lyc. GT.............(1929)	FA-9	FB-8	FC-8	FD-5	FE-10	FG-4	FH-18	HA-151
Roamer 8-80, Lyc. 4-HM...........(1929)	FA-9	FB-8	FC-8	FD-5	FE-10	FG-4	FH-18	HA-148
Roamer 8-88, Lyc. 4-H............(1929)	FA-5	FB-5	FC-8	FD-5	FE-10	FG-4	FH-26	HA-148
Star F, Cont. W5.................(1925)	FA-48	FB-44	FC-44	FD-34	FE-11	FG-14	FH-35	HA-72
Star M, Cont. W5.................(1926)	FA-48	FB-44	FC-44	FD-34	FE-11	FG-14	FH-35	HA-72
Star R, Cont. 14-L...............(1926)	FA-47	FB-45	FC-43	FD-34	FE-11	FG-14	FH-35	HA-72
Star M, Cont. W5..............(1927–28)	FA-48	FB-44	FC-44	FD-34	FE-11	FG-14	FH-35	HA-72
Star R, Cont. 14L.............(1927–28)	FA-47	FB-45	FC-43	FD-34	FE-11	FG-14	FH-35	HA-72
Stearns Knight B, 4 Cyl..........(1925)	FA-109	FB-113	FC-116	FD-90	FE-98	FG-20	FH-28	HA-9
Stearns Knight C, 6 Cyl..........(1925)	FA-119	FB-114	FC-117	FD-91	FE-99	FG-20	FH-28	HA-155
Stearns Knight S, 6 Cyl..........(1925)	FA-119	FB-114	FC-117	FD-91	FE-99	FG-20	FH-28	HA-173
Stearns Knight B, 4 Cyl..........(1926)	FA-109	FB-113	FC-116	FD-90	FE-98	FG-20	FH-28	HA-9
Stearns Knight C, 75.............(1926)	FA-119	FB-114	FC-117	FD-91	FE-99	FG-20	FH-52	HA-155
Stearns Knight S, 95.............(1926)	FA-119	FB-114	FC-117	FD-91	FE-99	FG-20	FH-52	HA-173
Stearns Knight F, 6-85...........(1927)	FA-126	FB-115	FC-118	FD-92	FE-100	FG-9	FH-21	HA-181
Stearns Knight 8-85..........(1927–28)	FA-127	FB-116	FC-119	FD-93	FE-101	FG-51	FH-10	HA-182
Stearns Knight F, 6-85...........(1928)	FA-126	FB-115	FC-118	FD-92	FE-100	FG-9	FH-52	HA-181
Stearns Knight H & J, 8-90.......(1928)	FA-127	FB-116	FC-119	FD-93	FE-101	FG-51	FH-18	HA-182
Stearns Knight H & J, 8-90.......(1929)	FA-127	FB-116	FC-119	FD-93	FE-101	Special	FH-18	HA-182
Stearns Knight M & N, 6-80...(1928–29)	FA-126	FB-115	FC-118	FD-92	FE-100	Special	FH-36	HA-196
Studebaker Big 6.................(1925)	FA-130	FB-118	FC-121	FD-84 FD-95	FE-103	FG-12	FH-32	HA-157
Studebaker Spec. 6...............(1925)	FA-130	FB-118	FC-121	FD-84 FD-95	FE-103	FG-12	FH-32	HA-157
Studebaker Std. 6................(1925)	FA-131	FB-119	FC-122	FD-96	FE-104*	FG-12	FH-69	HA-86
Studebaker Big 6.................(1926)	FA-130	FB-118	FC-121	FD-84 FD-95	FE-103	FG-12	FH-32	HA-7
Studebaker Std. 6................(1926)	FA-131	FB-119	FC-122	FD-96	FE-104*	FG-12	FH-69	HA-86
Studebaker Spec. 6...............(1926)	FA-130	FB-118	FC-121	FD-84 FD-95	FE-103	FG-12	FH-32	HA-7
Studebaker Big 6.................(1927)	FA-130	FB-118	FC-121	FD-84 FD-95	FE-103	FG-12	FH-32	HA-7
Studebaker Spec. 6...............(1927)	FA-130	FB-118	FC-121	FD-84 FD-95	FE-103	FG-12	GH-32	HA-7
Studebaker Std. 6................(1927)	FA-131	FB-119	FC-122	FD-96	FE-104	FG-12	FH-69	HA-86
Studebaker Com. 6................(1928)	FA-130	FB-118	FC-121	FD-84 FD-95	FE-103	FG-48	FH-56	HA-7
Studebaker Dict. 6...............(1928)	FA-132	FB-119	FC-122	FD-96	FE-104*	FG-48	FH-52	HA-93
Studebaker Pres. 8...............(1928)	FA-133	FB-121	FC-96	FD-97 FD-125	FE-105	FG-60	FH-36	HA-134
Studebaker Dict. 6...............(1929)	FA-132	FB-119	FC-122	FD-96	FE-104*	FG-48	FH-52	HA-93
Studebaker Com. 6................(1929)	FA-130	FB-118	FC-121	FD-96	FE-103	FG-48	FH-56	HA-93
Studebaker Com. 8................(1929)	FA-134	FB-118	FC-124	FD-124 FD-147	FE-104	FG-48	FH-56	HA-93
Studebaker Pres. 8...............(1929)	FA-133	FB-120	FC-125	FD-97 FD-125	FE-105	FG-60	FH-31	HA-134
Studebaker 6-53..................(1930)	FA-128	FB-41	FC-45	FD-25	FE-104*	FG-48	FH-52	HA-16
Studebaker Dict. 6...............(1930)	FA-132	FB-107	FC-106	FD-96	FE-104*	FG-48	FH-52	HA-64
Studebaker Dict. 8...............(1930)	FA-132	FB-107	FC-106	FD-124 FD-147	FE-104	FG-48	FH-56	HA-64
Studebaker Com. 6................(1930)	FA-130	FB-112	FC-94	FD-96	FE-104*	FG-48	FH-52	HA-93
Studebaker Com. 8................(1930)	FA-134	FB-117	FC-95	FD-124 FD-147	FE-104	FG-48	FH-56	HA-83
Studebaker Pres. 8...............(1930)	FA-133	FB-120	FC-110	FD-97 FD-125	FE-105	FG-60	FH-31	HA-126

COOLING SYSTEM and MUFFLER—Continued

Interchangeable Parts have the same CHILTON NUMBER in Any Column

Car Make and Model	WATER PUMP					Radiator Filler Cap	Fan Belt	Muffler
	Body Assembly	Shaft	Impeller	Bushings	Packing Nut or Gland			
Stutz 695 . . . .(1925)	FA-136	FB-122	FC-126	FD-98	FE-106	FG-20	FH-26	HA-105
Stutz AA . . . .(1926)	FA-137	FB-122	FC-126	FD-99	FE-107	FG-9	None	HA-108
Stutz AA . . . .(1927)	FA-137	FB-122	FC-126	FD-99	FE-107	FG-9	None	HA-108
Stutz BB . . . .(1928)	FA-137	FB-122	FC-126	FD-99	FE-107	FG-9	None	HA-17
Stutz Ser. M . . . .(1929)	FA-138	FB-122	FC-126	FD-10	FE-107	FG-31	None	HA-15
Stutz M . . . .(1930)	FA-138	FB-122	FC-126	FD-10	FE-107	FG-31	None	HA-15
Velie 60 . . . .(1925)	FA-139	FB-123	FC-127	FD-100	FE-108	FG-9	FH-46	HA-11
Velie 60 . . . .(1926)	FA-139	FB-123	FC-127	FD-100	FE-108	FG-9	FH-46	HA-137
Velie Spec. 60 . . . .(1927–28)	FA-139	FB-123	FC-127	FD-100	FE-108	FG-9	FH-40	HA-137
Velie Std. 50 . . . .(1927–28)	FA-4	FB-4	FC-4	FD-4	FE-4	FG-9	FH-4	HA-21
Velie 6-66 . . . .(1928)	FA-139	FB-123	FC-127	FD-100	FE-108	FG-1	FH-76	HA-21
Velie 6-77 . . . .(1928)	FA-139	FB-123	FC-127	FD-100	FE-108	FG-1	FH-76	HA-137
Velie 8-88, Lyc. 4 HM. . . . .(1928)	FA-9	FB-8	FC-8	FD-5	FE-10	FG-1	FH-8	NA-112
Viking . . . .(1927)	FA-140	FB-86	FC-88	FD-71 FD-101	FE-77	FG-35	FH-33	HA-184
Westcott 44, Cont. 8R . . . .(1925)	FA-3	FB-3	FC-3	FD-3	FE-3 FE-9	FG-2	FH-3	HA-116
Westcott 60, Cont. 8R . . . .(1925)	FA-3	FB-3	FC-3	FD-3	FE-3 FE-9	FG-2	FH-3	HA-116
Whippet 96, 4 Cyl . . . .(1927)	FA-97	FB-87	FC-89	FD-72	FE-78	FG-16	FH-26	HA-41
Whippet 93A, 6 Cyl . . . .(1927)	FA-97	FB-87	FC-89	FD-72	FE-78	FG-16	FH-52	HA-41
Whippet 96, 4 Cyl . . . .(1928)	FA-98	FB-88	FC-89	FD-73	FE-78	FG-16	FH-26	HA-41
Whippet 98, 6 Cyl . . . .(1928)	FA-99	FB-88	FC-89	FD-72 FD-73	FE-78	FG-16	FH-57	HA-124
Whippet 96A . . . .(1929)	FA-98	FB-88	FC-89	FD-149	FE-63	FG-16	FH-26	HA-191
Whippet 98A . . . .(1929)	FA-99	FB-88	FC-89	FD-149	FE-63	FG-16	FH-53	HA-10
Wills Ste. Claire 8 . . . .(1925)	FA-146	FB-127	FC-131	FD-104	FE-112	FG-9	None	HA-192
Wills Ste. Claire 6 . . . .(1925–26)	FA-147	FB-128	FC-128	FD-105	FE-113	FG-9	FH-57	HA-184
Wills Ste. Claire 8 . . . .(1926)	FA-146	FB-127	FC-131	FD-104	FE-112	FG-9	None	HA-192
Willys 6 . . . .(1930)	FA-135	FB-129	FC-83	FD-112	FE-110	FG-16	FH-9	HA-53
Willys 8 . . . .(1930)	FA-143	FB-130	FC-84	FD-103	FE-111	FG-63	FH-9	HA-89
Willys Knight 65 . . . .(1925)	None	None	None	None	None	FG-16	FH-12	HA-67
Willys Knight 66 . . . .(1925)	FA-141	FB-125	FC-129	FD-102	FE-109	FG-16	FH-36	HA-138
Willys Knight 66 . . . .(1926)	FA-141	FB-125	FC-129	FD-102	FE-109	FG-16	FH-36	HA-38
Willys Knight 70 . . . .(1926)	FA-142	FB-124	FC-130	FD-72	FE-78	FG-16	FH-21	HA-51
Willys Knight 66-A . . . .(1927)	FA-141	FB-125	FC-129	FD-102	FE-109	FG-16	FH-36	HA-196
Willys Knight 70-A . . . .(1927)	FA-142	FB-124	FC-130	FD-72	FE-78	FG-16	FH-21	HA-51
Willys Knight 66-A . . . .(1928)	FA-141	FB-125	FC-129	FD-102	FE-109	FG-16	FH-36	HA-196
Willys Knight Std. 6-56 . . . .(1928–29)	FA-142	FB-126	FC-123	FD-72	FE-78	FG-16	FH-29	HA-90
Willys Knight Spec. 6-70-A . . . . .(1928–29)	FA-142	FB-126	FC-123	FD-72	FE-78	FG-16	FH-21	HA-51
Willys Knight 66-A . . . .(1929)	FA-141	FB-125	FC-129	FD-102	FE-109	FG-16	FH-71	HA-196
Willys Knight 70-B . . . .(1929)	FA-142	FB-126	FC-123	FD-72	FE-78	FG-16	FH-21	HA-10
Willys Knight 66-B . . . .(1930)	FA-141	FB-125	FC-129	FD-102	FE-109	FG-16	FH-8	HA-136
Willys Knight 70-B . . . .(1930)	FA-142	FB-126	FC-123	FD-73	FE-78	FG-16	FH-21	HA-10

Key to Engine Abbreviations:
Cont.—Continental.   Lyc.—Lycoming.
*Studebaker Std. 6 1925, 26, also use FE-61 and FE-62.
Studebaker Dict. 6 1928, 29, 30, Com. 6, 6-53, Erskine 1930, also use FE-85 and FE-86.

INTERCHANGEABLE COUNT

Showing the exact number of times each Chilton Number occurs in the Cooling System and Muffler Table, beginning Page 211.

Body Assembly								
	FA-43-1	FA-87-3	FA-131-3	FB-24-1	FB-67-6	FB-111-2	FC-18-2	FC-61-2
	FA-44-1	FA-88-5	FA-132-4	FB-25-2	FB-68-1	FB-112-1	FC-19-4	FC-62-3
	FA-45-6	FA-89-2	FA-133-3	FB-26-7	FB-69-3	FB-113-2	FC-20-4	FC-63-1
FA-1-3	FA-46-1	FA-90-1	FA-134-2	FB-27-4	FB-70-4	FB-114-4	FC-21-2	FC-64-3
FA-2-5	FA-47-12	FA-91-1	FA-135-1	FB-28-2	FB-71-4	FB-115-3	FC-22-5	FC-65-2
FA-3-8	FA-48-5	FA-92-1	FA-136-1	FB-29-4	FB-72-4	FB-116-3	FC-23-3	FC-66-2
FA-4-2	FA-49-3	FA-93-3	FA-137-3	FB-30-1	FB-73-1	FB-117-1	FC-24-1	FC-67-1
FA-5-10	FA-50-1	FA-94-2	FA-138-2	FB-31-1	FB-74-3	FB-118-9	FC-25-2	FC-68-6
FA-6-1	FA-51-2	FA-95-3	FA-139-5	FB-32-2	FB-75-2	FB-119-5	FC-26-7	FC-69-3
FA-7-9	FA-52-2	FA-96-3	FA-140-1	FB-33-7	FB-76-1	FB-120-2	FC-27-4	FC-70-3
FA-8-4	FA-53-3	FA-97-4	FA-141-6	FB-34-8	FB-77-3	FB-121-1	FC-28-2	FC-71-4
FA-9-50	FA-54-1	FA-98-2	FA-142-6	FB-35-2	FB-78-5	FB-122-6	FC-29-4	FC-72-4
FA-10-9	FA-55-3	FA-99-2	FA-143-1	FB-36-1	FB-79-2	FB-123-5	FC-30-6	FC-75-3
FA-11-2	FA-56-4	FA-100-6	FA-144-1	FB-37-1	FB-80-1	FB-124-2	FC-31-2	FC-76-2
FA-12-3	FA-57-3	FA-101-2	FA-145-1	FB-38-2	FB-81-1	FB-125-6	FC-32-1	FC-77-1
FA-13-1	FA-58-2	FA-102-1	FA-146-2	FB-39-5	FB-82-3	FB-126-4	FC-33-3	FC-78-3
FA-14-1	FA-59-5	FA-103-1	FA-147-1	FB-40-1	FB-83-3	FB-127-2	FC-34-2	FC-79-1
FA-15-1	FA-60-3	FA-104-3		FB-41-2	FB-84-2	FB-128-1	FC-35-1	FC-80-5
FA-16-1	FA-61-3	FA-105-1	**Shaft**	FB-42-1	FB-85-3	FB-129-1	FC-36-1	FC-81-2
FA-17-1	FA-62-6	FA-106-3		FB-43-1	FB-86-4	FB-130-1	FC-37-2	FC-82-3
FA-18-1	FA-63-3	FA-107-4	FB-1-3	FB-44-5	FB-87-4	FB-131-1	FC-38-4	FC-83-1
FA-19-7	FA-64-1	FA-108-2	FB-2-5	FB-45-4	FB-88-4	FB-132-1	FC-39-1	FC-84-1
FA-20-1	FA-65-3	FA-109-3	FB-3-7	FB-46-10	FB-89-9	FB-133-1	FC-40-1	FC-85-3
FA-21-4	FA-66-1	FA-110-1	FB-4-2	FB-47-2	FB-90-1		FC-41-1	FC-86-2
FA-22-2	FA-67-3	FA-111-2	FB-5-11	FB-48-3	FB-91-1	**Impeller**	FC-42-6	FC-87-3
FA-23-8	FA-68-3	FA-112-4	FB-6-7	FB-49-3	FB-92-3		FC-43-16	FC-88-5
FA-24-4	FA-69-1	FA-113-3	FB-7-1	FB-50-1	FB-93-3	FC-1-3	FC-44-5	FC-89-8
FA-25-5	FA-70-1	FA-114-1	FB-8-62	FB-51-1	FB-94-2	FC-2-5	FC-45-2	FC-90-2
FA-26-1	FA-71-1	FA-115-1	FB-9-1	FB-52-2	FB-95-4	FC-3-8	FC-46-1	FC-91-10
FA-27-2	FA-72-6	FA-116-3	FB-10-9	FB-53-7	FB-96-1	FC-4-2	FC-47-5	FC-92-1
FA-28-8	FA-73-2	FA-117-2	FB-11-2	FB-54-3	FB-97-3	FC-5-8	FC-48-1	FC-93-3
FA-29-2	FA-74-3	FA-118-4	FB-12-3	FB-55-6	FB-98-3	FC-6-1	FC-49-2	FC-94-1
FA-30-2	FA-75-4	FA-119-4	FB-13-1	FB-56-1	FB-99-4	FC-7-4	FC-50-1	FC-95-1
FA-31-4	FA-76-4	FA-120-1	FB-14-1	FB-57-3	FB-100-3	FC-8-62	FC-51-3	FC-96-1
FA-32-1	FA-77-2	FA-121-2	FB-15-1	FB-58-3	FB-101-1	FC-9-3	FC-52-1	FC-97-2
FA-35-2	FA-78-4	FA-122-5	FB-16-11	FB-59-6	FB-102-2	FC-10-24	FC-53-3	FC-98-4
FA-36-7	FA-79-1	FA-123-1	FB-17-1	FB-60-2	FB-103-3	FC-11-2	FC-54-6	FC-99-1
FA-37-3	FA-80-3	FA-124-2	FB-18-2	FB-61-1	FB-104-2	FC-12-3	FC-55-3	FC-100-3
FA-38-1	FA-81-2	FA-125-1	FB-19-4	FB-62-2	FB-105-4	FC-13-1	FC-56-2	FC-101-3
FA-39-1	FA-83-5	FA-126-3	FB-20-2	FB-63-4	FB-107-2	FC-14-1	FC-57-1	FC-102-4
FA-40-1	FA-84-1	FA-127-3	FB-21-3	FB-64-3	FB-108-2	FC-15-1	FC-58-3	FC-103-3
FA-41-2	FA-85-9	FA-128-2	FB-22-5	FB-65-3	FB-109-5	FC-16-11	FC-59-3	FC-104-1
FA-42-2	FA-86-4	FA-130-9	FB-23-3	FB-66-1	FB-110-2	FC-17-1	FC-60-6	FC-105-2

COOLING SYSTEM and MUFFLER—Continued

Interchangeable Parts Have the Same CHILTON NUMBER in Any Column

INTERCHANGEABLE COUNT

Showing exact number of times each Chilton Number occurs in the Cooling System and Muffler Table, beginning Page 211.

FC-106-2	FD-38-6	FD-106-5	FE-22-4	FE-96-2	FG-53-6	FH-57-4	HA-48-2	HA-127-1
FC-107-2	FD-39-6	FD-107-11	FE-23-2	FE-98-2	FG-54-7	FH-58-1	HA-49-2	HA-128-1
FC-108-2	FD-40-3	FD-108-7	FE-24-8	FE-99-4	FG-55-6	FH-59-5	HA-50-2	HA-129-1
FC-109-4	FD-41-3	FD-109-6	FE-25-4	FE-100-3	FG-56-1	FH-60-1	HA-51-3	HA-130-3
FC-110-1	FD-42-6	FD-110-3	FE-26-1	FE-101-3	FG-57-2	FH-61-4	HA-52-1	HA-131-4
FC-111-1	FD-43-4	FD-111-1	FE-27-2	FE-103-8	FG-58-6	FH-62-4	HA-53-1	HA-132-4
FC-112-6	FD-44-1	FD-112-1	FE-28-11	FE-104-12	FG-60-3	FH-63-1	HA-54-1	HA-133-4
FC-113-2	FD-45-1	FD-113-12	FE-29-2	FE-105-3	FG-61-3	FH-64-1	HA-55-1	HA-134-3
FC-114-2	FD-46-1	FD-114-1	FE-30-4	FE-106-1	FG-62-2	FH-65-2	HA-56-2	HA-135-2
FC-115-1	FD-47-3	FD-115-7	FE-31-4	FE-107-5	FG-63-1	FH-66-1	HA-57-2	HA-136-6
FC-116-2	FD-48-3	FD-116-4	FE-32-1	FE-108-5		FH-67-1	HA-59-2	HA-137-7
FC-117-4	FD-49-2	FD-117-8	FE-34-1	FE-109-6	**Fan Belt**	FH-69-3	HA-60-2	HA-138-1
FC-118-3	FD-50-4	FD-118-3	FE-35-22	FE-110-1		FH-71-1	HA-61-4	HA-140-1
FC-119-3	FD-51-1	FD-119-3	FE-36-7	FE-111-1	FH-1-5	FH-72-2	HA-62-2	HA-141-1
FC-120-1	FD-52-1	FD-120-1	FE-37-11	FE-112-2	FH-2-4	FH-73-2	HA-63-2	HA-142-4
FC-121-8	FD-53-6	FD-121-2	FE-38-2	FE-113-1	FH-3-14	FH-74-1	HA-64-2	HA-143-3
FC-122-5	FD-54-3	FD-122-1	FE-39-6		FH-4-13	FH-75-3	HA-66-2	HA-144-1
FC-123-4	FD-55-3	FD-123-2	FE-40-1	**Radiator**	FH-5-17	FH-76-2	HA-67-2	HA-145-1
FC-124-1	FD-56-4	FD-124-3	FE-41-2	**Filler Cap**	FH-6-5		HA-68-1	HA-146-1
FC-125-1	FD-57-4	FD-125-3	FE-42-1		FH-7-2		HA-69-1	HA-147-1
FC-126-6	FD-58-1	FD-126-2	FE-43-2	FG-1-30	FH-8-13	**Muffler**	HA-70-4	HA-148-7
FC-127-5	FD-59-1	FD-127-4	FE-44-1	FG-2-2	FH-9-25		HA-71-1	HA-149-8
FC-128-1	FD-60-4	FD-128-2	FE-45-1	FG-3-13	FH-10-18	HA-1-3	HA-72-8	HA-150-2
FC-129-6	FD-61-3	FD-129-7	FE-46-1	FG-4-36	FH-11-15	HA-2-1	HA-73-2	HA-151-3
FC-130-2	FD-62-3	FD-130-6	FE-47-2	FG-5-21	FH-12-3	HA-4-1	HA-74-2	HA-152-4
FC-131-2	FD-63-5	FD-131-1	FE-48-2	FG-7-7	FH-13-4	HA-5-1	HA-75-2	HA-153-3
FC-132-1	FD-64-2	FD-132-1	FE-49-2	FG-8-5	FH-14-5	HA-6-4	HA-76-2	HA-154-1
	FD-65-3	FD-133-1	FE-50-4	FG-9-63	FH-15-19	HA-8-16	HA-77-14	HA-155-2
Bushings	FD-66-1	FD-134-1	FE-51-3	FG-10-5	FH-16-2	HA-9-6	HA-80-2	HA-156-1
	FD-67-1	FD-135-1	FE-52-4	FG-11-6	FH-17-2	HA-10-5	HA-81-2	HA-157-7
FD-1-3	FD-68-3	FD-136-1	FE-53-13	FG-12-30	FH-18-13	HA-11-6	HA-82-2	HA-158-1
FD-2-5	FD-69-4	FD-137-1	FE-54-13	FG-13-2	FH-20-18	HA-12-3	HA-83-1	HA-159-2
FD-3-9	FD-70-1	FD-138-2	FE-55-4	FG-14-17	FH-21-8	HA-13-3	HA-84-2	HA-160-2
FD-4-2	FD-71-4	FD-139-1	FE-56-2	FG-15-3	FH-22-4	HA-14-1	HA-85-1	HA-161-1
FD-5-68	FD-72-10	FD-140-1	FE-57-6	FG-16-46	FH-23-4	HA-15-4	HA-86-7	HA-162-6
FD-6-3	FD-73-3	FD-141-2	FE-58-6	FG-17-12	FH-24-2	HA-16-2	HA-87-4	HA-163-5
FD-7-9	FD-74-3	FD-142-3	FE-59-2	FG-18-11	FH-25-8	HA-17-5	HA-88-1	HA-164-1
FD-8-5	FD-75-9	FD-143-4	FE-60-3	FG-20-21	FH-26-20	HA-18-3	HA-89-1	HA-165-2
FD-9-2	FD-76-2	FD-144-1	FE-62-6	FG-21-1	FH-27-3	HA-19-1	HA-90-2	HA-166-1
FD-10-4	FD-77-5	FD-145-4	FE-63-2	FG-22-3	FH-28-18	HA-20-2	HA-91-1	HA-167-3
FD-11-1	FD-78-4	FD-146-5	FE-64-3	FG-23-3	FH-29-4	HA-21-6	HA-92-3	HA-168-1
FD-12-12	FD-79-4	FD-147-3	FE-65-4	FG-24-6	FH-30-6	HA-22-1	HA-93-5	HA-169-1
FD-13-1	FD-80-3	FD-148-3	FE-66-4	FG-25-7	FH-31-15	HA-23-1	HA-94-2	HA-170-1
FD-14-7	FD-81-1	FD-149-2	FE-67-1	FG-26-4	FH-32-6	HA-24-2	HA-95-3	HA-171-3
FD-15-4	FD-82-2		FE-68-3	FG-27-5	FH-33-21	HA-25-3	HA-96-3	HA-172-2
FD-16-2	FD-83-4	**Packing**	FE-69-2	FG-28-3	FH-34-4	HA-26-2	HA-99-1	HA-173-2
FD-17-8	FD-84-7	**Nut or Gland**	FE-70-5	FG-29-4	FH-35-10	HA-27-1	HA-101-13	HA-174-2
FD-18-4	FD-85-1		FE-71-2	FG-30-3	FH-36-17	HA-28-3	HA-102-4	HA-175-3
FD-19-2	FD-86-2	FE-1-3	FE-72-3	FG-31-7	FH-37-13	HA-29-2	HA-103-4	HA-176-2
FD-20-9	FD-87-5	FE-2-5	FE-73-2	FG-32-4	FH-39-4	HA-30-2	HA-104-3	HA-177-1
FD-21-4	FD-88-4	FE-3-9	FE-74-3	FG-34-4	FH-40-4	HA-31-1	HA-105-1	HA-178-2
FD-22-2	FD-89-2	FE-4-2	FE-75-6	FG-35-5	FH-41-1	HA-32-2	HA-108-2	HA-179-2
FD-23-3	FD-90-2	FE-6-6	FE-76-3	FG-36-4	FH-42-2	HA-33-1	HA-110-1	HA-180-1
FD-24-1	FD-91-4	FE-7-1	FE-77-5	FG-38-1	FH-43-1	HA-34-1	HA-111-2	HA-181-2
FD-25-2	FD-92-3	FE-8-1	FE-78-12	FG-39-1	FH-44-1	HA-35-1	HA-112-1	HA-182-3
FD-26-2	FD-93-3	FE-9-9	FE-79-8	FG-40-1	FH-45-2	HA-36-8	HA-113-1	HA-183-1
FD-27-7	FD-95-7	FE-10-73	FE-80-2	FG-41-1	FH-46-3	HA-37-4	HA-114-3	HA-184-7
FD-28-8	FD-96-8	FE-11-32	FE-81-1	FG-42-1	FH-47-1	HA-38-1	HA-115-8	HA-185-1
FD-29-3	FD-97-3	FE-12-3	FE-83-5	FG-43-1	FH-48-2	HA-39-2	HA-116-2	HA-187-1
FD-30-1	FD-98-1	FE-13-4	FE-84-4	FG-45-1	FH-49-3	HA-40-1	HA-117-2	HA-189-4
FD-31-6	FD-99-3	FE-14-7	FE-87-4	FG-46-1	FH-50-7	HA-41-8	HA-118-5	HA-190-1
FD-32-3	FD-100-5	FE-15-2	FE-88-3	FG-47-5	FH-51-2	HA-42-2	HA-120-3	HA-191-1
FD-33-1	FD-101-1	FE-16-3	FE-89-1	FG-48-15	FH-52-19	HA-43-1	HA-122-3	HA-192-2
FD-34-23	FD-102-6	FE-17-2	FE-90-2	FG-49-3	FH-53-5	HA-44-5	HA-123-3	HA-194-1
FD-35-2	FD-103-1	FE-18-12	FE-91-4	FG-50-1	FH-54-4	HA-45-2	HA-124-1	HA-196-8
FD-36-3	FD-104-2	FE-19-8	FE-93-2	FG-51-9	FH-55-2	HA-46-1	HA-125-1	HA-197-1
FD-37-4	FD-105-1	FE-20-2	FE-94-5	FG-52-7	FH-56-9	HA-47-3	HA-126-1	HA-198-1
		FE-21-4						

GENERATOR AND STARTER

HOW TO USE THIS TABLE

1. Locate in the first column the car and model for which the part is needed.
2. Follow this line across to the column pertaining to that part.
3. In this column opposite your car model you will find the CHILTON NUMBER for the part you want.
4. Look up and down the part column for the same CHILTON NUMBER. Wherever you find this same number you have an interchangeable part. The car make opposite tells you where to get the part—probably from a local dealer or a nearby jobber.

EXAMPLE: Suppose a Generator Armature is needed for an Auburn 4 (1925) car. Locate this car in the first column. Follow across to the column on Generator Armatures. Here you see the

CHILTON NUMBER for this part is KA-5. Checking through the CHILTON NUMBERS in this same column, you will find the number KA-5 opposite the Auburn 4-44 (1926), Elcar 4-40 (1925), and the Elcar 4-55 (1926). The Generator Armature used in all these cars is interchangeable with the one used in your Auburn 4 (1925) car.

5. At the end of this table, Pages 225, 226, you will find a count showing the number of times any part number appears in the table.

EXAMPLE: K-27 under Generator Assembly opposite the Cadillac 341A (1928) in this table will appear again in the count at the end of the table followed by the figure 4 under the heading Generator Assembly. This indicates that part number K-27 appears four times in this table.

Interchangeable Parts Have the Same CHILTON NUMBER in Any Column

Car Make and Model	GENERATOR					STARTER	
	Generator Assembly	Armature	Field Coils	Main Brushes	Third Brush	Starter Armature	Starter Drive Spring (Bendix Type) (See Footnote)
Ajax....................A.-L. (1925–26)	K-1	KA-1	KB-1	KC-1	KD-1	NA-1	*NE-4L
Apperson 6.................R. (1925)	K-4	KA-3	KB-3	KC-3	KC-3	NA-3	NE-2R
Apperson Str. 8...........R. (1925)	K-5	KA-3	KB 3	KC-3	KC-3	NA-3	NE-2R
Apperson 6.................R. (1926)	K-6	KA-3	KB-2	KC-3	KC-3	NA-3	NE-2R
Apperson Str. 8...........R. (1926)	K-5	KA-3	KB-3	KC-3	KC-3	NA-3	NE-2R
Auburn 4...................R. (1925)	K-7	KA-5	KB-4	KC-4	KC-4	NA-3	NE-2R
Auburn 6-43...............R. (1925)	K-8	KA-6	KB-3	KC-4	KC-4	NA-3	NE-2R
Auburn 8-88...............R. (1925)	{K-5 K-9	{KA-4 KA-7	KB-3	KC-3	KC-3	NA-3	NE-2R
Auburn 8-88...............R. (1926)	{K-5 K-9	{KA-4 KA-7	KB-3	KC-3	KC-3	NA-3	NE-2R
Auburn 4-44...............R. (1926)	K-7	KA-5	KB-4	KC-4	KC-4	NA-3	NE-2R
Auburn 6-66...............R. (1926)	K-9	KA-8	KB-3	KC-3	KC-4	NA-3	NE-2R
Auburn 6-66A.............R. (1927)	K-10	KA-8	KB-4	KB-4	KC-4	NA-3	NE-2R
Auburn 8-88...............R. (1927)	K-11	KA-8	KB-3	KC-3	KC-3	NA-3	NE-2R
Auburn 8-77...............R. (1927)	K-12	KA-9	KB-4	KC-3	KC-3	NA-9	NE-2R
Auburn 76.................D.-R. (1928)	K-12	KA-9	KB-4	KC-3	KC-3	NA-9	NE-2R
Auburn 88.................D.-R. (1928)	K-12	KA-9	KB-4	KC-3	KC-3	NA-9	NE-2R
Auburn 115................D.-R. (1929)	K-13	KA-7	KB-4	KC-3	KC-3	NA-3	NE-2R
Auburn 6-80..............D.-R. (1929)	K-14	KA-9	KB-4	KC-4	KC-4	NA-9	NE-2R
Auburn 8-90..............D.-R. (1929)	K-14	KA-9	KB-4	KC-4	KC-4	NA-9	NE-2R
Auburn 120................D.-R. (1929)	K-16	KA-7	KB-4	KC-4	KC-4	NA-3	NE-2R
Auburn 6-85..............D.-R. (1930)	K-14	KA-9	KB-4	KC-4	KC-4	NA-9	NE-2R
Auburn 8-95..............D.-R. (1930)	K-14	KA-9	KB-4	KC-4	KC-4	NA-9	NE-2R
Auburn 125................D.-R. (1930)	K-16	KA-7	KB-4	KC-4	KC-4	NA-3	NE-2R
Blackhawk L-6............D.-R. (1929)	K-18	KA-11	KB-4	KC-4	KC-4	NA-2	None
Blackhawk L-8............D.-R. (1929)	K-15	KA-164	KB-6	KC-4	KC-4	NA-9	NE-2R
Blackhawk L6.............D.-R. (1930)	K-18	KA-11	KB-4	KC-4	KC-4	NA-2	None
Blackhawk L8.............D.-R. (1930)	K-15	KA-164	KB-6	KC-4	KC-4	NA-9	NE-2R
Buick Master..................D. (1925)	K-19	KA-12	KB-7	KC-5	KD-4	KA-12	None
Buick Std.....................D. (1925)	K-20	KA-13	KB-8	KC-5	KD-4	KA-13	None
Buick Master.............D.-R. (1926)	K-21	KA-14	KB-9	KC-5	KD-4	NA-4	None
Buick Std.................D.-R. (1926)	K-21	KA-14	KB-9	KC-5	KD-4	NA-4	None
Buick 115.................D.-R. (1927)	K-21	KA-14	KB-9	KC-5	KD-4	NA-4	None
Buick 120, 128...........D.-R. (1927)	K-21	KA-14	KB-9	KC-5	KD-4	NA-4	None
Buick 115.................D.-R. (1928)	K-23	KA-15	KB-4	KC-5	KD-4	NA-5	None
Buick 120, 128...........D.-R. (1928)	K-23	KA-15	KB-4	KC-5	KD-4	NA-5	None
Buick 116.................D.-R. (1929)	K-24	KA-16	KB-4	KC-5	KD-4	NA-5	None
Buick 121, 129...........D.-R. (1929)	K-24	KA-16	KB-4	KC-5	KD-4	NA-5	None
Buick 40...................D.-R. (1930)	K-24	KA-16	KB-4	KC-5	KD-4	NA-2	None
Buick 50, 60..............D.-R. (1930)	K-24	KA-16	KB-4	KC-5	KD-4	NA-5	None
Buick 8-50................D.-R. (1930)	K-241	KA-89	KB-53	KC-5	KD-4	NA-6	None
Buick 8-60................D.-R. (1930)	K-242	KA-89	KB-53	KC-5	KD-4	NA-5	None
Buick 8-80, 8-90.........D.-R. (1930)	K-242	KA-89	KB-53	KC-5	KD-4	NA-5	None
Cadillac V-63...............D. (1925)	K-25	KA-17	KB-10	KC-6	KD-5	KA-17	None
Cadillac 314................D. (1926)	K-26	KA-18	KB-11	KC-7	KD-6	NA-4	None
Cadillac 314.............D.-R. (1927)	K-26	KA-18	KB-11	KC-7	KD-6	NA-4	None
Cadillac 341-A...........D.-R. (1928)	K-27	KA-19	KB-9	KC-4	KD-4	NA-7	None
Cadillac 341-B...........D.-R. (1929)	K-27	KA-19	KB-9	KC-4	KD-4	NA-7	None
Cadillac 353.............D.-R. (1930)	K-139	KA-19	KB-9	KC-5	KD-4	NA-9	None
Cadillac 452.............D.-R. (1930)	K-214	KA-132	KB-9	KC-5	KD-4	NA-8	None
Case JIC.................D.-R. (1925)	K-53	KA-41	KB-12	KC-5	KD-4	NA-10	NE-2R
Case X...................D.-R. (1925)	K-53	KA-41	KB-12	KC-5	KD-4	NA-10	NE-2R
Case Y...................D.-R. (1925)	K-53	KA-41	KB-12	KC-5	KD-4	NA-10	NE-2R
Case JIC.................D.-R. (1926)	K-53	KA-41	KB-12	KC-5	KD-4	NA-10	NE-2R
Case Y...................D.-R. (1926)	K-53	KA-41	KB-12	KC-5	KD-4	NA-10	NE-2R
Chandler 33..................B. (1925)	K-28	KA-20	KB-6	KC-8	KD-7	NA-11	NE-1R
Chandler 35..................B. (1926)	K-29	KA-21	KB-6	KC-8	KD-7	NA-11	NE-1R
Chandler Big 6...........D.-R. (1927)	K-29	KA-21	KB-6	KC-4	KC-4	NA-3	NE-5L
Chandler Royal 8.........D.-R. (1927)	K-30	KA-23	KB-6	KC-3	KC-3	NA-9	NE-2R
Chandler Spec. 6.........D.-R. (1927)	K-31	KA-24	KB-6	KC-4	KC-4	NA-16	NE-4L
Chandler Std. 6..........D.-R. (1927)	K-31	KA-24	KB-6	KC-4	KC-4	NA-16	NE-5L
Chandler Big 6...........D.-R. (1928)	K-29	KA-21	KB-6	KC-4	KC-4	NA-3	NE-2R
Chandler Royal 8.........D.-R. (1928)	K-33	KA-23	KB-6	KC-3	KC-3	NA-9	NE-2R
Chandler Spec. 6..........A.-L. (1928)	K-31	KA-24	KB-6	KC-4	KC-4	NA-16	NE-4L
Chandler Spec. In. 6........A.-L. (1928)	K-31	KA-24	KB-6	KC-4	KC-4	NA-16	NE-4L
Chevrolet K................R. (1925)	K-34	KA-25	KB-13	KC-4	KC-4	NA-3	†NE-2R
Chevrolet V................R. (1926)	K-35	KA-26	KB-4	KC-4	KC-4	NA-3	NE-1R
Chevrolet AA..............R. (1927)	K-35	KA-26	KB-4	KC-4	KC-4	NA-3	NE-1R
Chevrolet AB.............D.-R. (1928)	K-35	KA-26	KB-4	KC-4	KC-4	NA-3	NE-1R
Chevrolet AC.............D.-R. (1929)	K-36	KA-26	KB-4	KC-4	KC-4	NA-3	NE-1R
Chevrolet.................D.-R. (1930)	K-36	KA-26	KB-4	KC-4	KC-4	NA-3	NE-1R
Chrysler 6-B...............R. (1925)	K-37	KA-27	KB-3	KC-3	KC-3	NA-9	NE-2R
Chrysler 70................R. (1925)	K-37	KA-27	KB-3	KC-3	KC-3	NA-9	NE-2R
Chrysler 58................R. (1925)	K-38	KA-28	KB-13	KC-3	KC-3	NA-3	NE-2R
Chrysler 70................R. (1926)	K-39	KA-29	KB-4	KC-3	KC-3	NA-9	NE-2R
Chrysler 80................R. (1926)	K-40	KA-30	KB-6	KC-3	KC-3	NA-14	NE-8

Footnote: For corresponding starter spring numbers advertised, see page 221.

GENERATOR AND STARTER—Continued

Interchangeable Parts have the same CHILTON NUMBER in Any Column

Car Make and Model	GENERATOR					STARTER	
	Generator Assembly	Armature	Field Coils	Main Brushes	Third Brush	Starter Armature	Starter Drive Spring (Bendix Type) (See Footnote)
Chrysler 50..................R. (1927)	K-41 K-43	KA-31	KB-14	KC-4	KC-4	NA-3	NE-2R
Chrysler 60..................R. (1927)	K-42 K-44	KA-32	KB-4	KC-4	KC-4	NA-3	NE-2R
Chrysler 70..................R. (1927)	K-39	KA-29	KB-4	KC-3	KC-3	NA-9	NE-2R
Chrysler 80..................R. (1927)	K-40	KA-30	KB-6	KC-3	KC-3	NA-14	‡NE-2R
Chrysler 52..............D.-R. (1928)	K-43	KA-31	KB-14	KC-4	KC-4	NA-3	NE-2R
Chrysler 62..............D.-R. (1928)	K-44	KA-32	KB-4	KC-4	KC-4	NA-3	NE-2R
Chrysler 72..............D.-R. (1928)	K-44	KA-32	KB-4	KC-4	KC-4	NA-9	NE-2R
Chrysler Imp. 80.........D.-R. (1928)	K-45	KA-33	KB-4	KC-4	KC-4	NA-9	NE-2R
Chrysler 65..............D.-R. (1929)	K-46	KA-26	KB-15	KC-4	KC-4	NA-3	NE-2R
Chrysler 75..............D.-R. (1929)	K-47	KA-34	KB-4	KC-4	KC-4	NA-9	NE-9
Chrysler Imp. 80.........D.-R. (1929)	K-45	KA-33	KB-4	KC-4	KC-4	NA-9	NE-10
Chrysler 6........D.-R. N.-E. (1930)	K-57	KA-44	KB-21	KC-4	KC-4	NA-6	None
Chrysler 66..............D.-R. (1930)	K-46	KA-26	KB-15	KC-4	KC-4	NA-15	None
Chrysler 70..............D.-R. (1930)	K-215 K-218	KA-126 KA-165	KB-54	KC-4	KC-4	NA-15	None
Chrysler 77...............D.R. (1930)	K-215 K-218	KA-26 KA-165	KB-54	KC-4	KC-4	NA-9	None
Chrysler Imp. 80.........D.-R. (1930)	K-45	KA-33	KB-4	KC-4	KC-4	NA-9	None
Chrysler 8...............D.-R. (1930)	K-244	KA-26	KB-4	KC-4	KC-4	NA-9	None
Chrysler Imp. 8..........D.-R. (1930)	K-218	KA-165	KB-54	KC-4	KC-4	NA-9	None
Cleveland 31...............B. (1925)	K-32	KA-35	KB-6	KC-8	KC-7	NA-11	NE-4L
Cleveland 43...............B. (1925)	K-32	KA-35	KB-6	KC-8	KD-7	NA-18	NE-4L
Cleveland 31...............B. (1926)	K-48	KA-36	KB-6	KC-8	KD-7	NA-11	NE-4L
Cleveland 43...............B. (1926)	K-22	KA-36	KB-6	KC-8	KD-7	NA-18	NE-4L
Cord L29................D.-R. (1930)	K-95	KA-130	KB-4	KC-4	KC-4	NA-9	NE-2R
Davis 90....................D. (1925)	K-52	KA-40	KB-19	KC-5	KD-4	NA-19	NE-2R
Davis 91....................D. (1925)	K-53	KA-41	KB-12	KC-5	KD-4	NA-20	NE-2R
Davis 90....................D. (1926)	K-56	KA-108	KB-46	KC-5	KD-4	NA-21	NE-2R
Davis 91....................D. (1926)	K-53	KA-41	KB-12	KC-5	KD-4	NA-20	NE-2R
Davis 92....................D. (1926)	K-54	KA-42	KB-9	KC-11	KD-10	NA-27	NE-2R
Davis 93....................D. (1926)	K-54	KA-22	KB-9	KC-5	KD-4	NA-27	NE-2R
Davis 92....................D. (1926)	K-110	KA-123	KB-9	KC-11	KD-10	NA-27	NE-2R
Davis 94................D.-R. (1927)	K-10	KA-8	KB-4	KC-4	KC-4	NA-3	NE-2R
Davis 98................D.-R. (1927)	K-30	KA-23	KB-6	KC-4	KC-4	NA-9	NE-2R
Davis 99................D.-R. (1928)	K-55	KA-43	KB-3	KC-4	KC-4	NA-9	NE-2R
De Soto ................D.-R. (1928)	K-57	KA-44	KB-15	KC-4	KC-4	NA-3	NE-2R
De Soto ..................N.-E. (1929)	K-57	KA-44	KB-21	KC-12	KD-11	NA-22	NE-2R
De Soto Six.........N.-E. D.-R. (1930)	K-57	KA-44	KB-21	KC-33	KD-30	NA-6	None
De Soto Std. 8..........D.-R. (1930)	K-57	KA-44	KB-21	KC-33	KD-30	NA-6	None
Diana Str. 8................D. (1926)	K-54	KA-42	KB-9	KC-11	KD-10	NA-27	NE-2R
Diana Str. 8................D. (1927)	K-54	KA-42	KB-9	KC-13	KD-12	NA-27	NE-2R
Diana Str. 8................D. (1928)	K-110	KA-123	KB-9	KC-13	KD-12	NA-27	NE-2R
Dodge Brothers 4..........N.-E. (1925)	K-58	KA-48	KB-22	KC-14	KD-13	KA-48	None
Dodge Brothers 4..........N.-E. (1926)	K-59	KA-45	KB-22	KC-12	KD-14	NA-32	NE-2R
Dodge Bros. Series 128........(1927–28)	K-60	KA-46	KB-23	KC-12	KD-11	NA-32	NE-2R
Dodge Bros. Senior.........N.-E. (1928)	K-61	KA-47	KB-23	KC-12	KD-11	NA-34	NE-2R
Dodge Std. 6............N.-E. (1928)	K-61	KA-47	KB-23	KC-12	KD-11	NA-32	NE-2R
Dodge Brothers Vic. 6..N.-E. (1928–29)	K-61	KA-47	KB-23	KC-12	KD-11	NA-32	NE-2R
Dodge Brothers Senior.......N.-E. (1929)	K-61	KA-47	KB-23	KC-12	KD-11	NA-34	NE-2R
Dodge Brothers DA.........N.-E. (1929)	K-57	KA-44	KB-21	KC-9	KD-33	NA-32	NE-2R
Dodge DD6...........D.-R. N.-E. (1930)	K-57	KA-44	KB-21	KC-33	KD-30	NA-6	None
Dodge DC8..............D.-R. (1930)	K-57	KA-44	KB-21	KC-33	KD-30	NA-6	None
Dodge Senior.............N.-E. (1930)	K-61	KA-47	KB-23	KC-12	KD-11	NA-34	NE-2R
Durant A-22...............A.-L. (1925)	K-67	KA-54	KB-26	KC-17	KD-16	NA-38	NE-4L
Durant D-55...............A.-L. (1928)	K-68	KA-56	KB-27	KC-1	KD-1	NA-39	NE-4L
Durant D-65...............A.-L. (1928)	K-69 K-70	KA-56	KB-1 KB-27	KC-1	KD-1	NA-41	NE-4L
Durant M-2...............A.-L. (1928)	K-69 K-72	KA-56 KA-57	KB-1	KC-18	KD-17	NA 39	NE-4L
Durant 75.................A.-L. (1928)	K-71	KA-59	KB-27	KC-19	KD-18	NA-42	NE-5L
Durant 4-40...............A.-L. (1929)	K-72	KA-57	KB-1	KC-1	KD-1	NA-40	NE-4L
Durant 6-60...............A.-L. (1929)	K-70	KA-56	KB-27	KC-1	KD-1	NA-40	NE-4L
Durant 66.................A.-L. (1929)	K-70	KA-56	KB-27	KC-1	KD-1	NA-39	NE-4L
Durant 70.................A.-L. (1929)	K-73	KA-59	KB-27	KC-19	KD-18	NA-42	NE-5L
Durant 614................A.-L. (1930)	K-228	KA-137	KB-27	KC-34	KD-31	NA-37	NE-1R
Durant 617................A.-L. (1930)	K-71	KA-59	KB-27	KC-19	KD-18	NA-42	NE-5L
Elcar 4-40.................A.-L. (1925)	K-7	KA-5	KB-4	KC-4	KC-4	NA-3	NE-2R
Elcar 6-50.................A.-L. (1925)	K-74	KA-60	KB-27	KC-1	KD-1	NA-3	NE-1R
Elcar 6-60.................A.-L. (1925)	K-75	KA-61	KB-27	KC-1	KD-1	NA-3	NE-2R
Elcar 8-80....................D. (1925)	K-76	KA-58	KB-9	KC-5	KD-4	NA-27	NE-2R
Elcar 6-65....................R. (1926)	K-9	KA-7	KB-3	KC-3	KC-3	NA-3	NE-2R
Elcar 8-81....................D. (1926)	K-9	KA-58	KB-3	KC-9	KD-33	NA-27	NE-2R
Elcar 4-55....................R. (1926)	K-65	KA-5	KB-4	KC-1	KD-1	NA-3	NE-2R
Elcar 6-70................D.-R. (1927)	K-12	KA-9	KB-4	KC-3	KC-3	NA 9	NE-2R
Elcar 8-82................D.-R. (1927)	K-12	KA-9	KB-4	KC-3	KC-3	NA-9	NE-2R
Elcar 8-90................D.-R. (1927)	K-11	KA-7	KB-3	KC-3	KC-3	NA-3	NE-2R
Elcar 8-91................D.-R. (1928)	K-11	KA-7	KB-3	KC-3	KC-3	NA-3	NE-2R
Elcar 120.................D.-R. (1928)	K-16	KA-7	KB-4	KC-4	KC-4	NA-3	NE-2R
Elcar 6-70.............D.-R. (1928–29)	K-12	KA-9	KB-4	KC-3	KC-3	NA-9	NE-2R
Elcar 8-78.............D.-R. (1928–29)	K-12 K-14	KA-9	KB-4	KC-3 KC-4	KC-3 KC-4	NA-9	NE-2R
Elcar 8-82.............D.-R. (1928–29)	K-12 K-14	KA-9	KB-4	KC-3 KC-4	KC-3 KC-4	NA-9	NE-2R
Elcar 75..................D.-R. (1929)	K-14	KA-9	KB-4	KC-4	KC-4	NA-9	NE-2R
Elcar 95, 96.............D.-R. (1929)	K-12	KA-9	KB-4	KC-3	KC-3	NA-9	NE-2R
Elcar 120.................D.-R. (1929)	K-16	KA-7	KB-4	KC-4	KC-4	NA-9	NE-2R
Elcar 130, 140................(1930)	K-66	KA-133	KB-6	KC-4	KC-4	NA-15	NE-2R
Erskine 6-50.............D.-R. (1927)	K-77 K-78	KA-63	KB-4	KC-4	KC-4	NA-23	NE-2R
Erskine 6-51.............D.-R. (1928)	K-78	KA-63	KB-4	KC-4	KC-4	NA-23	NE-2R
Erskine 6-52.............D.-R. (1929)	K-78	KA-63	KB-4	KC-4	KC-4	NA-23	NE-2R
Erskine 53................D.-R. (1930)	K-219	KA-150	KB-56	KC-4	KC-4	NA-23	NE-2R
Essex 6......................B. (1925)	K-79	KA-64	KB-6	KC-8	KD-7	NA-24	NE-4L
Essex 6......................B. (1926)	K-79	KA-64	KB-6	KC-8	KD-7	NA-24	NE-4L
Essex Super 6.............A.-L. (1927)	K-80	KA-55	KB-6	KC-8	KD-7	NA-24	NE-4L
Essex Super 6.............A.-L. (1928)	K-156	KA-55	KB-6	KC-8	KD-7	NA-25	NE-4L
Essex Challenger...........A.-L. (1929)	K-81	KA-55	KB-6	KC-13	KD-17	NA-26	NE-4L
Essex Super Six...........A.-L. (1930)	K-227	KA-153	KB-57	KC-34	KD-31	NA-28	NE-4L
Falcon Knight 10..........A.-L. (1927)	K-82	KA-65	KB-1	KC-1	KD-1	NA-42	NE-5L
Falcon Knight 12..........A.-L. (1928)	K-83	KA-69	KB-1	KC-18	KD-17	NA-42	NE-5L
Flint E55.................DeJ. (1925)	K-85	KA-67	KB-27	KC-20	KC-19	NA-29	NE-5L

Footnote: For corresponding starter spring numbers advertised, see page 221.

BENDIX DRIVE SERVICE DATA
use only the genuine parts

The type of Bendix drive is designated by a number 13, 11, or 10 denoting the size of armature shaft, and by prefix "R" denoting Right Hand Screw Threads or "L" denoting Left Hand Screw Threads. The numbers 13, 11 and 10 also signify the standard number of teeth in pinion gear on these types, but if a special pinion is used, it is denoted by an addition, such as R-11-10 which means an R-11 drive with 10 tooth 8-10 pitch pinion.

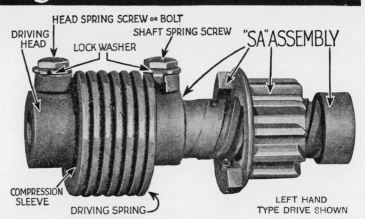

The R-13 or L-13 is mounted on an armature shaft, .802 (nearly $1\frac{3}{16}$ inch) in diameter.

The R-11 or L-11 is mounted on a shaft $\frac{5}{8}$ inch in diameter.

The R-10 or L-10 is mounted on a shaft $\frac{1}{2}$ inch in diameter.

An "X" added to the designation of a drive, such as "R-11X," means that a spring heavier than a regular is used.

The SA pinion and screw shaft assembly consists of shaft, gear and counterweight, stop nut, sleeve, and anti-drift pin and spring. It is strongly recommended that these parts *should not be purchased separately*—rebuilding of defective or worn sub-assemblies can be made quickly and easily at our factory at reasonable cost.

A Spring of Superior Quality—Look for the Red and Yellow Label

Bendix Part No.	Inside Diameter	Outside Diameter	Length	Diameter of Screws	Number of Coils	Interchangeable Multi-guide Nos.
	A	B	C	D	E	F
R-10-6	$1\frac{5}{16}''$	$1\frac{15}{16}''$	$1\frac{3}{4}''$	$\frac{5}{16}''$	7	NE-IR
L-10-6	$1\frac{5}{16}''$	$1\frac{15}{16}''$	$1\frac{3}{4}''$	$\frac{5}{16}''$	7	NE-4L
LA-10-6	$1\frac{3}{16}''$	$1\frac{13}{16}''$	$1\frac{3}{4}''$	$\frac{5}{16}''$	7	NE-6L
R-11-6x	$1\frac{5}{16}''$	$2\frac{1}{16}''$	$1\frac{3}{4}''$	$\frac{5}{16}''$	7	NE-2R
L-11-6x	$1\frac{5}{16}''$	$2\frac{1}{16}''$	$1\frac{3}{4}''$	$\frac{5}{16}''$	7	NE-5L
RB11xx-6	$1\frac{5}{16}''$	$2\frac{1}{8}''$	$2\frac{1}{4}''$	$\frac{5}{16}''$	8	
LB11xx-6	$1\frac{5}{16}''$	$2\frac{1}{8}''$	$2\frac{1}{4}''$	$\frac{5}{16}''$	8	
R-13-6	$1\frac{3}{8}''$	$1\frac{15}{16}''$	$2\frac{1}{8}''$	$\frac{3}{8}''$	8	
L-13-6	$1\frac{3}{8}''$	$1\frac{15}{16}''$	$2\frac{1}{8}''$	$\frac{3}{8}''$	8	
R-13-6x	$1\frac{3}{8}''$	$2\frac{3}{32}''$	$2\frac{1}{8}''$	$\frac{3}{8}''$	8	NE-3R
L-13-6x	$1\frac{3}{8}''$	$2\frac{3}{32}''$	$2\frac{1}{8}''$	$\frac{3}{8}''$	8	NE-7L
RC13xxx-6	$1\frac{3}{8}''$	$2\frac{3}{8}''$	$2\frac{1}{8}''$	$\frac{3}{8}''$	7	
LC13xxx-6	$1\frac{3}{8}''$	$2\frac{3}{8}''$	$2\frac{1}{8}''$	$\frac{3}{8}''$	7	

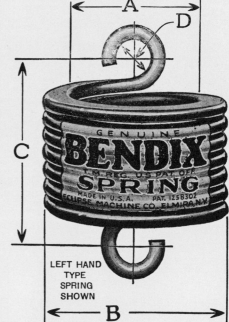

An "X" added to the designation of a spring, such as L-11-6X, means that a spring heavier than a regular is used—always use the same type if a replacement is made—a regular spring will not give service on an installation designed for the "X" spring. A slight permanent set in the spring does not interfere with its proper functioning. The regular and "X" type springs, even when used on Bendix drives otherwise identical, are not interchangeable unless the corresponding spring fastening screws are also used. Always use new lock washers when reassembling and make certain washer lip is bent up flush against the flat side of the head of the screw—this prevents screw coming loose.

With the Eclipse Bendix Drive it does no harm to engage the starter while the engine is running. However, it is recommended that care be taken in making a restart of the engine in case the first attempt does not result in the engine running. Wait and make certain that the engine and starting motor have both come to rest thus preventing the meshing of the pinion gear with the flywheel when the engine is back rocking just prior to its stopping.

Distorted springs can frequently be traced to engaging the drive for a restart without allowing a moment for the engine and starting motor to come to rest.

ECLIPSE MACHINE COMPANY, *Dept. 5,* ELMIRA, NEW YORK
Canadian Factory: Eclipse Machine Co., *Limited,* Walkerville, Ont.
(Subsidiaries of Bendix Aviation Corporation.)

GENERATOR AND STARTER—Continued

Interchangeable Parts Have the Same CHILTON NUMBER in Any Column

Car Make and Model	GENERATOR					STARTER	
	Generator Assembly	Armature	Field Coils	Main Brushes	Third Brush	Starter Armature	Starter Drive Spring (Bendix Type) (See Footnote)
Flint B-40............A.-L. (1925)	K-84	KA-66	KB-27	KC-33	KD-34	NA-30	NE-4L
Flint 60.............A.-L. (1926)	K-86	KA-66	KB-1	KC-1	KD-1	NA-31	NE-5L
Flint 80.............DeJ. (1926)	K-87	KA-67	KB-27	KC-1	KD-1	NA-30	NE-5L
Flint Jr.............A.-L. (1927)	K-88	KA-68	KB-1	KC-33	KD-34	NA-33	NE-2R
Flint Jr.............A.-L. (1927)	K-88	KA-68	KB-1	KC-33	KD-34	NA-33	NE-2R
Flint 60.............A.-L. (1927)	K-86	KA-68	KB-1	KC-1	KD-1	NA-31	NE-5L
Flint 80.............DeJ. (1927)	K-87	KA-67	KB-27	KC-1	KD-1	NA-30	NE-5L
Ford T.................(1925)	K-89	KA-70	KB-20	KC-21	KD-20	NA-52	NE-4L
Ford T.................(1926)	K-89	KA-70	KB-20	KC-21	KD-20	NA-52	NE-4L
Ford T.................(1927)	K-89	KA-70	KB-20	KC-21	KD-20	NA-52	NE-4L
Ford A.................(1928)	K-90	KA-71	KB-28	KC-17	KD-21	NA-51	§NE-6L
Ford A.................(1929)	K-91	KA-72	KB-29	KC-18	KD-17	NA-51	NE-5L
Ford A.................(1930)	K-91	KA-169	KB-29	KC-35	KD-32	NA-51	NE-5L
Franklin 11...........D.-Y. (1925)	K-92	KA-73	KB-30	KC-23	KD-22	NA-35	NE-5L
Franklin 11...........D.-Y. (1926)	K-92	KA-73	KB-30	KC-23	KD-22	NA-35	NE-5L
Franklin 11-B.........D.-Y. (1927)	K-92	KA-73	KB-30	KC-23	KD-22	NA-35	NE-5L
Franklin Series 12.....D.-Y. (1928)	K-93	KA-74	KB-31	KC-24	KD-23	NA-35	NE-5L
Franklin 130..........D.-R. (1929)	K-94	KA-75	KB-31	KC-24	KC-23	NA-9	NE-5L
Franklin 135, 137.....D.-R. (1929)	K-94	KA-75	KB-31	KC-4	KC-4	NA-9	NE-5L
Franklin 145, 147.....D.-R. (1930)	K-229	KA-75	KB-58	KC-4	KC-4	NA-9	NE-5L
Gardner 6-A...........R. (1925)	{ K-9 K-6	{ KA-4 KA-7	{ KB-2 KB-3	KC-3	KC-3	NA-3	NE-2R
Gardner 8-A...........R. (1925)	{ K-5 K-9	{ KA-3 KA-7	KB-3	KC-3	KC-3	NA-3	NE-2R
Gardner 6-B...........R. (1926)	{ K-9 K-6	{ KA-4 KA-7	{ KB-2 KB-3	KC-3	KC-3	NA-3	NE-2R
Gardner 8-B...........R. (1926)	{ K-5 K-9	{ KA-3 KA-7	KB-3	KC-3	KC-3	NA-3	NE-2R
Gardner 80............D.-R. (1927)	K-12	KA-9	KB-4	KC-3	KC-3	NA-9	NE-2R
Gardner 90............D.-R. (1927)	K-11	KA-7	KB-3	KC-3	KC-3	NA-3	NE-2R
Gardner 75............D.-R. (1928)	K-12	KA-9	KB-4	KC-3	KC-3	NA-9	NE-2R
Gardner 85............D.-R. (1928)	K-12	KA-9	KB-4	KC-3	KC-3	NA-9	NE-2R
Gardner 95............D.-R. (1928)	K-11	KA-7	KB-3	KC-3	KC-3	NA-3	NE-2R
Gardner 120...........D.-R. (1929)	K-14	KA-9	KB-4	KC-4	KC-4	NA-9	NE-2R
Gardner 125...........D.-R. (1929)	K-14	KA-9	KB-4	KC-4	KC-4	NA-9	NE-2R
Gardner 130...........D.-R. (1929)	K-11	KA-7	KB-3	KC-3	KC-3	NA-3	NE-2R
Gardner 136...........D.-R. (1930)	K-14	KA-9	KB-4	KC-4	KC-4	NA-9	NE-2R
Gardner 140...........D.-R. (1930)	K-14	KA-9	KB-4	KC-4	KC-4	NA-9	NE-2R
Gardner 150...........D.-R. (1930)	K-16	KA-7	KB-4	KC-4	KC-4	NA-3	NE-2R
Graham Paige 610......N.-E. (1928)	K-96	KA-76	KB-32	KC-9	KD-33	NA-36	NE-4L
Graham Paige 614......N.-E. (1928)	K-97	KA-77	KB-23	KC-12	KD-11	NA-32	NE-2R
Graham Paige 619......N.-E. (1928)	K-98	KA-77	KB-23	KC-12	KD-11	NA-43	NE-2R
Graham Paige 629......N.-E. (1928)	K-98	KA-77	KB-23	KC-12	KD-11	NA-43	NE-2R
Graham Paige 835......N.-E. (1928)	K-98	KA-77	KB-23	KC-4	KC-4	NA-43	NE-2R
Graham Paige 612......D.-R. (1929)	K-99	KA-78	KB-4	KC-4	KC-4	NA-44	NE-4L
Graham Paige 615......D.-R. (1929)	K-100	KA-79	KB-4	KC-4	KC-4	NA-3	NE-1R
Graham Paige 621......D.-R. (1929)	K-101	KA-80	KB-33	KC-4	KC-4	NA-15	NE-12
Graham Paige 827......D.-R. (1929)	K-101	KA-80	KB-33	KC-4	KC-4	NA-15	NE-13
Graham Paige 837......D.-R. (1929)	K-101	KA-80	KB-33	KC-4	KC-4	NA-15	NE-14
Graham Std. 6.........D.-R. (1930)	K-230	KA-78	KB-4	KC-4	KC-4	NA-32	NE-4L
Graham Spec. 6........D.-R. (1930)	K-100	KA-79	KB-4	KC-4	KC-4	NA-3	NE-2R
Graham Std. and Spec. 8..D.-R. (1930)	K-100	KA-79	KB-4	KC-4	KC-4	NA-15	None
Graham Custom 8.......D.-R. (1930)	K-101	KA-78	KB-33	KC-4	KC-4	NA-15	None
Hudson Super 6........B. (1925)	K-104	KA-83	KB-36	KC-26	KD-25	NA-45	None
Hudson Super 6........B. (1926)	K-105	KA-84	KB-36	KC-26	KD-25	NA-45	None
Hudson Super 6........B. (1927)	K-106	KA-85	KB-36	KC-26	KD-25	NA-45	None
Hudson Super 6O.......A.-L. (1928)	K-106	KA-85	KB-36	KC-26	KD-25	NA-45	None
Hudson Super 6S.......A.-L. (1928)	K-106	KA-85	KB-36	KC-26	KD-25	NA-45	None
Hudson Greater 6......A.-L. (1929)	K-106	KA-85	KB-36	KC-26	KD-25	NA-45	None
Hudson 8..............A.-L. (1930)	K-227	KA-153	KB-57	KC-34	KD-31	NA-47	NE-4L
Hupmobile Series R....A.-L. (1925)	K-108	KA-87	KB-37	KC-34	KD-35	NA-46	NE-4L
Hupmobile E1..........A.-L. (1925)	K-107	KA-86	KB-37	KC-1	KD-1	NA-48	NE-5L
Hupmobile A1..........A.-L. (1926)	K-109	KA-88	KB-1	KC-1	KD-1	NA-31	NE-5L
Hupmobile E2..........A.-L. (1926)	K-107	KA-86	KB-37	KC-1	KD-1	NA-48	NE-5L
Hupmobile A2..........A.-L. (1927)	K-109	KA-88	KB-1	KC-19	KD-18	NA-31	NE-5L
Hupmobile E3..........D.-R. (1927)	K-111	KA-90	KB-38	KC-1	KD-1	NA-49	NE-5L
Hupmobile Century 6...A.-L. (1928)	K-112	KA-91	KB-37	KC-19	KD-18	NA-31	NE-5L
Hupmobile Century 8...A.-L. (1928)	K-113	KA-92	KB-37	KC-19	KD-18	NA-49	NE-5L
Hupmobile Century 125..D.-R. (1928)	K-113	KA-92	KB-37	KC-19	KD-18	NA-49	NE-5L
Hupmobile M8.........A.-L. (1928–29)	K-113	KA-92	KB-37	KC-19	KD-18	NA-49	NE-5L
Hupmobile Century 6...A.-L. (1929)	K-112	KA-91	KB-37	KC-19	KD-18	NA-31	NE-5L
Hupmobile S...........A.-L. (1930)	K-232	KA-176	KB-58	KC-34	KD-34	NA-50	NE-5L
Hupmobile C...........A.-L. (1930)	K-233	KA-176	KB-58	KC-19	KD-18	NA-53	NE-2R
Hupmobile H, U........A.-L. (1930)	K-233	KA-178	KB-58	KC-19	KD-18	NA-48	NE-2R
Jewett 6-50...........A.-K. (1925)	K-114	KA-93	KB-39	KC-3	KC-3	NA-32	NE-5L
Jewett 6-55...........D.-R. (1926)	K-115	KA-93	KB-4	KC-4	KC-4	NA-32	NE-5L
Jordan A..............B. (1925)	K-116	KA-94	KB-36	KC-26	KD-25	NA-54	NE-2R
Jordan A..............B. (1926)	K-116	KA-94	KB-36	KC-26	KD-25	NA-54	NE-2R
Jordan J..............B. (1926)	K-117	KA-95	KB-36	KC-26	KD-25	NA-54	NE-2R
Jordan AA.............B. (1927)	K-116	KA-94	KB-36	KC-26	KD-25	NA-54	NE-2R
Jordan J..............A.-L. (1927)	K-118	KA-95	KB-36	KC-19	KD-18	NA-54	NE-2R
Jordan R..............A.-L. (1927)	K-119	KA-96	KB-1	KC-19	KD-18	NA-55	NE-4L
Jordan JJ.............A.-L. (1928)	K-118	KA-95	KB-36	KC-19	KC-18	NA-54	NE-2R
Jordan JE.............A.-L. (1928)	K-118	KA-95	KB-36	KC-19	KD-18	NA-54	NE-2R
Jordan E..............A.-L. (1929)	K-120	KA-97	KB-37	KC-19	KD-18	NA-56	NE-2R
Jordan G..............A.-L. (1929)	K-121	KA-166	KB-37	KC-19	KD-18	NA-54	NE-2R
Jordan 80.............A.-L. (1930)	K-120	KA-97	KB-37	KC-34	KD-31	NA-54	NE-2R
Jordan 90.............A.-L. (1930)	K-121	KA-166	KB-37	KC-34	KD-31	NA-54	NE-2R
Kissel 6-55...........R. (1925)	K-122	KA-167	KB-3	KC-4	KC-4	NA-3	NE-2R
Kissel 8-75...........R. (1925)	K-5	KA-4	KB-3	KC-3	KC-3	NA-3	NE-2R
Kissel 6-55...........R. (1926)	K-123	KA-168	KB-6	KC-4	KC-4	NA-3	NE-2R
Kissel 8-75...........R. (1926)	K-5	KA-4	KB-3	KC-3	KC-3	NA-3	NE-2R
Kissel 6-55...........R. (1927)	K-123	KA-168	KB-6	KC-4	KC-4	NA-3	NE-2R
Kissel 8-65...........D.-R. (1927)	K-12	KA-9	KB-4	KC-3	KC-3	NA-9	NE-2R
Kissel 8-75...........D.-R. (1927)	K-124	KA-98	KB-4	KC-3	KC-3	NA-3	NE-2R
Kissel 6-70...........D.-R. (1928)	K-12	KA-9	KB-4	KC-3	KC-3	NA-9	NE-2R
Kissel 8-80...........D.-R. (1928)	K-12	KA-9	KB-4	KC-3	KC-3	NA-9	NE-2R
Kissel 8-80S..........D.-R. (1928)	K-12	KA-9	KB-4	KC-3	KC-3	NA-9	NE-2R
Kissel 8-90...........D.-R. (1928)	K-124	KA-98	KB-4	KC-3	KC-3	NA-3	NE-2R
Kissel 6-73...........D.-R. (1929)	K-14	KA-9	KB-4	KC-4	KC-4	NA-9	NE-2R
Kissel 8-95...........D.-R. (1929)	K-14	KA-9	KB-4	KC-4	KC-4	NA-9	NE-2R
Kissel 8-126..........D.-R. (1929)	K-124	KA-98	KB-4	KC-3	KC-3	NA-3	NE-2R
La Salle 303..........D.-R. (1927)	K-125	KA-19	KB-9	KD-4	KD-4	NA-57	None

Footnote: For corresponding starter spring numbers advertised, see page 221.

GENERATOR AND STARTER—Continued

Interchangeable Parts Have the Same CHILTON NUMBER in Any Column

Car Make and Model	GENERATOR					STARTER	
	Generator Assembly	Armature	Field Coils	Main Brushes	Third Brush	Starter Armature	Starter Drive Spring (Bendix Type) (See Footnote)
La Salle 303............D.-R. (1928)	K-27	KA-19	KB-9	KD-4	KD-4	NA-15	None
La Salle 328............D.-R. (1929)	K-27	KA-19	KB-9	KD-4	KD-4	NA-15	None
La Salle 340............D.-R. (1930)	K-139	KA-19	KB-9	KC-5	KD-4	NA-9	None
Lincoln 8................D. (1925)	K-126	KA-99	KB-32	KC-27	KD-8	KA-99	None
Lincoln 8................D. (1926)	K-126	KA-99	KB-32	KC-27	KD-8	KA-99	None
Lincoln 8................D.-R. (1927)	K-126	KA-99	KB-32	KC-27	KD-8	KA-99	None
Lincoln 8................D.-R. (1928)	K-126	KA-99	KB-32	KC-27	KD-8	KA-99	None
Lincoln 8................D.-R. (1929)	K-126	KA-99	KB-32	KC-27	KD-8	KA-99	None
Lincoln 8................D.-R. (1930)	K-126	KA-99	KB-32	KC-36	KD-33	KA-99	None
Locomobile Jr. 8.........DeJ. (1925)	K-127	KA-100	KB-33	KC-20	KD-19	NA-58	NE-5L
Locomobile 48...........D. (1925)	K-128	KA-102	KB-34	KC-28	KD-26	NA-74	None
Locomobile 48...........D. (1926)	K-128	KA-102	KB-34	KC-28	KD-26	NA-74	None
Locomobile 90...........DeJ. (1926)	K-130	KA-103	KB-35	KC-20	KD-19	NA-75	None
Locomobile Jr. 8.........DeJ. (1926)	K-127	KA-100	KB-33	KC-20	KD-19	NA-58	NE-5L
Locomobile 48...........D. (1927)	K-128	KA-102	KB-34	KC-28	KD-26	NA-74	None
Locomobile 8-66.........DeJ. (1927)	K-131	KA-23	KB-35	KC-20	KD-19	NA-58	NE-5L
Locomobile 8-80.........DeJ. (1927)	K-132	KA-105	KB-36	KC-20	KD-19	NA-73	NE-2R
Locomobile 90...........DeJ. (1927)	K-130	KA-103	KB-35	KC-20	KC-19	NA-75	None
Locomobile 48...........D. (1927)	K-128	KA-102	KB-34	KC-28	KD-26	NA-74	None
Locomobile 8-70.........D.-R. (1928)	K-131	KA-104	KB-6	KC-4	KC-4	NA-9	NE-2R
Locomobile 8-80.........DeJ. (1928)	K-132	KA-105	KB-36	KC-20	KC-19	NA-73	NE-2R
Locomobile 90...........DeJ. (1928)	K-130	KA-103	KB-35	KC-20	KC-19	NA-75	None
Locomobile 8-80.........D.-R. (1929)	K-132	KA-105	KB-36	KC-20	KC-19	NA-73	NE-2R
Locomobile 88...........D.-R. (1929)	K-132	KA-105	KB-36	KC-20	KC-19	NA-73	NE-2R
Marmon 74..............D. (1925)	K-133	KA-106	KB-40	KC-5	KD-4	NA-73	None
Marmon 74..............D. (1926)	K-134	KA-106	KB-9	KC-5	KD-4	NA-73	None
Marmon, Little..........D.-R. (1927)	K-135	KA-107	KB-4	KC-4	KC-4	NA 60	None
Marmon E75.............D.-R. (1927)	K-134	KA-106	KB-9	KC-4	KC-4	NA-4	None
Marmon 68..............D.-R. (1928)	K-136	KA-26	KB-4	KC-4	KC-4	NA-3	NE-1R
Marmon E75.............D.-R. (1928)	K-134	KA-106	KB-9	KC-4	KC-4	NA-4	None
Marmon 78..............D.-R. (1928)	K-135	KA-107	KB-4	KC-4	KC-4	NA-60	None
Marmon 68..............D.-R. (1929)	K-136	KA-26	KB-4	KC-4	KC-4	NA-3	NE-1R
Marmon 78..............D.-R. (1929)	K-135	KA-107	KB-4	KC-4	KC-4	NA-60	None
Marmon, Roosevelt.......D.-R. (1929)	K-136	KA-26	KB-4	KC-4	KC-4	NA-3	NE-4L
Marmon, Roosevelt.......D.-R. (1930)	K-136	KA-26	KB-4	KC-4	KC-4	NA-3	NE-1R
Marmon 8-69............D.-R. (1930)	K-136	KA-26	KB-4	KC-4	KC-4	NA-3	NE-1R
Marmon 8-79............D.-R. (1930)	K-135	KA-107	KB-4	KC-4	KC-4	NA-3	NE-2R
Marmon Big 8...........D.-R. (1930)	K-135	KA-107	KB-4	KC-4	KC-4	NA-3	NE-2R
Marquette..............D.-R. (1929)	K-166	KA-26	KB-4	KC-4	KC-4	NA-3	None
Maxwell 25..............R. (1925)	K-38	KA-28	KB-13	KC-3	KC-3	NA-61	NE-2R
Moon Series A...........D. (1925)	K-137	KA-109	KB-9	KC-13	KD-12	NA-27	NE-2R
Moon Series A...........D. (1926)	{ K-137	{ KA-109	KB-9	KC-13	KD-12	NA-27	NE-2R
	{ K-138	{ KA-110					
Moon Series A...........D.-R. (1927)	K-137	KA-110	KB-9	KC-13	KD-12	NA-27	NE-2R
Moon 6-60..............D.-R. (1927)	K-140	KA-8	KB-4	KC-4	KC-4	NA-3	NE-2R
Moon Series A...........D.-R. (1928)	K-137	KA-110	KB-9	KC-13	KD-12	NA-27	NE-2R
Moon 6-60..............D.-R. (1928)	K-140	KA-8	KB-4	KC-4	KC-4	NA-3	NE-2R
Moon 6-72..............D.-R. (1928)	K-141	KA-111	KB-4	KC-4	KC-4	NA-3	NE-2R
Moon 8-80..............D.-R. (1928)	K-203	KA-43	KB-4	KC-4	KC-4	NA-9	NE-2R
Moon 6-72..............D.-R. (1929)	K-141	KA-111	KB-4	KC-4	KC-4	NA-3	NE-2R
Nash Adv. 6.............D. (1925)	K-142	KA-112	KB-9	KC-5	KD-4	NA-62	None
Nash Spec. 6............D. (1925)	K-143	KA-113	KB-9	KC-5	KD-4	NA-63	None
Nash Adv. 6.............D. (1926)	K-142	KA-171	KB-9	KC-5	KD-4	NA-64	None
Nash Spec. 6............D. (1926)	K-143	KA-113	KB-9	KC-5	KD-4	NA-64	None
Nash Adv. 6.............A.-L. (1927)	K-142	KA-171	KB-9	KC-11	KD-10	NA-2	None
Nash Spec. 6............A.-L. (1927)	K-144	KA-114	KB-9	KC-11	KD-10	NA-2	None
Nash Light 6............A.-L. (1927)	K-146	KA-1	KB-1	KC-1	KD-1	NA-1	NE-5L
Nash Adv. 6.............A.-L. (1928)	K-147	KA-116	KB-9	KC-5	KD-4	NA-2	None
Nash Spec. 6............A.-L. (1928)	K-148	KA-114	KB-4	KC-4	KC-4	NA-2	None
Nash Std. 6.............A.-L. (1928)	K-151	KA-115	KB-1	KC-18	KD-17	NA-1	NE-5L
Nash Adv. 6.............A.-L. (1929)	K-149	KA-117	KB-41	KC-18	KC-17	NA-65	None
Nash Spec. 6............A.-L. (1929)	K-150	KA-118	KB-41	KC-18	KC-17	NA-6	None
Nash Std. 6.............A.-L. (1929)	K-206	KA-115	KB-1	KC-18	KD-17	NA-6	NE-5L
Nash Single Ig. 6........A.-L. (1930)	K-206	KA-115	KB-49	KC-34	KD-31	NA-53	NE-5L
Nash Twin Ig. 6.........A.-L. (1930)	K-234	KA-179	KB-50	KC-34	KD-31	NA-67	NE-2R
Nash Twin Ig. 8.........A.-L. (1930)	K-235	KA-180	KB-50	KC-34	KD-31	NA-68	NE-2R
Oakland 6-54...........R. (1925)	K-152	KA-119	KB-3	KC-3	KC-3	NA-69	NE-2R
Oakland O6.............R. (1926)	{ K-152	{ KA-119	{ KB-3	KC-3	KC-3	NA-69	NE-2R
	{ K-153	{ KA-32	{ KB-4				
Oakland GO6............R. (1927)	K-153	KA-32	KB-4	KC-4	KC-4	NA-69	NE-1R
Oakland AA6............D.-R. (1928)	K-154	KA-26	KB-4	KC-4	KC-4	NA-3	NE-1R
Oakland AA6............D.-R. (1929)	K-154	KA-26	KB-4	KC-4	KC-4	NA-3	NE-1R
Oakland 8..............D.-R. (1930)	K-236	KA-181	KB-51	KC-4	KC-4	NA-70	None
Oldsmobile C............D. (1925)	K-155	KA-120	KB-9	KC-11	KD-10	NA-71	NE-2R
Oldsmobile D............D. (1926)	K-156	KA-120	KB-6	KC-13	KD-12	NA-72	¶NE-2R
Oldsmobile E............D.-R. (1927)	K-157	KA-172	KB-4	KC-4	KC-4	NA-72	NE-15
Oldsmobile F28..........D.-R. (1928)	K-158	KA-173	KB-4	KC-4	KC-4	NA-3	None
Oldsmobile F29..........D.-R. (1929)	K-158	KA-173	KB-4	KC-4	KC-4	NA-3	None
Oldsmobile F30..........D.-R. (1930)	K-158	KA-173	KB-4	KC-4	KC-4	NA-3	None
Overland 91.............A.-L. (1925)	K-145	KA-121	KB-1	KC-1	KD-1	NA-76	NE-4L
Overland 93.............A.-L. (1925)	K-159	KA-121	KB-1	KC-1	KD-1	NA-77	NE-4L
Overland 91.............A.-L. (1926)	K-160	KA-122	KB-1	KC-1	KD-1	NA-76	NE-4L
Overland 93.............A.-L. (1926)	K-159	KA-121	KB-1	KC-1	KD-1	NA-77	NE-4L
Packard 6 cyl., 326, 333......D.-Y. (1925)	K-164	KA-73	KB-30	KC-23	KD-22	NA-78	NE-2R
Packard 8 cyl., 236, 243......D.-Y. (1925)	K-165	KA-73	KB-30	KC-23	KD-22	NA-79	NE-2R
Packard 6 cyl., 326, 333......D.-Y. (1926)	K-164	KA-73	KB-30	KC-23	KD-22	NA-78	NE-2R
Packard 8 cyl., 236, 243......D.-Y. (1926)	K-165	KA-73	KB-30	KC-23	KD-22	NA-79	NE-2R
Packard 6 cyl., 426, 433......D.-Y. (1927)	K-164	KA-73	KB-30	KC-23	KD-22	NA-78	NE-2R
Packard 8 cyl., 336, 343......D.-Y. (1927)	K-164	KA-73	KB-30	KC-23	KD-22	NA-79	NE-2R
Packard 526, 533........D.-Y. (1928)	K-164	KA-51	KB-30	KC-23	KD-23	NA-78	NE-2R
Packard Std. 8-443......D.-Y. (1928)	K-164	KA-51	KB-30	KC-23	KD-22	NA-80	NE-2R
Packard 626, 633........D.-Y. (1929)	K-167	KA-51	KB-31	KC-24	KD-23	NA-81	NE-2R
Packard 640, 645........D.-Y. (1929)	K-167	KA-51	KB-31	KC-24	KD-23	NA-80	NE-2R
Packard 726, 733........D.-Y. (1930)	K-167	KA-51	KB-31	KC-24	KD-23	NA-81	NE-2R
Packard 740, 745........D.-Y. (1930)	K-167	KA-51	KB-31	KC-24	KD-23	NA-82	NE-2R
Paige 6-70..............R. (1925-26)	K-114	KA-93	KB-39	KC-3	KC-3	NA-83	NE-2R
Paige 6-72..............R. (1926)	K-222	KA-93	KB-4	KC-3	KC-3	NA-83	NE-5L
Paige 6-45..............D.-R. (1927)	K-168	KA-126	KB-4	KC-4	KC-4	NA-44	NE-5L
Paige 6-65..............D.-R. (1927)	K-169	KA-127	KB-4	KC-4	KC-4	NA-44	NE-5L
Paige 6-75..............D.-R. (1927)	K-169	KA-127	KB-4	KC-4	KC-4	NA-44	NE-5L
Paige 8-85..............D.-R. (1928)	K-170	KA-128	KB-4	KC-4	KC-4	NA-3	NE-2R
Peerless 70.............D. (1925)	K-171	KA-129	KB-9	KC-5	KD-4	NA-84	NE-2R
Peerless 80.............A.-L. (1926)	K-172	KA-68	KB-41	KC-19	KD-18	NA-85	NE-2R

Footnote: For corresponding starter spring numbers advertised, see page 221.

GENERATOR AND STARTER—Continued

Interchangeable Parts have the same CHILTON NUMBER in Any Column

Car Make and Model	GENERATOR Generator Assembly	Armature	Field Coils	Main Brushes	Third Brush	STARTER Starter Armature	Starter Drive Spring (Bendix Type) (See Footnote)
Peerless 69.............D. (1926)	K-53	KA-41	KB-12	KC-5	KD-4	NA-27	NE-2R
Peerless 60.............A.-L. (1927)	K-119	KA-96	KB-41	KC-1	KD-1	NA-86	NE-2R
Peerless 69.............D. (1927)	K-53	KA-41	KB-12	KC-5	KD-4	NA-27	NE-2R
Peerless 80.............A.-L. (1927)	K-172	KA-68	KB-41	KC-19	KD-18	NA-85	NE-2R
Peerless 72.............D. (1927)	K-171	KA-129	KB-9	KC-5	KD-4	NA-84	NE-2R
Peerless 60.............A.-L. (1928)	K-119	KA-96	KB-41	KC-1	KD-1	NA-86	NE-2R
Peerless 80.............A.-L. (1928)	K-120	KA-97	KB-41	KC-19	KD-18	NA-84	NE-2R
Peerless 91.............D.-R. (1928)	K-45	KA-33	KB-4	KC-4	KC-4	NA-23	NE-2R
Peerless 61.............A.-L. (1929)	K-141	KA-131	KB-41	KC-18	KD-17	NA-87	NE-2R
Peerless 81.............A.-L. (1929)	K-120	KA-97	KB-41	KC-19	KD-18	NA-88	NE-2R
Peerless 91.............D.-R. (1929)	K-174	KA-33	KB-42	KC-1	KD-1	NA-23	NE-2R
Peerless 125............D.-R. (1929)	K-223	KA-174	KB-47	KC-35	KD-36	NA-15	NE-2R
Peerless 61.............A.-L. (1930)	K-141	KA-131	KB-4	KC-18	KD-17	NA-3	NE-2R
Peerless A..............A.-L. (1930)	K-245 / K-246	KA-62	KB-59	KC-38	KD-36	NA-53	NE-2R
Peerless B..............A.-L. (1930)	K-247	KA-185	KB-60	KC-38	KD-36	NA-89	NE-2R
Peerless C..............A.-L. (1930)	K-247	KA-185	KB-60	KC-38	KD-36	NA-89	NE-2R
Pierce Arrow 80.........D.-R. (1925)	K-175	KA-134	KB-9	KC-5	KD-4	NA-90	None
Pierce Arrow 33.........D.-R. (1926)	K-176	KA-135	KB-9	KC-6	KD-8	NA-91	None
Pierce Arrow 80.........D.-R. (1926)	K-175	KA-134	KB-9	KC-5	KD-4	NA-90	None
Pierce Arrow 36.........D.-R. (1927)	K-177	KA-136	KB-43	KC-19	KD-18	NA-92	None
Pierce Arrow 80.........D.-R. (1927)	K-175	KA-134	KB-9	KC-5	KD-4	NA-93	None
Pierce Arrow 36.........D.-R. (1928)	K-177	KA-136	KB-43	KC-19	KD-18	NA-92	None
Pierce Arrow 81.........D.-R. (1928)	K-175	KA-134	KB-9	KC-5	KD-4	NA-93	None
Pierce Arrow A..........D.-R. (1929)	K-177	KA-182	KB-43	KC-4	KC-4	NA-9	None
Pierce Arrow B..........D.-R. (1930)	K-238	KA-183	KB-55	KD-4	KD-4	NA-9	None
Pierce Arrow C..........D.-R. (1930)	K-237	KA-182	KB-55	KC-4	KC-4	NA-9	None
Plymouth 4.............D.-R. (1929)	K-43	KA-31	KB-14	KC-4	KC-4	NA-3	NE-2R
Plymouth ..............D.-R. (1930)	K-43	KA-31	KB-14	KC-4	KC-4	NA-6	None
Pontiac 6..............D.-R. (1926)	K-35	KA-26	KB-4	KC-4	KC-4	NA-3	NE-1R
Pontiac 6..............D.-R. (1927)	K-35	KA-26	KB-4	KC-4	KC-4	NA-3	NE-1R
Pontiac 6..............D.-R. (1928)	K-35	KA-26	KB-4	KC-4	KG-4	NA-3	NE-4L
Pontiac Big 6...........D.-R. (1929)	K-36	KA-26	KB-4	KC-4	KC-4	NA-3	NE-4L
Pontiac................D.-R. (1930)	K-36	KA-26	KB-4	KC-4	KC-4	NA-94	None
Reo T6................N.-E. (1925)	K-180	KA-138	KB-44	KC-29	KD-27	NA-95	None
Reo T6................N.-E. (1926)	K-224	KA-138	KB-44	KC-29	KD-27	NA-95	None
Reo Flying Cloud........R. (1927)	K-181	KA-7	KB-4	KC-3	KC-3	NA-9	None
Reo Wolverine..........N.-E. (1927)	K-182	KA-47	KB-23	KC-12	KD-11	NA-32	NE-2R
Reo Flying Cloud........D.-R. (1928)	K-181	KA-7	KB-4	KC-3	KC-3	NA-9	None
Reo Wolverine..........N.-E. (1928)	K-182	KA-47	KB-23	KC-12	KD-11	NA-32	NE-2R
Reo Flying Cloud Master....D.-R. (1929)	K-183	KA-33	KB-4	KC-12	KD-11	NA-9	None
Reo Flying Cloud Mate......D.-R. (1929)	K-184	KA-33	KB-4	KC-12	KD-11	NA-32	None
Reo 15................D.-R. (1930)	K-183	KA-33	KB-4	KC-12	KD-11	NA-96	None
Reo 20................D.-R. (1930)	K-184	KA-33	KB-4	KC-12	KD-11	NA-9	None
Reo 25................D.-R. (1930)	K-184	KA-33	KB-4	KC-12	KD-11	NA-9	None
Rickenbacker 8-A........B. (1925)	K-186	KA-140	KB-6	KC-8	KD-7	NA-97	None
Rickenbacker 6-D........B. (1925)	K-186	KA-140	KB-6	KC-8	KD-7	NA-98	None
Rickenbacker 8-B........B. (1926)	K-187	KA-141	KB-6	KC-8	KD-7	NA-97	None
Rickenbacker 6-E........B. (1926)	K-187	KA-141	KB-6	KC-8	KD-7	NA-98	None
Rickenbacker 6-70.......B. (1927)	K-187	KA-141	KB-6	KC-8	KD-7	NA-98	None
Rickenbacker 8-80.......B. (1927)	K-187	KA-141	KB-6	KC-8	KD-7	NA-97	None
Rickenbacker 8-90.......B. (1927)	K-187	KA-141	KB-6	KC-8	KD-7	NA-97	None
Roamer 4-75E...........A.-L. (1925)	K-188	KA-142	KB-1	KC-1	KC-1	NA-100	NE-3R
Roamer 6-54E...........A.-L. (1925)	K-189	KA-142	KB-1	KC-18	KD-17	NA-99	NE-16
Roamer 6-50...........A.-L. (1925)	K-189	KA-143	KB-1	KC-18	KD-17	NA-99	NE-1R
Roamer 4-75E...........A.-L. (1926)	K-188	KA-142	KB-1	KC-1	KC-1	NA-100	NE-3R
Roamer 6-54E...........A.-L. (1926)	K-189	KA-142	KB-1	KC-18	KD-17	NA-99	NE-17
Roamer 8-80...........A.-L. (1926)	K-190	KA-144	KB-1	KC-18	KD-17	NA-77	NE-2R
Roamer 8-80...........A.-L. (1927)	K-190	KA-144	KB-1	KC-18	KD-17	NA-77	NE-2R
Roamer 8-88...........A.-L. (1927)	K-190	KA-144	KB-1	KC-18	KD-17	NA-77	NE-2R
Roamer 8-78...........A.-L. (1927)	K-190	KA-144	KB-1	KC-18	KD-17	NA-77	NE-2R
Roamer 8-78...........A.-L. (1928)	K-190	KA-144	KB-1	KC-18	KD-17	NA-77	NE-2R
Roamer 8-80...........A.-L. (1928)	K-190	KA-144	KB-1	KC-18	KD-17	NA-77	NE-2R
Roamer 8-88...........A.-L. (1928)	K-190	KA-144	KB-1	KC-18	KD-17	NA-77	NE-2R
Roamer 8-78 ..........A.-L. (1929)	K-190	KA-144	KB-1	KC-18	KD-17	NA-77	NE-2R
Roamer 8-80...........A.-L. (1929)	K-190	KA-144	KB-1	KC-18	KD-17	NA-77	NE-2R
Star F.................A.-L. (1925)	K-72	KA-57	KB-1	KC-1	KD-1	NA-101	NE-4L
Star M................A.-L. (1926)	K-72	KA-57	KB-1	KC-1	KD-1	NA-101	NE-4L
Star R................A.-L. (1926)	K-191	KA-57	KB-1	KC-1	KD-1	NA-101	NE-4L
Star M................A.-L. (1927–28)	K-72	KA-57	KB-1	KC-1	KD-1	NA-101	NE-4L
Star R................A.-L. (1927–28)	K-191	KA-57	KB-1	KC-1	KD-1	NA-101	NE-4L
Stearns Knight C........DeJ. (1925)	K-192	KA-145	KB-42	KC-20	KD-19	NA-102	NE-7L
Stearns Knight S........DeJ. (1925)	K-192	KA-145	KB-42	KC-20	KD-19	NA-103	NE-3R
Stearns Knight C75......DeJ. (1926)	K-192	KA-145	KB-42	KC-20	KD-19	NA-102	NE-7L
Stearns Knight S95......DeJ. (1926)	K-192	KA-145	KB-42	KC-20	KD-19	NA-103	NE-3R
Stearns Knight F6-85.....DeJ. (1927)	K-192	KA-145	KB-42	KC-20	KD-19	NA-104	NE-7L
Stearns Knight 8-85......DeJ. (1927–28)	K-193	KA-146	KB-27	KC-20	KD-19	NA-105	NE-5L
Stearns Knight F6-85......DeJ. (1928)	K-192	KA-145	KB-42	KC-20	KD-19	NA-104	NE-7L
Stearns Knight H & J 8-90.DeJ.(1928-29)	K-193	KA-146	KB-27	KC-20	KD-19	NA-106	NE-5L
Stearns Knight M & N 6-80.A.-L. (1928-29)	K-193	KA-146	KB-27	KC-20	KD-19	NA-107	NE-2R
Studebaker Big 6.........R. (1925)	K-195	KA-148	KB-4	KC-4	KC-4	NA-83	None
Studebaker Spec. 6.......R. (1925)	K-195	KA-148	KB-4	KC-4	KC-4	NA-83	None
Studebaker Std. 6........R. (1925)	K-196	KA-149	KB-4	KC-4	KC-4	NA-3	NE-2R
Studebaker Big 6.........R. (1926)	K-195	KA-148	KB-4	KC-4	KC-4	NA-83	None
Studebaker Spec. 6.......R. (1926)	K-195	KA-148	KB-4	KC-4	KC-4	NA-83	None
Studebaker Std. 6.....D.-R. (1926-27)	K-196	KA-149	KB-4	KC-4	KC-4	NA-3	NE-2R
Studebaker Big 6......D.-R. (1927)	K-195	KA-148	KB-4	KC-4	KC-4	NA-83	None
Studebaker Spec. 6....D.-R. (1927)	K-195	KA-148	KB-4	KC-4	KC-4	NA-83	None
Studebaker Com. 6.....D.-R. (1928)	K-195	KA-148	KB-4	KC-4	KC-4	NA-83	None
Studebaker Dic. 6......D.-R. (1928)	K-198	KA-151	KB-4	KC-4	KC-4	NA-3	NE-2R
Studebaker Pres. 8......D.-R. (1928)	K-197	KA-151	KB-4	KC-4	KC-4	NA-9	None
Studebaker Dic. 6......D.-R. (1929)	K-198	KA-151	KB-4	KC-4	KC-4	NA-3	NE-2R
Studebaker Com. 6.....D.-R. (1929)	K-197	KA-151	KB-4	KC-4	KC-4	NA-108	None
Studebaker Com. 8.....D.-R. (1929)	K-197	KA-151	KB-4	KC-4	KC-4	NA-108	None
Studebaker Pres.......D.-R. (1929)	K-197	KA-151	KB-4	KC-4	KC-4	NA-9	None
Studebaker Dict. 6.....D.-R. (1930)	K-219	KA-151	KB-4	KC-4	KC-4	NA-108	None
Studebaker Dict. 8.....D.-R. (1930)	K-239	KA-151	KB-4	KC-4	KC-4	NA-108	None / NE-2R
Studebaker Com. 6......D.-R. (1930)	K-198	KA-151	KB-4	KC-4	KC-4	NA-108	None
Studebaker Com. 8......D.-R. (1930)	K-197	KA-151	KB-4	KC-4	KC-4	NA-108	None / NE-2R
Studebaker 6-53.......D.-R. (1930)	K-219	KA-151	KB-4	KC-4	KC-4	NA-23	NE-2R
Studebaker Pres........D.-R. (1930)	K-197	KA-151	KB-4	KC-4	KC-4	NA-9	None

Footnote: For corresponding starter spring numbers advertised, see page 221.

GENERATOR AND STARTER—Continued

Interchangeable Parts have the same CHILTON NUMBER in Any Column

Car Make and Model	GENERATOR					STARTER	
	Generator Assembly	Armature	Field Coils	Main Brushes	Third Brush	Starter Armature	Starter Drive Spring (Bendix Type) (See Footnote)
Stutz AA..................D. (1926)	K-200	KA-152	KB-9	KC-13	KD-12	NA-109	None
Stutz AA..................D. (1927)	K-201	KA-11	KB-9	KC-11	KD-10	NA-109	None
Stutz BB...............D.-R. (1928)	K-202	KA-154	KB-9	KC-5	KD-4	NA-57	None
Stutz M................D.-R. (1929)	K-202	KA-154	KB-9	KC-5	KD-4	NA-110	None
Stutz Series M.........D.-R. (1930)	K-202	KA-154	KB-9	KC-5	KD-4	NA-110	None
Velie 60..................R. (1925)	K-204	KA-3	KB-3	KC-3	KC-3	NA-3	NE-2R
Velie 60..................R. (1926)	K-205	KA-155	KB-4	KC-3	KC-3	NA-3	NE-2R
Velie Std. 50.........A.-L. (1927)	K-226	KA-156	KB-1	KC-1	KD-1	NA-111	NE-2R
Velie Spec. 60........D.-R. (1927)	K-205	KA-155	KB-3	KC-3	KC-3	NA-3	NE-2R
Velie Std. 50.........A.-L. (1928)	K-226	KA-156	KB-1	KC-1	KD-1	NA-111	NE-2R
Velie 6-66............A.-L. (1928)	K-207	KA-156	KB-1	KC-1	KD-1	NA-111	NE-2R
Velie 6-77............D.-R. (1928)	K-226	KA-156	KB-1	KC-1	KD-1	NA-111	NE-2R
Velie 8-88............D.-R. (1928)	K-9	KA-7	KB-3	KC-3	KC-3	NA-3	NE-2R
Viking................D.-R. (1929)	K-217	KA-26	KB-4	KC-4	KC-4	NA-15	None
Viking................D.-R. (1930)	K-217	KA-26	KB-4	KC-4	KC-4	NA-15	None
Westcott 44..............D. (1925)	K-216	KA-163	KB-9	KC-5	KD-4	NA-20	NE-2R
Westcott 60..............D. (1925)	K-216	KA-163	KB-9	KC-5	KD-4	NA-27	NE-2R
Whippet 96, 4 cyl......A.-L. (1927)	K-160	KA-122	KB-1	KC-1	KD-1	NA-41	NE-4L
Whippet 93-A, 6 cyl....A.-L. (1927)	K-161 K-162	KA-121 KA-124	KB-1	KC-1	KD-1	NA-41	NE-4L
Whippet 96, 4 cyl......A.-L. (1928)	K-220 K-163	KA-123 KA-124	KB-1	KC-1	KD-1	NA-41	NE-4L
Whippet 98, 6 cyl......A.-L. (1928)	K-161 K-166	KA-121 KA-125	KB-1	KC-1	KD-1	NA-86 NA-112	NE-4L
Whippet 96-A .........A.-L. (1929)	K-163	KA-123	KB-1	KC-18	KD-17	NA-41	NE-4L
Whippet 98-A .........A.-L. (1929)	K-166	KA-125	KB-1	KC-18	KD-17	NA-112	NE-4L
Wills Ste. Claire, 8 cyl........B. (1925)	K-212	KA-160	KB-9	KC-27	KD-8	NA-54	None
Willl Ste. Claire, 6 cyl........B. (1925)	K-213	KA-161	KB-9	KC-5	KD-4	NA-64	None
Wills Ste. Claire W6.........D. (1926)	K-213	KA-161	KB-9	KC-5	KD-10	NA-64	None
Wills Ste. Claire, 8 cyl.......D. (1926)	K-212	KA-160	KB-9	KC-27	KD-8	NA-54	None
Willys Knight 66........A.-L. (1925)	K-208	KA-157	KB-1	KC-1	KD-1	NA-113	NE-2R
Willys Knight 65........A.-L. (1925)	K-208	KA-157	KB-1	KC-1	KD-1	NA-113	NE-2R
Willys Knight 66........A.-L. (1926)	K-209 K-211	KA-158	KB-1	KC-1	KD-1	NA-113	NE-2R
Willys Knight 70........A.-L. (1926)	K-221	KA-65	KB-1	KC-1	KD-1	NA-113	NE-5L
Willys Knight 66-A.......A.-L. (1927)	K-211 K-221	KA-158 KA-65	KB-1	KC-1	KD-1	NA-107	NE-2R
Willys Knight 70-A........A.-L. (1927)			KB-1	KC-1	KD-1	NA-107	NE-5L
Willys Knight 70-A.........A.-L. (1928)	K-83	KA-69	KB-1	KC-1	KD-1	NA-107	NE-5L
Willys Knight 66-A........A.-L. (1928)	K-211 K-231	KA-158	KB-1	KC-1	KD-1	NA-107	NE-2R
Willys Knight Std. 6-56......A.-L. (1928)	K-83	KA-69	KB-1	KC-18	KD-17	NA-107	NE-5L
Willys Knight Special 70A...A.-L. (1929)	K-83	KA-69	KB-1	KC-18	KD-17	NA-107	NE-5L
Willys Knight 66-B........A.-L. (1929)	K-231	KA-158	KB-1	KC-1	KD-1	NA-43	NE-2R
Willys Knight 6-56.......A.-L. (1929)	K-83	KA-69	KB-1	KC-18	KD-17	NA-107	NE-5L
Willys Knight 70-B.......A.-L. (1929)	K-83	KA-69	KB-1	KC-18	KD-17	NA-107	NE-5L
Willys Knight 70B........A.-L. (1930)	K-83	KA-69	KB-1	KC-34	KD-31	NA-107	NE-5L
Willys Knight 66B........A.-L. (1930)	K-231	KA-158	KB-1	KC-12	KD-11	NA-43	NE-5L
Willys Knight 87.........A.-L. (1930)	K-83	KA-69	KB-1	KC-34	KD-31	NA-107	NE-5L
Willys 6-98B.........A.-L. (1930)	K-240	KA-125	KB-1	KC-34	KD-31	NA-111	NE-2R
Willys 8.............A.-L. (1930)	....	....	....	....	....	NA-115	....

*Beginning with engine No. 23222.
†Spring NE-1R used beginning with engine No. 306444-K.

‡Beginning with engine No. L-1208-80.
§Spring NE-5L used after October, 1928.
¶Spring NE-1R used beginning with engine No. E-10700.

Footnote: For corresponding starter spring numbers advertised, see page 221.

INTERCHANGEABLE COUNT

Showing exact number of times each CHILTON NUMBER occurs in Generator and Starter Table, beginning Page 219.

Generator Assembly								
	K-33-1	K-71-2	K-105-1	K-138-1	K-170-1	K-208-1	K-244-1	KA-28-8
	K-34-1	K-72-2	K-106-4	K-139-3	K-171-2	K-209-1	K-245-1	KA-29-2
	K-35-6	K-73-4	K-107-2	K-140-2	K-172-2	K-211-3	K-246-1	KA-30-2
K-1-1	K-36-4	K-74-1	K-108-1	K-141-4	K-174-1	K-212-2	K-247-2	KA-31-4
K-4-1	K-37-2	K-75-1	K-109-1	K-142-3	K-175-4	K-213-2		KA-32-5
K-5-8	K-38-2	K-76-1	K-110-2	K-143-2	K-176-1	K-214-1	Armature	KA-33-10
K-6-3	K-39-2	K-77-1	K-111-1	K-144-1	K-177-3	K-215-2		KA-34-1
K-7-3	K-40-2	K-78-3	K-112-2	K-145-1	K-180-1	K-216-2	KA-1-2	KA-35-2
K-8-1	K-41-1	K-79-2	K-113-3	K-146-1	K-181-2	K-217-2	KA-3-7	KA-36-2
K-9-10	K-42-1	K-80-1	K-114-2	K-147-1	K-182-2	K-218-3	KA-4-6	KA-40-1
K-10-2	K-43-4	K-81-1	K-115-1	K-148-1	K-183-2	K-219-3	KA-5-4	KA-41-9
K-11-6	K-44-3	K-82-1	K-116-3	K-149-1	K-184-3	K-220-1	KA-6-1	KA-42-3
K-12-16	K-45-4	K-83-8	K-117-1	K-150-1	K-186-2	K-221-2	KA-7-21	KA-43-2
K-13-1	K-46-2	K-84-1	K-118-3	K-151-1	K-187-5	K-222-1	KA-8-6	KA-44-8
K-14-13	K-47-2	K-85-1	K-119-3	K-152-2	K-188-2	K-223-1	KA-9-27	KA-45-6
K-15-2	K-48-1	K-86-2	K-120-4	K-153-2	K-189-3	K-224-1	KA-11-3	KA-46-1
K-16-5	K-52-1	K-87-2	K-121-2	K-154-2	K-190-9	K-226-3	KA-12-2	KA-47-2
K-18-2	K-53-9	K-88-2	K-122-1	K-155-1	K-191-2	K-227-2	KA-13-2	KA-48-2
K-19-1	K-54-4	K-89-3	K-123-2	K-156-2	K-192-6	K-228-1	KA-14-4	KA-51-6
K-20-1	K-55-3	K-90-1	K-124-3	K-157-1	K-193-3	K-229-1	KA-15-2	KA-54-1
K-21-4	K-56-1	K-91-2	K-125-1	K-158-3	K-195-7	K-230-1	KA-16-4	KA-55-1
K-22-1	K-57-2	K-92-3	K-126-12	K-159-2	K-196-2	K-231-3	KA-17-2	KA-56-5
K-23-2	K-58-1	K-93-1	K-127-4	K-160-2	K-197-6	K-232-1	KA-18-2	KA-57-7
K-24-4	K-59-1	K-94-2	K-128-8	K-161-2	K-198-3	K-233-2	KA-19-7	KA-58-2
K-25-1	K-60-1	K-95-1	K-129-3	K-162-1	K-200-1	K-235-1	KA-20-1	KA-59-3
K-26-2	K-61-5	K-96-1	K-130-4	K-163-2	K-201-3	K-236-1	KA-21-3	KA-60-1
K-27-4	K-65-1	K-97-1	K-131-4	K-164-6	K-202-3	K-237-1	KA-22-1	KA-61-1
K-28-1	K-66-1	K-98-3	K-132-8	K-165-2	K-203-1	K-238-1	KA-23-4	KA-62-1
K-29-3	K-67-1	K-99-1	K-133-2	K-166-3	K-204-1	K-239-1	KA-24-4	KA-63-3
K-30-2	K-68-1	K-100-3	K-134-6	K-167-4	K-205-2	K-240-1	KA-25-1	KA-64-6
K-31-4	K-69-2	K-101-4	K-135-8	K-168-1	K-206-2	K-241-1	KA-26-24	KA-65-3
K-32-2	K-70-3	K-104-1	K-137-4	K-169-2	K-207-1	K-242-2	KA-27-2	KA-66-2

GENERATOR AND STARTER—Continued

INTERCHANGEABLE COUNT—Continued

Showing exact number of times each CHILTON NUMBER occurs in Generator and Starter Table, beginning Page 219.

KA-67-3	KA-110-3	KA-152-1	KB-11-2	KB-59-1	KD-7-16	NA-14-2	NA-55-1	NA-98-3
KA-68-5	KA-111-2	KA-153-2	KB-12-9	KB-60-2	KD-8-8	NA-15-13	NA-56-1	NA-99-3
KA-69-8	KA-112-1	KA-154-3	KB-13-3		KD-10-8	NA-16-4	NA-57-2	NA-100-3
KA-70-3	KA-113-2	KA-155-2	KB-14-4	**Main Brushes**	KD-11-18	NA-18-2	NA-58-3	NA-101-5
KA-71-1	KA-114-2	KA-156-4	KB-15-3		KD-12-8	NA-19-1	NA-60-3	NA-102-2
KA-72-2	KA-115-3	KA-157-2	KB-19-28	KC-1-52	KD-13-1	NA-20-3	NA-61-1	NA-103-2
KA-73-9	KA-116-1	KA-158-5	KB-20-3	KC-3-122	KD-14-1	NA-21-1	NA-62-1	NA-104-2
KA-74-1	KA-117-1	KA-160-2	KB-21-7	KC-4-293	KD-16-1	NA-22-1	NA-63-1	NA-105-1
KA-75-3	KA-118-1	KA-161-2	KB-22-2	KC-5-51	KD-17-26	NA-23-7	NA-64-4	NA-106-1
KA-76-1	KA-119-2	KA-163-2	KB-23-12	KC-6-2	KD-18-22	NA-24-3	NA-65-1	NA-107-11
KA-77-4	KA-120-2	KA-164-2	KB-26-1	KC-7-3	KD-19-14	NA-25-1	NA-67-1	NA-108-6
KA-78-3	KA-121-5	KA-165-3	KB-27-17	KC-8-17	KD-20-3	NA-26-1	NA-68-1	NA-109-2
KA-79-3	KA-122-2	KA-166-2	KB-28-1	KC-9-3	KD-21-1	NA-27-15	NA-69-3	NA-110-2
KA-80-3	KA-123-4	KA-167-1	KB-29-2	KC-11-7	KD-22-10	NA-28-1	NA-70-1	NA-111-5
KA-83-1	KA-124-2	KA-168-2	KB-30-11	KC-12-19	KD-23-6	NA-29-1	NA-72-1	NA-112-2
KA-84-1	KA-125-3	KA-169-1	KB-31-7	KC-13-8	KD-25-10	NA-30-3	NA-73-6	NA-113-4
KA-85-4	KA-126-2	KA-171-2	KB-32-7	KC-14-1	KD-26-4	NA-31-6	NA-74-4	NA-115-1
KA-86-2	KA-127-2	KA-172-1	KB-33-6	KC-17-4	KD-27-2	NA-32-8	NA-75-3	
KA-87-1	KA-128-1	KA-173-3	KB-34-4	KC-18-29	KD-30-4	NA-33-2	NA-76-2	**Starter Drive Spring (Bendix Type)**
KA-88-2	KA-129-2	KA-174-1	KB-35-4	KC-19-29	KD-31-11	NA-34-3	NA-77-11	
KA-89-3	KA-130-1	KA-176-2	KB-36-17	KC-20-20	KD-32-1	NA-35-4	NA-78-4	NE-4L-48
KA-90-1	KA-131-2	KA-178-1	KB-37-12	KC-21-3	KD-33-5	NA-36-1	NA-79-3	NE-5L-58
KA-91-2	KA-132-1	KA-179-1	KB-38-1	KC-23-12	KD-34-4	NA-37-1	NA-80-2	NE-6L-1
KA-92-3	KA-133-1	KA-180-1	KB-39-1	KC-24-6	KD-35-1	NA-38-1	NA-81-2	NE-7L-4
KA-93-4	KA-134-4	KA-181-1	KB-40-1	KC-26-10	KD-36-4	NA-39-3	NA-82-1	
KA-94-3	KA-135-1	KA-182-2	KB-41-9	KC-27-7		NA-40-2	NA-83-9	NE-1R-30
KA-95-4	KA-136-2	KA-183-1	KB-42-7	KC-28-4	**Starter Armature**	NA-41-5	NA-84-3	NE-2R-233
KA-96-3	KA-137-1	KA-185-2	KB-43-3	KC-29-2		NA-42-5	NA-85-2	NE-4R-3
KA-97-4	KA-138-2		KB-44-2	KC-33-7	NA-1-3	NA-43-5	NA-86-3	
KA-98-3	KA-140-2	**Field Coils**	KB-46-1	KC-34-14	NA-2-11	NA-44-4	NA-87-1	NE-8-1
KA-99-12	KA-141-5		KB-47-1	KC-35-2	NA-3-88	NA-45-6	NA-88-1	NE-9-1
KA-100-2	KA-142-4	KB-1-66	KB-49-1	KC-36-1	NA-4-8	NA-46-1	NA-89-2	NE-10-1
KA-102-4	KA-143-1	KB-2-3	KB-50-2	KC-38-3	NA-5-7	NA-47-1	NA-90-2	NE-12-1
KA-103-3	KA-144-9	KB-3-30	KB-51-1		NA-6-9	NA-48-3	NA-91-1	NE-13-1
KA-104-1	KA-145-6	KB-4-143	KB-53-3	**Third Brush**	NA-7-2	NA-49-4	NA-92-2	NE-14-1
KA-105-4	KA-146-3	KB-6-36	KB-54-3		NA-8-1	NA-50-1	NA-93-2	NE-15-1
KA-106-4	KA-148-7	KB-7-1	KB-55-2	KD-1-48	NA-9-65	NA-51-3	NA-94-1	NE-16-1
KA-107-5	KA-149-2	KB-8-1	KB-56-1	KD-4-61	NA-10-5	NA-52-3	NA-95-2	NE-17-1
KA-108-1	KA-150-1	KB-9-52	KB-57-2	KD-5-1	NA-11-4	NA-53-3	NA-96-1	
KA-109-2	KA-151-12	KB-10-1	KB-58-4	KD-6-2		NA-54-12	NA-97-4	

IGNITION SYSTEM

HOW TO USE THIS TABLE

1. Locate in the first column the car and model for which the part is needed.

2. Follow this line across to column pertaining to that part.

3. In this part column opposite your car model you will find the Chilton Number for the part you want.

4. Look up and down the part column for the same Chilton Number. Wherever you find this same number in the same column you have an interchangeable part. The car make opposite tells you where to get it—probably from a local repair shop or nearby jobber.

5. At the end of this table, pages 234, 235, you will find a count showing the number of times any part number appears in this table. Example: IB-1 under Contact Screw opposite Ajax (1925-26) in this table will appear again in the count at the end of the table followed by the figure 27 under the heading Contact Screw. This indicates part number IB-1 appears 27 times in this table.

Example: Suppose a distributor cap is needed for a (1928) Chevrolet AB car. Locate this car in the first column. Follow this line across to the column on Distributor Cap, which is the fourth column. Here you see the CHILTON NUMBER for the part is IC-24. Checking through the CHILTON NUMBERS in this same column, you will find that the number IC-24 opposite the Chrysler 50 (1927) and the Chrysler 52 (1928). The distributor cap used on these cars is interchangeable with the one in your Chevrolet car.

Interchangeable Parts have the same CHILTON NUMBER in Any Column

Car Make and Model	Contact or Breaker Arm	Contact Screw	Distributor Cap	Distributor Rotor	Coil	Automatic Advance Spring	Condenser	Distributor Shaft Gear or Coupling
Ajax.....................A.-L. (1925-26)	IA-1	IB-1	IC-1	ID-1	IE-1	IF-92	IG-1	IH-1
Apperson 6.....................R. (1925)	IA-4	IB-4	IC-4	ID-4	IE-2	IF-1	IG-3	IH-4
Apperson Str. 8.................R. (1925)	IA-4	IB-4	IC-5	ID-5	IE-2	IF-2	None	IH-8
Apperson 6.....................R. (1926)	IA-4	IB-4	IC-4	ID-4	IE-2	IF-3	IG-3	III-4
Apperson Str. 8.................R. (1926)	IA-4	IB-4	IC-5	ID-5	IE-2	IF-2	None	IH-8
Auburn 4.......................R. (1925)	IA-5	IB-5	IC-6	ID-6	IE-2	None	None	IH-8
Auburn 6-43....................R. (1925)	IA-5	IB-5	IC-7	ID-6	IE-2	None	None	IH-6
Auburn 8-88....................R. (1925)	IA-4	IB-4	IC-5	ID-5	IE-2	IF-2	None	IH-8
Auburn 8-88....................R. (1926)	IA-4	IB-4	IC-5	ID-5	IE-2	IF-2	None	IH-8
Auburn 4-44.................R. (1926-27)	IA-5	IB-5	IC-6	ID-6	IE-2	None	None	IH-8
Auburn 6-66.................R. (1926-27)	IA-4	IB-4	IC-9	ID-7	IE-3	IF-3	IG-3	IH-8
Auburn 6-66 A..................R. (1927)	IA-6	IB-6	IC-9	ID-8	IE-3	IF-4	IG-6	IH-6
Auburn 8-88.................R. (1927-28)	*IA-4	IB-7U. IB-31L.	IC-5	ID-5	IE-4	IF-5	None	IH-8
Auburn 8-77.................R. (1927-28)	*IA-4	IB-7U. IB-31L.	IC-5	ID-9	IE-3	IF-5	IG-7	IH-8
Auburn 76...................D.-R. (1928-29)	IA-4	IB-8	IC-10	ID-10	IE-4	IF-6	IG-8	IH-8
Auburn 88...................D.-R. (1928-29)	*IA-4	IB-7U IB-31L.	IC-2	ID-9	IE-4	IF-6 IF-7	IG-4	IH-8
Auburn 115..................D.-R. (1928-29)	*IA-4	IB-7U. IB-31L.	IC-2	ID-5	IE-4	IF-6 IF-7	IG-4	IH-8
Auburn 6-80.................D.-R. (1929)	IA-4	IB-8	IC-10	ID-10	IE-4	IF-6	IG-8	IH-8
Auburn 8-90.................D.-R. (1929)	*IA-4	IB-7U. IB-31L	IC-2	ID-9	IE-4	IF-8	IG-4	IH-8
Auburn 120..................D.-R. (1929)	*IA-4	IB-7U. IB-31L.	IC-2	ID-5	IE-4	IF-9 IF-10	IG-4	IH-8
Auburn 6-85.................D.-R. (1930)	*IA-4	*IB-8	IC-10	ID-10	IE-4	IF-6	IG-8	IH-8
Auburn 8-95.................D.-R. (1930)	*IA-4	IB-7U. IB-31L.	IC-2	ID-9	IE-4	IF-8	IG-4	IH-8
Auburn 8-125................D.-R. (1930)	*IA-4	IB-7U. IB-31L.	IC-2	ID-5	IE-4	IF-10 IF-9	IG-4	IH-8
Auburn 8-98.................D.-R. (1931)	*IA-4	IB-3 IB-32	IC-3	ID-80	IE-4	IF-10	IG-4	IH-8
Blackhawk L6............D.-R. (1929-30)	IA-4	†IB-10	IC-13	ID-12	IE-4	IF-12 IF-13	IG-10	IH-7
Blackhawk L8............D.-R. (1929-30)	*IA-4	IB-7U. IB-31L.	IC-5	ID-5	IE-4	IF-14	IG-7	IH-10
Buick Master.................D.-R. (1925)	IA-8	IB-10	IC-14	ID-13	IE-4	IF-15	IG-11	IH-11
Buick Std.....................D.-R. (1925)	IA-8	IB-10	IC-14	ID-13	IE-4	IF-15	IG-11	IH-11
Buick Master.................D.-R. (1926)	IA-8	IB-10	IC-14	ID-13	IE-3	IF-16 IF-17	IG-11	IH-12
Buick Std.....................D.-R. (1926)	IA-8	IB-10	IC-14	ID-13	IE-3	IF-16 IF-17	IG-11	IH-12
Buick 115.....................D.-R. (1927)	IA-8	IB-10	IC-14	ID-13	IE-3	IF-16 IF-17	IG-11	IH-12
Buick 120, 128...............D.-R. (1927)	IA-8	IB-10	IC-14	ID-13	IE-3	IF-16 IF-17	IG-11	IH-12
Buick 115.....................D.-R. (1928)	IA-4	IB-8	IC-15	ID-10	IE-3	IF-6 IF-18	IG-8	IH-13
Buick 120-128................D.-R. (1928)	IA-4	IB-8	IC-15	ID-10	IE-3	IF-6 IF-18	IG-8	IH-13
Buick 116.....................D.-R. (1929)	IA-4	IB-8	IC-16	ID-10	IE-4	IF-19	IG-8	IH-13
Buick 121, 129...............D.-R. (1929)	IA-4	IB-8	IC-16	ID-10	IE-4	IF-19	IG-8	IH-13
Buick Series 40..............D.-R. (1930)	IA-4	IB-8	IC-16	ID-10	IE-4	IF-19	IG-8	IH-13
Buick Series 50 and 60.......D.-R. (1930)	*IA-4	IB-7U. IB-32L.	IC-16	ID-10	IE-4	IF-20 IF-21	IG-56	IH-13
Buick 8-50....................D.-R. (1931)	*IA-4	IB-3 IB-32	IC-12	ID-80	IE-4	IF-19	IG-56	IH-2
Buick 8-60....................D.-R. (1931)	*IA-4	IB-3 IB-32	IC-12	ID-80	IE-4	IF-19	IG-56	IH-2
Buick 8-80....................D.-R. (1931)	*IA-4	IB-3 IB-32	IC-12	ID-80	IE-4	IF-19	IG-56	IH-3
Buick 8-90....................D.-R. (1931)	*IA-4	IB-3 IB-32	IC-12	ID-80	IE-4	IF-19	IG-56	IH-3
Cadillac V-63..................D. (1925)	*IA-9	*IB-10	IC-17	ID-14	IE-9	None	IG-62	IH-14
Cadillac 314...................D. (1926)	*IA-10	*IB-10	IC-17	ID-14	IE-9	IF-24	IG-10	IH-14
Cadillac 314.................D.-R. (1927)	*IA-10	*IB-10	IC-18	ID-15	IE-9	IF-24	IG-10	IH-7
Cadillac 341A................D.-R. (1928)	*IA-10	*IB-2	IC-18	ID-15	IE-9	IF-25	IG-64	IH-7
Cadillac 341B................D.-R. (1929)	*IA-10	*IB-2	IC-18	ID-15	IE-9	IF-12 IF-26	IG-64	IH-7
Cadillac 353.................D.-R. (1930)	*IA-4	IB-7U. IB-31L.	IC-96	ID-15	IE-5	IF-24	IG-10 IG-57	IH-7
Cadillac 452.................D.-R. (1930)	*IA-4	IB-33U. IB-34L.	IC-97	ID-83	*IE-8	IF-27	IG-58	IH-8
Cadillac 355.................D.-R. (1931)	*IA-4	IB-7 IB-31	IC-96	ID-15	IE-5	IF-24	IG-57	IH-7
Cadillac 370.................D.-R. (1931)	*IA-4	IB-33 IB-34	IC-34	ID-44	*IE-8	IF-28	IG-58	IH-8
Cadillac 452.................D.-R. (1931)	*IA-4	IB-33 IB-34	IC-97	ID-51	*IE-8	IF-27	IG-58	IH-8

IGNITION SYSTEM—Continued

Interchangeable Parts have the same CHILTON NUMBER in Any Column

Car Make and Model	Contact or Breaker Arm	Contact Screw	Distributor Cap	Distributor Rotor	Coil	Automatic Advance Spring	Condenser	Distributor Shaft Gear or Coupling
Case JIC.................D.-R. (1925)	IA-8	IB-10	IC-19	ID-16	IE-12	IF-29	IG-9	IH-16
Case X..................D.-R. (1925)	IA-8	IB-10	IC-19	ID-16	IE-12	IF-29	IG-9	IH-16
Case Y..................D.-R. (1925)	IA-11	IB-10	IC-19	ID-16	IE-2	IF-30	IG-9	IH-17
Case JIC.................D.-R. (1926)	IA-8	IB-10	IC-19	ID-16	IE-12	IF-29	IG-9	IH-16
Case Y..................D.-R. (1926)	IA-11	IB-10	IC-19	ID-16	IE-2	IF-30	IG-9	IH-17
Chandler 33................B. (1925)	IA-12	IB-11	IC-22	ID-17	IE-11	IF-91	IG-13	IH-18
Chandler 35................B. (1926)	IA-12	IB-12	IC-22	ID-17	IE-11	IF-91	IG-13	IH-19
Chandler Big 6.........D.-R. (1927)	IA-6	IB-6	IC-9	ID-11	IE-4	IF-4	IG-6	IH-5
Chandler Royal 8...........R. (1927)	*IA-4	{IB-7U. IB-31L}	IC-5	ID-5	IE-4	IF-31	IG-7	IH-20
Chandler Spec. 6.........D.-R. (1927)	IA-6	IB-6	IC-9	ID-8	IE-4	IF-4	IG-6	IH-21
Chandler Std. 6.........D.-R. (1927)	IA-6	IB-6	IC-9	ID-8	IE-4	{IF-32 IF-33}	{IG-6 IG-4}	IH-22
Chandler Big 6.............R. (1928)	IA-4	IB-6	IC-9	ID-8	IE-4	{IF-33 IF-34}	{IG-4 IG-8}	IH-5
Chandler Royal 8.........D.-R. (1928)	*IA-4	{IB-7U. IB-31L.}	IC-5	ID-5	IE-4	{IF-31 IF-35}	IG-4	IH-20
Chandler Spec. 6.........A.-L. (1928)	IA-13	IB-12	IC-20	ID-18	IE-1	IF-11	IG-14	IH-15
Chandler Spec. In. 6.......A.-L. (1928)	IA-13	IB-12	IC-20	ID-3	IE-1	IF-11	IG-14	IH-15
Chevrolet K...............R. (1925)	IA-5	IB-5	IC-6	ID-6	IE-2	None	None	IH-23
Chevrolet V...............R. (1926)	IA-5	IB-5	IC-6	ID-6	IE-2	None	None	IH-24
Chevrolet AA..............R. (1927)	IA-5	IB-5	IC-6	ID-6	IE-2	None	None	IH-24
Chevrolet AB...........D.-R. (1928)	IA-4	IB-6	IC-24	ID-8	IE-2	IF-36	None	IH-29
Chevrolet AC..............R. (1929)	IA-4	IB-6	IC-9	ID-8	IE-4	IF-27	IG-16	IH-30
Chevrolet 6............D.-R. (1930)	IA-4	IB-6	IC-9	ID-8	IE-4	IF-27	IG-16	IH-30
Chevrolet AE...........D.-R. (1931)	IA-4	IB-6	IC-9	ID-8	IE-4	IF-27	IG-16	IH-30
Chrysler 6B...............R. (1925)	IA-4	IB-4	IC-7	ID-7	IE-15	IF-37	{IG-3 IG-6}	IH-8
Chrysler 58........R. (Early 1926)	IA-4	IB-4	IC-25	ID-7	IE-2	IF-38	IG-3	IH-26
Chrysler 70...............R. (1926)	IA-4	IB-4	IC-10	ID-7	IE-2	IF-37	IG-6	IH-8
Chrysler 80...............R. (1926)	IA-4	IB-4	IC-10	ID-7	IE-6	{IF-39 IF-40}	IG-6	IH-8
Chrysler 50...............R. (1927)	IA-6	IB-6	IC-24	ID-8	IE-6	{IF-41 IF-42}	IG-6	IH-26
Chrysler 60...............R. (1927)	IA-6	IB-6	IC-9	ID-8	IE-6	{IF-42 IF-43}	IG-6	IH-8
Chrysler 70...............R. (1927)	*IA-4	{IB-7U. IB-32L.}	IC-10	ID-10	IE-2	{IF-44 IF-45}	IG-6	IH-8
Chrysler 80...............R. (1927)	*IA-4	{IB-7U. IB-32L.}	IC-10	ID-10	IE-15	IF-14	IG-6	IH-8
Chrysler 52.............D.-R. (1928)	IA-4	IB-6	IC-24	ID-8	IE-15	IF-42	IG-6	IH-26
Chrysler 62.............D.-R. (1928)	IA-4	IB-6	IC-9	ID-8	IE-15	IF-43	{IG-6 IG-6}	IH-8
Chrysler 72.............D.-R. (1928)	IA-4	{IB-7U. IB-32L.}	IC-10	ID-10	IE-15	IF-45	IG-6	IH-8
Chrysler Imp. 80.........D.-R. (1928)	*IA-4	{IB-7U. IB-32L.}	IC-10	ID-10	IE-6	IF-45	IG-6	IH-8
Chrysler 65.............D.-R. (1929)	IA-4	IB-6	IC-9	ID-8	IE-7	IF-43	IG-4	IH-25
Chrysler 75.............D.-R. (1929)	*IA-4	{IB-7U. IB-32L.}	IC-10	ID-10	IE-6	IF-45	IG-6	IH-8
Chrysler Imp. 80.........D.-R. (1929)	*IA-4	{IB-7U. IB-32L.}	IC-10	ID-10	IE-6	IF-45	IG-6	IH-8
Chrysler 6.............D.-R. (1930)	IA-4	IB-6	IC-11	ID-8	IE-10	IF-43	IG-7	IH-31
Chrysler 6.............N.-E. (1930)	IA-14	IB-14	IC-28	ID-81	IE-10	N.S.	IG-19	IH-25
Chrysler 66.............D.-R. (1930)	IA-4	IB-6	IC-9	ID-8	IE-7	IF-46	IG-7	IH-25
Chrysler 70.............D.-R. (1930)	IA-4	IB-6	IC-9	ID-8	IE-7	IF-46	IG-7	IH-25
Chrysler 77.............D.-R. (1930)	*IA-4	{IB-7U. IB-32L.}	IC-10	ID-10	IE-6	IF-21	IG-6	IH-8
Chrysler 6.............D.-R. (1931)	IA-4	IB-6	IC-11	ID-8	IE-13	IF-43	IG-7	IH-31
Chrysler 8.............D.-R. (1931)	*IA-4	{IB-3 IB-32}	IC-12	ID-80	IE-13	IF-14	IG-7	IH-32
Chrysler Imp. 8.........D.-R. (1931)	*IA-4	{IB-3 IB-32}	IC-97	ID-80	IE-13	IF-45	IG-65	IH-8
Cleveland 31................B. (1925)	IA-12	IB-12	IC-22	ID-17	IE-4	IF-91	IG-66	IH-21
Cleveland 43................B. (1925)	IA-12	IB-12	IC-22	ID-17	IE-12	IF-91	IG-13	IH-22
Cleveland 31................B. (1926)	IA-12	IB-12	IC-22	ID-17	IE-4	IF-91	IG-66	IH-21
Cleveland 43................B. (1926)	IA-12	IB-12	IC-22	ID-17	IE-12	IF-91	IG-13	IH-22
Cord L-29.............D.-R. (1929)	*IA-4	{IB-7U. IB-31L.}	IC-5	ID-9	IE-16	IF-8	IG-7	IH-8
Cord L-29.............D.-R. (1930)	IA-4	{IB-7U. IB-31L.}	IC-5	ID-9	IE-16	IF-8	IG-7	IH-8
Cord L-29.............D.-R. (1931)	IA-4	{IB-7 IB-31}	IC-5	ID-9	IE-16	IF-8	IG-7	IH-8
Davis 90................D. (1925)	IA-8	IB-10	IC-27	ID-19	IE-14	IF-29	IG-18	IH-33
Davis 91................D. (1925)	IA-8	IB-10	IC-27	ID-19	IE-14	IF-25	IG-18	IH-27
Davis 92................D. (1926)	IA-8	IB-10	IC-27	ID-19	IE-14	IF-25	IG-18	IH-39
Davis 93................D. (1926)	IA-8	IB-10	IC-27	ID-19	IE-14	IF-25	IG-18	IH-39
Davis 92................D. (1927)	IA-8	IB-10	IC-27	ID-19	IE-14	IF-25	IG-18	IH-39
Davis 94.............D.-R. (1927)	IA-6	IB-6	IC-9	ID-11	IE-3	IF-4	IG-6	IH-33
Davis 98.............D.-R. (1927)	IA-6	{IB-7U. IB-31L.}	IC-5	ID-5	IE-3	IF-31	IG-7	IH-20
Davis 99.............D.-R. (1928)	*IA-4	{IB-7U. IB-31L.}	IC-5	ID-5	IE-3	IF-14	IG-7	IH-20
De Soto 6..........D.-R. (1928-29)	IA-4	IB-6	IC-9	ID-11	IE-6	IF-50	IG-4	IH-25
De Soto 6..........N.-E. (1929-30)	IA-14	IB-14	IC-28	ID-20	IE-17	N.S.	IG-19	IH-25
De Soto 6.............D.-R. (1930)	IA-4	IB-6	IC-11	ID-8	IE-10	IF-43	IG-7	IH-25
De Soto 8.............D.-R. (1930)	*IA-4	{IB-3U. IB-32L.}	IC-98	ID-80	IE-18	IF-51	IG-7	IH-32
De Soto 76 Finer.........D.-R. (1931)	IA-4	IB-6U	IC-11	ID-8	IE-13	IF-33	IG-7	IH-25
De Soto 8.............D.-R. (1931)	*IA-4	{IB-3L IB-32}	IC-12	ID-80	IE-18	{IF-51 IF-50}	IG-7	IH-32
Diana Str. 8................D. (1926)	IA-8	IB-10	IC-98	ID-2	IE-20	IF-26	IG-10	IH-39
Diana Str. 8................D. (1927)	IA-10	IB-10	IC-99	ID-2	IE-20	{IF-24 IF-55}	IG-10	IH-39
Diana Str 8................D. (1928)	IA-10	IB-10	IC-99	ID-2	IE-20	IF-24	IG-10	IH-39
Dodge Brothers 4........N.-E. (1925)	IA-15	IB-15	IC-29	ID-21	IE-21	{IF-108 IF-109}	IG-20	IH-35
Dodge Brothers 4..........N.-E. (1926)	IA-16	IB-15	IC-30	ID-22	IE-22	‡IF-108	IG-21	IH-35
Dodge Brothers 4.........N.-E. (1927-28)	IA-16	IB-15	IC-30	ID-22	IE-22	IF-111	IG-21	IH-35
Dodge Brothers Senior....N.-E. (1928)	IA-16	IB-15	IC-31	ID-22	IE-23	IF-113	IG-21	IH-36
Dodge Brothers Std. 6...N.-E. (1928)	IA-14	IB-14	IC-32	ID-23	IE-23	N. S.	IG-19	IH-37
Dodge Brothers Victory 6...N.-E. (1928-29)	IA-14	IB-14	IC-32	ID-23	IE-23	N. S.	IG-19	IH-37
Dodge Brothers Senior....N.-E. (1929-30)	IA-16	IB-15	IC-31	ID-22	IE-23	IF-113	IG-21	IH-34
Dodge Brothers DA 6....N.-E. (1929-30)	IA-14	IB-14	IC-32	ID-23	IE-24	None	IG-19	IH-36
Dodge Brothers 8 Cyl......D.-R. (1930)	*IA-4	{IB-3U. IB-32L.}	IC-12	ID-80	IE-18	IF-50	IG-7	IH-32

IGNITION SYSTEM—Continued

Interchangeable Parts have the same CHILTON NUMBER in Any Column

Car Make and Model	Contact or Breaker Arm	Contact Screw	Distributor Cap	Distributor Rotor	Coil	Automatic Advance Spring	Condenser	Distributor Shaft Gear or Coupling
Dodge Brothers DD..........N.-E. (1930)	IA-14	IB-14	IC-11	ID-81	IE-19	IF-43	IG-19	IH-25
Dodge Brothers 6............D.-R. (1931)	IA-4	IB-6	IC-11	ID-8	IE-25	IF-33	IG-7	IH-25
Dodge Brothers 8............D.-R. (1931)	*IA-4	IB-3U IB-32L	IC-12	ID-80	IE-25	IF-14	IG-7	IH-32
Durant A-22...............A.-L. (1925)	IA-18	IB-1	IC-36	ID-27	IE-28	N. S.	IG-24	IH-23
Durant 55.................A.-L. (1928)	IA-13	IB-12	IC-33	ID-18	IE-29	N. S.	IG-25	IH-43
Durant 4..................A.-L. (1928)	IA-13	IB-12	IC-21	ID-18	IE-29	IF-11	IG-25 IG-26	IH-44
Durant 65.................A.-L. (1928)	IA-13	IB-12	IC-33	ID-18	IE-29	IF-22 IF-23	IG-14 IG-26	IH-43
Durant 75.............A.-L. (1928-29)	IA-13	IB-12	IC-33	ID-18	IE-29	IF-47	IG-26	IH-44
Durant 4-40..............A.-L. (1929)	IA-13	IB-12	IC-21	ID-18	IE-29	IF-47	IG-26	IH-44
Durant 6-60..............A.-L. (1929)	IA-13	IB-12	IC-33	ID-18	IE-29	IF-22 IF-48	IG-26	IH-43
Durant 66................A.-L. (1929)	IA-13	IB-12	IC-33	ID-18	IE-29	IF-23	IG-26	IH-43
Durant 70................A.-L. (1929)	IA-13	IB-12	IC-33	ID-18	IE-29	IF-47	IG-26	IH-44
Durant 63..............A.L. (1929-30)	IA-13	IB-12	IC-33	ID-18	IE-29	IF-22	IG-26	IH-43
Durant 614...............A.-L. (1930)	IA-13	IB-12	IC-33	ID-18	IE-27	IF-48	IG-26	IH-41
Durant 617...............A.-L. (1930)	IA-13	IB-12	IC-33	ID-18	IE-29	IF-47	IG-26	IH-44
Durant 610...............A.-L. (1931)	IA-13	IB-12	IC-80	ID-18	IE-27	IF-62	IG-6	IH-41
Durant 612...............A.-L. (1931)	IA-13	IB-12	IC-33	ID-18	IE-27	IF-48	IG-26	IH-41
Elcar 4-40...............A.-L. (1925)	IA-1	IB-1	IC-23	ID-6	IE-2	None	IG-1	IH-25
Elcar 6-50...............A.-L. (1925)	IA-1	IB-1	IC-37	ID-27	IE-2	None	IG-24	IH-8
Elcar 6-60...............A.-L. (1925)	IA-1	IB-1	IC-1	ID-29	IE-2	None	IG-1	IH-8
Elcar 8-80...................D. (1925)	IA-8	IB-10	IC-39	ID-30	IE-4	IF-55	IG-10	IH-8
Elcar 6-65...................R. (1926)	IA-4	IB-4	IC-7	ID-7	IE-2	IF-3	IG-67	IH-8
Elcar 8-81...................D. (1926)	IA-10	IB-10	IC-5	ID-31	IE-4	IF-55	IG-10	IH-8
Elcar 4-55................R. (1926 27)	IA-5	IB-5	IC-40	ID-6	IE-2	IF-26	IG-18	IH-8
Elcar 6-70..............D.-R. (1927)	IA-4	IB-4	IC-7	ID-7	IE 1	IF-56	IG-67	IH-8
Elcar 8-82..............D.-R. (1927)	*IA-4	IB-7U IB-31L	IC-5	ID-9	IE-4	IF-5	IG-7	IH-8
Elcar 8-90..............D.-R. (1927)	*IA-4	IB-7U IB-31L	IC-5	ID-5	IE-4	IF-5	IG-7	IH-8
Elcar 8-91..............D.-R. (1928)	*IA-4	IB-7U IB-31L	IC-5	ID-5	IE-4	IF-5	IG-7	IH-8
Elcar 8-120.............D.-R. (1928)	*IA-4	IB-7U IB-31L	IC-5	ID-9	IE-4	IF-54	IG-4	IH-8
Elcar 6-70..........D.-R. (1928-29)	IA-4	IB-4	IC-7	ID-7	IE-4	IF-56	IG-67	IH-8
Elcar 8-78..........D.-R. (1928-29)	*IA-4	IB-7U IB-31L	IC-5	ID-9	IE-4	IF-5	IG-7	IH-8
Elcar 8-82.............D.-R. (1928-29)	*IA-4	IB-7U IB-31L	IC-5	ID-9	IE-4	IF-5	IG-7	IH-8
Elcar 120..............D.-R. (1929)	*IA-4	IB-7U IB-31L	IC-5	ID-5	IE-4	IF-54	IG-7	IH-8
Elcar 75...............D.-R. (1929-30)	IA-4	IB-6	IC-9	ID-8	IE-6	IF-42	IG-4	IH-8
Elcar 95, 96...........D.-R. (1929-30)	*IA-4	IB-7U IB-31L	IC-5	ID-9	IE-4	IF-6	IG-4	IH-8
Elcar 130..............D.-R. (1930)	*IA-4	IB-3U IB-32L	IC-75	ID-60	IE-26	IF-21	IG-35	IH-8
Erskine 50.............D.-R. (1927)	IA-6	IB-6	IC-9	ID-8	IE-3	IF-41	IG-6	IH-45
Erskine 6-51...........D.-R. (1928)	IA-4	IB-6	IC-9	ID-8	IE-3	IF-57	IG-7	IH-45
Erskine 52.............D.-R. (1929)	IA-4	IB-6	IC-9	ID-8	IE-30	IF-57	IG-7	IH-45
Erskine 53.............D.-R. (1930)	IA-4	IB-6	IC-9	ID-8	IE-31	IF-33	IG-7	IH-40
Essex 6...................B. (1925)	IA-12	IB-12	IC-22	ID-17	IE-11	IF-91	IG-13	IH-46
Essex 6...................B. (1926)	IA-12	IB-12	IC-22	ID-17	IE-11	IF-91	IG-13	IH-46
Essex Super 6............A.-L. (1927)	IA-12	IB-12	IC-38	ID-32	IE-32	IF-91	IG-26 IG-31	IH-47
Essex Super 6............A.-L. (1928)	IA-13	IB-12	IC-38	ID-32	IE-32	IF-91 IF-65	IG-26 IG-31	IH-47
Essex Challenger .............A.-L. (1929)	IA-13	IB-12	IC-33	ID·18	IE-1	IF-70	IG-26	IH-48
Essex E....................A.-L. (1930)	IA-13	IB-12	IC-33	ID-18	IE-33	IF-70	IG-59	IH-28
Essex.....................A.-L. (1931)	IA-13	IB-12	IC-33	ID-18	IE-34	IF-70	IG-59	IH-28
Falcon Knight 10...........A.-L. (1927)	IA-1	IB-1	IC-1	ID-1	IE-1	IF-74 IF-92	IG-1	IH-49
Falcon Knight 12.........A.-L. (1928-29)	IA-1	IB-12	IC-1	ID-1	IE-1	IF-70	IG-1	IH-49
Flint B-40...........A.-L. (1925-26)	IA-1	IB-1	IC-37	ID-27	IE-35	None	IG-24	IH-44
Flint E-55.................DeJ. (1925)	IA-7	IB-1	IC-26	ID-48	IE-32	None	IG-68	IH-44
Flint B-60............A.-L. (1926)	IA-1	IB-1	IC-1	ID-1	IE-34	IF-47	IG-1	IH-50
Flint E-80............A.-L. (1926)	IA-1	IB-1	IC-1	ID-1	IE-36	None	IG-1	IH-50
Flint Jr.............A.-L. (1926)	IA-1	IB-1	IC-1	ID-1	IE-36	IF-47	IG-1	IH-50
Flint Jr.............A.-L. (1927)	IA-1	IB-1	IC-1	ID-1	IE-32	IF-47	IG-1	IH-50
Flint 60.............A.-L. (1927-28)	IA-1	IB-1	IC-1	ID-1	IE-36	IF-47	IG-1	IH-50
Flint 80.............A.-L. (1927-28)	IA-1	IB-1	IC-1	ID-1	IE-36	None	IG-1	IH-50
Ford T........................(1925)	IA-23	IB-20	IC-42	ID-33	IE-37	None	None	None
Ford T........................(1926)	IA-23	IB-20	IC-42	ID-33	IE-37	None	None	None
Ford T........................(1927)	IA-23	IB-20	IC-42	ID-33	IE-37	None	None	None
Ford A........................(1928)	IA-24	IB-21	IC-43	ID-34	IE-51	None	IG-33	IH-51
Ford A........................(1929)	IA-24	IB-21	IC-43	ID-34	IE-51	None	IG-33	IH-51
Ford A........................(1930)	IA-24	IB-21	IC-43	ID-34	IE-51	None	IG-33	IH-51
Ford A........................(1931)	IA-24	IB-21	IC-43	ID-34	IE-51	None	IG-33	IH-51
Franklin Series 11.............A.-K. (1925)	IA-25	IB-22	IC-44	ID-35	IE-38	None	IG-34	IH-52
Franklin Series 11.............A.-K. (1926)	IA-25	IB-22	IC-44	ID-35	IE-38	None	IG-34	IH-52
Franklin Series 11.............A.-K. (1927)	IA-25	IB-22	IC-44	ID-35	IE-38	None	IG-34	IH-52
Franklin Series 12............N.-E. (1928)	IA-16	IB-15	IC-31	ID-22	IE-39	IF-110 IF-93	IG-21 IG-63	IH-53
Franklin 130.............D.-R. (1929)	IA-4	IB-8	IC-16	ID-10	IE-40	IF-58	IG-8	IH-54
Franklin 135, 137.......D.-R. (1929)	IA-4	IB-8	IC-16	ID-10	IE-40	IF-58	IG-8	IH-54
Franklin 145, 147.......D.-R. (1930)	IA-4	IB-8	IC-16	ID-10	IE-40	IF-6	IG-8	IH-54
Franklin 155, 157.......D.-R. (1931)	IA-4	IB-8	IC-7	ID-10	IE-74	IF-6	IG-8	IH-54
Gardner 6A................R. (1925)	IA-4	IB-4	IC-4	ID-4	IE-2	IF-37	IG-67	IH-8
Gardner 8A................R. (1925)	IA-4	IB-4	IC-5	ID-5	IE-2	IF-2	None	IH-8
Gardner Series 5............R. (1925)	IA-4	IB-4	IC-48	ID-28	IE-2	IF-60	None	IH-8
Gardner 6A................R. (1926)	IA-4	IB-4	IC-4	ID-4	IE-2	IF-3	IG-67	IH-8
Gardner 8A................R. (1926)	IA-4	IB-4	IC-5	ID-5	IE-2	IF-2	None	IH-8
Gardner 80..............D.-R. (1927)	*IA-4	IB-7U IB-31L	IC-5	ID-9	IE-41	IF-5	IG-7	IH-8
Gardner 90..................D.-R. (1927)	*IA-4	IB-7U IB-31L	IC-5	ID-5	IE-41	IF-5	IG-7	IH-8
Gardner 75..................D.-R. (1928)	*IA-4	IB-7U IB-31L	IC-5	ID-9	IE-41	IF-5	IG-7	IH-8
Gardner 85..................D.-R. (1928)	*IA-4	IB-7U IB-31L	IC-5	ID-9	IE-41	IF-5	IG-7	IH-8
Gardner 95..................D.-R. (1928)	*IA-4	IB-7U IB-31L	IC-5	ID-5	IE-41	IF-54 IF-6	IG-7	IH-8
Gardner 120................D.-R. (1929)	*IA-4	IB-7U IB-31L	IC-5	ID-5	IE-42	IF-5	IG-7	IH-8

IGNITION SYSTEM—Continued

Interchangeable Parts have the same CHILTON NUMBER in Any Column

Car Make and Model	Contact or Breaker Arm	Contact Screw	Distributor Cap	Distributor Rotor	Coil	Automatic Advance Spring	Condenser	Distributor Shaft Gear or Coupling
Gardner 125...............D.-R. (1929)	*IA-4	{IB-7U. {IB-31L.	IC-5	ID-5	IE-42	IF-5	IG-7	IH-8
Gardner 130...............D.-R. (1929)	*IA-4	{IB-7U. {IB-31L.	IC-5	ID-5	IE-42	IF-6	IG-7	IH-8
Gardner 136...............D.-R. (1929-30)	IA-4	IB-8	IC-7	ID-10	IE-86	IF-6	IG-8	IH-8
Gardner 140...............D.-R. (1930)	*IA-4	{IB-7U. {IB-31L.	IC-5	ID-9	IE-86	IF-6	IG-69	IH-8
Gardner 150...............D.-R. (1930)	*IA-4	{IB-7U. {IB-31L.	IC-5	ID-5	IE-86	IF-6	IG-7	IH-8
Graham Paige 610.........N.-E. (1928-29)	IA-14	IB-14	IC-32	ID-23	IE-43	IF-114	IG-19	IH-55
Graham Paige 614.........N.-E. (1928)	IA-14	IB-14	IC-32	ID-23	IE-44	IF-79	IG-19	IH-55
Graham Paige 619.........N.-E. (1928)	IA-14	IB-14	IC-32	ID-23	IE-44	IF-115	IG-19	IH-56
Graham Paige 629.........N.-E. (1928)	IA-14	IB-14	IC-32	ID-23	IE-44	IF-115	IG-19	IH-56
Graham Paige 835.........N.-E. (1928)	IA-14	IB-14	IC-45	ID-37	IE-45	IF-79	IG-19	IH-8
Graham Paige 612.........D.-R. (1929)	IA-4	IB-6	IC-9	ID-8	IE-4	IF-33	IG-7	IH-8
Graham Paige 615.........D.-R. (1929)	IA-4	IB-6	IC-9	ID-10	IE-4	{IF-46 {IF-45	IG-7	IH-8
Graham Paige 621.........D.-R. (1929)	IA-4	IB-8	IC-7	ID-10	IE-4	IF-14	IG-8	IH-8
Graham Paige 827.........D.-R. (1929)	*IA-4	{IB-3U. {IB-32L.	IC-46	ID-60	IE-4	IF-4	IG-35	IH-8
Graham Paige 837...........D.-R. (1929)	*IA-4	{IB-3U. {IB-32L.	IC-46	ID-60	IE-4	IF-14	IG-35	IH-8
Graham Std. Six............D.-R. (1930)	IA-4	IB-6	IC-9	ID-8	IE-4	{IF-33 {IF-43	IG-7	IH-8
Graham Spec. Six..........D.-R. (1930)	IA-4	IB-8	IC-7	ID-10	IE-4	IF-45	IG-8	IH-8
Graham Std. and Spec. 8...D.-R. (1930)	*IA-4	{IB-3U. {IB-32L.	IC-12	ID-80	IE-4	IF-56	IG-7	IH-132
Graham Custom 8...........D.-R. (1930)	*IA-4	{IB-3U. {IB-32L.	IC-46	ID-60	IE-4	IF-14	IG-35	IH-133
Graham 6.................D.-R. (1930)	IA-4	IB-6	IC-9	ID-8	IE-4	IF-43	IG-7	IH-132
Graham 8.................D.-R. (1931)	*IA-4	{IB-3U {IB-32L	IC-12	ID-80	IE-4	IF-56	IG-7	IH-132
Graham Custom 8...........D.-R. (1931)	*IA-4	{IB-3U {IB-32L	IC-46	ID-60	IE-4	IF-14	IG-35	IH-132
Hudson Super 6............B. (1925)	IA-12	IB-12	IC-22	ID-17	IE-11	IF-91	IG-13	IH-46
Hudson Super 6............B. (1926)	IA-12	IB-12	IC-22	ID-17	IE-11	IF-91	IG-13	IH-46
Hudson Super 6............A.-L. (1927)	IA-1	IB-1	IC-1	ID-1	IE-32	IF-92	IG-1	IH-60
Hudson Super 6............A.-L. (1928)	IA-1	IB-12	IC-1	ID-1	IE-32	IF-48	IG-1	IH-60
Hudson Greater............A.-L. (1929)	IA-1	IB-12	IC-1	ID-1	IE-1	IF-94	IG-1	IH-60
Hudson 8.................A.-L. (1930)	*IA-41	{IB-12U. {IB-16L.	IC-55	ID-3	IE-98	IF-95	IG-60	IH-134
Hudson 8.................A.-L. (1931)	*IA-41	{IB-12U {IB-16L	IC-55	ID-3	IE-99	IF-95	IG-60	IH-134
Hupmobile E1..............D. (1925)	IA-10	IB-10	IC-98	ID-14	IE-4	IF-12	IG-10	IH-61
Hupmobile R...............D. (1925)	IA-27	IB-23	IC-50	ID-38	IE-46	None	IG-29	IH-62
Hupmobile E2..............D. (1926-27)	IA-10	IB-10	IC-98	ID-14	IE-4	IF-12	IG-10	IH-61
Hupmobile A1..............A.-L. (1926)	IA-1	IB-1	IC-1	ID-1	IE-1	IF-74	IG-1	IH-63
Hupmobile A2..............A.-L. (1927)	IA-1	IB-1	IC-1	ID-1	IE-1	IF-74	IG-1	IH-63
Hupmobile E3..............D.-R. (1927)	*IA-4	{IB-7U. {IB-31L.	IC-100	ID-15	IE-9	IF-25	IG-10	IH-61
Hupmobile Cent. 6.........A.-L. (1928)	IA-13	IB-12	IC-1	ID-1	IE-1	IE-96	IG-28	IH-63
Hupmobile Cent. M8........D.-R. (1928)	IA-10	IB-10	IC-5	ID-3	IE-1	IF-95	IG-27	IH-61
Hupmobile 125.............D.-R. (1928)	IA-10	IB-10	IC-5	ID-3	IE-1	IF-97	IG-27	IH-61
Hupmobile A6..............A.-L. (1929)	IA-13	IB-12	IC-1	ID-1	IE-1	IF-96	IG-28	IH-63
Hupmobile M8..............A.-L. (1929)	*IA-41	{IB-12U. {IB-16L.	IC-55	ID-3	IE-1	IF-97	IG-27	IH-41
Hupmobile C...............A.-L. (1930)	*IA-41	{IB-12U {IB-16L	IC-55	ID-3	IE-32	IF-95	IG-27	IH-41
Hupmobile H, U............A.-L. (1930)	*IA-41	{IB-12U. {IB-16L	IC-55	ID-3	IE-32	IF-95	IG-27	IH-41
Hupmobile S...............A.-L. (1930)	IA-13	IB-12	IC-1	ID-1	IE-69	IF-95	IG-28	IH-63
Hupmobile C...............A.-L. (1931)	IA-41	{IB-12U {IB-16L	IC-55	ID-3	IE-32	IF-95	IG-27	IH-41
Hupmobile H, U............A.-L. (1931)	*IA-41	{IB-12U {IB-16L	IC-55	ID-3	IE-32	IF-95	IG-27	IH-41
Hupmobile L...............A.-L. (1931)	*IA-41	{IB-12U {IB-16L	IC-55	ID-3	IE-70	IF-95	IG-27	IH-41
Hupmobile S...............A.-L. (1931)	IA-13	IB-12	IC-1	ID-1	IE-69	IF-95	IG-28	IH-63
Jewett 6-50...............A.-K. (1925)	IA-28	IB-24	IC-52	ID-40	IE-46	None	IG-36	IH-64
Jewett 6-55...............D.-R. (1926)	IA-6	IB-6	IC-9	ID-8	IE-3	None	IG-36	IH-65
Jordan, K. L..............D. (1925)	IA-8	IB-10	IC-53	ID-41	IE-47	IF-62	IG-9	IH-67
Jordan A.................B. (1925)	IA-12	IB-12	IC-54	ID-42	IE-48	IF-100	IG-13	IH-67
Jordan A.................B. (1926)	IA-12	IB-12	IC-54	ID-42	IE-48	IF-100	IG-13	IH-67
Jordan J.................B. (1926)	IA-12	IB-12	IC-54	ID-42	IE-48	IF-101	IG-13	IH-67
Jordan AA................B. (1927)	IA-12	IB-12	IC-54	ID-42	IE-48	IF-100	IG-13	IH-67
Jordan J.................A.-L. (1927)	IA-12	IB-12	IC-54	ID-24	IE-49	None	IG-31	IH-68
Jordan R.................A.-L. (1927-28)	IA-1	IB-1	IC-1	ID-1	IE-1	IF-98	IG-1	IH-41
Jordan JJ................B. (1928)	IA-12	IB-11	IC-56	ID-44	IE-49	IF-23	IG-31	IH-68
Jordan JE................A.-L. (1928)	IA-13	IB-12	IC-55	ID-24	IE-49	IF-98	IG-31	IH-68
Jordan E.................A.-L. (1929)	IA-12	IB-12	IC-33	ID-18	IE-29	IF-47	IG-26	IH-41
Jordan G.................A.-L. (1929)	*IA-41	{IB-12U. {IB-16L.	IC-57	ID-45	IE-50	IF-95	{IG-37 {IG-60	IH-43
Kissel 6-55...............R. (1925)	IA-29	IB-5	IC-4	ID-4	IE-2	IF-63	IG-23	IH-70
Kissel 8-75...............R. (1925)	IA-4	IB-4	IC-5	ID-5	IE-2	IF-2	None	IH-8
Kissel 6-55...............R. (1926)	IA-29	IB-5	IC-4	ID-4	IE-2	IF-63	IG-23	IH-70
Kissel 8-75...............R. (1926)	IA-4	IB-4	IC-5	ID-5	IE-2	IF-2	None	IH-8
Kissel 6-55...............R. (1927)	IA-29	IB-5	IC-4	ID-4	IE-2	IF-64	IG-23	IH-70
Kissel 8-65...............D.-R. (1927)	*IA-4	{IB-7U. {IB-31L.	IC-5	ID-9	IE-4	{IF-5 {IF-45	IG-7	IH-8
Kissel 8-75...............D.-R. (1927)	*IA-4	{IB-7U. {IB-31L.	IC-5	ID-5	IE-4	{IF-5 {IF-54	IG-7	IH-8
Kissel 6-70...............D.-R. (1928)	IA-4	IB-4	IC-7	ID-7	IE-9	{IF-56 {IF-6	IG-67	IH-8
Kissel 8-80...............D.-R. (1928)	*IA-4	{IB-7U. {IB-31L.	IC-5	ID-9	IE-4	{IF-5 {IF-45	IG-7	IH-8
Kissel 8-80 S.............D.-R. (1928)	*IA-4	{IB-7U. {IB-31L.	IC-5	ID-9	IE-4	{IF-5 {IF-45	IG-7	IH-8
Kissel 8-90...............D.-R. (1928)	*IA-4	{IB-7U. {IB-31L.	IC-5	ID-5	IE-9	{IF-5 {IF-54	IG-7	IH-8
Kissel 6-73...............D.-R. (1929)	IA-4	IB-8	IC-7	ID-10	IE-9	IF-6	IG-8	IH-8
Kissel 8-95...............D.-R. (1929-30)	*IA-4	{IB-7U. {IB-31L.	IC-5	ID-9	IE-9	IF-45	IG-7	IH-8
Kissel 8-126..............D.-R. (1929-30)	*IA-4	{IB-3U. {IB-32L.	IC-46	ID-25	IE-4	IF-16	IG-35	IH-8
La Salle 303..............D.-R. (1927)	IA-10	IB-2	IC-18	ID-15	IE-9	IF-12	IG-64	IH-7

IGNITION SYSTEM—Continued

Interchangeable Parts have the same CHILTON NUMBER in Any Column

Car Make and Model	Contact or Breaker Arm	Contact Screw	Distributor Cap	Distributor Rotor	Coil	Automatic Advance Spring	Condenser	Distributor Shaft Gear or Coupling
La Salle 303................D.-R. (1928)	IA-10	IB-2	IC-18	ID-15	IE-9	IF-25	IG-64	IH-7
La Salle 328................D.-R. (1929)	IA-10	IB-2	IC-18	ID-15	IE-9	IF-12	IG-64	IH-7
La Salle 340................D.-R. (1930)	*IA-4	IB-7U. / IB-31L.	IC-96	ID-15	IE-5	IF-24	IG-10 / IG-57	IH-7
La Salle 345................D.-R. (1931)	IA-4	IB-7U. / IB-31L.	IC-96	ID-15	IE-5	IF-24	IG-57	IH-7
Lincoln 8.....................D. (1925)	IA-11	IB-10	IC-58	ID-26	IE-20	IF-30 / IF-66	IG-38	IH-72
Lincoln 8.....................D. (1926)	IA-11	IB-10	IC-58	ID-26	IE-4	IF-30 / IF-66	IG-38	IH-72
Lincoln 8....................D.-R. (1927)	IA-11	IB-10	IC-59	ID-47	IE-4	IF-66	IG-38	IH-72
Lincoln 8....................D.-R. (1928)	IA-11	IB-10	IC-59	ID-47	IE-9	IF-66	IG-38	IH-72
Lincoln 8....................D.-R. (1929)	IA-11	IB-10	IC-59	ID-47	IE-9	IF-66	IG-38	IH-72
Lincoln 8.....................D. R. (1930)	*IA-11	*IB-10	IC-59	ID-36	IE-9	IF-66	IG-38	IH-72
Lincoln.....................D.-R. (1931)	*IA-11	*IB-10	IC-59	ID-36	IE-9	IF-66	IG-38	IH-72
Locomobile, Jr. 8.......DeJ. (1925)	IA-22	IB-1	IC-61	ID-49	IE-55	None	IG-68	IH-74
Locomobile 48...............D. (1925)	IA-9	IB-10	IC-62	ID-50	IE-56	IF-30 / IF-66	IG-40	IH-75
Locomobile 48...............D. (1926)	IA-9	IB-10	IC-62	ID-50	IE-56	IF-30 / IF-66	IG-40	IH-75
Locomobile 90..........DeJ. (1926)	IA-22	IB-1	IC-26	ID-48	IE-59	None	IG-68	IH-73
Locomobile, Jr. 8.......DeJ. (1926)	IA-22	IB-1	IC-61	ID-49	IE-55	None	IG-68	IH-74
Locomobile 48..............D.-R. (1927)	IA-9	IB-10	IC-62	ID-50	IE-56	IF-30 / IF-66	IG-40	IH-75
Locomobile 8-66..........DeJ. (1927)	IA-22	IB-1	IC-61	ID-49	IE-55	None	IG-68	IH-74
Locomobile 8-80..........DeJ. (1927)	IA-32	IB-12	IC-61	ID-53	IE-58	IF-47	IG-41	IH-8
Locomobile 90..........DeJ. (1927)	IA-22	IB-1	IC-26	ID-48	IE-59	None	IG-68	IH-73
Locomobile 48..............D.-R. (1928)	IA-9	IB-10	IC-62	ID-50	IE-56	IF-30 / IF-66	IG-40	IH-75
Locomobile 8-70..........D.-R. (1928)	*IA-4	IB-7U. / IB-31L.	IC-5	ID-5	IE-3	IF-14	IG-7	IH-20
Locomobile 8-80..........DeJ. (1928)	IA-32	IB-12	IC-61	ID-53	IE-58	IF-47	IG-41	IH-8
Locomobile 90..........DeJ. (1928)	IA-22	IB-1	IC-26	ID-48	IE-59	None	IG-68	IH-73
Locomobile 8-80..........DeJ. (1929)	IA-32	IB-12	IC-61	ID-53	IE-58	IF-47	IG-41	IH-8
Locomobile 86-88........DeJ. (1929)	IA-32	IB-12	IC-61	ID-53	IE-58	IF-47	IG-41	IH-8
Locomobile 90..........DeJ. (1929)	IA-22	IB-1	IC-26	ID-48	IE-59	None	IG-68	IH-73
Marmon 74........................D. (1925)	IA-11	IB-10	IC-65	ID-30	IE-60	IF-30	IG-9	IH-76
Marmon 74...................D.-R. (1926)	IA-10	IB-10	IC-65	ID-30	IE-20	IF-30	IG-9	IH-76
Marmon, Little.............D.-R. (1927)	*IA-4	IB-7U. / IB-31L.	IC-5	ID-5	IE-4	IF-5	IG-65	IH-8
Marmon E75...............D.-R. (1927)	IA-10	IB-10	IC-66	ID-54	IE-4	IF-12 / IF-67	IG-10	IH-76
Marmon 68...................D.-R. (1928)	*IA-4	IB-7U. / IB-31L.	IC-5	ID-5	IE-4	IF-5	IG-65	IH-8
Marmon E75...............D.-R. (1928)	IA-10	IB-10	IC-66	ID-54	IE-4	IF-12 / IF-67	IG-10	IH-8
Marmon 78...................D.-R. (1928)	*IA-4	IB-7U. / IB-31L.	IC-5	ID-5	IE-4	IF-5 / IF-31	IG-7 / IG-65	IH-8
Marmon 68...................D.-R. (1929)	*IA-4	IB-7U. / IB-31L.	IC-5	ID-5	IE-4	IF-6	IG-4	IH-8
Marmon 78...................D.-R. (1929)	*IA-4	IB-7U. / IB-31L.	IC-5	ID-5	IE-4	IF-5 / IF-31	IG-7 / IG-65	IH-8
Marmon Roosevelt........D.-R. (1929-30)	*IA-4	IB-7U. / IB-31L.	IC-5	ID-5	IE-79	IF-5	IG-7	IH-8
Marmon 69...................D.-R. (1930)	*IA-4	IB-7U. / IB-31L.	IC-5	ID-5	IE-100	IF-5	IG-65	IH-8
Marmon 79...................D.-R. (1930)	*IA-4	IB-7U. / IB-31L.	IC-5	ID-5	IE-100	IF-20	IG-65	IH-8
Marmon Big 8..............D.-R. (1930)	*IA-4	IB-7U. / IB-31L.	IC-5	ID-5	IE-100	IF-20	IG-65	IH-8
Marmon 69...................D.-R. (1931)	*IA-4	IB-7 / IB-31	IC-5	ID-5	IE-100	IF-15	IG-65	IH-8
Marmon 79...................D.-R. (1931)	*IA-4	IB-7U. / IB-31L.	IC-5	ID-5	IE-100	IF-20	IG-65	IH-8
Marmon Big 8..............D.-R. (1931)	*IA-4	IB-7 / IB-31	IC-5	ID-5	IE-100	IF-20	IG-65	IH-8
Marmon Roosevelt........D.-R. (1931)	*IA-4	IB-7 / IB-31	IC-5	ID-5	IE-79	IF-5	IG-7	IH-8
Marquette, Series 30...........D. (1930)	IA-4	IB-6	IC-9	ID-8	IE-53	IF-43	IG-7	IH-25
Maxwell.............................. (1925)	IA-5	IB-5	IC-101	ID-6	IE-2	None	IG-3	IH-26
Moon Series A..................D. (1925)	IA-8	IB-10	IC-27	ID-19	IE-4	IF-25	IG-18	IH-78
Moon Series A..................D. (1926)	IA-8	IB-10	IC-27	ID-19	IE-4	IF-25	IG-18	IH-78
Moon Series A..................D. (1927)	IA-8	IB-10	IC-27	ID-19	IE-4	IF-25	IG-18	IH-78
Moon 6-60........................D. (1927)	IA-4	IB-6	IC-9	ID-19	IE-3	IF-25 / IF-33	IG-7 / IG-18	IH-6
Moon Series A..................D. (1928)	IA-8	IB-10	IC-27	ID-19	IE-4	IF-25	IG-18	IH-78
Moon 6-60.....................D.-R. (1928)	IA-4	IB-6	IC-9	ID-19	IE-3	IF-33	IG-7	IH-6
Moon 6-72.....................D.-R. (1928)	IA-4	IB-8	IC-7	ID-10	IE-4	IF-31	IG-8	IH-79
Moon 8-80.....................D.-R. (1928)	*IA-4	IB-7U. / IB-31L.	IC-5	ID-5	IE-4	IF-14	IG-7	IH-20
Moon 6-72.....................D.-R. (1929)	IA-4	IB-8	IC-7	ID-10	IE-4	IF-31	IG-8	IH-79
Nash Adv. 6.....................D. (1925)	IA-8	IB-10	IC-68	ID-13	IE-10	IF-17	IG-11	IH-80
Nash Spec. 6....................D. (1925)	IA-8	IB-10	IC-27	ID-19	IE-14	IF-17	IG-18	IH-80
Nash Adv. 6.....................D. (1926)	IA-8	IB-10	IC-27	ID-13	IE-20	IF-17 / IF-26	IG-11 / IG-18	IH-80
Nash Spec. 6.................D.-R. (1926)	IA-8	IB-10	IC-27	ID-19	IE-4	IF-17	IG-18	IH-80
Nash Adv. 6.................D.-R. (1927)	IA-8	IB-10	IC-27	ID-19	IE-4	IF-26 / IF-56	IG-18 / IG-67	IH-80 / IH-81
Nash Spec. 6.................D.-R. (1927)	IA-8	IB-10	IC-27	ID-19	IE-4	IF-26 / IF-56	IG-18 / IG-67	IH-80 / IH-81
Nash Light 6.................A.-L. (1927)	IA-1	IB-1	IC-1	ID-1	IE-1	IF-92 / IF-74	IG-1	IH-1
Nash Std. 6..................A.-L. (1927)	IA-1	IB-1	IC-1	ID-1	IE-1	IF-74	IG-1	IH-1
Nash Adv. 6.................D.-R. (1928)	IA-4	IB-8	IC-7	ID-10	IE-4	IF-56	IG-8	IH-81
Nash Spec. 6.................D.-R. (1928)	IA-4	IB-8	IC-7	ID-10	IE-4	IF-56	IG-8	IH-81
Nash Std. 6...............A.-L. (1928-29)	IA-13	IB-12	IC-33	ID-18	IE-1	IF-23	IG-26	IH-1
Nash Adv. 6.................A.-L. (1929)	*IA-13	*IB-12	IC-69	ID-56	IE-1	IF-97	IG-28	IH-100
Nash Spec. 6.................A.-L. (1929)	IA-13	IB-12	IC-69	ID-56	*IE-1	IF-97	IG-28	IH-100
Nash Single 6...............A.-L. (1930)	IA-13	IB-12	IC-33	ID-18	IE-1	IF-23	IG-26	IH-1
Nash Twin Ign. 6...........A.-L. (1930)	*IA-13	*IB-12	IC-69	ID-56	*IE-1	IF-99	IG-28	IH-100
Nash Twin Ign. 8...........A.-L. (1930)	*IA-13	*IB-12	IC-100	ID-82	*IE-32	IF-98	IG-28	IH-100
Nash 6-60....................A.-L. (1931)	IA-13	IB-12	IC-33	ID-18	IE-1	IF-23	IG-26	IH-1
Nash 8-70....................A.-L. (1931)	*IA-41	IB-12U. / IB-16L.	IC-103	ID-29	IE-32	IF-65	IG-60	IH-1
Nash 8-80....................A.-L. (1931)	*IA-13	*IB-12	IC-102	ID-82	IE-32	IF-98	IG-28	IH-100

IGNITION SYSTEM—Continued

Interchangeable Parts have the same CHILTON NUMBER in Any Column

Car Make and Model	Contact or Breaker Arm	Contact Screw	Distributor Cap	Distributor Rotor	Coil	Automatic Advance Spring	Condenser	Distributor Shaft Gear or Coupling
Nash 8-90.....................A.-L. (1931)	*IA-13	*IB-12	IC-102	ID-82	IE-32	IF-98	IG-28	IH-100
Oakland 6-54..................R. (1925)	IA-4	IB-4	IC-7	ID-7	IE-2	IF-68	IG-3	IH-82
Oakland 6.....................R. (1926)	IA-4	IB-4	IC-7	ID-7	IE-2	{IF-68, IF-69	IG-67	IH-82
Oakland 6.....................R. (1927)	IA-4	IB-4	IC-7	ID-7	IE-2	IF-69	IG-67	IH-83
Oakland AA6................D.-R. (1928)	IA-4	IB-8	IC-7	ID-10	IE-2	IF-2	IG-8	IH-84
Oakland AA6................D.-R. (1929)	IA-4	IB-8	IC-7	ID-10	IE-4	IF-10	IG-8	IH-84
Oakland 101.................D.-R. (1930)	*IA-4	{IB-3U. IB-32L.	IC-104	ID-80	IE-86	IF-6	IG-7	IH-3
Oakland 301.................D.-R. (1931)	*IA-4	{IB-9U. IB-11L.	IC-104	ID-80	IE-86	IF-6	IG-7	IH-3
Oldsmobile 30..................D. (1925)	IA-8	IB-10	IC-27	ID-19	IE-4	IF-25	IG-18	IH-85
Oldsmobile 30..................D. (1926)	IA-8	IB-10	IC-27	ID-19	IE-42	IF-25	IG-18	IH-86
Oldsmobile 30E.............D.-R. (1927)	IA-6	IB-6	IC-27	ID-19	IE-42	{IF-41, IF-33	{IG-6, IG-7	IH-86
Oldsmobile F-28.............D.-R. (1928)	IA-4	IB-6	IC-9	ID-8	IE-42	IF-43	IG-7	IH-25
Oldsmobile F-29.............D.-R. (1929)	IA-4	IB-6	IC-9	ID-8	IE-42	IF-46	IG-7	IH-25
Oldsmobile F-30.............D.-R. (1930)	IA-4	IB-6	IC-9	ID-8	IE-4	IF-46	IG-7	IH-25
Oldsmobile F-31.............D.-R. (1931)	IA-4	IB-6	IC-9	ID-8	IE-63	IF-46	IG-7	IH-25
Overland 91...................A.-L. (1925)	IA-1	IB-1	IC-36	ID-27	IE-35	None	IG-24	IH-88
Overland 93...................A.-L. (1925)	IA-1	IB-1	IC-37	ID-1	IE-1	None	IG-1	IH-101
Overland 91...................A.-L. (1926)	IA-1	IB-1	IC-36	ID-27	IE-35	None	IG-24	IH-88
Overland 93...................A.-L. (1926)	IA-1	IB-1	IC-1	ID-1	IE-1	IF-74	IG-1	IH-101
Packard 6 Cyl., 326, 333.......D. (1925)	IA-11	IB-10	IC-65	ID-30	IE-54	‡IF-30	IG-9	IH-91
Packard 8 Cyl., 236, 243.......D. (1925)	IA-9	IB-10	IC-71	ID-14	IE-54	‡IF-30	IG-17	IH-91
Packard 6 Cyl., 326, 333.......D. (1926)	IA-11	IB-10	IC-65	ID-30	IE-54	‡IF-30	IG-9	IH-91
Packard 8 Cyl., 236, 243.......D. (1926)	IA-9	IB-10	IC-71	ID-14	IE-54	‡IF-30	IG-17	IH-91
Packard 6 Cyl., 426, 433.....D.-R. (1927)	IA-11	IB-10	IC-65	ID-16	IE-54	‡IF-30	{IG-9, IG-10	IH-91
Packard 8 Cyl., 336, 343.....D.-R. (1927)	IA-10	IB-10	IC-100	ID-15	IE-54	‡IF-30	{IG-10, IG-17	IH-91
Packard 6 Cyl., 526, 533.....D.-R. (1928)	*IA-4	{IB-7U. IB-32L	IC-10	ID-10	IE-9	IF-6	{IG-6, IG-10	IH-8
Packard Std. 8, 443...........D.-R. (1928)	*IA-4	{IB-7U IB-31L	IC-100	ID-15	IE-9	IF-24	IG-10	IH-91
Packard 8 Cyl., 626, 633......N.-E. (1929)	*IA-14	*IB-14	IC-73	ID-58	IE-67	N. S.	IG-71	IH-91
Packard 8 Cyl., 640, 645......N.-E. (1929)	*IA-14	*IB-14	IC-73	ID-58	IE-68	N. S.	IG-72	IH-91
Packard 726, 733.............N.-E. (1930)	*IA-14	*IB-14	IC-73	ID-58	IE-68	N. S.	IG-72	IH-91
Packard 740, 745.............N.-E. (1930)	*IA-14	*IB-14	IC-73	ID-58	IE-68	N. S.	IG-72	IH-91
Packard 826, 833.............N.-E. (1931)	*IA-14	*IB-14	IC-73	ID-58	IE-68	IF-104	IG-72	IH-102
Packard 840, 845.............N.-E. (1931)	*IA-14	*IB-14	IC-73	ID-58	IE-68	IF-104	IG-72	IH-102
Paige 6-70....................A.-K. (1925)	IA-28	IB-24	IC-52	ID-40	IE-57	None	IG-44	IH-92
Paige 6-70....................A.-K. (1926)	IA-28	IB-24	IC-52	ID-40	IE-57	None	IG-44	IH-92
Paige 6-45...................D.-R. (1927)	IA-6	IB-6	IC-9	ID-8	IE-3	{IF-72, IF-73	{IG-6, IG-7	IH-65
Paige 6-65...................D.-R. (1927)	IA-6	IB-6	IC-9	ID-8	IE-46	None	IG-6	IH-93
Paige 6-75...................D.-R. (1927)	IA-6	IB-6	IC-9	ID-8	IE-46	None	IG-6	IH-93
Paige 8-85..............D.-R. (1927-28)	*IA-4	{IB-7U. IB-31L.	IC-5	ID-5	IE-3	IF-5	IG-7	IH-8
Peerless 70.....................D. (1925)	IA-8	IB-10	IC-74	ID-59	IE-4	IF-17	IG-11	IH-94
Peerless 80...................A.-L. (1926)	IA-1	IB-1	IC-1	ID-1	IE-29	IF-47	IG-1	IH-50
Peerless 69.....................D. (1926)	IA-10	IB-10	IC-100	ID-15	IE-20	IF-25	IG-10	IH-95
Peerless 60...................A.-L. (1927)	IA-1	IB-1	IC-1	ID-1	IE-1	IF-98	IG-1	IH-41
Peerless 69.....................D. (1927)	IA-10	IB-10	IC-100	ID-15	IE-20	IF-25	IG-10	IH-95
Peerless 72.....................D. (1927)	IA-8	IB-10	IC-74	ID-59	IE-4	{IF-17, IF-15	IG-11	IH-94
Peerless 80...................A.-L. (1927)	IA-1	IB-1	IC-1	ID-1	IE-29	IF-47	IG-1	IH-50
Peerless 90...............A.-L. (1927-28)	IA-1	IB-1	IC-1	ID-1	IE-1	IF-92	IG-1	IH-41
Peerless 60...................A.-L. (1928)	IA-1	IB-1	IC-1	ID-1	IE-1	IF-98	IG-1	IH-41
Peerless 69..................D. (1928)	IA-10	IB-10	IC-18	ID-15	IE-20	IF-25	IG-10	IH-95
Peerless 80...................A.-L. (1928)	IA-1	IB-1	IC-1	ID-1	IE-29	IF-47	IG-1	IH-50
Peerless 91..................D.-R. (1928)	IA-4	IB-8	IC-7	ID-10	IE-4	IF-75	IG-8	IH-8
Peerless 81...................A.-L. (1929)	IA-13	IB-12	IC-33	ID-18	IE-29	IF-95	IG-14	IH-44
Peerless 91..................D.-R. (1929)	IA-4	IB-8	IC-7	ID-10	IE-1	IF-75	IG-8	IH-8
Peerless 125.................D.-R. (1929)	*IA-4	{IB-3U. IB-32L.	IC-75	ID-60	IE-26	{IF-14, IF-21	IG-35	IH-8
Peerless 61...................A.-L. (1929)	IA-13	IB-12	IC-33	ID-18	IE-1	IF-95	IG-4	IH-8
Peerless 91..................D.-R. (1930)	IA-4	IB-8	IC-7	ID-18	IE-6	IF-75	IG-8	IH-8
Peerless A...................A.-L. (1930)	*IA-41	{IB-12U. IB-16L.	IC-55	ID-3	IE-104	IF-95	IG-60	IH-43
Peerless B, C................A.-L. (1930)	*IA-41	{IB-12U. IB-16L.	IC-55	ID-3	IE-103	IF-23	IG-60	IH-41
Peerless A...................A.-L. (1931)	*IA-41	{IB-12U. IB-16L.	IC-55	ID-3	IE-104	IF-95	IG-60	IH-43
Peerless B, C................A.-L. (1931)	*IA-41	{IB-12U. IB-16L	IC-55	ID-3	IE-103	IF-23	IG-60	IH-41
Pierce Arrow 80...............D. (1925)	IA-11	IB-10	IC-65	ID-30	IE-20	{IF-30, IF-66	IG-9	IH-33
Pierce Arrow 33...............D. (1926)	IA-8	IB-10	IC-13	ID-12	IE-20	{IF-30, IF-71	IG-46	IH-103
Pierce Arrow 80.............D.-R. (1926)	IA-11	IB-10	IC-65	ID-30	IE-20	{IF-30, IF-66	IG-9	IH-33
Pierce Arrow 36.............D.-R. (1927)	IA-8	IB-10	IC-13	ID-62	IE-4	{IF-30, IF-71	IG-47	IH-103
Pierce Arrow 80.............D.-R. (1927)	IA-11	IB-10	IC-65	ID-30	IE-4	{IF-30, IF-66	IG-9	IH-74
Pierce Arrow 36.............D.-R. (1928)	IA-8	IB-10	IC-13	ID-62	IE-4	{IF-30, IF-71	IG-47	IH-103
Pierce Arrow 81.............D.-R. (1928)	IA-11	IB-10	IC-76	ID-48	IE-9	{IF-30, IF-66	IG-9	{IH-33, IH-74
Pierce Arrow 133, 143........D.-R. (1929)	*IA-4	{IB-3U. IB-32L.	IC-78	ID-60	IE-6	IF-76	IG-35	IH-133
Pierce Arrow A, B...........D.-R. (1930)	*IA-4	{IB-3U. IB-32L.	IC-78	ID-60	IE-6	IF-76	IG-35	IH-133
Pierce Arrow C.............D.-R. (1930)	*IA-4	{IB-7U. IB-31L.	IC-2	ID-80	IE-6	IF-20	IG-7	IH-133
Pierce Arrow A, B...........D.-R. (1931)	*IA-4	{IB-3U. IB-32L.	IC-78	ID-60	IE-6	IF-76	IG-35	IH-133
Pierce Arrow C.............D.-R. (1931)	*IA-4	{IB-3U. IB-32L.	IC-3	ID-80	IE-6	IF-45	IG-7	IH-133
Plymouth 4 Cyl............D.-R. (1929)	IA-4	IB-6	IC-77	ID-8	IE-7	IF-42	IG-7	IH-105
Plymouth..................D.-R. (1930)	IA-4	IB-6	IC-77	ID-8	IE-102	IF-42	IG-7	IH-105
Plymouth..................D.-R. (1931)	IA-4	IB-6	IC-77	ID-8	IE-102	IF-42	IG-7	IH-105
Pontiac 6..................R. (1926-27)	IA-6	IB-6	IC-9	ID-8	IE-4	IF-41	{IG-6, IG-7	{IH-82, IH-83

IGNITION SYSTEM—Continued

Interchangeable Parts have the same CHILTON NUMBER in Any Column

Car Make and Model	Contact or Breaker Arm	Contact Screw	Distributor Cap	Distributor Rotor	Coil	Automatic Advance Spring	Condenser	Distributor Shaft Gear or Coupling
Pontiac 6..................D.-R. (1928)	IA-4	IB-6	IC-9	ID-8	IE-4	IF-42	IG-7	IH-83
Pontiac 6..................D.-R. (1929)	IA-4	IB-6	IC-9	ID-8	IE-6	IF-46	IG-7	IH-83
Pontiac 6..................D.-R. (1930)	IA-4	IB-6	IC-9	ID-8	IE-86	IF-46	IG-7	IH-83
Pontiac 401................D.-R. (1931)	IA-4	IB-6	IC-9	ID-8	IE-86	IF-46	IG-7	IH-83
Reo T6....................N.-E. (1925)	IA-15	IB-15	IC-31	ID-21	IE-73	IF-93	IG-19	IH-97
Reo T6....................N.-E. (1926)	IA-14	IB-14	IC-31	ID-21	IE-73	{IF-93 IF-112	IG-19	IH-97
Reo T6....................N.-E. (1927)	IA-14	IB-14	IC-31	ID-21	IE-73	{IF-93 IF-112	IG-19	IH-97
Reo Flying Cloud..........R. (1927)	IA-4	IB-4	IC-10	ID-7	IE-6	IF-80	IG-67	IH-98
Reo Wolverine.............N.-E. (1927)	IA-16	IB-15	IC-31	ID-22	IE-44	{IF-113 IF-115	IG-21	IH-99
Reo Flying Cloud..........D.-R. (1928)	IA-4	IB-8	IC-10	ID-10	IE-6	IF-20	IG-8	IH-98
Reo Wolverine.............N.-E. (1928)	IA-16	IB-15	IC-31	ID-22	IE-44	{IF-113 IF-115	IG-63	IH-99
Reo Flying Cloud, Master...D.-R. (1929)	IA-4	IB-8	IC-10	ID-10	IE-6	IF-18	IG-8	IH-32
Reo Flying Cloud, Mate....D.-R. (1929)	IA-4	IB-8	IC-7	ID-10	IE-6	IE-6	IG-8	IH-8
Reo 15...................D.-R. (1930)	IA-4	IB-8	IC-7	ID-10	IE-6	IF-6	IG-8	IH-8
Reo 20, 25...............D.-R. (1930)	IA-4	IB-8	IC-10	ID-10	IE-6	IF-18	IG-8	IH-8
Reo 25...................D.-R. (1931)	IA-4	IB-8	IC-10	ID-10	IE-6	IF-18	IG-8	IH-32
Reo 30...................D.-R. (1931)	*IA-4	{IB-3U. IB-32L.	IC-97	ID-80	IE-6	IF-20	IG-7	IH-8
Reo 35...................D.-R. (1931)	*IA-4	{IB-3U. IB-32L.	IC-97	ID-80	IE-6	IF-20	IG-7	IH-8
Rickenbacker D-6..........B. (1925)	IA-12	IB-11	IC-22	ID-17	IE-11	IF-91	IG-13	IH-9
Rickenbacker 8-B..........D. (1926)	IA-10	IB-10	IC-71	ID-2	IE-14	IF-25	IG-10	IH-121
Rickenbacker 6-E..........B. (1926)	IA-12	IB-12	IC-22	ID-17	IE-11	IF-91	IG-13	IH-9
Rickenbacker 6-70.........B. (1926)	IA-12	IB-12	IC-22	ID-61	IE-1	IF-103	IG-66	IH-9
Rickenbacker 8-80.........A.-L. (1927)	IA-13	IB-12	IC-71	ID-66	IE-1	IF-104	IG-10	IH-121
Rickenbacker 8-90.........A.-L. (1927)	IA-13	IB-12	IC-71	ID-66	IE-1	IF-104	IG-10	IH-121
Roamer 4-75E..............A.-L. (1925)	IA-1	IB-1	IC-84	ID-67	IE-76	IF-105	IG-1	IH-49
Roamer 8-88...............A.-L. (1925-26)	IA-1	IB-1	IC-39	ID-14	IE-77	IF-74	IG-1	IH-49
Roamer 6-50...............D. (1925-26)	IA-8	IB-10	IC-12	ID-27	IE-77	None	IG-24	IH-42
Roamer 4-75E..............A.-L. (1926)	IA-1	IB-1	IC-84	ID-67	IE-76	IF-105	IG-1	IH-49
Roamer 8-80...............A.-L. (1926-27)	IA-1	IB-1	IC-39	ID-39	IE-77	IF-74	IG-1	IH-49
Roamer 8-88...............A.-L. (1927)	IA-1	IB-1	IC-39	ID-39	IE-77	IF-74	IG-1	IH-49
Roamer 8-78...............A.-L. (1927)	IA-1	IB-1	IC-39	ID-39	IE-77	IF-74	IG-1	IH-49
Roamer 8-78...............A.-L. (1928)	IA-1	IB-1	IC-5	ID-9	IE-77	IF-74	IG-1	IH-8
Roamer 8-80...............A.-L. (1928)	IA-1	IB-1	IC-39	ID-27	IE-77	IF-74	IG-1	IH-8
Roamer 8-88...............A.-L. (1928)	IA-1	IB-1	IC-39	ID-27	IE-77	IF-74	IG-1	IH-8
Roamer 8-78...............A.-L. (1929)	IA-1	IB-1	IC-5	ID-9	IE-77	IF-74	IG-1	IH-8
Roamer 8-80...............A.-L. (1929)	IA-1	IB-1	IC-39	ID-27	IE-77	IF-74	IG-1	IH-8
Roamer 8-88...............A.-L. (1929)	IA-1	IB-1	IC-39	ID-27	IE-77	IF-74	IG-1	IH-8
Star F....................A.-L. (1925)	IA-1	IB-1	IC-36	ID-27	IE-29	None	IG-24	IH-44
Star M....................A.-L. (1926)	IA-1	IB-1	IC-36	ID-27	IE-29	None	IG-24	IH-44
Star R....................A.-L. (1926)	IA-1	IB-1	IC-37	ID-27	IE-29	None	IG-24	IH-44
Star M....................A.-L. (1927)	IA-1	IB-1	IC-36	ID-27	IE-29	None	IG-24	IH-44
Star R....................A.-L. (1927)	IA-1	IB-1	IC-37	ID-27	IE-29	None	IG-24	IH-44
Stearns Knight B..........DeJ. (1925)	IA-22	IB-1	IC-21	ID-27	IE-80	None	None	IH-122
Stearns Knight C..........DeJ. (1925)	IA-22	IB-1	IC-26	ID-43	IE-80	None	IG-68	IH-122
Stearns Knight S..........DeJ. (1925)	IA-22	IB-1	IC-26	ID-48	IE-80	None	IG-68	IH-122
Stearns Knight B..........DeJ. (1926)	IA-22	IB-1	IC-21	ID-27	IE-80	None	None	IH-122
Stearns Knight C75........DeJ. (1926)	IA-22	IB-1	IC-26	ID-43	IE-80	None	IG-68	IH-122
Stearns Knight S95........DeJ. (1926)	IA-22	IB-1	IC-26	ID-48	IE-80	None	IG-68	IH-122
Stearns Knight F6-85......DeJ. (1927)	IA-32	IB-12	IC-26	ID-48	IE-80	IF-98	IG-41	IH-122
Stearns Knight 8-85.......DeJ. (1927)	IA-32	IB-12	IC-61	ID-53	IE-81	None	IG-41	IH-49
Stearns Knight F6-85......DeJ. (1928)	IA-32	IB-12	IC-26	ID-48	IE-80	IF-98	IG-41	IH-122
Stearns Knight HJ 8-90....DeJ. (1928)	IA-32	IB-12	IC-61	ID-53	IE-81	{IF-74 IF-47	{IG-41 IG-60	IH-49
Stearns Knight MN 6-80....A.-L. (1928)	IA-1	IB-12	IC-1	ID-1	IE-1	{IF-74 IF-47	IG-1	IH-49
Stearns Knight HJ 8-90....DeJ. (1929)	IA-32	IB-12	IC-61	ID-53	IE-81	{IF-74 IF-47	{IG-41 IG-60	IH-49
Studebaker Big 6..........R. (1925)	IA-29	IB-5	IC-4	ID-71	IE-62	IF-82	IG-23	IH-107
Studebaker Spec. 6........R. (1925)	IA-29	IB-5	IC-4	ID-71	IE-62	IF-82	IG-23	IH-107
Studebaker Std. 6.........R. (1925)	IA-29	IB-5	IC-4	ID-72	IE-83	IF-83	IG-23	IH-108
Studebaker Big 6..........R. (1926)	IA-4	IB-4	IC-4	ID-7	IE-83	‡IF-82	IG-23	IH-107
Studebaker Std. 6.........R. (1926)	IA-4	IB-4	IC-4	ID-72	IE-2	IF-83	IG-23	IH-108
Studebaker Spec. 6........R. (1926)	IA-4	IB-4	IC-4	ID-2	IE-83	‡IF-82	IG-23	IH-107
Studebaker Big 6..........D.-R. (1927)	IA-4	IB-4	IC-4	ID-7	IE-2	‡IF-82	{IG-23 IG-67	IH-107
Studebaker Spec. 6........R. (1927)	IA-4	IB-4	IC-4	ID-7	IE-2	‡IF-82	{IG-23 IG-67	IH-107
Studebaker Std. 6.........D.-R. (1927)	IA-4	IB-4	IC-4	ID-7	IE-2	{IF-83 IF-85	{IG-23 IG-67	IH-108
Studebaker Com. 6.........D.-R. (1928)	IA-4	IB-4	IC-7	ID-7	IE-6	IF-84	IG-67	IH-107
Studebaker Dict. 6........D.-R. (1928)	IA-4	IB-4	IC-7	ID-7	IE-3	‡IF-85	IG-67	IH-40
Studebaker Pres. 8........D.-R. (1928)	*IA-4	{IB-7U. IB-31L.	IC-5	ID-5	IE-6	{IF-14 IF-6	{IG-7 IG-35	IH-32
Studebaker Dict. 6........D.-R. (1929)	IA-4	IB-4	IC-7	ID-8	IE-6	{IF-6 IF-45	IG-3	IH-40
Studebaker Com. 6........D.-R. (1929-30)	*IA-4	*IB-4	IC-7	ID-5	IE-6	{IF-6 IF-45	IG-67	IH-40
Studebaker Com. 8........D.-R. (1929-30)	*IA-4	{IB-7U. IB-31L.	IC-5	ID-5	IE-6	IF-20	IG-7	IH-133
Studebaker Pres..........D.-R. (1929-30)	*IA-4	{IB-3U. IB-32L.	IC-46	ID-60	IE-6	IF-76	IG-35	IH-133
Studebaker Dict. 6........D.-R. (1930)	IA-4	IB-6	IC-9	ID-8	IE-6	IF-33	IG-7	IH-40
Studebaker Dict. 8........D.-R. (1930)	*IA-4	{IB-7U. IB-31L.	IC-2	ID-5	IE-6	IF-20	IG-7	IH-133
Studebaker 6-53...........D.-R. (1930)	IA-4	IB-6	IC-9	ID-8	IE-64	IF-33	IG-7	IH-40
Studebaker 6-54...........D.-R. (1931)	IA-4	IB-6	IC-11	ID-8	IE-64	IF-33	IG-7	IH-25
Studebaker Dict. 8-61.....D.-R. (1931)	*IA-4	{IB-7U. IB-31L.	IC-2	ID-5	IE-64	IF-20	IG-7	IH-133
Studebaker Com. 8-70......D.-R. (1931)	*IA-4	{IB-7U. IB-31L.	IC-2	ID-5	IE-6	IF-20	IG-7	IH-133
Studebaker Pres. 8-80.....D.-R. (1931)	*IA-4	{IB-3U. IB-32L.	IC-46	ID-60	IE-6	IF-76	IG-35	IH-133
Studebaker Pres. 8-90.....D.-R. (1931)	*IA-4	{IB-3U. IB-32L.	IC-46	ID-60	IE-6	IF-76	IG-35	IH-133
Stutz 695.................R. (1925)	IA-4	IB-4	IC-4	ID-4	IE-65	IF-1	IG-3	IH-111
Stutz AA..................D. (1926)	IA-10	IB-10	IC-89	ID-73	IE-54	{IF-12 IF-67	IG-10	IH-112
Stutz AA..................D. (1927)	IA-10	IB-10	IC-89	ID-73	IE-4	{IF-12 IF-67	IG-10	IH-112
Stutz BB..................D.-R. (1928)	IA-4	IB-10	IC-89	ID-73	IE-61	IF-25	IG-10	IH-7

IGNITION SYSTEM—Continued

Interchangeable Parts have the same CHILTON NUMBER in Any Column								
Car Make and Model	Contact or Breaker Arm	Contact Screw	Distributor Cap	Distributor Rotor	Coil	Automatic Advance Spring	Condenser	Distributor Shaft Gear or Coupling
Stutz Series M............D.-R. (1929-30)	IA-4	IB-10	IC-89	ID-73	IE-66	IF-25	IG-10	IH-7
Stutz M...................D.-R. (1931)	IA-4	IB-10	IC-89	ID-73	IE-66	IF-25	IG-10	IH-7
Velie 60....................R. (1925)	IA-4	IB-4	IC-7	ID-8	IE-3	IF-3	IG-67	IH-114
Velie 60....................R. (1926)	IA-6	IB-6	IC-9	ID-8	IE-3	IF-87	{IG-4 / IG-6	IH-114
Velie Spec. 60............D.-R. (1927)	IA-4	IB-6	IC-9	ID-8	IE-3	IF-87	{IG-4 / IG-6	IH-8
Velie Std. 50 ............A.-L. (1927)	IA-1	IB-1	IC-1	ID-1	IE-50	IF-62	IG-1	IH-116
Velie Spec. 60 ..........D.-R. (1928)	IA-4	IB-6	IC-9	ID-8	IE-3	IF-87	IG-7	IH-8
Velie 6-66................A.-L. (1928)	IA-1	IB-1	IC-1	ID-1	IE-50	IF-62	IG-1	IH-116
Velie 6-77................D.-R. (1928)	IA-4	IB-6	IC-9	ID-8	IE-3	IF-87	IG-7	IH-8
Velie 88..................D.-R. (1928)	*IA-4	{IB-7U. / IB-31L.	IC-5	ID-5	IE-3	IF-7	IG-4	IH-8
Viking...................D.-R. (1929-30)	*IA-4	{IB-7U. / IB-31L.	IC-5	ID-5	IE-42	IF-45	IG-7	IH-32
Westcott 44................D. (1925)	IA-8	IB-10	IC-27	ID-74	IE-85	IF-88	IG-39	IH-118
Westcott 60................D. (1925)	IA-8	IB-10	IC-27	ID-74	IE-85	IF-88	IG-39	IH-118
Whippet 96, 4 Cyl.........A.-L. (1927)	IA-13	IB-12	IC-80	ID-18	IE-1	IF-22	IG-26	IH-43
Whippet 93A, 6 Cyl.......A.-L. (1927)	IA-1	IB-1	IC-1	ID-18	IE-1	IF-74	IG-26	IH-57
Whippet 96, 4 Cyl.........A.-L. (1928)	IA-13	IB-12	IC-80	ID-18	IE-1	IF-47	IG-26	IH-43
Whippet 98, 6 Cyl.........A.-L. (1928)	IA-13	IB-12	IC-33	ID-18	IE-1	IF-47	IG-26	IH-57
Whippet 96A...............A.-L. (1929)	IA-13	IB-12	IC-80	ID-18	IE-1	IF-23	IG-26	IH-43
Whippet 98A...............A.-L. (1929)	IA-13	IB-12	IC-33	ID-18	IE-1	IF-47	IG-26	IH-57
Wills Ste. Claire 8...........D. (1925)	IA-11	IB-10	IC-92	ID-75	IE-20	{IF-30 / IF-71	IG-51	IH-125
Wills Ste. Claire 6...........D. (1925)	IA-11	IB-10	IC-65	ID-76	IE-60	{IF-89 / IF-90	IG-9	IH-126
Wills Ste. Claire 8...........D. (1926)	IA-11	IB-10	IC-92	ID-75	IE-20	{IF-30 / IF-71	IG-51	IH-125
Wills Ste. Claire 6...........D. (1926)	IA-11	IB-10	IC-65	ID-76	IE-60	{IF-89 / IF-90	IG-9	IH-126
Willys 6-98B...............A.-L. (1930)	IA-13	IB-12	IC-33	ID-18	IE-52	IF-11	IG-26	IH-136
Willys 8-80..................(1930)	*IA-41	{IB-12U. / IB-16L.	IC-55	ID-3	IE-71	IF-23	IG-60	IH-136
Willys 6-98D...............A.-L. (1931)	IA-13	IB-12	IC-33	ID-18	IE-71	IF-11	IG-26	IH-136
Willys 8-80D...............A.-L. (1931)	*IA-41	{IB-12U. / IB-16L.	IC-55	ID-3	IE-71	IF-23	IG-60	IH-136
Willys Knight 66............DeJ. (1925)	IA-7	IB-1	IC-1	ID-27	IE-1	IF-74	IG-1	IH-49
Willys Knight 65............A.-L. (1925)	IA-1	IB-1	IC-26	ID-1	IE-62	None	IG-24	IH-119
Willys Knight 66............A.-L. (1926)	IA-1	IB-1	IC-1	ID-1	IF-1	IF-74	IG-1	IH-49
Willys Knight 70............A.-L. (1926)	IA-1	IB-1	IC-1	ID-1	IE-1	IF-74	IG-1	IH-49
Willys Knight 66 A.........A.-L. (1927)	IA-1	IB-1	IC-1	ID-1	IE-1	IF-74	IG-1	IH-49
Willys Knight 70 A.........A.-L. (1927)	IA-1	IB-1	IC-1	ID-1	IE-1	IF-74	IG-1	IH-49
Willys Knight Great 6.......A.-L. (1928)	IA-1	IB-12	IC-1	ID-1	IE-1	IF-47	IG-1	IH-49
Willys Knight Std. 6-56.....A.-L. (1928-29)	IA-1	IB-12	IC-1	ID-1	IE-1	IF-77	IG-1	IH-49
Willys Knight Spec. 6-70A ..A.-L. (1928-29)	IA-1	IB-12	IC-1	ID-1	IE-1	IF-77	IG-1	IH-49
Willys Knight 66A..........A.-L. (1928-29)	IA-1	IB-12	IC-1	ID-1	IE-1	IF-47	IG-1	IH-49
Willys Knight 70B..........A.-L. (1929)	IA-13	IB-12	IC-1	ID-1	IE-1	IF-77	IG-28	IH-49
Willys Knight 66B..........A.-L. (1930)	IA-13	IB-12	IC-1	ID-1	IE-1	IF-65	IG-1	IH-49
Willys Knight 70B..........A.-L. (1930)	IA-13	IB-12	IC-1	ID-1	IE-1	IF-77	IG-28	IH-49
Willys Knight 87...........A.-L. (1930)	IA-13	IB-12	IC-1	ID-1	IE-1	IF-77	IG-28	IH-41
Willys Knight 66D..........A.-L. (1931)	IA-13	IB-12	IC-1	ID-1	IE-71	IF-78	IG-28	IH-58
Willys Knight 87...........A.-L. (1931)	IA-13	IB-12	IC-1	ID-1	IE-1	IF-77	IG-28	IH-41

KEY TO ABBREVIATIONS:

‡ Dodge 4-1926 also uses IF-109, IF-111
‡ Durant 617-1930 also uses IF-59, IF-61.
‡ Packard 326, 333; 236, 243 also use IF-66, IF-71
‡ Packard 426, 433 also use IF-24, IF-66, IF-71
‡ Packard 336, 343 also use IF-24, IF-66.
‡ Studebaker Big Six Special 6-1926-27 also use IF-64, IF-84
‡ Studebaker Dictator 6-1928 also uses IF-6, IF-45.
* Two used.

A.-L.—Auto-Lite.
A.-K-Atwater-Kent.
B.—Bosch.
D.—Delco.
DeJ.-DeJon.
D.-R.—Delco-Remy.

Dy.-Dyneto.
L.—Lower.
N.-E.—North East.
N. S.—Not Serviced.
R.—Remy.
U.—Upper.

IGNITION SYSTEM—Continued

INTERCHANGEABLE COUNT

Showing Exact Number of Times Each CHILTON NUMBER Occurs in the Ignition Table, Beginning Page 227.

Contact or Breaker Arm

IA-1-61
IA-4-230
IA-5-5
IA-6-15
IA-7-2
IA-8-37
IA-9-7
IA-10-24
IA-11-21
IA-12-20
IA-13-48
IA-14-19
IA-15-2
IA-16-7
IA-18-1
IA-22-13
IA-23-3
IA-24-4
IA-25-3
IA-27-1
IA-28-3
IA-29-6
IA-32-9
IA-41-16

Contact Screw

IB-1-27
IB-2-5
IB-3-28
IB-4-38
IB-5-14
IB-6-56
IB-7-77
IB-8-32
IB-9-1
IB-10-88
IB-11-4
IB-12-112
IB-14-19
IB-15-9
IB-16-16
IB-20-3
IB-21-4
IB-22-3
IB-23-1
IB-24-3
IB-30-1
IB-31-69
IB-32-28
IB-33-3
IB-34-3

Distributor Cap

IC-1-48
IC-2-10
IC-3-2
IC-4-17
IC-5-66
IC-6-5
IC-7-28
IC-9-46
IC-10-13
IC-11-7
IC-12-11
IC-13-4
IC-14-6
IC-15-2
IC-16-7
IC-17-2
IC-18-7
IC-19-5
IC-20-2
IC-21-4
IC-22-13
IC-23-1
IC-24-3
IC-25-1
IC-26-12
IC-27-19
IC-28-2
IC-29-1
IC-30-2
IC-31-8
IC-32-7
IC-33-13
IC-34-1
IC-36-6
IC-37-5
IC-38-2
IC-39-9
IC-40-1
IC-42-3
IC-44-3
IC-45-1
IC-46-8
IC-48-1
IC-50-1
IC-52-3
IC-53-1
IC-54-5
IC-55-15
IC-56-1
IC-57-1
IC-58-2
IC-59-5
IC-61-10
IC-62-4
IC-65-10
IC-66-2
IC-68-1
IC-69-3
IC-71-5
IC-73-6
IC-74-2
IC-75-2
IC-76-1
IC-77-3
IC-78-3
IC-80-4
IC-84-2
IC-89-5
IC-92-2
IC-96-4
IC-97-5
IC-98-2
IC-99-2
IC-100-6
IC-101-1
IC-102-2
IC-103-1
IC-104-2

Distributor Rotor

ID-1-47
ID-2-5
ID-3-18
ID-4-7
ID-5-52
ID-6-9
ID-7-19
ID-8-54
ID-9-22
ID-10-40
ID-11-3
ID-12-2
ID-13-8
ID-14-7
ID-15-16
ID-16-6
ID-17-12
ID-18-32
ID-19-18
ID-20-1
ID-21-4
ID-22-7
ID-23-7
ID-24-1
ID-25-1
ID-26-15
ID-27-4
ID-28-1
ID-29-2
ID-30-8
ID-31-1
ID-32-2
ID-33-3
ID-34-4
ID-35-3
ID-36-2
ID-37-1
ID-38-1
ID-39-3
ID-40-3
ID-41-1
ID-42-4
ID-43-2
ID-44-2
ID-45-1
ID-47-3
ID-48-9
ID-49-3
ID-50-4
ID-51-1
ID-53-7
ID-54-3
ID-58-6
ID-59-2
ID-60-12
ID-61-1
ID-62-2
ID-66-2
ID-67-2
ID-71-2
ID-72-2
ID-73-5
ID-74-2
ID-75-2
ID-76-2
ID-80-19
ID-81-2
ID-82-3
ID-83-1

Coil

IE-1-53
IE-2-43
IE-3-15
IE-4-77
IE-5-4
IE-6-37
IE-7-4
IE-8-3
IE-9-20
IE-10-3
IE-11-8
IE-12-5
IE-13-4
IE-14-7
IE-15-5
IE-16-3
IE-17-1
IE-18-4
IE-19-1
IE-20-15
IE-21-1
IE-22-2
IE-23-4
IE-24-1
IE-25-2
IE-26-2
IE-27-3
IE-28-1
IE-29-11
IE-30-1
IE-31-1
IE-32-14
IE-33-1
IE-34-2
IE-35-3
IE-36-4
IE-37-3
IE-38-3
IE-39-1
IE-40-3
IE-41-5
IE-42-8
IE-43-1
IE-44-5
IE-45-1
IE-46-4
IE-47-1
IE-48-1
IE-49-3
IE-50-3
IE-51-4
IE-52-1
IE-53-1
IE-54-7
IE-55-3
IE-56-4
IE-57-2
IE-58-4
IE-59-4
IE-60-3
IE-61-1
IE-62-3
IE-63-1
IE-64-3
IE-65-1
IE-66-2
IE-67-1
IE-68-5
IE-69-2
IE-71-4
IE-73-3
IE-74-1
IE-76-2
IE-77-11
IE-79-2
IE-80-8
IE-81-3
IE-83-3
IE-85-2
IE-86-7
IE-98-1
IE-99-1
IE-100-6
IE-102-2
IE-103-2
IE-104-2

Automatic Advance Spring

IF-1-1
IF-2-10
IF-3-5
IF-4-4
IF-5-26
IF-6-26
IF-7-3
IF-8-5
IF-9-2
IF-10-4
IF-11-5
IF-12-11
IF-13-1
IF-14-13
IF-15-4
IF-16-5
IF-17-10
IF-18-5
IF-19-7
IF-20-13
IF-21-3
IF-22-4
IF-23-11
IF-24-9
IF-25-20
IF-26-6
IF-27-5
IF-28-1
IF-29-4
IF-30-25
IF-31-7
IF-32-1
IF-33-13
IF-34-1
IF-35-1
IF-36-1
IF-37-3
IF-38-1
IF-39-1
IF-40-1
IF-41-4
IF-42-8
IF-43-10
IF-44-1
IF-45-16
IF-46-9
IF-47-24
IF-48-4
IF-50-3
IF-51-2
IF-54-5,
IF-55-3
IF-56-9
IF-57-2
IF-58-2
IF-60-1
IF-62-3
IF-63-2
IF-64-1
IF-65-3
IF-66-15
IF-67-4
IF-68-2
IF-69-2
IF-70-4
IF-71-5
IF-72-1
IF-73-1
IF-74-24
IF-75-3
IF-76-6
IF-77-6
IF-78-1
IF-79-2
IF-80-1
IF-82-6
IF-83-3
IF-84-1
IF-85-2
IF-87-4
IF-88-2
IF-89-2
IF-90-2
IF-91-12
IF-92-5
IF-93-4
IF-94-5
IF-95-15
IF-96-2
IF-97-4
IF-98-9
IF-99-1
IF-100-3
IF-101-1
IF-103-1
IF-104-4
IF-105-2
IF-108-2
IF-109-1
IF-110-1
IF-111-1
IF-112-2
IF-113-4
IF-114-1
IF-115-4

Condenser

IG-1-42
IG-3-9
IG-4-21
IG-6-29
IG-7-91
IG-8-32
IG-9-17
IG-10-30
IG-11-10
IG-13-14
IG-14-5
IG-16-3
IG-17-3
IG-18-18
IG-19-14
IG-20-1
IG-21-6
IG-23-12
IG-24-12
IG-25-2
IG-26-16
IG-27-8
IG-28-15
IG-29-1
IG-31-5
IG-33-4
IG-34-3
IG-35-14
IG-36-2
IG-37-1
IG-38-7
IG-39-2
IG-40-4
IG-41-9
IG-44-2
IG-46-1
IG-47-2
IG-51-2
IG-56-5
IG-57-4
IG-58-3
IG-59-3
IG-60-12
IG-62-1
IG-63-2
IG-64-5
IG-65-11
IG-66-3
IG-67-18
IG-68-12
IG-69-1
IG-71-1
IG-72-5

Distributor Shaft Gear or Coupling

IH-1-7
IH-2-2
IH-3-4
IH-4-2
IH-5-2
IH-6-4
IH-7-14
IH-8-129
IH-9-3
IH-10-1
IH-11-2
IH-12-4
IH-13-6
IH-14-2
IH-15-2
IH-16-3
IH-17-2
IH-18-1
IH-19-1
IH-20-5
IH-21-3
IH-22-3
IH-23-2
IH-24-2
IH-25-18
IH-26-4
IH-27-1
IH-28-2
IH-29-1
IH-30-3
IH-31-2
IH-32-12
IH-33-5
IH-34-1
IH-35-3
IH-36-2
IH-37-2
IH-39-6
IH-40-6
IH-41-18
IH-43-11
IH-44-13
IH-45-3
IH-46-4
IH-47-2
IH-48-1
IH-49-24
IH-50-9
IH-51-4
IH-52-3
IH-53-1
IH-54-4
IH-55-2
IH-56-2
IH-57-3
IH-58-1
IH-60-3
IH-61-5
IH-62-1
IH-63-6
IH-64-1
IH-65-2
IH-67-5
IH-68-3
IH-70-3
IH-72-7
IH-73-4
IH-74-5
IH-75-4
IH-76-3
IH-78-4
IH-79-2
IH-80-6
IH-81-4
IH-82-3
IH-83-6
IH-84-2
IH-85-1
IH-86-2
IH-88-2
IH-91-11
IH-92-2
IH-93-2
IH-94-2
IH-95-3
IH-97-3
IH-98-2
IH-99-2
IH-100-6
IH-101-2
IH-102-2
IH-103-3
IH-105-3
IH-107-7
IH-108-3
IH-111-1
IH-112-2
IH-114-2
IH-116-2
IH-118-2
IH-119-1
IH-121-3
IH-122-8
IH-125-2
IH-126-2
IH-132-4
IH-133-13
IH-134-2
IH-36-4

Clutch, Transmission, Front and Rear Axles

HOW TO USE THIS TABLE

1. Locate in the first column the car and model for which the part is needed.

2. Follow this line across to the column pertaining to that part.

3. In this part column opposite your car model you will find the CHILTON NUMBER for the part you want.

4. Look up and down the part column for the same CHILTON NUMBER. Wherever you find this same number you have an interchangeable part. The car make opposite tells you where to get the part—probably from a local dealer or a nearby jobber.

EXAMPLE: Suppose a King Pin is needed for a Gardner 95 (1928) car. Locate this car in the first column. Follow across to the column on King Pins. Here you see the CHILTON NUMBER for this part is AE-7. Checking through the CHILTON NUMBERS in this same column you will find the number AE-7 opposite the Auburn 115 (1928-29); 120 (Early and Late 1929); 125 (1930), Gardner 130 (1929), Jordan G (1930). The King Pin in all these cars is interchangeable with the one used in your Gardner 95 car.

5. At the end of this table, page 243, you will find the count showing the number of times any part appears in the table.

EXAMPLE: EG-4 under Clutch Facings opposite the Auburn 6-43 (1925), in this table will appear again in the count at the end of the table followed by the figure 4 under the heading Clutch Facings. This indicates part number EG-4 appears 4 times in this table.

Interchangeable Parts have the same CHILTON NUMBER in Any Column

Car Make and Model	CLUTCH			TRANSMISSION			FRONT AXLE		REAR AXLE					
	Clutch Facings (Lining)	Clutch Shaft	Clutch Discs	High and Intermediate Sliding or Coupling Gear	Low and Reverse or Second and Reverse Sliding Gear	Countershaft Gear Assembly	King Pins	King Pin Bushings	Differential Case	Differential Spider or Cross Pin	Differential Spider Pinions	Differential Side Gears	Drive Pinion and Ring Gear	Axle Shafts
Ajax...............(1925-26)	EG-1	EH-1	EI-26	PB-1	PC-1	PE-1	AE-1	AF-1	BD-1	BE-1	BF-1	BG-1	BI-1	BJ-1
Apperson, 6, Col..........(1925)	EG-2	EH-3	EI-56	PB-3	PC-3	PE-3	AE-4	AF-4	BD-4	BE-5	BF-5	BG-4	BI-5	BJ-4
Apperson Str. 8, Col........(1925)	EG-2	EH-3	EI-57	PB-3	PC-3	PE-3	AE-4	AF-4	BD-4	BE-5	BF-5	BG-4	BI-5	BJ-4
Apperson 6, Col..........(1926)	EG-2	EH-3	EI-56	PB-3	PC-3	PE-3	AE-4	AF-4	BD-4	BE-5	BF-5	BG-4	BI-5	BJ-4
Apperson Str. 8, Col........(1926)	EG-2	EH-3	EI-57	PB-3	PC-3	PE-3	AE-4	AF-4	BD-4	BE-5	BF-5	BG-4	BI-5	BJ-43
Auburn 4-44................(1925)	EG-4	EH-4	EI-2	PB-4	PC-4	PE-4	AE-8	AF-5	BD-11	BE-6	BF-6	BG-6	BI-6	BJ-6
Auburn 6-43, Col..........(1925)	EG-4	EH-5	EI-1	PB-4	PC-4	PE-4	AE-15	AF-4	BD-5	BE-5	BF-5	BG-7	BI-5	BJ-178
Auburn 8-88, Col....(Early) (1925)	EG-5	EH-6	EI-58	PB-4	PC-4	PE-4	AE-4	AF-4	BD-5	BE-5	BF-7	BG-7	BI-7	BJ-4
Auburn 8-88, Col......(Late 1925)	EG-5	EH-6	EI-58	PB-4	PC-4	PE-4	AE-4	AF-4	BD-5	BE-5	BF-7	BG-7	BI-7	BJ-65
Auburn 4-44............(1926)	EG-1	EH-4	EI-2	PB-4	PC-4	PE-4	AE-8	AF-5	BD-11	BE-6	BF-6	BG-2	BI-7	BJ-6
Auburn 6-66, Col..........(1926)	EG-4	EH-7	EI-59	PB-4	PC-4	PE-4	AE-4	AF-4	BD-3	BE-8	BF-8	BG-2	BI-7	BJ-7
Auburn 8-88, Col.....(Early 1926)	EG-5	EH-6	EI-58	PB-4	PC-4	PE-4	AE-4	AF-4	BD-5	BE-5	BF-7	BG-2	BI-7	BJ-65
Auburn 8-88, Col.....(Late 1926)	EG-5	EH-6	EI-58	PB-4	PC-4	PE-4	AE-4	AF-4	BD-5	BE-5	BF-7	BG-2	BI-7	BJ-8
Auburn 6-66A, Col........(1927)	EG-6	EH-7	EI-60	PB-2	PC-90	PE-2	AE-5	AF-6	BD-10	BE-7	BF-8	BG-8	BI-8	BJ-9
Auburn 8-88, Col........(1927)	EG-51	EH-8	EI-58	PB-4	PC-4	PE-4	AE-4	AF-4	BD-81	BE-8	BF-8	BG-2	BI-7	BJ-8
Auburn 8-77, Col........(1927-28)	EG-51	EH-7	EI-58	PB-4	PC-4	PE-4	AE-5	AF-6	BD-3	BE-8	BF-8	BG-2	BI-8	BJ-11
Auburn 8-88.............(1928)	EG-51	EH-8	EI-205	PB-4	PC-4	PE-4	AE-4	AF-4	BD-81	BE-8	BF-8	BG-2	BI-7	BJ-8
Auburn 115.............(1928)	EG-8	EH-9	EI-205	PB-4	PC-4	PE-4	AE-7	AF-8	BD-81	BE-8	BF-8	BG-2	BI-7	BJ-8
Auburn 76, Col...........(1928)	EG-6	EH-7	EI-60	PB-2	PC-90	PE-2	AE-6	AF-7	BD-10	BE-7	BF-8	BG-8	BI-8	BJ-5
Auburn 88, Col..........(1928)	EG-6	EH-8	EI-62	PB-6*	PC-4	PE-6*	AE-6	AF-7	BD-86	BE-3	BF-1	BG-9	BI-9	BJ-13
Auburn 115, Col..........(1929)	EG-8	EH-9	EI-63	PB-7	PC-6	PE-7	AE-7	AF-8	BD-81	BE-8	BF-8	BG-2	BI-7	BJ-8
Auburn 6-80*........(Early 1929)	EG-6	EH-7	EI-61	PB-5	PC-101	PE-5	AE-6	AF-7	BD-10	BE-7	BF-8	BG-8	BI-8	BJ-13
Auburn 6-80, Col.....(Late 1929)	EG-6	EH-7	EI-61	PB-2	PC-90	PE-2	AE-6	AF-7	BD-12	BE-29	BF-1	BG-10	BI-10	BJ-13
Auburn 8-90, Col.....(Early 1929)	EG-7	EH-8	EI-62	PB-6	PC-4	PE-6	AE-6	AF-7	BD-86	BE-76	BF-7	BG-9	BI-9	BJ-13
Auburn 8-90, Col.....(Late 1929)	EG-7	EH-8	EI-62	PB-6	PC-4	PE-6	AE-6	AF-7	BD-60	BE-76	BF-7	BG-10	BI-10	BJ-13
Auburn 120, Col.....(Early 1929)	EG-6	EH-9	EI-63	PB-7	PC-6	PE-7	AE-7	AF-8	BD-81	BE-8	BF-7	BG-2	BI-7	BJ-8
Auburn 120, Col.....(Late 1929)	EG-6	EH-9	EI-63	PB-7	PC-6	PE-7	AE-7	AF-8	BD-9	BE-69	BF-8	BG-5	BI-7	BJ-14
Auburn 6-85.........(Early 1930)	EG-6	EH-7	EI-61	PB-5	PC-101	PE-5	AE-6	AF-7	BD-12	BE-39	BF-8	BG-10	BI-10	BJ-13
Auburn 6-85.........(Late 1930)	EG-6	EH-7	EI-61	PB-5	PC-101	PE-5	AE-6	AF-7	BD-64	BE-88	BF-8	BG-3	BI-10	BJ-127
Auburn 8-95.........(1930)	EG-7	EH-8	EI-61	PB-6	PC-4	PE-6	AE-6	AF-7	BD-60	BE-76	BF-7	BG-10	BI-10	BJ-13
Auburn 125.........(1930)	EG-6	EH-9	EI-63	PB-7	PC-6	PE-7	AE-7	AF-8	BD-9	BE-69	BF-2	BG-5	BI-7	BJ-14
Blackhawk L6.......(1929-30)	EG-9	EH-11	EI-3	PB-10	PC-8	PE-10	AE-10	AF-10	BD-6	BE-9	BF-9	BG-11	BI-11	BJ-16
Blackhawk L8.......(1929-30)	EG-9	EH-11	EI-3	PB-10	PC-8	PE-10	AE-10	AF-10	BD-6	BE-9	BF-9	BG-11	BI-11	BJ-16
Buick Master........(1925)	EG-10	EH-12	EI-36	PB-11	PC-9	PE-12	AE-11	AF-11	BD-7	BE-4	BF-4	BG-12	BI-12	*BJ-17
Buick Std...........(1925)	EG-10	EH-13	EI-37	PB-12	PC-10	PE-11	AE-12	AF-12	BD-15	BE-10	BF-10	BG-13	BI-13	BJ-18
Buick Master........(1926)	EG-11	EH-12	EI-36	PB-13	PC-11	PE-12	AE-11	AF-11	BD-7	BE-4	BF-4	BG-12	BI-12	*BJ-17
Buick Std...........(1926)	EG-12	EH-14	EI-37	PB-12	PC-10	PE-11	AE-12	AF-12	BD-15	BE-10	BF-2	BG-13	BI-14	BJ-19
Buick 115...........(1927)	EG-12	EH-15	EI-37	PB-14	PC-12	PE-13	AE-12	AF-12	BD-15	BE-10	BF-2	BG-14	BI-14	BJ-19
Buick 120, 128......(1927)	EG-11	EH-16	EI-36	PB-15	PC-13	PE-14	AE-11	AF-11	BD-7	BE-4	BF-4	BG-15 BG-30	BI-15 BI- 3	*BJ-17
Buick 115...........(1928)	EG-12	EH-15	EI-37	PB-14	PC-12	PE-13	AE-12	AF-12	BD-15	BE-2	BF-2	BG-38 BG-39	BI-14	BJ-20
Buick 120,128.......(1928)	EG-11	EH-16	EI-36	PB-15	PC-13	PE-14	AE-11	AF-11	BD-7	BE-4	BF-4	BG-15 BG-30	BI-15 BI- 3	BJ-17
Buick 116...........(1929)	EG-12	EH-15	EI-37	PB-14	PC-12	PE-13	AE-12	AF-12	BD-16	BE-11	BF-2	BG-16	BI-37	BJ-21
Buick 121, 129......(1929)	EG-11	EH-16	EI-36	PB-15	PC-13	PE-14	AE-11	AF-11	BD-17	BE-12	BF-12	BG-17	BI-17	BJ-23
Buick 40............(1930)	EG-12	EH-10	EI-37	PB-34	PC-12	PE-32	AE-12	AF-12	BD-16	BE-11	BF-2	BG-16	BI-16	BJ-21
Buick 50, 60........(1930)	EG-36	EH-36	EI-36	PB-9	PC-13	PE-14	AE-11	AF-11	BD-17	BE-12	BF-12	BG-17	BI-17	BJ-23
Cadillac V-63......(Early 1925)	EG-13	EH-17	EI-38	PB-16	PC-14	PE-15	AE-13	AF-13	BD-8	BE-4	BF-4	BG-17	BI-17	BJ-24
Cadillac V-63.........(Late 1925)	EG-13	EH-17	EI-38	PB-16	PC-14	PE-15	AE-13	AF-13	BD-8	BE-4	BF-4	BG-18	BI-18	BJ-25
Cadillac 314........(1926)	EG-13	EH-18	EI-38	PB-17	PC-14	PE-15	AE-14	AF-14	BD-18	BE-4	BF-4	BG-40	BI-19	BJ-25
Cadillac 314........(1927)	EG-14	EH-18	EI-38	PB-17	PC-14	PE-15	AE-14	AF-14	BD-18	BE-4	BF-4	BG-40	BI-19	BJ-25
Cadillac 341-A......(1928)	EG-14	EH-19	EI-40	PB-18	PC-14	PE-15	AE-14	AF-14	BD-19	BE-4	BF-4	BG-40	BI-20	BJ-26
Cadillac 341-B......(1929)	EG-14	EH-19	EI-40	PB-18	PC-14	PE-15	AE-14	AF-14	BD-19	BE-4	BF-4	BG-40	BI-20	BJ-26
Cadillac 353........(1930)	EG-167	EH-167	EI-39	PB-117	PC-100	PE-16	AE-107	None	BD-96	BE-104	BF-3	BG-85	BI-20	BJ-27
Case JIC, Col.......(1925)	EG-15	EH-20	EI-64	PB-19	PC-17	PE-18	AE-4	AF-4	BD-20	BE-5	BF-5	BG-19	BI-21	BJ-28
Case X, Col.........(1925)	EG-15	EH-21	EI-64	PB-20	PC-18	PE-19	AE-15	AF-4	BD-22	BE-4	BF-4	BG-84	BI-7	BJ-28
Case Y, Col.........(1925)	EG-15	EH-22	EI-64	PB-21	PC-19	PE-20	AE-16	AF-15	BD-22	BE-4	BF-4	BG-20	BI-49	BJ-29
Case JIC, Col.......(1926)	EG-15	EH-20	EI-64	PB-19	PC-17	PE-18	AE-4	AF-4	BD-20	BE-5	BF-5	BG-19	BI-21	BJ-28
Case Y, Col.........(1926)	EG-15	EH-22	EI-64	PB-21	PC-19	PE-20	AE-16	AF-15	BD-22	BE-4	BF-4	BG-20	BI-49	BJ-29
Chandler 33.........(1925)	EG-2	EH-23	EI-66	PB-22	PC-20	PE-21	AE-17	AF-16	BD-23	BE-5	BF-5	BG-21	BI-24	BJ-30
Chandler 35.........(1926)	EG-2	EH-24	EI-4	PB-23	PC-21	PE-22	AE-17	AF-16	BD-23	BE-5	BF-5	BG-21	BI-24	BJ-30
Chandler Big 6......(1927)	EG-2	EH-24	EI-67	PB-23	PC-21	PE-22	AE-17	AF-16	BD-24	BE-5	BF-5	BG-21	BI-24	BJ-30
Chandler Royal 8....(1927)	EG-2	EH-24	EI-68	PB-23	PC-21	PE-22	AE-17	AF-16	BD-25	BE-5	BF-5	BG-21	BI-24	BJ-30
Chandler Spec. 6....(1927)	EG-2	EH-23	EI-5	PB-22	PC-20	PE-21	AE-18	AF-17	BD-26	BE-13	BF-10	BG-22	BI-25	BJ-31
Chandler Std. 6......(1927)	EG-1	EH-25	EI-6	PB-24	PC-22	PE-23	AE-20	AF-19	BD-39	BE-19	BF-13	BG-29	BI-57	BJ-32

CLUTCH, TRANSMISSION, FRONT AND REAR AXLES—Continued

	CLUTCH			TRANSMISSION			FRONT AXLE		REAR AXLE					
Car Make and Model	Clutch Facings (Lining)	Clutch Shaft	Clutch Discs	High and Intermediate Sliding or Coupling Gear	Low and Reverse or Second and Reverse Sliding Gear	Countershaft Gear Assembly	King Pins	King Pin Bushings	Differential Case	Differential Spider or Cross Pin	Differential Spider Pinions	Differential Side Gears	Drive Pinion and Ring Gear	Axle Shafts
Chandler Big 6............(1928)	EG-2	EH-24	EI-5	PB-23	PC-21	PE-22	AE-17	AF-16	BD-24	BE-5	BF-5	BG-21	BI-24	BJ-30
Chandler Royal 8...........(1928)	EG-2	EH-24	EI-5	PB-23	PC-21	PE-22	AE-17	AF-16	BD-25	BE-5	BF-5	BG-21	BJ-50	BJ-30
Chandler Spec. 6............(1928)	EG-1	EH-23	EI-5	PB-22	PC-20	PE-21	AE-19	AF-18	BD-26	BE-14	BF-10	BG-23	BI-26	BJ-31
Chandler Spec. Inv. 6.......(1928)	EG-1	EH-23	EI-5	PB-22	PC-20	PE-21	AE-19	AF-18	BD-26	BE-14	BF-10	BG-23	BI-26	BJ-31
Chevrolet K................(1925)	EG-16	EH-26	EI-43	PB-25	PC-23	PE-47	AE-21	AF-20	BD-27	BE-15	BF-15	BG-24	BI-27	BJ-33
Chevrolet V................(1926)	EG-16	EH-26	EI-43	PB-25	PC-23	PE-47	AE-21	AF-20	BD-27	BF-15	BF-15	BG-24	BI-27	BJ-33
Chevrolet AA...............(1927)	EG-16	EH-26	EI-43	PB-25	PC-23	PE-47	AE-21	AF-20	BD-27	BE-15	BF-15	BG-24	BI-27	BJ-33
Chevrolet AB...............(1928)	EG-16	EH-26	EI-43	PB-25	PC-23	PE-47	AE-22	AF-21	BD-27	BE-15	BF-15	BG-24	BI-27	BJ-33
Chevrolet AC...............(1929)	EG-16	EH-27	EI-44	PB-26	PC-24	PE-25	AE-22	AF-21	BD-28	BE-15	BF-15	BG-24	BI-28	BJ-33
Chevrolet AD...............(1930)	EG-16	EH-27	EI-44	PB-37	PC-23	PE-25	AE-22	AF-21	BD-21	BE-127	BF-11	BG-83	BI-52	BJ-98
Chrysler 6-B...............(1925)	EG-54	EH-28	EI-69	PB-27	PC-25	PE-26	AE-23	AF-22	BD-29	BE-16	BF-16	BG-25	BI-29	BJ-35
Chrysler 58................(1925)	Inter.	EH-29	EI-70	PB-28	PC-4	PE-27	AE-25	AF-112	BD-30	BE-17	BF-17	BG-130	BI-30	BJ-36
Chrysler 58................(1926)	Inter.	EH-29	EI-70	PB-28	PC-4	PE-27	AE-24	AF-23	BD-31	BE-18	BF-16	BG-25	BI-31	BJ-99
Chrysler 60................(1926)	Inter.	EH-32	EI-71	PB-28	PC-4	PE-27	AE-24	AF-23	BD-31	BE-18	BF-16	BG-25	BI-31	BJ-99
Chrysler 70................(1926)	Inter.	EH-28	EI-71	PB-27	PC-25	PE-17	AE-24	AF-23	BD-29	BE-16	BF-16	BG-25	BI-32	BJ-35
Chrysler 80................(1926)	Inter.	EH-30	EI-72	PB-30	PC-27	PE-28	AE-27	AF-24	BD-33	BE-5	BF-18	BG-26	BI-34	BJ-113
Chrysler 50................(1927)	Seg.	EH-31	EI-73	PB-31	PC-28	PE-29	AE-23	AF-5	BD-34	BE-20	BF-8	BG-27	BI-33	BJ-37
Chrysler 60................(1927)	Inter.	EH-165	EI-71	PB-29	PC-26	PE-27	AE-24	AF-23	BD-29	BE-16	BF-16	BG-25	BI-32	BJ-99
Chrysler 62................(1927)	EG-2	EH-33	EI-7	PB-32	PC-29	PE-30	AE-24	AF-23	BD-29	BE-16	BF-16	BG-25	BI-32	BJ-35
Chrysler 70................(1927)	Inter.	EH-28	EI-71	PB-27	PC-25	PE-17	AE-24	AF-23	BD-29	BE-16	BF-16	BG-25	BI-32	BJ-35
Chrysler 80................(1927)	Inter.	EH-30	EI-74	PB-30	PC-27	PE-28	AE-27	AF-24	BD-33	BE-5	BF-5	BG-26	BI-34	BJ-113
Chrysler 52................(1928)	Seg.	EH-31	EI-73	PB-31	PC-28	PE-29	AE-23	AF-5	BD-34	BE-20	BF-8	BG-27	BI-33	BJ-37
Chrysler 62................(1928)	EG-2	EH-33	EI-7	PB-32	PC-29	PE-30	AE-24	AF-23	BD-36	BE-21	BF-14	BG-28	BI-23	BJ-35
Chrysler 72................(1928)	EG-18	EH-33	EI-86	PB-32	PC-29	PE-30	AE-24	AF-23	BD-36	BE-21	BF-14	BG-28	BI-23	BJ-39
Chrysler Imp. 80...........(1928)	EG-17	EH-34	EI-74	PB-33	PC-30	PE-31	AE-27	AF-24	BD-37	BE-21	BF-14	BG-28	BI-35	BJ-40
Chrysler 65................(1929)	EG-2	EH-33	EI-7	PB-32	PC-29	PE-30	AE-26	AF-23	BD-36	BE-21	BF-14	BG-28	BI-23	BJ-41
Chrysler 75................(1929)	EG-18	EH-33	EI-86	PB-32	PC-29	PE-30	AE-26	AF-23	BD-36	BE-21	BF-14	BG-28	BI-23	BJ-41
Chrysler Imp. 80...........(1929)	EG-17	EH-34	EI-74	PB-33	PC-30	PE-31	AE-27	AF-24	BD-38	BE-21	BF-14	BG-28	BI-35	BJ-40
Chrysler 6.................(1930)	EG-1	EH-40	EI-10	PB-40	PC-5	PE-37	AE-30	AF-5	BD-47	BE-30	BF-24	BG-133	BI-91	BJ-55
Chrysler 66................(1930)	EG-2	EH-44	EI-7	PB-44	PC-7	PE-33	AE-30	AF-5	BD-32	BE-30	BF-24	BG-133	BI-55	BJ-55
Chrysler 70................(1930)	EG-2	EH-170	EI-7	PB-118	PC-30	PE-107	AE-26	AF-23	BD-35	BE-21	BF-14	BG-28	BI-56	BJ-38
Chrysler 77................(1930)	EG-18	EH-170	EI-86	PB-118	PC-30	PE-107	AE-26	AF-23	BD-35	BE-21	BF-14	BG-28	BI-56	BJ-38
Cleveland 31...............(1925)	EG-1	EH-25	EI-6	PB-24	PC-22	PE-23	AE-20	AF-19	BD-39	BE-23	BF-19	BG-29	BI-36	BJ-32
Cleveland 43...............(1925)	EG-2	EH-23	EI-15	PB-22	PC-20	PE-21	AE-18	AF-17	BD-26	BE-13	BF-10	BG-22	BI-25	BJ-31
Cleveland 31...............(1926)	EG-1	EH-25	EI-6	PB-24	PC-22	PE-23	AE-20	AF-19	BD-39	BE-19	BF-13	BG-29	BI-57	BJ-32
Cleveland 43...............(1926)	EG-2	EH-23	EI-5	PB-22	PC-20	PE-21	AE-18	AF-17	BD-26	BE-13	BF-10	BG-22	BI-25	BJ-31
Davis 92, Col..............(1925)	EG-2	EH-7	EI-1	PB-5	PC-5	PE-5	AE-29	AF-6	BD-3	BE-8	BF-7	BG-2	BI-7	BJ-50
Davis 90...............(1925-26)	EG-2	EH-39	EI-1	PB-38	PC-35	PE-5	AE-29	AF-26	BD-53	BE-28	BF-26	BG-33	BI-40	BJ-49
Davis 91...............(1925-26)	EG-2	EH-39	EI-1	PB-38	PC-35	PE-5	AE-29	AF-26	BD-53	BE-28	BF-26	BG-33	BI-40	BJ-49
Davis 92, Col..............(1926)	EG-2	EH-7	EI-1	PB-5	PC-5	PE-5	AE-29	AF-6	BD-10	BE-7	BF-7	BG-8	BI-8	BJ-54
Davis 93, Col..............(1926)	EG-1	EH-7	EI-6	PB-5	PC-5	PE-5	AE-5	AF-6	BD-10	BE-7	BF-8	BG-8	BI-8	BJ-51
Davis 92, Col..............(1927)	EG-2	EH-7	EI-8	PB-5	PC-5	PE-5	AE-4	AF-4	BD-10	BE-7	BF-8	BG-8	BI-8	BJ-54
Davis 93, Col..............(1927)	EG-1	EH-7	EI-6	PB-5	PC-5	PE-5	AE-5	AF-6	BD-10	BE-7	BF-8	BG-8	BI-8	BJ-51
Davis 94, Col..............(1927)	EG-1	EH-7	EI-6	PB-5	PC-5	PE-5	AE-5	AF-6	BD-10	BE-7	BF-8	BG-8	BI-8	BJ-51
Davis 98, Col..............(1927)	EG-2	EH-7	EI-78	PB-39	PC-36	PE-36	AE-4	AF-4	BD-10	BE-7	BF-8	BG-8	BI-41	BJ-54
Davis 99, Col..............(1928)	EG-2	EH-7	EI-79	PB-39	PC-36	PE-36	AE-4	AF-4	BD-10	BE-7	BF-8	BG-8	BI-42	BJ-54
De Soto 6..................(1929)	EG-1	EH-40	EI-10	PB-40	PC-5	PE-37	AE-30	AF-5	BD-47	BE-30	BF-8	BG-62	BI-91	BJ-55
De Soto Finer 6............(1930)	EG-1	EH-37	EI-10	PB-47	PC-31	PE-34	AE-30	AF-5	BD-47	BE-30	BF-8	BG-133	BI-91	BJ-55
De Soto 8..................(1930)	EG-1	EH-37	EI-76	PB-47	PC-31	PE-34	AE-30	AF-5	BD-115	BE-22	BF-65	BG-106	BI-53	BJ-132
Diana Str. 8, Col..........(1926)	EG-2	EH-41	EI-9	PB-4	PC-4	PE-4	AE-29	AF-6	BD-5	BE-10	BF-36	BG-7	BI-5	BJ-50
Diana Str. 8, Col..........(1927)	EG-2	EH-41	EI-9	PB-4	PC-4	PE-4	AE-29	AF-6	BD-5	BE-10	BF-36	BG-7	BI-5	BJ-50
Diana Str. 8, Col..........(1928)	EG-2	EH-41	EI-9	PB-4	PC-4	PE-4	AE-31	AF-27	BD-5	BE-10	BF-36	BG-7	BI-5	BJ-50
Dodge Brothers 4...........(1925)	EG-53	EH-42	EI-80	PB-41	PC-38	PE-38	AE-32	AF-28	BD-57	BE-31	BF-27	BG-34	BI-43	BJ-58
Dodge Brothers 4.....(Early 1926)	EG-53	EH-42	EI-81	PB-41	PC-38	PE-38	AE-32	AF-28	BD-57	BE-31	BF-27	BG-34	BI-43	BJ-58
Dodge Brothers 4......(Late 1926)	EG-53	EH-42	EI-81	PB-41	PC-38	PE-38	AE-33	AF-28	BD-57	BE-31	BF-27	BG-34	BI-43	BJ-139
Dodge Brothers 4...........(1927)	EG-2	EH-42	EI-11	PB-43	PC-39	PE-39	AE-33	AF-28	BD-57	BE-31	BF-27	BG-34	BI-43	BJ-139
Dodge Brothers Senior.(Early 1928)	EG-9	EH-42	EI-12	PB-43	PC-40	PE-40	AE-34	AF-23	BD-57, BD-58	BE-33	BF-28	BG-36	BI-45	BJ-140
Dodge Brothers Senior..(Late 1928)	EG-9	EH-42	EI-12	PB-43	PC-40	PE-40	AE-34	AF-23	BD-57, BD-58	BE-33	BF-28	BG-36	BI-45	BJ-145
Dodge Brothers Std. 6.......(1928)	EG-2	EH-43	EI-11	PB-43	PC-40	PE-40	AE-35	AF-29	BD-58	BE-33	BF-28	BG-36	BI-45	BJ-59
Dodge Brothers Vic. 6....(1928-29)	EG-2	EH-43	EI-11	PB-43	PC-40	PE-40	AE-35	AF-29	BD-58	BE-33	BF-28	BG-36	BI-45	BJ-59
Dodge Brothers Senior.......(1929)	EG-2	EH-44	EI-12	PB-43	PC-41	PE-40	AE-34	AF-23	BD-58	BE-33	BF-28	BG-36	BI-45	BJ-60
Dodge Brothers DA-6........(1929)	EG-2	EH-44	EI-7	PB-44	PC-41	PE-33	AE-37	AF-29	BD-58	BE-33	BF-28	BG-31	BI-45	BJ-61
Dodge Brothers DC-8........(1930)	EG-2	EH-37	EI-76	PB-47	PC-31	PE-34	AE-30	AF-5	BD-115	BE-22	BF-65	BG-106	BI-53	BJ-132
Dodge Brothers DD-6........(1930)	EG-1	EH-37	EI-10	PB-47	PC-31	PE-34	AE-30	AF-5	BD-115	BE-22	BF-65	BG-106	BI-53	BJ-132
Durant A-22................(1925)	Seg.	EH-50	EI-89	PB-50	PC-23	PE-47	AE-39	AF-31	BD-65	BE-1	BF-1	BG-41	BI-58	BJ-66
Durant D-55................(1928)	Seg.	EH-51	EI-90	PB-50	PC-23	PE-47	AE-41	AF-31	BD-10	BE-7	BF-8	BG-32	BI-59	BJ-67
Durant 65..................(1928)	Seg.	EH-165	EI-90	PB-50	PC-23	PE-47	AE-41	AF-31	BD-10	BE-7	BF-8	BG-32	BI-59	BJ-67
Durant M2..............(1928-29)	Seg.	EH-51	EI-91	PB-50	PC-23	PE-47	AE-41	AF-31	BD-10	BE-7	BF-8	BG-32	BI-59	BJ-67
Durant 75..............(1928-29)	Seg.	EH-51	EI-90	PB-42	PC-23	PE-47	AE-118	AF-98	BD-1	BE-1	BF-1	BG-41	BI-60	BJ-68
Durant 4-40................(1929)	Seg.	EH-51	EI-92	PB-50	PC-23	PE-47	AE-41	AF-31	BD-10	BE-7	BF-8	BG-8	BI-59	BJ-67
Durant 6-60................(1929)	Seg.	EH-51	EI-93	PB-50	PC-23	PE-47	AE-41	AF-31	BD-10	BE-7	BF-8	BG-32	BI-59	BJ-67
Durant 66..................(1929)	Seg.	EH-51	EI-13	PB-42	PC-23	PE-47	AE-41	AF-31	BD-10	BE-7	BF-8	BG-32	BI-59	BJ-67
Durant 70..................(1929)	Seg.	EH-166	EI-13	PB-42	PC-23	PE-47	AE-118	AF-98	BD-1	BE-1	BF-1	BG-41	BI-60	BJ-68
Durant 614.................(1930)	EG-1	EH-171	EI-75	PB-50	PC-23	PE-47	AE-41	AF-31	BD-64	BE-29	BF-32	BG-37	BI-61	BJ-69
Durant 617.................(1930)	EG-2	EH-168	EI-13	PB-122	PC-106	PE-35	AE-118	AF-98	BD-1	BE-1	BF-1	BG-41	BI-22	BJ-70
Elcar 4-40.................(1925)	EG-55	EH-39	EI-1	PB-38	PC-35	PE-5	AE-42	AF-32	BD-70	BE-5	BF-10	BG-45	BI-2	BJ-2
Elcar 6-50.................(1925)	EG-55	EH-39	EI-1	PB-38	PC-35	PE-5	AE-43	AF-33	BD-70	BE-5	BF-10	BG-45	BI-2	BJ-2
Elcar 6-60.................(1925)	EG-1	EH-39	EI-1	PB-38	PC-35	PE-5	AE-44	AF-34	BD-71	BE-5	BF-5	BG-46	BI-64	BJ-73
Elcar 8-80.................(1925)	EG-2	EH-6	EI-1	PB-4	PC-4	PE-4	AE-45	AF-35	BD-2	BE-5	BF-5	BG-46	BI-64	BJ-3
Elcar 4-55.................(1926)	EG-1	EH-39	EI-6	PB-38	PC-35	PE-5	AE-42	AF-32	BD-70	BE-5	BF-10	BG-45	BI-2	BJ-2
Elcar 6-65.................(1926)	EG-1	EH-6	EI-1	PB-38	PC-35	PE-5	AE-44	AF-34	BD-13	BE-5	BF-10	BG-14	BI-2	BJ-2
Elcar 8-81.................(1926)	EG-2	EH-6	EI-1	PB-4	PC-4	PE-4	AE-45	AF-35	BD-2	BE-5	BF-10	BG-46	BI-64	BJ-3
Elcar 6-70.................(1927)	EG-6	EH-6	EI-94	PB-4	PC-4	PE-4	AE-46	AF-36	BD-13	BE-37	BF-10	BG-47	BI-67	BJ-74
Elcar 8-82.................(1927)	EG-5	EH-6	EI-95	PB-4	PC-4	PE-4	AE-45	AF-35	BD-72	BE-10	BF-36	BG-48	BI-68	BJ-2
Elcar 8-90.................(1927)	EG-8	EH-8	EI-96	PB-6	PC-4	PE-6	AE-47	AF-37	BD-72	BE-41	BF-37	BG-48	BI-68	BJ-76
Elcar 8-91.................(1928)	EG-8	EH-8	EI-97	PB-6	PC-4	PE-6	AE-47	AF-37	BD-14	BE-53	BF-39	BG-51	BI-70	BJ-76
Elcar 120..................(1928)	EG-6	EH-8	EI-98	PB-6	PC-4	PE-6	AE-49	AF-39	BD-75	BE-59	BF-40	BG-52	BI-71	BJ-76
Elcar 6-70.............(1928-29)	EG-6	EH-6	EI-94	PB-4	PC-4	PE-4	AE-46	AF-36	BD-13	BE-127	BF-10	BG-47	BI-67	BJ-74
Elcar 8-78.............(1928-29)	EG-6	EH-52	EI-94	PB-5	PC-5	PE-5	AE-48	AF-38	BD-41	BE-130	BF-38	BG-48	BI-70	BJ-2
Elcar 8-82.............(1928-29)	EG-5	EH-6	EI-95	PB-4	PC-4	PE-4	AE-45	AF-35	BD-72	BE-10	BF-36	BG-48	BI-68	BJ-2
Elcar 75...................(1929)	EG-6	EH-8	EI-99	PB-4	PC-4	PE-4	AE-50	AF-40	BD-13	BE-40	BF-41	BG-53	BI-72	BJ-74
Elcar 95, 96...............(1929)	EG-51	EH-8	EI-100	PB-6	PC-4	PE-6	AE-51	AF-41	BD-14	BE-41	BF-37	BG-53	BI-70	BJ-81
Elcar 120..................(1929)	EG-6	EH-8	EI-98	PB-6	PC-4	PE-6	AE-47	AF-37	BD-75	BE-42	BF-40	BG-52	BI-71	BJ-76
Erskine 6-50...............(1927)	EG-6	EH-31	EI-101	PB-51	PC-47	PE-48	AE-52	AF-42	BD-76	BE-7	BF-8	BG-42	BI-75	BJ-83
Erskine 6-51...............(1928)	EG-6	EH-31	EI-101	PB-40	PC-5	PE-37	AE-52	AF-42	BD-76	BE-7	BF-8	BG-43	BI-69	BJ-83
Erskine 6-52...............(1929)	EG-6	EH-40	EI-101	PB-40	PC-5	PE-57	AE-52	AF-42	BD-40	BE-7	BF-8	BG-43	BI-69	BJ-83
Erskine 53.................(1930)	EG-52	EH-40	EI-127	PB-40	PC-5	PE-37	AE-112	AF-92	BD-40	BE-7	BF-8	BG-43	BI-69	BJ-198
Essex 6....................(1925)	None	EH-54	EI-45	PB-52	PC-48	PE-49	AE-53	AF-43	BD-77	BE-44	BF-5	BG-56	BI-76	BJ-84
Essex 6....................(1926)	None	EH-55	EI-45	PB-52	PC-48	PE-49	AE-53	AF-43	BD-77	BE-44	BF-5	BG-56	BI-76	BJ-84
Essex Super 6..............(1927)	None	EH-56	EI-46	PB-52	PC-48	PE-49	AE-54	AF-44	BD-77	BE-44	BF-5	BG-56	BI-66	BJ-84
Essex Super 6..............(1928)	None	EH-56	EI-46	PB-52	PC-48	PE-49	AE-54	AF-44	BD-78	BE-44	BF-5	BG-56	BI-65	BJ-84

CLUTCH, TRANSMISSION, FRONT AND REAR AXLES—Continued

Car Make and Model	CLUTCH			TRANSMISSION			FRONT AXLE		REAR AXLE					
	Clutch Facings (Lining)	Clutch Shaft	Clutch Discs	High and Intermediate Sliding or Coupling Gear	Low and Reverse or Second and Reverse Sliding Gear	Countershaft Gear Assembly	King Pins	King Pin Bushings	Differential Case	Differential Spider or Cross Pin	Differential Spider Pinions	Differential Side Gears	Drive Pinion and Ring Gear	Axle Shafts
Essex Challenger (1929)	None	EH-56	EI-46	PB-52	PC-48	PE-49	AE-54	AF-44	BD-78	BE-44	BF-5	BG-56	BI-63	BJ-84
Essex (1930)	None	EH-46	EI-46	PB-48	PC-33	PE-44	AE-54	AF-44	BD-42	BE-44	BF-5	BG-44	BI-62	BJ-46
Falcon Knight 10 (1927)	EG-1	EH-57	EI-14	PB-53	PC-49	PE-50	AE-55	None	BD-1	BE-1	BF-1	BG-1	BI-77	BJ-85
Falcon Knight 12 (1928)	Seg.	EH-57	EI-14	PB-53	PC-49	PE-50	AE-55	None	BD-1	BE-1	BF-1	BG-1	BI-73	BJ-86
Falcon Knight (1929)	Seg.	EH-58	EI-14	PB-54	PC-49	PE-51	AE-55	None	BD-1	BE-1	BF-1	BG-1	BI-73	BJ-86
Flint, Jr. (1925)	Seg.	EH-61	EI-105	PB-50	PC-23	PE-47	AE-39	AF-31	BD-10	BE-7	BF-8	BG-8	BI-59	BJ-67
Flint B40 (1925)	Seg.	EH-59	EI-102	PB-50	PC-23	PE-47	AE-56	AF-45	BD-1	BE-1	BF-1	BG-1	BI-79	BJ-88
Flint B40 (1926)	Seg.	EH-59	EI-102	PB-50	PC-23	PE-47	AE-56	AF-45	BD-1	BE-1	BF-1	BG-1	BI-79	BJ-90
Flint E55 (1925)	Seg.	EH-60	EI-103	PB-55	PC-50	PE-24	AE-57	AF-46	BD-80	BE-45	BF-44	BG-57	BI-80	BJ-89
Flint E55 (1926)	Seg.	EH-60	EI-103	PB-55	PC-50	PE-24	AE-57	AF-46	BD-80	BE-45	BF-44	BG-57	BI-80	BJ-91
Flint 60 (1926)	Seg.	EH-59	EI-104	PB-50	PC-23	PE-47	AE-56	AF-45	BD-1	BE-1	BF-1	BG-1	BI-79	BJ-90
Flint 80 (1926)	Seg.	EH-60	EI-103	PB-55	PC-50	PE-24	AE-58	AF-46	BD-43	BE-46	BF-44	BG-57	BI-80	BJ-91
Flint Jr. (1926)	Seg.	EH-61	EI-105	PB-50	PC-23	PE-47	AE-39	AF-31	BD-10	BE-7	BF-8	BG-8	BI-59	BJ-67
Flint 60 (1927)	Seg.	EH-59	EI-104	PB-50	PC-23	PE-47	AE-56	AF-45	BD-1	BE-1	BF-1	BG-1	BI-79	BJ-90
Flint 80 (1927)	Seg.	EH-60	EI-103	PB-55	PC-50	PE-24	AE-58	AF-46	BD-43	BE-46	BF-44	BG-57	BI-80	BJ-91
Flint Jr. (1927)	Seg.	EH-61	EI-105	PB-50	PC-23	PE-47	AE-39	AF-31	BD-10	BE-7	BF-8	BG-8	BI-59	BJ-67
Ford T (1925)	...	...	...	...	...	...	AE-59	AF-47	BD-82	BE-47	BF-45	BG-58	BI-81	BJ-93
Ford T (1926)	...	...	...	...	...	...	AE-59	AF-47	BD-82	BE-47	BF-45	BG-58	BI-81	BJ-93
Ford T (1927)	...	...	...	...	...	...	AE-59	AF-47	BD-82	BE-47	BF-45	BG-58	BI-81	BJ-93
Ford A (1928)	EG-22	EH-62	EI-47	PB-56	PC-51	PE-52	AE-60	AF-48	BD-83	BE-48	BF-46	BG-59	BI-82	BJ-94
Ford A (1929)	EG-23	EH-62	EI-42	PB-56	PC-51	PE-52	AE-60	AF-48	BD-83	BE-48	BF-46	BG-59	BI-82	BJ-94
Ford A (1930)	EG-23	EH-172	EI-42	PB-56	PC-51	PE-52	AE-60	AF-48	BD-83	BE-48	BF-46	BG-59	BI-82	BJ-94
Franklin 11 (1925)	EG-2	EH-63	EI-106	PB-57	PC-52	PE-53	AE-61	AF-49	BD-84	BE-49	BF-47	BG-60	BI-83	BJ-95
Franklin 11 (1926)	EG-2	EH-63	EI-106	PB-57	PC-52	PE-53	AE-61	AF-49	BD-84	BE-49	BF-47	BG-60	BI-83	BJ-95
Franklin 11-B (1027)	EG-2	EH-63	EI-106	PB-57	PC-52	PE-53	AE-61	AF-49	BD-84	BE-49	BF-47	BG-60	BI-83	BJ-95
Franklin Ser. 12 (1927-28)	EG-2	EH-64	EI-107	PB-57	PC-53	PE-54	AE-61	AF-49	BD-84	BE-49	BF-48	BG-60	BI-83	BJ-72
Franklin 130 (1929)	EG-2	EH-65	EI-107	PB-99	PC-53	PE-54	AE-62	AF-50	BD-86	BE-50	BF-48	BG-61	BI-84	BJ-96
Franklin 135, 137 (1929)	EG-24	EH-176	EI-108	PB-58	PC-104	PE-115	AE-62	AF-50	BD-86	BE-50	BF-48	BG-61	BI-84	BJ-96
Franklin 137* (1929)	EG-24	EH-177	EI-108	PB-132	PC-103	PE-116	AE-62	AF-50	BD-86	BE-50	BF-48	BG-61	BI-84	BJ-96
Franklin 145, 147 (1930)	EG-24	EH-47	EI-209	PB-119	PC-105	PE-45	AE-62	AF-50	BD-85	BE-50	BF-48	BG-61	BI-78	BJ-96
Franklin 145, 147* (1930)	EG-24	EH-177	EI-209	PB-132	PC-103	PE-116	AE-62	AF-50	BD-85	BE-50	BF-48	BG-61	BI-78	BJ-96
Gardner 6-A, Col. (1925)	EG-2	EH-66	EI-15	PB-4	PC-4	PE-4	AE-4	AF-4	BD-3	BE-38	BF-7	BG-2	BI-7	BJ-49
Gardner 8-A, Col. (1925)	EG-2	EH-67	EI-15	PB-4	PC-4	PE-4	AE-4	AF-4	BD-5	BE-8	BF-7	BG-2	BI-5	BJ-4
Gardner Ser. 5 (1925)	EG-2	EH-68	EI-109	PB-4	PC-4	PE-4	AE-63	AF-51	BD-88	BE-52	BF-10	BG-63	BI-86	BJ-100
Gardner 6-B, Col. (1926)	EG-2	EH-66	EI-9	PB-4	PC-4	PE-4	AE-4	AF-4	BD-3	BE-38	BF-7	BG-2	BI-7	BJ-49
Gardner 8-B, Col. (1926)	EG-2	EH-67	EI-9	PB-4	PC-4	PE-4	AE-4	AF-4	BD-5	BE-8	BF-7	BG-2	BI-5	BJ-4
Gardner 75, Col. (1927)	EG-1	EH-67	EI-18	PB-4	PC-4	PE-4	AE-5	AF-6	BD-10	BE-7	BF-8	BG-8	BI-8	BJ-9
Gardner 80, Col. (1927)	EG-1	EH-67	EI-18	PB-4	PC-4	PE-4	AE-5	AF-6	BD-10	BE-7	BF-8	BG-49	BI-8	BJ-9
Gardner 85, Col. (1927)	EG-1	EH-66	EI-18	PB-4	PC-4	PE-4	AE-6	AF-124	BD-3	BE-38	BF-7	BG-2	BI-7	BJ-11
Gardner 90, Col. (1927)	EG-2	EH-67	EI-9	PB-4	PC-4	PE-4	AE-4	AF-4	BD-5	BE-8	BF-7	BG-2	BI-5	BJ-4
Gardner 75, Col. (1928)	EG-1	EH-67	EI-18	PB-4	PC-4	PE-4	AE-5	AF-6	BD-10	BE-7	BF-8	BG-8	BI-8	BJ-11
Gardner 85, Col. (1928)	EG-1	EH-66	EI-18	PB-4	PC-4	PE-4	AE-6	AF-7	BD-3	BE-38	BF-7	BG-2	BI-7	BJ-13
Gardner 95, Col. (1928)	EG-2	EH-67	EI-16	PB-4	PC-4	PE-4	AE-7	AF-8	BD-5	BE-8	BF-7	BG-2	BI-5	BJ-8
Gardner 85, Col. (1929)	EG-1	EH-66	EI-18	PB-4	PC-4	PE-4	AE-6	AF-7	BD-3	BE-38	BF-7	BG-2	BI-7	BJ-13
Gardner 120, Col. (1929)	EG-1	EH-66	EI-19	PB-4	PC-4	PE-4	AE-6	AF-7	BD-12	BE-3	BF-1	BG-9	BI-10	BJ-13
Gardner 125, Col. (1929)	EG-1	EH-67	EI-19	PB-4	PC-4	PE-4	AE-6	AF-7	BD-12	BE-3	BF-8	BG-2	BI-7	BJ-13
Gardner 130, Col. (1929)	EG-2	EH-67	EI-17	PB-4	PC-4	PE-4	AE-7	AF-8	BD-12	BE-8	BF-1	BG-2	BI-7	BJ-14
Graham Paige 610 (Early 1928)	EG-6	EH-69	EI-110	PB-31	PC-28	PE-29	AE-44	AF-6	BD-89	BE-7	BF-8	BG-43	BI-87	BJ-103
Graham Paige 610 (Late 1928)	EG-6	EH-70	EI-110	PB-40	PC-5	PE-37	AE-44	AF-6	BD-89	BE-7	BF-8	BG-43	BI-87	BJ-103
Graham Paige 614 (1928-29)	EG-7*	EH-71	EI-111	PB-59	PC-54	PE-55	AE-44	AF-6	BD-41	BE-8	BF-8	BG-47	BI-88	BJ-81
Graham Paige 619 (1928-29)	EG-6	EH-72	EI-112	PB-60	PC-55	PE-56	AE-64	AF-53	BD-91	BE-4	BF-50	BG-66	BI-89	BJ-105
Graham Paige 629 (1928-29)	EG-6	EH-72	EI-112	PB-60	PC-55	PE-56	AE-64	AF-53	BD-91	BE-4	BF-50	BG-66	BI-89	BJ-105
Graham Paige 835 (1928-29)	EG-6	EH-72	EI-112	PB-60	PC-55	PE-56	AE-64	AF-53	BD-91	BE-4	BF-50	BG-66	BI-89	BJ-105
Graham Paige 612 (1929)	EG-6	EH-70	EI-110	PB-40	PC-5	PE-37	AE-65	AF-54	BD-89	BE-7	BF-8	BG-43	BI-85	BJ-107
Graham Paige 615 (1929)	EG-7	EH-71	EI-111	PB-123	PC-54	PE-55	AE-44	AF-6	BD-41	BE-8	BF-8	BG-47	BI-88	BJ-108
Graham Paige 621 (1929)	EG-6	EH-72	EI-111	PB-124	PC-55	PE-56	AE-66	AF-55	BD-91	BE-4	BF-50	BG-66	BI-89	BJ-105
Graham Paige 827 (1929)	EG-6	EH-72	EI-112	PB-124	PC-55	PE-56	AE-66	AF-55	BD-91	BE-4	BF-50	BG-66	BI-89	BJ-105
Graham Paige 837 (1929)	EG-6	EH-72	EI-112	PB-124	PC-55	PE-56	AE-66	AF-55	BD-91	BE-4	BF-50	BG-66	BI-89	BJ-105
Graham Std. 6 (Early 1930)	EG-52	EH-70	EI-88	PB-59	PC-5	PE-37	AE-65	AF-54	BD-89	BE-7	BF-8	BG-50	BI-74	BJ-107
Graham Std. 6 (Late 1930)	EG-52	EH-70	EI-88	PB-59	PC-5	PE-37	AE-65	AF-54	BD-44	BE-36	BF-71	BG-54	BI-84	BJ-10
Graham Spec. 6 (Early 1930)	EG-7	EH-71	EI-111	PB-123	PC-54	PE-55	AE-44	AF-6	BD-45	BE-37	BF-8	BG-47	BI-88	BJ-108
Graham Spec. 6 (Late 1930)	EG-7	EH-71	EI-111	PB-123	PC-54	PE-55	AE-129	AF-102	BD-45	BE-37	BF-8	BG-47	BI-88	BJ-15
Graham Std. 8 (1930)	EG-17	EH-173	EI-114	PB-125	PC-102	PE-114	AE-130	AF-103	BD-46	BE-80	BF-75	BG-55	BI-106	BJ-22
Graham Spec. 8 (1930)	EG-6	EH-174	EI-112	PB-124	PC-55	PE-56	AE-130	AF-103	BD-46	BE-80	BF-75	BG-55	BI-106	BJ-22
Graham Cust. 8 (1930)	EG-6	EH-72	EI-112	PB-124	PC-55	PE-56	AE-66	AF-55	BD-91	BE-4	BF-50	BG-66	BI-89	BJ-105
Hudson Super 6 (1925)	None	EH-75	EI-48	PB-63	PC-58	PE-59	AE-69	AF-57	BD-97	BE-5	BF-5	BG-68	BI-92	BJ-114
Hudson Super 6 (1926)	None	EH-75	EI-48	PB-63	PC-58	PE-59	AE-69	AF-57	BD-97	BE-5	BF-5	BG-68	BI-92	BJ-114
Hudson Super 6 (1927)	None	EH-76	EI-49	PB-63	PC-58	PE-59	AE-70	AF-58	BD-97	BE-5	BF-5	BG-68	BI-92	BJ-114
Hudson Super 6 (1928)	None	EH-76	EI-49	PB-63	PC-58	PE-59	AE-70	AF-58	BD-97	BE-5	BF-5	BG-68	BI-92	BJ-114
Hudson Greater 6 (1929)	None	EH-76	EI-50	PB-63	PC-58	PE-59	AE-70	AF-58	BD-98	BE-5	BF-5	BG-68	BI-93	BJ-114
Hudson 8 (1930)	None	EH-46	EI-204	PB-48	PC-33	PE-44	AE-54	AF-44	BD-42	BE-44	BF-5	BG-44	BI-62	BJ-46
Hupmobile E1 (1925–26)	EG-4	EH-77	EI-116	PB-64	PC-59	PE-60	AE-72	AF-59	BD-99	BE-54	BF-51	BG-69	BI-95	BJ-116
Hupmobile Ser. R. (1925)	EG-4	EH-78	EI-117	PB-65	PC-60	PE-61	AE-73	AF-60	BD-100	BE-13	BF-52	BG-13	BI-95	BJ-116
Hupmobile A1 (1926)	EG-1	EH-79	EI-18	PB-66	PC-6	PE-62	AE-74	AF-61	BD-102	BE-57	BF-54	BG-72	BI-97	BJ-118
Hupmobile E2 (1926-27)	EG-5	EH-77	EI-118	PB-64	PC-59	PE-60	AE-72	AF-59	BD-101	BE-13	BF-53	BG-71	BI-96	BJ-117
Hupmobile A2 (1927)	EG-1	EH-79	EI-18	PB-66	PC-6	PE-62	AE-74	AF-61	BD-102	BE-57	BF-54	BG-72	BI-97	BJ-118
Hupmobile E3 (1927-28)	EG-6	EH-80	EI-118	PB-64	PC-59	PE-60	AE-72	AF-59	BD-101	BE-56	BF-53	BG-71	BI-96	BJ-117
Hupmobile Cent. 6 (1928)	EG-1	EH-81	EI-20	PB-67	PC-6	PE-63	AE-74	AF-61	BD-102	BE-57	BF-54	BG-72	BI-97	BJ-119
Hupmobile Cent. 8 (1928)	EG-6	EH-82	EI-119	PB-67	PC-6	PE-63	AE-75	AF-61	BD-103	BE-56	BF-53	BG-64	BI-94	BJ-121
Hupmobile Cent. 125 (1928)	EG-6	EH-82	EI-119	PB-67	PC-6	PE-63	AE-75	AF-61	BD-101	BE-56	BF-53	BG-64	BI-94	BJ-117
Hupmobile Cent. 6 (1929)	EG-1	EH-81	EI-19	PB-67	PC-6	PE-63	AF-74	AF-61	BD-102	BE-57	BF-54	BG-72	BI-97	BJ-119
Hupmobile M8 (1929)	EG-7	EH-82	EI-120	PB-67	PC-6	PE-63	AE-76	AF-61	BD-103	BE-56	BF-53	BG-64	BI-94	BJ-121
Hupmobile S (1930)	EG-1	EH-53	EI-10	PB-62	PC-43	PE-100	AE-143	AF-128	BD-47	BE-30	BF-20	BG-133	BI-108	BJ-64
Hupmobile C (1930)	EG-7	EH-49	EI-115	PB-7	PC-6	PE-7	AE-144	AF-102	BD-48	BE-56	BF-53	BG-65	BI-118	BJ-77
Hupmobile H, U (1930)	EG-51	EH-48	EI-126	PB-49	PC-34	PE-95	AE-144	AF-104	BD-49	BE-58	BF-21	BG-67	BI-163	BJ-78
Jewett 6-50 (1925)	EG-8*	EH-83	EI-121	PB-4	PC-4	PE-4	AE-77	AF-52	BD-2	BE-2	BF-55	BG-48	BI-98	BJ-73
Jewett New Day 6-40 (1926)	Seg.	EH-84	EI-122	PB-38	PC-35	PE-5	AE-8	AF-5	BD-105	BE-10	BF-56	BG-74	BI-6	BJ-74
Jordan K, L. (1925)	EG-26	EH-85	EJ-123	PB-68	PC-6	PE-64	AE-78	AF-62	BD-106	BE-61	BF-5	BG-26	BI-34	BJ-123
Jordan A (1925)	EG-5	EH-79	EI-124	PB-64	PC-59	PE-60	AE-78	AF-62	BD-106	BE-61	BF-5	BG-26	BI-34	BJ-124
Jordan A (1926)	EG-5	EH-79	EI-124	PB-64	PC-59	PE-60	AE-78	AF-62	BD-106	BE-61	BF-5	BG-26	BI-34	BJ-124
Jordan J (1926-27)	EG-26	EH-87	EI-125	PB-69	PC-4	PE-65	AE-79	AF-5	BD-108	BE-8	BF-58	BG-76	BI-101	BJ-125
Jordan AA (1927-28)	EG-26	EH-86	EI-126	PB-64	PC-59	PE-60	AE-78	AF-62	BD-106	BE-61	BF-5	BG-26	BI-34	*BJ-124
Jordan J1 (1927-28)	EG-26	EH-87	EI-125	PB-69	PC-4	PE-65	AE-79	AF-5	BD-108	BE-8	BF-58	BG-76	BI-101	BJ-125
Jordan R, Col. (1927-28)	EG-6	EH-88	EI-127	PB-70	PC-62	PE-66	AE-80	AF-63	BD-109	BE-63	BF-59	BG-77	BI-102	BJ-126
Jordan JJ (1928-29)	EG-51	EH-87	EI-125	PB-69	PC-4	PE-65	AE-79	AF-5	BD-108	BE-8	BF-58	BG-76	BI-101	BJ-125
Jordan R. E. (1928-29)	EG-6	EH-88	EI-127	PB-70	PC-62	PE-66	AE-80	AF-63	BD-109	BE-63	BF-59	BG-77	BI-102	BJ-126
Jordan JE (1928-29)	EG-51	EH-87	EI-125	PB-69	PC-4	PE-65	AE-79	AF-5	BD-108	BE-8	BF-58	BG-76	BI-101	BJ-125
Jordan E, Col (1929)	EG-7	EH-87	EI-125	PB-69	PC-4	PE-65	AE-5	AF-6	BD-110	BE-64	BF-60	BG-78	BI-103	BJ-11
Jordan G, Col (1929)	EG-7	EH-87	EI-125	PB-69	PC-4	PE-65	AE-7	AF-8	BD-108	BE-8	BF-58	BG-76	BI-101	BJ-111
Kissel 6-55 (1925)	EG-2	EH-5	EI-1	PB-4	PC-4	PE-4	AE-78	AF-62	BD-50	BE-8	BF-5	BG-26	BI-34	BJ-124
Kissel 8-75 (1925)	EG-9	EH-6	EI-1	PB-4	PC-4	PE-4	AE-78	AF-62	BD-50	BE-8	BF-8	BG-26	BI-34	BJ-124
Kissel 6-55 (1926)	EG-2	EH-5	EI-1	PB-4	PC-4	PE-4	AE-78	AF-62	BD-50	BE-8	BF-5	BG-26	BI-34	BJ-124
Kissel 8-75 (1926)	EG-9	EH-6	EI-1	PB-4	PC-4	PE-4	AE-78	AF-62	BD-50	BE-8	BF-5	BG-26	BI-34	BJ-124

CLUTCH, TRANSMISSION, FRONT AND REAR AXLES—Continued

Car Make and Model	CLUTCH			TRANSMISSION			FRONT AXLE		REAR AXLE					
	Clutch Facings (Lining)	Clutch Shaft	Clutch Discs	High and Intermediate Sliding or Coupling Gear	Low and Reverse or Second and Reverse Sliding Gear	Countershaft Gear Assembly	King Pins	King Pin Bushings	Differential Case	Differential Spider or Cross Pin	Differential Spider Pinions	Differential Side Gears	Drive Pinion and Ring Gear	Axle Shafts
Kissel 6-55, Col. (1927)	EG-2	EH-5	EI-8	PB-4	PC-4	PE-4	AE-78	AF-4	BD-5	BE-8	BF-2	BG-2	BI-7	BJ-128
Kissel 6-70, Col. (1927)	EG-1	EH-6	EI-22	PB-4	PC-4	PE-4	AE-80	AF-125	BD-10	BE-7	BF-1	BG-8	BI-8	BJ-51
Kissel 8-65, Col. (1927)	EG-2	EH-5	EI-8	PB-4	PC-4	PE-4	AE-4	AF-4	BD-5	BE-8	BF-7	BG-2	BI-7	BJ-128
Kissel 8-75 (1927)	EG-9	EH-6	EI-8	PB-4	PC-4	PE-4	AE-78	AF-62	BD-5	BE-8	BF-5	BG-26	BI-34	BJ-124
Kissel 6-70, Col. (Early 1928)	EG-1	EH-6	EI-22	PB-4	PC-4	PE-4	AE-80	AF-63	BD-10	BE-7	BF-1	BG-8	BI-8	BJ-9
Kissel 6-70, Col. (Late 1928)	EG-1	EH-6	EI-22	PB-4	PC-4	PE-4	AE-5	AF-6	BD-10	BE-7	BF-1	BG-8	BI-8	BJ-9
Kissel 8-80, Col. (1928)	EG-2	EH-5	EI-6	PB-4	PC-4	PE-4	AE-4	AF-4	BD-5	BE-8	BF-7	BG-7	BI-103	BJ-128
Kissel 8-80-S (1928)	EG-2	EH-5	EI-6	PB-4	PC-4	PE-4	AE-4	AF-4	BD-5	BE-8	BF-7	BG-7	BI-103	BJ-128
Kissel 8-90 (1928)	EG-9	EH-6	EI-21	PB-4	PC-4	PE-4	AE-78	AF-62	BD-111	BE-66	BF-62	BG-80	BI-104	BJ-124
Kissel 6-73, Col. (1929)	EG-1	EH-6	EI-8	PB-4	PC-4	PE-4	AE-5	AF-6	BD-12	BE-7	BF-7	BG-9	BI-10	BJ-127
Kissel 8-95, Col. (1929)	EG-2	EH-5	EI-8	PB-4	PC-4	PE-4	AE-4	AF-4	BD-5	BE-8	BF-7	BG-7	BI-103	BJ-128
Kissel 8-126 (1929)	EG-9	EH-6	EI-21	PB-4	PC-4	PE-4	AE-81	AF-62	BD-112	BE-66	BF-62	BG-80	BI-104	BJ-124
La Salle 303 (1927)	EG-13	EH-18	EI-38	PB-18	PC-16	PE-17	AE-11	AF-11	BD-19	BE-67	BF-4	BG-40	BI-105	BJ-130
La Salle 303 (1928)	EG-13	EH-18	EI-40	PB-18	PC-16	PE-17	AE-11	AF-11	BD-19	BE-67	BF-4	BG-40	BI-105	BJ-130
La Salle 328 (1929)	EG-14	EH-19	EI-40	PB-18	PC-16	PE-17	AE-11	AF-11	BD-19	BE-67	BF-4	BG-40	BI-105	BJ-131
La Salle..340 (1930)	EG-50	EH-167	EI-206	PB-117	PC-100	PE-16	AE-107	None	BD-96	BE-104	BF-3	BG-85	BI-105	BJ-27
Lincoln 8 (1925)	EG-27	EH-91	EI-51	PB-71	PC-62	PE-67	AE-122	AF-64	BD-117	BE-4	BF-4	BG-18	BI-107	BJ-24
Lincoln 8 (1926)	EG-27	EH-91	EI-51	PB-71	PC-62	PE-67	AE-122	AF-64	BD-117	BE-4	BF-4	BG-18	BI-107	BJ-24
Lincoln 8 (1927)	EG-27	EH-91	EI-51	PB-71	PC-62	PE-67	AE-121	AF-64	BD-117	BE-4	BF-4	BG-18	BI-107	BJ-24
Lincoln 8 (1928)	EG-28	EH-91	EI-51	PB-71	PC-62	PE-67	AE-121	AF-64	BD-117	BE-4	BF-4	BG-18	BI-107	BJ-24
Lincoln 8 (1929)	EG-28	EH-91	EI-51	PB-71	PC-62	PE-67	AE-121	AF-64	BD-117	BE-4	BF-4	BG-18	BI-107	BJ-24
Lincoln 8 (1930)	EG-28	EH-91	EI-207	PB-120	PC-108	PE-67	AE-121	AF-64	BD-117	BE-4	BF-4	BG-18	BI-107	BJ-24
Locomobile Jr. 8 (1925)	Seg.	EH-92	EI-128	PB-72	PC-63	PE-68	AE-56	AF-45	BD-1	BE-1	BF-1	BG-1	BI-1	BJ-134
Locomobile 48 (1925)	Seg.	EH-93	EI-129	PB-73	PC-64	PE-69	AE-82	AF-65	BD-120	BE-71	BF-67	BG-87	BI-110	BJ-135
Locomobile 48 (1926)	Seg.	EH-93	EI-130	PB-73	PC-64	PE-69	AE-82	AF-65	BD-121	BE-71	BF-67	BG-87	BI-110	BJ-135
Locomobile 90 (1926)	Seg.	EH-94	EI-131	PB-74	PC-65	PE-70	AE-123	AF-105	BD-122	BE-72	BF-69	BG-88	BI-111	BJ-136
Locomobile Jr. 8 (1926)	Seg.	EH-92	EI-128	PB-72	PC-63	PE-68	AE-56	AF-45	BD-1	BE-1	BF-1	BG-1	BI-1	BJ-134
Locomobile 48 (1927)	Seg.	EH-93	EI-130	PB-73	PC-64	PE-69	AE-82	AF-65	BD-121	BE-71	BF-67	BG-87	BI-110	BJ-135
Locomobile 8-66 (1927)	Seg.	EH-9	EI-132	PB-7	PC-65	PE-7	AE-124	AF-106	BD-1	BE-1	BF-1	BG-1	BI-1	BJ-134
Locomobile 8-80 (1927)	Seg.	EH-9	EI-21	PB-7	PC-65	PE-7	AE-125	AF-107	BD-123	BE-72	BF-68	BG-89	BI-110	BJ-137
Locomobile 90 (1927)	Seg.	EH-94	EI-133	PB-74	PC-65	PE-70	AE-123	AF-105	BD-124	BE-73	BF-69	BG-88	BI-111	BJ-136
Locomobile 48 (1928)	Seg.	EH-93	EI-130	PB-73	PC-64	PE-69	AE-82	AF-65	BD-121	BE-71	BF-67	BG-87	BI-110	BJ-135
Locomobile 8-70 (1928)	EG-2	EH-9	EI-9	PB-7	PC-65	PE-7	AE-126	AF-108	BD-1	BE-1	BF-1	BG-1	BI-1	BJ-134
Locomobile 8-80 (1928)	EG-9	EH-9	EI-21	PB-7	PC-65	PE-7	AE-125	AF-107	BD-123	BE-72	BF-68	BG-89	BI-110	BJ-137
Locomobile 90 (1928)	Seg.	EH-94	EI-133	PB-74	PC-65	PE-70	AE-123	AF-105	BD-124	BE-73	BF-69	BG-88	BI-111	BJ-136
Locomobile 8-80 (1929)	EG-9	EH-9	EI-21	PB-7	PC-6	PE-7	AE-125	AF-107	BD-123	BE-72	BF-68	BG-89	BJ-110	BJ-137
Locomobile 86, 88 (1929)	EG-9	EH-9	EI-134	PB-7	PC-6	PE-7	AE-127	AF-109	BD-123	BE-72	BF-68	BG-89	BI-110	BJ-138
Locomobile 90 (1929)	Seg.	EH-94	EI-133	PB-74	PC-65	PE-70	AE-123	AF-105	BD-124	BE-75	BF-70	BG-88	BI-111	BJ-136
Marmon 74 (1925)	EG-29	EH-92	EI-135	PB-75	PC-61	PE-71	None	AF-110	BD-127	BE-4	BF-4	BG-12	BI-112	BJ-141
Marmon 74 (1926)	EG-27	EH-92	EI-135	PB-75	PC-61	PE-71	None	AF-110	BD-127	BE-4	BF-4	BG-12	BI-112	BJ-141
Marmon, Little (1927)	Seg.	EH-93	EI-136	PB-76	PC-66	PE-72	AE-118	AF-34	BD-125	BE-77	BF-72	BG-91	BI-113	BJ-142
Marmon E75 (1927)	EG-30	EH-92	EI-24	PB-77	PC-67	PE-73	AE-84	AF-67	BD-129	BE-4	BF-4	BG-12	BI-114	BJ-141
Marmon 68 (1928)	Seg.	EH-94	EI-137	PB-78	PC-68	PE-74	AE-118	AF-52	BD-130	BE-7	BF-8	BG-92	BI-115	BJ-74
Marmon E75 (1928)	EG-30	EH-92	EI-24	PB-77	PC-67	PE-73	AE-84	AF-67	BD-129	BE-4	BF-4	BG-12	BI-114	BJ-141
Marmon 78 (1928)	Seg.	EH-95	EI-138	PB-79	PC-69	PE-75	AE-119	AF-52	BD-51	BE-79	BF-74	BG-93	BI-116	BJ-144
Marmon 68 (1929)	Seg.	EH-94	EI-137	PB-40	PC-5	PE-74	AE-118	AF-52	BD-130	BE-7	BF-8	BG-8	BI-109	BJ-143
Marmon 78 (1929)	Seg.	EH-95	EI-138	PB-79	PC-69	PE-75	AE-119	AF-52	BD-51	BE-79	BF-74	BG-93	BI-116	BJ-144
Marmon, Roosevelt (1929)	Seg.	EH-138	EI-168	PB-40	PC-5	PE-97	AE-143	AF-128	BD-130	BE-7	BF-8	BG-8	BI-109	BJ-103
Marmon 69 (1930)	Seg.	EH-64	EI-210	PB-40	PC-5	PE-37	AE-118	AF-52	BD-52	BE-7	BF-8	BG-81	BI-99	BJ-80
Marmon 79 (1930)	Seg.	EH-98	EI-211	PB-99	PC-44	PE-75	AE-133	AF-78	BD-51	BE-37	BF-57	BG-73	BI-100	BJ-87
Marmon Big 8 (1930)	Seg.	EH-123	EI-211	PB-124	PC-109	PE-110	AE-133	AF-78	BD-54	BE-65	BF-57	BG-75	BI-171	BJ-92
Marquette (1930)	EG-21	EH-45	EI-155	PB-115	PC-117	PE-46	AE-91	AF-72	BD-55	BE-83	BF-61	BG-79	BI-127	BJ-34
Maxwell 25 (1925)	Inter.	EH-97	EI-70	PB-80	PC-70	PE-76	AE-85	AF-68	BD-30	BE-17	BF-17	BG-130	BI-30	BJ-36
Moon Series A, Sal. (1925)	EG-2	EH-39	EI-15	PB-38	PC-35	PE-5	AE-86	AF-52	BD-5	BE-10	BF-36	BG-48	BI-68	BJ-73
Moon Series A, Sal. (1926)	EG-2	EH-39	EI-15	PB-38	PC-35	PE-5	AE-86	AF-52	BD-5	BE-10	BF-36	BG-48	BI-68	BJ-54
Moon 6-60, Col. (1926)	EG-1	EH-7	EI-6	PB-5	PC-5	PE-5	AE-5	AF-6	BD-10	BE-7	BF-8	BG-8	BI-8	BJ-51
Moon Series A, Sal. (1927)	EG-2	EH-39	EI-15	PB-38	PC-35	PE-5	AE-86	AF-52	BD-5	BE-10	BF-7	BG-48	BI-68	BJ-54
Moon 6-60, Col. (1927)	EG-1	EH-7	EI-6	PB-5	PC-5	PE-5	AE-5	AF-6	BD-10	BE-7	BF-8	BG-8	BI-8	BJ-51
Moon Series A, Sal. (1928)	EG-2	EH-39	EI-15	PB-38	PC-35	PE-5	AE-86	AF-52	BD-5	BE-10	BF-7	BG-48	BI-68	BJ-54
Moon 6-60, Col. (1928)	EG-1	EH-7	EI-6	PB-5	PC-5	PE-5	AE-5	AF-6	BD-10	BE-7	BF-8	BG-8	BI-8	BJ-51
Moon 6-72, Col. (Early 1928)	EG-2	EH-99	EI-15	PB-5	PC-5	PE-5	AE-5	AF-6	BD-3	BE-38	BF-7	BG-2	BJ-7	BJ-148
Moon 6-72, Col. (Late 1928)	EG-2	EH-99	EI-15	PB-5	PC-5	PE-5	AE-5	AF-6	BD-3	BE-38	BF-7	BG-2	BI-7	BJ-127
Moon 8-80, Col. (1928)	EG-2	EH-6	EI-17	PB-4	PC-4	PE-4	AE-4	AF-4	BD-5	BE-8	BF-7	BG-2	BI-5	BJ-128
Moon 6-72, Col. (1929)	EG-2	EH-99	EI-25	PB-5	PC-5	PE-5	AE-5	AF-7	BD-3	BE-38	BF-7	BG-2	BI-7	BJ-127
Nash Adv. 6 (1925)	EG-2	EH-100	EI-28	PB-81	PC-71	PE-77	AE-87	AF-69	BD-135	BE-81	BF-76	BG-94	BI-122	BJ-150
Nash Spec. 6 (1925)	EG-2	EH-100	EI-27	PB-81	PC-71	PE-77	AE-88	AF-69	BD-136	BE-82	BF-77	BG-95	BI-123	BJ-150
Nash Adv. 6 (1926)	EG-9	EH-101	EI-28	PB-81	PC-71	PE-77	AE-87	AF-69	BD-135	BE-81	BF-76	BG-94	BI-122	BJ-150
Nash Spec. 6 (1926)	EG-2	EH-102	EI-27	PB-81	PC-71	PE-77	AE-88	AF-69	BD-137	BE-82	BF-77	BG-95	BI-123	BJ-150
Nash Adv. 6 (1927)	EG-9	EH-101	EI-28	PB-81	PC-71	PE-77	AE-87	AF-69	BD-135	BE-81	BF-76	BG-94	BI-122	BJ-150
Nash Spec. 6 (1927)	EG-2	EH-102	EI-29	PB-81	PC-71	PE-77	AE-88	AF-69	BD-137	BE-82	BF-77	BG-95	BI-123	BJ-150
Nash Light 6 (1927)	EG-1	EH-1	EI-26	PB-1	PC-1	PE-1	AE-1	AF-1	BD-1	BE-1	BF-1	BG-1	BI-1	BJ-1
Nash Adv. 6 (1928)	EG-9	EH-101	EI-28	PB-81	PC-71	PE-77	AE-87	AF-69	BD-135	BE-81	BF-76	BG-94	BI-122	BJ-150
Nash Spec. 6 (1928)	EG-2	EH-102	EI-29	PB-81	PC-71	PE-77	AE-88	AF-69	BD-137	BE-82	BF-77	BG-95	BI-123	BJ-150
Nash Std. 6 (1928)	EG-1	EH-1	EI-26	PB-1	PC-1	PE-1	AE-1	AF-1	BD-1	BE-1	BF-1	BG-1	BI-1	BJ-1
Nash Adv. 6 (1929)	EG-9	EH-103	EI-30	PB-82	PC-71	PE-78	AE-87	AF-69	BD-135	BE-81	BF-76	BG-94	BI-122	BJ-150
Nash Spec. 6 (1929)	EG-2	EH-103	EI-31	PB-82	PC-71	PE-78	AE-88	AF-69	BD-137	BE-82	BF-77	BG-95	BI-123	BJ-150
Nash Std. 6 (1929)	EG-1	EH-1	EI-26	PB-1	PC-1	PE-1	AE-1	AF-1	BD-56	BE-1	BF-1	BG-1	BI-1	BJ-1
Nash Single Ignition 6 (1930)	EG-1	EH-175	EI-85	PB-1	PC-1	PE-118	AE-1	AF-1	BD-56	BE-1	BF-1	BG-1	BG-1	BJ-1
Nash Twin Ignition 6 (1930)	EG-2	EH-103	EI-84	PB-82	PC-71	PE-78	AE-131	AF-69	BD-137	BE-82	BF-77	BG-95	BI-123	BJ-150
Nash Twin Ignition 8 (1930)	EG-9	EH-103	EI-208	PB-82	PC-71	PE-119	AE-145	AF-69	BD-135	BE-81	BF-76	BG-94	BI-122	BJ-106
Oakland 6-54 (1925)	EG-31	EH-104	EI-52	PB-83	PC-72	PE-79	AE-89	AF-70	BD-55	BE-83	BF-10	BG-79	BI-124	BJ-151
Oakland O6 (1926)	EG-31	EH-104	EI-52	PB-83	PC-72	PE-79	AE-89	AF-70	BD-55	BE-83	BF-10	BG-79	BI-124	BJ-151
Oakland GO6 (1927)	EG-31	EH-104	EI-52	PB-83	PC-72	PE-79	AE-89	AF-70	BD-55	BE-83	BF-10	BG-79	BI-124	BJ-151
Oakland AA-6 (1928)	EG-31	EH-105	EI-52	PB-84	PC-73	PE-80	AE-89	AF-70	BD-55	BE-83	BF-10	BG-79	BI-124	BJ-151
Oakland AA-6 (1929)	EG-31	EH-105	EI-52	PB-84	PC-73	PE-80	AE-89	AF-70	BD-55	BE-83	BF-10	BG-79	BI-125	BJ-151
Oakland 8 (1930)	EG-49	EH-129	EI-216	PB-84	PC-73	PE-80	AE-91	AF-72	BD-55	BE-83	BF-10	BG-79	BI-125	BJ-151
Oldsmobile C (1925)	EG-1	EH-106	EI-26	PB-85	PC-74	PE-81	AE-90	AF-71	BD-139	BE-84	BF-23	BG-97	BI-126	BJ-152
Oldsmobile D (1926)	EG-1	EH-107	EI-26	PB-86	PC-75	PE-82	AE-90	AF-71	BD-139	BE-84	BF-23	BG-97	BI-126	BJ-152
Oldsmobile E (1927)	EG-1	EH-108	EI-26	PB-86	PC-75	PE-82	AE-91	AF-72	BD-139	BE-84	BF-23	BG-97	BI-126	BJ-152
Oldsmobile F28 (1928)	EG-1	EH-109	EI-10	PB-84	PC-73	PE-80	AE-91	AF-72	BD-139	BE-84	BF-23	BG-97	BI-127	BJ-152
Oldsmobile F29 (1929)	EG-1	EH-109	EI-10	PB-84	PC-73	PE-80	AE-91	AF-72	BD-139	BE-84	BF-23	BG-97	BI-127	BJ-152
Oldsmobile F30 (1930)	EG-1	EH-109	EI-82	PB-84	PC-73	PE-80	AE-91	AF-72	BD-55	BE-83	BF-10	BG-79	BI-124	BJ-152
Overland 91 (1925)	EG-32	EH-110	EI-33	PB-53	PC-49	PE-50	AE-92	AF-73	BD-1	BE-3	BF-1	BG-1	BI-128	BJ-85
Overland 93 (1925)	EG-56	EH-111	EI-14	PB-53	PC-49	PE-50	AE-93	AF-74	BD-1	BE-3	BF-1	BG-1	BI-73	BJ-85
Overland 91 (1926)	EG-32	EH-110	EI-33	PB-53	PC-49	PE-50	AE-92	AF-73	BD-1	BE-3	BF-1	BG-1	BJ-128	BJ-85
Overland 93 (1926)	EG-1	EH-111	EI-14	PB-53	PC-49	PE-50	AE-93	AF-74	BD-1	BE-3	BF-1	BG-1	BI-73	BJ-85
Packard 6 Cyl. 326-333 (1925)	EG-34	EH-115	EI-140	PB-89	PC-77	PE-85	AE-96	None	BD-106	BE-5	BF-5	BG-68	BI-130	BJ-156
Packard 8 Cyl. 236-243 (1925)	EG-34	EH-115	EI-140	PB-89	PC-77	PE-85	AE-96	None	BD-142	BE-85	BF-78	BG-69	BI-131	BJ-157
Packard 6 Cyl. 326-333 (1926)	EG-34	EH-115	EI-140	PB-89	PC-77	PE-85	AE-96	None	BD-106	BE-5	BF-5	BG-68	BI-130	BJ-158
Packard 8 Cyl. 236-243 (1926)	EG-34	EH-115	EI-140	PB-89	PC-77	PE-85	AE-96	None	BD-142	BE-85	BF-79	BG-69	BJ-131	BJ-157
Packard 6 Cyl. 426-433 (1927)	EG-51	EH-116	EI-141	PB-89	PC-77	PE-85	AE-96	None	BD-106	BE-5	BF-79	BG-70	BI-132	BJ-158
Packard 6 Cyl. 336-343 (1927)	EG-34	EH-116	EI-142	PB-89	PC-77	PE-85	AE-96	None	BD-143	BE-85	BF-78	BG-69	BI-131	BJ-159

CLUTCH, TRANSMISSION, FRONT AND REAR AXLES—Continued

Car Make and Model	CLUTCH: Clutch Facings (Lining)	CLUTCH: Clutch Shaft	CLUTCH: Clutch Discs	TRANSMISSION: High and Intermediate Sliding or Coupling Gear	TRANSMISSION: Low and Reverse or Second and Reverse Sliding Gear	TRANSMISSION: Countershaft Gear Assembly	FRONT AXLE: King Pins	FRONT AXLE: King Pin Bushings	REAR AXLE: Differential Case	REAR AXLE: Differential Spider or Cross Pin	REAR AXLE: Differential Spider Pinions	REAR AXLE: Differential Side Gears	REAR AXLE: Drive Pinion and Ring Gear	REAR AXLE: Axle Shafts
Packard 6 Cyl. 526, 533......(1928)	EG-17	EH-116	EI-141	PB-89	PC-77	PE-85	AE-96	None	BD-141	BE-86	BF-79	BG-70	BI-133	BJ-158
Packard Std. 8, 443........(1928)	EG-57	EH-116	EI-142	PB-89	PC-77	PE-85	AE-96	None	BD-143	BE-85	BF-78	BG-69	BI-134	BJ-159
Packard 626, 633............(1929)	EG-17	EH-116	EI-143	PB-89	PC-77	PE-85	AE-96	None	BD-143	BE-85	BF-78	BG-69	BI-135	BJ-158
Packard 640-645............(1929)	EG-57	EH-116	EI-142	PB-89	PC-7	PE-85	AE-96	None	BD-143	BE-85	BF-78	BG-69	BI-134	BJ-159
Packard 726, 733.....(Early 1930)	EG-17	EH-181	EI-143	PB-126	PC-110	PE-120	AE-68	None	BD-61	BE-85	BF-78	BG-82	BI-4	BJ-160
Packard 726, 733.......(Late 1930)	EG-17	EH-181	EI-143	PB-126	PC-110	PE-120	AE-68	None	BD-61	BE-85	BF-78	BG-82	BI-4	BJ-161
Packard 740, 745.....(Early 1930)	EG-57	EH-182	EI-142	PB-127	PC-111	PE-121	AE-68	None	BD-62	BE-85	BF-78	BG-86	BI-38	BJ-159
Packard 740, 745.......(Late 1930)	EG-57	EH-182	EI-142	PB-127	PC-111	PE-121	AE-68	None	BD-62	BE-85	BF-78	BG-86	BI-38	BJ-162
Paige 6-70..........(1925-26)	EG-35	EH-116	EI-144	PB-45	PC-42	PE-42	AE-97	AF-77	BD-144	BE-5	BF-5	BG-68	BI-136	BJ-163
Paige 6-45..............(1926)	EG-35	EH-116	EI-145	PB-4	PC-4	PE-4	AE-8	AF-5	BD-105	BE-60	BF-56	BG-74	BI-6	BJ-74
Paige 6-72..............(1926)	EG-8	EH-117	EI-146	PB-4	PC-4	PE-4	AE-141	AF-126	BD-14	BE-87	BF-63	BG-53	BI-70	BJ-76
Paige 6-45..........(1927-28)	EG-35	EH-117	EI-145	PB-4	PC-4	PE-4	AE-8	AF-5	BD-105	BE-60	BF-56	BG-74	BI-6	BJ-74
Paige 6-65..........(1927-28)	EG-8	EH-117	EI-146	PB-4	PC-4	PE-4	AE-77	AF-43	BD-41	BE-10	BF-10	BG-47	BI-138	BJ-73
Paige 6-75..........(1927-28)	EG-8	EH-117	EI-146	PB-4	PC-4	PE-4	AE-133	AF-78	BD-14	BE-89	BF-63	BG-53	BI-70	BJ-76
Paige 8-85..........(1927-28)	EG-8	EH-118	EI-147	PB-91	PC-78	PE-87	AE-133	AF-78	BD-14	BE-89	BF-63	BG-53	BI-140	BJ-76
Peerless 70, Eat. Fr........(1925)	EG-15	EH-119	EI-148	PB-92	PC-79	PE-88	AE-71	AF-62	BD-148	BE-5	BF-5	BG-5	BI-141	BJ-124
Peerless 6-80, Col..........(1926)	EG-2	EH-9	EI-8	PB-7	PC-6	PE-7	AE-4	AF-4	BD-3	BE-8	BF-7	BG-2	BI-7	BJ-54
Peerless 8-69 Eat. Fr........(1926)	EG-9	EH-119	EI-21	PB-92	PC-79	PE-88	AE-71	AF-62	BD-149	BE-5	BF-5	BG-5	BI-142	BJ-79
Peerless 90,..............(1926)	EG-9	EH-9	EI-21	PB-116	PC-6	PE-7	AE-4	AF-4	BD-5	BE-8	BF-7	BG-2	BI-5	BJ-128
Peerless 6-60..............(1927)	EG-2	EH-9	EI-8	PB-116	PC-6	PE-7	AE-5	AF-5	BD-10	BE-7	BF-8	BG-8	BI-8	BJ-9
Peerless 8-69, Eat. Fr.......(1927)	EG-9	EH-119	EI-21	PB-92	PC-79	PE-88	AE-71	AF-62	BD-149	BE-5	BF-5	BG-5	BI-142	BJ-79
Peerless 6-80, Col.....(Early 1927)	EG-2	EH-9	EI-8	PB-116	PC-6	PE-7	AE-4	AF-4	BD-3	BE-8	BF-7	BG-2	BI-7	BJ-54
Peerless 6-80, Col......(Late 1927)	EG-2	EH-9	EI-8	PB-116	PC-6	PE-7	AE-4	AF-4	BD-3	BE-8	BF-7	BG-2	BI-7	BJ-128
Peerless 6-90..............(1927)	EG-9	EH-9	EI-21	PB-116	PC-6	PE-7	AE-4	AF-4	BD-5	BE-8	BF-7	BG-2	BI-5	BJ-128
Peerless 6-72, Eat. Fr.....(1927-28)	EG-9	EH-119	EI-154	PB-92	PC-79	PE-88	AE-71	AF-62	BD-148	BE-5	BF-5	BG-5	BI-141	BJ-79
Peerless 6-60, Col.....(Early 1928)	EG-2	EH-9	EI-8	PB-116	PC-6	PE-7	AE-5	AF-5	BD-10	BE-7	BF-8	BG-8	BI-8	BJ-9
Peerless 6-60, Col......(Late 1928)	EG-2	EH-9	EI-8	PB-116	PC-6	PE-7	AE-5	AF-5	BD-10	BE-7	BF-8	BG-8	BI-8	BJ-127
Peerless 8-69..............(1928)	EG-9	EH-119	EI-21	PB-92	PC-79	PE-88	AE-71	AF-62	BD-149	BE-5	BF-5	BF-5	BI-142	BJ-79
Peerless 6-80, Col..........(1928)	EG-2	EH-9	EI-8	PB-99	PC-6	PE-7	AE-4	AF-4	BD-3	BE-8	BF-7	BG-2	BI-7	BJ-128
Peerless 81, Col............(1928)	EG-2	EH-9	EI-8	PB-99	PC-6	PE-7	AE-142	AF-127	BD-1	BE-8	BF-7	BG-9	BI-9	BJ-127
Peerless 90, Col............(1928)	EG-9	EH-9	EI-21	PB-116	PC-6	PE-7	AE-4	AF-4	BD-5	BE-8	BF-7	BG-2	BI-5	BJ-128
Peerless 6-91, Col..........(1928)	EG-9	EH-9	EI-21	PB-99	PC-6	PE-7	AE-4	AF-4	BD-5	BE-8	BF-7	BG-2	BI-5	BJ-128
Peerless 6-61, Col.....(Early 1929)	EG-2	EH-9	EI-8	PB-99	PC-6	PE-7	AE-5	AF-6	BD-10	BE-7	BF-8	BG-8	BI-8	BJ-9
Peerless 6-61, Col......(Late 1929)	EG-2	EH-9	EI-8	PB-99	PC-6	PE-7	AE-5	AF-6	BD-10	BE-7	BF-8	BG-9	BI-8	BJ-127
Peerless 6-81, Col..........(1929)	EG-2	EH-9	EI-8	PB-99	PC-6	PE-7	AE-5	AF-6	BD-1	BE-8	BF-7	BG-9	BI-9	BJ-127
Peerless 6-91, Col..........(1929)	EG-9	EH-9	EI-21	PB-99	PC-6	PE-7	AE-4	AF-4	BD-5	BE-8	BF-7	BG-2	BI-5	BJ-128
Peerless 125, Col...........(1929)	EG-9	EH-9	EI-149	PB-99	PC-6	PE-7	AE-98	AF-79	BD-5	BE-8	BF-81	BG-2	BI-7	BJ-102
Peerless 125, Col...........(1930)	EG-9	EH-9	EI-149	PB-99	PC-6	PE-7	AE-98	AF-79	BD-5	BE-8	BF-81	BG-2	BI-7	BJ-14
Peerless A..................(1930)	Seg.	EH-130	EI-212	PB-103	PC-45	PE-111	AE-150	AF-131	BD-59	BE-74	BF-64	BG-90	BI-144	BJ-80
Peerless B..................(1930)	Seg.	EH-122	EI-213	PB-121	PC-112	PE-121	AE-151	AF-132	BD-63	BE-78	BF-66	BG-114	BI-143	BJ-87
Peerless C..................(1930)	Seg.	EH-132	EI-213	PB-121	PC-112	PE-121	AE-151	AF-132	BD-66	BE-78	BF-66	BG-134	BI-139	BJ-92
Pierce Arrow 80, Eat. Fr.....(1925)	EG-24	EH-124	EI-150	PB-93	PC-80	PE-89	AE-99	AF-80	BD-152	BE-91	BF-82	BG-76	BI-34	BJ-124
Pierce Arrow 33.............(1926)	EG-36	EH-125	EI-151	PB-94	PC-81	PE-90	AE-101	AF-81	BD-153	BE-92	BF-83	BG-77	BI-146	BJ-167
Pierce Arrow 80, Eat. Fr.....(1926)	EG-24	EH-124	EI-150	PB-93	PC-80	PE-89	AE-99	AF-80	BD-152	BE-91	BF-82	BG-76	BI-34	BJ-124
Pierce Arrow 36.............(1927)	EG-37	EH-125	EI-152	PB-94	PC-81	PE-90	AE-102	AF-82	BD-153	BE-92	BF-83	BG-77	BI-147	BJ-168
Pierce Arrow 80, Eat. Fr.....(1927)	EG-24	EH-124	EI-150	PB-93	PC-80	PE-89	AE-99	AF-80	BD-152	BE-91	BF-82	BG-76	BI-34	BJ-124
Pierce Arrow 36.............(1928)	EG-37	EH-125	EI-152	PB-94	PC-81	PE-90	AE-102	AF-82	BD-153	BE-92	BF-83	BG-77	BI-147	BJ-168
Pierce Arrow 81.............(1928)	EG-24	EH-124	EI-150	PB-95	PC-82	PE-91	AE-99	AF-80	BD-152	BE-91	BF-82	BG-76	BI-34	BJ-124
Pierce Arrow 133, 143.......(1929)	EG-57	EH-126	EI-153	PB-96	PC-83	PE-92	AE-113	AF-93	BD-154	BE-93	BF-84	BG-78	BI-148	BJ-199
Pierce Arrow A..............(1930)	EG-57	EH-178	EI-153	PB-49	PC-113	PE-123	AE-113	AF-93	BD-154	BE-93	BF-84	BG-135	BI-145	BJ-199
Pierce Arrow B..............(1930)	EG-57	EH-178	EI-153	PB-49	PC-113	PE-123	AE-113	AF-93	BD 154	BE-93	BF-84	BG-135	BI-145	BJ-199
Pierce Arrow C..............(1930)	EG-57	EH-178	EI-153	PB-49	PC-34	PE-95	AE-113	AF-93	BD-154	BE-93	BF-84	BG-135	BI-145	BJ-199
Pierce Arrow C*.............(1930)	EG-57	EH-178	EI-153	PB-128	PC-113	PE-123	AE-113	AF-93	BD-154	BE-93	BF-84	BG-135	BI-145	BJ-199
Plymouth, 4 Cyl.............(1929)	Seg.	EH-40	EI-155	PB-40	PC-5	PE-37	AE-30	AF-5	BD-47	BE-30	BF-24	BG-133	BI-91	BJ-55
Plymouth....................(1930)	Seg.	EH-40	EI-155	PB-40	PC-5	PE-37	AE-30	AF-5	BD-47	BE-30	BF-24	BG-133	BI-91	BJ-55
Pontiac 6...................(1926)	EG-16	EH-26	EI-53	PB-25	PC-23	PE-47	AE-21	AF-20	BD-27	BE-15	BF-15	BG-24	BI-27	BJ-33
Pontiac 6...................(1927)	EG-16*	EH-26	EI-53	PB-25	PC-23	PE-47	AE-21	AF-20	BD-27	BE-15	BF-15	BG-24	BI-27	BJ-33
Pontiac 6...................(1928)	EG-31	EH-26	EI-54	PB-25	PC-23	PE-47	AE-22	AF-21	BD-27	BE-15	BF-15	BG-24	BI-27	BJ-33
Pontiac Big 6...............(1929)	EG-31	EH-27	EI-55	PB-26	PC-24	PE-47	AE-22	AF-21	BD-55	BE-83	BF-10	BG-79	BI-125	BJ-151
Pontiac.....................(1930)	EG-31	EH-27	EI-55	PB-26	PC-24	PE-47	AE-22	AF-21	BD-55	BE-83	BF-10	BG-79	BI-125	BJ-151
Reo T6......................(1925)	EG-38	EH-127	EI-156	PB-97	PC-84	PE-93	AE-104	AF-84	BD-155	BE-96	BF-86	BG-97	BI-152	BJ-174
Reo T6..................(1926-27)	EG-38	EH-127	EI-156	PB-97	PC-84	PE-93	AE-104	AF-84	BD-155	BE-96	BF-86	BG-97	BI-152	BJ-174
Reo Flying Cloud............(1927)	EG-51	EH-128	EI-157	PB-98	PC-85	PE-94	AE-105	AF-85	BD-156	BE-97	BF-87	BG-98	BI-153	BJ-175
Reo Wolverine...............(1927)	EG-2	EH-6	EI-8	PB-4	PC-4	PE-4	AE-77	AF-52	BD-41	BE-8	BF-10	BG-47	BI-138	BJ-81
Reo Flying Cloud............(1928)	EG-51	EH-128	EI-158	PB-98	PC-85	PE-94	AE-105	AF-85	BD-156	BE-97	BF-87	BG-98	BI-153	BJ-175
Reo Wolverine...............(1928)	EG-2	EH-6	EI-23	PB-4	PC-4	PE-4	AE-77	AF-52	BD-41	BE-10	BF-10	BG-47	BI-138	BJ-81
Reo Flying Cloud Master.....(1929)	EG-51	EH-128	EI-158	PB-98	PC-85	PE-94	AE-105	AF-85	BD-156	BE-97	BF-87	BG-98	BI-153	BJ-175
Reo Flying Cloud Mate.......(1929)	EG-2	EH-6	EI-23	PB-4	PC-4	PE-4	AE-77	AF-52	BD-41	BE-8	BF-87	BG-47	BI-137	BJ-42
Reo 15......................(1930)	EG-2	EH-179	EI-23	PB-129	PC-114	PE-124	AE-77	AF-52	BD-41	BE-8	BF-87	BG-47	BI-137	BJ-42
Reo 20......................(1930)	EG-58	EH-180	EI-214	PB-130	PC-115	PE-125	AE-105	AF-85	BD-156	BE-94	BF-87	BG-98	BI-153	BJ-44
Reo 25......................(1930)	EG-51	EH-180	EI-214	PB-130	PC-115	PE-125	AE-105	AF-85	BD-156	BE-94	BF-87	BG-98	BI-153	BJ-44
Rickenbacker 8-A, Col.......(1925)	EG-28	EH-131	EI-161	PB-4	PC-4	PE-4	AE-4	AF-4	BD-3	BE-8	BF-7	BG-2	BI-5	BJ-28
Rickenbacker 6-D, Col.(Early 1925)	EG-51	EH-132	EI-162	PB-4	PC-4	PE-4	AE-4	AF-4	BD-3	BE-8	BF-7	BG-2	BI-7	BJ-178
Rickenbacker 6-D, Col..(Late 1925)	EG-51	EH-132	EI-162	PB-4	PC-4	PE-4	AE-4	AF-4	BD-3	BE-8	BF-7	BG-2	BI-7	BJ-179
Rickenbacker 8-B, Col.......(1926)	EG-28	EH-131	EI-163	PB-4	PC-4	PE-4	AE-4	AF-4	BD-20	BE-5	BF-5	BG-19	BI-21	BJ-28
Rickenbacker 6-E, Col.......(1926)	EG-51	EH-132	EI-164	PB-4	PC-4	PE-4	AE-4	AF-4	BD-5	BE-8	BF-7	BG-2	BI-7	BJ-128
Rickenbacker 6-70, Col......(1927)	EG-51*	EH-132	EI-164	PB-4	PC-4	PE-4	AE-4	AF-6	BD-10	BE-43	BF-8	BG-8	BI-8	BJ-9
Rickenbacker 8-80, Col (Early 1927)	EG-51*	EH-132	EI-164	PB-4	PC-4	PE-4	AE-4	AF-4	BD-10	BE-43	BF-8	BG-8	BI-8	BJ-128
Rickenbacker 8-80, Col..(Late 1927)	EG-51*	EH-132	EI-164	PB-4	PC-4	PE-4	AE-5	AF-6	BD-10	BE-8	BF-7	BG-8	BI-8	BJ-9
Rickenbacker 8-90, Col......(1927)	EG-40	EH-132	EI-165	PB-4	PC-4	PE-4	AE-4	AF-4	BD-20	BE-5	BF-7	BG-19	BI-21	BJ-28
Roamer 6-54-E...............(1925)	EG-2	EH-134	EI-167	PB-101	PC-88	PE-109	AE-106	AF-86	BD-159	BE-5	BF-5	BG-68	BI-136	BJ-181
Roamer 6-50.............(1925-26)	EG-2	EH-134	EI-167	PB-101	PC-88	PE-109	AE-106	AF-160	BD-160	BE-100	BF-90	BG-101	BI-158	BJ-182
Roamer 8-88.............(1925-26)	EG-41	EH-135	EI-167	PB-4	PC-4	PE-4	AE-138	AF-119	BD-162	BE-103	BF-93	BG-103	BI-161	BJ-184
Roamer 8-78.................(1926)	EG-41	EH-135	EI-18	PB-4	PC-4	PE-4	AE-140	AF-121	BD-163	BE-102	BF-92	BG-102	BI-159	BJ-149
Roamer 8-80.................(1926)	EG-2	EH-136	EI-18	PB-4	PC-4	PE-4	AE-139	AF-120	BD-161	BE-101	BF-91	BG-104	BI-160	BJ-183
Roamer 8-78.................(1927)	EG-41	EH-135	EI-18	PB-4	PC-4	PE-4	AE-140	AF-121	BD-163	BE-102	BF-92	BG-102	BI-159	BJ-149
Roamer 8-80.................(1927)	EG-2	EH-136	EI-18	PB-4	PC-4	PE-4	AE-139	AF-120	BD-161	BE-101	BF-91	BG-104	BI-160	BJ-183
Roamer 8-88.................(1927)	EG-41	EH-137	EI-18	PB-4	PC-4	PE-4	AE-138	AF-119	BD-162	BE-103	BF-93	BG-103	BI-161	BJ-184
Roamer 8-78.................(1928)	EG-1	EH-137	EI-18	PB-4	PC-4	PE-4	AE-140	AF-121	BD-163	BE-102	BF-92	BG-102	BI-159	BJ-149
Roamer 8-80.................(1928)	EG-2	EH-136	EI-18	PB-4	PC-4	PE-4	AE-139	AF-120	BD-161	BE-101	BF-91	BG-104	BI-160	BJ-183
Roamer 8-88.................(1928)	EG-41	EH-135	EI-18	PB-4	PC-4	PE-4	AE-138	AF-119	BD-162	BE-103	BF-93	BG-103	BI-161	BJ-184
Roamer 8-78.................(1929)	EG-1	EH-137	EI-18	PB-4	PC-4	PE-4	AE-140	AF-121	BD-163	BE-102	BF-92	BG-102	BI-159	BJ-149
Roamer 8-80.................(1929)	EG-2	EH-136	EI-18	PB-4	PC-4	PE-4	AE-139	AF-120	BD-161	BE-101	BF-91	BG-104	BI-160	BJ-183
Roamer 8-88.................(1929)	EG-41	EH-135	EI-18	PB-4	PC-4	PE-4	AE-138	AF-119	BD-162	BE-103	BF-93	BG-103	BI-161	BJ-184
Star F......................(1925)	Seg.	EH-139	EI-169	PB-50	PC-23	PE-47	AE-108	AF-88	BD-10	BE-7	BF-8	BG-32	BI-59	BJ-67
Star M......................(1926)	Seg.	EH-139	EI-170	PB-50	PC-23	PE-47	AE-41	AF-31	BD-10	BE-7	BF-8	BG-32	BI-59	BJ-67
Star R......................(1926)	Seg.	EH-139	EI-170	PB-50	PC-23	PE-47	AE-41	AF-31	BD-10	BE-7	BF-8	BG-32	BI-59	BJ-67
Star M..................(1927-28)	Seg.	EH-139	EI-170	PB-50	PC-23	PE-47	AE-41	AF-31	BD-10	BE-7	BF-8	BG-32	BI-59	BJ-67
Star R..................(1927-28)	Seg.	EH-139	EI-170	PB-50	PC-23	PE-47	AE-41	AF-31	BD-10	BE-7	BF-8	BG-32	BI-59	BJ-67
Stearns Knight B............(1925)	EG-43	EH-140	EI-171	PB-104	PC-91	PE-98	AE-110	AF-90	BD-148	BE-105	BF-96	BG-5	BI-164	BJ-79
Stearns Knight C, Eat. Fr....(1925)	EG-2	EH-141	EI-172	PB-104	PC-91	PE-98	AE-110	AF-90	BD-148	BE-106	BF-97	BG-108	BI-165	BJ-192
Stearns Knight S............(1925)	EG-43	EH-141	EI-173	PB-104	PC-91	PE-98	AE-71	AF-62	BD-169	BE-107	BF-98	BG-109	BI-166	BJ-192
Stearns Knight B............(1926)	EG-43	EH-140	EI-174	PB-104	PC-91	PE-98	AE-110	AF-90	BD-148	BE-105	BF-96	BG-5	BI-164	BJ-79

CLUTCH, TRANSMISSION, FRONT AND REAR AXLES—Continued

Car Make and Model	CLUTCH			TRANSMISSION			FRONT AXLE		REAR AXLE					
	Clutch Facings (Lining)	Clutch Shaft	Clutch Discs	High and Intermediate Sliding or Coupling Gear	Low and Reverse or Second and Reverse Sliding Gear	Countershaft Gear Assembly	King Pins	King Pin Bushings	Differential Case	Differential Spider or Cross Pin	Differential Spider Pinions	Differential Side Gears	Drive Pinion and Ring Gear	Axle Shafts
Stearns Knight C75..........(1926)	EG-2	EH-140	EI-175	PB-104	PC-91	PE-98	AE-110	AF-90	BD-148	BE-106	BF-97	BG-108	BI-165	BJ-192
Stearns Knight S95..........(1926)	EG-43	EH-141	EI-176	PB-105	PC-92	PE-99	AE-110	AF-90	BD-169	BE-107	BF-98	BG-109	BI-166	BJ-192
Stearns Knight F-6-85.......(1927)	EG-9	EH-142	EI-21	PB-105	PC-92	PE-99	AE-110	AF-90	BD-170	BE-108	BF-99	BG-110	BI-167	BJ-193
Stearns Knight G-8-85.......(1927)	EG-42	EH-143	EI-21	PB-105	PC-92	PE-99	AE-110	AF-90	BD-171	BE-109	BF-100	BG-111	BI-168	BJ-193
Stearns Knight F-6-85.......(1928)	EG-9	EH-142	EI-21	PB-105	PC-92	PE-99	AE-110	AF-90	BD-170	BE-108	BF-99	BG-110	BI-167	BJ-193
Stearns Knight H & J.......(1928)	EG-51	EH-145	EI-21	PB-105	PC-92	PE-99	AE-110	AF-90	BD-171	BE-110	BF-101	BG-112	BI-169	BJ-193
Stearns Knight H & J, 8-90..(1929)	EG-51	EH-145	EI-177	PB-105	PC-92	PE-99	AE-110	AF-90	BD-171	BE-110	BF-101	BG-112	BI-169	BJ-193
Stearns Knight M & N, 6-80.(1929)	EG-9	EH-146	EI-178	PB-105	PC-92	PE-99	AE-110	AF-90	BD-173	BE-111	BF-102	BG-113	BI-170	BJ-193
Studebaker Big 6...........(1925)	EG-44	EH-148	EI-180	PB-107	PC-94	PE-101	AE-111	AF-91	BD-175	BE-112	BF-103	BG-115	BI-172	BJ-197
Studebaker Spec. 6..........(1925)	EG-44	EH-148	EI-181	PB-107	PC-94	PE-101	AE-111	AF-91	BD-175	BE-112	BF-103	BG-115	BI-172	BJ-197
Studebaker Std. 6...........(1925)	EG-46	EH-149	EI-182	PB-108	PC-95	PE-102	AE-146	AF-66	BD-88	BE-113	BF-104	BG-116	BI-173	BJ-189
Studebaker Big 6...........(1926)	EG-44	EH-148	EI-181	PB-107	PC-94	PE-101	AE-111	AF-91	BD-175	BE-112	BF-103	BG-115	BI-172	BJ-197
Studebaker Std. 6...........(1926)	EG-46	EH-149	EI-183	PB-108	PC-95	PE-102	AE-146	AF-66	BD-88	BE-113	BF-104	BG-116	BI-173	BJ-198
Studebaker Spec. 6..........(1926)	EG-44	EH-148	EI-184	PB-107	PC-94	PE-101	AE-111	AF-91	BD-175	BE-112	BF-103	BG-115	BI-172	BJ-197
Studebaker Big 6...........(1927)	EG-17	EH-148	EI-185	PB-107	PC-94	PE-101	AE-111	AF-91	BD-175	BE-112	BF-103	BG-115	BI-172	BJ-197
Studebaker Spec. 6..........(1927)	EG-17	EH-148	EI-184	PB-107	PC-94	PE-101	AE-111	AF-91	BD-175	BE-112	BF-103	BG-115	BI-172	BJ-197
Studebaker Std. 6...........(1927)	EG-7	EH-149	EI-184	PB-108	PC-95	PE-102	AE-146	AF-66	BD-88	BE-113	BF-104	BG-116	BI-173	BJ-189
Studebaker Com. 6..........(1928)	EG-17	EH-150	EI-185	PB-109	PC-96	PE-103	AE-113	AF-93	BD-177	BE-112	BF-103	BG-99	BI-162	BJ-186
Studebaker Dict. 6..........(1928)	EG-7	EH-149	EI-186	PB-108	PC-95	PE-102	AE-112	AF-92	BD-177	BE-113	BF-103	BG-99	BI-174	BJ-173
Studebaker Pres. 8..........(1928)	EG-6	EH-151	EI-187	PB-109	PC-96	PE-103	AE-113	AF-93	BD-177	BE-112	BF-103	BG-99	BI-175	BJ-191
Studebaker Com. 6....(Early 1929)	EG-51	EH-150	EI-188	PB-109	PC-96	PE-103	AE-113	AF-93	BD-67	BE-112	BF-103	BG-99	BI-157	BJ-171
Studebaker Com. 6.....(Late 1929)	EG-51	EH-150	EI-188	PB-109	PC-96	PE-103	AE-147	AF-111	BD-67	BE-112	BF-103	BG-100	BI-156	BJ-171
Studebaker Com. 8..........(1929)	EG-51	EH-150	EI-188	PB-109	PC-96	PE-103	AE-147	AF-111	BD-67	BE-112	BF-103	BG-100	BI-156	BJ-170
Studebaker Dict. 6..........(1929)	EG-51	EH-149	EI-186	PB-108	PC-95	PE-102	AE-112	AF-92	BD-68	BE-113	BF-103	BG-105	BI-156	BJ-173
Studebaker Pres. 8..........(1929)	EG-6	EH-151	EI-187	PB-109	PC-96	PE-103	AE-113	AF-93	BD-69	BE-112	BF-103	BG-107	BI-155	BJ-199
Studebaker 6-53............(1930)	EG-52	EH-40	EI-127	PB-40	PC-5	PE-37	AE-147	AF-111	BD-40	BE-7	BF-8	BG-8	BI-69	BJ-198
Studebaker Dict. 6..........(1930)	EG-52	EH-137	EI-127	PB-103	PC-45	PE-111	AE-112	AF-92	BD-68	BE-112	BF-103	BG-105	BI-129	BJ-169
Studebaker Dict. 8..........(1930)	EG-52	EH-137	EI-127	PB-103	PC-45	PE-111	AE-147	AF-111	BD-68	BE-112	BF-103	BG-136	BI-129	BJ-169
Studebaker Com. 6..........(1930)	EG-51	EH-147	EI-188	PB-103	PC-45	PE-111	AE-147	AF-111	BD-67	BE-112	BF-103	BG-100	BI-129	BJ-165
Studebaker Com. 8..........(1930)	EG-51	EH-150	EI-188	PB-109	PC-96	PE-103	AE-147	AF-111	BD-67	BE-112	BF-103	BG-100	BI-129	BJ-165
Studebaker Pres.8...........(1930)	EG-6	EH-151	EI-187	PB-109	PC-96	PE-103	AE-113	AF-93	BD-69	BE-112	BF-103	BG-107	BI-155	BJ-199
Stutz 695....................(1925)	EG-2	EH-90	EI-1	PB-90	PC-42	PE-86	AE-13	AF-13	BD-144	BE-5	BF-5	BG-68	BI-34	BJ-124
Stutz AA.....................(1926)	EG-9	EH-153	EI-21	PB-110	PC-59	PE-104	AE-114	AF-94	BD-179	BE-114	BF-105	BG-117	BI-177	BJ-128
Stutz AA.....................(1927)	EG-9	EH-153	EI-21	PB-110	PC-59	PE-104	AE-114	AF-94	BD-179	BE-114	BF-105	BG-117	BI-177	BJ-128
Stutz BB.....................(1928)	EG-9	EH-86	EI-1	PB-80	PC-97	PE-84	AE-116	AF-96	BD-179	BE-114	BF-105	BG-117	BI-177	BJ-128
Stutz M......................(1929)	EG-9	EH-86	EI-3	PB-10	PC-8	PE-10	AE-115	AF-95	BD-180	BE-115	BF-106	BG-118	BI-178	BJ-147
Stutz M......................(1930)	EG-9	EH-152	EI-3	PB-10	PC-8	PE-10	AE-115	AF-95	BD-180	BE-115	BF-106	BG-118	BI-178	BJ-142
Velie 60.....................(1925)	EG-2	EH-154	EI-15	PB-102	PC-89	PE-96	AE-4	AF-4	BD-3	BE-8	BF-7	BG-2	BI-7	BJ-179
Velie 60.....................(1926)	EG-2	EH-154	EI-8	PB-102	PC-89	PE-96	AE-4	AF-5	BD-3	BE-8	BF-7	BG-2	BI-7	BJ-179
Velie Spec. 60...............(1927)	EG-1	EH-7	EI-6	PB-102	PC-89	PE-96	AE-4	AF-5	BD-10	BE-8	BF-8	BG-8	BI-8	BJ-179
Velie Std. 50................(1927)	EG-1	EH-155	EI-8	PB-5	PC-5	PE-5	AE-4	AF-5	BD-10	BE-7	BF-8	BG-8	BI-8	BJ-146
Velie 60.................(1927-28)	EG-1	EH-7	EI-6	PB-102	PC-89	PE-96	AE-4	AF-5	BD-10	BE-8	BF-8	BG-8	BI-8	BJ-179
Velie Std. 50................(1928)	EG-1	EH-7	EI-189	PB-5	PC-5	PE-5	AE-4	AF-5	BD-10	BE-7	BF-8	BG-8	BI-8	BJ-146
Velie 6-66...................(1928)	EG-1	EH-156	EI-189	PB-5	PC-5	PE-5	AE-117	AF-5	BD-10	BE-7	BF-8	BG-8	BI-8	BJ-146
Velie 6-77...................(1928)	EG-2	EH-157	EI-190	PB-5	PC-5	PE-5	AE-117	AF-5	BD-10	BE-7	BF-8	BG-8	BI-8	BJ-146
Velie 8-88...................(1928)	EG-9	EH-158	EI-21	PB-5	PC-5	PE-5	AE-4	AF-4	BD-181	BE-116	BF-107	BG-119	BI-179	BJ-146
Viking...................(1929-30)	EG-47	EH-159	EI-17	PB-111	PC-98	PE-105	AE-133	AF-113	BD-16	BE-117	BF-108	BG-16	BI-180	BJ-21
Westcott 44, Col............(1925)	EG-2	EH-5	EI-1	PB-4	PC-4	PE-4	AE-4	AF-4	BD-20	BE-5	BF-5	BG-19	BI-176	BJ-28
Westcott 60, Col............(1925)	EG-2	EH-5	EI-1	PB-4	PC-4	PE-4	AE-4	AF-4	BD-4	BE-5	BF-5	BG-5	BI-5	BJ-178
Whippet 96, 4 Cyl...........(1927)	EG-33	EH-112	EI-32	PB-87	PC-76	PE-83	AE-94	AF-75	BD-73	BE-7	BF-8	BG-1	BI-154	BJ-154
Whippet 93-A, 6 Cyl.........(1927)	EG-1	EH-111	EI-14	PB-53	PC-49	PE-50	AE-95	AF-75	BD-1	BE-3	BF-1	BG-1	BI-73	BJ-85
Whippet 96, 4 Cyl...........(1928)	EG-1	EH-113	EI-32	PB-87	PC-76	PE-83	AE-94	AF-75	BD-73	BE-7	BF-8	BG-8	BI-154	BJ-154
Whippet 98, 6 Cyl...........(1928)	EG-33	EH-58	EI-34	PB-54	PC-49	PE-51	AE-95	AF-75	BD-140	BE-7	BF-8	BG-8	BI-154	BJ-155
Whippet 96-A................(1929)	EG-33	EH-113	EI-32	PB-87	PC-76	PE-83	AE-94	AF-75	BD-73	BE-7	BF-8	BG-8	BI-154	BJ-154
Whippet 98-A................(1929)	Seg.	EH-114	EI-34	PB-88	PC-49	PE-84	AE-94	AF-75	BD-140	BE-7	BF-8	BG-8	BI-154	BJ-155
Wills Ste. Claire 6,Eat. Fr....(1925)	Inter.	EH-163	EI-197	PB-113	PC-100	PE-107	AE-71	AF-62	BD-74	BE-126	BF-117	BG-128	BI-34	BJ-124
Wills Ste. Claire 8, Eat. Fr...(1925)	....	....	....	....	....	....	AE-71	AF-62	BD-94	BE-5	BF-5	BG-128	BI-34	BJ-110
Wills Ste. Claire 6..........(1926)	Inter.	EH-163	EI-199	PB-113	PC-100	PE-107	AE-71	AF-62	BD-74	BE-126	BF-117	BG-128	BI-34	BJ-192
Wills Ste. Claire 8..........(1926)	Inter.	EH-162	EI-199	PB-113	PC-100	PE-107	AE-71	AF-62	BD-94	BE-5	BF-5	BG-129	BI-34	BJ-110
Willys 6.....................(1930)	EG-1	EH-114	EI-10	PB-106	PC-49	PE-84	AE-94	AF-75	BD-140	BE-7	BF-8	BG-127	BI-117	BJ-155
Willys 8.....................(1930)	EG-47	EH-181	EI-83	PB-131	PC-116	PE-112	AE-148	AF-87	BD-79	BE-55	BF-8	BG-131	BI-119	BJ-180
Willys Knight 66............(1925)	EG-48	EH-157	EI-191	PB-115	PC-46	PE-113	AE-55	AF-97	BD-183	BE-118	BF-109	BG-121	BI-181	BJ-188
Willys Knight 65............(1925)	EG-48	EH-157	EI-191	PB-115	PC-46	PE-113	AE-55	AF-97	BD-183	BE-119	BF-110	BG-122	BI-182	BJ-187
Willys Knight 66............(1926)	EG-48	EH-158	EI-192	PB-115	PC-46	PE-113	AE-134	None	BD-183	BE-120	BF-111	BG-123	BI-181	BJ-188
Willys Knight 70............(1926)	EG-1	EH-159	EI-14	PB-112	PC-99	PE-106	AE-55	AF-97	BD-186	BE-121	BF-112	BG-124	BI-184	BJ-185
Willys Knight 66-A.........(1927)	EG-9	EH-158	EI-193	PB-112	PC-99	PE-106	AE-135	None	BD-183	BE-122	BF-113	BG-125	BI-183	BJ-188
Willys Knight 70-A.........(1927)	EG-1	EH-159	EI-14	PB-112	PC-99	PE-106	AE-55	AF-97	BD-186	BE-121	BF-112	BG-124	BI-154	BJ-185
Willys Knight 66-A.........(1928)	EG-9	EH-160	EI-194	PB-112	PC-99	PE-106	AE-135	AF-114	BD-183	BE-123	BF-114	BG-125	BI-183	BJ-188
Willys Knight 70-A.........(1928)	EG-1	EH-159	EI-195	PB-112	PC-99	PE-106	AE-136	AF-116	BD-1	BE-3	BF-1	BG-1	BI-154	BJ-185
Willys Knight Std. 6-56.....(1928)	Seg.	EH-161	EI-14	PB-112	PC-49	PE-50	AE-55	AF-115	BD-1	BE-3	BF-1	BG-1	BI-77	BJ-86
Willys Knight 70-A.........(1929)	EG-1	EH-159	EI-195	PB-112	PC-99	PE-106	AE-136	AF-116	BD-1	BE-3	BF-1	BG-1	BI-154	BJ-185
Willys Knight 66-A.........(1929)	EG-9	EH-158	EI-193	PB-112	PC-99	PE-106	AE-135	AF-117	BD-187	BE-124	BF-115	BG-126	BI-183	BJ-188
Willys Knight 70-B.........(1929)	Seg.	EH-2	EI-196	PB-112	PC-99	PE-106	AE-137	AF-118	BD-92	BE-3	BF-116	BG-9	BI-149	BJ-180
Willys Knight 66-B.........(1930)	EG-9	EH-158	EI-193	PB-112	PC-99	PE-106	AE-135	AF-117	BD-187	BE-124	BF-115	BG-126	BI-183	BJ-172
Willys Knight 70-B.........(1930)	Seg.	EH-2	EI-215	PB-112	PC-99	PE-106	AE-137	AF-118	BD-92	BE-3	BF-116	BG-9	BI-149	BJ-180

* PB-6—1929; Use PB-4 on 1928 Cars.
* PE-6—Some PE-4 used also.
* Auburn 6-80 after serial No. 2982400.
* EG-7 after May 1928; use EG-6 before.
* EG-8 after September; use EG-5 before.
* EG-16—EG-31 also used.
* EG-51 First 700 cars; use EG-6 after.
* Franklin 135-145-147—4-speed cars.
* Pierce Arrow C: cars numbered 1002516 to 1003715.
* Buick Master 128 W. B. 1925, 26, 27 use BJ-97.
* Jordan AA 1927, 28 use BJ-79 for Eaton.

INTERCHANGEABLE COUNT

Showing the exact number of times each Chilton Number occurs in the CLUTCH, TRANSMISSION, FRONT AND REAR AXLE TABLE, beginning Page 236.

Clutch Facings	EG-9-41	EG-21-1	EG-32-2	EG-43-4	EG-54-1	EH-3-4	EH-13-1	EH-23-6	EH-33-5	EH-45-1	EH-56-3	EH-66-6
(Lining)	EG-10-2	EG-22-1	EG-33-3	EG-44-4	EG-55-2	EH-4-2	EH-14-1	EH-24-5	EH-34-2	EH-46-2	EH-57-2	EH-67-9
	EG-11-5	EG-23-2	EG-34-5	EG-46-2	EG-56-1	EH-5-10	EH-15-3	EH-25-3	EH-36-1	EH-47-1	EH-58-2	EH-68-1
EG-1-66	EG-12-5	EG-24-8	EG-35-3	EG-47-2	EG-57-9	EH-6-24	EH-16-3	EH-26-7	EH-37-4	EH-48-1	EH-59-4	EH-69-1
EG-2-102	EG-13-5	EG-26-4	EG-36-1	EG-48-3	EG-58-1	EH-7-22	EH-17-2	EH-27-4	EH-39-10	EH-49-1	EH-60-4	EH-70-4
EG-4-4	EG-14-4	EG-27-4	EG-37-2	EG-49-1		EH-8-12	EH-18-4	EH-28-3	EH-40-7	EH-50-1	EH-61-3	EH-71-4
EG-5-9	EG-15-6	EG-28-5	EG-38-2	EG-50-2	**Clutch Shaft**	EH-9-29	EH-19-3	EH-29-2	EH-41-3	EH-51-6	EH-62-2	EH-72-7
EG-6-37	EG-16-8	EG-29-1	EG-40-1	EG-51-27		EH-10-1	EH-20-2	EH-30-2	EH-42-6	EH-52-2	EH-63-3	EH-75-2
EG-7-13	EG-17-10	EG-30-2	EG-41-6	EG-52-6	EH-1-4	EH-11-2	EH-21-1	EH-31-4	EH-43-2	EH-54-1	EH-64-2	EH-76-3
EG-8-9	EG-18-3	EG-31-8	EG-42-1	EG-53-3	EH-2-2	EH-12-2	EH-22-2	EH-32-1	EH-44-3	EH-55-1	EH-65-1	EH-77-2

CLUTCH, TRANSMISSION, FRONT AND REAR AXLES—Continued

INTERCHANGEABLE COUNT—Continued

Showing the exact number of times each Chilton Number occurs in the CLUTCH, TRANSMISSION, FRONT AND REAR AXLE TABLE, beginning Page 236.

EH-78-1	EI-3-4	EI-112-7	PB-4-87	PB-115-4	PC-89-4	PE-78-3	AE-64-3	AF-26-2
EH-79-4	EI-4-1	EI-114-1	PB-5-21	PB-116-8	PC-90-3	PE-79-3	AE-65-3	AF-27-1
EH-80-1	EI-5-6	EI-115-1	PB-6-9	PB-117-2	PC-91-5	PE-80-6	AE-66-4	AF-28-4
EH-81-2	EI-6-14	EI-116-1	PB-7-12	PB-118-2	PC-92-7	PE-81-1	AE-68-4	AF-29-3
EH-82-3	EI-7-6	EI-117-1	PB-9-1	PB-119-1	PC-94-6	PE-82-2	AE-69-2	AF-31-15
EH-83-1	EI-8-20	EI-118-2	PB-10-4	PB-120-1	PC-95-5	PE-83-3	AE-70-3	AF-32-2
EH-84-1	EI-9-7	EI-119-2	PB-11-1	PB-121-2	PC-96-8	PE-84-3	AE-71-10	AF-33-1
EH-85-1	EI-10-8	EI-120-1	PB-12-2	PB-122-1	PC-97-1	PE-85-10	AE-72-3	AF-34-3
EH-86-3	EI-11-3	EI-121-1	PB-13-1	PB-123-3	PC-98-1	PE-86-1	AE-73-1	AF-35-4
EH-87-6	EI-12-3	EI-122-1	PB-14-3	PB-124-1	PC-99-10	PE-87-1	AE-74-4	AF-36-2
EH-88-2	EI-13-3	EI-123-1	PB-15-3	PB-125-1	PC-100-5	PE-88-5	AE-75-2	AF-37-3
EH-90-1	EI-14-9	EI-124-2	PB-16-2	PB-126-2	PC-101-3	PE-89-3	AE-76-1	AF-38-1
EH-91-6	EI-15-10	EI-125-6	PB-17-2	PB-127-2	PC-102-1	PE-90-3	AE-77-6	AF-39-1
EH-92-6	EI-16-1	EI-126-2	PB-18-5	PB-128-1	PC-103-2	PE-91-1	AE-78-11	AF-40-1
EH-93-5	EI-17-3	EI-127-6	PB-19-2	PB-129-1	PC-104-1	PE-92-1	AE-79-4	AF-41-1
EH-94-6	EI-18-19	EI-128-2	PB-20-1	PB-130-2	PC-105-6	PE-93-2	AE-80-4	AF-42-3
EH-95-2	EI-19-3	EI-129-1	PB-21-2	PB-131-1	PC-106-1	PE-94-3	AE-81-1	AF-43-3
EH-97-1	EI-20-1	EI-130-3	PB-22-6	PB-132-2	PC-108-1	PE-95-2	AE-82-4	AF-44-5
EH-98-1	EI-21-20	EI-131-1	PB-23-3		PC-109-1	PE-96-4	AE-84-2	AF-45-6
EH-99-3	EI-22-3	EI-132-1	PB-24-5	**Low and Re-**	PC-110-2	PE-97-1	AE-85-1	AF-46-4
EH-100-2	EI-23-3	EI-133-3	PB-25-7	**verse or Second**	PC-111-2	PE-98-5	AE-86-4	AF-47-3
EH-101-3	EI-24-2	EI-134-1	PB-26-3	**and Reverse**	PC-112-2	PE-99-7	AE-87-5	AF-48-3
EH-102-3	EI-25-1	EI-135-2	PB-27-3	**Sliding Gear**	PC-113-3	PE-100-1	AE-88-5	AF-49-4
EH-103-4	EI-26-7	EI-136-1	PB-28-3		PC-114-1	PE-101-6	AE-89-5	AF-50-5
EH-104-3	EI-27-2	EI-138-2	PB-29-1	PC-1-5	PC-115-2	PE-102-5	AE-90-2	AF-51-1
EH-105-2	EI-28-4	EI-140-4	PB-30-4	PC-3-4	PC-116-1	PE-103-8	AE-91-6	AF-52-14
EH-106-1	EI-29-2	EI-141-2	PB-31-5	PC-4-105	PC-117-1	PE-104-2	AE-92-2	AF-53-3
EH-107-1	EI-30-1	EI-142-5	PB-32-10	PC-5-33		PE-105-1	AE-93-2	AF-54-3
EH-108-1	EI-31-1	EI-143-3	PB-33-4	PC-6-33	**Countershaft**	PE-106-10	AE-94-5	AF-55-4
EH-109-3	EI-32-3	EI-144-1	PB-34-1	PC-7-2	**Gear Assembly**	PE-107-5	AE-95-2	AF-57-3
EH-110-2	EI-33-2	EI-145-2	PB-37-1	PC-8-4		PE-109-2	AE-96-10	AF-58-3
EH-111-3	EI-34-2	EI-146-3	PB-38-12	PC-9-1	PE-1-4	PE-110-1	AE-97-1	AF-59-3
EH-112-1	EI-36-6	EI-147-1	PB-39-2	PC-10-2	PE-2-3	PE-111-4	AE-98-2	AF-60-1
EH-113-2	EI-37-6	EI-148-1	PB-40-13	PC-11-1	PE-3-3	PE-112-1	AE-99-4	AF-61-7
EH-114-2	EI-38-5	EI-149-2	PB-41-3	PC-12-4	PE-4-87	PE-113-3	AE-101-1	AF-62-21
EH-115-4	EI-39-1	EI-150-4	PB-42-3	PC-13-4	PE-5-34	PE-114-1	AE-102-2	AF-63-3
EH-116-8	EI-40-4	EI-151-1	PB-43-6	PC-14-6	PE-6-9	PE-115-1	AE-104-2	AF-64-6
EH-117-4	EI-42-2	EI-152-2	PB-44-2	PC-16-3	PE-7-29	PE-116-2	AE-105-5	AF-65-4
EH-118-1	EI-43-4	EI-153-5	PB-45-1	PC-17-2	PE-9-1	PE-118-1	AE-106-2	AF-66-3
EH-119-5	EI-44-2	EI-154-1	PB-47-4	PC-18-1	PE-10-4	PE-119-1	AE-107-2	AF-67-2
EH-122-1	EI-45-2	EI-155-3	PB-48-2	PC-19-2	PE-11-2	PE-120-2	AE-108-1	AF-68-1
EH-123-1	EI-46-5	EI-156-2	PB-49-4	PC-20-6	PE-12-2	PE-121-4	AE-110-11	AF-69-12
EH-124-4	EI-47-1	EI-157-1	PB-50-19	PC-21-5	PE-13-3	PE-123-3	AE-111-6	AF-70-5
EH-125-3	EI-48-2	EI-158-2	PB-51-1	PC-22-3	PE-14-3	PE-124-1	AE-112-4	AF-71-2
EH-126-1	EI-49-2	EI-161-1	PB-52-5	PC-23-30	PE-15-6	PE-125-2	AE-113-10	AF-72-6
EH-127-2	EI-50-1	EI-162-2	PB-53-7	PC-24-3	PE-16-2		AE-114-2	AF-73-2
EH-128-3	EI-51-5	EI-163-1	PB-54-2	PC-25-3	PE-17-5	**King Pins**	AE-115-2	AF-74-2
EH-129-1	EI-52-5	EI-164-4	PB-55-4	PC-26-1	PE-18-2		AE-116-1	AF-75-7
EH-130-1	EI-53-2	EI-165-1	PB-56-3	PC-27-2	PE-19-1	AE-1-5	AE-117-2	AF-77-1
EH-131-2	EI-54-1	EI-167-3	PB-57-4	PC-28-3	PE-20-2	AE-4-52	AE-118-7	AF-78-4
EH-132-8	EI-55-2	EI-168-1	PB-58-1	PC-29-5	PE-21-6	AE-5-24	AE-119-2	AF-79-2
EH-134-2	EI-56-2	EI-169-1	PB-59-3	PC-30-4	PE-22-5	AE-6-14	AE-121-4	AF-80-4
EH-135-5	EI-57-2	EI-170-4	PB-60-3	PC-31-4	PE-23-3	AE-7-8	AE-122-2	AF-81-1
EH-136-4	EI-58-6	EI-171-1	PB-62-1	PC-33-2	PE-24-4	AE-8-5	AE-123-4	AF-82-2
EH-137-5	EI-59-1	EI-172-1	PB-63-5	PC-34-2	PE-25-2	AE-10-2	AE-124-1	AF-84-2
EH-138-1	EI-60-2	EI-173-1	PB-64-6	PC-35-12	PE-26-1	AE-11-9	AE-125-3	AF-85-5
EH-139-5	EI-61-5	EI-174-1	PB-65-1	PC-36-2	PE-27-4	AE-12-6	AE-126-1	AF-86-1
EH-140-3	EI-62-3	EI-175-1	PB-66-2	PC-38-3	PE-28-2	AE-13-3	AE-127-1	AF-87-1
EH-141-3	EI-63-4	EI-176-1	PB-67-5	PC-39-1	PE-29-3	AE-14-4	AE-129-1	AF-88-1
EH-142-2	EI-64-5	EI-177-1	PB-68-1	PC-40-4	PE-30-5	AE-15-2	AE-130-2	AF-90-11
EH-143-1	EI-66-1	EI-178-1	PB-69-6	PC-41-2	PE-31-2	AE-16-2	AE-131-1	AF-91-6
EH-145-2	EI-67-1	EI-180-1	PB-70-2	PC-42-2	PE-32-1	AE-17-6	AE-133-5	AF-92-4
EH-146-1	EI-68-1	EI-181-2	PB-71-5	PC-43-1	PE-33-2	AE-18-3	AE-134-1	AF-93-10
EH-147-1	EI-69-1	EI-182-1	PB-72-2	PC-44-1	PE-34-4	AE-19-2	AE-135-4	AF-94-2
EH-148-6	EI-70-3	EI-183-1	PB-73-4	PC-45-4	PE-35-4	AE-20-3	AE-136-2	AF-95-2
EH-149-5	EI-71-4	EI-184-3	PB-74-4	PC-46-3	PE-36-2	AE-21-5	AE-137-2	AF-96-1
EH-150-5	EI-72-1	EI-185-2	PB-75-2	PC-47-1	PE-37-13	AE-22-6	AE-138-4	AF-97-4
EH-151-3	EI-73-2	EI-186-2	PB-76-1	PC-48-5	PE-38-3	AE-23-3	AE-139-4	AF-98-3
EH-152-1	EI-74-3	EI-187-3	PB-77-2	PC-49-12	PE-39-1	AE-24-8	AE-140-4	AF-102-2
EH-153-2	EI-75-1	EI-188-5	PB-78-1	PC-50-4	PE-40-5	AE-25-1	AE-141-1	AF-103-2
EH-154-2	EI-76-2	EI-189-2	PB-79-2	PC-51-3	PE-42-1	AE-26-4	AE-142-1	AF-104-1
EH-155-1	EI-78-1	EI-190-1	PB-80-2	PC-52-3	PE-44-2	AE-27-4	AE-143-2	AF-105-4
EH-156-1	EI-79-1	EI-191-1	PB-81-8	PC-53-2	PE-45-1	AE-29-6	AE-144-2	AF-106-1
EH-157-3	EI-80-1	EI-192-1	PB-82-4	PC-54-4	PE-46-1	AE-30-9	AE-145-1	AF-107-3
EH-158-5	EI-81-2	EI-193-3	PB-83-1	PC-55-8	PE-47-31	AE-31-1	AE-146-3	AF-108-1
EH-159-5	EI-82-1	EI-194-1	PB-84-6	PC-58-5	PE-48-1	AE-32-2	AE-147-6	AF-109-1
EH-160-1	EI-83-1	EI-195-2	PB-85-1	PC-59-8	PE-49-5	AE-33-2	AE-148-1	AF-110-2
EH-161-1	EI-84-1	EI-196-1	PB-86-2	PC-60-1	PE-50-8	AE-34-3	AE-150-1	AF-111-6
EH-162-1	EI-85-1	EI-197-1	PB-87-3	PC-61-2	PE-51-2	AE-35-2	AE-151-2	AF-112-1
EH-163-2	EI-86-3	EI-199-2	PB-88-1	PC-62-7	PE-52-3	AE-37-1		AF-113-1
EH-165-2	EI-88-2	EI-204-1	PB-89-10	PC-63-2	PE-53-3	AE-39-4	**King Pin**	AF-114-1
EH-166-1	EI-89-1	EI-205-2	PB-90-1	PC-64-4	PE-54-2	AE-41-11	**Bushings**	AF-115-1
EH-167-2	EI-90-3	EI-206-1	PB-91-1	PC-65-8	PE-55-4	AE-42-2		AF-116-2
EH-168-1	EI-91-1	EI-207-1	PB-92-5	PC-66-1	PE-56-8	AE-43-1	AF-1-5	AF-117-2
EH-170-2	EI-92-1	EI-208-1	PB-93-3	PC-67-2	PE-57-1	AE-44-7	AF-4-59	AF-118-2
EH-171-1	EI-93-1	EI-209-2	PB-94-3	PC-68-1	PE-59-5	AE-45-4	AF-5-30	AF-119-4
EH-172-1	EI-94-3	EI-210-1	PB-95-1	PC-69-2	PE-60-6	AE-46-2	AF-6-30	AF-120-4
EH-173-1	EI-95-2	EI-211-2	PB-96-1	PC-70-1	PE-61-1	AE-47-3	AF-7-14	AF-121-4
EH-174-1	EI-96-1	EI-212-1	PB-97-2	PC-71-12	PE-62-2	AE-48-1	AF-8-8	AF-124-1
EH-175-1	EI-97-1	EI-213-1	PB-98-3	PC-72-3	PE-63-5	AE-49-1	AF-10-2	AF-125-1
EH-176-1	EI-98-2	EI-214-2	PB-99-11	PC-73-6	PE-64-1	AE-50-1	AF-11-9	AF-126-1
EH-177-2	EI-99-1	EI-215-1	PB-101-2	PC-74-1	PE-65-6	AE-51-1	AF-12-6	AF-127-1
EH-178-4	EI-100-1	EI-216-1	PB-102-4	PC-75-2	PE-66-2	AE-52-3	AF-13-3	AF-128-2
EH-179-1	EI-101-3		PB-103-4	PC-76-3	PE-67-6	AE-53-2	AF-14-4	AF-131-1
EH-180-2	EI-102-3		PB-104-5	PC-77-9	PE-68-2	AE-54-5	AF-15-2	AF-132-1
EH-181-3	EI-103-4	**High and**	PB-105-7	PC-78-1	PE-69-4	AE-55-8	AF-16-6	AF-160-1
EH-182-2	EI-104-2	**Intermediate**	PB-106-1	PC-79-5	PE-70-4	AE-56-6	AF-17-3	
	EI-105-3	**Sliding or**	PB-107-6	PC-80-3	PE-71-2	AE-57-2	AF-18-2	
	EI-106-3	**Coupling**	PB-108-5	PC-81-3	PE-72-1	AE-58-2	AF-19-3	**Differential**
Clutch	EI-107-2	**Gear**	PB-109-8	PC-82-1	PE-73-2	AE-59-3	AF-20-5	**Case**
Discs	EI-108-2		PB-110-2	PC-83-1	PE-74-2	AE-60-3	AF-21-6	
	EI-109-1	PB-1-5	PB-111-1	PC-84-2	PE-75-3	AE-61-4	AF-22-1	BD-1-27
EI-1-19	EI-110-3	PB-2-3	PB-112-11	PC-85-3	PE-76-1	AE-62-5	AF-23-15	BD-2-15
EI-2-2	EI-111-5	PB-3-4	PB-113-3	PC-88-2	PE-77-8	AE-63-1	AF-24-4	BD-3-8

CLUTCH, TRANSMISSION, FRONT AND REAR AXLES—Continued

INTERCHANGEABLE COUNT—Continued

Showing the exact number of times each Chilton Number occurs in the CLUTCH, TRANSMISSION, FRONT AND REAR AXLE TABLE, beginning Page 236.

BD-4-5	BD-121-3	BE-72-5	BF-61-1	BG-55-2	BI-24-5	BI-141-2	BJ-73-4
BD-5-31	BD-122-1	BE-73-2	BF-62-2	BG-56-5	BI-25-3	BI-142-3	BJ-74-7
BD-6-2	BD-123-4	BE-74-1	BF-63-3	BG-57-4	BI-26-2	BI-143-1	BJ-76-7
BD-7-2	BD-124-3	BE-75-1	BF-64-1	BG-58-3	BI-27-7	BI-144-1	BJ-77-1
BD-8-2	BD-125-1	BE-76-2	BF-65-3	BG-59-3	BI-28-1	BI-145-4	BJ-78-1
BD-9-2	BD-127-2	BE-77-1	BF-66-2	BG-60-4	BI-29-1	BI-146-1	BJ-79-6
BD-10-47	BD-129-2	BE-78-2	BF-67-4	BG-61-5	BI-30-2	BI-147-2	BJ-80-2
BD-11-2	BD-130-3	BE-79-2	BF-68-4	BG-62-2	BI-31-2	BI-148-1	BJ-81-4
BD-12-6	BD-135-6	BE-80-2	BF-69-3	BG-63-1	BI-32-4	BI-149-2	BJ-83-3
BD-13-4	BD-136-1	BE-81-6	BF-70-1	BG-64-3	BI-33-2	BI-152-2	BJ-84-5
BD-14-5	BD-137-5	BE-82-6	BF-71-1	BG-65-1	BI-34-20	BI-153-5	BJ-85-6
BD-15-4	BD-139-5	BE-83-10	BF-72-1	BG-66-7	BI-35-2	BI-154-8	BJ-86-3
BD-16-3	BD-140-3	BE-84-5	BF-74-2	BG-67-1	BI-36-1	BI-155-2	BJ-87-2
BD-17-2	BD-141-1	BE-85-10	BF-75-2	BG-68-10	BI-37-1	BI-156-3	BJ-88-1
BD-18-2	BD-142-2	BE-86-1	BF-76-6	BG-69-7	BI-38-2	BI-157-1	BJ-89-1
BD-19-5	BD-143-4	BE-87-1	BF-77-6	BG-70-2	BI-40-2	BI-158-1	BJ-90-3
BD-20-6	BD-144-2	BE-88-1	BF-78-9	BG-71-2	BI-41-1	BI-159-4	BJ-91-3
BD-21-1	BD-148-6	BE-89-2	BF-79-3	BG-72-4	BI-42-1	BI-160-4	BJ-92-2
BD-22-2	BD-149-3	BE-91-4	BF-81-2	BG-73-1	BI-43-4	BI-161-4	BJ-93-3
BD-23-2	BD-152-4	BE-92-3	BF-82-4	BG-74-3	BI-45-6	BI-162-1	BJ-94-3
BD-24-2	BD-153-7	BE-93-5	BF-83-3	BG-75-1	BI-49-2	BI-163-1	BJ-95-3
BD-25-2	BD-154-5	BE-94-2	BF-84-5	BG-76-9	BI-50-1	BI-164-2	BJ-96-5
BD-26-5	BD-155-2	BE-96-2	BF-86-2	BG-77-5	BI-52-1	BI-165-2	BJ-98-1
BD-27-7	BD-156-5	BE-97-3	BF-87-7	BG-78-2	BI-53-3	BI-166-2	BJ-99-3
BD-28-1	BD-159-1	BE-100-1	BF-90-1	BG-79-10	BI-55-1	BI-167-2	BJ-100-1
BD-29-5	BD-160-1	BE-101-4	BF-91-4	BG-80-2	BI-56-2	BI-168-1	BJ-102-1
BD-30-2	BD-161-4	BE-102-4	BF-92-4	BG-81-1	BI-57-2	BI-169-2	BJ-103-3
BD-31-2	BD-162-4	BE-103-4	BF-93-4	BG-82-2	BI-58-1	BI-170-1	BJ-105-7
BD-32-1	BD-163-4	BE-104-2	BF-96-2	BG-83-1	BI-59-14	BI-171-1	BJ-106-1
BD-33-2	BD-169-2	BE-105-2	BF-97-2	BG-84-1	BI-60-2	BI-172-6	BJ-107-2
BD-34-2	BD-170-2	BE-106-2	BF-98-2	BG-85-2	BI-61-1	BI-173-3	BJ-108-2
BD-35-2	BD-171-3	BE-107-2	BF-99-2	BG-86-2	BI-62-2	BI-174-1	BJ-110-2
BD-36-4	BD-173-1	BE-108-2	BF-100-1	BG-87-4	BI-63-1	BI-175-1	BJ-111-1
BD-37-1	BD-175-6	BE-109-1	BF-101-2	BG-88-4	BI-64-3	BI-176-1	BJ-113-2
BD-38-1	BD-177-3	BE-110-2	BF-102-1	BG-89-4	BI-65-1	BI-177-3	BJ-114-5
BD-39-3	BD-179-3	BE-111-1	BF-103-19	BG-90-1	BI-66-1	BI-178-2	BJ-116-2
BD-40-3	BD-180-2	BE-112-17	BF-104-3	BG-91-1	BI-67-2	BI-179-1	BJ-117-3
BD-41-8	BD-181-1	BE-113-5	BF-105-3	BG-92-1	BI-68-7	BI-180-1	BJ-118-2
BD-42-2	BD-183-5	BE-114-5	BF-106-2	BG-93-2	BI-69-4	BI-181-2	BJ-119-2
BD-43-2	BD-186-2	BE-115-2	BF-107-1	BG-94-6	BI-70-5	BI-182-1	BJ-121-2
BD-44-1	BD-187-2	BE-116-1	BF-108-1	BG-95-6	BI-71-2	BI-183-4	BJ-123-2
BD-45-2		BE-117-1	BF-109-1	BG-97-5	BI-72-1	BI-184-1	BJ-124-17
BD-46-2	**Differential**	BE-118-1	BF-110-1	BG-98-5	BI-73-5		BJ-125-4
BD-47-6	**Spider or**	BE-119-1	BF-111-1	BG-99-4	BI-74-1	**Axle Shafts**	BJ-126-2
BD-48-1	**Cross Pin**	BE-120-1	BF-112-2	BG-100-4	BI-75-1		BJ-127-8
BD-49-1		BE-121-2	BF-114-1	BG-101-1	BI-76-2	BJ-1-5	BJ-128-18
BD-50-4	BE-1-20	BE-122-1	BF-115-2	BG-102-4	BI-77-2	BJ-2-7	BJ-130-2
BD-51-3	BE-2-2	BE-123-1	BF-116-2	BG-103-4	BI-78-2	BJ-3-2	BJ-131-1
BD-52-1	BE-3-14	BE-124-2	BF-117-2	BG-104-4	BI-79-4	BJ-4-7	BJ-132-3
BD-53-2	BE-4-29	BE-126-2		BG-105-2	BI-80-4	BJ-5-1	BJ-134-4
BD-54-1	BE-5-49	BE-127-2	**Differential**	BG-106-3	BI-81-3	BJ-6-2	BJ-135-4
BD-55-10	BE-6-2	BE-130-1	**Side Gears**	BG-107-2	BI-82-3	BJ-7-1	BJ-136-4
BD-56-2	BE-7-62			BG-108-2	BI-83-4	BJ-8-6	BJ-137-3
BD-57-6	BE-8-56	**Differential**	BG-1-25	BG-109-2	BI-84-4	BJ-9-10	BJ-138-1
BD-58-6	BE-9-2	**Spider**	BG-2-45	BG-110-2	BI-85-1	BJ-10-1	BJ-139-2
BD-59-1	BE-10-15	**Pinions**	BG-3-1	BG-111-1	BI-86-1	BJ-11-4	BJ-140-1
BD-60-2	BE-11-2		BG-4-4	BG-112-2	BI-87-2	BJ-13-11	BJ-141-4
BD-61-2	BE-12-2	BF-1-36	BG-5-10	BG-113-1	BI-88-4	BJ-14-4	BJ-142-2
BD-62-2	BE-13-5	BF-2-7	BG-6-1	BG-114-1	BI-89-7	BJ-15-1	BJ-143-1
BD-63-1	BE-14-2	BF-3-2	BG-7-9	BG-115-6	BI-91-5	BJ-16-2	BJ-144-2
BD-64-2	BE-15-8	BF-4-25	BG-8-42	BG-116-3	BI-92-4	BJ-17-4	BJ-145-1
BD-65-1	BE-16-5	BF-5-52	BG-9-9	BG-117-3	BI-93-1	BJ-18-1	BJ-146-5
BD-66-1	BE-17-2	BF-6-2	BG-10-4	BG-118-2	BI-94-3	BJ-19-2	BJ-147-1
BD-67-5	BE-18-2	BF-7-47	BG-11-2	BG-119-1	BI-95-2	BJ-20-1	BJ-148-1
BD-68-3	BE-19-2	BF-8-82	BG-12-6	BG-120-1	BI-96-2	BJ-21-3	BJ-149-4
BD-69-2	BE-20-2	BF-9-2	BG-13-3	BG-122-1	BI-97-4	BJ-22-2	BJ-150-11
BD-70-3	BE-21-8	BF-10-26	BG-14-3	BG-123-1	BI-99-1	BJ-23-2	BJ-151-8
BD-71-1	BE-22-3	BF-11-1	BG-15-2	BG-124-2	BI-100-1	BJ-24-7	BJ-152-6
BD-72-3	BE-23-1	BF-12-2	BG-16-3	BG-125-2	BI-101-5	BJ-25-3	BJ-154-3
BD-73-3	BE-28-2	BF-13-2	BG-17-3	BG-126-2	BI-102-2	BJ-26-2	BJ-155-3
BD-74-2	BE-29-2	BF-14-8	BG-18-7	BG-127-1	BI-103-4	BJ-27-2	BJ-156-1
BD-75-2	BE-30-7	BF-15-8	BG-19-5	BG-128-3	BI-104-2	BJ-28-7	BJ-157-2
BD-76-2	BE-31-4	BF-16-7	BG-20-2	BG-129-1	BI-105-4	BJ-29-2	BJ-158-4
BD-77-3	BE-33-6	BF-17-2	BG-21-6	BG-130-2	BI-106-2	BJ-30-6	BJ-159-4
BD-78-2	BE-36-1	BF-18-1	BG-22-3	BG-131-1	BI-107-6	BJ-31-5	BJ-160-1
BD-79-1	BE-37-4	BF-19-1	BG-23-2	BG-133-6	BI-108-1	BJ-32-3	BJ-161-1
BD-80-2	BE-38-8	BF-20-1	BG-24-8	BG-134-1	BI-109-2	BJ-33-8	BJ-162-1
BD-81-5	BE-39-1	BF-21-1	BG-25-7	BG-135-8	BI-110-8	BJ-34-1	BJ-163-1
BD-82-3	BE-40-1	BF-23-5	BG-26-11	BG-136-1	BI-111-4	BJ-35-5	BJ-165-2
BD-83-3	BE-41-2	BF-24-4	BG-27-2		BI-112-2	BJ-36-2	BJ-167-1
BD-84-4	BE-42-1	BF-26-2	BG-28-8	**Drive Pinion**	BI-113-1	BJ-37-2	BJ-168-2
BD-85-2	BE-43-2	BF-27-4	BG-29-3	**and Ring Gear**	BI-114-2	BJ-38-2	BJ-169-2
BD-86-5	BE-44-7	BF-28-6	BG-30-2		BI-115-1	BJ-39-1	BJ-170-1
BD-88-4	BE-45-2	BF-32-1	BG-31-1	BI-1-9	BI-116-2	BJ-40-2	BJ-171-2
BD-89-4	BE-46-2	BF-36-7	BG-32-10	BI-2-4	BI-117-1	BJ-41-2	BJ-172-1
BD-91-7	BE-47-3	BF-37-2	BG-33-2	BI-3-2	BI-118-1	BJ-42-2	BJ-173-2
BD-92-2	BE-48-3	BF-38-1	BG-34-4	BI-4-2	BI-119-1	BJ-43-1	BJ-174-2
BD-94-2	BE-49-4	BF-39-1	BG-36-5	BI-5-20	BI-122-6	BJ-44-2	BJ-175-3
BD-96-2	BE-50-5	BF-40-2	BG-37-1	BI-6-4	BI-123-6	BJ-46-2	BJ-178-3
BD-97-4	BE-52-1	BF-41-1	BG-38-1	BI-7-38	BI-124-5	BJ-49-4	BJ-179-5
BD-98-1	BE-53-1	BF-44-4	BG-39-1	BI-8-32	BI-125-4	BJ-50-4	BJ-180-3
BD-99-1	BE-54-1	BF-45-3	BG-40-7	BI-9-4	BI-126-3	BJ-51-6	BJ-181-1
BD-100-1	BE-55-1	BF-46-3	BG-41-4	BI-10-7	BI-127-3	BJ-54-10	BJ-182-1
BD-101-3	BE-56-5	BF-47-3	BG-42-1	BI-11-2	BI-128-2	BJ-55-6	BJ-183-4
BD-102-4	BE-57-4	BF-48-6	BG-43-6	BI-12-2	BI-129-4	BJ-58-2	BJ-184-4
BD-103-2	BE-58-1	BF-50-7	BG-44-2	BI-13-1	BI-130-2	BJ-59-2	BJ-185-4
BD-105-3	BE-59-1	BF-51-1	BG-45-2	BI-14-3	BI-131-3	BJ-60-1	BJ-186-1
BD-106-7	BE-60-2	BF-52-1	BG-46-3	BI-15-2	BI-132-2	BJ-61-1	BJ-187-1
BD-108-5	BE-61-4	BF-53-6	BG-47-11	BI-16-1	BI-133-1	BJ-64-1	BJ-188-5
BD-109-2	BE-63-2	BF-54-4	BG-48-9	BI-17-3	BI-134-2	BJ-65-2	BJ-189-2
BD-110-1	BE-64-1	BF-55-1	BG-49-1	BI-18-1	BI-135-1	BJ-66-1	BJ-191-1
BD-111-1	BE-65-1	BF-56-3	BG-50-1	BI-19-2	BI-136-2	BJ-67-14	BJ-192-5
BD-112-1	BE-66-2	BF-57-2	BG-51-1	BI-20-3	BI-137-2	BJ-68-2	BJ-193-6
BD-115-3	BE-67-3	BF-58-5	BG-52-2	BI-21-4	BI-138-3	BJ-69-1	BJ-197-6
BD-117-6	BE-69-2	BF-59-2	BG-53-5	BI-22-1	BI-139-1	BJ-70-1	BJ-198-3
BD-120-1	BE-71-4	BF-60-1	BG-54-1	BI-23-4	BI-140-1	BJ-72-1	BJ-199-7

UNIVERSAL JOINTS

and

Gasoline-Tank Filler Caps

HOW TO USE THIS TABLE

1. Locate in the first column the car and model for which the part is needed.
2. Follow this line across to the column pertaining to that part.
3. In this part column opposite your car model you will find the CHILTON NUMBER for the part you want.
4. Look up and down the part column for the same CHILTON NUMBER. Wherever you find this same number you have an interchangeable part. The car make opposite tells you where to get the part—probably from a local dealer or nearby jobber.

EXAMPLE: Suppose a Front Universal Joint Assembly is needed for a Gardner 95 (1928) car. Locate this car in the first column. Follow across to the column on Front Universal Joint Assembly. Here you see the CHILTON NUMBER for the part is

Q-49F. Checking through the CHILTON NUMBERS in this same column you will find the number Q-49F opposite Gardner 130 (1929), the Jordan JE (1928), the Jordan JJ (1928), the Peerless 91 (1928-29). The Front Universal Joint Assembly used in these cars is interchangeable with the one used in your Gardner 95 (1928) car.

5. At the end of this table, page 250, you will find a count showing the number of times any part number appears in this table.

EXAMPLE: QA-5F under Rear Flange or Hub Yoke opposite the Auburn 76 (1928) in this table will appear again in the count at the end of the table followed by the figure 6 under the heading Front Flange or Hub Yoke. This indicates part number QA-5F appears 6 times in this table.

Interchangeable Parts have the same CHILTON NUMBER in Any Column

Car Make and Model	Front Universal Joint Assembly (Metal)	Rear Universal Joint Assembly (Metal)	Front Flange or Hub Yoke	Rear Flange or Hub Yoke	Sleeve Yoke on Propeller Shaft	Journal (cross) or Pins	Bushings or Balls	Inside Casing or Joint Body	Outside Casing	Fabric Disks	GAS-OLINE TANK FILLER CAPS
Ajax..................(1925–26)	None	None	None	None	None	None	None	None	None	QH-1	JA-1
Apperson 6...........M. (1925)	Q-1-F	Q-1-R	QA-3-F	QA-1-R	QB-1	QC-1	QD-1	QF-1	None	None	JA-2
Apperson Str. 8........M. (1925)	Q-1-F	Q-1-R	QA-3-F	QA-1-R	QB-1	QC-1	QD-1	QF-1	None	None	JA-2
Apperson 6...........M. (1926)	Q-1-F	Q-1-R	QA-3-F	QA-1-R	QB-1	QC-1	QD-1	QF-1	None	None	JA-2
Apperson Str. A8......M. (1926)	Q-1-F	Q-1-R	QA-3-F	QA-1-R	QB-1	QC-1	QD-1	QF-1	None	None	JA-2
Auburn 4............D. (1925)	Q-2-F	Q-2-F	QA-4-F	QA-4-F	None	QC-2	QD-2	QF-2	None	None	JA-1
Auburn 6-43..........D. (1925)	Q-2-F	Q-2-F	QA-4-F	QA-4-F	None	QC-2	QD-2	QF-2	None	None	JA-1
Auburn 8-88..........D. (1925)	Q-2-F	Q-2-F	QA-4-F	QA-4-F	None	QC-2	QD-2	QF-2	None	None	JA-1
Auburn 4-44..........D. (1926)	Q-2-F	Q-2-F	QA-4-F	QA-4-F	None	QC-2	QD-2	QF-2	None	None	JA-1
Auburn 6-66..........D. (1926)	Q-2-F	Q-2-F	QA-4-F	QA-4-F	None	QC-2	QD-2	QF-2	None	None	JA-1
Auburn 8-88..........D. (1926)	Q-2-F	Q-2-F	QA-4-F	QA-4-F	None	QC-2	QD-2	QF-2	None	None	JA-1
Auburn 6-66A.........D. (1927)	Q-2-F	Q-2-F	QA-4-F	QA-4-F	None	QC-2	QD-2	QF-2	None	None	JA-1
Auburn 8-88..........D. (1927)	Q-2-F	Q-2-F	QA-4-F	QA-4-F	None	QC-2	QD-2	QF-2	None	None	JA-1
Auburn 8-77........D. (1927–28)	Q-2-F	Q-2-F	QA-4-F	QA-4-F	None	QC-2	QD-2	QF-2	None	None	JA-1
Auburn 76..........D. (1928–29)	Q-7-F	Q-7-F	QA-5-F	QA-5-F	None	QC-3	QD-3	QF-3	None	None	JA-1
Auburn 88..........D. (1928–29)	Q-2-F	Q-2-F	QA-4-F	QA-4-F	None	QC-2	QD-2	QF-2	None	None	JA-1
Auburn 115.........D. (1928–29)	Q-2-F	Q-2-F	QA-4-F	QA-4-F	None	QC-2	QD-2	QF-2	None	None	JA-1
Auburn 6-80..........D. (1929)	Q-7-F	Q-7-F	QA-5-F	QA-5-F	None	QC-3	QD-3	QF-3	None	None	JA-3
Auburn 8-90..........D. (1929)	Q-2-F	Q-2-F	QA-4-F	QA-4-F	None	QC-2	QD-2	QF-2	None	None	JA-3
Auburn 120...........D. (1929)	Q-2-F	Q-2-F	QA-4-F	QA-4-F	None	QC-2	QD-2	QF-2	None	None	JA-3
Auburn 6-85..........D. (1930)	Q-7-F	Q-7-F	QA-5-F	QA-5-F	None	QC-3	QD-3	QF-3	None	None	JA-1
Auburn 8-95..........D. (1930)	Q-2-F	Q-2-F	QA-4-F	QA-4-F	None	QC-2	QD-2	QF-2	None	None	JA-1
Auburn 125...........D. (1930)	Q-2-F	Q-2-F	QA-4-F	QA-4-F	None	QC-2	QD-2	QF-2	None	None	JA-1
Blackhawk L6.........D. (1929)	Q-4-F	Q-4-F	QA-7-F	QA-7-F	None	QC-5	QD-5	QF-5	None	None	JA-5
Blackhawk L8.........D. (1929)	Q-4-F	Q-4-F	QA-7-F	QA-7-F	None	QC-5	QD-5	QF-5	None	None	JA-5
Blackhawk L6.........D. (1930)	Q-4-F	Q-4-F	QA-7-F	QA-7-F	None	QC-5	QD-5	QF-5	None	None	JA-5
Blackhawk L8.........D. (1930)	Q-4-F	Q-4-F	QA-7-F	QA-7-F	None	QC-5	QD-5	QF-5	None	None	JA-5
Buick Master...........(1925)	Q-5-F	None	QA-8-F	None	QB-2	QC-6	QD-6	QF-6	None	None	JA-1
Buick Std..............(1925)	Q-6-F	None	QA-9-F	None	QB-3	QC-7	QD-7	QF-7	None	None	JA-1
Buick Master...........(1926)	Q-5-F	None	QA-8-F	None	QB-2	QC-6	QD-6	QF-6	None	None	JA-1
Buick Std..............(1926)	Q-6-F	None	QA-9-F	None	QB-3	QC-7	QD-7	QF-7	None	None	JA-1
Buick 115.............(1927)	Q-6-F	None	QA-9-F	None	QB-3	QC-7	QD-7	QF-7	None	None	JA-1
Buick 120, 128........(1927)	Q-5-F	None	QA-8-F	None	QB-2	QC-6	QD-6	QF-6	None	None	JA-1
Buick 115.............(1928)	Q-6-F	None	QA-9-F	None	QB-3	QC-7	QD-7	QF-7	None	None	JA-1
Buick 120, 128........(1928)	Q-5-F	None	QA-8-F	None	QB-2	QC-6	QD-6	QF-6	None	None	JA-1
Buick 116.............(1929)	Q-6-F	None	QA-9-F	None	QB-3	QC-7	QD-7	QF-8	None	None	JA-5
Buick 121, 129........(1929)	Q-5-F	None	QA-8-F	None	QB-2	QC-6	QD-6	QF-9	None	None	JA-5
Buick 40..............(1930)	Q-6-F	None	QA-9-F	None	QB-3	QC-7	QD-7	QF-8	None	None	JA-1
Buick 50..............(1930)	Q-5-F	None	QA-8-F	None	QB-2	QC-6	QD-6	QF-9	None	None	JA-1
Buick 60..............(1930)	Q-5-F	None	QA-8-F	None	QB-2	QC-6	QD-6	QF-9	None	None	JA-1
Cadillac V63..........S. (1925)	Q-9-F	Q-5-R	QA-12-F	QA-12-F	QB-4	QC-8	QD-8	QF-10	QG-1	None	JA-6
Cadillac 314..........S. (1926)	Q-10-F	Q-5-R	QA-12-F	QA-12-F	QB-7	QC-8	QD-8	QF-10	QG-1	None	JA-6
Cadillac 314..........S. (1927)	Q-10-F	Q-5-R	QA-12-F	QA-12-F	QB-7	QC-8	QD-8	QF-10	QG-1	None	JA-6
Cadillac 341A..........(1928)	Q-5-F	None	QA-8-F	None	QB-2	QC-6	QD-6	QF-11	None	None	JA-3
Cadillac 341B..........(1929)	Q-8-F	None	QA-14-F	None	QB-11	QC-6	QD-6	QF-11	None	None	JA-3
Cadillac 353...........(1930)	Q-8F	None	QA-14-F	None	QB-11	QC-12	QD-6	QF-11	None	None	JA-3
Case JIC..............(1925)	None	None	None	None	None	None	None	None	None	QH-2	JA-7
Case X...............(1925)	None	None	None	None	None	None	None	None	None	QH-2	JA-7
Case Y...............(1925)	None	None	None	None	None	None	None	None	None	QH-3	JA-7
Case JIC..............(1926)	None	None	None	None	None	None	None	None	None	QH-2	JA-7
Case Y...............(1926)	None	None	None	None	None	None	None	None	None	QH-3	JA-7
Chandler 33............(1925)	None	None	None	None	None	None	None	None	None	QH-5	JA-1
Chandler 35............(1926)	None	None	None	None	None	None	None	None	None	QH-5	JA-1
Chandler Big 6.........(1927)	None	None	None	None	None	None	None	None	None	QH-5	JA-1
Chandler Royal 8.......(1927)	None	None	None	None	None	None	None	None	None	QH-4	JA-1
Chandler Spec. 6........(1927)	None	None	None	None	None	None	None	None	None	QH-14	JA-1
Chandler Std. 6......S. (1927)	Q-12-F	Q-74-R	QA-23-F	QA-23-F	QB-73	QC-8	QD-8	QF-10	QG-1	None	JA-1
Chandler Big 6.........(1928)	None	None	None	None	None	None	None	None	None	QH-5	JA-1
Chandler Royal 8.......(1928)	None	None	None	None	None	None	None	None	None	QH-4	JA-1
Chandler Spec. 6.....S. (1928)	Q-12-F	Q-74-R	QA-23-F	QA-23-F	QB-73	QC-8	QD-8	QF-10	QG-1	None	JA-1
Chandler Spec. In. 6..S. (1928)	Q-12-F	Q-74-R	QA-23-F	QA-23-F	QB-73	QC-8	QD-8	QF-10	QG-1	None	JA-1
Chevrolet K...........(1925)	Q-13-F	None	QA-19-F	None	QB-6	QC-9	QD-9	QF-12	QG-2	None	JA-8
Chevrolet V...........(1926)	Q-13-F	None	QA-19-F	None	QB-6	QC-9	QD-9	QF-12	QG-2	None	JA-8
Chevrolet AA..........(1927)	Q-13-F	None	QA-19-F	None	QB-6	QC-9	QD-9	QF-12	QG-2	None	JA-1

UNIVERSAL JOINTS—Continued

Interchangeable Parts have the same CHILTON NUMBER in Any Column

Car Make and Model	Front Universal Joint Assembly (Metal)	Rear Universal Joint Assembly (Metal)	Front Flange or Hub Yoke	Rear Flange or Hub Yoke	Sleeve Yoke on Propeller Shaft	Journal (cross) or Pins	Bushings or Balls	Inside Casing or Joint Body	Outside Casing	Fabric Disks	GAS-OLINE TANK FILLER CAPS
Chevrolet AB (1928)	Q-13-F	None	QA-19-F	None	QB-6	QC-9	QD-9	QF-12	QG-2	None	JA-1
Chevrolet AC (1929)	Q-13-F	None	QA-19-F	None	QB-6	QC-9	QD-9	QF-13	QG-3	None	JA-1
Chevrolet (1930)	Q-3-F	None	QA-6-F	None	QB-20	QC-4	QD-4	QF-4	None	None	JA-1
Chrysler 6B D. (1925)	Q-2-F	Q-2-F	QA-4-F	QA-4-F	None	QC-2	QD-2	QF-2	None	None	JA-9
Chrysler 70 D. (1926)	Q-2-F	Q-2-F	QA-4-F	QA-4-F	None	QC-2	QD-2	QF-2	None	None	JA-9
Chrysler 58 (1926)	None	None	None	None	None	None	None	None	None	QH-7	JA-9
Chrysler 70 D. (1926)	Q-2-F	Q-2-F	QA-4-F	QA-4-F	None	QC-2	QD-2	QF-2	None	None	JA-9
Chrysler 80 D. (1926)	Q-17-F	Q-17-F	QA-22-F	QA-22-F	None	QC-10	QD-10	QF-14	None	None	JA-9
Chrysler 50 (1927)	None	None	None	None	None	None	None	None	None	QH-8	JA-1
Chrysler 60 S. (1927)	Q-12-F	Q-74-R	QA-23-F	QA-23-F	QB-73	QC-8	QD-8	QF-10	QG-1	None	JA-9
Chrysler 70 D. (1927)	Q-2-F	Q-2-F	QA-4-F	QA-4-F	None	QC-2	QD-2	QF-2	None	None	JA-9
Chrysler 80 D. (1927)	Q-17-F	Q-17-F	QA-22-F	QA-22-F	None	QC-10	QD-10	QF-14	None	None	JA-9
Chrysler 52 (1928)	None	None	None	None	None	None	None	None	None	QH-8	JA-1
Chrysler 62 D. (1928)	Q-19-F	Q-19-F	QA-24-F	QA-24-F	None	QC-60	QD-60	QF-61	None	None	JA-1
Chrysler 72 D. (1928)	Q-2-F	Q-2-F	QA-4-F	QA-4-F	None	QC-2	QD-2	QF-2	None	None	JA-1
Chrysler Imp. 80 D. (1928)	Q-17-F	Q-17-F	QA-22-F	QA-22-F	None	QC-10	QD-10	QF-14	None	None	JA-5
Chrysler 65 D. (1929)	Q-19-F	Q-19-F	QA-24-F	QA-24-F	None	QC-60	QD-60	QF-61	None	None	JA-1
Chrysler 75 D. (1929)	Q-2-F	Q-2-F	QA-4-F	QA-4-F	None	QC-2	QD-2	QF-2	None	None	JA-5
Chrysler Imp. 80 D. (1929)	Q-17-F	Q-17-F	QA-22-F	QA-22-F	None	QC-10	QD-10	QF-14	None	None	JA-5
Chrysler 6 D. (1930)	Q-83-F	Q-83-F	QA-1-F	QA-1-F	None	QC-33	QD-33	QF-17	None	None	JA-1
Chrysler 66 S. (1930)	Q-12-F	Q-74-R	QA-23-F	QA-23-F	QB-73	QC-8	QD-8	QF-10	QG-1	None	JA-1
Chrysler 70 D. (1930)	Q-19-F	Q-19-F	QA-24-F	QA-24-F	None	QC-60	QD-60	QF-61	None	None	JA-1
Chrysler 77 D. (1930)	Q-19-F	Q-19-F	QA-24-F	QA-24-F	None	QC-60	QD-60	QF-61	None	None	JA-1
Cleveland 31 S. (1925)	Q-12-F	Q-74-R	QA-23-F	QA-23-F	QB-73	QC-8	QD-8	QF-10	QG-1	None	JA-1
Cleveland 43 (1925)	None	None	None	None	None	None	None	None	None	QH-14	JA-1
Cleveland 31 S. (1926)	Q-12-F	Q-74-R	QA-23-F	QA-23-F	QB-73	QC-8	QD-8	QF-10	QG-1	None	JA-1
Cleveland 43 (1926)	None	None	None	None	None	None	None	None	None	QH-14	JA-1
Davis 90 P. (1925)	Q-22-F	Q-9-R	QA-29-F	QA-7-R	QB-10	QC-12	QD-12	None	None	None	JA-4
Davis 91 P. (1925)	Q-22-F	Q-9-R	QA-29-F	QA-7-R	QB-10	QC-12	QD-12	None	None	None	JA-4
Davis 92 P. (1926)	Q-22-F	Q-9-R	QA-29-F	QA-7-R	QB-10	QC-12	QD-12	None	None	None	JA-4
Davis 93 P. (1926)	Q-22-F	Q-9-R	QA-29-F	QA-7-R	QB-10	QC-12	QD-12	None	None	None	JA-4
Davis 92 P. (1927)	Q-22-F	Q-9-R	QA-29-F	QA-7-R	QA-10	QC-12	QD-12	None	None	None	JA-4
Davis 94 U. (1927)	Q-24-F	Q-11-R	QA-31-F	QA-31-F	QB-13	QC-13	QD-13	QF-16	None	None	JA-4
Davis 98 P. (1927)	Q-25-F	Q-12-R	QA-32-F	QA-10-R	QB-14	QC-14	QD-14	None	None	None	JA-4
Davis 99 P. (1928)	Q-25-F	Q-12-R	QA-32-F	QA-10-R	QB-14	QC-14	QD-14	None	None	None	JA-4
De Soto 6 D. (1929)	Q-83-F	Q-83-F	QA-1-F	QA-1-F	None	QC-33	QD-33	QF-17	None	None	JA-1
De Soto Finer 6 D. (1930)	Q-83-F	Q-83-F	QA-1-F	QA-1-F	None	QC-33	QD-33	QF-17	None	None	JA-1
De Soto 8 D. (1930)	Q-83-F	Q-83-F	QA-1-F	QA-1-F	None	QC-33	QD-33	QF-17	None	None	JA-1
Diana Str. 8 M. (1926)	Q-1-F	Q-1-R	QA-3-F	QA-1-R	QB-1	QC-1	QD-1	QF-1	None	None	JA-13
Diana Str. 8 M. (1927)	Q-1-F	Q-1-R	QA-3-F	QA-1-R	QB-1	QC-1	QD-1	QF-1	None	None	JA-13
Diana Str. 8 M. (1928)	Q-1-F	Q-1-R	QA-3-F	QA-1-R	QB-1	QC-1	QD-1	QF-1	None	None	JA-13
Dodge Brothers 4 (1925)	Q-23-F	None	QA-33-F	None	QB-15	QC-15	QD-15	QF-18	QG-7	None	JA-14
Dodge Brothers 4 (1926)	Q-23-F	None	QA-33-F	None	QB-15	QC-15	QD-15	QF-18	QG-7	None	JA-14
Dodge Brothers 4 M. (1927)	Q-11-F	Q-13-R	QA-15-F	QA-12-R	QB-16	QC-16	QD-16	QF-19	None	None	JA-1
Dodge Brothers Sen. (1928)	Q-23-F	None	QA-33-F	None	QB-15	QC-15	QD-15	QF-20	QG-8	None	JA-1
Dodge Std. 6 M. (1928)	Q-11-F	Q-13-R	QA-15-F	QA-12-R	QB-16	QC-16	QD-16	QF-19	None	None	JA-1
Dodge Brothers Vic.6 M. (1928)	Q-14-F	Q-13-R	QA-16-F	QA-12-R	QB-17	QC-16	QD-16	QF-19	None	None	JA-1
Dodge Brothers Sen M. (1929)	Q-84-F	Q-15-R	QA-2-F	QA-13-R	QB-74	QC-1	QD-1	QF-1	None	None	JA-1
Dodge Brothers DA-6 M. (1929)	Q-85-F	Q-13-R	QA-10-F	QA-12-R	QB-75	QC-16	QD-16	QF-19	None	None	JA-1
Dodge DD6 D. (1930)	Q-83-F	Q-83-F	QA-1-F	QA-1-F	None	QC-33	QD-33	QF-17	None	None	JA-1
Dodge DC8 D. (1930)	Q-83-F	Q-83-F	QA-1-F	QA-1-F	None	QC-33	QD-33	QF-17	None	None	JA-1
Durant A22 S. (1925)	Q-32-F	Q-17-R	QA-40-F	QA-40-F	QB-23	QC-21	QD-21	QF-25	QG-12	None	JA-1
Durant 55 S. (1928)	Q-29-F	Q-18-R	QA-41-F	QA-41-F	QB-24	QC-21	QD-21	QF-25	QG-12	None	JA-1
Durant 65 S. (1928)	Q-30-F	Q-18-R	QA-41-F	QA-41-F	QB-12	QC-21	QD-21	QF-25	QG-12	None	JA-1
Durant M2 S. (1928–29)	Q-29-F	Q-18-R	QA-41-F	QA-41-F	QB-24	QC-21	QD-21	QF-25	QG-12	None	JA-8
Durant 75 S. (1928–29)	Q-31-F	Q-19-R	QA-42-F	QA-42-F	QB-25	QC-22	QD-22	QF-26	QG-13	None	JA-1
Durant 40 S. (1929)	Q-29-F	Q-18-R	QA-41-F	QA-41-F	QB-24	QC-21	QD-21	QF-25	QG-12	None	JA-8
Durant 60 S. (1929)	Q-29-F	Q-18-R	QA-41-F	QA-41-F	QB-24	QC-21	QD-21	QF-25	QG-12	None	JA-1
Durant 66 S. (1929)	Q-30-F	Q-20-R	QA-43-F	QA-43-F	QB-12	QC-21	QD-21	QF-25	QG-13	None	JA-1
Durant 70 S. (1929)	Q-31-F	Q-19-R	QA-42-F	QA-42-F	QB-25	QC-22	QD-22	QF-26	QG-13	None	JA-1
Durant 63 S. (1929)	Q-29-F	Q-18-R	QA-41-F	QA-41-F	QB-24	QC-21	QD-21	QF-25	QG-12	None	JA-1
Durant 614 S. (1930)	Q-29-F	Q-18-R	QA-41-F	QA-41-F	QB-24	QC-21	QD-21	QF-25	QG-12	None	JA-1
Durant 617 S. (1930)	Q-31-F	Q-19-R	QA-42-F	QA-42-F	QB-25	QC-22	QD-22	QF-26	QG-13	None	JA-1
Elcar 4-40 M. (1925)	Q-33-F	Q-21-R	QA-44-F	QA-16-R	QB-18	QC-1	QD-1	QF-1	None	None	JA-2
Elcar 6-50 M. (1925)	Q-33-F	Q-21-R	QA-44-F	QA-16-R	QB-18	QC-1	QD-1	QF-1	None	None	JA-2
Elcar 6-60 M. (1925)	Q-33-F	Q-21-R	QA-44-F	QA-16-R	QB-18	QC-1	QD-1	QF-1	None	None	JA-2
Elcar 8-80 S. (1925)	Q-34-F	Q-22-R	QA-45-F	QA-17-R	QB-26	QC-24	QD-24	QF-28	QG-15	None	JA-2
Elcar 6-65 M. (1926)	Q-36-F	Q-6-R	QA-11-F	QA-14-R	QB-28	QC-16	QD-16	QF-19	None	None	JA-2
Elcar 8-81 S. (1926)	Q-34-F	Q-22-R	QA-45-F	QA-17-R	QB-26	QC-24	QD-24	QF-28	QG-15	None	JA-2
Elcar 4-55 M. (1926)	Q-33-F	Q-21-R	QA-44-F	QA-16-R	QB-18	QC-1	QD-1	QF-1	None	None	JA-2
Elcar 6-70 S. (1927)	Q-12-F	Q-74-R	QA-23-F	QA-23-F	QB-27	QC-8	QD-8	QF-10	QG-1	None	JA-1
Elcar 8-82 S. (1927)	Q-35-F	Q-23-R	QA-46-F	QA-18-R	QB-29	QC-25	QD-25	None	None	None	JA-1
Elcar 8-90 S. (1927)	Q-34-F	Q-22-R	QA-45-F	QA-17-R	QB-26	QC-24	QD-24	QF-28	QG-15	None	JA-1
Elcar 8-91 S. (1928)	Q-34-F	Q-22-R	QA-45-F	QA-17-R	QB-26	QC-24	QD-24	QF-28	QG-15	None	JA-1
Elcar 120 S. (1928)	Q-34-F	Q-22-R	QA-45-F	QA-17-R	QB-26	QC-24	QD-24	QF-28	QG-15	None	JA-1
Elcar 6-70 S. (1928–29)	Q-12-F	Q-74-R	QA-23-F	QA-23-F	QB-27	QC-8	QD-8	QF-10	QG-1	None	JA-1
Elcar 8-78 S. (1928–29)	Q-12-F	Q-74-R	QA-23-F	QA-23-F	QB-27	QC-8	QD-8	QF-10	QG-1	None	JA-1
Elcar 8-82 S. (1928–29)	Q-35-F	Q-23-R	QA-46-F	QA-18-R	QB-29	QC-25	QD-25	None	None	None	JA-1
Elcar 75 S. (1929)	Q-12-F	Q-74-R	QA-23-F	QA-23-R	QB-27	QC-8	QD-8	QF-10	QG-1	None	JA-1
Elcar 95, 96 S. (1929)	Q-34-F	Q-22-R	QA-45-F	QA-17-R	QB-26	QC-24	QD-24	QF-28	QG-15	None	JA-1
Elcar 120 S. (1929)	Q-34-F	Q-22-R	QA-45-F	QA-17-R	QB-26	QC-24	QD-24	QF-28	QG-15	None	JA-1
Elcar 130 S. (1930)	Q-34-F	Q-22-R	QA-45-F	QA-17-R	QB-26	QC-24	QD-24	QF-28	QG-15	None	JA-1
Erskine 50 M. (1927)	Q-41-F	Q-30-R	QA-51-F	QA-20-R	QB-35	QC-26	QD-26	QF-30	None	None	JA-1
Erskine 6-51 S. (1928)	Q-42-F	Q-31-R	QA-52-F	QA-52-F	QB-36	QC-21	QD-21	QF-25	QG-12	None	JA-1
Erskine 6-52 S. (1929)	Q-42-F	Q-31-R	QA-52-F	QA-52-F	QB-36	QC-21	QD-21	QF-25	QG-12	None	JA-1
Erskine 53 S. (1930)	Q-42-F	Q-31-R	QA-52-F	QA-52-F	QB-36	QC-21	QD-21	QF-25	QG-12	None	JA-1
Essex 6 S. (1925)	Q-42-F	Q-18-R	QA-52-F	QA-52-F	QB-36	QC-21	QD-21	QF-25	QG-12	None	JA-11
Essex 6 S. (1926)	Q-42-F	Q-18-R	QA-52-F	QA-52-F	QB-36	QC-21	QD-21	QF-25	QG-12	None	JA-11
Essex Super 6 S. (1927)	Q-42-F	Q-18-R	QA-52-F	QA-52-F	QB-36	QC-21	QD-21	QF-25	QG-12	None	JA-11
Essex Super 6 S. (1928)	Q-42-F	Q-18-R	QA-52-F	QA-52-F	QB-36	QC-21	QD-21	QF-25	QG-12	None	JA-1
Essex Challenger S. (1929)	Q-42-F	Q-18-R	QA-52-F	QA-52-R	QB-36	QC-21	QD-21	QF-25	QG-12	None	JA-1
Essex S. (1930)	Q-42-F	Q-18-R	QA-52-F	QA-52-F	QB-36	QC-21	QD-21	QF-25	QG-12	None	JA-1
Falcon-Knight 10 M. (1927–28)	Q-86-F	Q-75-R	QA-18-F	QA-21-R	QB-5	QC-16	QD-16	QF-19	None	None	JA-16
Falcon-Knight 12 M. (1928–29)	Q-86-F	Q-75-R	QA-18-F	QA-21-R	QB-5	QC-16	QD-16	QF-19	None	None	JA-16
Flint B40 S. (1925–26)	Q-32-F	Q-17-R	QA-40-F	QA-40-F	QB-23	QC-21	QD-21	QF-25	QG-12	None	JA-1
Flint E55 S. (1925–26)	Q-34-F	Q-22-R	QA-45-F	QA-45-F	QB-26	QC-24	QD-24	QF-28	QG-15	None	JA-1
Flint B60 S. (1926)	Q-32-F	Q-17-R	QA-40-F	QA-40-F	QB-23	QC-21	QD-21	QF-25	QG-12	None	JA-1
Flint E80 S. (1926)	Q-34-F	Q-22-R	QA-45-F	QA-45-F	QB-26	QC-24	QD-24	QF-28	QG-15	None	JA-9
Flint, Jr. U. (1926)	Q-43-F	Q-35-R	QA-54-F	QA-54-F	QB-38	QC-28	QD-28	QF-31	None	None	JA-9
Flint 60 S. (1927)	Q-32-F	Q-17-R	QA-40-F	QA-40-F	QB-23	QC-21	QD-21	QF-25	QG-12	None	JA-1
Flint 80 S. (1927)	Q-34-F	Q-22-R	QA-45-F	QA-45-F	QB-26	QC-24	QD-24	QF-28	QG-15	None	JA-9
Flint, Jr. U. (1927)	Q-43-F	Q-35-R	QA-54-F	QA-54-F	QB-38	QC-28	QD-28	QF-31	None	None	JA-9
Ford T (1925)	Q-44-F	None	QA-55-F	None	QB-39	None	None	QF-32	QG-18	None	JA-17
Ford T (1926)	Q-44-F	None	QA-55-F	None	QB-39	None	None	QF-32	QG-18	None	JA-17

UNIVERSAL JOINTS—Continued

Interchangeable Parts have the same CHILTON NUMBER in Any Column

Car Make and Model	Front Universal Joint Assembly (Metal)	Rear Universal Joint Assembly (Metal)	Front Flange or Hub Yoke	Rear Flange or Hub Yoke	Sleeve Yoke on Propeller Shaft	Journal (cross) or Pins	Bushings or Balls	Inside Casing or Joint Body	Outside Casing	Fabric Disks	GAS-OLINE TANK FILLER CAPS
Ford T....................(1927)	Q-44-F	None	QA-55-F	None	QB-39	None	None	QF-32	QG-18	None	JA-17
Ford A....................(1928)	Q-45-F	None	QA-56-F	None	QB-40	None	None	QF-33	QG-19	None	JA-18
Ford A....................(1929)	Q-45-F	None	QA-56-F	None	QB-40	None	None	QF-33	QG-19	None	JA-18
Ford A....................(1930)	Q-45-F	None	QA-56-F	None	QB-40	None	None	QF-33	QG-19	None	JA-15
Franklin 11-A...........S. (1925)	Q-34-F	Q-22-R	QA-45-F	QA-45-F	QB-26	QC-24	QD-24	QF-28	QG-15	None	JA-16
Franklin 11.............S. (1926)	Q-34-F	Q-22-R	QA-45-F	QA-45-F	QB-26	QC-24	QD-24	QF-28	QG-15	None	JA-16
Franklin 11-B...........S. (1927)	Q-34-F	Q-22-R	QA-45-F	QA-45-F	QB-26	QC-24	QD-24	QF-28	QG-15	None	JA-1
Franklin Ser 12..........S. (1928)	Q-34-F	Q-22-R	QA-45-F	QA-45-F	QB-26	QC-24	QD-24	QF-28	QG-15	None	JA-1
Franklin 130............S. (1929)	Q-34-F	Q-22-R	QA-45-F	QA-45-F	QB-26	QC-24	QD-24	QF-28	QG-15	None	JA-1
Franklin 135, 137........S. (1929)	Q-34-F	Q-22-R	QA-45-F	QA-45-F	QB-26	QC-24	QD-24	QF-28	QG-15	None	JA-1
Franklin 145, 147........S. (1930)	Q-49-F	Q-40-R	QA-60-F	QA-60-F	QB-43	QC-52	QD-52	QF-54	QG-32	None	JA-1
Gardner 6-A..............(1925)	Q-40-F	Q-36-R	QA-57-F	QA-22-R	QB-41	QC-16	QD-16	None	None	None	JA-16
Gardner 8-A..............(1925)	Q-40-F	Q-36-R	QA-57-F	QA-22-R	QB-41	QC-31	QD-31	None	None	None	JA-16
Gardner Series 5..........(1925)	Q-46-F	Q-38-R	QA-53-F	QA-23-R	QB-37	QC-32	QD-32	None	None	None	JA-16
Gardner 6-B...........(1926–27)	Q-40-F	Q-36-R	QA-57-F	QA-22-R	QB-41	QC-31	QD-31	None	None	None	JA-16
Gardner 8-B...........(1926–27)	Q-40-F	Q-36-R	QA-57-F	QA-22-R	QB-41	QC-31	QD-31	None	None	None	JA-16
Gardner 80...............(1927)	Q-40-F	Q-36-R	QA-57-F	QA-22-R	QB-41	QC-31	QD-31	None	None	None	JA-16
Gardner 90...............(1927)	Q-87-F	Q-75-R	QA-58-F	QA-21-R	QB-76	QC-27	QD-27	None	None	None	JA-16
Gardner 75.............S. (1928)	Q-40-F	Q-36-R	QA-57-F	QA-22-R	QB-41	QC-31	QD-31	None	None	None	JA-16
Gardner 85.............S. (1928)	Q-40-F	Q-36-R	QA-57-F	QA-22-R	QB-41	QC-31	QD-31	None	None	None	JA-16
Gardner 95.............S. (1928)	Q-49-F	Q-40-R	QA-60-F	QA-60-F	QB-43	QC-52	QD-52	QF-54	QG-32	None	JA-16
Gardner 120............S. (1929)	Q-12-F	Q-74-R	QA-23-F	QA-23-F	QB-27	QC-8	QD-8	QF-10	QG-1	None	JA-16
Gardner 125............S. (1929)	Q-12-F	Q-74-R	QA-23-F	QA-23-F	QB-27	QC-8	QD-8	QF-10	QG-1	None	JA-16
Gardner 130............S. (1929)	Q-49-F	Q-40-R	QA-60-F	QA-60-F	QB-43	QC-52	QD-52	QF-54	QG-32	None	JA-16
Graham Paige 610....D. (1928–29)	Q-83-F	Q-83-F	QA-1-F	QA-1-F	None	QC-33	QD-33	QF-17	None	None	JA-1
Graham Paige 614....D. (1928–29)	Q-2-F	Q-2-F	QA-4-F	QA-4-F	None	QC-2	QD-2	QF-2	None	None	JA-1
Graham Paige 619....D. (1928–29)	Q-17-F	Q-17-F	QA-22-F	QA-22-F	None	QC-10	QD-10	QF-14	None	None	JA-1
Graham Paige 629....D. (1928–29)	Q-17-F	Q-17-F	QA-22-F	QA-22-F	None	QC-10	QD-10	QF-14	None	None	JA-1
Graham Paige 835....D. (1928–29)	Q-17-F	Q-17-F	QA-22-F	QA-22-F	None	QC-10	QD-10	QF-14	None	None	JA-1
Graham Paige 612.......D. (1929)	Q-83-F	Q-83-F	QA-1-F	QA-1-F	None	QC-33	QD-33	QF-17	None	None	JA-1
Graham Paige 615.......D. (1929)	Q-2-F	Q-2-F	QA-4-F	QA-4-F	None	QC-2	QD-2	QF-2	None	None	JA-1
Graham Paige 621.......D. (1929)	Q-17-F	Q-17-F	QA-22-F	QA-22-F	None	QC-10	QD-10	QF-14	None	None	JA-1
Graham Paige 827.......D. (1929)	Q-17-F	Q-17-F	QA-22-F	QA-22-F	None	QC-10	QD-10	QF-14	None	None	JA-1
Graham Paige 837.......D. (1929)	Q-17-F	Q-17-F	QA-22-F	QA-22-F	None	QC-10	QD-10	QF-14	None	None	JA-1
Graham Std. 6..........D. (1930)	Q-83-F	Q-83-F	QA-1-F	QA-1-F	None	QC-33	QD-33	QF-17	None	None	JA-1
Graham Spec. 6.........D. (1930)	Q-2F	Q-2-F	QA-4-F	QA-4-F	None	QC-2	QD-2	QF-2	None	None	JA-1
Graham Std. & Spec. 8..D. (1930)	Q-28-F	Q-28-F	QA-39-F	QA-39-F	None	QC-20	QD-20	QF-24	None	None	JA-1
Graham Cust. 8.........D. (1930)	Q-17-F	Q-17-F	QA-22-F	QA-22-F	None	QC-10	QD-10	QF-14	None	None	JA-1
Hudson Super 6..........S. (1925)	Q-34-F	Q-22-R	QA-45-F	QA-45-F	QB-26	QC-24	QD-24	QF-28	QG-15	None	JA-11
Hudson Super 6..........S. (1926)	Q-34-F	Q-22-R	QA-45-F	QA-45-F	QB-26	QC-24	QD-24	QF-28	QG-15	None	JA-11
Hudson Super 6..........S. (1927)	Q-34-F	Q-22-R	QA-45-F	QA-45-F	QB-26	QC-24	QD-24	QF-28	QG-15	None	JA-11
Hudson Super 6..........S. (1928)	Q-34-F	Q-22-R	QA-45-F	QA-45-F	QB-26	QC-24	QD-24	QF-28	QG-15	None	JA-1
Hudson Greater 6........S. (1929)	Q-34-F	Q-22-R	QA-45-F	QA-45-F	QB-26	QC-24	QD-24	QF-28	QG-15	None	JA-1
Hudson 8................S. (1930)	Q-42-F	Q-18-R	QA-52-F	QA-52-F	QB-36	QC-21	QD-21	QF-25	QG-12	None	JA-1
Hupmobile Ser. R.......D. (1925)	Q-2-F	Q-2-F	QA-4-F	QA-4-F	None	QC-2	QD-2	QF-2	QG-34	None	JA-14
Hupmobile E1...........D. (1925)	Q-2-F	Q-2-F	QA-4-F	QA-4-F	None	QC-2	QD-2	QF-2	None	None	JA-14
Hupmobile A1...........M. (1926)	Q-86-F	Q-42-R	QA-18-F	QA-11-R	QB-5	QC-16	QD-16	QF-19	None	None	JA-14
Hupmobile E2...........D. (1926)	Q-2-F	Q-2-F	QA-4-F	QA-4-F	None	QC-2	QD-2	QF-2	None	None	JA-14
Hupmobile A2...........M. (1927)	Q-86-F	Q-42-R	QA-18-F	QA-11-R	QB-5	QC-16	QD-16	QF-19	None	None	JA-1
Hupmoble E3............D. (1927)	Q-2-F	Q-2-F	QA-4-F	QA-4-F	None	QC-2	QD-2	QF-2	None	None	JA-1
Hupmobile Cent. 6......M. (1928)	Q-50-F	Q-43-R	QA-59-F	QA-25-R	QB-33	QC-16	QD-16	QF-34	None	None	JA-1
Hupmobile Cent. 8......D. (1928)	Q-2-F	Q-2-F	QA-4-F	QA-4-F	None	QC-2	QD-2	QF-2	None	None	JA-1
Hupmobile 125-8........D. (1928)	Q-2-F	Q-2-F	QA-4-F	QA-4-F	None	QC-2	QD-2	QF-2	None	None	JA-1
Hupmobile M8......D. (1928–29)	Q-2-F	Q-2-F	QA-4-F	QA-4-F	None	QC-2	QD-2	QF-2	None	None	JA-1
Hupmobile Cent. 6......M. (1929)	Q-50-F	Q-43-R	QA-59-F	QA-25-R	QB-33	QC-16	QD-16	QF-34	None	None	JA-1
Hupmobile S............M. (1930)	Q-50-F	Q-43-R	QA-59-F	QA-25-R	QB-33	QC-16	QD-16	QF-34	None	None	JA-1
Hupmobile C............D. (1930)	Q-16-F	Q-16-F	QA-37-F	QA-37-F	None	QC-19	QD-19	QF-23	None	None	JA-1
Hupmobile H & U........D. (1930)	Q-16-F	Q-16-F	QA-37-F	QA-37-F	None	QC-19	QD-19	QF-23	None	None	JA-1
Jewett 6-50............M. (1925)	Q-36-F	Q-24-R	QA-11-F	QA-19-R	QB-28	QC-16	QD-16	QF-19	None	None	JA-14
Jewett New Day 6-40...M. (1926)	Q-36-F	Q-77-R	QA-11-F	QA-15-R	QB-28	QC-16	QD-16	QF-19	None	None	JA-14
Jordan K-L.............T. (1925)	Q-52-F	Q-39-R	QA-65-F	QA-26-R	QB-44	QC-34	QD-34	None	None	None	JA-1
Jordan A...............T. (1925)	Q-52-F	Q-39-R	QA-65-F	QA-26-R	QB-44	QC-34	QD-34	None	None	None	JA-16
Jordan A...............T. (1926)	Q-52-F	Q-39-R	QA-65-F	QA-26-R	QB-44	QC-34	QD-34	None	None	None	JA-16
Jordan J...............A. (1926)	Q-88-F	Q-81-R	QA-47-F	QA-47-F	QB-77	QC-35	QD-35	QF-27	None	None	JA-16
Jordan J...............A. (1927)	Q-88-F	Q-81-R	QA-47-F	QA-47-F	QB-77	QC-35	QD-35	QF-27	None	None	JA-16
Jordan AA...........A. (1927–28)	Q-88-F	Q-81-R	QA-47-F	QA-47-F	QB-77	QC-35	QD-35	QF-27	None	None	JA-16
Jordan R.............S. (1927–28)	Q-42-F	Q-18-R	QA-52-F	QA-52-F	QB-36	QC-21	QD-21	QF-25	QG-12	None	JA-16
Jordan JJ..............S. (1928)	Q-49-F	Q-40-R	QA-60-F	QA-60-F	QB-43	QC-52	QD-52	QF-54	QG-32	None	JA-16
Jordan JE............S. (1928–29)	Q-49-F	Q-40-R	QA-60-F	QA-60-F	QB-43	QC-52	QD-52	QF-54	QG-32	None	JA-16
Jordan E...............S. (1929)	Q-54-F	Q-78-R	QA-67-F	QA-24-R	QB-46	QC-36	QD-36	None	None	None	JA-16
Jordan G...............S. (1929)	Q-54-F	Q-78-R	QA-67-F	QA-24-R	QB-46	QC-36	QD-36	None	None	None	JA-16
Kissel 6-55............S. (1925)	Q-32-F	Q-17-R	QA-40-F	QA-40-F	QB-23	QC-21	QD-21	QF-25	QG-12	None	JA-1
Kissel 8-75............S. (1925)	Q-32-F	Q-17-R	QA-40-F	QA-40-F	QB-23	QC-21	QD-21	QF-25	QG-12	None	JA-1
Kissel 6-55............S. (1926)	Q-32-F	Q-17-R	QA-40-F	QA-40-F	QB-23	QC-21	QD-21	QF-25	QG-12	None	JA-1
Kissel 8-75............S. (1926)	Q-32-F	Q-17-R	QA-40-F	QA-40-F	QB-23	QC-21	QD-21	QF-25	QG-12	None	JA-1
Kissel 6-55............S. (1927)	Q-32-F	Q-17-R	QA-40-F	QA-40-F	QB-23	QC-21	QD-21	QF-25	QG-12	None	JA-1
Kissel 8-65............M. (1927)	Q-55-F	Q-79-R	QA-64-F	QA-8-R	QB-45	QC-1	QD-1	QF-36	None	None	JA-1
Kissel 8-75............M. (1927)	Q-1-F	Q-1-R	QA-3-F	QA-1-R	QB-1	QC-1	QD-1	QF-1	None	None	JA-1
Kissel 6-70............M. (1928)	Q-86-F	Q-6-R	QA-18-F	QA-14-R	QB-5	QC-16	QD-16	QF-19	None	None	JA-1
Kissel 8-80............M. (1928)	Q-1-F	Q-1-R	QA-3-F	QA-1-R	QB-1	QC-1	QD-1	QF-1	None	None	JA-1
Kissel 8-80S...........M. (1928)	Q-1-F	Q-1-R	QA-3-F	QA-1-R	QB-1	QC-1	QD-1	QF-1	None	None	JA-1
Kissel 8-90............M. (1928)	Q-1-F	Q-1-R	QA-3-F	QA-1-R	QB-1	QC-1	QD-1	QF-1	None	None	JA-1
Kissel 6-73............M. (1929)	Q-86-F	Q-6-R	QA-18-F	QA-14-R	QB-5	QC-16	QD-16	QF-19	None	None	JA-1
Kissel 8-95............M. (1020)	Q-1-F	Q-1-R	QA-3-F	QA-1-R	QB-1	QC-1	QD-1	QF-1	None	None	JA-1
Kissel 8-126...........M. (1929)	Q-1-F	Q-1-R	QA-3-F	QA-1-R	QB-1	QC-1	QD-1	QF-1	None	None	JA-1
LaSalle 303..............(1927)	Q-5-F	None	QA-8-F	None	QB-2	QC-6	QD-6	QF-11	None	None	JA-3
LaSalle 303..............(1928)	Q-5-F	None	QA-8-F	None	QB-2	QC-6	QD-6	QF-11	None	None	JA-3
LaSalle 328..............(1929)	Q-5-F	None	QA-8-F	None	QB-2	QC-6	QD-6	QF-11	None	None	JA-3
LaSalle 340..............(1930)	Q-5-F	None	QA-8-F	None	QB-2	QC-6	QD-6	QF-11	None	None	JA-3
Lincoln 8................(1925)	Q-56-F	None	QA-70-F	None	QB-47	QC-37	QD-37	QF-37	None	None	JA-11
Lincoln 8................(1926)	Q-56-F	None	QA-70-F	None	QB-47	QC-37	QD-37	QF-37	None	None	JA-11
Lincoln 8................(1927)	Q-56-F	None	QA-70-F	None	QB-47	QC-37	QD-37	QF-37	None	None	JA-11
Lincoln 8................(1928)	Q-56-F	None	QA-70-F	None	QB-47	QC-37	QD-37	QF-37	None	None	JA-11
Lincoln 8................(1929)	Q-56-F	None	QA-70-F	None	QB-47	QC-37	QD-37	QF-37	None	None	JA-11
Lincoln 8................(1930)	Q-56-F	None	QA-70-F	None	QB-37	QC-37	QD-37	QF-37	None	None	JA-11
Locomobile J8..........U. (1925)	Q-43-F	Q-35-R	QA-54-F	QA-54-F	QB-38	QC-28	QD-28	QF-31	None	None	JA-1
Locomobile 48............(1925)	Q-57-F	Q-14-R	QA-71-F	QA-71-F	QB-38	QC-28	QD-28	QF-31	None	None	JA-10
Locomobile 48............(1926)	Q-57-F	Q-14-R	QA-71-F	QA-71-F	QB-38	QC-28	QD-28	QF-31	None	None	JA-1
Locomobile 90..........U. (1926)	Q-58-F	Q-48-R	QA-72-F	QA-72-F	QB-32	QC-38	QD-38	QF-38	None	None	JA-1
Locomobile Jr. 8.......U. (1926)	Q-43-F	Q-35-R	QA-54-F	QA-54-F	QB-38	QC-28	QD-28	QF-31	None	None	JA-1
Locomobile 48............(1927)	Q-57-F	Q-14-R	QA-71-F	QA-71-F	QB-32	QC-38	QD-38	QF-38	None	None	JA-1
Locomobile 8-66........U. (1927)	Q-43-F	Q-35-R	QA-54-F	QA-54-F	QB-32	QC-38	QD-38	QF-38	None	None	JA-1
Locomobile 8-80........S. (1927)	Q-34-F	Q-22-R	QA-45-F	QA-45-F	QB-26	QC-24	QD-24	QF-28	QG-15	None	JA-1
Locomobile 90..........U. (1927)	Q-58-F	Q-48-R	QA-72-F	QA-72-F	QB-26	QC-24	QD-24	QF-28	QG-15	None	JA-1

UNIVERSAL JOINTS—Continued

Interchangeable Parts have the same CHILTON NUMBER in Any Column

Car Make and Model	Front Universal Joint Assembly (Metal)	Rear Universal Joint Assembly (Metal)	Front Flange or Hub Yoke	Rear Flange or Hub Yoke	Sleeve Yoke on Propeller Shaft	Journal (cross) or Pins	Bushings or Balls	Inside Casing or Joint Body	Outside Casing	Fabric Disks	GAS-OLINE TANK FILLER CAPS
Locomobile 48............(1928)	Q-57-F	Q-14-R	QA-45-F	QA-45-F	QB-26	QC-24	QD-24	QF-28	QG-15	None	JA-1
Locomobile 8-70..........S. (1928)	Q-42-F	Q-18-R	QA-52-F	QA-52-F	QB-36	QC-21	QD-21	QF-25	OG-12	None	JA-1
Locomobile 8-80.........S. (1928)	Q-34-F	Q-22-R	QA-45-F	QA-45-F	QB-26	QC-24	QD-24	QF-28	QG-15	None	JA-1
Locomobile 90..........U. (1928)	Q-58-F	Q-48-R	QA-72-F	QA-72-F	QB-26	QC-24	QD-24	QF-28	QG-15	None	JA-1
Locomobile 8-80..........S. (1929)	Q-34-F	Q-22-R	QA-45-F	QA-45-F	QB-26	QC-24	QD-24	QF-28	QG-15	None	JA-1
Locomobile 86-88........S. (1929)	Q-34-F	Q-22-R	QA-45-F	QA-45-F	QB-26	QC-24	QD-24	QF-28	QG-15	None	JA-1
Locomobile 90..........U. (1929)	Q-58-F	Q-48-R	QA-72-F	QA-72-F	QB-26	QC-24	QD-24	QF-28	QG-15	None	JA-1
Marmon 74..............(1925)	Q-61-F	None	QA-75-F	None	QB-48	QC-39	QD-39	QF-39	QG-22	None	JA-1
Marmon 74..............(1926)	Q-61-F	None	QA-75-F	None	QB-48	QC-39	QD-39	QF-39	QG-22	None	JA-1
Marmon, Little 8........M. (1927)	Q-86-F	Q-6-R	QA-18-F	QA-14-R	QB-5	QC-16	QD-16	QF-19	None	None	JA-1
Marmon E75..............(1927)	Q-61-F	None	QA-75-F	None	QB-48	QC-39	QD-39	QF-39	QG-22	None	JA-14
Marmon 68..............S. (1928)	Q-12-F	Q-74-R	QA-23-F	QA-23-F	QB-27	QC-8	QD-8	QF-10	QG-1	None	JA-1
Marmon E75..............(1928)	Q-61-F	None	QA-75-F	None	QB-48	QC-39	QD-39	QF-39	QG-22	None	JA-14
Marmon 78..............S. (1928)	Q-12-F	Q-74-R	QA-23-F	QA-23-F	QB-27	QC-8	QD-8	QF-10	QG-1	None	JA-1
Marmon 68..............S. (1929)	Q-12-F	Q-74-R	QA-23-F	QA-23-F	QB-27	QC-8	QD-8	QF-10	QG-1	None	JA-1
Marmon Roosevelt.......S. (1929)	Q-12-F	Q-74-R	QA-23-F	QA-23-F	QB-27	QC-8	QD-8	QF-10	QG-1	None	JA-1
Marmon 78..............S. (1929)	Q-12-F	Q-74-R	QA-23-F	QA-23-F	QB-27	QC-8	QD-8	QF-10	QG-1	None	JA-1
Marmon 69..............S. (1930)	Q-12-F	Q-74-R	QA-23-F	QA-23-F	QB-27	QC-8	QD-8	QF-10	QG-1	None	JA-15
Marmon 79..............S. (1930)	Q-49-F	Q-40-R	QA-60-F	QA-60-F	QB-43	QC-52	QD-52	QF-54	QG-32	None	JA-15
Marmon Big 8..........S. (1930)	Q-34-F	Q-22-R	QA-45-F	QA-17-R	QB-26	QC-24	QD-24	QF-28	QG-15	None	JA-15
Marquette..............M. (1930)	Q-63-F	Q-53-R	QA-79-F	QA-30-R	QB-52	QC-16	QD-16	QF-19	None	None	JA-1
Maxwell..............(1925)	None	None	None	None	None	None	None	None	None	QH-7	JA-8
Moon Series A..........S. (1925)	Q-32-F	Q-17-R	QA-40-F	QA-40-F	QB-23	QC-21	QD-21	QF-25	QG-12	None	JA-13
Moon Series A..........S. (1926)	Q-32-F	Q-17-R	QA-40-F	QA-40-F	QB-23	QC-21	QD-21	QF-25	QG-12	None	JA-13
Moon Series A..........S. (1927)	Q-32-F	Q-17-R	QA-40-F	QA-40-F	QB-23	QC-21	QD-21	QF-25	QG-12	None	JA-13
Moon 6-60..............S. (1927)	Q-42-F	Q-18-R	QA-52-F	QA-52-F	QB-36	QC-21	QD-21	QF-25	QG-12	None	JA-13
Moon Series A..........S. (1928)	Q-32-F	Q-17-R	QA-40-F	QA-40-F	QB-23	QC-21	QD-21	QF-25	QG-12	None	JA-13
Moon 6-60..............S. (1928)	Q-42-F	Q-18-R	QA-52-F	QA-52-F	QB-36	QC-21	QD-21	QF-25	QG-12	None	JA-13
Moon 6-72..............M. (1928)	Q-86-F	Q-43-R	QA-18-F	QA-24-F	QB-5	QC-16	QD-16	QF-19	None	None	JA-13
Moon 8-80..............M. (1928)	Q-1-F	Q-1-R	QA-3-F	QA-1-R	QB-1	QC-1	QD-1	QF-1	None	None	JA-13
Moon 6-72..............M. (1929)	Q-86-F	Q-43-R	QA-18-F	QA-25-R	QB-5	QC-16	QD-16	QF-19	None	None	JA-9
Nash Adv. 6..............(1925)	Q-62-F	Q-52-R	QA-77-F	QA-77-F	QB-49	QC-40	QD-40	QF-40	QG-23	None	JA-1
Nash Spec. 6..............(1925)	Q-62-F	Q-52-R	QA-77-F	QA-77-F	QB-49	QC-40	QD-40	QF-40	QG-23	None	JA-1
Nash Adv. 6..............(1926)	Q-62-F	Q-52-R	QA-77-F	QA-77-F	QB-49	QC-40	QD-40	QF-40	QG-23	None	JA-1
Nash Spec..............(1926)	Q-62-F	Q-52-R	QA-77-F	QA-77-F	QB-49	QC-40	QD-40	QF-40	QG-23	None	JA-1
Nash Adv. 6..............(1927)	Q-62-F	None	QA-77-F	None	QB-49	QC-40	QD-40	QF-40	QG-23	None	JA-1
Nash Spec...............(1927)	Q-62-F	None	QA-77-F	None	QB-49	QC-40	QD-40	QF-40	QG-23	None	JA-1
Nash Light 6..............(1927)	None	None	None	NOne	None	None	None	None	None	QH-1	JA-1
Nash Adv. 6..............(1928)	Q-62-F	None	QA-77-F	None	QB-49	QC-40	QD-40	QF-40	QG-23	QH-11	JA-1
Nash Spec. 6..............(1928)	Q-62-F	None	QA-77-F	None	QB-49	QC-40	QD-40	QF-40	QG-23	QH-11	JA-1
Nash Std. 6..............(1928)	None	None	None	None	None	None	None	None	None	QH-1	JA-i
Nash Adv. 6..............(1929)	Q-62-F	None	QA-77-F	None	QB-49	QC-40	QD-40	QF-40	QG-23	QH-11	JA-1
Nash Spec. 6..............(1929)	Q-62-F	None	QA-77-F	None	QB-49	QC-40	QD-40	QF-40	QG-23	QH-11	JA-1
Nash Std. 6..............(1929)	None	None	None	None	None	None	None	None	None	QH-1	JA-1
Nash Single Ignition 6......(1930)	None	None	None	None	None	None	None	None	None	QH-1	JA-1
Nash Twin Ignition 6.......(1930)	Q-62-F	None	QA-77-F	None	QB-49	QC-40	QD-40	QF-40	QG-23	QH-11	JA-1
Nash Twin Ignition 8.......(1930)	Q-62-F	None	QA-77-F	None	QB-49	QC-40	QD-40	QF-40	QG-23	QH-11	JA-1
Oakland 6-54...........M. (1925)	Q-63-F	Q-21-R	QA-76-F	QA-16-R	QB-50	QC-1	QD-1	QF-1	None	None	JA-9
Oakland O6...........M. (1926)	Q-63-F	Q-6-R	QA-76-F	QA-14-R	QB-50	QC-1	QD-1	QF-1	None	None	JA-9
Oakland GO-6..........M. (1927)	Q-64-F	Q-6-R	QA-74-F	QA-14-R	QB-51	QC-16	QD-16	QF-19	None	None	JA-9
Oakland AA-6..........M. (1928)	Q-64-F	Q-6-R	QA-74-F	QA-14-R	QB-51	QC-16	QD-16	QF-19	None	None	JA-1
Oakland AA-6..........M. (1929)	Q-60-F	Q-53-R	QA-79-F	QA-30-R	QB-52	QC-16	QD-16	QF-19	None	None	JA-1
Oakland 8..............M. (1930)	Q-60-F	Q-53-R	QA-79-F	QA-30-R	QB-52	QC-16	QD-16	QF-19	None	None	JA-1
Oldsmobile C30............(1925)	None	None	None	None	None	None	None	None	None	QH-8	JA-9
Oldsmobile D30............(1926)	None	None	None	None	None	None	None	None	None	QH-8	JA-1
Oldsmobile E..............(1927)	None	None	None	None	None	None	None	None	None	QH-8	JA-1
Oldsmobile F28............(1928)	None	Q-54-R	None	QA-31-R	None	QC-41	QD-41	QF-41	None	QH-8	JA-1
Oldsmobile F29............(1929)	None	Q-54-R	None	QA-31-R	None	QC-41	QD-41	QF-41	None	QH-8	JA-1
Oldsmobile F-30............(1930)	None	Q-54-R	None	QA-31-R	None	QC-41	QD-41	QF-41	None	QH-8	JA-1
Overland 91..............(1925)	Q-59-F	None	QA-78-F	None	QB-53	QC-42	QD-42	QF-42	None	None	JA-16
Overland 93............M. (1925)	Q-86-F	Q-75-R	QA-18-F	QA-21-R	QB-5	QC-16	QD-16	QF-19	None	None	JA-16
Overland 91..............(1926)	Q-59-F	None	QA-78-F	None	QB-53	QC-42	QD-42	QF-42	None	None	JA-16
Overland 93............M. (1926)	Q-86-F	Q-75-R	QA-18-F	QA-21-R	QB-5	QC-16	QD-16	QF-19	None	None	JA-16
Packard 326-333........M. (1925)	Q-66-F	Q-56-R	QA-80-F	QA-34-R	QB-55	QC-44	QD-44	QF-44	None	None	JA-10
Packard 246-243........M. (1925)	Q-66-F	Q-56-R	QA-80-F	QA-34-R	QB-55	QC-44	QD-44	QF-44	None	None	JA-10
Packard 326-333........M. (1926)	Q-66-F	Q-56-R	QA-80-F	QA-34-R	QB-55	QC-44	QD-44	QF-44	None	None	JA-10
Packard 236-243........M. (1926)	Q-66-F	Q-56-R	QA-80-F	QA-34-R	QB-55	QC-44	QD-44	QF-44	None	None	JA-10
Packard 426-433........M. (1927)	Q-66-F	Q-56-R	QA-80-F	QA-34-R	QB-55	QC-44	QD-44	QF-44	None	None	JA-10
Packard 336-343........M. (1927)	Q-66-F	Q-56-R	QA-80-F	QA-34-R	QB-55	QC-44	QD-44	QF-44	None	None	JA-10
Packard 526-533........M. (1928)	Q-67-F	Q-57-R	QA-81-F	QA-35-R	QB-56	QC-45	QD-45	QF-45	None	None	JA-26
Packard 443............M. (1928)	Q-67-F	Q-57-R	QA-81-F	QA-35-R	QB-56	QC-45	QD-45	QF-45	None	None	JA-26
Packard 626-633........M. (1929)	Q-67-F	Q-57-R	QA-81-F	QA-35-R	QB-56	QC-45	QD-45	QF-45	None	None	JA-26
Packard 640-645........M. (1929)	Q-67-F	Q-57-R	QA-81-F	QA-35-R	QB-56	QC-45	QD-45	QF-45	None	None	JA-26
Packard 726-733........M. (1930)	Q-67-F	Q-57-R	QA-81-F	QA-35-R	QB-56	QC-45	QD-45	QF-45	None	None	JA-30
Packard 726-733........M. (1930)	Q-67-F	Q-57-R	QA-81-F	QA-35-R	QB-56	QC-45	QD-45	QF-45	None	None	JA-30
Packard 740-745........M. (1930)	Q-67-F	Q-57-R	QA-81-F	QA-35-R	QB-56	QC-45	QD-45	QF-45	None	None	JA-30
Paige 6-70..............M. (1925)	Q-68-F	Q-58-R	QA-82-F	QA-36-R	QB-57	QC-44	QD-44	QF-44	None	None	JA-14
Paige 6-72..............M. (1926)	Q-33-F	Q-80-R	QA-44-F	QA-37-R	QB-18	QC-1	QD-1	QF-1	None	None	JA-14
Paige 6-45...........M. (1927–28)	Q-86-F	Q-77-R	QA-18-F	QA-15-R	QB-5	QC-16	QD-16	QF-19	None	None	JA-1
Paige 6-65...........M. (1927–28)	Q-86-F	Q-77-R	QA-18-F	QA-15-R	QB-5	QC-16	QD-16	QF-19	None	None	JA-1
Paige 6-75...........M. (1927–28)	Q-86-F	Q-77-R	QA-18-F	QA-15-R	QB-5	QC-16	QD-16	QF-19	None	None	JA-1
Paige 8-85...........M. (1927–28)	Q-86-F	Q-77-R	QA-18-F	QA-15-R	QB-5	QC-16	QD-16	QF-19	None	None	JA-1
Peerless 70.............A. (1925)	Q-70-F	Q-22-R	QA-83-F	QA-83-F	QB-58	QC-46	QD-46	QF-46	None	None	JA-1
Peerless 69.............S. (1925)	Q-34-F	Q-22-R	QA-45-F	QA-45-F	QB-26	QC-24	QD-24	QF-28	QG-15	None	JA-1
Peerless 80.............A. (1926)	Q-70-F	Q-60-R	QA-83-F	QA-83-F	QB-58	QC-46	QD-46	QF-46	None	None	JA-1
Peerless 69.............A. (1926)	Q-34-F	Q-22-R	QA-45-F	QA-45-F	QB-26	QC-24	QD-24	QF-28	QG-15	None	JA-1
Peerless 60.............S. (1927)	Q-73-F	Q-29-R	QA-85-F	QA-5-R	QB-59	QC-47	QD-47	QF-47	QG-25	None	JA-1
Peerless 69.............S. (1927)	Q-34-F	Q-22-R	QA-45-F	QA-45-F	QB-26	QC-24	QD-24	QF-28	QG-15	None	JA-1
Peerless 80.............A. (1927)	Q-70-F	Q-60-R	QA-83-F	QA-83-F	QB-58	QC-46	QD-46	QF-46	None	None	JA-1
Peerless 72...........S. (1927–28)	Q-70-F	Q-22-R	QA-83-F	QA-83-F	QB-58	QC-46	QD-46	QF-46	None	None	JA-1
Peerless 90.............(1927–28)	Q-71-F	Q-40-R	QA-68-F	QA-60-F	QB-60	QC-48	QD-48	QF-48	None	None	JA-1
Peerless 60.............S. (1928)	Q-73-F	Q-29-R	QA-85-F	QA-5-R	QB-59	QC-47	QD-47	QF-47	QG-25	None	JA-1
Peerless 69.............S. (1928)	Q-34-F	Q-22-R	QA-45-F	QA-45-F	QB-26	QC-24	QD-24	QF-28	QG-15	None	JA-1
Peerless 80.............S. (1928)	Q-70-F	Q-60-R	QA-83-F	QA-83-F	QB-58	QC-46	QD-46	QF-46	None	None	JA-1
Peerless 91.............S. (1928)	Q-49-F	Q-40-R	QA-60-F	QA-60-F	QB-43	QC-52	QD-52	QF-54	QG-32	None	JA-1
Peerless 61.............S. (1929)	Q-70-F	Q-60-R	QA-83-F	QA-83-F	QB-58	QC-46	QD-46	QF-46	None	None	JA-1
Peerless 81.............S. (1929)	Q-70-F	Q-60-R	QA-83-F	QA-83-F	QB-58	QC-46	QD-46	QF-46	None	None	JA-1
Peerless 91.............S. (1929)	Q-49-F	Q-40-R	QA-60-F	QA-60-F	QB-43	QC-52	QD-52	QF-54	QG-32	None	JA-1
Peerless 125............S. (1929)	Q-74-F	Q-61-R	QA-86-F	QA-86-F	QB-61	QC-49	QD-49	QF-49	QG-27	None	JA-1
Peerless A..............S. (1930)	Q-12-F	Q-74-R	QA-23-F	QA-23-F	QB-27	QC-8	QD-8	QF-10	QG-1	None	JA-15
Peerless B..............S. (1930)	Q-49-F	Q-40-R	QA-60-F	QA-60-F	QB-43	QC-52	QD-52	QF-54	QG-32	None	JA-15
Peerless C..............S. (1930)	Q-34-F	Q-53-R	QA-79-F	QA-30-R	QB-52	QC-16	QD-16	QF-19	None	None	JA-15
Pierce Arrow 80.........S. (1925)	Q-34-F	Q-22-R	QA-45-F	QA-45-F	QB-26	QC-24	QD-24	QF-28	QG-15	None	JA-21

UNIVERSAL JOINTS—Continued

Interchangeable Parts have the same CHILTON NUMBER in Any Column

Car Make and Model	Front Universal Joint Assembly (Metal)	Rear Universal Joint Assembly (Metal)	Front Flange or Hub Yoke	Rear Flange or Hub Yoke	Sleeve Yoke on Propeller Shaft	Journal (cross) or Pins	Bushings or Balls	Inside Casing or Joint Body	Outside Casing	Fabric Disks	GAS-OLINE TANK FILLER CAPS
Pierce Arrow 33..........S. (1926)	Q-72-F	Q-62-R	QA-87-F	QA-87-F	QB-62	QC-50	QD-50	QF-50	QG-28	None	JA-21
Pierce Arrow 80..........S. (1926)	Q-34-F	Q-22-R	QA-45-F	QA-45-F	QB-26	QC-24	QD-24	QF-28	QG-15	None	JA-21
Pierce Arrow 36..........S. (1927)	Q-72-F	Q-62-R	QA-87-F	QA-87-F	QB-62	QC-50	QD-50	QF-50	QG-28	None	JA-21
Pierce Arrow 80..........S. (1927)	Q-34-F	Q-22-R	QA-45-F	QA-45-F	QB-26	QC-24	QD-24	QF-28	QG-15	None	JA-21
Pierce Arrow 36..........S. (1928)	Q-72-F	Q-62-R	QA-87-F	QA-87-F	QB-62	QC-50	QD-50	QF-50	QG-28	None	JA-21
Pierce Arrow 81..........S. (1928)	Q-34-F	Q-22-R	QA-45-F	QA-45-F	QB-26	QC-24	QD-24	QF-28	QG-15	None	JA-21
Pierce Arrow 133-143.....S. (1929)	Q-34-F	Q-62-R	QA-45-F	QA-88-F	QB-26	QC-24	QD-24	QF-28	QG-15	None	JA-1
Pierce Arrow A..........S. (1930)	Q-34-F	Q-62-R	QA-45-F	QA-88-F	QB-26	QC-24	QD-24	QF-28	QG-15	None	JA-1
Pierce Arrow B..........S. (1930)	Q-34-F	Q-62-R	QA-45-F	QA-88-F	QB-26	QC-24	QD-24	QF-28	QG-15	None	JA-1
Pierce Arrow C..........S. (1930)	Q-34-F	Q-62-R	QA-45-F	QA-88-F	QB-26	QC-24	QD-24	QF-28	QG-15	None	JA-1
Plymouth 4 Cyl............(1929)	None	None	None	None	None	None	None	None	None	QH-8	JA-1
Plymouth..................(1930)	None	None	None	None	None	None	None	None	None	QH-5	JA-1
Pontiac 6..................(1926)	Q-69-F	None	QA-66-F	None	QB-6	QC-9	QD-9	QF-51	QG-29	None	JA-8
Pontiac 6..................(1927)	Q-69-F	None	QA-66-F	None	QB-6	QC-9	QD-9	QF-51	QG-29	None	JA-1
Pontiac 6..................(1928)	Q-69-F	None	QA-66-F	None	QB-6	QC-9	QD-9	QF-51	QG-29	None	JA-1
Pontiac Big 6...........M. (1929)	Q-75-F	Q-53-R	QA-90-F	QA-30-R	QB-78	QC-16	QD-16	QF-19	None	None	JA-1
Pontiac.................M. (1930)	Q-75-F	Q-53-R	QA-90-F	QA-30-R	QB-78	QC-16	QD-16	QF-19	None	None	JA-1
Reo T6.....................(1925)	Q-76-F	None	QA-91-F	None	QB-65	QC-51	QD-51	QF-53	QG-31	QH-12	JA-22
Reo T6................(1926–27)	Q-76-F	None	QA-91-F	None	QB-65	QC-51	QD-51	QF-53	QG-31	QH-12	JA-22
Reo Flying Cloud.......D. (1927)	Q-2-F	Q-2-F	QA-4-F	QA-4-F	None	QC-2	QD-2	QF-2	None	None	JA-1
Reo Wolverine...........D. (1927)	Q-2-F	Q-2-F	QA-4-F	QA-4-F	None	QC-2	QD-2	QF-2	None	None	JA-1
Reo Flying Cloud.......D. (1928)	Q-2-F	Q-2-F	QA-4-F	QA-4-F	None	QC-2	QD-2	QF-2	None	None	JA-1
Reo Wolverine...........D. (1928)	Q-2-F	Q-2-F	QA-4-F	QA-4-F	None	QC-2	QD-2	QF-2	None	None	JA-1
Reo Fly. Cld. Master....D. (1929)	Q-2-F	Q-2-F	QA-4-F	QA-4-F	None	QC-2	QD-2	QF-2	None	None	JA-1
Reo Fly. Cld. Mate.......S. (1929)	Q-12-F	Q-74-R	QA-23-F	QA-23-F	QB-27	QC-8	QD-8	QF-10	QG-1	None	JA-1
Reo 15.....................S. (1930)	Q-12-F	Q-74-R	QA-23-F	QA-23-F	QB-27	QC-8	QD-8	QF-10	QG-1	None	JA-1
Reo 20, 25...............S. (1930)	Q-2-F	Q-2-F	QA-4-F	QA-4-F	None	QC-2	QD-2	QF-2	None	None	JA-1
Rickenbacker 8-A.......D. (1925)	Q-43-F	Q-35-R	QA-54-F	QA-54-F	QB-38	QC-28	QD-28	QF-31	QG-17	None	JA-1
Rickenbacker D6........M. (1925)	Q-89-F	Q-65-F	QA-89-F	QA-40-R	QB-79	QC-1	QD-1	QF-1	None	None	JA-1
Rickenbacker 8-B........M. (1926)	Q-89-F	Q-65-F	QA-89-F	QA-40-R	QB-79	QC-1	QD-1	QF-1	None	None	JA-1
Rickenbacker 6-E........M. (1926)	Q-89-F	Q-65-F	QA-89-F	QA-40-R	QB-79	QC-1	QD-1	QF-1	None	None	JA-1
Rickenbacker 6-70.......M. (1927)	Q-90-F	Q-65-F	QA-90-F	QA-40-R	QB-80	QC-1	QD-1	QF-1	None	None	JA-1
Rickenbacker 8-80.......M. (1927)	Q-90-F	Q-65-F	QA-90-F	QA-40-R	QB-80	QC-1	QD-1	QF-1	None	None	JA-1
Rickenbacker 8-90.......M. (1927)	Q-90-F	Q-65-F	QA-90-F	QA-40-R	QB-80	QC-1	QD-1	QF-1	None	None	JA-1
Roamer 6-54E..............(1925)	None	None	None	None	None	None	None	None	None	QH-3	JA-4
Roamer 6-50............(1925–26)	Q-66-F	Q-56-R	QA-80-F	QA-34-R	QB-55	QC-44	QD-44	QF-44	None	None	JA-4
Roamer 8-88.......M. (1925–26–27)	Q-66-F	Q-56-R	QA-80-F	QA-34-R	QB-55	QC-44	QD-44	QF-44	None	None	JA-4
Roamer 8-80..............M. (1926)	Q-66-F	Q-56-R	QA-80-F	QA-34-R	QB-55	QC-44	QD-44	QF-44	None	None	JA-4
Roamer 8-80..............M. (1927)	Q-66-F	Q-56-R	QA-80-F	QA-34-R	QB-55	QC-44	QD-44	QF-44	None	None	JA-4
Roamer 8-78..............M. (1927)	Q-66-F	Q-56-R	QA-80-F	QA-34-R	QB-55	QC-44	QD-44	QF-44	None	None	JA-4
Roamer 8-78..............M. (1928)	Q-66-F	Q-56-R	QA-80-F	QA-34-R	QB-55	QC-44	QD-44	QF-44	None	None	JA-4
Roamer 8-80..............M. (1928)	Q-66-F	Q-56-R	QA-80-F	QA-34-R	QB-55	QC-44	QD-44	QF-44	None	None	JA-4
Roamer 8-88..............M. (1928)	Q-66-F	Q-56-R	QA-80-F	QA-34-R	QB-55	QC-44	QD-44	QF-44	None	None	JA-4
Roamer 8-80..............M. (1929)	Q-66-F	Q-56-R	QA-80-F	QA-34-R	QB-55	QC-44	QD-44	QF-44	None	None	JA-4
Roamer 8-88..............M. (1929)	Q-66-F	Q-56-R	QA-80-F	QA-34-R	QB-55	QC-44	QD-44	QF-44	None	None	JA-4
Star F......................S. (1925)	Q-29-F	Q-18-R	QA-41-F	QA-41-F	QB-24	QC-21	QD-21	QF-25	QG-12	None	JA-1
Star M......................S. (1926)	Q-29-F	Q-18-R	QA-41-F	QA-41-F	QB-24	QC-21	QD-21	QF-25	QG-12	None	JA-1
Star R......................S. (1926)	Q-29-F	Q-18-R	QA-41-F	QA-41-F	QB-24	QC-21	QD-21	QF-25	QG-12	None	JA-1
Star M.................S. (1927–28)	Q-29-F	Q-18-R	QA-41-F	QA-41-F	QB-24	QC-21	QD-21	QF-25	QG-12	None	JA-8
Star R.................S. (1927–28)	Q-29-F	Q-18-R	QA-41-F	QA-41-F	QB-24	QC-21	QD-21	QF-25	QG-12	None	JA-8
Stearns Knight B 4 Cyl.....(1925)	None	None	None	None	None	None	None	None	None	QH-22	JA-16
Stearns Knight C 6 Cyl.....(1925)	None	None	None	None	None	None	None	None	None	QH-22	JA-16
Stearns Knight S 6 Cyl.....(1925)	None	None	None	None	None	None	None	None	None	QH-22	JA-16
Stearns Knight B 4 Cyl.....(1926)	None	None	None	None	None	None	None	None	None	QH-22	JA-16
Stearns Knight C75......M. (1926)	Q-68-F	Q-58-R	QA-82-F	QA-36-R	QB-57	QC-44	QD-44	QF-44	None	None	JA-16
Stearns Knight S95.......M. (1926)	Q-68-F	Q-58-R	QA-82-F	QA-36-R	QB-57	QC-44	QD-44	QF-44	None	None	JA-16
Stearns Knight F 6-85...M. (1927)	Q-68-F	Q-58-R	QA-82-F	QA-36-R	QB-57	QC-44	QD-44	QF-44	None	None	JA-16
Stearns Knight G 8-85...M. (1927)	Q-67-F	Q-57-R	QA-81-F	QA-35-R	QB-56	QC-45	QD-45	QF-45	None	None	JA-16
Stearns Knight F 6-85...M. (1928)	Q-1-F	Q-1-R	QA-3-F	QA-1-R	QB-1	QC-1	QD-1	QF-1	None	None	JA-16
Stearns Knight H-J 8-90.M. (1928)	Q-67-F	Q-57-R	QA-81-F	QA-35-R	QB-56	QC-45	QD-45	QF-45	None	None	JA-16
Stearns Knight H-J 8-90.M. (1929)	Q-67-F	Q-57-R	QA-81-F	QA-35-R	QB-56	QC-45	QD-45	QF-45	None	None	JA-5
Stearns Knight M-N 6-80.M. (1929)	Q-1-F	Q-1-R	QA-3-F	QA-1-R	QB-1	QC-1	QD-1	QF-1	None	None	JA-5
Studebaker Big 6.........S. (1925)	Q-34-F	Q-22-R	QA-45-F	QA-45-F	QB-26	QC-24	QD-24	QF-28	QG-15	None	JA-10
Studebaker Spec. 6........S. (1925)	Q-34-F	Q-22-R	QA-45-F	QA-45-F	QB-26	QC-24	QD-24	QF-28	QG-15	None	JA-10
Studebaker Std. 6..........(1925)	None	None	None	None	None	None	None	None	None	QH-13	JA-8
Studebaker Big 6..........S. (1926)	Q-34-F	Q-22-R	QA-45-F	QA-45-F	QB-26	QC-24	QD-24	QF-28	QG-15	None	JA-10
Studebaker Std. 6..........(1926)	None	None	None	None	None	None	None	None	None	QH-13	JA-8
Studebaker Spec. 6........S. (1926)	Q-34-F	Q-22-R	QA-45-F	QA-45-F	QB-26	QC-24	QD-24	QF-28	QG-15	None	JA-10
Studebaker Big 6..........S. (1927)	Q-34-F	Q-22-R	QA-45-F	QA-45-F	QB-26	QC-24	QD-24	QF-28	QG-15	None	JA-10
Studebaker Spec. 6........S. (1927)	Q-34-F	Q-22-R	QA-45-F	QA-45-F	QB-26	QC-24	QD-24	QF-28	QG-15	None	JA-10
Studebaker Std. 6..........(1927)	None	None	None	None	None	None	None	None	None	GH-13	JA-8
Studebaker Com...........S. (1928)	Q-34-F	Q-22-R	QA-45-F	QA-45-F	QB-26	QC-24	QD-24	QF-28	QG-15	None	JA-1
Studebaker Dict. 6........S. (1928)	Q-12-F	Q-74-R	QA-23-F	QA-23-F	QB-27	QC-8	QD-8	QF-10	QG-1	None	JA-1
Studebaker Pres. 8........S. (1928)	Q-34-F	Q-22-R	QA-45-F	QA-45-F	QB-26	QC-24	QD-24	QF-28	QG-15	None	JA-1
Studebaker Com. 6.........S. (1929)	Q-12-F	Q-74-R	QA-23-F	QA-23-F	QB-27	QC-8	QD-8	QF-10	QG-1	None	JA-1
Studebaker Com. 8.........S. (1929)	Q-12-F	Q-74-R	QA-23-F	QA-23-F	QB-27	QC-8	QD-8	QG-10	QG-1	None	JA-1
Studebaker Dict. 6........S. (1929)	Q-12-F	Q-74-R	QA-23-F	QA-23-F	QB-27	QC-8	QD-8	QF-10	QG-1	None	JA-1
Studebaker Dict. 8........S. (1929)	Q-12-F	Q-74-R	QA-23-F	QA-23-F	QB-27	QC-8	QD-8	QF-10	QG-1	None	JA-1
Studebaker Pres. 8........S. (1929)	Q-34-F	Q-22-R	QA-45-F	QA-45-F	QB-26	QC-24	QD-24	QF-28	QG-18	None	JA-1
Studebaker 6..............S. (1930)	Q-12-F	Q-31-R	QA-52-F	QA-52-F	QB-36	QC-21	QD-21	QF-25	QG-12	None	JA-1
Studebaker Dict. 6........S. (1930)	Q-12-F	Q-74-R	QA-23-F	QA-23-F	QB-27	QC-8	QD-8	QF-10	QG-1	None	JA-1
Studebaker Com. 6.........S. (1930)	Q-12-F	Q-74-R	QA-23-F	QA-23-F	QB-27	QC-8	QD-8	QF-10	QG-1	None	JA-1
Studebaker Dict. 8........S. (1930)	Q-12-F	Q-74-R	QA-23-F	QA-23-F	QB-27	QC-8	QD-8	QF-10	QG-1	None	JA-1
Studebaker Com. 8.........S. (1930)	Q-12-F	Q-74-R	QA-23-F	QA-23-F	QB-27	QC-8	QD-8	QF-10	QG-1	None	JA-1
Studebaker Pres. 8........S. (1930)	Q-34-F	Q-22-R	QA-45-F	QA-45-F	QB-26	QC-24	QD-24	QF-28	QG-18	None	JA-1
Stutz 695.................M. (1925)	Q-68-F	Q-58-R	QA-82-F	QA-36-R	QB-57	QC-44	QD-44	QF-44	None	None	JA-14
Stutz AA..................M. (1926)	Q-68-F	Q-58-R	QA-82-F	QA-36-R	QB-57	QC-44	QD-44	QF-44	None	None	JA-14
Stutz AA..................M. (1927)	Q-68-F	Q-29-R	QA-82-F	QA-36-R	QB-57	QC-44	QD-44	QF-44	None	None	JA-14
Stutz BB..................M. (1928)	Q-67-F	Q-57-R	QA-81-F	QA-35-R	QB-56	QC-45	QD-45	QF-45	None	None	JA-5
Stutz Series M...........M. (1929)	Q-67-F	Q-57-R	QA-81-F	QA-35-R	QB-56	QC-45	QD-45	QF-45	None	None	JA-5
Stutz M...................M. (1930)	Q-67-F	Q-57-R	QA-81-F	QA-35-R	QB-56	QC-45	QD-45	QF-45	None	None	JA-5
Velie 60...................P. (1925)	Q-40-F	Q-36-R	QA-57-F	QA-22-R	QB-41	QC-31	QD-31	None	None	None	JA-11
Velie 60...................P. (1926)	Q-79-F	Q-69-R	QA-94-F	QA-42-R	QB-69	QC-55	QD-55	None	None	None	JA-11
Velie Spec. 60............P. (1927)	Q-79-F	Q-69-R	QA-94-F	QA-42-R	QB-69	QC-55	QD-55	None	None	None	JA-1
Velie Std. 50..............P. (1927)	Q-80-F	Q-70-R	QA-95-F	QA-43-R	QB-70	QC-56	QD-56	None	None	None	JA-1
Velie 6-66.................P. (1928)	Q-81-F	Q-71-R	QA-96-F	QA-44-R	QB-71	QC-57	QD-57	None	None	None	JA-1
Velie 6-77.................P. (1928)	Q-81-F	Q-71-R	QA-96-F	QA-44-R	QB-71	QC-57	QD-57	None	None	None	JA-1
Velie 8-88.................P. (1928)	Q-81-F	Q-71-R	QA-96-F	QA-44-R	QB-71	QC-57	QD-57	None	None	None	JA-1
Viking....................M. (1929)	Q-1-F	Q-72-R	QA-3-F	QA-45-R	QB-1	QC-1	QD-1	QF-1	None	None	JA-1
Westcott 44................(1925)	Q-82-F	Q-73-R	QA-99-F	QA-46-R	QB-72	QC-58	QD-58	None	None	None	JA-13
Westcott 60................(1925)	Q-82-F	Q-73-R	QA-99-F	QA-46-R	QB-72	QC-58	QD-58	None	None	None	JA-13
Whippet 96 4 Cyl.......M. (1927)	Q-41-F	Q-30-R	QA-51-F	QA-20-R	QB-35	QC-26	QD-26	QF-30	None	None	JA-16
Whippet 93-A 6 Cyl......M. (1927)	Q-86-F	Q-75-R	QA-18-F	QA-21-R	QB-5	QC-16	QD-16	QF-19	None	None	JA-16
Whippet 96 4 Cyl.......M. (1928)	Q-41-F	Q-30-R	QA-51-F	QA-20-R	QB-35	QC-26	QD-26	QF-30	None	None	JA-16

UNIVERSAL JOINTS—Continued

Interchangeable Parts have the same CHILTON NUMBER in Any Column

Car Make and Model	Front Universal Joint Assembly (Metal)	Rear Universal Joint Assembly (Metal)	Front Flange or Hub Yoke	Rear Flange or Hub Yoke	Sleeve Yoke on Propeller Shaft	Journal (cross) or Pins	Bushings or Balls	Inside Casing or Joint Body	Outside Casing	Fabric Disks	GASOLINE TANK FILLER CAPS
Whippet 98 6 Cyl......M. (1928)	Q-86-F	Q-75-R	QA-18-F	QA-21-R	QB-5	QC-16	QD-16	QF-19	None	None	JA-16
Whippet 96-A...........M. (1929)	Q-65-F	Q-55-R	QA-69-F	QA-32-R	QB-54	QC-43	QD-43	QF-43	None	None	JA-1
Whippet 98-A;..........M. (1929)	Q-86-F	Q-75-R	QA-18-F	QA-21-R	QB-5	QC-16	QD-16	QF-19	None	None	JA-1
Wills Ste. Claire 8.......S. (1925)	Q-34-F	Q-22-R	QA-45-F	QA-36-R	QB-26	QC-24	QD-24	QF-28	QG-15	None	JA-25
Wills Ste. Claire 6.......S. (1925)	Q-34-F	Q-22-R	QA-45-F	QA-36-R	QB-26	QC-24	QD-24	QF-28	QG-15	None	JA-25
Wills Ste. Claire 8.......S. (1926)	Q-34-F	Q-22-R	QA-45-F	QA-36-R	QB-26	QC-24	QD-24	QF-28	QG-15	None	JA-25
Wills Ste. Claire 6.......S. (1926)	Q-34-F	Q-22-R	QA-45-F	QA-36-R	QB-26	QC-24	QD-24	QF-28	QG-15	None	JA-25
Willys 6...............M. (1930)	Q-86-F	Q-6-R	QA-18-F	QA-14-R	QB-5	QC-16	QD-16	QF-19	None	None	JA-1
Willys 8...............M. (1930)	Q-86-F	Q-6-R	QA-18-F	QA-14-R	QB-5	QC-16	QD-16	QF-19	None	None	JA-1
Willys Knight 66.........(1925)	None	None	None	None	None	None	None	None	None	QH-2	JA-16
Willys Knight 65.........(1925)	None	None	None	None	None	None	None	None	None	QH-2	JA-16
Willys Knight 66.......M. (1926)	Q-1-F	Q-1-R	QA-3-F	QA-1-R	QB-1	QC-1	QD-1	QF-1	None	None	JA-16
Willys Knight 70.......M. (1926)	Q-86-F	Q-75-R	QA-18-F	QA-21-R	QB-5	QC-16	QD-16	QF-19	None	None	JA-16
Willys Knight 66-A.....M. (1927)	Q-1-F	Q-1-R	QA-3-F	QA-1-R	QB-1	QC-1	QD-1	QF-1	None	None	JA-16
Willys Knight 70-A.....M. (1927)	Q-86-F	Q-6-R	QA-18-F	QA-14-R	QB-5	QC-16	QD-16	QF-19	None	None	JA-16
Willys Knight 66.......M. (1928)	Q-86-F	Q-6-R	QA-18-F	QA-14-R	QB-5	QC-16	QD-16	QF-19	None	None	JA-1
Willys Knight 6-56.....M. (1928)	Q-86-F	Q-6-R	QA-18-F	QA-14-R	QB-5	QC-16	QD-16	QF-19	None	None	JA-16
Willys Knight 70-A.....M. (1928)	Q-86-F	Q-6-R	QA-18-F	QA-14-R	QB-5	QC-16	QD-16	QF-19	None	None	JA-16
Willys Knight 66-A.....M. (1929)	Q-1-F	Q-72-R	QA-3-F	QA-45-R	QB-1	QC-1	QD-1	QF-1	None	None	JA-1
Willys Knight 70-B.....M. (1929)	Q-86-F	Q-75-R	QA-18-F	QA-21-R	QB-5	QC-16	QD-16	QF-19	None	None	JA-1
Willys Knight 66B......M. (1930)	Q-1-F	Q-72-R	QA-3-F	QA-45-R	QB-1	QC-1	QD-1	QF-1	None	None	JA-1
Willys Knight...........M. (1930)	Q-86-F	Q-75-R	QA-18-F	QA-21-R	QB-5	QC-16	QD-16	QF-19	None	None	JA-1

Abbreviations: F—Front.   R—Rear.   A—Almetal.   D—Detroit.   M—Mechanics.   P—Peters   S—Spicer.   T—Thicmer.
U—Universal Machine.

INTERCHANGEABLE COUNT

Showing exact number of times each CHILTON NUMBER occurs in the UNIVERSAL JOINT TABLE, beginning Page 245.

Front Universal Joint Assembly (Metal)

Q-1F-21
Q-2F-74
Q-3F-1
Q-4F-8
Q-5F-12
Q-6F-6
Q-7F-6
Q-8F-2
Q-9F-1
Q-10F-2
Q-11F-2
Q-12F-32
Q-13F-5
Q-14F-1
Q-16F-4
Q-17F-22
Q-19F-8
Q-22F-5
Q-23F-3
Q-24F-1
Q-25F-2
Q-28F-2
Q-29F-21
Q-30F-2
Q-31F-3
Q-32F-13
Q-33F-5
Q-34F-54
Q-35F-2
Q-36F-3
Q-40F-8
Q-41F-3
Q-42F-14
Q-43F-6
Q-44F-3
Q-45F-3
Q-46F-1
Q-49F-9
Q-50F-3
Q-52F-3
Q-54F-2
Q-55F-1
Q-56F-6
Q-57F-4
Q-58F-4
Q-59F-2
Q-60F-2
Q-61F-4
Q-62F-12
Q-63F-3
Q-64F-2
Q-65F-7
Q-66F-16
Q-67F-13
Q-68F-7
Q-69F-3
Q-70F-7

Q-71F-1
Q-72F-3
Q-73F-2
Q-74F-1
Q-75F-2
Q-76F-2
Q-79F-2
Q-80F-1
Q-81F-3
Q-82F-2
Q-83F-18
Q-84F-1
Q-85F-1
Q-86F-27
Q-87F-1
Q-88F-3
Q-89F-3
Q-90F-3

Rear Universal Joint Assembly (Metal)

Q-1R-18
Q-5R-3
Q-6R-13
Q-9R-5
Q-11R-1
Q-12R-2
Q-13R-4
Q-14R-4
Q-15R-1
Q-17R-13
Q-18R-22
Q-19R-3
Q-20R-1
Q-21R-3
Q-22R-51
Q-23R-2
Q-24R-1
Q-29R-3
Q-30R-3
Q-31R-4
Q-35R-6
Q-36R-8
Q-38R-1
Q-39R-3
Q-40R-10
Q-42R-2
Q-43R-5
Q-48R-4
Q-52R-4
Q-53R-6
Q-54R-3
Q-55R-1
Q-56R-17
Q-57R-13
Q-58R-6
Q-59F-3
Q-60R-5
Q-61R-1
Q-62R-7
Q-69R-2

Q-70R-1
Q-71R-3
Q-72R-3
Q-73R-2
Q-74R-31
Q-75R-11
Q-77R-5
Q-78R-2
Q-79R-1
Q-80R-1
Q-81R-3

Front Flange or Hub Yoke

QA-1F-18
QA-2F-1
QA-3F-21
QA-4F-74
QA-5F-6
QA-6F-1
QA-7F-8
QA-8F-12
QA-9F-6
QA-10F-1
QA-11F-3
QA-12F-6
QA-14F-2
QA-15F-2
QA-16F-1
QA-18F-27
QA-19F-5
QA-22F-22
QA-23F-61
QA-24F-9
QA-29F-5
QA-31F-2
QA-32F-2
QA-33F-3
QA-37F-4
QA-39F-1
QA-40F-28
QA-41F-24
QA-42F-6
QA-43F-2
QA-44F-5
QA-45F-91
QA-46F-2
QA-47F-6
QA-51F-3
QA-52F-29
QA-53F-1
QA-54F-12
QA-55F-3
QA-56F-3
QA-57F-8
QA-58F-1
QA-59F-3
QA-60F-18
QA-64F-1
QA-65F-3
QA-66F-3

QA-67F-2
QA-68F-1
QA-69F-1
QA-70F-6
QA-71F-6
QA-72F-8
QA-74F-2
QA-75F-4
QA-76F-2
QA-77F-16
QA-78F-2
QA-79F-4
QA-80F-16
QA-81F-13
QA-82F-7
QA-83F-14
QA-85F-2
QA-86F-2
QA-87F-6
QA-88F-4
QA-89F-3
QA-90F-5
QA-91F-2
QA-94F-2
QA-95F-1
QA-96F-3
QA-99F-2

Sleeve Yoke on Propeller Shaft

QB-1-21
QB-2-12
QB-3-6
QB-4-1
QB-5-27
QB-6-8
QB-7-2
QB-10-5
QB-11-2
QB-12-2
QB-13-1
QB-14-2
QB-15-3
QB-16-2
QB-17-1
QB-18-5
QB-20-1
QB-23-13
QB-24-11
QB-25-3
QB-26-57
QB-27-24
QB-28-3
QB-29-2
QB-32-3
QB-33-3
QB-35-3
QB-36-15
QB-37-2
QB-38-7
QB-39-3
QB-40-3
QB-41-8
QB-43-9
QB-44-3
QB-45-1
QB-46-2
QB-47-5
QB-48-4
QB-49-12
QB-50-2
QB-51-2
QB-52-4
QB-53-2
QB-54-1
QB-55-16
QB-56-13
QB-57-7
QB-58-7
QB-59-2
QB-60-1
QB-61-1

QB-62-3
QB-65-2
QB-69-2
QB-70-1
QB-71-3
QB-72-2
QB-73-7
QB-74-1
QB-75-1
QB-76-1
QB-77-3
QB-78-2
QB-79-3
QB-80-3

Journal (cross) or Pins

QC-1-36
QC-2-37
QC-3-3
QC-4-1
QC-5-4
QC-6-14
QC-7-5
QC-8-34
QC-9-8
QC-10-11
QC-12-6
QC-13-1
QC-14-2
QC-15-3
QC-16-46
QC-19-2
QC-20-1
QC-21-41
QC-22-3
QC-24-57
QC-25-2
QC-26-3
QC-27-1
QC-28-7
QC-31-7
QC-32-1
QC-33-9
QC-34-3
QC-35-3
QC-36-2
QC-37-6
QC-38-3
QC-39-4
QC-40-12
QC-41-3
QC-42-2
QC-43-1
QC-44-23
QC-45-13
QC-46-7
QC-47-2
QC-48-1
QC-49-1

QC-50-3
QC-51-2
QC-52-9
QC-55-2
QC-56-1
QC-57-3
QC-58-2
QC-60-4

Bushings or Balls

QD-1-36
QD-2-37
QD-3-3
QD-4-1
QD-5-4
QD-6-14
QD-7-6
QD-8-34
QD-9-8
QD-10-11
QD-12-5
QD-13-1
QD-14-2
QD-15-3
QD-16-46
QD-19-2
QD-20-1
QD-21-41
QD-22-3
QD-24-57
QD-25-2
QD-26-3
QD-27-1
QD-28-7
QD-31-7
QD-32-1
QD-33-9
QD-34-3
QD-35-3
QD-36-2
QD-37-6
QD-38-3
QD-39-4
QD-40-12
QD-41-3
QD-42-2
QD-43-1
QD-44-23
QD-45-13
QD-46-7
QD-47-2
QD-48-1
QD-49-1
QD-50-3
QD-51-2
QD-52-9
QD-55-2
QD-56-1
QD-57-3

QD-58-2
QD-60-4

Inside Casing or Joint Body

QF-1-35
QF-2-37
QF-3-3
QF-4-1
QF-5-4
QF-6-4
QF-7-4
QF-8-2
QF-9-3
QF-10-34
QF-11-7
QF-12-4
QF-13-1
QF-14-11
QF-16-1
QF-17-9
QF-18-2
QF-19-42
QF-20-1
QF-23-2
QF-24-1
QF-25-40
QF-26-3
QF-27-3
QF-28-57
QF-30-3
QF-31-7
QF-32-3
QF-33-3
QF-34-3
QF-36-1
QF-37-6
QF-38-3
QF-39-4
QF-40-12
QF-41-3
QF-42-2
QF-43-1
QF-44-23
QF-45-13
QF-46-7
QF-47-2
QF-48-1
QF-49-1
QF-50-3
QF-51-3
QF-53-2
QF-54-9
QF-61-4

Outside Casing

QG-1-34
QG-2-4

QG-3-1
QG-7-2
QG-8-1
QG-12-40
QG-13-4
QG-15-55
QG-17-1
QG-18-5
QG-19-3
QG-22-4
QG-23-12
QG-25-2
QG-27-1
QG-28-3
QG-29-3
QG-31-2
QG-32-9
QG-34-1

Fabric Disks

QH-1-5
QH-2-5
QH-3-3
QH-4-2
QH-5-5
QH-7-2
QH-8-9
QH-11-6
QH-12-2
QH-13-3
QH-14-3
QH-22-4

GASOLINE TANK FILLER CAPS

JA-1-263
JA-2-11
JA-3-10
JA-4-19
JA-5-14
JA-6-3
JA-7-5
JA-8-11
JA-9-17
JA-10-13
JA-11-14
JA-13-13
JA-14-15
JA-15-17
JA-16-53
JA-17-3
JA-18-2
JA-21-7
JA-22-2
JA-25-4
JA-26-4
JA-30-3

BRAKE ASSEMBLIES

Section 1

HOW TO USE THIS TABLE

Only Bendix brakes are covered in the first section. Lockheed brakes are covered in the second section. Molded brake lining data by makes and car models are given in the third section. To find interchangeability of Bendix parts:

1. Locate in the first column of the Bendix table the car and model for which the part is needed.
2. Follow this line across to column pertaining to that part.
3. In this part column opposite your car model you will find the CHILTON NUMBER for the part you want.
4. Look up and down the part column for the same CHILTON NUMBER. Wherever you find this same number in this same column you have an interchangeable part. The car make opposite tells you where to get it—probably from another local dealer.

Example: Suppose a Reinforcement Plate for a Bendix Brake is needed for an Erskine with Serial Number after 5021764.

Locate this car in the first column. Follow across to the column on Reinforcement Plate, which is the sixth column. Here you see the CHILTON NUMBER for this part is DFA-5. Checking through the CHILTON NUMBERS in this same column, you will find the number DFA-5 opposite the Durant M and R, Essex 1927-28 and Studebaker Dictator 8, 1929. The Reinforcement Plate used in the brakes of all these cars is interchangeable with the one in your Erskine car.

5. At the end of this Table, page 257, you will find a count showing the number of times any part appears in this table. Example: DAA-5 under Carrier Bracket, opposite Durant 6 (California), in this table will appear again in the count at the end of this table, followed by the figure 10 under the heading Carrier Bracket. This indicates part DAA-5 appears ten times in this table.

Instructions for finding interchangeability of Lockheed brake parts in second section are the same as above.

BENDIX BRAKE PARTS

Interchangeable Parts have the same CHILTON NUMBER in Any Column

Car Make and Model	Control Shaft and Carrier Bracket [1] Assembly	Carrier [2] Bracket	Operating Cam	Brake Shoes Less Lining	Reinforcement Plate	Eccentric Adjusting Cam	Articulating Pin	Primary and Auxiliary or Primary and Secondary Shoe Spring	Primary or Secondary Shoe Spring
Cunningham, 8......(1926-27-28) 16x2 Aluminum 3 Shoe	*DA-2-Lf.Fr. *DA-3-Rg.Fr. ‡DA-1-Fr.	§DAA-1-Fr. ¶DAA-2 DAA-3-Rr.	*DAB-4 ‖DAB-1-Fr. †DAB-2-Fr. DAB-3-Rr.	DD-1-Pri. DD-2-Sec. DD-1-Aux.	DFA-1-Lf DFA-2-Rg.	DFB-1	DFC-1	DFD-1	DFE-1
*Used on 1926 cars. † Used on 1927 cars. ‡ Used on 1927-28 cars. § Used with Unflanged Cam. ¶ Used with Flanged Cam. ‖ Used with DAA-2 Bracket.									
Cunningham, 8........(1929-30) 16x2½ Duo Servo 2 Shoe	DA-67	DAA-4	DAB-5	DD-3-Pri. DD-3-Sec.	DFA-3	DFB-2	....	DFD-2	DFE-2
Durant, 6 (California)........... 11x1½ Standard 3 Shoe.....		DAA-5	DAB-6	DD-4-Pri. DD-5-Sec. DD-4-Aux.	DFA-4	DFB-3	DFC-2	DFD-3	DFE-3
Durant, M (4 Cyl.), R (6 Cyl.) Star 11x1½ Super Servo 3 Shoe			DAB-7-Lf.Fr. DAB-8-Rg.Fr. DAB-9-Rr. * Used with Steel Shoes.	DD-6-Pri. DD-7-Sec. DD-8-Aux.	DFA-5	DFB-4	DFC-3	*DFC-4	DFE-4
Durant, 40, 60, 66........(1929) 11x1½ Duo Servo 2 Shoe		DAA-6	DAB-12	DD-12-Pri. DD-12-Sec.	DFA-7	DFB-5	....	DFD-4	DFE-5
Durant, 70 Series 607......(1929) 13x1¾ Duo Servo 2 Shoe		DAA-7	DAB-12	DD-13-Pri. DD-13-Sec.	DFA-7	DFB-5	....	DFD-4	DFE-5
Erskine........ 11x1½ Standard 3 Shoe		DAA-5-Fr. DAA-8-Rr.	DAB-6-Fr. *DAB-15-Rr.	DD-4-Pri. DD-5-Sec. DD-4-Aux.	*DFA-8-Lf. *DFA-9-Rg. * Used before car Serial 5021764.	DFB-3	*DFC-2	DFD-3	DFE-3
Erskine........ 11x1½ Super Servo 3 Shoe			DAB-13-Lf. DAB-14-Rg. * Used after car Serial 5021764.	DD-6-Pri. DD-7-Sec. DD-8-Aux.	*DFA-5 † Used with Steel Shoes.	DFB-4	*DFC-3	†DFD-4	DEE-4
Erskine, 53.............(1930) 12x1½ Duo Servo 2 Shoe	DA-84-Fr. DA-85-Rr.	DAA-41-Lf. DAA-44-Rg.	DAB-16 Cable and Conduit Control.	DD-14-Pri. DD-14-Sec.	....	DFB-5	....	DFD-4	DFE-6
Essex................(1927-28) 11x1½ Super Servo 3 Shoe			DAB-17-Lf. DAB-9-Rg. * Used with Steel Shoes.	DD-6-Pri. DD-7-Sec. DD-8-Aux.	DFA-5	DFB-4	DFC-3	*DFD-4	DFE-4
Essex, Challenger.........(1929) 11x1½ Duo Servo 2 Shoe		DAA-6	DAB-16	DD-12-Pri. DD-12-Sec.	DFA-7	DFB-5	....	DFD-4	DFE-5
Essex, Super 6...........(1930) 11x1½ Duo Servo 2 Shoe		DAA-9	DAB-16	DD-12-Pri. DD-12-Sec.	DFA-7	DFB-5	....	DFD-4	DFE-5
Falcon Knight................ 12x1¾ Standard 3 Shoe	DA-4-Rr.	DAA-5	DAB-18-Fr. DAB-6-Rr.	DD-15-Pri. DD-16-Sec. DD-15-Aux	DFA-10	DFB-3	DFC-4	DFD-5	DFE-1
Hudson, 6.........(1926-27-28) 14x2 Standard 3 Shoe	DA-5-Fr. DA-4-Rr.	*DAA-2-Fr. DAA-10-Rr.	DAB-1-Fr.	DD-17-Pri. DD-18-Sec. DD-17-Aux.	†DFA-11-Lf. †DFA-12-Rg. ‡DFA-13-Lf. ‡DFA-14-Rg.	DFB-3	DFC-4	DFD-6	DFE-1
* Used with Flanged Cam. † Used on 1926 Cars. ‡ Used on 1927-28 Cars.									

BENDIX BRAKE PARTS—Continued

Interchangeable Parts have the same CHILTON NUMBER in Any Column

Car Make and Model	Control Shaft and Carrier Bracket [1]Assembly	Carrier [2]Bracket	Operating Cam	Brake Shoes Less Lining	Reinforcement Plate	Eccentric Adjusting Cam	Articulating Pin	Primary and Auxiliary or Primary and Secondary Shoe Spring	Primary or Secondary Shoe Spring
Hudson, 6..........(Early 1929) 14x2 Duo Servo 2 Shoe	....	DAA-11	DAB-12	DD-19-Pri. DD-19-Sec.	DFA-15	DFB-6	....	DFD-7	DFE-7
Hudson, 6...........(Late 1929) 14x2 Duo Servo 2 Shoe	....	DAA-12	DAB-12	DD-19-Pri. DD-19-Sec.	DFA-16	DFB-6	....	DFD-7	DFE-7
Hudson, 8...............(1930) 12x1½ Duo Servo 2 Shoe	....	DAA-9	DAB-12	DD-20-Pri. DD-20-Sec.	DFA-7	DFB-5	....	DFD-4	DFE-5
Hupmobile, 6.................. 12x1¾ Standard 3 Shoe	DA-6	*DAA-1 †DAA-2	DAB-2 ‡DAB-1 DAB-15-Rr.	DD-15-Pri. DD-16-Sec. DD-15-Pri.	DFA-10	DFB-1	DFC-1	DFD-5	DFE-1
	* Used with Unflanged Cam. † Used with Flanged Cam. ‡ Used with DAA-2 Bracket and after car Serial 65000. Front Brakes only except Cam.								
Jordan, U................(1930) 12x1¾ Duo Servo 2 Shoe	....	....	DAB-16	DD-21-Pri. DD-21-Sec.	....	DFB-5	....	DFD-4	DFE-6
	Cable and Conduit Control.								
Lincoln....................... 16x2½ Standard 3 Shoe	DA-7-Lf.Fr. DA-8-Rg.Fr. DA-9-Lf.Rr. DA-10-Rg.Rr. *DA-11-Lf.Rr. *DA-12-Rg.Rr.	DAA-13-Fr. DAA-14-Rr. †DAA-15-Lf.Rr.	DAB-19-Lf.Fr. DAB-20-Rg. Fr. DAB-21-Lf.Rr. DAB-22-Rg.Rr. DAB-23-Lf.Rr. DAB-24-Rg.Rr.	DD-22-Pri. DD-23-Sec. DD-23-Aux.	†DFA-17-Rr. †DFA-18-Rr.	DFB-7 †DFB-8-Fr.	DFC-5	DFD-8	DFE-8
	* Used on 1928 Cars. † Used on 1929-30 Cars.								
Locomobile, Junior 8.......(1926) 12x1¾ Standard 3 Shoe	DA-13-Lf.Fr. DA-14-Rg.Fr. DA-15-Rr.	*DAA-1-Fr. †DAA-2-Fr. DAA-16-Rr.	DAB-2-Fr. ‡DAB-1-Fr. DAB-25-Rr.	DD-15-Pri. DD-16-Sec. DD-15-Aux.	DFA-19	DFB-1	§DFC-4 ¶DFC-1	DFD-5 DFD-9-Rr.	
	* Used with Unflanged Cam. † Used with Flanged Cam. ‡ Used with DAA-2 Bracket. § Used with Take-up Cam with groove in head. ¶ Used with Take-up Cam with plain head.								
Locomobile, 33-90...(1925-26-27) 16x2 Standard 3 Shoe	*DA-18-Fr. †DA-19-Lf.Fr. †DA-20-Rg.Fr.	‡DAA-1-Fr. §DAA-2-Fr. DAA-16-Rr.	*DAB-2-Fr. ¶DAB-1-Fr. DAB-26-Rr. †DAB-4-Fr.	DD-24-Pri. DD-25-Sec. DD-24-Aux.	DFA-1-Lf.Fr. DFA-2-Rg.Fr.	DFB-1	‖DFC-1 **DFC-4	††DFD-1 ‡‡DFD-10	DFE-1
	* Used on 1925 cars. † Used on 1926-27 cars. ‡ Used with Unflanged Cam. § Used with Flanged Cam. ¶ Used with DAA-2 Brackets. ‖ Used with Take-up Cam with plain head. ** Used with Take-up Cam with groove in head. †† Used with Aluminum Shoes. ‡‡ Used with Steel Shoes.								
Locomobile, 8-70.......(1928-29) 12x1¾ Standard 3 Shoe	DA-16-Fr. DA-4-Rr.	*DAA-17-Fr. DAA-10-Rr.	DAB-1-Fr. DAB-15-Rr.	DD-15-Pri. DD-16-Sec. DD-15-Aux.	DFA-10	DFB-3	DFC-4	DFD-5 DFD-6	DFE-1
	* Interchangeable with DAA-2 Brackets.								
Locomobile, 8-80....(1927-28-29) 14x2 Standard 3 Shoe	DA-17-Fr. DA-4-Rr.	*DAA-2-Fr. DAA-10-Rr.	DAB-1-Fr. DAB-15-Rr.	DD-17-Pri. DD-18-Sec. DD-17-Aux.	DFA-13-Lf. DFA-14-Rg.	DFB-3	DFC-4	DFD-6	DFE-1
	* Used with Flanged Cam.								
Marmon, Little...........(1927) 12x1¾ Standard 3 Shoe	*DA-21-Fr. †DA-22-Fr. ‡DA-23-Fr. §DA-24-Fr. DA-25-Rr.	¶DAA-1-Fr. ‖§DAA-2-Fr. DAA-10-Rr. DAA-18-Rr.	DAB-2-Fr. **DAB-1-Fr. DAB-15-Rr.	DD-15-Pri. DD-16-Sec. DD-15-Aux.	DFA-10-Fr DFA-19-Rr.	DFB-3	DFC-4	DFD-5	DFE-1
	* Used from January to April, 1927. † Used from April to July, 1927. ‡ Used from June to August, 1927. § Used after June, 1927. ¶ Used with Unflanged Cam. ‖ Used with Flanged Cam. ** Used with DAA-2 Bracket and after car Serial 606.								
Marmon, E 75............(1928) 16x2 Standard 3 Shoe	....	DAA-19-Fr. DAA-5	DAB-27-Fr. DAB-28-Rr.	DD-24-Pri. DD-25-Sec. DD-24-Aux.	DFA-20-Lf DFA-21-Rg.	DFB-3	DFC-4	DFD-10	DFE-1
Marmon, 68...........(1928-29) 12x1¾ Standard 3 Shoe.	DA-4	DAA-10	DAB-15	DD-15-Pri. DD-16-Sec. DD-15-Aux.	DFA-10	DFB-3	DFC-4	DFD-5	DFE-1
Marmon, 78...........(1928-29) 12x1¾ Standard 3 Shoe	DA-23-Fr. DA-4	DAA-2-Fr. DAA-10	*DAB-1-Fr. DAB-15	DD-15-Pri. DD-16-Sec. DD-15-Aux.	DFA-10	DFB-3	DFC-4	DFD-5	DFE-1
	* Used with DAA-2 Bracket.								
Marmon, Roosevelt........(1929) 11x1½ Duo Servo 2 Shoe	....	DAA-6	DAB-12	DD-12-Pri. DD-12-Sec.	DFA-7	DFB-5	....	DFD-4	DFE-5-Fr. DFE-6-Rr.
Marmon, Big 8............(1930) 15x2 Duo Servo 2 Shoe	DA-68-Fr. DA-69-Rr.	DAA-47-Lf. DAA-48-Rg.	DAB-16	DD-26-Pri. DD-26-Sec.	....	DFB-6	....	DFD-2	DFE-7
	Cable and Conduit Control.								
Marmon, 69.............(1930) 12x1½ Duo Servo 2 Shoe	DA-70-Fr. DA-71-Rr.	DAA-45-Lf. DAA-46-Rg.	DAB-16	DD-20-Pri. DD-20-Sec.	....	DFB-5	....	DFD-4	DFE-6
	Cable and Conduit Control.								
Marmon, 79.............(1930) 14x2 Duo Servo 2 Shoe	DA-72-Fr. DA-73-Rr.	DAA-49-Lf. DAA-50-Rg.	DAB-16	DD-27-Pri. DD-27-Sec.	....	DFB-6	....	DFD-7	DFE-7
	Cable and Conduit Control.								
Marquette............(1929-30) 12x1¾ Duo Servo 2 Shoe	....	DAA-7	DAB-12	DD-28-Pri. DD-28-Sec.	DFA-7	DFB-5	....	DFD-4	DFE-5
Nash, Special 6...........(1930) 13x1¾ Duo Servo 2 Shoe	DA-75-Fr. DA-76-Rr. [3]DA-74-Rr.	DAA-51-Lf. DAA-52-Rg.	DAB-16	DD-13-Pri. DD-13-Sec.	....	DFB-5	....	DFD-4	DFE-6
	Cable and Conduit Control.								
Nash, Adv. 8 (490 Twin Ign.)(1930) 15x2 Duo Servo 2 Shoe	DA-77-Fr. DA-78-Rr. [3]DA-79-Rr.	DAA-11	DAB-12	DD-29-Pri. DD-29-Sec.	DFA-16	DFB-6	....	DFD-2	DFE-7

BENDIX BRAKES PARTS—Continued

Interchangeable Parts have the same CHILTON NUMBER in Any Column

Car Make and Model	Control Shaft and Carrier Bracket [1] Assembly	Carrier [2]Bracket	Operating Cam	Brake Shoes Less Lining	Reinforcement Plate	Eccentric Adjusting Cam	Articulating Pin	Primary and Auxiliary or Primary and Secondary Shoe Spring	Primary or Secondary Shoe Spring
Oldsmobile, F-28(1928),F-29.(1929) 12x1¾ Standard 3 Shoe	....	DAA-5	DAB-6	DD-15-Pri. DD-16-Sec. DD-15-Aux. Front Brakes only.	DFA-10	DFB-3	DFC-4	DFD-5	DFE-1
Oldmobile, F-30..........(1930) 12x1½ Duo Servo 2 Shoe	DA-80-Fr. DA-81-Rr.	DAA-51-Lf. DAA-52-Rg.	DAB-16	DD-20-Pri. DD-20-Sec. Cable and Conduit Control.	....	DFB-5	....	DFD-4	DFE-6
Overland, 93.............(1926) 12x1¾ Standard 3 Shoe	....	DAA-5	....	....	DFA-10-Fr.	DFB-1 DFB-3- Rr.	*DFC-1 †DFC-4	DFD-5	DFE-1
		* Used with Take-up Cam with plain head. † Used with Take-up Cam with groove in head.							
Packard, (6 Cyl.) 326,333.(1925-26) 14x2¼ Standard 3 Shoe	*DA-27-Lf.Fr. *DA-28-Rg.Fr. *DA-29-Rr.	*DAA-21-Fr. *DAA-22-Rr.	*DAB-29-Lf.Fr. *DAB-30-Rg.Fr.	DD-17-Pri. DD-18-Sec. DD-17-Aux.	DFA-13-Lf. DFA-14-Rg.	DFB-3	†DFC-4	DFD-6	DFE-1
		* Used with Straight Backing Plate. † Used with Take-up Cam with groove in head.							
Packard, (6 Cyl.) 426, 433 .(1927) 14x2 Standard 3 Shoe	DA-30-Lf.Fr. DA-31-Rg.Fr. DA-33-Rr.	*DAA-21-Fr. *DAA-22-Rr. †DAA-23-Lf.Fr. †DAA-24-Rg.Fr	DAB-31-Lf.Fr. DAB-32-Rg. Fr.	DD-17-Pri. DD-18-Sec. DD-17-Aux.	DFA-13-Lf. DFA-14-Rg.	DFB-3	‡DFC-4	DFD-6	DFE-1
		* Used with Straight Backing plate. † Used with Flanged Backing Plate. ‡Used with Take-up Cam with groove in head.							
Packard, (6 Cyl.) 526, 533 . (1928) 14x2 Standard Welded 3 Shoe	DA-30-Lf.Fr. DA-31-Rg.Fr. DA-33-Rr.	*DAA-23-Lf.Fr. *DAA-24-Rg.Fr. DAA-25-Rr.	DAB-31-Lf.Fr. DAB-32-Rg. Fr. DAB-33-Rr.	DD-17-Pri. DD-18-Sec. DD-17-Aux.	DFA-22-Lf DFA-23-Rg.	DFB-3	DFC-9	DFD-6	DFE-9
		* Used with Flanged Backing plate.							
Packard, (8 Cyl.) 236, 243..(1926)	DA-32-Lf.Fr. DA-34-Rg.Fr. DA-35-Rr.	*DAA-26-Fr. †DAA-22-Rr. DAA-27-Rr.	DAB-33-Rr. DAB-34-Rr. *DAB-35-Lf *DAB-36-Rg. Fr.	DD-24-Pri. DD-25-Sec. DD-27-Aux.	....	DFB-3	‡DFC-4	DFD-1	DFE-1
		* Used with Straight Backing Plate. † Used with Flanged Backing Plate. ‡ Used with Take-up Cam with groove in head.							
Packard, (8 Cyl.) 336, 343..(1927) 16x2 Standard 3 Shoe	*DA-36-Lf.Fr. *DA-37-Rg.Fr. DA-35-Rr. DA-38-Lf.Fr. DA-39-Rg.Fr.	*DAA-26-Fr. *DAA-22-Rr. DAA-27-Rr. DAA-28-Lf.Fr. DAA-29-Rg.Fr	DAB-33-Rr *DAB-29-Lf.Fr. *DAB-30-Rg.Fr. DAB-34-Rr. DAB-31-Lf.Fr. DAB-32-Rg.Fr.	DD-24-Pri. DD-25-Sec. DD-27-Aux.	....	DFB-3	†DFC-4	‡DFD-1	DFE-1
		* Used with Straight Backing Plate. † Used with Take-up Cam with groove in head. ‡ Used with Aluminum Shoes.							
Packard, (8 Cyl.) 443......(1928) 16x2 Welded 3 Shoe	DA-38-Lf.Fr. DA-39-Rg.Fr. DA-35-Rr.	*DAA-30-Lf.Fr. *DAA-31-Rg.Fr. DAA-25-Rr. DAA-28-Lf.Fr. DAA-29-Rg.Fr.	DAB-31-Lf.Fr. DAB-32-Rg. Fr. DAB-37-Lf.Fr. DAB-38-Rg.Fr. DAB-34-Rr.	DD-31-Pri. DD-32-Sec. DD-33-Aux.	DFA-1-Lf. DFA-2-Rg.	DFB-3	DFC-9	DFD-11	DFE-9
		* Used with Flanged Backing Plate.							
Packard, (8 Cyl.) 640, 645..(1929) 16x2 Welded 3 Shoe	DA-40-Lf.Fr. DA-41-Rg.Fr. DA-35-Rr.	DAA-32-Lf.Fr. DAA-34-Rg.Fr. *DAA-33-Lf.Fr. *DAA-35-Rg.Fr DAA-36-Lf.Fr DAA-37-Rg.Fr. *DAA-27-Rr.	*DAB-37-Lf.Fr. *DAB-38-Rg. Fr. DAB-40-Lf.Fr. DAB-41-Rg. Fr. *DAB-34-Rr.	DD-31-Pri. DD-32-Sec. DD-33-Aux.	DFA-24	DFB-7	DFC-10	DFD-10	DFE-1
		* Also used on 6th Series 1928.							
Packard, (8Cyl.) 626,633.(1929-30) 726, 733.............(1930) 16x1¾ Welded 3 Shoe	DA-40-Lf.Fr. DA-41-Rg.Fr. DA-35-Rr. *DA-42-Lf.Fr. *DA-43-Rg.Fr.	DAA-32-Lf.Fr. DAA-34-Rg.Fr †DAA-33-Lf.Fr. †DAA-35-Rg.Fr DAA-36-Lf.Fr. DAA-37-Rg.Fr DAA-27-Rr.	DAB-37-Lf.Fr. DAB-38-Rg. Fr. DAB-40-Lf.Fr. DAB-41-Rg. Fr. DAB-34-Rr.	DD-34-Pri. DD-35-Sec. DD-36-Aux.	DFA-24	DFB-7	DFC-10	DFD-10 DFD-11	DFE-1
		* Used on Models 726, 733. † Also used on 6th Series 1928.							
Packard, (8 Cyl.) 745, 747..(1930) 16x2 Welded 3 Shoe	DA-44-Lf.Fr. DA-45-Rg.Fr. DA-35-Rr.	DAA-36-Lf.Fr. DAA-37-Rg.Fr. DAA-27-Rr.	DAB-40-Lf.Fr. DAB-41-Rg. Fr. DAB-34-Rr.	DD-31-Pri. DD-32-Sec. DD-33-Aux.	DFA-24	DFB-7	DFC-10	DFD-10	DFE-1
Peerless, Std.............(1930) 12x1½ Duo Servo 2 Shoe	DA-82-Fr. DA-83-Rr.	DAA-45-Lf. DAA-46-Rg.	DAB-16	DD-20-Pri. DD-20-Sec. Cable and Conduit Control.	....	DFB-5	....	DFD-4	DFE-6
Peerless, Master 8.........(1930) 14x2 Duo Servo 2 Shoe	DA-72-Fr. DA-73-Rr.	DAA-49-Lf. DAA-50-Rg.	DAB-16	DD-37-Pri. DD-37-Sec. Cable and Conduit Control.	....	DFB-6	....	DFD-7	DFE-7
Peerless, Custom 8........(1930) 15x2 Duo Servo 2 Shoe	DA-68-Fr. DA-69-Rr.	DAA-47-Lf. DAA-48-Rg.	DAB-16	DD-29-Pri. DD-29-Sec. Cable and Conduit Control.	....	DFB-6	....	DFD-2	DFE-7
Pierce Arrow, 133, 143..(1929-30) 15x2¼ Servo Welded 3 Shoe	*DA-46	DAA-8	DAB-42	DD-38-Pri. DD-39-Sec. DD-40-Aux.	DFA-25	DFB-7	DFC-10	DFD-10	DFE-1
		* Interchangeable with DA-4							

BENDIX BRAKE PARTS—Continued

Interchangeable Parts have the same CHILTON NUMBER in Any Column

Car Make and Model	Control Shaft and Carrier Bracket [1] Assembly	Carrier [2] Bracket	Operating Cam	Brake Shoes Less Lining	Reinforcement Plate	Eccentric Adjusting Cam	Articulating Pin	Primary and Auxiliary or Primary and Secondary Shoe Spring	Primary or Secondary Shoe Spring
Stearns Knight, F-685..(1927-28) 14x2 Standard 3 Shoe	*DA-47-Lf.Fr. *DA-48-Rg.Fr. †DA-49-Lf.Fr. †DA-50-Rg.Fr. †DA-51-Fr. §DA-52-Fr. DA-53-Lf.Rr. DA-54-Rg.Rr.	¶DAA-1-Fr. ∥DAA-2 DAA-39-Rr. DAA-5 *DAA-40-Fr.	‡DAB-2-Fr. **DAB-1-Fr. ††DAB-43-Rr. ‡‡DAB-44-Rr. §§DAB-45-Rr. *DAB-4-Fr.	DD-17-Pri. DD-18-Sec. DD-17-Aux.	§DFA-11-Lf. §DFA-12-Rg.	§DFB-1 DFB-3	¶¶DFC-1 ∥∥DFC-4	DFD-6	DFE-1

* Used on 1925 and early in 1927.   ‡ Used on late 1926 cars.   ‡ Used before car Serial 606.   § Used on cars after Serial 606.   ¶ Used with Unflanged Cam.   ∥ Used with Flanged Cam.   ** Used with DAA-2 Brackets.   †† Used on early cars using brackets with two studs.   ‡‡ Used on cars using brackets with bronzed bushings.   ¶¶ Used with Take-up Cam with plain head.   ∥∥ Used with Take-up with groove in head.   §§ Used on late 1927 and on 1928 cars.

Car Make and Model	Control Shaft	Carrier	Operating Cam	Brake Shoes	Reinforcement	Eccentric	Articulating Pin	Pri./Aux. Spring	Pri./Sec. Spring
Stearns Knight, 8-85....(1927-28) 16x2½ Standard 3 Shoe	†DA-55-Lf.Fr. †DA-56-Rg.Fr. †DA-57-Lf.Fr. †DA-58-Rg.Fr. *DA-59-Lf.Rr. *DA-60-Rg.Rr. †DA-61-Lf.Rr. †DA-62-Rg.Rr.	*DAA-13-Fr. †DAA-42-Fr. DAA-43-Rr.	*DAB-46-Lf.Rr. *DAB-47-Rg.Rr. *DAB-19-Lf.Fr. †DAB-20-Rg.Fr. †DAB-21-Lf.Rr. †DAB-22-Rg.Rr.	DD-22-Pri. DD-23-Sec. DD-41-Aux.	DFA-26-Lf. DFA-27-Rg.	DFB-7	DFC-5	DFD-8	DFE-8

* Used before car Serial 650.   † Used after car Serial 650.

Car Make and Model	Control Shaft	Carrier	Operating Cam	Brake Shoes	Reinforcement	Eccentric	Articulating Pin	Pri./Aux. Spring	Pri./Sec. Spring
Stearns Knight, 8-90.......(1929) 16x2½ Duo Servo 2 Shoe	DA-67	DAA-4	DAB-5	DD-3-Pri. DD-3-Sec.	DFA-3	DFB-2	....	DFD-2	DFE-2
Studebaker, Dictator 6.....(1927) 12x1¾ Super Servo	....	....	DAB-50	DD-9-Pri. DD-10-Sec. DD-11-Aux.	DFA-6	DFB-4	DFC-3	*DFD-4	DFE-4

* Used with Steel Shoes.

Car Make and Model	Control Shaft	Carrier	Operating Cam	Brake Shoes	Reinforcement	Eccentric	Articulating Pin	Pri./Aux. Spring	Pri./Sec. Spring
Studebaker, Dictator 6..(1927-28) 12x1¾ Super Servo	....	....	*DAB-7-Lf.Fr. *DAB-8-Rg.Fr. *DAB-9-Rr. †DAB-51-Lf. †DAB-52-Rg.	DD-9-Pri. DD-10-Sec. DD-11-Aux.	DFA-28	DFB-4	DFC-3	DFD-4	DFE-4

* Used on cars not having bracket with bronzed bushing.   † Used on cars having bracket with bronzed bushing.

Car Make and Model	Control Shaft	Carrier	Operating Cam	Brake Shoes	Reinforcement	Eccentric	Articulating Pin	Pri./Aux. Spring	Pri./Sec. Spring
Studebaker, Com. 6 BG....(1928) 14x2 Standard 3 Shoe	*DA-63-Fr. *DA-64-Fr. ‡DA-46-Rr.	§DAA-2-Fr. DAA-8-Rr.	¶DAB-39-Fr. DAB-42-Rr.	DD-17-Pri. DD-18-Sec. DD-17-Aux.	DFA-13-Lf. DFA-14-Rg.	DFB-3	DFC-4	DFD-6	DFE-1

* Used before car Serial GH 4063817.   † Used after car Serial GH 4063817.   ‡ Interchangeable with DA-4.   § Used with Flanged Cam.   ¶ Interchangeable with DAB-1 on this car.

Car Make and Model	Control Shaft	Carrier	Operating Cam	Brake Shoes	Reinforcement	Eccentric	Articulating Pin	Pri./Aux. Spring	Pri./Sec. Spring
Studebaker, President 8 FA (1928) 14x2 Standard 3 Shoe	*DA-65 †DA-66-Fr. †‡DA-46-Rr.	§DAA-2-Fr. DAA-8-Rr.	¶DAB-39-Fr. DAB-42-Rr.	DD-17-Pri. DD-18-Sec. DD-17-Aux.	DFA-13-Lf. DFA-14-Rg.	DFB-3	DFC-4	DFD-6	DFE-1

* Used before car Serial 6009298 Rg. Side and 6009596 Lf. Side.   † Used after car Serial 6009298 Rg. Side and 6009596 Lf. Side.   ‡ Interchangeable with DA-4.   § Used with Flanged Cam.   ¶ Interchangeable with DAB-1 on this car.

Car Make and Model	Control Shaft	Carrier	Operating Cam	Brake Shoes	Reinforcement	Eccentric	Articulating Pin	Pri./Aux. Spring	Pri./Sec. Spring
Studebaker, President 8 FE(1929) 15x2¼ Servo Welded 3 Shoe	*DA-46	DAA-10	DAB-42	DD-38-Pri. DD-45-Sec. DD-40-Aux.	DFA-25	DFB-7	DFC-10	DFD-10	DFE-1

* Interchangeable with DA-4.

Car Make and Model	Control Shaft	Carrier	Operating Cam	Brake Shoes	Reinforcement	Eccentric	Articulating Pin	Pri./Aux. Spring	Pri./Sec. Spring
Studebaker, Com. 6 GJ....(1929) 12x1¾ Steel Servo	....	....	*DAB-50 DAB-51-Lf. DAB-52-Rg.	DD-9-Pri. DD-10-Sec. DD-11-Aux.	DFA-29	DFB-4	DFC-3	DFD-4	DFE-4

* Used with Super Servo type Brakes.

Car Make and Model	Control Shaft	Carrier	Operating Cam	Brake Shoes	Reinforcement	Eccentric	Articulating Pin	Pri./Aux. Spring	Pri./Sec. Spring
Studebaker, Dictator 8.....(1929) 11x1½ Super Servo	....	....	DAB-13-Lf. DAB-14-Rg.	DD-6-Pri. DD-46-Sec. DD-47-Aux.	DFA-5	DFB-4	DFC-3	DFD-4	DFE-4
Viking.............(1929-30) 14x2 Duo Servo 2 Shoe	....	DAA-11	DAB-12	DD-19-Pri. DD-19-Sec.	DFA-16	DFB-6	....	DFD-7	DFE-7
Whippet 93A.........(1927) 11x1½ Standard 3 Shoe *Front Brakes only.*	....	DAA-5	DAB-6	DD-4-Pri. DD-5-Sec. DD-4-Aux.	DFA-4	DFB-3	DFC-2-Pri. DFC-8-Aux.	DFD-3 DFD-5	DFE-3 DFE-1
Whippet, 96..........(1928-29) 11x1½ 2 Shoe	DA-26	DAA-20	....	DD-30-Pri. DD-30-Sec.	....	DFB-9	*DFC-6 †DFC-7	DFD-4	DFE-4

* Used before 1929 cars.   † Used on 1929 cars.   Front Brakes only.

Car Make and Model	Control Shaft	Carrier	Operating Cam	Brake Shoes	Reinforcement	Eccentric	Articulating Pin	Pri./Aux. Spring	Pri./Sec. Spring
Whippet, 98A..........(1929-30) 11x1½ Duo Servo 2 Shoe *Front Brakes only.*	....	DAA-6	DAB-12	DD-12-Pri. DD-12-Sec.	DFA-7	DFB-5	....	DFD-4	DFE-5
Willys-Knight 56.......(1928-29) 12x1¾ Standard 3 Shoe *Front Brakes only.*	....	DAA-5	DAB-18	DD-15-Pri. DD-16-Sec. DD-15-Aux.	DFA-10	DFB-3	DFC-4	DFD-5	DFE-1
Willys-Knight, 70B.......(1929) 12x1¾ Standard *Front Brakes only.*	....	DAA-5	DAB-18	DD-15-Pri. DD-16-Sec. DD-15-Aux.	DFA-30	DFB-3	DFC-4	DFD-5	DFE-1
Willys-Knight, 70B.......(1930) 12x1¾ Duo Servo	....	DAA-7	DAB-12	DD-21-Pri. DD-21-Sec.	DFA-7	DFB-5	....	DFD-4	DFE-5
Willys-Knight, 66B.......(1930) 14x2 Duo Servo 2 Shoe	....	DAA-11	DAB-12	DD-19-Pri. DD-19-Sec.	DFA-16	DFB-6	....	DFD-7	DFE-7
Willys Six, 98B..........(1930) 11x1½ Duo Servo 2 Shoe	....	DAA-6	DAB-12	DD-12-Pri. DD-12-Sec.	DFA-7	DFB-5	....	DFD-4	DFE-5

Abbreviations: Fr.—Front. Rr.—Rear. Lf.—Left. Rg.—Right. Pri.—Primary. Sec.—Secondary. Aux.—Auxiliary.
[1] Number refers to cable and conduit assembly if brakes are so operated.
[2] Number refers to anchor pin plate and crank assembly if brakes are cable operated.   [3] Long wheelbase.

BENDIX BRAKE PARTS—Continued

INTERCHANGEABLE COUNT

Showing exact number of times each Chilton Number occurs in Bendix table starting Page 251.

Control Shaft and Carrier Bracket Assembly	DA 34–1	DA 72–2	DAA 20–1	DAB 4–3	DAB 44–1	DD 27– 4	DFA 16–4	DFC 5–2
	DA 35–6	DA 73–2	DAA 21–2	DAB 5–2	DAB 45–1	DD 28– 2	DFA 17–1	DFC 6–1
	DA 36–1	DA 74–1	DAA 22–4	DAB 6–5	DAB 46–1	DD 29– 4	DFA 18–1	DFC 7–1
	DA 37–1	DA 75–1	DAA 23–2	DAB 7–2	DAB 47–1	DD 30– 2	DFA 19–2	DFC 8–1
	DA 38–2	DA 76–1	DAA 24–2	DAB 8–2	DAB 50–2	DD 31– 3	DFA 20–1	DFC 9–2
DA 1–1	DA 39–2	DA 77–1	DAA 25–2	DAB 9–3	DAB 51–2	DD 32– 3	DFA 21–1	DFC 10–5
DA 2–1	DA 40–2	DA 78–1	DAA 26–2	DAB 12–13	DAB 52–2	DD 33– 3	DFA 22–1	
DA 3–1	DA 41–2	DA 79–1	DAA 27–5	DAB 13–2		DD 34– 1	DFA 23–1	**Primary and Auxiliary or Primary and Secondary Shoe Spring**
DA 4–6	DA 42–1	DA 80–1	DAA 28–2	DAB 14–2	**Brakes Shoes Less Lining**	DD 35– 1	DFA 24–3	
DA 5–1	DA 43–1	DA 81–1	DAA 29–2	DAB 15–7		DD 36– 1	DFA 25–2	
DA 6–1	DA 44–1	DA 82–1	DAA 30–1	DAB 16–12		DD 37– 2	DFA 26–1	
DA 7–1	DA 45–1	DA 83–1	DAA 31–1	DAB 17–1	DD 1– 2	DD 38– 2	DFA 27–1	
DA 8–1	DA 46–3	DA 84–1	DAA 32–2	DAB 18–3	DD 2– 1	DD 39– 1	DFA 28–1	DFD 1–4
DA 9–1	DA 47–1	DA 85–1	DAA 33–2	DAB 19 2	DD 3– 4	DD 40– 2	DFA 29–1	DFD 2–5
DA 10–1	DA 48–1		DAA 34–2	DAB 20–2	DD 4– 6	DD 41– 1	DFA 30–1	DFD 3–3
DA 11–1	DA 49–1	**Carrier Bracket**	DAA 35–2	DAB 21–2	DD 5– 3	DD 45– 1		DFD 4–24
DA 12–1	DA 50–1		DAA 36–3	DAB 22–2	DD 6– 4	DD 46– 1	**Eccentric Adjusting Cam**	DFD 5–12
DA 13–1	DA 51–1		DAA 37–3	DAB 23–1	DD 7– 3	DD 47– 1		DFD 6–9
DA 14–1	DA 52–1	DAA 1–6	DAA 39–1	DAB 24–1	DD 8– 3			DFD 7–6
DA 15–1	DA 53–1	DAA 2–11	DAA 42–1	DAB 25–1	DD 9– 3	**Reinforcement Plate**		DFD 8–2
DA 16–1	DA 54–1	DAA 3–1	DAA 43–1	DAB 26–1	DD 10– 3		DFB 1–6	DFD 9–1
DA 17–1	DA 55–1	DAA 4–2	DAA 44–1	DAB 27–1	DD 11– 3		DFB 2–2	DFD 10–7
DA 18–1	DA 56–1	DAA 5–10	DAA 45–2	DAB 28–1	DD 12–12	DFA 1–3	DFB 3–24	DFD 11–2
DA 19–1	DA 57–1	DAA 6–5	DAA 46–2	DAB 29–2	DD 13– 4	DFA 2–3	DFB 4–7	
DA 20–1	DA 58–1	DAA 7–3	DAA 47–2	DAB 30–2	DD 14– 2	DFA 3–2	DFB 5–16	**Primary or Secondary Shoe Spring**
DA 21–1	DA 59–1	DAA 8–4	DAA 48–2	DAB 31–4	DD 15–20	DFA 4–2	DFB 6–9	
DA 22–1	DA 60–1	DAA 9–2	DAA 49–2	DAB 32–4	DD 16–10	DFA 5–4	DFB 7–7	
DA 23 2	DA 61–1	DAA 10–7	DAA 50–2	DAB 33–3	DD 17–16	DFA 6–1	DFB 8–1	
DA 24 1	DA 62–1	DAA 11–4	DAA 51–2	DAB 34–6	DD 18– 8	DFA 7–8	DFB 9–1	DFE 1–28
DA 25–1	DA 63–1	DAA 12–1	DAA 52–2	DAB 35–1	DD 19–13	DFA 8–1		DFE 2– 2
DA 26–1	DA 64–1	DAA 13–2		DAB 36–1	DD 20– 8	DFA 9–1	**Articulating Pin**	DFE 3– 3
DA 27–1	DA 65–1	DAA 14–1	**Operating Cam**	DAB 37–3	DD 21– 4	DFA 10–9		DFE 4– 8
DA 28–1	DA 66–1	DAA 15–1		DAB 38–3	DD 22– 2	DFA 11–2		DFE 5–10
DA 29–1	DA 67–1	DAA 16–2		DAB 39–2	DD 23– 3	DFA 12–2	DFC 1–6	DFE 6– 7
DA 30–2	DA 68–2	DAA 17–1	DAB 1–10	DAB 40–3	DD 24– 6	DFA 13–6	DFC 2–3	DFE 7– 9
DA 31–2	DA 69–2	DAA 18–1	DAB 2–6	DAB 41–3	DD 25– 4	DFA 14–6	DFC 3–21	DFE 8–12
DA 32–1	DA 70–1	DAA 19–1	DAB 3–1	DAB 42–4	DD 26– 2	DFA 15–1	DFC 4–21	DFE 9– 2
DA 33–2	DA 71–1			DAB 43–1				

BRAKE ASSEMBLIES
Section 2

LOCKHEED HYDRAULIC BRAKE PARTS—First Group
See instructions at beginning of BRAKE ASSEMBLIES, page 251

Interchangeable Parts have the same CHILTON NUMBER in any Column

NOTE: In this table the same CHILTON NUMBERS occur frequently in both the forward and the reverse brake shoe columns. In such instances the forward and reverse shoes are interchangeable.

CAR MAKE AND MODEL	MASTER CYLINDER					BRAKE SHOES**		Anchor Pin or Stud (All Wheels)	Brake Shoe or Band Return Spring
	Complete Assembly	Cylinder Casting or Head and Bbl.	Piston Cup	Piston Stop	Master Piston Assembly	Complete Brake Shoe Assembly (Forward)	Complete Brake Shoe Assembly (Reverse)		
Auburn, 4-44..........................(1926)	DI-1	DIA-1	DIB-1	DIC-1	DID-1	....	....	....	DOB-1
Auburn, 76, 88 (Early)................(1928)	DI-2	DIA-2	DIB-2	{DIC-2 DIC-3	DID-2	DL-1	DL-14	DOA-1	DOB-2
Auburn, 76, 88 (Late)...............(1928)	DI-3	DIA-3	DIB-2	DIC-4	DID-3	DL-27	DL-63	DOA-1	DOB-2
Auburn, 115 (Early)................(1928)	DI-2	DIA-2	DIB-2	DIC-3	DID-2	DL-50	DL-64	DOA-2	DOB-3
Auburn, 115 (Late)................(1928)	DI-3	DIA-3	DIB-2	DIC-4	DID-3	DL-2	DL-15	DOA-2	DOB-3
Auburn, 6-80, 8-90 (Channel Shoes).......(1929)	DI-3	DIA-3	DIB-2	DIC-4	DID-3	{DL-33F. DL-3R.	{DL-33F. DL-3R.	DOA-3	DOB-4
Auburn, 120 (Channel Shoes)..........(1929)	DI-3	DIA-3	DIB-2	DIC-4	DID-3	DL-4	DL-4	DOA-4	DOB-5
Auburn 6-85 (Channel Shoes)..........(1930)	DI-3	DIA-3	DIB-2	DIC-4	DID-3	DL-58	DL-58	DOA-3	DOB-4
Auburn 8-95 (Channel Shoes)..........(1930)	DI-3	DIA-3	DIB-2	DIC-4	DID-3	DL-58	DL-58	DOA-3	DOB-4
Auburn 125 (Channel Shoes)..........(1930)	DI-3	DIA-3	DIB-2	DIC-4	DID-3	DL-59	DL-59	DOA-4	DOB-5
Case (Columbia Axle)...............(1926-27)	DI-1	DIA-1	DIB-1	DIC-1	DID-1	....	....	....	DOB-1
Chalmers (Eaton Axle)...............(1925)	DI-1	DIA-1	DIB-1	DIC-1	DID-1	....	....	....	DOB-1
Chrysler, 58.......................(1925)	DI-4	DIA-4	DIB-3	DIC-5	DID-4	....	....	....	DOB-1
Chrysler, 70.......................(1925)	{*DI-5 DI-8	{DIA-5 DIA-6	DIB-3	DIC-5	DID-4	....	....	....	DOB-1
Chrysler, 58.......................(1926)	DI-11	DIA-7	DIB-4	DIC-6	DID-5	....	....	....	DOB-1
Chrysler, 80.......................(1927)	DI-16	DIA-10	DIB-9	DIC-7	DID-6	....	....	....	DOB-1
Chrysler 60, 1926-27, †62.............(1928)	DI-12	DIA-8	DIB-4	DIC-6	DID-5	....	....	....	DOB-1
Chrysler 70, 1926-27, †72.............(1928)	DI-14	DIA-9	DIB-4	DIC-6	DID-5	....	....	....	DOB-1
Chrysler, 80.......................(1928-29)	DI-17	DIA-11	DIB-2	{DIC-3 DIC-2	DID-2	{DL-5-Lf. DL-6-Rg.	{DL-16-Rg. DL-17-Lf.	....	DOB-6
Chrysler, 65 (Back-to-Back Shoes).......(1929)	DI-18	DIA-12	DIB-2	DIC-4	DID-3	DL-7	DL-18	DOA-5	DOB-7
Chrysler, 66 (T-Section Shoes)........(1929-30)	DI-19	DIA-13	DIB-2	DIC-4	DID-3	DL-8	DL-19	DOA-6	DOB-8
Chrysler, 70, 77 (T-Section Shoes)....(1929-30)	DI-19	DIA-13	DIB-2	DIC-4	DID-3	DL-9	DL-20	DOA-5	DOB-7
Chrysler, 75 (3 Piece Pressed Steel Shoes)..(1929)	DI-18	DIA-12	DIB-2	DIC-4	DID-3	DL-10	DL-21	DOA-7	DOB-7
Chrysler 6 (T-Section Shoes)..........(1930)	DI-6	DIA-25	DIB-2	DIC-4	DID-14	DL-8	DL-19	DOA-6	DOB-8
Cord (Front Drive).................(1929-30)	DI-23	DIA-3	DIB-2	DIC-4	DID-3	DL-53	DL-61	DOA-16	DOB-16
Davis, 92, 93 (1926-27); 94, 98........(1927)	DI-1	DIA-1	DIB-1	DIC-1	DID-1	....	....	....	DOB-1
De Soto 6.......................(1929-30)	DI-20	DIA-12	DIB-2	DIC-4	DID-3	DL-8	DL-19	DOA-6	DOB-8
De Soto 8.......................(1930)	DI-6	DIA-25	DIB-2	DIC-4	DID-14	DL-8	DL-19	DOA-6	DOB-8
Diana, Str. 8....................(1926-27-28)	DI-1	DIA-1	DIB-1	DIC-1	DID-1	....	....	....	DOB-1
Dodge, Senior 6..................(1928)	DI-2	DIA-2	DIB-2	{DIC-2 DIC-3	DID-2	{DL-23F. DL-13R.	{DL-24F. DL-25R.	DOA-2	{DOB-9 DOB-10
Dodge, Victory 6, 130...............(1928)	DI-2	DIA-2	DIB-2	{DIC-2 DIC-3	DID-7	DL-11	DL-48	DOA-1	DOB-2
Dodge, DA (Channel Shoes)............(1929)	DI-20	DIA-12	DIB-2	DIC-4	DID-3	DL-26	DL-26	DOA-3	DOB-4
Dodge, Senior.....................(1929)	DI-21	DIA-14	DIB-2	{DIC-2 DIC-3	DID-2	DL-51	DL-65	DOA-2	DOB-9
Dodge DD-6.......................(1930)	DI-6	DIA-25	DIB-2	DIC-4	DID-14	DL-8	DL-19	DOA-6	DOB-8
Dodge DC-8.......................(1930)	DI-6	DIA-25	DIB-2	DIC-4	DID-14	DL-34	DL-35	DOA-6	DOB-8
Elcar, 6-65 (1926); 8-80............(1926-27) 8-85, 8-91, 92, 120...............(1927-28)	DI-1	DIA-1	DIB-1	DIC-1	DID-1	....	....	....	DOB-1
Elcar, 6-70, 8-82 (1927-28); 8-78........(1928)	DI-22	DIA-15	DIB-5	DIC-8	DID-8	....	....	....	DOB-1
Elcar, 6-75 (Die Cast Shoes)........(1929-30)	DI-23	DIA-3	DIB-2	DIC-4	DID-3	DL-27	DL-63	DOA-1	DOB-2
Elcar, 95, 120 (Malleable Shoes).......(1929-30)	DI-23	DIA-3	DIB-2	DIC-4	DID-3	DL-2	DL-15	DOA-8	DOB-3
Flint, 40, 55, 60 (1925); 80......(1925-26-27)	DI-24	DIA-16	DIB-6	....	DID-9	DL-30	DL-30	{DOA-9 DOA-10	{DOB-11 DOB-12
Franklin, Airman..................(1927-28)	DI-25	DIA-2	DIB-2	{DIC-2 DIC-3	DID-2	{DL-31F. DL-32R.	DL-31	DOA-2	DOB-3
Franklin 130, 135, 137 (Die Cast Shoes)...(1929)	DI-25	DIA-2	DIB-2	{DIC-2 DIC-3	DID-2	DL-54	DL-54	DOA-2	DOB-5
Franlin 130,135,137 (Late) (Channel Shoes)..(1929)	DI-25	DIA-2	DIB-2	DIC-2	DID-2	DL-33	DL-33	DOA-4	DOB-5
Franklin, 145, 147.................(1930)	DI-26	DIA-2	DIB-2	DIC-4	DID-3	DL-33	DL-33	DOA-4	DOB-5
Gardner, 8-85....................(1928)	DI-2	DIA-2	DIB-2	{DIC-2 DIC-3	DID-2	DL-1	DL-14	DOA-1	DOB-2
Gardner, 8-95....................(1928)	DI-2	DIA-2	DIB-2	{DIC-2 DIC-3	DID-2	DL-50	DL-64	DOA-2	DOB-3
Gardner, 120, 125.................(1929)	DI-23	DIA-3	DIB-2	DIC-4	DID-3	DL-27	DL-63	DOA-1	DOB-2
Gardner, 130.....................(1929)	DI-23	DIA-3	DIB-2	DIC-4	DID-3	DL-2	DL-15	DOA-2	DOB-3
Gardner, 120, 125 (1929); 136, 140 (Channel Shoes)......................(1929-30)	DI-23	DIA-3	DIB-2	DIC-4	DID-3	{DL-33F. DL-3R.	{DL-33F. DL-3R.	DOA-3	DOB-4
Gardner, 130 (1929); 150 (Channel Shoes)(1929-30)	DI-23	DIA-3	DIB-2	DIC-4	DID-3	DL-4	DL-4	DOA-4	DOB-5
Graham Paige, 610.................(1928-29)	{DI-27 °DI-28	{DIA-17 DIA-18	DIB-5	DIC-8	DID-8	....	....	....	DOB-1
Graham Paige, 614.................(1928-29)	DI-30	DIA-20	DIB-7	DIC-2	DID-10	....	....	....	DOB-1
Graham Paige, 615, Spec. 6, Std. and Spec. 8 (1929-30).....................	DI-29	DIA-19	DIB-2	DIC-4	DID-3	DL-28	DL-29	DOA-8	DOB-3
Graham Paige, 619, 629, 835..........(1928-29)	DI-2	DIA-2	DIB-2	{DIC-2 DIC-3	DID-2	DL-38	DL-39	DOA-12	DOB-13
Graham Paige, 612, Std. 6...........(1929-30)	DI-29	DIA-19	DIB-2	DIC-4	DID-3	DL-36	DL-37	DOA-11	DOB-2
Graham Paige, 621, 827, 837 Cust. 8....(1929-30)	DI-29	DIA-19	DIB-2	DIC-4	DID-3	DL-12	DL-40	DOA-12	DOB-13
Hupmobile, 8......................(1925)	DI-1	DIA-1	DIB-1	DIC-1	DID-1	....	....	....	DOB-1
Jewett, 23, 25....................(1925)	DI-31	DIA-21	DIB-8	DIC-8	DID-11	....	....	....	DOB-1
Jewett, New Day, Paige 6-45..........(1926-27)	DI-32	DIA-1	DIB-1	DIC-8	DID-11	....	....	....	DOB-1
Jordan, R Small 6.................(1927-28)	DI-22	DIA-15	DIB-5	DIC-8	DID-8	....	....	....	DOB-1
Jordan, K, L (1925); Line 8 A (1925-26); J (1926-27); JE, JJ.............(1928-29)	DI-1	DIA-1	DIB-1	DIC-1	DID-1	....	....	....	DOB-1
Jordan, G, T, E...................(1929)	DI-23	DIA-3	DIB-2	DIC-4	DID-3	DL-4	DL-4	DOA-4	DOB-5
Kissel, 8-75 (1925-26-27); 6-80 (1926); 6-55 (1926-27); 8-65 (1927); 8-80, 8-90....(1928)	DI-1	DIA-1	DIB-1	DIC-1	DID-1	....	....	....	DOB-1
Kissel, 6-70.....................(1928)	DI-22	DIA-15	DIB-5	DIC-8	DID-8	....	....	....	DOB-1
Kissel, 6-73 (Die Cast Shoes).........(1929)	DI-23	DIA-3	DIB-2	DIC-4	DID-3	DL-27	DL-63	DOA-1	DOB-2
Kissel, 8-95 (Die Cast Shoes).........(1929)	DI-23	DIA-3	DIB-2	DIC-4	DID-3	DL-2	DL-15	DOA-2	DOB-3

LOCKHEED HYDRAULIC BRAKE PARTS—First Group

Interchangeable Parts have the same CHILTON NUMBER in any Column

CAR MAKE AND MODEL	MASTER CYLINDER					BRAKE SHOES**		Anchor Pin or Stud (All Wheels)	Brake Shoe or Band Return Spring
	Complete Assembly	Cylinder Casting or Head and Bbl.	Piston Cup	Piston Stop	Master Piston Assembly	Complete Brake Shoe Assembly (Forward)	Complete Brake Shoe Assembly (Reverse)		
Kissel, 126 (3 Piece Pressed Steel Shoes)...(1929)	DI-23	DIA-3	DIB-2	DIC-4	DID-3	{DL-41R. DL-42L.	{DL-41R. DL-42L.	....	DOB-6
Kissel, 8-126 (Channel Shoes)............(1929)	DI-23	DIA-3	DIB-2	DIC-4	DID-3	DL-43	DL-43	DOA-13	DOB-14
McFarlan, Light 6 (1925-26); TV6 (1925-26-27-28); 8 in Line................(1926-27-28)	DI-1	DIA-1	DIB-1	DIC-1	DID-1	....	....		DOB-1
Moon, London, Metropolitan, Newport (1925) Series A.............(1925-26-27-28)	DI-1	DIA-1	DIB-1	DIC-1	DID-1	....	....		DOB-1
Moon, 6-60, 6-62, 6-72..........(1926-27-28-29)	DI-33	DIA-15	DIB-5	DIC-8	DID-12	....	....		DOB-1
Moon, 8-80, 8-82.................(1928-29)	DI-30	DIA-20	DIB-7	DIC-2	DID-10	....	....		DOB-1
Moon 6-72 (Int. Brakes) 6-75, 6-77, 8-92 (1929-30)	DI-23	DIA-3	DIB-2	DIC-4	DID-3	{DL-33F. DL-3R.	....	DOA-3	DOB-4
Paige, 21 (1924-25); 6-70 (1925-26); 24.....(1926)	DI-31	DIA-21	DIB-8	DIC-8	DID-11	....	....		DOB-1
Paige, 8-85....................(1927-28)	DI-34	DIA-15	DIB-5	DIC-8	DID-13	....	....		DOB-1
Paige, 6-45 After Chassis 320537 6-65 After Chassis 167138 }...(1927-28) 6-75 After Chassis 117138	DI-22	DIA-15	DIB-5	DIC-8	DID-8	....	....		DOB-1
Peerless, 60.................(1927)	DI-22	DIA-15	DIB-5	DIC-8	DID-8	....	....		DOB-1
Peerless, 6-80 (1926); 80, 90.........(1927-28)	DI-1	DIA-1	DIB-1	DIC-1	DID-1	....	....		DOB-1
Peerless, 61.......................(1929)	DI-35	DIA-3	DIB-2	DIC-4	DID-3	DL-11	DL-26	DOA-1	DOB-2
Peerless, 81.......................(1929)	DI-36	DIA-2	DIB-2	{DIC-2 DIC-3	DID-2	DL-11	DL-26	DOA-1	DOB-2
Peerless, 91.....................(1928-29)	DI-36	DIA-2	DIB-2	{DIC-2 DIC-3	DID-2	DL-55	DL-22	DOA-2	DOB-3
Peerless, 8-125 (Channel Shoes).......(1929-30)	DI-2	DIA-2	DIB-2	{DIC-2 DIC-3	DID-2	{DL-56F. DL-44R.	{DL-56F. DL-44R.	DOA-13	DOB-14
Plymouth.......................(1928)	DI-37	DIA-3	DIB-2	DIC-4	DID-3	DL-57	DL-46	DOA-6	DOB-8
Plymouth.....................(1929-30)	DI-38	DIA-3	DIB-2	DIC-4	DID-3	DL-8	DL-19	DOA-6	DOB-8
Reo, Wolverine B..............(1927)	DI-2	DIA-2	DIB-2	{DIC-2 DIC-3	DID-2	DL-1	DL-14	DOA-1	DOB-2
Reo, Flying Cloud, Series "A".........(1927-28)	DI-2	DIA-2	DIB-2	{DIC-2 DIC-3	DID-2	DL-45	DL-45	DOA-14	DOB-9
Reo, Flying Cloud (1928) Master......(1929)	DI-2	DIA-2	DIB-2	{DIC-2 DIC-3	DID-2	DL-50	DL-49	DOA-2	DOB-3
Reo, Wolverine B (1928); Mate..........(1929)	DI-2	DIA-2	DIB-2	DIC-2	DID-2	DL-1	DL-14	DOA-1	DOB-2
Reo 15......................(1930)	DI-2	DIA-2	DIB-2	DIC-2	DID-2	DL-1	DL-14	DOA-1	DOB-2
Reo 20, 25 (Early)...................(1930)	DI-2	DIA-2	DIB-2	DIC-2	DID-2	DL-50	DL-49	DOA-2	DOB-3
Reo 20, 25 (Late)....................(1930)	DI-21	DIA-2	DIB-2	{DIC-2 DIC-3	DID-2	DL-60	DL-62	DOA-2	DOB-3
Stutz, 6.....................(1925)	DI-1	DIA-1	DIB-1	DIC-1	DID-1	....	....		DOB-1
Stutz, AA....................(1926-27)	DI-23	DIA-3	DIB-2	DIC-4	DID-3	{DL-41R. DL-42L.	{DL-41R. DL-42L.		DOB-6
Stutz, BB.....................(1927)	DI-2	DIA-2	DIB-2	DIC-3	DID-2	{DL-41R. DL-42L.	{DL-41R. DL-42L.		DOB-15
Stutz, BB.....................(1928)	DI-2	DIA-2	DIB-2	{DIC-2 DIC-3	DID-2	{DL-41R. DL-42L.	{DL-41R. DL-42L.		DOB-6
Stutz, L (Channel Shoes)...............(1929)	DI-39	DIA-2	DIB-2	DIC-2	DID-2	DL-52	DL-52	DOA-4	DOB-5
Stutz, M....................(1929)	DI-30	DIA-20	DIB-7	DIC-2	DID-10	DL-56	DL-56	DOA-15	DOB-14
Velie, 59 (1925-26); 60...........(1925-26-27)	DI-1	DIA-1	DIB-1	DIC-1	DID-1	....	....		DOB-1
Velie, 6-50.....................(1927-28)	DI-33	DIA-15	DIB-5	DIC-8	DID-12	....	....		DOB-1
Velie, 66, 77, 88....................(1928)	DI-2	DIA-2	DIB-2	{DIC-2 DIC-3	DID-2	DL-50	DL-49	DOA-2	DOB-3
Wills St. Claire......................(1926)	DI-1	DIA-1	DIB-1	DIC-1		....	....		DOB-1

** Complete brake shoe assemblies have lining attached. Bare brake shoes are not available.
* Master Cylinder Assembly with high mounting base.
† Late 62 and 72 models use DI-13 master cylinder assembly and casting DIA-24 with plug for stop light switch (Piston cup DIB-4, Piston stop DIC-6 and Piston assembly DID-5).

° Used after 3000 cars.
F—Front.
R—Rear.
Lf—Left Side.
Rg—Right Side.

INTERCHANGEABLE COUNT

Showing exact number of times each CHILTON NUMBER occurs in Lockheed Brake Table—First Group beginning opposite.

Complete Assembly								Brake Shoe or Band Return Spring
	DI-28-1	DIA-8-1	DIB-7-3	DID-6-1	DL-13-1	DL-38-1	DL-64-2	
	DI-29-3	DIA-9-1	DIB-8-2	DID-7-1	DL-14-6	DL-39-1	DL-65-1	
	DI-30-3	DIA-10-1	DIB-9-1	DID-8-6	DL-15-4	DL-40-1		
DI-1-15	DI-31-2	DIA-11-1		DID-9-1	DL-16-1	DL-41-4		DOB-1-34
DI-2-17	DI-32-1	DIA-12-4	**Piston Stop**	DID-10-3	DL-17-1	DL-42-8	**Anchor Pin or Stud (All wheels)**	DOB-2-13
DI-3-7	DI-33-3	DIA-13-2		DID-11-3	DL-18-1	DL-43-2		DOB-3-14
DI-4-1	DI-34-1	DIA-14-1	DIC-1-15	DID-12-2	DL-19-6	DL-44-2		DOB-4-6
DI-5-1	DI-35-1	DIA-15-8	DIC-2-26	DID-13-1	DL-20-1	DL-45-2	DOA-1-12	DOB-5-7
DI-6-4	DI-36-2	DIA-16-1	DIC-3-20	DID-14-4	DL-21-1	DL-46-1	DOA-2-14	DOB-6-4
DI-8-1	DI-37-1	DIA-17-1	DIC-4-38		DL-22-1	DL-48-1	DOA-3-6	DOB-7-3
DI-11-1	DI-38-1	DIA-18-1	DIC-5-2		DL-23-1	DL-49-3	DOA-4-7	DOB-8-8
DI-12-1	DI-39-1	DIA-19-3	DIC-6-3	**Brake Shoes**	DL-24-1	DL-50-5	DOA-5-2	DOB-9-3
DI-14-1		DIA-20-3	DIC-7-1		DL-25-1	DL-51-2	DOA-6-8	DOB-10-1
DI-16-1		DIA-21-2	DIC-8-12	DL-1-5	DL-26-4	DL-52-1	DOA-7-1	DOB-11-1
DI-17-1	**Cylinder Casting or Head & Bbl.**	DIA-25-4		DL-2-4	DL-27-3	DL-53-1	DOA-8-2	DOB-12-1
DI-18-2				DL-3-5	DL-28-1	DL-54-2	DOA-9-1	DOB-13-2
DI-19-2		**Piston Cup**	**Master Piston Assembly**	DL-4-6	DL-29-1	DL-55-1	DOA-10-1	DOB-14-3
DI-20-2				DL-5-1	DL-30-2	DL-56-4	DOA-11-1	DOB-15-1
DI-21-2	DIA-1-16	DIB-1-16	DID-1-14	DL-6-1	DL-31-2	DL-57-1	DOA-12-2	DOB-16-1
DI-22-5	DIA-2-24	DIB-2-64	DID-2-25	DL-7-1	DL-32-1	DL-58-4	DOA-13-2	
DI-23-14	DIA-3-25	DIB-3-2	DID-3-34	DL-8-6	DL-33-9	DL-59-2	DOA-14-1	
DI-24-1	DIA-4-1	DIB-4-3	DID-4-2	DL-9-1	DL-34-1	DL-60-1	DOA-15-1	
DI-25-3	DIA-5-1	DIB-5-9	DID-5-3	DL-10-1	DL-35-1	DL-61-1	DOA-16-1	
DI-26-1	DIA-6-1	DIB-6-1		DL-11-3	DL-36-1	DL-62-1		
DI-27-1	DIA-7-1			DL-12-1	DL-37-1	DL-63-4		

LOCKHEED HYDRAULIC BRAKE PARTS—Second Group

Interchangeable Parts have the same CHILTON NUMBER in Any Column

Note: In this table, the same CHILTON NUMBERS for the front-wheel cylinder assemblies and their component parts occur frequently in the columns covering the rear-wheel cylinders. In such instances the front and rear parts are interchangeable.

CAR, MAKE AND MODEL	FRONT WHEEL CYLINDER, RIGHT AND LEFT				REAR WHEEL CYLINDER, RIGHT AND LEFT				Hose Assembly Front and Rear ††
	Cylinder Assembly	Cylinder Casting	Piston Cup	Piston Boot	Cylinder Assembly	Cylinder Casting	Piston Cup	Piston Boot	
Auburn, 4-44...........................(1926)	DJ-1-R / DJ-39-L	DJA-1-R / DJA-2-L	DJB-1	DJC-1	DJ-23-R / DJ-33-L	DJA-20-R / DJA-21-L	DJB-1	DJC-1	DOC-5-F / DOC-6-R
Auburn, 76, 88........................(1928)	DJ-2	DJA-3	DJB-2	DJC-2	DJ-2	DJA-3	DJB-2	DJC-2	DOC-1
Auburn, 115..........................(1928)	DJ-2	DJA-3	DJB-2	DJC-2	DJ-2	DJA-3	DJB-2	DJC-2	DOC-1
Auburn, 6-80, 8-90 (Channel Shoes).......(1929)	DJ-2	DJA-3	DJB-2	DJC-2	DJ-2	DJA-3	DJB-2	DJC-2	DOC-1
Auburn, 120 (Channel Shoes)...........(1929)	DJ-2	DJA-3	DJB-2	DJC-2	DJ-2	DJA-3	DJB-2	DJC-2	DOC-1
Auburn 6-85 (Channel Shoes)...........(1930)	DJ-2	DJA-3	DJB-2	DJC-2	DJ-2	DJA-3	DJB-2	DJC-2	DOC-1
Auburn 8-95 (Channel Shoes)...........(1930)	DJ-2	DJA-3	DJB-2	DJC-2	DJ-2	DJA-3	DJB-2	DJC-2	DOC-1
Auburn 125 (Channel Shoes)...........(1930)	DJ-2	DJA-3	DJB-2	DJC-2	DJ-2	DJA-3	DJB-2	DJC-2	DOC-1
Case (Columbia Axle)................(1926-27)	DJ-1-R / DJ-39-L	DJA-1-R / DJA-2-L	DJB-1	DJC-1	DJ-23-R / DJ-33-L	DJA-20-R / DJA-21-L	DJB-1	DJC-1	DOC-2
Chalmers (Eaton Axle)...............(1925)	DJ-3	....	DJB-1	DJC-1	DJ-3	....	DJB-1	DJC-1	DOC-4
Chrysler, 58.........................(1926)	DJ-4	DJA-4	DJB-3	....	DJ-26	DJA-22	DJB-3	....	DOC-4
Chrysler, 70.........................(1926)	DJ-4	DJA-4	DJB-3		DJ-4	DJA-4	DJB-3	....	DOC-7
Chrysler, 58.........................(1927)	DJ-5	DJA-5	DJB-4	DJC-3	DJ-5	DJA-5	DJB-4	DJC-3	DOC-5
Chrysler, 60 (1927); 62............(1928)	DJ-5	DJA-5	DJB-4	DJC-3	DJ-5	DJA-5	DJB-4	DJC-3	DOC-5
Chrysler, 70 (1927); 72............(1928)	DJ-5	DJA-5	DJB-4	DJC-3	DJ-5	DJA-5	DJB-4	DJC-3	DOC-5
Chrysler, 80.........................(1927)	DJ-6	DJA-6	DJB-3	DJC-1	DJ-6	DJA-6	DJB-3	DJC-1	DOC-5
Chrysler, 80.......................(1928-29)	DJ-7	DJA-7	DJB-5	DJC-4	DJ-19	DJA-3	DJB-2	DJC-4	DOC-1
Chrysler, 65 (Back-to-back Shoes).........(1929)	DJ-8	DJA-8	DJB-5	DJC-4	DJ-40	DJA-9	DJB-2	DJC-4	DOC-1
Chrysler, 66 (T-Section Shoes)........(1929-30)	DJ-40	DJA-9	DJB-2	DJC-4	DJ-40	DJA-9	DJB-2	DJC-4	DOC-1
Chrysler, 70, 77 (T-Section Shoes)....(1929-30)	DJ-8	DJA-8	DJB-5	DJC-4	DJ-40	DJA-9	DJB-2	DJC-4	DOC-1
Chrysler, 75 (3-Piece Pressed Steel Shoes)...(1929)	DJ-8	DJA-8	DJB-5	DJC-4	DJ-40	DJA-9	DJB-2	DJC-4	DOC-1
Chrysler 6 (T-Section Shoes).........(1929-30)	DJ-40	DJA-9	DJB-2	DJC-4	DJ-40	DJA-9	DJB-2	DJC-4	DOC-1
Cord.............................(1929-30)	DJ-42	DJA-36	DJB-5	DJC-2	DJ-2	DJA-3	DJB-2	DJC-2	DOC-1
Davis, 92, 93 (1926-27); 94, 98.........(1927)	DJ-1-R / DJ-39-L	DJA-1-R / DJA-2-L	DJB-1	DJC-1	DJ-23-R / DJ-33-L	DJA-20-R / DJA-21-L	DJB-1	DJC-1	DOC-6
De Soto 6.........................(1929-30)	DJ-40	DJA-9	DJB-2	DJC-4	DJ-40	DJA-9	DJB-2	DJC-4	DOC-2
De Soto 8............................(1930)	DJ-40	DJA-9	DJB-2	DJC-4	DJ-40	DJA-9	DJB-2	DJC-4	DOC-1
Diana, Str. 8.................(1926-27-28)	DJ-1-R / DJ-39-L	DJA-1 / DJA-2	DJB-1	DJC-1	DJ-23-R / DJ-33-L	DJA-20-R / DJA-21-L	DJB-1	DJC-1	DOC-2
Dodge Senior 6.......................(1928)	DJ-2	DJA-3	DJB-2	DJC-2	DJ-2	DJA-3	DJB-2	DJC-2	DOC-1
Dodge, Victory 6, 130.................(1928)	DJ-2	DJA-3	DJB-2	DJC-2	DJ-2	DJA-3	DJB-2	DJC-2	DOC-1
Dodge, DA (Channel Shoes)............(1929)	DJ-2	DJA-3	DJB-2	DJC-2	DJ-2	DJA-3	DJB-2	DJC-2	DOC-1
Dodge, Senior........................(1929)	DJ-2	DJA-3	DJB-2	DJC-2	DJ-2	DJA-3	DJB-2	DJC-2	DOC-1
Dodge DD6...........................(1930)	DJ-40	DJA-9	DJB-2	DJC-4	DJ-40	DJA-9	DJB-2	DJC-4	DOC-1
Dodge DC 8..........................(1930)	DJ-8	DJA-8	DJB-5	DJC-4	DJ-40	DJA-9	DJB-2	DJC-4	DOC-1
Elcar, 6-65 (1926); 8-80 (1926-27); 8-85 8-91, 92, 120...(1927-28)	DJ-1-R / DJ-39-L	DJA-1-R / DJA-2-L	DJB-1	DJC-1	DJ-23-R / DJ-33-L	DJA-20-R / DJA-21-L	DJB-1	DJC-1	DOC-2
Elcar, 6-70, 8-82 (1927-28); 8-78.........(1928)	DJ-9-R / DJ-10-L	DJA-10-R / DJA-11-L	DJB-6	DJC-3	DJ-27	DJA-24	DJB-6	DJC-3	DOC-1-F / DOC-2-R
Elcar, 6-75 (Die Cast Shoes)..........(1929-30)	DJ-2	DJA-3	DJB-2	DJC-2	DJ-2	DJA-3	DJB-2	DJC-2	DOC-1
Elcar, 95, 120 (Malleable Shoes).......(1929-30)	DJ-2	DJA-3	DJB-2	DJC-2	DJ-2	DJA-3	DJB-2	DJC-2	DOC-1
Flint, 40, 55, 60 (1925); 80.........(1925-26-27)	DJ-11-R / DJ-12-L	DJA-12-R / DJA-13-L	DJB-6	DJC-5	DJ-28-R / DJ-37-L	DJA-25-R / DJA-26-L	DJB-6	DJC-5	DOC-1
Franklin, Airman...................(1927-28)	DJ-2	DJA-3	DJB-2	DJC-2	DJ-2	DJA-3	DJB-2	DJC-2	DOC-1
Franklin, 130, 135, 137 (Die Cast Shoes).(1929)	DJ-2	DJA-3	DJB-2	DJC-2	DJ-2	DJA-3	DJB-2	DJC-2	DOC-1
Franklin, 130, 135, 137 (Late)(Channel S.).(1929)	DJ-2	DJA-3	DJB-2	DJC-2	DJ-2	DJA-3	DJB-2	DJC-2	DOC-1
Franklin, 145, 147....................(1930)	DJ-2	DJA-3	DJB-2	DJC-2	DJ-2	DJA-3	DJB-2	DJC-2	DOC-1
Gardner, 8-85........................(1928)	DJ-2	DJA-3	DJB-2	DJC-2	DJ-2	DJA-3	DJB-2	DJC-2	DOC-1
Gardner, 8-95........................(1928)	DJ-2	DJA-3	DJB-2	DJC-2	DJ-2	DJA-3	DJB-2	DJC-2	DOC-1
Gardner, 120, 125...................(1929)	DJ-2	DJA-3	DJB-2	DJC-2	DJ-2	DJA-3	DJB-2	DJC-2	DOC-1
Gardner, 130........................(1929)	DJ-2	DJA-3	DJB-2	DJC-2	DJ-2	DJA-3	DJB-2	DJC-2	DOC-1
Gardner, 120, 125 (1929); 136, 140 (Channel Shoes)...(1929-30)	DJ-2	DJA-3	DJB-2	DJC-2	DJ-2	DJA-3	DJB-2	DJC-2	DOC-1
Gardner, 130, (1929); 150 (Channel S.).(1929-30)	DJ-2	DJA-3	DJB-2	DJC-2	DJ-2	DJA-3	DJB-2	DJC-2	DOC-1
Graham Paige, 610...................(1928-29)	DJ-13-R / DJ-14-L	DJA-14-R / DJA-15-L	DJB-6	DJC-3	DJ-29	DJA-27	DJB-6	DJC-3	DOC-1
Graham Paige, 612, Std. 6.........(1929-30)	DJ-2	DJA-3	DJB-2	DJC-2	DJ-2	DJA-3	DJB-2	DJC-2	DOC-1
Graham Paige, 614................(1928-29)	DJ-13-R / DJ-14-L	DJA-14-R / DJA-15-L	DJB-6	DJC-3	DJ-29	DJA-27	DJB-6	DJC-3	DOC-1
Graham Paige, 615, Spec. 6, Std. and Spec. 8 (1929-30)........................	DJ-2	DJA-3	DJB-2	DJC-2	DJ-2	DJA-3	DJB-2	DJC-2	DOC-1
Graham Paige, 619, 629, 835.......(1928-29)	DJ-2	DJA-3	DJB-2	DJC-2	DJ-2	DJA-3	DJB-2	DJC-2	DOC-1
Graham Paige, 621, 827, 837 Cust. 8..(1929-30)	DJ-2	DJA-3	DJB-2	DJC-2	DJ-2	DJA-3	DJB-2	DJC-2	DOC-1
Hupmobile, 8 (Before Serial 9925)........(1925)	DJ-16-R / DJ-15-L	DJA-16-R / DJA-17-L	DJB-1	DJC-6	DJ-30-R / DJ-38-L	DJA-28-R / DJA-29-L	DJB-1	DJC-6	DOC-1-F / DOC-2-R
Hupmobile, 8 (After Serial 9925).......(1925-26)	DJ-17	DJA-18	DJB-1	DJC-6	DJ-17	DJA-18	DJB-1	DJC-6	DOC-1-F / DOC-2-R
Jewett, 23, 25..........................(1925)	DJ-1-R / DJ-39-L / DJ-39-L	DJA-1-R / DJA-2-L / DJA-2-L	DJB-1	DJC-1	DJ-31	DJA-30	DJB-1	DJC-1	DOC-2
Jewett, New Day...................(1926-27)	DJ-1-R / DJ-39-L	DJA-1-R / DJA-2-L	DJB-1	DJC-1	DJ-31	DJA-30	DJB-1	DJC-1	DOC-1
Jordan, K, L.......................(1925)	DJ-18	....	DJB-7	DJC-1	DJ-32	....	DJB-7	DJC-1	DOC-4
Jordan, Line 8A (1925-26); J.........(1926-27)	*DJ-18	....	DJB-7	DJC-1	*DJ-32	....	DJB-7	DJC-1	DOC-2
Jordan, R Small 6...................(1927-28)	DJ-9-R / DJ-10-L	DJA-10-R / DJA-11-L	DJB-6	DJC-3	DJ-24-R / DJ-27-L	DJA-32-R / DJA-24-L	DJB-6	DJC-3	DOC-1-F / DOC-2-R
Jordan, E.............................(1929)	DJ-2	DJA-3	DJB-2	DJC-2	DJ-2	DJA-3	DJB-2	DJC-2	DOC-1-F / DOC-2-R
Jordan, G, T...........................(1929)	DJ-2	DJA-3	DJB-2	DJC-2	DJ-2	DJA-3	DJB-2	DJC-2	DOC-1-F / DOC-2-R
Jordan, JE, JJ.....................(1928-29)	DJ-18	....	DJB-7	DJC-1	DJ-32	....	DJB-7	DJC-1	DOC-2
Kissel, 6-80 (1926); 8-90..............(1928)	DJ-18	....	DJB-7	DJC-1	DJ-32	....	DJB-7	DJC-1	DOC-2
Kissel, 8-75 (1925-26-27); 6-55 (1926-27); 8-65 (1927); 8-80...............(1928)	DJ-1-R / DJ-39-L	DJA-1-R / DJA-2-L	DJB-1	DJC-1	DJ-33-R / DJ-23-L	DJA-20-R / DJA-21-L	DJB-1	DJC-1	DOC-1-F / DOC-2-R
Kissel, 6-70.........................(1928)	DJ-9-R / DJ-10-L	DJA-10-R / DJA-11-L	DJB-6	DJC-3	DJ-27	DJA-24	DJB-6	DJC-3	DOC-1
Kissel, 6-73 (Die Cast Shoes)...........(1929)	DJ-2	DJA-3	DJB-2	DJC-2	DJ-2	DJA-3	DJB-2	DJC-2	DOC-1
Kissel, 8-95 (Die Cast Shoes)...........(1929)	DJ-2	DJA-3	DJB-2	DJC-2	DJ-2	DJA-3	DJB-2	DJC-2	DOC-1
Kissel, 126 (3-Piece Pressed Steel Shoes)...(1929)	DJ-19	DJA-3	DJB-2	DJC-2	DJ-19	DJA-3	DJB-2	DJC-2	DOC-1
Kissel, 8-126 (Channel Shoes)..........(1929)	DJ-2	DJA-3	DJB-2	DJC-2	DJ-2	DJA-3	DJB-2	DJC-2	DOC-1
McFarlan, Light 6 (1925-26); TV6 (1925-26-27-28); 8 in Line.........(1926-27-28)	DJ-18	....	DJB-7	DJC-1	DJ-32	....	DJB-7	DJC-1	†DOC-4 / DOC-6
Moon, London, Metropolitan, Newport (1925), Series A (1925-26-27-28).................	DJ-1-R / DJ-39-L	DJA-1 / DJA-2	DJB-1	DJC-1	DJ-23-R / DJ-33-L	DJA-20-R / DJA-21-L	DJB-1	DJC-1	DOC-2

LOCKHEED HYDRAULIC BRAKE PARTS—Second Group

Interchangeable Parts have the same CHILTON NUMBER in Any Column

CAR, MAKE AND MODEL	FRONT WHEEL CYLINDER, RIGHT AND LEFT				REAR WHEEL CYLINDER, RIGHT AND LEFT				Hose Assembly Front and Rear ††
	Cylinder Assembly	Cylinder Casting	Piston Cup	Piston Boot	Cylinder Assembly	Cylinder Casting	Piston Cup	Piston Boot	
Moon, 6-60, 6-62, 6-72.........(1926-27-28-29)	DJ-9-R / DJ-10-L	DJA-10-R / DJA-11-L	DJB-6	DJC-3	DJ-27	DJA-24	DJB-6	DJC-3	DOC-1
Moon, 8-80, 8-82.................(1928-29)	DJ-9-R / DJ-10-L	DJA-10-R / DJA-11-L	DJB-6	DJC-3	DJ-27	DJA-24	DJB-6	DJC-3	DOC-1
Moon, 6-72 Int. Brakes, 6-72, 6-77, 8-92.(1929-30)	DJ-2	DJA-3	DJB-2	DJC-2	DJ-2	DJA-3	DJB-2	DJC-2	DOC-1
Paige, 21 (1924-25); 24 (1926); 6-70....(1925-26)	DJ-1-R / DJ-39-L	DJA-1 / DJA-2	DJB-1	DJC-1	DJ-31	DJA-30	DJB-1	DJC-1	DOC-2
Paige, 8-85.....................(1927-28)	DJ-9-R / DJ-10-L	DJA-10-R / DJA-11-L	DJB-6	DJC-3	DJ-34	DJA-33	DJB-6	DJC-3	DOC-1
Paige, 6-45 After Chassis 320537 / 6-65 After Chassis 167138 / 6-75 After Chassis 117138 ......(1927-28)	DJ-9-R / DJ-10-L	DJA-10-R / DJA-11-L	DJB-6	DJC-3	DJ-34	DJA-33	DJB-6	DJC-3	DOC-1
Peerless, 6-80.....................(1926)	DJ-1-R / DJ-39-L	DJA-1-R / DJA-2-L	DJB-1	DJC-1	DJ-33-R / DJ-23L	DJA-20-R / DJA-21-L	DJB-1	DJC-1	DOC-1
Peerless, 60......................(1927)	DJ-9-R / DJ-10-L	DJA-10-R / DJA-11-L	DJB-6	DJC-3	DJ-27	DJA-24	DJB-6	DJC-3	DOC-5
Peerless, 80, 90..................(1927-28)	DJ-1-R / DJ-39-L	DJA-1-R / DJA-2-L	DJB-1	DJC-1	DJ-23-R / DJ-33-L	DJA-20-R / DJA-21-L	DJB-1	DJC-1	DOC-1
Peerless, 61.....................(1929)	DJ-2	DJA-3	DJB-2	DJC-2	DJ-2	DJA-3	DJB-2	DJC-2	DOC-1
Peerless, 81.....................(1929)	DJ-2	DJA-3	DJB-2	DJC-2	DJ-2	DJA-3	DJB-2	DJC-2	DOC-1
Peerless, 91..................(1928-29)	DJ-2	DJA-3	DJB-2	DJC-2	DJ-2	DJA-3	DJB-2	DJC-2	DOC-1
Peerless, 8-125 (Channel Shoes).......(1929-30)	DJ-2	DJA-3	DJB-2	DJC-2	DJ-2	DJA-3	DJB-2	DJC-2	DOC-1
Plymouth.....................(1928-29)	DJ-40	DJA-9	DJB-2	DJC-4	DJ-40	DJA-9	DJB-2	DJC-4	DOC-1
Plymouth.....................(1929-30)	DJ-40	DJA-9	DJB-2	DJC-4	DJ-40	DJA-9	DJB-2	DJC-4	DOC-1
Reo, Flying Cloud Series A............(1927-28)	DJ-2	DJA-3	DJB-2	DJC-2	DJ-2	DJA-3	DJB-2	DJC-2	DOC-1
Reo, Wolverine B.................(1927)	DJ-2	DJA-3	DJB-2	DJC-2	DJ-2	DJA-3	DJB-2	DJC-2	DOC-1
Reo, Flying Cloud (1928); Master........(1929)	DJ-2	DJA-3	DJB-2	DJC-2	DJ-2	DJA-3	DJB-2	DJC-2	DOC-1
Reo, Wolverine B (1928); Mate..........(1929)	DJ-2	DJA-3	DJB-2	DJC-2	DJ-2	DJA-3	DJB-2	DJC-2	DOC-1
Reo 15.........................(1930)	DJ-2	DJA-3	DJB-2	DJC-2	DJ-2	DJA-3	DJB-2	DJC-2	DOC-1
Reo 20, 25 (Early)................(1930)	DJ-2	DJA-3	DJB-2	DJC-2	DJ-2	DJA-3	DJB-2	DJC-2	DOC-1
Reo 20, 25 (Late).................(1930)	DJ-2	DJA-3	DJB-2	DJC-2	DJ-2	DJA-3	DJB-2	DJC-2	DOC-1
Stutz, 6.......................(1925)	DJ-18	....	DJB-7	DJC-1	DJ-32	....	DJB-7	DJC-1	DOC-4
Stutz, AA....................(1926-27)	DJ-19	DJA-3	DJB-2	DJC-2	DJ-19	DJA-3	DJB-2	DJC-2	DOC-5
Stutz, BB....................(1927-28)	DJ-19	DJA-3	DJB-2	DJC-2	DJ-2	DJA-3	DJB-2	DJC-2	DOC-1
Stutz, L (Channel Shoes)...............(1929)	DJ-20	DJA-7	DJB-5	DJC-2	DJ-2	DJA-3	DJB-2	DJC-2	DOC-1
Stutz, M.......................(1929)	DJ-21	DJA-19	DJB-8	DJC-7	DJ-20	DJA-7	DJB-5	DJC-2	DOC-1
Velie, 59 (1925-26); 60............(1925-26-27)	DJ-1-R / DJ-39L	DJA-1-R / DJA-2-L	DJB-1	DJC-1	DJ-35-R / DJ-25-L	DJA-34-R / DJA-35-L	DJB-1	DJC-1	DOC-2
Velie, 6-50.....................(1927-28)	DJ-9-R / DJ-10L	DJA-10-R / DJA-11-L	DJB-6	DJC-3	DJ-27	DJA-24	DJB-6	DJC-3	DOC-1
Velie, 66, 77, 88...................(1928)	DJ-2	DJA-3	DJB-2	DJC-2	DJ-2	DJA-3	DJB-2	DJC-2	DOC-1
Wills Ste. Claire...................(1926)	‡DJ-18 / °DJ-22	....	DJB-7 / DJB-1	DJC-1	‡DJ-32 / °DJ-22	....	DJB-7 / DJB-1	DJC-1	‡DOC-6 / °DOC-4

* 1,000 cars between serials 63935 and 65035 were equipped with Eaton axles using Wheel Cylinder assembly DJ-41 (Piston cup DJB-1 and Piston Boot DJC-1).
† For ⅝″ frame hose bracket.
‡ Used on Timken Axles.
° Used on Eaton Axles.
†† Hose assemblies should be matched with sample in all cases.

ABBREVIATIONS:
F. —Front.
R. —Rear.
Lf. —Left Side.
Rg. —Right Side.

INTERCHANGEABLE COUNT

Showing exact number of times each CHILTON NUMBER occurs in Lockheed Brake Table—Second Group beginning opposite.

Cylinder Assembly				Cylinder Casting			Piston Cup	Piston Boot	Hose Assembly Front & Rear
	DJ-11-1	DJ-24-1	DJ-39-14	DJA-6-2	DJA-19-1	DJA-34-1	DJB-7-14		
	DJ-12-1	DJ-25-1	DJ-40-18	DJA-7-3	DJA-20-9	DJA-35-2	DJB-8-1		
	DJ-13-2	DJ-26-1	DJ-42-1	DJA-8-4	DJA-21-9	DJA-36-1			
DJ-1-13	DJ-14-2	DJ-27-8		DJA-9-18	DJA-22-1				DOC-1-77
DJ-2-92	DJ-15-1	DJ-28-1		DJA-10-9	DJA-24-7		Piston Boot		DOC-2-18
DJ-3-2	DJ-16-1	DJ 29-2	Cylinder Casting	DJA-11-9	DJA-25-1	Piston Cup		DJC-1-44	DOC-4-6
DJ-4-3	DJ-17-2	DJ-30-1		DJA-12-1	DJA-26-1		DJC-2-101	DOC-5-8
DJ-5-6	DJ-18-7	DJ-31-3	DJA-1-13	DJA-13-1	DJA-27-2	DJB-1-34	DJC-3-28	DOC-6-4
DJ-6-2	DJ-19-7	DJ-32-7	DJA-2-14	DJA-14-2	DJA-28-1	DJB-2-117	DJC-4-24	DOC-7-1
DJ-7-1	DJ-20-2	DJ-33-9	DJA-3-99	DJA-15-2	DJA-29-1	DJB-3-6	DJC-5-2	
DJ-8-4	DJ-21-1	DJ-34-2	DJA-4-3	DJA-16-1	DJA-30-3	DJB-4-6	DJC-6-4	
DJ-9-9	DJ-22-2	DJ-35-1	DJA-5-6	DJA-17-1	DJA-32-1	DJB-5-8	DJC-7-1	
DJ-10-9	DJ-23-9	DJ-38-1		DJA-18-2	DJA-33-2	DJB-6-24		

RIVETS—Brass Tubular Type

Here are listed, by CHILTON NUMBER, the thirty brake-lining rivets found, in the preparation of the Chilton Brake Book, to be most important. Corresponding numbers used by ten rivet manufacturers are shown under each CHILTON NUMBER. Illustrations and dimensions on page opposite.

No. 1
Chicago 304
J.M. ....C-4⁄16″
Man. B.H. ...38-4⁄16″
Multi. 1
Penn 4B
Raybestos 1
Rusco .....30-4⁄16″
Shelton 1
Thermoid 1
Tubular 1

No. 2
Chicago 404
J.M. ....A-4⁄16″
Man. B.H. ...12-4⁄16″
Multi. 2
Penn 4A
Raybestos 2
Rusco .....40-4⁄16″
Shelton 2
Thermoid 2
Tubular 2

No. 3
Chicago 906
J.M. ....D-9⁄16″
Man. B.H. ...48-9⁄16″
Multi. 3
Penn 6D
Raybestos 3
Rusco .....90-9⁄16″
Shelton 3
Thermoid 3
Tubular 3

No. 4
Chicago 806
J. M. ....
Man. B.H. ...22-9⁄16″
Multi. 4
Penn 6C
Raybestos 4
Rusco ....
Shelton 4
Thermoid 4
Tubular 4

No. 5
Chicago 808
J.M. ....
Man. B.H. ...22-8⁄16″
Multi. 5
Penn 8C
Raybestos 5
Rusco ....
Shelton 5
Thermoid 5
Tubular 5

No. 6
Chicago 908
J.M. ....D-8⁄16″
Man. B.H. ...48-8⁄16″
Multi. 6
Penn 8D
Raybestos 6
Rusco .....90-8⁄16″
Shelton 6
Thermoid 6
Tubular 6

No. 7
Chicago 405
J.M. ....A-5⁄16″
Man. B.H. ...12-5⁄16″
Penn 5A
Raybestos 7
Rusco .....40-5⁄16″
Shelton 7
Thermoid 7
Tubular 7

No. 8
Chicago 305
J.M. ....C-5⁄16″
Man. B.H. ...38-5⁄16″
Multi. 8
Penn 5B
Raybestos 8
Rusco .....30-5⁄16″
Shelton 8
Thermoid 8
Tubular 8

No. 9
Chicago 306
J.M. ....C-6⁄16″
Man. B.H. ...38-6⁄16″
Multi. 9
Penn 9B
Raybestos 9
Rusco .....30-6⁄16″
Shelton 9
Thermoid 9
Tubular 9

No. 10
Chicago 406
J.M. ....A-6⁄16″
Man. B.H. ...12-6⁄16″
Multi. 10
Penn 6A
Raybestos 10
Rusco .....40-6⁄16″
Shelton 10
Thermoid 10
Tubular 10

No. 11
Chicago 9010
J.M. ....D-10⁄16″
Man. B.H. ...48-10⁄16″
Multi. 11
Penn 10D
Raybestos 11
Rusco .....90-10⁄16″
Shelton 11
Thermoid 11
Tubular 11

No. 12
Chicago 8010
J.M. ....
Man. B.H. ...22-10⁄16″
Multi. 12
Penn 10C
Raybestos 12
Rusco ....
Shelton 12
Thermoid 12
Tubular 12

No. 13
Chicago 4010
J.M. ....A-10⁄16″
Man. B.H. ...12-10⁄16″
Multi. 13
Penn 10A
Raybestos 13
Rusco .....40-10⁄16″
Shelton 13
Thermoid 13
Tubular 13

No. 14
Chicago 4012
J.M. ....A-12⁄16″
Man. B.H. ...12-12⁄16″
Multi. 14
Penn 12A
Raybestos 14
Rusco .....40-12⁄16″
Shelton 14
Thermoid 14
Tubular 14

No. 15
Chicago 408
J.M. ....A-8⁄16″
Man. B.H. ...12-8⁄16″
Multi. 15
Penn 8A
Raybestos 15
Rusco .....40-8⁄16″
Shelton 15
Thermoid 15
Tubular 15

No. 16
Chicago 308
J.M. ....C-8⁄16″
Man. B.H. ...38-8⁄16″
Multi. 16
Penn 8B
Raybestos 16
Rusco .....30-8⁄16″
Shelton 16
Thermoid 16
Tubular 16

No. 17
Chicago 9012
J.M. ....D-12⁄16″
Man. B.H. ...48-12⁄16″
Multi. 17
Penn 12D
Raybestos 17
Rusco .....90-12⁄16″
Shelton 17
Tubular 17
Thermoid 17

No. 18
Chicago 8012
J.M. ....
Man. B.H. ...22-12⁄16″
Multi. 18
Penn 12C
Raybestos 18
Rusco ....
Shelton 18
Thermoid 18
Tubular 18

No. 19
Chicago 9014
J.M. ....D-14⁄16″
Man. B.H. ...48-14⁄16″
Multi. 19
Penn 14D
Raybestos 19
Rusco .....90-14⁄16″
Shelton 19
Thermoid 19
Tubular 19

No. 20
Chicago 8014
J.M. ....
Man. B.H. ...22-14⁄16″
Multi. 20
Penn 14C
Raybestos 20
Rusco ....
Shelton 20
Thermoid 20
Tubular 20

No. 21
Chicago 9016
J.M. ....D-16⁄16″
Man. B.H. ...48-16⁄16″
Multi. 21
Penn 16D
Raybestos 21
Rusco .....90-16⁄16″
Shelton 21
Thermoid 21
Tubular 21

No. 22
Chicago 8016
J.M. ....
Man. B.H. ...22-16⁄16″
Multi. 22
Penn 16C
Raybestos 22
Rusco ....
Shelton 22
Thermoid 22
Tubular 22

No. 23
Chicago 3010
J.M. ....C-10⁄16″
Man. B.H. ...38-10⁄16″
Multi. 23
Penn 10B
Raybestos 23
Rusco .....30-10⁄16″
Shelton 23
Thermoid 23
Tubular 23

No. 24
Chicago 106
J.M. ....
Man. B.H. ....2-9⁄16″
Multi. 24
Penn ......2800-9⁄16″
Raybestos 24
Rusco .....10-9⁄16″
Shelton 24
Thermoid 24
Tubular 24

No. 25
Chicago 186
J. M. ....
Man. B.H. ...32-9⁄16″
Multi. 25
Penn 6G
Raybestos 25
Rusco .....18-9⁄16″
Shelton 25
Thermoid 25
Tubular 25

No. 26
Chicago 545
J.M. ....
Man. B.H. ..33-4½⁄16″
Multi. 26
Penn 9F
Raybestos 26
Rusco ....5-4½⁄16″
Shelton 26
Thermoid 26
Tubular 26

No. 27
Chicago 105
J.M. ....
Man. B.H. ....2-5⁄16″
Multi. 27
Penn ......2800-5⁄16″
Raybestos 27
Rusco .....10-5⁄16″
Shelton 27
Thermoid 27
Tubular 27

No. 28
Chicago 107
J.M. ....
Man. B.H. ....2-7⁄16″
Multi. ....
Penn ......2800-7⁄16″
Raybestos 28
Rusco 28
Shelton 28
Thermoid 28
Tubular 28

No. 200
Chicago 9645
J.M. ....
Man. B.H. ....9-5⁄16″
Multi. ....2970-5⁄16″
Penn ......5200-5⁄16″
Raybestos ....
Rusco ....9645-5⁄16″
Shelton 200
Thermoid 200
Tubular ....2970-5⁄16″

No. 201
Chicago 9648
J.M. ....
Man. B.H. ....9-8⁄16″
Multi. ....2970-8⁄16″
Penn ......5200-8⁄16″
Raybestos ....
Rusco ....964-8⁄16″
Shelton 201
Thermoid 201
Tubular ....2970-8⁄16″

KEY TO ABBREVIATIONS

Chicago—Chicago Rivet & Machine Company
J.M.—Johns-Manville Corporation
Man. B. H.—Manufacturers Belt Hook Company
Multi.—Multibestos Co.
Penn—Penn Rivet Corp.

Raybestos—Raybestos Company
Rusco—Russel Manufacturing Company
Shelton—Shelton Tubular Rivet Company
Thermoid—Thermoid Rubber Company
Tubular—Tubular Rivet & Stud Company

RIVETS—Brass Tubular Type

ILLUSTRATIONS—SIIZES—CHILTON NUMBERS

For Corresponding Manufacturers' Numbers of Various Makes, See Page Opposite

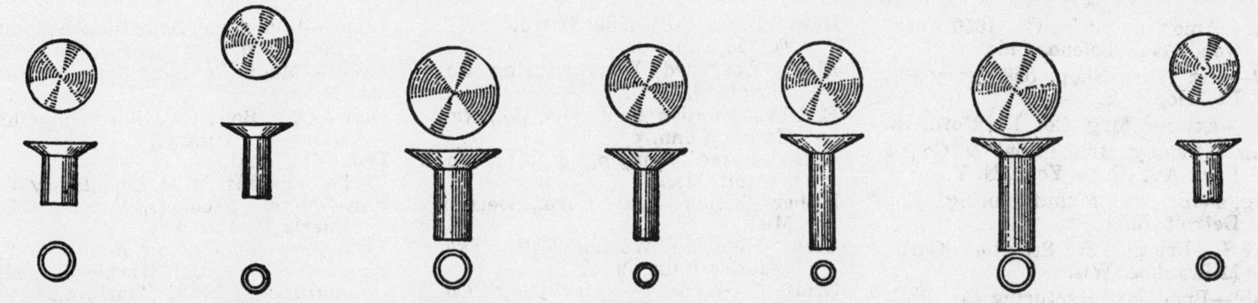

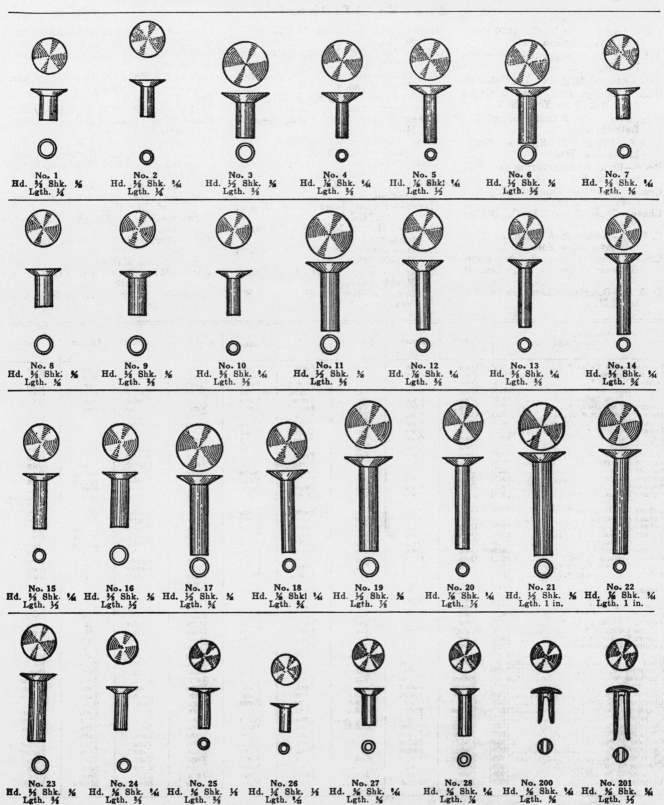

No. 1 Hd. 3/8 Shk. 5/16 Lgth. 1/4

No. 2 Hd. 3/8 Shk. 9/64 Lgth. 1/4

No. 3 Hd. 1/2 Shk. 5/16 Lgth. 3/8

No. 4 Hd. 7/16 Shk. 9/64 Lgth. 3/8

No. 5 Hd. 7/16 Shk. 9/64 Lgth. 1/2

No. 6 Hd. 1/2 Shk. 5/16 Lgth. 1/2

No. 7 Hd. 3/8 Shk. 9/64 Lgth. 5/16

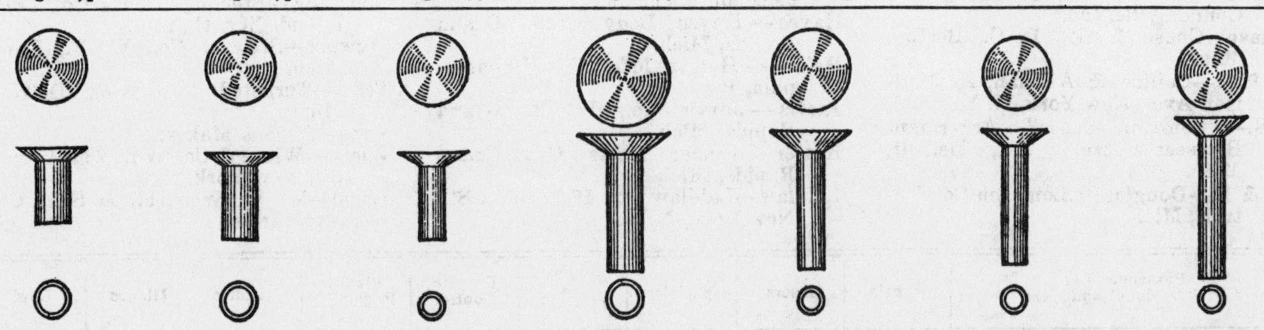

No. 8 Hd. 3/8 Shk. 5/16 Lgth. 5/16

No. 9 Hd. 3/8 Shk. 5/16 Lgth. 3/8

No. 10 Hd. 3/8 Shk. 9/64 Lgth. 3/8

No. 11 Hd. 1/2 Shk. 5/16 Lgth. 5/8

No. 12 Hd. 7/16 Shk. 9/64 Lgth. 5/8

No. 13 Hd. 3/8 Shk. 9/64 Lgth. 5/8

No. 14 Hd. 3/8 Shk. 9/64 Lgth. 3/4

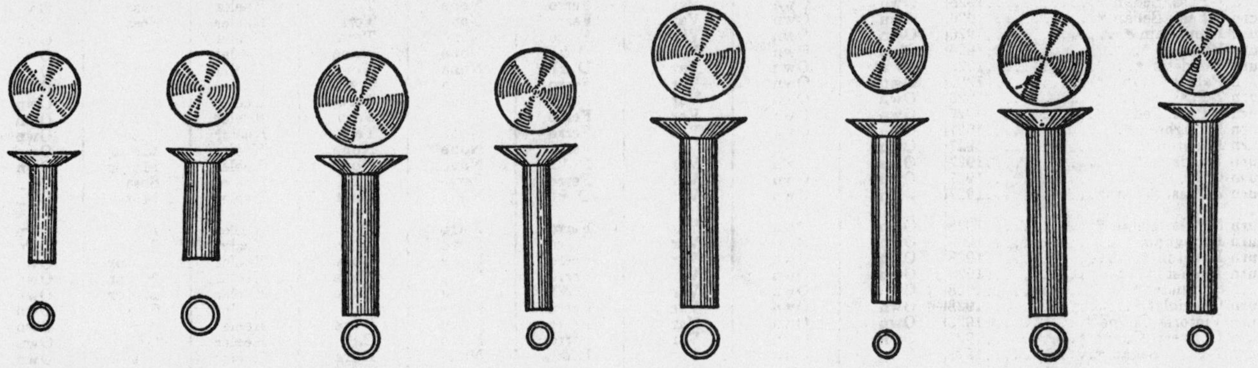

No. 15 Hd. 3/8 Shk. 9/64 Lgth. 1/2

No. 16 Hd. 3/8 Shk. 5/16 Lgth. 1/2

No. 17 Hd. 1/2 Shk. 5/16 Lgth. 3/4

No. 18 Hd. 7/16 Shk. 9/64 Lgth. 3/4

No. 19 Hd. 1/2 Shk. 5/16 Lgth. 7/8

No. 20 Hd. 7/16 Shk. 9/64 Lgth. 7/8

No. 21 Hd. 1/2 Shk. 5/16 Lgth. 1 in.

No. 22 Hd. 7/16 Shk. 9/64 Lgth. 1 in.

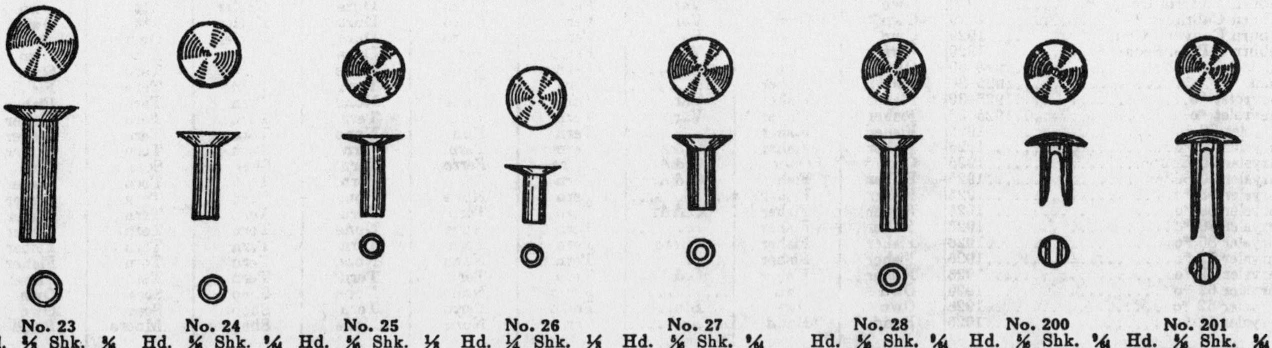

No. 23 Hd. 3/8 Shk. 5/16 Lgth. 5/8

No. 24 Hd. 5/16 Shk. 9/64 Lgth. 3/8

No. 25 Hd. 5/16 Shk. 1/8 Lgth. 3/8

No. 26 Hd. 1/4 Shk. 1/8 Lgth. 9/32

No. 27 Hd. 5/16 Shk. 9/64 Lgth. 5/16

No. 28 Hd. 5/16 Shk. 9/64 Lgth. 7/16

No. 200 Hd. 5/16 Shk. 9/64 Lgth. 5/16

No. 201 Hd. 5/16 Shk. 9/64 Lgth. 1/2

Body Materials and Equipment

Here the Supply House and Body Service Department Can Find the Make of Each of Nine Items in Body Construction of Passenger Car Models from 1925-1930

ABBREVIATIONS USED:

A.S.—American Swiss Co., 1650 Fernwood Ave., Toledo, Ohio.

Art—Art Work Shop, 828 Ferry St., Buffalo, N. Y.

Att.—Atwood Mfg. Co., Rockford, Ill.

Blum.—Sidney Blumenthal & Co., 1 Park Ave., New York, N. Y.

Briggs—Briggs Manufacturing Co., Detroit, Mich.

B. & S.—Briggs & Stratton Corp., Milwaukee, Wis.

Budd—Budd Manufacturing Co., Philadelphia, Pa.

Central—Central Manufacturing Co., Connersville, Ind.

Chase—Chase & Co., L. C., Boston, Mass.

C. & A.—Collins & Aikman, 25 Madison Ave., New York, N. Y.

C.S.—"Common Sense"—Ackerman-Blaesser-Fezzey, Inc., Detroit, Mich.

D. & L.—Douglas & Lomason Co., Detroit, Mich.

Dura—Dura Co., 4500 Detroit Ave., Toledo, Ohio.

Eber.—Eberhard Manufacturing Co., Cleveland, Ohio.

E. & M.—English & Mersick Co., New Haven, Conn.

Ferro—Ferro Stamping & Mfg. Co., Detroit, Mich.

Fisher—Fisher Body Corp., Detroit, Mich.

Glen.—Glenside Woolen Mills, Skaneateles Falls, N. Y.

Greist — Greist Manufacturing Co., New Haven, Conn.

Han. — Hancock Manufacturing Co., Jackson, Mich.

Hayes—Hayes Body Corp., Grand Rapids, Mich.

Heintz — Heintz Mfg. Co., Philadelphia, Pa.

Jarvis — Jarvis Co., W. B., Grand Rapids, Mich.

Keeler — Keeler Brass Co., Grand Rapids, Mich.

Laidlaw—Laidlaw Co., 16 W. 60th St., New York, N. Y.

Limo.—Limousine Body Co., Kalamazoo, Mich.

Motor—Motor Products Corp., Detroit, Mich.

Ohio—Ohio Body Co., Cleveland, Ohio. (Out of business.)

Opt.—Optional.

Pacific—Pacific Mills Upholstery Co.

Par.—Motor Products Corp. (Formerly Parsons.)

Perf.—Perfect Window Regulator Co.

Shep.—Deverau Co. (formerly Shephard Co.), 11831 Charlevoix Ave., Detroit, Mich.

Soss—Soss Mfg. Co., Roselle, N. J.

Sterl. Br.—Sterling Bronze Co., Long Island City, N. Y.

Stewart—Stewart Co., W. F., Flint, Mich.

Tern.—Ternsted Mfg. Co., Detroit, Mich.

Var.—Various Makes.

Wiese—Wiese & Co., Wm., 234 W. 56th St., New York, N. Y.

Wood—W. W. Woodruff & Sons Co., Mt. Carmel, Conn.

Passenger Car Make, Model and Year	Panels	Doors	Upholstery	Locks	Remote Control	Window Regulator	Handles	Hinges	Cowl
Auburn 5-Pass. Sedan * 1925	Own	Own	Var	Ferro	None	Tern	Keeler	Soss	Own
Auburn Brougham * 1925	Own	Own	Var	Ferro	None	Tern	Keeler	Soss	Own
Auburn Phaeton * 1925	Own	Own	Var	D. & L.	None	None	Keeler	Par	Own
Auburn Roadster * 1925	Own	Own	Var	E.&M.	None	None	Keeler	Par	Own
Auburn 7-Pass. Sedan * 1925	Own	Own	Var	Ferro	None	Tern	Keeler	Soss	Own
Auburn 5-Pass. Sedan * 1926	Own	Own	Var	Ferro	None	Tern	Keeler	Soss	Own
Auburn Brougham * 1926	Own	Own	Var	Ferro	None	Tern	Keeler	Soss	Own
Auburn Phaeton * 1926	Own	Own	Var	D.&L.	None	None	Keeler	Par	Own
Auburn Roadster * 1926	Own	Own	Var	D.&L.	None	None	Keeler	Par	Own
Auburn Fabric Coupe * 1926	Own	Own	Var	Ferro	None	Tern	Keeler	Motor	Own
Auburn 7-Pass. Sedan * 1926	Own	Own	Var	Ferro	None	Tern	Keeler	Tern	Own
Auburn 5-Pass. Sedan * 1927	Own	Own	Var	Ferro	None	Tern	Keeler	Att	Own
Auburn Brougham * 1927	Own	Own	Var	Ferro	None	Tern	Keeler	Att	Own
Auburn Phaeton * 1927	Own	Own	Var	Ferro	None	None	Keeler	Motor	Own
Auburn Roadster * 1927	Own	Own	Var	D.&L.	None	None	Keeler	Motor	Own
Auburn Cabriolet * 1927	Own	Own	Var	Ferro	Ferro	C.S.	Keeler	Soss	Own
Auburn 7-Pass. Sedan * 1927	Own	Own	Var	D.&L.	None	Dura Tern	Keeler	Motor	Own
Auburn 5-Pass. Sedan * 1928	Own	Own	Var	Ferro	Ferro	Dura	Keeler	Att	Own
Auburn Brougham * 1928	Own	Own	Var	Ferro	Ferro	Dura	Keeler	Att	Own
Auburn Phaeton * 1928	Own	Own	Var	Ferro	None	None	Keeler	Motor	Own
Auburn Roadster * 1928	Own	Own	Var	Ferro	None	None	Keeler	Motor	Own
Auburn Speedster * 1928	Own	Own	Var	D.&L.	None	None	Keeler	Motor	Own
Auburn Cabriolet * 1928	Own	Own	Var	Ferro	Ferro	C.S.	Keeler	Soss	Own
Auburn Victoria Coupe * 1928	Own	Own	Var	Ferro	Ferro	Dura	Keeler	Att	Own
Auburn Convert. Coupe * 1928	Own	Own	Var	Ferro	Ferro	C.S.	Keeler	Own	Own
Auburn 7-Pass. Sedan * 1928	Own	Own	Var	D.&L.	None	Dura Tern	Keeler	Att	Own
Auburn 5-Pass. Sedan * 1929	Own	Own	Var	Ferro	Ferro	Dura	Keeler	Att	Own
Auburn Brougham * 1929	Own	Own	Var	Ferro	Ferro	Dura	Keeler	Att	Own
Auburn Phaeton * 1929	Own	Own	Var	Ferro	None	None	Keeler	Motor	Own
Auburn Speedster * 1929	Own	Own	Var	Ferro	None	None	Keeler	Motor	Own
Auburn Victoria Coupe * 1929	Own	Own	Var	Ferro	Ferro	Dura	Keeler	Att	Own
Auburn Cabriolet * 1929	Own	Own	Var	Ferro	Ferro	Dura	Keeler	Att	Own
Auburn Convert. Coupe * 1929	Own	Own	Var	Ferro	Ferro	Dura	Keeler	Own	Own
Auburn 7-Pass. Sedan * 1929	Own	Own	Var	Ferro	Ferro	Dura	Keeler	Att	Own
Buick *o 1925-30	Own	Own	....	Tern	None	None	Tern	Tern	Own
Buick *c 1925-30	Fisher	Fisher	....	Tern	Tern	Tern	Tern	Tern	Fisher
Chevrolet *o 1925-30	Fisher	Fisher	Var	Tern	None	None	Tern	Tern	Fisher
Chevrolet *c 1925-30	Fisher	Fisher	Var	Tern	Tern	Tern	Tern	Tern	Fisher
Chrysler 70 *o 1925	Fisher	Fisher	....	Tern	None	None	Tern	Tern	Fisher
Chrysler 70 *c 1925	Fisher	Fisher	C.&A.	Tern	Tern	Tern	Tern	Tern	Fisher
Chrysler 60 Coupe...................1925	Own	Own	C.&A.	Ferro	Ferro	Tern	Shep	Soss	Own
Chrysler 60 Sedan...................1925	Fisher	Fisher	C.&A.	Tern	Tern	Tern	Tern	Tern	Fisher
Chrysler 58 *o 1925	Fisher	Fisher	....	Tern	None	None	Tern	Tern	Fisher
Chrysler 58 *c 1925	Fisher	Fisher	C.&A.	Tern	Tern	Tern	Tern	Tern	Fisher
Chrysler 80 *o 1926	Fisher	Fisher	....	Tern	None	None	Tern	Tern	Fisher
Chrysler 80 *c 1926	Fisher	Fisher	Wiese	Tern	Tern	Tern	Tern	Tern	Fisher
Chrysler 72 *o 1926	Fisher	Fisher	....	Tern	None	None	Tern	Tern	Fisher
Chrysler 72 *c 1926	Fisher	Fisher	C.&A.	Tern	Tern	Tern	Tern	Tern	Fisher
Chrysler 62 *o 1926	Own	Own	....	Ferro	None	None	Shep	Soss	Own
Chrysler 62 *c 1926	Own	Own	Blum	Ferro	Ferro	Tern	Shep	Soss	Own
Chrysler 52 *o 1926	Budd	Budd	....	Ferro	None	None	Shep	Moore	Budd

*—All models: *O—All open models: *C—All closed models.

BODY MATERIALS AND EQUIPMENT—Continued

Passenger Car Make, Model and Year	Panels	Doors	Upholstery	Locks	Remote Control	Window Regulator	Handles	Hinges	Cowl
Chrysler 52 *c............1926	Budd	Budd	C.&A.	Ferro	Ferro	E&M	Shep	Moore	Budd
Chrysler 80 *c............1927	Own	Own	....	Tern	None	None	Tern	Tern	Own
Chrysler 80 *c............1927	Own	Own	Glen	Tern	Tern	Tern	Tern	Tern	Own
Chrysler 72 *c............1927	Fisher	Fisher	....	Tern	None	None	Tern	Tern	Fisher
Chrysler 72 *c............1927	Fisher	Fisher	C.&A.	Tern	Tern	Tern	Tern	Tern	Fisher
Chrysler 62 *c............1927	Own	Own	....	A.S.	None	None	Jarvis	Soss	Own
Chrysler 62 *c............1927	Own	Own	Blum	A.S.	A.S.	Tern	Jarvis	Soss	Own
Chrysler 58 *c............1927	Briggs	Briggs	....	A.S.	None	None	Jarvis	Soss	Briggs
Chrysler 58 *c............1927	Briggs	Briggs	Blum	A.S.	A.S.	Dura	Jarvis	Soss	Briggs
Chrysler 80 *c............1928	Briggs	Own	....	Tern	None	None	Tern	Att	Own
Chrysler 80 *c............1928	Briggs	Own	Weise	Tern	Tern	Tern	Tern	Att	Own
Chrysler 75 *c............1928	Mullin Heintz	Own	....	A.S.	None	None	Jarvis	Soss	Own
Chrysler 75 *c............1928	Mullin Heintz	Own	Blum	A.S.	A.S.	Tern Dura	Jarvis	Soss	Own
Chrysler 65 *c............1928	Briggs	Briggs	....	A.S.	None	None	Jarvis	Soss	Briggs
Chrysler 65 *c............1928	Briggs	Briggs	Blum	A.S.	A.S.	Dura	Jarvis	Soss	Briggs
Chrysler 80 *c............1929	Briggs	Own	....	Tern	None	None	Tern	Att	Own
Chrysler 80 *c............1929	Briggs	Own	Weise	Tern	Tern	Tern	Tern	Att	Own
Chrysler 77 *c............1929	Murray	Own	....	A.S.	None	None	Jarvis	Att	Own
Chrysler 77 *c............1929	Murray	Own	Glen	A.S.	A.S.	Tern	Jarvis	Att	Own
Chrysler 70 *c............1929	Murray	Murray	....	A.S.	None	None	Jarvis	Soss	Murray
Chrysler 70 *c............1929	Murray	Murray	Blum	A.S.	A.S.	Tern	Jarvis	Soss	Murray
Chrysler 66 *c............1929	Briggs	Briggs	....	A.S.	None	None	Jarvis	Soss	Briggs
Chrysler 66 *c............1929	Briggs	Briggs	Blum	A.S.	A.S.	Tern	Jarvis	Soss	Briggs
Cord Sedan.............1929	Own	Own	Var	Tern	Tern	Tern	Keeler	Att	Own
Cord Sport Sedan........1929	Own	Own	Var	Tern	Tern	Tern	Keeler	Att	Own
Cord Cabriolet..........1929	Own	Own	Var	Tern	Tern	Tern	Keeler	Central	Own
Cord Convertible........1929	Own	Own	Var	Tern	Tern	Tern	Keeler	Central	Own
De Soto *c..............1928	Hayes Briggs	Hayes Briggs	....	A.S.	None	None	Jarvis	Soss	Hayes Briggs
De Soto *c..............1928	Hayes Briggs	Hayes Briggs	Blum	A.S.	A.S.	Dura	Jarvis	Soss	Hayes Briggs
De Soto *c..............1929	Briggs	Briggs	....	A.S.	None	None	Jarvis	Soss	Briggs
De Soto *c..............1929	Briggs	Briggs	Blum	A.S.	A.S.	Tern	Jarvis	Soss	Briggs
De Soto *c..............1930	Budd	Budd	....	B.&S.	None	None	Jarvis	Att	Budd
De Soto *c..............1930	Budd	Budd	Blum	B.&S.	Dura	Dura	Jarvis	Att	Budd
Dodge *c............1925–26	Budd	Budd	....	E.&M.	None	None	Jarvis	Att	Budd
Dodge *c............1925–26	Budd	Budd	....	E.&M.	Dura	Dura	Jarvis	Att	Budd
Dodge *c..............1927	Budd	Budd	....	E.&M.	Dura	Dura	Jarvis	Att	Budd
Dodge *c..............1928	Budd	Budd	....	E.&M.	Dura	Dura	Jarvis	Att	Budd
Dodge Victory 6 *c......1928	Budd	Budd	....	E.&M.	Dura	Dura	Jarvis	Att	Budd
Dodge 6 *c..........1928–29	Budd	Budd	....	Ferro	None	None	Jarvis	Moore	Budd
Dodge 6 *c..........1928–29	Budd	Budd	....	Ferro	Ferro	E.&M.	Jarvis	Moore	Budd
Erskine *c........1927–28–29	Budd	Budd	Budd	Dura	Dura	Dura	Dura	Budd	Budd
Gardner *c..............1925	Ohio	Ohio	Opt	Ferro	None	None	N.&J.	Soss	Ohio
Gardner *c..............1925	Ohio	Ohio	Opt	Ferro	None	Dura	N.&J.	Soss	Ohio
Gardner *c..............1926	Ohio	Ohio	Opt	Ferro	None	None	N.&J.	Soss	Ohio
Gardner *c..............1926	Ohio	Ohio	Opt	Ferro	Ferro	Dura	N.&J.	Soss	Ohio
Gardner *c..............1927	Limo	Limo	Opt	Ferro	None	None	Ferro Tern	Soss	Limo
Gardner *c..............1927	Limo	Limo	Opt	Ferro	Ferro	Dura	Ferro Tern	Soss	Limo
Gardner *c........1928–29–30	Centra	Central	Opt	Tern	None	None	Ferro Tern	Soss	Central
Gardner *c........1928–29–30	Centra	Central	Opt	Tern	Tern	Dura	Ferro Tern	Soss	Centra
Graham-Paige *c.......1928–30	Briggs Heintz Mullin	Own	....	Ferro	None	None	Dura	Soss	Briggs
Graham-Paige *c.......1928–30	Briggs Heintz Mullin	Own	Chase	Ferro	None	Dura	Dura	Soss	Briggs
Jordan Model A *o....1925–27	Ohio	Ohio	....	E.&M.	None	None	E.&M.	Eber	Ohio
Jordan Model A *c....1925–27	Ohio	Ohio	Wiese	E.&M.	E.&M.	Per	E.&M.	Eber	Ohio
Jordan Model J *o....1925–27	Budd	Budd	....	E.&M.	E.&M.	None	E.&M.	Att	Budd
Jordan Model J *c....1925–27	Budd	Budd	Chase	E.&M.	E.&M.	Dura	E.&M.	Att	Budd
Jordan Model R Coupe..1927–28	Murray	Murray	....			Dura	Greist	....	Murray
Jordan Model R Sedan.1927–28	Murray	Murray	Wiese			Dura	Greist	....	Murray
Jordan Model R Salon..1927–28	Ohio	Ohio	....	Ferro	None	None	Greist	....	Ohio
Jordan Model R Touring.1927–28	Ohio	Ohio	Wiese	Ferro	Ferro	Dura	Greist	....	Ohio
Jordan Model JE *o...1927–28	Murray	Murray	....			None	Greist	....	Murray
Jordan Model JE *c...1927–28	Murray	Murray	Wiese			Dura	Greist	....	Murray
Jordan Model T *o....1929–30	Murray	Murray	....	A.S.	None	None	Dura	....	Murray
Jordan Model T *c....1929–30	Murray	Murray	Wiese	A.S.	A.S.	B.&S.	Dura	....	Murray
Jordan Model G *o....1929–30	Murray	Murray	....	A.S.	None	None	Art	....	Murray
Jordan Model G *c....1929–30	Murray	Murray	Wiese	A.S.	A.S.	B.&S.	Art	....	Murray
Jordan Model E *c.......1929	Murray	Murray	....	Dura	None	None	Art	....	Murray
Jordan Model E *c.......1929	Murray	Murray	Pacific	Dura	Art	Art	Art	....	Murray
Lincoln *o............1926–28	Own	Own	....	E.&M.	None	None	Wood Sterl Br	E.&M.	Own
Lincoln *c............1926–28	Own	Own	Laidlaw Weise	E.&M.	Own	Perf Tern	Wood Sterl Br	E.&M.	Own
Lincoln *o..............1929	Own	Own	....	E.&M.	None	None	Wood Sterl Br	Att	Own
Lincoln *c..............1929	Own	Own	Laidlaw Weise	E.&M.	E.&M.	C.S.	Wood Sterl Br	Att	Own
Marquette *o..........1929–30	Own	Own	....	Tern	None	None	Tern	Tern	Own
Marquette *c..........1929–30	Fisher	Fisher	....	Tern	Tern	Tern	Tern	Tern	Own
Oakland *o............1925–30	Stewart	Stewart	....		None	None	....	....	....
Oakland *c............1925–30	Fisher	Fisher	....	Tern	Tern	Tern	Tern	Tern	Fisher
Oldsmobile *o.........1925–30	Fisher	Fisher	Var	Tern	None	None	Tern	Tern	Fisher
Oldsmobile *c.........1925–30	Fisher	Fisher	Var	Tern	Tern	Tern	Tern	Tern	Fisher
(Except Convert. Roadster...1929–30)									
Oldsmobile Convertible Roadster.1929–30	Hayes	Hayes	Var	Ferro	Ferro	C.S.	Tern	Att	Own
Packard 6 *o..........1925–30	Own	Own	....	E.&M.	None	None	Tern	Att	Own
Packard 6 *c. (Except 4-Pass. Coupe....1926–28)	Own	Own	Laidlaw Wiese	E.&M.	E.&M.	C.S.	Tern	Att	Own
Packard 6 Cyl. 4-Pass. Coupe....1926–28	Budd	Budd	....	Budd	Dura	Dura	Dura	Att	Budd
Packard 8 *o..........1925–29	Own	Own	....	E.&M.	None	None	Tern	Att	Own
Packard 8 *c. (Except 4-Pass. Coupe....1926–28)	Own	Own	Laidlaw Wiese	E.&M.	E.&M.	C.S.	Tern	Att	Own
Packard 8 Cyl. 4-Pass. Coupe.1926–28	Budd	Budd	....	Budd	Dura	Dura	Dura	Att	Budd
Peerless *c..............1930	Hayes	Hayes	....	Tern	None	None	Tern	Att	Hayes
Peerless *c..............1930	Hayes	Hayes	Laidlaw C.&A.	Tern	Tern	B.&S.	Tern	Att	Hayes
Pierce-Arrow *o........1925–28	Own	Own	....	E.&M.	None	None	Sterl Br	Eber	Own
Pierce-Arrow *c........1925–28	Own	Own	Laidlaw Wiese	E.&M.	E.&M.	C.S.	Sterl Br	Eber	Own

*—All models: *O—All open models: *C—All closed models.

BODY MATERIALS AND EQUIPMENT—Continued

Passenger Car Make, Model and Year	Panels	Doors	Upholstery	Locks	Remote Control	Window Regulator	Handles	Hinges	Cowl
Pierce-Arrow *o...................1929	Murray	Own	....	Han	None	None	Dura	Att	Own
Pierce-Arrow *c...................1929	Murray	Own	Wiese Laidlaw	Han	Han	Dura	Dura	Att	Own
Pierce-Arrow 132 2-4 Pass. Coupe....1930	Murray	Own	Wiese Laidlaw	Han	Han	Dura	Dura	Att	Own
Pierce-Arrow 132 5-Pass. Brougham..1930	Budd	Budd	Wiese Laidlaw	Han	Han	Dura	Dura	Budd	Budd
Pierce-Arrow 132 5-Pass. Sedan.....1930	Budd	Budd	Wiese Laidlaw	Han	Han	Dura	Dura	Budd	Budd
Pierce-Arrow 125 2-Pass. Runabout..1930	Murray	Own	....	Han	None	None	Dura	Att	Own
Pierce-Arrow 125 4-Pass. Phaeton...1930	Murray	Own	....	Han	None	None	Dura	Att	Own
Pierce-Arrow 125 4-Pass. Sp. Phat'n.1930	Murray	Own	....	Han	None	None	Dura	Att	Own
Pierce-Arrow 125 2-Pass. Convt. Cp.1930	Murray	Own	Wiese Laidlaw	Han	Han	Dura	Dura	Att	Own
Pierce-Arrow 139 5-Pass. Sedan.....1930	Murray	Own	Wiese Laidlaw	Han	Han	Dura	Dura	Att	Own
Pierce-Arrow 139 5-Pass. Club Sed....1930	Murray	Own	Wiese Laidlaw	Han	Han	Dura	Dura	Att	Own
Pierce-Arrow 139 5-Pass. Club Ber...1930	Murray	Own	Wiese Laidlaw	Han	Han	Dura	Dura	Att	Own
Pierce-Arrow 139 5-Pass. Victoria....1930	Murray	Own	Wiese Laidlaw	Han	Han	Dura	Dura	Att	Own
Pierce-Arrow 139 7-Pass. Sedan.....1930	Murray	Own	Wiese Laidlaw	Han	Han	Dura	Dura	Att	Own
Pierce-Arrow 139 7-Pass. Enc.Dr.Lim.1930	Murray	Own	Wiese Laidlaw	Han	Han	Dura	Dura	Att	Own
Plymouth *o......................1928	Hayes Briggs	Hayes Briggs	....	A.S.	None	None	Jarvis	Soss	Hayes Briggs
Plymouth *c......................1928	Hayes Briggs	Hayes Briggs	C.&A.	A.S.	A.S.	Tern Dura	Jarvis	Soss	Hayes Briggs
Plymouth *o......................1929	Briggs	Briggs	....	A.S.	None	None	Jarvis	Soss	Briggs
Plymouth *c......................1929	Briggs	Briggs	C.&A.	A.S.	A.S.	Tern	Jarvis	Soss	Briggs
Pontiac *o......................1925–30	Stewart	Stewart	....	....	None	None	....	....	Stewart
Pontiac *c......................1925–30	Fisher	Fisher	....	Tern	Tern	Tern	Tern	Tern	Fisher
V king *o......................1929–30	Fisher	Fisher	....	Tern	None	None	Tern	Tern	Fisher
V king *c......................1929–30	Fisher	Fisher	....	Tern	Tern	Tern	Tern	Tern	Fisher

*—All models;   *O—All open models;   *C—All closed models.

REPLACEMENT PARTS SIZES

AND OTHER SERVICE DATA

The next 40 pages contain important dimensional data on service parts. These were selected by taking from the Replacement Parts Section of the last Chilton Catalog and Directory the parts on which size information is most needed. Other service material which the trade found of particular value in the old Yellow Book also is included.

The primary use of most of the following tables is to find the actual size of the part required for replacement in the vehicle being serviced. What car models, and how many, use this same size of any particular part can also be determined.

Used in conjunction with the data on Interchangeability of parts immediately preceding, many of these size tables have merchandising and stock-control value.

The information on Serial Numbers tells you the age of a car from its manufacturer's number. Here also is a guide to the location of the number plate on each model.

You can determine also the year and model of any car so as to use the data in the interchangeable and replacement size tables. In some cases these serial numbers indicate the models made by a particular company, how many of each model were made and how long they were in the market.

INDEX TO PARTS SHOWN IN THESE TABLES

(See also detailed index to all contents pages 7, 9, and index to parts interchangeability on page 162)

For Manufacturers of Parts See Page 309

CLEARANCE STANDARDS

These tolerances are for general use *only* when the specific instructions of the manufacturer are not available. Measurements in inches unless otherwise specified.

Measure king pin clearance in bushing with micrometer calipers and telescoping gage.
Desirable .... .001-.002
Serviceable .... .005
Repair or replace ..... .007

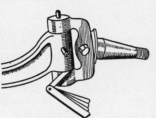

Measure end clearance of spindle thrust bearings with feeler gage.
Desirable .... .010
Serviceable .... .015 .025
Repair or replace ..... .030

Measure clearance between spring eye bolt and bushing with micrometer calipers and telescoping gage.
Desirable .... .001-.002
Serviceable .... .010
Repair or replace ..... .015

Measure variation in distance between spring eye bolt and axle on each side with steel scale.
Desirable 1/64
Serviceable 1/32
Repair 1/16

Measure variation in camber of front wheels on each side with camber gage.

	DEGREES	INCHES
Desirable	0	1/32
Serviceable	1/4	1/16
Repair	1/2	1/8

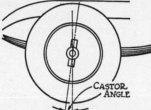

Measure caster of front axle with caster gage, (variation from specifications).

DEGREES

Desirable 0
Serviceable 1/4
Repair 1/2

Measure clearance between pitman arm shaft and bushing with micrometer calipers and telescoping gage.
Desirable .... .001-.002
Serviceable .... .004
Repair or replace ..... .006

Measure looseness of steering gear at rim of wheel with pointer and steel scale.
Desirable .... 1/2-1 in.
Serviceable .... 2 in.
Repair .... 3 in.

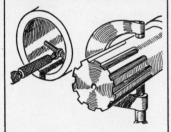

Measure clearance between sliding sleeve and clutch shaft with micrometer calipers and telescoping gage.
Desirable .... .001-.002
Serviceable .... .005
Repair or replace ..... .007

Measure clearance beween clutch hub and clutch shaft splines with dial gage.
Desirable .... .002-.003
Serviceable .... .006
Repair or replace ..... .010

Measure difference in pressure between clutch springs with spring pressure testing gage.
Desirable .... 1-2 lb.
Serviceable .... 3 lb.
Replace .... 5 lb.

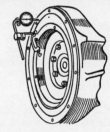

Measure alignment of clutch-bell housing with flywheel face, using dial gage.
Desirable .... .002-.003
Serviceable .... .005
Repair or replace ..... .010

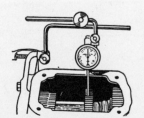

Measure clearance between transmission gear teeth with dial gage.
Desirable .... .003-.005
Serviceable .... .012
Repair or replace ..... .015

Measure clearance between gear hub and splines of shaft with dial gage.
Desirable .... .001-.002
Serviceable .... .004
Repair or replace ..... .005

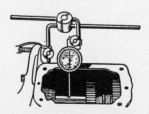

Measure diametral clearance of transmission bearings with dial gage.
Desirable .... .0005-.001
Serviceable .... .004
Repair or replace .... .005

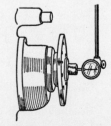

Measure end clearance of transmission bearings with dial gage.
Desirable .... .001-.003
Serviceable .... .005
Repair or replace ..... .010

Compiled by J. A. Purvis for *Automobile Trade Journal*

FOR CHECKING PARTS

These tolerances are for general use *only* when the specific instructions of the manufacturer are not available.

Measure clearance of piston rings in grooves with feeler gage.
Desirable .... .001-.0015
Serviceable .... .0025
Repair or replace.... .004

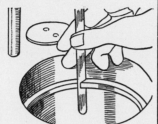

Measure clearance between ends of rings in cylinders (clearance per inch of piston diameter).
Desirable .... .003
Serviceable .... .004
Repair or replace .... .006

Measure fit of floating pin in alloy piston with spring scale.
Desirable..5-7 lb. pull when cold
Serviceable when worn .... .001
Repair or replace when worn .002

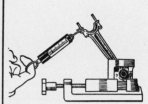

Measure fit of pin using bronze bushings with spring scale.
Desirable..3-5 lb. pull when cold
Serviceable when worn .... .001
Repair or replace when worn .002

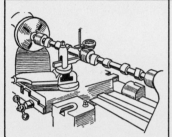

Measure straightness of camshaft with dial gage.
Desirable .... .0005-.001
Serviceable .... .002
Repair or replace .... .004

Measure camshaft bearing to journal clearance with micrometer calipers and telescoping gage.
Desirable .... .001-.002
Serviceable .... .003
Repair or replace ..... .005

Measure lateral trueness of camshaft timing gear with dial gage.
Desirable .... .001-.002
Serviceable .... .003
Repair or replace .... .005

Measure clearance between teeth on camshaft and crankshaft timing gears with feeler gage.
Desirable .... .001-.002
Serviceable .... .004
Repair or replace ..... .006

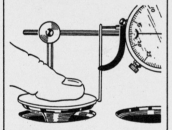

Measure clearance between valve stem and valve guide with dial gage.
Desirable .... .002-.004
Serviceable .... .005
Repair or replace ..... .006

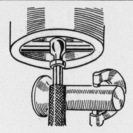

Measure clearance between valve lifter and lifter guide with micrometer calipers and telescoping gage.
Desirable .... .001-.002
Serviceable .... .003
Repair or replace ..... .005

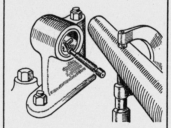

Measure clearance between rocker arm shaft and bushings with micrometer calipers and telescoping gage.
Desirable .... .001-.002
Serviceable .... .003
Repair or replace ..... .005

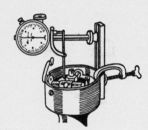

Measure sidewise movement of ignition distributor cam with dial gage.
Desirable .... .001-.002
Serviceable .... .004
Repair or replace ..... .006

Measure clearance between oil pump gear teeth and housing with feeler gage.
Desirable .... .001-.002
Serviceable .... .004
Repair or replace ..... .006

Measure clearance between oil pump housing cover and face of gears with feeler gage.
Desirable .... .001-.002
Serviceable .... .004
Repair or replace ..... .006

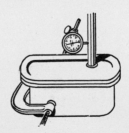

Measure clearance between oil pump shaft and bushings with dial gage.
Desirable .... .001-.002
Serviceable .... .004
Repair or replace ..... .006

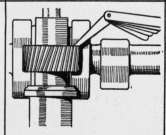

Measure clearance between oil pump drive gear and camshaft gear teeth with feeler gage.
Desirable .... .003-.005
Serviceable .... .007
Repair or replace ..... .010

CLEARANCE STANDARDS

These tolerances are for general use *only* when the specific instructions of the manufacturer are not available. Measurements in inches unless otherwise specified.

Measure straightness of crankshaft with dial gage.
Desirable .... .0005-.001
Serviceable .... .002
Repair or replace .... .004

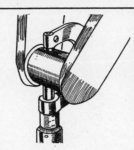

Measure crankpin for taper and roundness with micrometer calipers.
Desirable .... .0005-.001
Serviceable .... .002
Repair or replace .... .003

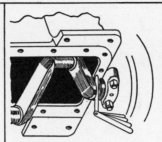

Measure end clearance of crankshaft with feeler gage.
Desirable .... .006-.008
Serviceable .... .012
Repair or replace ..... .018

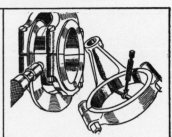

Measure clearance of forked-type outside bearing with micrometer calipers and telescoping gage.
Desirable .... .004-.005
Serviceable .... .006
Replace under.. .004 or over .007

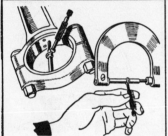

Measure roundness of bearings with micrometer calipers and telescoping gage.
Desirable .... .0005-.001
Serviceable .... .002
Repair or replace .... .003

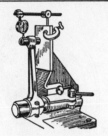

Measure connecting rod bearing for parallelism with piston pin, using aligning fixture and dial gage.
Desirable .... .0005
Serviceable .... .001
Repair or replace .... .002

Measure bearing to shaft clearance with micrometer calipers and telescoping gage.
Desirable .... .0015-.0025
Serviceable .... .003-.004
Repair or replace ... .005

Measure end clearance of connecting rod bearing with feeler gage.
Desirable .... .005-.007
Serviceable .... .010
Repair or replace ..... .015

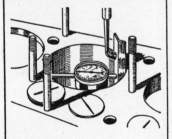

Measure roundness of cylinder bore with dial gage.
Desirable .... .0005-.001
Serviceable .... .002-.003
Repair or replace .... .004

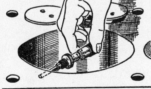

Measure cylinder bore for taper with inside micrometer.
Desirable .... .001-.002
Serviceable .... .003
Repair or replace ..... .005

Measure squareness of bore with top of block, using Vee edge protractor and feeler gage.
Desirable .... .001-.002
Serviceable .... .004
Repair or replace ..... .006

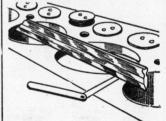

Measure flatness of top of block with steel straightedge and feeler gage.
Desirable .... .003-.005
Serviceable .... .007
Repair or replace ..... .010

Measure clearance of piston in cylinder with feeler gage (clearance per inch of piston diameter).

	IRON	ALUMINUM
Desirable ...	.001	.001-.0015
Serviceable .	.0015	.0015-.002
Replace	.0025	.003

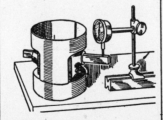

Measure piston pin boss bore for parallelism with head, using surface plate and dial gage.
Desirable .... .001
Serviceable .... .002
Repair or replace .... .003

Measure variation in compression height with surface plate and dial gage.
Desirable .... .003-.005
Serviceable .... .010
Repair or replace ..... .020

Measure difference in weight between pistons with balance scale.
Desirable .... 1/16 oz.
Serviceable .... 1/8 oz.
Repair or replace ...... 1/4 oz.

Compiled by J. A. Purvis for *Automobile Trade Journal*

FOR CHECKING PARTS

These tolerances are for general use *only* when the specific instructions of the manufacturer are not available.

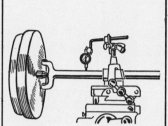

Measure straightness of propeller shaft with dial gage.
Desirable .... .002-.004
Serviceable .... .006
Repair .... .010

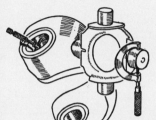

Measure clearance between universal joint pins and bushings with micrometer calipers and telescoping gage.
Desirable .... .001-.002
Serviceable .... .005 if quiet
Replace .... .007 if noisy

Measure end clearance of universal joint pins in bushings with feeler gage.
Desirable .... .001-.002
Serviceable .... .005
Repair or replace ..... .010

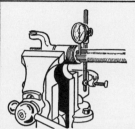

Measure fit of propeller shaft splines in universal joint yoke with dial gage.
Desirable .... .002-.004
Serviceable .... .005
Repair or replace ..... .010

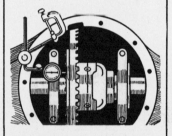

Measure lateral trueness of differential case flange with dial gage before installing ring gear.
Desirable ..... .001-.002 variation
Serviceable ...... .003 variation
Repair or replace. .004 variation

Measure lateral trueness of assembled ring gear with dial gage.
Desirable ... .002-.003 variation
Serviceable ...... .006 variation
Replace .... .010 variation

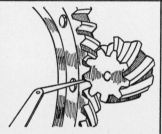

Measure clearance between pinion and ring gear teeth with feeler gage.
Desirable .... .006-.008
Serviceable .... .010
Repair or replace ..... .015

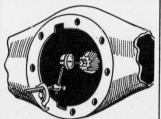

Measure endwise clearance of pinion shaft with dial gage.
Desirable .... .001-.002
Serviceable .... .003
Repair or replace ..... .005

Measure brake drum for roundness and concentricity with hub, using dial gage mounted in hub.
Desirable .... .002-.004
Serviceable .... .008
Repair or replace ..... .010

Measure brake drum for taper or bell-mouth with dial gage mounted in hub.
Desirable .... .001-.002
Serviceable .... .004
Replace .... .006

Measure endwise clearance of axle shaft with dial gage.
Desirable .... .002-.004
Serviceable .... .005
Repair or replace ..... .010

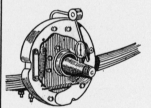

Measure wheel bearing clearance with dial gage.
Desirable .... .001-.002
Serviceable .... .005
Repair or replace ..... .008

Measure all splined shafts for straightness with dial gage.
Desirable .... .001-.0015
Serviceable .... .002
Repair .... .003

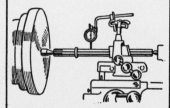

Measure all axle shafts for straightness with dial gage.
Desirable .... .001-.002
Serviceable .... .004
Repair .... .005

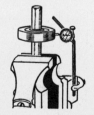

Measure all ball bearings for radial or diametral clearance with dial gage, (clearance per inch of diameter).
Desirable .... .0005-.001
Serviceable .... .003
Replace .... .005

Measure all ball bearings for endwise clearance with dial gage, (clearance per inch of diameter).
Desirable .... .001-.002
Serviceable .... .004
Replace .... .006

TUNE-UP and SERVICE SPECIFICATIONS

Line Number	CAR, MAKE AND MODEL	No. Cylinders, Bore and Stroke	VALVE TIMING: Inlet Opens °TC	VALVE TIMING: Inlet Opens Flywheel Teeth—TC	VALVE TIMING: Inlet Tappet Gap (Ins.)	OPERATING TAPPET CLEARANCE: Inlet (Ins.)	OPERATING TAPPET CLEARANCE: Exhaust (Ins.)	VALVE SPRINGS: Outer Free Length (Ins.)	VALVE SPRINGS: Inner Free Length (Ins.)	VALVE SPRINGS: Pressure (Lbs. at Ins.) Outer	VALVE SPRINGS: Pressure (Lbs. at Ins.) Inner	IGNITION: Spark Plug Gap (Ins.)	IGNITION: Breaker Point Gap (Ins.)	IGNITION: Timing: Spark Occurs °TC	IGNITION: Timing: No. Flywheel Teeth Spark Occurs—TC	IGNITION: Timing: Breaker Housing	Coil Draw Engine Stopped (Amps.)	FRONT AXLE: Total Caster (Deg.)	FRONT AXLE: Wheel Cam. (Deg.) 1 Wh.	FRONT AXLE: Wheel Camber (Ins.) 1 Wheel	FRONT AXLE: Toe in (Ins.)	Line Number
1	Auburn 6-66......1927	6-3¼x4½	TC	TC	.010	.007 H	.007 H	2¾	....	60-2	......	.025	.022	TC	TC	Ret	....	2¼	2	....	¼	1
2	Auburn 6-66A.....1927	6-2⅞x4¾	4A	1A	.012	.006 H	.008 H	....	....	......	......	.028	.020	TC	TC	Ret	....	2½	2	....	¼	2
3	Auburn 8-88......1927	8-3¼x4½	TC	TC	.010	.005 H	.007 H	2¾	....	62.5-2	......	.028	.020	6B	2B	Adv	....	2½	2	....	¼	3
4	Auburn 8-77...1927-28	8-2¾x4¾	TC	TC	.010	.007 H	.007 H	2⅝	....	89-1 27/32	......	.028	.020	TC	TC	Ret	....	2½	2	....	¼	4
5	Auburn 6-66......1928	6-2⅞x4¾	4A	1A	.012	.006 H	.006 H	....	....	......	......	.028	.020	TC	TC	Ret	....	....	....	....	....	5
6	Auburn 8-88......1928	8-3¼x4½	TC	TC	.010	.005 H	.007 H	2⅝	....	89-1 27/32	......	.028	.020	6B	2B	Adv	....	2½	2	5/16	¼	6
7	Auburn 76.....1928-29	8-2⅞x4¾	TC	TC	.010	.007 H	.007 H	2⅝	....	89-1 27/32	......	.025	.022	TC	TC	Adv	....	2½	2	....	¼	7
8	Auburn 88.....1928-29	8-2⅞x4¾	TC	TC	.010	.007 H	.007 H	2⅝	....	89-1 27/32	......	.028	.022	TC	TC	Adv	....	2½	2	....	¼	8
9	Auburn 115....1928-29	8-3¼x4½	TC	TC	.010	.007 H	.007 H	2⅝	....	83.5-1 27/32	......	.028	.022	6B	2B	Adv	....	2¼	2	....	¼	9
10	Auburn 6-80......1929	6-2⅞x4¾	TC	TC	.010	.007 H	.007 H	2⅝	....	89-1 27/32	......	.025	.022	10B	3B	Adv	4.6	2½	2	....	⅛-¼	10
11	Auburn 8-90......1929	8-2⅞x4¾	TC	TC	.010	.007 H	.007 H	2⅝	....	89-1 27/32	......	.028	.022	TC	TC	Adv	4.6	2½	2	....	⅛-¼	11
12	Auburn 120.......1929	8-3¼x4½	TC	TC	.010	.007 H	.007 H	2⅝	....	83.5-1 27/32	......	.028	.022	6B	2B	Adv	4.6	2½	2	....	¼	12
13	Auburn 6-85......1930	6-2⅞x4¾	5B	1½B	.	.006 H	.008 H	2⅝	....	89-1 27/32	......	.030	.020	0A	3A	Ret	4.6	2½	2	....	⅛-¼	13
14	Auburn 8-95......1930	8-2⅞x4¾	5B	1½B	.	.006 H	.008 H	2⅝	....	89-1 27/32	......	.030	.022	6A	3A	Ret	4	2½	2	....	⅛-¼	14
15	Auburn 125.......1930	8-3¼x4½	5B	1½B	.	.006 H	.008 H	2⅝	....	83.5-1 27/32	......	.030	.022	6A	3A	Ret	4	2½	2	5/16	¼	15
16	Auburn 8-98......1931	8-3x4¾	5B	1½B	.	.006 H	.006 H	2⅝	....	89-1 27/32	......	.020	.018	3½A	......	Ret	4.6	....	2	....	....	16
17	Austin.........1930-31	4-2.2x3	TC	TC	.	.002 H	.004 H	....	....	......	......	.020	.020	......	......	......	....	....	....	....	....	17
18	Blackhawk L-6. 1929-30	6-3⅜x4½	7A	3A	....	.028	.028	....	....	102-2 5/64	......	.022	.017	15B	5B	Adv	10	3	1½	....	⅛-3/16	18
19	Blackha'7k L-8. 1929-30	8-3x4¾	8A	2½A	....	.008	.008	....	....	103-1 15/16	......	.022	.017	8B	2½B	Adv	10	3	1½	....	⅛-3/16	19
20	Buick Std.........1925	6-3x4½	5/6B	¼B	....	.007 H	.007 H	2 3/16	....	84-2 1/32	......	.025	.020	......	......	......	....	....	....	....	....	20
21	Buick Master 6....1925	6-3⅜x4¾	½B	......	.010	.008 H	.008 H	2 13/16	2⅜	84-2 1/32	45-1 25/32	.025	.020	17B	5½B	Adv	....	....	....	....	....	21
22	Buick Std. 6......1926	6-3⅛x4½	5/6B	¼B	....	.007 H	.007 H	2¾	....	100-1⅞	......	.025	.020	17B	5½B	Adv	....	....	....	....	....	22
23	Buick Master 6...1926	6-3½x4¾	½B	½B	.010	.008 H	.008 H	2¾	2⅜	100-1⅞	45-1 25/32	.025	.020	17B	5½B	Adv	....	....	....	....	....	23
24	Buick 115.........1928	6-3⅛x4½	26B	9B	.008	.008 H	.008 H	2 15/16	1⅞	90-1 19/32	55-1⅜	.025	.020	17B	6B	Adv	....	....	2½	....	....	24
25	Buick 128, 120.. 1927-28	6-3½x4¾	26B	8B	.012	.008 H	.008 H	2 15/16	1⅞	90-1 19/32	55-1⅜	.025	.020	17B	6B	Adv	....	....	2½	....	....	25
26	Buick 116.........1929	6-3 5/16x4⅝	10½B	3½B	.012	.008 H	.008 H	....	....	......	......	.025	.020	17B	6B	Adv	10	1-2½	2½	....	⅛-3/16	26
27	Buick 129, 121....1929	6-3⅝x5	12½A	4½A	.012	.008 H	.008 H	....	....	......	......	.025	.020	17B	6B	Adv	3	1	2½	....	⅛-3/16	27
28	Buick 40..........1930	6-3 5/16x4⅝	10½B	1½B	.012	.008 H	.008 H	....	....	80-1 19/32	......	.025	.020	15B	5B	Adv	....	1-2½	2	⅜-⅝	⅛-3/16	28
29	Buick 50, 60......1930	6-3¾x5	12½A	4½A	.012	.008 H	.008 H	....	....	80-1 19/32	......	....	.020	17B	6B	Adv	....	1-2½	2	⅜-⅝	⅛-3/16	29
30	Buick 8-50........1931	8-2⅞x4¼	1½B	½B	.012	.008 H	.008 H	....	....	77-1 19/32	27-1 15/32	.030	.013	12B	4B	Adv	5	1½	1¾	5/16-½	⅛-3/16	30
31	Buick 8-60........1931	8-3 1/16x4⅝	1½B	½B	.012	.008 H	.008 H	....	....	......	......	.025	.024	11B	3¾B	Adv	5	1½	2	....	....	31
32	Buick 8-80, 8-90...1931	8-3 5/16x5	1½B	½B	.012	.008 H	.008 H	....	....	......	......	.025	.024	10B	3½B	Adv	5	1½	2	....	....	32
33	Cadillac V-63.....1925	8-3⅛x5⅛	......	......	....	.004 C	.006 C	....	....	......	......	.023	.018	......	......	Adv	....	....	....	....	....	33
34	Cadillac 314....1926-27	8-3⅛x5⅛	18B	5½B	....	.004 C	.006 C	....	....	72-3¼	......	.032	.022	......	......	......	....	¾	2½	....	3/16	34
35	Cadillac 341-A....1928	8-3 5/16x4 15/16	9½B	3B	....	.004 C	.006 C	....	....	160-2 5/32	......	.026	.022	......	......	......	2	2½	2½	....	3/16	35
36	Cadillac 341-B....1929	8-3 5/16x4 15/16	9½B	3B	....	.004 C	.006 C	....	....	160-2 5/32	......	.026	.022	......	......	......	2	1½	2½	....	⅛	36
37	Cadillac 353......1930	8-3⅜x4 15/16	11B	3½B	....	.004 C	.066 C	....	....	160-2 5/32	......	.028	.020	71/3B	2¼B	Adv	2	2½	1½	7/16	3/16	37
38	Cadillac 452....1930-31	16-3x4	TC	TC	....	AA	AA	2.089	1.94	50-1⅞	20-1¾	.025	.018	10½B	3½B	Adv	2	2½	1½	1/16	3/16	38
39	Cadillac 370......1931	12-3⅛x4	TC	TC	....	AA	AA	2.089	1.94	50-1⅞	20-1¾	.025	.020	15B	4¾B	Adv	2	3	1½	....	3/16	39
40	Cadillac 355......1931	8-3⅜x4 15/16	9B	2¾B	....	.004 C	.006 C	2 27/32	....	79-2½	......	.025	.022	71/3B	2¼B	Adv	2	3	1½	....	3/16	40
41	Chandler Std. 6 ...1927	6-3x4¼	4B	1B	.004	.007 H	.007 H	....	....	......	......	.027	.022	TC	TC	Adv	....	1½	2½	....	1/16	41
42	Chandler Sp. 6.....1927	6-3⅛x4¾	2B	½B	.006	.006 H	.006 H	2 5/16	....	70-1 11/32	......	.027	.020	......	......	......	....	1½	2½	....	1/16	42
43	Chand. Big 6-35 1927-28	6-3½x5	2B	¾B	.004	.004 H	.004 H	4⅛	....	70-2⅝	......	.025	.020	......	......	......	....	....	2¼	....	1/16	43
44	Chand. Roy 8..1927-28	8-3¼x4¾	......	1½A	.009	.007 H	.007 H	3¼	....	82-2⅜	......	.028	.020	......	......	......	....	....	2¼	....	1/16	44
45	Chand. Sp. 6-31A.1928	6-3x4¼	TC	TC	.009	.006 H	.006 H	2 5/16	....	70-1 11/32	......	.028	.022	TC	TC	Adv	....	1½	2½	....	1/16	45
46	Chand. Sp. In. 6....1928	6-3⅛x4¼	TC	TC	.009	.006 H	.006 H	2 5/16	....	70-1 11/32	......	.028	.022	TC	TC	Adv	....	1½	2½	....	1/16	46
47	Chand. Big6-135 1928-29	6-3¾x5	TC	TC	.009	.007 C	.007 C	3¼	....	95-2⅜	......	.025	.020	......	......	......	4	....	2¼	....	1/16	47
48	Chand. Roy. 8-137 1928	8-3⅜x4¾	......	1½A	.009	.007 H	.007 H	3¼	....	82-2⅜	......	.028	.020	......	......	......	....	....	2¼	¾	1/16	48
49	Chandler 65.......1929	6-3⅛x4¼	TC	TC	.009	.006 H	.006 H	2 5/16	....	70-1 11/32	......	.028	.022	TC	TC	Adv	4	....	2½	....	....	49
50	Chandler Roy. 75..1929	8-3x4½	TC	TC	....	.007 C	.007 C	3 1/16	....	80-2 9/32	......	.027	.022	5B	......	Adv	4	....	2	....	....	50
51	Chandler Roy. 85..1929	8-3⅜x4¾	TC	TC	....	.007 C	.007 C	3¼	....	95-2⅜	......	.027	.022	2A	......	Ret	4	....	2 3	....	....	51
52	Chevrolet Sup. F..1925	4-3 11/16x4	......	......	....	......	......	....	....	......	......	....	....	......	......	......	....	3½	2½	....	3/16-5/16	52
53	Chevrolet Sup. K 1925-26	4-3 11/16x4	16A	5A	....	.008 H	.010 H	....	....	......	......	.025	.020	TC	TC	Ret	....	3½	2½	....	3/16-5/16	53
54	Chevrolet Ser. V 1926-27	4-3 11/16x4	16A	5A	....	.008 H	.010 H	....	....	......	......	.025	.020	TC	TC	Ret	....	3½	2½	....	3/16-5/16	54
55	Chevrolet Cap. AA 1927	4-3 11/16x4	16A	5A	....	.006 H	.008 H	....	....	......	......	.027	.018	TC	TC	Ret	....	3½	1½	½	3/16-5/16	55
56	Chevrolet Nat. AB 1928	4-3 11/16x4	......	......	....	.006 H	.008 H	....	....	......	......	.023	.019	TC	TC	Ret	....	3½	1½	½	....	56
57	Chev. Inter. AC 1929-30	6-3 5/16x3¾	4A	1A	.010	.006 H	.008 H	....	....	......	......	.025	.021	TC	TC	Ret	3	3½	1½	½	....	57
58	Chevrolet Uni. AD 1930	6-3 5/16x3¾	4A	1A	.010	.006 H	.008 H	....	....	......	......	.025	.030	TC	TC	Ret	3	....	....	....	....	58
59	Chevrolet.........1931	6-3 5/16x3¾	4A	1A	.010	.006 H	.008 H	....	....	......	......	.025	.030	TC	TC	Ret	3	....	....	....	....	59
60	Chrysler B.......1925	6-3x4¾	......	......	....	......	......	....	....	......	......	....	....	......	......	......	....	....	....	....	....	60
61	Chrysler 58.......1926	4-3⅝x4½	......	......	.008	.004 H	.006 H	....	....	......	......	.028	.020	1/16 B	......	Adv	....	....	....	....	....	61
62	Chrysler 60.......1927	6-3x4½	6A	2A	.008	.004 H	.006 H	....	....	44-2⅜	......	.028	.020	.030"B	......	Adv	....	2	2	....	⅛-3/16	62
63	Chrysler 70....1926-27	6-3⅛x4¾	6A	2A	.008	.004 H	.006 H	....	....	52-2¾	......	.028	.022	.087"B	......	Adv	....	2	2	5/32	⅛-3/16	63
64	Chrysler Imp. 80 1926-27	6-3½x5	6A	2A	.010	.006 H	.008 H	....	....	57-3 1/16	......	.028	.022	.046"B	......	Adv	....	2	2	....	⅛-3/16	64
65	Chrysler 50.......1927	4-3⅝x4⅛	......	......	....	......	......	....	....	37-1 13/16	......	....	....	......	......	......	....	2	2	½	⅛-3/16	65
66	Chrysler 52.......1928	4-3⅝x4⅛	.010"A	1½A	.008	.004 H	.006 H	....	....	40-1 13/16	......	.028	.018	.063"B	......	Adv	....	2	2	....	⅛-3/16	66
67	Chrysler 62.......1928	6-3x4¼	.014"A	2A	.008	.004 H	.006 H	....	....	44-2⅜	......	.028	.020	.030"B	......	Adv	....	2	2	....	⅛-3/16	67
68	Chrysler 72.......1928	6-3¼x5	.017"A	2A	.008	.004 H	.006 H	....	....	52-2¾	......	.028	.020	.067"B	......	Adv	....	1½	2	5/32	⅛-3/16	68
69	Chry. Imp. 80 1928-29-30	6-3⅝x5	6A	2A	.010	.006 H	.008 H	....	....	58-3 1/16	......	.030	.022	.046"B	......	Adv	....	2	2	....	⅛-3/16	69
70	Chrysler 65.......1929	6-3⅛x4¼	.014"A	2A	.008	.004 H	.006 H	....	....	44-2⅜	......	.028	.018	.010"B	......	Adv	....	1-2	2	....	⅛-3/16	70
71	Chrysler 75.......1929	6-3¼x5	6A	2A	.008	.004 H	.006 H	....	....	52-2¾	......	.028	.022	.067"B	......	Adv	....	1-2	2	....	⅛-3/16	71
72	Chrysler 66.....1930-31	6-3⅛x4¾	6A	2A	....	.005 H	.007 H	....	....	44-2⅜	......	.030	.020	.035"B	......	Adv	....	....	2	....	⅛	72
73	Chrysler 70....1930-31	6-3⅜x5	6A	2A	....	.005 H	.007 H	....	....	52-2¾	......	.030	.022	.068"B	......	Adv	....	....	2	....	⅛	73
74	Chrysler Six....1930-31	6-3⅛x4¼	......	......	....	......	......	....	....	42-2 1/16	......	....	....	......	......	......	....	....	....	....	⅛	74
75	Chrysler 77.......1930	6-3⅜x5	6A	2A	....	.005 H	.007 H	....	....	52-2¾	......	.030	.022	.068"B	......	Adv	....	....	2	....	⅛	75
76	Chrysler Eight....1931	8-3x4¼	6A	2A	....	.005 H	.007 H	....	....	42-2 1/16	......	.025	.020	.018"B	......	Adv	....	1½	2	....	⅛	76
77	Chrysler Imp. 8...1931	8-3½x5	6A	2A	....	.005 H	.007 H	....	....	52-2¾	......	.025	.020	.047"B	......	Adv	....	1½	2	....	⅛	77
78	Cleveland 31......1925	6-2⅞x4¼	......	......	....	......	......	2¾	2 11/32	49-1 21/32	21-1 11/32	....	....	......	......	......	....	....	....	....	....	78
79	Cleveland 31......1926	6-3x4¼	......	......	....	......	......	2¾	2 11/32	49-1 21/32	21-1 11/32	....	....	......	......	......	....	....	....	....	....	79
80	Cord L-29......1930-31	8-3¼x4½	5B	1½B	....	.006 H	.008 H	....	....	......	......	.030	.020	12.8B	4B	Adv	4.6	½	1½	11/32	0	80
81	Cunningham V-7..1928	8-3¾x5	......	......	....	......	......	3⅝	....	75-2⅝	......	....	....	......	......	......	....	....	2½	....	1/16	81
82	Cunningham V-8..1929	8-3¾x5	5A	......	....	.003 C	.0015C	3⅝	....	75-2⅝	......	.031	.018	10A	......	Ret	3	....	1	....	0-1/16	82
83	Cunningha' V-9 1930-31	8-3¾x5	5A	2A	....	.001 C	.003 C	3⅝	....	75-2⅝	......	.028	.020	......	6A	Ret	3	1	6	....	....	83
84	Davis 94-27.......1927	6-2⅞x4¾	......	......	....	......	......	....	....	......	......	....	....	......	......	......	....	....	....	....	....	84
85	Davis 99.........1928	8-3x4¾	......	......	....	......	......	....	....	......	......	....	....	......	......	......	....	2	2	1	⅛	85
86	DeSoto...........1929	6-3x4⅛	.014"A	......	.008	.004 H	.006 H	....	....	......	......	.028	.020	.030"B	......	Adv	....	1-2	2	....	⅛-3/16	86
87	DeSoto Six.......1930	6-3⅛x4⅛	6A	2A	....	.005 H	.007 H	2 1/16	....	42-2 1/16	......	.030	.020	.035"B	......	Adv	....	1-2	2	....	⅛-3/16	87
88	DeSoto Str. 8...1930-31	8-2⅞x4¼	6A	2A	....	.005 H	.007 H	2 1/16	....	42-2 1/16	......	.025	.022	......	......	Adv	....	2	2	....	1/16-⅛	88
89	De Soto 6 SA.....1931	6-3¼x4⅛	6A	2A	....	.005 H	.007 H	....	....	......	......	.025	.022	......	......	......	....	1½	2	....	....	89
90	Diana Str. 8...1926-7-8	8-3x4¼	......	......	....	.004 H	.006 H	....	....	......	......	.028	.020	TC	TC	Ret	....	2	2	1	⅛	90
91	Dodge......1925-26-27	4-3⅞x4½	3A	1A	.005	.004 H	.005 H	....	....	......	......	.028	.020	12B	4B	Adv	....	2-2/3	2½	....	⅛	91
92	Dodge 124.........1920	4-3⅞x4½	3A	1A	.005	.004 H	.006 H	3¾	....	40-2¼	......	.028	.020	12B	4B	Adv	....	....	....	....	....	92
93	Dodge Senior......1928	6-3¼x4½	TC	TC	....	.005 H	.005 H	2 7/16	....	110-1 13/16	......	.025	.020	10B	3¼B	Adv	....	2-2/3	2½	¾	⅛	93
94	Dodge Sen...1928-29-30	6-3⅜x4½	TC	TC	....	.005 H	.005 H	2 7/16	....	110-1 13/16	......	.025	.020	10B	3¼B	Adv	6	2-2/3	2½	¾	⅛	94
95	Dodge 128.........1928	4-3⅞x4½	......	......	....	......	......	3¾	....	40-2¼	......	....	....	......	......	......	....	....	....	....	....	95
96	Dodge Vict. 6 1928-29	6-3⅜x3⅞	TC	TC	.005	.005 H	.005 H	2 9/16	....	44-2⅛	......	.027	.018	4B	......	Adv	....	2-2/3	2½	¾	⅛	96
97	Dodge Std. 6...1928-29	6-3⅜x3⅞	TC	TC	....	.005 H	.005 H	2 9/16	....	44-2⅛	......	.028	.018	4B	1B	Adv	6	2-2/3	2½	¾	⅛	97
98	Dodge 6 DA....1929-30	6-3⅜x3⅞	TC	TC	.005	.005 H	.005 H	2 7/16	....	110-1 13/16	......	.025	.020	4B	1½B	Adv	6	2-2/3	2½	¾	⅛	98
99	Dodge DD 6...1930-31	6-3⅛x4⅛	6A	2A	....	.006 H	.006 H	2 7/16	....	78-1¾	......	.025	.020	5B	......	Adv	5	2	2	....	1/16-⅛	99
100	Dodge DC 8....1930-31	8-2⅞x4¼	6A	1½A	....	.007 H	.007 H	2 7/16	....	78-1¾	......	.025	.020	10B	......	Adv	5	2	2	....	1/16-⅛	100
101	Dodge Six.........1931	6-3¼x4¼	6A	2A	....	.005 H	.007 H	....	....	......	......	.022	.020	.032"B	......	Adv	5	1½	2	21/32	1/32-3/32	101
102	Dodge Eight.......1931	8-3x4¼	6A	2A	....	.005 H	.007 H	....	....	......	......	.022	.020	.019"B	......	......	5	1½	2	21/32	1/32-3/32	102
103	Duesenberg J 1929-30-31	8-3¾x4¾	6B	2B	....	.022	.022	2¾	2 11/32	65-1 21/32	37-1 19/32	.025	.018	15A	5A	Ret	6	1	1	⅜	⅛	103

ABBREVIATIONS

A—Above
A—After (Valve & Ignition Timing)
AA—Automatic Adjustment
AD—Adjustable
Adv—Advance
Al—Aluminum
Als—Aluminum Alloy with strut
B—Before (Valve & Ignition Timing)
B—Below
C—Cold
CI—Cast Iron
F—Full Floating
H—Hot
IN—Interchangeable

TUNE-UP and SERVICE SPECIFICATIONS

Line Number	CAR, MAKE AND MODEL	No. Cylinders, Bore and Stroke	Inlet Opens °TC	Inlet Opens Flywheel Teeth—TC	Inlet Tappet Gap (Ins.)	Inlet (Ins.)	Exhaust (Ins.)	Outer Free Length (Ins.)	Inner Free Length (Ins.)	Pressure Outer	Pressure Inner	Spark Plug Gap (Ins.)	Breaker Point Gap (Ins.)	Spark Occurs °TC	No. Flywheel Teeth Spark Occurs—TC	Breaker Housing	Coil Draw Engine Stopped (Amps.)	Total Caster (Deg.)	Wheel Cam. (Deg.) 1 Wh.	Wheel Camber (Ins.) 1 Wheel	Toe in (Ins.)	Line Number
1	du Pont E...1927-28-29	6-3⅜x5																				1
2	du Pont F.....1928	6-3⅜x5																				2
3	du Pont G.1929-30-31	8-3⅜x4½	5A			.006	.008					.023	.022	TC	TC	Ret	4					3
4	Durant 55.....1928-29	6-2⅜x4¼	4A	1A	.012	.007 H	.007 H					.026	.018	TC	TC	Ret		1	2	⅝	⅛	4
5	Durant 65.....1928-29	6-2⅜x4¼	4A	1A	.012	.007 H	.007 H					.026	.017	TC	TC	Ret		1	2	⅝	⅛	5
6	Durant 75.....1928-29	6-3⅜x4⅝	4A	1½A	.010	.006 H	.006 H					.025	.020	8B	2½B	Adv		1	2	1⅛	⅛	6
7	Durant 40.....1929-30	4-3⅜x4½	4A	1¼A	.012	.006 H	.006 H					.027	.018	TC	TC	Ret		1	2	⅝	⅛	7
8	Durant 60.....1929-30	6-2⅜x4¼	4A	1A	.008	.006 H	.006 H					.025	.020	16B	5B	Adv	4½	1	2	⅝	⅛	8
9	Durant 66.....1929-30	6-2⅜x4¼	4A	1A	.012	.006 H	.006					.025	.020	8½B	2½B	Adv		1	2	⅝	⅛	9
10	Durant 70.....1929-30	6-3⅜x4⅝	5A	1½A	.010	.006 H	.008 H					.025	.020	8B	2½B	Adv		1	2	1⅛	⅛	10
11	Durant 6-14..1930-31	6-3¼x4	5A	1.84A		.006 H	.008					.025	.020	6	2			1½	1¼	⅞	⅛-⅜	11
12	Durant 6-17..1930-31	6-3¼x4	5A	2A		.006 H	.008 H					.025	.020	6½	2			1½	1¼	⅞	⅛-⅜	12
13	Elcar 6-70..1927-28-29	6-2⅞x4¾	TC	TC	.010	.008 H	.008 H					.025	.021	TC	TC	Ret		1½	2	⅝	⅛	13
14	Elcar 8-82...1927	8-2⅞x4¼	TC	TC	.010	.006 H	.006 H					.028	.020	TC	TC	Ret		1½	2	⅝	⅛	14
15	Elcar 90, 91, 92.1927-29	8-3¼x4¼	TC	TC	.010	.006 H	.008 H	2⅜		89-1⅝		.028	.021	6B	2B	Ret		1½	2	⅝	⅛	15
16	Elcar 8-78...1928-29	8-2⅜x4¾	TC	TC	.010	.006 H	.008 H	2⅜		89-1⅝		.028	.020	TC	TC	Ret		1½	2	1¼	⅛	16
17	Elcar 8-82...1928-29	8-2⅞x4¼	TC	TC	.010	.006 H	.008 H	2⅜		89-1⅝		.028	.020	TC	TC	Ret		1½	2	⅝	⅛	17
18	Elcar 75.....1928-29	6-3¼x4½	TC	TC	.010	.006 H	.008 H	2⅜		89-1⅝		.025	.021	TC	TC	Ret		1½	2	⅝	⅛	18
19	Elcar 95, 96..1929-30	8-3¼x4½	TC	TC	.010	.008 H	.008 H	2⅜		80 1⅝		.028	.020	TC	TC	Ret	4					19
20	Elcar 120.....1929-30	8-3¼x4½	TC	TC	.010	.008 H	.008 H	2⅜		83½-1⅝		.028	.020	6B	2B	Adv	4					20
21	Elcar 130, 140..1930	8-3¼x4½	TC	TC		.006 H	.006 H	2⅜		83½-1⅝		.030	.024	8B		Adv						21
22	Elcar 75-A....1930	6-3¼x4½	TC	TC		.006 H	.008 H	2⅜		89-1⅝		.030	.018	TC	TC	Adv	4					22
23	Erskine Six 51..1928	6-2⅞x4½	5A	1½A	.008	.008 H	.008 H					.025	.018	7½A	2A	Ret		1	1½	¾	⅛	23
24	Erskine Six 52..1929-30	6-3¼x4½	5A	1½A	.008	.008 H	.006 H					.026	.019	7½A	2A	Ret	4½	1-1⅛	1	⅞	⅛	24
25	Erskine Six 53...1930	6-3¼x4½	5A	1½A	.004	.004 H	.006 H					.020	.020	7½A	2¼A	Ret		1	1	⅞	⅛	25
26	Essex....1925-26-27-26	6-2⅜x4⅜	7A	2A		.004 H	.006 H					.026	.018					1½	1	½	0-⅛	26
27	Essex Super 6..1928-29	6-2⅜x4¼	7A	2A		.004 H	.006 H					.026	.018					1	1	½	0-⅛	27
28	Essex Challenger 6 1929	6-2⅜x4¼	7A	2A		.004 H	.006 H	2⅝		50-2		.027	.020	7½A	2A	Adv		1	1	½	0-⅛	28
29	Essex Super 6...1930	6-2⅜x4¼				.006 H	.006 H	2⅝		50-2		.022	.020	TC	TC	Adv	5	1	1	½	0-⅛	29
30	Essex Super 6...1931	6-2⅜x4¼				.004 H	.006 H	2⅜				.022	.020	TC	TC	Adv		1	1	½	⅛	30
31	Falcon Knl. 12.1928-29	6-2⅛x3⅞		1½A	SI	SI	SI	SI	SI	SI	SI	.023		8B	2B	Adv		1½		⅛	⅛	31
32	Ford T....1925-26-27	4-3¾x4	⅛°A			.015 C	.015 C					.025						2	2	¾	¾	32
33	Ford A....1928	4-3⅞x4	7½B	2B	.014	.014 C	.014 C					.035	.022	TC	TC	Ret		5	2	⅞	⅛	33
34	Ford A....1929-30-31	4-3⅞x4	7½B	2B	.014	.014 C	.013 C					.035	.022				4½	5	2	⅞	⅛	34
35	Franklin 11....1925-26	6-3¼x4¼	TC	TC	.031	.010 C	.010 C					.020	.027	6B	2B	Adv		3	2	⅛	0-⅛	35
36	Franklin 11B...1927-28	6-3¼x4	TC	TC	.031	.010 C	.010 C	2½		28-1¾		.020	.027	6B	2B	Adv		3	2	⅛	0-⅛	36
37	Franklin 12 Air...1928	6-3¼x4¾	TC	TC	.031	.010 C	.010 C	2½	2¼	21-1¼	10-1½	.028	.020	6B	3B	Adv		3	2	⅛	0-⅛	37
38	Franklin 130....1929	6-3¼x4¾	TC	TC	.031	.012 C	.012 C					.025	.020	13B		Adv	3¼	2	2	⅛	0-⅛	38
39	Franklin 137....1929	6-3¼x4¾	TC	TC	.031	.012 C	.012 C	2⅛	2⅜	26⅛-1⅜	13⅛-1⅜	.025	.020	13B		Adv	3¼	2	2	⅛	0-⅛	39
40	Franklin 145, 147..1930	12A	4A		.007	.007	2⅛	2⅜	32-2⅜	17-2	.025	.020	8B	2¾B	Adv	4	4	2	⅛	0-⅛	40
41	Franklin Ser. 15...1931	28A	9¾A		.003	.006					.025	.020	8B	2¾B	Adv	4	1		⅛	0-⅛	41
42	Gardner 6-B....1927	6-3¼x4½	TC	TC	.010	.007 H	.007 H					.027	.025	TC	TC	Ret		2	2	¾	⅛	42
43	Gardner Ser. 90 1927-29	8-2⅜x4¼	TC	TC	.010	.007 H	.007 H					.027	.020	6B	2B	Adv		2	2	¾	⅛	43
44	Gardner 75, 80..1928-29	8-2⅜x4¼	TC	TC	.010	.007 H	.007 H	2⅜		89-1⅝		.027	.021	TC	TC	Ret		2	2	¾	⅛	44
45	Gardner 95....1928	8-2⅜x4¼	TC	TC	.010	.007 H	.007 H	2⅜		89-1⅝		.027	.021	6B	2B	Adv		2	2	¾	⅛	45
46	Gardner 85,125.1928-29	8-2⅞x4¼	TC	TC	.010	.007 H	.007 H	2⅜		89-1⅝		.027	.021	6B	2B	Ret	4½	2	2	¾	⅛	46
47	Gardner 130,150.1929-30	8-3¼x4½	TC	TC	.010	.007 H	.007 H	2⅜		83½-1⅝		.027	.021	6B	2B	Adv	4½	2	2	¾	⅛	47
48	Gardner 136...1930-31	6-2⅞x4¾	5B	1½B		.006 H	.008 H	2⅜		89-1⅝		.030	.022	TC	TC	Adv	4½	2	2	¾	⅛	48
49	Gardner 140....1930	8-2⅜x4¼	TC	TC		.006 H	.008 H	2⅜		89-1⅝		.030	.022	6B	1½B	Adv	4½	2	2	¾	⅛	49
50	Gardner 148....1931	8-2⅜x4¾	TC	TC		.006 H	.008 H	2⅜		89-1⅝		.030	.022	6B	1½B	Adv	4½	2	2	¾	⅛	50
51	Gardner 150,158,1930-31	8-3¼x4½	TC	TC		.006 H	.008 H	2⅜		83½-1⅝		.030	.022	6B	1½B	Adv	4½	2	2	¾	⅛	51
52	Graham Std. 6..1930	6-3⅛x4½	TC	TC	.010	.010	.010	2⅜		53-2⅜		.025	.020	1B	1/3B	Adv	4	1½	1¼	¼-⅛		52
53	Graham Std. 8...1930	8-3x4½	TC	TC	.010	.010	.010	2⅜		53-2⅜		.025	.020	8B	3B	Adv		1½	1¼	⅜-⅛		53
54	Graham Cus. 8..1930	8-3⅜x4⅝	2A	½A	.010	.010	.010	2⅝		43-2⅜		.023	.020	2B	1½B	Adv		1½	1¼	⅜-⅛		54
55	Graham Std.Spec.6.1931	6-3¼x4½	TC	TC		.010	.010	2⅝				.025	.020	1B		Adv	4	2	1½	¼-⅛		55
56	Graham Spec. 8-20 1931	8-3x4½	TC	TC								.025	.020	6B	1½B	Adv		2	1½	⅜-⅛		56
57	Graham Cus. 8-34 1931	8-3⅜x4⅝	TC	TC								.025	.020	5B	1½B	Adv		2	1½	⅜-⅛		57
58	Grah.-Paige 610 1928-29	6-2⅞x4¼	TC	TC		.006 H	.010 H	2⅝		53-2⅛		.026	.019	7B	2B	Adv		2	1½	¾-⅛		58
59	Grah.-Paige 614 1928-29	6-2⅞x4¼	TC	TC		.006 H	.010 H	2⅝		53-2⅛		.024	.019	6B	2B	Adv		3¼	1½	¾-⅛		59
60	Grah.-Paige 619 1928-29	8-3x5	TC	TC		.010 H	.010 H	3⅛		53-2⅛		.024	.019	6B	2B	Adv		2	1½	¾-⅛		60
61	Grah.-Paige 835 1928-29	8-3⅜x4⅝	2A	½A	.008	.008 H	.008 H	2⅝		43-2⅜		.024	.018	8B	3B	Adv	4	4	1½	¾-⅛		61
62	Graham-Paige 612 1929	6-3x4½	TC	TC		.006 H	.010 H	2⅝		52-2⅛		.027	.020	7B	2B	Adv		2	1½	⅜-⅛		62
63	Graham-Paige 612 1930	6-3x4½	TC	TC		.006 H	.010 H	2⅝		52-2⅛		.023	.019	6B	2B	Adv		1½	1½	⅜-⅛		63
64	Graham-Paige 615 1929	6-3⅛x4½	TC	TC		.006 H	.010 H	2⅝		52-2⅛		.024	.019	6B	2B	Adv		1½	1½	⅜-⅛		64
65	Graham-Paige 621 1929	8-3⅛x5	TC	TC	.010	.006 H	.010 H	3⅛		52-2⅛		.024	.018	6B	2B	Adv	4		1½	½	⅛	65
66	Graham-Paige 827 1929	8-3⅜x4⅝	2A	½A	.008	.008 H	.008 H	2⅝		43-2⅜		.024	.019	8B	3B	Adv		4	1½	¾-⅛		66
67	Hudson....1925-26-27	6-3⅜x5	TC	TC		.005 H	.007 H	3	3	75-1⅛	26-1⅛	.025	.017	TC	TC	Ret		1	2½	1¼	0-⅛	67
68	Hudson Super 6...1927	6-3½x5	TC	TC		.005 H	.007 H	3	3	75-1⅛	26-1⅛	.028	.020	3A	3A	Adv		1	2½	1¼	0-⅛	68
69	Hudson O. S....1928	6-3½x5	TC	TC		.005 H	.007 H	3	3			.028	.020	3A	3A	Adv		1	2½	1¼	0-⅛	69
70	Hudson Greater...1929	6-3½x5	TC	TC		.005 H	.007 H	3	3	75-1⅛	26-1⅛	.028	.020	3A	3A	Adv		1	2½	1¼	0-⅛	70
71	Hudson Great 8..1930	8-2⅞x4½	TC	TC		.005	.007	2⅝		50-2		.022	.020	TC	TC	Adv	5	1	2½	1¼	0-⅛	71
72	Hudson Great 8..1931	8-2⅞x4½	TC	TC		.004	.006					.022	.020	TC	TC	Adv		1	2½	1¼	0-⅛	72
73	Hupmobile R....1925	4-3⅜x5½	TC	TC		.006 H	.006 H					.023		TC	TC	1/3A		3	2	½	⅛	73
74	Hupmobile E-1....1925	8-3⅜x4¼																	3	¾	⅛	74
75	Hupmobile A-1. 1926-27	6-3⅞x4¾	4A	1A	.010	.008 H	.008 H			55-2⅛		.023	.022	TC	TC	½ Adv			3	¾	⅛	75
76	Hupmobile E-2....1926	8-3¾x4¼	TC	TC	.010	.007 H	.007 H					.025	.018	TC	TC	½ Adv			3	¾	⅛	76
77	Hupmobile E-3....1927	8-3⅜x4¼	TC	TC	.010	.007 H	.007 H					.025	.025	TC	TC	½ Adv			3	¾	⅛	77
78	Hupmobile A-5....1928	6-3⅝x4¼																2⅛	3	¾	⅛	78
79	Hup.Cent.6,A6.1928-29	8-3⅜x4¾	4A	1A	.010	.008 C	.008 C			55-2⅜		.023	.017	TC	TC	Ret		2⅛	3	¾	⅛	79
80	Hup.Cent.8,M.-1928-29	8-3⅜x4¾	4A	1A	.010	.007 H	.007 H	3⅝		81-2⅛		.029	.020	TC	TC	Adv		3F		¾	⅛	80
81	Hup. 125 (E-4) 1928	8-3⅜x4¾				.007 H	.007 H					.027	.020	TC	TC	Ret		¾	3	¾	⅛	81
82	Hupmobile S....1930	6-3⅛x4¾	4A	1A		.008 C	.008 C			80-2⅛		.025	.018	9B		Adv			3	½	⅛	82
83	Hupmobile S....1930	8-3⅛x4¾	4A	1½A		.008 C	.009 C	2⅛	2⅛	46-2⅛	44-2⅛	.030	.020	9B	2¾B	Adv			3	½	⅛	83
84	Hupmobile H. U.1930	8-3⅛x4¾				.008 C	.008 C	2⅛	2⅛	46-2⅛	44-2⅛	.030	.020						3	½	⅛	84
85	Hupmobile S-2..1931	8-3⅛x4¾	4A	1A		.007 C	.015 C					.025	.018					3-1/3	3	½	⅛	85
86	Hupmobile L...1931	8-2⅜x4¾	1A			.007 C	.015 C					.030	.020					3	3	½	⅛	86
87	Hupmobile C...1931	8-3¼x4¾	1A			.007 C	.015 C					.030	.020					3	1½	½	⅛	87
88	Hupmobile H. U.1931	8-3⅛x4¾	1A			.007 C	.015 C					.030	.020									88
89	Jewett 6-50....1925-6	6-3⅝x4¾	TC	TC		.006 H	.010 H	2⅛		52-2⅛		.025	.017	10B	3½B	Adv		2	2½	¾	⅛	89
90	Jordan K, L...1925	6-3⅛x4¾	12A	4A	.008	.004 C	.006 C			52-2⅛		.025	.018	TC	TC	½Ad		2-1/3	2½	⅞	⅛	90
91	Jordan A....1926	8-2⅛x4¾			.008	.004 C	.006 H			52-2⅛		.025	.018	TC	TC	Adv		2½	2½	⅞	⅛	91
92	Jordan J, J-1..1927-28	8-2⅞x4¾			.008	.004 C	.006 H			61-1⅛	26-1⅛	.025	.018	TC	TC	½ Adv		2½	2½	⅞	⅛	92
93	Jordan AA....1927	8-3¼x4¾			.008	.004 C	.006 H			52-2⅛		.025	.018	TC	TC	½ Adv		2½	2½	⅞	⅛	93
94	Jordan R....1927-28	6-3¼x4			.008	.005 H	.006 H			99-2		.028	.020			Adv		1¾	2½	⅞	⅛	94
95	Jordan JE....1928	8-3x4¾			.008	.004 H	.006 H			103-1⅛		.030	.019			Adv		2½	2½	⅞	⅛	95
96	Jordan E....1929	8-3x4¾	5A		.008	.004	.006			103-2		.030	.024	8B		Adv	4	2½	2½	⅞	⅛	96
97	Jordan Gt. 90...1929	8-3⅝x4⅝	8A		.008	.004	.006			103-1⅛		.030	.024	8B		Adv	4	2½	2½	⅞	⅛	97
98	Jordan RE....1929	6-3⅜x4⅜			.008	.006 H	.006 H			99-2		.030	.024			Adv		1¾	2½	⅞	⅛	98
99	Jord. U 70, 80, 1930, 31	8A	2¼A		.006	.007			103-1⅛		.030	.024	8B	2½B	Adv	4	2			0-⅛	99
100	Jordan 90....1930-31	8A	2¼A		.006	.0075			103-1⅛		.030	.024	15B		Adv		2				100
101	Jordan Z Speedway 1930	2A	1½A		.010	.010	2⅝		43-2⅜		.030	.024	8B		Adv		2			0-⅛	101
102	Kissel 6-55 1925-6-7-8	6-3⅜x5	TC	TC								.027	.021					2		⅛		102
103	Kissel 8-75..1925-6-7	8-3x5	TC	TC	.010	.007 H	.007 H					.027	.021	6B	2B	Adv		2		⅛		103
104	Kissel 8-65....1927	8-2⅜x4¼	TC	TC	.010	.007 H	.007 H	2⅝		89-1⅝		.027	.021	TC	TC	Ret		2		⅛		104
105	Kissel 6-70....1928	6-3¼x4½	TC	TC	.010	.007 H	.007 H	2⅝		89-1⅝		.027	.021	TC	TC	Ret		2		⅛		105
106	Kissel 8-90....1928	8-2⅜x4¼	TC	TC	.010	.007 H	.007 H	2⅝		89-1⅝		.027	.021	TC	TC	Ret		2		⅛		106
107	Kissel 6-73....1929-30	6-2⅜x4¾	TC	TC	.010	.007 H	.007 H	2⅝		89-1⅝		.027	.021	TC	TC	Ret				¼		107

N—Negative (Battery terminal grounded)
N—No
NA—Not Adjustable

NI—Not Interchangeable
P—Piston
P—Positive Battery terminal grounded

R—Rod
Ret—Retarded
s—Sectors

SI—Sleeve Valve
SS—Semi-Steel
Y—Yes

TUNE-UP and SERVICE SPECIFICATIONS

Line Number	CAR, MAKE AND MODEL	No. Cylinders, Bore and Stroke	VALVE TIMING			OPERATING TAPPET CLEARANCE		VALVE SPRINGS				IGNITION						FRONT AXLE				Line Number
			Inlet Opens °TC	Inlet Opens Flywheel Teeth—TC	Inlet Tappet Gap (Ins.)	Inlet (Ins.)	Exhaust (Ins.)	Outer Free Length (Ins.)	Inner Free Length (Ins.)	Pressure (Lbs. at Ins.) Outer	Inner	Spark Plug Gap (Ins.)	Breaker Point Gap (Ins.)	Spark Occurs °TC	No. Flywheel Teeth Spark Occurs—TC	Breaker Housing	Coil Draw Engine Stopped (Amps.)	Total Caster (Deg.)	Wheel Cam. (Deg.) 1 Wh.	Wheel Camber (Ins.) 1 Wheel	Toe in (Ins.)	
1	Kissel 8-95.....1929-30	8-2⅞x4¾	TC	TC	.010	.007 H	.007 H	2⅝		89-1¾		.027	.021	TC	TC	Ret		2			¼	1
2	Kissel 8-126..1929-30	8-3¼x4½	TC	TC	.010	.007 H	.007 H	2⅝		83½-1¾		.027	.021	6B	2B	Adv			2½		¼	2
3	LaSalle 303....1927-28	8-3⅜x4⅞	9½B	3B		.004 C	.006 C	2⅛		79-2½		.027	.023			Adv		2½	2½		⅛	3
4	LaSalle 328......1929	8-3⅜x4⅞	9½B	3B		.004 C	.006 C	2⅛		79-2½		.027	.023			Adv	2	1½	1½		⅛	4
5	LaSalle 340......1930	8-3⅜x4⅞	11B	3½B		.004 C	.006 C	2⅛		79-2½		.028	.022	7-1/3B	2¾B	Adv	2	1½	1½		⅛	5
6	LaSalle 345......1931	8-3⅜x4⅞	9B	2¾B		.004 C	.006 C	2⅛		79-2½		.025	.022	7-1/3B	2¾B	Adv	2	3	1½		⅛	6
7	Lincoln.....1925-6-7	8-3½x5	2½B	1B	.004	.004 C	.004 C					.028	.020	5A	1½A	Ret		2	2		0-⅛	7
8	Lincoln....1928-29-30	8-3½x5	2½B	1B	.004	.004 C	.004 C					.028	.020			Ret		2	1			8
9	Lincoln.......1931	8-3½x5	22½B	8B		.004 C	.004 C					.028	.020									9
10	Locomobile 48....1925	6-4⅛x5½	TC			.005 H	.007 H					.025	.019		3A	Ret		0	1½	⅞	⅜	10
11	Locomobile Jr. 8 1925-26	8-2⅛x4	TC	TC	.007	.005 H	.007 H					.027	.020	10A	3A	Ret		0	1½	1½	¼	11
12	Loco. 48-9-10 1926-7-8	6-4⅛x5½	20B			.002 C	.002C					.027	.020	10A	TC	Ret		0	1½	1½	⅜	12
13	Locomo. 90 1927-28-29	6-3⅜x5½	TC	TC		.003 C	.003 C					.018	.018	TC	TC	Ret	6.3	0	1½	1½	¾	13
14	Locomobile 8-66..1927	8-2⅛x4	TC		.007	.005 H	.007 H					.025	.019		3A	Ret		0	2½		¼	14
15	Loco. 8-70.....1928-29	8-2⅛x4	8A	2½A	.007	.004 H	.006 H					.025	.018	TO	TO	Ret		0	2½	1½	¼	15
16	Locomobile 86, 88..1929	8-3⅜x4½	TC	5A		.010 C	.010 C	2⅛		83½-1¾		.018	.017	TC	TC	Ret	6.3					16
17	Marmon 74..1925-26-27	8-3¾x5½	13A	5A	.014	.008 H	.008 H	2⅜	2¼	69-1¾	63-1¾	.030	.026	18B	7B	Adv		4	2½		½	17
18	Marmon Little....1927	8-2¾x4	6B	1½B	.013	.006 H	.006 H	2⅜	2¼	70-2½	5-1¾	.026	.021		7B	Adv		2	1½		½	18
19	Marmon E-75..1927-28	6-3¾x5½	13A	5A	.014	.008 H	.008 H	3¾	2¾	69-1¾	64-1¾	.030	.026	18B	7B	Adv		4	2½		½	19
20	Marmon 68......1928	8-3¼x4¾	6B	1½B	.010	.008 H	.008 H	2⅛		80-1½		.025	.020	7½ B	2B	Adv	4.5	4½	1½	1½	½	20
21	Marmon 68......1929	8-3¼x4¾	6B	1½B	.010	.007 H	.007 H	2⅛		80-1½		.025	.020	7½ B	2B	Adv	4.5	4½	1½	1½	½	21
22	Marmon 78....1928-29	8-2⅛x4	6B	1½B		.007 H	.007 H	2⅛	2¾	79-2¾	5-1¾	.025	.020	7½ B	2B	Adv	4.7	4½	1½	1½	½	22
23	Mar. Roosev. 1930-31	8-3¼x4¾	6B	1½B		.007 H	.007 H	2⅛		80-1½		.025	.022	7½ B	2B	Adv	4.7	4½	1½	1½	½	23
24	Mar. Big Eight 1930-31	8-3¼x4¾	TC	TC		.008 H	.008 H	2⅛		100-2½		.025	.022		2B	Adv	4.7	4½	1½	1½	½	24
25	Mar. 69, 70...1930-31	8-2⅛x4¾	6B	1½B		.007 H	.007 H	2⅛		80-1½		.025	.022	7½ B	2B	Adv	4.7	4½	1½	1½	½	25
26	Mar. Eight 79 1930-31	8-3¼x4¾	TC	TC		.008 H	.008 H	2¼		100-2½		.028	.022	5-2/3	2B	Adv	4.7	4½	1½	1½	½	26
27	Marmon 88......1931	8-3¼x4¾	TC	TC		.008 H	.008 H	2¼		100-2½		.028	.022	5-2/3B	2B	Adv	4.7	3¼	1½	1½	½	27
28	Marmon 16.......1931	16-3⅛x4	6B	2B		.008	.008															28
29	Marquette....1929-30	6-3¼x4½	5B	1½B		.006	.006					.022	.022	7A	2¼A	Ret	5	1¾	1¾	⅜-½	⅛-½	29
30	McFarlan SV..1925-26	6-3½x5																2½				30
31	McFarlan TV 1925-6-7-8	6-4⅛x6																2½				31
32	McFarlan Str. 8 1925-6-7-8	8-3⅛x4½	TC	TC	.010	.008 H	.008 H	2½		83½-1¾		.028	.020	6B	2B	Adv		2½				32
33	Moon Ser. A 1925-6-7-8	6-3⅛x4½	4A	1A	.008	.004 H	.006 H					.027	.017			Adv		2½				33
34	Moon 6-60....1927-28-9	6-2⅞x4½	4A	1A	.008	.004 H	.006 H					.027	.020									34
35	Moon 6-72....1928-29	6-3⅛x4	5A	2A	.008	.004 H	.006 H	2⅛		103-2		.025	.018			Ret		2	2½	1	⅛-⅜	35
36	Moon 8-80....1928-29	8-3⅛x4	8A	2A	.008	.004 H	.006 H	2⅛		103-1½		.028	.018			Adv		2	2½	1	⅛-⅜	36
37	Nash Adv. 6..1925-26	6-3⅛x5	15A	5A	.010	.010 H	.010 H					.028	.017	TC	TC	Ret		2				37
38	Nash Spec. 6..1925-26	6-3⅛x4½	15A	5A	.010	.010 H	.010 H					.026	.022	TC	TC	Ret		2				38
39	Nash Light 6 1925-6-7	6-3x4	5A	1½A	.005	.005 H	.005 H					.023	.017	TC	TC	Ret		2				39
40	Nash Adv. 6..1926-7-8	6-3⅛x5	15A	5A	.010	.010 H	.010 H					.025	.017	TC	TC	Ret						40
41	Nash Adv.......1929	6-3⅛x5	15			.012	.012					.024	.015				8	1½	1½		¼	41
42	Nash Spec...1927-28	6-3¼x4½	15A		.010	.010 H	.010 H					.028	.017				8	1½	1½		⅛	42
43	Nash Spec......1929	6-3¼x4½															4	1½	1½		⅛	43
44	Nash Std. 6...1928-29	6-3⅛x4	5A	1A		.005 H	.005 H					.025	.020				4	1½			⅛	44
45	Nash Twin Ign. 8 1930	8-3¼x4½	15A	4¾A		.012	.012					.020	.020	15B	4½ B	Adv	10					45
46	Nash Twin Ign. 6 1930	6-3½x4½	15A	4¾A		.012	.012					.020	.020	15B	4½ B	Adv	4					46
47	Nash 6, 6-60..1930-31	6-3½x4½	5A	1½A		.008	.008			72-1¾		.020	.022			Ret	4	2				47
48	Nash 8-70......1931	8-2½x4½	5A	1½A		.008	.008			72-1¾		.020	.022			Ret	4	1½	1½		¼	48
49	Nash 8-80......1931	8-3x4¼	15A	4¾A		.012	.012			90-1¾	20-1½	.015	.025	15B	TC	Adv		1½	1½		¼	49
50	Nash 8-90......1931	8-3¼x4½	15A	4¾A		.012	.012			90-1¾	20-1½	.019	.025	TC	TC	Ret		0	1½		¼	50
51	Oakland Six.....1926	6-2⅞x4¾	5A	2A		.007 H	.007 H					.025	.018					½	2½	1¾	⅜	51
52	Oakland Greater Six 1927	6-2⅞x4¾	5A	2A	.008	.008 B	.008 H	2⅛		35-2½		.025	.018					½	2½	1¾	⅜	52
53	Oakland AA Six...1928	6-2⅞x4¾	5A	1½A	.010	.008 H	.008 H	2⅛		35-2½		.025	.022	4B	1½B	Ret		1½-2	2½	1¾	⅜-⅝	53
54	Oakland AA Six...1928	6-2⅞x4¾	5A	1½A	.010	.008 H	.008 H	2⅛		35-2½		.025	.022	4B	1½B	Ret	4	1½-2	2½	1¾	⅜-⅝	54
55	Oakland 101, 8. 1930-31	8-3x3⅞	TC	TC		.012 H	.012 H	2⅜		105-1⅞		.025	.022	7B	TC	Adv		1½-2	2½	1¾	⅜-⅝	55
56	Oldsmobile 30...1925	6-2¾x4¾	2A	1A	.005	.005 H	.005 H					.027	.024	TC	TC	Ret		2¾	1¾		¼	56
57	Oldsmobile D....1926	6-2¾x4¾	2A	1A	.005	.005 H	.005 H					.027	.024	TC	TC	Ret		2¾	1¾		¼	57
58	Oldsmobile E....1927	6-2¾x4¾	2A	1A	.005	.005 H	.005 H					.027	.021	TC	TC	Ret		2¾	1¾		¼	58
59	Oldsmobile F-28..1928	6-3⅛x4½	TC	TC	.010	.008 H	.008 H	2⅞		43-2¼		.027	.021	8A	2½A	Ret		3	1¾	¼	½	59
60	Oldsmobile F-29..1929	6-3⅛x4½	TC	TC	.008	.010 H	.010 H	2⅞		43-2¼		.025	.022	8A	2½A	Adv	4.5	3	1¾	½	½	60
61	Oldsmobile F-30, F-31	6-3⅛x4½	TC	TC		.010 H	.010 H					.025	.024	8B	2½B	Adv	4.5					61
62	Overland 91, 92 1925-26	4-3⅛x4	12A	3½A		.004 H	.004 H	2		22-1½		.025	.018					1-9	2			62
63	Overland 93...1925-26	6-3x4	5A	1½A		.004 H	.004 H	2¾		48-2¼		.025	.018	6B	1½B	Adv		1-2	2		¼	63
64	Over. Whip. 96 1927-8	4-3⅛x4½	5A			.004 H	.006 H	2¾		48-2		.025	.018	7B	2B	Adv		1-2	2		¼	64
65	Over. Whip. 93-A 1927	6-3x4	5A	1½A		.004 H	.006 H	2¾		42-1½		.025	.018	6B	1½B	Adv		1-2	2		¼	65
66	Over. Whip. 98 1928-29	6-3½x3⅞	7A	2A		.004 H	.006 H	2¾		75-2		.025	.018	10B	3B	Adv		1-2	2		¼-⅜	66
67	Packard 2-26, 2-33 1925	6-3⅜x5	9A	3A	.004	.004 H	.004 H					.032	.023			Adv		1	1½		⅛	67
68	Packard 1-36, 1-43 1925	8-3⅜x5	10A	3A	.004	.004 H	.004 H					.032	.023			Adv		1	1½		⅛	68
69	Pack. 2-36, 2-43 1925-26	8-3⅜x5	TC	TC	.004	.004 H	.004 H			60-3¼		.030	.018			Adv		1	1½		⅛	69
70	Packard 4-26, 4-33 1927	6-3½x5	TC	TC	.004	.004 H	.004 H			69-3¼		.028	.018			Adv		1	1½		⅛	70
71	Packard 3-36, 3-43 1927	8-3½x5	TC	TC	.004	.004 H	.004 H			69-3¼		.028	.018			Adv		1	1½		⅛	71
72	Packard 5-26, 5-33 1928	6-3⅜x5	TC	TC	.004	.004 H	.004 H					.028	.018			Adv		1	1½		⅛	72
73	Packard 626, 633..1929	8-3⅜x5	TC	TC	.004	.004 H	.004 H			43-3½		.028	.018			Adv		1	1½		⅛	73
74	Packard 4-43,640. 1928-9	8-3½x5	TC	TC	.004	.004 H	.004 H			43-3½		.028	.018			Adv		1	1½		⅛	74
75	Packard 645.....1929	8-3½x5	TC	TC	.004	.004 H	.004 H			43-3½		.028	.018			Adv		1	1½		⅛	75
76	Packard 726, 733..1930	8-3⅛x5	20B	6½B		.004 H	.004 H			43-3½		.025	.020	1½"B	2B	Adv		1	1½		⅛	76
77	Packard 740, 745..1930	8-3½x5	20B	6½B		.004 H	.004 H			43-3½		.025	.020	1½"B	2B	Adv		1	1½		⅛	77
78	Packard 826, 833..1931	8-3⅛x5	20B	6½B		.004 H	.004 H					.025	.020	1½"B	2B	Adv		1	1½		⅛	78
79	Packard 840, 845..1931	8-3½x5	20B	6½B		.004 H	.004 H					.025	.020	1½"B	2B	Adv		1	1½		⅛	79
80	Paige 6-70.....1925-26	6-3¾x5	12A	4A		.005 H	.005 H					.026	.016	12A	4A	Ret						80
81	Paige 6-72......1926	6-3¾x5	TC	TC		.006 H	.010 H					.026	.016	10B	3½B	Adv						81
82	Paige 6-65.....1927-28	6-3⅛x5	TC	TC		.006 H	.010 H	2⅛		52-2⅜		.026	.016	10B	3½B	Adv						82
83	Paige 6-75.....1927-28	6-3¾x5	TC	TC		.006 H	.010 H	3⅛		52½-2½		.028	.021	11A	3A	Ret						83
84	Paige 6-45.....1927-28	6-2⅛x4¾	4A	TC	.012	.006 H	.006 H	2⅛		7½-2½		.027	.021	6B	2B	Adv						84
85	Paige 8-85.....1927-28	8-3⅛x4½	TC	TC	.008	.008 C	.008 C	2¾		36-2½		.025	.019	10B	3½B	Adv						85
86	Peerless 67.....1925	6-3⅛x5	TC	TC		.008 C	.008 C			87-1½		.027	.019	10B	4½B	Adv		4	2			86
87	Peerless 72 1925-6-7-8	6-3⅛x5	TC	TC		.008 C	.006 C					.027	.019	10B	4½B	Adv		4	2		¼	87
88	Peerless 69 1925-6-7-8	6-3⅜x5	TC	TC	.008	.008 H	.006 H			120-1¾		.026	.018			Adv			2		¼	88
89	Peerless 80 1926 7-8	6-3⅛x4½	4A	1A	.008	.004 H	.006 H					.025	.021	15B	5B	Adv			2		¼	89
90	Peerless 90, 91..1927-28	8-3x4½	TC	TC		.004 H	.006 H					.025	.021	15B	5B	Adv					¼	90
91	Peerless 60..1927-28-29	6-3⅛x4½	5A	1½A	.008	.004 H	.006 H	2⅛		103-2		.026	.021			Adv					¼	91
92	Peerless 81......1929	6-3⅜x4½	4A	1A	.008	.004 H	.006 H	2⅛		103-2		.025	.018	.010"A		Adv	4.5	1½			¼	92
93	Peerless 61-A..1929-30	6-3⅜x4½	5A		.008	.006 H	.008 H	2⅛		103-2		.025	.018	¾"B		Adv	4.5				¼	93
94	Peerless 125..1929-30	8-3x4½	2A	2/3 A	.012	.006 H	.008 H	2⅛		110-1¾		.025	.020	¾"B		Adv	4.5	1½	1½		¼	94
95	Peerless Mast. 8 1930-31	8-3¼x4½	2A	2½A		.006 H	.008 H	2⅛		106-1¾		.028	.020	¾"B		Adv		2	1½		¼	95
96	Peerless Std. 8.....1931	8-2⅛x4½	8A	2½A		.007	.007			75-2½		.027				Adv	4.5	2	1½		¼	96
97	Pierce-Arrow 33 1925-26	6-4x5½								71-2¾		.029	.022	20A	7A	Ret		2½	3		¼	97
98	Pier'-A. Ser. 80 1925-6-7	8-3-½x5	TC	TC	.007	.003 H	.003 H	2⅛				.029	.022	20A	7A	Ret		2½	2½		¼	98
99	Pier'-A. Ser. 81 1928	8-3-½x5	TC	TC	.007	.003 H	.003 H					.025	.017			Adv		2½	2½		¼	99
100	Pier'-A. 133, 143 1929-30	8-3½x4½				.003 C	.007 C	2¾		55-2¾		.018		8½ B	2B			1½	1½		¼	100
101	Pierce-Arrow 132..1930	8-3½x4½	5A	1½A		.003	.007	2¾		55-2⅝		.018		8½ B	2B			1½	1		¼	101
102	Pierce-A. 125, 139 1930	8-3¼x4½	5A	1½A		.003	.007	2¾		55-2⅝		.018		8½ B	2B			1½	1½		¼	102
103	Pierce-Arrow 43...1931	8-3½x4½	5A	1½A		.003	.007	2¾		55-2⅝		.018		8½ B	2B			1½	1½		¼	103
104	Pierce-A. 126,41-42, 1931	8-3⅛x5	5A	1½A		.003	.007	2¾		55-2⅝		.028				Adv		1½	1-4		¼-½	104
105	Plymouth......1928-29	4-3⅝x4½	2A		.008	.004 H	.006 H			39-1¾		.025				Adv		1½	1½		¼	105

ABBREVIATIONS

A—Above
A—After (Valve & Ignition Timing)
AA—Automatic Adjustment
AD—Adjustable
Adv—Advance
Al—Aluminum
Als—Aluminum Alloy with strut
B—Before (Valve & Ignition Timing)
B—Below
C—Cold
CI—Cast Iron
F—Full Floating
H—Hot
IN—Interchangeable

TUNE-UP and SERVICE SPECIFICATIONS

Line Number	CAR, MAKE AND MODEL	No. Cylinders, Bore and Stroke	VALVE TIMING		Inlet Tappet Gap (Ins.)	OPERATING TAPPET CLEARANCE		VALVE SPRINGS		Pressure (Lbs. at Ins.)		IGNITION		Timing			Coil Draw Engine Stopped (Amps.)	FRONT AXLE				Line Number
			Inlet Opens °TC	Inlet Opens Flywheel Teeth—TC		Inlet (Ins.)	Exhaust (Ins.)	Outer Free Length (Ins.)	Inner Free Length (Ins.)	Outer	Inner	Spark Plug Gap (Ins.)	Breaker Point Gap (Ins.)	Spark Occurs °TC	No. Flywheel Teeth Spark Occurs—TC	Breaker Housing		Total Caster (Deg.)	Wheel Cam. (Deg.) 1 Wh.	Wheel Camber (Ins.)	Toe in (Ins.)	
1	Plymouth........1929-30	4-3⅝x4⅛	5A	1½A	.008	.004 H	.006 H			39-1⅞		.028	.020			Adv		1-2	4		⅛-₃₂	1
2	Plymouth........1930	4-3⅝x4⅛	5A	1¼A	.008	.004 H	.006 H			39-1⅞		.027	.018	.050″B		Adv		1½-2	4		₃₂	2
3	Plymouth........1931		TC	TC		.005 H	.007 H					.025	.020	.050″B		Adv		1½	2		⅞	3
4	Pontiac 6-27...1926-27	6-3¼x3¾	7A	2A	.009	.009 H	.009 H	2½		35-1¾		.022	.022					4½	1½		⅛	4
5	Pontiac 6-28....1928	6-3¼x3¾	7A	2A	.008	.008 H	.008 H	2½		35-1¾		.023	.023	7B	2B			4½	1½		⅛	5
6	Pontiac......1929-30-31	6-3₁₆x3⅞	7A	2A		.008 H	.008 H	2½		35-1¾		.025	.022	4B	1¼B	Ret	5	1½-2½	1½		⅛	6
7	Reo T-6......1925-6-7	6-3¼x5				.005 H	.005 H	2₈		51-2½		.026	.019	TC	TC	Ret						7
8	Reo Fly. Cld. A 1927-28	6-3¼x5	TC	TC	.007	.004 H	.006 H	3		90-2₃₂		.029	.018			Adv		2¼	1½		¾	8
9	Reo Wolverine B 1927-28	6-3¾x4				.005 H	.007 H	2₁₆		93-2		.028	.020					2	1½		¾	9
10	Reo F.Cld.C,Mt.1929-30	6-3¼x5	TC	TC	.007	.005 H	.007 H	3		90-2₃₂		.028	.018			Adv		3½	1½		¾	10
11	Reo Wolverine B.....1929	6-3¾x4				.005 H	.007 H					.028	.020			Adv		2	1½		¾	11
12	Re F. C., B2,Mt.1929-30	6-3¾x4				.005 H	.007 H					.025	.020			Adv		2	1½		¾	12
13	Reo 15......1930	6-3¼x4				.007 H	.007 H					.025	.020					2	1½		¾	13
14	Reo 25N......1931	6-3¼x5	TC	TC		.007 H	.007 H	3		90-2₃₂		.025	.020			Adv		3½	1½		¾	14
15	Reo 30N, Roy. 35N 1931	8-3¼x4¾	TC	TC		.008 H	.008 H	3		85-2₃₂		.025	.020	15A		Ret	4.5	3½	1½			15
16	Rickenbacker D....1925	6-3¼x4¾	TC	TC															2			16
17	Rickenbacker 0-70.1927	6 3⅛x4¾	TC	TC															2			17
18	Rickenbacker 8-80.1927	8-3x4¾	TC	TC															2			18
19	Rickenbacker 8-90.1927	8-3¼x4¾	TC	TC		.008 H	.008 H					.028	.021	6B	2B	Adv				2			19
20	Roamer 8-88....1926-30	8-3¼x4½	TC	TC	.010	.005 H	.007 H					.028	.021	6B	2B	Adv						20
21	Roa. 8-80, 1927-8-9-30	8-3¼x4½	TC	TC	.010	.005 H	.007 H					.028	.021	5A	2B	Ret						21
22	Roa. 8-78, 1927-8-9-30	8-2¾x4½										.025	.021	7½B	2B	Adv						22
23	Roosevelt.......1929	8-2¾x4¼	6B	1½B	.010	.006 C	.006 C					.025	.018					4½	1½	₃₂		23
24	Star F........1925	4-3⅜x4¼	4A	1¼A		.007 H	.007 H					.027						3	2	1₃₂		24
25	Star F........1925-26	4-3⅜x4¼																3		₃₂		25
26	Star M......1926-27	6-2¾x4¾	4A	1¼A		.006 H	.006 H					.028	.018	TC	TC	Ret		3	2	1₃₂		26
27	Star R......1926-27-28	6-2¾x4¾	4A	1¼A	.012	.006 H	.006 H					.028	.020	TC	TC	Ret		3	2	1₃₂		27
28	Stearns-Knight C. 1925	4-3¾x5		Sl	Sl	Sl	Sl	Sl	Sl	Sl	Sl											28
29	Stearns-Kni. B.1925-26	4-3¾x5⅝		Sl	Sl	Sl	Sl	Sl	Sl	Sl	Sl											29
30	Stearns-Kni. S-6..1925	6-3¼x5		Sl	Sl	Sl	Sl	Sl	Sl	Sl	Sl											30
31	Stearns-Kni. 8-95. 1926	8-3¼x5		Sl	Sl	Sl	Sl	Sl	Sl	Sl	Sl											31
32	Stearns-Kni. C-75..1926	6-3¼x5		Sl	Sl	Sl	Sl	Sl	Sl	Sl	Sl											32
33	Stearn'-K. F6-851927-28	6-3¼x5		Sl	Sl	Sl	Sl	Sl	Sl	Sl	Sl							1	2½	2₁₆	0-₁₆	33
34	Stearn'-K.G8-851927-28	8-3¼x5		Sl	Sl	Sl	Sl	Sl	Sl	Sl	Sl							1	1	1₁₆	0-₁₆	34
35	St.-K. HJ8-90 1928-9-30	8-3¼x5	6A		Sl	Sl	Sl	Sl	Sl	Sl	Sl	.028	.018	8B		Adv	4	1	1		0-₁₆	35
36	St.-K. MN6-80. 1928-29	6-3¼x5	10A		Sl	Sl	Sl	Sl	Sl	Sl	Sl	.028	.018	12B		Adv	4					36
37	Stu. Std. 6,ER 6 1925-6-7	6-3⅜x4¾				.006 H	.006 H			87-1₁₆		.026	.019					1-1½	1		⅜	37
38	Stu. Sp. 6, EQ 6 1925-26	6-3⅜x4½				.006 H	.006 H			57-1₁₆		.026	.019					1-1½	1		¾	38
39	Stu. Big 6, EP 6 1925-26	6-3⅞x5				.006 H	.006 H			57-1₁₆		.026	.019					1-1½	1		¾	39
40	Studebaker Big 6..1927	6-3⅞x5	TC	TC	.006	.006 H	.006 H			87-1₁₆		.026	.020	TC	TC	½ Adv		1-1½	1		⅜	40
41	Stude. Dict. EU 1928	6-3⅜x4½				.006 H	.006 H			57-1₁₆		.026	.019					1-1½	1		₃₂	41
42	Stude. Com. EW...1928	6-3⅞x5	TC	TC		.006 H	.006 H			57-1₁₆		.026	.021	TC	TC	½ Adv		1-1½	1		₃₂	42
43	Stude. Dict. GE 6 1929	6-3⅜x4½	5A	1½A	.010	.004 C	.006 C			57-1₁₆		.025	.021	7¼A	2¼A	Adv	4	1-1½	1		₃₂	43
44	Stude. Pres. 6 ES 1927-28	6-3⅞x5	TC	TC	.006	.006 H	.006 H			57-1₁₆		.026	.020	TC	TC	½ Adv		1-1½	1		₃₂	44
45	Stude. Pres. 8 FA 8 1928	8-3¼x4½	5A	1½A	.010	.003 C	.007 C			98-1₁₆		.025	.020	17A	5½A	Ret	4½	1-1½	1		₃₂	45
46	Stude. Pres. FA, FB 1929	8-3¼x4½	5A	1½A	.010	.003 C	.007 C			98-1₁₆		.025	.020	17A	5½A	Ret	4½	1-1½	1		₃₂	46
47	Stude.Com.6GJ1929-30	6-3⅜x4½	5A	1½A		.004 H	.006 H			65-1₁₆		.025	.020	7¼A	2A	Ret	4½	1-1½	1		₃₂	47
48	Stu Com. 8 FD 1929-30	8-3¼x4½	TC	TC		.004 H	.006 H			65-1₁₆		.025	.020	17A	5A	Ret	4½	1-1½	1		₃₂	48
49	Stu. Pres. 8 FE,F H1930	8-3¼x4½	5A	1½A	.010	.004 H	.006 H			98-1₁₆		.025	.020	17A	5½A	Ret	4½	1-1½	1		₃₂	49
50	Stude. Dict. 6 GL 1930	6-3₁₆x4½	5A	1½A		.004 H	.006 H			65-1₁₆		.025	.020	5B	1½B	Adv	4	1-1½	1		₃₂	50
51	Stude. Dict. 8 FC 1930	8-3x3½	TC	TC		.004 H	.006 H			65-1₁₆		.025	.020	17A	5A	Ret		1-1½	1		₃₂	51
52	Studebaker Six 54.1931	6-3¼x4½	5A	1½A		.004 H	.006 H					.025	.020	7¼A	2¼A	Adv	4	1-1½	1		₃₂	52
53	Stude. Dict. 8 1931	8-3¼x4½	5A	1½A		.004 H	.006 H					.025	.020	9B	2½B	Adv		1-1½	1		₃₂	53
54	Stude. Com. 70....1931	8-3₁₆x4½	15B	4½B		.004 H	.006 H					.025	.020	7B	2B	Adv	4½	1-1½	1		₃₂	54
55	Studebaker Pres...1931	8-3¼x4½	5A	1½A		.004 H	.006 H					.025	.020	17A	5¼A	Ret	4½	1-1½	1		₃₂	55
56	Stutz 693-4......1925	6-3½x5	10A	3½A	.004	.007 H	.007 H					.026	.021								⅛	56
57	Stutz 695.......1925	6-3½x5	10A	3½A	.004	.007 H	.007 H					.026	.021								⅛	57
58	Stutz AA........1926	8-3¼x4½	10A	3A	.028	.028 C	.028 C	2₁₆		90-2½		.025	.019	TC	TC	Ret		2½	2½	½-¾	½-¼	58
59	Stutz AA........1927	8-3¼x4½	10A	3A	.028	.028 C	.028 C	2₁₆		90-2½		.025	.019	TC	TC	Ret		2½	2½	½-¾	½-¼	59
60	Stutz BB........1928	8-3¼x4½	10A	3A	.028	.028 C	.028 C					.02	.017	TC	TC	Ret		2½	2½	¼	½-₃₂	60
61	Stutz M......1929-30	8-3¼x4½	7A	2½A		.028 C	.028 C					.025	.017	15B	3B	Adv	10	1	1		½-₃₂	61
62	Stutz LA........1931	8-3¼x4½	7A	2½A		.028	.028					.022	.017	15B	5B	Adv	10	2½			½	62
63	Stutz MA........1931	8-3¼x4½	7A	2½A		.028 C	.028 C					.022	.017	15B	3B	Adv	10	1			½	63
64	Stutz MB........1931	8-3¼x4½	7A	2¼A		.028 C	.028 C					.022	.017	15B	5B	Adv		2½			½	64
65	Velie 60......1925-26	6-3₁₆x4½	7A	2A	.009	.007 H	.007 H					.025	.020	8B	2B	Adv		2	2		½	65
66	Velie Sp. 60....1927-28	6-3₁₆x4½	7A	2A	.009	.007 H	.007 H					.025	.020	8B	2B	Adv		2	2		½	66
67	Velie Std. 50....1927-28	6-3₁₆x4½	7A	2A	.009	.007 H	.007 H					.025	.020	8B	2B	Adv		2	2		½	67
68	Velie 6-77, 6-78...1928	6-3₁₆x4½	7A	2A	.009	.007 H	.007 H					.025	.020	8B	2B	Adv		2	2	1½	0-₃₂	68
69	Velie 6-66, 6-68...1928	6-3¼x4¼	7A	2A	.009	.007 H	.007 H					.025	.020	8B	2B	Adv		2	2	1½	0-₃₂	69
70	Velie 8-88, 8-90..1928	8-3¼x4½	TC	TC	.010	.007 H	.007 H					.028	.021	6B	2B	Adv		2	2	1½	0-₃₂	70
71	Viking........1929	8-3¼x4⅝	1-1/3 B	1/3B	.010	.008 H	.012 H	2₁₆		40-2¼		.026	.021			Adv		3R	2		½	71
72	Viking V-30.....1930	8-3¼x4⅝	1-1/3 B	¾ B		.010 H	.010 H	2₁₆		40-2¼		.024	.022	.045″B		Adv	5	3R	2		½	72
73	Whippet 96-A..1929-30	4-3⅛x4¼	7A	2A		.004 H	.006 H	2₁₆		75-2		.025	.018	TC	TC	Adv	4	1-2	2		½	73
74	Whippet 98-A..1929-30	6-3⅛x3¾	7A	2A	.008	.004 H	.006 H	2₁₆		75-2		.025	.018	8B	2¼B	Adv	4	1-2	2		½	74
75	Willys-Kni. 65....1925	4-3¼x4¾	15A	Sl	Sl	Sl	Sl	Sl	Sl	Sl	Sl	.025	.017			Adv		1-2	2½		½	75
76	Willys-Kni. 66.1925-26	6-3⅛x4¼	25A	8A	Sl	Sl	Sl	Sl	Sl	Sl	Sl	.028	.017	12B	4B	Adv		1-2	2½		½	76
77	Willys-Kni. 70-...1927	6-2₁₆x4¼	10A	3A	Sl	Sl	Sl	Sl	Sl	Sl	Sl	.026	.017	8B	2B	Adv		1-2	2½		½	77
78	Willys-Kni. 66-A..1927	6-3⅜x4¼	10A	3A	Sl	Sl	Sl	Sl	Sl	Sl	Sl	.028	.018	12B	4B	Adv		1-2	2½		½	78
79	Willys-Kni. 70A..1927	6-2₁₆x4¼	10A	3A	Sl	Sl	Sl	Sl	Sl	Sl	Sl	.025	.018	8B	2B	Adv		1-2	2½		½	79
80	Willys-K. Great 6 1929-9	6-3⅜x4½	10A	3A	Sl	Sl	Sl	Sl	Sl	Sl	Sl	.025	.018	12B	4B	Adv		1-2	2½		½	80
81	Willys-K. Sp. 6.1928-9	6-2₁₆x4¼	10A	2½A	Sl	Sl	Sl	Sl	Sl	Sl	Sl	.025	.018	8B	2B	Adv		1-2	2½		½	81
82	Willys-K. Std. 6.1928-9	6-2₁₆x3⅞	10A	2½A	Sl	Sl	Sl	Sl	Sl	Sl	Sl	.026	.017	8B	2B	Adv		1-2	2½		½	82
83	Willys-Kni. 70B 1929-30	6-2₁₆x4¼	10A	2½A	Sl	Sl	Sl	Sl	Sl	Sl	Sl	.025	.018	8B	2¼B	Adv		1-2	2½		½	83
84	Willys-Knight 66B 1930	6-3⅜x4½	5A	1½A	Sl	Sl	Sl	Sl	Sl	Sl	Sl	.025	.018	16B	5B	Adv	4	1-2	2½		½	84
85	Willys-Knight 87. 1930	6-2₁₆x4¼	TC	TC	Sl	Sl	Sl	Sl	Sl	Sl	Sl	.025	.018	8B	2¼B	Adv	4	1-2	2½	₃₂	₃₂	85
86	Willys-Knight 66D 1931	6-3⅜x4½	5A	1½A	Sl	Sl	Sl	Sl	Sl	Sl	Sl	.025	.018	16B	5B	Adv	4	1-2	2½		₃₂	86
87	Willys Six 98B...1930	6-3⅛x3⅞	7B	2-1/3 B	.004 H	.006 H			2₁₆		83-1₁₆		.025	.018	TC	TC	Adv	4	1-2	2½		½	87
88	Willys Six 97...1931	6-3⅛x3⅞	7B	2-1/3 B		.004 H	.006 H					.025	.018	TC	TC	Adv	4½	1-2	2½		½	88
89	Willys Six 98D...1931	6-3⅛x3⅞	7B	2-1/3 B		.004 H	.006 H					.025	.018	TC	TC	Adv	4½	1-2	2½		½	89
90	Willys Eight 8-80. 1930	8-3⅛x4	TC	TC		.006 H	.008 H					.025	.018	TC	TC	Adv		1-2	2½		½	90
91	Willys Eight 8-80D 1931	8-3⅛x4	TC	TC		.006 H	.008 H					.025	.018	6B	1¼B	Adv	4½	1-2	2½		½	91
92	Wills Ste. Cla. A-68 1925	8-3¼x4	10A	3½A								.016	.021					2½			₃₂	92
93	Wills Ste. Cla. B-68 1925	8-3¼x4	10A	3½A								.016	.021					2½			₃₂	93
94	Wills Ste. Cla. C-68 1925	8-3¼x4	10A	3½A								.016	.021					2½			₃₂	94
95	Wills Ste. Cla. W-6 1925	6-3¼x4										.031	.022	7B	2B	Ret		2½			₃₂	95
96	Wills Ste. Cla. W-61926	6-3¼x5½										.031	.022	7B	2B	Ret		2½			₃₂	96
97	Wills Ste. Cla. T-6 1926	6-3¼x5½										.031	.022	7B	2B	Ret		2½			₃₂	97
98	Wills Ste. Cla. D68 1928	8-3¼x4										.026	.021					2½			₃₂	98
99	Windsor 8-82....1929	8-3x4¾	8A	2A	.008	.006 H	.008 H					.025	.021			Adv	4½	2½	1		½-₃₂	99
100	Windsor 8-92...1929-30	8-3x4¾	8A	2A	.008	.006 H	.008 H					.025	.018	8½B	2¼B	Adv	4½	2½	1		½-₃₂	100
101	Windsor 6-72....1929	6-3¼x4¾	5A	1½A		.004 H	.006 H					.025	.018			Ret	4½	2½	1		½-₃₂	101
102	Windsor 6-77....1929	6-3¼x4¾	5A	1½A		.004 H	.006 H					.025	.018			Ret	4½	2½	1		½-₃₂	102
103	Windsor 6-69...1929-30	6-3¼x4¾	4A	1A		.004 H	.006					.015	.020	8½B	2¼B	Ret	4½	2½	1		½-₃₂	103
104	Windsor 6-75....1930	6-3¼x4¾	5A	1¼A		.004 H	.006 H					.025	.018	8½B	2¼B	Ret	4½	2½			½	104
105	Windsor 8-85....1930	8-3x4¾	8A	2A		.006	.008					.025	.020	8½B	2¼B	Ret	4½	2½			½	105

N—Negative (Battery terminal grounded)
N—No
NA——Not Adjustable

NI—Not Interchangeable
P—Piston
P—Positive (Battery terminal grounded)

R—Rod
Ret—Retarded
s—Sectors

Sl—Sleeve Valve
SS—Semi-Steel
Y—Yes

Piston Ring Sizes

Car, Model and Year	Diameter	Compression: Width	Compression: No. Rings Used Per Car	Oil Control: Width	Oil Control: No. Rings Used Per Car
Auburn 6-66A (1927)	2 7/8	1/8	12	3/16	6
Auburn 8-88 (1927-28)	3 1/4	1/8	16	1/8	16
Auburn 8-77 (1927-28)	2 3/4	1/8	24	1/8	8
Auburn 76 (1928-29)	2 7/8	1/8	12	3/16	6
Auburn 88 (1928-29)	2 7/8	1/8	16	1/8	16
Auburn 115 (1928-29)	3 1/4	1/8	16	3/16	8
Auburn 6-80 (1929)	2 7/8	1/8	12	3/16	6
Auburn 8-90 (1929)	2 7/8	1/8	24	3/16	8
Auburn 120 (1929)	3 1/4	1/8	24	3/16	8
Auburn 6-85 (1930)	2 7/8	1/8	12	*	12
Auburn 8-95 (1930)	2 7/8	1/8	12	*	16
Auburn 125 (1930)	3 1/4	1/8	16	3/16	16
Blackhawk L6 (1929-30)	3 3/8	1/8	18	3/16	6
Blackhawk L8 (1929-30)	3	1/8	24	3/16	8
Buick 115 (1927-28)	3 1/8	1/8	12	1/8	6
Buick 120, 128 (1927-28)	3 1/2	1/8	12	3/16	6
Buick 116 (1929)	3 5/16	1/8	12	3/16	6
Buick 121, 129 (1929)	3 5/8	1/8	12	3/16	6
Buick Series 40 (1930)	3 7/16	1/8	12	3/16	6
Buick-Series 50, 60 (1930)	3 3/4	1/8	12	3/16	6
Cadillac 314 (1927)	3 1/8	3/16	16	3/16	8
Cadillac 341 A, B (1928-29)	3 5/16	3/16	16	3/16	8
Cadillac 353 (1930)	3 3/8	1/8	24	3/16	8
Cadillac 452 (1930)	3	1/8	48	3/16	16
Chandler Big 6 (1927-28)	3 1/2	1/8	12	3/16	6
Chandler Royal 8 (1927-28)	3 1/4	1/8	16	3/16	8
Chandler Spec. 6 (1927)	3 1/8	1/8	12	3/16	6
Chandler Std. 6 (1927)	3	1/8	12	3/16	6
Chandler Spec. 6 (1928)	3 1/8	1/8	12	3/16	6
Chevrolet AA (1927)	3 11/16	3/16	12	..	..
Chevrolet AB (1928)	3 11/16	5/32	8	5/32	4
Chevrolet AC (1929-30)	3 5/16	5/32	12	5/32	6
Chrysler 50 (1927)	3 5/8	1/8	8	1/8	4
Chrysler 60 (1927)	3	1/8	12	1/8	6
Chrysler 70 (1927)	3 1/8	1/8	12	1/8	6
Chrysler 80 (1927)	3 1/2	1/8	12	1/8	6
Chrysler 52 (1928)	3 5/8	1/8	8	1/8	4
Chrysler 62 (1928)	3	11/64	12	1/8	6
Chrysler 72 (1928)	3 1/4	9/64	24	1/8	6
Chrysler Imp. 80 (1928-30)	3 5/8	5/32	24	9/64	6
Chrysler 65 (1929)	3 1/8	9/64	18	1/8	6
Chrysler 75 (1929)	3 1/4	9/64	24	1/8	6
Chrysler 66 (1930)	3 1/8	9/64	12	1/8	6
Chrysler 70 (1930)	3 1/8	9/64	12	1/8	6
Chrysler 77 (1930)	3 3/8	9/64	24	1/8	6
Cord (1929-30)	3 1/4	1/8	24	3/16	8
Davis 92 (1927)	3 1/4	3/16	12	3/16	6
Davis 94 (1927)	2 7/8	3/16	12	3/16	6
Davis 98 (1927)	2 7/8	3/16	16	3/16	8
Davis 99 (1928)	3	1/8	24	3/16	8
De Soto 6 (1928-30)	3	9/64	12	1/8	6
De Soto 8 (1930)	2 7/8	3/32	24	1/8	8
Diana Str. 8 (1927-28)	3	3/16	16	3/16	8
Dodge Brothers 4 (1927-28)	3 7/8	1/8	12	5/32	4
Dodge Bros. Senior (1927-28)	3 1/4	1/8	18	5/32	6
Dodge Bros. Vict. Std. 6 (1928-29)	3 3/8	1/8	18	5/32	6
Dodge Bros. Senior (1929-30)	3 3/8	1/8	18	5/32	6
Dodge Bros. D A6 (1929-30)	3 3/8	1/8	18	5/32	6
Dodge Bros. 8 (1930)	2 7/8	3/32	24	1/8	8
Dodge Bros. D D (1930)	3 1/8	11/64	12	1/8	6
Durant D-55 (1928)	2 3/4	3/16	12	3/16	6
Durant 4 (1928-29)	3 3/8	1/8	18	3/16	4
Durant D-65 (1928)	2 7/8	1/8	12	3/16	6
Durant 70, 75 (1928-29)	3 3/8	1/8	18	5/32	6
Durant 60 (1929)	2 7/8	1/8	18	5/32	6
Durant 66 (1929)	2 7/8	1/8	18	3/16	6
Durant 614 (1930)	3 1/4	1/8	18	5/32	6
Durant 617 (1930)	3 3/8	1/8	18	5/32	6
Elcar 6-70 (1927-29)	2 7/8	1/8	18	1/8	6
Elcar 8-78 (1927-29)	2 3/4	1/8	24	1/8	8
Elcar 8-90, 8-91 (1927)	3 1/4	1/8	24	1/8	8
Elcar 8-82 (1928-29)	2 7/8	1/8	16	1/8	16
Elcar 120 (1929)	3 1/4	1/8	16	3/16	16
Elcar 75 (1929-30)	2 7/8	1/8	12	1/8	6
Elcar 95, 96 (1929-30)	2 7/8	1/8	16	1/8	8
Elcar 130 (1930)	3 3/8	1/8	16	3/16	8
Erskine 50 (1927)	2 5/8	1/8	18	3/16	6
Erskine (1928-29)	2 3/4	1/8	18	3/16	6
Erskine 53 (1930)	3 1/4	1/8	18	3/16	6
Essex Super 6 (1927-28)	2 11/16	1/8	12	1/8	6
Essex (1929)	2 3/4	1/8	6	1/8	12
Essex E (1930)	2 3/4	1/8	12	1/8	12
Falcon Knight 10 (1927-28)	2 15/16	1/8	18	..	..
Falcon Knight 12 (1928-29)	2 15/16	1/8	18	1/8	6
Flint Jr. (1927)	2 3/4	3/16	18	..	..
Flint 60 (1927-28)	3 1/4	3/16	18	..	..
Flint 80 (1927-28)	3 3/8	3/16	18	..	..
Ford T (1927)	3 3/4	1/4	12	..	..
Ford A (1928)	3 7/8	1/8	8	1/8	4
Ford A (1929-30)	3 7/8	1/8	8	5/32	4
Franklin Series 11B 12, 130 (1927-29)	3 1/4	1/8	18	1/8	6
Franklin 135, 137 (1929)	3 1/2	1/8	12	1/8	12
Franklin 145, 147 (1930)	3 1/2	1/8	12	3/16	12
Gardner 80 (1927)	2 3/4	1/8	24	1/8	8
Gardner 90 (1927)	3 1/4	1/8	24	1/8	8
Gardner 75 (1928)	2 3/4	1/8	16	1/8	16
Gardner 85 (1928)	2 7/8	1/8	16	1/8	16
Gardner 95 (1928)	3 1/4	3/16	24	1/8	8
Gardner 120 (1929)	2 3/4	1/8	24	1/8	8
Gardner 125 (1929)	2 7/8	1/8	16	3/16	8
Gardner 130 (1929)	3 1/4	1/8	16	1/8	16
Gardner 136 (1929-30)	2 7/8	1/8	12	3/16	12
Gardner 140 (1930)	2 7/8	1/8	16	3/16	16
Gardner 150 (1930)	3 1/4	1/8	16	3/16	16
Graham Paige 610 (1928-29)	2 7/8	1/8	12	3/16	6
Graham Paige 614 (1928-29)	3 1/8	1/8	12	3/16	6
Graham Paige 619, 629, 621 (1928-29)	3 1/2	1/8	12	3/16	6
Graham Paige 835, 827, 837 (1928-29)	3 3/8	1/8	16	3/16	8
Graham Paige 612 (1929)	3	1/8	12	3/16	6
Graham Paige 615 (1929)	3 1/4	1/8	12	3/16	6
Graham Std. 6 (1930)	3 1/8	1/8	12	3/16	6
Graham Spec. 6 (1930)	3 1/4	1/8	12	3/16	6
Graham Std., Spec. 8 (1930)	3 1/4	1/8	16	3/16	8
Graham Custom 8 (1930)	3 3/8	1/8	16	3/16	8
Hudson (1927)	3 1/2	1/8	18	..	..
Hudson (1928-29)	3 1/2	1/8	6	1/8	12
Hudson 8 (1930)	2 3/4	1/8	16	1/8	16
Hupmobile A2 (1927)	3 1/8	1/8	12	3/16	6
Hupmobile E3 (1927)	3	1/8	16	3/16	8
Hupmobile 6 (1928)	3 1/4	1/8	12	3/16	6
Hupmobile M8, 125 (1928-29)	3	1/8	16	3/16	8
Hupmobile A6 (1929)	3 1/4	1/8	12	3/16	6
Hupmobile H, U (1930)	3 1/2	9/64	32	1/8	8
Hupmobile S (1930)	3 1/4	1/8	12	3/16	6
Hupmobile C	3	1/8	16	3/16	8
Jordan AA (1927)	3	3/16	16	3/16	8
Jordan J (1927)	2 7/8	3/16	16	3/16	8
Jordan R (1927-28)	3 1/4	1/8	18	5/32	6
Jordan JE, JJ (1928-29)	3	1/8	16	3/16	16
Jordan E (1929)	3 3/8	5/32	8	1/8	24
Jordan G (1929)	3	1/8	24	3/16	8
Kissel 6-55 (1927)	3 5/16	1/8	18	1/8	6
Kissel 8-65 (1927)	2 7/8	1/8	24	1/8	8
Kissel 8-75 (1927)	3 5/16	1/8	16	1/8	16
Kissel 6-70, 673 (1928-30)	2 7/8	1/8	12	1/8	12
Kissel 8-80, 880S, 8-95 (1928)	2 7/8	1/8	16	1/8	16
Kissel 8-90 (1928)	3 5/16	1/8	16	1/8	8
Kissel 8-126 (1929-30)	3 1/4	1/8	16	1/8	8
La Salle 303 (1927-28)	3 1/8	3/16	16	3/16	8
La Salle 328 (1929)	3 1/4	3/16	16	3/16	8
La Salle 340 (1930)	3 5/16	1/8	24	3/16	8
Lincoln 8 (1927)	3 3/8	1/8	24	..	..
Lincoln 8 (1928-30)	3 1/2	1/8	16	1/8	8
Locomobile 48 (1927-28)	4 1/2	1/4	12	1/4	6
Locomobile Jr. 8 (1927)	2 13/16	1/8	24	3/16	8
Locomobile 8-80 (1927)	3 1/4	1/8	16	1/8	16
Locomobile 90 (1927-29)	3 7/8	3/16	12	3/16	6
Locomobile 8-70 (1928)	2 7/8	1/8	24	3/16	8
Locomobile 8-80, 86, 88 (1928-29)	3 1/4	1/8	24	1/8	8
Marmon, Little, 68 (1927-28)	2 3/4	1/8	16	3/16	8
Marmon E75 (1927-28)	3 3/4	3/16	12	3/16	6
Marmon 78 (1928-29)	2 15/16	1/8	16	3/16	8
Marmon 68 (1929)	2 13/16	1/8	16	3/16	8
Marmon Roosevelt (1929-30)	2 3/4	1/8	16	3/16	8
Marmon 69 (1930)	2 13/16	1/8	16	3/16	8
Marmon 79 (1930)	3 5/16	1/8	24	3/16	8
Marmon Big 8 (1930)	3 1/4	1/8	24	3/16	8
Marquette, Series 30 (1930)	3 1/8	1/8	12	3/16	6
Moon Series A (1927)	3 1/8	3/16	12	3/16	6
Moon 6-60 (1927-28)	2 7/8	1/8	12	3/16	6
Moon 6-72 (1928-29)	3 3/8	1/8	18	5/32	6
Moon 8-80 (1928)	3	1/8	24	3/16	8
Nash Adv. 6 (1927)	3 7/16	3/16	18	3/16	6
Nash Spec. (1927)	3 1/4	1/8	18	1/8	6
Nash Light 6 (1927)	3	1/8	12	1/8	6
Nash Std. 6 (1927-28)	3 1/8	1/8	18	3/16	6
Nash Adv. 6 (1928)	3 7/16	3/16	18	3/16	6
Nash Spec. 6 (1928)	3 1/4	1/8	18	1/8	6
Nash Std. 6 (1928-29)	3 1/8	1/8	12	3/16	12
Nash Adv. 6 (1929)	3 7/16	1/8	18	3/16	6
Nash Spec. 6 (1929)	3 1/4	1/8	18	3/16	6
Nash Single 6 (1929-30)	3 1/8	1/8	12	3/16	12
Nash Twin Ign. 6 (1929-30)	3 3/8	1/8	12	3/16	12
Nash Twin Ign. 8 (1929-30)	3 1/4	1/8	16	3/16	16
Oakland 6 (1927)	2 7/8	1/8	12	1/8	6
Oakland AA6 (1928)	3 1/4	3/16	12	3/16	6
Oakland AA6 (1929)	3 3/8	3/16	12	3/16	6
Oakland 101 (1930)	3 7/16	1/8	24	3/16	8
Oldsmobile 30E (1927)	2 7/8	1/8	12	3/16	6
Oldsmobile (1928-30)	3 3/16	1/8	12	3/16	6
Packard 6 (1927)	3 1/2	1/8	18	..	..
Packard 8 (1927)	3 1/2	1/8	16	1/8	8
Packard 6 (1928)	3 1/2	1/8	18	1/8	6
Packard 8 (1928)	3 1/2	1/8	24	1/8	8
Packard 626, 633 (1929)	3 3/16	1/8	24	1/8	8
Packard 640, 645 (1929)	3 1/2	1/8	24	1/8	8
Packard 726, 733 (1930)	3 3/16	1/8	24	1/8	8
Packard 740, 745 (1930)	3 1/2	1/8	24	1/8	8
Paige 6-45 (1927-28)	2 7/8	1/8	12	3/16	6
Paige 6-65 (1927-28)	3 1/4	3/16	12	3/16	6
Paige 6-75 (1927-28)	3 3/8	1/8	18	3/16	12
Paige 8-85 (1927-28)	3 1/4	1/8	24	1/8	8
Peerless 69 (1927-28)	3 1/4	1/8	16	1/8	8
Peerless 72 (1927)	3 1/2	1/8	18	1/8	6
Peerless 80 (1927)	3 1/4	3/16	18	3/16	6
Peerless 90 (1927-28)	3 1/2	1/8	18	1/8	6
Peerless 60 (1928)	3 1/4	1/8	18	5/32	6
Peerless 80 (1928)	3 1/4	1/8	18	5/32	6
Peerless 91 (1928-29)	3 1/2	1/8	12	1/8	6
Peerless 81 (1929)	3 3/8	1/8	12	5/32	12
Peerless 125 (1929)	3 3/8	1/8	16	3/16	8
Peerless B, C (1930)	3 3/8	1/8	24	5/32	8
Peerless A (1930)	2 7/8	1/8	16	1/8	8
Pierce Arrow 36 (1927)	4	3/16	12	3/16	6
Pierce Arrow 80 (1927)	3 1/2	3/16	12	3/16	6
Pierce Arrow 36 (1928)	4	3/16	12	3/16	6
Pierce Arrow 81 (1928)	3 1/2	3/16	12	1/8	6
Pierce Arrow 133, 143 (1929)	3 1/2	3/16	16	1/8	8
Pierce Arrow 125, 126, 139 (1930)	3 1/2	1/8	16	3/16	16
Pierce Arrow 132 (1930)	3 3/8	1/8	24	3/16	8
Plymouth 4 cyl. (1929-30)	3 5/8	1/8	4	1/8	8
Pontiac 6 (1927-28)	3 1/4	3/16	12	3/16	6
Pontiac 6 (1929-30)	3 5/16	3/16	12	3/16	6
Reo Flying Cloud (1927)	3 1/4	3/16	12	3/16	6
Reo Wolverine (1927-28)	3 1/4	1/8	18	5/32	6
Reo Flying Cloud (1928)	3 1/4	3/16	12	3/16	6
Reo, All (1929-30)	3 3/8	1/8	18	3/16	6
Rickenbacker 6-70 (1927)	3 1/4	1/8	12	1/8	12
Rickenbacker 8-80 (1927)	3	1/8	16	1/8	16
Rickenbacker 8-90 (1927)	3 1/4	1/8	16	1/8	16
Roamer 8-80, 8-88 (1927-29)	3 1/4	1/8	16	1/8	16
Roamer 8-78 (1927-29)	2 3/4	1/8	16	1/8	16
Star Four (1927-28)	3 3/8	3/16	8	3/16	4
Star Six (1927-28)	2 3/4	3/16	12	3/16	6
Stearns Knight F 6-85 (1927)	3 1/2	1/8	24	..	..
Stearns Knight 885, 8-90 (1927-28)	3 1/2	1/8	24	1/8	8
Stearns Knight F 6-85 (1928)	3 1/2	1/8	32	..	..
Stearns Kni. MN 6-80 (1928-29)	3 3/8	1/8	18	3/16	6
Studebaker Big 6 (1927)	3 7/8	3/16	12	3/16	12
Studebaker Spec. 6 (1927)	3 1/2	3/16	12	3/16	12
Studebaker Std. 6 (1927)	3 3/8	3/16	12	3/16	12
Studebaker Com. 6 (1928)	3 7/8	3/16	12	3/16	12
Studebaker Dict. 6 (1928)	3 3/8	1/8	18	3/16	12
Studebaker Pres. 8 (1928)	3 3/8	1/8	24	3/16	8
Studebaker Dict., Com. 6 (1929)	3 3/8	1/8	24	3/16	6
Studebaker Com. 8 (1929)	3 1/16	1/8	24	3/16	8
Studebaker Pres. (1929-30)	3 1/2	1/8	24	3/16	8
Studebaker Dict., Com. 6 (1930)	3 3/8	1/8	24	3/16	6
Studebaker Dict., Com. 8 (1930)	3 1/16	1/8	24	3/16	8
Stutz AA, BB (1927-28)	3 1/4	1/8	16	1/8	8
Stutz, Series M (1929-30)	3 3/8	1/8	24	3/16	8
Velie Std. 50 (1927-28)	3 1/8	1/8	18	3/16	6
Velie 6-77 (1928)	3 5/16	1/8	18	1/8	6
Velie 88 (1928)	3 1/4	1/8	24	1/8	8
Viking (1929-30)	3 3/8	5/32	16	3/16	8
Whippet 96, 4 cyl. (1927)	3 1/8	1/8	8	1/8	4
Whippet 93A, 6 cyl. (1927)	3	1/8	12	1/8	6
Whippet 96, 4 cyl. (1928)	3 1/8	1/8	8	1/8	4
Whippet 98, 98A (1928-30)	3 1/8	1/8	12	5/32	6
Whippet 96A (1929)	3 1/8	1/8	8	5/32	4
Willys 6 (1930)	3 1/4	1/8	12	3/16	6
Willys Knight 66A (1927)	3 1/4	1/8	18	1/8	6
Willys Knight 70A (1927)	2 15/16	1/8	12	1/8	6
Willys Knight 66A (1928)	3 3/8	1/8	18	3/16	6
Willys Knight Std. 6-56 (1928-29)	2 15/16	1/8	18	1/8	6
Willys Knight 70B (1930)	2 15/16	1/8	18	1/8	6
Willys Knight 166B (1930)	3 3/8	1/8	18	3/16	6

* Auburn 6-85, 6 3/16, 6 1/8.
Auburn 8-95, 8 3/16, 8 1/8

Hose Connections, Passenger Cars

Year	Model	Upper Hose Length	Upper Hose Inner Diam.	Lower Hose Length	Lower Hose Inner Diam.
Auburn					
1925-26	6-66	8½	1½	13½	1⅜
1925-26	8-88	8	1½	8½	1⅜
1927	6-66	6½	1¼	7¾	1¼
1927	8-77	....	...	....	...
1927	8-88	5½	1½	13½	1⅜
1928	76	9	1½	5¼	1½
1928	88	7½	1½	4¼	1½
1928	115	6	1½	15¼	1⅜
1929	6-80	9	1½	5¼	1½
1929	8-90	6	1½	15¼	1½
1929	120	5½	1½	15¾	1¾
1930	6-85	9	1½	5¼	1½
1930	8-95	6	1½	15¼	1½
1930	125	5½	1½	15¾	1¾
1931	8-98	9	1½	11	1½
Austin					
1930-31		9	1¼	10½	1¼
Blackhawk					
1929-30	L6	3½	1½	3½	1½
1929-30	L8	3	1¼	3	1¼
Buick					
1923-25	6	7	1¼	13	1¼
1925-26j	Std. 6	9	1¼	3¼	1¼
1925-26	Master 6	7¾	1¼	3¼	1¼
1926	115	9⅛	1¼	3¼	1¼
1927-28	115	8⅞	1⅛	3¼	1⅛
1927-29	Others	6¾	1¼	3¼	1⅛
1929	116	8⅞	1⅛	3¼	1⅛
1930	40	....	1⅛	....	1⅛
1930	50, 60	....	1¼	....	1¼
1931	8-50	3⅞	1 5/16	4¾	1 5/16
1931	8-60	6¼	1 7/16	5¾	1 7/16
1931	8-80, 8-90	6¼	1 7/16	6¼	1 7/16
Cadillac					
1925-26	314	14½	1¼	4½	1⅝
1927	314	14½	1¼	11	1⅞
1928	341	16¾	1¼	12⅜	1⅞
1929	341B	16¾	1¼	12⅛	1⅞
1930	353	12 5/16	1¼	11	1⅞
1930-31	452	8¾	1¼	3½	1¾
1931	355	10¼	1¼	10⅜	1⅞
1931	370	7¼	1¼	3½	1¾
Chandler					
1926	35-Big 6	6⅝	1⅜	7¼	1⅜
1926-27	Std. 6	10⅜	1⅜	3½	1⅛
1926-27	Spec. 6	12	1 7/16	3½	1⅛
1927	Royal St. 8	2⅜	Sp.	8⅛	1½
		2	1⅜		
1927	Big 6	6⅝	1⅜	7¼	1⅜
1928	Spec. & Inv. 6	7¼	1⅜	3½	1⅛
1928	Big 6	6⅝	1⅜	7¼	1⅜
1928	Roy. St. 8	2⅜	Spe.	8½	1½
		2	1⅜		
1929	65	12¼	1½	3½	1⅛
1929	Royal 75	8¼	1½	6¼	1½
1929	Big 6	7¼	1⅜	1⅞	1⅛
1929	Royal 85	1¾	1⅜	8⅛	1½
Chevrolet					
1924-25	Sup.	7½	1¼	5⅜	1¼
1926	"K"	8	1¼	5⅞	1¼
1927	AA	8	1¼	5¼	1¼
1928		11⅜	1¼	8	1¼
1929-31		10⅜	1¼	5⅛	1¼
Chrysler					
1924-26	6-G, 70	4¾	1½	6¾	1¼
1925-26	4-58	8½	2⅛	7	2⅛
1926-27	6-80	5½	1½	6¼	1¼
1926	60	7⅜	1¼	5½	1¼
1927	50	8¼	2⅛	3½	2⅛
1927-28	62	7⅜	1¼	5½	1¼
1927	70	4¾	1½	6¾	1¼
1928	52	8¼	2⅛	7	2⅛
1928	72	5¾	1½	6½	1¼
1928-30	Imp. 80	6½	1½	5½	1½
1929-30	65, 66	7⅜	1¼	5½	1¼
1929	75	1½	5¾	1¼	2⅜
1930	70	8⅝	1½	2¾	...
1930	77	7⅝	1½	2¾	1½
Cleveland					
1925-26	6-43	12	1 7/16	3½	1⅛
1925-26	31	10⅜	1⅜	3½	1⅛
Cunningham					
1925-28	All	5½	1¼	2¾	1¾
1929	V-8	5½	1¼	3¼	1¾
1930-31	V-9	5	1¼	3¼	1¾
Davis					
1926	92	8	1½	12	1¼
1926	93	2	1¼	3	1¼
1927	92-27	8	1½	13	1¼
1927	94-27	6	1¼	3	1¼
1927	98-27	12	1½	13	1½
1928	99	3	1¼	13½	1¼
De Soto					
1929-30	Six	10¾	1⅝	2¾	1⅝
De Vaux					
1931	Six	....	1½	....	1½
Diana					
1925	St. 8	8	1¼	12	1½
1926-28	St. 8	7¾	1½	7¾	1½
Dodge					
1922-26	4	9	1½	7¼	1 5/16
1927	4	9	1½	2¾	1¼
1928	Senior 6	4⅞	1 15/16	3¼	1 7/16
1928	Std. 6	....	...	....	...
1928	Victory 6	9	1½	3¼	1 7/16
1929-30	Senior	7	1 15/16	3¼	1 7/16
1929-30	6	10	1 9/16	2½	1 9/16
1930-31	DD6	10¾	1¼	2°	1¼
1930-31	DC8	10⅜	1¼	2¾°	1¼
Duesenberg					
1922-26	S	8	1½	7½	1½
1930-31	J	....	1¾	....	1¾
du Pont					
1925	D	6½	1¾	12	1¼
1926	D	4½	1¾	12	1¼
1927	E	4	1¾	12	1¼
1928-29	E&F	5	1¾	12	1¼
1929	G	6	1¾	4½	1½
1930	G	6	1¾	4	1¾
1931	G	6	1¾	4	1¾
				4½	1½
Durant					
1925-26	4	4½	1¼	15	1¼
1928	55	6½	1¼	5	1¼
1928-29	65, 60, 66	5	1¼	5	1¼
1928-29	75, 70	6	1¼	5	1¼
1929	40	5	1¼	5	1¼
1930-31	6-14	8¾	1½	2¾	1½
1930-31	6-17	8	1½	4½	1¼
Elcar					
1925	6-51	12	1½	21	1½
1925	8-80	12½	1½	12½	1½
1926	4-55	10	2¼	21	2¼
1926	6-65	12½	1½	22	1½
1926	8-81	12½	1½	12½	1½
1927	6-70	9½	1½	11¼	1½
1927	8-82	12	1½	13	1½
1927	8-90	11½	1½	15	1½
1928	6-70	10¼	1½	11¼	1½
1928	8-78	10	1½	....	1½
1928	8-82	10	1½	13	1½
1928	8-91, 120	11½	1½	15	1½
1929-30	75, 75A	10	1¾	8	1¾
1929-30	95, 96	11	1¾	9	1¾
1929-30	120	11½	1¾	9	1¾
Erskine Six					
1928	51	9	1¼	3	1¼
1929	52	7¼	1¼	3	1¼
1930	53	8	1¼	2½	1¼
Essex					
1925-26	6	5½	2¼	14½	2¼
1927	6	5½	2¼	15 5/16	2¼
1928-29	Super 6	5½	2¼	15 5/16	2¼
1930-31	Super 6	7½	2¼	14½	2¼
Falcon Knight					
1927		8½	1 5/16	3 13/16	1 1/16
1928	12	8½	1 5/16	3 13/16	1 5/16
Flint					
1925-26	55, E80	8	1½	13¼	1¼
1926	B-60	5½	1¼	4	1¼
1926	Z-18	5¾	1¼	2⅛	1¼
1927	Z-18	5¼	1¼	1⅛	1¼
1927	60	5½	1¼	4	1¼
1927	80	8	1½	13¼	1¼
Ford					
1925-27	T	4	2	2¾	1¾
1928	A	6½	2	2¾	1¾
1929	A	6¼	2	2¾	1¾
1930-31	A	8½	2	2¾	1¾
Gardner					
1925	6A	12	1½	3	1½
1926	6A	9	1½	6	1½
1925	8-A-B	12	1½	11	1½
1926	8-A	9	1½	11	1½
*1926	8-B	9	1½	17	1½
1927	80	10	1½	20½	1½
1927	90	9	1½	20	1½
1928	75, 85	10	1½	....	1½
1928	95	9	1½	....	1½
1929	120, 125	9½	1½	....	1½
1929	130	9	1½	....	1½
1930-31	136	8½	1½	7	1½
1930-31	140, 148	9½	1½	11	1½
1930-31	150, 158	9	1½	6	1½
Graham					
1930	Std. 6	3½	1½	3½	1½
1930	Spec. 6	3½	1½	3½	1½
1930	Spec., Std. 8	3½	1¾	3¼	2
1930	Cus. 8	3½	1¾	3½	1¾
1931	Std., Spec. 6	5	1¾	3	2
1931	Spec. 8-20	5	1¾	3	2⅛
1931	Cus. 8-34	5	1¾	3	2⅛
Graham-Paige					
1928	610	9½	1 13/16	3½	1 13/16
1928	614	11	1 13/16	3½	1 13/16
1928	619, 629	3½	1¾	3½	1¾
1928	835	3½	1¾	3½	1¾
1929	612	10½	1½	3½	1½
1929	615	3½	1½	3½	1½
1929	621	3½	1¾	3½	1¾
1929	827, 837	3½	1¾	3½	1¾
Hudson					
1925-26	Super 6	7	1½	10½	1½
1927	Super 6	6	1½	10½	1½
1928-29		7	1½	10½	1½
1930	Great 8	9⅜	1 5/16	5	1 5/16
1931	Great 8	10¾	1 5/16	5	1 5/16
Hupmobile					
1925-26j	A-1	11½	1¼	6½	1¼
j1926-27	A	8¼	1¼	6½	1¼
1925-26	E	7⅛	1½	3	1½
1927-28	E, 125-8	7⅛	1½	3	1½
1928	Cent. 6	10¾	1¼	6½	1¼
1928	Cent. 8	6⅜	1½	3⅝	1½
1929-30	A, S	10¾	1¼	6½	1¾
1929-30	M, C	6⅜	1½	3⅜	1½
1931	C	....	1½	....	1½
1931	H, V	....	1½	....	1½
Jewett					
1926	New Day	7½	1¼	6	1¼
Jordan					
1924-25	K, L	11	1¼	9½	1¼
1925-26	"A," J	12½	1¼	7⅜	1¼
1927	AA	12½	1¼	7⅜	1¼
1927	J-1	12½	1¼	7⅜	1¼
1928	JJ	....	...	7⅜	1¼
1928	JE	....	...	6⅜	1¼
1929	E	9	1½	4⅜	1¼
1929	G	8	1¼	8	1¼
1930	70, 80, 90	8	1¼	8	1¼
1930	Z Speed.	3¼	1¾	3¾	1½
1931	80, 90	4¾	1¼	4¾	1¼
Kissel					
1925	55	8⅝	1¼	11 5/16	1¾
1926	55	7 5/16	1¾	10 5/16	1½
1925-26	75	7 5/16	1¾	3¾	1½
*1926-27	55	7 5/16	1¾	10 5/16	1¾
*1926	75	7 5/16	1¾	3¾	1¾
1927	75	7 5/16	1¾	3¾	1¾
1928	6-70	12	1¾	12	1¾
1928	8-80, 8-80S	8¼	1¾	10¾	1¾
1928	8-90	7 5/16	1¾	3¾	1¾
1929-30	6-73	10½	1¾	11	1¾
1929-30	8-95	10	1¾	10¾	1¾
1929-30	8-126	8¼	1¾	10⅛	1¾
La Salle					
1927-28		10¾	1¼	12⅛	1⅞
		12 5/16	1¼	....	...
1929	340	14½	1¼	12⅛	1⅞
1930	340	11¼	1¼	11	1⅞
1931	345	11¾	1¼	11	1⅞
Lincoln					
1922-30	8	16¼	1¾	11¼	1¾
1931	8	12⅛	1⅜	3¼	1¾
Locomobile					
1925-29	48	2¾	1⅜	5	1⅜
1925	Jr. 8	3¼	1¼	13	1¼

HOSE CONNECTIONS, Passenger Cars—Continued

Year	Model	Upper Hose Length	Upper Hose Inner Diam.	Lower Hose Length	Lower Hose Inner Diam.
Locomobile—Cont.					
1926	Jr. 8	13	1¼	7⅛	1¼
1926	90	9¼	1½	8½	1½
1927-29	90	9¼	1½	8	1½
1927	8-70	6½	1½	3¼	1¼
1927	8-80	8¼	1½	11½	1½
1928	8-70	6½	1½	3¼	1¼
1928-29	8-80	8¼	1½	10¾	1½
1929	86, 88	9½	1½	10¾	1½
McFarlan					
1925	6	6	1¼	1½	¼
1925-26	St. 8	13	1½	9¼	...
1926	TV	4	2	11¼	¾
1927	TV	4	2	10¾	¾
1927	St. 8	10	1½	9¼	½
1928	St. 8	10	1½	9¼	1½
1928	TV6	4	2	10¾	1¾
Marmon					
1925-26	34, 74	3⅞	1¼	3⅞	1¼
1927	Little	3⅞	1¼	3⅞	1¼
1927-28	E-75	3⅞	1¼	3⅞	1¼
1928-29	68	5½	1½	8	1½
1928-29	78	4	1½	4	1½
1930-31	Roosevelt	5½	1½	8	1½
1930-31	Eight 69	5½	1½	8	1½
1930-31	Eight 79	7½	1¾	17	1¾
1930-31	Big Eight	7½	1¾	17	1¾
1931	70	5½	1½	8	1½
1931	88	7½	1¾	3¼	1¾
Marquette					
1929-30		2⅝	1 7/16	8¾	1 7/16
Moon					
1925	Newport	14	1½	4	1¼
1925-26	London	10	1¼	12	1¼
1925-28	A	12	1½	4	1¼
1926-28	6-60	7¾	1½	4	1¼
1928	6-72	9	1½	4	1¼
1928	8-80	9	1½	4	1¼
1929	6-72	9	1½	4	1¼
				5	1¼
Nash					
1926	Special	4	1½	13½	1¼
†1926	Adv.	7½	1½	4	1½
1927	Light 6	10¾	1¼	7½	1¼
1927-28	Adv.	3⅝	1½	3⅝	1½
1927-28	Special	3⅜	1½	4⅛	1¼
1928-29	Std. 6	9¾	1¼	5¾	1¼
1929	Adv.	5½	1½	3	1½
1929	Special	4¾	1½	2⅞	1½
1930	Single 6	8¾	1¼	5¾	1¼
1930	Twin Ign. 6	4⅜	1½	2⅞	1½
1930	Twin Ign. 8	3¼	1½	3¼	1½
1931	6-60	11½	1¼	6¼	1¼
1931	8-70	10¾	1¼	5	1½
1931	8-80	5⅜	1½	6¼	1¾
1931	8-90	3¼	1½	3¼	1¾
Oakland					
1925-26	6-54	8¼	1¼	9¼	1¼
1927	6	8¼	1¼	9¼	1¼
1928-29	AA6	9¼	1¼	11	1¼
1931	8	6½	1½	5¾	1½
Oldsmobile					
1925-26	30	10¼	1½	9½	1½
j1926-27	30E	10	1½	10	1½
1928	F-28	....	...	....	...
1929	F-29	10	1½	8½	1½
1930	F-30	12	1½	8½	1½
1931	F-31	12½	1½	6	1½
Overland					
1925-26	4	12	2	7¼	1¾
1925	6-93	9¼	1¼	4⅝	1¼
1926	6-93	4½	1¼	4¾	1¼
1927	4	....	...	....	...
1927	6	4½	1¼	4¾	1¼
Packard					
1925-28	All	3⅞	1½	6¼	1½
1929	All	3¼	1½	6¾	1½
1930-31	All	4⅞	1½	8¾	1½
Paige					
1925-26	Super 6	7	1½	10½	1½
1925	6	9	2	10	1 11/16
1927	6-45	7½	1¼	6	1¼
1927	6-65, 6-75	9	1¾	8¾	1 11/16
1927	8-85	8½	1¾	8	1½
Peerless					
1926	6-80	8⅝	1 7/16	8⅝	1 3/16
1926	8-69	7	1⅜	6⅛	1 9/16
1927	6-72	12½	1 5/16	7⅞	1 7/16
1927-28	6-80	8⅝	1 7/16	8⅝	1 3/16
1927-29	6-90, 6-91	8⅝	1 7/16	7⅜	1 7/16
1927-28	8-69	8	1⅜	6⅛	1 11/16
1928-29	6-60, 6-61	8⅝	1⅞	8⅝	1⅝
1929	6-81	8⅝	1 7/16	3	1 3/16
1929-30	61-A	7	1⅞	8⅝	1⅝
1930-31	Mas., Cus. 8	7⅞	1 11/16	3	1 7/16
1931	Std. 8	7¼	1 7/16	7¾	1 3/16
Pierce-Arrow					
1925-26	33	3	2	14¼	1½
1925-28	80, 81	3¼	1¾	3¼	1½
1927-28	36	3	2	14¼	1½
1929	All	14	1½	2⅝	1½
1930	All	14	1½	5	2
Plymouth					
1929-30		8¼	2⅛	7	2⅛
Pontiac					
1926-27	Six	9¼	1¼	5	1¼
1928	Six	5	1¼	11	1¼
1929	Big Six	11	1½	2⅝	1¼
1930-31		11	1¼	2⅝	1½
Reo					
1925	T-6	12	1½	8¾	1¼
1926	T-6	12	1½	9½	1⅜
j1926	T-6	14½	1½	12	1¼
1927-29	F. C., Mas.	8½	1½	11½	1¼
1927-29	Wol., Mate	8¾	1½	9½	1¼
1930	15	8¾	1½	9½	1¼
1930	20, 25	8½	1½	11½	1¼
1931	25N	10¾	1½	10¼	1½
1931	30N, 35N	11	1¾	....	1½
Rickenbacker					
1925	A-8	9¾	1¼	12½	1¼
1925	D	9¾	1	14¾	1¼
1926	E&B	9¾	1¼	11½	1¾
1927	6-70	11¼	1¼	19½	1¾
1927	8-80	3½	1¼	11½	1¾
1927	8-90	5⅛	1¼	11½	1¼
Roamer					
1925-26	6-50	13	1½	3½	1¼
1925-26	6-54	8	1½	16	1½
1925-26	8-88-80	12½	1¼	10	1¼
1927	8-80, 8-88	14	1½	9¼	1½
1928-30	8-78	12	1½	10	...
1928-30	8-80	14	1½	10	1½
1928-30	8-88	14	1½	12	1½
Rolls-Royce					
1925-26	40-50	5	1½	2	1½
1927-30	S. Gh.	5	1½	2	1½
1927-31	N. Phan.	6½	1½	2½	1½
Roosevelt					
1929		5½	1½	8	1½
Star					
1926-27	4	4½	1¼	3¼	1¼
1925-27	6	6	1¼	3¼	1¼
1928	4	5	1¼	5	1¼
Stearns-Knight					
1926	B, 75, 95	6½	1⅜	9	1⅜
1927-28	F6-85	7½	1⅜	9	1⅜
1927	G8-85	9	1⅜	11½	1⅜
1928	H&J	10	1⅜	11½	1⅜
1929	M&N 6-80	7½	2	8	2
1929	H&J 8-90	8½	1⅜	10¾	1⅜
Studebaker					
1925-26	Std. 6	5	1	2	1
1925-26	Spec. 6	10½	1½	9	1½
				5½	1⅛
1925-26	Big 6	11	1½	9½	1½
1928-29	Dic.	7⅞	1¼	2½	1¼
1928	Com.	10½	1½	9	1½
1928	Pres. 8	12⅜	1½	3	1½
1929	Com. 6	7⅞	1¼	2½	1¼
1929	Com. 8	7⅞	1¼	2½	1¾
1929	Pres.	12	1½	3	1½
1930	Dic. 6	9	1¼	2½	1¼
1930-31	Dic. 8	10¼	1¼	2½	1¾
1930	Com. 6	7⅞	1¼	2½	1¼
1930	Com. 8	7⅞	1¼	2½	1¾
1930-31	Pres.	12	1½	3	1½
1931	Six	8	1¼	2½	1¼
1931	Com. 70	12	1½	2½	1¾
Stutz					
1926	AA	4	1½	6	1½
*1926	AA	3	1½	3	1½
1927	AA	3½	1½	2	1½
1928-31	All	3½	1½	3½	1½
Velie					
1925	60	9	2¼	12¾	2¼
1926	60	12¾	2¼	12¾	2¼
1927-28	Std. 50	8¼	2¼	12¾	2¼
1927	Spec. 60	11½	2¼	12¾	2¼
1928	6-66	8½	2¼	12¾	2¼
1928	6-77	11½	2¼	12¾	2¼
1928	8-88	8¼	1½	8	1½
Viking					
1929-30	V-29, 30	16¾	1¼	3	1½
Wills Sainte Claire					
1925-26	68	5¾	2¼	5½	2
1925-26	6	5½	3¼	5½	2¾
1926-27	T-6	5½	3¼	5½	2¾
Willys-Knight					
1925	64-67	6	2¼	6	2¼
1926	66	5	2	7½	2
1926-27	70	2	1¼	7¼	1⅛
1927	66-A	5	2	7½	2
Windsor					
1929	6-72, 6-77	9	1½	4	1¼
				5	1¼
1929-30	6-69	13	1½	9	1¼
				4½	1¼
1929-30	8-82, 8-92	9	1½	10	1¼
1930	8-85	9	1½	10	1¼

† May a—August * June j—July s—September

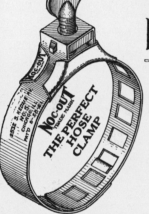

Hose Connections, Commercial Cars

Year	Model and Capacity	Upper Hose		Lower Hose	
		Length	Inner Diam.	Length	Inner Diam.
Acme					
1923-25	40L-2-60-2½-3	11½	1½	12½	1½
1923-25	60L-3	11½	1½	12½	1½
1923-25	90-3½-4½	10	1½	12	1½
1923-25	90L-4-4½-125-5, 6¼	10	1½	10	1½
1924-25	20L-1½	7	1¼	11	1¼
1925	K (Bus)	12¾	1 7/16	12¾	1 7/16
1925	40L-2	10	1½	10	1½
1925	116-Bus-16, 118-Bus-18	9	1¾	11	1½
1925-26	21-1, 41-2	9	1½	10	1¼
1925-26	20L-1½	8½	1¼	11½	1¼
1925-26	60-3	10	1½	10	1½
1925-26	60L-3	10	1½	8	1½
1925-26	90-4½	10	1½	12½	1½
1925-26	90L-5	10	1½	10	1½
1925-26	125-6¼	10	1½	12	1⅜
1926	60LS-3	9	1¾	11¼	1½
1926-27	116-Bus-16	9	1¾	11¼	1½
1926-27	118-Bus-21	9¼	2¼	9½	1¾
1927-29	14-¾-1	10	1½	23	1¼
1927	16-¾-1	4	1½	7	1¼
1927	24-1¼	6½	1½	10	1¼
1927	36-1½	7	1¼	9¼	1¼
1927	54-2½	11	1½	9½	1¼
1927-28	56-2½	9	1¾	11¼	1½
1927	74-3½	9	1½	9	1½
1927	76-3½, 106-6¼	9¼	2¼	9½	1¾
1927	104-6¼	9	1½	9	1½
Acorn					
1927	15	11	1½	9	1¼
1927	30, 40, 45	6	2	6	1½
1927	50	13½	2	18	1½
1927	70, 80	13½	2	15	1½
American-LaFrance					
1925	W	5½	1½	10½	1½
1925	V&Y	9	1½	11½	1½
1926-28	W	11½	1½	11½	1½
1926-28	V&Y	10½	1½	11½	1½
1928	Chief 1½	18	1¾	8¼	1¼
1928	S-4-5	10½	1½	11½	1½
1929	Chief 1½-2	13	2	5½	1½
1929	Big Chief	13	2	5½	1½
Armleder					
1924-25	30-1½	10	1¾	16½	1¼
1924-25	50-2½	12	2	17¾	1¼
1926-28	30	10	1¾	16½	1¼
1926	30B	10	1¾	16½	1¼
1926	30-6	10	1¼	21	1¾
1926	50, 60	12	2	17¾	1¼
1926	50-6, 60-6	16½	2	17	1½
1926	55	14¼	1½	17¾	1¼
1926	70	9½	2	16½	1¼
1928	30-6	21	1¾	10	1¼
1928	40	10	1¼	16½	1¼
1928	50	12	2	17¾	1¼
1928	50-6	16½	2	11	1½
1928	60	16½	2	17¾	1½
1928	70	12	2	16½	1¼
1930-31	M-31	16½	1¾	15	1¼
1930-31	M-41	16½	1¾	16½	1¼
1930-31	M-61	16½	1¾	16½	1¼
Atterbury					
1922-27	22C-2½, 22D-3½	10½	1½	16	1½
1924-27	24E	10½	1½	16	1½
1925-27	24-R	10½	1½	16	1½
1927	26B-1, 26-G	9	1½	18	1½
Autocar					
1917-26	F-G	3	1⅛	4	1⅛
1920-25	Y-B-M-L-LA	3½	1½	3½	1½
1922-27	H-K-KA-FH-GK-HT	3½	1½	3½	1½
1925-27	HPDS-HS-KS KAS-HST	3½	1½	3½	1½
1926-27	M-L-LA-MT	3½	1½	3½	1½
1926-27	CH-CK-CKA-CFH-CGK-CHS-CKS-CKAS-CHPDS	6	1½	11	1½
1926-27	CM-CL	8	1½	11	1½
1926-27	A-AA	4¼	1½	9	1½
1929	SA-1½-2	3½	1½	3½	1½
1929	H-3, HS-3½	3½	1½	3½	1½
1929	CH-3, CHS-3½	11	1½	10½	1½
1929	SCH-3, TA-3	11	1½	3½	1½
1929	SHS-3½	3½	1½	3½	1½
1929	SCM-5	9	1½	3½	1½
Available					
1922-25	H-1½, 2½	11	1⅝	14	1⅝
1921-25	H-1½, 2, 2½, 3	12	1⅝	14	1⅝
1922-24	H-3½, 5	12	1⅝	14	1⅝
1925	J-H5	12	2	16	2
1931	T-10, 11, 12	10	1½	17	1¼
1931	T-13, 15, 20, 22	10	1½	6	1¼
1931	T-23, 24, 25, 27, 30, 32, 35, 37	14	1½	8	1½
1931	T-36V, 38V	14	1½	8	1½
1931	T-39, 43, 40V, 44V	8	2¼	10	1½
1931	T-45	14	1½	12	1½
1931	T-50	12	2	10	2
Biederman					
1921-27	20, 30, 40, 50, 60	13	1¼	15½	1¼
1921-27	70, 80	13	1½	15½	1¼
1931	10, 20, 30, 40, 50, 60	10	1¾	16	1¾
Brockway					
1919-25	S-2-1½	10½	2¼	5½	2¼
1919-25	K4-2½	6½	1¾	13	1¼
1919-25	R2-3½	9½	1¾	14	1¼
1919-25	T-6-5	13	2	22	2
1927-29	Wis Y	....	1½	....	1½
1928	SW, SY, J-1	7	1½	14	1½
1928-29	EN	9½	2	7½	1¼
1928-29	SG	7	1¾	14	1¼
1928-29	EG	7	1½	6	1¾
1928-29	JF, CJBF	8½	1½	5	1¼
1929-30	K, R	11	1½	15	1½
1930	65,75,90,90-B,91	12½	1½	4¼	1¼
1930	290, 640	9	2¼	12	1¾
Chevrolet					
1925	All	7½	1¼	3⅜	1¼
1926	All	8	1¼	4¾	1¼
1927-28	Util. Exp.	6 7/16	1¼	5¼	1¼
1927	Comm.	8	1¼	5¼	1¼
1928	Comm.	11⅜	1¼	5¼	1¼
		....	...	4	1¼
1929	U.E., Comm.	10⅜	1¼	10¼	2½
Clinton					
1923-25	20-1¼	8	1¾	14	1¼
1923-25	45-2	11	1¾	17½	1¼
1923-25	65-3	11	2	19	1¼
1923-25	90-90M-4	13¼	2	19	1¼
1923-25	120L-120LM-5-120S-120SM 5-7	12	2	18	1½
1926	20-1¼, 30-1½, 45-2	8½	1¼	14	1¼
1926	65-3	7	1½	11½	1½
1926	90-4-5	10	1½	11½	1½
1926	120-6-7	10	1½	11½	1½
Clydesdale					
1922-25	120B-5-6	9	2	18½	2
1921-25	90-3½-4½	9	1½	14	1½
1922-25	65EX-2½-3	9	1½	14	1½
1922-25	65X-2½-3	11	1½	11	1½
1922-25	42-1½-2	15	2	12	2
1922-25	20-1-1½	15	2	12	2
1922-25	18-¾-1¼	15	2	12	2
1922-25	10-¾-1¼	9	2	9	2
1922-25	10A-1-¾-1¼	9	2	9	2
1927-29	4X, 4, 6, "6"	11	1½	16	1½
1927-29	6B, 12, 14	11	1¼	17	1¼
1927-29	9, 10A, 16, "4"	8	1½	16	1½
1927-29	4, "4"	11	1½	16	1½
1927-29	6T, "6"	11	2¼	16	1¾
1927-29	8, "4"	11	1½	15	1½
Columbia					
1925	H-1½, G-2½	10	1¼	12	1¼
1925	K-3	11	1½	13	1½
Commerce					
1923-25	14B-1½	10	2	9½	1½
1923-25	25B-2½	9½	1½	15½	1½
1924-25	11-25-1	10	2	10	2
1926-27	7-1	12	1½	4	1¼
1926-27	S-11-1½	9½	1½	10½	1½
1926-27	SD-11-1½	9½	1½	10½	1½
1926-27	S-14-2	10	2	9½	1½
1926-27	25-2½	9½	1½	16½	1½
1926-27	26-3	12	¾	16½	1½
1926-27	27-2½	9½	1½	16½	1½
1926-27	28-3	12	¾	16½	1½
1926-27	30-3½	12	¾	16½	1½
1928	1-1½ Ser. 1	3	2⅛	4	1¼
1928	1-1½ Ser. 2	10¾	1¾	4	1¼
1928	1½-2 Ser. 2	3	2⅛	10	1¼
1928-29	2½-4	3	2⅛	17½	1½
1929	1, 1½	12	1¾	6½	1¼
1929	1½, 2	10¾	1¾	10	1¼
Concord					
1924-26	E1, G2, H2, J2½,JL2½	7	1⅞	9½	1⅜
1926-27	GX2, K1	8	1¾	9	1¼
1926-27	JX3, JLX3, JBX3	8	1⅞	14	1½
1926-27	BUS-25P	8	2	14	1½
Corbitt					
1924-25	E1	9	2	12	2
1924-25	D1½	11	1¼	15	1¼
1924-25	B2½, C-2	13	1¼	15	1¼
1924-25	A3½-4, R2½-3	14	1¼	8	1¼
1924-25	AA-5	13	2	14	2
1925	S-¾	8	2	14	2
1927-28	20-21-6	13	1¼	12	1¼
1927-28	A4, R4, 60, 80, 70	13	1½	12	1½
1927-28	28, 25, 40, 50	13	1½	12	1½
Day-Elder					
1925	G-1½, H2	....	1¾	....	1¼
1925	I-2½	....	1¾	....	1¼
1925	J3, K4	....	2	....	1¼
1925	L5	....	2	....	1¼
1924-27	G, H	10	1¾	10	1⅜
....	I	10	1¾	14	1⅜
....	HSM	10	1¾	14	1⅜
1925-27	J	14	2	17	1½
1924-28	K	14	2	12	1½
1924-28	L	15¼	2	12	1½
....	20 BUS	....	1⅜	....	1¼
....	30 BUS	15¼	2	14	1½
1928	M-1	8	1½	20	1¼
1928	HB6-2	8	1½	20	1¼
Defiance					
1926	F	14	1½	13½	1¼
1926	HC	10½	1½	12	1¼
1926	EV	8½	1½	13	1¼
1928	F1	9	1½	11	1¼
1928	FT1-O2	11	1½	11	1¼
1928	E2	....	1½	....	1½
1928	B3	9	1¾	4	1¼
Diamond T					
1922-25	TK-3½	10	½	10	1½
1922-25	TS-5	9	2	21	2
1923-25	TU2-2½	9	1¼	8	1¼
1924-25	T75, ¼-1	8	1½	10½	1¼
1925	T04-1-1¼, T-T-1½	9	1¼	6	1¼
1926-27	76	13¼	1¼	12½	1½
1926-27	T-3-4-5	13¼	1¼	13	1½
1926-27	U-4-5-6	6¾	1½	15½	1½
1926-27	K-2-3, S-2-3-7	9	2	15½	1½
1928-29	76, T-3-4-5	13½	1½	13	1½
1930	200, 215	15	1¾	9	1⅝
1930	290	17½	1½	4½	1½
1930	303, 503, 551	3½	1½	5	1½
Dixon					
1923-25	D	11	1½	8	1½
1923-25	C	11	1½	9	1½
1923-25	A	12	1½	10	1½
Dodge					
1926	¾	9	1½	8	1 5/16
1928	Senior 2	4⅞	1 15/16	3¾	1 7/16
1929	½	8½	1½	3¼	1 7/16
1929	¾, 1, ½	4⅜	1 15/16	2⅞	1 7/16
1929	2, 3	4⅜	1 15/16	2⅞	1 7/16
1929-30	½-1	12	2⅛	4	1¼
1929-30	1½	8⅝	2¼	4½	1¼
1929-30	¾, 1½	4½	2	3	1⅝
1931	UF10, UF30	10⅞	2⅛	3¼	1¼
1931	F10, F30	4½	2⅛	2¾	1¼
Double Drive					
1927	TT	12	2	19	1½
1927-28	FT	13¾	1¾	17	1⅜
1928	HF	17½	1¾	22½	1¼
1931	HE, 3½-5	11½	1¾	15½	1¼
Douglas					
1926	B-4	10	1¾	16½	1¼
1926	B-6	18½	1¾	11	1¼
1926	C-4, GC	9½	2	16	1½
1926	C-6	19	1¾	12	1¼
1926	D-4	10	2	18	1½
1926	D-6	15	2	17	1½
1926	BUS	20	1¾	13	1¼
1928	B-4, GC	9	1¾	13	1½
1928	B-6	4	1¾	8	1¼
1928	C-4, GC	11	1¾	10	1½
1928	D-4	13	2	10	1¾
1928	D-6, DS6	14	2	10	1½
1928	DS 4	14	2	10	1½

HOSE CONNECTIONS, COMMERCIAL CARS—Continued

Year	Model and Capacity	Upper Hose		Lower Hose	
		Length	Inner Diam.	Length	Inner Diam.
Erskine					
1928	Del	9	1¼	5	1¼
Fageol					
1922-25	2½-3	10	1¼	14¾	1¼
1922-25	3½, 5, 6	9	1½	17½	1½
1924-25	1½-2	10	2½	20	2½
1925	235-2, 340-3	7	1½	15½	1½
1925-26	445-4, 645-6	10	1½	17	1½
1926	Flyer-1½	7¾	1¼	12	1¼
1926	230-B-2	8	1¼	11½	1¼
1926	340-3	7	1½	15½	1½
1928	130-1½	7¾	1¼	13	1¼
1928	135-2	14	1¼	18½	1¼
1928	250-2½	15½	1¼	18½	1¼
1928	340-3	7	1½	15½	1½
1928	370-3	9½	1½	22	1½
1928	445, 645	17	1½	10	1½
1928	485, 685	10¾	1½	20	1½
1928	10-66	10¾	1½	20	1½
1928-29	130, 1½	7¾	1¼	13	1¼
1928-29	340, 3	7	1½	15½	1½
1928-29	445, 645	17	1½	10	1½
Federal					
1924-26	1W6, 1K6, 2K6	13⅜	1¼	5	1¼
1924-26	U2, U3	8¾	1½	14 7/16	1½
1924-27	FK, FK2, S25, S26, S27, S30, S1, S2	5½	2¼	7½	2¼
1924-27	R2, R3, S23	8¾	1½	15	1½
1924-28	W2, W3, X2, X3, X4, X5, X6, X7	10	1¾	14 7/16	1½
1924-30	T2B, T2W, T20, T21	10¾	2½	12¾	2½
1925	T6B, T6W	8	1½	5½	1¼
1925-26	UB6	9	1¾	8¾	1½
1926-28	1B6, 2B6, 3B6	14	1¾	9¾	1½
1926-29	U4, U5	13	1½	13¾	1½
1926-31	X8	14	1¾	13	1½
1926-31	T6B, T6W, T7W, T8, A6, A6T, A6TW	8	1½	3½	1¼
1927	BB6	8¾	1½	8¾	1½
1927	F6	9⅞	1¼	3½	1¼
1927-29	F6, 2F6, 3F6	9⅞	1¼	2½	1¼
1927-30	FW, 2FW, 3FW, 4FW	7½	2	11¾	2
1927-30	UL4, UL5, UL7, W4	14	1¾	14 7/16	1½
1928-30	3C6, 4C6, 4C6SW, U6, U6SW	5	2	3 9/16	1¾
1929-30	T3W, T22	9	1¼	9⅞	1¼
1929-30	X8R	14	1¾	3¼	2
1929-31	F7	7	1½	3½	1¼
1930	T10B, T10W	6⅞	2	3 9/16	1¾
1930-31	D	8	1½	3	1½
1930-31	E6	7	1½	3	1½
1931	T10B, T10W	5	2	3 9/16	1¾
1931	3C6, 4C6, 4C6A, 4C6SW, U6 U6SW, X8R	3¼	2	3 9/16	1¾
Ford					
1922-27	T-1	4	2	2¾	1¾
1928-29	A	6¼	2	2¾	1¾
F. W. D.					
1918-27	B-3	4	2	5	1½
1929	U6	3½	1½	5	1½
1929	H6	3½	1½	4	1½
Garford					
1928	20Z	3	1¾	4	1¼
1928	80C-80Z	3	2⅛	17	1½
1928	1-1½ Ser. 1	3	2⅛	4	1¼
1928	1-1½ Ser. 2	10¾	1¾	4	1¼
1928	1½, 2 Ser. 2	3	2⅛	10	1¼
1928-29	2½-4	3	2⅛	17½	1½
1929	1, 1½	12	1¾	6½	1¼
1929	40Z-2	10¾	1¾	10	1¼
Gary					
1924	W-1-1½	....	2	....	...
1924	I-2	13½	2	12	1¼
1924	J-2½	10	2	12	1¼
1924	K-3½	13	2	16½	1¼
1924	M-5	14	2	18	1⅜
1925	WLD-1-1½	....	2	....	...
1925	G15-1½	13½	2	12	1¼
1925	E25-2½	10	2	12	1¼
1925	Y35-2½	13	2	16½	1¼
1925	B50-5	14	2	18	1⅜
G. M. C.					
1921-25	K-16	8¾	1½	8 5/16	1½
1922-25	K-41	10	1¾	9½	1¾
1922-25	K-71	11¾	1¾	9½	1¾
1922-25	K-101	11¾	1¾	9½	1¾
Gotfredson					
1925	20B-1, 30-1½	10¼	1¾	10½	1¼
1925	41-2	8½	1¾	4	1¼
1925	60-3	11	2	16¼	1¼
1925	80-4	14	2	18	1¼
1925	100-5	14	2	19	1½
1929-30	RB-36	11	1½	5¾	1⅜
1929-30	RB-46, RW-46, 54	15½	1⅞	4	1½
Graham Brothers					
1925	All Models	9	1½	7¼	1¼
1926	All Models	9	1½	8	1 3/16
1928	½, ¾	9	1½	3	1¼
1928	½, ¾, 1¼, 1¾	4½	2	4¼	1½
1928	1, 1½	9	1½	3	1¼
1928-29	2-3	5	2	4½	1½
1928-29	2 & 3	5	2	4¼	1½
1928-29	½, 1¾	4½	2	4¼	1½
Gramm-Bernstein					
1920-25	15-65-1½	10¼	2	6	2
1920-25	2½-75P-3½-40-4	11	1½	9	1½
1922-25	50-5-6	23¼	2	13¾	1⅞
1925	125-2½	4½	1½	12	1½
1925	30-3	11	1½	9	1½
1926	10-1	9	2¼	14½	2¼
1926	115-1½	9	2¼	10	1¼
1926	115-S-1½-2	7½	1½	5	1¼
1926	125-2½	9	1½	12½	1½
1926	30-3-3½	11	1½	15	1½
1926	40-4-5	11	1½	15	1½
1926	50-5-6	12½	1½	15	1½
Grass Premier					
1925	40A	12	2¼	14½	2¼
1925	60A1½, 70A2½	14	2½	16	2½
1925	90A3½	11	1½	11	1½
Hahn					
1925	B2	10	1¼	16	1¼
1926	0	10	1¼	16	1¼
1926	K & K Spec.	10	1¼	16	1¼
1926	L &M	12	1½	16	1½
1926	N & R	12	1½	18	1½
1928	26, 36	8	1½	8	1¼
1928	56	13	1½	8	1½
1928	76	14	2	12	1¼
Harvey					
1922-25	WHB-3½	10	2	14	1¼
1922-24	WOA2, WFB2½	7	2	14	1¼
1925	WFC2½, WTT6	7	2	14	1½
1926	WHB3½	10	2	15	1½
1926-29	WG2½, WTT6	7	2	14	1½
1928-29	WG6-2½	16	1¾	6	1¼
1929-30	WG, 2½	13	1½	7	2
Hawkeye.					
1922-25	N	14	2½	12	1½
1924-25	K, O	12	2	9	1¼
1924-25	M	12	2¼	9	1½
1926	50	12	2	9½	1¼
1926	30	12	1¾	9½	1½
1925-26	50	9	2	17	1½
1925-26	K	9	1¾	12	1¼
1925-27	2½	....	2	....	1½
1926-27	A-B	11	1¾	15	1¼
1928-29	30-4	9½	1¾	10½	1½
1928-29	50-4	8½	2	15	1½
1928-29	50-6	13	2	14	1½
Hendrickson					
1929	ST-2½	15	2	14	1½
1929	T-3	15	2	16	1½
1929	U-4	16	2	16	1½
1929	V-5	13	1½	17	1½
1929	SSW-6	18	2	17	1½
1929	MSW-8	19	2	17	1½
1929	SW-10	19	1½	17	1½
1929	SW-6-10	19	2	....	1½
1930	ST, T-6	14	1¾	10 6	1¼ 1¼
1930	U, SW-6	18	2	17	1½
1930	MSW	18	2	17	1½
1930	SW	13	1½	17	1½
1931	24-S	14	1¾	10 6	1¼ 1¼
1931	32-S, 36-S	20	2	19	1½
1931	44-D	18	2	17	1½
Hug					
1925	HA-H4-HA2	12	1¾	11½	1¼
1925-26	H4K	13	1¾	F. 4 R. 4	1¼
1926	HA2-HA4-TA-H4	12	1¾	11½	1¼
1926	HD6	F. 4 R. 4	1¾	9	1¼
1927	HA4-20-60	12	1¾	11½	1¼
1927	H4K-80-88	14	1¾	F. 4 R. 4	1¼
1927	40-90	F. 5 R. 5	1¾	9	1¼
1927	25-30	F. 5 R. 5	1¾	7	1¼
1928-29	60	12	1¾	11½	1¼
1928-29	81-84	14	1¾	F. 4 R. 4	1¼
1928	21-25-22-66	F. 5 R. 5	1¾	7	1¼
1928-29	40-86-90-486-846-40A	F. 5 R. 5	1¾	9	1¼
1929	66-22	F. 5 R. 5	1¾	7	1¼
1929	87-C 87-96-C96-26-41	F. 5 R. 5	1¾	9	1¼
1929	82-85	14	1¾	F. 4 R. 4	1¼
Indiana					
1920-25	12-1½	17	1¼	14	1¼
1920-25	20-2-25-2½-35-3½	6	1¼	13	1¼
1922-25	51-5	10	1½	17½	1½
1923-26	15	7	1¾	15	1¼
1925-26	25, 26, 27	9½	2	11	1½
1925-26	41	10	1½	13	1½
1926-27	11, 111	7	1¾	12½	1¼
1927	126	6	2	11	1½
1927	41	10½	2	8½	1½
1927	115	7	1¾	15	1¼
1928	111X	8½	1¾	13	1¼
1928	200-300	7¾	1½	9½	1¼
1928	115-A	8½	1¼	15¼	1¼
1928	400	7¼	1¾	14	1¼
1928	615-A	7¼	1¾	14	1¼
1928	126, 127, 127A, 138	9½	2	3	1¼
1928	41	6	2	8½	1¾
1928	641	13½	2	4	1½
1929	T-101	9⅞	1 5/16	6⅜	1 5/16
1929	T-101	9½	1 5/16	6⅜	1 5/16
1929	T-103	9	1 5/16	4½	1 5/16
International Harvester					
1921-25	SD-1½	9¾	2¼	17¾	2¼
1924-26	33-1½, 43-2	5	2¼	6	2½
1924-26	63-3	5	3	9	2½
1924-26	103-5	5	3	9	2½
1926	Spec. Del. ¾	13¼	2	6½	2
1926	S-26-1¼, SL-36-1½	5	2¼	F2¼ R3	1½ 1½
1926	S-24-1¼, SL-34-1½	10½	2¼	3½	2¼
1928	Spec. Del.	6½	2	11½	2
1928	S-24-SL34-SF34-SD-F44	10½	2¼	3½	2¼
1928	S-26-SL36-SF36-15B	5	2¼	5	1½
1928	SD46-SF46	5	2¼	5½	1½
1929	¾, 1	6½	2	11½	2
1929	S-24, SF-34, SD-44	10½	2¼	3½	2¼
1929	1¼, 1½, 2, SD-46	5	2¼	5	1½
1929	2½, 3½, 5	9⅜	†1¾	18	2
Kelly-Springfield					
1924-25	K33-1½	12¼	1½	26¾	1½
1924-25	K41-3½-5, K61-5-7	6¼	1⅝	24	1½
1924-25	K75-K76-2½	7	1½	13	1½
1925	K70-1½-2	12¼	1½	16	1½
1926-27	KS-15-1½ KS-20-2	16	1½	12¼	1½
1926-27	KS-25-2½, KS-35-3½	9	1½	12¼	1½
1926-27	KS-50-5, KS-70-7	24	1½	12	1⅝
Kenworth					
1925	O-1	12½	1¼	18½	1¼
1925	M-2	12½	2	17	1½
1925	KS3, L4	11½	2	17	1½
1925	RS-5	10	2	15	1½
King Zeitler					
1925	1-1½	11	1½	16	1½
1925	2½	12	1½	16	1½
1925	3½	12	1½	16	1½
1925	5	14	2	22	2
1926-27	25, 30, 40, 45	....	1½	....	1½
1926-27	42-A	....	1½	....	1½
1926-27	60	....	1½	....	1½
1926-27	75	....	1½	....	1½
1926-27	90	....	2	....	2
Kleiber					
1925-26	1	3	1¼	2½	1½
1925-26	1½	9½	1¼	13	1¼
1925-26	1½-2, 2-2½	12	1½	14	1½
1925-26	2½-3	12	1½	14	1½
1925-26	3½-5	12	1½	14	1½
1928	1½, 2	11	1¼	13	1¼
1928	Spec. 2	21	1¾	8	1¼
1928	2½	11	1¾	10	1¼
1928	2, 2½	13	1½	14	1½
1928	Spec. 3	15	2	14	1¾
1928	3½-5	14	1½	15½	1¼
1931	52	9	1½	3	1¼
1931	54, 56	14	1¾	3½	1¾
1931	58, 65, 657	7	2	3½	1¾

HOSE CONNECTIONS, COMMERCIAL CARS—Continued

Year	Model and Capacity	Upper Hose		Lower Hose	
		Length	Inner Diam.	Length	Inner Diam.
Kleiber—Cont.					
1931	66, SW100	7	2	3½	1¾
1931	SW200, 300	7	2	3½	1¾
1931	SW400	13	2	3½	1½
Krebs					
1925	J-24	8	1½	17	1½
1925	50, K-45	10	1½	17	1½
1925	L75, 80, 100, L-110-130, B-120	11	1½	17	1½
Lange					
1920-22	B-2	2¾	2¼	11¼	2
1921-28	E-2½	7	1½	14	1½
1923-26	F-3½	4	1½	14	1½
1924-30	G-1½	5½	1½	13	1½
1925-28	H	5	1¾	14	1½
1926-29	K-1¼	5½	1½	3	1¼
1929-31	R-1½	13½	1½	13½	1½
1927-31	L-2, O-2½	6	1¾	10	1¾
1928-31	H, M-3	6	1¾	10	1¾
1929-31	F16-4, T-5	6	1¾	10	1¾
1930-31	V-3½	6	1¾	10	1¾
Larrabee-Deyo					
1922-25	X2-1-1½	6	1½	14	1½
1923-25	J4-1½, 2½	6½	1¼	10	1½
1924-27	K5-2½-3½-L4-3½-4½	6	1½	11	1½
1925-27	X Series	Spec.		14	1¼
1926-27	XH	9	1¾	5	1½
				12	1½
1926-27	A-3	7	1½	9	1¼
Lehigh					
1926	S4, SR	8½	2	14	1⅝
1926	6S	9	1¼	17	1¾
Maccar					
1924-25	EX-1¼	4½	1½	15	1½
1924-25	V-1-2	4	1¾	19	1¼
1924-25	H-1-3	4	1¾	19	1½
1924-25	M-2-4	4	1¾	19	1½
1924-25	G-1-5	8	1¾	16½	1¾
1926	36-1¼	4	1¾	10	1¼
1926	46-2	14	1¼	6½	1¾
1926	64-3	9½	1½	4	1¾
1926	66-3	17	1½	13½	2
1926	94-4	9½	1½	4	1¾
1926	96-4	13½	2	7	1¼
				11¼	1½
1929	36-1½	4	1¾	10	1¼
1929	46-2½	14	1¼	6½	1¾
Mack					
1924-25	AC-3½, 5-6½, 7½	5	1¾	3¼	2
1924-25	AC-Tr., 7-10-13-15	5	1¾	3¼	2
1925	AB1½, 2, 2½-T-Ch D.R. 1½, 2, 2½ Tr-5	7½	1¼	5⅜	1¼
1928-29	AB	7¼	1½	5⅜	1¼
Menominee					
1922-25	D-2	3	1¾	3	1½
1924-25	H-1-1½	6	1½	12	1¼
1924-25	HT-1¼	6	½	12	1¼
1924	J-3-5	3	1¾	3	1¾
1925-27	T-Bus	7	1½	12	1¼
Moreland					
1925	EX-2	9	1½	14	1½
1925	RX-5	8	1½	14½	1½
1925	EC&AC Bus, AX-3	9	1½	13	1½
1926	RR, BX	6	2	4	1¼
1926	EXX4	9	1½	14	1½
1926	EXX6	8	1¼	14	1¼
1926	AXX4	9	1½	13	1½
1926	AXX6	9½	1¾	14	1½
1926	SX4, TX4	9	1½	14½	1½
1926	SX6	12½	2¼	14½	1¾
1926	TX6	8	2¼	14½	1¾
1926-29	TX	8	2¼	14½	1¾
1926	EXX	9	1½	14	1½
1927	RB6, BS6	6	2	4	1¼
1929	RR-RC	7	2	4	1¼
1929	ACE	6	1¼	4	1¼
National					
1924-27	M	16	2½	14	2½
1924-27	T	12	1½	18	1½
Nelson & Le Moon					
1924	G-1, 1½	8	1⅜	3½	1⅜
1925	GP-1, 1½, 2, G3, 4, 5	12	1⅜	10	1⅜
1926-27	L4, B5, B7	9	1⅜	13	1⅜
1926-27	S4, K4	8	1⅜	13	1⅜
1927-28	650, H-15, H-20	10	1½	12	1¼
1927-28	H-30	10	1¾	13½	1⅜
1927-28	MP-3 Ton	8	1⅜	13	1⅜
1927-28	MP 4-5 Ton	9	1⅜	13	1⅜
Nevin					
1928	A	14	2	9	1½
Noble					
1922-25	B31-1½	7	1⅞	16½	1¼
1922-25	D51-2½, 52-3	9½	2	12	1¼
1922-25	E71-3½, 72-4	14½	2	16	1¼
1924-25	A76-1½	12	1¾	12½	1¼
1924-25	A21-1½	12	1¾	12½	1¼
1926-27	RS-24, A-76, A-21	12	1¾	16	1¼
1926-27	B-31, 2 Ton	7	1⅞	13	1¼
1926-27	D-51, 52, 2½-3	9½	2	16	1¼
1926-27	E71, E-72, 3½-5	14	2	16	1¼
Oakland					
1927	Six	8¼	1¼	9¼	1¼
Oshkosh					
1920-25	AA-2	16	2	17	2
1922-25	B, BB-2½	9¾	1½	12	1½
1923-25	AW, AAW	3½	1½	7½	1¼
1924-25	BO, BBO	9¾	1½	12	1½
1924-25	F	9¾	1½	F3½	1½
				R3½	1½
1925	H, HH	8	2	12	1½
1925	M, MM	10½	1½	12	1½
1926	R, RR	5	1½	12	1½
1928	A	17	2	16	2
1928	AW	7½	1¼	4	1½
1928	B	13	1½	11	1½
1928	F	9	1½	9½	1½
1928	H6	13	1½	9	2
1928	H6	14¾	1½	6	2
1928	K	13	1½	11	1½
1928	R	12	1½	9½	1½
1928	R6	8	1½	4½	1¾
1929	L-2½, H-3	14	1½	10	2
1929-30	HC, HXC, FHX	13	1½	9	2
1930	L, H	14	1½	10	2
Patriot					
1923-25	1	8	2	9	2
1923-25	2	6	1¼	8	1½
1923-25	3	11	1½	10	2
Pierce-Arrow					
1924-28	XA-2, XB-3-TT	16⅜	2	14¼	1¾
1924-28	WC, RD, RF, WD	11	2	15½	1¾
1928	Z	3	2	14¼	1½
1928	FA	3¼	1¾	3¼	1½
1931	PT-2	17	1½	19	1½
1931	PW-3	12	1½	19	1½
1931	PX, PY	10½	2½	20	1¾
1931	PZ-8	12½	2½	19⅜	2½
Pontiac					
1927		9¼	1¼	5	1¼
Rainier					
1923-25	R31-¾, R29-1	9	2	6	2
1923	R36-1½	8	1½	14	1½
1923-25	R28-2-2½, R20-2½-3	9½	1½	14	1½
1923-25	R25-3½-5	9½	1½	14	1½
1924-25	R36-1½	8	1½	14	1½
1924-25	R27-6-7	9½	1½	14	1½
Rehberger					
1924-28	A-2	13½	1¾	16	1½
1924-26	B-3, C-4	14	2	16	1¼
1924-26	D-5	14	2	17	1½
1924-26	B-2, B-3	14	2	13	1½
1928	B-3, C-4	15	2	16	1½
1928	D-5	15	2	17	1½
1928	B-4	15	2	9½	1½
Relay					
1928	30A-1½	3	2⅛	10	1¼
1928	40A-2	3	2⅛	10	1¼
1928	50C-2½	3	2⅛	17½	1½
1928	60C-3	3	2⅛	17½	1½
1928	70C-3½	3	2⅛	17½	1½
1928	80C-4	3	2⅛	17½	1½
1929	20B-1	12	1¾	6½	1¼
1929	S11B-1½	12	1¾	6½	1¼
1929	30A-1½	10¾	1¾	10	1¼
1929	40A-2	10¾	1¾	10	1¼
1929	50C-2½	3	2⅛	17½	1½
1929	60C-3	3	2⅛	17½	1½
1929	70C-3½	3	2⅛	17½	1½
1929	80C-4	3	2⅛	17½	1½
1930-31	15A	8¼	1¾	10	1½
1930-31	S11B	3	1¾	4	1¼
1930-31	40A, 50D	3	2⅛	10	1¼
1930-31	60D	3	2⅛	17	1½
1930-31	100A	9	2	10	1½
1931	40D Bus	10	1¾	15	1½
1931	100B	8	2⅛	10	1½
Reo					
1925	F¾, 1¼	5½	1	5½	1
1926	F-1¼	5½	1	5½	1
1926	F-6-1¼	14½	1½	12	1¼
1926	G-2, W-Bus	16¼	1½	12	1¼
1930	GA, GB, GC	11	1¾	14 15/16	1½
1930	FC, FD, FH	11	1¾	14 15/16	1½
1930	DF	9¾	1¾	6¾	1½
1930	FA, FB, FE, FF	11	1¾	14 15/16	1½
Rowe					
1924-25	CDW-GSW-HW-2½-3-4	18	1¾	16	1½
1924-25	HW5-FW5	11	1¾	17	1¾
Royal					
1924	C	11	2	21½	1¼
1925	D	11	2	21½	1¼
1926-27	E	11	2	20	1¼
Rugby					
1928	Fast Mail	5	1¼	5	1¼
1928	Express	6½	1¼	5	1¼
1929	401	5	1¼	3½	1¼
Safeway					
1928	92-4	....	2¼	4½	1¾
1928	64-66	....	2¼	3	1¾
1928-29	63	7	2	3	1¾
Sandow					
1924-25	G-CG1-1½	9	2	7	2
1924-25	J-2½	7	1¼	13	1¼
1924-25	M-3½	9	1½	13	1¼
1925	L-5	10	2	13	¼
1926	G-GA-CG-JS	9	1¾	13	1¼
1926	J-JD	10	1¾	13	1¼
Sanford					
1923-25	W15-1½	9	2¼	11	1½
1923-25	2½-35-3½-50-5	8	1½	11	1½
1924-25	2½	8	1½	11	1½
1924-25	35-50-3½-5	9	1½	11	1½
Schacht					
1926	L	17	2	15	1½
1926	M, LM	10½	2	18	1¾
1926	LO, MP, LN	10½	2	15	1¾
1928	H-1½	5	1¾	14¾	1¼
1928	HS-2	5	1¾	14¾	1¼
1928	T-2½	15	1¾	16	1¼
1928	N, R	11	2	20½	1½
1928	H-1, 1½	5	1¾	14¾	1¼
1928-29	T, 2½	15	1¾	16	1¼
1928-29	HS-2	5	1¾	14¾	1¼
1928-29	N. R.	11	2	20½	1½
1929-30	20	9	1¾	4	1¼
1929-30	25	15	1¾	14¼	1¼
1929-30	30	5	1¾	14½	1¼
Selden					
1923-25	50-B	8⅜	1½	14¾	1½
1923-25	52-70	8⅜	1½	16¼	1½
1923-25	53-B	11½	1½	16¼	1½
1924-25	70-B	8⅜	1½	16¾	1½
1924-25	73-B	9	1¾	14¾	1½
1924-25	90-B	7	1¾	16¾	1½
1925	30C	6	1½	11½	1½
1929-30	17C, 1¼	9	1½	4	1¼
Service					
1924-25	33-34-1½	8	1¾	10	1¼
1924-25	42-61-2-2½-3	10	2	10	1¼
1924-25	81-103-4-5-6	10	2	11½	1¼
1925	25F, 25C	12½	1¾	10	1¼
1926-27	25H	8	1¾	10	1¼
1926-27	34	8	1¾	10	1¼
1926-27	61	10	2	10	1¼
1926-27	81-103	10	2	11½	1¼
1928	20-Z, 25-Z, S-11-Z	10¾	1¾	4	1¼
1928	30-Z, 40-Z	3	2⅛	10	1¼
1928-29	50-Z, 60-Z, 70-Z, 80-Z	3	2⅛	17½	1½
1928	Ser. 1 20-Z, 25-Z, S-11-Z	3	2⅛	4	1¼
1929	20Y, S-11-Y	12	1¾	6½	1¼
1929	30Z, 40-Z	10¾	1¾	10	1¼
Six Wheel					
....	55	7	2	3	1¾
....	63, 64	7	2	3	1¾
....	66	9	2¼	3	1¾
Sterling					
1925	GB2, DW10, 12, 14, 16, DWS14	10	1½	18	1½
1925	GB4-6	....	1½	....	1½
1925	DW8	11½	1¼	....	1¼
1925	EW20, 23, EC29	13½	1½	22	1½
1925	EW25, EW27, EC23, ECS24, 26, 29	10	1½	18	1½
Stewart					
1923-28	16, 17	15	2¼	11	2¼
1923-28	16X, 17X	3½	1½	11¼	1½
1924	17	4	1¼	7¼	2¼
1924-25	18	4	1¼	6	2¼

HOSE CONNECTIONS, COMMERCIAL CARS—Continued

Year	Model and Capacity	Upper Hose Length	Upper Hose Inner Diam.	Lower Hose Length	Lower Hose Inner Diam.
Stewart—Cont.					
1925	10X	12	1¼	11½	2
1927-29	22, 22X	9½	1½	8¼	1½
1928	21, 21X	4	1¼	11	1¼
1928-29	24, 25	4	1¼	6½	2¼
1928-29	24X, 25X	3½	1½	9½	1½
1928-30	16, 16A	15	2¼	6½	2¼
1928-30	16X, 16XA	3½	1½	9½	1½
1928-30	18X	9½	1½	9½	1½
1928-30	19X	9½	1½	8¼	1½
1929	24X, 25X	3½	1½	11	1½
1929-30	26X, 26XW	9½	1½	9½	1½
1929-30	28, 29, 29W	4	1¼	6½	2¼
1929-31	30, 40	3	2¼	3	2¼
1929-31	30X, 40X	3½	1½	11	1½
1930-31	21, 21X	3½	1½	9½	1½
1930	32X	3½	1¾	9	1½
1930	33X	9½	1½	8¼	1½
1930-31	27X, 31	3½	1½	10	2¼
Stoughton					
1925-26	C	14	2½	14	2½
1925-26	B-Jr. & J	13½	1¾	12½	1¼
1925-26	D-2	9	2	14	1¼
1925-26	F-3	10	2	15	1¼
Studebaker					
1928	Dic. Del	7⅞	1¼	2½	1¼
1928	75-76	10½	1½	9	1½
1929	99, 88	12	1½	3	1½
1929	GK	9	1¼	2½	1¼
1931	S1	8	1¼	3	1¼
1931	S20, 30, 40	10¼	1¼	2½	1¾
1931	S50, S60	10¼	1¼	2½	1¾
Traylor					
1923-27	B	10	2	6	1¼
1923-27	C-D	12	2	12	1¼
1923-27	F	14	2	14	1¼
Twin City					
1926	2½	8	1⅝	4	1⅝
United					
1925	25, 30, 35, 50, 60	10	2	13½	2
1925	80	8⅝	2	13¾	1½
U. S.					
1920-25	3½-4	9	1½	8	1½
1922-28	U-1¼	11½	1¾	11½	1¼
1922-28	N-1½	11½	2	9	1¼
1920-25	R-2½-3	10	1¼	10	1¼
1923-25	NW23-1½	10¾	1¾	11½	1¼
1923-25	T-5-7	15	2	13	1½
1923-25	S-4-5	9	1½	8	1½
1928-29	20, L	21	1¾	8	1¼
1928-29	21	10¾	1¾	11	1¼
1928-29	31, 40	11½	2	12	1¼
1928-29	30	21	1¾	8	1¼
Velie					
1928	33	8	2¼	12½	2¼
1928	40	8	2¼	12½	2¼
Victor					
1924-25	25-X-1	10	2	14½	2
1924-25	40-1½	8½	2	12½	1½
1924-25	50-2	8½	2	12½	1½
1924-25	60-2½	8½	2	12½	1½
1924-25	70-2½	8½	2	12½	1½
1924-25	80-3½	10	1½	12½	1½
1925	90-6	....	1½	....	1½
1927	40, 50, 60, 70	8½	2	12½	1½
1927	25	10½	2	14½	2
1927	80	10	1½	12½	1½
Wachusett					
1924-25	S-1	9½	1¼	11	1¼
1924-25	J-1½	10	1½	10½	1½
1924-25	K-2	11	1½	11	1½
1924-25	L-2½	10	1½	11	1½
Walter					
1920-25	S-5	10	1½	18	1½
1925-28	FH, FHR	10	1½	22	1½
Ward La France					
1920-25	2-B-2½, 3½	7	1½	16	1½
1920-25	4A-3½, 5	8½	1½	18	1½
1925	5A-5-7	9¼	1½	18	1½
White					
1919-27	15-¾, 20-2	7¼	1	6½	1¼
1919-25	20D-2	7¼	1	6½	1¼
1919-26	15-45-¾, 40D-3-3½, 45D-5	12¾	1½	12¾	1½
1919-24	20-45-2	12¾	1½	12¾	1½
1919-26	40-3-3½, 45-5	12¾	1½	12¾	1½
1922-23	50-Bus	12¾	1½	12¾	1½
1923-25	50A-Bus	12¾	1½	12¾	1½
1925-26	51-2½	12¾	1½	12¾	1½
1926	40A-3-3½, 45A-5, 50B-Bus	12¾	1½	12¾	1½
1926-29	52-HD, 52D-HD, 53-Bus	9½	1½	12¾	1½
1927-29	15B-1	7¼	1	6½	1¼
1927-29	20A-1-½	7¼	1	6½	1¼
1927-29	51A-2½	12½	1½	12¾	1½
1927-29	52T-3-5	9½	1½	12¾	1½
1927-29	55-3-3½	9½	1½	12¾	1½
1927-29	56, 57-1¼-2	12¼	1½	12¾	1½
1928-29	58-3	9½	1½	12¾	1½
1927-29	50B-Bus	9½	1½	12¾	1½
1927-29	54-Bus	7	2	3	1½
1929	60-1, 61-1	11	1¼	3½	¼
Wichita					
1931	6-95-4	14	2¼	7	1
				7	1
1931	6-21, 6-60	16¾	1¼	4	1¼
				4	1¼
Willys					
1930	C-101	13	1 5/16	2¼	1 5/16
1930	T-103	9	1 5/16	2¼	1 5/16
Willys-Knight					
1928	15, 16	11½	1 5/16	5¼	1 5/16
1928	20-21-25-26	9	2	8	2
Witt-Will					
1925	P-2, N-1½	8	1½	12	1¼
1925	SS-3, S2½	8	1½	12	1¼
1926-27	1½, 3	10	1½	14	1½
1926-27	5	10	1½	18	1½
1928	NN	10	1½	16	1½
1928	S, SS	10	1½	14	1½
1928	L, A, AS	10	1½	18	1½
Yellow Cab					
1922-25	A2, O3, O4	8¼	2	10⅛	2
1925-27	D-1	9¼	1½	2¼	1¼
1925-27	O5	7	2	9¼	2
1925-27	X	....	2⅝	7⅛	1½
1925-27	Y	....	2⅝	4⅛	1¾
1925-27	Z-4	11	2⅝	4	2⅝
1925-27	YZ	5	2⅝	4⅛	1¾
1925-27	K17-1, K32-1½	10½	1½	9½	1¼
1925-27	K52-2½	12¼	1¾	9½	1¾
1925-27	K72-3½, K102-5, K10T-3½, K15T-5	14⅛	1¾	11.2	1¾
1925-26	T2-1	9¼	2	7	2

*—Outside
D—Diameter
F—Front
R—Rear
V—"V" Type
†—Double Outlet, 2 required

Brake Lining Sizes—Passenger Cars

For Commercial Car, Motor Truck Brake Lining Sizes See Page 286.
For Rivet Sizes, Interchangeability and Specifications See Page 262.

Passenger Car, Make, Model and Year	Brake Lining: Front, Total Length (Ins.)	Front, Width (Ins.)	Front, Thickness (Ins.)	Rear, Total Length (Ins.)	Rear, Width (Ins.)	Rear, Thickness (Ins.)	Hand, Total Length (Ins.)	Hand, Width (Ins.)	Hand, Thickness (Ins.)
Auburn 6-66.....1927	61	1 5/8	5/32	65 1/2	2	5/32	18 1/2	2	5/32
Auburn 8-88.....1927	76	1 5/8	5/32	84	2	5/32	24 5/8	2	5/32
Auburn 8-77...1927-28	61	1 5/8	5/32	65	2	5/32	24 5/8	2	5/32
Auburn 8-88.....1928	....	1 3/4	3/16	....	1 3/4	3/16	24 5/8	2	5/32
Auburn 76....1928-29	....	1 3/4	3/16	....	1 3/4	3/16	18 1/2	2	5/32
Auburn 88....1928-29	....	1 3/4	3/16	....	1 3/4	3/16	24 5/8	2	5/32
Auburn 115...1928-29	....	1 3/4	3/16	....	1 3/4	3/16	24 5/8	2	5/32
Auburn 6-80.....1929	42	1 3/4	5/32	42	1 3/4	3/16	18	2	5/32
Auburn 8-90.....1929	42	1 3/4	5/32	42	1 3/4	3/16	24 5/8	2	5/32
Auburn 120......1929	50	1 3/4	5/32	50	1 3/4	3/16	22 3/4	2 1/2	3/16
Auburn 6-85.....1930	42	1 3/4	5/32	42	1 3/4	5/32	18 9/16	2	5/32
Auburn 8-95.....1930	42	1 3/4	5/32	42	1 3/4	5/32	24 5/8	2	5/32
Auburn 125......1930	50	1 3/4	5/32	50	1 3/4	5/32	22 3/4	2 1/2	3/16
Auburn 8-98.....1931	67 1/2	1 3/4	13/64	67 1/2	1 3/4	13/64	....	....	
Austin........1930-31	24	1 1/8	3/16	24	1 1/8	3/16	48	1 1/8	3/16
Blackhawk L-6 1929-30	73	1 3/4	3/16	73	1 3/4	3/16	20	2 1/4	1/8
Blackhawk L-8 1929-30	73	1 3/4	3/16	73	1 3/4	3/16	20	2 1/4	1/8
Buick Master 6...1925	....	2	3/16	....	2	3/16	81	1 5/8	5/32
Buick Master 6...1926	....	2	3/16	....	2	3/16	72	1 5/8	5/32
Buick 115.......1928	....	2	3/16	....	2	3/16	82	1 5/8	5/32
Buick 128,120 1927-28	....	2	3/16	....	2	3/16	82	1 5/8	5/32
Buick 116.......1929	77 1/4	1 3/4	3/16	77 1/4	1 3/4	3/16	71 1/8	1 3/8	3/16
Buick 129, 121...1929	78 1/2	2	3/16	78 1/4	2	3/16	....	1 5/8	5/32
Buick 40........1930	....	1 3/4	3/16	....	1 3/4	3/16	....	1 3/4	3/16
Buick 50, 60.....1930	....	2		....	2		....	2	
Buick 8-50.......1931	52	1 3/4	3/16	52	1 3/4	3/16	104	1 3/4	3/16
Buick 8-60.......1931	44 3/8	1 3/4	3/16	44 3/8	1 3/4	3/16	88	1 3/4	3/16
Buick 8-80, 8-90..1931	47 9/32	2	3/16	47 9/32	2	3/16	93 1/2	2	3/16
Cadillac V-63....1925	98	2 1/2	3/16	71	2 1/4	3/16	97	2 1/2	3/16
Cadillac 314...1926-27	98	2 1/2	3/16	71	2 1/4	3/16	97	2 1/2	3/16
Cadillac 341-A...1928	77 7/8	2 1/4	3/16	89 7/8	2 1/2	3/16	80 3/4	2	3/16
Cadillac 341-B...1929	48 1/4	2 1/4	3/16	48 1/4	2 1/4	3/16	20 5/8	2 1/4	3/16
Cadillac 353......1930	47 1/2	2 1/4	3/16	47 1/2	2 1/4	3/16	47 1/2	2 1/4	3/16
Cadillac 452...1930-31	47 1/2	2 1/4	3/16	47 1/2	2 1/4	3/16	47 1/2	2 1/4	3/16
Cadillac 370......1931	43 1/2	2	3/16	43 1/2	2	3/16	43 1/2	2	3/16
Cadillac 355......1931	43 1/2	2	3/16	43 1/2	2	3/16	43 1/2	2	3/16
Chandler Std. 6..1927	....	1 3/4	5/32	....	1 3/4	5/32	22 1/8	1 3/4	5/32
Chandler Sp. 6...1927	....	2	5/32	....	2	5/32	32 1/8	1 3/4	5/32
Chan. Big 6-35 1927-28	....	2	3/16	....	2	3/16	21	1 3/4	5/32
Chan. Roy 8..1927-28	....	2	3/16	....	2	3/16	21	1 3/4	5/32
Chan. Sp. 6-31A..1928	....	1 3/4	5/32	....	1 3/4	5/32	22 1/8	1 3/4	5/32
Chan. Sp. In. 6...1928	....	1 3/4	5/32	....	1 3/4	5/32	22 1/8	1 3/4	5/32
Chan.Big6-135 1928-29	79	2	3/16	79	2	3/16	20 3/4	1 3/4	5/32
Chan. Roy. 8-137.1928	....	2	3/16	....	2	3/16	21	1 3/4	5/32
Chandler 65.... 1929	72	1 3/4	5/32	72	1 3/4	5/32	22 1/8	1 3/4	5/32
Chandler Roy.75..1929	72	1 3/4	5/32	72	1 3/4	5/32	22 1/8	1 3/4	5/32
Chandler Roy.85..1929	79	.	3/16	79	2	3/16	20 3/4	1 3/4	5/32
Chevrolet Sup.F..1925	....	1 1/2	5/32	....	1 1/2	5/32	58	1 1/4	5/32
Chev. Sup.K..1925-26	....	1 1/2	5/32	....	1 1/2	5/32	58	1 1/4	5/32
Chev. Cap. AA...1927	....	2	5/32	....	2	5/32	56	1 1/4	5/32
Chev. Nat. AB....1928	36 1/8	1 1/2	5/32	67 7/8	2	5/32	56	1 1/4	5/32
Chev.Inter.AC 1929-30	34 1/4	1 1/2	5/32	60 3/4	2	3/16	56	1 1/4	5/32
Chev. Uni. AD...1930	34 1/4	1 1/2	5/32	60 3/4	2	3/16	56	1 1/4	5/32
Chrysler B.......1925	....	1 1/2	3/16	....	1 1/2	3/16	19	2 1/2	3/16
Chrysler 58......1926	....	1 1/2	3/16	....	1 1/2	3/16	25	2	5/32
Chrysler 70...1926-27	....	1 1/2	3/16	....	1 1/2	3/16	24 5/8	2	5/32
Chrys.Imp.80..1926-27	....	2	3/16	....	2	3/16	24 5/8	2	5/32
Chrysler 50......1927	....	1 3/4	3/16	....	1 3/4	3/16	21 3/8	2	5/32
Chrysler 52......1928	....	2	3/16	....	2	3/16	21 3/8	2	5/32
Chrysler 62......1928	....	1 1/2	3/16	....	1 1/2	3/16	24 5/8	2	5/32
Chrysler 72......1928	....	1 1/2	3/16	....	1 1/2	3/16	24 5/8	2	5/32
Chry.Im.80.1928-29-30	....	1 3/4	3/16	....	1 3/4	3/16	24 5/8	2	5/32
Chrysler 65......1929	....	1 3/4	3/16	....	1 3/4	3/16	24 5/8	2	5/32
Chrysler 75......1929	....	1 3/4	3/16	....	1 3/4	3/16	24 5/8	2	5/32
Chrysler 66...1930-31	....	1 1/2	3/16	....	1 1/2	3/16	19 1/4	2 1/2	5/32
Chrysler 70...1930-31	29	1 3/4	3/16	25 3/16	1 3/4	3/16	24 5/8	2	..
Chrysler Six...1930-31	....	1 1/2		....	1 1/2		....	2	..
Chrysler 77......1930	29	1 3/4	3/16	25 3/16	1 3/4	3/16	24 5/8	2	5/32
Chrysler Eight...1931	43 3/16	1 3/4	3/16	43 3/16	1 3/4	3/16	21 13/32	2	5/32
Chrysler Imp. 8..1931	55 3/16	1 3/4	3/16	55 3/16	1 3/4	3/16	24 5/8	2	5/32
Cleveland 31.....1925	....	1 3/4	5/32	....	1 3/4	5/32	22	1 3/4	5/32
Cleveland 31.....1926	....	1 3/4	5/32	....	1 3/4	5/32	22	1 3/4	5/32
Cord L-29....1930-31	....	2 1/4	3/16	28	1 3/4	3/16	28	1 3/4	3/16
Cunningham V-7.1928	....	2	3/16	....	2	3/16	184	2	3/16
Cunningham V-8.1929	92	2	3/16	92	2	3/16	184	2	3/16
Cunning'mV-9.1930-31	69 1/2	2 1/2	1/4	69 1/2	2 1/2	1/4	139	2 1/2	1/4
Davis 94-27......1927	....	1 3/4	3/16	....	1 3/4	3/16	25	2	3/16
Davis 99........1928	....	2	3/16	....	2	3/16	19	2	3/16
DeSoto..........1929	....	1 1/2	3/16	....	1 1/2	3/16	21 3/8	2	5/32
DeSoto Six......1930	22 5/32	1 1/2	3/16	18 9/32	1 1/2	3/16	21 3/8	2	5/32
DeSoto Str. 8..1930-31	22 5/32	1 1/2	3/16	18 9/32	1 1/2	3/16	21 13/32	2	5/32
DeSoto 6 SA......1931	40 7/16	1 1/2	3/16	40 7/16	1 1/2	3/16	21 3/8	2	5/32
Diana Str. 8..1926-7-8	57 3/4	1 3/4	3/16	57 3/4	1 3/4	3/16	24 3/8	2	5/32
Dodge.....1925-26-27	....	2 1/4	3/16	....	2 1/4	3/16	71	1 3/4	3/16
Dodge 124........1920	....	2 1/4	3/16	....	2 1/4	3/16	70 5/8	1 3/4	3/16
Dodge Senior.....1928	....	1 3/4	3/16	....	1 3/4	3/16	17 15/32	2 1/2	3/16
Dodge Sen..1928-29-30	26 3/4	1 3/4	3/16	26 3/4	1 3/4	3/16	17 15/32	2 1/2	3/16
Dodge 128....... 1928	....	2	3/16	....	2	3/16	17 15/32	2 1/2	3/16
Dodge Vict. 6..1928-29	....	1 3/4	3/16	....	1 3/4	3/16	17 15/32	2 1/2	3/16
Dodge Std. 6..1928-29	....	1 1/4	3/16	....	1 3/4	3/16	18 1/8	2 1/2	5/32
Dodge 6 DA..1929-30	27 5/8	1 3/4	3/16	27 5/8	1 3/4	3/16	19 1/8	2 1/2	5/32
Dodge DD 6..1930-31	20 7/8	1 1/2	11/64	20 7/8	1 1/2	11/64	21 13/32	2	5/32
Dodge DC 8..1930-31	22 11/32	1 3/4	11/64	22 11/32	1 3/4	11/64	21 13/32	2	5/32
Dodge Six.......1931	40 7/16	1 1/2	3/16	40 7/16	1 1/2	3/16	21 3/8	2	5/32
Dodge Eight.....1931	43 7/16	1 3/4	3/16	43 7/16	1 3/4	3/16	21 13/32	2	5/32
Duesenberg J..1929-31	64	2 1/4	1/4	64	2 1/4	1/4	18 1/2	3	1/4
du Pont E..1927-28-29	....	2	3/16	....	2	3/16	23 1/4	1 3/4	5/32
du Pont F.......1928	....	2	3/16	....	2	3/16	23 1/4	1 3/4	5/32
du Pont G..1929-30-31	68	2 1/4	1/4	....	2 1/4	1/4	23 1/2	2	5/32
Durant 55....1928-29		1 1/2	5/32	....	1 1/2	5/32	118 1/2	1 1/2	5/32
Durant 65....1928-29	59 1/4	1 1/2	5/32	59 1/4	1 1/2	5/32	118 1/2	1 1/2	5/32
Durant 75....1928-29	64 1/4	1 3/4	3/16	64 1/4	1 3/4	3/16	128 1/2	1 3/4	3/16
Durant 40....1929-30	59 1/4	1 1/2	5/32	59 1/4	1 1/2	5/32	118 1/2	1 1/2	5/32
Durant 60....1929-30	49 1/4	1 1/2	5/32	49 1/4	1 1/2	5/32	118 1/2	1 1/2	5/32
Durant 66....1929-30	....	1 1/2	5/32	....	1 1/2	5/32	....	1 1/2	5/32
Durant 70....1929-30	.	1 3/4	3/16	....	1 3/4	3/16	....	1 3/4	3/16
Durant 6-14...1930-31	59 1/8	1 1/2	3/16	29 9/16	1 1/2	3/16	118 1/4	1 1/2	3/16
Durant 6-17...1930-31	....	2	3/16	....	2	3/16	153	2	3/16
Elcar 6-70..1927-28-29	....	1 1/2	3/16	....	1 1/2	3/16	18 1/4	2	5/32
Elcar 8-82........1927	....	2	3/16	....	2	3/16	24 5/8	2	5/32
Elcar 90,91,92.1927-29	....	2	3/16	....	2	3/16	24 5/8	2	5/32
Elcar 8-78.....1928-29	59	.	3/16	59	...	3/16	18 1/4	2	5/32
Elcar 8-82.....1928-29	70	1 3/4	3/16	70	1 3/4	3/16	24 5/8	2	5/32
Elcar 75......1929-30	43 7/16	1 3/4	3/16	43 7/16	1 3/4	3/16	18 1/4	2	5/32
Elcar 95, 96...1929-30	51 1/4	1 3/4	3/16	51 1/4	1 3/4	3/16	24 5/8	2	5/32
Elcar 75-A.......1930	43 7/16	1 3/4	3/16	43 7/16	1 3/4	3/16	18 1/4	2	5/32
Erskine Six 51...1928	....	1 1/2	5/32	....	1 1/2	5/32	118 5/8	1 1/2	5/32
Erskine Six 52.1929-30	59 5/16	1 1/2	5/32	59 5/16	1 1/2	5/32	118 5/8	1 1/2	5/32
Erskine Six 53...1930	53 9/16	1 1/2	5/32	53 9/16	1 1/2	5/32	107 1/8	1 1/2	5/32
Essex...1925-26-27-28	....	1 3/4	3/16	....	1 3/4	3/16	70	1 1/2	3/16
Essex Super 6..1928-29	60 1/2	1 1/2	5/32	60 1/2	1 1/2	5/32	121	1 1/2	5/32
Essex Challeng.6..1929	36 1/2	1 1/2	5/32	36 1/2	1 1/2	5/32	18 1/4	1 1/2	5/32
Essex Super 6....1930	49	1 1/2	5/32	49	1 1/2	5/32	98	1 1/2	5/32
Essex Super 6....1931	49	1 1/2	5/32	49	1 1/2	5/32	98	1 1/2	5/32
Falcon Kni.12.1928-29	62	1 3/4	5/32	62	1 3/4	5/32	31	1 3/4	5/32
Ford T....1925-26-27	....	1 15/16		....	1 15/16	.	64	1 1/2	5/32
Ford A...........1928	....	1 1/2	3/16	....	1 1/2	3/16	66	1 1/2	3/16
Ford A.....1929-30-31	56	1 1/2	3/16	56	1 1/2	3/16	57 1/2	1 1/32	3/16
Franklin 11...1925-26	....	3 1/2	3/16	....	3 1/2	3/16	65	2	5/32
Franklin 11B..1927-28	....	3 1/2	3/16	....	3 1/2	3/16	56	2	5/32
Franklin 12 Air...1928	....	1 3/4	3/16	....	1 3/4	3/16	23 7/8	2	5/32
Franklin 130.....1929	42 1/2	1 3/4	3/16	50 7/8	1 3/4	3/16	23 7/8	2	5/32
Franklin 137.....1929	42 1/4	1 3/4	3/16	50 7/8	1 3/4	3/16	22 1/2	2	5/32
Franklin 145, 147.1930	66 3/4	1 3/4	3/16	66 3/4	1 3/4	3/16	22 1/4	2	5/32
Franklin Ser. 15..1931	66 3/4	1 3/4	3/16	66 3/4	1 3/4	3/16	22 1/2	2	5/32
Gardner 6-B......1927	....	1 5/8	5/32	....	1 5/8	5/32	68	1 5/8	5/32
Gardner Ser.90 1927-28	....	1 5/8	5/32	....	1 5/8	5/32	18 9/16	2	5/32
Gardner 75, 80 1928-29	....	1 5/8	5/32	....	1 5/8	5/32	24	2	5/32
Gardner 95.......1928	....	..		....	....	.	24	2	5/32
Gardner 85,125 1928-29	43 7/16	1 3/4	3/16	43 7/16	1 3/4	3/16	24	2	5/32
Gard. 130, 150.1929-30	50 7/8	1 3/4	3/16	50 7/8	1 3/4	3/16	24	2	5/32
Gardner 136...1930-31	43 1/2	1 3/4	3/16	43 1/2	1 3/4	3/16	18	2	5/32
Gardner 140......1930	43 1/2	1 3/4	3/16	43 1/2	1 3/4	3/16	18	2	5/32
Gardner 148......1931	43 1/2	1 3/4	3/16	43 1/2	1 3/4	3/16	18	2	5/32
Gard. 150,158..1930-31	50 3/4	1 3/4	3/16	50 3/4	1 3/4	3/16	24 1/2	2	5/32
Graham Std. 6....1930	43 7/8	1 3/4	3/16	43 7/8	1 3/4	3/16	18 9/16	2	5/32
Graham Std. 8....1930	53 7/16	1 3/4	3/16	53 7/16	1 3/4	3/16	24 5/8	2 1/2	5/32
Graham Cus. 8....1930	53 3/16	1 3/4	3/16	53 1/16	1 3/4	3/16	24 5/8	2 1/2	5/32
Graham Std.Sp.6.1931	43 7/8	1 3/4	3/16	43 7/8	1 3/4	3/16	24 5/8	2 1/2	5/32
Graham Sp.8-20..1931	53 7/16	1 3/4	3/16	53 7/16	1 3/4	3/16	24 5/8	2 1/2	5/32
Graham Cus.8-34.1931	53 7/16	1 3/4	3/16	53 7/16	1 3/4	3/16	24 5/8	2 1/2	5/32
Gra.-Paige 610 1928-29	57 1/4	1 1/2	3/16	57 1/4	1 1/2	3/16	18 9/16	2	5/32
Gra.-Paige 614 1928-29	69 3/4	1 1/2	3/16	69 3/4	1 1/2	3/16	18 9/16	2	5/32
Gra.-Paige 619 1928-29	53 1/8	1 3/4	3/16	53 1/8	1 3/4	3/16	24 5/8	2	5/32
Gra.-Paige 835 1928-29	53 1/8	1 3/4	3/16	53 1/8	1 3/4	3/16	24 5/8	2	5/32
Graham-Paige612 1929	43 7/8	1 3/4	3/16	43 7/8	1 3/4	3/16	18 9/16	2	5/32
Graham-Paige612 1930	43 7/8	1 3/4	3/16	43 7/8	1 3/4	3/16	18 9/16	2	5/32
Graham-Paige615 1929	53 7/16	1 3/4	3/16	53 7/16	1 3/4	3/16	18 9/16	2 1/2	5/32
Graham-Paige621 1929	53 1/16	1 3/4	3/16	53 1/16	1 3/4	3/16	24 5/8	2 1/4	5/32
Graham-Paige827 1929	53 1/16	1 3/4	3/16	53 1/16	1 3/4	3/16	24 5/8	2 1/4	5/32
Hudson....1925-26-27	....	2 1/2	3/16	....	2 1/2	3/16	80	2 1/2	3/16
Hudson Super 6..1927	....	2	3/16	....	2	3/16	76 7/16	2	3/16
Hudson O. S.....1928	....	2	3/16	....	2	3/16	76 7/16	2	3/16
Hudson Greater..1929	30 1/4	2	3/16	30 1/4	2	3/16	....	....	..
Hudson Great 8..1930	53 3/4	1 1/2	5/32	53 3/4	1 1/2	5/32	107 1/2	1 1/2	5/32
Hudson Great 8..1931	53 3/4	1 1/2	5/32	53 3/4	1 1/2	5/32	107 1/2	1 1/2	5/32
Hupmobile R.....1925	....	2	3/16	....	2	3/16	81	1 3/4	5/32
Hupmobile E-1...1925	....	2	3/16	....	2	3/16	23	2	3/16
Hupmob. A-1..1926-27	66	2	3/16	67	1 3/4	3/16	66	2	3/16
Hupmobile E-2...1926	....	2	3/16	....	2	3/16	23	2	3/16
Hupmobile E-3...1927	....	2	3/16	....	2	3/16	22 5/8	2	3/16
Hupmobile A-5...1928	....	....	....	....	....	....	....	....	..
Hup.Ct.6,A6..1928-29	66	2	3/16	67	1 3/4	3/16	66	2	3/16
Hup.Ct.8,M...1928-29	....	....	....	....	....	....	....	....	..
Hup. 125 (E-4)...1928	....	2	3/16	....	2	3/16	22 5/8	2	3/16
Hupmobile H,U...1930	....	1 3/4		....	1 3/4		....	1 3/4	..
Hupmobile S-2...1931	72	2	3/16	72	2	3/16	144	2	3/16
Hupmobile L.....1931	72	2	3/16	72	2	3/16	144	2	3/16
Hupmobile C.....1931	82	2	3/16	82	2	3/16	164	2	3/16
Hupmobile H, U..1931	78 3/4	2	7/32	78 3/4	2	7/32	157 1/2	2	7/32
Jewett 6-50......1925	....	1 3/4	3/16	....	1 3/4	3/16	25	2	3/16
Jordan K, L......1925	....	2	3/16	....	2	3/16	23 1/2	2 1/2	3/16
Jordan A.........1926	....	2	3/16	....	2	3/16	23 1/2	2 1/2	3/16
Jordan J, J-1..1927-28	....	2	3/16	....	2	3/16	23 1/2	2 1/2	3/16
Jordan AA.......1927	....	2	3/16	....	2	3/16	24	2 1/2	3/16
Jordan R.....1927-28	....	1 3/4	5/32	....	1 3/4	5/32	16	2	5/32
Jordan JE........1928	....	2	3/16	....	2	3/16	24	2 1/2	3/16
Jordan E.........1929	34 1/2	1 3/4	3/16	34 1/2	1 3/4	3/16	17 5/8	2	3/16
Jordan Gt. 90.....1929	34 1/2	1 3/4	3/16	34 1/2	1 3/4	3/16	24 1/4	2	3/16
Jord.U, 70, 80.1930-31	52	1 3/4	3/16	52	1 3/4	3/16	52	1 3/4	3/16
Jordan 90.....1930-31	....	1 3/4	3/16	....	1 3/4	3/16	....	2	3/16
Jord. Z Speedway.1930	....	1 3/4	3/16	....	1 3/4	3/16	....	2	3/16
Kissel 6-55..1925-6-7-8	....	2	3/16	....	2	3/16	26	2	3/16
Kissel 8-75.1925-26-27	....	2	3/16	....	2	3/16	26	2	3/16
Kissel 8-65.......1927	....	2	3/16	....	2	3/16	25 1/2	2	3/16
Kissel 6-70.......1928	....	1 3/4	3/16	....	1 3/4	3/16	19	1 3/4	3/16
Kissel 8-80.......1928	....	2	3/16	....	2	3/16	25 1/2	2	3/16
Kissel 6-73....1929-30	23	1 3/4	3/16	23	1 3/4	3/16	19	2	3/16
Kissel 8-95....1929-30	35	1 3/4	3/16	35	1 3/4	3/16	19	2	3/16
Kissel 8-126...1929-30	40	1 3/4	3/16	40	1 3/4	3/16	19	2	3/16
LaSalle 303....1927-28	....	2	3/16	....	2	3/16	81 3/8	1 5/8	5/32
LaSalle 328......1929	43 15/16	2	3/16	43 15/16	2	3/16	18 1/2	2	3/16
LaSalle 340......1930	43 1/4	2	3/16	43 1/4	2	3/16	43 1/4	2	3/16
LaSalle 345......1931	43 1/4	2	3/16	43 1/4	2	3/16	43 1/4	2	3/16
Lincoln....1928-29-30	46 9/16	2 1/2	1/4	46 9/16	2 1/2	1/4	46 9/16	1 3/4	1/4
Lincoln..........1931	35	2 1/2	1/4	25	2 1/2	1/4	....	....	..
Locomobile 48...1925	98	3	3/16	50	2 1/2	3/16	58	2 1/2	3/16
Loco. Jr. 8....1925-26	68	1 3/4	3/16	68	1 3/4	3/16	68	1 3/4	3/16
Loco. 48-9-10.1926-7-8	98	3	3/16	50	2 1/2	3/16	58	2 1/2	3/16
Loco. 90...1927-28-29	90	2	3/16	90	2	3/16	90	2	3/16
Locomobile 8-66..1927	68	1 3/4	3/16	68	1 3/4	3/16	68	1 3/4	3/16
Loco. 8-70.....1928-29	68	1 3/4	3/16	68	1 3/4	3/16	68	1 3/4	3/16
Locomobile 86,88.1929	77	2	3/16	77	2	3/16	77	2	3/16
Marmon 74.1925-26-27	....	2	3/16	....	2	3/16	95	1 1/2	3/16
Marmon Little....1927	....	2	3/16	....	2	3/16	144	2	3/16
Marmon E-75.1927-28	90	2	3/16	90	2	3/16	90	2	3/16
Marmon 68.......1928	....	1 3/4	3/16	....	1 3/4	3/16	128 1/4	1 3/4	3/16
Marmon 68.......1929	64 1/8	1 3/4	3/16	64 1/8	1 3/4	3/16	128 1/4	1 3/4	3/16
Marmon 78....1928-29	64 1/8	1 3/4	3/16	64 1/8	1 3/4	3/16	128 1/4	1 3/4	3/16
Mar. Roosev..1930-31	48 7/8	1 1/2	5/32	48 7/8	2 1/2	5/32	97 3/4	1 1/2	5/32
Mar.Big Eight.1930-31	60	2	3/16	66	2	3/16	132	2	3/16
Mar. 69, 70....1930-31	53	1 1/2	5/32	53	1 1/2	5/32	106	1 1/2	5/32
Mar. Eight 79.1930-31	60 3/4	2	3/16	60 3/4	2	3/16	121 1/2	2	3/16
Marmon 88.......1931	66	2	3/16	66	2	3/16	132	2	3/16
Marmon 16.......1931	72	2 1/2	1/4	72	2 1/2	1/4	144	2 1/2	1/4
Marquette....1929-30	52 1/2	1 3/4	3/16	52 1/2	1 3/4	3/16	....	....	.
McFarlan SV.1925-26	....	2	3/16	....	2	3/16	25	2	5/32
McFar.TV..1925-6-7-8	....	2 1/2	3/16	....	2 1/2	3/16	94	2 1/2	3/16
McFar. Str.8..1926-7-8	....	2	3/16	....	2	3/16	25	2	5/32
Moon Ser. A1925-6-7-8	....	...	3/16	....	...	3/16	18	2	3/16
Moon 6-60..1927-28-29	....	1 3/4	5/32	....	1 3/4	5/32	18	2	3/16
Moon 6-72.....1928-29	57	1 3/4	5/32	57	1 3/4	5/32	18 5/8	2	5/32
Moon 8-80.....1928-29	....	1 3/4	5/32	....	1 3/4	5/32	24 5/8	2	3/16
Nash Adv. 6...1925-26	....	....	5/32	....	...	5/32	17	3 1/2	3/16
Nash Spec. 6..1925-26	....	...	5/32	....	...	5/32	19	2 1/2	3/16
Nash Light 6..1925-6-7	....	1 3/4	5/32	....	1 3/4	5/32	16 1/8	1 3/4	5/32
Nash Adv. 6..1926-7-8	....	...	5/32	....	...	5/32	....	3 1/2	3/16
Nash Adv.........1929	63 1/4	2	5/32	89	2 1/2	5/32	13 11/16	2 1/2	3/16

BRAKE LINING SIZES—Passenger Cars—Continued

PASSENGER CAR, MAKE, MODEL AND YEAR	BRAKE LINING								
	Front			Rear			Hand		
	Total Length (Ins.)	Width (Ins.)	Thickness (Ins.)	Total Length (Ins.)	Width (Ins.)	Thickness (Ins.)	Total Length (Ins.)	Width (Ins.)	Thickness (Ins.)
Nash Spec....1927-28	...	2	5/32	...	2	5/32	13½	2½	3/16
Nash Spec.......1929	50	2	5/32	72⅝	2	5/32	13¾	2½	3/16
Nash Std. 6...1928-29	38⅝	1¾	5/32	66½	1¾	5/32	66½	1¾	5/32
Nash Twin Ign.8..1930	63¼	2	3/16	63¼	2	3/16	...	...	...
Nash Twin Ign.6..1930	56	1¾	3/16	56	1¾	3/16	...	...	...
Nash 6, 6-60...1930-31	67½	1¾	3/16	67½	1¾	3/16	...	...	...
Nash 8-70.......1931	62¼	1 23/32	13/64	62¼	1 23/32	13/64	...	...	...
Nash 8-80.......1931	62¼	1 23/32	13/64	62¼	1 23/32	13/64	...	...	...
Nash 8-90.......1931	64⅝	2	3/16	64⅝	2	3/16	...	...	...
Oakland Six.....1926	...	1⅞	5/32	...	1⅞	5/32	17	2½	3/16
Oakland Gr. 6....1927	...	1⅞	5/32	...	1⅞	5/32	17	2½	3/16
Oakland AA Six..1928	72½	2	3/16	72½	2	3/16	37	2	3/16
Oakland AA Six..1929	72½	2	3/16	72½	2	3/16	37	2	3/16
Oakland 101,8.1930-31	67 5/16	1¾	3/16	67 5/16	1¾	3/16	134⅝	1¾	3/16
Oldsmobile 30....1925	...	1¾	5/32	...	1¾	5/32	19	2	3/16
Oldsmobile D....1926	...	1¾	5/32	...	1¾	5/32	19	2	3/16
Oldsmobile E....1927		1¾	3/16		1¾	3/16	75	1¾	3/16
Oldsmobile F-28..1928	...	1¾	3/16	...	1¾	3/16	...	...	...
Oldsmobile F-29..1929	64⅛	1¾	3/16	74	1¾	3/16	74	1¾	3/16
Oldsmobile F-30, F-31	53½	1½	3/16	53½	1½	3/16	107	1½	3/16
Overland 91,92 1925-26	...	1½	5/32	...	1½	5/32	55	1¼	5/32
Overland 93...1925-26	...	1⅞	5/32	...	1⅞	5/32	18	2	3/16
Over.Whip.96..1927-28	...	1½	5/32	...			...	...	
Over.Whip.98..1928-29	...	...		...	1⅞	5/32	69¾	1⅞	5/32
Packard 2-26,2-33 1925	...	2	¼	...	2	¼	85	2	¼
Packard 1-36,1-43 1925	54	2	¼	83	2½	¼	54	2	¼
Pack.2-36,2-43.1925-26	62	2	¼	83	2½	¼	62	2	¼
Packard 4-26,4-33 1927	...	2	¼	...	2	¼	79	2	¼
Packard 3-36,3-43 1927	...	2	¼	...	2	¼	90	2	¼
Packard 5-26,5-33 1928	...	2	3/16	...	2	3/16	77	2	3/16
Packard 626, 633.1929	...	2	3/16	...	2	3/16	90⅛	2	3/16
Pack. 4-43, 640.1928-9	...	2	3/16	...	2	3/16	90⅛	2	3/16
Packard 645.....1929	...	2	3/16	...	2	3/16	90⅛	2	3/16
Packard 726, 733.1930	90 7/16	1¾	3/16	90 7/16	1¾	3/16	90 7/16	1¾	3/16
Packard 740, 745.1930	90 7/16	2	3/16	90 7/16	2	3/16	90 7/16	2	3/16
Packard 826, 833.1931	90 7/16	1¾	3/16	90 7/16	1¾	3/16	90 7/16	1¾	3/16
Packard 840, 845.1931	90 7/16	2	3/16	90 7/16	2	3/16	90 7/16	2	3/16
Paige 6-70....1925-26	...	2	3/16	...	2	3/16	24⅝	2	5/32
Paige 6-72......1926	...	2	3/16	...	2	3/16	24⅝	2	5/32
Paige 6-65.....1927-28	...	1¾	3/16	...	1¾	3/16	24⅝	2	5/32
Paige 6-75....1927-28	...	1¾	3/16	...	1¾	3/16	24⅝	2	5/32
Paige 6-45....1927-28	...	1½	3/16	...	1½	3/16	18 9/16	2	5/32
Paige 8-85....1927-28	...	1¾	3/16	...	1¾	3/16	24⅝	2	5/32
Peerless 67......1925	...	2	3/16	...	2	3/16	44	2½	3/16
Peerless 72..1925-6-7-8	...	1¾	¼	...	1¾	¼	78	1¾	5/32
Peerless 69..1925-6-7-8	...	2	3/16	...	2	3/16	...		
Peerless 80..1926-7-8-9	...	2	5/32	...	2	5/32	19⅜	1¾	5/32
Peerless 90, 91.1927-28	...	2	5/32	...	2	5/32	19⅜	1¾	5/32
Peerless **81**......1929	...	...		...	...		19⅜	1¾	5/32
Peerless 61-A..1929-30	22	1¾	3/16	22	1¾	3/16	19⅜	1¾	5/32
Peerless 125...1929-30	...	...		...	...		19⅜	1¾	5/32
Peerless M.8...1930-31	...	2	3/16	...	2	3/16	...	2	3/16
Peerless Std. 8....1931	54	1½	5/32	54	1½	5/32	108	1½	5/32
Pierce-A. 33...1925-26	...	3¼	3/16	...	3¼	3/16	68	2¾	3/16
Pier'-A.Ser.80.1925-6-7	...	2	3/16	...	2	3/16	58	2	3/16
Pierce-A. Ser.81..1928	...	2	3/16	...	2	3/16	58	2	3/16
Pier'-A.133,1431929-30	77¾	2¼	3/16	77¾	2¼	3/16	24 1/16	2	3/16
Pierce-Arrow 132.1930	49	2¼	3/16	49	2¼	3/16	98	2¼	3/16
Pierce-A. 125,139.1930	49	2¼	3/16	49	2¼	3/16	98	2¼	3/16
Pierce-Arrow 43..1931	65½	2¼	11/64	65½	2¼	11/64	131	2¼	3/16
Pier'-A.126,41-42.1931	65½	2¼	11/64	65½	2¼	11/64	131	2¼	3/16
Plymouth.....1928-29	...	1½	...	...	1½	...	21⅜	2	5/32
Plymouth.....1929-30	...	1½		...	1½		21⅜	2	5/32
Plymouth.......1930	40 7/16	1½	11/64	40 7/16	1½	11/64	21⅜	2	5/32
Plymouth.......1931	40 7/16	1½	11/64	40 7/16	1½	11/64	21⅜	2	5/32
Pontiac 6-27...1926-27	...	2	5/32	...	2	5/32	56	1¼	5/32
Pontiac 6-28.....1928	36⅛	1½	5/32	67⅝	2	5/32	66	2	5/32
Reo T-6.. 1925-26-27	...	2½	3/16	...	2½	3/16	81	2½	3/16
Reo Fly.Cld.A.1927-28	...	1¾	3/16	...	1¾	3/16	19 11/16	2½	3/16
ReoWolver. B.1927-28	...	1¾	3/16	...	1¾	3/16	23	2	3/16
ReoF.Cld.C.M 1929-30	...	1¾	3/16	...	1¾	3/16	19 11/16	2½	3/16
Reo Wolverine B.1929	...	...		...	...	...	...	...	...
Reo B2, M...1929-30	...	1¾	3/16	...	1¾	3/16	23	2	3/16
Reo 15..........1930	...	1¾	3/16	...	1¾	3/16	23	2	3/16
Reo 25N.........1931	51⅜	1¾	11/64	51⅜	1¾	11/64	20½	2½	3/16
Reo30N,Roy. 35N1931	62¼	2¼	3/16	62¼	2¼	3/16	20½	2½	3/16
Rickenbacker D..1925	...	1⅝	5/32	...	1⅝	5/32	23	2	5/32
Rickenbacker6-70 1927	...	1⅝	5/32	...	1⅝	5/32	67	1⅝	5/32
Rickenbacker8-80 1927	...	1⅝	5/32	...	1⅝	5/32	67	1⅝	5/32
Rickenbacker8-90 1927	...	1⅝	5/32	...	1⅝	5/32	22	2	5/32
Roamer 8-88..1926-30	...	2	3/16	...	2	3/16	22	2	3/16
Roosevelt.......1929	48⅞	1½	5/32	48⅞	1½	5/32	24 7/16	1½	5/32
Star F..........1925	...	2	5/32	...	2	5/32	62	1¾	5/32
Star F........1925-26	...	2	5/32	...	2	5/32	62	1¾	5/32
Star M....1926-27-28	...	2	5/32	...	2	5/32	62	1¾	5/32
Star R... 1926-27-28	...	2	5/32	...	2	5/32	62	1¾	5/32
Stearns-Knight C.1925	...	2½	3/16	...	2½	3/16	74	1½	7/32
Stearns-Kni.B. 1925-26	...	2½	3/16	...	2½	3/16	83	1¾	7/32
Stearns-Kni. S-6..1925	...	2½	3/16	...	2½	3/16	74	1½	7/32
Stearns-Kni. S-95.1926	...	2	3/16	...	2	3/16	79	2	3/16
Stearns-Kni. C-75 1926	...	2	3/16	...	2	3/16	79	2	3/16
Ster'-K. F6-85 1927-28	...	2	3/16	...	2	3/16	78	2	3/16
Stear'-K.G8-851927-28	...	2½	¼	...	2½	¼	88¾	2½	¼
St.-K.HJ8-901928-9-30	88⅞	2½	¼	...	2½	¼	177¾	2½	¼
St.-K.MN6-80.1928-29	63¾	2	3/16	...	2	3/16	80⅞	1⅝	5/32
Stu.Std.6,ER61925-6-7	...	2¼	3/16	...	2¼	3/16	24⅝	2	3/16
Stu. Sp. 6, EQ 6 1925-26	...	2½	3/16	...	2½	3/16	24⅝	3	3/16
Stude. Dict. EU..1928	64⅛	1¾	3/16	64⅛	1¾	3/16	24 1/16	2	3/16
Stude. Com. EW.1928	76½	2	3/16	76½	2	3/16	24 1/16	2	3/16
Stude. Dict. GE 6 1929	59¼	1½	5/32	59¼	1½	5/32	118½	1½	5/32
Stu. Pres. 8 FA 8 1928	76½	2	3/16	76½	2	3/16	24 1/16	2	3/16
Stu. Pres. FA, FB 1929	80	2¼	3/16	80	2¼	3/16	40	2¼	3/16
Stu. Com. 6 GJ 1929-30	67½	1¾	3/16	67½	1¾	3/16	135	1¾	3/16
Stu. Com. 8 FD 1929-30	67½	1¾	3/16	67½	1¾	3/16	135	1¾	3/16
Stu. Pres.8FE, FH 1930	80	2¼	3/16	80	2¼	3/16	40	2¼	3/16
Stu. Dict. 6 GL 1930	59¼	1½	5/32	59¼	1½	5/32	118½	1½	5/32
Stu. Dict. 8 FC 1930	59¼	1½	5/32	59¼	1½	5/32	118½	1½	5/32
Studebaker Six 54.1931	49½	1½	5/32	49½	1½	5/32	99	1½	5/32
Stude. Dict. 8 1931	49½	1½	5/32	49½	1½	5/32	99	1½	5/32
Stude. Com. 70..1931	57 11/16	1¾	3/16	57 11/16	1¾	3/16	115⅜	1¾	3/16
Studebaker Pres..1931	65	2¼	3/16	64	2¼	3/16	128	2¼	3/16
Stutz 693-4......1925	...	2	3/16	...	2	3/16	88	1¾	3/16
Stutz 695........1925	...	2	3/16	...	2	3/16	88	2½	3/16
Stutz AA........1926	...	1¾	3/16	...	1¾	3/16	19	2½	3/16
Stutz AA........1927	...	1⅞	⅛	...	1⅞	⅛	18½	2½	3/16
Stutz BB........1928	...	1¾	3/16	...	1¾	3/16	20	2½	3/16
Stutz M.......1929-30	68	1¾	3/16	68	1¾	3/16	20	2¼	⅛
Stutz LA........1931	68	1¾	3/16	68	1¾	3/16	20	2¼	⅛
Stutz MA........1931	68	1¾	3/16	68	1¾	3/16	20	2¼	⅛
Stutz MB........1931	68	1¾	3/16	68	1¾	3/16	20	2¼	⅛
Velie 60......1925-26	...	2	5/32	...	2	5/32	...	2	5/32
Velie Sp. 60...1927-28	...	2	5/32	...	2	5/32	24½	2	5/32
Velie Std. 50..1927-28	...	1¾	5/32	...	1¾	5/32	19	2	5/32
Velie 6-77, 6-78...1928	...	1¾	3/16	...	1¾	3/16	23	2	5/32
Velie 6-66, 6-68...1928	...	1¾	3/16	...	1¾	3/16	19	2	5/32
Velie 8-88, 8-90...1928	...	1¾	3/16	...	1¾	3/16	23	2	5/32
Viking..........1929	30⅜	2	3/16	30⅜	2	3/16	30⅜	2	3/16
Viking V-30.....1930	30⅜	2	3/16	30⅜	2	3/16	30⅜	2	3/16
Whippet 96-A.1929-30	39½	1½	5/32	69¾	1½	5/32	69¾	1⅞	5/32
Whippet 98-A.1929-30	49	1½	5/32	69¾	1⅞	5/32	69¾	1⅞	5/32
Willys-Kni. 65...1925	...	2	3/16	...	2	3/16	81	1⅝	5/32
Willys-Kni. 66.1925-26	...	2	3/16	...	2	3/16	81	1⅝	5/32
Willys-Kni. 70...1926	...	1¾	3/16	...	1¾	3/16	...	...	3/16
Willys-Kni. 66-A.1927	...	...	3/16	...	...	3/16	81	1⅝	5/32
Willys-Kni. 70A..1927	...	1¾	3/16	...	1¾	3/16	...	...	...
Willys-K. Gre. 6 1928-9	...	...	3/16	...	...	3/16	31	1⅝	5/32
Willys-K. Sp. 6 1928-9	...	1¾	3/16	...	1¾	3/16	...	...	3/16
Willys-K. Std. 6 1928-9	64⅛	1¾	3/16	69¾	1⅞	5/32	69¾	1⅞	5/32
Willys-Kni70B1929-30	64⅛	1¾	3/16	69¾	1⅞	5/32	69¾	1⅞	5/32
Willys-Kni. 66B 1930	60 9/16	2	3/16	60 9/16	2		21⅛	2	3/16
Willys-Kni. 87...1930	53½	1¾	3/16	53½	4¾	3/16	107	1¾	3/16
Willys-Kni. 66D..1931	51 15/16	1¾	3/16	51 15/16	1¾	3/16	103⅝	1¾	3/16
Willys-Six 98B...1930	49	1½	5/32	49	1½	5/32	98	1½	5/32
Willys Six 97.....1931	...	1½	5/32	...	1½	5/32	...	1½	5/32
Willys Six 98D...1931	...	1½	5/32	...	1½	5/32	...	1½	..
WillysEight 8-80..1930	53½	1¾	3/16	53½	1¾	3/16	107	1¾	3/16
WillysEight8-80D1931	51 15/16	1¾	3/16	51 15/16	1¾	3/16	103⅝	1¾	3/16
WillsSte.Cla.A-681925	...	2¼	3/16	...	2¼	3/16	12⅝	6	3/16
WillsSte.Cla.B-681925	...	2¼	3/16	...	2¼	3/16	12⅝	6	3/16
WillsSte.Cla.C-681925	...	2¼	3/16	...	2¼	3/16	12⅝	6	3/16
WillsSte.Cla.W-61925	...	2¼	3/16	...	2¼	3/16	12⅝	6	3/16
WillsSte.Cla.W-61926	...	2¼	3/16	...	2¼	3/16	12⅝	6	3/16
Wills Ste. Cla. T-6 1926	...	2¼	3/16	...	2¼	3/16	12⅝	6	3/16
WillsSte.Cla.D681926	...	2¼	3/16	...	2¼	3/16	12⅝	6	3/16
Windsor 8-82.....1929	55¼	1¾	3/16	55¼	1¾	3/16	24⅝	2	5/32
Windsor 8-92..1929-30	55¼	1¾	3/16	55¼	1¾	3/16	18⅝	2	5/32
Windsor 6-72.....1926	55¼	1¾	3/16	55¼	1¾	3/16	18⅝	2	5/32
Windsor 6-77.....1929	55¼	1¾	3/16	55¼	1¾	3/16	18⅝	2	5/32
Windsor 6-69..1929-30	57	1¾	5/32	57	1¾	5/32	18⅝	2	5/32
Windsor 6-75.....1930	55¼	1¾	3/16	55¼	1¾	1/32	18⅝	2	5/32
Windsor 8-85....1930	72	2	5/32	72	2	5/32	24⅝	2	5/32

Brake Lining Sizes—Commercial Vehicles

For Passenger Car Brake Lining Sizes See Page 282.
For Rivet Sizes, Interchangeability and Specifications See Page 262.

Commercial Vehicle Make, Year and Model		Service Total Length	Service Width	Service Thickness	Emergency Total Length	Emergency Width	Emergency Thickness
Acason							
1919–22	1	90	3	¼	90	3	¼
1919–22	1½	96	3¼	¼	96	3¼	¼
1919–20	2	108	3½	¼	108	3½	¼
1919–24	5	146	4	¼	146	4	¼
1923–24	2½	132	3½	¼	132	3½	¼
Ace							
1920–26	1½	48	3¼	1¼	48	3¼	1¼
1920–26	3	204	2¼	¼	204	2¼	¼
1921–26	2½	52	3½	¼	52	3½	¼
1926	Bus	124	3¾	¼	124	3¾	¼
Acme							
1922–24	40, 40L	192	3¼	¼	192	3¼	¼
1922–26	60, 60L	208	3½	¼	208	3½	¼
1922–24	125	72	4	¼	72	4	¼
1920	1	44	3	¼	44	3	¼
1921–23	G, 20	44	2½	¼	44	2½	¼
1921–24	B, 30	44	3	¼	44	3	¼
1921	F	46	3¼	¼	46	3¼	¼
1922–26	90, 90L	63	3¾	¼	63	3¾	¼
1923–24	K	63	3¾	¼	63	3¾	¼
1925–26	21	85	2½	¼	47	2¼	¼
1925–26	20L	46	3¾	¼	46	3	¼
1925–26	41	48	3¼	¼	48	3¼	¼
1925–26	116-118	48	2½	5/16	48	2½	5/16
Acorn							
1927	15	68	2½	5/16	68	1¼	5/16
1927	30, 40, 45	90½	3¼	¼	.....	.....	.....
1927	50	104	3½	¼	.....	.....	.....
1927	70, 80	121	3¾	¼	.....	.....	.....
American La France							
1923–26	W	.....	.....	¼	68	3½	¼
1923–26	Y-S-V-Z-U	23½	8	¼	84	4	¼
1926	4R	63	3½	5/16	D	D	D
		68	3½	¼			
1928–29	Big Chief	D	D	D	68	3½	½
Armleder							
1920–25	1½	47	3¼	¼	47	3¼	¼
1920–25	2½	54	3½	¼	54	3½	¼
1920–26	3½	37	3	5/16	126	3¾	¼
1926–27	30, 30B	47	3¼	¼	47	3¼	¼
1926–27	50, 55	54	3½	¼	54	3½	¼
1926–27	70	20¼	6	¼	126	3¾	¼
1926–27	60	63	3¾	¼	63	3¾	¼
1928	30, 30-6, 40	48	3¼	¼	48	3¼	¼
1928	50, 50-6	52	3½	¼	52	3½	¼
1928	60	62	3¾	¼	62	3¾	¼
1928	70	23	6	¼	124	3¾	¼
1930	31	123½	2¼	5/16	22	2½	5/16
1930	41	61¾	2¼	5/16	.....	.....	.....
		63½	4	¼			
1930	61	61¾	2¼	5/16	.....	.....	.....
		63½	4	¼			
Atterbury							
1917–21	7R. 7C	106	3½	¼	106	3½	¼
1920–26	1½	90	3¼	¼	90	3¼	¼
1922–26	22C	106	3½	¼	106	3½	¼
1919–26	3½	121	3¾	¼	121	3¾	¼
1924–25	24E	68¾	4	¼	68¾	4	¼
1930	A	48	1¾	5/16	24	2	5/16
1930	K	48	1¾	5/16	24	2	5/16
1930	G	60	2¼	5/16	24	2	5/16
1930	H	60	2¼	5/16	24	2½	5/16
1930	R	60	2¼	5/16	24	2½	5/16
1930	C	48	5	¼	24	3¼	¼
Autocar							
1917–26	F-1½	65	2½	7/32	54	2½	7/32
1920–27	M-5	94	2¾	¼	94	2¾	¼
1922–27	H-2½	82	2	¼	82	2	¼
1925–27	H-3-3½	94	2¾	¼	94	2¾	¼
1926	A-1½	181	2½	5/16	.....	.....	.....
1927	A-1½-2	181	F2½ R-3	¼	.....	.....	.....
1929–30	SA-1½, 2	31	2¼	5/16	40	4	¼
		40	4	¼			
1929–30	H-3, HS-3½	82	2	¼	41	2	¼
1929–30	CH-3	40	4	¼	.....	3	¼
1929–30	HS-3½	92	2¾	¼	46	2¾	¼
1929–30	CHS-3½, TA-3, TAS-3	40	5½	¼	.....	3	¼
1929–30	SCM-5	92	2¾	¼	.....	3	¼
Available							
1920–22	2½	108	3½	¼	108	3½	¼
1920–23	7	144	3½	¼	144	3½	¼
1922–25	1½-2	96	2½	¼	72	2½	¼
1923–25	2½	108	3½	¼	108	3½	¼
1919–25	3-3½	128	3¾	¼	128	3¾	¼
1919–25	5	144	4	¼	144	4	¼
Bessemer							
1919–21	K2	117	3½	5/16	30¼	4½	5/16
1919–21	J, H	113	2½	¾	110	2¼	5/16
1919–21	G-1	95	2½	5/16	91	2¼	5/16
1922–25	G-1	92	2½	5/16	88	2¼	5/16
1922–24	K2-4	110	3½	¼	33	4½	¼
1922–25	H2-1½	66	2	¼	66	2	¼
1922–25	J2-2½	74	2¼	¼	74	2¼	¼
Bethlehem (See Lehigh 1926)							
1920–22	KN-1	99	2¼	5/16	78	2¼	5/16
1922	SM-2	104	2½	5/16	74	2½	5/16
1922–25	HM-3	103	2½	5/16	94	2½	5/16
1923–25	KN-1	82	1¾	5/16	82	1¾	5/16
1923–25	GN-2-L	102	2½	5/16	74	2½	5/16
Biederman							
1925	20-1-1½	86	2¼	5/16	86	2¼	5/16
1925–26	30-1¼-2	96	3	¼	96	3	¼
1925–26	40-1½-2½	96	3¼	¼	96	3¼	¼
1925	60-2½-3½	104	3¼	¼	104	3¼	¼
1925–26	80-3½-5	124	3¾	¼	124	3¾	¼
1926	20	84	2	5/16	84	2	5/16
1926	60	108	3½	¼	108	3½	¼
1931	10, 20, 30	71	2	¼	.....	2½	3/16
1931	40, 50, 60	73	3	¼	.....	2½	3/16
Brockway							
1919–22	K	96	3⅜	5/16	96	3⅜	5/16
1919–22	T	144	4	5/16	144	4	5/16
1919–24	S2-1½	160	2	5/16	160	2	5/16
1923–26	K4-2½	104	3½	¼	104	3½	¼
1919–26	R2-2½	120	2¾	¼	120	2¾	¼
1920–26	T-5	142	4	¼	142	4	¼
1925	S-1½	80	3¼	¼	80	3¼	¼
1926	S-2	90	3¼	¼	90	3¼	¼
Buck							
1925–26	J-24, 34	90	2½	¼	90	2½	¼
1925–26	K-45, 44	96	3¼	¼	96	3¼	¼
1925	50, 80, L75	108	3½	¼	108	3½	¼
1925	L-110, 100	128	3¾	¼	128	3¾	¼
1925	B-120, 130	128	3¾	¼	128	3¾	¼
1926	64-3	108	3½	¼	108	3½	¼
1926	84-5	128	3¾	¼	128	3¾	¼
1925–27	34-36	46	3¼	¼	46	3¼	¼
1925–27	44-46	46	3½	¼	46	3½	¼
1925–27	64-66	52	3½	¼	52	3½	¼
1925–27	84-86	60	3¾	¼	60	3¾	¼
1925–27	94-96	.....	4	¼	.....	4	¼
Chevrolet							
1923–25	Sup. Comm. Chassis.	59¼	1½	5/32	57¼	1¼	5/32
1923–25	Util. Exp.	74	2	3/16	65¼	1¾	3/16
1925–26	X	74	2	3/16	67	1¾	5/32
1927	Com.	67	2	5/32	56	1¼	5/32
1927–28	LM-1	74	2	3/16	67	1¾	5/32
1928	Util. Exp.	34¼	½	.145	.....	.....	.....
		74	2	3/16			
1928	Comm. Chassis	34¼	1½	.145	56	1¼	5/32
		67 3/16	2	3/16			
1929	Comm. Chassis	34¼	1¼	.145	56	1¼	5/32
		59 25/32	2	3/16			
1929	1½	34¼	1½	.145	66 11/16	1¾	5/32
		74	2	3/16			
Chicago							
1919–22	1½-2½	96	3¼	¼	96	3¼	¼
1923–24	1½-2½	84	2½	¼	84	2½	¼
1923–24	3½-5	100	3¼	¼	96	2¼	¼
1925–26	10-1	109	3¼	5/16	109	3¼	5/16
1925–26	15-1½	95	3¼	¼	95	3¼	¼
1925–26	25-2½	106	3½	¼	106	3½	¼
1925–26	35-3½	121	3¾	¼	121	3¾	¼
1925–26	50-5	144	4	¼	144	4	¼
Clinton							
1923	1¼	87	2½	¼	87	2½	¼
1922–26	2	94	3¼	¼	94	3¼	¼
1923–26	3	106	3½	¼	106	3½	¼
1923–26	4	125	3¾	¼	125	3¾	¼
1922–26	5-7	144	4	¼	144	4	¼
1924–26	1¼	94	3¼	¼	94	3¼	¼
Clydesdale							
1922–24	20-18 ¾-1 1¼	92	3	¼	92	3	¼
1924–25	10-¾-1¼	92	2½	¼	92	2½	¼
1922–25	¾-1¼	92	2½	¼	92	2½	¼
1918–25	5-6	144	4	¼	144	4	¼
1921–25	3½-4¼	128	3¾	¼	128	3¾	¼
1918–25	2½-3	106	3½	¼	106	3½	¼
Columbia							
1919–22	F-1	80	2½	5/16	81	1¾	5/16
1919–23	G-2½	110	3	5/16	100	2	5/16
1924–25	H-1½	92	1¾	¼	92	1¾	¼
1924–25	G, K-2½, 3	104	2	¼	104	2	¼
Commerce							
1919–21	EP-16	90	2½	5/32	87	2¼	5/32
1920–25	T, 9, 11	100	2	5/32	97	2	5/32
1922	12-18	101	2½	5/16	97	2¼	5/16
1923–26	25	104	3½	¼	104	3½	¼
1923–26	14	91	3¼	¼	91	3¼	¼
1926	7-11	42	2	5/16	42	2	5/16
1926	30	61	3	¼	16	6½	¼
1928	20Z, 25Z, S11Z	121	2¼	¾	24⅜	4	¼
1928–29	30Z	60½	2¼	5/16	24⅜	4	¼
		57⅝	3½	¼	.....	.....	.....
1928–29	40Z	60½	2¼	5/16	24⅜	4	¼
		57⅝	3½	¼	.....	.....	.....
1928–29	50Z	60½	2¼	5/16	60	3	¼
		99	5	5/16	.....	.....	.....
1928–29	60Z	60½	2¼	5/16	60	3	¼
		99	5	5/16	.....	.....	.....
1928–29	70Z	121	3¾	¼	39½	4½	¼
1928–29	80Z	121	3¾	¼	39½	4½	¼
1929	20Y	121	2¼	¼	22⅞	2	5/16
1929	S11Y	121	2¼	¼	22⅞	2	5/16
Concord							
1919–26	A, H-2	96	3¼	¼	96	3¼	¼
1920–26	2-3	108	3½	¼	108	3½	¼
1924–25	E-1	96	3	¼	96	3	¼
1926	EO	88	3	¼	88	3	¼
1926	Bus	52	5	¼	52	5	¼
Corbitt							
1919–23	AA-5	139	3	¼	139	3	¼
1924–25	AA-5	124	4	5/16	124	4	5/16
1919–23	BC-2½	103	2¼	¼	103	2¼	¼
1919–23	H, E, S	76	2	5/16	76	2	5/16
1919–23	A-3½	128	2½	¼	128	2½	¼
1919–23	D-1½	91	2	¼	91	2	¼
1924–26	D-1½	72	2	¼	72	2	¼
1924–26	C, B, R-2-3	89	2¼	¼	89	2¼	¼
1924–25	¾-1	134	1¾	5/16	134	1¾	5/16
1926	A, AA	84	4	¼	84	3	¼
1927	20	.....	2¼	¼	.....	2¼	¼
1927	25	72	2	¼	72	2	¼
1927	40	.....	3¼	¼	.....	4	¼
1927	50	.....	3½	¼	.....	4	¼
1927	A	.....	3¾	¼	.....	3¾	¼
1927	70	.....	4	¼	.....	4	¼
C. T. Electric							
1924–26	C6-7 A7-10	74	2½	¼	74	2½	¼
1925–26	H, F1-2-5	86	3	¼	86	3	¼
1925–26	F-4	106	3½	¼	106	3½	¼
1925–26	F7-10	126	3¾	¼	126	3¾	¼
Day-Elder							
1920–22	A-B	176	2	¼	176	2	¼
1920–22	D-2	90	2	¼	90	2	¼
1920–22	C-2½	104	2¼	¼	104	2¼	¼
1920–22	F-3½	112	2½	¼	112	2½	¼
1920–22	E-5	138	3	¼	138	3	¼
1923–24	AN-1½	84	3	¼	84	3	¼
1923–25	BN, G, H, 1½-2	94	3¼	¼	94	3¼	¼
1923–25	CN, DN, I, J, 2-3	106	3½	¼	106	3½	¼
1923–25	FM, K, 4	125	3¾	¼	125	3¾	¼
1923–26	EN, L, 5-6	144	4	¼	144	4	¼
1926	20 Bus, G, H	91	3¼	¼	91	3¼	¼
1926	25 Bus, I	104	3½	¼	104	3½	¼
1926	30 Bus, J, K	121	3¾	¼	121	3¾	¼
1926–27	G	47	3¼	¼	47	3¼	¼
1926–28	H	47	3¼	¼	47	3¼	¼
1926–28	I	52¾	3½	¼	52¾	3½	¼
1926–28	J	52¾	3½	¼	52¾	3½	¼
1926–27	K	62½	3¾	¼	61½	3¾	¼
1926–28	L	71¾	4	¼	71¾	4	¼
1927	M	94	2½	¼	93	2¼	5/16
1928	M	47	2¼	¼	45	2¼	¼
1928	G, HB6	44	2¼	5/16	44	2¼	5/16
1928	K	63	3¾	¼	63	3¾	¼
1928	30 Bus	71¾	3¾	¼	71¾	3¾	¼
1929–30	MF	51¾	1¾	5/16	23½	2	5/16
		61⅜	2¼	5/16			
1929–30	GF	122¾	2¼	5/16	23½	2	5/16
1929–30	HF	122¾	2¼	5/16	25	2½	5/16
1929–30	HBF	122¾	2¼	5/16	25	2½	5/16
1929–30	JF	61¼	4	5/16	21	2 11/16	¼
		61⅜	2¼	5/16			
1929–30	KF	102¼	5	5/16	23¼	2 11/16	¼
		69½	3	5/16			

BRAKE LINING SIZES—Commercial Vehicles—Continued

COMMERCIAL VEHICLE MAKE, YEAR AND MODEL		SERVICE			EMERGENCY		
		Total Length	Width	Thickness	Total Length	Width	Thickness
Day Elder—Cont.							
1929-30	30 Bus	122½	5	5/16	23¼	2 11/16	¼
Defiance							
1920-22	B-E-EL	90	2½	5/32	87	2¼	5/32
1920-22	C-D	109	2½	5/32	105	2¼	5/32
1923	E-2	94	2½	3/16	66	2½	3/16
1923-24	EL	109	2½	3/16	105	2¼	3/16
1922-24	G, GL2-1¼	80	1¾	3/16	80	1¾	3/16
1924	H-HL2-3	122	2½	3/16	94	2½	3/16
1925-26	A-1½	72	2¼	3/16	72	1½	3/16
1926	F-1½	39	2½	3/16	39	1¼	3/16
1926	H-3	103	2¼	¼	103	2¼	¼
1928	FT-1	42	2¼	3/16	42	2¼	3/16
1928	O2-E2	48	3	5/16	36	2½	3/16
1928	B3	49	5	5/16	36	2½	3/16
Dixon							
1921-26	D	96	3¼	¼	96	3¼	¼
1923-26	C	104	3½	¼	104	3½	¼
1923-26	A, B	124	3¾	¼	124	3¾	¼
Denby							
1919-21	12-1	87	2½	3/16	79	1¾	3/16
1919-21	13-1½	103	2½	3/16	94	2	3/16
1919-21	25-2½	112	3	3/16	102	2	3/16
1920-21	27	103	3	3/16	90	2¼	3/16
1920-21	210-5	178	2¼	3/16	178	2¼	3/16
1921-22	33-1½	17	4	¼	92	1½	3/16
1921-22	31	98	2½	3/16	95	2¼	3/16
1922-24	33	98	2½	3/16	21	4	¼
1922-23	36	102	3	3/16	21	4	¼
1923-24	27	116	2½	3/16	26	6	¼
1923-24	210	178	2¼	3/16	26	6	¼
1922-24	41-1	92	2½	¼	97	2¼	3/16
1923-24	43-35, 2½-3	98	3	3/16	21	4	¼
Diamond T							
1921-26	T-1½	92	3¼	¼	92	3¼	¼
1923-26	U2-U3, 2-2½	106	3½	¼	106	3½	¼
1921-26	3½-K	125	3¾	¼	125	3¾	¼
1922-25	O3, 1-1¼	96	2½	3/16	66	2½	3/16
1921-26	EL-S, 5	144	4	¼	144	4	¼
1923-26	75, 1	44	2½	¼	47	2¼	5/32
1926	T4, 1½-2	82	2¼	¼	82	2¼	¼
1926-27	76	88	2½	¼	94	2¼	5/32
1926-27	T3	46	3¼	¼	46	3¼	¼
1926-27	T4	82	2¼	3/16	82	2¼	3/16
1926-27	U4-5	53	3½	¼	53	3½	¼
1926-27	K2-3	63	3¾	¼	63	3¾	¼
1926-27	S2-3-7	72	4	¼	72	4	¼
Dodge Brothers							
1919-25	¾	77	2¼	3/16	58	1¾	3/16
1925-26	¾	79½	2¼	3/16	71	1¾	3/16
1928	Senior	107	1¾	3/16	17 15/32	2½	3/16
1929	½	142⅜	2	3/16	17 15/32	2½	3/16
1929	¾	60¼	1¼	3/16	17 15/32	2½	3/16
		46½	1¾	3/16			
1929	1	111¼	2	3/16	21½	2	3/16
1929	1½, 2	61¼	2	3/16	21½	2	3/16
		54½	2¼	3/16			
1929	3	116¾	3½	¼	21½	2	3/16
Double-Drive							
1931	HF3½-5	45	4¼	¼	52	4	¼
Douglas							
1928	B4-B6	98	5	¼	72	2½	3/16
1928	C4-C6	98	5	¼	72	2½	3/16
1928	D4-D6	94	3	¼	65	2½	3/16
1928	DS4-6	114	3	¼	85	2½	3/16
Duplex							
1920-22	A-1½	78	2	3/16	78	2	3/16
1923-26	A-2	89	2¼	¼	89	2¼	¼
1920-26	AB-2	89	2¼	¼	89	2¼	¼
1920-24	AC-2½-3	104	2	¼	104	2	¼
1925	AC-3	89	2¼	¼	89	2¼	¼
1926	AC-3	61	3¾	¼	61	3¾	¼
1917-24	E, EL-3½	19*	2½	¼	104	2¼	¼
1925-30	EF, EFL-3½	19*	4	¼	19*	4	¼
1927-30	FAC-3	61	3¾	¼	61	3¾	¼
1920-26	FB-3	104	2	¼	104	2	¼
1920-30	G-1	44	2½	¼	44	2½	¼
1920-25	GH-1½	78	2	3/16	78	2	3/16
1926	GH-1½	46	3¼	¼	46	3¼	¼
1927-30	GF, GS-1½	46	3¼	¼	46	3¼	¼
1927-28	S-2	52	3½	¼	52	3½	¼
1929-30	S-2	50	4	5/16	50	4	5/16
1929-30	S-2	62	2¼	3/16	....	....	....
		62	4	5/16	35½*	3¾	¼
1927-29	SAC-3	61	3¾	¼	61	3¾	¼
		94	5	¼	35½*	3¾	¼
1930	SAC-3	50	5	5/16	50	5	5/16
		99	5	5/16	35½*	3¾	¼
1928-30	M-5-7	71	4	¼	71	4	¼
*Denotes propeller shaft brake							
Eagle							
1921-25	100-104 2-3	99	3	3/16	92	2	3/16
22-25	101-1¼	84	2½	3/16	84	2¼	3/16
25	105-2-3	116	2½	3/16	88	2½	3/16
Erskine							
1928	Del.	118¾	1½	5/16	118¾	1½	5/16
Fageol							
1919-24	1½-2	154	1¾	3/16	77	1¾	3/16
1922-24	2½-3	106	3½	¼	106	3¼	¼
1922-24	5-6	142	4	5/16	142	4	5/16
1925-26	1½-2	96	3¼	¼	96	3¼	¼
1925-26	3 ton Buses	108	3½	¼	108	3½	¼
1925-26	4	126	3¾	¼	126	3¾	¼
1925-26	6	144	4	¼	144	4	¼
1926	360-3	104	3½	¼	104	3½	¼
1927	1½	156	2¼	3/16	....	....	....
1927	2½	104	3½	¼	....	....	....
1927	3	121	3¾	¼	....	....	....
1927-28	3	104½	5	¼	35½	3½	¼
1927-28	4	121	3¾	¼	40¼	4	¼
1927	5½	132	4	¼	....	....	....
1928	1½-2	78	2¼	3/16	78	2¼	3/16
1928	2½	48	3¼	¼	48	3¼	¼
1928	485, 685	142	4	¼	40¼	4	¼
Federal							
1920-23	SD-1	87	3	¼	87	3	¼
1922-26	R-¾-1¼	87	2½	¼	87	2½	¼
1919-23	2½	106	3½	¼	106	3½	¼
1919-26	Series X	144	4	¼	144	4	¼
1922	Light	106	3½	¼	106	3½	¼
1918-26	Series W	125	3¾	¼	125	3¾	¼
1922-25	Series S	90	3¼	¼	90	3¼	¼
1923	Heavy	125	3¾	¼	125	3¾	¼
1923-26	Series U	106	3½	¼	106	3½	¼
1926	Series S	163	2¼	3/16	163	2¼	3/16
1927-28	FW, F6	171¼	2¼	3/16	171¼	2¼	3/16
1927-28	T2B, T6B	94¾	2½	3/16	94¾	2	3/16
1927-28	T2W-T6W	100	3½	¼	29⅝	3½	¼
1927-28	U5-UL5 2B6, 1K6	90⅞	3½	¼	29⅝	3½	¼
1927-28	W4	123¾	3¾	¼	29 17/32	4½	¼
1927-28	X8	142	4	¼	29 17/32	4½	¼
1928	A6	133	2¼	3/16	18¼	3	3/16
1928	T20	90½	3¼	¼	90½	3¼	¼
1928	UL7-3B6-2K6	93⅝	5	¼	29⅝	3½	¼
1928	T3W-T7	66½	2¼	3/16	29⅝	3½	¼
		66⅜	3½	¼			
1928	2FW-2F6	66½	2¼	3/16	18¼	3	3/16
		55⅛	2	3/16			
1929	2FW, 2F6 1	66½	2¼	3/16	18¼	3	3/16
		55⅛	2				
1929	A6, 2	133	2¼	3/16	18¼	3	3/16
1929	T22, 2	45¼	3¼	¼	45¼	3¼	¼
1929	T3W, 2½	100	3½	¼	34¾	3½	¼
1929	T8, 2½	100	3½	¼	18¼	3	3/16
1929	U5, 2½	90⅞	3½	¼	29⅝	3½	¼
1929	UL7, 3C6, 3	129⅝	5	¼	29⅝	3½	¼
1929	W4, 4	123¾	3¾	¼	29 17/32	4½	¼
1929	X8, 7½	142	4	¼	29 17/32	4½	¼
1930	4FW-D-DSW E6-E6SW	56	2	3/16	23½	2½	3/16
1930	F7	31	2	3/16	27½	2½	3/16
		27	2¼	3/16	....	....	....
1930	A6	58	2¼	3/16	18¼	3	3/16
1930	T3W-T7W-T8	33	2¼	3/16	18¼	3	3/16
		24½	3½	¼	....	....	....
1930	A6T-A6TW-T10W	33	2¼	3/16	18¼	3	3/16
		26½	4	5/16	....	....	....
1930	U6SW	33	2¼	3/16	22⅛	4½	¼
		26½	4	5/16	....	....	....
1930	U6	33	2¼	3/16	22⅛	4½	¼
		29	5	5/16			
1930	4C6	33	3½	¼	25	3½	¼
		29	5	5/16			
1930	4CA	33	3½	¼	34	4½	¼
		29	5	5/16			
1930	U6SWAB	34¼	3	5/16	22⅛	4½	¼
		68½	4	5/16			
1930	4C6SW	34¼	3	5/16	22⅛	4½	¼
		36½	4	¾			
1930	4C6ABS	34¼	3	5/16	34	4½	¼
		37	5½	¾			
1930	X8R	122	3¾	¼	34	4½	¼
1930	X8	142	4	¼	34	4½	¼
Fifth Avenue Coach							
1925	J	52	3½	¼	52	3½	¼
1925-26	L	117	2¾	3/16	46	4½	¼
1925	2L	119	4½	¼	46	4½	¼
1926	2L	46	4½	¼	106	4½	¼
Ford							
1919-25	T-1	23⅜	1 3/16	5/32	....	....	....
1926	T-1	23½	1 5/16	5/32	48	1⅝	3/16
Front Drive							
1920-25	C-1½	....	4	¼	....	4	¼
1926	FT	72	4	¼	17½	4	¼
F. W. D.							
1917-25	B	27½	3½	¼	86	2¾	¼
1925	Late 3	109	3½	¼	22	7	¼
1929	U6, H6	32	7	¼	48	3	¼
Garford							
1921-25	15, ¾-1	88	2½	¼	88	2½	¼
1919-26	25-30, 1½	94	3¼	¼	94	3¼	¼
1920-26	70-50, 2½	106	3½	¼	106	3½	¼
1917-26	77-80, 4	125	3¾	¼	125	3¾	¼
1922-26	68D-5	142	3½	¼	142	3½	¼
1917-26	151-5	21	4	⅜	86	4	¼
1926	KB Bus	162	2½	3/16	88	2½	3/16
1926	CB Bus	192	3½	¼	100	2	¼
1928	20Z, 25Z, S11Z	121	2¼	¾	24⅜	4	¼
1928-29	30Z	60½	2¼	3/16	24⅜	4	¼
		57⅝	3½	¼			
1928-29	40Z	60½	2¼	3/16	24⅜	4	¼
		57⅝	3½	¼			
1928-29	50Z	60½	2¼	3/16	60	3	¼
		99	5	5/16			
1928-29	60Z	60½	2¼	3/16	60	3	¼
		99	5	5/16			
1928-29	70Z, 80Z	121	3¾	¼	39½	4½	¼
1929	20Y, S11Y	121	2¼	¼	22⅞	2	3/16
Gary							
1922-23	F-1-1½	88	3	¼	88	3	¼
1922-25	1½-2	96	3¼	¼	96	3¼	¼
1922-25	2½	108	3½	¼	108	3½	¼
1922-25	3½	126	3¾	¼	126	3¾	¼
1922-24	5	146	4	¼	146	4	¼
1925	5	100	4	¼	100	4	¼
1925	1	92	3	¼	92	3	¼
G. M. C.							
1922-24	K15-16-20	100	2⅜	3/16	94	2⅛	3/16
1917-26	K-41-52	104	3½	¼	104	3½	¼
1917-26	K-71-72	121	3¾	¼	121	3¾	¼
1921-26	K-101-102	142	4	¼	142	4	¼
1925	K-17-32	86	2⅜	3/16	94	2½	3/16
1926	K-17-32	172	2½	3/16	94	2¼	3/16
1930	T-11	.....	1½	3/16	.....	1½	3/16
			1½	3/16			
1930	T-15, T-17	.....	1¾	3/16	.....	1½	3/16
			2	3/16			
1930	T-19	.....	2	3/16	.....	2	¼
			2	¼			
1930	T-25	.....	2	3/16	.....	3	¼
			2	¼			
1930	T-30	.....	2	¼	.....	3	¼
			2½	¼			
1930	T-42, T-44	.....	2	¼	.....	3	¼
			3	3/16			
1930	T-60	.....	2½	¼	.....	3	¼
			4	⅜			
1930	T-82	.....	2½	¼	.....	4	⅜
			5	⅜			
1930	T-90	.....	.....	.....	.....	4	⅜
			4	⅜			
Gotfredson							
1924-26	20-1	85	3¼	3/16	22	2	3/16
1924-26	30-41, 1½-2	47	3¼	3/16	....	....	....
1926	30B-1½	168	2¼	3/16	168	2¼	3/16
1925	60-3	23½	5	3/16	56	3¼	¼
1925-26	80-4	23½	7	5/16	62	3¾	¼
1924-26	100-5	25½	7	3/16	73	4	¼
1926	51-2½	106	3½	¼	106	3½	¼
Graham Brothers							
1923-24	All	100	2½	3/16	80	2½	3/16
1925-26	BB-1	87	2	3/16	87	2	3/16
1925-26	CB, FD, JB, LB, YB	87	2¼	3/16	87	2¼	3/16
Gramm-Bernstein							
1920-22	20-2-2½	90	2	¼	90	2	¼
1920-21	25-30-2½	182	2¼	¼	182	2¼	¼
1921	35-3½	115	2¾	¼	115	2¾	¼
1922-25	10, Speed	98	2	3/16	52	2	3/16
1922-25	15-1½-2	97	2	3/16	94	1½	3/16
1922-25	65-1½-2	17½	5	¼	39½	1¾	3/16
1922-25	30-3	17½	5	¼	91	2¼	¼
1922-25	40-4	115	2¾	¼	115	2¾	¼
1920-25	50-5-6	132	2¾	¼	132	2¾	¼
1923-25	125-2-2½	16	5	¼	90	2	3/16
1925	75P-3½	91	2¼	¼	91	2¼	¼
Hahn							
1921-24	CD, EE, KS, L	112	3½	¼	112	3½	¼
1921-25	FN M M2	128	3¾	¼	128	3¾	¼
1921-25	FE, N, R	72	4	¼	72	4	¼
1922-23	B2	68	1¾	3/16	68	1¾	3/16
1922	O	72	2	3/16	72	2	3/16
1922	K	96	3¼	¼	96	3¼	¼
1924	B2	88	2½	¼	88	2½	¼
1924	O, K	96	3¼	¼	96	3¼	¼
1925	B2	36	2¼	3/16	36	2¼	3/16
1925	O	80	2¾	¼	56	2¾	¼
1925	L	106	3½	¼	106	3½	¼
1926	O-1½	80	2½	3/16	56	2½	3/16
1926	K-2	94	3¼	¼	94	3¼	¼
1926	K-2½	106	3½	¼	106	3½	¼
1926	L-M, 3-5	125	3¾	¼	125	3¾	¼
1928	26	40	2¼	3/16	40	2¼	3/16
1928	36	45	2¼	3/16	45	2¼	3/16
1928	56	34	4½	¼	16	2½	¼
1928	76	32	3¾	¼	32	3¾	¼

BRAKE LINING SIZES—Commercial Vehicles—Continued

Commercial Vehicle Make, Year and Model	Service			Emergency		
	Total Length	Width	Thickness	Total Length	Width	Thickness
Harvey						
1917–21 WKA-5	138	3	5/16	138	3	5/16
1917–23 WHA	112	2½	¼	112	2½	¼
1917–21 WSA-2½	104	2¼	¼	104	2¼	¼
1919–21 WEA, 1½-2	92	2	¼	92	2	¼
1922–25 WFB-2, WFT	100	2¼	¼	100	2¼	¼
1922–25 WOA-2	180	2	¼	180	2	¼
1924–25 WHB, WHT	42	4	¼	42	3	¼
1925–26 WTT	52	3½	¼	52	3½	¼
1925–27 WFC	52	3½	¼	52	3½	¼
1926–29 WG	62	4	¼	62	4	¼
1927–29 WTT	62	4	¼	62	4	¼
Hendrickson						
1919–23 I-2½	96	3½	3/16	96	3½	3/16
1919–23 J-3½	128	3¾	3/16	128	3¾	3/16
1919–23 K-5	144	4	3/16	144	4	3/16
1929 ST 2½	13½	3½	¼	13½	3½	¼
1929 T3, U4	15½	3¾	¼	15½	3¾	¼
1929 V5	18	4	¼	18	4	¼
1929 SSW-6	48	3	¼	36½	3½	¼
1929 SW-10	58½	4½	¼	36½	3½	¼
1930 U-6	15½	3¾	¼	36½	3½	¼
1930 MSW	18	4	¼	36½	3½	¼
1930 SW	58½	4½	¼	36½	3½	¼
1930 SW-6	58½	4½	¼	36½	3½	¼
1931 24S	138	4	¼	36½	3½	¼
1931 32-S, 36-S	138	4	¼	36½	3½	¼
1931 44-D	152	5	5/16	36½	3½	¼
Huffman						
1919–22 C-1½-2	92	2½	5/32	88	2¼	⅛
1921–22 B-1½-2	76	2¼	3/16	76	1½	3/16
1926 EH, Speed	68	2½	3/16	68	1¼	3/16
1926 BH	78	2¼	3/16	78	1½	3/16
Hug						
1922 C-T	97	2½	3/16	80	1½	3/16
1923-24-25 T-TA	97	2½	3/16	80	1½	3/16
1923 C-H-HA	94	2½	3/16	66	2½	3/16
1924 HA-C	94	2½	3/16	66	2½	3/16
1924 H4	94	2½	3/16	66	2½	3/16
1925 H4-HA H4K-HA2	94	2½	3/16	66	2½	3/16
1926 H4-H4K-HA2-HA4-TA	94	2½	3/16	66	2½	3/16
1926–27 HD6-90	53	4	¼	39½	2½	3/16
1927 HA4	94	2½	3/16	66	2½	3/16
1926–27 HD6-90	53	4	¼	39½	2½	3/16
1927 HA4	94	2½	3/16	66	2½	3/16
1927 H4K-80-88	52½	4	¼	39	2½	3/16
1927–28 25–60	50	3	3/16	35½	2½	3/16
1927 30-40	47	2½	3/16	47	2½	3/16
1927 20	44	2¼	3/16	44	2¼	3/16
1928 21	44	2¼	3/16	44	2¼	3/16
1928–29 40	47	2½	3/16	47	2½	3/16
1928 66	50	3	3/16	35½	2½	3/16
1928 81-84-86-90 486-846-40A	52½	4	¼	39	2½	3/16
1928–29 22-41	16	2¼	3/16	Tru	Stop	
		Brak	e Li	ning	No.	C4
1929 60-66-26	50	3	3/16	35½	2½	3/16
1929 81-84-86-87 C87-486-90-96-C96-846-40A	52½	4	¼	39	3½	3/16
1930 97-C97-98	.....	3	3/16	Tru	Stop	....
		5	½			
Indiana						
1920–26 12-15-1½	152	2	3/16	152	2	3/16
1920–26 20-25-26	180	2¼	¼	180	2¼	¼
1920–25 35-3½	83	4	¼	83	3	¼
1920–25 51-5	261	3	⅜	261	3	⅜
1926 41-4	83	3	¼	83	3	¼
1926 52	138	4	¼	138	3	¼
1927 11-11X	83½	2	3/16	83½	2	3/16
1927 111X-111A 111-6111	83½	2¼	3/16	83½	2¼	3/16
1927 628-115A, 127-627	93	2½	3/16	93	2½	3/16
1927 115-615	48	3¼	¼	48	3¼	¼
1927 126-626	64	3¾	¼	64	3¾	¼
1927 41	145	4	¼	39½	4½	¼
1928 200-300	68	1¾	3/16	.....	.....	....
	76½	2¼	¼			
1928 111X	169	2¼	3/16	.....	.....	....
1928 400 Shuler	90	2	¼	.....	.....	....
1928 400 Clark	90	2½	¼	.....	.....	....
1928 400 Tim.	92½	3	¼	.....	.....	....
1928 115A-615A 127-127A	185	2½	3/16	.....	.....	....
1928 627-627A 628	185	2½	3/16	.....	.....	....
1928 126-626	121	3¾	¼	.....	.....	....
	96½	5	¼	34¾	3½	¼
1928 138-638	91½	3¾	¼	.....	.....	....
138-638	123¼	3¾	¼	39½	4½	¼
1928 41-641	142	4	¼	39½	4½	¼
1928 SG	76½	2¼	¼	.....	.....	....
	98	3	¼			
International (Harvester) Truck						
1917–23 1½	175	2¼	3/16	89	2¼	3/16
1918–23 2-3	101	2¼	3/16	101	2¼	3/16
1919–23 5	147	2½	3/16	147	2½	3/16
1924–26 5	43	2¼	¼	148	4	3/16
1921–25 ¾-1-1½	76	2	5/32	72	2	5/32
1926–27 1-1½	89	2¼	3/16	89	2¼	3/16
1924–26 2-3	43	2¼	¼	101	3	3/16
1928 Spec. Del.	72	2	5/32	22	2	5/32
1928 1¼-1½	78	2¼	3/16	78	2¼	3/16
1928 SD-SF44	85⅝	3	¼	85⅝	2	3/16
1928 SD-F46	85⅝	3	¼	85⅝	2	¼
1929 ¾	64⅛	1¾	3/16	36	2	5/32
	36	2	5/32			
1929 1	64⅛	1¾	3/16	36	2¼	5/32
	36	2¼	5/32			
1929 ¼, ½, 2	160 1/16	2¼	3/16	78½	2¼	3/16
1929 SD-44, SD-46	166 1/16	2¼	3/16	84½	2¼	¼
1929 2½	65⅝	3¾	¼	65⅝	3¾	¼
	66	5	¼	66	5	¼
1929	65⅝	3¾	¼	65⅝	3¾	¼
	92 9/16	4½	¼	92 9/16	4½	¼
1929 3½	65⅝	3¾	¼	65⅝	3¾	¼
	111	5	¼	111	5	¼
1929 3½, 5	65⅝	3¾	¼	65⅝	3¾	¼
	97⅞	4½	¼	97⅞	4½	¼
International (Harvester) Bus						
1922–24 52-53	43	2¼	¼	101	3	3/16
1925 54L	97	2½	3/16	81	2½	3/16
	102	2	3/16			
1926 54M	96	3	¼	68	2½	¼
1926 54H, H	118	4	¼	78	3	3/16
1926 54L	84	2¼	¼	84	2¼	¼
1928 54 D.R.	86	5	¼	21½	5	¼
1928 54 Chain	92 9/16	4½	¼	21½	5	¼
1928 74 D.R.	111	5	¼	21½	5	¼
1928 74-C	97⅞	4½	¼	21½	5	¼
Kelly Springfield						
1917–24 K-32-33-36-380	139	1⅞	3/16	139	1⅞	3/16
1918–22 K-32-34	85	2	¼	85	2	¼
1918–22 K-36	99	2¼	¼	99	2¼	¼
1918–22 K-40	84	2⅞	3/16	84	2⅜	3/16
1920–22 K-41	38½	4½	¼	123	3	3/16
1923–26 K-39, K-75	38½	4½	¼	85	2½	3/16
1923–24 K-41, K-61	38½	4½	¼	102	2½	3/16
1920–25 K-42	110	2¾	¼	110	2¾	¼
1924–25 K-76, K-70	70	2⅜	3/16	70	1⅞	3/16
1925–26 K-41, K-61	38½	4½	¼	116	2½	3/16
1925–26 K-100	93	3	3/16	93	2½	3/16
Kenworth						
1923–24 M1½, KS 2½	80	2¼	¼	80	2¼	¼
1923 SK-2½	92	2	¼	92	2	¼
1923–24 L-3	112	2½	¼	112	2½	¼
1925–26 O-1	72	2	3/16	72	2	3/16
1925–26 M2, KS3	89	2¼	¼	89	2¼	¼
1925–26 L4	93	4	¼	93	3	¼
1925–26 RS5	139	3	¼	139	3	¼
Kimball						
1922 AB-2	90	2	¼	90	2	¼
1922 2½-3	90	2¼	¼	90	2¼	¼
1922 AF-4	112	2½	¼	112	2½	¼
1922 AF-5	138	3	¼	138	3	¼
1924 AB-2	80	3¼	¼	80	3¼	¼
1924 AC-2½	112	3½	¼	112	3½	¼
1924 4	132	3¾	¼	132	3¾	¼
1924 AF, S	148	4	¼	148	4	¼
King Zeitler						
1920–24 1	88	3	¼	88	3	¼
1920–24 ¾	88	2½	¼	88	2½	¼
1924 5	156	4	¼	156	4	¼
1924–26 1½	49	3¼	¼	49	3¼	¼
1924–26 2½	53	3½	¼	53	3½	¼
1924–26 3½	64	3¾	¼	64	3¾	¼
1924–26 5	72	4	¼	72	4	¼
1927 42A	84	3¼	3/16	84	3¼	3/16
1927 62A	64	3¾	¼	64	3¾	¼
Kissel						
1919–25 4	112	2½	3/16	112	2½	3/16
1919–23 Gen	76	2	3/16	76	2	3/16
1921–22 1	88	3	¼	88	3	¼
1919–25 2	112	3½	¼	112	3½	¼
1924–25 1	88	3	¼	96	3¼	¼
1924–25 ½	76	2	3/16	72	3¼	¼
Kleiber						
1922–24 1½	96	3¼	¼	96	3¼	¼
1922–26 2-2½	108	3½	¼	108	3¼	¼
1920–26 3½	128	3¾	¼	128	3¾	¼
1920–26 5	144	4	¼	144	4	¼
1925–26 1½	104	3¼	¼	104	3¼	¼
Krebs						
1922–25 J	90	2½	¼	90	2½	¼
1922–25 50-80-75	108	3½	¼	108	3½	¼
1924–25 K-L-45	96	3¼	¼	96	3¼	¼
1922–25 B-L	144	3¾	¼	144	3¾	¼
Lange						
1922 B-2½	54	2	¼	72	3	¼
1921–28 E	54	3½	¼	54	3½	¼
1923–26 F	63	3¾	¼	63	3¾	¼
1924–30 G	48	3¼	¼	48	3¼	¼
1925–28 H	63	3¾	¼	63	3¾	¼
1926–29 K	78	2¼	3/16	78	2¼	3/16
1929–31 R	121	2¼	3/16	....	....	....
1927–31 L	100	5	¼	....	....	....
1928–31 O	100	5	¼	....	....	....
1928–31 H	104	4	¼	....	....	....
1928–31 M	119	4½	¼	....	....	....
1929–31 F16, T	119	4½	¼	....	....	....
Lansden Electric						
1922–26 M-1	72	2½	¼	72	2½	¼
1922–26 M-2	88	3	¼	88	3	¼
1922–26 M-3½	94	3	¼	94	3	¼
1922–26 M-5	104	3½	¼	104	3½	¼
Larrabee Deyo						
1919–23 U-X2, 1-1½	96	2	¼	96	2	¼
1922–23 J4-1½	96	2	¼	96	2	¼
1922–23 K4-2½	108	2¼	¼	108	2¼	¼
1919–23 L4-3½	120	2½	¼	120	2½	¼
1918–23 5-7	144	3	¼	144	3	¼
1924–25 X2-1-1¼	100	2	3/16	100	2	3/16
1924–25 J4-1½-2½	76	2	5/16	76	2	5/16
1924–25 K5-2½-3½	84	2¼	¼	84	2¼	¼
1924–26 L4-6, 3½-4½	84	4	¼	84	3	¼
1926 1¼-1½	82	2¼	3/16	82	2¼	3/16
1926 1½-2¼, XH	78	2	3/16	78	2	3/16
1926 K5-2½-3½	98	2¼	¼	98	2¼	¼
Le Moon						
1925 GP-1	92	2½	3/16	92	2½	3/16
1925 GP-1½	92	3	3/16	92	3	3/16
1925 GP-2	96	3¼	¼	96	3¼	¼
1925 G-3	108	3½	¼	108	3½	¼
1925 G-4	132	3¾	¼	132	3¾	¼
1925 G-5	144	4	¼	144	4	¼
1930 HB10	26	1¼	3/16	24	2	3/16
	31	2¼	3/16			
1930 HB17	62	2¼	3/16	24	2	3/16
HB21	31	2¼	3/16	24	2½	3/16
	31	3¼	¼			
1930 HB26	31	2¼	3/16	24	2½	3/16
	32	4	¼			
1930 HB30	31	2¼	3/16	36	3½	¼
	32	5	5/16			
1930 HB46	31	2¼	3/16	....	....	....
	31	3½	¼			
1930 HB60	37	4	¾	....	....	....
1930 HB100	37	4	¾	....	....	....
Luedinghaus						
1920–23 K2-LS2	107	2½	¼	77	2½	¼
1924 1-2½	96	2½	3/16	66	2½	3/16
1924 D-3½	114	2½	3/16	86	2½	3/16
Maccar						
1920–26 Series G	144	4	¼	144	4	¼
1917–25 Series L&V	93	3¼	¼	93	3¼	¼
1917–25 Series H	106	3½	¼	106	3½	¼
1917–26 Series M	118	3¾	¼	118	3¼	¼
1917–23 Series S	87	2	3/16	87	2	3/16
1924–26 EX	100	2	3/16	96	2	3/16
1926 46	100	2½	3/16	71	2½	3/16
Mack						
1921–22 AB-1½-2-5-Tr	24½	4	¼	66	2½	¼
1923–25 AB Ch-Tr	23¼	4	¼	66	2½	¼
1924–26 AB-1½-2-2½ (Chain)	23¼	4	¼	66	2½	¼
1924–25 AB-Tr. 5	23¼	4	¼	66	2½	¼
1922 AC-Tr.	75	2½	⅛	75	2½	¼
1922–25 AC-Tr.-7-10	32¼	3	¼	84	3½	¼
1924–26 AC-3½ to 7½	32¼	3	¼	84	3½	¼
1924–25 AC-13-15	32¼	3	¼	84	3½	¼
1924–25 AB-1½-2-2½ (Dual-R'dn)	73	3½	¼	24	6	¼
1925–26 AB-Bus	24	6	¼	73	3½	¼
Master						
1919–26 1½	96	3¼	¼	96	3¼	¼
1920–22 2½-6	17¼	4½	3/16	107	3	3/16
1919–22 2½-5	106	3½	¼	106	3½	¼
1922–23 3½	128	3¾	¼	128	3¾	¼
1923–25 61-64, 5-6	106	4	¼	108	4	¼
1923 11, 21, 31	94	2½	¼	94	2¼	¼
1923 41-51	94	2½	¼	94	2¼	¼
1925–26 41-2½	106	3½	¼	106	3½	¼
1925–26 51-3½	128	3¾	¼	128	3¾	¼
1925–26 11	84	2½	¼	84	2½	¼
Maxwell						
1922–25 1½	69	1½	3/16	24½	2	3/16
Menominee						
1919–23 D-H, 1-1½-2	106	3½	¼	84½	2½	5/32
1922–24 HT-1¼	95	2½	3/16	67	2½	3/16
1922–24 J-3-5	138	3½	3/16	104	2½	3/16

BRAKE LINING SIZES—Commercial Vehicles—Continued

COMMERCIAL VEHICLE MAKE, YEAR AND MODEL	SERVICE			EMERGENCY		
	Total Length	Width	Thick-ness	Total Length	Width	Thick-ness
Menominee—Cont.						
1922-24 G-3 1/2	125	3 3/4	1/4	125	3 3/4	1/4
1924-25 1-Hurryton	96	2 1/2	5/16	88	2 1/2	5/16
1924-25 D-2	108	3 1/2	5/16	67	2 1/2	5/16
1925 H-HT	95	2 1/2	5/16	67	2 1/2	5/16
1926 J3	144	4	1/4	144	4	1/4
1926 Hurryton	98	2 1/2	5/16	94	2 1/4	5/16
1927 Hurryton	108	2 1/2	5/16	92	2 1/4	5/16
1927 T Bus	102	4	1/4	86	3 1/2	1/4
Moreland						
1917-25 BX-EX, 1 1/2-2	96	3 1/4	1/4	96	3 1/4	1/4
1919-25 AX-3, EC	108	3 1/2	1/4	108	3 1/2	1/4
1923-25 RX-5, AC	124	3 3/4	1/4	124	3 3/4	1/4
1922-25 RR-1	98	2 1/2	1/4	92	2 1/2	1/4
1926-27 RR	84	2 1/4	5/16	84	2 1/4	5/16
1926 EX-AX	106	3 1/2	1/4	38 1/2	4	1/4
1927 BX	48	3 1/4	1/4	48	3 1/4	1/4
1927 EXX	54	3 1/2	1/4	54	3 1/2	1/4
1927 AXX	105 1/2	5	1/4	38 1/4	4	1/4
1927 SX	211	3 1/2	1/4	48	3 1/2	5/16
1927 TX	251	5	1/4	48	3 1/2	5/16
1930-31 Ace	.....	.....	....	11	2	5/16
1930-31 RR7, RC7 B-7, BD7	.....	.....	....	11 1/2	2 1/2	5/16
1930-31 E-7, EX7 ED7, HD7	.....	.....	....	38 1/4	4	1/4
1930-31 H-7	.....	.....	....	38 1/4	4 1/2	1/4
1930-31 SD7, TD7	.....	.....	....	12	3 1/2	5/16
Nash						
1917-26 4017Qd	99	2 1/2	1/4	25 1/2	2 1/2	1/4
1919-26 3018	120	3	5/16	20 1/2	2 1/2	5/16
1918-26 2017-18	99	2	5/16	20 1/2	2 1/2	5/16
National						
1924-27 M	96	3 1/4	1/4	96	3 1/4	1/4
1924-27 T	108	3 1/2	1/4	108	3 1/2	1/4
Nelson & Le Moon						
1922-26 G2-GP, 1 1/2	96	3 1/4	1/4	96	3 1/4	1/4
1922-26 2 1/2-3	55	3 1/2	1/4	55	3 1/2	1/4
1922-26 3 1/2-4	62	3 3/4	1/4	62	3 3/4	1/4
1922-26 5	72	4	5/16	72	4	5/16
Noble						
1922-25 A-1 1/4-1 1/2	76	2	1/4	76	2	1/4
1920-24 B-1 1/2-2	172	2	1/4	172	2	1/4
1922-25 D-2 1/2-3	84	2 1/4	1/4	84	2 1/4	1/4
1920-26 E-3 1/2-4	114	2 1/2	1/4	114	2 1/2	1/4
1924-25 A-76-1 1/2	94	2 1/2	1/4	90	2 1/2	1/4
1926 A-1	80	2 1/4	5/16	80	2 1/4	5/16
1926 A-1 1/2	144	2	5/16	144	2	5/16
1926 D-2	171	2	1/4	171	2	1/4
1926 D-2 1/2-3	196	2 1/4	1/4	196	2 1/4	1/4
Ogden						
1922-25 A-2	88	2 1/2	1/4	88	2 1/2	1/4
1922-25 D-1 1/2	88	3	1/4	88	3	1/4
1922-25 E-2 1/2	104	2 1/4	1/4	104	2 1/4	1/4
1922-25 F-3 1/2	125	3 3/4	1/4	83	3 3/4	1/4
1922-25 G-5	.....	6	1/4	100	4	1/4
Old Reliable						
1919-24 KLM-7 1/2	108	3 1/2	1/4	60	4	1/4
1919-22 A	96	2 1/2	1/4	96	2 1/2	1/4
1920-23 B-2 1/2	164	2	1/4	164	2	1/4
1920-23 C-3 1/2	86	3	1/4	86	2	1/4
1920-24 D	144	3	1/4	144	3	1/4
1920-25 K-7 1/2	80	5	1/4	94	3 1/2	1/4
1924-25 B-2 1/2	108	2	1/4	108	2	1/4
1924-25 C-3 1/2	120	2 1/4	1/4	120	2 1/2	1/4
Oneida						
1920-26 A-B-9, 3/4	96	2 1/2	5/16	68	2 1/2	5/16
1920-26 C-9, 2 1/2	116	2 1/2	5/16	86	2 1/2	5/16
1920-26 D-9, 3 1/2	128	3 3/4	5/16	86	2 1/2	5/16
1920-26 E-9, 5	144	4	5/16	144	4	5/16
1927-30 SFF15	94	3	1/4	.....	.....	....
1927-30 SFF10	94	3	1/4	65	2 1/2	5/16
1927-30 B9	94	3	1/4	65	2 1/2	5/16
1927-30 C9	97	5	1/4	65	2 1/2	5/16
1927-30 D9	104	4	1/4	74	2 1/2	5/16
Oshkosh						
922-26 AW, AAW, A, AA	23 5/8	3 1/2	1/4	87	2 1/2	5/16
1922-26 B, BB, BO, BBO	24	4 1/2	3/8	87	2 1/2	5/16
1925-26 F	30	4 1/2	3/8	82	4	1/4
1925-26 H	30	4 1/2	3/8	71	3 1/2	1/4
1925-26 M	66	2 1/2	5/16	94	2 1/2	5/16
1928 K	24	4 1/2	3/8	71	2 1/2	1/4
1928 F	30	4 1/2	3/8	82	4	1/4
1928 H	30	4 1/2	3/8	68	3 1/2	1/4
1928 M	94 5/8	3	5/16	66 1/2	2 1/2	5/16
1928 R	94	3	1/4	65	2 1/2	5/16
1929-30 L, H	30	4 1/2	3/8	32	3 1/2	1/4
1929-30 HC, HXC	30	4 1/2	3/8	32	3 1/2	1/4
1929-30 FHX	28	6	3/8	32	3 1/2	1/4
Overland						
24-26 1/2	63	1 1/2	5/32	54 1/2	1 1/4	5/32
Packard						
1920-23 EC-EX	15 1/2	4 3/4	1/4	56	2	5/16
1917-23 ED	19 1/8	4 3/4	1/4	68	3	5/16
1917-23 EF-E 4-6	19 1/8	6 1/2	1/4	75	3 1/2	5/16
Parker						
1919-24 J-20-24	21 1/2	5	1/4	76	3 1/2	1/4
1920-24 M-20	21 1/2	5	1/4	98	4	1/4
1922 G-22	42	3	1/4	42	3	1/4
1920-24 G-1, F-20	21 1/2	5	1/4	76	2 1/2	1/4
1923-24 B-23	82	2 3/4	5/16	84	2 3/4	5/16
1923 E-23	47	3 1/4	1/4	47	3 1/4	1/4
1924 E-24, F-24	94	2 1/2	5/16	66	2 1/2	5/16
Patriot						
1919-24 Lin-Rev	82	1 3/4	5/16	82	1 3/4	5/16
1922-25 Wash	116	2 1/2	5/16	86	2 1/2	5/16
1924-25 7R-9L 1-2	91	1 3/4	5/16	91	1 3/4	5/16
Pierce-Arrow						
1921-27 5-6-7 1/2	19 5/8	6	1/4	83 3/8	4 3/4	7/32
1921-24 2-3	180 1/2	2 1/4	1/4	180 1/2	2 1/4	1/4
1921-27 3 1/2-4	19 5/8	6	1/4	72	4 3/4	7/32
1924-25 XA-XB-TT	121	3 3/4	1/4	121	3 3/4	1/4
1925-26 Z Bus	54 3/4	5	1/4	103	5	1/4
1928 XA-XB	26 7/8	5	1/4	103	5	1/4
1928 WC	19 5/8	6	1/4	72	4 3/4	7/32
1928 RD-RF	19 5/8	6	1/4	83 3/8	4 3/4	7/32
1928 Z Bus	53 3/4	5	1/4	103	5	1/4
1928 FA	125	2 1/4	5/16	24 3/8	3	1/4
		2 3/4	5/16	.....	.....	
Pittsburgher						
1921-23 2 1/2	104	2 1/4	1/4	104	2 1/4	1/4
1922-24 C&D	104	2	1/4	104	2	1/4
1924 A	96	2	1/4	96	2	1/4
Pontiac						
1927	67 7/8	2	5/32	56	1 1/4	5/32
Rainier						
1919-22 R8-9-2	89	2	1/4	89	2	1/4
1922 R6-19, 1-1/2	76	2	1/4	76	2	1/4
1922 R11-3/4	90	3	5/16	90	3	5/16
1923-25 R29-31, 3/4-1	88	2 1/2	1/4	88	2 1/2	1/4
1923-25 R36-1 1/2	94	3 1/4	1/4	88	3 1/4	1/4
1923-25 R28-2	160	2 1/4	1/4	160	2 1/4	1/4
1923-25 R20-2 1/2	104	3 1/2	1/4	104	3 1/2	1/4
1923-25 R25-3 1/2	124	3 3/4	1/4	124	3 3/4	1/4
1923-25 R27-6	144	4	1/4	144	4	1/4
Rehberger						
1924-26 B-3, B2 Bus	106	3 1/2	1/4	106	3 1/2	1/4
1924-26 C-4	125	3 3/4	1/4	125	3 3/4	1/4
1924-26 D-5	144	4	1/4	144	4	1/4
1926 A-2	91	3 1/4	1/4	91	3 1/4	1/4
1927-30 B-4	124	3 3/4	1/4	124	3 3/4	1/4
Relay						
1928-29 30A	60 1/2	2 1/4	5/16	24 3/8	4	1/4
	79 1/2	3	1/4			
1928-29 40A	60 1/2	2 1/4	5/16	24 3/8	4	1/4
	79 1/2	3	1/4			
1928-29 50C	60 1/2	2 1/4	5/16	60	3	1/4
	77	4	1/4			
1928-29 60C	60 1/2	2 1/4	5/16	60	3	1/4
	77	4	1/4			
1928-29 70C	192	4	1/4	17 1/2	6 1/2	1/4
1928-29 80C	192	4	1/4	17 1/2	6 1/2	1/4
1929 S11B, 20B	60 1/2	2 1/4	1/4	24 3/8	4	1/4
	62 1/2	2 1/2	5/16			
1930-31 15A	62 1/2	2 1/2	5/16	24 5/8	2 1/2	....
1930-31 S11B	62 1/2	2 1/2	5/16	11 7/16	2	....
1930-31 40A	79 1/2	3	1/4	24 3/8	4	1/4
1930-31 50D	77	4	1/4	24 3/8	3	1/4
1930-31 60D	77	4	1/4	60	3	1/4
1930-31 100A	72	4	3/4	60	3	1/4
1931 40D Bus	72 1/2	3	1/4	60	3	1/4
1931 100B	62	4	3/8	60	3	1/4
Reo						
1919-23 F	86	2 1/4	5/16	83	2	5/16
1923-26 F	93	3	5/16	81	3	5/16
1930 B2	86 7/8	1 3/4	.177	....	....	....
1930 DA, DC	62 1/4	2 1/4	.192	....	....	....
1930 FA, FB, FC,	31 1/8	2 1/4	.192	....	....	....
FD,FE,FF,FH	33 1/8	2 1/4	.182			
1930 GA, GB, GC,	31 1/8	2 1/4	.192	....	....	....
GD, GE	34	3	.245			
1930 DF	31 1/8	2 1/4	.192	....	....	....
	31 1/8	2 1/4	.182			
Republic						
1922-23 10,-E, 1	85	2 1/2	5/32	79	2 1/4	5/32
1920-23 20-3 1/2	112	3 1/2	5/32	31	4 1/2	5/32
1922-23 3/4	76	2	5/32	72	2	5/32
1922-23 1 1/2-2 1/2	101	2 1/2	5/16	97	2 1/4	5/16
Rowe						
1919-23 FW-5	136	3	5/16	136	3	5/16
1924-26 FW-5	136	3	1/4	136	3	1/4
1919-23 CW-1 1/2	72	2	5/16	72	2	5/16
1919-22 CDW-2	90	2	1/4	90	2	1/4
1919-22 CDW-2 1/2-3	103	2 1/2	1/4	103	2 1/2	1/4
1919-22 HW-4	113	2 1/2	1/4	113	2 1/2	1/4
1924-25 CDW-2 1/2	80	2 1/4	1/4	80	2 1/4	1/4
1924-25 GSW-3	80	2 1/4	1/4	80	2 1/4	1/4
1924-25 HW-4	88	4	1/4	88	3	1/4
Rugby						
1928 Fast Mail	118 1/2	1 1/2	5/32	118 1/2	1 1/2	5/32
1928 Express	166 1/2	2	5/16	166 1/2	2	5/16
Ruggles						
1924-25 15-16, 3/4-1	88	2	5/32	78	1 3/4	5/32
1924-26 1 1/4-1 1/2	96	2 1/2	5/32	94	2 1/4	5/16
1924-26 2	95	2 1/2	5/16	67	2 1/2	5/32
1924-26 2 1/2	116	2 1/2	5/16	88	2 1/2	5/16
Safeway						
1924-25 37C	96	3 1/2	1/4	88	2	1/4
1924-25 55, 63-66	96	3 1/2	1/4	88	2	1/4
1926 55,63-66	99	5	5/16	99	5	5/16
1927 55, 64, 92	99	5	5/16	99	5	5/16
1927 66	99	5	3/4	99	5	3/4
1928 92	104	5	3/8	104	5	3/8
Sandow						
1919-23 G, CG	80	2	5/16	80	2	5/16
1919-23 J	108	3 1/2	1/4	108	3 1/2	1/4
1919-23 L	96	4 1/2	1/4	96	4 1/2	1/4
1919-23 M	74	4	1/4	74	4	1/4
1924-25 G-CG, 1-1 1/2	89	2 1/4	1/4	89	2 1/4	1/4
1924-25 J-2 1/2	94	3 1/2	1/4	94	3 1/2	1/4
1924-26 M-L, 3 1/2-5	108	4	1/4	94	3 1/2	1/4
1925-26 GA	88	2 1/2	5/16	88	2 1/2	5/16
1925-26 JS	90	2 1/2	1/4	90	2 1/2	1/4
Sanford						
1923-24 25-2 1/2	83	2 1/4	1/4	83	2 1/4	1/4
1925-26 W4-2 1/2	89	2 1/4	1/4	89	2 1/4	1/4
1924-25 W4-2 1/2	112	4	1/4	112	2 1/2	1/4
1926 W4-2 1/2	84	4	1/4	84	3	1/4
1923-25 W-1 1/2	89	2 1/4	1/4	89	2 1/4	1/4
1926 W-15-1 1/2	78	2	5/16	78	2	5/16
1925-26 1 1/4	89	2 1/4	5/16	89	2 1/4	5/16
1925-26 W6-2 1/2	78	2	5/16	78	2	5/16
1923-26 W4-5	136	3	1/4	136	3	1/4
Schacht						
1922-25 F2-3, G2-3	33	3	1/4	52	3	1/4
1922-25 E4-5, G4-5	33	3	1/4	60	4	3/8
1924-25 H-1 1/2, J-2	66	2 1/2	5/16	96	2 1/2	5/16
1925 Bus	122	4	5/16	26 1/2	4	1/4
(Front Wh.)	63	2 1/2	5/16			
1926-27 H-1 1/2, J-2	106	4	5/16	79	2 1/2	5/16
1926 2 1/2-3 1/2, L-M	33	3	1/4	54	3	1/4
1926 M-5-7	33	3	1/4	60	4	3/8
1926 Bus	118	4 1/2	5/16	26 1/2	4	1/4
(Front Wh.)	100	3	1/4			
1927 LO, LN MP, N	45	3	1/4	98	5	3/8
1928 H-HS	106	4	5/16	79	2 1/2	5/16
1928 T	104	4	1/4	77 1/2	2 1/2	5/16
1928 N, R	45	3	1/4	98	5	3/8
Schwartz						
1922 A-1	80	1 3/4	5/16	80	1 3/4	5/16
1922 K-2	81	2 1/4	1/4	81	2 1/4	1/4
1922 L-3	103	2 1/4	1/4	103	2 1/4	1/4
1922 M-4	139	3	1/4	139	3	1/4
1923-24 20	87	2 1/2	1/4	87	2 1/2	1/4
1923 45	94	3 1/4	1/4	94	3 1/4	1/4
1923 65	106	3 1/2	1/4	106	3 1/2	1/4
1923 90	125	3 3/4	1/4	125	3 3/4	1/4
1923 120	144	4	1/4	144	4	1/4
Selden						
1922-26 30-33	91	3 1/4	1/4	91	3 1/4	1/4
1922-26 50-53, 3	104	3 1/2	1/4	104	3 1/2	1/4
1922-23 31-51	104	3 1/2	1/4	104	3 1/2	1/4
1922-26 70-70B, 73	125	3 3/4	1/4	125	3 3/4	1/4
1923-25 52	125	3 3/4	1/4	125	3 3/4	1/4
1923-25 53	104	3 1/2	1/4	104	3 1/2	1/4
1926 Pacem.	83	2 1/4	5/16	83	2 1/4	5/16
1926 Roadm.	89	2 1/2	5/16	89	2 1/2	5/16
1922-26 90-90B	144	4	1/4	144	4	1/4
Service						
1919-26 230-40, 31-61	108	3 1/2	1/4	108	3 1/2	1/4
1919-26 71-275-81	124	3 3/4	1/4	124	3 3/4	1/4
1919-26 101-3, 300	144	4	1/4	144	4	1/4
1921-23 12	88	2 1/2	1/4	88	2 1/2	1/4
1919-26 21-42-34	94	3 1/4	1/4	94	3 1/4	1/4
1923-24 33	88	3	1/4	88	3	1/4
1921-24 15-25	80	1 3/4	5/16	80	1 3/4	5/16
1925-26 25	160	2	5/16	160	2	5/16
1928 20-Z, 25-Z	121	2 1/4	5/16	24 3/8	4	1/4
1928-29 S11-Z	121	2 1/4	5/16	24 3/8	4	1/4
1928-29 30-Z	60 1/2	2 1/4	5/16	24 3/8	4	1/4
	57 5/8	3 1/2	1/4			
1928-29 40Z	60 1/2	2 1/4	5/16	24 3/8	4	1/4
	57 5/8	3 1/2	1/4			

BRAKE LINING SIZES—Commercial Vehicles—Continued

Commercial Vehicle Make, Year and Model	Service Total Length	Service Width	Service Thickness	Emergency Total Length	Emergency Width	Emergency Thickness
Service—Cont.						
1928–29 50-Z, 60-Z	60½	2¼	3/16	60	3	¼
	99	5	5/16			
1928–29 70-Z, 80 Z	121	3¾	¼	39½	4½	¼
1929 20-Y, S-11-Y	121	2¼	¼	22⅞	2	3/16
Signal						
1922–24 NF-1	90	3	¼	90	3	¼
1919–24 H-1½	94	3¼	¼	94	3¼	¼
1919–24 J-2½	105	3½	¼	105	3½	¼
1919–24 M-3½	125	3¾	¼	125	3¾	¼
1919–24 R-5	144	4	¼	144	4	¼
Standard						
1919–26 66, K-3½	125	3¾	¼	125	3¾	¼
1919–26 86, K-5-7	144	4	¼	144	4	¼
1922–26 75-¾-1-1¼	94	2½	¼	94	2½	¼
1920–25 K-1½	87	3	¼	87	3	¼
1919–25 70K-2½	108	3½	¼	108	3½	¼
1925–26 K-1½	96	3¼	¼	96	3¼	¼
Sterling						
1919–24 3½	126	3¾	¼	126	3¾	¼
1919–24 5-Worm	142	4	¼	142	4	¼
1919–24 5-7½ Ch.	113	3½	¼	113	3½	¼
1919–24 1½	94	3¼	¼	94	3¼	¼
1919–25 2-2½	107	3½	¼	107	3½	¼
1924–25 7½	113	3½	¼	90	4	¼
1925–26 GB-2-4-6	121	3¾	¼	121	3¾	¼
1925–26 DW 8-10-12	89	3¼	¼	89	3¼	¼
1925–26 DW-23-25-27	142	4	¼	142	4	¼
1925–26 EW-20	121	3¾	¼	121	3¾	¼
1926 DW-12-14	107	3½	¼	107	3½	¼
1926 Series EC	118	4½	¼	29	4	¼
Stewart						
1918–25 M7-M7X	101	2	3/16	16	5	3/16
1918–25 M11-15	83	2	3/16	22¾	2	5/32
1918–25 9-1½-2	97	2	3/16	16	5	3/16
1919–25 10-10X	120	3	3/16	16	5	3/16
1925–26 16, 16X	84	3	3/16	22	4	¼
1925–26 17-17X, 18	84	3	3/16	22	4	¼
1925–26 10X	106	2½	3/16	16	5	3/16
1925–26 20, Bus	93	4	3/16	22	4	¼
1926 21, Bus	77	2	¼	24⅝	2	5/32
1929 25XW-25W	67	2	¼	22¾	5	5/16
	68½	3	⅜			
1930 30-30X	118	2	3/16	24⅝	2½	5/32
1930 34X-40-40X	59	2	3/16	24⅝	2½	5/32
	67	2	¼			
1930 32X	67	2	¼	22¾	5	5/16
	69½	3	¼			
1930 32XW	67	2	¼	22¾	5	5/16
	68½	4	⅜			
1930 29X-29XS	67	2	¼	20⅜	4	¼
	67	2½	¼			
1930 29XW	67	2	¼	20⅜	4	¼
	68½	3	⅜			
1930 18X-19X-33X	67	2½	¼	22¾	5	5/16
	68½	4	⅜			
1930 31X	67	2½	¼	28¾	5	5/16
	100	5	5/16			
1930 27X	69½	3	¼	28¾	5	5/16
	123	3¾	¼			
1930 28X	59	2	3/16	20⅜	4	¼
	134	2½	¼			
Stoughton						
1922–23 C-¾	113	2½	⅛	110	2¼	⅛
1922–23 A-1	67	1¾	3/16	67	2	3/16
1919–23 B-1½	76	2	3/16	76	2	3/16
1922–23 D-F, 2-3	104	2¼	¼	104	2¼	¼
1926 C-1¼	88	2½	¼	96	2½	5/32
1926 B Jr	88	2½	¼	96	2¼	5/32
1926 B	76	2	3/16	76	2	3/16
1926 D-F, 2-3	94	2¼	¼	94	2¼	¼
1927 K-2, C-1¼	88	2½	¼	96	2¼	5/32
Studebaker						
1926 N, A	150	2½	3/16	24⅝	3	3/16
1926 D	60	3½	3/16	24⅝	3	3/16
(Front Wh.)	58	2½	3/16			
1928 75 H. D	178½	3	¼	17	2½	¼
1928 75 Jr-76 Sp.	177¾	1½	¼	17	2½	¼
1928 Dic. Del.	124¼	1	3/16	25	2	3/16
1929 99	178½	3	¼	21	2½	¼
1929 88, 77	177¾	2½	¼	21	2½	¼
1929 GK	155	2¼	3/16	24	2	3/16
1930 99, 111	167⅛	3	¼	....	....	....
1930 77, 88	177¾	2½	¼	....	....	....
1930 GN-N	154⅞	2¼	3/16	24⅝	2	5/32
1930 GN-S	154⅞	2¼	3/16	24 1/16	2	3/16
1930 GN-P	129¾	1¾	3/16	129¾	1¾	3/16
1930 FJ-H	154⅞	2¼	3/16	24 1/16	2	3/16
1930 FL-H	154⅞	2¼	3/16	154⅞	2¼	3/16
1931 S1	95¾	1½	13/64	95¾	1½	13/64
1931 S20, S30	47⅞	1¾	13/64	48⅝	1¾	13/64
	56¼	2¼	15/64	56¼	2¼	15/64
1931 S40, S50, S60	56⅝	2	13/64	56⅝	2	13/64
	63⅞	2½	13/64	63⅞	2½	13/64
Super Truck						
1919–23 30-3½	96	2½	3/16	63	2½	3/16
1919–23 40-2	106	2½	3/16	76	2½	3/16
1920–26 50-2½	103	2¼	¼	103	2¼	¼
1920–26 70-3½	111	2½	¼	111	2½	¼
1920–26 100-5	136	3	¼	103	3	¼
1925–26 60-3	115	2½	3/16	85	2½	3/16
Traffic						
1922–23 Speedboy	99	2½	3/16	79	1¾	3/16
1924–25 Speedboy	93	2	3/16	81	2	3/16
1922–26 6000	106	3	3/16	94	2	3/16
1925 C-2	87	2½	3/16	76	1¾	3/16
1926 2½	91	3¼	¼	91	3¼	¼
1926 3½	104	3½	¼	104	3½	¼
Transport						
1919–24 20	97	2	3/16	93	1½	3/16
1922–24 15-1	96	2½	5/32	93	2¼	5/32
1922 35	22	3	5/16	93	1½	3/16
1920–23 36	20½	3⅛	5/16	93	1½	3/16
1924 36-2	20½	3½	5/16	93	1½	3/16
1921–24 75	24	3	5/16	116	2½	3/16
1924 61-2½	24	3	5/16	97	2½	3/16
Traylor						
1922–25 1½-2	100	2	¼	100	2	¼
1920–25 3-3½	113	2¼	¼	113	2¼	¼
1922–25 5-6	118	2½	¼	118	2½	¼
1926 B-1½	144	2	3/16	144	2	3/16
1926 D-3	160	2¼	¼	16	2¼	¼
1926 F-5	90	4	¼	90	3	¼
Twin City						
1924 BW-2½	113	3½	¼	113	3½	¼
1924–26 AW-3½	128	3¾	¼	128	3¾	¼
1925 BW-2½	104	3	3/16	100	2½	3/16
1926 BW-2½	106	3½	3/16	102	3	3/16
1926 DW-Bus	107	5	5/16	28	5	5/16
Union						
1922–25 FW-2½	26½	4½	¼	104	3	¼
1922–25 HW-4	26	4½	¼	48	4	¼
1921–25 H-4	114	3½	3/16	32	4½	3/16
U. S.						
1918–22 H-S	100	2½	¼	100	2½	¼
1922 NW-1½	78	2	3/16	78	2	3/16
1922–26 NW-R, 2-3	84	2¼	3/16	84	2¼	3/16
1922–25 N-1½	101	2½	3/16	93	1½	3/16
1920–26 T-5-6-7	124	3	¼	33	4	¼
1922–25 U-1¼	101	2½	3/16	80	1½	3/16
1923–26 S-3½-4-5	84	4	¼	84	3	¼
1926 U-¼	84	2¼	3/16	84	2¼	3/16
1927 N	101	2½	3/16	93	1½	3/16
1927 U	84	2¼	3/16	84	2¼	3/16
1927–29 20, 21	11½	3¼	¼	11½	3¼	¼
1927–29 30, 31	53	5	¼	36	3¾	5/16
1927 40	63	3¾	5/16	41	4½	5/16
1928–29 40	15¼	3¾	¼	15¼	3¾	¼
1928–29 U	41¾	2¼	3/16	41¾	2¼	3/16
1928–29 N, L	50½	2½	3/16	46¾	1½	3/16
United						
1920–23 1½	96	2	3/16	96	1½	3/16
1920–23 2-2½	98	2½	3/16	98	2½	3/16
1920–22 5	88½	2¼	3/16	88½	2¼	3/16
1920–23 3½-5	124	3	3/16	116	2½	3/16
1924–25 25–30	96	2½	5/32	94	2¼	5/32
Velie						
1920–24 46-1½	109	2½	5/32	105	2¼	5/32
1928 33	103	1¾	3/16	17½	2	5/32
1928 40	127	2	3/16	23	2	3/16
Victor						
1924 25-¾-1	90	2½	3/16	21	2½	3/16
1924–26 40-50-1½-2	96	2½	3/16	68	2½	3/16
1924–25 60-70-80	116	2½	3/16	89	2½	3/16
1925 25-1¼	44	2½	3/16	46	2½	3/16
1925 85-90, 5-6	142	2½	3/16	110	2½	3/16
1926 25-1¼	44	2½	3/16	112	2½	3/16
1926 60-70-80	115	2½	3/16	85	2½	3/16
1926 85-90, 5-6	148	3½	3/16	120	3½	3/16
Walter						
1918–25 S-5-F	60	5	¼	112	2½	¼
1925–28 FH	120	5	¼	60	5	¼
1928 FHR	120	5	¼	60	3	¼
Ward Electric						
1921–23 WS-2	119	1½	3/16	119	1½	3/16
1924 WS-2	58	1½	3/16	15¾	1½	3/16
1921–26 WA, WM, C	72	2	3/16	72	2	3/16
1921–24 WD	79	2	¼	79	2	¼
1924–26 B-222	67	1¾	3/16	67	1¾	3/16
1921–24 WD	100	2¼	¼	100	2¼	¼
1921–24 WF	112	2½	¼	112	2½	¼
1921–24 WH	138	3	¼	138	3	¼
1924–26 A-211	67	2	3/16	64	1½	3/16
1924–26 E-G-211	89	2¼	¼	89	2¼	¼
1924–26 J-211	83	4	¼	83	3	¼
1924–25 35-50	95	2½	3/16	33¼	2½	3/16
1924–25 60	115	2½	3/16	85	2½	3/16
1924–25 80	120	3	¼	120	3	¼
Ward LaFrance						
1918–26 2A-2B	104	2½	¼	104	2½	¼
1918–26 3½-4A, 4-5B	128	3¾	¼	128	3¾	¼
1920–26 5A, 7B, 5-7	144	4	¼	144	4	¼
White						
1921–26 15	92	2½	3/16	82⅝	2½	3/16
1927 15	90¼	2½	¼	82⅝	2½	3/16
1923–25 15A	92	2½	3/16	82⅝	2½	3/16
1927–30 15B	90¼	2½	¼	82⅝	2½	3/16
1923–24 15-45	107¾	2½	3/16	101¾	2½	3/16
1925 15-45	108¼	2½	3/16	101¾	2½	3/16
1926 15–45	109	2½	¼	101¾	2½	3/16
1921–27 20 & 20D	111¾	3½	¼	101¾	3½	3/16
1927–30 20A	111¾	3½	¼	101¾	3½	3/16
1923 20-45	45½	5	5/16	101¾	3½	3/16
1924–25 20-45	47	5	5/16	101¾	3½	3/16
1921–26 40 & 40D	47	4	5/16	104	5	5/16
1926–27 40A, 45A	47	5	5/16	104	5	5/16
1921–26 45, 45D	47	5	5/16	104	5	5/16
1922–23 50	47	5	5/16	101¾	3½	3/16
1924 50A	111¾	3½	3/16	98	3½	3/16
1925–26 50A	47	5	5/16	98	3½	¼
1925–27 51	47	5	5/16	98	3½	¼
1927–30 51A	66¼	5	5/16	47	5	5/16
1926–30 52, 52T	47	5	5/16	104	5	5/16
1926 53	71¼	4	5/16	48	5	5/16
1927–30 53	66¼	4	5/16	48	5	5/16
1927–30 55	47	5	5/16	104	5	5/16
1927–30 56	66¼	4	5/16	24	5	5/16
1927–30 57	90¼	2½	¼	82⅝	2½	3/16
1928–30 58	47	5	5/16	61½	5	5/16
1929–30 60	133	2¼	3/16	24	5	5/16
1929–30 61	115¼	3½	¼	24	5	5/16
1929–30 65	133¾	5	5/16	24	5	5/16
Wilcox						
1920–25 C-E	115	2½	3/16	85	2½	¼
1920–25 F	139	3½	¼	104	3½	¼
1920–25 AA1-B1½	95	2½	3/16	67	2½	3/16
1925 Bus	114	5	¼	96	2½	¼
Willys-Knight						
1927-8-9 F100	85⅝	2¼	3/16	85⅝	2¼	3/16
	64⅛	1¾				
1929 T-101-T-103	65	1¾	3/16	80⅞	1⅝	5/32
	78½	2	3/16			
1929 15, 16, 20, 21	66	2	3/16	70	2¼	3/16
	90	2¼	3/16			
1929 25, 26	86	2¼	3/16	70	2½	3/16
	98	5	¼			
1929–31 T-103	53⅜	1¾	3/16	69¼	2	¼
	69¼	2	¼			
	64⅛	1¾	3/16	80⅞	1⅞	5/32
	80⅞	1⅞	3/16			
Witt-Will						
1920–24 N-1½	104	3¼	¼	104	3¼	¼
1920–26 S-SS	104	3½	¼	104	3½	¼
1923–26 A-5	148	4	¼	148	4	¼
1924–25 N-P, 1½-2	104	3¼	¼	96	3¼	¼
1926 N	104	3¼	¼	104	3¼	¼
1926 P	104	3½	¼	104	3½	¼
Yellow Cab						
1923 T1	44½	2½	¼	22	2½	¼
1920–25 M-22-¾	98	2½	¼	90	2½	¼
1924–25 M-42-1¾	44	3	¼	22	3	¼
1924–25 Express	44	3½	¼	22	2½	¼
1925 T1	44	3½	¼	23	2½	3/16
1925 T2	44	2½	3/16	45	2½	3/16
1925 T3	44	2¾	¼	23	2	3/16

Exhaust Pipe Diameters—Passenger Cars

For Fitting Mufflers, Muffler Cutouts and Car Heaters

Make and Model	INCHES 1926	1927	1928	1929	1930	1931
Ajax	1¾	D	D	D	D	D
Apperson 6	2	D	D	D	D	D
Apperson 8	2	D	D	D	D	D
Auburn-Open & 6-66, 76	2¾	1¾	2	D	D	D
Auburn 8-88, 115	2¼	2¼	2¼	D	D	D
Auburn 8-77, 88	N	2½	2¼	D	D	D
Auburn 6-80, 6-85	N	N	N	2	2	D
Auburn 8-90, 120, 8-95, 125, 8-98	N	N	N	2¼	2¼	2¼
Blackhawk L6, L8	N	N	N	2¼	2¼	D
Buick, others	2¼	2¼	2¼	2½	....	2½
Buick, Std. 115, 116, 8-50	2	2	2	2¼	....	2
Buick 8-60	N	N	N	N	N	2¼
Cadillac	1¾	1¾	2⅛	2½	2½	2½
Case, Y	2½	....	D	D	D	D
Case, J. I. C.	2¼		D	D	D	D
Chandler	2¼	2¼	2¼	2¼	D	D
Chandler Std., Spec., 65	2	2	2	2	D	D
Chevrolet	2 1/16	2	2	2	2	2
Chrysler 6 G, 70, 72	2 1/16	2	2	....	....	2¼
Chrysler 58	1⅝	D	D	D	D	D
Chrysler 80, Imp. 80	2½	2½	2½	2½	2½	2½
Chrysler 50, 52	1⅝	1⅝	1⅝	D	D	D
Chrysler 60, 62	N	1¾	1¾	D	D	D
Cleveland	2	D	D	D	D	D
Cunningham	2¾	2½	2½	2¾	2¾	2¾
Dagmar	2½	2½	D	D	D	D
Davis, 90, 93	1¾	D	D	D	D	D
Davis, 91, 92	2¼	D	D	D	D	D
Davis, 92-27	2¼	2¼	D	D	D	D
Davis, 94-27	N	1¾	D	D	D	D
Davis, 98-27, 99	N	2	2	D	D	D
De Soto Six	N	N	N	1⅝	1⅝	....
De Soto St. 8	N	N	N	N	....	....
Diana, Str. 8	2¼	2¼	2¼	D	D	D
Dodge Brothers	2	2	2	2	2	2
Dodge Brothers DD6	N	N	N	N	1⅝	1⅝
Duesenberg	2⅜	....	D	....	4¾	4¾
duPont G	2¼	2¼	2½	2½	2½	2½
Durant, A-22, 4	1¾	D	D	D	D	D
Durant, others, 6-14	N	N	1¾	1¾	2	2
Durant 75, 70, 6-17	N	N	2¼	2¼	2¼	2¼
Elcar 6-70, 75, 75-A	N	2	2	2	2	D
Elcar 95, 96, 120	2¼	2¼	2¼	2¼	2¼	D
Erskine Six 53	N	....	1¾	1¾	1¾	D
Essex 6, Super 6	1¾	1¾	1¾	1¾	2	2
Falcon-Knight	N	1⅝	1⅝	D	D	D
Flint Z-18	1¾	1¾	D	D	D	D
Flint, all others	2¼	2¼	D	D	D	D
Ford	1½	1½	2	2	2	2
Franklin	2	2	2⅛	2⅛	2½	2½
Gardner	2¼	2¼	2¼	2¼	2¼	2¼
Gardner 80	N	2	D	D	D	D
Gardner 136	N	N	N	N	2	2
Graham, Std. 6, Spec. 6	N	N	N	N	2	2
Graham, Spec. 8, Std. 8, Cus. 8, Cus. 8-34	N	N	N	N	2½	2½
Graham-Paige 612, 615	N	N	N	2	D	D
Graham-Paige, all others	N	N	2½	2½	D	D
Gray	1¾	D	D	D	D	D
Hertz D-1	2¼	....	D	D	D	D
Hudson	2¼	2¼	2¼	2¼	2	2
Hupmobile, all others	2	2	2	2	2	2
Hupmobile H, U	N	N	N	N	....	3
Hupmobile L, C	N	N	N	N	N	2½
Jewett	1¾	D	D	D	D	D
Jordan	2¼	2¼	2¼	2¼	2¼	2¼
Jordan, J. R.	2	2	2	D	D	D
Jordan, Z Speedway	N	N	N	N	2½	D
Kissel, 45 & 75	2¼	2¼	D	D	D	D
Kissel 6-73, 8-95	N	N	N	2	2	D
Kissel, all others	2¼	2¼	2¼	2¼	2¼	D
La Salle	N	2⅛	2⅛	2½	2⅛	2½
Lexington	2¼	D	D	D	D	D
Lincoln 8	2½	2½	2½	2½	2½	2½
Locomobile, 48	2¾	2¾	2¾	2¾	D	D
Locomobile, 8	2	2	2¼	2¼	D	D
Locomobile, 90	2¼	2¼	2¼	2¼	D	D
Locomobile, 8-70	N	2	2	D	D	D
Marmon	2½	2½	2½	D	D	D
Marmon, Little, 68, 78, Roosevelt, Eight 69, 70	N	2	2	2	2	2
Marmon, Eight 79, Big Eight, 88	N	N	N	N	2¼	2¼
Marquette	N	N	N	....	....	D
McFarland, TV	3	3	3	D	D	D
McFarland, SV, St. 8	2¼	2¼	2¼	D	D	D
Moon 6-60	1¾	1¾	1¾	D	D	D
Moon Series A, Newp.	2	2	2	D	D	D
Moon, Metro, London	2¼	D	D	D	D	D
Moon 6-72, 8-80	N	N	2¼	2¼	D	D
Nash 6, Std. Single 6, 6-60	2	1¾	1¾	1¾	1¾	1¾
Nash, others	2	2	2	2	2	2
Nash Spec.	1¾	1¾	1¾	1¾	D	D
Nash 8-90	N	N	N	N	N	2½
Oakland	2¼	2¼	1½	1½	2	2
Oldsmobile	2	1¾	2	2	2	2
Overland 4, Whippet 4	2	1⅝	1⅝	1⅝	D	D
Overland 6, Whippet	1⅝	1⅝	D	1¾	D	D
Packard 6, 626, 633, 726, 733, 826, 833	2¼	2¼	2¼	2¼	2¼	2¼
Packard 8, 740, 745, 840, 845	2¼	2⅝	2⅝	2⅝	2⅝	2⅝
Paige 6-45	N	1¾	D	D	D	D
Paige 6-65-75	2	2	D	D	D	D
Paige 8-85	N	2½	D	D	D	D
Paige 6-66-70, etc.	2	D	D	D	D	D
Peerless 6-80, 6-81, 61-A	2½	2¼	2¼	2¼	2¼	D
Peerless, all others	2¼	2¼	2¼	2¼	2½	2½
Peerless Std. 8	N	N	N	N	N	2
Pierce-Arrow 33, 36	2⅞	2⅞	2⅞	D	D	D
Pierce-Arrow 132	N	N	N	N	2½	D
Pierce-Arrow, all others	2¼	2¼	2¼	2¼	2¼	2¼
Plymouth	N	N	....	....	1⅝	1⅝
Pontiac	1⅞	1⅞	2	2	2	2
Reo 15, 20, 25, 25N	2	2¼	2¼	2¼	2¼	2¼
Reo 30N, 35N	N	N	N	N	N	2½
Revere	3	D	D	D	D	D
Rickenbacker D & E	2¼	D	D	D	D	D
Rickenbacker 8	1¾	2¼	D	D	D	D
Rickenbacker 6-70	N	2¼	D	D	D	D
Roamer 8-88, 8-80	2¼	2¼	2¼	2¼	2½	D
Roamer 4-75	2½	D	D	D	D	D
Rolls-Royce	3	3	3	3	3	....
Roosevelt	N	N	N	2	D	D
Star	1¾	1¾	1¾	D	D	D
Stearns-Knight 4	2¼	D	D	D	D	D
Stearns-Knight 6, M & N	2½	2½	2½	2¼	D	D
Stearns-Knight C, 75	2¼	D	D	D	D	D
Stearns-Knight 8, H & J	N	2½	2½	2½	D	D
Studebaker L6	1¾	D	D	D	D	D
Studebaker Std., Big 6	2	....	D	D	D	D
Studebaker Dic. 6, 8, Six	N	N	1¾	1¾	1¾	1¾
Studebaker Com. 6, 8	N	N	2	1¾	1¾	1¾
Studebaker Pres. 8	N	N	2¼	2¼	2¼	2¼
Stutz Series M, MA, MB	2½	2½	2¾	2¾	2¾	2¾
Stutz LA	N	N	N	N	N	2¼
Velie 60, 56	2¼	D	D	D	D	D
Velie Std. 50	2	2	2	D	D	D
Velie, all others	2¼	2¼	2¼	D	D	D
Viking	N	N	N	2¼	2¼	D
Whippet 96A	N	N	N	N	1⅝	D
Whippet 98A	N	N	N	N	1¾	D
Wills Ste. A, B, C	2	D	D	D	D	D
Wills Ste. Claire W6	2¼	D	D	D	D	D
Wills Ste. Claire T6	2¼	2¼	D	D	D	D
Willys Eight	N	N	N	N	2	2
Willys-Knight 70, Spec. 6, 70B, 87	1¾	1¾	1¾	1¾	1¾	D
Willys-Knight 66, Great 66B, 66D	2 1/16	2¼	....	2¼	2¼	2¼
Willys Six 98B, 97, 98D	N	N	N	N	2	2
Windsor, 8-85, 8-92	N	N	N	2¼	2¼	D
Windsor, 6-75, 6-69	N	N	N	1¾	2¼	D

D—Discontinued. N—Not manufactured.

Mazda Lamp Numbers—Passenger Cars

Key to Mazda Lamp Numbers

Lamp number ...	61	62	63	64	67	68	81	82	89	90	1129	1130	1141	1142	1158	1101	1110
Base	S.C.	D.C.	S.C.	D.C.	S.C.	D.C.	S.C.	D.C.	S.C.	D.C.	S.C.	D.C.	S.C.	D.C.	D.C.	S.C.	D.C. *
Volts	3-4	3-4	6-8	6-8	12-16	12-16	6-8	6-8	12-16	12-16	6-8	6-8	12-16	12-16	6-8	6-8	6-8
Candlepower	2	2	3	3	3	3	6	6	6	6	21	21	21	21	21	21	21

S.C.—Single Contact. D.C.—Double Contact. * Double Filament.

MAKE OF CAR	Year	Mazda Lamp Numbers				
		Head	Aux. Head	Cowl	Tail	Instr. Bd.
Ajax	25-26	1129	N	63	63	..
Anderson	25	1129	..	63	63	63
Apperson	25	1129	N	63	63	64
Auburn	25	1129	81	63	63	64
Auburn	26	1158	N	63	63	63
Auburn 6-66, 8-77	27	1110	63	N	63	63
Auburn 8-88	27	1110	N	N	63	63
Auburn 6-80, 120	29	1129	N	63	63	63
Auburn 8-90	29	1158	N	63	63	63
Auburn	30	1129	N	63	63	63
Auburn 8-98	31	1110	..	63	..	63
Austin	30	....	..	..	63	63
Blackhawk	29-30	1133	..	63	63	63
Buick	25	1129	63	63	63	63
Buick	26	1110	63	63	63	63
Buick 115	27-29	1110	63	63	63	63
Buick 120-128	27-29	1110	N	63	63	63
Cadillac	25	1129	63	N	63	63
Cadillac	26	1110	63	N	63	63
Cadillac	27-31	1110	N	63	63	63
Case	25-26	1129	N	63	63	63
Chandler Std. & Sp.	a26-27	1129	N	63	63	63
Chandler, Others	25-27	1129	81	63	63	63
Chandler, All	28	1129	N	63	63	63
Chandler, All	29	1110	N	63	63	63
Chev. G & Sup.	25-26	1129	N	63	63	63
Chevrolet	27-28	1129	N	63	63	63
Chevrolet	29-31	1110	N	63	63	63
Chrysler	25-26	1129	63	63	63	63
Chrysler 80	26	1110	63	..	63	..
Chrysler 50, 62	27	1129	..	..	63	63
Chrysler 70	27	1129	..	63	63	63
Chrysler 80	27-28	1110	N	63	63	63
Chrysler 52	28	1129	..	63	..	63
Chrysler 62	28	1110	..	..	63	63
Chrysler 72	28	1110	..	63	..	63
Chrysler, All	29-30	1110	N	63	63	63
Chrysler 70	31	1110	..	63	..	63
Cleveland	25-26	1129	63	63	63	63
Cord L-29	30-31	1110	..	63	63	63
Cunningham	26-31	1129	N	81	63	..
Dagmar	22-26	1129	81	64	63	64
Dagmar 6-60	27	1129	81	64	63	64
Dagmar 6-70	27	1129	81	N	63	64
Davis	25	1129	81	64	63	..
Davis	26	1110	N	..	..	..
Davis	27-28	1110	N	81	63	63
De Soto Six	29-30	1110	..	63	63	63
Diana	25-26	1129	63	63	63	63
Diana	27-28	1129	N	63	63	63
Dodge	25-26	1141	N	67	67	67
Dodge	27	1129	N	63	63	63
Dodge Sr. 6	28	1129	63	..	63	63
Dodge Vic. 6	28	1110	..	..	63	63
Dodge Bros. Sr. 6	29-30	1110	..	63	63	63
Dodge Bros.	30-31	1110	..	63	..	63
Dodge Eight	31	1120	..	63	..	63
Duesenberg	25-26	1129	81	63	63	63
duPont	25-26	1129	81	64††	63	63
duPont G	27-31	1129	81	63	63	63
Durant	25-26	1129	N	63	63	64
Durant 55, 40, 60	28-29	1129	N	N	63	64
Durant	30-31	....	..	63	63	63
Elcar	25-26	1129	81	63†	63	64
Elcar 8	26	1110	81	81	63	64
Elcar 6-70, 8-90	27-28	1110	81	N	63	63
Elcar 8-82	27-28	1110	81	N	..	81
Elcar 8-91, 120	28	1110	81	N	63	63
Elcar 75, 95 & 96	29-30	1110	..	..	..	64
Elcar 120	29	1110	..	..	..	..
Erskine	27	1110	81	N	63	63
Erskine	28-29	1110	..	N	63	63
Essex	25-26	1129	N	63	61	61
Essex	27	1129	N	63	63	63
Essex	28-31	1110	N	63	63	63
Flint	25-26	1129	..	63	63	63
Flint	27	1129	N	63	63	63
Ford T	25-26	1158	N	N	63	63
Ford T	27	1158	N	N	63	63
Franklin	25-26	1129	81	N	61	61
Franklin	27	1110	N	N	61	61
Franklin 130	29	1110	N	63	63	63
Franklin 135, 137	29	1129	N	63	61	63
Franklin	30-31	1110	..	63	63	63
Gardner	25-26	1129	N	63	63	63
Gardner	27	1110	63	N	63	63
Gardner	28	1110	63	N	63	83
Gardner	29	1110	63	81	63	83
Gardner	30-31	1110	N	81	63	63
Graham	30-31	1110	..	63	63	63
Graham-Paige 619, 629	28	1110	..	81	81	81
Graham-Paige	29	1110	..	63	63	63
Gray	25-26	1129	N	63	63	63
Hertz	25-26	1129	N	63	63	63
Hudson	25-26	1129	N	63	61	61
Hudson	27	1129	N	63	63	63
Hudson	28-29	1110	N	63	63	63
Hudson Great 8	30-31	1110	..	63	63	63
Hupmobile	25-26a	1129	..	63	63	63
Hupmobile	a26	1110	N	63	63	63
Hupmobile A, Cent. 6	27-28	1110	N	N	63	63
Hupmobile, Others	27-29	1110	N	63	63	63
Hupmobile A, S	29-31	1110	N	..	63	63
Hupmobile C	30-31	1110	N	N	63	63
Jewett	25	1129	..	63	63	64
Jewett	26	1129	N	64	63	..
Jordan	25-28	1129	81	63	63	63
Jordan R	27-28	1110	..	..	..	..
Kissel	25	1129	81	64	63	64
Kissel 55-75	24-26a	1129	..	63	63	64
Kissel	a26-30	1110	N	63	63	64
LaSalle	27-31	1110	N	63	63	63
Lexington	25-26	1129	81	63	63	64
Lincoln	25-26	1129	81	61	61	61
Lincoln	27-30	1110	81	61	61	61
Lincoln	31	1110	..	63	63	63
Locomobile 6	25-26	1141	67	67	67	67
Locomobile Jr. 8	26	1129	81	63	63	63
Locomobile 48	27-29	1141	67	67	67	67
Locomobile 90, 8-66	27-28	1129	63	63	63	63
Locomobile 8-80	27-29	1129	63	63	63	63
Locomobile 8-70	27-28	1129	63	63	63	63
Locomobile 90	29	1129	63	63	63	63
Locomobile 86, 88	29	1129	..	63	63	63
McFarlan	25	1129	81	63	64	63
McFarlan	26	1129	..	81	63	64
McFarlan TV	27	1129	81	81	81	63
McFarlan Str. 8	27	....	..	81	81	63
McFarlan Str. 8	28	1110	..	81	63	63
McFarlan TV6	28	1129	81	81	63	63
Marmon	25-26	1129	81	81	63	63
Marmon, Little	27	1110	N	..	..	63
Marmon E-75	27-28	1110	N	81	63	63
Marmon 78	28	1110	N	..	..	..
Marmon 78	29	1129	N	..	..	..
Marquette	30	1110	..	63	63	63
Maxwell	25	1129	63	63	63	63
Mercer	25	1129	81	..	63	63
Moon	25-26	1129	81	63	63	63
Moon Series A	27-28	1129	N	63	63	63
Moon 6-60	27	1129	N	63	63	63
Moon 6-60	28	1130	N	63	63	63
Moon 6-72	28-29	1110	N	63	63	63
Nash	25-27	1129	N	63	63	63
Nash Adv.	a26-29	1110	N	63	63	63
Nash Spec.	27-29	1110	N	63	63	63
Nash Std. 6	28	1129	N	63	63	63
Nash Std. 6	29	1110	N	63	63	63
Nash Single 6	30	1110	..	63	63	63
Nash Twin Ign.	30	1120	..	63	63	63
Nash 6-60, 8-70	31	1110	..	63	63	63
Nash 8-80, 8-90	31	1120	..	63	63	63
Oakland	25-26	1129	81	63	63	63
Oakland	27-29	1110	N	63	63	63
Oakland 8	30-31	1110	..	63	63	63
Oldsmobile	25-26J	1129	63	63	63	63
Oldsmobile	J26-27	1110	N	63	63	63
Oldsmobile	29-30	1110	..	N	63	63
Oldsmobile	31	1110	63	N	63	63
Overland	25-26	1129	N	N	61	61
Overland	27-28	1129	N	N	63	63
O'land-Whip.	29	1110	N	N	63	63
O'land-Whip.	29	1110	N	63	63	63
Packard 8	25-26M	1129	..	63	63	63
Packard 8	M26	1158	..	..	63	63
Packard 6	25	1129	81	63	63	63
Packard 6	26	1110	81	N	63	63
Packard 6	27-28	1110	63	N	63	63
Packard 8	28-31	1110	63	63	63	63
Paige	25	1129	81	..	63	81
Paige	26	1129	N	64	63	64
Paige	27	1129	N	63	63	64
Peerless 8	25	1101	81	81	61	61
Peerless 6	25-26	1129	63	63	63	63
Peerless 8	26	1110	81	..	61	61
Peerless 6-72	27	1129	R	63	63	63
Peerless 6-80	27-28	1110	N	81	63	63
Peerless 6-90, 8-69, 6-91, 61-A	27-30	1110	N	63	63	63
Pierce-Arrow	25-28	1129	81	81	81	81
Pierce-Arrow 90	25	1129	81	81	81	63
Pierce-Arrow 133, 143	29	1129	..	81	81	63
Plymouth	29-31	1110	..	..	..	63
Pontiac	26-27	1129	N	63	63	63
Pontiac	28	1110	N	63	63	63
Pontiac Six	29-31	1110	..	63	63	63
Reo	25	1129	63	63	63	63
Reo	26-31	1110	N	63	63	63
Revere 25	25	1129	81	63	63	64
Rickenbacker	25	1158	..	63	63	63
Rickenbacker	26	1110	..	63	63	63
Rickenbacker	27	1110	N	63	63	63
Roamer	26	1129	63	63	63	64
Roamer	27-30	1129	63	81	81	64
Rollin	25	1129	81	63	63	63
Rolls Royce	25	1140	..	82	63	63
Rolls Royce	26-27	1130	82	82	82	64
Rolls Royce S.G.	28-30	1129	81	81	81	64
Rolls Royce N.P.	28	1110	..	81	81	64
Rolls Royce N.P.	29-31	1116	..	63	63	64
Star	25-26	1129	N	..	63	64
Star	27-28	1129	N	N	63	64
Stearns-Knight	25-26	1141	89	67	67	67
Stearns-Kn. 6-85	a26	1110	89	89	67	67
Stearns-Knight	27	1110	89	63	63	63
Stearns-Knight	28-29	1110	..	63	63	63
Stevens Duryea	25	1129	81	..	63	63
Studebaker	25	1129	..	81	63	62
Studebaker	26-28	1110	N	81	63	63
Studebaker	a26	1110	N	81	81	81
Studebkr. Com. 6 & 8	29-31	1110	..	63	63	63
Studebkr. Dict.	29	1110	N	81	63	63
Studebkr. Dict.	30	1110	N	63	63	63
Studebkr. Pres.	29-31	1110	N	63	63	63
Stud'kr. Dic. 8	31	1110	..	63	63	..
Stutz	25	1129	81	63	63	63
Stutz	26-27	1110	63	N	63	63
Stutz	28	1110	63	81	63	63
Stutz	29-31	1133	N	63	63	63
Velie	25-26	1129	81	63	63	63
Velie Std. 50	27-28	1129	..	..	63	63
Velie, Others	28	1129	..	63	63	63
Viking	29-30	1110	N	N	63	63
Whippet 96A	30	1110	N	N	..	63
Whippet 98A	30	1110	N	63	..	63
Wills St. Claire	25	1101	..	63	63	63
Wills St. Claire	26	1129	N	N	63	63
Wills St. Claire	27	1110	N	N	63	63
Willys-Knight	25	1129	81	63	61	61
Willys-Kn. 66	26	1129	N	81	63	63
Willys-Kn. 70	26	1110	..	..	..	..
Willys-Kn. 66-A	27	1129	R	63	63	63
Willys-Kn. 70-A	27	1110	N	63	63	63
Willys-Knight Std. 6	28	1110	N	..	..	..
Willys-Kn. Gt. 6	28	1129	..	63	63	63
Willys-Knight Spe. 6	28	1110	N	63	63	63
Willys-Kn. 66B	29	1129	N	63	63	63
Willys-Kn. 70B	29-30	1110	N	63	63	63
Willys-Kn. 66B	30	1110	N	63	63	63
Willys-Kn. 66D	31	1110	N	63	..	63
Willys Six	30-31	1110	N	63	..	63
Willys Eight	31	1110	N	63	..	63
Windsor 8-82, 8-92	29	1110	N	63	63	63
Windsor	30	1110	N	63	63	63

† 64 on 1926 models. †† 63 on 1925-26 models. N None. J July. a August. M May.

Headlight Lens Sizes—Passenger Cars

MAKE AND MODEL	LENS DIAMETER (In.)					
	1926	1927	1928	1929	1930	1931
Ajax	8	D	D	D	D	D
Apperson "6"	8¾	D	D	D	D	D
Apperson "8"	8¾	D	D	D	D	D
Auburn "6"	8½	D.	D	D	D	D
Auburn "8-88"	8½	8½	D	D	D	D
Auburn "6-66" & "8-77"	N	8½	D	D	D	D
Auburn 76, 88 & 115	N	N	11½	D	D	D
Auburn, All Others	N	N	N	11½	11½	10¾
Blackhawk L6, L8	N	N	N	11½	11½	D
Buick Master 6	8¾	8¾	8¼	D	D	D
Buick Std. 6, 116, 121, 129	8¼	8¼	7¾	10	10	D
Buick 8-50, 8-60	N	N	N	N	N	10½
Buick 8-80, 8-90	N	N	N	N	N	9½
Cadillac	9⅝ 10⅜	10½	10¼	10¼	12½	10¼
Cadillac 452, 370	N	N	N	N	11¼	11¼
Case V, W, Y, JIC	9⅜	9⅜	D	D	D	D
Chandler Big 6, Roy. 75	a9	9½	9½	9½	D	D
Chandler Spec. 6	9	9	9	D	D	D
Chandler Roy. 8	N	9½	9½	9½	D	D
Chandler 65	N	N	N	D	D	D
Chevrolet	a8	8⅜	8½	9	9	9
Chrysler "70"	8	8	8	D	D	D
Chrysler "4"	8⅞	8½	8½	D	D	D
Chrysler "60"	7⅝	7⅝	D	D	D	D
Chrysler "62", 65, 75	N	7⅝	7⅝	D	D	D
Cleveland "43"	8½	D	D	D	D	D
Cleveland "31"	8½	D	D	D	D	D
Cord L-29	N	N	N	N	10¼	10¼
Cunningham	11	11	11	11	11	11
Dagmar	10	10	D	D	D	D
Davis	8⅝ b7½	8¾	8¾	D	D	D
Diana	9⅜	9⅜	9⅜	D	D	D
Dodge Brothers 4		8¾	D	D	D	
Dodge Bros. Sen. 6	N	9	9	9½	9½	D
Dodge Bros. Vic. 6	N	N	9	D	D	D
Dodge Bros. 6	N	N	N	9	8½	8½
Dodge Bros. DD6	N	N	N	N	8½	8½
Dodge Bros. DC8	N	N	N	N	9	9
Duesenberg	10				11½	11½
duPont	8¾	8¾	8¾	8¾	D	D
duPont G	N	N	N		9½	9½
Durant	8½	D	D	D	D	D
Durant 55	N	N	7¾	7	D	D
Durant 40	N	N	N	7	D	D
Durant 60	N	N	N	9⅞	D	D
Durant 66	N	N	N	9	D	D
Durant 70	N	N	N	9½	D	D
Durant 6-14, 6-17	N	N	N	N	8½	8½
Elcar "4"	8	D	D	D	D	D
Elcar "6"	8	D	D	D	D	D
Elcar "8"	9⅝	D	D	D	D	D
Elcar 6-70	N	8	8	D	D	D
Elcar 8-82	N	9	9⅝	D	D	D
Elcar 8-90, 120	N	9½	9½	D		D

MAKE AND MODEL	LENS DIAMETER (In.)					
	1926	1927	1928	1929	1930	1931
Elcar 75, 95 & 96	N	N	N	9⅜	9⅜	D
Erskine	N	8	8	8	9	D
Essex "6"	8	8	8	8	8½	8½
Falcon Knight	N	7⅛	7⅛	D	D	D
Flint 55-80	9½	9	D	D	D	D
Flint 40-60-Z18	8½	8½	D	D	D	D
Ford	8½	8½	8½	8½	8½	8½
Franklin	10¼	10¼	10⅝	9⅝	10⅝	D
Franklin	N	N	N	11¼	11½	12
Gardner 130	9½	9¾	9¾	9¾	D	D
Gardner 120, 125, 140, 148	N	N	N	N	9½	9½
Gardner 136	N	N	N	N	9⅞	9⅞
Gardner 150, 158	N	N	N	N	9¾	9¾
Graham Std., Spec. 6	N	N	N	N	9½	9½
Graham, All Others	N	N	10	D	10¾	10¾
Graham-Paige 629	9½	9¾	9¾	9¾	D	D
Graham-Paige 612, 615	N	N	N	9½	D	D
Graham-P. 621, 827, 837	N	N	N	10¾	D	D
Gray	8⅛	D	D	D	D	D
Hertz	7	D	D	D	D	D
Hudson	9	9	9	10	10	
Hupmobile E, 125-8	8¾	9	9	9	9	
Hupmobile A-1, 6, S, S-2	N	7⅝	7⅝	9½	9½	9½
Hupmobile 8, C	N	N	9⅞	9½	9½	9½
Jewett	8½	D	D	D	D	D
Jordan	8¾	8¾	D	D	D	D
Jordan J	8	8	8	D	D	D
Jordan 70, 80	N	N	N	N	10¾	10¾
Jordan 90	N	N	N	N	10⅛	10⅛
Kissel	8¾	8¾	10¾	11	11	
Lexington	9	D	D	D	D	D
LaSalle	N	9⅝	9⅝	9⅝	10¼	10¼
Lincoln	9¼	10¾	10¾	10¾	10¼	10¼
Locomobile 48	11	11	11	11	D	D
Locomobile 8	8⅞	D	D	D	D	D
Locomobile 90	10	10⅞	10⅞	10⅞	D	D
Locomobile 8-66, 8-70	N	8	8	9	D	D
Locomobile 8-80	N	9	9	9	D	D
Locomobile 86, 88	N	N	N	10⅛	D	D
McFarlan TV	9½	9	D	D	D	D
McFarlan 8	N	8½	9⅞	D	D	D
McFarlan Str. 8	9⅞	9⅞	9⅞	D	D	D
Marmon Six	N	8½	D	D	D	D
Marmon, Little	N	N	N	10¾	D	D
Marmon 68, 78	N	N	N	10¾	10⅝	10⅝
Marmon Roosevelt	N	N	N		10⅝	10⅝
Marmon Eight 69	N	N	N	N	10⅝	10⅝
Marmon, 8-79, Big 8, 88	N	N	N	N	12	12
Marmon 70	N	N	N	N	N	10
Marquette	N	N	N	N	9½	D
Moon 6-58, London	9	D	D	D	D	
Moon "A"	8⅝	8⅝	8⅝	D	D	D
Moon 6-60	8	8	8	D	D	D
Moon 6-72	N	N	9⅝	9⅝	D	D
Moon 8-80	N	N	9⅝	D	D	D
Nash	8¾	D	D	D	D	

MAKE AND MODEL	LENS DIAMETER (In.)					
	1926	1927	1928	1929	1930	1931
Nash Spec., Single6, 60, 70	8	8	8	9⅝	9⅜	9⅜
Nash Lt., Std., T6, 8-80	8	8	8	9¼	9	9
Nash Adv., Twin 8, 8-90	9	9	9	9½	9½	9⅞
Oakland "44 & 54"	8⅛	D	D	D	D	D
Oakland 6, 8	8⅛	8⅜	8⅜	8⅜	9¾	10½
Oldsmobile	7⅝	8⅜	8⅜	8⅜	8¾	8¾
Overland	8⅛	8⅛	8⅛	10⅛	D	D
Packard 6	8½	8½	8½	D	D	D
Packard "Twin", 8	9	9	9	9	D	D
Packard 726, 733, 826, 833	N	N	N	N	10¼	10¼
Packard 740, 745, 840, 845	N	N	N	N	11¼	11¼
Paige	8½	9	D	D	D	D
Paige 6-45	8½	8½	D	D	D	D
Peerless	9	9	9	D	D	D
Peerless 6-80, 6-81, 61, 61A	8¼	8¼	8¼	8¼	D	D
Peerless 6-91	N	N	N	9	9	D
Peerless 8-69, 125	9½	10⅛	10⅛	10⅛	D	D
Peerless Std., Mas., Cus	N	N	N	N	12	12
Pierce-Arrow	9¼	9¼	9¼			9¼
Pierce-Arrow "80", 81	8⅜	8⅜	8⅜	8¾	8¾	D
Pontiac	8⅛	8¼	8⅜	8⅝	9¾	10¼
Reo, Mas., 20, 25, 25N	9	9½	9½	9½	9½	10¼
Reo Wol., Mate, 15, 30, 35	N	8⅜	8⅜	8⅜	8⅜	8½
Revere	8	D	D	D	D	D
Rickenbacker	9	D	D	D	D	D
Rickenbacker 6-70	N	9	D	D	D	D
Rickenbacker 8-80, 8-90	N	8⅜	D	D	D	D
Roamer	8⅞	9	9	9	D	D
Roamer 6-50	7¼	D	D	D	D	D
Roll-Royce	10⅜	10⅜	10⅜	10⅜	10⅜	10⅜
Roosevelt	N	N	N	10⅝	D	D
Star	7	7	7	D	D	D
Star 6	7¾	7¾	D	D	D	D
Stearns-Knight	9¼	10¼	10¼	10¼	D	D
Stearns-Knight 6-80	N	N	N	9	D	D
Studebaker Big 6, Com. 6 and 8	9½		9⅝	9⅞	9⅞	
Studebaker Std., Dic., Six	8½	9½	9½	D	D	9
Studebaker Pres. 8	N	N	11⅜	11⅜	11⅜	
Stutz	9½	9½	9½	11⅜	11⅜	11
Velie "Std. 50	8⅜	8	8	D	D	D
Velie "60, 6-77	8⅜	8⅜	11	D	D	D
Velie 8-88	N	N	11	D	D	D
Viking	N	N	N	11	11	
Whippet	N	N	N	10⅛	10⅛	D
Wills Ste. Claire	8	8	D	D	D	D
Willys-Knight 66-A, Great	N	8⅛	8⅛	8⅛	D	D
Willys-Knight 70-A, Spec	N	8¾	8⅛	D	D	D
Willys-Knight Std. 6	N	8⅛	8⅛	D	D	D
Willys-Knight	8½	D	D	D	D	D
Willys-Knight 66B, 66D	N	N	8⅛	10¾	10⅛	
Willys-Knight 70B	N	N	10⅛	10⅛	D	
Willys Six 97, 98D	N	N	N	10⅛	10⅛	
Windsor 8-82, 8-92, 8.85	N	N	N	11¼	11¼	D
Windsor 6-69, 6-75	N	N	N	N	9⅝	D

a—from Sept., 1925   b—from June, 1926   D—Discontinued   N—Not manufactured.

Information on Lamps or Bulbs for Motor Vehicle Lights

(Supplementing the Mazda Lamp Data on Opposite Page)

Bulbs fall into two general classes, as determined by the base. Using the correct base is most important in headlight adjusting, because using the wrong base makes focusing and elimination of glare practically impossible.

Standard Base: With base pins at right angles to plane of filaments.

Ford Base (commonly so called): With base pins in plane of filaments.

If you remember that the plane on the "V" filament must always be horizontal, you won't go wrong.

Bulbs also fall into five classes according to voltage:

3–4 Volts made only with Standard Base.

6–8 Volts made both with Standard and Ford Bases.

9 Volts made only with Ford Base for old magneto light Fords. (Bulb 1160.)

12–16 Volts made only with Standard Base for Dodges up to 1927.

18–24 Volts made only with Ford Base for spotlight on old magneto-light Fords. (Bulb 1146.)

Practically all demands will be for the 6-8 and the 12-16 volt groups.

What Bulb Numbers Indicate

All numbers over 100 are for headlights.

All numbers from 61 to 94 are for auxiliary lights.

Even numbers indicate double contact (D.C.)

Odd numbers indicate single contact (S.C.)

Numbers 61 and 62 are the only 2 cp. bulbs and are always used on instrument board in series with the tail light. **Bulb Interchangeability—21 cp. and 32 cp.**

	Standard Base				Ford Base		
	6–8 Volts		12–16 Volts		6–8 Volts		
21 cp.	1110	1129	1141	1142	1158*	1114*	1130
32 cp.	1116*	1133	1143	1144	None	1118*	1134

*These headlight bulbs can be accidentally put in upside down. Notice particularly how you put them in.

These data can be used in changing headlight bulbs from standard equipment 21 cp. bulb to 32 cp. bulb in all states which now permit the higher cp. light. As of May, 1931, only Massachusetts, Nevada, and District of Columbia had not legalized the use of the 32-32 cp. bulb.

Anti-Freeze Requirements

Cooling System Capacities by Makes and Models

Make and Model	Cap.
Auburn 6-66,1926	17½
Auburn 6-66, 1927	14
Auburn 8-77, 8-88, 1926-7	20
Auburn 76, 1928	15
Auburn 88, 1928	16
Auburn 115, 1928	20
Auburn 6-80, 1929, 1930	19
Auburn 8-90, 1929, 1930	22
Auburn 120, 1929, 1930	25
Auburn 8-98, 1931	21
Austin 1930, 31	6
Blackhawk L6, 1929, 1930	24
Blackhawk L8, 1929, 1930	26
Buick Std., 1926, 1927	12
Buick Mstr., 1926, 27	18
Buick 115, 1928; 40, 1930	16
Buick 120 & 128, 1928	20
Buick 116, 40, 1928, 29, 30	17
Buick 121, 129, 1928, 29	22
Buick 50, 60, 1930	22½
Buick 8-50	12
Buick 8-60	15
Buick 8-80, 8-90	19
Cadillac 314	22
Cadillac 341A, 341B, 353, 355	24
Cadillac 370	26
Cadillac 452	28
Chandler 35, 1926, 27	20
Chandler Spec. 6	16
Chandler Std. 6	10
Chandler Roy. 8, Big 6	22
Chandler 65	12
Chandler Royal 75	17
Chevrolet, 1929, 30, 31	10
Chevrolet, 1926, 27, 28	8
Chrysler, 50, 52, 60, 62, 66	14
Chrysler 58, 1925, 26	13
Chrysler 70, 1926, 27	17
Chrysler 72, 1928	15
Chrysler Imp. 80, 1926	20½
Chrysler 65, 1928, 29	13
Chrysler 75, 1929	15
Chrysler 70, 1930	18
Chrysler 77, 1930	21
Chrysler 70, 1931	21
Chrysler Imp. 80, 1927, 28, 29	19
Chrysler 6, 1930	12
Chrysler 6, 8, 1930, 31	16
Chrysler Imp. 8, 1931	26
Cleveland 31, 1925, 26	10
Cleveland 43, 1925, 26	16
Cord L-29, 1930, 31	22
Cunningham, 1929-31	29
Davis 6, 1926, 27	13
Davis 8, 1927, 28	20
De Soto 6, 1929	10
De Soto 8, 1930	13
De Vaux, 1931	15
Diana, 1926, 27, 28	18
Dodge Bros. 4, 1926	11
Dodge Bros. 4, 1927-28	12½
Dodge Std. Vic., 1928	12
Dodge Senior, 1928, 30	18
Dodge Senior, 1929	17
Dodge Std. Vic. 6, 1929	14
Dodge DC8, 1930	14
Dodge DD6, 1930, 31	12
Dodge DA6, Six, 1929-31	14
Dodge 8, 1931	16
Duesenberg 8, 1929-30	28
Duesenberg J, 1931	34
duPont G, 1929, 30, 31	26
Durant 65, 60, 66,1928, 29, 30	12
Durant 75, 6-17	14½
Durant 40, 55, 1928, 29	8
Durant 6-14, 1930, 31	14
Elcar 6-70, 1927, 28, 29	12
Elcar 8-82, 1928, 29	17
Elcar 8-90, 91, 92, 95, 96	18
Elcar 8-78, 1928, 29	16
Elcar 120	22
Elcar 75, 75-A, 1930	14
Erskine 51, 52, 1928-30	13
Erskine 53, 1930	12½
Essex Six All	19
Falcon-Knight 1927-29	15
Flint E-80 and 55	19
Flint Z-18	11
Flint 60	13½
Flint 80	18
Ford T, 1924 to 27	12½
Ford A, 1928 to 31	12
Gardner 75, 80, 90, 136	17
Gardner 140, 148	19
Gardner 85, 120, 125, 150, 158	23
Graham Std. 6, 1930	18
Graham Std. 6, 1931	20
Graham Spe. 6, 1930,31	20
Graham Spe. 8-20, 1931	26
Graham Spec. & Std. 8	26
Graham Cus. 8-34, 1931	26
Grah. Paige 610, 614, 615	20
Grah. Paige 619, 629, 835	26
Graham Paige 612, 1929	18
Graham Paige 621, 1929	25
Graham Paige 827, 837	27
Hudson, 1924 to 1927	16
Hudson, 1928, 1929	22
Hudson Gt. 8, 1930, 31	18
Hupmobile 6, 1926, 27, 28	13
Hupmobile 8, 1925, 26, 27	19
Hupmobile M-8, M, 1929	22
Hupmobile S, 1929	13
Hupmobile S, S-2, '30, 31	28
Hupmobile C, 1930, 31	20
Hupmobile H, U, '30, 31	28
Hupmobile L, 1931	16
Jewett New Day, '26, 27	12
Jordan A, AA, 1925-27	20
Jordan J, J-1, JJ, JE, E	17
Jordan R, RE	14
Jordan G, T, U, 70, 80, 90	18
Kissel 55, 65, 75	27
Kissel 6-73	16
Kissel 70, 80, 80S, 95	20
Kissel 8-90, 8-126	24
LaSalle 303, 1927, 28	20
LaSalle 328, 1929	21
LaSalle 340, 345, '30, 31	24
Lincoln 1925 to 1930	30
Lincoln 8, 1931	32
Locomobile Jr. 8, 8-66	18
Loco. 8-70, 1928, 29	21
Loco. 6-90, 8-80, 86, 88	23
Locomobile 48	27
Marmon 74, 75, E75	22
Marmon 68, 78, Little	20
Marmon 69, 70, Roosvlt.	16
Marmon 79, Big 8, 88	28
Marmon 16, 1931	29
Marquette, 1929, 1930	12
McFarlan St. 8 and TV	20
Moon A, 1924-28	15
Moon 6-60, 6-62	12
Moon 6-72, 1928, 29	14
Moon 8-80, 1928, 29	16
Nash Light and Std. 6, 1926, 27, 28	11
Nash Adv. & Spec., 1926	22
Nash Adv., 1927, 28	22
Nash Spec., 1927	20
Nash Spec., 1928	16
Nash Adv. 400, Adv. 6, 1929	19
Nash Std. 6, 1929	10
Nash Spec. 6, 1929	17
Nash Single 6, 6-60, 1930-31	12
Nash Twin Ign. 6, 8-80	16
Nash Twin Ign. 8, 8-90	22
Nash 8-70, 1931	15
Oakland, 1925, 26, 27	12
Oakland 6, 1928	11
Oakland AA6, 1928	12
Oakland AA6, 1929	22
Oakland 8, 1930, 31	25
Olds. 6, 1925, 26, 27	12
Oldsmobile, 1929, 30, 31	13
Overland 4 Whippet 96	11
Overland 6 Whip. 93, 93A, 98	12½
Packard 226, 233, 426, 433	17
Packard 526, 533, 626, 633	20
Packard 336, 343, 1927	24
Packard 443, 640, 645, 840, 845	25
Packard 726, 733, 826, 833	20
Packard 740, 745, 1930	26
Paige 6-45, 1927, 28	12
Paige 6-72, 6-65, 6-75	22
Paige 6-70, 8-85	23
Peerless 6-72, 1925-27	12
Peerless 6-72, 1928	13
Peerless 6-80, 6-90, 6-91	14
Peerless 8-69, 1926-28	24
Peerless 6-60, 1927-29	12
Peerless 6-61, 6-61A	12½
Peerless 6-81, 1929	13½
Peerless 125, 1929	20
Peerless Mas., Cus.	23½
Peerless Std. 8, 1930	21
Peerless Std. 8, 1931	14
Pierce-Arrow, 1929-31	26
Pierce-Arrow 80 All	22
Pierce-Arrow 81	21
Plymouth, 1929	14
Plymouth, 1930	13½
Plymouth, 1931	9
Pontiac, 1929, 30, 31	14
Reo T6, 1924, 25, 26	14
Reo Flying Cloud	16
Reo Wolverine, B2 Fl. Cloud, 1929, 15-1929	14
Reo C Fl. Cloud, 1929	19
Reo 20, 25, 1930	19
Reo 25N, 1931	17
Reo 30N, Roy 35N, 1931	23
Rolls-Royce S.G.	36
Rolls-Royce N.P.	32
Roosevelt 1929	22
Star 4, 1924, 25, 26, 27, 28	8
Star 6, 1926, 27	12
Stearns-Kni. 75, 1925-26	20
Stearns-Kni. 95, 1925-26	28
Stearns-Knight F6-85	26
Stearns-Knight G8-85	28
Stearns-Knight H&J	28
Stearns-Knight H&J, 8-90	30
Stearns-Knight M&N 6-80	18½
Studebaker Std. 6	17
Studebaker Spec. Big 6, 1925, 26	18
Studebaker Big 6, 1927	19
Studebaker Dict., 1928	14
Studebaker Pres. 6	19
Studebaker, Com., 1928	20
Studebaker Pres. 8, 1928	20
Studebaker Dic. 6&8, 1929, 30	15
Studebaker Com. 6	17
Studebaker Com. 8	14
Studebaker Pres. 8	21
Studebaker Six 54, 1931	12½
Studebaker Dict 8, 1931	18
Stutz 1926-31	28
Stutz LA, 1931	24
Velie 60, 1925, 26	19
Velie Std. 50, 1927, 28	19
Velie Spec. 60, 1927	20
Velie 77, 66-1928	20
Viking V-29, V-30	32
Whippet 96-A, 1929, 30	11½
Whippet 98-A, 1929, 30	15½
Wills Ste. Claire T6&W6	32
Wills Ste. Claire C&D-68	26
Willys Eight, 8-80, 1930	20
Willys Eight, 8-80D, '31	15½
Willys-Knight 4-65	22
Willys-Kni. 66, 1925, 26	23
Willys-Knight 66-A, 1927, 28; 66-8, 1929, 1930	21
Willys-Kni. 70, 1925, 26, 27, 70-B, 1929, 1930	17
Willys-Knight 56	14
Willys-Kni. 70-A, 1928	16
Willys-Knight 66-D	17½
Willys Six, 98-B, 1930	14
Willys Six, 97, 98-D, '31	13½
Windsor 6-69, 1929, 1930	12
Windsor 6-72, 6-77, 6-75	14
Windsor 8-82, 8-92, 8-85	16

# of Current Passenger Cars

Quarts of Anti-Freeze Required

(With Specific Gravity of Solutions)

TEMPERATURE EXPECTED (FAHR.)

Cooling System Capacity in Qts.	20°ABOVE ALCOHOL Sp. Gr. .978	20°ABOVE E. GLYCOL Sp. Gr. 1.030	10°ABOVE ALCOHOL Sp. Gr. .9700	10°ABOVE GLYCERINE Sp. Gr. 1.080	10°ABOVE E. GLYCOL Sp. Gr. 1.040	ZERO ALCOHOL Sp. Gr. .9600	ZERO GLYCERINE Sp. Gr. 1.108	ZERO E. GLYCOL Sp. Gr. 1.050	10°BELOW ALCOHOL Sp. Gr. .9500	10°BELOW GLYCERINE Sp. Gr. 1.120	10°BELOW E. GLYCOL Sp. Gr. 1.060	20°BELOW ALCOHOL Sp. Gr. .9400	20°BELOW GLYCERINE Sp. Gr. 1.130	20°BELOW E. GLYCOL Sp. Gr. 1.065	30°BELOW ALCOHOL Sp. Gr. .9200	30°BELOW GLYCERINE Sp. Gr. 1.144	30°BELOW E. GLYCOL Sp. Gr. 1.070
6	1¼	1	1¾	3	1½	2½	4	2¼	2¾	4½	2½	3	4¾	2¾	3¾	5½	3
7	1½	1¼	2¼	3½	1¾	2¾	4½	2½	3½	5¼	3	3½	5½	3¼	4¼	6½	3½
8	1½	1½	2½	4	2	3¼	5½	2¾	4	6	3¼	4	6½	3½	5	7¼	4
9	1¾	1¾	2¾	4½	2¼	3½	6	3	4½	7	3½	4½	7¼	4	5½	8	4½
10	2	1¾	3	5	2½	4	6½	3½	4¾	7½	4	5½	8	4½	6	9	5
11	2¼	2	3½	5½	2¾	4½	7¼	3¾	5¼	8½	4½	5¾	9	5	6½	10	5½
12	2½	2¼	3¾	6	3	4¾	7¾	4¼	5½	9	4¾	6½	9½	5½	7½	11	6
13	2½	2½	4	6½	3¾	5¼	8½	4½	6	10	5¼	7	10½	6	8½	11½	6½
14	2¾	2½	4¼	7	3½	5½	9	5¼	6½	10½	5½	7½	11	6½	9	12½	7
15	3	2¾	4½	7½	3¾	6	9¾	5½	7	11½	6	8	12	6¾	9½	13½	7½
16	3¼	2¾	4¾	8	4	6½	10½	5¾	7½	12	6½	8½	13	7¼	10	14½	8
17	3½	3	5¼	8½	4¼	6¾	11	6	8	13	7	9	13½	7½	10½	15½	8½
18	3¾	3¼	5½	9	4½	7¼	11¾	6¼	8½	13½	7¼	9½	14½	8	11	16	9
19	4	3½	5¾	9½	4¾	7½	12½	6½	9	14½	7½	10	15	8½	11½	17	9½
20	4	3½	6	10	5	8	13	7	9½	15	8	10½	16	9	12	18	10
21	4¼	3¾	6½	10½	5¼	8½	13½	7½	10	16	8½	11	17	9½	13	19	10½
22	4½	4	6¾	11	5½	8¾	14½	7¾	10½	16½	8¾	11½	17½	10	13½	20	11
23	4½	4¼	7	11½	5¾	9¼	15	8	11	17½	9¼	12	18½	10½	14	21	11½
24	4¾	4¼	7¼	12	6	9½	15½	8½	11¼	18	9½	12½	19	10¾	14½	21½	12
25	5	4½	7½	12½	6¼	10	16½	8¾	11½	19	10	13	20	11¼	15	22½	12½
26	5¼	4¾	7¾	13	6½	10½	17	9	12	19½	10½	13½	21	11¾	16	23½	13
27	5½	5	8¼	13½	6¾	11	17½	9½	12½	20	11	14	22	12	16½	24½	13½
28	5¾	5	8½	14	7	11¼	18¼	9¾	13	21	11¼	14½	22½	12½	17	25	14
29	5¾	5¼	8¾	14½	7¼	11¾	19	10	13½	22	11½	15	23½	13	18	26	14½
30	6	5½	9	15	7½	12	19½	10½	14	22½	12	15½	24	13½	18½	27	15
31	6¼	5¾	9½	15½	7¾	12½	20	10¾	14½	23½	12½	16	25	14	19	28	15½
32	6½	5¾	9¾	16	8	13	21	11¼	15	24	13	16½	25	14½	19½	29	16

To determine the amount of anti-freeze required for any car, find the cooling system capacity of the car in question in the list opposite. Then, by selecting the corresponding figure in the first column above, the amount of any anti-freeze for the temperature anticipated may be found by following the column across the page.

Crankcase Oil Capacities—Passenger Cars

For Tools and Equipment Needed in Lubrication Service, see List Page 145.

Make and Model	1926	1927	1928	1929	1930	1931
Auburn 6-63, 8	7	D	D	D	D	D
Auburn 6-66, 8-77, 88	N	6	7	N	D	D
Auburn 8-88, 115	8	8	8	8	D	D
Auburn 6-80, 6-85	N	N	6	6	6	D
Auburn 8-90, 8-95	N	N	N	7	7	D
Blackhawk L6	N	N	N	9	9	D
Blackhawk L8	N	N	N	8	8	D
Buick 6	5	D	D	D	D	D
Buick Master 6	6	D	D	D	D	D
Buick 120, 128, 121, 129, 40	6	6	6	6½	7½	D
Buick Std., 116, 50, 60	5	5	5	5½	6½	D
Buick 8-50	N	N	N	N	N	7
Buick 8-60	N	N	N	N	N	8
Buick 8-80, 8-90	N	N	N	N	N	9
Cadillac	8	8	8	8	8	D
Cadillac 452	N	N	N	N	10	10
Cadillac 370	N	N	N	N	N	9
Case Y, JIC	7	.	D	D	D	D
Chandler Big 6, Roy. 75	8	8	8	8	D	D
Chandler Spec. 6, 65	7	7	8	7	D	D
Chandler Std. 6	6	6	D	D	D	D
Chandler Roy. Std. 8	N	N	9	9	D	D
Chevrolet	4	4	4	5	5	5
Chrysler 62, 65, 75, 66, 70, 77	N	6	6	6	6	6
Chrysler 6-70, 72	6	6	6	D	D	D
Chrysler 4, 52	4	4	4	D	D	D
Chrysler 60	6	6	D	D	D	D
Chrysler 80, Imperial	8	8	8	8	8	8½
Chrysler Six, Eight	N	N	N	N	N	6
Cleveland	6	D	D	D	D	D
Cleveland 43	7	D	D	D	D	D
Cord L-29	N	N	N	N	8	8
Cunningham V-9	8	8	8	8	8	D
Dagmar	.	6	D	D	D	D
Davis 98, 99	N	8	8	D	D	D
Davis	.	6	D	D	D	D
De Soto Six	N	N	N	N	6	6
De Soto St. 8	N	N	N	N	7	D
Diana Str. 8	8	7½	7½	D	D	D
Dodge Bros. 4	5	5	5	D	D	D
Dodge Bros. Senior 6	N	7	7	7	7	D
Dodge Bros	N	N	6	6	6	D
Duesenberg	6	D	D	12	12	12
duPont	7	10	10	10	D	D
duPont G	N	N	N	12	12	12
Durant 40	N	N	N	4	D	D
Durant	5	D	D	D	D	D
Durant 55, 65, 60, 66, 6-14	N	N	6	6	6	6
Durant 75, 70, 6-17	N	N	7	7	7	7
Elcar 4	5	D	D	D	D	D
Elcar 6, 75-A	6	5	6	7	D	D
Elcar 8-82, 8-78	N	6	7	D	D	D
Elcar 8-90, 8-91, 120, 130, 140	8	8	8	8	8	D

Make and Model	1926	1927	1928	1929	1930	1931
Elcar 95, 96	N	N	N	8	8	D
Erskine Six 53	N	5	5	8	8	D
Essex Super 6	5½	6	6	6	5	5
Falcon Knight 12	N	8	8	D	D	D
Flint	6	D	D	D	D	D
Flint B-60	6½	6	D	D	D	D
Flint Z-18	5	5	D	D	D	D
Flint 80	N	6	D	D	D	D
Ford A	4	4	5	5	5	5
Franklin 145, 147, 15	5	5	6	6	6	6
Gardner 90, 95, 75, 85	N	8	8	D	D	D
Gardner 8, 80	7	7	D	D	D	D
Gardner 6	6	D	D	D	D	D
Gardner 120, 125, 130, 140, 150, 148, 158	N	N	N	8	8	8
Gardner 136	N	N	N	7	7	7
Graham, Std. 6, Sp. 6 and 8-20	N	N	N	N	6	6
Graham Spec. 8, Std. 8, Cus. 8, 8-34	N	N	N	N	8	8
Graham-Paige 612, 615	N	N	N	6	D	D
Graham-Paige 621	N	N	N	7	D	D
Graham-Paige 827, 837	N	N	N	8	D	D
Hertz	7	.	D	D	D	D
Hudson Great 8	9	9	9	7	8	8
Hupmobile A, S, L	6	6	6	6	6	6
Hupmobile E, M, C	8	8	8	8	8	9
Hupmobile H, U	N	N	N	N	12	12
Jewett	6	D	D	D	D	D
Jordan St. 8	7	D	D	D	D	D
Jordan R, E	N	5	5	5	D	D
Jordan, All Others	8	8	8	8	8	8
Kissel 55	11	10	D	D	D	D
Kissel 8-65, 6-70, 6-73	N	7	7	7	D	D
Kissel 8-80, 8-80S 8-95	N	N	11	11	11	D
Kissel 75, 8-90, 8-126	13	12	12	12	12	D
La Salle	N	8	8	8	8	8
Lincoln 8	10	10	10	.	10	10
Locomobile 48	6	6½	6½	6½	D	D
Locomobile 8-66, 8-70	6	6	8	D	D	D
Locomobile Jr. 8	7	D	D	D	D	D
Locomobile 80, 90, 86, 88	8	8	8	D	D	D
McFarlan TV	10	10	10	D	D	D
McFarlan St. 8	8	8	D	D	D	D
Marmon, Little	N	6	D	D	D	D
Marmon E-75, 68, 78 Eight 69, Roosevelt, 70	N	10	6	6	6	6
Marmon, Others	N	N	N	N	10	10
Moon A, 6-60	6	6	6	D	D	D
Moon 6-72	N	N	5	5	D	D
Moon 8-80	N	N	8	D	D	D
Nash Adv., Twin 8	8	8	8	8	8	D
Nash Lt. 6, Twin 6, 70	4	7	D	8	8	6
Nash Spec., 8-80	N	7	7	7	8	7
Nash Std. 6 Single 6, 60	N	N	5	5	5	5

Make and Model	1926	1927	1928	1929	1930	1931
Nash 8-90	N	N	N	N	N	10
Oakland 8	6	6	6	6	7	7
Oldsmobile	6	6	7	6	6	6
Overland 4, 93, 96A	6	5	5	5	D	D
Overland Whippet 96	N	6	6	D	D	D
Overland Whippet 93-A	N	7	D	D	D	D
Overland Whippet 98	N	N	5	5	D	D
Packard 6	7½	6	7	D	D	D
Packard 8, 626, 633, 726, 733, 826, 833	8½	7½	8	8	8	8
Packard 640, 645, 740, 745, 840, 845	N	N	N	10	10	10
Paige	6	6	6	D	D	D
Paige 6-70	8	.	D	D	D	D
Peerless 6-60, 6-61, 61-A	N	6	6	5	D	D
Peerless 6-80, 6-81	6	6	6	7	D	D
Peerless 6-72, 6-90, 6-91	9	9	9	9	D	D
Peerless 8, 69, Mas., Cus	10	10	10	10	10	10
Peerless Std. 8	N	N	N	N	N	8
Pierce Arrow 33, 36	10½	10½	10½	D	D	D
Pierce Arrow, Others	9	9	9	9	9	9
Plymouth	N	N	N	4	6	6
Pontiac	6	6	6	6	6	6
Reo T-6, A, C, 20, 25, 25N	7	6	6	6	6	6
Reo B, B2, Mate, 15	N	5	5	5	5	D
Reo, 30N, Roy. 35N	N	N	N	N	N	8
Revere	6	D	D	D	D	D
Roamer 8-80, 8-88	8	8	8	8	8	D
Roamer 8-78	8	7	7	7	7	D
Rolls Royce Si. Ghost	6	6	6	6	6	D
Rolls Royce Phantom	N	N	N	7	7	7
Roosevelt	N	N	N	6	D	D
Star	4	4	4	D	D	D
Star 6	6	5	D	D	D	D
Stearns Knight	10	10	10	10	10	D
Stearns-Kni. 75, 95, 6-80	8	.	8	D	D	D
Studebaker Big 6	8	9½	D	D	D	D
Studebaker, All Others	8	8	8	8	8	D
Studebaker Pres. 6	N	9½	9½	D	8	D
Studebaker Pres. 8	N	N	8	8	8	8
Studebaker Dict. 8	N	N	N	N	6½	6½
Studebaker Six 54	N	N	N	N	N	D
Stutz	12	12	12	12	12	12
Stutz LA	N	N	N	N	D	9
Velie	6	8	8	D	D	D
Whippet 96-A	N	N	N	5	D	D
Whippet 98-A	N	N	N	6	D	D
Wills St. Claire	10	8	D	D	D	D
Willys Eight 8-80, 8-80D	N	N	N	N	8	8
Willys Knight	N	8	8	8	8	8
Willys Six 98B, 97, 98D	N	N	N	N	7	7
Windsor 8-85, 8-92, 8-82	N	N	N	8	8	D
Windsor 6-69	N	N	N	6	5	D
Windsor 6-72, 6-75, 6-77	N	N	N	5	D	D

D—Discontinued.　　　　N—Not manufactured.

Engines—Commercial Vehicles

The Make and Model of Engine Used in Any Commercial Vehicle Can Be Determined Here By Looking Up the Name, Tonnage, and Year of the Vehicle in Its Alphabetical Order. For Abbreviations See End of List.

Make of Commercial Vehicle	Tonnage	Year	Make of Engine Used
Ace	1-1½	23	Midw. 412
Ace	2-3	23	Midw. 402
Ace	1½	24	Buda WU
Ace	3	24	Buda HU
Ace	2½	25-26	Buda EBU
Acme	¾-1½	18-23	Cont. NA
Acme	2½	22-23	Cont. B5
Acme	2	22-24	Cont. J4
Acme	2-3	22-24	Cont. K4
Acme	4½	22-25	Cont. L4
Acme	1½	24-27	Cont. 8R
Acme	3	24-25	Cont. 6B
Acme	4	24	Cont. B5
Acme	1-2	25-26	Cont. S4
Acme	6	25-26	Cont. B7
Acme	3	26	Cont. L4
Acme	5	26	Cont. B7
Acme 14	1	27-29	Cont. H8
Acme 16	1	27-28	Cont. 20L
Acme 16	1	29	Cont. 29L
Acme 24	1¼	27-28	Cont. S4
Acme 44, 54	2-2½	27-28	Cont. S4
Acme 56	2½	27-28	Cont. 6B
Acme 74	3½	27-28	Cont. L4
Acme 76	3½	27-28	Cont. 7T
Acme 90L, 104	4½-5	27-28	Cont. B7
Acme 36	1½	28	Cont. 8R
Acme 46	2	28	Cont. 15C
Acme 106	5	28	Cont. 8T
Acme 44, 340	2	29	Cont. S4
Acme 46, 341	2	29	Cont. 16C
Acme 52, 56 Spec.	2½	29-31	Cont. 18R
Acme 64	3	29-30	Cont. L4
Acme 66, 120	3	29-31	Cont. 20R
Acme 90L, 150	4½-5½	29-31	Cont. B7
Acme 151	5½	29-30	Cont. 15H
Acme 17	1	30-31	Cont. 29L
Acme 24	1½	30	Cont. S4
Acme 26, 47	1½-2	30-31	Cont. 16C
Acme 45D	3½	31	Her OXC
Acorn	2½	25-26	Buda ETU
Acorn	4	25-26	Buda YBUI
Acorn	1-1½	27-28	Cont. S4
Acorn	2-2½	27-28	Cont. S4
Acorn 50	2½-3	27-28	Buda ETU
Acorn	4-5	27-29	Buda YBUI
Acorn	1-2	28	Cont. 15C
Acorn	2½-3	28-29	Buda DW6
Acorn 20P, 30P, 40P	1-1½	29	Cont. 15C
Acorn 30, 40, 45	1½-2-2½	29-30	Cont. S4
Acorn 20P, 30P, 40P	1-1½-2	30	Cont. 16C
Acorn 50	3	30	Buda ETU
Acorn 50P	2½-3	30	Buda DW6
Acorn 70, 100	4-5	30	Buda YBU-I
Amer. La Fr. Chief	1½-2½	28-29	Buda DW6
Amer. La Fr.	Others	24-29	Own
Amer. La Fr. Big Chief	5	29	Buda GL6
Amer. La Fr.	5-15	29	Own
Amer. La Fr. 12R, 12, Ch.	3-3½-4	30-31	Own
Amer. La Fr. W.	3-3½-4	30-31	Own 2R
Amer. La Fr. Chief, Big Ch.	2-2½-5	30-31	Own
Amer. La Fr. V, Z6½, U7½	3-6½-7½	30-31	Own 5R
Amer. La Fr. W 2R	3½	30-31	Opt.
Amer. La Fr. 5, 7T	TT	30	Own 2R
Amer. La Fr. 10, 13, 15T	TT	30	Own 5R
Armleder	1½	25	Herc. OX
Armleder	1½	26	Buda KAJ
		26-27	Herc. OX
Armleder	2½	25	Buda EBUI
Armleder	2½	26-29	Cont. K4
		26-29	Buda EBUI
Armleder	3½-4	25-26	Buda YBUI
Armleder	3	26-29	Buda EBUI
Armleder 30B	1½	27-30	Buda KBU-I
Armleder 30-6	1½	27-29	Buda HS6
Armleder 40	2	27-28	Herc. OX
Armleder 50-6	2½	27-29	Buda BUS
Armleder 60-6	3	27-29	Buda BUS
Armleder 70	4, TT	27-30	Buda YBUI
Armleder 70-6	4	27-30	Buda BUS
Armleder 40-6	2	28-29	Buda HS
Armleder 50, 60	2½-3, TT	28-30	Buda EBU-J
Armleder 30	1½, TT	28-29	Herc. OX
Armleder 30, 40	1½-2, TT	30	Herc. OX
Armleder 30-6, 40-6	1½-2	30	Buda HS6
Armleder 55	2½	30	Cont. K4
Armleder 50-6, 60-6	2½-3	30	Buda BUS
Armleder 31	3	31	Her WXB
Armleder 41	4	31	Her WXC
Armleder 61	5	31	Her WXC2
Atterbury	2½-3	22-29	Cont. K4
Atterbury	3½-4	22-29	Cont. L4
Atterbury	1½-2	24-27	Buda KTU
Atterbury	5	24-29	Cont. B7
Atterbury 26B	1-1¼	27-29	Lyc. S
Atterbury 26G4	1½	27-29	Lyc. C4
Atterbury 26G6	1½	27-29	Lyc. 4S
Atterbury 24R	2	28	Buda KBU-I
Atterbury 27R6	2½	28	Lyc. TF
Atterbury 27C6	3	28-29	Lyc. TS
Atterbury 27R6	2½	29	Lyc. TS
Atterbury A6	1	30	Lyc. WRG
Atterbury K6, G6	1½-2	30-31	Lyc. 4SL
Atterbury H6	2½	30	Cont. 16R
Atterbury 22C	3	30	Cont. K4
Atterbury R6, 65	3	30-31	Cont. 18R
Atterbury 22D	4	30	Cont. L4
Atterbury C6, 70	3½-4	30-31	Cont. 20R
Atterbury 24E	5	30	Cont. B7
Atterbury A, K	1-1½	31	Lyc. WTG
Atterbury 45	2	31	Lyc. ASB
Atterbury 50, 60	2½-3	31	Lyc. ASD
Atterbury 100	5	31	Con. 21R
Autocar All	1¼-5-TT	18-31	Autocar
Available	1-2½	24-26	Herc. O
Available	3½	24	Herc. MU3
Available	5	24	Herc. T-3
Available	3½	25-26	Herc. L-3
Available	4	25-26	Herc. L
Available	5	25-26	Wau. EU
Available T-10	1	31	Cont. 18 E
Available T-13, T-20	1½-2	31	Cont. 16 C
Available T-23, T-27	2	31	Wau. MS
Available T-30	2½	31	Wau. ML
Available T-37	2½	31	Wau. MK
Available T-39, T-40V	3	31	Wau. SRL
Available T-34, T-44V	3	31	Wau. SRL
Available T-45	4	31	Wau. 6AB
Available T-50	5	31	Wau. 6RB
Bessemer	1-1½	24-25	Cont. N
Bessemer	2-2½	24-25	Hink. HA500
Bessemer	4	24	Cont. E-7
Bessemer	1½	25	Cont. J4
Bessemer	1½	25	Hink. 400
Bessemer	2½	25	Cont. K4
Bethlehem	All	18-27	Bethlehem
Betz	1	19-21	Buda RU
Betz	1	24-26	Betz
Betz	2½	24-26	Betz
Betz J3, F3	1-1½	29	Buda WTU
Betz J3-6	1	29	Buda HS6
Betz D-3	2½	29	Buda ETU
Betz D3-6	2½	29	Buda DW6
Biederman	1	25-28	Cont. 8R
Biederman	1¼-1½-2½	25-27	Cont. 6M
Biederman	3½	25-28	Cont. 6B
Biederman	5	26-27	Cont. 6B
Biederman	1-1¼-1½	28-30	Cont. 8R
Biederman	2½-3½	28-30	Cont. 6B
Biederman	5	28-30	Cont. 7T
Bridgeport	1½	21-25	Buda HU, HTU, WTU
Bridgeport	2-2½	21-25	Buda YU, YTU, ETU
Bridgeport	4	24-25	Buda YTU
Bridgeport	2	27	Buda WTU
Bridgeport	3	27	Buda ETU
Bridgeport G7		27	Buda BTU
Brinton	1½	24-26	Cont. N
Brinton	2½	24-26	Cont. C4
Brockway	1-1½-2	24-26	Wis. SU
Brockway	2-2½-3	24-26	Cont. K4
Brockway	3-3½-4	24-26	Cont. L4
Brockway	1¼	25-26	Wis. 6Y
Brockway	4	25-26	Cont. B5
Brockway	5	24-27	Cont. B7
Brockway Jr., CJB	1¼-1½	27-31	Wis. C
Brockway	1½	27-29	Wis. SU
Brockway EY, SY, EYW	1½	27-30	Wis. Y
Brockway S, E	1½-2	27-31	Wis. SU
Brockway SK	2	27	Cont. K4
Brockway	2-2½	27-29	Wis. Y
Brockway K	3	27-30	Cont. K4
Brockway KR, R	3	27	Cont. LR
Brockway KHB	3	27	Wis. HB
Brockway	4	27	Cont. LR
Brockway RT	4	27-28	Cont. B5
Brockway RH	4	27	Wis. H
Brockway BT	5½ up	27	Buda BTU
Brockway KW	3	28-30	Wis. H
Brockway	3-4	28-29	**Cont. L4**
Brockway	4-5	28-29	Cont. B7
Brockway BT	5½ up	28-30	Buda BBU
Brockway	1¼-1½	29	Wis. F
Brockway EN	1½	29	Wis. N
Brockway 75, 90	1¼-1½	30-31	Wis. C
Brockway 120, 140	2½-3½-4	30-31	Cont. 30B
Brockway T	5	30	Cont. B7
Brockway 290, 640-6	5½, TT	30-31	Cont. 16H
Brockway 60, 65	1	31	Cont.
Brockway 141-4	2½	31	Her.
Brockway 141-6	2½	31	Cont.
Brockway 170	2½	31	Cont.
Brockway 175, 190, 195	3-3½	31	Cont.
Brockway 220, 250	3½-4-5	31	Cont.
Brockway 640-6wh.		31	Cont.
Buck	1½-2	26-27	Cont. S4
Buck	1½-2	26	Cont. 8R
Buck	2½	26	Cont. K4
Buck	3-4	26	Cont. L4
Buck	5	26	Cont. B5
Buck	7½	26	Cont. B7
Buck 44	2	27	Cont. S4
Buck 46	2	27	Cont. 8R
Buck 64	3	27	Cont. L4
Buck 66	3	27	Cont. 6B
Buck 84	5	27	Cont. B5
Buck 86	5	27	Cont. 7T
Buck 94		27	Cont. B7
Buck 96		27	Cont. 14H
Chevrolet	All	18-31	Own
Chicago	1-2½	26-27	Herc. OX
Chicago	3½-5	26-27	Herc. L
Chicago	1½-3	27	Herc. OX
Chicago	3½-4	27	Herc. L
Chicago 70-7, 40C, 70C	4	27	Wau. EU
Chicago	1	28	Wau. XA
Chicago	1½-3	28-30	Wau. V
Chicago 20XL	2	28	Wau. XL
Chicago, 31B, 35C	3-3½	28-30	Wau. CU
Chicago	4	28	Wau. DU
Chicago 64D	5-5½	28-30	Wau. EU
Chicago 16A, 21A, 26A	1½-2½	29-30	Wau. XK
Chicago 32B, 36D, 46D	3-5½ up	29-30	Wau. KU
Chicago	4-5½ up	29	Wau EU
Chicago 66D	5½ up	29-30	Wau. 6AB
Chicago 15A, 20A, 25A	1½-2-2½	30	Wau. V
Chicago 56D	5½	30	Wau. AB
Chicago 1-18-A	2	31	Wau. 6TL
Chicago 1-24-A, 1-30-A	2½-3	31	Wau. 6ML
Chicago 1-50-B, 1-56-D (6 wh)	4	31	Wau. 6SRL
Clinton	1¼	25-26	Buda WTU
Clinton	2	25-26	Buda KTU
Clinton	3	25-26	Buda ETU
Clinton	4	25-26	Buda YTU
Clinton	5-7½	25-26	Buda BTU
Clinton	1¼-1½	27-28	Wau. V
Clinton	2	27-28	Wau. V
Clinton	2½-3	27-29	Buda DW6
Clinton 65	3	27-28	Wau. CU
Clinton	4	27-28	Wau. DU
Clinton	5	27-28	Wau. EU
Clinton 120SM	5½ up	27-28	Wau. EU
Clinton	3½	28-29	Buda BUS
Clinton 20B, 32	1¼-1½	29-30	Buda WTU
Clinton 45	2	29-30	Buda KTU
Clinton 65	3	29-30	Buda ETU
Clinton 90, 90M	4	29	Buda YTU
Clinton	5-5½ up	29-30	Buda BTU
Clinton 65-6	3	30	Buda DW6
Clinton 85-6	3½	30	Buda BUS
Clydesdale	2½-3	23-26	Cont. K4
Clydesdale	3½-4	23-25	Cont. L4
Clydesdale	5-7	23-25	Cont. B5

ENGINES—Commercial Vehicles—Continued

Make of Commercial Vehicle	Tonnage	Year	Make of Engine Used
Clydesdale 16, 10A	1-1¼	26-30	Cont. S4
Clydesdale	1¼	25-26	Cont. J4
Clydesdale	1½	25-29	Cont. 8R
Clydesdale 9	2	25-30	Cont. S4
Clydesdale	3½	25-29	Cont. B5
Clydesdale 2	5	26-30	Cont. B-7
Clydesdale	1¼-2	27-29	Cont. S4
Clydesdale 8	2½	27-29	Cont. K4
Clydesdale 6	3	27-29	Cont. L4
Clydesdale 6X	3	27-29	Cont. K4
Clydesdale 4X	3½	27-29	Cont. L4
Clydesdale 12, 14	1½	30	Cont. 8-R
Clydesdale 8, 6X	2½	30	Cont. K-R
Clydesdale 6, 4X	3-3½	30	Cont. L-R
Clydesdale 4	3½	30	Cont. B5
Coleman	5	26	Buda YBUI
Coleman	2½	27	Buda HS
Coleman 4	5	27-28	Buda YBUI
Coleman	5	27-28	Buda BUS
Coleman	2	28	Buda HS6
Coleman D-40	3	28-30	Buda DW6
Coleman C-25, C-25D	2-2½	30	Buda DW6
Coleman D 40X	3½-5	30	Buda BA
Coleman X100F, F75	5-5½	30	Buda GL
Coleman F75S	5½	30	Buda GF
Commerce	1	26	Cont. 7U
Commerce	1½-2	25-28	Cont. S4
Commerce	2½	25	Cont. 6B
Commerce	2½	26	Cont. K4
Commerce 8A	1	27-28	Cont. 11U
Commerce	3-3½	27	Cont. 6B
Commerce S11	1-1½-2	29-31	Buda HS6
Commerce	1½-2	29	Buda DS6
Commerce	2½-3	29	Buda BUS
Commerce 80, 60	2½-4	29-31	Buda BA6
Commerce 40Z, 40	1½-2½-2	30-31	Buda DS6
Commerce 60	1½-3	30	Buda BUS
Commerce 100, 100Z B	5-5½	31	Buda BA6
Concord	1-1½-2	24-25	Buda GBU
Concord	1½	26	Buda KBU
Concord	2	26-27	Buda GBU
Concord	2-2½-3	24-26	Buda EBU
Concord K	1	27-28	Buda WTU
Concord	3	27-28	Buda EBU
Concord	1¼	28	Buda HS6
Concord GX	2	28	Buda KBU
Concord GX6, JX6	2	28-31	Buda DW6
Concord JLX-6	3½	30-31	Buda BA6
Corbitt	2-2½	22-26	Cont. K4
Corbitt	3-3½-4	22-26	Cont. L4
Corbitt	1	24-25	Cont. N
Corbitt	1¼	25-26	Cont. S4
Corbitt	1½	25	Cont. J4
Corbitt	5	25	Cont. B7
Corbitt	5	26	Buda BTU
Corbitt 20	1	27-28	Cont. 20L
Corbitt 21	1	27-28	Cont. 11U
Corbitt 25	1½	27-28	Cont. S4
Corbitt	2	27-28	Cont. S4
Corbitt	2-2½	27-29	Cont. K4
Corbitt	3-4	27-29	Cont. L4
Corbitt 70	5	27	Buda BTU
Corbitt	1	28	Cont. 31L
Corbitt 620, 7B6	1¼-1½	28-31	Cont. 18E
Corbitt	1½-2	28	Cont. 15C
Corbitt 56	2½	28	Cont. 6B
Corbitt 70	5	28-29	Cont. B7
Corbitt 630, 9B6	1½-2	29-31	Cont. 16C
Corbitt	2½-3	29-30	Cont. 16R
Corbitt 66, 18W6	3-4	29-31	Cont. 18R
Corbitt 70S, 86	4-5	29-30	Cont. 20R
Corbitt 8B4	1½	31	Cont. W10
Corbitt 8B6, 10B6	1½-2	31	Cont. 25A
Corbitt 12W6, 12B6	2-2½	31	Cont. 16R
Corbitt 15B6, 15W6	2½-3	31	Cont. 16R
Corbitt 24W6	4-5	31	Cont. 20R
Corbitt 33W6	5-7	31	Cont. 21R
Day-Elder	1½-2	25-28	Buda WTU
Day-Elder	2-2½	25-28	Buda KBU
Day-Elder	3	25-26	Buda EBU
Day-Elder	4	25-26	Buda YBU
Day-Elder	5	25-26	Buda BTU
Day-Elder M	1	27	Cont. 11U
Day-Elder H	2	27	Buda WTU
Day-Elder HSM	2	27	Buda KBU
Day-Elder	2½	27	Buda KBU
Day-Elder	3	27-28	Buda EBU
Day-Elder	4	27-28	Buda YBU
Day-Elder	5	27	Buda BTU
Day-Elder	1-2	28-29	Cont. 16C
Day-Elder	3	28	Cont. 6B
Day-Elder	5	28-29	Buda BBU
Day-Elder	3	29	Buda DW6
Day-Elder	4	29	Buda BA6
Day-Elder MF, GF	1¼-1½	30	Cont. 16C
Day-Elder HF	2	30	Cont. 16C
Day-Elder HBF	2	30	Cont. 16C
Day-Elder JF, 160, 200	3-4	30-31	Cont. 18R
Day-Elder KF, 240	4-5	30-31	Cont. 21R
Day-Elder 60	1	31	Cont. 25A
Day-Elder 85, 110	1½-2	31	Cont. 16C
Day-Elder 130	2½	31	Cont. 16R
Day-Elder 285, 345	8-10	31	Cont. 21R
Day-Elder 402 302-3	12	31	Cont. 16H
Defiance	1½-2	24-26	Cont. J4
Defiance	3	24-26	Cont. K4
Defiance	1½	25-26	Wis. CAU
Defiance	1½	26	Cont. S4
Defiance FRT	1½	27	Defiance
Defiance EVT	2	27	Herc.
Defiance	1¼	28	Cont. 18E
Defiance	1½-2½	28	Cont. 15C
Defiance E2	2½	28	Cont. S4
Defiance	3½	28	Cont. 6B
Defiance RV-45	1¼	30	Cont.
Defiance TT50C	1½	30	Cont.
Defiance TT62T	2	30	Cont. S4
Defiance OX	2½	30	Cont. 6B
Defiance OXH	2½	30	Herc. WXC
Denby	2	24-26	Cont. J4
Denby	1-1½	24-29	Herc. O
Denby	3	24-28	Cont. K4
Denby 27	4	24-30	Cont. L4
Denby 210	5	24-30	Cont. B5
Denby	2½	26-29	Herc. O
Denby 41, 41A, 43	1-1½-2½	30	Herc. OX
Diamond T	¾-1	24-26	Herc. OX
Diamond T	1¼-1½	24-25	Hink. 700
Diamond T	1-2	26-28	Herc. OX
Diamond T	2½	24-25	Hink. 1400
Diamond T	2½	26	Hink. 1500
Diamond T	3½	24-25	Hink. 1500
Diamond T	3½	26	Hink. 200
Diamond T	5	24-26	Hink. B, B-2
Diamond T-U4	2½	27-28	Herc. K
Diamond T-U6	2½	27-28	Herc. L
Diamond T	3-3½	27-28	Herc. L
Diamond T-S2	5	27-28	Herc. G
Diamond T	7½	27-28	Herc. G
Diamond T	1	28-29	Cont. 18E
Diamond T-77	1¼-1½	28-29	Herc. WXA
Diamond T 302-3	2	28-31	Herc. W¾B
Diamond T-U56	2½	28	Herc. YXB
Diamond T	3-4	28-30	Herc. YXC
Diamond TS7	7½	28	Buda BTU
Diamond T550-1, T505-4	2½	29-31	Herc. WXC
Diamond T	5½ up	29	Wau. RB
Diamond T-215	1	30	Buda
Diamond T-200	1	30	Buda
Diamond T-290-1	1½	30-31	Herc. WXA2
Diamond T-1000	5	30	Herc. YXC2
Diamond T-1600, 6 Whl.	8	30-31	Herc. YXC3
Diamond T-2500, 6 Whl.	5½	30	Wau. 6RB
Diamond T-200	1	31	Buda H199
Diamond T-216	1	31	Herc. JXA
Diamond T-506	2½	31	Herc. WXC3
Diamond T-603	3	31	Herc. YXC
Diamond T-606	3	31	Herc. YXC2
Diamond T-750	4	31	Herc. YXC4
Diamond T-801 6wh.	4	31	Herc. YXC
Diamond T-1200 6-wh.	6	31	Herc. YXC2
Diamond T-1601	8	31	Wau. 6RB
Dixon	1½-2	23-25	Cont. J4
Dixon	1½-2	26	Cont. S4
Dixon	2½	23-26	Cont. K4
Dixon	3½-5	23-25	Cont. L4
Dixon	3½	26	Herc.
Dixon	5	26	Herc.
Dixon	2	27-29	Herc. OX
Dixon	3-3½	27-30	Herc. G
Dixon	5	27-30	Herc. G
Dodge	All	18-31	Own
Douglas	1½	20-29	Weid.
Douglas	2-3	20-29	Buda HTU
Douglas	1½	27-31	Buda WTU
Douglas	1½	27-31	Buda HS6
Douglas	2	27-31	Buda KBUI
Douglas	3	27	Buda EBUI
Douglas	3	27-31	Buda BUS
Douglas	5	27-31	Buda BBU
Douglas	2	28-31	Buda DW6
Douglas	3	28-29	Buda YBUI
Douglas	3-5	28-29	Buda BA6
Douglas 6 Whl.	5	29-31	Buda GL6
Douglas A6	1	31	Buda J214
Douglas F6	5	31	Buda GL6
Duplex	1-1½	23-29	Buda WTU
Duplex	1½	20-24	Hink. 400
Duplex	2	24-26	Hink. HAA
Duplex	3½	24	Buda ETU
Duplex	3-3½	25-26	Buda EBUI
Duplex GS	1½	27-31	Buda HS6
Duplex S	2	27-31	Buda DW6
Duplex FAC	3	27-31	Buda EBUI
Duplex SAC	3	27-31	Buda BA6
Duplex EF	3½	27-31	Buda EBUI
Duplex M5-7	5	29-31	Buda GL6
Duplex GF	1½	31	Buda WTU
Durant Com. Ch.	½	29-30	Cont.
Eagle	1¼	24-26	Buda WTU
Eagle	2	24	Buda GTU
Eagle	2-2½	25-26	Buda KTU
Eagle	3½	26	Buda YTU
Eagle 102	2	27-28	Buda WTU
Eagle 105	3	27-28	Buda KTU
Eagle 106	5	27-28	Buda YTU
Eagle 107	5½ up	27-28	Buda BTU
Eagle 10	1	28	Lyc. CT
Eagle 6-10, 6-25	1½-2½	30	Cont. 18E
Eagle 6-20	3	30	Herc. WXB
Eagle 6-30	4	30	Herc. WXC
Eagle 6-40	5	30	Herc. YXC
Fageol	1½	26-28	Wau. V
Fageol	2½-3	22-25	Wau. CU
Fageol	3½-6	18-26	Wau. DU
Fageol	2	24-26	Wau. FU
Fageol	3	26	Wau. CV
Fageol	2	24-26	Ha-S 360
Fageol	2½	27	Wau. V
Fageol 340	3	27-30	Wau. CU
Fageol 370	3	27	Wau. KL
Fageol 445	4	27-31	Wau. DU
Fageol 485	4	27-31	Wau. AB
Fageol 10-66, A-C	5½ up	27-30	Wau. AB
Fageol 645	5½ up	27-29	Wau. DU
Fageol 685	5½ up	27-29	Wau. AB
Fageol 135	2	28-30	Wau. XL
Fageol 250	2½	28-30	Wau. XK
Fageol 370-365	3	28-30	Wau. KS
Fageol	1¼	29	Wau. XA
Fageol 130	2	29-31	Wau. V
Fageol	3	29-31	Wau. KU
Fageol 106	1¼-1½	30-31	Wau. TS
Fageol 370, 470	3-4	30-31	Wau. SRL
Fageol 101	1½	31	Wau. XAK
Fageol 135	2	31	Wau. TL
Fageol 250	2½	31	Wau. MK
Fageol 10-66 A&C, 6wh.		31	Wau. AB
Fageol 6-66, 6 wh.	6	31	Wau. SRL
Fargo	2	19-22	Cont. NA
Fargo Packet	½-1	29-31	Own
Fargo Clipper	¾	29-31	Own
Fargo Freighter	1	31	Own
Federal	1-1½	19-26	Cont. J4
Federal	2-3	22-29	Cont. K4
Federal	3	26-27	Cont. 6B
Federal	2-3½	22-24	Cont. L4
Federal Knight	1	25-27	Federal-Knight
Federal Knight	1½-2	26-27	Federal-Knight
Federal	4	25-26	Cont. L4
Federal	5-6	25-26	Cont. B5
Federal Scout	1	27-29	Wau. X
Federal 51	2	27	Knight
Federal	4	27-29	Cont. L4
Federal X8	5½ up	27-29	Cont. B7
Federal F6	1	28	Cont. 30L
Federal A6, F7	1½-2½	28-31	Cont. 16C
Federal	2-2½	28-29	Wau. V
Federal UL7	3½	28-29	Cont. L4
Federal 2K6	3½	28	Wau. 6KS
Federal 3B6	3½	28	Cont. 6B
Federal LD	TT	28-29	Cont. K4
Federal HD	TT	28-29	Cont. L4
Federal 4FW	1	30	Wau. XA
Federal E6	1	30-31	Cont. 17E
Federal T10B, T10W	2½-3	30-31	Cont. 16R
Federal U6	3-3½	30-31	Cont. 18R
Federal 4C6-A, 4CAB	4-5	30-31	Cont. 20R
Federal X8	7½	30-31	Cont. B7
Federal X8R	7½	30-31	Cont. 21R
Federal D	1½	31	Cont. W10
Federal A6, A6TW	2½	31	Cont. 16C
Federal DSW	2½-3	31	Cont. W10
Federal E6SW	2½-3	31	Cont. 17E
Federal U6SW, U6SWAB	6	31	Cont. 20R
Federal 4C6SW	8	31	Cont. 21R
Fisher F.F.	1½	26-30	Cont. S4
Fisher Jr. Exp.	1	27	Cont. 20L
Fisher M. Exp.	2	27-28	Cont. S4
Fisher H. D.	2½	27-29	Cont. 6B
Fisher Jr. Exp.	1	28-30	Cont. 31L
Fisher Mer. Ex.	2	29	Cont. 15C
Fisher Mer. Ex.	2	30	Cont. 16C
Fisher Heavy Duty	2½	30	Cont. 16R
Fisher Super 6	3½	30	Cont. 18R
Fisher Super 6	3½	30	Cont. 20R
Fisher Std, Jr. B, Spc. X	¾-1½	31	Cont. W10
Fisher Std, Jr. B 15A	¾-1½	31	Cont. 17E
Fisher-Std. 16A, 20A	1½-2	31	Cont. 16C

ENGINES—Commercial Vehicles—Continued

Make of Commercial Vehicle	Tonnage	Year	Make of Engine Used
Fisher-Std. 17A, 23A	1½-2	31	Cont. S4
Fisher-Std. Mer EX	2-2½	31	Cont. 16C
Fisher-Std. 10AK	2	31	Cont. 17E
Fisher-Std. H.D.6	2½	31	Cont. 16R
Fisher-Std. T10W	2½-3	31	Cont. 16R
Fisher-Std. H.D.6	3	31	Cont. 18R
Fisher-Std. Super 6	3½-4	31	Cont. 18R
Fisher-Std. Super 6	3½-4	31	Cont. 18R
Fisher-Std. 100C, 150A (6 wh.)	5	31	Cont. 21R
Flint	1½	26	Herc. O
Ford	½-1	18-29	Own
Ford AA	1½	30-31	Own
Freeman DW 144	3	29-31	Buda DW6
Freeman BA	4-5	29-31	Buda BA6
Freeman GL	5½-7½	30-31	Buda GL6
Freeman DW 186	3-3½	31	Buda DW6
Freeman BASP	3½-4	31	Buda BA6
Freeman BAS	5½-7	31	Buda BA6
Front Drive	1½	20-26	Buda CTU
Front Drive	1½	27-29	Buda WTU
F. W. D., H, H4, BTL	1½-2	27-31	Wis. SU
F.W.D.	3	18-26	Wis. A
F.W.D.	3-3½	27-29	Own
F.W.D.	3½-5-5½ up	29-30	Wau.
F. W. D. H6	2	30	Wau. XL
F. W. D. HH6	2½	30	Wau. XL
F. W. D. B	3	30-31	Own A
F.W.D. BTL-6	2	31	Wau. MS
F.W.D. H6	2	31	Wau. MS
F.W.W. HH6	2½	31	Wau. MS
F.W.D. CU6	3½	31	Wau. SRS
F.W.D. SSU	4	31	Wau. SRL
F.W.D. M5	5	31	Wau. SRL
F.W.D. M7	7½	31	Wau. RB
F.W.D. X6	6TT	31	Own 331
Garford	1-1¼	20-23	Buda WU
Garford	2-4½	20-23	Buda HTU
Garford	3½	20-24	Buda YTU
Garford	¾	22-24	Buda MU
Garford	5-7½	22	Buda BTU
Garford	1½-2	24-28	Buda KTU
Garford	1½	25	Buda KBUI
Garford	1	26	Buda MU
Garford	2½	25-28	Buda EBUI
Garford	3½	25	Buda YBUI
Garford	4-7, TT	26-28	Buda BTU
Garford 20	1	27-28	Buda WTU
Garford 100	5	27	Buda BTU
Garford 150W		27	Buda BTU
Garford 20-6	1	28	Buda HS6
Garford 30-6	1½-2	28	Wis. Y
Garford 50-6, 60	2½-3	28-30	Buda BUS
Garford 50	TT	28	Buda EBU-I
Garford S11	1-2	29-31	Buda HS6
Garford 40	1½-2½	29-31	Buda DS6
Garford	3½-5½	29-30	Buda BA6
Garford 60, 80, 100, 100ZB	2½-5½	31	Buda BA6
Gen. Mot.	1	21-26	G. M. C.
Gen. Mot.	2-2½	21-26	G. M. C.
Gen. Mot.	3½-5	21-26	G. M. C.
Gen. Mot.	1-1½	27	G. M. C.
Gen. Mot.	1-1½	27-29	Buick Std.
Gen. Mot.	2-2½	27-28	G. M. C.
Gen. Mot.	2	27-29	Buick Master
Gen. Mot.	3½ up	27-28	G. M. C.
Gen. Mot.	½-1	28-29	Pontiac
Gen. Mot.	3	29	Buick
Gen. Mot.	5TT	29	Own 89
Gen. Mot.	½-1½	30	Pontiac
Gen. Mot.	¾-5½	30	Buick
Gen. Mot.	5	30	Own
Gen. Mot.	5½	30	Own RB-36
Gen. Mot. T11, T15, T17, T19	½-2	31	Pontiac
Gen. Mot. T25, T30, T42, T44 T60	1½-6½	31	Buick
Gen. Mot. T26	2½-3	31	Own 257
Gen. Mot. T51, T55, T61, T82 T90	4-7½	31	Own 331
Gen. Mot. T85, T95, T96	5-10	31	Own 468
Gotfredson	1-1½	24-28	Buda WTU
Gotfredson	2-2½	24-29	Buda KBUI
Gotfredson	3	24-29	Buda EBUI
Gotfredson RW84A	3½-4	24-30	Buda YBUI
Gotfredson	5	24-26	Buda BTU
Gotfredson A6	2	27	Buda BUS
Gotfredson 56	2½	27	Buda BUS
Gotfredson 66	3	27	Buda BUS
Gotfredson 86	4	27-28	Buda GL6
Gotfredson 100	5-5½ up	27-29	Buda BBU
Gotfredson 106	5-5½ up	27-29	Buda GL6
Gotfredson 36B	1½	28	Buda HS6A
Gotfredson	2-3-3½	28-29	Buda BA6
Gotfredson RB 24	1¼	29-31	Buda WTU
Gotfredson	1½	29	Buda HS6
Gotfredson	2½-3	29	Buda DW6
Gotfredson	1¼-5	30-31	Own
Gotfredson RW44, RW54	2½-3	30-31	Buda KBU-I
Gotfredson RW64A	3½	30-31	Buda EBU-I
Gotfredson RW104A	5½	30-31	Buda BBU
Gotfredson RW106A	5½	30	Buda GL6
Gotfredson RW56	3	31	Herc. WXC
Gotfredson RW66A	3-4	31	Herc. YXC
Gotfredson RW84A	4	31	Buda YBUI
Gotfredson RW86A	5	31	Herc. YXC3
Gotfredson RB34	1½	31	Buda H199
Gotfredson RB36	1½	31	Buda J214
Gotfredson RB46	2	31	Buda H298
Gotfredson RB56	2½	31	Buda K358
Gotfredson	3	31	Buda K381
Gotfredson	3½	31	Buda K428
Gotfredson	4½	31	Buda K479
Graham Bros.	1½	19-21	Cont. NA
Graham Bros.	All	22-27	Dodge
Gramm	1-1½	27	Lyc. CT
Gramm 263N	1-1¼	27	Cont. 8R
Gramm	1½-2	27	Cont. 8R
Gramm	2-2½	27	Lyc. C4
Gramm 564N	2½	27	Cont. 8R
Gramm	2½-3	27	Cont. 6B
Gramm	3-4	27-29	Herc. L
Gramm	4-5	27	Cont. 6B
Gramm 60	5-5½	27-31	Herc. G
Gramm	1-2	28-29	Lyc. S
Gramm	2½-5½	28-29	Lyc. TS
Gramm	TT	28-30	Lyc. TS
Gramm	TT	28-29	Herc. L
Gramm	TT	28-29	Herc. G
Gramm	5½ up	29	Lyc. TS
Gramm	5½ up	29	Herc. G
Gramm	5½ up	29	Cont. B7
Gramm B140	1½	30	Lyc.
Gramm	2-4	30-31	Lyc. TS
Gramm E-150	3	30	Lyc. ST
Gramm EY	3	30-31	Cont. 20R
Gramm AX4, BX4	1-1½	31	Cont. W-10
Gramm AX6, BX6	1-1½	31	Cont. 25A
Gramm B	1¾	31	Lyc. 4SL
Gramm CX4	2	31	Cont. W-20
Gramm CX6	2	31	Cont. 16C
Gramm C, D	2-2½	31	Lyc. ASD
Gramm GW, GY	4	31	Cont. 21R
Gramm HY	5	31	Cont. 16H
Gramm 60	5-5½	31	Lyc. TS
Gramm-Bern.	2	23-25	Cont. J4
Gramm-Bern. 10	1-1¼	24-31	Lyc. CT
Gramm-Bern.	1½	24-26	Lyc. C4
Gramm-Bern. 125	2½	26-30	Cont. S4
Gramm-Bern.	3½-4	24	Hink. HA200
Gramm-Bern.	3-4	24-26	Cont. L4
Gramm-Bern.	5	25-26	Cont. B2
Gramm-Bern.	1-1¼	27-29	Lyc. CT
Gramm-Bern. 115	1½-2	27-31	Lyc. C4W
Gramm-Bern.	2	27	Cont. 11U
Gramm-Bern. 30, 40	3-4	27-30	Cont. L4
Gramm-Bern. 50	5-5½	27-30	Cont. B7
Gramm-Bern. 115S	2	28-31	Cont. 15C
Gramm-Bern.	2½-3	28-30	Cont. K4
Gramm-Bern. C6	2½-3	28-31	Cont. 6B
Gramm-Bern. B6, B6X	2-2½-3	29-31	Cont. 16C
Gramm-Bern.	3½-4-5	29	Cont. L4
Gramm-Bern. J	1½	31	Buda 214
Gramm-Bern. K	2½	31	Buda H298
Gramm-Bern. D, DX	2½-3	31	Cont. 16R
Gramm-Bern. A	3-3½	31	Cont. 18R
Gramm-Bern. HV	5	31	Cont. 21R
Gramm-Kinc.	1-1½	26	Lyc. CT (4)
Gramm-Kinc.	1-1½	26	Cont. 8R (6)
Gramm-Kinc.	2-2½	26	Lyc. C4 (4)
Gramm-Kinc.	2-2½	26	Cont. 8R (6)
Gramm-Kinc.	3-4	26	Herc. L
Grass Premier	1-1½	25-29	Lyc. CT
Grass Premier	1½-2½	25-27	Lyc. C
Grass Premier	1½-2	25	Wau. V
Grass Premier	1½	26	Wau. FU
Grass Premier	2	26	Wau. V
Grass Premier	2½	25-26	Wau. CU
Grass Premier	2½	26	Lyc. C
Grass Premier	3½	25-26	Wau. DU
Grass Prem. 50	2	27	Lyc. C
Grass Premier 50-6	2	27	Lyc. TF
Grass Prem. 55	2½	27	Lyc. C
Grass Premier 52-6	2-2½-3	27-29	Lyc. TS
Grass Prem. 80	3-4	27-29	Wau. CU
Grass Premier 80-6	3-4	27-29	Wau. 6KU
Grass Prem. 90	4	27-28	Wau. DU
Grass Premier 90-6	4	27-29	Wau. 6D
Grass Premier	1-1½	28-29	Lyc. S
Grass Prem. 45	1½-2-3	28-29	Lyc. C4
Grass Premier 51-4	2½	28	Wis. X
Grass Premier 90-6	4-5	28-29	Wau. 6AB
Grass Premier	2½	29	Wau. CR
Grass Premier	2½	29	Wau. 6-KS
Grass Premier	5	29	Wau. ER
G-P 42-6	1½	30	Lyc. 4SL
G-P 47-6	2	30	Lyc. TH
G-P 48-8	2	30	Lyc. HD
G-P 57-6	2½-3½	30	Wau. KU
G-P 54-8	3	30	Own
G-P 100 S-W	5½	30	Wau. 6RB
G-P 52-6	3	30	Lyc. TS
G-P 57-4	2½	30	Wau. CR
G-P 92-4	5	30	Wau. ER
G-P 45-6, 45-8	2-3	31	Lyc. ASD
G-P 55-6	3-4	31	Lyc. ASD
G-P 55-8, 65-8	3-5	31	Lyc. HF
G-P 65-6	3½-5	31	Lyc. TS
G-P 75-6	4-6	31	Wau. SRL
G-P 75.8	4-6	31	Lyc. AEC
G-P 85-6	5-7	31	Wau. 6AB
G-P 85-8SW	8-10	31	Lyc. AED
G-P 95-65SW	10-12	31	Wau. 6RB
Guilder	1¼	25-26	Buda WTU (4)
Guilder	1¼-1½	25-26	Cont. 8R (6)
Guilder	1½	25	Buda KTU
Guilder	2	25	Buda GTU
Guilder E	2	26-30	Buda KBUI
Guilder	2¼	26	Cont. 6B
Guilder	3	25	Buda ETU
Guilder H	3	26-30	Buda EBUI
Guilder J	4-5	25-30	Buda YTU
Guilder	5-7	25-26	Buda BTU
Guilder B	1¼-1½	27-29	Buda WTU
Guilder B6, C6	1¼-1½	27	Cont. 8R
Guilder D6	2-2½	27-28	Buda HS-6
Guilder E	2	27-29	Buda KBUI
Guilder E6	2½	27	Cont. 6B
Guilder H	3	27-29	Buda EBUI
Guilder J, K5	4-5	27-29	Buda YTU
Guilder L6	5½-7	27-30	Buda BTU
Guilder	1½-2½	28-29	Buda HS6
Guilder E6	3	28-29	Buda DW6
Guilder B6	1½	30	Herc. WXA
Guilder C6	2	30	Herc. WXA2
Guilder E6	2½	30	Herc. WXB
Guilder H6, J6	3-4	30	Herc. WXC
Guilder K6	5	30	Herc. YXC2
Hahn	2-2½	23-28	Cont. K4
Hahn	3-5	23-26	Cont. L4
Hahn	1¼-1½	25-26	Herc. OX
Hahn	5	25-26	Cont. B5
Hahn	1-2	27-29	Herc. O
Hahn B2	1	27	Herc. OX
Hahn O	1½	27	Herc. OX
Hahn K	2-2½	27-28	Cont. K4
Hahn L	3	27-29	Cont. L4
Hahn M	4	27-29	Cont. L
Hahn R	5	27-29	Cont. B5
Hahn N	5½ up	27-29	Cont. B5
Hahn	1-1½	28-29	Buda HS6
Hahn	2	28-29	Buda HS
Hahn 56	2½	28-29	Cont. 6B
Hahn	2½	29	Herc. L
Hahn	3½	29	Herc. YXC
Hahn 37H, 37HL	2	30	Cont. 15C
Hahn 39H, 39HL	3	30	Cont. 16R
Hahn 47HB	3½-4	30	Cont. 18R
Hahn 17H, 67	5	30	Cont. 21R
Hahn 7H, 37HL	1	30-31	Cont. 29L
Hahn 17H	1½	30-31	Cont. 18E
Hahn 317H	1½	31	Cont. 16C
Hahn 37	2	31	Cont. 16C
Hahn 39	2½	31	Cont. 16R
Hahn 47B, 47D	3-4	31	Cont. 18R
Harvey WG	2½	25-30	Buda EBUI
Harvey WHC	3½, TT	25-30	Buda YBUI
Harvey	3, TT	27-29	Buda EBUI
Harvey WG6	2½	28-30	Buda DW6
Hawkeye	2	19-23	Buda HU, HTU
Hawkeye	1½	23	Buda CTU
Hawkeye	3½	21-24	Buda YU, YTU
Hawkeye	1	23	Buda MU
Hawkeye	1½	24	Buda WTU
Hawkeye	2½	24	Buda ETU
Hawkeye 36	1½	27-30	Buda HS6
Hawkeye 30	1½	27-30	Buda WTU

ENGINES—Commercial Vehicles—Continued

Make of Commercial Vehicle	Tonnage	Year	Make of Engine Used
Hawkeye 56	2½	27-28	Buda BUS
Hawkeye 50-48	2½	27-30	Buda EBUI
Hawkeye 50-60	2½	28-30	Buda DW6
Hawkeye 50-75	2½	29-30	Buda BA6
Hendrickson 5Q	2	27	Buda KTU
Hendrickson	2½-3	27-29	Buda ETU
Hendrickson U4	4	27-28	Buda YTU
Hendrickson V4	5	27-29	Wau. EU
Hendrick. SW10		27-29	Wau. EU
Hendrick. SW6		28-29	Buda BA6
Hendrick. SW10		28-29	Buda GL6
Hendrickson	3	29	Buda EBUI
Hendrickson	4	29	Buda YBUI
Hendrickson ST6, T-6	2½-3	30-31	Buda DW6
Hendrick. U-6	4	30-31	Buda BA6
Hendrickson SSW, MSW	5½	30-31	Buda BA6
Hendrick, SW	5½	30-31	Wau. EU
Hendrickson SW6	5½	30-31	Buda GL6
Huffman EH	1½	27-30	Herc. OX
Huffman EW	1½	27-30	Wis.
Huffman BC	2	27-30	Cont. S4
Huffman BH	2	27-30	Herc. OX
Hug 22	1½-2	28-31	Buda HS6
Hug	2-2½	25	Buda WTU
Hug 60	2	26-31	Buda WTU
Hug	2½	26	Buda KTU
Hug	1½-2	27-29	Buda WTU
Hug 30	2½	27	Buda HS6
Hug 81, 84	2½	27-30	Buda KBUI
Hug	3-3½	27	Buda DS6
Hug	2½-3½-5	28-31	Buda DW6
Hug 66, 67	2	30	Buda HS6
Hug 98, 6 whl.	8-10	30-31	Buda GF6
Hug C97, 6 Whl	5	30-31	Buda BA6
Hug 486	3 TT	30-31	Buda DW6
Hug 85, 85D	2½-3	31	Buda KBU-I
Hug 67	3	31	Buda H298
Hug 85-6, 85D6	3	31	Buda DW 6
Hug 97	5	31	Buda BA6
Indiana	1-2½	24-30	Herc. OX
Indiana	2½-3	26	Herc. L
Indiana	3½-4	24-26	Wau. DU
Indiana	5	25-26	Wau. EU
Indiana 611	1	27	Cont. 11U
Indiana 115	2-2½	27	Herc. O
Indiana 615	2-2½	27-30	Wis. Y
Indiana	3	27-28	Wis. HB
Indiana	3-4	27-30	Wis. H
Indiana	3-3½	27-28	Herc. L
Indiana 41	5	27-30	Herc. G
Indiana	1¼-1½	28	Cont. 12C
Indiana 127AW	3	28-31	Herc. K
Indiana 641	5½	28-30	Wis. Z
Indiana 200, 300	1½	30	Wis. F
Indiana	2½-4	30	Herc. L
Indiana 627W	3	30	WXC
Indiana	5½-TT	30	Cont. 16T
Indiana 60,64 74	1-1¼	31	Cont.
Indiana 11,11X	1¼	31	Herc.
Indiana 111	1½	31	Herc.
Indiana 89, 170	1½-2½	31	Cont.
Indiana 111XW	2	31	Herc.
Indiana 120,140, 141-6	2-2½	31	Cont.
Indiana 115A, 141-4	2½	31	Herc.
Indiana 615A	2½	31	Wis.
Indiana 175,190, 195	3-3½	31	Cont.
Indiana 627AW	3	31	Wis.
Indiana 220	3½-4	31	Cont.
Indiana 250, 290	5-7½	31	Cont.
Indiana 640	6 wheel	31	Cont.
International	¾-1-1½	31	Wau. XA
International	1¼-2	31	Lyc. CT
International	1¼-2	31	Lyc. 4SL
Internat'l AL-3	1½	31	Lyc. 4SLH
Internat'l A4, A5, A6	2-3	31	Own FBB
International	2½	31	HaS 151
Internat'l W2	3½	31	HaS 151
International	3½-5	31	HaS 152
Inter. Harv.	¾-1	21-26	Lyc. Spec.
Inter. Harv.	1-5	21-26	Int. Harv.
Inter. Harv.	1½	26	Lyc. Spec.
Inter. Harv. Del.	¾	27-28	Wau. X
Inter. Harv. S-24	1¼	27-30	Lyc. CT
Inter. Harv. S-26	1¼	27	Lyc. 4SG
Inter. Harv. 33	1½	27-28	Own 33
Inter. Harv. 34	1½	27-30	Lyc. CT
Inter. Harv. 36	1½	27	Lyc. 4SG
Inter. Harv. 43	2	27	Own
Inter. Harv.	2	27-30	Lyc. CT
Inter. Harv. SF46	2	27	Lyc. 4SG
Inter. Harv.	Others	27-29	Own
Inter. Harv.	3½-5	27	Own
Inter. Harv.	1¼-2	28-30	Lyc. 4SL
Inter. Harv.	¾-1	29-30	Wau. XA
Inter. Harv.	2½-TT	29-30	HaS 151
Inter. Harv.	3½-5, TT	29-30	HaS 152
Kearns	1	24	H-SP. 7000
Kearns	2	24-26	Herc. O
Kearns	3½-5	24-26	Wis. VAU
Kearns	1½	25-26	Herc. OX
Kearns	2½	25-26	Herc. L
Kelly-Springfld.	All	19-26	Kelly-Spr.
Kelly-Springfld.	2½	24-26	Cont. L5
Kelly-Springfld.	1½	25-26	Cont. K4
Kelly-Springfld.	1½-2	27-28	Herc. OX
Kelly-Springfld.	2½	27-28	Herc. K
Kelly-Springfld.	3½	27-28	Herc. L
Kelly-Springfld.	5-5½	27-28	Own
Kenworth	2½	23	Buda HTU
Kenworth	1½	23	Buda ITU
Kenworth	3½	23	Buda YTU
Kenworth	2	24-26	Buda KBU
Kenworth	3	24-29	Buda EBU
Kenworth	4	24-30	Buda YBU
Kenworth	1-1½	25-29	Buda WTU
Kenworth	5	25-29	Buda BTU
Kenworth	2	28-29	Buda HS6
Kenworth	2½	28	Buda KBUI
Kenworth G	3	28-29	Buda DW6
Kenworth	10	28-30	Wau. GU
Kenworth 145	2½-3	29-31	Herc. WXC
Kenworth	5½ up	29	Wau. GU
Kenworth 70, 85	1-1¼	30-31	Cont. 18E
Kenworth 100	1½	30	Buda HS-6
Kenworth 125	2	30-31	Herc. WXB
Kenworth 185	3	30-31	Herc. YXC
Kenworth 345,	10-6 whl.	30	HaS 155
Kenworth NT	TT	30	Buda GL-6
Kenworth 100	1½	31	Buda H260
Kenworth 165, 184	3	31	Herc. WXC2
Kenworth 205	3½	31	Buda GL6
Kenworth 220	3½	31	HaS 160
Kenworth 240	4	31	Herc. YXC3
Kenworth 345	6 wheel	31	HaS 160
Kenworth 385	6 wheel	31	HaS 175
Kimball	1½-2	19-24	Wis. EAU
Kimball	4	21-24	Wis. RAU
Kimball	3-4	21-24	Wis. VAU
Kimball	2½	24	Wis. WAU
Kimball	5	24	Wis. RBU
Kimball	2½	25-26	Wis. UAU
King-Zeitler	1-1½	24-25	Cont. J4
King-Zeitler	2½	24-25	Cont. K4
King-Zeitler	3½	24-26	Cont. L4
King-Zeitler	5	24-26	Cont. B5
King-Zeitler	1-2½	25-30	Cont. S4
King-Zeitler	2	26	Cont. 6M (6)
King-Zeitler	3	26-29	Cont. K4
King-Zeit. 22A	1	27	Cont. 20L
King-Zeit. 42A	2	27	Cont. 11U
King-Zeit. 62A	3	27-29	Cont. 6B
King-Zeitler 75	3½	27-29	Cont. L4
King-Zeitler 90	5	27	Cont. B5
King-Zeit. 22A	1	28	Cont. 31L
King-Zeitler	2	29-30	Cont. 15C
King-Zeitler 60	3	30	Cont.
King-Zeit. 62A	3	30	Cont. 18R
King-Zeitler 75	3½	30	Cont. 20R
Kissel	2-5	19-24	Kissel
Kissel	1-1½-2½	24-30	Kissel
Kissel	4	26-27	Kissel
Kissel	5	25-26	Buda BTU
Kissel	4-5	27-30	Wau. DU
Kleiber	1	23-26	Cont. J4
Kleiber	1½	23-26	Cont. K4
Kleiber	2½-3½-4	23-25	Cont. L4
Kleiber	2½-3	26	Cont. L4
Kleiber	3½-5	26	Cont. B5
Kleiber	5	24-25	Cont. B5
Kleiber	1½-2	27-28	Cont. 8R
Kleiber	2	27-31	Cont. K4
Kleiber	2½-3	27-30	Cont. L4
Kleiber Spec.	3	27-30	Buda BUS
Kleiber	3½	27-30	Cont. B5
Kleiber	5	27-30	Cont. B5
Kleiber	¾-1-1½-2	28-30	Cont.
Kleiber Speed	1½-2½	28-30	Buda
Kleiber Speed	3	28	Cont. 6B
Kleiber Speed	3	29-30	Cont. 18R
Kleiber	4	29-31	Buda BA6
Kleiber 22DD	5, 6-whl.	30-31	Cont. 18R
Kleiber 28DD	6 wheel	30-31	Cont. 20R
Kleiber 34DD	6 wheel	30-31	Cont. 21R
Kleiber 34DDT	6 wheel	30-31	Buda GF6
Kleiber 51	1½	31	Cont. 18E
Kleiber 64	2½	31	Cont. 16R
Kleiber 54, 56	2½	31	Buda
Kleiber 58	3	31	Cont.
Kleiber 65	3½	31	Cont. 18R
Kleiber 66	5	31	Cont. 21R
Krebs	1¼	24	Cont. J4
Krebs	2½-3-4	24-25	Cont. L4
Krebs	5	24-25	Cont. B5
Krebs	1½-2	25	Cont. S4
Krebs	1½-2	25	Cont. 8R
Krebs	2½	25	Cont. K4
Krebs	6	25	Cont. B7
LaFrance-Rep.	1	31	Lyc. WTG
LaFrance-Rep.	1¼-2	31	Lyc. 4SL
LaFrance-Rep.	2½-3	31	Lyc. TF
LaFrance-Rep.	3½	31	Lyc. TS
LaFrance-Rep.	4	31	Wau. SRL
LaFrance-Rep.	5½	31	Wau. 6AB
Lange	1½	24-28	Cont. J4
Lange	2½	26	Cont. J4
Lange	3	26	Cont. 6B
Lange	3½	26	Cont. L4
Lange K	1½	27	Cont. 11U
Lange G	2	27	Cont. J4
Lange E	2½-3	27-28	Cont. K4
Lange H	3	27-28	Cont. 6B
Lange F	3½	27-28	Cont. L4
Lange K	1½	28	Cont. 15C
Lange M	3-4	28-31	Herc. YXC
Lange H-1, F-6	3	28-30	Herc. YXB
Lange L	2	28	Buda DW6
Lange R	1½	29-31	Herc. WXB
Lange L	2	29-30	Herc. YXA
Lange T, TA	5	30-31	Herc. YXC2
Lange L	2	31	Herc. WXC
Lange O	2½	31	Herc. YXB
Lange H,F16	3-4	31	Herc. YXC
Larrabee	1-1¼-1½	23-26	Cont. 8R
Larrabee	2½-3½-5	23-25	Cont. L4
Larrabee	2¼	25-26	Cont. 6B
Larrabee	2½	26	Cont. L-4
Larrabee	3½	26	Cont. B-5
Larrabee A3	1	27-28	Cont. 11U
Larrabee	1½-2	27-28	Cont. 8R
Larrabee	2½	27	Cont. L4
Larrabee XH25	3	27-28	Cont. 6B
Larrabee X33S	2	28	Cont. 15C
Larrabee	1-1½	29-30	Cont. 16C
Larrabee	2-2½	29	Cont. 16R
Larrabee Deyo	3	29-31	Cont. 18R
Larrabee	3½-4	29-31	Cont. 20R
Larrabee 80	5	30	Cont. 21R
Larrabee 40, 50	2-2½	30	Cont. 15R
Larrabee 25, 35	1½-2	31	Cont. 16C
Larrabee 45	2½	31	Cont. 16R
Larrabee 65	3½	31	Cont. 18R
Larrabee 85	4½	31	Cont. 21R
Lehigh	2	26	Herc. OX
Lehigh	2	27	Herc. O
Lehigh 6S	2	27	Buda HS-6
LeMoon	1-1½-2	25-26	Cont. S4
LeMoon	2½	25-28	Cont. K4
LeMoon	3½	25-28	Cont. L4
LeMoon	5	25-26	Cont. B5
LeMoon	1-1½-2	28	Cont. 12C
LeMoon	2-3	28	Cont. 6B
LeMoon	3½	28	Cont. 8T
LeMoon	5	28	Cont. B7
LeMoon	1½	29-31	Cont. 16C
LeMoon	2-2½	29-30	Wau. 6XK
LeMoon	2½-5	29	Wau. 6KU
LeMoon	5½ up	29	Wau. 6AU
LeMoon	5½ up	29	Wau. 6KB
LeMoon H100	5½	30	Wau. 6AB
LeMoon HB10	1	31	Cont. 16C
LeMoon HB21, 26	2-2½	31	Wau. 6MS
LeMoon HB27	2½	31	Wau. 6KU
LeMoon HB30	3	31	Wau. 6SRL
LeMoon HB46, 56, 60	6 wheel	31	Wau. 6SRL
LeMoon HWB100	6 wheel	31	Wau. 6AB
LeMoon HWB120	6 wheel	31	Wau. 6RB
Luedinghaus	3½-5	23-25	Wau. DU
Luedinghaus	1	24	Wis. X
Luedinghaus	1½	24-26	Wau. Y
Luedinghaus	2½	24-25	Wau. RU4R
Luedinghaus	5	24-26	Wau. EU
Luedinghaus	1	25	Wau. X
Luedinghaus	1-1½	26-30	Wau. V
Luedinghaus	2½	26-30	Wau. FU
Luedinghaus	3½	26-30	Wau. DU
Luedinghaus	5	27-30	Wau. EU
Maccar	3-4	25-28	Wis. VAU
Maccar	1¼	24-26	Wis. SU
Maccar	2	24-25	Wis. TAU
Maccar	2-2½	26-29	Wis. Y
Maccar	2-3	24-25	Wis. UAU
Maccar	5	24-31	Wis. RBU
Maccar	1¼-2	27-31	Buda HS
Maccar 64	3	27	Wis. UAU
Maccar	3-4	27-28	Buda BUS
Maccar 96	4	27	Wis. H6
Maccar 64	3-4	28-30	Buda YBUI
Maccar	3-4-5½	29-31	Buda BA6
Maccar 66	3	30	Buda BA
Maccar 36A	1½	31	Buda H-298
Maccar 40A	2	31	Buda 298
Maccar 56	3	31	Buda DW6
Maccar 66A, 86A	4-5	31	Herc. YXC3
Maccar 126	6, 6 whl.	31	Buda BA6
Mack	All	18-31	Mack
Master	1-1½	24-29	Buda WTU
Master	2½-3½	24-25	Buda EBU
Master	5-6	24-26	Buda YBU
Master	1½	25-29	Buda KBUI
Master	2½-4	25-29	Jackson
Master	3	26	Buda EBUI
Master	3½	26-28	Buda YBUI
Master	5½	26	Buda BTU
Master 41A	2½	27-29	Buda ETU
Master 61	3½	27-29	Buda BTU
Master	5	27-28	Buda BTU
Menominee	1-2	23-29	Wis. SU
Menominee	2½	25-27	Wis. TAU

ENGINES—Commercial Vehicles—Continued

Make of Commercial Vehicle	Tonnage	Year	Make of Engine Used
Menominee HX	2	28-29	Wis. W
Menominee N	3½	28	Wis. HB
Menominee	2½	29	Wau. 6XK
Menominee	3½	29	Wau. 6KS
Moreland	2-2½	22-26	Cont. K4
Moreland	3½-5	20-21	Cont. B2
Moreland	3-3½	22-26	Cont. L4
Moreland	5	22-26	Cont. B5
Moreland	1-1½	24-26	Herc. OBX
Moreland	1½-2	27	Cont. 11U
Moreland	2½	27-28	Cont. 6B
Moreland	4	27	Cont. 6B
Moreland SX4	6	27	Buda B5
Moreland SX6	6	27	Cont. 14T
Moreland TX4	10	27	Cont. B7
Moreland TX6	10	27	Cont. 14H
Moreland	1½-3	28-31	Cont. 16C
Moreland HD6	4-5½	28-30	Herc. YXC
Moreland SB6-10		28	Cont. 16T
Moreland TD6-10		28	Cont. 15H
Moreland Ace	1¼	30	Cont. 34L
Moreland	3½-5½	30	Herc. WXC
Moreland SD6	5½	30	Herc. YXC2
Moreland TD6	5½	30	Cont. 15H
Moreland Ace	1¼	31	Cont. 18E
Moreland B7	3	31	Herc. WXB
Moreland E7, EX-7	3½-5	31	Herc. WXC2
Moreland BD7	4	31	Herc. WXB
Moreland ED7	6 wheel	31	Herc. WXC2
Moreland HD, SD7	6 wheel	31	Herc. YXC3
Moreland TD7	6 wheel	31	Cont. 16H
Nash	1-2	24-27	Nash
Nash	2	24-25	Buda HU
National	2	24-26	Wau. Y
National	3	24-26	Wau. CU
National	3½	24-26	Wau. DU
National	1½-2-2½	27-28	Wau. V
National	3-3½	27-28	Wau. CU
Nelson Le Moon	1	18-23	Cont. NA
Nelson Le Moon	1½-2½	18-23	Cont. C4
Nelson Le Moon	3-5	18-23	Cont. E, E4
Nelson Le Moon	5	19-24	Cont. B2
Nelson Le Moon	1-3½	24	Cont. J4, L4
Nelson Le Moon	1½-2½	24	Cont. K4
Netco	2	22-24	Cont. K4
Netco	2½-3	22-25	Cont. L4
Netco	4	24-25	Hink. 200
Netco AB	1½-2	31	Wau. 6TL
Netco E, J	3½-5	31	Wau. 6SRL
Noble	3½-5	20-26	Buda YTU
Noble	1-1½	24-27	Buda WTU
Noble	2	24-26	Buda GTU, KTU
Noble	2½-3	24-26	Buda ETU
Noble 124	1¼	27	Buda WYU
Noble	2	27-31	Buda HS6
Noble 154	2	27	Buda KBU
Noble 156	2½	27	Buda DS6
Noble 164	3	27-28	Buda EBU
Noble 166	3	27-28	Buda BUS
Noble 184	4	27-28	Buda YBU
Noble 134	1½	28	Buda KBU
Noble 156	2½	28-30	Buda DW6
Noble	3	29-30	Buda BA6
Noble 156C	3	31	Cont. 18R
Noble 166C	4	31	Cont. 20R
Northway	All	22-26	Northway
Ogden	3½	22-26	Cont. L4
Ogden	1-1½	24-25	Cont. J4
Ogden	1½	26	Cont. J4
Ogden	2½-5	24-25	Cont. B5
Ogden	1	25-27	Cont. N
Ogden	2½	25-27	Cont. K4
Ogden	5	26	Cont. B-5
O. K.	3½	20-25	Buda YTU
O. K.	1	23-25	Buda MU
O. K.	1-1½	24-25	Buda WTU, CTU
O. K.	2-2½	24-25	Buda ITU, ETU
O. K.	1¼	27	Buda WTU
O. K.	1½	27	Buda CTU
O. K.	2	27	Buda KBUI
O. K.	2½	27	Buda EBUI
O. K. Oil	2½	27	Buda YBUI
O. K.	3	27	Buda BUS
O. K.	3½	27	Buda YTU
Old Reliable	1½	20-23	Wis. SU
Old Reliable	3½	23-24	Wis. VAU
Old Reliable	5	21-24	Wis. RAU
Old Reliable	2½	24	Wis. EAU
Old Reliable	5½-7	24	Wau. P
Old Reliable	2½	27	Wis. VAU
Old Reliable	3½	27	Wau. DU
Old Reliable	5	27	Wau. EU
Omort 200, 250	2-2½	31	Herc. OX
Omort 25	2½	31	Herc. WXB
Omort 300	3	31	Herc. OXC
Omort 30, 3005	3	31	Herc. WXB
Omort 35	3½	31	Herc. WXC
Oneida	1½-2	27-28	Herc.OX
Oneida C9	2½	27-28	Herc. K
Oneida D9	3½	27-28	Herc. L
Oneida E9	5	27-28	Herc. G
Oneida BB9	2	28	Cont. 12C
Oneida CC9	3	28	Wis. HB

Make of Commercial Vehicle	Tonnage	Year	Make of Engine Used
Oneida	1½	29-30	Cont. 16C
Oneida	2-2½	29-30	Wau. V
Oneida	2½	29	Wau. CK
Oneida	3	29-30	Wau. 6XL
Oneida	3½	29-30	Wau. DU
Oneida	5	29-30	Wau. GU
Oneida	TT	29-30	Wau. 6KU
Oneida	TT	29-30	Wau. 6AB
Oneida C9	3	30	Wau. CR
Oshkosh	2	24-28	Wis. SU
Oshkosh	2½	24-28	Herc. O, OX
Oshkosh	3	26-28	Herc. L
Oshkosh	5	26-28	Wau. EU
Oshkosh	4	24-25	Wau. O
Oshkosh Exp.	1½-2	27-30	Herc. OX
Oshkosh	2	28	Wis. Y
Oshkosh	3½-4	28-30	Herc. YXC
Oshkosh R6	2	30	Herc. WXB
Oshkosh L, M	2½-3	30-31	Herc. WXB
Oshkosh H, S	3-3½	30	Herc. G
Oshkosh H6	3	30	Herc. YXB
Oshkosh FHX	5	30	Herc. YXC
Oshkosh H	3½	31	Herc. YWC
Oshkosh HC	3	31	Herc. WXC2
Oshkosh HXC	4	31	Herc. YXC2
Oshkosh FHX	5	31	Herc. YXC3
Overland	½	24-26	Overland 91
Packard	All	18-23	Packard
Paige	1¾	31	Own
Parker	1	24	Buda WTU
Parker	1½	24	Wis. SU
Parker	2	24	Wis. TAU
Parker	2½	24	Wis. UAU
Parker	5	24	Wis. RBU
Parker	1-1½	27	Wis. SU
Parker	2½	27	Wis. UAU
Parker	3½	27	Wis. VAU
Patriot	1½-2-3	20-25	Hink. 400
Patriot	1	24	Cont. N
Patriot	1¼	25-26	Buda WTU
Patriot	1½	26	Buda WTU
Patriot	2-2½	26	Hink. 400
Patriot	3	25-26	Hink. 200
Pendell	1½	26-27	Herc.
Penn	2	22	Buda MU
Penn	1	24	Penn
Penn	2	23-26	Buda WTU, WU
Penn	1	25-26	Overland
Penford	2	25-28	Himico
Pierce-Arrow	All	18-31	Pierce-Arrow
Pontiac	½	26-27	Pontiac
Rainier	6	22-24	Cont. B2
Rainier	¾-1	24-26	Cont. N
Rainier	1¼	24-25	Cont. J4
Rainier	1½	26	Cont. K4
Rainier	2-2½	24-26	Cont. K4
Rainier	3½	24-25	Cont. L4
Rainier	3½-6	26	Cont. B7
Rainier	5½-7	24-25	Cont. B5
Rehberger	2	25-29	Buda KTU
Rehberger	3-4	25-30	Buda YBU
Rehberger	3	25-26	Buda BUS
Rehberger	5	25-30	Buda BTU
Rehberger A-6	2	30	Wau. XK
Relay	1½-2½	28-31	Buda DS6
Relay	2-3	28-31	Buda DW6
Relay	2½-3½	28-30	Buda BUS
Relay	1-2	29-31	Buda HS6
Relay	3½-4	29-31	Buda BA6
Relay 15AA,AB	¾-1	31	Cont. 17E
Relay 100B	5	31	Buda GF6
Relay 100C	5	31	Cont. 21R
Relay 50SW	5, 6 whl.	31	Buda DW6
Relay 60SW	7, 6 whl.	31	Buda BA6
Reo	1¼-2	22-29	Reo
Reo	½	28	Cont.
Reo	½-1	29-30	Cont. 16E
Reo	1½-3	29-31	Own
Reo Jr. 15	½	31	Cont. 19E
Reo DF	1	31	Own
Republic	¾-2	21-24	Lyc. LC
Republic	1½-2	23-25	Cont. J4
Republic	2½-3	23-25	Cont. K4
Republic	3½-4-5	23-25	Cont. L4
Republic	1½	24	Lyc. K
Republic	1¼-1½	25-30	Lyc. CT
Republic	2	26-28	Cont. J4
Republic	2	26-30	Wau. V
Republic	3	26-29	Cont. K4
Republic	3	26	Wau. FU
Republic	4½	26-30	Wau. CU
Republic	5	26-30	Wau. DU
Republic	2-2½	27-30	Lyc. 4SG
Republic 60	2½	27-30	Lyc. TF
Republic 25W	3	27	Wau. F4
Republic 30	4½	27-29	Cont. L4
Republic	1¼-2½	28-30	Lyc. 4SL
Republic	2-2½	28-30	Lyc. C4
Republic 25W	3-3½	28-30	Wau. CU
Republic 65	2½-3½	28-30	Lyc. TS
Rowe	2-3	19-25	Wis. TAU
Rowe	5	20-23	Wis. VAU
Rowe	5	24-26	Wis. RAU
Rowe	3	25	Wis. UAU
Rowe	4	25	Wis. VAU
Rugby	½-¾-1	28-30	Cont.
Rugby 614, 615	½-1½	31	Cont. 22A
Ruggles	¾	23-25	H-SP. 30

Make of Commercial Vehicle	Tonnage	Year	Make of Engine Used
Ruggles	1¼-2½	24	Ruggles
Ruggles	1	25-26	Lyc. CT
Ruggles	1¼-3	25-26	Herc. O
Ruggles 18	1¼	27-28	Lyc. CT
Ruggles 18	1¼	27	Lyc. SG
Ruggles	1½-3	27-28	Herc. OX
Ruggles 25	2	27-28	Lyc. TF
Ruggles	1¼-1½	28	Lyc. 4SG
Rumely	1½	24-27	Buda CTU
Safeway	4	27-28	Cont. 15H
Sandow	1	24	Cont. N
Sandow	1-1½	24-26	Buda WTU
Sandow	2	24-26	Herc. O
Sandow	2½	24-26	Buda ETU
Sandow	3½	24-26	Buda YTU
Sandow	5	24-26	Buda BTU
Sandow	1-2	25-28	Herc. OX
Sandow	2½	27	Herc. K
Sandow M	3½	27	Herc. L
Sandow L	5	27	Herc. G
Sandow JS6	2	28	Herc. HS6
Sandow	2½	28	Buda EBU-I
Sandow M	3½	28	Buda YBU-I
Sandow L	5	28	Buda BTU
Sanford	1-1½	22-27	Cont. 8R
Sanford	2½-3½	24-26	Cont. L4
Sanford	3½-5	24-26	Cont. B7
Sanford	2	27	Cont. 8R
Sanford	3	27	Cont. 6B
Sanford	4-5	27	Cont. B7
Sanford	¾-1	29-30	Cont. 31L
Sanford	1¼	29-30	Cont.
Sanford	1½	29	Cont. 18C
Sanford	2-2½	29-30	Cont. 16C
Sanford	3-4	29	Buda
Sanford AX	1¾	30	Cont. 18E
Sanford F	3	30	Cont. 16R
Sanford FL	3	30	Buda 16R
Sanford O	4	30	Cont. 18R
Saurer	All	24-29	Saurer
Schacht	1-1½-2	23-28	Wis. SU
Schacht	2-2½-3	24-25	Wis. UAU
Schacht	3½-4-5	25	Wis. VAU
Schacht	7	25-26	Wis. RBU
Schacht	2½	26-27	Wis. UAU
Schacht	2½-5	26-27	Wis. RCU
Schacht	7½	27	Wis. RBU
Schacht HS	2	28	Wis. Y
Schacht	2½-5TT	28-29	Wis. XK
Schacht	All others	28-30	Wau. KU
Schacht	1½-2½	29-30	Cont.
Schacht	2	29	Wau. XL
Schacht	5-5½ up	29-31	Wau. SRL
Schacht	3, TT	29-30	Wau. XK
Schacht 40	5	30	Herc.
Schacht	TT	29	Wau. SRL
Schacht	1½-2½	31	Cont. 16C
Schacht	3	31	Herc. WXB
Schacht	4	31	Herc. WXC
Schacht	5	31	Herc. WXC2
Selden	5	23-25	Cont. B5, B6, B7
Selden	1¼-2	24-28	Cont. 8R
Selden	1¼	26	Herc. O
Selden	2-2½	23-25	Cont. J4, K4
Selden	2-2½	26	Cont. K4
Selden	2¼	26	Cont. 6B
Selden	3-3½	24-25	Cont. K4,L4
Selden	1½	25	Herc. O
Selden	4	25-27	Cont. B5
Selden	5	26-28	Cont. B7
Selden	1¼-2	27-29	Cont. S4
Selden	3-4	27-29	Cont. 6B
Selden	3-3½	27	Cont. L4
Selden	1¼-2½	28-30	Cont. C15
Selden	4-5	28	Cont. 8T
Selden	1½	29-31	Cont. 18E
Selden	5	29	Buda GF6
Selden 7	1	30-31	Cont. 29L
Selden 39C, 39	3	30-31	Cont. 16R
Selden Roadmaster 47CB1	3½	30	Cont. 18R
Selden 67C	5	30	Cont. 21R
Selden 77	5½	30	Cont. 16H
Selden 317, 37	1½-2	31	Cont. 16C
Selden 47D	4	31	Cont. 18R
Service	1	26-28	Buda WTU
Service	1¼-1½	24-25	Buda WTU
Service	1½	24	Buda GBUI
Service	2-2½-3	24-26	Buda EBUI
Service	3½-6	24-26	Buda YBUI
Service	1½	25-26	Buda KBUI
Service	2½-TT	27-28	Buda EBUI
Service	1-1½-2	29-31	Buda HS6
Service	1½-2-2½	29-31	Buda DS6
Service	2½-3	29-30	Buda BUS
Service	3½-5½	29-30	Buda BA6
Service 81	3½-TT	27-28	Buda YBUI
Service 103	5-TT	27-28	Buda YBUI
Service 61	2½	28	Buda DW6
Service 60	2½	31	Buda BA6
Service All	3-5½	31	Buda BA6
Signal	2½-3½	23	Cont. K4
Signal	5	23	Cont. L4
Signal	7½	23	Cont. B5
Signal	1	23-24	Cont. J4
Signal	1½-2½	24	Cont. K4
Signal	3½	24	Cont. L4

ENGINES—Commercial Vehicles—Continued

Make of Commercial Vehicle	Tonnage	Year	Make of Engine Used
Signal	5	24	Cont. B5
Standard	2½-3½	23-30	Cont. K4, L4
Standard	5-6	23-26	Cont. B5
Standard	1-1¼-1½	24-26	Cont. N, J4
Standard	5-7	27-31	Cont. B5
Standard	3½-5	28-29	Cont. L4
Star 4	½	26-27	Cont. Spec.
Star 6	1	27	Cont.
Steinkoenig A	1½	27	Wau. V
Steinkoenig	2½	27	Wau. CU
Sterling	All	24-29	Sterling
Sterling	1¼	29-30	Cont. 18E
Sterling	3	29-30	Own 6XK
Sterling DB9-64	1½-2	30-31	Cont. 16C
Sterling DB11-64	2-2½	30-31	Wau. 6XL
Sterling DW13-65	3-3½	30-31	Wau. 6XK
Sterling	3½-4½	30-31	Wau. 6XK
Sterling	4-4½	30-31	Wau. 6KS
Sterling DB7-64	1½	31	Cont. 18E
Sterling EW, DC 23	5½-7	31	Wau. 6KS
Sterling DW	5-6	31	Wau. 6SRL
Sterling EW, DC26	7-8½	31	Wau. 6SRL
Sterling DC27	7-8½	31	Wau. 6HB
Sterling EC	8½-12	31	Wau. 6AB
Stewart	1	25-26	Lyc. CT
Stewart	1¼	26	Lyc. (6)
Stewart	1½-2	25-26	Lyc. C
Stewart	2½	25-26	Buda HTU
Stewart	3½	25-26	Buda YTU
Stewart Buddy	¾-1	27-28	Cont.
Stewart 16-25X	1¼-2	27-30	Lyc. CT
Stewart	1½-2	27	Lyc. C
Stewart 19	2½	27-30	Lyc.
Stewart 22	3½	27-30	Lyc.
Stewart 16X	1¼	28-30	Lyc.
Stewart 24-25	1½-2	28-29	Lyc. C4
Stewart 24X	1½	28-30	Lyc.
Stewart 18X	2-2½	28-30	Lyc. TF
Stewart	3-4	28-30	Lyc. TS
Stewart	2	29-30	Lyc. 4SL
Stewart	2	29	Lyc. C4W
Stewart Buddy	¾-1	29-30	Lyc.
Stewart	2	29	Lyc. 4
Stewart	3½-5½	30	Wau.
Stewart 30, 40	1-1½	31	Lyc. AFE
Stewart 30X	1	31	Lyc. WSG
Stewart 40X	1½	31	Lyc.
Stewart 34X, 28X	1½-2	31	Lyc. 4SL
Stewart 29S, 32X	2-2½	31	Lyc. ASA
Stewart 35X	3	31	Lyc. ASD
Stewart 31X, 27X	5-6-7	31	Wau. 6SRL
Stoughton	1¼-2-3	25-26	Stoughton
Stoughton	1½	25-26	Wau.
Stoughton	1½-2-3	27	Stoughton
Studebaker	¾	28	Studebaker
Stud. Erskine	½	29	Cont. 9F
Studebaker	¾-3½	29-31	Own
Super-Truck	2½	20-26	Wis. EAU, TAU
Super-Truck	5	20-23	Wis. A, AI, AU
Super-Truck	3-3½	24-26	Wis. VAU, UAU
Super-Truck	5	24-26	Wis. RAU
Traffic	1½-4	20-25	Cont. NA
Traffic	1½-2-3	25	Cont. N4
Traffic	2-3½	26-27	Cont. S4
Traffic 6000	3	27	Cont. S4
Transport	1-1½	20-25	Cont. NA
Transport	2½-3	20-23	Cont. C4
Transport	3½	20-23	Cont. E, E4
Transport	1½-5	22-25	Buda WTU, YTU
Transport	2-3½	24-25	Buda KTU, ETU
Traylor	1-1½	20-27	Buda WU
Traylor	2½-3	20-24	Buda HTU
Traylor	5-6	20-27	Buda YTU
Traylor	3	25-27	Buda ETU
Twin City	2	22-23	Buda IU, ITU
Twin City	2-2½-3½	24-28	Twin City
Union	4	19-26	Wis. VAU
Union	1½	24	Cont. 6M
Union	2½	24-26	Wis. TAU
Union	1½	25-26	Wis. Y
United	1¼-3	25-26	Herc. OX
United	2	26	Wis. Y (6)
United	5	25	Herc. L
United	5	26	Herc. G
United 16	1	27-30	Wau. X
United 20	1¼	27-30	Herc. OX
United	1¼-2	27-30	Herc. OX
United 40	2	27	Wis. Y6
United	2-4	27-30	Herc. OX
United 70	3½	27-30	Herc. L
United 100	5-5½	27-30	Herc. G
United 16C6	1	28	Cont. 20L
United 20C6	1¼	28	Cont. 12C
United 30C6	1½	28-30	Cont. 8R
United	2-2½	28-30	Cont. 6B
United 70C6	3½	28-30	Cont. 8T
United	1	29-30	Cont. 29L
United	1¼	29-30	Cont. 16C
United States	1½-2	20-23	Cont. NA
United States	1¼-2	22-26	Buda WTU
United States	3	21-26	Hink. 400
United States	4-5	24-26	Hink. 200, 230
United States	5-7	24-25	Buda ATU
United States	7	26	Buda ATU
United States U	1	27-30	Buda WTU
United States L	1½	27-30	Buda HS
United States N	1½	27-30	Buda
United States 21	2	27-30	Buda WTU
United States 20	2	27-30	Buda HS
United States 31	2½-3	27-30	Buda EBUI
United States 30	3	27-30	Buda DS
United States 40	3½-4	27-30	Buda YBUI
United States	3	28-29	Buda DW
United States	5½	28-30	Buda BTU
U. S. T.	5½ up	29-30	Buda BTU
Valley Disp.	1¼-2½	27-30	Herc. OX
Valley	3-4	28	Herc. K
Valley	1¼-3-4	29	Herc.
Velie	1½	20-23	Cont. NA
Velie	2½	23	Herc. CU3
Velie	¾-1½	28-29	Velie
Victor	1¼-2½	25-28	Herc. O, OX
Victor	3½-5	25-26	Cont. L4
Victor	6	25-26	Cont. B5
Victor 70	2½	27-28	Herc. K
Victor 80	3½	27-28	Herc. L
Victor 90		27-28	Herc. G
Victor 25	1¼	28-29	Cont.
Victor	1½	29	Cont. 18E
Victor	2-2½	29	Herc. WXB
Victor	3-3½	29	Herc. WXC
Wachusett	1	25-29	Cont. 8R
Wachusett	1½	25-29	Cont. J4
Wachusett	2	25-26	Cont. K4
Wachusett	2½	25-29	Cont. L4
Wachusett K	1½	27-29	Cont. K4
Walter, 4.W.D.	5	21-23	Wau. MU7
Walter, 4.W.D.	2-3	23	Wau. FU, DU
Walter	TT	28	Walter
Walter	TT	29-31	Own 6
Ward LaFrance	2½-5	20-23	Wau. RU, DU, EU
Ward LaFrance	2½-5	24-25	Wau. CU
Ward LaFrance	2½-3½	26	Wau. CU
Ward LaFrance	7	25	Wau. EU
Ward LaFrance	5-7	26	Wau. EU
Ward LaFrance	2½	27-29	Wau. V
Ward LaFrance	3	27-30	Wau. CU
Ward LaFrance	3½-4	27-30	Wau. DU
Ward LaFrance	3½	27-29	Wau. 6QL
Ward LaFrance	5	27-30	Wau. EU
Ward LaFrance	5-5½ up	27-29	Wau. 6AL
Ward LaFrance	5½ up	27-30	Wau. GU
Ward LaFrance	5-5½ up	27-29	Wau. 6AL
Ward LaFrance	3	28	Wau. 6KL
Ward LaFrance	4	29	Wau. 6KW
Ward LaFrance	2-2½	30	Wau. XK
Ward LaFrance	3-4	30	Wau. KU
Ward LaFrance	5-7½	30-31	Wau. AB
Ward LaFrance	3-3½	30-31	Own
Ward LaFrance 25R	3	31	Wau. 6ML
Ward LaFrance 30RU	3½	31	Wau. 6MK
Ward LaFrance	4-5-7	31	Wau. SRL
Whippet 96A	½	30	Own
Whitcomb	5-10	31	Wis. Z
White	All	20-31	White
Wichita	1½	26	Wau. BUX
Wichita	3	26	Wau. CU
Wichita 20	1½	30	Wau. V
Wichita 6-50	2	30	Wau. 6XL
Wichita 6-60	2½	30	Wau. 6XK
Wichita 6-90	3½	30	Wau. 6KU
Wichita 6-21	1½	31	Wau. MS
Wichita 6-50	2	31	Wau. 6XK
Wichita 6-60	2½	31	Wau. ML
Wichita 6-95	3½	31	Wau. SRL
Wilcox	1	20-23	Buda CTU
Wilcox	3½	20-26	Buda YTU
Wilcox	1	24-26	Buda WTU
Wilcox	1½-2½	24-26	Wilcox
Wilcox	5	24-26	Buda ATU
Willys-Knight	Taxi	23-25	Own
Willys-Knight	1-2½	28-30	Own
Willys-Knight	1½	31	Own 87
Willys Six C-101	1½	30	Own
Willys Six C-113	½	31	Own C-113
Willys Six C-131	1½	31	Own C-131
Winther	1½-2½	25-26	Wis. SU
Winther	3	25-26	Wis. UAU
Winther	3½	25-26	Wis. VAU
Winther	5	25-26	Wis. RAU
Winther	5-7	25-26	Wis. RBU
Wisconsin	1½	25-26	Wau. Y
Witt-Will	1½-2	19-26	Cont. C4
Witt-Will	1-2½-3	22-26	Cont. K4
Witt-Will	1½-2	26-31	Cont. S4
Witt-Will	2½-3	27-30	Cont. K4
Witt-Will	3-3½	27-30	Cont. L4
Witt-Will	4-5½	24-30	Cont. B5
Witt-Will	1½	29	Cont. 15C
Witt-Will P6	2	29	Cont.
Witt-Will S6	2½-3	29	Cont. R18
Witt-Will	1½-2	30-31	Cont. 16C
Witt-Will	2-2½	30-31	Cont. 16R
Witt-Will	3-3½	30-31	Cont. 18R
Witt-Will	3½-5	29-31	Cont. 20R
Witt-Will R4X	4	31	Cont. 21R
Witt-Will R55	5½ up	31	Cont. 21R
Woods	1¼	27	Buda WTU
Woods 31B4	1½	27	Buda WTU
Woods 31B6	1½	27	Buda HS6
Woods 36W4	2	27	Buda KBUI
Woods 51W4	2½	27-29	Buda KBUI
Woods 56W4	3	27	Buda YTU
Woods 20B6	1¼	28-29	Cont. 31L
Woods 40B6	2	28-29	Buda HS6A
Woods 52W6	3	28-29	Buda DW6
Woods 60W4	3½	28-29	Buda YBU
Woods	1¼	29	Buda WTU
Woods 32	1½	30	Herc. WXA2
Woods 41	2	30	Herc. WXB
Woods	2½-3	30-31	Herc. WXC
Woods 61	3½	30	Herc. G
Woods 90	4	30	Herc. YXC2
World	1½-2½	28	Cont. 15S
World	1½-3	30	Lyc.
World D-60	1	30	Lyc. 4SL
World DA-60	1	31	Lyc. WTG
World	1½-2	31	Lyc. 4SL
World	2-2½	31	Lyc. GR
World	3-4-5	31	Lyc. HD
Yellow Cab	¾-1-1½	22-25	Cont. V4, V7
Yellow Cab	¾	26-27	Cont. V7
Yellow Cab	1	26-28	Cont. V4
Yellow Coach	2½-4	28	Own
Yellow Knight	1	27-28	Yell. V.

ABBREVIATIONS

Cont.—Continental
G.M.C.—General Motors Corp.
HaS—Hall Scott
Herc.—Hercules
Hink.—Hinkley
H-SP—Herschell-Spillman
Int. Harv.—International Harvester
Kelly-Spr.—Kelly-Springfield
Lyc.—Lycoming
Midw.—Midwest
Spec.—Special
TT—Tractor Truck
Wau.—Waukesha
Weld.—Weldley
Wis.—Wisconsin
Yell.—Yellow Sleeve

Engines—Motor Bus

The Make and Model of Engine Used in Any Motor Bus Can Be Determined Here By Looking Up the Name, Model, Year, etc., of the Vehicle in Its Alphabetical Order.

Make and Model of Bus	Seating Capacity	Year	Make of Engine Used
ACF All	..	27-28	Hall-S
ACF 30, 40	29-34	30-31	Hall-S 160
ACF 45, 64	38	30-31	Hall-S 175
ACF 85	21	31	Own WXC-2
ACF 216	25	31	Own WXC-3
Ace C	30	25	Cont 6B
Ace C	30	26	Cont 7T
Acme 116-118	16-18	26-29	Cont 6B
Acme 121	21-22	26-29	Cont 7T
Acme 120	29	30-31	Cont 20R
Amer. La Fr., 4R	25-29	26	Own 4R
Bridgeport	29	27	Buda BUS
Brockway FB	18-20	24-30	Wisc SU
Brockway EB4	18-20	26-30	Wisc Y
Brockway H	22	25-26	Cont 6B
Brockway H	22	20-27	Wisc HB
Brockway I	40	26	Wisc Z
Brockway JI	29	26-27	Wisc H
Brockway J3-6	25	24-26	Cont SB
Brockway EB4	20	25	Wisc SU
Brockway JB	16	28-30	Wisc C
Brockway SW	22-24	28-30	Wisc Y
Brockway ZL	30	28	Wisc Y
Brockway H	25-28	28-29	Wisc H
Brockway JBF	16-29	29	Wisc F
Brockway JI	32	29	Wisc H
Brockway H	22	30	Wisc HB
Brockway JI-2	30	30	Wisc H
Brockway 90B	16	30	Cont 16C
Brockway 17B	..	31	Cont 27B
Brockway 90B	..	31	Cont 27B
Brockway 120B	21	31	Cont 30B
Brockway 140B	..	31	Cont 30B
Brockway 170B	..	31	Cont 33B
Brockway 195B	..	31	Cont 33B
Brockway 220B	..	31	Cont 34B
Clinton 65B	30	25-26	Buda EBU
Clinton 65B	30	26-28	Wauk CU
Clinton 65BS	35	25-26	Buda YBU
Clinton 65BS	35	26-27	Wauk DU
Clinton 65BS	35	27-28	Wauk 6Q
Corbitt SB 630	15	28	Cont 15C
Corbitt SB 620	15	29	Cont 18E
Corbitt SB 630	18	29	Cont 16C
Corbitt SB 646	21	29	Cont 16C
Day-Elder 20	..	26-27	Buda KBU
Day-Elder 25	25	25-26	Cont 6B
Day-Elder 30	30	25-27	Buda BUS
Day-Elder 20,30	20	27-28	Cont 6B
Day-Elder 20,30	30	28-29	Buda BA6
Day-Elder 30A	30	31	Cont 21R
Denby 36	30	30-31	Cont 6B
Dodge Bros. All	16-21	29-30	Own
Douglas	21	27-28	Buda DS6
Douglas	21	29-31	Buda DW6
Douglas	29	31	Buda BA-6
Fageol (St. Car)	22-29	24-27	Hall-S 50
Fageol	26-29	24-27	Hall-S 75
Fageol Dbl. Deck	58	26	Hall-S 75C
Fageol 503 (Kent)	29	27-29	Hall-S
Fageol Par. Car	26	28-29	Wauk
Fageol St. Car	29	28-29	Wauk
Fageol Dbl. Deck	58	28-29	Wauk
Fargo CG2R-172	..	31	Own CG-2
Federal S 26	17-21	26	Knight 64
Federal BB6, UB6	25	25-26	Cont 6B
Fifth Ave. J	29-25	24-29	Yell EZ
Fifth Ave. L	53-55	24-27	Yell EZ
Fifth Ave. I, L	55	28-29	Yell EZ
Flxible 81-H2	14	31	Buick St. 8
Flxible 81-H3	17	31	Buick St. 8
Garford KB	17-21	25-29	Wisc Y
Garford 51D	29	26-27	Buda BUS
Garford CB	29-30	26-29	Wisc Z
Gary 45B	40	26	Buda GL6
Gotfredson 56-B-60	60	26-27	Buda GL6
Gotfredson 50-B-29	29	26	Buda BUI
Gotfredson 50-B-29	29	27	Buda GL6

Make and Model of Bus	Seating Capacity	Year	Make of Engine Used
Graham Bros. All	16-21	25-28	Dodge
Gramm N	15	27	Cont 8R
Gramm R	21	27	Cont 6R
Gramm 363N	15	28-29	Lyc S
Gramm RA	17	28-29	Lyc TS
Gramm 30	21	28-29	Buda BA-6
Gramm 31	25	28-29	Buda BA-6
Gramm EYB	21	31	Cont 20R
Gramm GYB	25	31	Cont 21R
Gramm HYB	35	31	Cont 16H
Gramm Kincaid	15	25-26	Cont 8R
Gramm Kincaid	18-25	25-26	Cont 6R
Guilder CB20	18	31	Herc WXB
Guilder EB26	21	31	Herc WXC
Guilder GB35	25	31	Herc WXC
Guilder GB36	30	31	Herc YXC
Hahn KB	27	26-28	Cont 6B
Hahn LB	35-36	26-28	Cont 14H
Hahn DB, OB	18-20	26-28	Herc OX
Hahn OB	18	29-30	Cont 6B
Hahn KB	27	29-30	Cont 16T
Hahn LB	36	29-30	Cont 15H
Hahn 39C	21	31	Cont 16R
Hahn 47B, 47D	25-29	31	Cont 18R
Indiana 17B, 90B	..	31	Cont 27B
Indiana 120B	21	31	Cont 30B
Indiana 140B	..	31	Cont 30B
Indiana 170, 195B	..	31	Cont 33B
Indiana 220B	..	31	Cont 34B
Int. Harv. 54-M	24	26	Buda
Int. Harv. S L	16	25-26	Lyc KB
Int. Harv. 54-L	18	25-26	Own Spec.
Int. Harv. 54-M	24	25	Own Spec.
Int. Harv. 54-H	30	25	Own Spec.
Int.Harv.54-H-1	34	25-26	Own Spec.
Int. Harv.54-DD	60	25	Own Spec.
Int. Harv. 15	16	27-28	Lyc 4-SG
Int. Harv. 15	16	29	Lyc 4-SL
Kenw'th BU 21	21	28-29	Buda BA6
Kenw'th BU 29	21	28-29	Buda GL6
Kissel 55	20	26	Own 55
Kissel	20	26-27	Own CB6
Kissel	21	28-29	Own CB6
Kissel 55	21	30-31	Own 55
Larrabee X42	17	26	Cont 8R
Larrabee XH4	25-30	26	Cont 6B
Lar'bee X2, L10	16	23-26	Cont 8R
Lar'bee XH3, 31	21	25-27	Cont 6B
Larrabee XH31	21	28-29	Cont 6B
Maccar H3	40	26	Buda BUS
Mack AB	25-29	23-27	Own
Mack (Sed) AB	24	25-27	Own AB
Mack AL	25-29	27-29	Own AL
Mack AB	25-29	28-29	Own AB
Mack City AB	29-33	31	Own AB
Mack City BC	29-33	31	Own BC
Mack Inter. BC	25	31	Own BC
Mack City BK	33-40	31	Own BK
Mack Inter. BK	29	31	Own BK
Menominee T	16-23	24-30	Wisc Y
Menominee T	25	26	Wisc H
Menominee T	21	27	Wisc H
Menominee T2	17-21	28-30	Wisc HB
Menominee T	16-21	31	Wauk ML
Moreland RC	16	26	Herc OBX
Moreland EC	20	24-26	Cont K4
Moreland AC	25	24-26	Cont L4
Pierce-Arrow Z	25-30	25-26	Own Z
Pierce-Arrow Z	25-30	28-29	Own
Rehberg'r B-2-3	25	25-28	Buda BUS
Rehberger B4	29-31	29-30	Buda BA6
Relay KBR	19-21	30-31	Buda DS6
Reo GB	21	28-31	Own
Reo FB	12	29	Own
Reo Sedan	16	26-27	Own T6
Reo (St.Car) W	21	25-27	Own W
Republic 81	15-20	26-27	Lyc C-4
Ruggles 70	25	25-26	Own
Ruggles 60	20	26	Wisc Y
Ruggles 60	19	26-27	Lyc
Ruggles 65-70	25-29	26-28	Wisc
Ruggles 60	19	28	Lyc
Safeway 63-4	29	26	Cont 12T
Safeway 66	61	26-27	Cont 14H
Safeway 36-37	27	25	Cont 6B
Safeway 55	27	25-26	Cont 14H

Make and Model of Bus	Seating Capacity	Year	Make of Engine Used
Safeway 64	29	27	Cont 12T
Safeway 6 Wh. 64	29	28	Cont 12H
Safeway 6 Wh. 66	63	28	Cont 15H
Schacht O	27	25-26	Wisc Z
Schacht	25	26-27	Buda
Schacht N	25	27-28	Buda BA-6
Schacht 60	25	29	Wauk KU
Selden Pace	18	26-28	Cont 8R
Selden R'dm'str	21-25	26-28	Cont 6B
Selden Century	29	26	Cont 14H
Selden 42	21-25	29-30	Cont 18R
Selden 39C	21	31	Cont 16R
Selden 47B, 47D	25-29	31	Cont 18R
Sterling GB2	29	24-26	Wauk CU
Sterling GB4	29	26	Own DU
Sterling GB6	29	26-27	Own 6Q
Sterling GB6	..	25-26	Wauk 6A
Stewart 20	25	26	Cont 6B
Stewart N	29	27	Cont
Studebaker N	15	26-27	Own
Studebaker A	20	26-27	Own
Studebaker D	21	26-27	Own
Studebaker 75, 75 Jr., 76 Spec.	15-22	28-29	Own
Studebaker All	15-25	30-31	Own 8
Til'ng-Stev's*X	33	26	Wauk 6Q
Til'ng-Stev's*W	27	26	Wauk 6A
Til'ng-Stev's*Z	64	26	Wauk 6A
Twin City DW	25	26-28	Own TW
Twin Coach	40	28	Wauk
Twin Coach	37-40	29-30	Own
Twin Coach	21	30	Own WXG
Twin Coach	37-40	31	2-Own WXE
Twin Coach	20-24	31	Own WXO
Union GW	30	26	Wisc Z
Union EC	19	26	Wisc Y & H
Uppercu Sig. 220-80	30	25-26	Cont 6B
Uppercu S, S2	32	26-29	Wauk 6A
Ward LaFr. 3B	25	25-27	Wauk DU
Ward LaFr.4B6	25	27-29	Wauk 6QL
Ward LaFr.4B6	25	28-29	Wauk 6HB
Ward LaFr.29B	29	29	Wauk 6AB
White 54	25-29	23-27	Own
White 54, 54A	25-35	28-30	Own 1A1
White 53, 50B	25-29	28-31	Own GRB
White 65	14-21	30	Own 3AI
White 65, 65A	14-21	31	Own 3A
White 613	..	31	Own 4A
White 54	25-35	31	Own 1A
White 54A	38-41	31	Own 1A
W.M.C. GX	29-38	28-29	Wauk 6AB
W.M.C. NL	21	30	Wauk 6-KU
W.M.C. NTB, GN	29-38	30	Wauk 6-RB
Yellow XZ	17-21	26-28	Own X
Yellow Z & YZ (Double)	67	24-28	Own Z & YZ
Yellow Y & YZ (Single)	29-67	25-28	Own Y & YZ
Yellow Y	29	28-30	Own Y
Yellow Z	67	28	Own Z
Yellow W	17-23	29	Cad 341
Yellow Z-200, 230, 240	29-39	29-30	Own YZ
Yellow W	17-21	30	Cad 343
Yellow Coach 365, 366	17-21	31	Cad 353
Yellow Coach 378	38	31	Own YZ
Yellow Coach 600	29	31	Own YZ
Yellow Coach 603	21	31	Cad 353
Yellow Coach 605	16	31	Buick 50-60
Yellow Coach 607	21	31	Buick 50-60
Yellow Coach 610	38	31	Own 616
Yellow Coach 612	21	31	Buick 50-60
Yellow Coach 614	29	31	Own 616
Yellow Coach 617	38	31	Own 616

Cad—Cadillac
Cont—Continental
Hall-S—Hall-Scott
Herc—Hercules
Her-S—Herschell-Spillman

Hink—Hinkley
Lyc—Lycoming
Midw—Midwest
R & V K—R. & V. Knight
TT—Tractor Truck

Wauk—Waukesha
Wisc—Wisconsin
WSM—W. S. Morgan
Yell—Yellow Sleeve

Serial Numbers—Passenger Cars

The Information Here Enables You to Determine the Year the Automobile Was Built So You Can Fix Its Value for Trade-In Purposes or to Secure Proper Replacement Parts. The Model Designation Also Is Shown and Where You Can Locate the Serial Number Plate.

Prices Given Are for Standard Touring or Sedan Models

AUBURN—Auburn Automobile Co., Auburn, Ind.

Year	Model	Cyls.	Price	Serial Numbers
1925	6-43	6	....	54501-54976
1925	6-66	6	$1395	2555501-2556750
1925	8-63	8	1895	38791-29094
1925	8-88	8	1995	2539200-2540294
1926	6-66	6	1395	2656751-2659977
1926	8-88	8	1695	2640301-2744311
1926	4-44	4	1145	2670001-2670990
1927	4-44	4	....	2744312 upward
1927	6-66	6	....	2759981-2761000
1927	6-66A	6	....	2771501 upward
1927	8-77	8	....	2761001 upward
1927	8-88	8	....	2744312 upward
1928	76	8	....	2878301 upward
1928	88	8	....	2866901 upward
1928	115	8	....	2848001 upward

Number stamped on serial name plate on dash

Year	Model	Cyls.	Price	Serial Numbers
1929	120	8	....	2948001 and up
1929	8-90	8	$1395	2948001 and up
1929	6-80	6	995	284800l and up
1930	6-85	6	995	1001 and up
1930	8-95	8	1195	1001 and up
1931	8-98	8	945	1001 and up

Number stamped on plate under front floor mat at R. H. door

AUSTIN—American Austin Motor Car Co., Butler, Pa.

Year	Model	Cyls.	Price	Serial Numbers
1930-31	....	4	....	1 and up

Number stamped on top of frame on left side beside oil level rod on motor

BLACKHAWK—Stutz Motor Car Co. of America, Inc., Indianapolis, Ind.

Year	Model	Cyls.	Price	Serial Numbers
1929	L6	6	....	16001 and up
1929	L8	8	....	28001 and up
1930	L6	6	$2535	16001 and up
1930	L8	8	2535	28001 and up

Number on Fedco plate

Discontinued

BUICK—Buick Motor Co., Flint, Mich.

Year	Model	Cyls.	Price	Serial Numbers
1925*	Standard 6		$1175	1239259 and up
1925*	Master	6	1395	1211720 and up
1926*	Standard 6		1150	1398244 and up
1926*	Master	6	1295	1412093 and up

Number on left frame at rear

Year	Model	Cyls.	Price	Serial Numbers
1927*	114½	6	$1225	1638800 and up
1927*	120	6	....	1661435 and up
1927*	128	6	....	1677210 and up

Number on right frame at front
Numbers run according to body style
*Indicates Model. Serial Nos. begin July of preceding year

Year	Model	Cyls.	Price	Serial Numbers
1928	114	6	$1195	1888911 and up
1928	120	6	1495	1911026 and up
1928	128	6	....	1921026
1929	116	6	$1225	2123926-2137873
1929	121	6	....	2151760-2159907
1929	129	6	3990	2166412-2175065
1931	55	8	1055	2461629 and up
1931	65	8	1335	2467537 and up
1931	95	8	1620	2486273 and up

Number stamped on plate under right front fender

CADILLAC—Cadillac Motor Car Co., Detroit, Mich.

Year	Model	Cyls.	Price	Serial Numbers
1925	314	8	$3250	100001 and up
1926	314	8	3450	114284 and up

Number stamped on generator bolt boss and on plate on dash and on crankcase at base of oil filler

Year	Model	Cyls.	Price	Serial Numbers
1927	314	8	$3450	142040 and up

Number stamped on name plate on dash and on crankcase either just below the

---

fan bracket or to the left of the distributor support

Year	Model	Cyls.	Price	Serial Numbers
1928	341	8	$3450	300001 and up
1929	341-B	8	3450	320101 and up

Motor number on name plate on left side of dash and crankcase below water inlet

Year	Model	Cyls.	Price	Serial Numbers
1930	353	8	....	500001 and up
1930-31	452	16	....	700001 and up
1931	355	8	....	800001 and up
1931	370	12	....	1000001 and up

Number on crankcase just below water inlet on right hand side

CHANDLER—Chandler - Cleveland Motors Corp., Cleveland, Ohio

Year	Model	Cyls.	Price	Serial Numbers
1925	33A	6	$1595	147001-159624
1926	35	6	1490	159624-174000
1926-27	*Big 6	6	1545	174001 and up
1926-27	*Spec. 6	6	1145	77526 and up
1926-27	*Std. 6	6	945	15998 and up

Number stamped on right hand frame rail behind front fender iron

* Beginning August, 1926

Year	Model	Cyls.	Price	Serial Numbers
1927	Std. 6	6	$945	15998-C30000
1927	Spec. 6	6	1145	77527-80032
1927	Big 6	6	1695	174001-180100
1927	Royal 8	8	2195	E100001-E103000
1928	Spec. 6	6	995	C30001 and up
1928	Big 6	6	1725	18010 and up
1928	Royal 8	8	1995	E103001 and up

Number on frame rail R

Year	Model	Cyls.	Price	Serial Numbers
1929	65	6	....	C46001 and up
1929	Big 6	6	....	188001 and up
1929	Roy. 75	8	....	1001 and up
1929	Roy. 85	8	....	E-108001 and up

Number stamped on right front side member

Discontinued

CHEVROLET—Chevrolet Motor Co., Detroit, Mich.

Year	Model	Cyls.	Price	Serial Numbers
1925	K	4	$525	*F-*K
1926	Superior	4	525	*K-*V
1927	V & X	4	510	*V-*X
1927	Capitol	4	525	*AA
1927	LM	4	490	*LM
1928	National	4	495	AB
1928	Capitol	4	495	LO

Number on plate on left of right side of front seat frame

As Chevrolet cars are numbered by manufacturing zones it is not possible to reproduce the numbers in such a way as to be of use to the dealer
* Where further information is required on a specific car write to the plant where the car was manufactured, addressing your letter to the Chevrolet Motor Co. The numerical prefix in the serial number denotes the plant where the cars are manufactured. These plants are located as follows:

Up to and including 1923	Since 1923
1. Flint, Michigan	1. Flint, Michigan
2. Tarrytown, N. Y.	2. Tarrytown, N. Y.
3. St. Louis, Missouri	3. St. Louis, Mo.
6. Oakland, California	6. Oakland, Cal.
7. Fort Worth, Texas	9. Cincinnati, Ohio
9. Oshawa, Ontario	12. Buffalo, N. Y.
	21. Janesville, Wis.
1929 Intern'l 6	.... AC
1930 Universal 6	.... AD 1000 and up

Number on right side of dash under cowl

CHRYSLER—Chrysler Corporation, Detroit, Mich.

Year	Model	Cyls.	Price	Serial Numbers
1925	B	6	$1395	32813 and up
1925	G	6	1395	WY580P and up
1926	G-70	6	1395	WE585E and up
1926	E-80	6	2545	EW000P and up
1926	H-60	6	1075	YR500D and up
1926	I-50	4	750	FW000P and up

Number on plate on front of dash, also on left frame side member at rear spring horn

Year	Model	Cyls.	Price	Serial Numbers
1927	50	4	$750	FH556D and up
1927	60	6	1075	YD243W and up
1927	70	6	1395	PH679C and up
1927	80	8	2495	EW655L and up
1928	52	4	695	HH738Y and up
1928	62	6	1095	LH448Y and up
1928	72	.	....	CC339Y and up
1928	80	.	....	EP066E and up
1929	65	6	1075	LS400P and up
1929	75	6	1795	CY050P and up
1929	Imp.	6	3095	EP320W and up

Number stamped Fedco System on instrument board

Year	Model	Cyls.	Price	Serial Numbers
1930	Six	6	$785	6514920 and up
1930	66	6	1025	H-252-SS and up
1930	70	6	1295	P-180-YD and up
1930	Eight	8	1525	7500001 and up
1930	Imp. 8	8	2745	7800001 and up
1931	Six	6	895	6520501 and up
1931	Eight	8	1945	6510539 and up

CORD—Auburn Automobile Co., Auburn, Ind.

Year	Model	Cyls.	Price	Serial Numbers
1930	......	8	$3295	2925001 and up
1931	L-39	8	2595	2928720 and up

Number stamped under right hand front door

CUNNINGHAM—Jas. Cunningham Son & Co., Rochester, N. Y.

Year	Model	Cyls.	Price	Serial Numbers
1925	V-4	8	$6150	......
1928	V-7	8	6150	......
1928	V-8	8		......

Number on left frame member near radiator
Do not use consecutive numbers
No yearly models

Year	Model	Cyls.	Price	Serial Numbers
1930	V-9	8	....	......

DAVIS—G. W. Davis Motor Car Co., Richmond, Ind.

Year	Model	Cyls.	Price	Serial Numbers
1925	90	6	$1395	12518-13100
1925	91	6	1695	15124-15268
1926	90	6	1395	13101-13521
1926	91	6	1695	15269-15356
1926	92	6	1395	20000-20168
1926	93	6	1285	25000-25301

Numbers on left side of crankcase

Year	Model	Cyls.	Price	Serial Numbers
1927*	92	6	$1395	20169-20324
1927*	93	6	1285	25302 to 25492
1927*	94	6	1285	25515-25912
1927	98	8	1795	30101-30186

* Beginning July, 1926

Number stamped on motor name plate

Year	Model	Cyls.	Price	Serial Numbers
1928	99	8	$1795	30201-30240

Numbers on left side of crankcase

Discontinued

DE SOTO—De Soto Motor Corp. (Div. Chrysler Corp.), Detroit, Mich.

Year	Model	Cyls.	Price	Serial Numbers
1929	Six	6	$1035	KH255C
1930	Six	6	845	KL300E and up
1930	Six	6	830	5000001-5006932
1930	Eight	8	1035	L661WP and 6000001 up
1931	Six	6	830	5006933 and up
1931	Eight	8	1035	6000801 and L185PH up

DIANA—Moon Motor Car Co., St. Louis, Mo.

Year	Model	Cyls.	Price	Serial Numbers
1925	8	8	....	80001 and up
1926	8	8	....	80001-82500
1927	8	8	....	82501 and up
1928	8	8	$1695	84000 and up

Discontinued

SERIAL NUMBERS, Passenger Cars—Continued

DODGE BROTHERS—Dodge Brothers Corp. (Div. Chrysler Corp.), Detroit, Mich.

Year	Series	Cyls.	Price	Serial Numbers
1925	25 & 26*	4	$875	A232221-A494124
1926	26 & 27*	4	795	A494125 and up

* Beginning July 1

Number on plate on toeboard, also on right frame member back of front spring rear bracket

1927	....	4	$795	A702243 and up
1927	Senior	6	....	A910000 and up
1929-30	Senior	6	1595	DB-1 and up
1929-30	Senior	6	1025	DA-83715
1930	DD6	6	875	D001WPand 3500001 up
1930	DC8	8	1225	E001 WC and 4500001 up
1931	DD6	6	775	3504189 and up
1931	DC8	8	1125	4501084 and up
1931	Six	6	845	3518001 and up
1931	Eight	8	1135	4508001 and up

DUESENBERG—Duesenberg, Inc., Indianapolis, Ind.

Year	Model	Cyls.	Price	Serial Numbers
1925	St. 8	8	$6650	1001 and up

Number on right hand side front dash

1929	J	8	....	2000 and up
1930	J	8	....	2000 and up
1931	J	8	....	2000 and up

Number stamped on front dash

duPONT—duPont Motors, Inc., Wilmington, Del.

Year	Model	Cyls.	Price	Serial Numbers
1925	C	6	$2090	1 to 480
1925	D	6	2600	481 and up
1926	E	6	2800	510 and up

Number on dash under cowl
Serial numbers do not run consecutively

1927-29	E	6	$2800	510 and up

Number stamped on R. H. side engine block. Serial under cowl on dash

1929	G	8	$4560	800 and up

Number stamped on L. H. rear spring horn. Also inside of dash

1930	G	8	....	....

DURANT—Durant Motor Co. of Michigan, Lansing, Mich.

Year	Model	Cyls.	Price	Serial Numbers
1929	40	4	....	1001 and up
1929	60	6	....	1001 and up
1929	66	6	....	1001 and up
1929	70	6	....	1001 and up
1930-31	6-14	6	....	1001 and up
1930-31	6-17	6	....	1001 and up
1931	6-10	6	....	1001 and up

Number on upper toe board

ERSKINE—Studebaker Corp., South Bend, Ind.

Year	Model	Cyls.	Price	Serial Numbers
1927	50	6	$915	5000001 and up
1928	51	6	835	5025001 and up

Discontinued

ESSEX—Hudson Motor Car Co., Detroit, Mich.

Year	Model	Cyls.	Price	Serial Numbers
1925	All	6	$765	177751-337949
1926	All	6	765	337950-442675
1926-27*	Coach	6	795	442676-500000

Serial number on dash
* Beginning July, 1926

1927	Coach	6	$735	500001-610276
1928†	Coach 6	6	735	610276-706270

† Beginning July, 1927

1928	Super Six	6	....	706270 and up
1928	(Model 1929)	6	....	816865-928658
1929	Chalg.	6	695	928658 and up
1930	Sup. Six	6	....	1165674 and up
1931	Sedan	6	695	1234267 and up

FALCON-KNIGHT—Falcon Motors Corp., Detroit, Mich.

Year	Model	Cyls.	Price	Serial Numbers
1927	10	6	$975	1000-12000
1928	12	6	....	12000 and up

Discontinued

FORD—Ford Motor Co., Dearborn, Mich.

Year	Model	Cyls.	Price	Serial Numbers
1925	T	4	$290	10999901-12990055
1926	T	4	380	12990056 and up

Number stamped on left side cylinder block just above water inlet connection. Car and engine number the same from May 1, 1915

FRANKLIN—Franklin Automobile Co., Syracuse, N. Y.

Year	Model	Cyls.	Price	Serial Numbers
1925	11	6	$2650	151501-158872
1926	11	6	2635	158873-164801
1927	11	6	2635	164801-172001

Number stamped on dash under hood

1928	12	6	$3060	172001-182440
1929	130	6	....	30-183001-30-197260
1929	135	6	....	35-183001-35-197260
1929	137	6	2870	37-183001-37-197260
1930	145	6	2750	45-198000 and up
1930	147	6	2885	47-198000 and up
1931	15	6	2495	204000 and up

Number on left side gas tank bracket on dash under hood

GARDNER—Gardner Motor Co., Inc., St. Louis, Mo.

Year	Model	Cyls.	Price	Serial Numbers
1925	6-A	6	$1395	32500-34525
1925	8-A	8	1795	32500-34525
1926	6-B	6	1395	34526-41765
1926	8-B	8	1795	34526-41765
1927*	6-B	6	1395	41766 and up
1927*	8-B	8	1795	41766 and up

*Beginning June, 1926

Number under front seat cushion and left side of motor block

1927	90	8	$1995	5DD01
1927	80	8	1395	5DD01
1927	85	8	1695	5DD01
1928	90	8	....	5T.U.-16 and up
1928	85	8	....	5T.F.-64 and up
1928	80	8	....	5S.P.-74 and up
1928	75	8	....	5T.F.-33 and up

Number stamped on instrument board and L. H. of motor block

1928-29	85-95	8	....	GRR-01 and up
1928-29	75	8	....	5-AE-01 and up
1929	130	8	....	GUU-857 and up
1929	125	8	....	GUU-857 and up
1929	120	8	....	GUU-857 and up

Fedco number plate on right hand side of instrument board

1930	150	8	....	SST-827 and up
1930	140	8	....	SST-827 and up
1930	136	6	....	SST-827 and up

Fedco number plate

GRAHAM—Graham-Paige Motors Corp., Detroit, Mich.

Year	Model	Cyls.	Price	Serial Numbers
1930	127	8	$2295	558001 and up
1930	137	8	2295	508001 and up
1930	Std. 6	6	1015	900001 and up
1930	Spec. 6	6	....	736001 and up
1930	Std. 8	8	....	660001 and up
1930	Spec. 8	8	....	615001 and up
1931	Std. 6	6	955	1510001 and up
1931	Spec. 6	6	1035	1200001 and up
1931	Spec.8-20	8	1245	1000001 and up
1931	Cus. 8-34	8	1845	626001 and up

Number stamped on plate on body floor inside right rear door

GRAHAM-PAIGE—Graham-Paige Motors Corp., Detroit, Mich.

Year	Model	Cyls.	Price	Serial Numbers
1928	610	6	....	800001
1928	614	6	....	700001
1928	619	6	....	600001
1928	629	6	....	550001
1928	835	8	....	503001
1929	612	6	$935	848001 and up
1929	615	6	1195	713001 and up
1929	621	6	1865	608001 and up
1929	827	8	2195	555001 and up
1929	837	8	2195	506001 and up

Number stamped on plate on engine
Name changed to Graham

HUDSON—Hudson Motor Car Co., Detroit, Mich.

Year	Model	Cyls.	Price	Serial Numbers
1925	6	6	$1200	562017-672227
1926†	6	6	1250	672228-713809
1926-27*	Coach	6	1195	713810 and up
1926-27*	Bro'm	6	1495	716440 and up
1926-27*	Sedan	6	1595	714674 and up

Number on plate on front of dash
*Beginning July, 1926
†To July, 1926

1927	Coach	6	$1285	750001 and up
1927-28	S 6	6	....	1001-12269
1927-28	O 6	6	....	730399-803569
1929	Coach	6	1095	825415 and up
1929	139" W.B.	6	1850	41384 and up
1931*	119"W.B.	8	1095	914293 and up
1931*	126"W.B.	8	1295	57115 and up

Beginning Nov. 26, 1930

HUPMOBILE—Hupp Motor Car Corp., Detroit, Mich.

Year	Model	Cyls.	Price	Serial Numbers
1925	R	4	$1225	150001 and up
1925	E	8	1795	15000
1926	A-1	6	1325	5000 and up
1926	E-2	8	1945	15001 and up
1926	A-2	..	....	15001-35000
1926-27	A-3	..	....	35001-55000
1927	A-4	..	....	55000-65000
1927	A-5	..	....	65001 and up
1926-27	E-2	8	....	15001-25000
1927	E-3	8	....	25001 and up
1927-28	A-6	6	....	75001 and up
1928	M-1	8	....	5001 and up
1929	A-11	6	$1425	130001-150000
1929	M-3	8	1935	8501-18500

Number stamped on plate where steering joins dash

1930	S	6	$1135	1-5001-30200
1930	C	8	1750	C-5001-10000
1930	H	8	2190	H-5001-6000
1930	U	8	....	U-5001-5100
1931	S	6	1050	30201
1931	L	8	1350	5001
1931	C	8	1685	10001
1931	H	8	2005	6001
1931	U	8	....	5101

Number stamped on plate on right side of dash under hood

JORDAN—Jordan Motor Car Co., Cleveland, Ohio

Year	Model	Cyls.	Price	Serial Numbers
1925	K	6	$2385	51401-52649
1925	L	6	2095	41801-42310
1925	A	8	2275	60001-64200
1926	A & AA	8	....	64201-66825
1926	J	8	....	70001-79920

Number left front side of dash on plate

1927	J	8	$1695	DY-992-S-DY999E
1927	AA	8	2495	DL-682-L-DL739E
1927-28	R	8	1595	DE-000-S and up
1927	J & J1	8	1645	DN000D-DN424E
1928	J E	8	....	ST500S and up

Number stamped on L. H. side of instrument board

1929	E	6	$1795	95001 and up
1929	G	8	2195	130001 and up

Number plate riveted to left toe board riser

1930	G90	8	$2295	130153 and up
1930	T80	8	1795	96001 and up
1930	U70	8	1495	170001 and up
1930-31	Z	8	5550	200001 and up
1931	80	8	1795	96400 and up
1931	90	8	2295	131800 and up

Number stamped on plate riveted L. H. toe board riser

KISSEL—Kissel Motor Car Co., Hartford, Wis.

Year	Model	Cyls.	Price	Serial Numbers
1925	55	6	$1685	......
1925	75	8	1985	......
1926	55	6	1585	55-10001 and up
1926	75	8	1985	75-3501 and up

Number stamped on front end right frame member adjacent to right head lamp. Engine number on right front motor arm.

1927	55	6	$1785	55-13038 and up
1927	65	8	1985	65-1001 and up
1927	75	8	2285	75-5645 and up

Number on rignt front frame member

1929	6-73	6	$1595	73-1001 and up
1929	6-95	8	1995	95-1001 and up
1929	8-126	8	3275	126-1001 and up
1930	6-73	6	1595	73-3001-73-4001
1930	8-95	8	1995	95-4501-95-5501
1930	8-126	8	3275	126-5001-126-6001

Number stamped on right front frame casting

LASALLE—Cadillac Motor Car Co., Detroit, Mich.

Year	Model	Cyls.	Price	Serial Numbers
1927	303	8	$2495	200001 and up

Engine number stamped on name plate on front of dash and on crankcase just below water inlet on right hand side

1929	328	8	$2295	400001 and up
1930	340	8	....	600000 and up
1931	345	8	3245	900001 and up

LINCOLN—Lincoln Motor Co. (Div. Ford Motor Co.), Detroit, Mich.

Year	Model	Cyls.	Price	Serial Numbers
1923-26	8	8	$....	8709-40000

Number on left side crankcase between No. 1 and No. 2 cylinder

SERIAL NUMBERS, Passenger Cars—Continued

Year	Model	Cyls.	Price	Serial Numbers
1927-28	8	8	....	40001-52999
1929	8	8	....	53000 and up

Number on plate on dash under hood

Year	Model	Cyls.	Price	Serial Numbers
1930	8	8	$4200	61500 and up

Number stamped on left side crankcase below No. 1 cylinder

| 1931 | 8 | 8 | $4400 | 66001 and up |

LOCOMOBILE—Locomobile Co. of America, Inc., Bridgeport, Conn.

Year	Model	Cyls.	Price	Serial Numbers
1925	48	6	$7460	1900 and up

Number on right side of dash column

| 1925 | Jr. 8 | 8 | $1785 | 101 and up |

Number on engine side of dash

1927	48	6	$7460	19350
1927	90	6	6000	33325
1927	80	8	2850	101
1927	70	8	1975	5601

Number on name plate on dash
Discontinued

MARMON—Marmon Motor Car Co., Indianapolis, Ind.

Year	Model	Cyls.	Price	Serial Numbers
1925	74	6	$3165	D8-1-D8-5171
1926	74	6	3295	D8-5172 and up
1926	75	6	3565	Fedco Nos.

Numbers on heel board of driver's seat and on left side of main frame
Serial numbers run according to body style and not consecutively

| 1927 | 75 | 6 | .... | Fedco Nos. |
| 1927 | Little | 8 | .... | Fedco Nos. |

Number on name plate located on dash just above the toe board

1928	68	8	$1395	Fedco Nos.
1928	78	8	1895	Fedco Nos.
1928	75	6	....	Fedco Nos.

Fedco plates on left side instrument panels

| 1929 | 78 | 8 | .... | Fedco Nos. |
| 1929 | 68 | 8 | .... | Fedco Nos. |

Numbers on Fedco plates on left side instrument panels

1930-31	Roosevelt	8	$1075	7020001 and up
1930-31	Eight 69	8	1610	130501 and up
1930-31	Eight 79	8	2020	100501 and up
1930-31	Big 8	8	3170	110501 and up
1931	70	8	......	120-501 up
1931	88	8	2275	160-501 up
1931	16	16	4775	16-501 up

MOON—Moon Motor Car Co., St. Louis, Mo.

Year	Model	Cyls.	Price	Serial Numbers
1928	6-60	6	$995	11000 and up
1928	Series A6	6	1195	16000 and up
1928	6-72	6	....	10A01 and up
1929	6-72	6	....	EOWOU and up

Fedco number plate welded to metal dash
Discontinued

NASH—Nash Motors, Kenosha, Wis.

Year	Model	Cyls.	Price	Serial Numbers
1925	Advanced	6	$1375	288001 and up
1925	Special	6	1095	51001 and up

On the 6-cyl. models the numbers do not run consecutively, but by body styles
Number on left front cross member, just back of radiator

1926-27	Advanced	6	$1340	386972 and up
1926-27	Special	6	1135	A26276 and up
1926-27	Light	6	865	R28374 and up

Number on top of right side member

1928	Standard	6	....	169914 and up
1928	Special	6	....	B15230 and up
1928	Advanced	6	....	478937 and up
1929	460	6	....	478937 and up
1929	430	6	....	B15230 and up
1929	420	6	....	169914 and up
1930	490	8	$1845	496400
1930	480	6	1475	B37582
1930	450	6	995	R216590
1931	6-60	6	895	R-249708 and up
1931	8-70	8	955	X-1001 and up
1931	8-80	8	1295	B-54928 and up
1931	8-90	8	1595	509201 and up

OAKLAND—Oakland Motor Car Co., Pontiac, Mich.

Year	Model	Cyls.	Price	Serial Numbers
1925	6-54B	6	$1095	3710054-6452354
1926	O-6	6	1025	6460154 and up

Number on frame opposite right rear wheel

1927		6	1025	120801-54 and up
1928	AA-6	6	1095	170001 and up
1929	AA-6	6	1145	After 227001
1930	O8	8	1065	273501 and up
1931	O8	8	895	296001 and up

Number on plate on left frame side member under front fender

OLDSMOBILE—Olds Motor Works, Lansing, Mich.

Year	Model	Cyls.	Price	Serial Numbers
1925	30	6	$875	Series C
1925*	30	6	875	Series D
1926†	30	6	875	Series E

Numbers on plate on body sill at right of the boards
Numbers do not run in consecutive order, but according to body styles
* Beginning July 14, 1925
† Beginning June 14, 1926

1926-27	Touring	6	....	T23001 and up
1926-27	DeL. Tg.	6	....	DT12001 and up
1926 27	Sedan	6	....	S16001 and up
1926-27	DeL. Sed.	6	....	DS22001 and up
1926-27	Coach	6	....	K19001 and up
1926-27	DeL. C.	6	....	DK18001 and up
1926-27	Coupe	6	....	C6001 and up
1926-27	DeL.Cpe.	6	....	DC8001 and up
1926-27	DeL.Rds.	6	....	DR3001 and up
1926-27	Land.Sed.	6	....	LS1001 and up
1926-27	Spt.Coupe	6	....	SC1001 and up

Number on brass plate under front passenger seat

1928	Spt. Rd.	6	....	R-1-1602
1928	Spt. Phaeton	6	....	T-1-84
1928	Std. Coupe	6	....	C-1-8906
1928	Spt. Coupe	6	....	SC-1-4039
1928	Sedan 2 dr.	6	....	K-1-23129
1928	Sedan 4 dr.	6	....	S-1-25956
1928	Landau	6	....	LS-1-9214
1928	DeL. Rd.	6	....	DR-1-100
1928	DeL. Phaeton	6	....	DT-1-21
1928	DeL. Sedan	6	....	DS-1-1962
1928	DeL.Spt.Cpe.	6	....	DSC-1-539
1928	DeL. Landau	6	....	DLS-1-1603
1928	Spec.Coupe	6	....	ZC-1-728
1928	Spec.Sed.2 dr.	6	....	ZK 1-1-61

STANDARD

1929	Phaeton	6	....	T-1001-1018
1929	Roadster	6	....	R-2001-2309
1929	Conv.Rd.	6	....	CR-101-740
1929	Coupe	6	....	C-9001-17134
1929	Spt. Coupe	6	....	SC-5001-9634
1929	Sedan 2-dr.	6	....	K-24001-45266
1929	Sedan 4-dr.	6	....	S-26001-51445
1929	Landau	6	....	L-10001-12484

SPECIAL

1929	Phaeton	6	....	ZT-1-9
1929	Roadster	6	....	ZR-1-128
1929	Conv. Rd.	6	....	ZCR-101-313
1929	Coupe	6	....	ZC-1001-3011
1929	Spt. Coupe	6	....	SZC-1-1287
1929	Sedan 2-dr.	6	....	ZK-101-4386
1929	Sedan 4-dr.	6	....	ZS-1-6622
1929	Landau	6	....	ZL-1-601

DE LUXE

1929	Phaeton	6	....	DT-101-151
1929	Roadster	6	....	DR-201-594
1929	Conv. Rd.	6	....	DCR-101-725
1929	Coupe	6	....	DC-1-647
1929	Spt. Coupe	6	....	DSC-601-3471
1929	Sedan 2-dr.	6	....	DK-1-1548
1929	Sedan 5-dr.	6	....	DS-2001-9198
1929	Landau	6	....	DL-1701-3475

Number stamped on plate on floor board or beneath seat.

1930	Std. Phaeton	6	....	T-1101-1122
1930	Std.Conv.Rd.	6	....	CR-1001-2186
1930	Std.Bus.Cpe.	6	....	C-18001-22069
1930	Std.Spt.Cpe.	6	....	SC-10001-12798
1930	Std.2-Dr.Sed.	6	....	K-46001-56649
1930	Std.4-Dr.Sed.	6	....	S-52001-65084
1930	Std. Pat. Sed.	6	....	PS-1-1321
1930	Spec.Phaeton	6	....	ZT-21-25
1930	Spec.Conv.Rd.	6	....	ZCR-401-633
1930	Spec.Bus.Cpe.	6	....	ZC-4001-4633
1930	Spec.Spt.Cpe.	6	....	ZSC-1301-1781
1930	Spec.2-Dr.Sed.	6	....	ZK-5001-6598
1030	Spec.4-Dr.Sed.	6	....	ZS-7001-10032
1930	Spec.Pat.Sed.	6	....	ZPS-1-431
1930	DeL.Phaeton	6	....	DT-201-276
1930	DeL.Conv.Rd.	6	....	DCR-1001-2186
1930	DeL.Bus.Cpe.	6	....	DC-1001-1307
1930	DeL.Spt.Cpe.	6	....	DSC-4001-6592
1930	DeL.2-Dr.Sed.	6	....	DK-2001-2615
1930	DeL.4-Dr.Sed.	6	....	DS-10001-12972
1930	DeL.Pat.Sed.	6	....	DPS-1-2525

Note—Models equipped with (5) wire wheels have serial number and letters prefixed by the letter "w"

STANDARD

1931	Conv.Rdster	6	$935	CR-2201 up
1931	Bus. Coupe	6	845	C-25001 up
1931	Spt. Coupe	6	895	SC-13001 up
1931	Sedan 2-dr.	6	845	K-57001 up
1931	Sedan 4-dr.	6	925	S-66001 up
1931	Pat. Sedan	6	960	P-1401

DELUXE

Year	Model	Cyls.	Price	Serial Numbers
1931	Conv. Rdster	6	$1000	DCR-2601 up
1931	Bus. Coupe	6	910	DC-1401 up
1931	Spt. Coupe	6	960	DSC-5601 up
1931	Sedan, 2 Door	6	910	DK-2701 up
1931	Sedan, 4 Door	6	990	DS-13001 up
1931	Pat. Sedan	6	1025	DP-2601 up

Number stamped on pad, stamped on block above water pump and on plate on right-hand side of front floor board

PACKARD—Packard Motor Car Co., Detroit, Mich.

Year	Model	Cyls.	Price	Serial Numbers
1925	326-333	6	$2585	49501 and up
1925	236-243	8	3750	20900 and up

Number on plate at left rear side of dash

1927	426-433	6	$2585	95007 and up
1927	336-343	8	3750	220007 and up
1928	526-533	6	2275	125013 and up
1928	443	8	3550	225013 and up
1929	626	8	....	233013 and up
1929	633	8	2475	233013 and up
1929	640	8	3275	167013 and up
1929	645	8	4585	167013 and up
1930	726-733	8	2525	277013 and up
1930	740	8	3325	179013 and up
1930	745	8	4585	179013 and up
1930	734	8	5200	179013 and up

Number on metal plate on motor side of dash

PAIGE—Paige-Detroit Motor Car Co., Detroit, Mich.

Year	Model	Cyls.	Price	Serial Numbers
1925	6	6	$2165	149897-163956
1926	6-75	6	1695	415501 and up
1926	6-65	6	1395	160001 and up

Number under right hand front seat

1927	6-45	6	$1095	318983 and up
1927	6-65	6	1395	166461 and up
1927	6-75	6	1695	417122 and up
1927	8-85	8	2295	500001 and up

Number under right hand front seat
Discontinued

PEERLESS—Peerless Motor Car Corp., Cleveland, Ohio

Year	Model	Cyls.	Price	Serial Numbers
1925	70	6	$2185	301701 and up
1925	67	8	2945	329626 and up
1925	72	6	1895	302501-304420
1926	72	6	1895	304421 and up
1926	80	6	1395	350501 and up
1926	69	8	....	335501 and up
1927	60	6	1295	A400501 and up
1927	80	6	1395	A350001 and up
1927	90	6	1695	A390001 and up
1927	72	6	1895	A302001 and up
1927	69	8	....	A335001 and up

Number stamped on metal plate attached to dash

1928	60	6	$1195	B600001 and up
1928	80	6	1295	B800001 and up
1928	91	6	....	B910001 and up
1928	69	8	....	B6900001 and up
1929	61	6	....	610501 and up
1929	80	6	....	803309 and up
1929	81	6	....	810001 and up
1929	125	6	....	125501 and up
1930	61	6	....	615451 and up
1930	81	6	....	812901 and up
1930	61A	6	....	616501 and up
1930	125	6	....	126291 and up
1930	Std.	8	1495	A10001 and up
1930	Mast.	8	1995	B40001 and up
1930	Cus.	8	2795	C70001 and up
1931	Std.	8	1495	1001 and up
1931	Mast.	8	1995	4001 and up
1931	Cus.	8	2795	7001 and up

Number stamped on plate right body sill, inside door

PIERCE-ARROW—Pierce-Arrow Motor Car Co., Buffalo, N. Y.

Year	Model	Cyls.	Price	Serial Numbers
1925	80	6	$2895	8010000-8022501
1925-26	33	6	5250	340001-340999
*1927-28	36	6	5875	361000-362871

Number on plate below driver's seat
Numbers are not allotted on a yearly basis but according to series
*Sept. 15, 1926

SERIAL NUMBERS, Passenger Cars—Continued

Year	Model	Cyls.	Price	Serial Numbers
1927	80	6	$2895	8010000-8022501
1928	81	6	3100	8101001-8106501
1929	133	8	2950	2000001-2007885
1929	143	8	3750	3000001-3001972
1930	132	8	2695	1000001-1003883
1930	125	8	3125	2025001-2025510
1930	139	8	3475	2500001-2503129
1930	126	8	3975	3025001-3026036
1931	43-134	8	2685	1025001-
1931	43-137	8	2685	1500001-
1931	42-142	8	3450	2525001-
1931	41-147	8	4275	3050001-

Number stamped on right side of frame rear of front spring

PLYMOUTH—Plymouth Motor Corp. (Div. Chrysler Corp.), Detroit, Mich.

Year	Model	Cyls.	Price	Serial Numbers
1929	Touring	4	....	RH584Y
1930	....	4	....	Y000WW and up
1930	*Touring	4	$625	1500001 and up
1931	Phaeton	4	625	1530245 and up

*Beginning May 10, 1930

Number stamped on plate mounted over right front door hinge pillar

PONTIAC—Oakland Motor Car Co., Pontiac, Mich.

Year	Model	Cyls.	Price	Serial Numbers
1926-27	....	6	$825*	1-27 and up

*2-door Sedan

Number on rear frame cross member

| 1928 | 6-28 | 6 | $775 | 204001 and up |
| 1929 | Big 6 | 6 | 745 | 410101-591501 |

Number on plate on left frame side member below front fender

| 1930 | Series B | 6 | $775 | 591501 |
| 1931 | | 6 | 675 | 649001 and up |

Number stamped on left frame side member below front fender

REO—Reo Motor Car Co., Lansing, Mich.

Year	Model	Cyls.	Price	Serial Numbers
1925*	T-6	6	$1595	75850-83993
1925	T-6	6	1395	83994-97753

Number on right forward end of sub frame

| 1926 | T6 | 6 | $1395 | 97754 |

Number on left forward end of sub frame

*To Aug. 1

| 1927 | A | 6 | $1685 | 1 |
| 1927 | B | | 1195 | 2 |

Number on top left side rail opposite steering gear

1929	C	6	....	C1-C999
1929	C3⅜ Bore	6	....	C1000 and up
1929	B2	6	....	2B1400 and up
1930	25	6	$1795	100
1930	20	6	1595	102
1930	15	6	1195	22465
1930†	15	6	1195	2B-24254
1930†	20	6	1595	2289
1930†	25	6	1795	2C-2227
1931*	25N	6	1695	25N-1
1931*	30N	8	1995	30N-1
1931*	35N	8	2485	35N1

†Aug. 1930.

*Beginning Sept. 1930.

RICKENBACKER — Rickenbacker Motor Co., Detroit, Mich.

Year	Model	Cyls.	Price	Serial Numbers
1925	D	6	$1395	40001-46999
1925	8-A	8	2195	25924-27499
1925-26*	E	6	1495	47000 and up
1925-26*	B	8	1995	27500 and up

Number on plate at heel board, left side front seat

*Beginning Aug., 1925
Discontinued

ROAMER — Roamer Consolidated Corp., Kalamazoo, Mich.

Year	Model	Cyls.	Price	Serial Numbers
1925	6-50	6	$1295	35000-35746
1925	8-88	8	2495	80000-80057
1926	6-50	6	1295	35746-35999
1926	8-80	8	2495	80057-80999
1926	8-80	8	$1895	81000-81999
1927	8-78	8	1395	86000-86999

Number on front right side rail

| 1930 | 8-85 | 8 | $1450 | 92000 and up |
| 1930 | 8-125 | 8 | 2975 | 88500 and up |

STEARNS-KNIGHT—F. B. Stearns Co., Cleveland, Ohio

Year	Model	Cyls.	Price	Serial Numbers
1925	B	4	$1595	B1214-B1315
1925	C	6	1875	C1-C1249
1925	S	8	2395	S2693-S3989

Number on first floor board near right side

1926	D6-85	6	$3250	D1-D433
1927	F6-85	6	3250	F600 and up
1927	G8-85	8	3950	G1 and up

Number on left hand side of engine

| 1928 | H8-90 | 8 | .... | H650 and up |

Number on first floor board near right side

1928	M6-80	6	....	M21550 and up
1928	N6-80	6	....	N51550 and up
1929	J8-90	8	$5500	J11773 and up
1929	H8-90	8	5500	H15696 and up
1929	N6-80	6	2195	M-21572 and up
1929	N6-80	6	2345	N51595 and up

Discontinued

STUDEBAKER—Studebaker Corp., South Bend, Ind.

Year	Model	Cyls.	Price	Serial Numbers
1925	Std. 6 ER	6	$1495	4202101 and up
1925	Spec. 6 EQ	6	1895	3120001 and up
1925	Big 6 EP	6	2245	2060001 and up
1926	Std. 6 ER	6	1395	1284001 and up
1926	Spec. 6 EQ	6	1895	3161001 and up
1926	Big 6 EP	6	2145	2073001 and up
1927	Dic. EU	6	1195	1346101 and up
1927	Com.	6	1495	4000001 and up
1927	Com. EW	6	1895	3173001 and up
1927	Pres. 6 ES	6	2180	2102301 and up
1928	Dic. GE	6	1265	1410001 and up
1928	Com. GB	6	1495	4039801 and up
1928	Pres. 6 ES	6	1985	2114903 and up
1928	Pres. 8 FA	8	2085	6000001 and up
1929	Dic. GE	6	1265	1437601 and up
1929	Com. 6 GJ	6	1325	4070501 and up
1929	Com. 8 FD	8	1475	8000001 and up
1929	Com. GH	6	1665	4062101 and up
1929	Pres. FH	8	1735	7013501 and up
1929	Pres. FB	8	1885	7000001 and up
1929	Pres. FE	8	1995	6013001 and up
1929	Pres. FA	8	2085	6008601 and up
1930	Dic. 6 GL	6	1165	1460001 and up
1930	Dic. 8 FC	8	1285	2120001 and up
1930	Com. 6 GJ	6	1425	4081001 and up
1930	Com. 8 FD	8	1515	7011001 and up
1930	Pres. FH	8	1765	7021001 and up
1930	Pres. FE	8	1995	6016001 and up
1930	Six 53	6	895	5073001 and up
1931	Six 53	6	895	5085001 and up
1931	Six 54	6	895	5096001 and up
1931	Dic. 61	6	1150	9000001 and up
1931	Dic. FC	6	1295	2134001 and up
1931	Com. 70	8	1585	8025001 and up
1931	Pres. 80	8	1850	7031001 and up
1931	Pres. 90	8	2150	6022001 and up

STUTZ—Stutz Motor Car Co. of America, Inc., Indianapolis, Ind.

Year	Model	Cyls.	Price	Serial Numbers
1925	693, 694	6	$2395	6-2601 and up
1925	695		3070	14001 and up

Number on left side of dash

| 1926 | AA | 8 | $2995 | 80001 and up |

Number on forward right side of dash

1927	AA	8	$3180	80001 and up
1928	BB	8	3595	87226 and up
1929	M	8	....	30001 and up
1929	M	8	....	40001 and up

Number stamped on forward right side of dash

| 1930 | 134½M | 8 | $3345 | 30001 |
| 1930 | 145M | 8 | 3745 | 40001 |

Number stamped on Fedco plate

VELIE—Velie Motors Corp., Moline, Ill.

Year	Model	Cyls.	Price	Serial Numbers
1925	60	6	$1275	144100-150989
1926	60	6	1450	150990 and up

Number on name plate right side seat box Engine number left side crankcase

1927	50	6	....	160100 and up
1927	60	6	....	154250 and up
1928	6-66	6	....	166001 and up
1928	6-77	6	....	157001 and up
1928	8-88	8	....	180101 and up

Discontinued

VIKING—Olds Motor Co., Lansing, Mich.

Year	Model	Cyls.	Serial Numbers
1930	4-d. Sedan	8	VS3001 and up
1930	Brougham	8	VB3001 and up
1930	Conv't. Coupe	8	VCC3001 and up
1930	Sp. 4-d. Sed.	8	VZS3001 and up
1930	Sp. Broug.	8	VZB3001 and up
1930	Sp. Con. C'pe	8	VZCC3001 and up
1930	DeL. Broug.	8	VDB3001 and up

WHIPPET—Willys-Overland, Toledo, Ohio

Year	Model	Cyls.	Price	Serial Numbers
1930	96-A	4	$475	435093
1930	08-A	6	635	109336

Number stamped on plate on right rear frame member and on plate under driver's seat cushion

WILLS STE. CLAIRE—Wills Sainte Claire, Inc., Marysville, Mich.

Year	Model	Cyls.	Price	Serial Numbers
1925	A-68	8	$2475	7697 and up
1925	B-68	8	2885	12190 and up
1925	W-6	6	2600	20000-21897
1925-27	C-68	8	2900	14000-15000
1926-27	T-6	6	2700	23000 and up
1926-27	W-6	6	2600	21897-23000
1926-27	D-68	8	3000	15000 and up

Number in driver's compartment on dash above steering column
Discontinued

WILLYS EIGHT—Willys-Overland, Inc., Toledo, Ohio

Year	Model	Cyls.	Price	Serial Numbers
1931	8-80D	8	$995	1001 and up

WILLYS-KNIGHT—Willys-Overland, Inc., Toledo, Ohio

Year	Model	Cyls.	Price	Serial Numbers
1930	66-B	6	$1795	43001
1930	70-B	6	975	110366

66-B stamped on left side frame member under front fender and on plate under driver's seat cushion

70-B stamped on plate on top of right rear front member and under driver's seat cushion

| 1931 | 66D | 6 | $1095 | 1001 and up |
| 1931 | 87 | 6 | .... | 4627 and up |

WILLYS-SIX—Willys-Overland, Inc., Toledo, Ohio

Year	Model	Cyls.	Price	Serial Numbers
1930	98B	6	$735	131000 and up

Number stamped on plate on right rear front member and on plate under driver's seat cushion

| 1931 | 97 | 6 | $545 | 1001 and up |
| 1931 | 98D | 6 | 795 | 1001 and up |

WINDSOR—Windsor Corp., St. Louis, Mo.

Year	Model	Cyls.	Price	Serial Numbers
1929	8-82	8	....	COWOU and up
1929	8-92	8	....	POWOU and up

Fedco number plate welded to metal dash

Orphan Car or Truck Parts Sources

Where Parts Can Be Obtained
for Repairing Orphan Vehicles

HOW TO USE THIS INFORMATION

1. Locate your orphan car in the first alphabetically-arranged list below.
2. Note the numbers following the name of your car. They correspond with numbers preceding names of sources in the list immediately following.
3. An asterisk (*) in front of a number means an original source of supply—one that has taken over the manufacturer's patterns, blueprints, etc., or stock on hand.
4. Letters following a number indicate that only certain parts are handled by that source: ep—Engine Parts; fsg—Flywheel Starter Gears; rag—Rear Axle Gears.

LIST OF ORPHAN CARS WITH KEY TO PARTS SOURCES

Abbreviations: ep—Engine Parts   fsg—Flywheel Starter Gears   rag—Rear Axle Gears

ACE—45, 5 ep, 6 rag & fsg.
ALL AMERICAN TRUCK—*1, 24, 45.
ALLEN—7, *24, 25, 6 rag & fsg.
ALTER—*2, 5 ep.
AMERICAN—*2, 7, 24, 5 ep, 6 rag & fsg.
ANDERSON—24, 25, 5 ep, 6 rag & fsg.
APPERSON—*3, 6 rag & fsg.
ATTERBURY TRUCK—48.
BARLEY—37, 6 rag & fsg.
BAY STATE—7, 45, 5 ep, 6 rag & fsg.
BRINTON—24.
BRISCOE—7, *13, 28, 45, 46, 48, 5 ep, 6 rag & fsg.
C. T. ELECTRIC—47.
CHALMERS—*8, 5 ep.
CHANDLER—17, *21.
CLEVELAND—17, *21.
COLE—44, 45, 5 ep.
COLUMBIA—*9, 37, 45, 5 ep.
COMET—7, 45, 5 ep.
COURIER—5 ep.
CROW-ELKHART—7, *10, 24, 45, 46, 5 ep.
DANIELS—*24, 45, 5 ep.
DETROITER—24, 45, 5 ep.
DIANA—*17.
DIXIE FLYER—24, 45, 5 ep.

DORRIS—45.
DORT—*12, 28, 44, 5 ep.
EARL—7, *13, 28, 45, 48, 5 ep.
ECONOMY—5 ep.
ELGIN—7, *14, 24, 45, 46, 5 ep.
ELKHART—45, 5 ep.
EMPIRE—5 ep.
FALCON-KNIGHT—51.
FLANDERS—24.
FLINT—*16, 27, 44.
G. V. ELECTRIC TRUCK—47.
GRANT—7, *18, 24, 45, 46, 48, 5 ep.
GRAY—*2, *19.
H.C.S.—*2, 5 ep.
HALLADAY—5 ep.
HATFIELD—24, 45.
HAYNES—20, 44, 45, 5 ep.
HOLLIER—45.
HUDFORD TRUCK UNIT—*24, 45.
INTER-STATE—45, 46, 5 ep.
JACKSON—7, *22, 37, 45, 46, 5 ep, 6 rag & fsg.
JEFFERY—45, 5 ep, 6 rag.
KING—28, 45.
KREBS TRUCK—24.
LAFAYETTE—28, 31.
LEXINGTON—*25, 28, 44.
LIBERTY—*26, 45, 46.
LOCOMOBILE—26a.
LOZIER—45.

MAIBOHM—7, 24, 45, 46, 5 ep.
MARION—*2.
MARION-HANDLEY—5 ep.
MASON—*16, 33, 6 fsg.
MAXWELL—*8.
MERCER—45, 6 fsg.
METEOR—5 ep.
MITCHELL—*30, 44, 45, 5 ep.
MOLINE-KNIGHT—*23.
MONROE—*2, 45, 5 ep.
MOON—*17.
MURRAY—45.
NATIONAL—28, *32, 45, 5 ep.
NOMA—5 ep.
PARTIN-PALMER—5 ep.
PATERSON—*34, 5 ep.
PILOT—45, 5 ep.
PREMIER—*2, 45, 48, 5 ep.
R & V KNIGHT—*23, 6 fsg.
RAINIER—24.
RAUCH & LANG—*28.
REGAL—24, 45, 5 ep.
RELIANCE TRUCK—*24.
RICKENBACKER—27, 36, 44.
RIKER—*24.
ROLLIN—38.
ROSS—45.
RUGGLES TRUCK—*39.
RUXTON—30a.
SAMSON TRUCK—40, 45.
SAXON—24, 45, 5 ep.

SCRIPPS-BOOTH—7, 25, 45, 5 ep.
SENECA—23, 6 rag & fsg.
SHERIDAN—*33, 45, 5 ep, 6 rag.
SIGNAL TRUCK—*24.
SMITH FORM A TRUCK—24, *35, 45.
STANDARD—24, *41, 45, 5 ep.
STANLEY STEAMER—11.
STEARNS-KNIGHT—42.
STEPHENS—24, *43, 45, 5 ep, 6 rag
STERLING—5 ep.
STEVENS-DURYEA—*28, 6 fsg.
TEMPLAR—28, 45, 5 ep, 6 rag & fsg.
TONFORD TRUCK UNIT—45.
TRANSPORT TRUCK—*24.
TRUCKFORD UNIT—45.
U. S. TRUCKS—43a.
UNION TRUCK UNIT—45.
VELIE—*15, 6 rag & fsg.
VIM TRUCK—*24.
WESTCOTT—45, *49, 6 rag & fsg.
WILLS SAINTE CLAIRE—27, 28, 44, *50, 6 rag & fsg.
WINDSOR—*17.
WINTHER—45, 6 rag & fsg.
WINTON—27, 44, 45, *52, 5 ep, 6 rag & fsg.
WOLVERINE—*24.

INDEX OF CONCERNS MAKING PARTS FOR ORPHAN CARS LISTED ABOVE

1. All-American Truck Service Co., Flint, Mich.
2. American Motor Parts Co., Washington Ave. & Geisendorff St., Indianapolis, Ind.
3. Apperson Automobile Co., Kokomo, Ind.
4. Appleton Motor Truck Co., 924 W. Spencer St., Appleton, Wis.
5. Arrow Head Steel Products Co., 1101 Stinson Blvd., Minneapolis, Minn.
6. Automotive Gear Works, Eighth & S. O Sts., Richmond, Ind.
7. Autoparts Co., 705 Beacon St., Boston, Mass.
8. Chrysler Sales Corp., Service Parts Dept., Dayton, Ohio.
9. Columbia Motors Co., Flint, Mich.
10. Crow-Elkhart Motor Car Co., Flint, Mich.
11. Cruban Machine & Steel Corp., 54 Varick St., New York, N. Y.
12. Dort Motors, Inc., Flint, Mich.
13. Earl Motors Mfg. Service Co., Flint, Mich.
14. Elgin Motor Car Service Corp., Flint, Mich.
15. Falls Motor Corp., Flint, Mich.
16. Flint Motor Service Co., Flint, Mich.
17. General Parts Corp., Flint, Mich.
18. Grant Motor Service Co., Flint, Mich.

19. Gray Engineering Co., Flint, Mich.
20. Haynes Automobile Co., 1142 S. Main St., Kokomo, Ind.
21. Hupp Motor Car Co., Cleveland, Ohio.
22. Jackson Auto Service Co., Flint, Mich.
23. Knight Auto Parts Co., 917 Fifth Ave., East Moline, Ill.
24. Levene Motor Co., 2200 Diamond St., Philadelphia, Pa.
25. Lexington Motor Co., Kokomo, Ind.
26. Liberty Motor Car Co., Flint, Mich.
26a. Locomobile Co. of America, Inc., Bridgeport, Conn.
27. Madson & Richards, 1674 Pacific Ave., San Francisco, Cal.
28. Magnetic Auto Parts Co., Fifth Ave. & 142nd St., New York, N. Y.
29. Mason Motor Truck Co., Flint, Mich.
30. Mitchell Motor Car Co., 725 Louisa St., Flint, Mich.
30a. Moon Motor Car Co., St. Louis, Mo.
31. Nash Motors Co., Racine Div., Packard Ave., Racine, Wis.
32. National Motor Service Co., Kokomo, Ind.
33. Olds Motor Works, Division St., Lansing, Mich.
34. Paterson Motor Car Co., Flint, Mich.
35. Perfection Brake Co., 2426 Spring Grove Ave., Cincinnati, Ohio.
36. Rickenbacker Motor Co., Flint, Mich.

37. Roamer Consolidated Corp., Kalamazoo, Mich.
38. Rollin Motors Service Co., E. 193rd St. & Euclid Ave., Cleveland, Ohio.
39. Ruggles Motor Truck Co., Flint, Mich.
40. Samson Tractor Co., Janesville, Wis.
41. Standard Motor Car Co., Flint, Mich.
42. Stearns Knight Corp., Lakeview Rd. at Euclid Ave., Cleveland, Ohio.
43. Stephens Service Co., Freeport, Ill.
43a. Stewart Iron Works Co. (U. S. Truck Service Div.), 1700 Madison Ave., Covington, Ky.
44. United Automobile Specialists, Inc., 801 W. Washington St., Los Angeles, Cal.
45. United Motive Parts Co., 302 W. 53rd St., New York, N. Y.
46. United Parts Co., 121 N. High St., Muncie, Ind.
47. Walker Vehicle Co., 101 W. 87th St., Chicago, Ill.
48. Weske, Ad., 830 38th Ave., San Francisco, Cal.
49. Westcott Motor Car Co., Kokomo, Ind.
50. Wills Sainte Claire Co., Flint, Mich.
51. Willys-Overland, Inc., Walcott Blvd., Toledo, Ohio.
52. Winton Service, Inc., 1143 S. Main St., Kokomo, Ind.

BUYERS' GUIDE

Classified Directory of Important Sources of Supply for the Trade, Arranged Alphabetically by Product

Except for advertisers, whose complete names and addresses are shown, all companies are listed by numbers.

For names and addresses which these numbers represent see numerical-alphabetical index to all manufacturers, starting page 364.

For TRADE NAMES see alphabetical list, starting page 384.

NOTE: This directory of supplies includes only those selling to the trade. It does not include many well-known manufacturers of automobile products who sell only to other manufacturers, as for original equipment, etc.

ABRASIVES

(Bulk material used for tool sharpening, surface grinding, etc.; see also Cloth, Abrasive; Dressers; Emery Wheel; Paper, Emery & Sand; Wheels, Grinding)

11	152	1031	2336	3267
3921	4351	4761	6159a	6827

Accelerometers
See Instruments, Brake Testing

Accessories, Buyers of Surplus
See Parts and Accessories, Buyers of Surplus

Accounting Books
See Books and Forms, Accounting

Accounting Systems
See Systems, Accounting

Acetylene Gas
See Gas, Acetylene (In Tanks)

Acid, Battery
See Electrolyte, Storage Battery

Acid, Soldering
See Flux, Soldering

ADAPTERS to Accommodate Alemite Fittings for Model A Fords
518

ADAPTERS, Battery Post
35

ADAPTERS, Lamp (Electric)
(For converting gas or oil lamps into electric lamps)
5179

Addressing Machines
See Machines, Addressing

ADJUSTERS, Brake and Reverse Band for Fords
2795

ADJUSTERS, Coach Seat
720   1624   4677   6218

Aligning Gages, Running Gear
See Gages, Wheel and Axle Aligning

Aligning Jigs, Camshaft
See Reamers and Jigs, Camshaft Aligning, for Fords

Aligning Reamers, Camshaft for Fords
See Reamers and Jigs, Camshaft Aligning, for Fords

ALUMINUM, Sheet, Rod and Ingot
120   2044   2419   4222A

Ambulances, Motor
See Automobiles (Ambulances)

Ambulances, Wrecking
See Trucks, Casters and Spare Wheels, Wrecking

AMMETERS, Instrument Board

Moto Meter Gauge & Equipment Corp., Toledo, Ohio—*See adv. p.* 60

Simmons Mfg. Co., 3405-11 Perkins Ave., Cleveland, Ohio. (For Ford & Chevrolet Cars)—*See adv. p.* 62

6	1257	2818	3992	5563
5687	6336	6667		

Anti-Freeze, Radiator
See Compounds, Anti-Freezing

ANTI-RATTLERS, Brake Rod

Loock & Co., R. J., 343-45 N. Gay St., Baltimore, Md. "Lightnin"—*Illustration & prices, p.* 51

Williams Products Co., H. E., 100 S. Main St., Carthage, Mo.—*See adv. p.* 32

ANTI-RATTLERS, Brake Rod Clevis, for Fords

Loock & Co., R. J., 343-45 N. Gay St., Baltimore, Md. "Lightnin"—*Illustrated, p.* 51

Williams Products Co., H. E., 100 S. Main St., Carthage, Mo. "Reliance"—*See adv. p.* 32

2053   2634   5051   6733

ANTI-RATTLERS, Door

(Rubber or spring bumpers to prevent rattling of car doors)

Loock & Co., R. J., 343-45 N. Gay St., Baltimore, Md. "Lightnin"—*Illustration, description & prices, p.* 51

131	203	297	346	1178
1580	1829	1840	2053	2634
3324	3537	3892	3903	5627
6627				

ANTI-RATTLERS, Hood

Continental Rubber Works, 1902 Liberty St., Erie, Pa.—*See adv. p.* 64

Loock & Co., R. J., 343-45 N. Gay St., Baltimore, Md. "Lightnin"—*Illustrated, p.* 51

Anti-Rattlers, Mud Guard
See Braces, Mud Guard or Fender

ANTI-RATTLERS, Radius Rod
295

ANTI-RATTLERS, Radius Rod, for Fords
224   1842

ANTI-RATTLERS, Steering Rod

Loock & Co., R. J., 343-45 N. Gay St., Baltimore, Md. "Lightnin"—*Illustration & prices, p.* 51

Williams Products Co., H. E., 100 S. Main St., Carthage, Mo. "Reliance." (For Fords)—*See adv. p.* 32

295

ANTI-RATTLERS, Window

35	295	1309	1829	1840
1842	2412	2604	3120	3805
3903	4240	4327	5627	6627

Anti-Shimmy Devices
See Checks, Steering Gear

Anti-Squeak, Body
See Lining, Body or Frame

ANVILS, Rim
6611

APRONS, Acid Resisting

Gates Rubber Co., 999 S. Broadway, Denver, Colo.—*See adv. p.* 62

559	644	1318	1829	2324
4525	5597	5617	6344	

APRONS, Wash

291	644	1035	1192	1318
1573	1905	2415	2773	5617
6133	6344			

Arbors, Expanding
See Mandrels, Expanding

ARMATURES

Armature Co., 7510 Stanton Ave., Cleveland, Ohio. "Ar-Nu"—*Illustrated, p.* 59

Jambor Tool & Stamping Co., 1261 30th St., Milwaukee, Wis. "Bull Dog"—*See adv. p.* 64

See Page 364 for Names of Companies Represented by Above Numbers

ARMATURES—Continued
Simmons Mfg. Co., 3405-11 Perkins Ave., Cleveland, Ohio—*See adv. p. 62*

241   1242   2477   5513   5563
6324A 6354

Arm Rests
See Rests, Arm

ARMS, Breaker
Jambor Tool & Stamping Co., 1261 30th St., Milwaukee, Wis. "Bull Dog"—*See adv. p. 64*

Niehoff & Co., C. E., 230 W. Superior St., Chicago, Ill.—*See adv. p. 63*

Simmons Mfg. Co., 3405-11 Perkins Ave., Cleveland, Ohio. (For Ford & Chevrolet Cars)—*See adv. p. 62*

1827   5550

ARRESTERS, Flame
6   66

Ash Receivers or Trays
See Receptacles, Ash

Asphalt Distributors
See Automobiles (Oil, Tar and Asphalt Distributors)

Assist Cords
See Cords, Assist

ATTACHMENTS, Lathe Milling
4726   4779

ATTACHMENTS, Six Wheel, for Trucks
1637   1885   2012   3521a   4775
5195   5585   5828   6203a   6351
6377

ATTACHMENTS, Snow, for Fords
(Runners and Traction Treads)
5616

AUTOMOBILES (Ambulances)
1340   2094   3300   5442   6691

AUTOMOBILES (Buses)
8	141	363	632a	636a
731	1142	1293	1614	1630
2011	2023	2040	2094	2351
2433	2476	3029	3048	3300
3753	3968	4244	5081	5085
5402a	5434	5498	5747	6225
6376	6562	6572	6691	

AUTOMOBILES, Commercial (Electric)
4500   6562   6574

AUTOMOBILES, Commercial (Gasoline)
Reo Motor Car Co., 1331 S. Washington Ave., Lansing, Mich.—*Prices, p. 16*

Stewart Motor Corp., Dept. 16, 93 Dewey Ave., Buffalo, N. Y.—*Illustration, specifications & prices, p. 28*

Willys-Overland, Inc., Walcott Blvd., Toledo, Ohio. "Willys," "Whippet," "Willys-Knight"—*Distributors, p. 22*

8	28	245	294	309
363	632A	636A	707	731
1073	1110	1163	1194	1202
1216	1254a	1293	1346	1558a
1586	1593	1609a	1611	1614
1630	1657	1665	1808	1876a
2011	2040	2102	2119	2136
2351	2406	2423	2430	2431
2433	2440a	2476	2667	2679
2731	2824	2827	3029	3043
3048	3259	3300	3307	3409a
3436	3458	3558	3705	3753
3938	3968	4244	4273a	4290
4325	4552	4627	4640	4732
5061	5081	5083a	5085	5099
5141	5402a	5434	5498	5688
5713	5747	5760	5778	6376
6572	6691	6705	6738	6742
6748	6765	6795a		

AUTOMOBILES, Delivery (Frequent Stop)
1607   2094   5736

AUTOMOBILES (Fire Apparatus)
8	61	165	703	777
2119	2612	2813	3048	3704
4290	4718	5149	5486	5498
6592				

AUTOMOBILES (Hearses and Funeral Cars)
1340   2094   3300   3860   5442
5791

AUTOMOBILES (Oil, Tar and Asphalt Distributors)
1911   3290

AUTOMOBILES, Passenger (Gasoline)
Auburn Automobile Co., S. Main St., Auburn, Ind. ("Auburn" rear drive; "Cord" front drive)—*Prices, p. 130*

Buick Motor Co., Flint, Mich.—*Description, prices & zone offices, p. 15*

Cadillac Motor Car Co., 2830 Clark Ave., Detroit, Mich. "Cadillac," "La Salle"—*See adv. p. 24*

Hudson Motor Car Co., 12601 E. Jefferson Ave., Detroit, Mich. "Essex," "Hudson"—*Description & prices, p. 30*

Reo Motor Car Co., 1331 S. Washington Ave., Lansing, Mich.—*Prices, p. 16*

Willys-Overland, Inc., Walcott Blvd., Toledo, Ohio. "Willys," "Whippet," "Willys-Knight"—*Distributors, p. 22*

130a	298	785	1008	1110
1138	1340	1567	1586	1614
1641	1662	1665	1853	2094
2102	2128	2315	2430	2824
2844	3017a	3148	3300	3504
3792	3843	3901	3938	4207
4505	4535	4611	4650	4704
4732	5099	5141	5168	5791
5796	6742			

AUTOMOBILES (Street Sweepers, Flushers and Sprinklers)
818   1874   1911   2430

AUTOMOBILES (Taxicabs)
707   1105   2102   2351   2844
3938   4704   4732

AWNINGS, Fabric, Door and Window
(See also Awnings and Shades Combined; also Ventilators, Closed Car)
Williams Products Co., H. E., 100 S. Main St., Carthage, Mo.—*Illustrated, p. 32*

291	621	644	740	1192
1225	1318	1651	1905	2139
2614	2748	2758	3718	3895
5178	5191	5448	5460	5554
6133	6150	6733		

AWNINGS AND SHADES COMBINED
6500   6659

Axle Parts, Repair Tools, etc.
See following heads:
Bars, Axle Straightening
Cages, Pinion Shaft Bearing
Mills, Steering Knuckle Bushing, for Fords
Nuts, Axle Shaft Adjusting
Presses, Axle
Pullers, Axle Housing for Fords
Retainers, Rear Axle Grease
Rods, Rear Axle Truss, for Fords
Shafts, Propeller and Rear Axle
Shims, Axle Caster
Spindles, Emergency Rear Axle, for Fords
Stands, Axle Repair (Rear)
Trucks, Rear Axle

Axle Rethreading Dies
See Tools, Thread Restoring

AXLES, Front, for Fords
Simmons Mfg. Co., 3405-11 Perkins Ave., Cleveland, Ohio — *See adv. p. 62*

AXLES, Rear
(Complete Rear Axle Units; for Axle Parts—See Specific Article)
2406   4227   6157

AXLES, Rear (Two Speed)
2389a

Babbitt Metal
See Metals, Bearing

Babbitt Peining Tools
See Tools, Babbitt Peining

Babbitting Jigs
See Jigs, Main Bearing and Connecting Rod Babbitting

Babbitting Machines
See Machines, Babbitting (Main Bearing and Connecting Rod)

Back Rests
See Rests, Cushion Back

BACKS, Metal Seat
1885   3872

Bags, Curtain
See Cases, Curtain

Bags, Grease
See Boots, Steering Knuckle and Joint

BAGS, Steam Tire Curing
532   2355   3894   6649

BAGS, Water Carrying
(See also Buckets, Collapsible)
621   740   1225   4798
5448   6679

BAGS or ROLLS, Tool
291	602	644	1035	1132
1318	1573	1583	1905	3027
3147	4308	4798	6200	

Balancing Machines
See Machines, Balancing, Crankshaft; also Machines, Balancing (Wheel)

Ball Bearings
See Bearings, Ball

Ball Shims, for Fords
See Bearings, Crankshaft Thrust, for Fords

BALLS, Gear Shift Lever (Composition)
Loock & Co., R. J., 343-45 N. Gay St., Baltimore, Md. 'Lightnin'—*Illustration, description & prices, p. 51*
582   2396   3018   3352   3537
4731   6145   6218   6832

BALLS, Gear Shift Lever (Onyx)

| 2809 | 4334 | 5639 | 6145 |

BALLS, Gear Shift Lever (Wood)

584

BALLS, Steel

C & C Sales Corp., General Motors Bldg., Broadway at 57th St., New York, N. Y. "F & S" (Importers) —*Warehouse stocks, p. 58*

SKF Industries, Inc., 40 E. 34th St., New York, N. Y. "Atlas"—*Distributors, p. 171*

299	580	1000a	2480	2656
2702	2803	4286	5025	5401
5788	6589			

BANDS, Brake

Jambor Tool & Stamping Co., 1261 30th St., Milwaukee, Wis. "Bull Dog"—*See adv. p. 64*

| 281 | 1669 | 1905 | 3104 | 3858 |
| 4353 | 4702 | 6806 | | |

BANDS, Transmission, for Fords

| 1672 | 1905 | 2338 | 3891A | 5049 |
| 6361 | | | | |

Bar Cutters

See Cutters, Rod and Bar

BAROMETERS, Altitude Indicating

(For dash attachment)

| 6109 | 6125 |

Barrel Faucets

See Faucets, Drum or Barrel

BARS, Axle Straightening

Bear Mfg. Co., 21st St. & Fifth Ave., Rock Island, Ill.—*See adv. p. 123*

National Machine & Tool Co., 801 S. Water St., Jackson, Mich.—*See adv. p. 120*

| 581 | 4005 |

BARS, Axle Straightening, for Fords

| 581 | 6745 |

BARS, Boring

(See also Tools, Cylinder Reboring (Portable))

| 250 | 1130 | 1178 | 3512a | 5058 |
| 5192 | 5485 | 6461 | 6730 | |

Bars, Cored and Solid

See Metals, Bearing

BARS, Grease Rack

(For freeing frozen shackles)

5059

BARS, Straightening

| 100 | 3256 | 4005 | 6745 |

BARS, Towing (One-Man Type)

(See also Ropes, Chains and Bars, Tow)

National Machine & Tool Co., 801 S. Water St., Jackson, Mich.—*Illustration & prices, p. 120*

| 100 | 3256 | 3974 | 4258 |

BATTERIES, Dry

| 684 | 729 | 798 | 2141 | 2342 |
| 2761 | 4223 | 4258 | 5495 | 6300 |

BATTERIES, Storage

235	684	1182	1219	1222
1260	1286	1322	1548a	1868
1892	2110	2348	2366	2398
2425	2438	2770	2794	2795
2836	3451	3573	3790	3951

4221	4690	4771	4773	5062
5092	5495	5600	5671	5677
6300	6355	6476	6646	6726
6760	6803			

Battery Chargers, Auto

See Generators, Electric Lighting and Battery Charging (Auto)

Battery Parts, Supplies, Boxes, etc.

See Bolts; Boxes; Cables; Compounds; Connectors; Covers; Electrolyte; Handles; Jars; Locks, Cabinet and Pad; Paints; Parts, Storage Battery Repair; Separators; Shims, Battery Post; Terminals; Zincs

Battery Shop Equipment

See Adapters; Carriers; Chargers; Clamps, Clips; Drills and Bits; Fillers; Heaters; Hydrometers; Indicators; Instruments; Jumpers; Molds; Motor Generators; Openers; Plugs; Presses; Rheostats; Tools, Storage Battery Repair; Vises

Batting, Cotton

See Wadding and Batting, Cotton

Bearing Caps, Adjustable Center, for Fords

See Caps, Adjustable Main Bearing, for Fords

Bearing Metals

See Metals, Bearing

Bearing Repair Tools

See following heads:
Drivers, Bearing Cup
Jigs, Connecting Rod Aligning
Jigs, Main Bearing and Connecting Rod Aligning
Machines, Babbitting
Machines, Boring
Mandrels, Connecting Rod
Pullers, Bearing
Reamers, Main Bearing and Connecting Rod
Scrapers, Bearing
Tools, Bearing Shaving and Burnishing
Tools, Piston Pin and Connecting Rod Bushing Honing

BEARINGS and BUSHINGS, Bronze-Backed

(See also Bearings and Bushings, Die Cast (Babbitt, Etc.); also Bushings, Bronze; for bearing or bushing metal—See Metals, Bearing)

Federal-Mogul Corp., 11031 Shoemaker Rd., Detroit, Mich.—*Illustration & warehouses, p. 189*

Johnson Bronze Co., S. Mill St., New Castle, Pa.—*Illustration & warehouses, p. 60*

McQuay-Norris Mfg. Co., Cooper & Southwest Aves., St. Louis, Mo.—*See adv. p. 88*

| 764 | 790 | 2039 | 2853 | 3129 |
| 3728 | 3911 | 4605 | 5210 | |

BEARINGS and BUSHINGS, Die Cast (Babbitt, etc.)

(See also Bearings and Bushings, Bronze-backed; for bearing or bushing metal—See Metals, Bearing)

Federal-Mogul Corp., 11031 Shoemaker Rd., Detroit, Mich.—*Illustration & warehouses, p. 189*

McQuay-Norris Mfg. Co., Cooper & Southwest Aves., St. Louis, Mo.— *See adv. p. 88*

Simmons Mfg. Co., 3405-11 Perkins Ave., Cleveland, O. (For Fords & Chevrolet cars)—*See adv. p. 62*

| 2039 | 2853 | 3728 | 3911 | 3975 |
| 4605 | 5563 | | | |

BEARINGS, Ball

(For bearing parts—See Balls, Steel; also Cups and Cones, Ball; also Retainers, Ball)

Biglow & Co., L. C., 250 W. 54th St., New York, N. Y. (New York representatives for Bearings Co. of America)—*See adv. p. 129*

C & C Sales Corp., General Motors Bldg., Broadway at 57th St., New York, N. Y. "F & S" (Importers). —*Illustration & warehouse stocks, p. 58*

Fafnir Bearing Co., New Britain, Conn.—*Illustration & distributors, p. 167*

Federal Bearings Co., 17 Fairview Ave., Poughkeepsie, N. Y.—*Illustration & warehouse stocks, p. 173*

New Departure Mfg. Co., 269 N. Main St., Bristol, Conn.—*Illustration & control branches, p. 165*

Norma - Hoffmann Bearings Corp., Stamford, Conn. — *Illustrated, p. 169*

SKF Industries, Inc., 40 E. 34th St., New York, N. Y. "Hess-Bright," "SKF"—*Distributors, p. 171*

Simmons Mfg. Co., 3405-11 Perkins Ave., Cleveland, Ohio. (For Ford & Chevrolet cars)—*See adv. p. 62*

60	299	341	535	580
641	1000a	2010	2034	2480
2803	3272	4286	4312	4335
5025	5026	5130	5400	5401
5403	5563	5648	5683	5695a
5786	6177	6634		

BEARINGS, Ball (Reground)

| 60 | 4604 | 5400 |

BEARINGS, Clutch Throwout (Composition)

Hygrade Products Co., 333 W. 52nd St., New York, N. Y.—*See adv. p. 86*

Dorman Star Washer Co., 219 E. Eighth St., Cincinnati, Ohio—*Illustrated & described, p. 102*

Es-M-Co Auto Products Corp., 31 34th St., Brooklyn, N. Y. (For Chevrolet cars) — *Illustration & warehouses, p. 70*

| 1626 | 1906 | 2033 | 2619 | 4556 |
| 5494A | 5687 | | | |

BEARINGS, Crankshaft Thrust, for Fords

| 43 | 81 | 295 | 3418 | 3537 |

Bearings, Intermediate

See Boxes, Propeller Shaft

BEARINGS, Oilless

Dorman Star Washer Co., 219 E. Eighth St., Cincinnati, Ohio—*See adv. p. 102*

Es-M-Co Auto Products Corp., 31 34th St., Brooklyn, N. Y.—*Illustration & warehouses, p. 70*

| 3129 | 4279a |

BEARINGS, Rebabbitted

(Advertisers in this publication only)

Clawson & Bals, Inc., 4701-09 W. Lake St., Chicago, Ill. "C & B"— *Illustration & plants, p. 95*

Federal-Mogul Corp., 11031 Shoemaker Rd., Detroit, Mich. "Watkins"—*Babbitting plants, p. 189*

See Page 364 for Names of Companies Represented by Above Numbers

BEARINGS, Roller
(See also Bearings, Roller (Tapered))
Biglow & Co., L. C., 250 W. 54th St., New York, N. Y. (New York representatives for Roller Bearing Co. of America)—*See adv. p.* 129
Norma-Hoffmann Bearings Corp., Stamford, Conn. — *Illustrated, p.* 169
Roller Bearing Co. of America (Replacement Div.), Whitehead Rd., Trenton, N. J. "Heliflex"—*Illustration & sizes, p.* 175
Rollway Bearing Co., 541 Seymour St., Syracuse, N. Y.—*See adv. p.* 185
SKF Industries, Inc., 40 E. 34th St., New York, N. Y.—*Distributors, p.* 171
Simmons Mfg. Co., 3405-11 Perkins Ave., Cleveland, Ohio. (For Ford & Chevrolet cars)—*See adv. p.* 62
Timken Roller Bearing Service & Sales Co., 19th St. & Dueber Ave., S. W., Canton, Ohio—*Illustrated, p.* 57

299	535	580	641	697
2480	2849	3272	3717	4335
4544	4757	5025	5167	5170
5201	5400	5401	5563	5648
5683	6106	6159	6644	

BEARINGS, Roller (Tapered)
Simmons Mfg. Co., 3405-11 Perkins Ave., Cleveland, Ohio. (For Ford & Chevrolet cars)—*See adv. p.* 62
Timken Roller Bearing Service & Sales Co., 19th St. & Dueber Ave., S. W., Canton, Ohio — *Illustrated, p.* 57

2803	4544	4757

BEARINGS, Steel-Backed
2039

BEDS or BERTHS, Car and Camp

44	307	644	740	2408
3069	3222	3718	3895	3993
4798	5773			

BELLS and BUZZERS, Bus Passenger Signal

1262	1866	5476

Belt Fasteners
See Fasteners, Belt
Belt Lacers
See Lacers, Belt
Belt Tighteners, Automatic Fan, for Fords
See Tighteners, Automatic Fan Belt, for Fords

BELTING, Leather

23	692	763	1027	1111
1124	2441	2808	3128	3408
3455	3725	4725	5046	5075
5113	5612	5672	6657	6696
6734				

BELTS, Fabric
Continental Rubber Works, 1902 Liberty St., Erie, Pa. "Vitalic"—*See adv. p.* 64
Durkee-Atwood Co., 40 Wilder St., Minneapolis, Minn.—*Illustrated & described, p.* 63
Emsco Asbestos Co., 206 S. Crawford St., Downey, Calif.—*Illustration & warehouse stocks, p.* 84
Gates Rubber Co., 999 S. Broadway, Denver, Colo. "Gates Vulco"—*Illustrated & described, p.* 62

Holfast Rubber Co., Lakewood Ave., Atlanta, Ga.—*See adv. p.* 65

115	258	808	1274	1534
1667	1829	1889	2324	2378
2412	2416	2758	2781	3903
4556	5182	5214	5598	5612
6344	6361			

BELTS, Rubber
Emsco Asbestos Co., 206 S. Crawford St., Downey, Calif.—*Illustration & warehouse stocks, p.* 84

3903	5612

BELTS, V
Continental Rubber Works, 1902 Liberty St., Erie, Pa. "Vitalic"—*Illustrated, p.* 64
Durkee-Atwood Co., 40 Wilder St., Minneapolis, Minn.—*See adv. p.* 63
Gates Rubber Co., 999 S. Broadway, Denver, Col. "Gates Vulco"—*Illustrated & described, p.* 62
Holfast Rubber Co., Lakewood Ave., Atlanta, Ga.—*See adv. p.* 65

1027	1111	1124	1274	1534
1667	1829	2324	2378	2412
2416	2441	2781	3903	5046
5049	5075	5113	5214	5612
6361				

Benches, Electric Test
See Stands, Electric Test

BENCHES, Work
Lyon Metal Products, Inc., 2931 Montgomery St., Aurora, Ill.—*Illustrated, p.* 106
Manley Mfg. Co., 929 Connecticut Ave., Bridgeport, Conn. — *Illustrated, p.* 38

3571	3774	4741	5635	5690
6621				

BENDERS, Angle (Hand)

6565	6701

Billing Systems
See Systems, Accounting
Binders, Loose Leaf
See Books and Forms, Accounting

BINS, Parts Storage
Berger Mfg. Co., Div. Republic Steel Corp., 1038 Belden Ave., N.E., Canton, Ohio. "Berloy"—*Illustration, description & specifications, p.* 105
Lyon Metal Products, Inc., 2931 Montgomery St., Aurora, Ill.—*Illustrated, p.* 106

213	304	622	1555	2345
3564	3571	3782b	3840	4253
4654	5728	6124		

Bits, Battery Strap
See Drills and Bits, Battery Strap

BLADES, Saw (Hack)
(See also Frames, Hack Saw)

275	726	1052	1592	1604
2107	2410	2835	3905	3918
4205	4649	5029	5565	5602
5719	6142	6208	6485	

Blocks, Car Extracting
See Winches and Blocks, Car Extracting

BLOCKS or HOISTS, Chain
(For portable cranes—See Cranes, Portable)

36	1070	1134	1876	2101
3546	4306	5193	5649	6778
6799				

Blow Guns
See Nozzles, Air

BLOW PIPES, Brazing, Welding & Cutting
Linde Air Products Co., 30 E. 42nd St., New York, N. Y. "Oxweld," "Prest-O-Weld" — *Illustration, description & branch offices, p.* 125

157	4708	5821	6171	6176

Blow Torches
See Torches and Furnaces, Gasoline or Kerosene

BLOWERS, Heat
See Tools, Heat Blowing (Electric)

BLUE, Mechanics'
(For use when adjusting bearings)

1667	2616	2661	3922	4347
4673	5120	6143	6456	

BOARDS, Display (Wooden)

152	2841	5654	5814

BOARDS, Floor or Foot

5654	5814

BOARDS, Running
Simmons Mfg. Co., 3405-11 Perkins Ave., Cleveland, Ohio. (For Ford and Chevrolet cars)—*See adv. p.* 62

209	1294	1919	3035a	3263
3448	3872	4751	5563	5654
5814	6460	6814a		

BODIES, Armored
(Advertisers in this publication only)
National Steel Products Co., 1611 Crystal Ave., Kansas City, Mo.—*Illustrated, p.* 130

BODIES, Dump (Stock Models)
(Advertisers in this publication only)
(Automatic, rocking, elevating, gravity and hoisting types)
National Steel Products Co., 1511 Crystal Ave., Kansas City, Mo.—*Illustrated, p.* 130

Body Hoists
See Hoists, Truck Body
Body Surfacing Machines
See Tools, Metal Finishing, Portable Electric
Bolt and Screw Cases
See Cases, Bolt and Screw
Bolt Clippers
See Clippers, Bolt and Rivet
Bolt Extractors
See Extractors, Bolt and Screw

BOLTS, Anchor
2338A

BOLTS, Battery Hold Down

2338a	2861	5213	6323a

BOLTS, Bumper End
284

BOLTS, Clip

284	774	1128	1158	2338a
3420	5538	5815	6644	

BOLTS, Connecting Rod
(See also Bolts and Nuts, Automatic Connecting Rod Bearing)
Cleveland Cap Screw Co., 3004 E. 79th St., Cleveland, Ohio—*Warehouse stocks, p.* 95

16	284	774	1128	1173
2056	2338a	3420	4688	5213
5789	6323a	6644		

See Page 364 for Names of Companies Represented by Above Numbers

BOLTS, Coupling

Cleveland Cap Screw Co., 3004 E. 79th St., Cleveland Ohio—*Warehouse stocks, p. 95*

774	1128	1173	2338a	2663
5538	5612	5815	6483	6644

BOLTS, Demountable Rim

Russell, Burdsall & Ward Bolt & Nut Co., Port Chester, N. Y. "Empire" —*Illustration & branch offices, p. 61*

284	774	1158	2338a	2858
3420	5213	6139	6568	6677

Bolts, King

See Bolts, Steering Knuckle

BOLTS, Machine and Carriage

Dorman Star Washer Co., 219 E. Eighth St., Cincinnati, Ohio—*See adv. p. 102*

Russell, Burdsall & Ward Bolt & Nut Co., Port Chester, N. Y. "Empire" (Also "Eagle" carriage)—*Illustration & branch offices, p. 61*

284	295	691	774	1095
1158	1234	1626	2338a	2669
2680	3420	4239	4254	4536
4688	5114	5156	5213	5815
6139	6221			

Bolts, Plow

See Bolts, Machine and Carriage

Bolts, Shackle

See Bolts, Spring Shackle

BOLTS, Special, for Fords

Cleveland Cap Screw Co., 3004 E. 79th St., Cleveland, Ohio—*Warehouse stocks, p. 95*

Jambor Tool & Stamping Co., 1261 30th St., Milwaukee, Wis. "Bull Dog"—*See adv. p. 64*

Simmons Mfg. Co., 3405-11 Perkins Ave., Cleveland, Ohio — *See adv. p. 62*

284	1173	3104	5563	5815
6139	6677			

BOLTS, Spring Center

Dorman Star Washer Co., 219 E. Eighth St., Cincinnati. Ohio.—*See adv. p. 102*

284	1081	1128	1626	2056
2338a	2680	3420	5213	5538
5789	5815	6568	6644	

BOLTS, Spring Shackle

(Complete bolt with oil or grease cup attached)

Cleveland Cap Screw Co., 3004 E. 79th St., Cleveland, Ohio—*Warehouse stocks, p. 95*

Jambor Tool & Stamping Co., 1261 30th St., Milwaukee, Wis. "Bull Dog"—*See adv. p. 64*

McQuay-Norris Mfg. Co., Cooper & Southwest Aves., St. Louis, Mo.— *See adv. p. 88*

Monmouth Products Co., 882 E. 72nd St., Cleveland, Ohio—*See adv. p. 72*

Russell, Burdsall & Ward Bolt & Nut Co., Port Chester, N. Y. "Empire"—*See adv. p. 61*

Simmons Mfg. Co., 3405-11 Perkins Ave., Cleveland, Ohio—*See adv. p. 62*

Thompson Products, Inc., 2196 Clarkwood Rd., Cleveland, Ohio.—*Illustrated, p. 89*

696	1128	1158	1173	2056
2116	2338a	2619	3104	3284
3728	3954	4000	5114	5213
5563	6141	6192	6644	6686
6806				

BOLTS, Steering Knuckle

Aluminum Industries, Inc., 2416 Beekman St., Cincinnati, Ohio. "Permite."—*See adv. p. 10*

Jambor Tool & Stamping Co., 1261 30th St., Milwaukee, Wis. "Bull Dog"—*See adv. p. 64*

McQuay-Norris Mfg. Co., Cooper & Southwest Aves., St. Louis, Mo.— *See adv. p. 88*

Monmouth Products Co., 882 E. 72nd St., Cleveland, Ohio—*See adv. p. 72*

Simmons Mfg. Co., 3405-11 Perkins Ave., Cleveland, Ohio—*See adv. p. 62*

Thompson Products, Inc., 2196 Clarkwood Rd., Cleveland, Ohio.—*Illustrated, p. 89*

121	1128	2056	2116	2338a
2619	3104	3284	3728	3954
4000	4536	5114	5563	6141
6192	6323a	6644	6686	6806

Bolts, Step

See Bolts, Machine and Carriage

BOLTS, Stove and Tire

Russell, Burdsall & Ward Bolt & Nut Co., Port Chester, N. Y. "Empire"—*Illustration & branch offices, p. 61*

185	284	774	1158	1234
1292	2338A	2472	2680	2702
3420	4239	4254	4522	4688
5056	5156	5213	5815	6221

Bolts, Tie Rod

See Bolts, Steering Knuckle

BOLTS and NUTS, Automatic Connecting Rod Bearing

(See also Bolts, Connecting Rod)

Federal-Mogul Corp., 11031 Shoemaker Rd., Detroit, Mich.—*Illustration & warehouses, p. 189*

BOOKS and FORMS, Accounting

(Advertisers in this publication only)

Comfort Printing Specialty Co., 107 N. Eighth St., St. Louis, Mo.—*See adv. p. 108*

St. Louis Tag Co., 217 Locust St., St. Louis, Mo.—*See adv. p. 114*

Unique Printed Products Co., 2224 N. 13th St., Terre Haute, Ind.— *See adv. p. 127*

BOOKS, Sales

(Advertisers in this publication only)

Comfort Printing Specialty Co., 107 N. Eighth St., St. Louis, Mo.—*See adv. p. 108*

BOOSTERS, Battery

503A

Boosters, Brake

See Brakes, Power

Boosters, Clutch

See Brakes, Power

Boosters, Grease

See Drivers, Grease

BOOSTERS, Vacuum Tank

5761

BOOTHS, Spraying (Paint and Varnish)

Lyon Metal Products, Inc., 2931 Montgomery St., Aurora, Ill.—*See adv. p. 106*

646	1587	3016	4603

BOOTS, Steering Knuckle and Joint

(Leather, oilcloth and fabric covers for enclosing steering connections and universal joints)

1124	1573	1829	2441	3027
3455	6821			

BOOTS, Steering Knuckle, for Fords

(Leather, oilcloth and fabric covers for enclosing steering connections)

1575

Boots, Tire Repair

See Patches, Tire Repair

Boots, Top

See Covers, Top

Boring Machines

See Machines, Boring, Main Bearing and Connecting Rod

Bow Clamps or Holders

See Holders, Top

Bow Sockets

See Sockets, Bow

BOWS, Side (Ornamental)

6134

BOWS, Top

1020	1319	1552	2407	**3459**
6145				

Box Locks

See Locks, Cabinet and Pad

BOXES, Battery (Composition)

(For encasing cell jars)

59	161	2789	5117A	5207

BOXES, Battery (Metal)

(For carrying battery on running board of car)

1603	2392	3294	5725

BOXES, Battery (Metal), for Fords

2392

BOXES, Battery (Rubber)

(For encasing cell jars)

Continental Rubber Works, 1902 Liberty St., Erie, Pa. "Vitalic"— *See adv. p. 64*

Gates Rubber Co., 999 S. Broadway, Denver, Colo. "Gates Vulco."—*See adv. p. 62*

1829	2412

BOXES, Battery (Wood)

(For encasing cell jars)

4288A	5671	6355

BOXES, Battery (Wood)

(For carrying battery on running board of car)

2451

BOXES, Fare

4528

Boxes, Propeller Shaft

See Propeller Shaft Boxes

Boxes, Rubber Battery Cell

See Jars, Battery Cell (Rubber)

Boxes, Spare Lamp Bulb

See Cases, Lamp Bulb

BOXES, Tool (Metal)

(For tool bags—See Bags or Rolls, Tool)

Lyon Metal Products, Inc., 2931 Montgomery St., Aurora, Ill.—*See adv. p. 106*

114	304	656	1150	1247
1658	1668	2392	2769	3252
3294	3571	3872	4726	5511
5611	5725	5753	6108	6306
6814a				

BOXES, Tool (Metal), for Fords

1294   2392

BOXES, Tool (Wood)

(For tool bags—See Bags or Rolls, Tool)

6306

BOXES, Tote (Metal)

(Shop Boxes and Barrels)

Lyon Metal Products, Inc., 2931 Montgomery St., Aurora, Ill.—*See adv. p. 106*

213	1164	1555	1668	1845
2009	2362	3252	3294	3571
3782b	4017	4248	4751	5725
6566				

BOXES, Tote (Wood)

1164

Braces, Headlight

See Brackets, Headlight (Stationary)

BRACES, Mud Guard or Fender

3530   3855

BRACES, Mud Guard or Fender (For Model T Fords)

Williams Products Co., H. E., 100 S. Main St., Carthage, Mo.—*See adv. p. 32*

1905   6559   6733

BRACES, Running Board (For Model T Fords)

1905

BRACKETS, Headlight (Stationary)

1823

BRACKETS, Lamp (Side and Tail)

76   1603   4757   5731

BRACKETS, Mirror

720   3212

Brads

See Tacks, Upholstery

Brake Band Repair Equipment

See Adjusters, Brake and Reverse Band, for Fords; Machines, Brake Relining; Tools, Brake Band

Brake Cleaning Compounds, Hydraulic

See Compounds, Hydraulic Brake Cleaning

Brake Cleaning Machines, Hydraulic

See Machines, Brake Cleaning (Portable Hydraulic)

Brake Compounds

See Dressing, Brake

Brake Drum Repair Equipment

See Drums, Brake Dummy; Gages, Brake Drum; Gages, Brake and Drum Concentricity; Lathes, Brake Drum; Machines, Grinding, Brake Drum

Brake Fluid

See Fluid, Hydraulic Brake and Shock Absorber

Brake Parts and Attachments

See Bands, Brake; Brakes, Power; Cable; Drums, Brake; Equalizers, Brake; Lining, Brake; Screws, Brake; Shoes, Brake

Brake Relining Equipment

See Clamps, Brake Lining; Cutters, Brake Lining; Machines, Grinding, Brake Lining; Machines, Brake Relining

Brake Testing Equipment

See Depressors, Brake Pedal; Instruments, Brake Testing; also Machines; also Tools

BRAKES, Air

Bendix-Westinghouse Automotive Air Brake Co. (Div. of Bendix Aviation Corp.), 5001 Centre Ave., Pittsburgh, Pa.—*See Front Cover*

BRAKES, Hydraulic

Duplex Brake Engineering Co., 54 Garfield Ave., Trenton, N. J. "Mackenzie." — *Illustrated & described, p. 58*

Hydraulic Brake Co. (Div. of Bendix Aviation Corp.), 2843 Grand Blvd., E., Detroit, Mich. "Lockheed."—*See Front Cover*

6553

BRAKES, Mechanical

Bendix Brake Co. (Div. of Bendix Aviation Corp.), 401 Bendix Drive, South Bend, Ind.—*See Front Cover*

138a   5761

BRAKES, Power (Amplifying Unit Only) (Compressed Air)

6597

BRAKES, Power (Amplifying Unit Only) (Hydraulic)

5723

BRAKES, Power (Amplifying Unit Only) (Mechanical)

Duplex Brake Engineering Co., 54 Garfield Ave., Trenton, N. J. "Duplex Brakeaid."—*Illustration, description & prices, p. 58*

BRAKES and CLUTCHES, Power (Amplifying Unit Only) (Vacuum)

Bragg-Kliesrath Corp. (Div. of Bendix Aviation Corp.), 401 Bendix Drive, South Bend, Ind. "B-K"— *Illustration & distributors, p. 1; also see Front Cover*

5761

BRAKES, Power (Complete With Brakes)

5761

Brazing Flux or Compounds

See Fluxes, Brazing and Welding

Breaker Arms

See Arms, Breaker

Breaker Points

See Points, Contact

Breather Caps

See Caps, Crankcase Breather

BROADCLOTH, Upholstery

725   2387   3411   6563   6710

Bronze, Bearing

See Metals, Bearing

Bronze Bushings

See Bushings, Bronze

Bronze Paints

See Paints, Aluminum and Bronze

Brush Holders, for Generators, etc.

See Parts, Starting Motor Drive

Brushes, Air

See Sprayers, Paint, Varnish and Lacquer

Brushes, Buffing, Wire

See Brushes, Rotary Wire

BRUSHES, Carbon Cleaning (Hand)

1895a   3905   4721a   6461   6792

BRUSHES, Carbon Removing

(With arbors to fit electric drill chucks)

1342a   2721   3271   6332   6459
6461

Brushes, Car Washing

See Washers, Automobile (Brushes); also Washers, Automobile (Fountain Brushes and Mops)

BRUSHES, File Cleaning

1148	1895A	3781	4314	4550
4694	5129	6199		

BRUSHES, Floor

2721	3026	3781	3912	4550
4721a	5144	6791		

Brushes, Fountain

See Washers, Automobile (Fountain Brushes and Mops)

BRUSHES, Generator, Horn and Starter

(Carbon, metal and woven wire)

Jambor Tool & Stamping Co., 1261 30th St., Milwaukee, Wis. "Bull Dog"—*See adv. p. 64*

Niehoff & Co., C. E., 230 W. Superior St., Chicago, Ill.—*See adv. p. 63*

337	1092	1257	1548a	1827
2472	2619	3202	4317	4517
4601	5739			

BRUSHES, Rotary Wire

83	655	1342a	1525	2721
3781	3905	3912	4550	4709
4721a	5129	5783	6459	6461
6619	6792			

BRUSHES, Spark Plug

(Small wire or bristle brushes for cleaning spark plugs)

138   1040   2721   4721a   6619

BRUSHES, Timer, for Fords

Simmons Mfg. Co., 3405-11 Perkins Ave., Cleveland, Ohio — *See adv. p. 62*

5212

Brushes, Wheel

See Washers, Automobile (Brushes); also Washers, Automobile (Fountain Brushes and Mops)

Brushes, Wool Dusting

See Dusters, Wool and Cotton

BUCKETS, Collapsible

4798   5448

Buckets, Grease

See Lubricators, Portable, High Pressure

BUCKETS, Tank Body

3713   4784

Buffers, Electric Portable

See Drills, Grinders and Polishers, Electric Portable

Buffing Machines, Tire

See Machines, Tire Buffing (Electric)

Bulbs, Incandescent

See Lamps or Bulbs, Miniature Incandescent

Bumper End Bolts

See Bolts, Bumper End

BUMPER PARTS

Bumpers, Inc., 340 W. 70th St., New York, N. Y.—*See adv. p. 67*

Bumper Shields

See Shields, Bumper

BUMPERS, Automobile

(Front and rear)

Bumpers, Inc., 340 W. 70th St., New York, N. Y. (Distributors) — *See adv. p. 67*

113	142	639	789	1141
1603	1819	2042	2694	3327
3410	3445	3721	3794	3943
5692	5761	5772	6347	6503
6582				

Bumpers, Door

See Anti-Rattlers, Door

BUMPERS, Spring

(Rubber or spiral spring bumpers to prevent car frame from striking axle)

634	1146	1240	1274	1829
1909	3903	5049	6344	

Bumping Hammers

See Tools, Body and Fender Repair

BURLAP

602   2157   3422

BURNERS, Acetylene Lamp

166   3293

BURNERS, Lead

Imperial Brass Mfg. Co., 1225 W. Harrison St., Chicago, Ill. — *See adv. p. 126*

221	555	559	2654	3016
3507	3891	3928a	4708	4801a
4803	5419	5608	5811	6171
6176	6217	6622		

Burning-In Machines

See Machines, Burning-In

Burning Machines, Lead

See Burners, Lead

BURRS, Rivet

292   5765   6323a

Buses

See Automobiles (Buses)

Bushing Extractors

See Extractors, Bushing; also Saws, Bushing Removing

Bushings, Babbitt-Lined Bronze-Backed

See Bearings and Bushings, Bronze-backed

Bushings for Breaker Arms

See Parts, Starting Motor Drive

BUSHINGS, Bronze

(For cored bushing bars—See Metals, Bearing; for die cast bearings—See Bearings and Bushings, Die Cast (Babbitt, etc.); for bronze-backed, babbitt-lined bearings and bushings—See Bearings and Bushings, Bronze-backed)

Aluminum Industries, Inc., 2416 Beekman St., Cincinnati, Ohio. "Permite."—*See adv. p. 10.*

Es-M-Co Auto Products Corp., 31 34th St., Brooklyn, N. Y. (For Chevrolet c a r s)—*Illustration & warehouses, p. 70*

Federal-Mogul Corp., 11031 Shoemaker Rd., Detroit, Mich.—*Illustration & warehouses, p. 189*

Jambor Tool & Stamping Co., 1261 30th St., Milwaukee, Wis. "Bull Dog"—*See adv. p. 64*

Johnson Bronze Co., S. Mill St., New Castle, Pa. — *Illustration & warehouses, p. 60*

Monmouth Products Co., 882 E. 72nd St., Cleveland, Ohio. "Steelclad" —*Described, p. 72*

Simmons Mfg. Co., 3405-11 Perkins Ave., Cleveland, Ohio. (For Chevrolet & Ford cars) — *See adv. p. 62*

Thompson Products, Inc., 2196 Clarkwood Rd., Cleveland, Ohio.—*Illustrated, p. 89*

Williams Products Co., H. E., 100 S. Main St., Carthage, Mo. (For Chevrolet cars)—*See adv. p. 32*

121	174	285	764	790
806	1618	1906	2039	2116
2655	3104	3129	3954	4000
4011	4215	4506	4605	4700
4782	5563	5674	6141	6192
6223	6315	6356		

Bushings, Graphite

See Bearings, Oilless

BUSHINGS, Rubber

1829   2412   3903   4750

BUSHINGS, Steel

Aluminum Industries, Inc., 2416 Beekman St., Cincinnati, Ohio. "Permite."—*See adv. p. 10.*

Jambor Tool & Stamping Co., 1261 30th St., Milwaukee, Wis. "Bull Dog"—*See adv. p. 64*

McQuay-Norris Mfg. Co., Cooper & Southwest Aves., St. Louis, Mo.—*See adv. p. 88*

Monmouth Products Co., 882 E. 72nd St., Cleveland, Ohio. "Steelclad." (Bronze lined)—*Illustrated & described, p. 72*

Simmons Mfg. Co., 3405-11 Perkins Ave., Cleveland, Ohio. (For Ford & Chevrolet cars)—*See adv. p. 62*

Thompson Products, Inc., 2196 Clarkwood Rd, Cleveland, Ohio—*Illustrated, p. 89*

91A	121	2116	3104	3284
3728	3954	4000	5563	6141
6192	6323A			

BUTTONS, Push

(Special push buttons for use with electric horns—See also Controls, Horn)

Fitzgerald Mfg. Co., 691 Main St., Torrington, Conn.—*See adv. p. 76*

Hackett Products Co., 407 Pine St., Providence, R. I. (For Chevrolet, Essex & Fords cars)—*See adv. p. 40*

Schwarze Electric Co., Grace, Church & Payne Sts., Adrian, Mich.—*Illustrated p. 47*

224	337	614	1257	1844
2079	2347	2604	3002	3035a
3119	3202	4731	5179	5476
6314a				

BUTTONS, Quick Start, for Fords

(Fits over Ford starter button)

224

BUTTONS, Upholstery

Auto-Vehicle Parts Co., 1040 Saratoga St., Newport, Ky. "Au-Ve-Co"—*See adv. pp. 34 & 35*

292   4271

Buyers of Surplus Parts

See Parts and Accessories, Buyers of Surplus

Buzzers, Bus Passenger Signal

See Bells and Buzzers, Bus Passenger Signals

Cabinet Locks

See Locks, Cabinet and Pad

CABINETS, Accessory

(See also Cases, Bolt and Screw)

Lyon Metal Products, Inc., 2931 Montgomery St., Aurora, Ill.—*Illustrated, p. 106*

147	304	622	656	2705
2767	3571	4654	5753	6632

Cabinets, Tool

Lyon Metal Products, Inc., 2931 Montgomery St., Aurora, Ill.—*Illustrated, p. 106*

Cabinets, Wash Rack Equipment

Lyon Metal Products, Inc., 2931 Montgomery St., Aurora, Ill.—*Illustrated, p. 106*

CABLE, Brake Control (With Conduit)

138a   2480

CABLE, Brake or Cutout Control

Dorman Star Washer Co., 219 E. Eighth St., Cincinnati, Ohio—*See adv. p. 102*

138a   5163

CABLE, Ignition, Starting and Lighting

(In bulk length on spools, rolls, etc.)

Hygrade Products Co., 333 W. 52nd St., New York, N. Y.—*See adv. p. 86*

Manhattan Insulated Wire Co., 17-23 W. 60th St., New York, N. Y.—*Illustrated & described, p. 65*

190	202	339	592	653
1321	1851	2327	2341a	2343
2390	2411	2686	3028	3202
3771	3948	4533	4610	5163
5425	5577	5655	5687	5739
6139	6314a	6344	6681	6725

Cable Wire

See Rope or Cable, Bronze Wire

CABLES (Sets)

(Ignition and lighting assemblies made up to fit different makes of cars)

General Electric Co., Merchandise Dept., Bridgeport, Conn. "G-E"—*Illustration & prices, p. 109*

Hygrade Products Co., 333 W. 52nd St., New York, N. Y.—*Illustrated, p. 86*

Manhattan Insulated Wire Co., 17-23 W. 60th St., New York, N. Y.—*Illustrated & described, p. 65*

Simmons Mfg. Co., 3405-11 Perkins Ave., Cleveland, Ohio.—*See adv. p. 62*

337	541	592	1214	1257
1321	1548a	2327	2343	2411
2619	2858	3202	3771	3948
4610	5563	5687	5739	6193
6678	6681	6725		

CABLES (Sets), for Fords

Manhattan Insulated Wire Co., 17-23 W. 60th St., New York, N. Y.—*Illustrated & described, p. 65*

1321   2411   3948   6725

Cables, Spark Plug

See Cables (Sets)

CABLES, Storage Battery

(Complete with terminals and cut in proper lengths to fit different makes of cars)

Manhattan Insulated Wire Co., 17-23 W. 60th St., New York, N. Y.—*Illustrated & described, p. 65*

339	560	592	1219	1321
1927	2343	2477	2686	2861
3028	3202	3771	3948	4523
4610	4672	4785	5425	5577
5687	5739	6107	6139	6193
6561	6646	6678	6681	6725

CABS, Metal Truck

Weatherproof Body Corp., 480 Shiawassee St., Corunna, Mich.—*Illustrated & described, p. 32*

129	136	252	1162	1196
1517	1522	2339	2357	2603
2720	2743	3251	3294	3715
3861	3908	3937	5547	5658
5668	5778	5792	6609	

CABS, Wood Truck

Weatherproof Body Corp., 480 Shiawassee St., Corunna, Mich.—*Illustrated & described, p. 32*

136	252	1196	1282	1517
1522	2339	2357	2603	2720
2743	3024	3069	3251	3715
3861	3908	3937	3962	5547
5570	5658	5778	6609	6618
6815				

CAGES, Pinion Shaft Bearing

4662

Calcium Carbide

See Carbide, Calcium

CALIPERS and DIVIDERS

(See also Micrometers)

752	2084	2410	3032	3256
3559	4644	5719	6311	6730

Camp Equipment

See Beds or Berths, Car and Camp.

Camshaft Aligning Reamers, for Fords

See Reamers and Jigs, Camshaft Aligning, for Fords

CAMSHAFTS, Special

(For racing cars)

3986A   4030

Cane Seats

See Pads, Seat

Can Holders

See Holders, Oil Can

CANS, Gasoline

Brookins Mfg. Co., 770 Hawthorne St., Dayton, Ohio — *Illustrated & described, p. 117*

139	279	590	704A	734
817	1067	1231	1597	1632
1807	1885a	2362	2826	3159
3448	3727	3882	4784	6611

Cans, Measuring

See Measures, Metal

CANS, Oiling

Imperial Brass Mfg. Co., 1225 W. Harrison St., Chicago, Ill. (For springs)—*See adv. p. 126*

590	600	786	1523	1632
1668	1807	3016	3495	3806
4327	4757	6130	6193	6566
6679				

CANS, Radiator Filling

Brookins Mfg. Co., 770 Hawthorne St., Dayton, Ohio—*Illustrated & described, p. 117*

279	590	704A	734	1632
2362	2826	3448	3713	4784

CAPS, Adjustable Main Bearing, for Fords

(Adjustable center bearing cap to permit taking up end play in crankshaft)

42

CAPS, Crankcase Breather

Williams Products Co., H. E., 100 S. Main St., Carthage, Mo. (For Model T Fords)—*See adv. p. 32*

518	1620	5559	6502

CAPS, Dash Lamp

3278

CAPS, Gasoline Tank (Aluminum)

Jambor Tool & Stamping Co., 1261 30th St., Milwaukee, Wis. "Bull Dog"—*See adv. p. 64*

Loock & Co., R. J., 343-45 N. Gay St., Baltimore, Md. "Lightnin"—*Illustration & prices, p. 51*

Williams Products Co., H. E., 100 S. Main St., Carthage, Mo.—*See adv. p. 32*

723	1906	2053	2121	3104
3537	4556	5210	6145	6559
6733				

CAPS, Gasoline Tank (Automatic)

Shepard & Moore, Inc., Advance Bldg., Cleveland, Ohio "Shur-On" —*See adv. p. 47*

CAPS, Gasoline Tank (Brass)

295	723	2121	3727	3992
4327	5710	6145	6626	

CAPS, Gasoline Tank (Bronze)

723	2121	6686

CAPS, Gasoline Tank (Steel)

Williams Products Co., H. E., 100 S. Main St., Carthage, Mo. — *Illustrated, p. 32*

134	295	723	1247	1819
2121	2700	3992	5496	5710
6559	6626			

CAPS, Gasoline Tank (White Metal)

Jambor Tool & Stamping Co., 1261 30th St., Milwaukee, Wis. "Bull Dog"—*See adv. p. 64*

Simmons Mfg. Co., 3405-11 Perkins Ave., Cleveland, Ohio. (For Chevrolet & Ford cars) — *See adv. p. 62*

131	357a	518	2121	3104
3992	5563	5710		

CAPS, Hub

Williams Products Co., H. E., 100 S. Main St., Carthage, Mo.—*See adv. p. 32*

76	723	1095	1257	1624
2033	2121	2138	4327	4702
6458a	6642			

CAPS, Radiator (Aluminum)

Williams Products Co., H. E., 100 S. Main St., Carthage, Mo.—*See adv. p. 32*

295	723	2121	6145

CAPS, Radiator (Brass)

Simmons Mfg. Co., 3405-11 Perkins Ave., Cleveland, Ohio. (For Ford & Chevrolet cars) — *See adv. p. 62*

295	339	723	1132	2018
2121	2396	3349	3992	4327
5563	5710	6145	6626	6686

CAPS, Radiator (Bronze)

723	2121	4506	6686

CAPS, Radiator (Rubber or Composition)

1829

CAPS, Radiator (Steel)

Simmons Mfg. Co., 3405-11 Perkins Ave., Cleveland, Ohio. (For Ford & Chevrolet cars) — *See adv. p. 62*

Williams Products Co., H. E., 100 S. Main St., Carthage, Mo. — *Illustrated, p. 32*

723	2121	3992	5710

CAPS, Radiator (White Metal)

Simmons Mfg. Co., 3405-11 Perkins Ave., Cleveland, Ohio. (For Ford & Chevrolet cars) — *See adv. p. 62*

131	311	1294	1339	1905
2018	2053	2121	3537	3992
5563	5710	6686		

Caps, Tank

See Caps, Gasoline Tank

CAPS, Tire Valve Dust

Continental Rubber Works, 1902 Liberty St., Erie, Pa. "Vitalic"— *See adv. p. 64*

Dill Mfg. Co., 686 E. 82nd St., Cleveland, Ohio "Instanton" — *Illustrated, p. 43*

Peck Spring Co., 68 Broad St., Plainville, Conn. — *Illustrated & described, p. 55*

Schrader's Son, A., 470 Vanderbilt Ave., Brooklyn, N. Y.—*Prices, p. 29*

22	210	1274	1602	1664
1829	2033	2795	4643	5465
6615	6634			

CARBIDE, Calcium

Linde Air Products Co., 30 E. 42nd St., New York, N. Y. "Carbic," "Carbolite," "Union"—*Branch offices, p. 125*

67	792

Carbon Removers

See Brushes, Carbon Removing; Machines, Engine Decarbonizing; Scraper, Carbon

Carborundum Paper

See Paper, Emery and Sand

Carborundum Wheels

See Wheels, Grinding

Carburetor Choker Springs, for Fords

See Springs, Carburetor Choker, for Fords

Carburetor Controls

See Controls, Dash

Carburetor Floats

See Floats, Cork; also Floats, Metal

Carburetor Intake Silencers

See Silencer, Carburetor Intake

Carburetor Intake Strainers
See Cleaners, Air

Carburetor Regulators
See Regulators, Carburetor (Thermostatic)

CARBURETORS, Gasoline

Bendix Stromberg Carburetor Co., Div. of Bendix Aviation Corp., 701 Bendix Drive, South Bend, Ind. "Stromberg" — See adv. Front Cover

Marvel Carbureter Co., 2300 St. John St., Flint, Mich. — Illustration & distributors, p. 68

Simmons Mfg. Co., 3405-11 Perkins Ave., Cleveland, Ohio. (For Chevrolet cars)—See adv. p. 62

611	1047	1642	1894	2783
3207	3529	3803	4652	5563
5761	6676	6753	6823	

Card Cases
See Cases, Toilet, Vanity, Card and Smoking

Card Holders
See Holders, Card and Label

Cards, File
See Brushes, File Cleaning

CARPET, Coach and Motor Car
(See also Mats, Carpet)

Biltmore Mfg. Co., 1747 Central Ave., Cincinnati, Ohio—See adv. p. 40

291	644	725	1318	1583
1646	1905	2006	2139	2418
2758	2763	2773	3411	3811
3932	5803	6469	6710	

Carriers, Golf Bag
See Holders, Golf Bag

CARRIERS, Luggage
(For attaching to rear of car)

Fostoria Pressed Steel Corp., Dept. CM-2, N. Maine St., Fostoria, Ohio —Prices & warehouse stocks, p. 71

Williams Products Co., H. E., 100 S. Main St., Carthage, Mo.—See adv. p. 32

35	539	595	1667	2033
3252	3316	3410	3526	4681
5191	6597	6626		

CARRIERS, Luggage
(For attaching to running board)

Biltmore Mfg. Co., 1747 Central Ave., Cincinnati, Ohio—See adv. p. 40

Fostoria Pressed Steel Corp., Dept. CM-1, N. Main St., Fostoria, Ohio —Illustration, prices & warehouse stocks, p. 71

Williams Products Co., H. E., 100 S. Main St., Carthage, Mo. "Foldaway"—Illustrated, p. 32

44	146	352	644	704A
720	765	1132	1905	2115
2384	3212	3252	3526	3718
3772	3794	3966	3987	4551
4757	4798	5191	5773	6498
6559	6615	6733		

CARRIERS, Luggage, for Fords
(For attaching to front of cars)

Williams Products Co., H. E., 100 S. Main St., Carthage, Mo.—See adv. p. 32

CARRIERS, Luggage (Folding)

2384　3222　3409

CARRIERS, Parcel
(For interior of car)

6731

CARRIERS, Storage Battery

35	100	142	559	1842
3015	3537	3989	4523	4708
5425	6107	6355	6586a	6825

CARRIERS, Tire

131	1842	2694	2802	4682
4751	5697	5757	6139	6197
6559	6677			

Carriers, Trunk
See Racks, Trunk

Cases, Battery
See Boxes, Battery

CASES, Bolt and Screw

Lyon Metal Products, Inc., 2931 Montgomery St., Aurora, Ill.—Illustrated, p. 106

2705　2767　4284　6581　6632

Cases, Card
See Cases, Toilet, Vanity, Card and Smoking

CASES, Curtain

1573

CASES, Lamp Bulb
(Cases or boxes for carrying spare lamp bulbs on car)

1632　5461

CASES, Medical Emergency

3132

Cases, Screw
See Cases, Bolt and Screw

Cases, Smoking
See Cases, Toilet, Vanity, Card and Smoking

CASES, Spark Plug
(Leather or fabric cases for holding spare plugs)

4787

CASES, Toilet, Vanity, Card and Smoking
(For limousines or other closed cars)

2121	3018	3103	3765	3885
3892	3990	4321	4334	4507
4731	5094	5604	6464	

Cases, Tool
See Bags or Rolls, Tool

CASES, Tube Fitting

Lincoln Brass Works, 2067 12th St., Detroit, Mich.—See adv. p. 73

Casing, Flexible Metallic
See Shafting, Flexible

CASTERS, for Repair Creepers

2621

CASTERS, Truck

1608	2621	3268	3429	4312
5409A	5504			

Casters, Wrecking
See Trucks, Casters and Spare Wheels, Wrecking

Celluloid, Sheet
See Sheets, Transparent

CEMENT, Celluloid
(For repairing curtain lights)

1660　5413

CEMENT, Gasket
(Advertisers in this publication only)

Bell Co., 407-11 N. Lincoln St., Chicago, Ill.—Illustrated, p. 93

Liquid Veneer Corp., 822 Liquid Veneer Bldg., Buffalo, N. Y. "Neverleak"—Illustration & prices, p. 66

Cement, Glass Setting
See Putty, Bedding

CEMENT, Leather

763　1619　2441　5413　6734

CEMENT, Linoleum

1619　5413　6456

CEMENT, Radiator Repair
(For repairing or sealing leaks in radiators)
(Advertisers in this publication only)

Bell Co., 407-11 N. Lincoln St., Chicago, Ill.—Illustrated, p. 93

Holfast Rubber Co., Lakewood Ave., Atlanta, Ga.—See adv. p. 65

Liquid Veneer Corp., 822 Liquid Veneer Bldg., Buffalo, N. Y. "Neverleak"—Illustration & prices, p. 66

CEMENT, Rubber (Liquid)

1829	2412	2416	2773	3247
3903	5413	6344		

CEMENT, Tire Repair
(Rubber cement for repairing or patching shoes and tubes; for cement for filling cuts in shoes—See Compounds, Tire Repair)
(Advertisers in this publication only)

Bell Co., 407-11 N. Lincoln St., Chicago, Ill.—Illustrated, p. 93

CEMENT, Top Repair

2773　2784　5120　5413　6456

CENTERS, Lathe and Grinder

1847　2684　3986　5613　5700

CHAIN ADJUSTMENTS, Automatic or Manual

3510

Chain Appliers
See Tools, Tire Chain Attaching

Chain Blocks
See Blocks or Hoists, Chain

Chain Cutters
See Cutters, Chain; also Cutters, Shear

Chain Drills
See Drills, Chain

Chain Drives, Front End Silent
See Chains, Timing

Chain, Driving
See Chain, Transmission or Driving

Chain Fasteners, Tire
See Fasteners, Tire Chain

Chain Hoists
See Blocks or Hoists, Chain

Chain Links
See Links, Tire Chain Repair

Chain, Silent
See Chain, Transmission or Driving

Chain Tighteners
See Tighteners, Tire Chain

CHAIN, Transmission or Driving

530　3510　6699

CHAINS, Sling

142　1237　3256　3721　3774

CHAINS, Timing

Biglow & Co., L. C., 250 W. 54th St., New York, N. Y. (Silent) (New York representatives for Whitney Mfg. Co.)—See adv. p. 129

See Page 364 for Names of Companies Represented by Above Numbers

CHAINS, Timing—Continued

Link-Belt Co., Indianapolis, **Ind.** (Silent)—*Illustrated, p. 70*

Morse Chain Co. (Div. Borg-Warner Corp.), Ithaca, N. Y.—*Illustration & Chilton & Morse numbers, p. 203*

Whitney Mfg. Co., 237 Hamilton St., Hartford, Conn. (Silent)—*Illustration, warehouse stocks & Chilton & Whitney numbers, p. 201*

530	641	1504	3510	3982
4665	5040	6699		

Chains, Tire

See Chains or Grips, Non-Skid for Pneumatic Tires; also Chains or Grips, Non-Skid, for Solid Tires

Chains, Tire Locking

See Locks, Spare Tire and Wheel

Chains, Tow

See Ropes, Chains and Bars, Tow

CHAINS or GRIPS, Non-Skid for Pneumatic Tires

(For repair links, see Links, Tire Chain Repair)

American Chain Co., 929 Connecticut Ave., Bridgeport, Conn. "Weed"—*See adv. p. 38*

Cleveland Chain & Mfg. Co., Penna. R. R. & Henry Rd., Cleveland, Ohio. "Wear-Well"—*Illustrated & described, p. 39*

Columbus - McKinnon Chain Corp., Tonawanda, N. Y. "Dreadnaught," "Claw"—*Illustration, sizes & prices, p. 36*

Gates Rubber Co., 999 S. Broadway, Denver, Col. (Rubber)—*See adv. p. 62*

Lion Chain Co., 3124 W. 51st St., Chicago, Ill. "Cub"—*Illustrated & described, p. 37*

McKay Co., Union Trust Bldg., Pittsburgh, Pa. (Steel & rubber; licensees)—*Illustrated, p. 33*

United States Chain & Forging Co. —See McKay Co.

Woodworth Specialties Co., 121-25 Montgomery St., Binghamton, N. Y. —*See adv. p. 36*

142	724	1077	1127	1174
1237	2324	2355	2364	3015
3040	3150	3468	3512	3526
4203	4647	4792	4806	5420
5457	6101	6647	6711	6778
6787				

CHAINS or GRIPS, Non-Skid for Solid Tires

(For repair links, see Links, Tire Chain Repair)

American Chain Co., 929 Connecticut Ave., Bridgeport, Conn. "Weed"—*See adv. p. 38*

Cleveland Chain & Mfg. Co., Penna. R. R. & Henry Rd., Cleveland, Ohio. "Trax-Yun," "Duo-Wear"—*Illustrated & described, p. 39*

Columbus - McKinnon Chain Corp., Tonawanda, N. Y. "Dreadnaught" —*Illustration, prices & sizes, p. 36*

Lion Chain Co., 3124 W. 51st St., Chicago, Ill. "Cub"—Illustrated & described, p. 37

McKay Co., Union Trust Bldg., Pittsburgh, Pa.—*See adv. p. 33*

United States Chain & Forging Co. —See McKay Co.

142	724	1077	1174	1237
2364	3015	3040	3468	3512
4203	4647	4806	5457	6647
6778				

CHAINS or HOOKS, Mud Extricating

Cleveland Chain & Mfg. Co., Penna. R. R. & Henry Rd., Cleveland, Ohio. "Double Grip"—*See adv. p. 39*

Lion Chain Co., 3124 W. 51st St., Chicago, Ill. "Cub"—*See adv. p. 37*

Woodworth Specialties Co., 121-25 Montgomery St., Binghamton, N. Y. "Easyon," "Handichains"— *Illustration, description & prices, p. 36*

142	350	1077	1174	2694
3468	3512	3721	3950	4792
6787				

Chairs, Folding

See Seats, Auxiliary

Chamois

See Sponges and Chamois

CHANNELS, Adjustable

(Steel spring, leather or fabric covered)

Auto-Vehicle Parts Co., 1040 Saratoga St., Newport, Ky. "Snugger." (Sole distributors) — *Illustrated, pp. 34 & 35*

CHANNELS, Felt

Felt Products Mfg. Co., 1510 Carroll Ave., Chicago, Ill.—*See adv. p. 75*

2046	2047	2625	3426	4607
6651				

CHANNELS, Metal

343	521	1309	3294

CHANNELS, Rubber

Continental Rubber Works, 1902 Liberty St., Erie, Pa. "Vitalic"— *See adv. p. 64*

634	751	1274	1580	1591
2047	2625	2773	3903	

Chargers, Battery (Auto)

See Generators, Electric Lighting and Battery Charging (Auto)

CHARGERS, Battery Service Station (Bulb Type)

(See also Chargers, Battery Service Station, Constant Potential; also Motor Generators, Battery Charging; also Rheostats)

General Electric Co., Merchandise Dept., Bridgeport, Conn. "Tungar" —*Illustration & prices, p. 109*

36	100	559	576a	665
1226	1860	2103	2123	2343
2409	2438	3060	3323	3890
4670	4708	5079	6193	6454
6616	6664			

CHARGERS, Battery Service Station (Constant Potential)

Hobart Brothers, Box C51, Canal Locks Square, Troy, Ohio. "HB"— *Illustrated, p. 108*

100	1865	2766	3798	5190
6616	6664		

CHARGERS, Magneto Magnet

(For remagnetizing magneto magnets)

100	576a	1226	2103	5511
6314a	6616		

Charging Apparatus, Service Station

See Chargers, Battery, Service Station; Motor Generators, Battery Charging; Panels & Switchboards, Charging; Rheostats

Charging Clips

See Clips, Battery Charging

Charts, Headlight Testing

See Testers, Headlight (Chart Type)

Check Valves

See Valves, Ball Check

CHECKS, Brass, Time, Tool and Pay

2643	3227	3542	3822	3869
3988	5816		

CHECKS, Car Door

(See also Anti-Rattlers, Door)

Auto- Vehicle Parts Co., 1040 Saratoga St., Newport, Ky.—*Illustrated & described, pp. 34 & 35*

360	692	1048	1580	1829
1840	2773	2860	3027	3151
3324	5075			

CHECKS, Steering Gear

(Spring, hydraulic or friction attachments for steering gear to eliminate sidesway and reduce the shock transmitted to the steering wheel by the road wheels)

Hackett Products Co., 407 Pine St., Providence, R. I.—*See adv. p. 40*

224	228	1840	2604	2671
4005			

CHECKS, Steering Gear, for Fords

2033	2634

Chemicals, Metal Cleaning

See Cleaners, Metal

Chemicals, Rust Preventing and Removing

See Compounds, Rust Preventing and Removing

Chimes, Exhaust

See Horns, Exhaust

CHISELS, Cold and Cape

National Machine & Tool Co., 801 S. Water St., Jackson, Mich.—*See adv. p. 120*

Truth Tool Co., 711 S. Front St., Mankato, Minn.—*See adv. p. 128*

9	635	643	726	1148
1299	1324	1604	1921	2410
2841	2846	3830	3918	4003
4241	4600	4726	5035	5602
5611	5709	5777	6208	6491
6497				

CHISELS, Glass Removing

4644

Choke Rod Holders for Fords

See Holders, Choke Rod, for Fords

Choker Extensions, for Fords

See Extensions, Choker, for Fords

Chucks, Air

See Connections, Tire Pump

CHUCKS, Drill

116a	1130	1815	2410	3101
3905	3986	4338	4755	4778
6611				

CHUCKS, Lathe

116a	1253a	2778	5629	6643
6702				

Cigar Lighters

See Lighters, Electric Cigar

Cigarette Cases

See Cases, Toilet, Vanity Card and Smoking

CLAMPS, Battery Hold Down

35	559	2861	4523	4708
6107			

See Page 364 for Names of Companies Represented by Above Numbers

Clamps, Body Builders
See Clamps, Woodworkers'

Clamps, Bow
See Holders, Top

CLAMPS, Brake Lining
(For holding lining tight against shoe for riveting and drilling)
Chicago Rivet & Machine Co., 1830 S. 54th Ave. (Cicero P. O.), Chicago, Ill.—*See adv. p. 92*
1929 5214 5721

Clamps, Differential Assembly, for Fords
See Plates, Differential Assembly, for Fords

CLAMPS, Hose
(For radiator hose or tire pump tubing)
(Advertisers in this publication only)
Jambor Tool & Stamping Co., 1261 30th St., Milwaukee, Wis. "Bull Dog"—*See adv. p. 64*
Rex Metal Products Co., 365 First Ave., New York, N. Y.—*Illustration, description & prices, p. 114*
Simmons Mfg. Co., 3405-11 Perkins Ave., Cleveland, Ohio. (For Ford & Chevrolet cars)—*See adv. p. 62*
Wittek Mfg. Co., 4305-9 W. 24th Place, Chicago, Ill. "Noc-Out," "Star"—*Illustration & sizes, p. 279*
Williams Products Co., H. E., 100 S. Main St., Carthage, Mo. — *Illustrated, p. 32*

CLAMPS, Machinists'
Armstrong Bros. Tool Co., 304 N. Francisco Ave., Chicago, Ill. — *Illustrated, p. 119*
Columbian Vise & Mfg. Co., 9017 Bessemer Ave., Cleveland, Ohio— *See adv. p. 122*

43	250	591a	643	1148
1232	1887	2410	3461	3767
4623	4694	4757	5719	6112
6483	6497	6660	6730	

Clamps, Piston
See Vises, Piston

Clamps, Top Bow
See Holders, Top

CLAMPS, Transmission Band Assembling, for Fords
134 681

CLAMPS, Welders' (Oxy-Acetylene)
2391

CLAMPS, Woodworkers'
Columbian Vise & Mfg. Co., 9017 Bessemer Ave., Cleveland, Ohio.—*See adv. p. 122*

643	1148	1232	1887	4537
4694	6112	6730	6783	

CLEANERS, Air
(Device to attach to air intake of carburetors to remove sand and dust from the entering air)

6	66	611	1620	1651
2619	3872	4546	6314	6502

Cleaners, Auto
See Cleaners, Vacuum (Portable); also Cleaners, Vacuum, Stationary; also Washers, Automobile (Brushes); also Washers, Automobile (Systems)

Cleaners, Chemical
See Compounds, Glass Windshield

CLEANERS, Differential and Transmission

86	1212	1300	3151	3846
5112a	5178	5510	6604	6611

CLEANERS, Engine
(For cleaning oil and grease from engines and chassis by gasoline, kerosene, compressed air, or employing stream and cleaning compounds; also Washers, Automobile (Systems)
Kellogg Mfg. Co., 65 Humboldt St., Rochester, N. Y.—*Illustration & prices, p. 2*
Brunner Mfg. Co., 1800 Broad St., Utica, N. Y.—*Illustrated, p. 113*

759	1831	2394	2766	2792
3241	3774	3826	3894	4353
5173	5568	6217	6324	6745

CLEANERS, Engine (Attachments)
Imperial Brass Mfg. Co., 1225 W. Harrison St., Chicago, Ill. — *See adv. p. 126*

1168	1587	2641	3016	3767
5173				

CLEANERS, Fabric
(Compounds for cleaning upholstery or slip covers)
(Advertisers in this publication only)
Bell Co., 407-11 N. Lincoln St., Chicago, Ill.—*See adv. p. 93*

CLEANERS, Glass (Rubber)
3829 6190 6615

CLEANERS, Metal
(Advertisers in this publication only)
American Chemical Paint Co., Brookside Ave. & Reading R. R., Ambler, Pa. "Deoxidine"—*Described, p. 126*

CLEANERS, Spark Plug
(See also Brushes, Spark Plug; also Machines, Spark Plug Cleaning)
1604

Cleaners, Upholstery
See Cleaners, Fabric

CLEANERS, Vacuum (Portable)
Bean Mfg. Co., John, 18 Hosmer St., Lansing, Mich. "Bean Air-Vac"— *Illustrated, p. 31*
Fitzgerald Mfg. Co., 691 Main St., Torrington, Conn. "Star-Rite"— *See adv. p. 76*
General Electric Co., Merchandise Dept., Bridgeport, Conn. "G-E"— *Illustration & prices, p. 109*

237	525	719	1170	1290
1842	1917	2079	2331	2343
2646	3003	3062	3254	3271
3765a	3856	4501	4765	6324
6350				

CLEANERS, Vacuum, Stationary
(Advertisers in this publication only)
Bean Mfg. Co., John, 18 Hosmer St., Lansing, Mich.—*Illustrated, p. 31*

CLEANERS, Windshield, Electric
Tot Industries of Detroit, 2270 First National Bank Bldg., Detroit, Mich—*Illustration, description & prices, p. 46*
United American Bosch Corp., 3664 Main St., Springfield, Mass. (Also sole American representatives for Robert Bosch, A. G., Stuttgart, Germany)—*See adv. p. 69*

208	611	1800	2631	3708
4561	4754	5774	6178	6314a

CLEANERS, Windshield (Hand and Automatic)
(For chemical cleaners or preventives—see Compounds, Glass Windshield)
Hackett Products Co., 407 Pine St., Providence, R. I. — *Illustrated & described, p. 40*
Trico Products Corp., 807 Washington St., Buffalo, N. Y.—*Illustrated, p. 55*

131	1139	1257	1500	1669
2384	2449	2604	3445	3765A
3772	3950	6190		

CLEANERS and POLISHERS, Overhead Electric (Automobile)
(Consisting of liquid containers, flexible shaft, brushes and polishers)
2670

Cleaning Compounds, Auto Body
See Cleaners, Metal.

Cleansers, Hydraulic Brake
See Compounds, Hydraulic Brake Cleaning

CLEATS, Fibre Wiring
1270 3067 4266 4607 6744

Clevis Pins
See Pins, Yoke

Clevises
See Yokes, Special

Clip Bolts
See Bolts, Clip

CLIPPERS, Bolt and Rivet
(Hand power)
591a 4743

Clips, Battery Charging

339	559	2665A	2766	4012
4708	5751	6139	6355	

Clips, Battery Holding Down
See Clamps, Battery Hold Down

CLIPS, Electrical Test
(For testing electrical circuits at any point without removing insulation from wire or disconnecting)
2665a 4012 6561

CLIPS, Spring

686	720	1081	1234	1885
6307				

Clock and Mirror Combinations
See Mirror and Clock Combinations

CLOCKS, Electrically Wound
Sterling Clock Co., Div. of Western Clock Co., La Salle, Ill.—*Illustration, description & prices, p. 41*

796	3034	4321	5740	6132
6570				

CLOCKS, Hand Wound

1842	3103	3464	3566	3776
4292	4692	5430a	6464	6570
6648				

CLOCKS, Time Recording
(For time stamps—see Stamps, Time)
Simplex Time Recorder Co., 50 Time Ave., Gardner, Mass. "Telechron" *Illustrated & described, p. 127*
1147 3056

CLOCKS, Watchmen's
Simplex Time Recorder Co., 50 Time Ave., Gardner, Mass.—*See adv. p. 127*

CLOTH, Abrasive
591 1031 1198

Cloth, Emery and Sand
See Cloth, Abrasive

See Page 364 for Names of Companies Represented by Above Numbers

CLOTH, Enameled or Oiled

259	704	1235	2728	3422
5699	6179			

Cloth, Leather
See Leather, Artificial or Imitation

CLOTH, Mohair

725	5433

CLOTH, Rubber Coated

53	693	1045	1304	1646
1659	1829	2602	3221	3422
4734	5055	5413	6344	

Cloth, Upholstery
See Cloth, Mohair; Broadcloth; Corduroys; Plush; Whipcord; Velours; Velvets

Clothing, Mechanics'
See Coveralls and Service Coats

Cloths, Dusting, Polishing and Wiping
See Wipers and Polishing Cloths

Clutch Collar Oilers, for Chevrolets
See Oilers, Chevrolet Clutch Collar

Clutch Disc Drum Pullers, for Fords
See Pullers, Clutch Disc Drum, for Fords

Clutch Discs, Fabric and Composition
See Lining, Brake (Woven)

Clutch Discs, Steel
See Discs, Clutch (Steel)

Clutch Facings
See Lining, Brake

Clutch Leather
See Leather, Friction

Clutch Linings
See Linings, Brake (Woven)

Clutch Pilot Tools
See Tools, Clutch Pilot Alignment

Clutch Plates
See Discs, Clutch (Steel)

Clutch Shafts
See Shafts, Transmission, Clutch and Pump

Clutch Spiders
See Discs, Clutch (Composition)

Clutch Throwout Bearings
See Bearings, Clutch Throwout (Composition)

CLUTCHES, Automatic (For Model A Fords)

319b

CLUTCHES, Automobile Friction

2156	2747	3141	5653

CLUTCHES, Free Wheeling
See Free Wheeling Units

Coat Rails
See Rails, Robe or Coat

COCKS, Pet (Drain, Gasoline, Air, etc.)
Imperial Brass Mfg. Co., 1225 W. Harrison St., Chicago, Ill. — *See adv. p. 126*
Lincoln Brass Works, 2067 12th St., Detroit, Mich.—*See adv. p. 73*
Simmons Mfg. Co., 3405-11 Perkins Ave., Cleveland, Ohio. (For Ford and Chevrolet cars)—*See adv. p. 62*

1249	1261	1618	1842	3016
3502	3935	5142A	5563	6608
6663				

Cocks, Reserve Fuel
See Valves, Two-Way Tank

Coil Locks
See Locks, Ignition

Coil Parts
See Parts, Magneto, Coil and Distributor

COILS, Generator Field

2477	4304	6324a

COILS, Ignition (Non-Vibrating)
(See also Systems, Ignition (Complete))
Jambor Tool & Stamping Co., 1261 30th St., Milwaukee, Wis. "Bull Dog"—*See adv. p. 64*
Jefferson Electric Co., 1508 S. Laflin St., Chicago, Ill.—*Illustration & prices, p. 75*
Niehoff & Co., C. E., 230 W. Superior St., Chicago, Ill.—*See adv. p. 63*
United American Bosch Corp., 3664 Main St., Springfield, Mass. "American Bosch." (Also sole American representatives for Robert Bosch, A. G., Stuttgart, Germany)—*See adv. p. 69*

228	1257	1547	1548a	1857
2472	3104	3114	3202	3207
3287	3768	4019	4304	4317
4601	6314a	6631		

COILS, Ignition (Vibrating)
Jefferson Electric Co., 1508 S. Laflin St., Chicago, Ill. — *Illustration & prices, p. 75*
Simmons Mfg. Co., 3405-11 Perkins Ave., Cleveland, Ohio. (For Ford & Chevrolet cars)—*See adv. p. 62*
United American Bosch Corp., 3664 Main St., Springfield, Mass. "Bosch." (Sole American representatives for Robert Bosch, A. G., Stuttgart, Germany)—*See adv. p. 69*

3207	3287	4304	5563	6314a

COILS, Tube Bending (Wire)
Imperial Brass Mfg. Co., 1225 W. Harrison St., Chicago, Ill.—*See adv. p. 126*

Collar Oilers, Clutch, for Chevrolets
See Oilers, Chevrolet Clutch Collar

Commutator Insulation Undercutting Machines
See Machines, Commutator Turning and Insulation Undercutting

COMMUTATORS, Electric Motor
Jambor Tool & Stamping Co., 1261 30th St., Milwaukee, Wis. "Bull Dog"—*See adv. p. 64*
Simmons Mfg. Co., 3405-11 Perkins Ave., Cleveland, Ohio. (For Ford & Chevrolet cars)—*See adv. p. 62*

1017	1864	6168

COMPASSES, Automobile
(For car mounting or pocket)

1873	4328	6125

Compasses, Striping
See Tools, Striping

COMPOUNDS, Anti-Freezing
(Advertisers only in this publication)
McKay Co., Union Trust Bldg., Pittsburgh, Pa.—*Illustrated, p. 33*
United States Chain & Forging Co.—*See* McKay Co.

COMPOUNDS, Battery Corrosion Preventing

1099

Compounds, Brake
See Dressing, Brake

COMPOUNDS, Carbon Removing

86	534	1138	1239	2616
3405	3922	4347	4519	5413
6113				

COMPOUNDS, Glass Windshield
(For keeping glass clear in rain, fog or snow; for mechanical cleaners—see Cleaners, Windshield)

1667	2323	3046	3922	6143
6773				

COMPOUNDS, Glazing

652	5514	5541

Compounds, Grinding
See Compounds, Valve Grinding

COMPOUNDS, Hydraulic Brake Cleaning

4009

COMPOUNDS, Masking
(To prevent lacquer overspray)

1268	3921	4622a	5541	5604a

COMPOUNDS, Radiator Cleaning
(For radiator cement—see Cement, Radiator Repair)
(Advertisers in this publication only)
Bell Co., 407-11 N. Lincoln St., Chicago, Ill.—*See adv. p. 93*
Liquid Veneer Corp., 822 Liquid Veneer Bldg., Buffalo, N. Y. "Purgo"—*Illustration & prices, p. 66*
Loock & Co., R. J., 343-45 N. Gay St., Baltimore, Md. "Lightnin." *Illustration & prices, p. 51*

Compounds, Radiator Sealing
See Cement, Radiator Repair

COMPOUNDS, Rubbing and Polishing
(Especially for use with pyroxylin painting systems)

586	1022	1660	1850	2773
3702	3921	4622a	5514	5566
5604a	6143	6727	6780	

COMPOUNDS, Rust Preventing and Removing
(Advertisers in this publication only)
American Chemical Paint Co., Brookside Ave. & Reading R. R., Ambler, Pa. "Deoxidine," "Lithoform," "Peroline," "Deoxylyte."—*Described, p. 126*

Compounds, Spoke Tightening
See Compounds, Wood Wheel Tightening

Compounds, Storage Battery Terminal
See Paints, Storage Battery Terminal

COMPOUNDS, Tar Removing
(For removing tar or road oils from bodies)
(Advertisers in this publication only)
Bell Co., 407-11 N. Lincoln St., Chicago, Ill.—*See adv. p. 93*

COMPOUNDS, Tire Repair
(For filling cuts in outer casings or shoes)

1286	1667	2071	2412	2616
2773	3903	3983	5413	6160
6456				

See Page 364 for Names of Companies Represented by Above Numbers

COMPOUNDS, Valve Grinding
(Advertisers in this publication only)
Bell Co., 407-11 N. Lincoln St., Chicago, Ill.—*See adv. p. 93*

Compounds, Waterproofing
See Finish, Top, Waterproofing

COMPOUNDS, Wood Wheel Tightening
(For swelling and tightening loose spokes in wood wheels)
4558

Compression Testers
See Gages, Cylinder Compression

COMPRESSORS, Air (Automobile Driven)
(Mounted on front of service car or truck, driven from motor crankshaft through power take-off)
2394

COMPRESSORS, Air (Electric)
Bean Mfg. Co., John, 18 Hosmer St., Lansing, Mich.—*Illustrated, p. 31*
Brunner Mfg. Co., 1800 Broad St., Utica, N. Y.—*Illustration, description & prices, p. 113*
Champion Pneumatic Machinery Co., 8170 S. Chicago Ave., Chicago, Ill. —*Illustrated & described, p. 112*
Curtis Pneumatic Machinery Co., 1927 Kienlen Ave., St. Louis, Mo. —*Illustrated & described, p. 111*
Hobart Brothers, Box C 51, Canal Locks Square, Troy, Ohio. "HB" —*Illustrated, p. 108*
Imperial Brass Mfg. Co., 1225 W. Harrison St., Chicago, Ill. — *See adv. p. 126*
Kellogg Mfg. Co., 65 Humboldt St., Rochester, N. Y. — *Illustration, specifications & prices, p. 2*
Manley Mfg. Co., 929 Connecticut Ave., Bridgeport, Conn—*Illustrated, p. 38*
Service Station Equipment Co., Conshohocken, Pa. "Eco"—*Illustrated & described, p. 121*

176	310	525	559	577
646	759	1086	1141	1169
1345	1527	1568	1587	2394
2681	2731	2766	3033	3123
3241	3406	3513	3553	3774
3859	3910	4222	4658	4713
4775	4784	5004	5140	5510
5524	5568	6324	6604	6612
6745				

CONDENSERS, Electric
Jambor Tool & Stamping Co., 1261 30th St., Milwaukee, Wis. "Bull Dog"—*See adv. p. 64*
Niehoff & Co., C. E., 230 W. Superior St., Chicago, Ill. "All-In-One"—*See adv. p. 63*
Simmons Mfg. Co., 3405-11 Perkins Ave., Cleveland, Ohio. (For Ford & Chevrolet cars)—*See adv. p. 62*

228	337	1257	2472	3104
3202	3761	3768	4304	4317
4601	5513	5563	5626	6314a

CONDENSERS AND RELIEF VALVES, Radiator
311

CONDUIT, Flexible Car Wiring
(Metal and fabric conduit; see also Tubing, Flexible Metallic)
American Metal Hose Co., 67 Jewelry St., Waterbury, Conn. — *Branch offices, p. 100*

Chicago Tubing & Braiding Co., 210 N. Clinton St., Chicago, Ill. "Rex-Tube"—*See adv. p. 102*
International Metal Hose Co., 10109-15 Quincy Ave., Cleveland, Ohio— *Specifications, p. 99*

171	718	1133	1815	2343
2723	3045	4656	5443	

Cones, Ball
See Cups and Cones, Ball

Connecting Rod Bearings
See Bearings and Bushings, Bronzebacked; also Bearings and Bushings, Die Cast (Babbitt, etc.)

Connecting Rod Bolts
See Bolts, Connecting Rod

Connecting Rod Bearing Repair Tools
See following heads:
Jigs, Connecting Rod Aligning
Jigs, Main Bearing and Connecting Rod Babbitting
Machines, Babbitting
Machines, Boring
Mandrels, Connecting Rod
Pullers, Bearing
Reamers, Main Bearing and Connecting Rod
Scrapers, Bearing
Tools, Bearing Shaving and Burnishing
Tools, Piston Pin and Connecting Rod Bushing Honing

Connecting Rods
See Rods, Connecting

Connecting Rods, Rebabbitted
See Bearings, Rebabbitted

Connections, Steering
See Links, Steering

CONNECTIONS, Tire Pump
Dill Mfg. Co., 686 E. 82nd St., Cleveland, Ohio—*Illustrated, p. 43*

1095	1297	1602	1801	1817
1842	1893	2415	2479	3774
5173	5178	5465	5753	

Connections, Tubing
See Fittings, Tube (Copper or Brass)

Connector Drills
See Drills and Bits, Battery Strap

Connectors, Belt
See Fasteners, Belt

CONNECTORS, Dry Battery
(See also Terminals, Wire)
Fitzgerald Mfg. Co., 691 Main St., Torrington, Conn. "Perfection"— *See adv. p. 76*
3002

CONNECTORS, Lamp (Electric)
Pines Winterfront Co., 1125 N. Cicero Ave., Chicago, Ill.—*See adv. p. 54*

1214	1553	1629	1804	2723
3202	3856	4712	4735	5179
5604	5687			

Connectors, Storage Battery
See Terminals, Storage Battery

Connectors, Storage Battery Repair
See Parts, Storage Battery Repair

CONNECTORS, Terminal (Storage Battery Charging)
576a 4708

Contact Point Cleaning Stones
See Stones, Contact Point Cleaning

Contact Point Files
See Files, Contact Point

Contact Point Synchronizers
See Synchronizers, Ignition Contact Point

Contact Points
See Points, Contact

Contact Resurfacing Tools
See Tools, Contact Resurfacing

Control Cable and Casing
See Cable, Brake Control (with conduit)

CONTROLLERS, Vulcanizer Steam Pressure
(Automatic valve to regulate the flow of gas to the burner on a steam vulcanizer and to control the steam pressure)
510 532

CONTROLS, Automatic Spark (For Model A Fords)
Hackett Products Co., 407 Pine St., Providence, R. I.—*Illustrated & described, p. 40*

Controls, Bus Door
See Openers, Bus Door

Controls, Carburetor
See Controls, Dash; also Regulators, Carburetor (Thermostatic)

CONTROLS, Dash
(For changing adjustment of carburetor from seat or operating choker for starting, muffler cut-out, exhaust heater, exhaust horn, ventilator, radiator shutter, etc.)
Imperial Brass Mfg. Co., 1225 W. Harrison St., Chicago, Ill. — *See adv. p. 126*

224	268	718	1197	1201
1287	2074	2384	2392	3016
3985	4682	5720	5733	6608
6825				

CONTROLS, Horn
(Inner wheel installed over steering wheel, allowing horn to be sounded at touch of thumb; see also Buttons, Push)
6822

CONVERTERS, Chassis
(For lengthening or reinforcing frame members; for six wheel units—see Attachments, Six Wheel, for Trucks)
2406 3521A 5162 6815

CONVERTERS, Chassis, for Ford and Chevrolet Cars
2000 5076 5195 5828

CONVERTERS, Ignition
(High frequency, connected in series on spark plug wires)
3478

Converters, Truck
See Converters, Chassis

Conveyors, Oil
See Dispensers, Oil; also Tanks, Oil (Portable)

CORD, Service (Portable Tool)
General Electric Co., Merchandise Dept., Bridgeport, Conn. "G-E."— *Illustration & prices, p. 109*
592 653 4610 6344

CORDS, Assist
725 1035 2860 4358 5206a

CORDUROYS, Upholstery
3411

Cored Bars
See Metals, Bearing

CORES, Radiator

584	2032	2089	2304	2659
2733	3402	3709	3724	4228
5172	6187	6750		

Cores, Valve
See Valves, Tire

Cork Carpet
See Linoleum

CORK, Sheet
Felt Products Mfg. Co., 1510 Carroll Ave., Chicago, Ill. "Fel-Pro"
—See adv. p. 75

251	4021	4607	5115

Cost System Books
See Books and Forms, Accounting

Cotter Pins
See Pins, Cotter

COTTON, Dusters
See Dusters, Wool and Cotton

COUNTERBALANCES, Crankshaft
1651

COUNTERBORES

124	756	1253A	2388	3986
4261	4263	4758	6697	

Counters, Revolution
See Tachometers

COUNTERS, Store
Berger Mfg. Co., Div. Republic Steel Corp., 1038 Belden Ave., N. E., Canton, Ohio. "Berloy" — Illustrated, p. 105

Lyon Metal Products, Inc., 2931 Montgomery St., Aurora, Ill.—Illustrated, p. 106

304	622	1555	2345	2705
2767	3564	3571	3782b	5728
6228				

COUPLERS, Trailer

1584	1823	2151	3503	3845
5668	6182	6685		

Couplings, Belt
See Fasteners, Belt

Couplings, Compression
See Fittings, Tube (Copper or Brass)

Couplings, Generator
See Couplings, Magneto, Generator and Water Pump

COUPLINGS, Hose
Hansen Mfg. Co., 1786 E. 27th St., Cleveland, Ohio — Illustration, prices & sizes, p. 112

International Metal Hose Co., 10109-15 Quincy Ave., Cleveland, Ohio—Specifications, p. 99

1179	1842	2641	2842	3045
4014	5173	6344		

COUPLINGS, Magneto, Generator and Water Pump
Continental Rubber Works, 1902 Liberty St., Erie, Pa. "Vitalic"—See adv. p. 64

Gates Rubber Co., 999 S. Broadway, Denver, Col. "Gates Vulco."—See adv. p. 62

Holfast Rubber Co., Lakewood Ave., Atlanta, Ga.—See adv. p. 65

Thermoid Rubber Co., Whitehead Rd., Trenton, N. J. "Hardy." —See adv. p. 85

United American Bosch Corp., 3664 Main St., Springfield, Mass. "American Bosch." (Also sole American representatives for Robert Bosch, A. G., Stuttgart, Germany)—See adv. p. 69

228	1274	1603	1667	1829
1851	1889	2106	2324	2412
2781	3202	4702	5612	5687
6129	6314a	6484		

Couplings, Tube
See Fittings, Tube (Copper or Brass)

COVERALLS and Service Coats
(Advertisers in this publication only)

Motor Suit Mfg. Co., 816 Central Ave., Kansas City, Mo. "Allova" —Illustrated & described, p. 119

Covers, Automatic Radiator
See Shutters, Automatic Radiator

COVERS, Automobile
(For covering automobiles when in storage)

223	291	602	621	740
1192	1225	2157	2728	3250
3422	3766	4308	4798	5052
5448	5773	6123	6639	

COVERS, Coil
Loock & Co., R. J., 343 N. Gay St., Baltimore, Md. "Lightnin"—Illustrated, p. 51
812

COVERS, Crankcase
(Metal cover lined with heat retaining material to keep crankcase oil warm over prolonged periods)
6616

COVERS, Distributor
(To prevent short circuits caused by rain and water)

Loock & Co., R. J., 343-45 N. Gay St., Baltimore, Md. "Ducksback"—Illustrated, p. 51

Rajah Co., Locust Ave. & Nelson St., Bloomfield, N. J.—See adv. p. 100

592	812	1827	4707

Covers, Joint
See Boots, Steering Knuckle and Joint

COVERS, Lamp
338   2157

COVERS, Louvre
(Heat retaining engine boards; see also Lining, Hood (Insulated))
3514

COVERS, Luggage Carrier
1035   1905   4308   5460

COVERS, Magneto
1124   1573   3027

COVERS, Oil Hole
(Stamped or turned metal dustproof covers for oil holes)
568   696   6212

COVERS, Repairmen's
(Fabric covers designed to place over fenders, seats, doors, cowls or other parts of car to protect them from being scratched when car is being worked on; for paper covers—see Paper,, Upholstery Covering)

85	142	291	338	597
602	644	652	1066	1184
1192	1573	1583	1905	2157
2758	2773	3237	3305	4220
4615	4663a	5139	5460	6133

Covers, Seat
See Covers, Slip; also Covers, Repairmen's

COVERS, Slip
Auto-Matic Seat Cover Corp., 120 E. 16th St., New York, N. Y. "Auto-Matic," "Zip-O-Matic," "Simplex," "Marvel"—Illustration, description & prices, p. 44

Biltmore Mfg. Co., 1747 Central Ave., Cincinnati, Ohio — Illustrated & described, p. 40

Williams Products Co., H. E., 100 S. Main St., Carthage, Mo. — Illustrated, p. 32

223	291	324	338	597
644	652	1032	1035	1066
1184	1192	1318	1319	1333
1573	1666	1905	2006	2418
2628	2758	2773	2860	3027
3112	3147	3221	3237	3514
4220	4308	4663a	4787	5460
5785	5803	6123	6133	6346
6469				

COVERS, Spark Plug
Loock & Co., R. J., 343-45 N. Gay St., Baltimore, Md. "Lightnin"—Illustrated, p. 51

Rajah Co., Locust Ave. & Nelson St., Bloomfield, N. J.—See adv. p. 100

812   2343a   2412   6344

COVERS, Spoke (Stainless Steel Snap)
770

COVERS, Spring
(See also Covers, Spring Leaf Lubricating; also Oilers, Spring)

210	602	727	1177	3112
3441	3724	4615		

COVERS, Spring Leaf Lubricating
(Lubricant retaining covers to be applied to springs to keep them lubricated; see also Covers, Spring; also Oilers, Spring)

Woodworth Specialties Co., 121-25 Montgomery St., Binghamton, N. Y.—Illustration, description & prices, p. 36

1666	2305	2773	3112	3410
3854	6787			

Covers, Starting Crank
See Holders, Starting Crank

Covers, Steering Knuckle
See Boots, Steering Knuckle and Joint

COVERS, Steering Wheel Rim

291	338	1066	2773	4615
4626	5460	6133		

COVERS, Storage Battery
161   2798   5207

COVERS, Tire (Fabric)
Biltmore Mfg. Co., 1747 Central Ave., Cincinnati, Ohio. "Snug-Fit"—See adv. p. 40

Williams Products Co., H. E., 100 S. Main St., Carthage, Mo. — Illustrated, p. 32

97	223	291	338	644
652	819a	1035	1066	1184
1192	1200	1218	1319	1333
1573	1583	1666	1905	2006
2418	2628	2758	2773	2860
3027	3237	4220	4308	4615
4663a	4787	5139	5147	5469
6133	6469	6797b		

COVERS, Tire (Illuminated)
45

COVERS, Tire (Metal)

Biltmore Mfg. Co., 1747 Central Ave., Cincinnati, Ohio—*See adv. p. 40*

Tropic-Aire, Inc., 36 11th Ave., N.E., Minneapolis, Minn. "TA"—*Illustrated, p. 50.*

Williams Products Co., H. E., 100 S. Main St., Carthage, Mo. — *Illustrated, p. 32*

1177	2042	2773	3569	5219

COVERS, Top

(See also Enclosures, Panel Top)

223	291	652	1192	1319
1583	1905	2006	2758	2773
3221	3422	4308	4787	5460

Covers, Universal Joint
See Boots, Steering Knuckle **and** Joint

Covers, Upholstery
See Covers, Slip

Cowl Protectors
See Covers, Door, Fender, Hood, Cowl, Seat, etc.

CRANES, DRAGS and JACKS, Truck Wheel Removing

3240	3256

CRANES, Hand Traveling

1134	2649	3546	5193	5649
6695	6799	6808		

CRANES, Portable (Hand Operated)

(For chain blocks or hoists—see Blocks or Hoists, Chain)

Manley Mfg. Co., 929 Connecticut Ave., Bridgeport, Conn. — *Illustrated, p. 38*

526	709	1023	1025	3256
3774	4741	5193	6611	

CRANES, Truck

144	274	336	526	564
589	1876	2649	2772	2786
3256	3309	3774	3794	3831
3833	4258	4741	5438	5557
6611	6745			

Crankcase Covers
See Covers, Crankcase

Crankcase Draining Systems, for Pits
See Systems, Crankcase Draining Disposal

Crankcase Draining Tanks
See Tanks, Crankcase Draining (Portable)

Crankcase Oil Drain Plugs
See Plugs, Crankcase Oil Drain

Crankcase Oil Heaters
See Heaters, Crankcase Oil

Crankcase Supports, for Fords
See Supports, Engine, for Fords

Crank Holders
See Holders, Starting Crank

Crankpin Gages
See Gages, Crankpin

Crank Ratchet Pins, for Fords
See Pins, Crank Ratchet, for Fords

Crankshaft Counterbalances
See Counterbalances, Crankshaft

Crankshaft Straightening Presses
See Presses, Straightening (Crankshaft)

Crankshaft Truing Tools
See Tools, Crankpin Truing

CRANKSHAFTS (For Ford and Chevrolet Cars)

Simmons Mfg. Co., 3405-11 Perkins & Chevrolet cars) — *See adv. p. 62*

CRANKSHAFTS, Special

(For racing cars)

2308	3896a

CRANKS, Starting

Simmons Mfg. Co., 3405-11 Perkins Ave., Cleveland, Ohio. (For Ford & Chevrolet cars)—*See adv. p. 62*

1885	2439	2453a	5748	6141

CREEPERS, Repair

National Machine & Tool Co., 801 S. Water St., Jackson, Mich. "Hovey" —*Illustration & prices, p. 120*

352	538	704a	720	1104
1233	1259	2109	2384	2786
2826	3256	3350	4241	4258
4531	4621	5428	6554	6745

Crests, Hand Painted
See Monograms, Hand Painted

Cribs
See Hammocks, Baby

CRIBS, Tools

Lyon Metal Products, Inc., 2931 Montgomery St., Aurora, Ill.—*Illustrated, p. 106*

CUPS, Leather

1124	2441	2702	3151	5134

CUPS, Oil and Grease

(Advertisers in this publication only)

Simmons Mfg. Co., 3405-11 Perkins Ave., Cleveland, Ohio. (For Ford & Chevrolet cars) — *See adv. p. 62*

Lincoln Brass Works, 2067 12th St., Detroit, Mich.—*See adv. p. 73*

CUPS, Priming

1261	1842	3016	3502	3563
5142A	6568	6608		

CUPS and CONES, Ball

Simmons Mfg. Co., 3405-11 Perkins Ave., Cleveland, Ohio. (For Ford & Chevrolet cars)—*See adv. p. 62*

Curb Boxes
See Stations, Air or Water

Curtain Bags or Cases
See Cases, Curtain

Curtain Fasteners
See Fasteners, Curtain

Curtain Lights
See Lights, Curtain

Curtain Openers
See Openers, Curtain

Curtain Rollers
See Rollers, Curtain

Curtain Windows
See Lights, Curtain; also Windows, Glass Curtain

Curtains, Window
See Shades, Closed Car

Cushions, Back Rest
See Rests, Cushion Back

CUSHIONS, Seat

(Including springs and upholstery)

219	1319	1905	2006	2421
2773	3221	3329	4305	5803
6133	6352	6615		

Cutout Pedals
See Pedals, Horn and Cutout

Cutouts, Muffler
See Valves, Cutout

CUTOUTS, Reverse Current

(For automatically connecting generator to battery when the voltage is high enough to charge battery and disconnecting it when voltage is too low)

Jambor Tool & Stamping Co., 1261 30th St., Milwaukee, Wis. "Bull Dog"—*See adv. p. 64*

Simmons Mfg. Co., 3405-11 Perkins Ave., Cleveland, Ohio—*See adv. p. 62*

337	339	1257	1547	1548a
1827	2472	2858	3104	3202
3287	4304	4317	4601	5563
5626	5655	5687		

Cutter Grinders
See Machines, Grinding (Reamer and Cutter)

Cutters, Bar
See Cutters, Rod and Bar

CUTTERS, Belt

1195	1570

CUTTERS, Brake Lining

Chicago Rivet & Machine Co., 1830 S. 54th Ave. (Cicero P.O.), Chicago, Ill—*See adv. p. 92*

635	1126	1195	2338	2410
3518	4018	4338	4644	5049
5214	5567			

CUTTERS, Chain

4743

Cutters, Gasket
See Cutters, Washer or Gasket

CUTTERS, Milling

Morse Twist Drill & Machine Co., 163 Pleasant St., New Bedford, Mass. *Illustrated, p. 118*

124	752	1130	2684	3877
3986	4261	4263	4758	5044
5700	5808	6102	6312	6697

CUTTERS, Pipe

(Hand power)

Imperial Brass Mfg. Co., 1225 W. Harrison St., Chicago, Ill.—*See adv. p. 126*

250	253	548	1842	3016
3048a	4649	5068	6166	6458

CUTTERS, Rod and Bar

(Hand power)

249	591a	4346	4743	6212
6565				

Cutters, Rotary
See Saws and Cutters, Rotary

CUTTERS, Shear

4743

CUTTERS, Washer and Gasket

Rex Metal Products Co., 365 First Ave., New York, N. Y. "Rex Hole in One"—*Illustration & prices, p. 114*

1148	2410	2778	4549	5529
5777				

Cylinder Compression Gages
See Gages, Cylinder Compression

Cylinder Gages
See Gages, Cylinder

See Page 364 for Names of Companies Represented by Above Numbers

Cylinder Heads
See Heads, Cylinder

Cylinder Hones
See Tools, Cylinder Honing

Cylinder Reamers
See Reamers and Jigs, Cylinder

Cylinder Reboring Machines
See Machines, Cylinder Reboring

Cylinder Reboring Tools
See Tools, Cylinder Reboring

Cylinder Regrinding Tools
See Tools, Cylinder Regrinding (Portable)

Cylinder Sleeves
See Sleeves, Cylinder

Decalcomania Transfers
See Transfers, Decalcomania

DECARBONIZERS, Engine
(Device which automatically feeds liquid or gas to cylinders while car is running; see also Compounds, Carbon Removing; also Machines, Engine Decarbonizing)

1028   4019

Decelerometers
See Instruments, Brake Testing

Deflators, Tire
See Tools, Tire Deflating; also Machines, Tube Deflating and Valve Removing

Deflectors, Wind
See Shields, Wing (For Open and Closed Cars)

DEPRESSORS, Brake Pedal
Bear Mfg. Co. 21st St. & Fifth Ave., Rock Island, Ill.—*See adv. p. 123*
Bendix-Cowdrey Brake Tester, Inc. (Div. of Bendix Aviation Corp.), South Bend, Ind. "Cowdrey" (Gage equipped)—*Illustrated, p. 107; also Front Cover*
Muther Mfg. Co., 44 Binford St., Boston, Mass. — *Illustration, description & prices, p. 115*

577	581	610	1929	3817
4034	4353	4531	4681	5133
5214	6153	6208		

Derricks
See Cranes, Truck

DERRICKS, Transmission
(To enable one man to remove bell housing on transmission or fly wheel)
Shepard & Moore, Inc., Advance Bldg., Cleveland, Ohio. "S & M." —*See adv. p. 47*
718   5410   5562

Die Sets
See Taps, Dies and Screw Plates

Die Stocks
See Stock, Die

Dies, Marking
See Stamps, Steel

Dies, Standard
See Punches and Dies, Standard

Dies, Thread Cutting
See Taps, Dies and Screw Plates

Differential Assembly Plates, for Fords
See Plates, Differential Assembly, for Fords

Differential Cleaners
See Cleaners, Differential and Transmission

Differential Repair Stands
See Stands, Transmission and Differential Repair

DIFFERENTIALS, Auto
(For individual gears—see Gears and Pinions, Metal; also Axles, Rear)
New Process Gear Co., 500 Plum St., Syracuse, N. Y.—*See adv. p. 237*
Simmons Mfg. Co., 3405-11 Perkins Ave., Cleveland, Ohio. (For Ford & Chevrolet cars)—*See adv. p. 62*
Warner Gear Co., Clerk & Penn Sts., Muncie, Ind.—*Illustration & warehouse stocks, p. 20*

149	747	3348	4297	4665
5563	6577			

DIMMERS, Glare (Rear View Mirror)
(Attachment to dim the glare of headlights from cars approaching from the rear)
Cuno Engineering Corp., 80 S. Vine St., Meriden, Conn. "Glar-Dim"— *Illustration, description & prices, p. 37*

4682

DIMMERS, Glare (Windshield)
(Colored glass, celluloid or steel attachment to dim the glare from approaching headlights)
Signal Mfg. Co., 587 Washington St., Lynn, Mass. "Lion"—*Illustrated, p. 45*
Woodworth Specialties Co., 121-25 Montgomery St., Binghamton, N. Y. —*See adv. p. 36*

1257	2007	2053	2158	2796
2809	2819	3291	4651	5556
5604	5779a	6185	6787	

DIMMERS or DEFLECTORS, Headlight
(Cups to attach to bulbs to deflect light; also metal shutters, etc. For other dimming devices—see Reflectors, Deflecting or Dimming; Switches, Headlight Dimming (Dash); Visors, Headlight)

5604   6197

Disc Wheel Straightening Machines
See Machines, Wheel Straightening (Disc)

DISCS, Clutch (Composition)

5214

DISCS, Clutch (Steel)
Burgess-Norton Mfg. Co., 517 Peyton St., Geneva, Ill. "B-N"—*Branch offices, p. 187*
Es-M-Co Auto Products Corp., 31 34th St., Brooklyn, N. Y.—*Illustration & warehouses, p. 70*
Jambor Tool & Stamping Co., 1261 30th St., Milwaukee, Wis. "Bull Dog"—*See adv. p. 64*
Monmouth Products Co., 882 E. 72nd St., Cleveland, Ohio — *Illustrated, p. 72*
Warner Gear Co., Clerk & Penn Sts., Muncie, Ind.—*Illustration & warehouse stocks, p. 20*

16	800	1906	2799	3104
3775	3954	4665	5214	5684
6577	6652			

DISCS, Universal Joint
Continental Rubber Works, 1902 Liberty St., Erie, Pa. "Vitalic"— *Illustrated, p. 64*
Holfast Rubber Co., Lakewood Ave., Atlanta, Ga.—*See adv. p. 65*
Thermoid Rubber Co., Whitehead Rd., Trenton, N. J. "Hardy"—*See adv. p. 85*

204	1124	1274	1670	1829
2412	2441	2781	5612	6129

Dispensers, Grease
See Lubricators, Portable High Pressure

DISPENSERS, Oil
(Trays, bottles and spouts for dispensing oil in quarts; for oil tanks on wheels—see Tanks, Oil (Portable)
Brookins Mfg. Co., 770 Hawthorne St., Dayton, Ohio. "Rapid"—*Illustrated & described, p. 117*

128	304	700	734	817
2635	2826	3713	3794	4784
6465	6586	6827		

Distributor Covers
See Covers, Distributor

Distributor Parts
See Parts, Magneto, Coil and Distributor

DISTRIBUTORS, Ignition

1547   1857   3768

Dividers and Calipers
See Calipers and Dividers

DOGS, Lathe
Armstrong Bros. Tool Co., 304 N. Francisco Ave., Chicago, Ill.— *Illustrated, p. 119*

250	3461	4694	5058	6660
6670	6730			

Dollies, Car
See Jacks on Wheels

Dolly Blocks
See Tools, Body and Fender Repair

Dome Lights
See Lamps, Dome

DOORS, Commercial Car (Steel)

3294

DOORS, Garage
(Including fire-proof and rolling doors)

319a	1296	3054	3134	3289
3764a	3850	4559	4753	6814

Drag Links
See Links, Steering

Drags, Truck Wheel Removing
See Cranes, Drags and Jacks, Truck Wheel Removing

Drain Plug Wrenches
See Wrenches, Drain Plug

DRESSERS, Emery Wheel

568	1128	1566	2693	4346
5700	5744	6483	6492	6660

DRESSING, Brake
Bell Co., 407-11 N. Lincoln St., Chicago, Ill.—*See adv. p. 93*

243	534	562	565	593
698	1245	2616	2648	2784
3922	4673	4801	5120	5413
5566	5707	6143		

DRESSING, Leather
(Advertisers in this publication only)
Bell Co., 407-11 N. Lincoln St., Chicago, Ill.—*See adv. p. 93*
Holfast Rubber Co., Lakewood Ave., Atlanta, Ga.—*See adv. p. 65*

DRESSING, Top (Weatherproof)
(Advertisers in this publication only)
Bell Co., 407-11 N. Lincoln St., Chicago, Ill.—*Illustrated, p. 93*
Holfast Rubber Co., Lakewood Ave., Atlanta, Ga.—*See adv. p. 65*
Liquid Veneer Corp., 822 Liquid Veneer Bldg., Buffalo, N. Y. "Neverleak"—*Illustration & prices, p. 66*

Drill, Enameled
See Cloth, Enameled or Oiled
Drill Stands, Electric
See Stands, for Portable Electric Drills and Grinders
Drilling Machines, Bench
See Machines, Drilling, Bench
Drilling Machines, Pneumatic (Portable)
See Machines, Drilling, Pneumatic, (Portable)
Drilling Machines, Vertical
See Machines, Drilling (Vertical)

DRILLS AND BITS, Battery Strap
124   4708

DRILLS, Breast

1143	2410	3905	4338	5034
5676	5709	5783		

DRILLS, Centering

3986	4758	5596	6312	6697

DRILLS, Chain
2410   3905   4338

DRILLS, Cotton
1659   2728   3422

DRILLS, GRINDERS and POLISHERS, Electric Portable
(For complete portable outfits—see Tools, Metal Finishing, Portable Electric)
United States Electrical Tool Co., Dept. T, 2483 W. Sixth St., Cincinnati, Ohio. "U. S."—Illustration, branch offices & prices, p. 25

83	633	645	655	678
1123	1143	1161	1266	1644
2372	2410	2764	3271	3457
3769	3902	3905	4252	4269
4670	5452	5511	5676	5708
5782	5783	5784	5833	6118
6332	6454	6459	6571	6684
6745				

Drills, Portable
See Drills, Grinders and Polishers, Electric Portable; also Machines, Drilling, Pneumatic (Portable)

DRILLS, Ratchet
Armstrong Bros. Tool Co., 304 N. Francisco Ave., Chicago. Ill.—See adv. p. 119

250	643	2410	3270	3905
3986	5777	6697		

Drills, Tapping
See Machines, Drilling (Vertical)

DRILLS, Twist
Morse Twist Drill & Machine Co., 163 Pleasant St., New Bedford, Mass. —Illustrated, p. 118

124	201	569	767	1148
1185	2456	3986	4263	5700
6312	6679	6697		

Drive Shaft Bearing End Mills, for Fords
See Mills, Drive Shaft Bearing End, for Fords
Drive Shafts
See Shafts, Propeller

DRIVERS, Bearing Cup
3256

DRIVERS, Bushing
National Machine & Tool Co., 801 S. Water St., Jackson, Mich.—Illustration & prices, p. 120
2841

DRIVERS, Grease
(Pressure developed by tap of hammer)
1212   1669   5100   5165   6108

DRIVERS, Screw (Hand)
(Advertisers in this publication only)
Peck, Stow & Wilcox Co., 217-313 Center St., Southington, Conn. "Pexto"—See adv. p. 124

DRIVERS, Screw (Portable Electric)

633	655	1143	2764	3905
5452	5708	5783	6332	6459
6766				

DRIVES, Reamer
Dall Motor Parts Co., P.O. Station D (Dept. CAM), Cleveland, Ohio. "Dall"—Branch offices, p. 187
663   1503   2448   4547

DRIVES, Starter and PARTS (Bendix)
(For automatically meshing pinion on starter motor with flywheel gear)
Eclipse Machine Co. (Div. of Bendix Aviation Corp.), Dept. 5, Elmira, N. Y. "Bendix"—See illustration & service instructions, p. 221; also Front Cover

Drum Faucets
See Faucets, Drum or Barrel

DRUMS, Brake (Dummy)
(For use in adjusting brakes)
3907A

DRUMS, Brake (Iron)
4   1535   2478   2843   3230
3474

DRUMS, Brake (Pressed or Stamped Steel)
Simmons Mfg. Co., 3405-11 Perkins Ave., Cleveland, Ohio (For Ford & Chevrolet cars)—See adv. p. 62
623a   3410   3474   5607

Duck, Enameled or Oiled
See Cloth, Enameled or Oiled

DUSTERS, Wool and Cotton
3924   6619

DYE, Top Lining
702   1922   4025   4347   4673
5566

DYNAMOMETERS, Chassis Testing
3857

DYNAMOMETERS, Engine Testing
1596   2343a   3857   6664

Dynamos, Battery Charging (Auto)
See Generators, Electric Lighting and Battery Charging (Auto); also Motor Generators, Battery Charging

ELECTROLYTE, Storage Battery
2440   3211

ELEVATORS, Automobile and Parts
2369   3054   3280   3510   5493
5555   5649   6576

Emblems
See Flags, Pennants and Emblems
Emblems, Radiator
See Monograms, Initials and Emblems, Ornamental

EMBLEMS, Tire Cover
338   1200

Emergency Cases
See Cases, Medical Emergency
Emery Cloth
See Cloth, Abrasive
Emery Paper
See Paper, Emery and Sand
Emery, Powdered
See Abrasives; also Compounds, Valve Grinding
Emery Wheel Dressers
See Dressers, Emery Wheel
Emery Wheels
See Wheels, Grinding
Enamel Paints
See Paints
Enamel Removers
See Removers, Paint, Enamel and Varnish
Enameled Cloth
See Cloth, Enameled or Oiled

ENAMELS
(See also Lacquer; also Paints)
American Chemical Paint Co., Brookside Ave. & Reading R. R., Ambler, Pa. "Paradox"—Description, p. 126
Sherwin-Williams Co., Dept. 733, 101 Prospect Ave., N. W., Cleveland, Ohio—See adv. p. 21

38	78	143	236	534
593	702	1022	1660	1667
2616	2689	2751	2860	3066
3122	3922	4347	4508	4529
4673	4696	4756	5120	5541
5625	5704	5727	6143	6456
6789				

Enamels, Engine
See Paints, Exhaust Pipe, Muffler and Cylinder

ENAMELS, High Bake
American Chemical Paint Co., Brookside Ave. & Reading R. R., Ambler, Pa. "Paradox"—Description, p. 126

78	143	236	244	1186
1660	2389	2751		

ENCLOSURES, Panel Top
652   2628   5045

ENCLOSURES, Panel Top, for Ford and Chevrolet Cars
1905   2773   3332   6133

ENDS, Rod
Es-M-Co Auto Products Corp., 31 34th St., Brooklyn, N. Y. (For Ford & Chevrolet cars)—Illustration & warehouses, p. 70
528b   643   720   6730

Ends, Yoke
See Yokes, Special
Engine Logs
See Logs, Engine
Engine Revolution Counters
See Tachometers

ENGINES, Automobile (Gasoline)
Continental Motors Corp., 12801 E. Jefferson Ave., Detroit, Mich. "Argyll," "Continental"—Illustration & description, p. 19

4	769	779	1272	2351
2716	3498	3567	3848	3901
5430	5742	6599	6759	

See Page 364 for Names of Companies Represented by Above Numbers

EQUALIZERS, Brake
2694

EQUALIZERS, Trailer Brake
5049

Expanders, Piston Ring
See Rings, Piston Ring Expanding or Packing

EXTENSIONS, Brake Lever, for Fords
3992   5105

EXTENSIONS, Choker, for Fords
1257   2158   5567

EXTENSIONS, Door Latch, for Fords
2053   2604

EXTENSIONS, Gear Shift Lever
2018   2396   2404   2809   3018
3349   3750   6145   6221   6686

EXTENSIONS, Pedal
2158

EXTENSIONS, Starter Button
224   620   3120   3150   5567
6218

EXTINGUISHERS, Automobile Fire
165   515   765   777   1905
2164   2350   3276   3727   4806
5407

EXTINGUISHERS, Factory Fire
165   515   777   1597   1643a
1905   2164   2350   3276   3320
3727   4693   4718   4806   5407
5617

EXTRACTORS, Bolt and Screw
1002   1185   2456   2841

EXTRACTORS, Bushing
(See also Saws, Bushing Removing)
National Machine & Tool Co., 801 S. Water St., Jackson, Mich.—Illustration & prices, p. 120
Truth Tool Co., 711 S. Front St., Mankato, Minn.—See adv. p. 128
35   100   336   756   1253a
2723   2795   2841   3256   3276
3989   4241   4600   5035   5181
5611   6208   6491   6503   6559

EXTRACTORS, Bushing, for Fords
Truth Tool Co., 711 S. Front St., Mankato, Minn.—See adv. p. 128
681   1185   6208   6745

Extractors, Car
See Winches and Blocks, Car Extracting

Eye Protectors
See Goggles, Mechanics' and Welders'

Eyelets
See Grommets and Eyelets

Fabrics, Upholstery and Top
See Broadcloth; Cloth; Corduroys; Plush; Velours; Velvets

Facings, Brake
See Lining, Brake

Fan Belts
See Belts, Rubber; also Belts, Fabric; also Belts, V; also Belting, Leather

Fan Pulley Pins, For Fords
See Pins, Fan Pulley, for Fords

FANS, Electric
(For closed cars)
3313

FANS, Exhaust Drying
(For use in connection with drying room equipment)
646   778   1587   3007   3294
4269   6745

FANS, Radiator
Simmons Mfg. Co., 3405-11 Perkins Ave., Cleveland, Ohio. (For Ford & Chevrolet cars)—See adv. p. 62
2647

Fare Boxes
See Boxes, Fare

Fare Registers
See Registers, Fare

FASTENERS, Belt
1195   2087   2454   2758   3780
3983   5046   5214   5599   6586

Fasteners, Chain
See Fasteners, Tire Chain

FASTENERS, Curtain
Auto-Vehicle Parts Co., 1032 Saratoga St., Newport, Ky. "Au-Ve-Co."—See adv. pp. 34 & 35
United-Carr Fastener Corp., 31 Ames St., Cambridge, Mass. "Dot"—Illustration & prices, p. 72
360   1139   1192   2773   2860
3857   4271   6318

FASTENERS, Hood
295   331   1603   1823   2384
5627   6627

FASTENERS, License Tag
Bellevue Mfg. Co., Ashford Ave., Bellevue, Ohio—See adv. p. 52
131   224   595   1257   2033
2643   3756b   4677   4791   6559

Fasteners, Storage Battery Holding Down
See Clamps, Battery Hold Down

FASTENERS, Tire Chain
Cleveland Chain & Mfg. Co., Penna. R. R. & Henry Rd., Cleveland, Ohio —See adv. p. 39
McKay Co., Union Trust Bldg., Pittsburgh, Pa.—Illustrated, p. 33
United States Chain & Forging Co.— See McKay Co.
1077   1237

FASTENERS, Top
(Fastener or clamp to hold top to windshield)
295   720   1309   6783

FAUCETS, Drum or Barrel
(For oil, gasoline and anti-freezing solution)
Imperial Brass Mfg. Co., 1225 W. Harrison St., Chicago, Ill. — See adv. p. 126

FAUCETS, Radiator Filling
2826   3713   5173   5197

FAUCETS, Tank Body
817   3846

Felloes, Steel
See Rims or Felloes, Steel

FELT, Polishing and Rubbing
Felt Products Mfg. Co., 1510 Carroll Ave., Chicago, Ill. "Fel-Pro" —See adv. p. 75
47   509   717   1250   2047
4607   6651

FELT, Upholstery
(See also Hair, Upholstery; also Moss, Upholstery)
Felt Products Mfg. Co., 1510 Carroll Ave., Chicago, Ill.—See adv. p. 75
801   1159   1250   2047   4607
5471

Fender Braces
See Braces, Mud Guard or Fender

Fender Indicators
See Indicators, Fender

Fender Repair Tools
See Tools, Body and Fender Repair

Fender Shrinking Clamps
See Tools, Body and Fender Repair

FENDERS or MUD GUARDS, Metal
Fostoria Pressed Steel Corp., Dept. CM-1, N. Main St., Fostoria, Ohio —Illustration & warehouse stocks, p. 71
Simmons Mfg. Co., 3405-11 Perkins Ave., Cleveland, Ohio. (For Ford & Chevrolet cars)—See adv. p. 62
209   1233   1294   2115   3294
3448   5563   6814a

FENDERS or GUARDS, Truck Radiator
1584   3263   3500   3870

Fibre Board
See Fibre, Hard

Fibre Cleats
See Cleats, Fibre Wiring

FIBRE, Hard
(Sheets, rods and tubes)
27   258   1270   3067   4266
4607   6744

Fifth Wheels
See Wheels, Fifth

File Cleaning Brushes
See Brushes, File Cleaning

FILES, Contact Point
339   3202   5753   6103

Files, Spark Plug
See Cleaners, Spark Plug

FILES and RASPS
275   1604   1895a   1921   4314
5565   5611   6679

FILLERS, Storage Battery
(See also Hydrometers)
Loock & Co., R. J., 343-45 N. Gay St., Baltimore, Md. "Lightnin"— Illustrated, p. 51
559   1842   2132   2412   2623
2826   2860   3202   3537   4707
4708   5482   6125   6586a   6825

Filters, Air
See Cleaners, Air

Filters, Gasoline or Oil
See Strainers, Gasoline or Oil

Filters, Oil
See Purifiers, Oil, for Attaching to Engines; also Reclaimers or Rectifiers, Oil (Garage or Repair Shop)

See Page 364 for Names of Companies Represented by Above Numbers

FINDERS, Traffic Signal
Shepard & Moore, Inc., Advance Bldg., Cleveland, Ohio. "Moonbeam"—*See adv. p. 47*
4791

FINISH, Top (Waterproofing)
(See also Dressing, Top (Weatherproof)
Holfast Rubber Co., Lakewood Ave., Atlanta, Ga.—*See adv. p. 65*
1660   2602   4802   5497

Fire Apparatus
See Automobiles (Fire Apparatus)

Fire Extinguishers
See Extinguishers, Automobile Fire; also Extinguishers, Factory Fire

Fire Pots
See Furnaces, Soldering

Fishing Tools, Tire Valve
See Tools, Tire Valve Fishing

Fittings, Automobile and Truck Body
See Hardware, Automobile and Truck Body; also Hardware, Convertible Cabriolet

FITTINGS, Bus
(Including all hardware and irons used in bus body construction, such as enameled pipes, stanchions, seat irons, etc.)
295   1823   1866   5411   6145
6627   6783

Fittings, Curtain Opening
See Openers, Curtain

FITTINGS, Lubricating
(For guns for use with fittings—see Lubricators, Hand)
39   86   696   1141   1623

Fittings, Pipe
See Fittings, Tube (Copper or Brass)

FITTINGS, Tube (Copper or Brass)
(Unions, tees, ells, etc., for connecting small size brass and copper tubing)
Dole Valve Co., 1913-33 Carroll Ave., Chicago, Ill.—*Illustrated & described, p. 42*
Imperial Brass Mfg. Co., 1225 W. Harrison St., Chicago, Ill.—*See adv. p. 126*
Lincoln Brass Works, 2067 12th St., Detroit, Mich.—*Illustration & sizes, p. 73*
103   295   1095   1249   1618
1842   3016   3202   3337   3502
3563   4011   4296   5142a   5589a
6608

FITTINGS and FIXTURES, Top
(See also Bows, Top; also Fasteners, Curtain; also Irons, Slat; also Sockets, Bow)
2407   6627   6783

FLAGS, PENNANTS and EMBLEMS
(See also Ornaments, Radiator)
218   268   295   1225   1585
1886   5679

Flame Arresters
See Arresters, Flame

Flaps, Fender
See Guards, Fender Splash

FLAPS, Tire
Continental Rubber Works, 1902 Liberty St., Erie, Pa. "Vitalic"—*See adv. p. 64*

Gates Rubber Co., 999 S. Broadway, Denver, Colo. "Gates Vulco"—*See adv. p. 62*
Holfast Rubber Co., Lakewood Ave., Atlanta, Ga.—*See adv. p. 65*
766   812   1274   1286   1589
1829   2324   2355   2412   2416
2781   3469   3903   4736   5046
6160   6344

FLASHERS, Stop Light
2337

FLASHLIGHTS or LANTERNS
684   729   798   1553   2141
2761   4223   4311   5496

Flint Paper
See Paper, Abrasive

FLOATS, Cork
Simmons Mfg. Co., 3405-11 Perkins Ave., Cleveland, Ohio (For Ford & Chevrolet cars)—*See adv. p. 62*
251   4021   4607   4612

FLOATS, Metal
Es-M-Co Auto Products Corp., 31 34th St., Brooklyn, N. Y. (For Chevrolet cars) — *Illustration & warehouses, p. 70*
Hygrade Products Co., 333 W. 52nd St., New York, N. Y.—*Illustrated, p. 86*
1053   1906   2619   2655   2858
3016   5816

Floor Boards
See Boards, Floor or Foot

Floor Pads, Felt
See Pads, Floor (Felt, Jute, etc.)

Floor Scrubbing and Polishing Machines
See Machines, Floor (Electric)

FLUID, Hydraulic Brake and Shock Absorber
Bell Co., 407-11 N. Lincoln St., Chicago, Ill.—*See adv. p. 93*
702   1667   2773   4673   4801
5707   6143

FLUIDS, Priming
2616

FLUXES, Brazing
Imperial Brass Mfg. Co., 1225 W. Harrison St., Chicago, Ill. — *See adv. p. 126*
Linde Air Products Co., 30 E. 42nd St., New York, N. Y.—*Branch offices, p. 125*
222   287   1609   3345   4617
4678   5608

FLUX, Soldering
(For self-fluxing solder—see Solder, Self-Fluxing)
(Advertisers in this publication only)
American Chemical Paint Co., Brookside Ave. & Reading R. R., Ambler, Pa. "Flosol"—*Described, p. 126*

Flywheel Gear Heaters
See Heaters, Flywheel Gear

Foot Boards
See Boards, Floor or Foot

Foot Rests or Rails
See Rests or Rails, Foot

Foot Warmers
See Heaters, Automobile

Footman Loops
See Loops, Brass Snap and Strap

Forms, Accounting
See Books and Forms, Accounting

FORMS, Printed
(Advertisers in this publication only)
Unique Printed Products Co., 2224 N. 13th St., Terre Haute, Ind.—*See adv. p. 127*

FOUNDATIONS, Body Upholstery
263   3959   6773A

Fountain Brushes and Mops
See Washers, Automobile (Fountain Brushes and Mops)

Frame Extensions
See Converters, Chassis

Frame Padding
See Lining, Body or Frame

FRAMES, Hack Saw
(For hack saw blades—see Blades, Saw, Hack)
81   275   726   1324   1604
2107   2410   2841   3201   3905
3918   5034   5611   5719   6142
6146a   6311

FRAMES, License Plate
Hackett Products Co., 407 Pine St., Providence, R. I.—*Illustrated & described, p. 40*
Rex Metal Products Co., 365 First Ave., New York, N. Y.—*Illustrated & described, p. 114*
131   2129   2604   3002   3349
4506   6643a

Free Wheeling Units
4297

FREE-WHEELING UNITS (For Model A Ford Cars)
50   1855   4297   4651b   5040a
6197a

Freezometers
See Hydrometers

FRONTS, Store
(Glass fronts for stores and motor sales rooms)
3054   3228   3850

Frost Eliminators
See Heaters, Windshield; also Shields, Frost

Fuel Feed Systems
See Systems, Fuel Feed

Fuel Level Indicators
See Gages, Gasoline

Fuel Mixers
See Mixers, Economizers or Agitators and Auxiliary Air Valves

Fuel Pump Parts
See Parts, Fuel Pump

Fuel Reserve Cocks
See Valves, Two-Way Tank

Funeral Cars
See Automobiles (Hearses and Funeral Cars.)

Funnel and Crankcase Wrench Combined
2158

Funnels, Hard Rubber
Continental Rubber Works, 1902 Liberty St., Erie, Pa.—*See adv. p. 64*
559

FUNNELS, Metal
(For gasoline or oil)
279   590   817   1067   1523
1632   2826   3342   3448   3713
4784

Furnaces, Gasoline
See Torches and Furnaces, Gasoline
or Kerosene

FURNACES, Soldering

157	221	320	626	1831
2674	2793	3131	5789	6483
6817				

FURNITURE, Metal
Lyon Metal Products, Inc., 2931
Montgomery St., Aurora, Ill.—See
adv. p. 106

213	622	5690	5728

FUSES, Electric
Bussmann Mfg. Co., University at
Jefferson, St. Louis, Mo. "Buss"—
Illustration, description & prices,
p. 74
Jefferson Electric Co., 1508 S. Laflin
St., Chicago, Ill. "Union"—Illus-
tration & prices, p. 75
Killark Electric Mfg. Co., 3940 East-
on Ave., St. Louis, Mo.—Illustra-
tion & prices, p. 76

337	816	1227	1905	2300
2343	3114	3202	3279	3296
4556	4706	6189a	6664	

Gage Lamps
See Lamps, Dash or Gage

Gages, Air
See Gages, Steam and Air

Gages, Axle Aligning
See Gages, Wheel and Axle Aligning

Gages, Battery
See Hydrometers

GAGES, Brake Drum

4531	4791

**GAGES, Brake and Drum Concen-
tricity**
(See also Tools, Brake Testing)
3907A

Gages, Compression
See Gages, Cylinder Compression

GAGES, Crank Pin
200

GAGES, Cylinder
(See also Micrometers)
Maxwell Automotive Engineering Co.,
44 Binford St., Boston, Mass. "M-
A-E-C-O"—Illustration, descrip-
tion & prices, p. 115

169	200	2084	3256	5719

GAGES, Cylinder Compression

1842	3018	3106	3452	6336

GAGES, Drill and Wire

752	3986	4758	5700	5719
6312				

GAGES, Gasoline Auto (Dash Type)
King-Seeley Corp., 294 Second St.,
Ann Arbor, Mich. "K-S Telegage"
—Illustrated, p. 45
Moto Meter Gauge & Equipment
Corp., Toledo, Ohio. "R.K.D.,"
"Nagel," "Neco"—See adv. p. 60

6	2305	3285	3299	3992
5154				

**G A G E S, Gasoline Auto (Tank
Type)**
Moto Meter Gauge & Equipment
Corp., Toledo, Ohio—See adv. p. 60

76	1257	5154

GAGES, Muffler Back Pressure
Powell Muffler Co., 316 Catherine St.,
Utica, N. Y.—Illustrated, p. 86

GAGES, Oil, for Fords
Simmons Mfg. Co., 3405-11 Perkins
Ave., Cleveland, Ohio—See adv. p.
62

224	1257	1842	2051	5105
5563	6130			

GAGES, Oil Level
Moto Meter Gauge & Equipment
Corp., Toledo, Ohio.—See adv. p.
60

76	2305	5154

GAGES, Oil Pressure
Moto Meter Gauge & Equipment
Corp., Toledo, Ohio.—See adv. p.
60

6	1257	3018	3503	3915
3992	5154	5567	5687	5761
6336				

GAGES, Piston Pin, for Fords
6745

GAGES, Plug and Ring

364	752	2456	2684	3986
5536	6104	6358		

Gages, Pump
See Gages, Tire Pressure

Gages, Ring
See Gages, Plug and Ring

GAGES, Screw Pitch

752	2084	2410	3559	4758
5719				

GAGES, Steam and Air
Moto Meter Gauge & Equipment
Corp., Toledo, Ohio.—See adv. p.
60

1895A	3018	3774	3992	6336
6586A				

**GAGES, Storage Tank (Distance
Reading)**
King-Seeley Corp., 294 Second St.,
Ann Arbor, Mich. "K-S Telegage"
—Illustrated & described, p. 45

3515	6604

GAGES, Surface

200	2410	3559	5719

Gages, Tank
See Gages, Gasoline Auto

GAGES, Thickness (Pocket)
Hygrade Products Co., 333 W. 52nd
St., New York, N. Y. — See adv.
p. 86

116A	200	337	339	752
1063	1257	2084	2410	2619
2841	2858	3018	3202	3256
3559	3918	5611	5687	6208
6311	6717A			

GAGES, Tire Pressure
Dill Mfg. Co., 686 E. 82nd St., Cleve-
land, Ohio—Illustrated, p. 43
Moto Meter Gauge & Equipment
Corp., Toledo, Ohio.—See adv. p.
60
Schrader's Son, A., 470 Vanderbilt
Ave., Brooklyn, N. Y.—Illustration
& prices, p. 29
Syracuse Gauge Mfg. Corp., 212 Bear
St., Syracuse, N. Y. "Hand-D"—
Illustration, description & prices,
p. 44

22	1602	2412	2723	3018
3241	3330	3800	3992	5465
5505	5834	6336		

GAGES, Wheel and Axle Aligning
Bear Mfg. Co., 21st St. & Fifth Ave.,
Rock Island, Ill.—Illustrated, p. 123
Manley Mfg. Co., 929 Connecticut
Ave., Bridgeport, Conn.—See adv.
p. 38

577	581	2835	3256	3774
3805	4005	4775	6611	

GAGES, Windshield Glass
3426

Gages, Wire
See Gages, Drill and Wire

Gaps, Spark
See Intensifiers, Spark

GAS, Acetylene (In Tanks)
(For acetylene lighting and welding)
Linde Air Products Co., 30 E. 42nd
St., New York, N. Y. "Prest-O-
Lite"—Branch offices, p. 125

67	792	1244	1871	3049
4245	4527	4636	4801a	5636

Gas Generators
See Generators, Acetylene, Gas

GAS, Oxygen (In Tanks)
(For oxy-acetylene welding)
Linde Air Products Co., 30 E. 42nd
St., New York, N. Y.—Branch of-
fices, p. 125

67	792	1030	1244	1871
3049	3507	4245	4527	4636
4801a	5636			

Gasket Cement
See Cement, Gasket

Gasket Cutters
See Cutters, Washer or Gasket

Gasket Shellac
See Cement, Gasket

GASKETS, Asbestos
Advance Packing & Supply Co., 806
Washington Blvd., Chicago, Ill.
—See adv. p. 87
Felt Products Mfg. Co., 1510 Carroll
Ave., Chicago, Ill. "Wirepak"—
Illustrated, p. 75
Fitzgerald Mfg. Co., 691 Main St.,
Torrington, Conn.—See adv. p. 76
Victor Mfg. & Gasket Co., 5750
Roosevelt Rd., Chicago, Ill. "Vic-
tor," "Victorpac"—See adv. p. 77

27	49	204	1263	1513
1591	1670	1829	1889	2047
2054	2079	2322	2338	2412
3127	3234	4607	4697	6325
6480				

GASKETS, Copper
Fitzgerald Mfg. Co., 691 Main St.,
Torrington, Conn.—Illustrated &
described, p. 76
Victor Mfg. & Gasket Co., 5750
Roosevelt Rd., Chicago, Ill. "Vic-
tor," "H-B-A"—See adv. p. 77

2079	4697	6480

GASKETS, Copper-Asbestos
Fitzgerald Mfg. Co., 691 Main St.,
Torrington, Conn.—Illustrated &
described, p. 76
Victor Mfg. & Gasket Co., 5750
Roosevelt Rd., Chicago, Ill. "Blue
Edge," "H-B-A"—Illustrated, p.
77

27	258	1314	1670	2079
3709	4607	4697	6480	

See Page 364 for Names of Companies Represented by Above Numbers

GASKETS, Cork
Advance Packing & Supply Co., 806 Washington Blvd., Chicago, Ill. —See adv. p. 87
Felt Products Mfg. Co., 1510 Carroll Ave., Chicago, Ill. "Fel-Pro," "Carrocork"—Illustrated, p. 75
Fitzgerald Mfg. Co., 691 Main St., Torrington, Conn.—Illustrated & described, p. 76
Simmons Mfg. Co., 3405-11 Perkins Ave., Cleveland, Ohio. (For Ford and Chevrolet cars) — See adv. p. 62
Thermoid Rubber Co., Whitehead Rd., Trenton, N. J.—See adv. p. 85
Victor Mfg. & Gasket Co., 5750 Roosevelt Rd., Chicago, Ill. — See adv. p. 77

27	47	49	251	258
1670	2047	2079	2322	3709
4021	4607	4612	5563	6129
6480				

Gaskets, Felt
See Washers, Felt

GASKETS, Fibrous
Advance Packing & Supply Co., 806 Washington Blvd., Chicago, Ill. —See adv. p. 87
Felt Products Mfg. Co., 1510 Carroll Ave., Chicago, Ill. "Karropak," "Felpak"—See adv. p. 75
Vellumoid Co., 54 Rockdale St., Worcester, Mass.—See adv. p. 78
Victor Mfg. & Gasket Co., 5750 Roosevelt Rd., Chicago, Ill. "Victorite," "Ferropac"—See adv. p. 77

27	49	204	1270	1670
1891	2047	2322	4607	6475
6480	6744			

GASKETS, Flexible Metallic
Felt Products Mfg. Co., 1510 Carroll Ave., Chicago, Ill. "Alupak"—See adv. p. 75

Gaskets, Hard Fibre
See Fibre, Hard

GASKETS, Leather
Advance Packing & Supply Co., 806 Washington Blvd., Chicago, Ill. —See adv. p. 87
Felt Products Mfg. Co., 1510 Carroll Ave., Chicago, Ill.—Illustrated, p. 75

27	49	1111	1124	2047
2441	2702	3027	3455	4607
4697	5571	5612		

GASKETS, Paper
Advance Packing & Supply Co., 806 Washington Blvd., Chicago, Ill. "Adpasco"—Illustration & sizes, p. 87
Felt Products Mfg. Co., 1510 Carroll Ave., Chicago, Ill.—Illustrated, p. 75
Vellumoid Co., 54 Rockdale St., Worcester, Mass.—See adv. p. 78
Victor Mfg. & Gasket Co., 5750 Roosevelt Rd., Chicago, Ill. — See adv. p. 77

27	47	49	258	1263
1532	1670	2047	2322	4607
4697	6475	6480		

GASKETS, Paste
4673　5425

GASKETS, Plastic
698　4801　5425　6725A

Gaskets, Rubber
See Packing, Rubber

Gasoline Economizers
See Mixers, Economizers or Agitators and Auxiliary Air Valves

Gasoline Hose
See Hose, Gasoline (Metal Lined Rubber and Fabric)

Gasoline Mileage Testers
See Testers, Gasoline Mileage

Gear Cutting
See Gears and Pinions, Metal

Gear Pullers
See Pullers, Gear and Wheel

Gear Shift Grease and Oil Protectors
See Protectors, Gear Shift Grease and Oil

Gear Shifters, Automatic
See Shifters, Gear (Automatic)

GEARS, Auxiliary Transmission (For Model A Fords)
1605	3503	4020	4775	5209
6575				

Gears, Differential
See Differentials, Auto

GEARS, Generator and Ignitor
339	1827	1857	2073	2472
3202	3401	4317	4601	4620
5687				

Gears, Ring
See Gears, Starter

GEARS, Special Ratio (Rear Bevel), for Fords
(Rear bevels and pinions of higher ratio than standard for increasing speed of car for racing purposes)

3914　5101

Gears, Speedometer
See Gears and Pinions, Speedometer

GEARS, Starter
(For attaching to flywheel)
Springfield Mfg. Co., Bechtle Ave. & Columbia St., Springfield, Ohio. "Excelsior"—Illustrated p. 78
Warner Gear Co., Clerk & Penn Sts., Muncie, Ind.—Illustration & warehouse stocks, p. 20

15	332	558	1224	2448
2825	3106	3534	3775	3914A
4323	4556	4665	5101	5199
5664	6652	6577	6820	

GEARS, Steering
(Complete steering gear units)
New Process Gear Co., 500 Plum St., Syracuse, N. Y.—See adv. p. 237
Simmons Mfg. Co., 3405-11 Perkins Ave., Cleveland, Ohio (For Chevrolet cars)—See adv. p. 62

5183

GEARS, Steering, for Fords
Simmons Mfg. Co., 3405-11 Perkins Ave., Cleveland, Ohio — See adv. p. 62

GEARS, Timing (Metallic and Non-Metallic)
Biglow & Co., L. C., 250 W. 54th St., New York, N. Y. (New York representatives for Timing Gears Corp.)—See adv. p. 129
Continental-Diamond Fibre Co., Newark, Del. "Celoron"—Illustration & warehouses, p. 8

641	1199	1224	1270	1504
1605	2343	4323	4657	4665
6156	6664			

Gears, Transmission
See Transmissions (Auto)

GEARS, Worm Drive
Cleveland Worm & Gear Co., 3261 E. 80th St., Cleveland, Ohio — Illustrated & described, p. 79

563　3401　3474　3842a

GEARS and PINIONS, Metal
(Metal gear cutting on contract to sample or blueprint; also stock gears)
Jambor Tool & Stamping Co., 1261 30th St., Milwaukee, Wis. "Bull Dog"—See adv. p. 64
New Process Gear Co., 500 Plum St., Syracuse, N. Y.—Illustrated, p. 237
Simmons Mfg. Co., 3405-11 Perkins Ave., Cleveland, Ohio (For Ford & Chevrolet Cars)—See adv. p. 62
Warner Gear Co., Clerk & Penn Sts., Muncie, Ind.—Illustration & warehouse stocks, p. 20

82	332	563	630	747
1199	2073	2156	3104	3401
3510	3534	3842a	3914	3914a
4297	4621	4657	4665	5101
5563	5663	6110	6216a	6652
6653	6577	6793	6806	

Gears and Pinions, Non-Metallic (Timing)
See Gears, Timing (Metallic and Non-Metallic)

GEARS and PINIONS, Speedometer
1270	2073	2799	3401	4620
5759	5761	5832		

Generator Bracket Savers
See Tools, Generator Bracket Saving

Generator Brushes
See Brushes, Generator, Horn and Starter

Generator Brush Holders
See Parts, Starting Motor Drive

Generator Couplings
See Couplings, Magneto, Generator and Water Pump

Generator Cutouts
See Cutouts, Reverse Current

Generator Field Coils
See Coils, Generator Field

Generator Gear Pullers
See Pullers, Gear and Wheel

Generator Gears
See Gears, Generator and Ignitor

Generator Parts
See Parts, Magneto, Coil and Distributor

GENERATORS, Acetylene Gas
(For use on car; for Generators for Welding—see Machines and Equipment, Oxy-Acetylene Welding; for Acetylene in Tanks—see Gas, Acetylene (In Tanks)
67　3928A　5608　5811

GENERATORS, Electric Lighting and Battery Charging (Auto)
(See also Motors, Starting; also Systems, Electric Lighting)
Simmons Mfg. Co., 3405-11 Perkins Ave., Cleveland, Ohio (For Ford & Chevrolet cars)—See adv. p. 62
United American Bosch Corp., 3664 Main St., Springfield, Mass. "Bosch" (Also sole American representatives for Robert Bosch, A. G., Stuttgart, Germany)—See adv. p. 69

1547	1548A	1857	3462	4561
5563	6314A			

Generators, Motor Driven Battery Charging
See Motor Generators, Battery Charging

Glare Dimmers or Preventers
See Dimmers, Glare (Windshield); also Visors, Headlight; also Visors, Windshield

Glass Beveling Machines
See Machines, Glass Beveling and Grinding

Glass, Bullet-Proof
See Glass, Non-Shatterable

Glass Cleaners, Rubber
See Cleaners, Glass (Rubber)

Glass Grinders
See Machines, Glass Beveling and Grinding

GLASS, Non-Shatterable

1655	3022	3137a	4794	5406
6194				

GLASS, Polished Plate and Flat Drawn
(For windshield and closed body work; also for lamp, clock, gage and meter glasses)

506	1536	2809	3000	3137a
3489	4362	4721	4744	4748
5047	5198	5406	6131	

Glass, Window, Windshield and Visor
See Glass, Polished Plate and Flat Drawn

Glazing Compounds
See Compounds, Glazing

GLOVES, Rubber
(Acid proof gloves for storage battery workers)

559	2029	2324	2412	2415
3903	5617	6205	6344	6747

GOGGLES, Mechanics' and Welders'
Linde Air Products Co., 30 E. 42nd St., New York, N. Y.—*Illustration & branch offices, p. 125*

48	192	792	1115	5597
5608	6125	6176	6741	

Golf Bag Carriers
See Holders, Golf Bag

GOVERNORS, Engine
Handy Governor Corp., 3921 W. Fort St., Detroit, Mich. "KP"—*Illustrated, p. 79*

629	1253	2631	3287	3310
3946			

Governors, Load
See Meters, Truck Load Indicating

Grade Indicators
See Meters, Grade

Graphite Cylinder Lubricators
See Lubricators, Cup Cylinder

Grease Bags
See Boots, Steering Knuckle and Joint

Grease Cups
See Cups, Oil and Grease

Grease Guns, Pumps, Cabinets and Buckets
See Lubricators.

Grease Rack Bars
See Bars, Grease Rack

Grease Rams
See Drivers, Grease

Grease Retainers
See Retainers, Rear Axle Grease

Grinder Centers
See Centers, Lathe and Grinder

Grinding Equipment
See following heads:
Compounds, Valve Grinding
Drills, Grinders and Polishers
Machines, Glass Beveling and Grinding
Machines, Grinding
Refacers, Valve
Tools, Reamer Sharpening
Tools, Valve Grinding
Wheels, Grinding

Gripping Straps
See Straps, Gripping

Grips, Non-Skid
See Chains or Grips, Non-Skid, for Solid Tires; also Chains or Grips, Non-Skid, for Pneumatic Tires.

Grips, Pedal
See Pads, Pedal

Grips, Steering Wheel
See Covers, Steering Wheel Rim

GRIPS or JAWS, Vise
6321

GROMMETS and EYELETS
Auto-Vehicle Parts Co., 1042 Saratoga St., Newport, Ky.—*See adv. pp. 34 & 35*

360	1139	1274	1664	1829
1893	2412	5126	5765	6323A
6344				

GUARDS, Fender Splash
Signal Mfg. Co., 587 Washington St., Lynn, Mass. "Lion" — *Illustrated & described, p. 45*
Williams Products Co., H. E., 100 S. Main St., Carthage, Mo.—*See adv. p. 32*
Woodworth Specialties Co., 121-25 Montgomery St., Binghamton, N. Y. — *Illustration, description & prices, p. 36*

224	338	692	1667	1905
2628	3221	4677	5556	6133
6469	6787			

Guards, Machinery (Wire)
See Guards, Safety, for Machines

Guards, Radiator (Truck)
See Fenders or Guards, Truck Radiator

GUARDS, Safety, for Machines

301	782	3294

Guards, Store Window (Wire)
See Wire, for Enclosures, Fences, Window Guards, etc.

GUARDS, Transmission Lever, for Fords
224

GUIDES, Valve
Thompson Products, Inc., 2196 Clarkwood Rd., Cleveland, Ohio.—*Illustrated, p. 89*

2799	3709	3775	5718

Guns, Blow
See Nozzles, Air

Guns, Grease and Oil (Hand)
See Lubricators, Hand

GUNS, Heated Air (Electric)
(For draining crankcase and differentials, thawing radiators, etc.)
5185A

Guns, Portable Grease
See Lubricators, Portable High Pressure

GUNS, Radiator Cleaning (High Pressure)
4347

Guns, Spring Leaf Spray
See Lubricators, Spring Leaf

Guns, Wash Spray (Auto)
See Washers, Automobile (Equipment)

Hack Saw Blades
See Blades, Saw (Hack)

Hack Saw Frames
See Frames, Hack Saw

Hack Saws, Rotary
See Saws and Cutters, Rotary

HAIR, Upholstery
(See also Moss, Upholstery; also Felt, Upholstery)

246	668	801

Hammers, Bumping
See Tools, Body and Fender Repair

Hammers, Copper
See Hammers, Soft Face

HAMMERS, Machinists'
(Advertisers in this publication only)
Peck, Stow & Wilcox Co., 217-313 Center St., Southington, Conn.—*See adv. p. 124*

HAMMERS, Portable Electric

655	5708	5833	6459

HAMMERS, Soft Face
(Including brass, copper, rubber, etc., for use on finished surfaces)
Continental Rubber Works, 1902 Liberty St., Erie Pa. "Vitalic"—*See adv. p. 64*
Peck, Stow & Wilcox Co., 217-313 Center St., Southington, Conn. "Pexto"—*See adv. p. 124*

726	1124	1274	1591	1829
1921	2410	2416	2429	2454
2622	2627	2841	2846	3010
3256	3903	4214	4525	4644
5611	6197	6208	6344	6717A

HAMMOCKS, Baby

291	692	1035	1905	2139
2420	3334	3772	3787	4308
4666				

HANDLES, Car Door

295	1095	1117	1309	1823
3992	5627	6145	6627	6783

HANDLES, Storage Battery

100	2022	6162

HANGERS and HINGES, Garage Door

110	3546	4036	5118

Hangers, License
See Holders, License

HARDWARE, Automobile and Truck Body
(For top holders—see Holders, Top; for bus hardware—see Fittings, Bus)

295	356	720	1309	1823
2407	4507	4630	5543	5627
6145	6627	6783	6808	

HARDWARE, Convertible Cabriolet
720

HASPS, Hinge
1291 3816 4695

Hat Holders
See Holders, Hat

Headlight Dimming Switches
See Switches, Headlight Dimming

Headlight Focusing Instruments
See Testers, Headlight

Headlight Reflectors, for Fords
See Reflectors, Headlight, for Fords

Headlight Shades, Dimmers or Deflectors
See Dimmers or Deflectors, Headlight; also Visors, Headlight

Headlights
See Lamps, Head

Headlights, Turning
See Lamps, Road Light (Turning)

HEADS, Cylinder
Jambor Tool & Stamping Co., 1261 30th St., Milwaukee, Wis. "Bull Dog"—See adv. p. 64
Simmons Mfg. Co., 3405-11 Perkins Ave., Cleveland, Ohio. (For Ford and Chevrolet cars) — See adv. p. 62

558	1109	1885	1906	3986A
5037	5209	5563	5779a	

HEADS, Special Cylinder (For Model A Fords)
Martin & Stoner Co., 2326 S. Michigan Ave., Chicago, Ill. "Hi-Turb" —Illustrated & described, p. 80

558	1310a	1885	5563	5779a

Hearses
See Automobiles (Hearses and Funeral Cars)

Heat Deflectors, for Fords
See Shields, Air Draft Pedal, for Fords

Heater Motors, Electric
See Motors, Electric Heater

Heaters, Air, for Melting Grease, etc.
See Guns, Heated Air (Electric)

HEATERS, Automobile, Truck and Bus
Francisco Auto Heater Co., Essex & Cleveland Aves., Columbus, Ohio. —Illustrated & described, p. 46
Noblitt-Sparks Industries, Inc., 9th Floor, Spink Bldg., 603 E. Washington St., Indianapolis, Ind. "Arvin"—Illustration, distributors & prices, p. 27
Powell Muffler Co., 316 Catherine St., Utica, N. Y.—See adv. p. 86
Schoedinger, F. O., 322-58 Mt. Vernon Ave., Columbus, Ohio. "Fosco"—See adv. p. 48
Shepard & Moore, Inc., Advance Bldg., Cleveland, Ohio "Purozone," (Hot water, also manifold heaters for Ford & Chevrolet cars)—Illustration & prices, p. 47
Tropic-Aire, Inc., 36 11th Ave., N. E., Minneapolis, Minn. (Hot water)— Illustrated, p. 50

268	1262	1547	1620	1651
1819	1866	1905	2108	2124
2384	2402	2659	2812	3010
3065	3207	3355	3493	3509
3544	3855	3857	3926	3943
4326	4557	4681	4682	4750
4782	4800	5172	5191	5458A
5720	6198	6664		

HEATERS, Crankcase Oil
(Attached to car; for crankcase oil heating tools—see Tools, Heat Blowing (Electric)
3752 4674 5745

HEATERS, Engine Cooling System
(Permanently installed in cooling system—plug in type, for keeping radiators from freezing or quickly warming them in garages; see also Heaters, Radiator and Under Hood)
Durkee-Atwood Co., 40 Wilder St., Minneapolis, Minn.—Illustrated & described, p. 63

1861	1867a	2711	6223	6642

HEATERS, Flywheel Gear
15 56 2448

HEATERS, Garage

135	361	1045A	1156	1262
1604A	1885	2090	2465	3007
3266	4303	4669	5176	5458A
5479	5795	6184	6754	6819

HEATERS, Mixture
Simmons Mfg. Co., 3405-11 Perkins Ave., Cleveland, Ohio. (For Ford and Chevrolet cars) — See adv. p. 62

2401	2749	3119	4681	5563
5761				

HEATERS, Radiator and Under Hood
(Removable, plug-in type, for keeping radiators from freezing in garages; see also Heaters, Engine Cooling System)
1262 3856 5745

Heaters, Steering Wheel
See Warmers, Hand (Electric)

HEATERS, Storage Battery (Electric)
(Apparatus for softening sealing compound on storage batteries)
35

HEATERS, Windshield (Electric)
(See also Shields, Frost)
Casco Products Corp., 1333 Railroad Ave., Bridgeport, Conn.—See adv. p. 39
Signal Mfg. Co., 587 Washington St., Lynn, Mass. "Lion Sleet-Skat"— Illustrated & described, p. 45
Tot Industries of Detroit, 2270 First National Bank Bldg., Detroit. Mich. — Illustration, description & prices, p. 46
Trico Products Corp., 807 Washington St., Buffalo, N. Y.—See adv. p. 55
Williams Products Co., H. E., 100 S. Main St., Carthage, Mo.—See adv. p. 32

679	1053	1341	1907	2158
5094	5556	6133a	6178	6190

HEATERS, Windshield (Warm Air)
5496 6197

Heel Plates
See Plates, Heel and Pedal

Heel Rests
See Rests, Heel

HINGES, Door (Auto)
297 343 1823 6783 6814

Hinges, Door (Garage)
See Hangers and Hinges, Garage Door

HINGES, Hood
295 2453a 5627 6472 6783

HINGES, Windshield
(For shields on closed cars)
295 1823 5627 6472 6783

Hitches, Trailer
See Couplers, Trailer

HOISTS
Manley Mfg. Co., 929 Connecticut Ave., Bridgeport, Conn.—Illustrated, p. 38
1134 5142 6611

Hoists, Chain
See Blocks or Hoists, Chain

Hoists, Portable
See Cranes, Portable (Hand Operated)

Hoists, Transmission
See Derricks, Transmission

HOISTS, Truck Body
(Power and hand hoists for dumping bodies)
National Steel Products Co., 1611 Crystal Ave., Kansas City, Mo.— Illustrated, p. 130

194	587	1584	1811	2080
2307	2697	2829	3251	3521a
3794	3965	4259	4741	5162
5418	5570	6363	6460	6576
6779				

Holders, Bouquet
See Vases, Bouquet

HOLDERS, Bow
See Holders, Top

HOLDERS, Card and Label

556	652	1243	1291	1583
2773	3212	4615	5163	

HOLDERS, Choke Rod, for Fords
Loock & Co., R. J., 343-45 N. Gay St., Baltimore, Md. "Lightnin"—Illustration & prices, p. 51

Holders, Crank
See Holders, Starting Crank

HOLDERS, Door (Garage)
(For garage door openers—see Openers, Garage Door)

1669	4687	5105	5118	5451
5694	5697			

HOLDERS, Flag, Pennant and Emblem

218	736	1585	1905	5176
5679	6559			

HOLDERS, Golf Bag
6174

HOLDERS, Hat
Woodworth Specialties Co., 121-25 Montgomery St., Binghamton, N. Y.—See adv. p. 36
1561 2092 6498

HOLDERS, Lathe, Planer, Shaper and Slotter
Armstrong Bros. Tool Co., 304 N. Francisco Ave., Chicago, Ill. —Illustrated, p. 119

250	1178	2684	3512A	5058
6660	6730			

HOLDERS, License
(Advertisers in this publication only)
Signal Mfg. Co., 587 Washington St., Lynn, Mass. "Lion"—See adv. p. 45

Holders, Luggage
See Carriers, Luggage

HOLDERS, Match Box
3772

HOLDERS, Oil Can
1669 3992 5654 5697

HOLDERS, Starting Crank
(Leather strap and holder to prevent starting crank swinging)
692 1048 1575 2053 2758
5612

Holders, Tire
See Carriers, Tire

Holders, Tool
See Holders, Lathe, Planer, Shaper and Slotter

HOLDERS, Top
(For holding or clamping top securely when in folded or down position; see also Straps, Leather)
356 720 1309 1823 2407

HOLDERS, Watch
3103 4507

Hones
See Tools, Cylinder Honing

Hood Anti-Rattlers
See Anti-Rattlers, Hood

Hood Fastener Silencers
See Silencers, Hood Fastener

Hood Hinges
See Hinges, Hood

Hood Lacing
See Lacing, Hood; also Leather, Rawhide Lace

HOODS, Engine
Simmons Mfg. Co., 3405-11 Perkins Ave., Cleveland, Ohio (For Ford & Chevrolet cars)—*See adv. p. 62*
209 347 1087 1233 3294
5563 5725 6814A

HOOKS, Car Lifting
3256 4241 6745

HOOKS, Door (Ventilating)
295

HOOKS, Lacing
5765

Hooks, Mud Extricating
See Chains or Hooks, Mud Extricating

Hooks, Tire Chain
See Fasteners, Tire Chain

Horn Buttons
See Buttons, Push

Horn Controls
See Controls, Horn

Horn Pedals
See Pedals, Horn and Cut-out

HORNS, Bulb (French Type)
2161 4321 5478

HORNS, Electric
Moto Meter Gauge & Equipment Corp., Toledo, Ohio "Moto Vox"—*See adv. p. 60*
Schwarze Electric Co., Dept. 3, Church St. at Payne Ave., Adrian, Mich.—*Illustration, description & prices, p. 47*
Sparks-Withington Co., Jackson, Mich. "Sparton" — *Illustrated, p. 48*

United American Bosch Corp., 3664 Main St., Springfield, Mass. "Bosch" (Also sole representatives for Robert Bosch, A. G., Stuttgart, Germany)—*See adv. p. 69*
701 1800 2347 3303 3992
4321 4677 5112 5476 5496
5641 5761 6314A 6319

HORNS, Exhaust
(Tube horns or chimes and whistles)
163 772 1541 2158 3119

HORNS, Mechanical
(Hand-operated diaphragm horns)
1800 3303 5496 5641 5733

HORNS, Pneumatic
612 772 5112 6663

HORNS, Siren
(For ambulances and police and fire department apparatus)
701 2035 5749

HORNS, Vacuum Operated
Trico Products Corp., 807 Washington St., Buffalo, N. Y. "Trico Claireon"—*Illustration & prices, p. 55*

HORSES and TRESTLES
352 3256 3774 4741 4531
5155 5536 6166A 6478 6611

HOSE, Air, Pneumatic Tool (Armored)
277 718 759 1591 1829
2412 3844 4014 6796

HOSE, Air, Pneumatic Tool (Rubber and Fabric)
Continental Rubber Works, 1902 Liberty St., Erie, Pa. "Vitalic"—*Illustrated, p. 64*
700 1123 1146 1274 1513
1591 1829 2412 2416 3844
4525 5049 5102 5617 6344
6796

HOSE, Air, Tire Inflating (Armored)
Continental Rubber Works, 1902 Liberty St., Erie, Pa. "Vitalic"—*Illustrated, p. 64*
277 718 1274 1591 1829
3844 6501 6796

HOSE, Air, Tire Inflating (Rubber and Fabric)
Gates Rubber Co., 999 S. Broadway, Denver, Col. "Gates-Vulco"—*See adv. p. 62*
Holfast Rubber Co., Lakewood Ave., Atlanta, Ga.—*See adv. p. 65*
Thermoid Rubber Co., Whitehead Rd., Trenton, N. J.—*See adv. p. 85*
277 700 759 1591 1817
1829 1862 2324 2378 2412
2416 2773 2781 3324 3844
5049 5102 5612 6129 6344
6501 6796

HOSE ASSEMBLIES, Pump
1274 1801 1829 1907 3002
3151 5178

Hose Clamps
See Clamps, Hose

Hose Connections
See Connections, Tire Pump

Hose Couplings
See Couplings, Hose

Hose, Flexible Armored
See Hose, Air, Pneumatic Tool (Armored); also Hose, Air, Tire Inflating (Armored)

Hose, Flexible Metallic
See Tubing, Flexible Metallic

HOSE, Gasoline (Metal Lined Rubber and Fabric)
Continental Rubber Works, 1902 Liberty St., Erie, Pa. "Vitalic"—*Illustrated, p. 64*
International Metal Hose Co., 10109-15 Quincy Ave., Cleveland, Ohio—*Specifications, p. 99*
700 718 1133 1274 1591
1829 2412 3045 3324 3853
4014 4525 4656 5049 5102
6344

HOSE, Metal
(See also Tubing, Flexible Metallic)
American Metal Hose Co., 67 Jewelry St., Waterbury, Conn.—*Branch offices, p. 100*
Chicago Tubing & Braiding Co., 210 N. Clinton St., Chicago, Ill. "Rex Tube"—*See adv. p. 102*
International Metal Hose Co., 10109-15 Quincy Ave., Cleveland, Ohio—*Description & specifications, p. 99*
171 277 718 1133 3045
4014 4656 6163

HOSE, Radiator (Rubber and Fabric)
Continental Rubber Works, 1902 Liberty St., Erie, Pa. "Vitalic"—*Illustrated, p. 64*
Durkee-Atwood Co., 40 Wilder St., Minneapolis, Minn.—*Illustrated & described, p. 63*
Emsco Asbestos Co., 206 S. Crawford St., Downey, Cal.—*Illustration, description & warehouse stocks, p. 84*
Gates Rubber Co., 999 S. Broadway, Denver, Col. "Gates Vulco"—*Illustrated, p. 62*
Holfast Rubber Co., Lakewood Ave., Atlanta, Ga.—*See adv. p. 65*
Simmons Mfg. Co., 3405-11 Perkins Ave., Cleveland, Ohio. (For Ford & Chevrolet cars)—*See adv. p. 62*
Thermoid Rubber Co., Whitehead Rd., Trenton, N. J. "Rexoid," "Testoid," "Thermoid"—*See adv. p. 85*
204 693 812 1003 1146
1240 1274 1591 1664 1667
1829 1889 1893 1909 2324
2378 2412 2416 2773 2781
2860 3324 3713 3844 3903
4716 5046 5049 5102 5563
5612 5617 6129 6187 6344
6484 6796

HOSE, Water (Rubber and Fabric)
Continental Rubber Works, 1902 Liberty St., Erie, Pa. "Vitalic"—*Illustrated, p. 64*
Gates Rubber Co., 999 S. Broadway, Denver, Col. "Gates Vulco"—*See adv. p. 62*
Thermoid Rubber Co., Whitehead Rd., Trenton, N. J.—*See adv. p. 85*
1146 1274 1591 1829 1862
2324 2378 2412 2416 2773
4525 5049 5102 5612 5617
6129 6344 6796

HOSE, Welding (Rubber and Fabric)
Continental Rubber Works, 1902 Liberty St., Erie, Pa. "Vitalic"—*Illustrated, p. 64*

See Page 364 for Names of Companies Represented by Above Numbers

Gates Rubber Co., 999 S. Broadway, Denver, Col. "Gates Vulco"—*See adv. p. 62*

Linde Air Products Co., 30 E. 42nd St., New York, N. Y.—*Illustration & branch offices, p. 125*

Thermoid Rubber Co., Whitehead Rd., Trenton, N. J.—*See adv. p. 85*

1146	1274	1591	1817	1829
1862	2324	2412	2416	2781
5049	5102	5608	6129	6344

Hose, Wire Wound
See Hose, Air, Pneumatic Tool (Armored); also Hose, Air, Tire Inflating (Armored)

HOUSINGS, Starting Motor
Es-M-Co Auto Products Corp., 31 34th St., Brooklyn, N. Y.—*Illustration & warehouses, p. 70*

Jambor Tool & Stamping Co., 1261 30th St., Milwaukee, Wis. "Bull Dog"—*See adv. p. 64*

Hub Caps
See Caps, Hub

Hub Drums
See Winches and Blocks, Car Extracting

Hub Odometers
See Meters or Odometers, Distance Recording

HUBS, Demountable, for Fords
6689

HUBS, Wheel
(Advertisers in this publication only)
Simmons Mfg. Co., 3405-11 Perkins Ave., Cleveland, Ohio (For Chevrolet cars)—*See adv. p. 62*

U. S. Axle Co., Water St.. Pottstown, Pa.—*Warehouses, p. 59*

HUBS, Wheel, for Fords
Simmons Mfg. Co., 3405-11 Perkins Ave., Cleveland, Ohio—*See adv. p. 62*

4515	5563	5828

HYDROMETERS
(For testing battery electrolyte, gasoline, etc.)

559	1099	1137	1842	2132
2623	3018	3120	3202	4708
5217	5482	5687	5733	6125
6314A				

Ignition Point Refinishing Tools
See Tools, Ignition Point Refinishing

Ignition Systems, Battery
See Systems, Ignition (Complete)

Ignitor Gears
See Gears, Generator and Ignitor

IMPELLERS, Water Pump
Aluminum Industries, Inc., 2416 Beekman St., Cincinnati, Ohio—"Permite"—*See adv. p. 10*

121	2073	2439	3775

INDICATORS, Battery Condition
(Device to show water level, specific gravity charge, etc.)

2305	4601	5822	6737

INDICATORS, Fender
2053

INFLATORS, Tire (Automatic)
(Permanently attached to each wheel)
6811

INSERTS, Spring Leaf
(To eliminate interleaf friction need for oiling between leaf springs and to avoid squeaks)
6596

Initials, Ornamental
See Monograms, Initials and Emblems, Ornamental

INSTRUMENTS, Brake Testing
(See also Machines, Brake Testing; also Tools, Brake Testing)
Muther Mfg. Co., 44 Binford St., Boston, Mass. "Stopmeter"—*Illustration, description & prices, p. 115*

164	270	1311	2146	4034
4353	5049			

INSTRUMENTS, Electrical Circuit Testing
Hobart Brothers, Box C-51, Canal Locks Square, Troy, Ohio. "HB" —*See adv. p. 108*

Maxwell Automotive Engineering Co., 44 Binford St., Boston, Mass. "M-A-E-C-O" — *Illustration, description & prices, p. 115*

100	228	559	576A	1226
1860	2343A	2384	2766	2818
3114	3121	3256	3768	3798
3825	3890	4007	4304	4317
4601	5511	6193	6616	6664
6745				

INSTRUMENTS, Engine Testing

160	200	228	336	349
588	2120	2627	3256	4007
5787A	6616			

Instruments, Headlight Testing
See Testers, Headlight

Instruments, Ignition Contact Point Synchronizing
See Synchronizers, Ignition Contact Point

Instruments, Insulation Testing
636

INSTRUMENTS, Storage Battery Testing
(See also Instruments, Electric Circuit Testing; also Hydrometers)
General Electric Co., Merchandise Dept., Bridgeport, Conn. "Tungar"—*Illustration & prices, p. 109*

98	100	576A	1860	2103
2343	2766	3121	3202	3890
4352	4708	5511	6107	6586A
6616	6667	6745		

Instruments, Truck Load Indicating
See Meters, Truck Load Indicating

Insulation Undercutting Machines, Commutator
See Machines, Commutator Turning and Insulation Undercutting

Insulators, Rubber Shock
See Shackles, Spring (Rubber Cushioned)

INTENSIFIERS, Spark
(Auxiliary spark gaps, intensifiers or indicators; see also Converters, Ignition)

131	6314A

Irons, Body
See Hardware, Automobile and Truck Body

IRONS, Slat
(For Bow Sockets—see Sockets, Bow)

720	2407

IRONS, Soldering (Acetylene)
3507

IRONS, Soldering (Electric)

587	1510	1653	1923	2343A
2409	3014	6353	6504	

Irons, Tire
See Tools, Tire

Irons, Top
See Hardware, Automobile and Truck Body; also Hardware, Convertible Cabriolet

JACKS, Car Lifting
(For wheeled lifting jacks—see Jacks On Wheels; see also Jacks, Hydraulic)
Auto Specialties Mfg. Co., 557 Graves St., St. Joseph, Mich. "Drednaut"—*Illustrated, p. 50*

Bellevue Mfg. Co., Ashford Ave., Bellevue, Ohio—*See adv. p. 52*

35	41	71	356	595
656	765	1259	1643	1876
3149	3774	3905	3913	3979
4258	4757	5103	5424	5529
6121	6122	6497	6560	6611
6745				

JACKS, Garage Repair

71	656	3774	3979	4258

JACKS, Hydraulic
Silver King Hydraulic Jack Co., 5604 Cedar Ave., Cleveland, Ohio—*Illustration, description, specifications & prices, p. 49*

Simmons Mfg. Co., 3405-11 Perkins Ave., Cleveland, Ohio—*See adv. p. 62*

71	656	1905	2379	2673
2700	3774	3905	4258	4531
4757	5165	5560	5563	6560

JACKS, Hydraulic (On Wheels)

1876	3417	3774	3794	4258
6478				

JACKS, Hydraulic (Permanently Attached to Car)
5562

JACKS, On Wheels
(See also Jacks, Car Lifting; also Jacks, Tire Saving)
Manley Mfg. Co., 929 Connecticut Ave., Bridgeport, Conn.—*Illustrated, p. 38*

71	2786	3240	3774	3794
4241	4258	4757	6560	6611
6811	6825			

JACKS On WHEELS (Electric)
3979

Jacks, Pedal Depressing
See Depressors, Brake Pedal

JACKS, Pneumatic
5049

JACKS, Pulling
6559A

JACKS, Spring
(For use in removing spring shackle bolts)
Thompson Products, Inc., 2196 Clarkwood Rd., Cleveland, Ohio—*See adv. p. 89*

2116	3256	6717A

JACKS, Tire Saving
(For holding car off the floor when not in use)

71	656	1876	3149	4551
4757	6811			

Jacks, Truck Wheel Removing
See Cranes, Drags and Jacks, Truck Wheel Removing

See Page 400 for Names of Companies Represented by Above Numbers

JARS, Battery Cell (Rubber)
161 1829 2412 2798 6344

Jaws, Vise
See Grips or Jaws, Vise.

JEWELS, Lamp
506 2809 3002 3293 4677

JIGS, Connecting Rod Aligning
Shoemaker Automotive Equipment Co., Henney Bldg., Freeport, Ill.—Illustrated, p. 106

100	336	663	1023	1806
2113	3140	3256	3774	3831
5039	5218	5441	5536	5545
5578	5580	5753	5775	6745

JIGS, Crankcase Aligning, for Fords
(For repairing bent or buckled crank-cases)

6745

JIGS, Main Bearing and Connecting Rod Babbitting
(See also Machines, Babbitting (Main Bearing and Connecting Rod))
Shoemaker Automotive Equipment Co., Henney Bldg., Freeport, Ill.—Illustrated, p. 106

2707 5218 5441 5545 5775
6551

Jigs, Piston Aligning
See Jigs, Connecting Rod Aligning

JOBBERS OF RADIO PARTS
(Advertisers in this publication only)
Continental Tire Corp., Dept. C, 1508-15 Michigan Ave., Chicago, Ill.—See adv. p. 82

JOBBERS and SUPPLY DEALERS
(Advertisers in this publication only)
Continental Tire Corp., Dept. C, 1508-15 Michigan Ave., Chicago, Ill.—See adv. p. 82

JOINTS, Ball
(For spark and throttle connections)
Hygrade Products Co., 333 W. 52nd St., New York, N. Y.—See adv. p. 86

1128 1842 2619 2702 2858
3202 5219

JOINTS, Speedometer Swivel
1053 5759 5832

JOINTS, Universal
(For complete drive shaft assemblies—see Shafts, Propeller)
Almetal Universal Joint Co., 1553 E. 55th St., Cleveland, Ohio—Illustration, specifications & prices, p. 81
Jambor Tool & Stamping Co., 1261 30th St., Milwaukee, Wis. "Bull Dog"—See adv. p. 64
Simmons Mfg. Co., 3405-11 Perkins Ave., Cleveland, Ohio — See adv. p. 62

116 1906 2033 3104 3838
4288 4702 5563 5576 5653
5783

JUMPERS, Battery
559 665 3771 5425

Key Cutting Tools
See Tools, Key Cutting

KEYS, Acetylene Gas Tank
1823 6559

KEYS, Machine
Dorman Star Washer Co., 219 E. Eighth St., Cincinnati, Ohio—Illustrated & described, p. 102
1626 3453 3987 4254 5093
5696

Keys, Split
See Pins, Cotter

KEYS, Switch, for Fords
Loock & Co., R. J., 343-45 N. Gay St., Baltimore, Md. "Lightnin"—Illustrated, p. 51
35 339 3537 4735 5687

KEYS, Switch and Starting
3202 4735 5687

Keys, Valve Spring
See Retainers, Valve Spring

KEYSEATERS, Portable
809

Kick Plates
See Plates, Kick or Scuff

KITS, Cable
Hygrade Products Co., 333 W. 52nd St., New York, N. Y.—Illustrated, p. 86

Kits, First Aid
See Cases, Medical Emergency

KITS, Tire and Tube Repair
(Advertisers in this publication only)
(See also Cement, Tire Repair; also Patches, Tube Repair; also Plugs, Tire Repair)
Bell Co., 407-11 N. Lincoln St., Chicago, Ill.—See adv. p. 93

KITS, Tool (Ignition)
Hygrade Products Co., 333 W. 52nd St., New York, N. Y.—See adv. p. 86
4317

KNIVES, Rubber
2850 6214

KNIVES, Tire Repair
2850

Knobs, Control Lever
See Balls, Gear Shift Lever

KNOCKERS, Wheel
National Machine & Tool Co., 801 S. Water St., Jackson, Mich.—See adv. p. 120
3201 3831

Knuckle Boots or Cases
See Boots, Steering Knuckle and Joint

Label Holders
See Holders, Card and Label

LABELS
(Advertisers in this publication only)
Unique Printed Products Co., 2224 N. 13th St., Terre Haute, Ind.—See adv. p. 127

LACERS, Belt
1195 1570

LACING, Hood (Fabric)
231 1829 2378 3485 3891A
5182 5214 5598 5612 5637

Lacing, Hood (Leather)
See Leather, Rawhide Lace

LACING, Hood (Rubber)
Gates Rubber Co., 999 S. Broadway, Denver, Col. "Gates Vulco"—See adv. p. 62
1829 2324 2723

Lacing Hooks
See Hooks, Lacing

Lacing Machines, Belt
See Lacers, Belt

LACQUER
(Nitro-cellulose and pyroxylin materials for spray gun application)
Sherwin-Williams Co., Dept 733, 101 Prospect Ave., N. W., Cleveland, Ohio "Opex"—See adv. p. 21

33	38	177	244	520
586	642	737	1022	1186
1524	1588	1660	1850	2059
2142	2389	2689	2751	3046
3231	3555	4313	4319	4508
4558	4756	5136	5174	5541
5704	5727	6453	6822B	

Lacquer Polishing Discs
See Polishers, Disc, for Lacquer

Lacquer Sprayers
See Sprayers, Paint, Varnish and Lacquer

Lacquer Spraying Booths
See Booths, Spraying (Paint and Varnish)

Lamp Parts and Fittings
See following heads:
Adapters, Electric Lamp
Brackets, Lamp (Side and Tail)
Burners, Acetylene Lamp
Caps, Dash Lamp
Cases, Lamp Bulb
Connectors, Lamp (Electric)
Covers, Lamp
Dimmers or Deflectors, Headlight
Jewels, Lamp
Lamps or Bulbs, Miniature Incandescent
Lenses, Lamp (Flat and Ground)
Rims, Headlamp Door
Sockets, Electric Lamp
Washers, Felt

Lamp Posts
See Posts, Lamp (Filling Station)

LAMPS, Cowl, Fender, Tail, Parking, Running Board and Clearance
K-D Lamp Co., 108-18 W. Third St., Cincinnati, Ohio—Illustrated, p. 49
Pines Winterfront Co., 1125 N. Cicero Ave., Chicago, Ill.—See adv. p. 54
Schwarze Electric Co., Grace, Church & Payne Sts., Adrian, Mich.—See adv. p. 47
Simmons Mfg. Co., 3405-11 Perkins Ave., Cleveland, Ohio. (For Ford and Chevrolet cars) — See adv. p. 62

57	131	225	750	1150
1233	1257	1309	1553	1599
1624	1866	2475	3002	3025
3200	3278	3759	3772	3809
4227	4352A	4712	4735	5176
5179	5402	5476	5496	5563
5604	6326	6810		

LAMPS, Dash or Gage
Pines Winterfront Co., 1125 N. Cicero Ave., Chicago, Ill.—See adv. p. 54
Simmons Mfg. Co., 3405-11 Perkins Ave., Cleveland, Ohio. (For Ford and Chevrolet Cars) — See adv. p. 62

1135	1553	1599	1629	2461
2475	2723	3278	3349	3856
3992	4712	4735	5179	5563
5604	6810			

LAMPS, Dome

Pines Winterfront Co., 1125 N. Cicero Ave., Chicago, Ill.—*See adv. p. 54*

1233	1257	1309	1553	2475
3278	4352A	4507	4712	4735
5179	5604	6326	6810	

LAMPS, Dome (Bus)

1309   1866   4352A

LAMPS, Flood, for Display

128   614   700   2646   5402

Lamps, Gage

See Lamps, Dash or Gage

LAMPS, Garage Floor

2448   3311   3774   6683   6825

Lamps, Hand

See Lamps, Trouble

LAMPS, Head (Acetylene)

K-D Lamp Co., 108-18 W. Third St., Cincinnati, Ohio—*Illustrated, p. 49*

750   1150   1599   1624   3200
6810

LAMPS, Head (Electric)

K-D Lamp Co., 108-18 W. Third St., Cincinnati, Ohio—*Illustrated, p. 49*
Simmons Mfg. Co., 3405-11 Perkins Ave., Cleveland, Ohio. (For Ford & Chevrolet cars)—*See adv. p. 62*

750	1150	1599	1624	1866
2475	3025	3200	3278	4321
5402	5563	5692	6326	6674
6810				

LAMPS, Head (Electric Bus)

57   1866   5179

Lamps, Incandescent

See Lamps or Bulbs, Miniature Incandescent

Lamps, Instrument Board

See Lamps, Dash or Gage

Lamps, Parking

See Lamps, Cowl, Fender, Tail, Parking, Running Board and Clearance

Lamps, Reel

See Lamps, Trouble; also Lamps, Spot

LAMPS, Road (Courtesy)

K-D Lamp Co., 108-18 W. Third St., Cincinnati, Ohio—*See adv. p. 49*

131	1150	1553	1624	2162
3278	3759	4037	4712	5405
5496	6196			

LAMPS, Road Light (Turning)

(Interconnected with steering gear so as to turn headlights or roadlights with front wheels and illuminate the road around turn ahead of car)

4639

Lamps, Running Board

See Lamps, Cowl, Tail, Parking, Running Board and Clearance

LAMPS, Running Board (Searchlights)

K-D Lamp Co., 108-18 W. Third St., Cincinnati, Ohio—*See adv. p. 49*

57   1034   3200   5402   6326
6810

Lamps, Side and Tail (Electric)

See Lamps, Cowl, Fender, Tail, Parking, Running Board and Clearance

LAMPS, Side and Tail (Electric Bus)

1866

LAMPS, Spot

K-D Lamp Co., 108-18 W. Third St., Cincinnati, Ohio—*See adv. p. 49*
Pines Winterfront Co., 1125 N. Cicero Ave., Chicago, Ill.—*See adv. p. 54*

57	225	229	750	1150
1233	1553	1624	1819	2033
2162	2475	3200	3278	3541
3759	3772	4037	4321	4712
4735	5137	5179	5761	6145
6314a	6326	6353	6810	

Lamps, Stop

See Signals, Direction Indicating or Traffic

LAMPS, Tail (Acetylene)

(For electric tail lamps—see Lamps, Fender, Cowl, Tail, Parking, Running Board and Clearance)

1599

LAMPS, Tell Tale

(Special lamp and coil for dash attachment to indicate when rear signal or tail lamp fails to light)

5822

LAMPS, Trouble (Electric)

(Lamp and flexible cord for work around car)

General Electric Co., Merchandise Dept., Bridgeport, Conn. "G-E" —*Illustration & prices, p. 109*
Pines Winterfront Co., 1125 N. Cicero Ave., Chicago, Ill. "Griptite"—*Illustrated & described, p. 54*

224	229	614	1053	1629
1804	1817	2024	2033	2334
2343	2383	2723	3311	3507
3771	3856	3948	3983	4610
4712	4735	5179	5604	6810

LAMPS, Trouble (Magnetic)

Hackett Products Co., 407 Pine St., Providence, R. I.—*See adv. p. 40*

2604   3278   4230   5179

Lamps, Tungsten

See Lamps or Bulbs, Miniature Incandescent

LAMPS or BULBS, Miniature Incandescent

1843   3819   4223   4237   6216
6665

Lanterns, Hand

See Flashlights

Lapping Compounds, Valve

See Compounds, Valve Grinding

Latches, Hood

See Fasteners, Hood

Lathe Attachments

See Centers, Lathe and Grinder; Chucks, Lathe; Dogs, Lathe; Holders, Lathe, Planer, Shaper and Slotter; Attachments, Lathe

Lathe Tools

See Tools, Lathe, Planer, Shaper and Slotter

LATHES, Bench or Precision

South Bend Lathe Works, 373 E. Madison St., South Bend, Ind.— *Illustration, description & prices, p. 124*

100   364   670   1875   2410
4758   5502   5629   6461

LATHES, Brake Drum (Automatic)

Bean Mfg. Co., John, 18 Hosmer St., Lansing, Mich.—*Illustrated, p. 31*
Chicago Rivet & Machine Co., 1830 S. 54th Ave. (Cicero P. O.), Chicago, Ill.—*See adv. p. 92*

South Bend Lathe Works, 373 E. Madison St., South Bend, Ind.— *Illustration, description & prices, p. 124*

56	577	1126	2448	3779
4775	5049	5212	5629	5763
6551				

Lathes, Commutator

See Machines, Commutator Turning and Insulation Undercutting

LATHES, Crankshaft

3457   3532

LATHES, Engine

South Bend Lathe Works, 373 E. Madison St., South Bend, Ind.— *See adv. p. 124*

545	701a	1046	1145	2708
3457	3532	4758	5033	5157
5490	5502	5629	5662	

LATHES, Extension and Gap

South Bend Lathe Works, 373 E. Madison St., South Bend, Ind.— *See adv. p. 124*

3457   5033   5502   5629

LATHES, Flywheel

623a

Lathes, Precision

See Lathes, Bench or Precision

Lathes, Valve

See Refacers, Valve

LAUNDRIES, Auto

(Including complete equipment, such as car washers, vacuum cleaners, hot water heaters, air compressors, conveyors, etc.; see also Washers, Automobile (Systems); also Cleaners and Polishers, Overhead Electric (Automobile)

Bean Mfg. Co., John, 18 Hosmer St., Lansing, Mich.—*See adv. p. 31*

577   2147

Lead Burners

See Burners, Lead

LEATHER, Artificial or Imitation

259	1041	1045	1304	1661
1829	2036	3262	3411	3422
4618	5433	5699	6128	6673

Leather Cement

See Cement, Leather

Leather Dressing

See Dressing, Leather

LEATHER, Friction

(For lining brakes and clutches)

1124   2441   2808   3408   5113
5612   6734

LEATHER, Natural

694   1183   1809   2349   2691
3447   5031   5044a   5084   5180

Leather Packing

See Packing, Leather

LEATHER, Rawhide Lace

(For preventing motor hoods from rattling; for fabric lacing—see Lacing, Hood (Fabric); for rubber lacing— see Lacing, Hood (Rubber)

1124   2441   2808   5612   6734

LEATHER, Reconstructed

182A

Leather, Upholstery

See Leather, Natural; also Leather, Artificial or Imitation

Leathers, Pump

See Gaskets, Leather

LEGS, Bench

213	352	685	1668	3294
3409	3564	3782B	4284	5690
6621				

LENSES, Lamp (Composition)
2064

LENSES, Lamp (Flat and Ground)
Simmons Mfg. Co., 3405-11 Perkins Ave., Cleveland, Ohio (For Ford & Chevrolet cars)—*See adv. p. 62*

617	1297	1536	1624	2475
2787	2809	3111	3115	3137A
3421	3463	3752a	3956	4748
5563	5601	5687	6337	

Lever Balls
See Balls, Gear Shift Lever

Lever Extensions
See Extensions, Gear Shift Lever; also Extensions, Brake Lever, for Fords

License Holders
See Holders, License

License Plate Frames and Fittings
See Fasteners, License Tag; Frames, License Plate; Screws, License Plate

LIFTERS, Special Valve, for Fords
5212

Lifters, Storage Battery
See Carriers, Storage Battery

LIFTS, Auto (Electric)

132	701	2027	2786	3793
3794	4530			

LIFTS, Auto (Hydraulic)
Curtis Pneumatic Machinery Co., 1927 Kienlen Ave., St. Louis, Mo. *Illustrated & described, p. 111*
Manley Mfg. Co., 929 Connecticut Ave., Bridgeport, Conn. — *Illustrated, p. 38*

1169	1345	2393	2785	2786
3149	3406	3774	3794	3842
4530	4538	5185a	5408	6324
6604	6611			

LIFTS, Auto (Pneumatic)
Bean Mfg. Co., John, 18 Hosmer St., Lansing, Mich.—*Illustrated, p. 31*
Curtis Pneumatic Machinery Co., 1927 Kienlen Ave., St. Louis, Mo. *Illustrated & described, p. 111*

LIFTS, Auto (Self Operated)
701

LIGHTERS, Electric Cigar
(For use on car from regular lighting battery)
Casco Products Corp., 1333 Railroad Ave., Bridgeport, Conn. (Also combination ash receiver and cigar lighter) — *Illustration, description & prices, p. 39*
Cuno Engineering Corp., 80 S. Vine St., Meriden, Conn. (Also combination ash receiver and cigar lighter) — *Illustration, description & prices, p. 37*
Hackett Products Co., 407 Pine St., Providence, R. I. "Shur-Lite"— *See adv. p. 40*

1053	1341	1666	1905	2033
2604	3018	3065	3119	3464
3856	3992	4321	4507	4764
5112	5581	5626	5761	5822

Lighting Systems, Auto
See Systems, Electric Lighting

LIGHTS, Curtain
(For glass curtain lights—see Windows, Glass Curtain)

291	644	1905	2773	4271

Lights, Flash
See Flashlights

Lights, Flood, for Display
See Lamps, Flood, for Display

LIGHTS, Motor Meter
3445

Lights, Reel
See Lamps, Trouble; also Lamps, Spot

Lights, Stop
See Signals, Direction Indicating or Traffic

Liners, Leather
See Shims and Liners, Leather

LINING, Body or Frame
(For use between body sill and steel frame to prevent squeaking)
Felt Products Mfg. Co., 1510 Carroll Ave., Chicago, Ill. "Fel-Pro." *See adv. p. 75*

47	251	1124	1250	1829
2046	2047	2378	2412	3422
3903	5214	5598	5612	5637
6651				

LINING, Brake (Liquid)
(For resurfacing worn brake lining)
3516

LINING, Brake (Molded)
Biglow & Co., L. C., 250 W. 54th St., New York, N. Y. (New York representatives for Multibestos Co.) —*See adv. p. 129*
Emsco Asbestos Co., 206 S. Crawford St., Downey, Calif. — *Illustration, description & warehouse stocks, p. 84*
Ferodo and Asbestos, Inc., Extension of Codwise Ave., New Brunswick, N. J.—*Described p. 82*
Johns-Manville, 292 Madison Ave., New York, N. Y.—*Illustration, description & branch offices, p. 83*
Multibestos Co., 235 Harvey St., Cambridge B, Mass.—*Prices, p. 255*
Raybestos Div. of Raybestos-Manhattan, Inc., Bridgeport, Conn.—*Illustrated, p. 253*
Thermoid Rubber Co., Whitehead Rd., Trenton, N. J.—*Illustrated, p. 85*
United States Asbestos Div. of Raybestos-Manhattan, Inc., Manheim, Pa. "Grey-Rock" — *Illustrated & described, p. 81*
United States Rubber Co. (Fibre Products Dept.), 1790 Broadway, New York, N. Y. "U. S. Royal LB" —*Described, p. 84*

95	115	137	265	265a
267	281	641	775	808
1672	1889	2054	2325	3127
3234	3410	4018	4616	5049
5182	5214	5445	5544	6129
6325	6344	6795		

LINING, Brake (Woven)
(For lining brakes or clutches—See also Lining, Brake (Molded); also Leather, Friction)
Biglow & Co., L. C., 250 W. 54th St., New York, N. Y. (New York representatives for Multibestos Co.) —*See adv. p. 129*
Emsco Asbestos Co., 206 S. Crawford St., Downey, Calif. — *Illustration & warehouse stocks, p. 84*

Ferodo and Asbestos, Inc., Extension of Codwise Ave., New Brunswick, N. J.—*Described, p. 82*
Johns-Manville, 292 Madison Ave., New York, N. Y.—*Illustration, description & branch offices, p. 83*
Multibestos Co., 235 Harvey St., Cambridge B, Mass.—*Prices, p. 255*
Raybestos Div. of Raybestos-Manhattan, Inc., Railroad Ave., Bridgeport, Conn. "Hycoe," "Vel-Coe"— —*Illustrated & described, p. 253*
Thermoid Rubber Co., Whitehead Rd., Trenton, N. J. "Rexold," "Thermoid"—*Illustrated, p. 85*
United States Asbestos Div. of Raybestos-Manhattan, Inc., Manheim, Pa. "Motobestos," "Durabestos," "Grey-Rock," "U. S. Asbestos," "Grey-Rock Eagle"—*Illustrated & described, p. 81*

95	101	115	130	146
204	265	265a	267	281
641	768	808	1670	1672
1889	2054	2325	2338	2378
3104	3119	3127	3234	3410
3797	3891a	4018	4218	4616
5046	5049	5182	5214	5425
5445	5457	5563	5598	5612
5633	5637	6129	6304	6325
6628	6795	6796		

Lining, Frame
See Lining, Body or Frame

LINING, Hood (Insulating)
(See also Covers, Louvre)

3234	4786

LININGS, Head

291	1516	4618	6801

LINKS, Spring Shackle

720	3268	6307

LINKS, Steering

1141	6141

LINKS, Tire Chain Repair
American Auto Products Co., 219 Ascot Place, N.E., Washington, D. C. "Klinch-Linx" — *Illustration & prices, p. 93*
Cleveland Chain & Mfg. Co., Penna. R. R. & Henry Rd., Cleveland, Ohio —*See adv. p. 39*
Flower City Specialty Co., 250 Mill St., Rochester, N. Y. "Monkey Links"—*Illustration, description & prices, p. 17*
Lion Chain Co., 3124 W. 51st St., Chicago, Ill. "Cub"—*See adv. p. 37*
Loock & Co., R. J., 343-45 N. Gay St., Baltimore, Md. "Lightnin"—*Illustration & prices, p. 51*
McKay Co., Union Trust Bldg., Pittsburgh, Pa.—*Illustrated, p. 33*
United States Chain & Forging Co. *See* McKay Co.

134	724	1077	1174	2092
3150	3512	3537	5046	5051
5420	5556	6162	6586	

LINOLEUM
(For covering floors and running boards)

251	1075	4607	5595

Linoleum Cement
See Cement, Linoleum

Load Governors or Indicators
See Meters, Truck Load Indicating

Load Plates
See Plates, Load Data

See Page 364 for Names of Companies Represented by Above Numbers

Lock Nuts
See Nuts, Lock
Lock Switches
See Locks, Ignition
Lock Washers
See Washers, Lock
LOCKERS, Metal Clothes
Lyon Metal Products, Inc., 2931 Montgomery St., Aurora, Ill.—Illustrated, p. 106

114	622	1247	3113	3571
3782B	3840	4350	4654	5112A
6124				

LOCKS, Cabinet and Pad

523	727	1117	1291	1805
2122	2346	2845	3816	3899
5072	5593	6808		

Locks, Cap
See Locks, Radiator Cap and Thermometer
Locks, Chain
See Locks, Spare Tire and Wheel
LOCKS, Door (Automobile)

1809	1805	1823	3014	3287
3750	5627	6783	6808	

LOCKS, Gasoline Tank Cap
334A
LOCKS, Ignition

727	1201	1257	1291	1548a
1857	3926			

Locks, Nut
See Nuts, Lock
LOCKS, Radiator Cap and Thermometer
96   131   3464
LOCKS, Robe
508
LOCKS, Spare Tire and Wheel
(Including locks, locking chains, cables, etc.)

142	523	724	1077	1174
1237	1291	1537	1640	1669
1805	1905	2120	2122	2312
2845	3468	3816	3855	3899
4503	5072	5105	5593	5692
6100	6808			

LOCKS, Spare Tire and Wheel, for Fords

1291	1669	2120	2158	2845
3509	5072	5692	5697	5745

LOCKS, Steering (Towing)
3794   4258
LOCKS, Steering Wheel
1603   3794   4670   5593
Locks, Switch
See Switches, Lock
Locks, Thermometer
See Locks, Radiator Cap and Thermometer
Locks, Tire
See Locks, Spare Tire and Wheel
LOCKS, Tool Box

1291	1805	2122	5072	5593
6808				

LOCKS, Transmission
1291   1537   2845   6808
Locks, Valve Spring
See Retainers, Valve Spring
Locks, Wheel
See Locks, Spare Tire and Wheel

LOGS, Engine
1311
Loom Tubing
See Tubing, Spaghetti and Loom
LOOPS, Brass Snap and Strap
(See also Fittings & Fixtures, Top)
Auto-Vehicle Parts Co., 1040 Saratoga St., Newport, Ky. "Au-Ve-Co"—Illustration & sizes, pp. 34 & 35

295	360	1309	1823	4271
6627	6783			

Lubricants
See Oils, Lubricating
Lubricants for Combustion Chamber Oilers
See Oils, Lubricating (For Combustion Chamber Oilers)
LUBRICANTS, Spring
(Advertisers in this publication only)
Bell Co., 407-11 N. Lincoln St., Chicago, Ill.—Illustrated, p. 93
Emerol Mfg. Co., 242 W. 69th St., New York, N. Y. "Marvel Mystery"—Illustration, description & prices, p. 4
Lubricator Systems, for Fords
See Lubricators and Oil Pumps, for Fords
Lubricators, Chassis
See Fittings, Lubricating
LUBRICATORS, Combustion Chamber
Emerol Mfg. Co., 242 W. 69th St., New York, N. Y. "Marvel Mystery"—Illustration, description & prices, p. 4
Opco Co., 1894 Niagara St., Buffalo, N. Y.—Illustration, description & prices, p. 52

35	529	1316	1539	1888
2617	3110	3209	3218	4007
4301	4543	5064	5720	6161
6193	6580			

LUBRICATORS, Hand
(Including type commonly known as grease and oil guns; also high pressure type; see also Lubricators, Portable, High Pressure; for car lubricators—see Lubricators or Oil Pumps, Hand; also Fittings, Lubricating)
Gray Co., 120 S. Tenth St., Minneapolis, Minn. "Graco"—Illustrated, p. 18
Rogers Products Co., 198 Pacific Ave., Jersey City, N. J. "Everready"—Illustrated, p. 110

39	44	58	86	131
696	723	1141	1632	1842
1905	2445	2656	2760	3151
3846	3950	4327	5165	5178
5753	6217	6679		

LUBRICATORS, Portable, High Pressure (Compressed Air)
(See also Lubricators, Hand)
Gray Co., 120 S. Tenth St., Minneapolis, Minn. "Graco"—Illustrated, p. 18
Kellogg Mfg. Co., 65 Humboldt St., Rochester, N. Y.—Illustration, description & prices, p. 2
Rogers Products Co., 198 Pacific Ave., Jersey City, N. J. "Everready"—Illustrated, p. 110

39	86	254A	704A	1141
2445	3241	3298	3553	3554
3774	4603	5100	5112a	5165
6161	6477			

LUBRICATORS, Portable, High Pressure (Electric)
Rogers Products Co., 198 Pacific Ave., Jersey City, N. J. "Everready"—Illustrated, p. 110

39	86	254a	1141	5165
6324				

LUBRICATORS, Portable, High Pressure (Hand Operated)
Rogers Products Co., 198 Pacific Ave., Jersey City, N. J. "Everready"—Illustrated, p. 110

86	254A	295	1141	2760
3241	3846	3942	5100	5165
5510	6604	6611		

LUBRICATORS, Spring Leaf
(For service station use; for automobile spring leaf lubricators—see Covers, Spring Leaf Lubricating; also Oilers, Spring)
Champion Pneumatic Machinery Co., 8170 S. Chicago Ave., Chicago, Ill.—See adv. p. 112
Gray Co., 120 S. Tenth St., Minneapolis, Minn. "Graco"—Illustrated, p. 18
Hansen Mfg. Co., 1786 E. 27th St., Cleveland, Ohio — Illustration, description & prices, p. 112
Imperial Brass Mfg. Co., 1225 W. Harrison St., Chicago, Ill.—See adv. p. 126
Kellogg Mfg. Co., 65 Humboldt St., Rochester, N. Y. — Illustration & prices, p. 2
Rogers Products Co., 198 Pacific Ave., Jersey City, N. J. "Everready"—Illustrated, p. 110

39	1086	1141	2394	2445
2617	2641	2826	3241	4603
5165	5173	5185a	5524	6161
6324				

LUBRICATORS, Stationary, High Pressure (Compressed Air)
254A   1141   2445   5112A
LUBRICATORS or OIL PUMPS, Hand
(Auxiliary hand oil pumps)
Imperial Brass Mfg. Co., 1225 W. Harrison St., Chicago, Ill. — See adv. p. 126
LUBRICATORS or OIL PUMPS, for Fords
(Supplementary oiling devices)

224	2795	3119	5105	5166
5715				

Luggage Carrier Covers
See Covers, Luggage Carrier
Luggage Carriers
See Carriers, Luggage; also Racks, Trunk
Luggage Nets
See Nets, Luggage
LUGS, Wheel
Bear Mfg. Co., 21st St. & Fifth Ave., Rock Island, Ill.—See adv. p. 123
Lumber Rollers
See Rollers, Lumber
Machinery Guards
See Guards, Safety, for Machines
MACHINES, Addressing
(Advertisers in this publication only)
Elliott Addressing Machine Co., Cambridge, Mass.—Illustrated, p. 74

MACHINES, Babbitting (Main Bearing and Connecting Rod)

(See also Jigs, Main Bearing and Connecting Rod Babbitting)

Shoemaker Automotive Equipment Co., Henny Bldg., Freeport, Ill.—*See adv. p. 106*

4547

MACHINES, Balancing (Crankshaft)

4351   6477a   6745

MACHINES, Balancing (Wheel)

Bear Mfg. Co., 21st St. & Fifth Ave., Rock Island, Ill.—*See adv. p. 123*

2786

Machines, Bearing Reaming

See Reamers, Main Bearing and Connecting Rod

MACHINES, Boring (Main Bearing and Connecting Rod)

Shoemaker Automotive Equipment Co., Henny Bldg., Freeport, Ill.— *Illustrated, p. 106*

2113	2707	2821	3256	4332
5218	5545	5650	5775	6104

MACHINES, Brake Cleaning (Portable Hydraulic)

3939   4009   6153

Machines, Brake Drum Grinding

See Machines, Grinding Brake Drum

Machines, Brake Lining Grinding

See Machines, Grinding (Brake Lining)

MACHINES, Brake Relining

(For performing all operations in relining external and internal brakes)

Bean Mfg. Co., John, 18 Hosmer St., Lansing, Mich.—*Illustrated, p. 31*

Biglow & Co., L. C., 250 W. 54th St., New York, N. Y. (New York representatives for Multibestos Co.) —*See adv. p. 129*

Chicago Rivet & Machine Co., 1830 S. 54th Ave. (Cicero P. O.), Chicago, Ill.—*See adv. p. 92*

Manufacturer's Belt Hook Co., 1315-21 W. Congress St., Chicago, Ill. "L-X"—*Illustration & prices, p. 94*

Multibestos Co., 235 Harvey St., Cambridge B, Mass.—*See adv. p. 255*

Thermoid Rubber Co., Whitehead Rd., Trenton, N. J.—*See adv. p. 85*

101	115	577	641	718
1082	1126	1518	1669	2338
2437	3256	3417	3518	3774
3780	3891a	4018	4655	5046
5049	5132	5212	5214	5721a
5363	6129	6144a	6611	6719
6797a				

MACHINES, Brake Testing

(See also Instruments, Brake Testing; also Tools, Brake Testing)

Bean Mfg. Co., John, 18 Hosmer St., Lansing, Mich.—*Illustrated, p. 31*

Bendix-Cowdrey Brake Tester, Inc. (Div. of Bendix Aviation Corp.), South Bend, Ind. "Cowdrey"— *Illustrated, p. 107; also Front Cover*

577	610	712	1930	4029
4775	5049	5132	5133	5408
6611	6819A			

MACHINES, Burning-in

3106   3256

MACHINES, Commutator Turning and Insulation Undercutting

Cedar Rapids Engineering Co., 901 N. 17th St., Cedar Rapids, Iowa. "Kwik-Way"—*See adv. p. 110*

100	533	645	1058	2384
3003	5441	6616	6745	

MACHINES, Cylinder Reboring

(See also Bars, Boring; also Tools, Cylinder Regrinding (Portable); also Tools, Cylinder Reboring (Portable))

5775   6745

MACHINES, Drilling, Bench (Hand)

3905   4338

MACHINES, Drilling, Bench (Power)

200	545	778	1023	2764
5809	6756			

MACHINES, Drilling, Pneumatic, (Portable)

1123   1179   3033

MACHINES, Drilling (Vertical)

81	545	778	1023	1082
2112	4514	5117	5157	5553
5809	6339a			

MACHINES, Engine Decarbonizing

(Oxygen carbon burning outfits; for chemical carbon removers—see Compounds, Carbon Removing)

Imperial Brass Mfg. Co., 1225 W. Harrison St., Chicago, Ill. — *See adv. p. 126*

555	792	2654	3016	3507
3891	5419	5608	5811	6171
6176	6622			

MACHINES, Floor (Electric)

(For polishing, sandpapering and scrubbing floors)

2068   3254   3505

MACHINES, Glass Beveling and Grinding

3426   5624

MACHINES, Grinding (Automotive Parts)

1144

MACHINES, Grinding (Bench)

United States Electrical Tool Co. Dept. T, 2483 W. Sixth St., Cincinnati, Ohio—*Illustration, branch offices & prices, p. 25*

272	559	655	670	1143
2764	3264	3271	3326	3547
3783	3795	5064	5452	5578
5676	5708	5741	5783	6118
6332	6459	6571	6616	6745
6756				

MACHINES, Grinding, Brake Drum

5132

MACHINES, Grinding (Brake Lining)

Biglow & Co., L. C., 250 W. 54th St., New York, N. Y. (New York representatives for Multibestos Co.) —*See adv. p. 129*

Chicago Rivet & Machine Co., 1830 S. 54th Ave. (Cicero P.O.), Chicago, Ill.—*See adv. p. 92*

Multibestos Co., 235 Harvey St., Cambridge B, Mass.—*See adv. p. 255*

577	1126	5049	5212	5763

Machines, Grinding (Piston)

See Machines, Piston Turning and Grinding

MACHINES, Grinding (Plain Tool)

Hobart Brothers, Box C-51, Canal Locks Square, Troy, Ohio. "HB" —*See adv. p. 108*

752	1107	1143	1161	1197
1590	2309	2384	2766	3986
4019a	4346	4634	5043	5201
6102	6331			

MACHINES, Grinding (Portable Pneumatic)

1123

MACHINES, Grinding (Reamer and Cutter)

Cedar Rapids Engineering Co., 901 N. 17th St., Cedar Rapids, Iowa. "Kwik-Way"—*See adv. p. 110*

752	1058	1308	1918	2113
2309	3457	4351	4514	6312
6461				

MACHINES, Grommetting and Eyeletting

5765

Machines, Lead Burning

See Burners, Lead

MACHINES, Milling (Hand)

752	2145	3249	5800	6339a
6461				

MACHINES, Piston Rechamfering

Dall Motor Parts Co., P.O. Station D (Dept. CAM), Cleveland, Ohio— —*Branch offices, p. 187*

5775   6461

MACHINES, Piston Turning and Grinding

Cedar Rapids Engineering Co., 901 N. 17th St., Cedar Rapids, Iowa. "Kwik-Way"—*See adv. p. 110*

1058	5578	5748	5775	6461

Machines, Reboring

See Machines, Cylinder Reboring

MACHINES, Rubbing (Pneumatic)

5800

Machines, Running-In

See Machines, Burning-In

MACHINES, Sanding (Portable Electric)

633	645	655	1031	1123
1154	3769	4252	4269	645Q
6756				

MACHINES, Sanding (Portable Pneumatic)

5800

MACHINES, Score Filling (Electric)

3728

Machines, Service Station

See Tools and Machines, Service Station

MACHINES, Spark Plug Cleaning

62

MACHINES, Spring (Elliptic)

1920

MACHINES, Tire Buffing (Electric)

Hobart Brothers, Box C-51, Canal Locks Square, Troy, Ohio. "H-B" See adv. p. 108

36	83	186	510	645
1143	1161	2670	2766	3239
3250	3894	5741	5782	5783
5784	6331			

MACHINES, Tire Cutting Off (Solid)

(For cutting or sawing worn-out solid tires so that they may be readily removed)

5029

MACHINES, Tire Inspecting

(For spreading the shoe or opening it to permit more careful examination of the inner surface; for tire spreading tools —see Tools, Tire Spreading)

Kellogg Mfg. Co., 65 Humboldt St., Rochester, N. Y. — *Illustration & prices, p. 2*

1876	3239	3241	3774	5038
6611				

MACHINES, Tire Removing and Replacing

Manley Mfg. Co., 929 Connecticut Ave., Bridgeport, Conn. — *Illustrated, p. 38*

510	718	3519	3774	6611
6649				

Machines, Valve Refacing

See Refacers, Valve (Electric)

MACHINES, Washing (Metal Parts)

1227	1831	2768	2817	3446
5635				

MACHINES, Wheel Straightening (Disc)

770

MACHINES and EQUIPMENT, Electric Welding (Arc)

Hobart Brothers, Box C-51, Canal Locks Square, Troy, Ohio. "HB" —*Illustrated, p. 108*

94	1856	2343a	2766	4349
5833	6300	6301	6664

MACHINES and EQUIPMENT, Oxy-Acetylene Welding

Imperial Brass Mfg. Co., 1225 W. Harrison St., Chicago, Ill.—*Illustration & prices, p. 126*

Linde Air Products Co., 30 E. 42nd St., New York, N. Y. "Oxweld," "Carbic," "Prest-O-Weld"—*Branch offices, p. 125*

67	555	559	792	2654
3016	3049	3891	3928a	4565
4708	4803	5419	5608	5811
6171	6176	6487	6622	

Magnet Remagnetizers

See Chargers, Magneto Magnet

Magneto Couplings

See Couplings, Magneto, Generator and Water Pump

Magneto Parts

See Parts, Magneto, Coil and Distributor

MAGNETOS, Ignition

Scintilla Magneto Co., Div. of Bendix Aviation Corp., Sherman Ave., Sidney, N. Y.—*See adv. Front Cover.*

Simmons Mfg. Co., 3405-11 Perkins Ave., Cleveland, Ohio. (For Ford & Chevrolet cars)—*See adv. p. 62*

United American Bosch Corp., 3664 Main St., Springfield, Mass. "American Bosch." (Also sole American representatives for Robert Bosch, A.G., Stuttgart, Germany) "Bosch"—*See adv. p. 69*

228	624	1851	3207	5563
5655	6314a		

MAGNETS, Lifting

(For picking small parts out of oil pans, gear cases, etc.)

682a

Mallets, Brass, Copper or Rubber

See Hammers, Soft Face

MANDRELS, Connecting Rod

6605

MANDRELS, Expanding

3986	5218	5700	6660

Manifold Heaters

See Heaters, Mixture

MANIFOLDS, Intake, for Fords

Simmons Mfg. Co., 3405-11 Perkins Ave., Cleveland, Ohio—*See adv. p. 62*

5563	6676

Market Reports, Used Car

See Reports, Used Car Market

Marketing Service

See Service, Marketing

Masking Compounds, Pastes and Paints

See Compounds, Masking

Masking Tape

See Tape, Masking

Master Vibrators

See Coils, Ignition (Vibrating)

MATS, Carpet

(See also Carpet, Coach and Motor Car)

1035	2139	3236	4308	5460
6133				

MATS, Floor Board, for Fords

634	693	812	1667	1909
2006	2324	3324	4308	5460
6344	6484	6615		

MATS, Leather

5681

Mats, Linoleum

See Linoleum

MATS and MATTING, Rubber

Continental Rubber Works, 1902 Liberty St., Erie, Pa. "Vitalic"—*See adv. p. 64*

Gates Rubber Co., 999 S. Broadway, Denver, Colo. "Gates Vulco"—*See adv. p. 62*

131	634	649	812	1240
1274	1286	1583	1829	1893
1909	2324	2412	2416	2773
2860	3327	3844	4302	4525
4613a	4676	5049	5102	5207
6205	6344	6484	6615	

MATS, Running Board

812	1591	1829	1889	1909
2412	2416	2773	2860	3324
4613a	4676	6205	6344	6484

MATTING, Aluminum

1896	5654	6822a

MATTRESSES, Pneumatic

278	1893	3208	3862	4305

MEASURES, Metal

(For gasoline or oil)

Brookins Mfg. Co., 770 Hawthorne St., Dayton, Ohio — *Illustrated & described, p. 117*

590	734	817	1067	1233
1523	1632	2362	2826	3342
3448	3713	5831		

Medical Emergency Cases

See Cases, Medical Emergency

METAL, Body Filling

(For repairing steel and aluminum body parts)

2017

METAL, Perforated

1328	2652	2709

METALS, Bearing

(Advertisers in this publication only)

Federal-Mogul Corp., 11031 Shoemaker Rd., Detroit, Mich. "Mogul" —*Illustration & warehouses, p. 189*

Johnson Bronze Co., S. Mill St., New Castle, Pa.—*Warehouses, p. 60*

METERS, Air Tower (Automatic)

5510

Meters, Cylinder Compression

See Gages, Cylinder Compression

METERS or ODOMETERS, Distance Recording

(For combined odometers and speedometers, see Speedometers)

Veeder-Root, Inc., 22 Sargeant St., Hartford, Conn.—*Illustrated, p. 54*

4528	5761

METERS or ODOMETERS, Distance Recording, for Fords

Veeder-Root, Inc., 22 Sargeant St., Hartford, Conn.—*Illustrated, p. 54*

3321

METERS, Gasoline or Oil

(For use in connection with gasoline or oil storage systems to indicate or record the amount drawn out)

700	780	1899	2467	3238
6827				

METERS, Grade

(For attaching to car to indicate degree of grade)

5131

METERS, Truck Load Indicating

655

METERS, Water Temperature Indicating

(For attachment to radiator cap or dash to show temperature of cooling water)

Moto Meter Gauge & Equipment Corp., Toledo, Ohio. "Boyce Moto-Meter," "Safe-T-Stat," "Nagel," "Red Ball"—*See adv. p. 60*

6	208	1257	2018	2132
3992	5105	5761		

MICA SHEETS, TUBES, WASHERS and CORES

27	1270	4607	5125

Mica, Tire

See Talc, Tire

MICROMETERS

(See also Gages, Cylinder)

116a	752	2084	2410	3559
5596	5719			

Milling Attachments
See Attachments, Lathe Milling

Milling Cutters
See Cutters, Milling

Milling Machines
See Machines, Milling (Hand)

MILLS, Drive Shaft Bearing End, for Fords
6745

MILLS, Steering Knuckle Bushing, for Fords
6745

Mirror Brackets
See Brackets, Mirror

Mirror Glare Shields
See Dimmers, Glare (Rear View Mirror)

MIRROR and CLOCK COMBINATIONS
3776   4292   5430a   5685

MIRRORS, Closed Car
506   720   4321   6218

MIRRORS, Panel (for Buses)
5685

MIRRORS, Rear Vision
(Advertisers in this publication only)
K-D Lamp Co., 108-18 W. Third St., Cincinnati, Ohio—*Illustrated, p. 49*
Trico Products Corp., 807 Washington St., Buffalo, N. Y.—*See adv. p. 55*

MIXERS, ECONOMIZERS or AGITATORS and AUXILIARY AIR VALVES
Simmons Mfg. Co., 3405-11 Perkins Ave., Cleveland, Ohio—(For Ford & Chevrolet cars)—*See adv. p. 62*
5105   5559   5563

Mohair Cloth
See Cloth, Mohair

Molds, Battery
See Molds, Lead

MOLDS, Lead
559   1009   3437   4708   6355
6586a

MONEY CHANGERS
2306

MONOGRAMS, Celluloid
3525

Monograms, Decalcomania
See Transfers, Decalcomania

MONOGRAMS, Hand Painted
3525

MONOGRAMS, INITIALS and EMBLEMS, Ornamental
Biltmore Mfg. Co., 2234 Ogden Ave., Chicago, Ill.—*Branch offices, p. 40*
1323   1905   2121   3016   3018
3227   3828a   3955   4215   4321
6151   6217   6464

Mops, Fountain
See Washers, Automobile (Fountain Brushes and Mops)

MOSS, Upholstery
(See also Hair, Upholstery; Felt, Upholstery)
153   505   801

Motor Commutators
See Commutators, Electric Motor

MOTOR GENERATORS, Battery Charging
(For garages and battery charging plants; for automobile generators—see Generators, Electric Lighting and Battery Charging, Auto)
Hobart Brothers, Box C-51, Canal Locks Square, Troy, Ohio. "HB" —*See adv. p. 108*
802   1596   2014   2343a   2384
2724   2766   3017   4349   5142
5190   6664

Motor Mountings, Rubber Insulated
See Mountings, Motor (Rubber Insulated)

MOTORS, Electric, for Driving Machinery
107   802   1161   1644   1865
2014   2343   2701   2724   3282a
3783   4349   4518   5030   5142
5190   5741   5783   6331   6454
6553   6664

MOTORS, Electric Heater
1547   2701   3313   5066

MOTORS, Starting
United American Bosch Corp., 3664 Main St., Springfield, Mass. "Bosch." (Sole American representatives for Robert Bosch, A.G., Stuttgart, Germany)—*See adv. p. 69*
1857   3462   4561   6314a

MOULDING, Drip
Auto-Vehicle Parts Co., 1040 Saratoga St., Newport, Ky. "Au-Vecolite"—*Illustration & sizes, pp. 34 & 35*
120   343   360   521   1048
1628   2625   2722   3294   3465
5041   5543   5654   6783

MOULDING, Finish
Auto-Vehicle Parts Co., 1042 Saratoga St., Newport, Ky. —*Illustration & sizes, pp. 34 & 35*
120   343   521   1048   2625
2682   2722   3294   5041   5104
5543   5654   6214a   6783

MOULDING, Running Board
Auto-Vehicle Parts Co., 1040 Saratoga St., Newport, Ky. "Au-Vecolite" — *Illustration & sizes, pp. 34 & 35*
120   343   360   521   1628
2722   3294   3465   5654   6783

MOUNTINGS, Motor (Rubber Insulated)
Powell Muffler Co., 316 Catherine St., Utica, N. Y.—*See adv. p. 86*

Mountings, Spring (Rubber Insulated)
See Shackles, Spring (Rubber Cushioned)

Mud Extricating Chains or Hooks
See Chains or Hooks, Mud Extricating

Mud Guard Braces
See Braces, Mud Guard or Fender

Mud Guards
See Fenders or Mud Guards, Metal

Muffler Cut-Out Pedals
See Pedals, Horn and Cut-Out

Muffler Cut-Outs
See Valves, Cut-Out

Muffler Pressure Gages
See Gages, Muffler Back Pressure

MUFFLERS, By-Pass
1287   1541   2402   4534

MUFFLERS, Exhaust (Auto)
Aluminum Industries, Inc., 2416 Beekman St., Cincinnati, Ohio. "Permatite"—*See adv. p. 10*
Jambor Tool & Stamping Co., 1261 30th St., Milwaukee, Wis. "Bull Dog"—*See adv. p. 64*
Powell Muffler Co., 316 Catherine St., Utica, N. Y.—*Illustrated, p. 86*
Simmons Mfg. Co., 3405-11 Perkins Ave., Cleveland, Ohio. — *See adv. p. 62*
121   798   1541   1603   1905
2334   2402   2795   3104   3872
4534   4750   4755   5563   6675

Mufflers, Intake Carburetor
See Silencers, Carburetor Intake

Nails, Upholstery
See Tacks, Upholstery

NETS, Luggage
4358

Nippers
See Pliers

Nipples, Pipe
See Fittings, Tube (Copper or Brass)

Nipples, Pump
See Connections, Tire Pump

Nipples, Rubber
See Covers, Distributor; also Covers, Spark Plug

Nitro-Cellulose Finishes
See Lacquer

NOZZLES, Air
(Blow gun for blowing dust and dirt from chassis and body)
Bean Mfg. Co., John, 18 Hosmer St., Lansing, Mich.—*Illustrated, p. 31*
Imperial Brass Mfg. Co., 1225 W. Harrison St., Chicago, Ill.—*Illustrated, p. 126*
525   1141   6633

Nozzles, Automobile Washing
See Washers, Automobile (Equipment)

NOZZLES, Lubricating
86   1587

Nozzles, Paint Spray
See Sprayers, Paint, Varnish and Lacquer

Nut Splitters
See Splitters, Nut

NUTS
Aetna Metal Products Co., 1824 Washington Ave., St. Louis, Mo.—*Illustration & prices, p. 97*
Auto-Vehicle Parts Co., 1040 Saratoga St., Newport, Ky.—*See adv. pp. 34 & 35*
Dill Mfg. Co., 686 E. 82nd St., Cleveland, Ohio. (Tire valve)—*Illustrated, p. 43*
Dorman Star Washer Co., 219 E. Eighth St., Cincinnati, Ohio—*Illustrated, p. 102*

See Page 364 for Names of Companies Represented by Above Numbers

Jambor Tool & Stamping Co., 1261 30th St., Milwaukee, Wis. "Bull Dog"—See adv. p. 64
Russell, Burdsall & Ward Bolt & Nut Co., Port Chester, N. Y. "Empire" —Illustration & branch offices, p. 61
Simmons Mfg. Co., 3405-11 Perkins Ave., Cleveland, Ohio. (For Ford & Chevrolet cars)—See adv. p. 62

16	24	52	284	295
323	351	543	630	728
774	1128	1158	1173	1234
1602	1626	2056	2338a	2472
2655	2663	2669	2680	2702
3104	3420	3944	4011	4211
4254	4271	4536	4688	5069
5213	5538	5563	5815	6195
6221	6309	6323a	6559	6644
6658				

NUTS, Axle Shaft Adjusting
Dorman Star Washer Co., 219 E. Eighth St., Cincinnati, Ohio.—See adv. p. 102
1626   4662

Nuts, Bearing
See Bolts & Nuts, Automatic Connecting Rod Bearing

NUTS, Lock
(For Lock Washers—See Washers, Lock)
Auto-Vehicle Parts Co., 1040 Saratoga St., Newport, Ky. "Au-Ve-Co"—Illustrated, pp. 34 & 35
Dorman Star Washer Co., 219 E. Eighth St., Cincinnati, Ohio.—Illustrated, p. 102

295	360	691	1626	1633
2338a	4746	5093	6323a	

NUTS, Semi-Finished
Cleveland Cap Screw Co., 3004 E. 79th St., Cleveland, Ohio—Warehouse stocks, p. 95
Jambor Tool & Stamping Co., 1261 30th St., Milwaukee, Wis. "Bull Dog"—See adv. p. 64
Russell, Burdsall & Ward Bolt & Nut Co., Port Chester, N. Y. "Empire" —Illustration & branch offices, p. 61

16	24	284	323	774
1128	1173	2056	2663	2669
2702	3104	3420	4254	4688
5114	5213	5538	6195	6309
6323a	6644			

NUTS, Spindle Bolt, for Fords
Simmons Mfg. Co., 3405-11 Perkins Ave., Cleveland, Ohio—See adv. p. 62

NUTS, Thumb
295	643	1158	3268	6323a
6730				

NUTS, Wing
295	1823	2663	3268	4254
4688	5069	6323a	6483	

Odometers or Distance Meters
See Meters or Odometers, Distance Recording

Oil Can Holders
See Holders, Oil Can

Oil Cans
See Cans, Oiling

Oil Cups
See Cups, Oil and Grease

Oil Dispensers
See Dispensers, Oil; also Tanks, Oil (Portable)

Oil Distributors
See Automobiles (Oil, Tar and Asphalt Distributors)

Oil Drip Pads (Floor)
See Pads, Oil Drip (Floor)

Oil Filters
See Reclaimers or Rectifiers, Oil (Garage or Repair Shop); also Purifiers, Oil (For Attaching to Engine)

Oil Funnels
See Funnels, Metal

Oil Gages
See Gages, Oil Pressure; also Gages, Oil Level

Oil Gages, for Fords
See Gages, Oil, for Fords

Oil Guns
See Lubricators, Hand

Oil Hole Covers
See Covers, Oil Hole

Oil Level Gages
See Gages, Oil Level

Oil Level Indicators, for Fords
See Gages, Oil, for Fords

Oil Line Tubing
See Tubing, Oil and Gasoline Line

Oil Measures
See Measures, Metal

Oil Pans
See Pans, Engine

Oil Reclaimers
See Reclaimers or Rectifiers, Oil (Garage or Repair Shop)

Oil Rectifiers
See Reclaimers or Rectifiers, Oil (Garage or Repair Shop); also Purifiers, Oil (for Attaching to Engine)

Oil Retainers
See Retainers, Rear Axle Grease

Oil Retaining Rings
See Washers, Felt

Oil Rod Wipers
See Wipers, Oil Rod

Oil Stills
See Purifiers, Oil (For Attaching to Engine); also Reclaimers or Rectifiers, Oil (Garage or Repair Shop)

Oil Tanks
See Tanks & Systems, Gasoline and Oil Storage; also Tanks, Oil (Portable)

Oil Test Cocks, for Fords
See Gages, Oil, for Fords

Oiled Duck
See Cloth, Enameled or Oiled

OILERS, Chevrolet Clutch Collar
3530

Oilers, Cup
See Cups, Oil and Grease

OILERS, Spring
(Oil cups or retainers to be applied to springs to keep them lubricated; see also Covers, Spring Leaf Lubricating)
2668   3018

Oilers, Squirt
See Cans, Oiling

Oiling Systems, for Fords
See Lubricators and Oil Pumps, for Fords

OILS, Lubricating
(Advertisers in this publication only)
Bell Co., 407-11 N. Lincoln St., Chicago, Ill.—See adv. p. 93

Bijur Lubricating Corp., 22-08 43rd Ave., Long Island City, N. Y.—Distributors, p. 87
Emerol Mfg. Co., 242 W. 69th St., New York, N. Y. "Marvel Mystery"—Illustration, description & prices, p. 4

OILS, Lubricating (For Combustion Chamber Oilers)
Opco Co., 1894 Niagara St., Buffalo, N. Y. "Opco"—See adv. p. 52

226	1006a	1667	4007	4543
5001	5064	5549	5625	6161
6580				

Oils, Penetrating
See Lubricants, Spring

Oldham Couplings
See Couplings, Magneto, Generator and Water Pump

OPENERS, Bus Door
295   1262   1823

OPENERS, Curtain
(A device to be attached to doors of open cars so that storm curtains may be opened with the doors)
295   652

OPENERS, Electric Battery
(See Heaters, Storage Battery (Electric))
559   3890   6825

OPERATORS, Garage Door (Electric)
128   2675   4753   5118   6814

OPERATORS, Garage Door (Mechanical)
3865

OPERATORS, Garage Door (Pneumatic)
3874   5459

ORNAMENTS, Radiator
(See also Flags, Pennants and Emblems; Holders, Flag, Pennant and Emblem; Monograms, Initials and Emblems, Ornamental)

131	261	556	1323	1339
2121	2404	3349	4321	5687
6145	6151			

Orphan Car Repair Parts
See page 308

Overalls
See Coveralls and Service Coats

Oxygen Gas
See Gas, Oxygen (In Tanks)

Oxygen Tank Trucks
See Trucks, Acetylene and Oxygen Tank

PACKING, Asbestos
Advance Packing & Supply Co., 806 Washington Blvd., Chicago, Ill. "Tenax"—Illustration & sizes, p. 87
Emsco Asbestos Co., 206 S. Crawford St., Downey, Calif.—Illustration & warehouse stocks, p. 84
Felt Products Mfg. Co., 1510 Carroll Ave., Chicago, Ill. "Asbesto-pak," "Grafel"—See adv. p. 75
Ferodo and Asbestos, Inc., Extension of Codwise Ave., New Brunswick, N. J. "Permanite" — See adv. p. 82
Thermoid Rubber Co., Whitehead Rd., Trenton, N. J.—See adv. p. 85

PACKING, Asbestos—Continued

United States Asbestos Div. of Ray-bestos-Manhattan, Inc., Manheim, Pa. "Duraco," "Duraplastic" — *Illustrated & described*, p. 81
Victor Mfg. & Gasket Co., 5750 Roosevelt Rd., Chicago, Ill. "Victo-pac," "Victor"—*See adv. p. 77*

27	49	204	267	1108
1263	1513	1591	1829	1889
2038	2047	2054	2338	2412
2416	3127	3234	4302	4607
4697	5115a	6129	6325	6344
6480	6797a			

PACKING, Felt

Advance Packing & Supply Co., 806 Washington Blvd., Chicago, Ill. —*See adv.* p. 87
Felt Products Mfg. Co., 1510 Carroll Ave., Chicago, Ill.—*See adv.* p. 75
Victor Mfg. & Gasket Co., 5750 Roosevelt Rd., Chicago, Ill.—*See adv.* p. 77

27	47	49	258	717
1250	2046	2047	4607	6480
6651				

PACKING, Fibrous

Advance Packing & Supply Co., 806 Washington Blvd., Chicago, Ill. "Tanpac," "Adpasco"—*Illustrated*, p. 87
Felt Products Mfg. Co., 1510 Carroll Ave., Chicago, Ill. "Felpak," "Karropak," "Wirepak"—*See adv.* p. 75
Vellumoid Co., 54 Rockdale St., Worcester, Mass.—*See adv. p. 78*
Victor Mfg. & Gasket Co., 5750 Roosevelt Rd., Chicago, Ill. "Victorite"—*See adv. p. 77*

27	49	204	1146	1670
1829	1891	2047	3127	4607
5115a	6344	6475	6480	

PACKING, Graphite

Emsco Asbestos Co., 206 S. Crawford St., Downey, Calif.—*Illustration & warehouse stocks*, p. 84

PACKING, Leather

Advance Packing & Supply Co., 806 Washington Blvd., Chicago, Ill. —*See adv.* p. 87
Felt Products Mfg. Co., 1510 Carroll Ave., Chicago, Ill.—*See adv.* p. 75

27	49	1111	1124	1207
2047	2441	2808	4607	5571
5612	6696			

PACKING, Metallic

Felt Products Mfg. Co., 1510 Carroll Ave., Chicago, Ill. "Fel-Pro," "Alupak"—*Illustrated*, p. 75

204	1255	1314	2038	2047
2439	3709	4607	5115a	6344

Packing, Paper

See Gaskets, Paper

PACKING, Plastic Metallic

Advance Packing & Supply Co., 806 Washington Blvd., Chicago, Ill. —*See adv.* p. 87

1255

PACKING, Rubber

Advance Packing & Supply Co., 806 Washington Blvd., Chicago, Ill. —*See adv.* p. 87
Felt Products Mfg. Co., 1510 Carroll Ave., Chicago, Ill.—*See adv.* p. 75

27	49	204	1146	1263
1274	1513	1591	1829	1893
2047	2322	2412	2416	3844
4607	4697	5049	6344	

PADS, Body Foundation

Felt Products Mfg. Co., 1510 Carroll Ave., Chicago, Ill. — *See adv.* p. 75

47	549	801	2047	3422
4218	4607	6651		

PADS, Felt, Anti-Squeak

See Lining, Body or Frame

PADS, Floor (Felt, Jute, etc.)

Felt Products Mfg. Co., 1510 Carroll Ave., Chicago, Ill. — *See adv.* p. 75

47	652	717	1159	6651

PADS, Filling

(For service station use to absorb overflow in filling tank or radiator)

3995

PADS, Oil Drip (Floor)

6133

PADS, Pedal

(For applying to clutch and brake pedals to prevent feet from slipping)

131	649	1829	2158	3324
3855	3892	3903		

PADS, Seat

(Cane, rubber, wicker or straw seats to be used over regular cushions)

291	1035	1893	1905	1926
2773	6615			

Pads, Top

See Protectors, Top

Padding, Body

See Pads, Body Foundation

Padding, Frame

See Lining, Body or Frame

Padlocks

See Locks, Cabinet and Pad

Pails, Folding

See Buckets, Collapsible

Paint, Masking

See Compounds, Masking

Paint Removers

See Removers, Paint, Enamel and Varnish

Paint Sprayers

See Sprayers, Paint, Varnish and Lacquer

Paint Spraying Booths

See Booths, Spraying (Paint and Varnish)

PAINTS

(See also Enamels; also Lacquer)
Sherwin-Williams Co., Dept. 733, 101 Prospect Ave., N. W., Cleveland, Ohio—*See adv.* p. 21

33	38	78	177	244
520	642	699	702	1022
1075	1186	1588	1667	2142
2689	2773	3231	3523	3555
3714	3925	4313	4529	4673
4696	4711	4756	5136	5174
5514	5541	5566	6505	

PAINTS, Aluminum and Bronze

Sherwin-Williams Co., Dept. 733, 101 Prospect Ave., N. W., Cleveland, Ohio—*See adv.* p. 21

38	120	177	236	520
534	647	699	1022	1588
2144	2860	3046	3122	4022
4347	5120	5435	5541	5750
6206	6456	6725a		

PAINTS, Exhaust Pipe, Muffler and Cylinder

American Chemical Paint Co., Brookside Ave. & Reading R.R., Ambler, Pa. "Kemick"—*Described*, p. 126
Bell Co., 407-11 N. Lincoln St., Chicago, Ill.—*See adv.* p. 93
Sherwin-Williams Co., Dept. 733, 101 Prospect Ave., N. W., Cleveland, Ohio—*See adv.* p. 21

33	38	143	177	531
534	593	699	1006a	1022
1303	2144	2389	2616	2648
2751	2773	2789	3046	3523
4347	4696	4711	5120	5413
5541	5667	6456		

PAINTS, Rim

1667	2355	2416	2616	3523
4564	4673	4722	5413	

PAINTS, Rubber

(For refinishing rubber mats and matting and painting tires)

534	698	1006a	1508	1667
1922	2355	2412	2416	2616
2648	2773	2784	3247	3523
3903	4347	4529	4673	5120
5413	5667	5707	5727	5750
6456				

PAINTS, Storage Battery Terminal

536	3925	5425

PAINTS, Tire

See Paints, Rubber

PANELS, Door (For Model A Fords)

1319

Panels, Fibre

See Fibre, Hard; also Foundations, Body Upholstery

PANELS, Instrument Board, for Fords

1651

PANELS and SWITCHBOARDS, Charging

Hobart Brothers, Box C51, Canal Locks Square, Troy, Ohio. "HB" —*See adv.* p. 108

98	665	2343a	2724	2766
6573	6664			

PANS, Drip

(For placing under cars in garages or sales rooms to catch any oil or grease that may drip)
Brookins Mfg. Co., 770 Hawthorne St., Dayton, Ohio — *Illustrated & described*, p. 117

347	352	590	704A	734
1135	1632	1668	2362	2826
3294	3409	3448	5635	5725
6611				

PANS, Engine

Simmons Mfg. Co., 3405-11 Perkins Ave., Cleveland, Ohio (For Ford & Chevrolet cars)—*See adv.* p. 62

1233	1668	3294	4751	5563
6814a				

Pans, Tote

See Boxes, Tote (Metal)

PAPER, Abrasive

591	1031	1198	3921	6345

PAPER (Corrugated Sheets and Rolls)

2328   5572

Paper Gaskets

See Gaskets, Paper

See Page 364 for Names of Companies Represented by Above Numbers

PAPER, Upholstery Covering
(Placed over upholstery to keep it from being soiled when car is being repaired)
354

Paper Washers
See Gaskets, Paper

Parcel Carriers
See Carriers, Parcel

Parking Lights
See Lamps, Cowl, Fender, Tail, Parking, Running Board and Clearance

PARTS and ACCESSORIES, Buyers of Surplus
(Advertisers in this publication only)
Manufacturers Surplus Outlet Co., 542 S. Dearborn St., Chicago, Ill.—*See adv. p. 66*
Warshawsky & Co., 1915-35 S. State St., Chicago, Ill.—*See adv. p. 68*

Parts, Battery Repair
See Parts, Storage Battery Repair

Parts, Bumper
See Bumper Parts

PARTS, Fuel Pump
Hygrade Products Co., 333 W. 52nd St., New York, N. Y. (Glass bowls, gaskets, etc.)—*Illustrated, p. 86*
Brunswick Engineering Co., 30 Cortlandt St., New Brunswick, N. J. "C & H"—*Illustration & prices, p. 42*

PARTS, Magneto, Coil and Distributor
Holfast Rubber Co., Lakewood Ave., Atlanta, Ga.—*See adv. p. 65*
Niehoff & Co., C. E., 230 W. Superior St., Chicago, Ill.—*See adv. p. 63*
Shurhit Products, Inc., Waukegan, Ill.—*Illustrated, p. 80*
Simmons Mfg. Co., 3405-11 Perkins Ave., Cleveland, Ohio. (For Ford & Chevrolet cars)—*See adv. p. 62*

161	178	228	337	339
1063	1257	1827	2073	2472
2619	2781	3202	4317	4556
4601	4620	5550	5563	5612
5626	6707			

Parts, Orphan Car Repair
See page 308

Parts, Radio (Jobbers)
See Jobbers of Radio Parts

PARTS, Rim
Hubco Mfg. Co., 404 W. Conway St., Baltimore, Md.,—*Illustrated, p. 104*
Simmons Mfg. Co., 3405-11 Perkins Ave., Cleveland, Ohio. (For Ford & Chevrolet cars)—*See adv. p. 62*

337	1602	2070	2822	5563
6139	6677			

PARTS, Speedometer
(Gears, swivel joints, etc.; for a flexible casing and cable — see Shafting, Flexible)

2073	4556	4620	5759	5832

PARTS, Starting Motor Drive
(See also Drives, Starter)
Es-M-Co Auto Products Corp., 31 34th St., Brooklyn, N. Y. (For Ford & Chevrolet cars) — *Illustration & warehouses, p. 70*
Jambor Tool & Stamping Co., 1261 30th St., Milwaukee, Wis. "Bull Dog"—*See adv. p. 64*
Niehoff & Co., C. E., 230 W. Superior St., Chicago, Ill.—*See adv. p. 63*

Simmons Mfg. Co., 3405-11 Perkins Ave., Cleveland, Ohio. (Springs)—*See adv. p. 62*
Williams Products Co., H. E., 100 S. Main St., Carthage, Mo. (Screws & washers)—*See adv. p. 32*

16	337	339	1827	1906
2033	2472	2619	2858	3104
3202	4317	4601	5494a	5563
5687				

PARTS, Storage Battery Repair

235	560	684	1182	1219
1267	1286	1322	1892	1904
2110	2130	2366	2438	3573
4317	4773	5062	5092	5207
5425	5671	6107	6139	6355
6646	6760			

PARTS, Universal Joint
16   116   4288

PARTS, Used
(Advertisers in this publication only)
Warshawsky & Co., 1915-35 S. State St., Chicago, Ill.—*See adv. p. 68*

Parts Washing Machines
See Machines, Washing (Metal Parts)

PARTS, Wheel
Hubco Mfg. Co., 404 W. Conway St., Baltimore, Md. (Dual truck)—*See adv. p. 104*
Jambor Tool & Stamping Co., 1261 30th St., Milwaukee, Wis. "Bull Dog"—*See adv. p. 64*
337

PARTS, Windshield Cleaner
Hackett Products Co., 407 Pine St., Providence, R. I.—*Illustrated & described, p. 40*
Signal Mfg. Co., 587 Washington St., Lynn, Mass. "Lion"—*See adv. p. 45*
Trico Products Corp., 807 Washington St., Buffalo, N. Y.—*Description & prices, p. 55*

89	131	208	224	812
1135	1257	1500	2604	2773
3014	3150	3151	3324	3563a
3708	3841	3892	5207	5451
5556	5687	6190		

Paste, Masking
See Compounds, Masking

PATCHES, Blowout (Wing)
(Advertisers in this publication only)
Gates Rubber Co., 999 S. Broadway, Denver, Colo. "Gates Vulco"—*See adv. p. 62*

PATCHES, Tire Repair
(Advertisers in this publication only)
Continental Rubber Works, 1902 Liberty St., Erie, Pa. "Vitalic"—*See adv. p. 64*
Gates Rubber Co., 999 S. Broadway, Denver, Colo. "Gates Vulco"—*See adv. p. 62*

PATCHES, Top Repair
(For repairing mohair or other fabric tops)
Biltmore Mfg. Co., 1747 Central Ave., Cincinnati, Ohio. "Stik-Tite"—*See adv. p. 40*
Holfast Rubber Co., Lakewood Ave., Atlanta, Ga.—*See adv. p. 65*

291	644	1905	2602	2616
2758	2773	2781	2784	2860
4025	4711	5413	5722	6143
6456				

PATCHES, Tube Repair
(Advertisers in this publication only)
Gates Rubber Co., 999 S. Broadway, Denver, Colo.—*See adv. p. 62*
Holfast Rubber Co., Lakewood Ave., Atlanta, Ga.—*See adv. p. 65*

Pedal Depressors
See Depressors, Brake Pedal

Pedal Extensions
See Extensions, Pedal

Pedal Pads
See Pads, Pedal

Pedal Plates
See Plates, Heel and Pedal

Pedal Shields, for Fords
See Shields, Air Draft Pedal, for Fords

Pedals, Accelerator
See Pedals, Special Accelerator

PEDALS, Horn and Cut-Out
1287   1823   4682   4757   5733

PEDALS, Special Accelerator
40	131	1656	1823	2158
2404	4215	6134	6151	6218

PEDALS, Starter, for Fords
224   5105   6218

Pencils, Striping
See Tools, Striping

Pennant Holders
See Holders, Flag, Pennant and Emblem

Pennants
See Flags, Pennants and Emblems

Photometers, Headlight Testing
See Testers, Headlight, Photometric

Pinion Shaft Bearing Cages
See Cages, Pinion Shaft Bearing

Pinion Shafts
See Shafts, Propeller and Rear Axle

Pinions, Metal
See Gears and Pinions, Metal

Pinions, Speedometer
See Gears and Pinions, Speedometer

Pins, Clevis
See Pins, Yoke

PINS, Cotter
Simmons Mfg. Co., 3405-11 Perkins Ave., Cleveland, Ohio. (For Ford & Chevrolet cars)—*See adv. p. 62*

142	739	2033	2472	2702
2756	3420	4254	5563	5599
5753	6559	6586	6662	

PINS, Crank Ratchet, for Fords
134

PINS, Fan Pulley, for Fords
Loock & Co., R. J., 343-45 N. Gay St., Baltimore, Md. "Lightnin"—*Illustration & prices, p. 51*

Pins, King
See Bolts, Steering Knuckle

PINS, Piston
Aluminum Industries, Inc., 2416 Beekman St., Cincinnati, Ohio. "Permatite"—*Illustrated, p. 10*
Burgess-Norton Mfg. Co., 517 Peyton St., Geneva, Ill. "B-N"—*Illustration, branch offices, Chilton & Burgess-Norton numbers, p. 187*
Emsco Asbestos Co., 206 S. Crawford St., Downey, Calif. "Jadson"—*Illustration & warehouse stocks, p. 84*

See Page 364 for Names of Companies Represented by Above Numbers

PINS, Piston—Continued

Jambor Tool & Stamping Co., 1261 30th St., Milwaukee, Wis. "Bull Dog"—*See adv. p. 64*

McQuay-Norris Mfg. Co., Cooper & Southwest Aves., St. Louis, Mo.—*See adv. p. 88*

Simmons Mfg. Co., 3405-11 Perkins Ave., Cleveland, Ohio. (For Ford & Chevrolet cars)—*See adv. p. 62*

Thompson Products, Inc., 2196 Clarkwood Rd., Cleveland, Ohio—*Illustrated, p. 89*

14	121	170	256	800
1128	1569	1872	1889	3104
3284	3728	3755	3775	3913
3954	4000	4515	5563	5652
6141	6192	6482		

PINS, Taper

351	598	1128	2663	2702
3453	3986	4255	4758	5093
5696	5700	6323A	6644	6794

PINS, Yoke

Dorman Star Washer Co., 219 E. Eighth St., Cincinnati, Ohio.—*Illustrated, p. 102*

Es-M-Co Auto Products Corp., 31 34th St., Brooklyn, N. Y. (For Ford & Chevrolet cars) — *Illustration & warehouses, p. 70*

Simmons Mfg. Co., 3405-11 Perkins Ave., Cleveland, Ohio. (For Ford & Chevrolet cars)—*See adv. p. 62*

1626	1906	2056	2702	4665
4688	5049	5563	6309	6644

Pipe Cutters
See Cutters, Pipe

Pipe Fittings
See Fittings, Tube (Copper or Brass)

Pipe Flaring Tools
See Tools, Tube Flaring

Pipe Vises
See Vises, Pipe

Pipe Wrenches
See Wrenches, Pipe

Pipes, Blow
See Blow Pipes, Brazing, Welding and Cutting

PIPES, Tail
Powell Muffler Co., 316 Catherine St., Utica, N. Y.—*Illustrated, p. 86*

Piston Pin Repair Tools
See Tools, Piston Pin

Piston Pins
See Pins, Piston

Piston Repair Tools
See Jigs, Connecting Rod Aligning; Machines, Piston Rechamfering; Machines, Piston Turning and Grinding; Tools, Piston Fitting

Piston Ring Expanding Springs
See Rings, Piston Ring Expanding or Packing

Piston Ring Repair Tools
See Gages, Piston Ring; Tools, Piston Ring

Piston kings
See Rings, Piston

PISTONS
Aluminum Industries, Inc., 2416 Beekman St., Cincinnati, Ohio. "Permite," "Unitype"—*Illustrated, p. 10*

Dall Motor Parts Co., P.O. Station D (Dept. CAM), Cleveland Ohio—*Illustration, branch offices, Chilton & Dall numbers, p. 187*

DeLuxe Products Corp., 2001 Lake St., La Porte, Ind.—*Illustrated, p. 90*

Emsco Asbestos Co., 206 S. Crawford St., Downey, Cal. "Jadson-Emsco" —*Illustration & warehouse stocks, p. 84*

McQuay-Norris Mfg. Co., Cooper & Southwest Aves., St. Louis, Mo. (Also sole distributors of "Nelson Bohnalite" pistons, for Bohn Aluminum & Brass Corp., 2512 E. Grand Blvd., Detroit, Mich.)—*See adv. p. 88*

Simmons Mfg. Co., 3405-11 Perkins Ave., Cleveland, Ohio. (For Ford & Chevrolet cars)—*See adv. p. 62*

Thompson Products, Inc., 2196 Clarkwood Rd., Cleveland, Ohio.—*Illustrated, p. 89*

14	120	121	169	170
256	682	1229	1503	1556
1569	1889	3284	3728	3913
3986A	4000	4214	4515	4524
5050	5199	5563	5652	5748
5779A	6141	6165A	6209	6320
6728	6758			

PITS, Crankcase Service
3793   5526

Planer Tool Holders
See Holders, Lathe, Planer, Shaper and Slotter

Planer Tools
See Tools, Lathe, Planer, Shaper and Slotter

Plate Glass
See Glass, Polished Plate

Plates, Clutch
See Discs, Clutch (Steel)

PLATES, Demountable Rim Wedge
(Small stamped plates or shims to be used under the rim wedges to insure their tightness)
6677

PLATES, Differential Assembly, for Fords
6745

PLATES, Heel and Pedal
4215   4506   5654

PLATES, Hub, for Fords
2018   2033

PLATES, Kick or Scuff

1842	2121	2404	2412	2773
3016	3828A	3988	4215	4506
6145	6627	6643A		

PLATES, Load Data
2121   4764A

PLATES, Step
Imperial Brass Mfg. Co., 1225 W. Harrison St., Chicago, Ill. "Fits-All"—*See adv. p. 126*

131	649	1648	1842	2384
2404	2412	2773	3016	3263
3988	4215	4506	4525	5108
5654	6145	6151	6217	6218
6627	6643A			

PLATES, Surface
2113   3256   5536   6104

PLATES, Town

3966	3988	4215	5522	5666
6145	6151			

PLIERS
(Advertisers in this publication only)

Peck, Stow & Wilcox Co., 217-313 Center St., Southington, Conn. "Pexto"—*See adv. p. 124*

Truth Tool Co., 711 S. Front St., Mankato, Minn.—*See adv. p. 128*

Pliers, Fender Repair
See Tools, Body and Fender Repair

Pliers, Terminal
See Tools, Storage Battery Repair

PLIERS, Tire Chain
(See also Tools, Tire Chain Repair)

McKay Co., Union Trust Bldg., Pittsburgh, Pa.—*Illustrated, p. 33*

United States Chain & Forging Co., —*See* McKay Co.

142   1077   1237   2714   5420

PLOWS, Snow
(For attaching to trucks)

28	527	2413	2697	3433
3764	5133A	5187	6569	6601

Plug Gages
See Gages, Plug and Ring

PLUGS, Charging
(For electric vehicles)
2343A   3311   5215

PLUGS, Crankcase Oil Drain
Martin & Stoner Co., 2326 S. Michigan Ave., Chicago, Ill. "M & S"—*Illustration, description & prices, p. 80*

PLUGS, Expansion
Dorman Star Washer Co., 219 E. Eighth St., Cincinnati, Ohio.—*Illustrated, p. 102*
720

Plugs, Lamp
See Connectors, Lamp (Electric)

PLUGS, Radiator Testing
Thermoid Rubber Co., Whitehead Rd., Trenton, N. J.—*See adv. p. 85*
1.00   1343   1895A   5032   6187

PLUGS, Spark
Champion Spark Plug Co., Upton Ave., Toledo, Ohio — *Illustrated, Back Cover*

Rajah Co., Locust Ave. & Nelson St., Bloomfield, N. J.—*See adv. p. 100*

Simmons Mfg. Co., 3405-11 Perkins Ave., Cleveland, Ohio. (For Ford & Chevrolet cars)—*See adv. p. 62*

United American Bosch Corp., 3664 Main St., Springfield, Mass. "American Bosch" (Also sole American representatives for Robert Bosch, A. G., Stuttgart, Germany. "Bosch"—*See adv. p. 69*

6	70	93	616	679
1005	1088	1326	1542	1615
1894	2162	2361	2619	2861
3158	3477	3492	3992	4019
4515	4613	4631	5036	5078
5563	5655	5767	6314a	6672
6679				

PLUGS, Tire Repair
1589   2033   2416   3903   6615

PLUSH, Upholstery
725   4542

POCKETS, Door, for Fords
1192   1905   2139   2773   4787

POINTS, Contact
(Contact points and screws of platinum or platinum substitute)

Jambor Tool & Stamping Co., 1261 30th St., Milwaukee, Wis. "Bull Dog"—*See adv. p. 64*

See Page 364 for Names of Companies Represented by Above Numbers

Shurhit Products, Inc., Waukegan, Ill—*See adv. p. 80*
Niehoff & Co., C. E., 230 W. Superior St., Chicago, Ill. "A. E. S"—*See adv. p. 63*

178	228	337	1063	1827
2073	2472	3104	3202	3207
3287	4317	4556	4601	

POLISHERS, Disc, for Lacquer
(Felt, sheepskin or lamb's wool, for use in electric drills)

1031	3271	3921	6727

Polishers, Electric Portable
See Drills, Grinders and Polishers, Electric Portable; also Tools, Metal Finishing (Portable Electric)

POLISHERS, Hydraulic Brake Cylinder
2462

POLISHES, Automobile Body
(Advertisers in this publication only)
Bell Co., 407-11 N. Lincoln St., Chicago, Ill.—*Illustrated, p. 93*
Liquid Veneer Corp., 822 Liquid Veneer Bldg., Buffalo, N. Y. "Washine"—*Illustration & prices, p. 66*

POLISHES, Metal
(Advertisers in this publication only)
Bell Co., 407-11 N. Lincoln St., Chicago, Ill.—*See adv. p. 93*

Polishing Cloths
See Wipers and Polishing Cloths

Polishing Compounds
See Compounds, Rubbing and Polishing

Polishing Discs
See Polishers, Disc, for Lacquer

Polishing Felt
See Felt, Polishing and Rubbing

Polishing Machines, Floor
See Machines, Floor (Electric)

POSTS, Lamp (Filling Station)

817	3793	3850	4784	6308

Pots, Solder Melting
See Furnaces, Soldering

Power Take-Offs
See Take-Offs, Power

Preheaters, Engine
See Heaters, Engine Cooling System

PRESSES, Arbor
Manley Mfg. Co., 929 Connecticut Ave., Bridgeport, Conn.—*Illustrated, p. 38*

35	290	545	551	1023
1082	2640	2786	2835	3256
3439	3549	3774	3794	3831
5531	6611	6745		

PRESSES, Axle
(For wheel alignment)
Bear Mfg. Co., 21st St. & Fifth Ave., Rock Island, Ill.—*See adv. p. 123*

814	2835

Presses, Broaching
See Presses, Forcing

Presses, Crankshaft Straightening
See Presses, Straightening (Crankshaft)

PRESSES, Forcing

545	2712

PRESSES, Sheet Metal Working

46	664	2041	3439	3774
3543a	4282	4309	5683	6567

PRESSES, Solid Truck Tire Applying

1650	2854	6629	6671

Presses, Stamping
See Presses, Sheet Metal Working

PRESSES, Storage Battery Plate
559

PRESSES, Straightening
Bear Mfg. Co., 21st St. & Fifth Ave., Rock Island, Ill.—*Illustrated, p. 123*

290	2835	3256	3986	5662
6611				

PRESSES, Straightening (Crankshaft)

3774	5662

PRIMERS, Engine (Automatic)

35	270	344	4681	4705

PRIMERS, Engine (Hand)
(See also Heaters, Mixers; also Mixers, Economizers or Agitators and Auxiliary Air Valves)
Dole Valve Co., 1913-33 Carroll Ave., Chicago, Ill.—*Illustrated, p. 42*
Imperial Brass Mfg. Co., 1225 W. Harrison St., Chicago, Ill. "Primeur"—*See adv. p. 126*

1327	1618	3016	3563	5219

Priming Cups
See Cups, Priming

Priming Fluids
See Fluids, Priming

PROPELLER SHAFT BOXES
SKF Industries, Inc., 40 E. 34th St., New York, N. Y.—*Distributors, p. 171*

Propeller Shafts
See Shafts, Propeller

Protectors, Car (Repairmen's)
See Covers, Repairmen's

PROTECTORS, Door
(Leather or fabric pads to protect the finish of the door)

338	644	692	1192	1319
1905	2773	2860		

PROTECTORS, Gear Shift Grease and Oil
Loock & Co., R. J., 343-45 N. Gay St., Baltimore, Md. "Lightnin"—*Illustrated, p. 51*

Protectors, Spring
See Covers, Spring

PROTECTORS, Top
(Strips of felt or other soft material to be placed between top bow and top covering)

291	2860	4663a	6133

PULLERS, Axle Housing, for Fords
Truth Tool Co., 711 S. Front St., Mankato, Minn.—*See adv. p. 128*
100

Pullers, Battery Connector
See Tools, Storage Battery Repair

PULLERS, Bearing
National Machine & Tool Co., 801 S. Water St., Jackson, Mich. (Generator, for Model A Ford cars)—*Illustration & prices, p. 120*
Truth Tool Co., 711 S. Front St., Mankato, Minn.—*See adv. p. 128*

100	1019	1625	2841	3256
3989	4241	4317	6208	6616
6745				

PULLERS, Bearing (Front Wheel), for Fords
National Machine & Tool Co., 801 S. Water St., Jackson, Mich.—*See adv. p. 120*

Pullers, Bushing
See Extractors, Bushing

Pullers, Car
See Winches and Blocks, Car Extracting

PULLERS, Clutch Disc Drum, for Fords

4241	6745

PULLERS, Cotter Pin

643	720	2017	2410	4549
4726	5777	6559	6825	

PULLERS, Driveshaft
Truth Tool Co., 711 S. Front St., Mankato, Minn.—*See adv. p. 128*

PULLERS, Gear and Wheel
National Machine & Tool Co., 801 S. Water St., Jackson, Mich.—*Illustration & prices, p. 120*
Simmons Mfg. C., 3405 Perkins Ave., Cleveland, Ohio—*See adv. p. 62*
Truth Tool Co., 711 S. Front St., Mankato, Minn.—*See adv. p. 128*

5	26	35	91	169
224	681	765	1063	1505
1625	1669	2033	2676	2723
2795	2822	2835	2841	3201
3203	3256	3774	3831	3887
3989	4241	4600	4672	4726
5049	5155	5214	5451	5481
5536	5563	5611	5665A	5753
6185	6208	6559	6586A	6616
6717A	6745	6825		

Pullers, Piston Pin
See Tools, Piston Pin Removing and Installing

Pullers, Separator
See Tools, Storage Battery Repair

PULLERS, Spring Perch (For Model A Fords)
National Machine & Tool Co., 801 S. Water St., Jackson, Mich.—*See adv. p. 120*
6745

Pullers, Wheel
See Pullers, Gear and Wheel

Pulleys and Sheaves
See Sheaves and Pulleys

Pulling Jacks
See Jacks, Pulling

Pump Parts and Fittings
See following heads:
Connections, Tire Pump
Couplings, Magneto, Generator and Water Pump
Cups, Leather
Hose, Air, Tire Inflating (Rubber & Fabric)
Hose Assemblies, Pump
Gaskets
Impellers, Water Pump
Packing
Shafts, Transmission, Clutch and Pump

Pumps, Air
See Pumps, Tire; also Stations, Air or Water

See Page 364 for Names of Companies Represented by Above Numbers

PUMPS, Barrel Emptying

(For emptying oil or gasoline barrels or transferring contents to tanks)

86	295	600	658	700
817	1141	1212	1300	2000
2467	3713	3846	4538	5175
5510	6165	6604	6656	

Pumps, Fuel Feed

See Systems, Fuel Feed (Pump Type)

PUMPS, Gasoline (Curb)

35	176	600	700	817
1169	1231	1300	1533	1899
2370	2422	2681	3155	3238
3406	3713	3846	3917	4246
4260	5112A	5510	5526	5640
5698	6165	6604	6656	

Pumps, Gasoline and Oil

See Tanks and Systems, Gasoline and Oil Storage; also Tanks, Gasoline (Portable); also Tanks, Oil (Portable)

Pumps, Grease (Portable)

See Lubricators, Portable (High Pressure); also Lubricators, Hand

Pumps, Oil Circulating

See Lubricators or Oil Pumps, Hand

Pumps, Tire (Automatic)

See Inflators, Tire (Automatic)

PUMPS, Tire (Engine Driven)

3241   3513

PUMPS, Tire (Hand)

Imperial Brass Mfg. Co., 1225 W. Harrison St., Chicago, Ill. "Wixon" —*See adv. p.* 126

221	723	1207	1505	1801
2394	3002	3016	3151	3958
4326	4327	4757	5178	5529
6497				

PUMPS, Water Circulating

Es-M-Co Auto Products Corp., 31 34th St., Brooklyn, N. Y. (For Chevrolet Cars)—*Illustration & warehouses, p.* 70

656	1906	2384	2700	3534

PUMPS, Water Circulating, for Fords

(Auxiliary water circulators)

Jenkins Vulcan Spring Co., Eighth & N. G Sts., Richmond, Ind. "Miami," "Vulcan"—*See adv. p.* 97

656	2000	2672	2700	3116
5135	5166	5212	5715	

PUNCHES, Arch or Washer

3336   4549

PUNCHES, Center, Prick and Drift

National Machine & Tool Co., 801 S. Water St., Jackson, Mich.—*See adv. p.* 120

Truth Tool Co., 711 S. Front St., Mankato, Minn.—*See adv. p.* 128

9	643	681	1063	1132
1148	1299	1324	1921	2017
2084	2410	2841	2846	3336
3833	3918	4549	4600	4644
4726	5002	5035	5602	5611
5709	5719	5777	6208	6214
6311	6470	6489	6491	6497
6503	6679			

PUNCHES AND DIES, Standard

6701

PUNCHES, Hand

Truth Tool Co., 711 S. Front St., Mankato, Minn.—*See adv. p.* 128

778	1921	2826	3336	3905
4287	4309	4644	6208	6701

Punches, Standard

See Punches and Dies, Standard

Punches, Washer

See Punches, Arch or Washer

PURIFIERS, Oil (For Attaching to Engine)

(See also Reclaimers or Rectifiers, Oil, Garage or Repair Shop)

Cuno Engineering Corp., 80 S. Vine St., Meriden, Conn.—*Illustration, description & prices, p.* 37

6	1027A	1341	1840	2024
2630	3205	3872	3998	5589
5761	6823			

PURIFIERS, Oil, for Fords

6	224	1840	2033	2384

Push Rods

See Rods, Valve Lift (Adjustable)

PUTTY, Bedding

(For setting stationary lights in closed cars)

33	652	1619	2049	2773
5136				

Putty, Rubber

See Compounds, Tire Repair

PUTTY, Top

(Advertisers only in this publication)

Holfast Rubber Co., Lakewood Ave., Atlanta, Ga.—*See adv. p.* 65

Pyroxylin Finishes

See Lacquer

Races, Ball

See Cups and Cones, Ball

Racks, Battery Burning

See Tools, Storage Battery Repair

RACKS, Bus Baggage

295   6145   6627

Racks, Luggage

See Racks, Trunk

RACKS, Metal Tool, Stock and Tire

Lyon Metal Products, Inc., 2931 Montgomery St., Aurora, Ill.—*Illustrated, p.* 106

213	304	622	1555	1668
1893	2345	2705	3113	3488
3533	3564	3571	3782B	3840
4253	4284	4315	4350	4654
5635	5725	5728	5753	6124
6228	6621	6660		

Racks, Parts or Tool

See Racks, Metal Tool, Stock and Tire

RACKS, Service and Greasing (Automobile)

(See also Lifts, Auto)

Bear Mfg. Co., 21st St. & Fifth Ave., Rock Island, Ill. "Teeterack"— *Illustrated, p.* 123

581	2474	3256	3309	3774
3793	4784	5635	6611	

RACKS, Trunk

Bellevue Mfg. Co., Ashford Ave., Bellevue, Ohio—*Illustrated & described, p.* 52

Williams Products Co., H. E., 100 S. Main St., Carthage, Mo. — *Illustrated, p.* 32

595	640a	644	708	1576
2003	2058	2384	2392	2628
2773	2802	3410	3540	3556
3870	3943	4270	4288B	4751
5552	5692	6370	6556	

Radiator Parts, Attachments, Compounds, Service Station Equipment, etc.

See following heads:

Alcohol, Denatured
Cans, Radiator Filling
Caps, Radiator
Cement, Radiator Repair
Compounds, Radiator Cleaning
Condensers and Relief Valves, Radiator
Cores, Radiator
Fans, Radiator
Faucets, Radiator Filling
Fenders or Guards, Truck Radiator
Guns, Radiator Cleaning (High Pressure)
Heaters, Radiator and Under Hood
Hose, Radiator (Rubber and Fabric)
Lacing, Hood
Leather, Rawhide Lace
Lights, Motor Meter
Locks, Radiator Cap & Thermometer
Meters, Water Temperature Indicating
Monograms, Initials and Emblems
Ornaments, Radiator
Pans, Engine
Plugs, Radiator Testing
Screens, Radiator Protection
Shutters
Spouts, Radiator and Gasoline Tank
Tongs, Radiator Fin Straightening

RADIATORS, Engine Cooling

Simmons Mfg. Co., 3405-11 Perkins Ave., Cleveland, Ohio. (For Ford & Chevrolet cars)—*See adv. p.* 62

584	1294	2032	2089	2304
2659	2733	3402	3709	3724
3929	4669	5172	5537	5563
6187	6750	6814a	6819	

RADIO SETS

(Advertisers in this publication only)

Sparks - Withington Co., Jackson, Mich. "Sparton"—*See adv. p.* 48

United American Bosch Corp., 3664 Main St., Springfield, Mass. "American Bosch"—*See adv. p.* 69

Radius Rod Silencers

See Anti-Rattlers, Radius Rod

Rags, Wiping

See Wipers and Polishing Cloths

Rails, Coat

See Rails, Robe or Coat

Rails, Foot

See Rests or Rails, Foot

RAILS, Robe or Coat

(Metal rails or leather or fabric straps for attaching to back of front seats)

295	692	725	1048	1124
1309	2453A	3027	4296	4358
5206A	5627	5731	6783	

RAILS or STRIPS, Trunk

(Metal rails or strips to fasten to back of car to prevent trunk or other luggage from marring the finish of the body)

131	295	1628	2003	2404
2773	4215	5654	5731	6145
6627	6783			

Rams, Grease

See Drivers, Grease

Rasps

See Files and Rasps

Reamer Drives

See Drives, Reamer

Reamer Grinders

See Machines, Grinding, Reamer and Cutter

Reamer Stones
See Tools, Reamer Sharpening
Reamers, Battery Connector
See Tools, Storage Battery Repair
Reamers, Camshaft Aligning, for Fords
See Reamers and Jigs, Camshaft Aligning, for Fords
Reamers, Connecting Rod Bearing
See Reamers, Main Bearing and Connecting Rod
Reamers, Cylinder
See Reamers and Jigs, Cylinder

REAMERS (Expansion, Solid and Adjustable)
Morse Twist Drill & Machine Co., 163 Pleasant St., New Bedford, Mass.—*Illustrated, p. 118*
National Machine & Tool Co., 801 S. Water St., Jackson, Mich.—*See adv. p. 120*

124	201	756	767	819
1076	1130	1185	1253A	1918
2113	2311	2388	2456	2640
3256	3271	3830	3904	3986
4241	4263	4300	4758	5065
5083	5453	5485	5700	5753
6104	6208	6312	6343	6471
6593	6605	6679	6697	6745

REAMERS, Main Bearing and Connecting Rod

124	336	756	3271	3904
3986	5536	6104	6343	6593
6745				

REAMERS, Power
6461

REAMERS (Service Sets)

124	756	1076	2113	3256
3271	3904	5753	6343	6593
6605				

Reamers, Valve Seat
See Tools, Valve Seat Refinishing

REAMERS and JIGS, Camshaft Aligning, for Fords
3256   6745

REAMERS and JIGS, Cylinder
124   1076   2113   3271
Rebabbitting Connecting Rods
See Bearings, Rebabbitted
Rebabbitting Jigs
See Jigs, Main Bearing and Connecting Rod Babbitting
Rebabbitting Machines
See Machines, Babbitting (Main Bearing and Connecting Rod)
Reboring Machines
See Machines, Cylinder Reboring
Rebound Straps
See Straps, Rebound

RECEPTACLES, Ash
(Advertisers in this publication only)
Casco Products Corp., 1333 Railroad Ave., Bridgeport, Conn. (Combination ash receiver and cigar lighter) — *Illustration, description & prices, p. 39*
Cuno Engineering Corp., 80 S. Vine St., Meriden, Conn. (Combination ash receiver and cigar lighter)— *Illustration, description & prices, p. 37*
Rechargers, Magnet
See Chargers, Magneto Magnet

RECLAIMERS or RECTIFIERS, Oil (Garage or Repair Shop)

1545	2747	3138	4211	5525
5589				

RECORDERS, Vehicle Movement
(For recording time vehicle is used)
1311   1869   4528   5508
Records, Sales (Forms)
See Books and Forms, Accounting

Rectifiers, Alternating Current
See Chargers, Battery Service Station (Bulb Type)
Rectifiers, Oil
See Purifiers, Oil, for Attaching to Engine; also Reclaimers or Rectifiers, Oil (Garage or Repair Shop)
Reducers, Battery Post
See Tools, Storage Battery Repair
Reel Lights
See Lamps, Trouble

REELS, Automatic Extension Lamp
229

REFACERS, Valve (Electric)
(For grinding engine valves; for hand valve refacers—see Refacers, Valve (Hand); also Tools, Valve Grinding)
United States Electrical Tool Co., Dept. T, 2483 W. Sixth St., Cincinnati, Ohio. "U. S."—*Illustration, branch offices & prices, p. 25*

83	655	1058	2384	3256
3271	3518	5134	5441	5536
5578	6332	6459	6461	6745
6825				

REFACERS, Valve, Hand (Cutters)
83   1327   6825

REFACERS, Valve, Hand (Grinders)
5134   5753

REFLECTORS, Deflecting or Dimming
(For other dimming devices—see Dimmers or Deflectors, Headlight; also Visors, Headlight)
Simmons Mfg. Co., 3405-11 Perkins Ave., Cleveland, Ohio. (For Ford & Chevrolet cars)—*See adv. p. 62*

131	154	1624	3200	3759
5563				

REFLECTORS, Headlight, for Fords
Simmons Mfg. Co., 3405-11 Perkins Ave., Cleveland, Ohio—*See adv. p. 62*
1624

REFLECTORS, Safety
(For attaching to cars)

131	1553	1624	3002	4677
5134				

Reflectors, Traffic Signal
See Finders, Traffic Signal

REGISTERS, Autographic and Manifold

182	315	1849	2620	4224
4528	5110	5691	6316	

REGISTERS, Fare
1866   3050   4224   4528
Regrinding of Ball Bearings
See Bearings, Ball (Reground)

REGULATORS, Carburetor (Thermostatic)
4705
Regulators, Steam Pressure
See Controllers, Vulcanizer Steam Pressure

REGULATORS, Water Circulating
(See also Shutters, Automatic Radiator)
1190   1528   1618

REGULATORS, Window
1309   2642

Reliners, Brake
See Machines, Brake Relining
Remagnetizers, Magnet
See Chargers, Magneto Magnet
Removers, Bushing
See Extractors, Bushing; also Saws, Bushing Removing

REMOVERS, Paint, Enamel and Varnish
American Chemical Paint Co., Brookside Ave. & Reading R.R., Ambler, Pa. "Stripple"—*See adv. p. 126*

33	38	143	196	531
627	699	737	1075	1079
1524	1588	1667	2689	3041
3555	4225	4313	4504	4722
4756	5413	5514	5541	5704
5727	6746			

REPORTS, Used Car Market
National Used Car Market Report, Inc., 1315 S. Michigan Ave., Chicago, Ill.—*Illustration, description & prices, p. 128*
Reseaters, Valve
See Tools, Valve Seat Refinishing

RESTS, Arm
620   751   5670   6686

RESTS, Cushion Back
(Special removable cushions for back rests for drivers' seats)

278	291	338	664	671
1035	1192	1318	1319	1666
1838	1905	2006	2139	2628
2758	2773	3208	3849	3862
3996	4305	4308	4663A	4787
5460	6133	6615		

RESTS, Heel

1648	1829	1909	2404	3324
3349	4215	5654		

RESTS or RAILS, Foot
(For heated foot rests—see Heaters, Automobile, Truck and Bus)

40	295	1616	1648	2404
3453a	3016	3855	4296	5654
5731	6559	6627	6783	

RETAINERS, Ball
4312

RETAINERS, Rear Axle Grease
(For preventing leakage of grease from rear axle on to brakes, wheels or tires)
Jambor Tool & Stamping Co., 1261 30th St., Milwaukee, Wis. "Bull Dog"—*See adv. p. 64*
Loock & Co., R. J., 343-45 N. Gay St., Baltimore, Md. "Lightnin" (For Chevrolet cars)—*Illustrated & described, p. 51*
1111   2047   3537

RETAINERS, Rear Axle Grease, for Fords

Loock & Co., R. J., 343-45 N. Gay St., Baltimore, Md. "Lightnin"—*Illustrated & described, p. 51*

| 1002 | 1111 | 2053 | 2634 | 3537 |
| 4607 | 5051 | 5692 | 5715 | 6185 |

RETAINERS, Valve Spring

Dorman Star Washer Co., 219 E. Eighth St., Cincinnati, Ohio.—*Illustrated & described, p. 102*

| 4665 | 5051 | 5718 |

Reverse Current Cutouts

See Cut-Outs, Reverse Current

RHEOSTATS

(Used with rectifiers or motor generator sets—see also Chargers, Battery Service Station)

Hobart Brothers, Box C51, Canal Locks Square, Troy, Ohio. "HB" —*See adv. p. 108*

| 636 | 2123 | 2343A | 2724 | 2766 |
| 6573 | 6664 |

Rim Anvils

See Anvils, Rim

Rim Bolts

See Bolts, Demountable Rim

Rim Paints

See Paints, Rim

Rim Parts

See Parts, Rim

Rim Shims

See Plates, Demountable Rim Wedge

Rim Tools

See Tools, Demountable Rim Contracting

Rim Wedge Plates

See Plates, Demountable Rim Wedge

RIMS, Demountable

| 1187 | 2070 | 3534 | 6677 |

RIMS, Headlamp Door

K-D Lamp Co., 108-18 W. Third St., Cincinnati, Ohio—*See adv. p. 49*

| 644 | 1624 | 1905 | 3025 | 3200 |

RIMS, Quick Detachable

| 1187 | 2070 | 2416 |

Rims, Removable

See Rims, Demountable

RIMS or FELLOES, Steel

| 2070 | 3534 |

Ring Gages

See Gages, Plug and Ring

Ring Gears, Starter

See Gears, Starter

RINGS, Piston

Aluminum Industries, Inc., 2416 Beekman St., Cincinnati, Ohio. "Permalite"—*Illustrated, p. 10*

American Auto Products Co., 219 Ascot Place, N. E., Washington, D. C. "Nu-Life"—*Illustration, description & sizes, p. 93*

Continental Piston Ring Co., 276 Walnut St., Memphis, Tenn. "Elastic"—*Illustrated & described, p. 94*

Hebert Mfg. Co., Central St., Franklin, N. H.—*Illustrated & described, p. 91*

McQuay-Norris Mfg. Co., Cooper & Southwest Aves., St. Louis, Mo. "Superoyl," "Step Cut Compression"—*See adv. p. 88*

Ohio Hammered Piston Ring Co., 2401 Superior Ave., N. W., Cleveland, Ohio—*Illustrated, p. 88*

Piston Ring Co., Sanford & Keating Sts., Muskegon, Mich. "Quality," "Drainoil," "Sta-Tite," "Double-Slot"—*Illustrated & described, p. 14*

Renu Heteprufe Co., Holland, Mich. "Re-Nu," "Hete-Pruf" — *Illustrated & described, p. 23*

Simmons Mfg. Co., 3405-11 Perkins Ave., Cleveland, Ohio. (For Ford & Chevrolet cars)—*See adv. p. 62*

Superior Piston Ring Co., 6423 Epworth Blvd., Detroit, Mich. "Mor-Power" — *Illustrated & described, p. 90*

Wel-Ever Piston Ring Co., Speilbusch Ave., near Jackson, Toledo, Ohio. "Flexo"—*Illustrated & described, p. 92*

121	160	312	544	794
1090	1273	1654	2637	2672
2690	3136	3284	3492	3728
3817	4000	4299	4520	4556
4619	4663	4719	5039	5098
5123	5199	5440	5563	5573
5715	5726	5766	5812	6144
6192	6338	6602	6625	6689
6717	6723

RINGS, Piston Ring Expanding or Packing

(Spring or fabric ring designed to be placed under old piston ring to give increased pressure or prevent leakage)

Dorman Star Washer Co., 219 E. Eighth St., Cincinnati, Ohio.—*See adv. p. 102*

Loock & Co., R. J., 343-45 N. Gay St., Baltimore, Md. "Lightnin"—*Illustrations & prices, p. 51*

Wel-Ever Piston Ring Co., Speilbusch Ave., near Jackson, Toledo, Ohio. "Flexo"—*Described, p. 92*

16	134	312	1626	1654
3492	3537	4665	5039	5051
5098	5199	5210	5425	5573
6144	6192	6343	6625

RINGS, Wire Wheel

Globe Machine & Stamping Co., 1212 W. 76th St., Cleveland, Ohio.—*Illustrated & described, p. 53*

Rivet Burrs

See Burrs, Rivet

Rivet Clippers

See Clippers, Bolt and Rivet

Rivet Sets

See Sets, Rivet.

RIVETERS, Ring Gear

3774

Riveting Machines

See Machines, Brake Relining

Riveting Tools, Gear Ring

See Tools, Gear Ring Riveting

RIVETS, Aluminum

Chicago Rivet & Machine Co., 1830 S. 54th Ave. (Cicero P. O.), Chicago, Ill.—*See adv. p. 92*

Emsco Asbestos Co., 206 S. Crawford St., Downey, Cal.—*Illustration & warehouse stocks, p. 84*

Jambor Tool & Stamping Co., 1261 30th St., Milwaukee, Wis. "Bull Dog"—*See adv. p. 64*

Manufacturer's Belt Hook Co., 1315-21 W. Congress St., Chicago, Ill. "L-X"—*Illustrated, p. 94*

120	284	1126	1889	2702
3104	3780	3891A	4248	4655
5049	5214	5520	5533	5765

RIVETS, Brass and Copper

Chicago Rivet & Machine Co., 1830 S. 54th Ave. (Cicero P. O.), Chicago, Ill.—*See adv. p. 92*

Emsco Asbestos Co., 206 S. Crawford St., Downey, Calif.—*Illustration & warehouse stocks, p. 84*

Jambor Tool & Stamping Co., 1261 30th St., Milwaukee, Wis. "Bull Dog"—*See adv. p. 64*

Manufacturer's Belt Hook Co., 1315-21 W. Congress St., Chicago, Ill. "L-X"—*Illustrated, p. 94*

Thermoid Rubber Co., Whitehead Rd., Trenton, N. J.—*See adv. p. 85*

284	292	1083	1095	1126
1889	2702	3104	3780	3891A
4248	4655	4688	5049	5104
5214	5520	5533	5765	6129

RIVETS, Iron and Steel

Chicago Rivet & Machine Co., 1830 S. 54th Ave. (Cicero P. O.), Chicago, Ill.—*See adv. p. 92*

Dorman Star Washer Co., 219 E. Eighth St., Cincinnati, Ohio—*See adv. p. 102*

Emsco Asbestos Co., 206 S. Crawford St., Downey, Calif.—*Illustration & warehouse stocks, p. 84*

284	691	1126	1158	1234
1626	1889	3780	4248	4254
4536	4655	4688	5069	5213
5533

RIVETS, Tubular and Clinch

Auto-Vehicle Parts Co., 1040 Saratoga St., Newport, Ky. "Au-Ve-Co"—*Illustrated, pp. 34 & 35*

Chicago Rivet & Machine Co., 1830 S. 54th Ave. (Cicero P. O.), Chicago, Ill.—*See adv. p. 92*

Manufacturer's Belt Hook Co., 1315-21 W. Congress St., Chicago, Ill. "L-X"—*Illustrated, p. 94*

Tubular Rivet & Stud Co., 87 Lincoln St., Boston, Mass. "T. R. & S."—*Illustrated, p. 91*

101	292	360	1126	1518
3780	3891A	4018	4248	4655
5049	5214	5520	5533	5765
6144A	6211	6797A

Roadlights, Turning

See Lamps, Road Light (Turning)

Robe Cords or Rails

See Rails, Robe or Coat

Robe Locks

See Locks, Robe

Rod, Aluminum

See Aluminum, Sheet, Rod and Ingot

Rod Cutters

See Cutters, Rod and Bar

Rod Ends

See Ends, Rod

RODS, Connecting

Simmons Mfg. Co., 3405-11 Perkins Ave., Cleveland, Ohio. (For Chevrolet cars)—*See adv. p. 62*

| 790 | 2308 | 2693 | 4310 |

RODS, Connecting, for Fords

Simmons Mfg. Co., 3405-11 Perkins Ave., Cleveland, Ohio — *See adv. p. 62*

| 2693 | 4310 |

Rods, Connecting, Rebabbitted

See Bearings, Rebabbitted

Rods, Fibre

See Fibre, Hard

Rods, Push

See Rods, Valve Lift (Adjustable)

RODS, Rear Axle Truss, for Fords
(For reinforcing or strengthening rear axle)
774   5731   6559

Rods, Rebabbitted Connecting
See Bearings, Rebabbitted

Rods, Steering
See Links, Steering

Rods, Truss, for Fords
See Rods, Rear Axle Truss, for Fords

RODS, Valve Lift (Adjustable)
Jambor Tool & Stamping Co., 1261 30th St., Milwaukee, Wis. "Bull Dog"—*See adv. p. 64*
Simmons Mfg. Co., 3405-11 Perkins Ave., Cleveland, Ohio. (For Ford & Chevrolet cars)—*See adv. p. 62*
1128   2799   3954   5718   6717

RODS, Welding
Imperial Brass Mfg. Co., 1225 W. Harrison St., Chicago, Ill.—*See adv. p. 126*
Linde Air Products Co., 30 E. 42nd St., New York, N. Y.—*Branch offices, p. 125*
94   287   1069   2684   3016
3049   3345   3774   4011   5104
5503   5730   5811   6176   6301

ROLLERS, Curtain
1309   2665   5116   6500   6659

ROLLERS, Lumber
(Roller bed equipment for trucks and trailers)
4694   5446   5668

Rolls, Tool
See Bags or Rolls, Tool

ROPE or CABLE, Bronze Wire
(For operating brakes or cutouts)
4700

ROPES, CHAINS and BARS, Tow
(Advertisers in this publication only)
Cleveland Chain & Mfg. Co., Penna. R. R. & Henry Rd., Cleveland, Ohio —*See adv. p. 39*
Lion Chain Co., 3124 W. 51st St., Chicago, Ill. "Cub" — *See adv. p. 37*

Rotors, Timer, for Fords
See Brushes, Timer, for Fords

Rubbing Compounds
See Compounds, Rubbing and Polishing

Rubbing Felt
See Felt, Polishing and Rubbing

Rubbing Machines, Pneumatic
See Machines, Rubbing (Pneumatic)

RULES, Steel
116a   752   2410   3559   3988
5719   6311

Rumble Seats
See Seats, Rumble

Rumble Seat Slickers
See Slickers, Rumble Seat

Running Board Shields
See Shields, Running Board

Running Boards
See Boards, Running

Running Gear Aligners
See Gages, Wheel and Axle Aligning

Running-In Machines
See Machines, Burning-In

Runways, Service
See Racks, Service and Greasing

Rust Preventing and Removing Chemicals
See Compounds, Rust Preventing and Removing

Salts, Soldering
See Flux, Soldering

Sand Paper
See Paper, Emery and Sand

Sandpapering Machines, Floor
See Machines, Floor (Electric)

Sanding Machines, Portable
See Machines, Sanding (Portable Pneumatic)

Saw Blades
See Blades, Saw (Hack)

SAWS, Bushing Removing
2092

Saws, Hack
See Frames, Hack Saw

SAWS, Portable Electric
5588   5833   6178A   6766

SAWS and CUTTERS, Rotary (For Use With Portable Electric Drills)
(For cutting holes in instrument boards for mounting instruments)
655   3256   3271   3905   5708
5753   6459

SCALES, Dial
6167

Score Filling Machines
See Machines, Score Filling (Electric)

SCRAPERS, Bearing
9   1299   1324   1604   2017
2410   3336   3905   4549   4600
4726   5035   5602   5709   5753
5777   6208   6214   6491   6497
6679

SCRAPERS, Carbon
2410   2841   4241   4549   4600
4726   5035   6208   6497   6503
6717a

SCRAPERS, Garage Floor
5449

Scrapers, Storage Battery Box
See Tools, Storage Battery Repair

SCREENS, Door and Window
307

Screens, Gasoline or Oil
See Strainers, Gasoline or Oil

SCREENS, Radiator Protection
Globe Machine & Stamping Co., 1212 W. 76th St., Cleveland, Ohio—*Illustrated & described, p. 53*
163   644   782   1624   2392
2404   2819   3278   4321   4677
6810

SCREENS, Radiator Protection, for Model A Fords
2278   4557

SCREENS, Windshield Ventilating
84

SCREENS, Wire (Commercial Body)
6310

Screw Assortments, for Magnetos, Distributors, etc.
See Parts, Magneto, Coil and Distributor

Screw Cases
See Cases, Bolt and Screw

Screw Drivers
See Drivers, Screw

Screw Extractors
See Extractors, Bolt and Screw

SCREW-EYES, Brass and Iron
2756   6586

Screw Pitch Gages
See Gages, Screw Pitch

Screw Plates
See Taps, Dies and Screw Plates

Screws, Body (Assortments)
Auto-Vehicle Parts Co., 1040 Saratoga St., Newport, Ky. "Au-Ve-Co"—*Illustrated, pp. 34 & 35*

SCREWS, Brake
Dorman Star Washer Co., 219 E. Eighth St., Cincinnati, Ohio—*Illustrated & described, p. 102*
1906   1919   2619   4665

SCREWS, Cap and Set
(Advertisers in this publication only)
Cleveland Cap Screw Co., 3004 E. 79th St., Cleveland, Ohio — *Illustration & warehouse stocks, p. 95*
Jambor Tool & Stamping Co., 1261 30th St., Milwaukee, Wis. "Bull Dog"—*See adv. p. 64*

SCREWS, Coach and Lag
284   630   774   1158   1234
1854   2669   3420   4239   4254
4536   5815

SCREWS, Connecting Rod Clamp
16

SCREWS, Drive
Auto-Vehicle Parts Co., 1040 Saratoga St., Newport, Ky.—*Illustration & sizes, pp. 34 & 35*
4239   4625

SCREWS, License Plate
(See also Fasteners, License Tag)
3002

SCREWS, Machine
(Advertisers in this publication only)
Aetna Metal Products Co., 1824 Washington Ave., St. Louis, Mo.—*Illustration, prices & sizes, p. 97*

SCREWS, Thumb
295   643   1128   1158   1823
2472   3268   4688   4694   6323a
6483   6559   6730

SCREWS, Valve Adjusting
2799

Screws, Valve Tappet
See Screws, Valve Adjusting

SCREWS, Wood
Aetna Metal Products Co., 1824 Washington Ave., St. Louis, Mo.—*Illustration, prices & sizes, p. 97*
52   185   295   1095   1292
1805   1854   2702   4239   4254
4624   5056   5069   6221

Scrubbing Machines, Floor
See Machines, Floor (Electric)

Scuff Plates
See Plates, Kick or Scuff

SEALS, Lead, for Taxicab Meters
4745

SEALS, Paper
Unique Printed Products Co., 2224 N. 13th St., Terre Haute, Ind.—*See adv. p. 127*

SEALS, Rim
6615

Searchlights
See Lamps, Head (Acetylene); Lamps, Head (Electric); Lights, Spot; Lamps, Running Board (Searchlight)

Seat Adjusters
See Adjusters, Coach Seat

Seat Backs
See Backs, Metal Seat

Seat Covers
See Covers, Slip

Seat Cushions
See Cushions, Seat

Seat Pads
See Pads, Seat

Seat Protectors
See Covers, Slip; also Covers, Repairmen's

SEATS, Auxiliary
(Including folding chairs and stools)

352	2734	3724	3772	3872
5185	5570			

SEATS, Babies'
1543

SEATS, Mechanics'
(Metal chairs, with tool box on casters for use by repairman under hoisted car)
352

SEATS, Reclining (Adjustable)
307

SEATS, Rumble
2628

SEATS, Rumble, for Fords
2628

SEATS, Valve
(For insertion in worn cylinders)
794   2821   3467

Semaphores
See Signals, Direction indicating or Traffic

Separators, Gasoline or Oil
See Strainers, Gasoline or Oil

Separators, Oil
See Reclaimers or Rectifiers, Oil (Garage or Repair Shop); also Purifiers, Oil (For Attaching to Engine)

SEPARATORS, Storage Battery

161	1829	1904	1919	5609
5671	5758	6355		

SETS, Rivet

2839	2841	3336	4241	4644
6323A	6470			

Shackle Bolts
See Bolts, Spring Shackle

SHACKLES, Spring (Ball Bearing)
2010

SHACKLES, Spring (Rubber Cushioned)
Powell Muffler Co., 316 Catherine St., Utica, N. Y.—*See adv. p. 86*

SHACKLES, Spring (Self-Adjusting)
Thompson Products, Inc., 2196 Clarkwood Rd., Cleveland, Ohio. "Tryon" (Sole distributors)—*Illustrated, p. 89*
6741A

SHADES, Closed Car
(See also Awnings and Shades Combined)

644	725	1318	1319	1905
2614	3895	5116	5178	5411
5460	5762	6150	6659	

Shades, Headlight
See Dimmers or Deflectors, Headlight; also Visors, Headlight

Shades, Sun
See Visors, Windshield

Shaft Couplings
See Couplings, Magneto, Generator and Water Pump

SHAFTING, Flexible
(For driving speedometers, odometers or taximeters; also for drilling, grinding, polishing machines, etc.)
Hygrade Products Co., 333 W. 52nd St., New York, N. Y. (Speedometer)—*Illustrated, p. 86*

83	537	633	645	718
1603	2074	2085	2858	3202
3769	5759	5782	5783	5784
5832				

Shafts, Cam, for Racing Cars
See Camshafts, Special

Shafts, Clutch
See Shafts, Transmission, Clutch and Pump

Shafts, Crank, for Racing Cars
See Crankshafts, Special

Shafts, Flexible
See Shafting, Flexible; also Tubing, Flexible, Metallic

SHAFTS, Propeller
(Complete propeller shaft assemblies to blue print or specification; for universal joints only—see Joints, Universal)
Biglow & Co., L. C., 250 W. 54th St., New York, N. Y. (New York representatives for U. S. Axle Co.)—*See adv. p. 129*
U. S. Axle Co., Water St., Pottstown, Pa.—*Illustration & warehouses, p. 59*

116	641	3838	4288	4702
5576	5635			

SHAFTS, Propeller and Rear Axle
(Shafts only; for complete axles—see Axles, Rear)
Simmons Mfg. Co., 3405-11 Perkins Ave., Cleveland, Ohio. (For Ford & Chevrolet cars—*See adv. p. 62*
Spencer Mfg. Co., Main St., Spencer, Ohio—*Illustrated & described, p. 96*

714	1166	1605	2104	3474
3986a	4515	5096	5563	5651
5711	5731	6328		

SHAFTS, Transmission, Clutch and Pump
Aluminum Industries, Inc., 2416 Beekman St., Cincinnati, Ohio. "Permite"—*Illustrated, p. 10*

746	2073	2439	3775	3954

SHEARS and SNIPS, Metal

623	682A	778	1082	1324
1921	4309	4644	5420	5516

SHEAVES and PULLEYS
(For horn and cut-out cables)
1287   4266a

SHEETS, Transparent
(For windows in curtains and storm fronts)

300	1060	1663	1816	1905
2059	2773	2860	3221	6133

Shellac
See Cement, Gasket

SHELVING, Metal
Lyon Metal Products, Inc., 2931 Montgomery St., Aurora, Ill.—*Illustrated, p. 106*

304	622	1555	1668	2345
2705	3564	3571	3782b	3840
4253	4654	5728	6124	6632

SHIELDS, Air Draft Pedal, for Fords
(Rubber or metal deflectors to attach to front floor board to prevent heat from motor entering body)

291	1667	1905	2139	2773
4308	4788	6132		

SHIELDS, Bumper
(To keep bumpers and front of car free from splash)
Woodworth Specialties Co., 121-25 Montgomery St., Binghamton, N. Y.—*Illustration & prices, p. 36*
2628

SHIELDS, Frost
(To prevent frosting of windshield; see also Heaters, Windshield)
Durkee-Atwood Co., 40 Wilder St., Minneapolis, Minn.—*Illustrated & described, p. 63*
Trico Products Corp., 807 Washington St., Buffalo, N. Y. "Pilot Glass"—*See adv. p. 55*

644	2158	4651	6646

Shields, Radiator
See Screens, Radiator Protection

Shields, Rain
See Visors, Top; also Visors, Windshield

SHIELDS, Rumble Seat
163   6174

SHIELDS, Running Board
1294   2115

SHIELDS, Tonneau
(Special adjustable shields for the protection of rear seat passengers in open cars)

2404	2407	2664	3897	6131
6174				

SHIELDS, Wind
2664   5668

SHIELDS, Wing (For Open and Closed Cars)
Dole Valve Co., 1913-33 Carroll Ave., Chicago, Ill.—*Illustration, description & prices, p. 42*
Trico Products Corp., 807 Washington St., Buffalo, N. Y.—*See adv. p. 55*

163	617	1536	1557	1618
2404	2664	2773	2809	3885
3897	4503	4744	4748	5094
5406	5685	6131	6174	6190

See Page 364 for Names of Companies Represented by Above Numbers

SHIFTERS, Gear (Automatic)

6362

Shimmy Eliminators

See Checks, Steering Gear

SHIMS, Axle Caster (Aluminum)

Bear Mfg. Co., 21st St. & Fifth Ave., Rock Island, Ill.—*See adv. p. 123*

2835

SHIMS, Battery Post

Loock & Co., R. J., 343-45 N. Gay St., Baltimore, Md. "Lightnin"— *Illustration & prices, p. 51*

SHIMS, Connecting Rod

4243

SHIMS, Connecting Rod, for Fords

Loock & Co., R. J., 343-45 N. Gay St., Baltimore, Md. "Lightnin"—*Illustrated, p. 51*
Simmons Mfg. Co., 3405-11 Perkins Ave., Cleveland, Ohio — *See adv. p. 62*
Victor Mfg. & Gasket Co., 5750 Roosevelt Rd., Chicago, Ill. — *See adv. p. 77*

27   3418

Shims, Crankshaft, for Fords

See Bearings, Crankshaft Thrust, for Fords

Shims, Demountable Rim

See Plates, Demountable Rim Wedge

SHIMS, Drive Shaft Universal Ball Joint, for Fords

Loock & Co., R. J., 343-45 Gay St., Baltimore, Md. "Lightnin"—*Illustration & prices, p. 51*

SHIMS, Laminated

Federal-Mogul Corp., 11031 Shoemaker Rd., Detroit, Mich. "Laminum," "Fit-All" (Brass; distributors for Laminated Shim Co.)—*Illustration & warehouses, p. 189*

2039   3418   4243

SHIMS, Radius and Steering Rod Ball Cap, for Fords

3537

SHIMS, Rear Axle Taper, for Fords

Loock & Co., R. J., 343-45 N. Gay St., Baltimore, Md. "Lightnin" — *Illustrated, p. 51*

2795   5697

SHIMS and LINERS, Brass and Copper

Fitzgerald Mfg. Co., 691 Main St., Torrington, Conn.—*See adv. p. 76*

27   790   2079   2795   3018
3212   3275   3418   3709   4005
4243   6323a   6480

SHIMS and LINERS, Leather

1124   2441   3455

SHIMS and LINERS, Steel

Victor Mfg. & Gasket Co., 5750 Roosevelt Rd., Chicago, Ill. — *See adv. p. 77*
Williams Products Co., H. E., 100 S. Main St., Carthage, Mo.—*See adv. p. 32*

3418   6323

Shock Absorbers, Oil

See Fluid, Hydraulic Brake and Shock Absorber

SHOCK ABSORBERS, Friction, Hydraulic and Pneumatic

31   142   203   529   765
1179   1180   1548   2053   2305
2668   2671   2807   3010   3410
3423   3721   3805   3958   5653
5761   6596

SHOCK ABSORBERS, Rubber, for Coach Front Seats

3805   4677

SHOCK ABSORBERS, Spring

2671

SHOCK ABSORBERS, Spring, for Coach Front Seats

20   2707a   5051

SHOCK ABSORBERS, Spring, for Fords

224   2671

Shock Absorbers, Spring Shackle

See Shackles, Spring

SHOES, Brake, for Fords

(Including both lined or faced and unlined shoes)

115   1669   1906   2338   2411
3958   5049   5082   5159   5212
5697   6689

Shoes, Inner Tire

See Patches, Blowout (Wing)

Show Cases

See Counters, Store

Show Windows

See Fronts, Store

SHUTTERS, Automatic Radiator

(Metal shutter automatically opened or closed by a thermostat—see also Regulators, Water Circulating; for hand operated shutters—see Shutters, Metal and Fibre Radiator)

Pines Winterfront Co., 1125 N. Cicero Ave., Chicago, Ill. "Winterfront"—*Illustrated, p. 54*

SHUTTERS, Metal and Fibre Radiator

(Metal and fibre shutters for protecting the radiator in cold weather; for automatic shutters—see Shutters, Automatic Radiator)

Globe Machine & Stamping Co., 1212 W. 76th St., Cleveland, Ohio. —*Illustrated, p. 53*

97   720   1319   2402   2659
3027   3065   3857   4757

SIGHT-FEEDS, Independent

(For installing on dash or instrument boards to show when oil is feeding or flowing properly)

3016

Signal Indicators, Dash

See Lamps, Tell-Tale

Signal Rings

See Controls, Horn

SIGNALS, Direction Indicating or Traffic

(Devices for attaching to a car to enable operator to indicate when a turn or stop is about to be made)

K-D Lamp Co., 108-18 W. Third St., Cincinnati, Ohio—*Illustrated, p. 49*
Pines Winterfront Co., 1125 N. Cicero Ave., Chicago, Ill.—*See adv. p. 54*

United American Bosch Corp., 3664 Main St., Springfield, Mass. "Bosch" (Sole American representatives for Robert Bosch, A. G., Stuttgart, Germany)—*See adv. p. 69*

131   1150   2018   3115   3200
3278   3992   4538   4712   4735
5176   5212   6117   6314a   6810

SIGNS, Electric

730   2088   3311   3344   3730
5048   5522

SIGNS, Illuminated Destination, for Buses

1866

SILENCERS, Carburetor Intake

6   798   6314

SILENCERS, Hood Fastener

Continental Rubber Works, 1902 Liberty St., Erie, Pa. "Vitalic Jorgensen"—*See adv. p. 64*

31   280

SILENCERS, Overhead Valve

Dorman Star Washer Co., 219 E. Eighth St., Cincinnati, Ohio—*See adv. p. 102*

1651   2799   3805   3950   4665

Silencers, Radius Rod

See Anti-Rattlers, Radius Rod

Silencers, Steering Rod

See Anti-Rattlers, Steering Rod

Silent Chain Drives

See Chains, Timing

SILK, Curtain

725   3411   5477   6710

Silk Thread

See Thread, Silk

Siren Horns

See Horns, Siren

Six Wheel Attachments, for Trucks

See Attachments, Six Wheel, for Trucks

Slat Irons

See Irons, Slat

Sleet Eliminators

See Shields, Frost; also Heaters, Windshield

SLEEVES, Cylinder

(Sleeve inserts for use in connection with regrinding or reboring of heads in cylinders)

Dall Motor Parts Co., P.O. Station D Dept. CAM), Cleveland, Ohio— *Branch offices, p. 187*

14   4000   5779a   6758

SLICKERS, Rumble Seat

1666

Smoking Cases

See Cases, Toilet, Vanity, Card and Smoking

Snow Plows

See Plows, Snow

Snubbers

See Shock Absorbers, Spring; also Straps, Rebound

Soapstone, Tire

See Talc, Tire

SOCKETS, Bow

(For slat irons—see Irons, Slat)

720   2407

SOCKETS, Electric Lamp

Pines Winterfront Co., 1125 N. Cicero Ave., Chicago, Ill.—*See adv.* 54

1214	1553	1629	1804	2723
3856	4712	4735	5179	5604

Sockets, Wrench

See Wrenches, Socket

SOLDER

(See also Solder, Self-Fluxing)

1530	1810	2044	2384	2632
2732	3210	3265	3762	4238
4337	6315	6637		

SOLDER, Aluminum

120	1895a	2044	4541	4617
5608	5811	6637	

SOLDER, Self-Fluxing

(See also Solder)

330	2313	3265	4238	4689

Soldering Acid, Fluid, Flux, Paste and Salts

See Flux, Soldering

Soldering Furnaces

See Furnaces, Soldering

Spark Coil Covers

See Covers, Coil

Spark Coils

See Coils, Ignition

Spark Controls, Automatic

See Controls, Automatic Spark (For Model A Fords)

Spark Intensifiers

See Intensifiers, Spark

Spark Plug Equipment

See Brushes, Spark Plug; Cables (Sets); Cases, Spark Plug; Cleaners, Spark Plug; Covers, Spark Plug; Machines, Spark Plug Cleaning; Terminals, Wire; Testers, Spark Plug

Sparking Points

See Points, Contact

Speedometer Gears

See Gears and Pinions, Speedometer

Speedometer Joints

See Joints, Speedometer Swivel

Speedometer Parts

See Parts, Speedometer

Speedometer Shaft, Cable and Casing

See Shafting, Flexible

SPEEDOMETERS

6	1311	1547	5761	6570

Spindle Bolt Nuts, for Fords

See Nuts, Spindle Bolt, for Fords

SPINDLES, Emergency Rear Axle, for Fords

100	4241	6825

Splitters, Nut

4743

Spoke Covers

See Covers, Spoke

Spoke Straighteners

See Tools, Spoke Straightening (For Model A Fords)

Spoke Tighteners

See Tighteners, Spoke

Spoke Tightening Compounds

See Compounds, Wood Wheel Tightening

SPOKES, Wire

4254

SPONGES and CHAMOIS

104	188	666	667	1334
2091	2450	3064	4209	4316
4738	5115	5468	6463	

Spoons, Body and Fender

See Tools, Body and Fender Repair

Spotlights

See Lamps, Spot

SPOUTS, for Oil Dispensers

3989

SPOUTS, Radiator and Gasoline Tank

1139	5710

SPRAYERS, Paint, Varnish and Lacquer

Brunner Mfg. Co., 1800 Broad St., Utica, N. Y.—*Illustration, description & prices, p.* 113

Champion Pneumatic Machinery Co., 8170 S. Chicago Ave., Chicago, Ill. —*See adv. p.* 112

Hobart Brothers, Box C-51, Canal Locks Square, Troy, Ohio. "HB"— *Illustrated, p.* 108

Imperial Brass Mfg. Co., 1225 W. Harrison St., Chicago, Ill.—*Illustration & prices, p.* 126

Kellogg Mfg. Co., 65 Humboldt St., Rochester, N. Y. — *Illustration, specifications & prices, p.* 2

Manley Mfg. Co., 929 Connecticut Ave., Bridgeport, Conn. — *Illustrated, p.* 38

35	212	310	570	646
719	759	1086	1141	1331
1587	1830	1837	1867	2394
2766	3014	3016	3123	3151
3513	3774	3823	3856	3891
3950	4301	4319	4353	4501
4603	4713	4729	4801	5524
5568	5656	5781	5811	6324
6745	6767			

Spreaders, Spring

See Tools, Spring Spreading

Spreaders, Tire

See Tools, Tire Spreading

Spring Parts, Repair Equipment, etc.

See Bolts; Bumpers; Clips; Covers; Jacks, Spring; Links; Lubricators; Machines, Spring (Elliptic); Oilers; Pins, Cotter; Pullers; Shackles; Tools, Spring

SPRINGS, Auxiliary (Truck)

3

Springs, Brake

See Springs, Small (Flat or Coil)

SPRINGS, Carburetor Choker, for Fords

3855

Springs, Coil

See Springs, Small (Flat or Coil)

Springs, Engine Valve

See Springs, Small (Flat or Coil)

SPRINGS, Leaf

Jenkins Vulcan Spring Co., Eighth & N. G Sts., Richmond, Ind. "Vulcan"—*Illustrated, p.* 96

St. Louis Spring Co., 3129-39 Washington Ave., St. Louis, Mo. "Moog" —*Illustrated, p.* 97

Service Spring Co., 735 St. Paul St., Indianapolis, Ind.—*Illustrated, p.* 98

3	85	618	632	810
1016	1081	1089	1152	1582
1819	2653	2668	2802	3116
3410	3497	3543	3786	4720
5196	5414	5509	6119	6183
6188	6222	6347		

Spring Leaf Inserts

See Inserts, Spring Leaf

SPRINGS, Seat or Upholstery

Chicago Coil Spring Co., 3101 Carroll Ave., Chicago, Ill. "Chicago-Quality"—*Illustrated, p.* 98

190	1113	1269	1514	2421
2634	3996	4242	5111	5202

SPRINGS, Small (Flat or Coil)

Chicago Coil Spring Co., 3101 Carroll Ave., Chicago, Ill. "Chicago-Quality"—*Illustrated, p.* 98

Dorman Star Washer Co., 219 E. Eighth St., Cincinnati, Ohio—*Illustration & description, p.* 102

Es-M-Co Auto Products Corp., 31 34th St., Brooklyn, N. Y. — *Illustration & warehouses, p.* 70

Jambor Tool & Stamping Co., 1261 30th St., Milwaukee, Wis. "Bull Dog"—*See adv. p.* 64

Loock & Co., R. J., 343-45 N. Gay St., Baltimore, Md. "Lightnin"—*Illustrated, p.* 51

Peck Spring Co., 68 Broad St., Plainville, Conn.—*Illustrated, p.* 55

Simmons Mfg. Co., 3405-11 Perkins Ave., Cleveland, Ohio. (For Ford & Cheverolet cars)—*See adv. p.* 62

16	190	339	632	1016
1113	1287	1514	1626	1906
2053	2619	2702	2834	2838
3104	3146	3327a	3537	4010
4556	4643	4649	4665	4680
5049	5563	5687	5718	6134
6214	3347	6586	6818	

Springs, Starting Motor Drive

See Parts, Starting Motor Drive

Springs, Upholstery

See Springs, Seat or Upholstery

Springs, Valve

See Springs, Small (Flat or Coil)

SPROCKETS

3510	3982	6699

SQUARES, Machinists'

752	2410	3559	5719	6311

Stabilizers, Engine, for Fords

See Supports, Engine, for Fords

Stabilizers, Steering

See Checks, Steering Gear

STAMPS, Steel

(For numbering or lettering parts)

682a	2643	2778	3227	3542
3822	3869	3988	4026	4708
5816	6311	6586a		

STAMPS, Time

Simplex Time Recorder Co., 50 Time Ave., Gardner, Mass.—*See adv. p.* 127

325	1147	2096	5816

STANDS, Axle Repair (Rear)

685	3256	5635	6745

Stands, Burning-In

See Machines, Burning-In

STANDS, Display
(Painted, enameled or lithographed advertising)
2095   4735

STANDS, Display, for Oil Dispensers
128   2635

STANDS, Electric Test
(For testing starting and lighting equipment)
Hobart Brothers, Box C-51, Canal Locks Square, Troy, Ohio "H-B" —*Illustrated, p. 108*

100	559	576a	1226	1625
2766	3256	3282a	5511	5635
5676	6616	6745		

STANDS, Engine Repair
100	685	1082	3256	3774
4241				

STANDS, for Portable Electric Drills and Grinders
Sunnen Products Co., 7900 Manchester St., St. Louis, Mo.—*Illustration, description & prices, p. 26*

336	655	1123	1161	2764
2848	3271	3409	3564	3730
5708	6118	6312	6332	6459
6571				

STANDS, Portable Tool and Parts
Lyon Metal Products, Inc., 2931 Montgomery St., Aurora, Ill.—*See adv. p. 106*

114	213	304	352	685
2848	3409	3564	3571	3730
3782b	4284	4741	5635	5690
5753	5833	6660		

Stands, Repair
See Stands, Axle Repair (Rear); also Stands, Engine Repair; also Stands, Portable Tool and Parts

Stands, Running-In
See Machines, Burning-In

STANDS, Tire Building
532	3894	4233a	4249	4250

STANDS, Transmission and Differential Repair
3256   4241

STAPLES, Insulated
(Fibre insulated staples for car wiring)
661   5532   6816

Starter Equipment
See Brushes; Buttons; Cable; Drives; Extensions, Starter Button; Keys; Pedals

STARTERS, Hand, for Fords
1064a   3855

Starting Crank Holders
See Holders, Starting Crank

Starting Cranks
See Cranks, Starting

Starting Motor Drive Parts
See Drives, Starter and Parts (Bendix); also Parts, Starting Motor Drive

Starting Motors
See Motors, Starting

Starting Motor Housings
See Housings, Starting Motor

STATIONS, Air or Water
(For installing at curb for free air and water service)
Brunner Mfg. Co., 1800 Broad St., Utica, N. Y. (Distributors)—*Illustrated & described, p. 113*
Champion Pneumatic Machinery Co., 8170 S. Chicago Ave., Chicago, Ill. —*Illustrated & described, p. 112*
Curtis Pneumatic Machinery Co., 1927 Kienlen Ave., St. Louis, Mo. —*Illustrated & described, p. 111*
Hobart Brothers, Box C-51, Canal Locks Square, Troy, Ohio. "HB" —*See adv. p. 108*
Service Station Equipment Co., Conshohocken, Pa. "Eco"—*Illustrated & described, p. 121*

176	700	759	1086	1345
1568	2384	2394	2646	2681
2766	3245	3406	3513	3774
3794	4741	4784	5408	5505
5510	6324	6604	6798	

Steel Wool
See Wool, Steel

Steering Apparatus
See Anti-Rattlers; Bolts; Boots, Checks; Gears; Links; Locks; Wheels

Steering Knuckle Bushing Mills, for Fords
See Mills, Steering Knuckle Bushing, for Fords

STENCILS
2643	3227	3542	3822	3869
3988	5816	6586a		

Step Lights
See Lamps, Cowl, Fender, Tail, Parking, Running Board and Clearance

Step Plates
See Plates, Step

STEPS, Rumble Seat
1616	1829	2412	4215	6151
6218	6627			

Stethoscopes, Engine Testing
See Instruments, Engine Testing

Stills, Oil
See Purifiers, Oil (for Attaching to Engines); also Reclaimers or Rectifiers, Oil (Garage or Repair Shop)

STILLS, Water
(For distilling water for use in storage batteries)
Atlas Copper & Brass Mfg. Co., 2724-42 High St., Chicago, Ill. "Polarstill" — *Illustrated & described, p. 117*

286	550	559	5771	5821

STOCKS, Die
250	1253a	2694	4758	6146a

STONES, Contact Point Cleaning
4735

STOOLS, Steel Shop
213	1668	3294	3782b	4284
5690	6495			

Stop Light Flashers
See Flashers, Stop Light

Stop Lights
See Signals, Direction Indicating or Traffic

Storage Battery Flushers
See Flushers, Storage Battery

STORAGE SYSTEMS, Shop
(Consisting of platform-trucks, lifting devices, sectional bins, folding stakes, racks, etc.)
Lyon Metal Products, Inc., 2931 Montgomery St., Aurora, Ill.—*Illustrated, p. 106*
2009

Storage Tanks and Systems
See Tanks and Systems, Gasoline and Oil Storage

Store Counters
See Counters, Store

Store Fronts
See Fronts, Store

STRAIGHTENERS, Frame
Bear Mfg. Co., 21st St. & Fifth Ave., Rock Island, Ill.—*Illustrated & described, p. 123*
Utility-Strate Mfg. Co., 105 Glasgow Ave., Fort Wayne, Ind. "Utili-Strate" — *Illustration, description & prices, p. 118*
100

Straightening Equipment
See Bars, Axle Straightening; Bars, Straightening; Machines, Wheel Straightening (Disc); Presses, Straightening; Straighteners, Frame

Strainers, Carburetor Air Intake
See Cleaners, Air

STRAINERS, Gasoline or Oil
(For use between tank and carburetor and in oil pumps to remove dirt and water; for strainer funnels—see Funnels, Metal)
Hygrade Products Co., 333 W. 52nd St., New York, N. Y.—*See adv. p. 86*
Imperial Brass Mfg. Co., 1225 W. Harrison St., Chicago, Ill. — *See adv. p. 126*

6	86	224	611	613
1341	1894	2018	2619	2858
3016	3202	3563	4503	4791
6145	6823			

Strap Loops
See Loops, Brass Snap and Strap

STRAPS, Gripping
(For removing or tightening hub and radiator caps, headlight rims, etc.)
518   5059   5134   5135

STRAPS, Leather
Auto-Vehicle Parts Co., 1040 Saratoga St., Newport, Ky. "Au-Ve-Co"—*See adv. pp. 34 & 35*

23	360	692	1048	1111
1124	2441	2773	3027	3455
5075	5113	5191	5214	5612
5672	6734			

STRAPS, Rebound
(See also Shock Absorbers, Friction, Hydraulic and Pneumatic)
1124   2441   3891a   5637

Straps, Starting Crank
See Holders, Starting Crank

Straps, Tire and Top
See Straps, Leather; also Straps, Web

STRAPS, Web
Williams Products Co., H. E., 100 S. Main St., Carthage, Mo.—*See adv. p. 32*

146	644	692	781	1048
1192	1318	2360	2378	3455
5182	5214	5598	5637	5794

See Page 364 for Names of Companies Represented by Above Numbers

Street Sweepers
See Automobiles (Street Sweepers, Flushers and Sprinklers)

STRETCHERS, Brake Lining

2116   4791   5214   5721a

STRIPS, Sill

(For setting door and window glass)

251

STRIPS, Windshield Weather

Continental Rubber Works, 1902 Liberty St., Erie, Pa. "Vitalic"— *See adv. p. 64*

1274   1580   1829   1893   2412
2625   3324   3903   4607

Striping Pencils
See Tools, Striping

Strut Rods, for Fords
See Rods, Rear Axle Truss, for Fords

STUDS

Cleveland Cap Screw Co., 3004 E. 79th St., Cleveland, Ohio—*Warehouse stocks, p. 95*

774   1128   1158   1173   2056
2663   2680   3420   3756   4211
4239   4536   4555   6221   6309
6323a   6483   6568   6644

SUPERCHARGES

6574a

Supplies, Dealers and Jobbers
See Jobbers and Supply Dealers

Supports, Car
See Jacks, Tire Saving

SUPPORTS, Engine, for Fords

720   2795   5567   6825

Supports, Top
See Fasteners, Top

Surface Gages
See Gages, Surface

Surface Plates
See Plates, Surface

Surplus Parts and Accessories, Buyers of
See Parts and Accessories, Buyers of Surplus

Sweepers, Street
See Automobiles (Street Sweepers, Flushers and Sprinklers)

Switch Keys
See Keys, Switch and Starting

Switch Locks
See Locks, Ignition

Switchboards, Charging
See Panels and Switchboards, Charging

SWITCHES, Floor or Foot

(For signals, horns, headlight dimming, etc.)

542   1201

SWITCHES, Headlight Dimming (Dash)

(For other dimming devices—see Dimmers or Deflectors, Headlight; also Switches, Light; also Switches, Headlight Dimming, Steering Wheel)

1257   2723   4304   5179

SWITCHES, Headlight Dimming, for Fords

(Extensions on steering wheels)

5105

SWITCHES, Headlight Dimming, Steering Wheel

3539   5105   6218

SWITCHES, Ignition

United American Bosch Corp., 3664 Main St., Springfield, Mass. "Bosch." (Sole American representatives for Robert Bosch, A.G., Stuttgart, Germany)—*See adv. p. 69*

1201   1257   1629   3856   5179
5604   5655   5687   6314a

SWITCHES, Light

(For turning on and off electric lights on car; see also Switches, Headlight Dimming, Steering Wheel)

Pines Winterfront Co., 1125 N. Cicero Ave., Chicago, Ill.—*See adv. p. 54*
United American Bosch Corp., 3664 Main St., Springfield, Mass. "Bosch." (Sole American representatives for Robert Bosch, A.G., Stuttgart, Germany)—*See adv. p. 69*

131   582   1201   1214   1257
1548a   1553   1629   2347   2723
3278   3809   3856   3935   4712
4735   5179   5604   5687   6314a

SWITCHES, Rear Signal

Pines Winterfront Co., 1125 N. Cicero Ave., Chicago, Ill.—*See adv. p. 54*
Signal Mfg. Co., 587 Washington St., Lynn, Mass. "Eveready" — *See adv. p. 45*
Simmons Mfg. Co., 3405-11 Perkins Ave., Cleveland, Ohio. (For Ford and Chevrolet cars) — *See adv. p. 62*

1201   1214   1553   1629   2053
3278   3926   4712   5556   5563
5604   6810

SWITCHES, Starter

Es-M-Co Auto Products Corp., 31 34th St., Brooklyn, N. Y.—*Illustration & warehouses, p. 70*
Jambor Tool & Stamping Co., 1261 30th St., Milwaukee, Wis. "Bull Dog"—*See adv. p. 64*
United American Bosch Corp., 3664 Main St., Springfield, Mass. "Bosch." (Sole American representatives for Robert Bosch, A.G., Stuttgart, Germany)—*See adv. p. 69*

322   337   339   1257   1547
1548a   1857   1906   2472   2858
3104   3202   3462   4317   4601
5687   6314a   6634

SWITCHES, Starter, for Fords

Es-M-Co Auto Products Corp., 31 34th St., Brooklyn, N. Y. — *Illustration & warehouses, p. 70*

5210

Switches, Stop Light
See Switches, Rear Signal

SYNCHRONIZERS, Ignition Contact Point

Brunswick Engineering Co., 30 Cortlandt St., New Brunswick, N. J. "C & H"—*Illustration & prices, p. 42*

100   228   533   559   760
3702a   4007   4601   6616

SYSTEMS, Accounting

Comfort Printing Specialty Co., 107 N. Eighth St., St. Louis, Mo.—*See adv. p. 108*

Systems, Brake
See Brakes, Air

Systems, Chassis Lubricating
See Fittings, Lubricating

SYSTEMS, Crank Case Drainage Disposal

(For storing and disposing of crank case oil in pits)

700

SYSTEMS, Fuel Feed (Pump Type)

6   345   3709   5002a   5761
6464

SYSTEMS, Fuel Feed (Vacuum Tank Type)

5761

Systems, Ignition
See Coils, Ignition; also Magnetos, Ignition

SYSTEMS, Ignition (Complete)

(See also Coils, Ignition; also Magnetos, Ignition—For combined ignition and starting systems—see also Motors, Starting; also Magnetos, Ignition; also Distributors, Ignition)

United American Bosch Corp., 3664 Main St., Springfield, Mass. "Bosch." (Sole American representatives for Robert Bosch, A.G., Stuttgart, Germany)—*See adv. p. 69*

1547   1548a   1857   3462   6314a

SYSTEMS, Lighting (Electric)

(See also Generators, Electric Lighting and Battery Charging (Auto)

1547   1548a   1857   3462   6314a

Systems, Lubricator, for Fords
See Lubricators and Oil Pumps, for Fords

Systems, Monorail
See Systems, Overhead Carrying

Systems, Oil Purifying
See Reclaimers or Rectifiers, Oil (Garage or Repair Shop)

SYSTEMS, Overhead Carrying

110   1134   1254   2649   2840
3510   3546   4306   5118   5193
5535   6799

SYSTEMS, Tire Repair

2071   2416   3239

Systems, Trolley
See Systems, Overhead Carrying

TACHOMETERS

Veeder-Root, Inc., 22 Sargeant St., Hartford, Conn.—*Illustrated, p. 54*

TACKS, Upholstery

Auto-Vehicle Parts Co., 1040 Saratoga St., Newport, Ky. "Hit 'em" —*Illustration & sizes, pp. 34 & 35*

292   305a   360   528a   720
725   2358   2750   2773   2782
3821   3916   4254   4271   5552
6180   6816

TAGS, Paper Shipping

(Advertisers in this publication only)

Comfort Printing Specialty Co., 107 N. Eighth St., St. Louis, Mo.—*See adv. p. 108*

TAGS, for Storage, Repair Work, Battery Charging, etc.

(Advertisers in this publication only)

Comfort Printing Specialty Co., 107 N. Eighth St., St. Louis, Mo.—*Illustration, description & prices, p. 108*

See Page 364 for Names of Companies Represented by Above Numbers

St. Louis Tag Co., 217 Locust St., St. Louis, Mo.—*Illustration & price, p. 114*
Unique Printed Products Co., 2224 N. 13th St., Terre Haute, Ind.—*See adv. p. 127*

TAKE-OFFS, Power
(Attachments to permit the use of the car motor for general power purposes)

144	748	1305	2744	4020
4020a	5418	6779		

TAKE-OFFS, Power, for Fords
6203   6575

TALC, Tire
(Including soapstone and mica tire powders)

1211	1667	1829	1833	2412
2416	3046	3247	3523	3903
3922	5046	5413	6340	6344
6702a	6729			

Tank Body Equipment
See Buckets, Tank Body; also Vents, Tank Body; also Faucets, Tank Body

Tank Equipment
See Floats; Gages; Keys; Locks; Spouts; Trucks

TANKS, Chemical Fire
(For installation on motor propelled fire apparatus)

165   703   4718   5407

TANKS, Compressed Air (Portable)
69   1345

TANKS or CANS, Emergency or Reserve
(For carrying a reserve supply of gasoline or oil; for reserve cocks—see Valves, Two-Way Tank)

1632   5559   5831   6790

TANKS or CANS, Emergency or Reserve, for Fords
2795

TANKS, Crankcase Draining (Portable)
734

Tanks, Fire
See Tanks, Chemical Fire

TANKS, Gasoline (Portable)
(Tanks and pumps on wheels, for dispensing gasoline in gallons)

176	700	1231	2370	5510
6604	6656			

TANKS, Inner Tube Testing

704a	1632	2826	3894	3930
4757	4784	5178	6649	

Tanks, Metal Parts Washing
See Machines, Washing (Metal Parts)

TANKS, Oil (Portable)
(Tanks and pumps on wheels, for dispensing oil in quarts; for oil dispensing trays, bottles and spouts—see Dispensers, Oil)

176	700	2370	3513	8846
5510	6604		

Tanks, Reserve
See Tanks or Cans, Emergency or Reserve

Tanks, Storage
See Tanks and Systems, Gasoline and Oil Storage

Tanks, Vacuum and Compression Gasoline
See Systems, Fuel Feed (Vacuum Tank Type)

TANKS and SYSTEMS, Gasoline and Oil Storage
(For storing and handling oil in filling stations; for Portable Tanks—see Tanks, Gasoline (Portable); also Tanks, Oil (Portable)

69	176	295	347	600
640	650	677	700	704a
753	817	1112	1129	1523
1533	1820	1899	2027	2051a
2370	2697	3238	3294	3846
3917	4016	4246	4260	4691
4784	5000	5112a	5122	5444
5510	5526	5584	6165	6604
6656				

Tap Sharpening Tools
See Tools, Tap Sharpening

TAPE, Insulating and Tire
Holfast Rubber Co., Lakewood Ave., Atlanta, Ga.—*See adv. p. 65*

204	205	231	693	1007
1589	1653	1667	1829	2071
2416	2343	2355	2773	2781
3127	3247	3469	3903	3925
3983	4525	4533	4613a	4733
5046	5413	5612	5807	6344
6456	6664			

TAPE, Masking

561	1667	1816	1829	3883
3921	3925	5514		

Tape, Tire
See Tape, Insulating and Tire

Taper Pins
See Pins, Taper

TAPS, DIES and SCREW PLATES
Morse Twist Drill & Machine Co., 163 Pleasant St., New Bedford, Mass.—*Illustrated, p. 118*
National Machine & Tool Co., 801 S. Water St., Jackson, Mich.—*Illustration & prices, p. 120*

124	364	569	756	819
1033	1082	1253a	2317	2456
3256	3271	3986	4241	4758
5083	5212	5214a	5700	6146a
6312	6745	6755	6679	6830

Tappet Screws
See Screws, Valve Adjusting

Tappet Silencers, Overhead Valve
See Silencers, Overhead Valve

Tappet Wrenches
See Wrenches, Tappet

Tappets, Valve
See Rods, Adjustable Valve Lift

Tar Distributors
See Automobiles (Oil, Tar and Asphalt Distributors)

Tar Removing Compounds
See Compounds, Tar Removing

Taxicab Meter Seals
See Seals, Lead, for Taxicab Meters

Taxicabs
See Automobiles (Taxicabs)

TAXIMETERS
4528   4723

Tees, Pipe
See Fittings, Tube (Copper or Brass)

TELEPHONES, Closed Car
1257   1548a   1595

Tell-Tale Lights
See Lamps, Tell-Tale

TENTS, Touring

621	740	1192	1225	1318
2157	2728	3277	3862	4698
4798	5448	5773	6200	6639

Terminal Connectors
See Connectors, Terminal (Storage Battery Charging)

Terminal Forming Tools
See Tools, Wire Terminal Forming

Terminal Paints
See Paints, Storage Battery Terminal

Terminal Tongs
See Tools, Storage Battery Repair

TERMINALS, Storage Battery

153a	559	760	1321	1868
1927	2735	2861	3244	3331
3437	4215	4299a	4523	4556
4610	4672	4785	5034a	5425
5687	5739	6107	6139	6355
6561	6678	6681	6772	

TERMINALS, Wire
(See also Connectors, Dry Battery; also Tools, Wire Terminal Forming)
Fitzgerald Mfg. Co., 691 Main St., Torrington, Conn.—*See adv. p. 76*
Manhattan Insulated Wire Co., 17-23 W. 60th St., New York, N. Y.—*See adv. p. 65*
Rajah Co., Locust Ave. & Nelson St., Bloomfield, N. J.—*Illustration, description, specifications & prices, p. 100*
Wittek Mfg. Co., 4305-9 W. 24th Place, Chicago, Ill. "Tab"—*Illustrated & described, p. 279*

541	1063	1257	1851	2079
3002	3202	3349a	3771	4556
4735	5036	5494a	5539	6681
6763				

Test Benches or Stands, Electric
See Stands, Electric Test

Test Clips
See Clips, Electrical Test

Testers, Acid
See Hydrometers

Testers, Battery
See Hydrometers; also Instruments, Storage Battery Testing

Testers, Brake
See Machines, Brake Testing; also Instruments, Brake Testing; also Tools, Brake Testing

Testers, Electrical
See Instruments, Electrical Circuit Testing

Testers, Engine
See Instruments, Engine Testing; also Dynamometers

Testers, Gasoline
See Hydrometers

TESTERS, Gasoline Mileage
6823

TESTERS, Headlight (Chart Type)
2436

TESTERS, Headlight (Optical)
4353   6611

TESTERS, Headlight (Photometric)
1526

Testers, Insulation
See Instruments, Insulation Testing

TESTERS, Spark Plug

62	100	337	1226	2120
3849	4775	5179	5511	6686

TESTERS, Valve Seat
3271

See Page 364 for Names of Companies Represented by Above Numbers

TESTERS, Valve Spring
5134

Testing Tanks
See Tanks, Inner Tube Testing

Thermometer Lights, Radiator
See Lights, Motor Meter

Thermometer Locks, Radiator
See Lock, Radiator Cap and Thermometer

Thermometers, Radiator
See Meters, Water Temperature Indicating

THERMOMETERS, Vulcanizer
1091a　3992　6109

Thermostats, Water Circulating
See Regulators, Water Circulating

Thread Cutting Dies
See Taps, Dies and Screw Plates

Thread Restoring Tools
See Tools, Thread Restoring

THREAD, Silk
3868a

THREAD, Top and Upholstery
3868a

TICKETS, Bus Passenger
2397　4799　5042

Tie Rod Bolts
See Bolts, Steering Knuckle

TIGHTENERS, Automatic Fan Belt, for Fords
134

Tighteners, for Chain Drives
See Chain Adjustments, Automatic or Manual

TIGHTENERS, Spoke
(For chemical tighteners—see Compounds, Wood Wheel Tightening)
Hubco Mfg. Co., 404 W. Conway St., Baltimore, Md.—*Illustrated, p. 104*
2469a　2795　6213

TIGHTENERS, Tire Chain
Cleveland Chain & Mfg. Co., Penna. R. R. & Henry Rd., Cleveland, Ohio —*See adv. p. 39*
Continental Rubber Works, 1902 Liberty St., Erie, Pa. — *See adv. p. 64*
Gates Rubber Co., 909 S. Broadway, Denver, Colo. "Gates Vulco"—*See adv. p. 62*
Lion Chain Co., 3124 W. 51st St., Chicago, Ill. "Cub" — *See adv. p. 37*
McKay Co., Union Trust Bldg., Pittsburgh, Pa.—*Illustrated, p. 33*
Signal Mfg. Co., 587 Washington St., Lynn, Mass. "Lion" — *Illustrated & described, p. 45*
United States Chain & Forging Co. See McKay Co.

142	508	1174	1274	1347
1906	2053	2074	2324	2860
3040	3468	3512	5051	5420
5556	6586			

Tightening Compounds, Wood Wheel
See Compounds, Wood Wheel Tightening

Time Checks
See Checks, Brass, Time, Tool and Pay

Time Recording Clocks
See Clocks, Time Recording

Time Stamps
See Stamps, Time

Timer Brushes, for Fords
See Brushes, Timer, for Fords

Timer Points
See Points, Contact

Timer Rings, Fibre
See Fibre, Hard

Timer Rotors, for Fords
See Brushes, Timer, for Fords

Timers, Ignition
See Distributors, Ignition

TIMERS, Ignition or Spark (For Model T Fords)
Jambor Tool & Stamping Co., 1261 30th St., Milwaukee, Wis. "Bull Dog"—*See adv. p. 64*

208	620	690	2795	2861
3104	3207	3545	4515	6170
6218				

Timing Chains
See Chains, Timing

Timing Gears
See Gears, Timing (Metallic and Non-Metallic)

Tire Bolts, Carriers, Covers, Cover Emblems, Gages, Jacks, Locks, Racks, Straps, Wells, etc.
See specific heads, such as Bolts, Stove and Tire

Tire Chains and Equipment
See Chains; Fasteners; Links; Pliers; Tighteners; Tools, Tire Chain Repair

Tire Curing Bags
See Bags, Steam Tire Curing

Tire Pump Connections
See Connections, Tire Pump

Tire Pumps
See Inflators, Tire (Automatic); also Pumps, Tire (Hand)

Tire Repair Materials
See Cement; Compounds; Flaps; Kits; Patches; Plugs; Talc; Tape

Tire Repair Tools and Machines
See following heads:
Knives, Tire Repair
Machines, Tire Buffing
Machines, Tire Cutting Off
Machines, Tire Inspecting
Machines, Tire Removing and Replacing
Presses, Solid Tire Truck Applying
Stands, Tire Building
Systems, Tire Repair
Tools, Tire
Tools, Tire Deflating
Tools, Tire Spreading
Tools, Tire Tread Rolling
Tools, Tire Vulcanizing

Tire Valves, Parts and Tools
See following heads:
Caps, Tire Valve Dust
Tools, Tire Valve Fishing
Tools, Tire Valve Rethreading
Valves, Tire

TIRES, Pneumatic
(See also Tubes, Inner)
Continental Tire Corp., Dept. C, 1508-15 Michigan Ave., Chicago, Ill. (Distributors)—*See adv. p. 82*

Gates Rubber Co., 999 S. Broadway, Denver, Colo. "Gates Vulco"—*See adv. p. 62*

1003	1039	1205	1240	1276
1286	1295	1342	1534	1560a
1591	1649	1829	2019	2071
2076	2324	2355	2365	2412
2416	2740	2798	3031	3247
3260	3469	3706	3710	3778
3903	3934	3949	4028	4342
4354	4360	4560	4659	4686
5426	5495	6205	6344	

TIRES, Solid

1649	1829	2071	2076	2355
2412	2416	2798	3247	3469
4560	6344			

Toilet Cases
See Cases, Toilet, Vanity, Card and Smoking

TOILETS, Bus
1825

TONGS, Radiator Fin Straightening
1895a

Tongs, Terminal
See Tools, Storage Battery Repair

Tool Bags
See Bags or Rolls, Tool

Tool Boxes
See Boxes, Tool (Metal); also Boxes, Tool (Wood)

Tool Cribs
See Cribs, Tool

Tool Grinders, Plain
See Machines, Grinding (Plain Tool)

Tool Holders
See Holders, Lathe, Planer, Shaper and Slotter.

Tool Racks
See Racks, Metal Tool, Stock and Tire

Tool Rolls
See Bags or Rolls, Tool

TOOLS, Babbitt Peining
6745

Tools, Bearing Pulling
See Pullers, Bearing

TOOLS, Bearing Shaving and Burnishing (Main and Connecting Rod)
5218

TOOLS, Body and Fender Repair, (Hand)
Fostoria Pressed Steel Corp., Dept. CM-1, N. Main St., Fostoria, Ohio —*Illustration, prices & warehouse stocks, p. 71*
Peck, Stow & Wilcox Co., 217-313 Center St., Southington, Conn. "Pexto'—*Illustration, description prices, p. 124*

35	1921	2017	2115	2627
2841	3256	3509	4549	4644
4726	5709	5763	6191	6717a
6745				

TOOLS, Body and Fender Repair (Portable Electric)
3779

TOOLS, Brake Band
5709　6717a

Tools, Brake Lining Stretching
See Stretchers, Brake Lining

See Page 364 for Names of Companies Represented by Above Numbers

TOOLS, Brake Testing

(See also Gages, Brake and Drum Concentricity)

3240 3817 4353 5049 6551

TOOLS, Clutch Pilot Alignment

National Machine & Tool Co., 801 S. Water St., Jackson, Mich.—*Illustration & prices, p. 120*

Shepard & Moore, Inc., Advance Bldg., Cleveland, Ohio. "Shur-Shot"—*See adv. p. 47*

TOOLS, Contact Resurfacing

5039

Tools, Cotter Pin

See Pullers, Cotter Pin

TOOLS, Crank Pin Truing

336 5441 5578

TOOLS, Cylinder Honing

(Abrasive tools for use in drill presses for cylinder refinishing work)

Sunnen Products Co., 7900 Manchester St., St. Louis, Mo.—*Illustration, description & prices, p. 26*

336	1019	1307	2113	2436a
2615	3270	3271	3472	3794
3879	4662	5775	5801	6745

TOOLS, Cylinder Reboring (Portable)

(See also Machines, Cylinder Reboring; also Bars, Boring; also Tools, Cylinder Honing)

349	2113	2436a	2615	4762
5192	5416	5456	5578	5715
5775	6461			

TOOLS, Cylinder Regrinding (Portable)

(See also Tools, Cylinder Honing)

349 2848 5578

TOOLS, Demountable Rim Contracting

510	686	765	1669	1905
2717	2841	3015	3794	3894
4757	5038	5135	5410	5424
6197	6630	6733		

Tools, Fender Repair

See Tools, Body and Fender Repair

Tools, Frame Straightening

See Straighteners, Frame

TOOLS, Front Axle Bushing Removing and Replacing

5489a

TOOLS, Gear Ring Riveting

3256 6611

TOOLS, Generator Bracket Saving

35

TOOLS, Heat Blowing (Electric)

(For thawing gas or oil lines, melting, grease, etc.)

719

TOOLS, Ignition Point Refinishing

2626

TOOLS, Key Cutting

1201

TOOLS, Lathe, Planer, Shaper and Slotter

250	1589b	2684	3986	5058
5629	6730			

TOOLS, Metal Finishing (Portable Electric)

(Portable flexible shaft machines with attachments for grinding, polishing, sanding, etc.)

83	532	633	645	1031
3769	4252	4269	5783	6616

TOOLS, Piston Fitting

3256

TOOLS, Piston Pin Hole Grinding

2848

TOOLS, Piston Pin Honing

336 756 3271 6593

TOOLS, Piston Pin and Connecting Rod Bushing Honing

336 2615

TOOLS, Piston Pin Removing and Installing

National Machine & Tool Co., 801 S. Water St., Jackson, Mich. (For Model A Fords) — *Illustration & prices, p. 120*

35	2084	2627	2841	3201
4241	5753			

TOOLS, Piston Ring Compressing

(To facilitate the entering of piston and ring into cylinder)

National Machine & Tool Co., 801 S. Water St., Jackson, Mich. — *See prices, p. 120*

26	35	62	100	131
681	1499	2795	3492	4241
4299	5039	5105	5451	5753
6208	6491	6559		

TOOLS, Piston Ring Groove Cleaning

National Machine & Tool Co., 801 S. Water St., Jackson, Mich. — *See adv. p. 120*

Truth Tool Co., 711 S. Front St., Mankato, Minn.—*See adv. p. 128*

35	2627	2676	2795	3918
4241	4726	5753	6208	6471
6717a				

TOOLS, Piston Ring Removing

(Special pliers or tongs for installing or removing rings from pistons)

Truth Tool Co., 711 S. Front St., Mankato, Minn.—*See adv. p. 128*

35	4241	4663	5212	6208
6717a			

Tools, Planer

See Tools, Lathe, Planer, Shaper and Slotter

TOOLS, Reamer Sharpening

3256 6630

TOOLS, for Replacing Lubricating Fittings

6197

Tools, Rim Contracting

See Tools, Demountable Rim Contracting

Tools, Service Station

See Tools and Machines, Service Station

Tools, Soldering

See Irons, Soldering

TOOLS, Spoke Straightening (For Model A Fords)

6197

TOOLS, Spring Coiling

5817

TOOLS, Spring Leaf Separating

1178

TOOLS, Spring Service Station

336 1920

TOOLS, Spring Shackle

(For use in removing or replacing shackle bolt bushings)

336 3256 6208

TOOLS, Spring Spreading

(For lengthening springs so that shackles and bolts slip easily into place)

National Machine & Tool Co., 801 S. Water St., Jackson, Mich. (For Fords only)———*Illustration, prices, p. 120*

TOOLS, Starter Ring Gear Aligning

2754

TOOLS, Storage Battery Repair

35	100	559	560	576a
623	756	1084	1219	1324
2703	2714	2814	3256	3537
3794	3839	4523	4672	4708
6107	6208	6355	6374	6461
6561	6585a			

TOOLS, Striping

3999 4603

TOOLS, Tap Sharpening

6630

TOOLS, Thread Restoring

National Machine & Tool Co., 801 S. Water St., Jackson, Mich. (Axle) —*Illustration & prices, p. 120*

2841 5083

TOOLS, Tire

(For taking off and putting on tires; for rim tools—see Tools, Demountable Rim Contracting)

Jenkins Vulcan Spring Co., Eighth & N. G Sts., Richmond, Ind.—*See adv. p. 97*

510	532	656	726	1089
1132	1604	2017	2158	2676
2714	3116	3786	3794	4549
5038	6197	6222	6503	

TOOLS, Tire Chain Attaching

(Screw or toggle clamps to draw ends of tire chains together when putting on wheel so they may be easily hooked or fastened)

1077 4791

TOOLS, Tire Chain Repair

(For removing old and applying new cross sections on tire chains; see also Pliers, Tire Chain)

142	623	1077	1237	3518
3721	3774		

TOOLS, Tire Deflating

(For holding down valve plunger to allow air to escape without removing the plunger)

5534

TOOLS, Tire Spreading

(For tire spreading machines—see Machines, Tire Inspecting)

Loock & Co., R. J. 343-45 N. Gay St., Baltimore Md. "Lightnin"—*Illustrated & prices, p. 51*

See Page 364 for Names of Companies Represented by Above Numbers

TOOLS, Tire Spreading—Cont'd.

Manley Mfg. Co., 929 Connecticut Ave., Bridgeport, Conn. — *Illustrated & described*, p. 38
Shepard & Moore, Inc., Advance Bldg., Cleveland, Ohio "Little Inspector"—*See adv.* p. 47

510	532	1253a	1549	2841
3537	3774	4233a	4277	6151
6197	6649			

TOOLS, Tire Tread Rolling

3894

TOOLS, Tire Valve Fishing

5465

TOOLS, Tire Valve Rethreading

Dill Mfg. Co., 686 E. 82nd St., Cleveland, Ohio—*See adv.* p. 43
5465

TOOLS, Tire Vulcanizing

510	3894	5520

TOOLS, Tube Flaring

Imperial Brass Mfg. Co., 1225 W. Harrison St., Chicago, Ill.—*See adv. p.* 126
National Machine & Tool Co., 801 S. Water St., Jackson, Mich.—*Illustration & prices*, p. 120

35	2841	3016	3256	3918
5753				

TOOLS, Valve Grinding

(For valve grinding machines—see Refacers, Valve (Electric); also Refacers, Valve (Hand)

26	83	224	656	681
696	726	759	812	1063
1107	1669	2410	3201	3905
3998	4249	5105	5134	5451
5611	5657	5720	5753	5783
6208	6221	6559	6825	

TOOLS, Valve Grinding (Air)

759

Tools, Valve Grinding (Portable Electric)

See Drills, Grinders and Polishers, Electric Portable

TOOLS, Valve Guide Cleaning

5485

TOOLS, Valve Key Inserting and Removing

1160	3201	3205	3818a

TOOLS, Valve Lifting and Spring Compressing

Simmons Mfg. Co., 3405-11 Perkins Ave., Cleveland, Ohio. (For Ford & Chevrolet cars)—*See adv.* p. 62
Sunnen Products Co., 7900 Manchester St., St. Louis, Mo. — *Illustration, description & prices*, p. 26
Truth Tool Co., 711 S. Front St., Mankato, Minn.—*See adv.* p. 128

224	681	726	1160	1627
1639	1905	2017	2410	2795
2841	3002	3201	3220	3256
3818a	4241	4600	4726	4757
5105	5155	5212	5563	5611
5775	5801	6208	6497	6559
6825				

Tools, Valve Refacing

See Refacers, Valve; also Tools, Valve Grinding

TOOLS, Valve Seat Refinishing

(Special reamers for refinishing worn or pitted valve seats; for tools for installing new valve seats—see Tools, Valve Seat Renewing)

National Machine & Tool Co., 801 S. Water St., Jackson, Mich. — *See adv. p.* 120

83	124	501	518	655
756	1019	1058	1063	1327
1669	1918	2113	3256	3271
4241	4348a	4804	5484	5578
5580	5611	5657	6221	6459
6461	6471	6593	6605	6745
6825				

TOOLS, Valve Seat Renewing

(For installing new valve seats; for valve seat refinishing tools—see Tools, Valve Seat Refinishing)

83	553	1019	2821	4348a
5218	5578			

TOOLS, Wheel Retaining, Ring Removing and Replacing

6197

TOOLS, Wire Stripping

3003

TOOLS, Wire Terminal Forming.

1851

TOOLS and MACHINES, Service Station

(Special tools or machines for servicing one or more certain makes of cars)

100	3256	3907a

Top Lining Dye

See Dye, Top Lining

Top Materials

See Cloth; also Leather

Top Parts and Fittings

See Bows; Covers; Enclosures; Fasteners; Fittings; Hardware; Holders; Irons; Protectors, Sockets; Straps

Top Patches

See Patches, Top Repair

Top Putty

See Putty, Top

Top Repair Cement

See Cement, Top Repair

TOPS, Rumble Seat

Williams Products Co., H. E., 100 S. Main St., Carthage, Mo.—*Illustrated, p.* 32

TORCHES, Welding, Cutting and Brazing

(For complete oxy-acetylene outfits—see Machines and Equipment, Oxy-Acetylene Welding)

Imperial Brass Mfg. Co., 1225 W. Harrison St., Chicago, Ill.—*Illustrated, p.* 126
Linde Air Products Co., 30 E. 42nd St., New York, N. Y. "Orweld," "Prest-O-Weld" — *Illustration & branch offices*, p. 125

67	555	626	792	2654
3016	3049	3507	3891	4708
4801a	4803	5419	5608	5811
6171	6176	6487	6586a	

TORCHES and FURNACES, Gasoline or Kerosene

221	626	1168	1343	1597
1923	2674	2826	3159	5091
5129	5419	5608	6217	6566

Tote Boxes

See Boxes, Tote (Metal)

Towers, Air

See Stations, Air or Water

Towing Equipment

See Bars, Towing, One-Man Type; Ropes, Chains and Bars, Tow; Trucks, Casters and Spare Wheels, Wrecking

Town Plates

See Plates, Town

Tracks, Overhead Carrying

See Systems, Overhead Carrying

Trailer Parts

See Couplers; Equalizers; Wheels

TRAILERS, Automobile Transport

2720	3258

TRAILERS, Commercial

316	1106	1157	1540	1584
1870	2012	2151	2153	2720
2731	2744	2772	3258	3283
3431	3511a	3802	3832	4201
4285	4325	4540	4640	5071
5095	5103a	5164	5446	5654a
5665	5668	5701	6129a	6182
6377	6638	6685		

TRAILERS, Tourists'

316	1106	1157	3511a	5654a
5701				

TRANSFERS, Decalcomania

148	3868	4614	5605

Transmission Lever Guards, for Fords

See Guards, Transmission Lever, for Fords

Transmission Linings, for Fords

See Lining, Brake, for Fords

Transmission Locks

See Locks, Transmission

Transmission Repair Equipment

See following heads

Clamps, Transmission Band Assembling
Cleaners, Differential and Transmission
Derricks, Transmission
Stands, Transmission and Differential Repair

Transmission Shafts

See Shafts, Transmission, Clutch and Pump

TRANSMISSIONS, Auto

(For individual gears—see Gears and Pinions, Metal)

New Process Gear Co., 500 Plum St., Syracuse, N. Y.—*See adv. p.* 237
Simmons Mfg. Co., 3405-11 Perkins Ave., Cleveland, Ohio (For Ford & Chevrolet cars)—*See adv. p.* 62

733	1305	1574	1605	1671
2119	2156	3775	3838	4020
4297	4665	5101	5563	6577

Transparent Sheeting

See Sheets, Transparent

TRANSPORTING SYSTEMS, Shop

(Consisting of platform-trunks, lifting device, sectional bins, folding stakes, racks, etc.)

2009

TRAPS, Refuse (For Cylinder Hones)

35

Trays, Ash

See Receptacles, Ash

See Page 364 for Names of Companies Represented by Above Numbers

Trestles
See Horses and Trestles

Trimmers, Battery Post and Separator
See Tools, Storage Battery Repair

TRIMMINGS, Metal
(See Fasteners, Curtain; Fittings, Top; Handles, Car Door; Hinges, Door; Locks, Door (Automobile); Irons, Slat)

Auto-Vehicle Parts Co., 1040 Saratoga St., Newport, Ky.—*See adv. pp. 34 & 35*

295	360	720	3016	5543
5654	6783			

TRUCK-TRACTORS

28	636a	1164	1346	1593
1881	2040	2119	2351	2433
2667	2679	2731	3029	3048
3458	3558	5747	6569	6691
6795a				

TRUCKS, Acetylene and Oxygen Tank

555

TRUCKS, CASTERS and SPARE WHEELS, Wrecking
(For towing in cars with damaged wheels or axles)

3774	3845	4258	6611

TRUCKS, Factory

87	180	213	507	1881
2009	2814	3010	3429	3570
4253	5409a	5446	5504	5505
5690	6808			

Trucks, Motor
See Automobiles, Commercial

TRUCKS, Rear Axle

3256

Trucks, Repair
See Creepers, Repair

Trunk Carriers and Racks
See Racks, Trunk

TRUNKS, Leather, Fabric and Board

Williams Products Co., H. E., 100 S. Main St., Carthage, Mo. (Steel skeleton frame)—*Illustrated, p. 32*

10	75	576	640a	1200
1675	1928	2003	2058	2319
2628	2773	3410	3540	3556
3720	3978	4262	4270	4701
5003	5515	5552	5706	5814
5819	6114	6556		

TRUNKS, Metal
(See also Carriers, Luggage Folding)

1576	1667	1675	2003	2319
2384	2773	3277	3409	3540
3794	4701	4747	5552	6597

Trusses, Rear Axle, for Fords
See Rods, Rear Axle Truss, for Fords

Tube Bending Coils
See Coils, Tube Bending (Wire)

Tube Deflators
See Tools, Tire Deflating

Tube Patches
See Patches, Tube Repair

TUBES, Inner
(For outer casings or shoes — See Tires, Pneumatic)
(Advertisers in this publication only)

Gates Rubber Co., 999 S. Broadway, Denver, Colo. "Gates Vulco"—*See adv. p. 62*

Tubes, Mica
See Mica Sheets, Tubes, Washers and Cores

TUBING, Brass and Copper

Imperial Brass Mfg. Co., 1225 W. Harrison St., Chicago, Ill. — *See adv. p. 126*

295	3016	3507a	4011	4228
4653	5510a	6629a		

Tubing Connections
See Fittings, Tube (Copper or Brass)

TUBING, Engine

Powell Muffler Co., 316 Catherine St., Utica, N. Y.—*Illustrated, p. 86*

5702	5731

Tubing, Fibre
See Fibre, Hard

Tubing Fittings
See Fittings, Tube (Copper or Brass)

Tubing, Flexible Control
See Conduit, Flexible Car Wiring

TUBING, Flexible Metallic
(Crimped or wound tubing for exhaust piping, carburetors, heaters, speedometer shaft covering, wire covering, etc.; see also Tubing, Oil and Gasoline Line)

American Metal Hose Co., 67 Jewelry St., Waterbury, Conn.—*Branch offices, p. 100*

Chicago Tubing & Braiding Co., 210 N. Clinton St., Chicago, Ill. "Rex-Tube" — *Illustrated & described, p. 102*

International Metal Hose Co., 10109-15 Quincy Ave., Cleveland, Ohio—*Specifications, p. 99*

116a	171	280	718	1133
1177	1815	2037	2108	3045
4014	4656	6163	6335	6818

TUBING, Oil and Gasoline Line
(Brass, copper, aluminum, etc.)

American Metal Hose Co., 67 Jewelry St., Waterbury, Conn.—*Branch offices, p. 100*

Chicago Tubing & Braiding Co., 210 N. Clinton St., Chicago, Ill. "Rex-Tube"—*See adv. p. 102*

1133	4228	4653	5702	5731
6163	6210		

TUBING, Soft Rubber

Continental Rubber Works, 1902 Liberty St., Erie, Pa. "Vitalic"—*See adv. p. 64*

Thermoid Rubber Co., Whitehead Rd., Trenton, N. J.—*See adv. p. 85*

280	634	812	1146	1240
1274	1591	1664	1829	1862
1893	1909	2029	2071	2365
2412	2416	2773	3324	3844
3903	4302	4525	5049	5451
6129	6160	6344		

TUBING, Spaghetti and Loom

1815

Tubing Unions
See Fittings, Tube (Copper or Brass)

TURN-BUCKLES, Wrought

41	1234	1823	5156

TURNTABLES, Automobile
(See also Casters, Garage)

1025	2711	6324	6695

TWINE, Tufting

801

UNDERCOATS, Fender and Hood

American Chemical Paint Co., Brookside Ave. & Reading R. R., Ambler, Pa. "Paradox"—*Description, p. 126*

Sherwin-Williams Co., Dept. 733, 101 Prospect Ave., N. W., Cleveland, Ohio—*See adv. p. 21*

38	2389	5541

Undercoats, Nitro-Cellulose Base
See Lacquer

UNDERCOATS, Oil-Base
(For nitro-cellulose and pyroxylin finishes)

Sherwin-Williams Co., Dept. 733, 101 Prospect Ave., N. W., Cleveland, Ohio—*See adv. p. 21*

38	177	586	1022	1186
2389	4756	5136	5514	5541

UNDERCOATS, Pyroxylin Base
(For nitro-cellulose and pyroxylin finishes)

Sherwin-Williams Co., Dept. 733, 101 Prospect Ave., N. W., Cleveland, Ohio—*See adv. p. 21*

33	38	1660	2389

Undercutters
See Machines, Commutator Turning and Insulation Undercutting

Unions, Hose
See Connections, Tire Pump

Unions, Tubing
See Fittings, Tube (Copper or Brass)

Universal Joint Covers
See Boots, Steering Knuckle and Joint

Universal Joint Discs
See Discs, Universal Joint

Universal Joint Parts
See Parts, Universal Joint

Universal Joints
See Joints, Universal

Upholstery Dressing
See Dressing, Leather; also Dressing, Top (Weatherproof)

Upholstery Fabrics
See Broadcloth, Upholsterery; also Corduroys, Upholstery; also Whipcord, Upholstery; also Plush, Upholstery; also Velvet, Upholstery; also Velours, Upholstery

Vacuum Brakes
See Brakes, Power

Vacuum Cleaners
See Cleaners, Vacuum

Vacuum Tank Boosters
See Boosters, Vacuum

Vacuum Tanks
See Systems, Fuel Feed (Vacuum Tank Type)

Valve Cores
See Valves, Tire

Valve Dust Caps
See Caps, Tire Valve Dust

Valve Fittings, Engine
See Guides, Valve; Retainers, Valve Spring; Rods, Valve Lift (Adjustable); Seats, Valve; Silencers, Overhead Valve

Valve Repair Equipment, Engine
See Compounds, Valve Grinding; Lifters; Refacers; Tools, Valve

Valve Seat Testers
See Testers, Valve Seat

Valve Spring Testers
See Testers, Valve Spring

See Page 364 for Names of Companies Represented by Above Numbers

VALVES, Ball Check

(Small ball check valves with tubing connections; see also Fittings, Tube (Copper or Brass)

Imperial Brass Mfg. Co., 1225 W. Harrison St., Chicago, Ill. — *See adv. p. 126*

1249	1618	3337	3713	6735

VALVES, Cut-Out

(For mufflers, heaters, etc.; for cut-out pedals—see Pedals, Horn and Cut-Out)

169	268	1287	2402	2411
3544	3985	4682	4757	5212
5720	5733	6675		

VALVES, Engine Poppet

Aluminum Industries, Inc., 2416 Beekman St., Cincinnati, Ohio. "Permite"—*Illustrated, p. 10*

Burgess-Norton Mfg. Co., 517 Peyton St., Geneva, Ill. "B-N"—*Branch offices, p. 187*

Emsco Asbestos Co., 206 S. Crawford St., Downey, Calif. "Jadson"—*Illustration, description & warehouse stocks, p. 84*

McQuay-Norris Mfg. Co., Cooper & Southwest Aves., St. Louis, Mo. "Rich" (Distributors for Wilcox-Rich Corp., 9771 French Rd., Detroit, Mich.)—*See adv. p. 88*

Simmons Mfg. Co., 3405-11 Perkins Ave., Cleveland, Ohio. (For Ford & Chevrolet cars)—*See adv. p. 62*

Thompson Products, Inc., 2196 Clarkwood Rd., Cleveland, Ohio—*Illustrated, p. 89*

Wilcox-Rich Corp., 9771 French Rd., Detroit, Mich (McQuay - Norris Mfg. Co., Cooper & Southwest Aves., St. Louis, Mo., and King Quality Products Co., 2320 Cooper St., St. Louis, Mo., sole distributors)—*Illustrated, p. 101*

121	705	800	1063	1229
1889	3102	3728	3873	4000
4556	4665	5563	6141	6169
6192	6717			

Valves, Gasoline Reserve

See Valves, Two-Way Tank

VALVES, Hose (Radiator Filling)

Hansen Mfg. Co., 1786 E. 27th St., Cleveland, Ohio — *Illustration, description & prices, p. 112*

VALVES, Needle

Lincoln Brass Works, 2067 12th St., Detroit, Mich.—*See adv. p. 73*

1249	1618	3502	3563	6171
6735				

Valves, Relief (Radiator)

See Condensers and Relief Valves, Radiator

VALVES, Safety or Emergency

(For safeguarding contents of tanks—protection in case of fire or broken off faucets)

2697	3713

VALVES, Tire

Dill Mfg. Co., 686 E. 82nd St., Cleveland, Ohio—*See adv. p. 43*

Peck Spring Co., 68 Broad St., Plainville, Conn. — *Illustrated & described, p. 55*

Schrader's Son, A., 470 Vanderbilt Ave., Brooklyn, N. Y.—*See adv. p. 29*

22	1602	1840	4643	5173
5465	6615	6663		

VALVES, Two-Way Tank

(Fuel reserve valves or cocks)

Imperial Brass Mfg. Co., 1225 W. Harrison St., Chicago, Ill. — *See adv. p. 126*

Lincoln Brass Works, 2067 12th St., Detroit, Mich.—*See adv. p. 73*

5142a

Vanity Cases

See Cases, Toilet, Vanity, Card and Smoking

Vaporizers, Electric

See Heaters, Mixture

Varnish Removers

See Removers, Paint, Enamel and Varnish

Varnish Sprayers

See Sprayers, Paint, Varnish and Lacquer

Varnish Spraying Booths

See Booths, Spraying (Paint and Varnish)

VASES, Bouquet

131	617	2678	2809	3772
4507	4735	5179	5604	6337
6810				

VELOURS, Upholstery

725	3485	4542	5200

VELVETS, Upholstery

3411

Ventilating Door Hooks

See Hooks, Door Ventilating

VENTILATORS, Bus

1866

VENTILATORS, Closed Car

1309	1651	2668	2758	2809
2819	2860	3426	4748	4800
5451				

VENTILATORS, Cowl

713a	3974	4215	5105	5421
5592				

VENTS, Tank Body

2697	3713

VISCOSIMETERS

197	1587	6493

Vise Grips or Jaws

See Grips or Jaws, Vise

VISES, Battery

559	6818

VISES, Machinists' Bench

Columbian Vise & Mfg. Co., 9017 Bessemer Ave., Cleveland, Ohio — *Illustration, specifications & prices, p. 122*

Manley Mfg. Co., 929 Connecticut Ave., Bridgeport, Conn. "Acco"—*Illustrated, p. 38*

Parker Co., Charles, 48 Elm St., Meriden, Conn. — *Illustrated & described, p. 120*

142	184	272	635	1232
1887	2113	2159	2346	2410
3010	3048a	3774	3905	4338
4624	4694	4766	5068	5159
5709	6660	6799	6817	

VISES, Pipe

Armstrong Bros. Tool Co., 304 N. Francisco Ave., Chicago, Ill. — *Illustrated, p. 119*

250	1632	2456	3048a	3107
4624	4649	4694	4766	5068
5159	6166	6191	6730	6799
6817				

VISES, Piston

National Machine & Tool Co., 801 S. Water St., Jackson, Mich. — *See adv. p. 120*

35	91	100	1307	3256
4241	5039	5753	6825	

VISES, Piston, for Fords

91

Visors, Door

See Ventilators, Closed Car

VISORS, Headlight

(See also Dimmers or Deflectors, Headlight; also Reflectors, Deflecting or Dimming)

96

VISORS, Top

(Leather or fabric strip to attach to top to close up space between top and windshield)

2139	2773

VISORS, Windshield

338	778	1905	2139	2404
2614	2664	2809	2819	3294
6150	6733			

Voltmeters

See Ammeters, Instrument Board

Vulcanizer Steam Pressure Controllers

See Controllers, Vulcanizer Steam Pressure

VULCANIZERS, Portable

510	3239	3894	4764

VULCANIZERS, Shop

36	211	510	532	640
1097	2699	3894	4202	4233a
4241	4277	5520	6333	6616
6649				

Vulcanizing Cement

See Cement, Tire Repair

Vulcanizing Tools, Tire

See Tools, Tire Vulcanizing

WADDING and BATTING, Cotton

153	549	801	3422	3528
4218				

Warmers, Foot

See Heaters, Automobile

WARMERS, Hand (Electric)

(Electric heating device to attach to steering wheel)

5176

Wash Aprons

See Aprons, Wash

Washer Cutters

See Cutters, Washer or Gasket

Washer Punches

See Punches, Arch or Washer

Washers, Air

See Cleaners, Air

WASHERS, Automobile (Brushes)

138	811	1040	2154	2482
3912	4550	4721a	6461	

WASHERS, Automobile (Equipment)

(Overhead attachments, nozzles, etc.)

1141	2075	2329	3794	4353
4661	5197	6145		

WASHERS, Automobile (Fountain Brushes and Mops)

1040	1055	2154	3002	6344a
6619				

See Page 364 for Names of Companies Represented by Above Numbers

WASHERS, Automobile (Systems)

(Water, steam and compressed air)

Bean Mfg. Co., John, 18 Hosmer St., Lansing, Mich.—*Illustrated,* p. 31

Brunner Mfg. Co., 1800 Broad St., Utica, N. Y. (Hydraulic)—*Illustration, description & prices,* p. 113

Champion Pneumatic Machinery Co., 8170 S. Chicago Ave., Chicago, Ill. —*Illustrated & described,* p. 112

Curtis Pneumatic Machinery Co., 1927 Kienlen Ave., St. Louis, Mo. (Air and hydraulic) — *Illustrated & described,* p. 111

Hobart Brothers, Box C-51, Canal Locks Square, Troy, Ohio—*Illustrated,* p. 108

Imperial Brass Mfg. Co., 1225 W. Harrison St., Chicago, Ill.—*See adv.* p. 126

Manley Mfg. Co., 929 Connecticut Ave., Bridgeport, Conn. — *Illustrated,* p. 38

Service Station Equipment Co., Conshohocken, Pa. "Eco"—*Illustrated & described,* p. 121

577	759	1086	1213	1345
1559	1587	1831	2025	2051a
2147	2394	2646	2766	2792
3016	3406	3513	3774	4036
4222	4603	4775	5188	5510
6324	6604	6611	6745	

WASHERS, Brass and Copper

Aetna Metal Products Co., 1824 Washington Ave., St. Louis, Mo.— *Illustration & prices,* p. 97

Auto-Vehicle Parts Co., 1040 Saratoga St., Newport, Ky. "Au-Ve-Co"—*Illustrated,* pp. 34 & 35

Victor Mfg. & Gasket Co., 5750 Roosevelt Rd., Chicago, Ill. — *See adv.* p. 77

27	52	175	295	360
1095	1158	2702	3212	4607
4688	4697	5104	5765	6323a
6480				

WASHERS, Bronze

27	174	2039	6323a	6480

Washers, Cork
See Gaskets, Cork

Washers, Engine
See Cleaners, Engine

WASHERS, Felt

Advance Packing & Supply Co., 806 Washington Blvd., Chicago, Ill. —*See adv.* p. 87

Felt Products Mfg. Co., 1510 Carroll Ave., Chicago, Ill. "Fel-Pro" —*Illustrated,* p. 75

Fitzgerald Mfg. Co., 691 Main St., Torrington, Conn. "Fitz-Rite"—*Illustrated & described,* p. 76

Simmons Mfg. Co., 3405-11 Perkins Ave., Cleveland, Ohio (For Ford & Chevrolet cars)—*See adv.* p. 62

Victor Mfg. & Gasket Co., 5750 Roosevelt Rd., Chicago, Ill. — *See adv.* p. 77

27	47	49	258	509
717	1250	1271	2046	2047
2079	2322	3709	4607	4697
5563	6480	6651		

WASHERS, Finishing

27	4607	5053

Washers, Hard Fibre
See Fibre, Hard

WASHERS, Iron & Steel

16	27	175	1158	1234
2702	3201	3212	3817	4536
4665	4688	4697	5213	6221
6323a				

Washers, Leather
See Gaskets, Leather

WASHERS, Lock

(See also Nuts, Lock)

Aetna Metal Products Co., 1824 Washington Ave., St. Louis, Mo.— *Illustration, prices & sizes,* p. 97

Dorman Star Washer Co., 219 E. Eighth St., Cincinnati, Ohio—*See adv.* p. 102

National Umbrella Frame Co., Penn St. & Belfield Ave., Philadelphia, Pa. "Never Slip"—*Illustrated & described,* p. 104

Williams Products Co., H. E., 100 S. Main St., Carthage, Mo.—*Illustrated,* p. 32

175	575	1626	2033	2472
2702	3212	3777	4240	4243
4264	4271	4746	4763	5093
5519	5753	6139	6559	6586
6662	6679			

Washers, Mica
See Mica Sheets, Tubes, Washers and Cores

Washers, Paper
See Gaskets, Paper

Washers, Pump
See Gaskets, Leather

WASHERS, Spacing

Aetna Metal Products Co., 1824 Washington Ave., St. Louis, Mo. —*Illustration, prices & sizes,* p. 97

Auto-Vehicle Parts Co., 1040 Saratoga St., Newport, Ky. "Au-Ve-Co"—*See adv.* pp. 34 & 35

Dorman Star Washer Co., 219 E. Eighth St., Cincinnati, Ohio—*See adv.* p. 102

52	175	337	360	1626
2472	2702	3212	5753	6323a

Washers, Steel
See Washers, Iron and Steel

Washers, Thrust
See Shims and Liners

WASHERS, Windshield and Window

(With water reservoir, self-fed felt pad and rubber squeegee)

1050

WASHERS, Wrought

175	4536	5156	6323a

Washing Brushes
See Washers, Automobile (Brushes); also Washers, Automobile (Fountain Brushes and Mops)

Washing Machines, Metal Parts
See Machines, Washing (Metal Parts)

WASTE, Cotton

(For wiping rags—see Wipers and Polishing Cloths)

651	2157	2607	2608	2777
3814	3820	5628	5705	6776

Watch Holders
See Holders, Watch

Watches
See Clocks

Watchmen's Clocks
See Clocks, Watchmen's

Water Circulating Pumps
See Pumps, Water Circulating

Water Circulating Regulators
See Regulators, Water Circulating

Water Pump Impellers
See Impellers, Water Pump

Water Stations
See Stations, Air or Water

Water Temperature Indicators
See Meters, Water Temperature Indicating

Weather Strips
See Strips, Windshield Weather

WEBBING, Jute and Cotton

231	781	801	2360	2378
2773	3422	5182	5214	5637
5794				

Wedge Plates
See Plates, Demountable Rim Wedge

Weight Plates
See Plates, Load Data

Welders' Clamps
See Clamps, Welders (Oxy - Acetylene)

Welding Machines
See Machines and Equipment, Electric Welding (Arc); also Machines and Equipment (Oxy - Acetylene Welding)

Welding Rods
See Rods, Welding

Welding Torches
See Torches, Welding, Cutting and Brazing

WELLS, Tire (Fender)

2115

Wheel Dressers
See Dressers, Emery Wheel

Wheel Lugs
See Lugs, Wheel

Wheel Parts and Accessories
See Locks; Parts, Wheel; Rings, Wire Wheel

Wheel Removing Equipment
See Cranes; Knockers; Pullers

Wheel Testing Equipment
See Gages, Wheel and Axle Aligning; Machines, Balancing, Wheel

Wheel Tightening Compounds
See Compounds, Wood Wheel Tightening

WHEELS, Cast Metal

Motor Wheel Corp., Lansing, Mich. "Spoksteel" — *Illustration & distributors,* p. 103

198	1262a	1535	1898	2359
2800	3021	3230	3873a	4005
4629	6466	6506	6670	6685

WHEELS, Change-Over Unit

2070	3021	3967

WHEELS, Disc (Steel)

Motor Wheel Corp., Lansing, Mich. "Tuarc," "Disteel" — *Illustration & distributors,* p. 103

770	3021

WHEELS, Dual Pneumatic

198	770	1262a	1535	1584
1898	2143	2800	3021	4629
5417	6351	6506	6685	

Wheels, Emergency
See Wheels, Special Pneumatic Spring and Emergency

Wheels, Emery
See Wheels, Grinding

See Page 364 for Names of Companies Represented by Above Numbers

WHEELS, Fifth
(For mounting on rear of chassis or vehicle platform so that semi-trailer can be attached)
3802

WHEELS, Grinding

11	152	633	1031	4235
4351	4761	5565a	5663	5744
6332	6459	6461		

WHEELS, Malleable Iron
6351

WHEELS, Special Pneumatic, Spring and Emergency
4648

Wheels, Spoked
See Wheels, Cast Metal

WHEELS, Steering, Non-Locking (Non-Tilting)
584   3035a

WHEELS, Steering, Non-Locking (Non-Tilting) (For Ford and Chevrolet Cars)
1905   3035a

WHEELS, Trailer

770	1535	2359	2800	4275
5417	6506			

Wheels, Trailing, for Trucks
See Attachments, Six Wheel, for Trucks

WHEELS, Wire
Motor Wheel Corp., Lansing, Mich.—*Illustration & distributors, p. 103*
770   1603

WHEELS, Wood
Motor Wheel Corp., Lansing, Mich.—*Illustration & distributors, p. 103*
234   1824a   2800   4275   5417

WHIPCORD, Upholstery
3411   3422

Whistles, Exhaust
See Horns, Exhaust

WICKING, Candle
Advance Packing & Supply Co., 806 Washington Blvd., Chicago, Ill. "Adpasco"—*Illustrated, p. 87*
1889   3466   6668

WICKING, Felt Lubricator
(For felt washers—see Washers, Felt)
Felt Products Mfg. Co., 1510 Carroll Ave., Chicago, Ill. "Fel-Pro" —*See adv. p. 75*
47   717   1250   2046   6651

Wicks, Lamp
See Washers, Felt

WINCHES and BLOCKS, Car Extracting
564   5764

WINCHES, Truck

144	564	589	706	2744
2772	3283	3754	3774	3833
4031	5193	5446	5472	5557
5668	5764	6654		

WINCHES, Truck (Gas or Electric Operated)
3833   5764

Windings, Generator Field Coil
See Coils, Generator Field

Windings, Generator and Starter Armature
See Armatures

Windings, Magneto Armature
See Armatures

Windlace, Rubber
See Strips, Windshield Weather

Window Channels
See Channels, Metal; also Channels, Rubber; also Channels, Felt

Window Regulators
See Regulators, Window

Window Washers
See Washers, Windshield and Window

Windows, Curtain
See Windows, Glass Curtain; also Lights, Curtain

WINDOWS, Glass Curtain
(Bevel glass window with metal and wood frame for use in place of celluloid lights in top curtains)

720	1520	1536	2672	2773
5627				

Windows, Show
See Fronts, Store

Windshield Cleaner Parts
See Parts, Windshield Cleaner

Windshield Fittings
See Cleaners; Heaters; Hinges; Screens; Shields, Wing; Visors; Washers, Windshield and Window

Windshield Glass Gages
See Gages, Windshield Glass

Windshields
See Shields, Wind

Wings, Glass Windshield
See Shields, Wing (For Open and Closed Cars)

Winter Top Enclosures
See Enclosures, Panel Top

WIPERS, Oil Rod
224   6218

WIPERS and POLISHING CLOTHS
(For cotton waste—see Waste, Cotton)
(Advertisers in this publication only)
Consumers Paper Co., 6301-31 E. Lafayette Ave., Detroit, Mich. — *Described, p. 56*
Flower City Specialty Co., 250 Mill St., Rochester, N. Y. "Elcaro," "Mon Kloth"—*Illustration, description & prices, p. 17*
Kozak, Inc., 1 Park Pl., Batavia, N. Y.—*See adv. p. 56*

Wire Cable
See Rope or Cable, Bronze Wire; also Cable, Brake or Cutout Control

WIRE, for Enclosures, Fences, Window Guards, etc.
782

Wire Gages
See Gages, Drill and Wire

Wire Guards
See Guards, Safety, for Machinery; also Wire, for Enclosures, for Window Guards, etc.

WIRE, Phosphor Bronze, Brass and Copper

112	723	1289	4011	4236
4662a	4700			

Wire Rope
See Rope or Cable, Bronze Wire

WIRE, Steel Spring
190   1287   2665   3143   5163

Wire Strippers
See Tools, Wire Stripping

Wires, Spark Plug
See Cables (Sets)

Wiring Cleats
See Cleats, Fibre Wiring

Wiring Conduit
See Conduit, Flexible Car Wiring

Wiring Sets, Ignition, Starting and Lighting
See Cables (Sets)

Woodworkers' Clamps
See Clamps, Woodworkers'

Wool Dusters
See Dusters, Wool and Cotton

WOOL, Steel
5129

Work Benches
See Benches, Work

Worms and Worm Gears
See Gears, Worm Drive

Wrecking Casters, Dollies, Spare Wheels, Trucks, etc.
See Trucks, Casters and Spare Wheels, Wrecking

Wrecking Cranes
See Cranes, Truck

Wrenches, Crankcase Plug
See Funnel and Crankcase Wrench Combined

WRENCHES, Drain Plug
1063   5753

WRENCHES, Hub Cap
Hubco Mfg. Co., 404 W. Conway St., Baltimore, Md. (For Chevrolet cars)—*Illustrated & described, p. 104*
Loock & Co., R. J., 343-45 N. Gay St., Baltimore, Md. "Lightnin" (For Chevrolet cars) — *Illustration & prices, p. 51*

35	224	656	1842	2822
2841	3256	3509	4757	5059
5753	6559			

WRENCHES, Magneto and Distributor
Hygrade Products Co., 333 W. 52nd St., New York, N. Y.—*See adv. p. 86*
Loock & Co., 343-45 N. Gay St., Baltimore, Md. "Lightnin" — *Illustrated, p. 51*

337	339	1063	2472	2858
3537	4317	4556	4601	5687
6634				

WRENCHES, Nut and Bolt
(See also Wrenches, Socket)
Loock & Co., R. J., 343-45 N. Gay St., Baltimore, Md. "Lightnin"—*Illustration & prices, p. 51*
Peck, Stow & Wilcox Co., 217-313 Center St., Southington, Conn. "Pexto"—*See adv. p. 124*

Simmons Mfg. Co., 3405-11 Perkins Ave., Cleveland, Ohio — *See adv. p. 62*

Truth Tool Co., 711 S. Front St., Mankato, Minn.—*See adv. p. 128*

Woodworth Specialties Co., 121-25 Montgomery St., Binghamton, N. Y. —*See adv. p. 36*

35	224	250	603	643
656	681	686	1132	1148
1299	1324	1589a	1669	2017
2158	2410	2714	3104a	3256
3270	3336	3438	3476	3537
3719	3918	4556	4600	4632
4644	5002	5114	5148	5462
5563	5647	5753	6191	6208
6374	6491	6497	6557	6679
6730	6787			

WRENCHES, Pipe

Armstrong Bros. Tool Co., 304 N. Francisco Ave., Chicago, Ill.—*Illustrated, p. 119*

Peck, Stow, & Wilcox Co., 217-313 Center St., Southington, Conn. "Pexto"—*See adv. p. 124*

250	591a	603	643	686
2456	3048a	2711	4644	6191
6679	6730			

WRENCHES, Portable Electric

655	3905	6332	6459

Wrenches, Reamer

See Wrenches, Tap and Reamer

WRENCHES, Socket

Blackhawk Mfg. Co., Dept. C, 120 N. Broadway, Milwaukee, Wis.—*Illustrated & described, p. 122*

Truth Tool Co., 711 S. Front St., Mankato, Minn. "Cyclone" — *See adv. p. 128*

224	643	656	681	686
1132	1148	1299	1669	1813
2017	2846	3270	3438	3918
4284	4288b	4556	4600	4632
4726	4741	5611	5655	5719
5753	6208	6491	6557	6730

Wrenches, Spark Plug

See Wrenches, Nut & Bolt

WRENCHES, Special, for Fords

National Machine & Tool Co., 801 S. Water St., Jackson, Mich. — *See adv. p. 120*

Simmons Mfg. Co., 3405-11 Perkins Ave., Cleveland, Ohio—*See adv. p. 62*

Truth Tool Co., 711 S. Front St., Makato, Minn.—*See adv. p. 128*

538	681	765	4241	4694
5103	5563	6208	6491	6497
6730	6745			

WRENCHES, Tap and Reamer

National Machine & Tool Co., 801 S. Water St., Jackson, Mich. — *See adv. p. 120*

623	756	1033	1082	1253a
2410	3270	3271	3986	4241
4338	5700	5719	6146a	6311
6497				

WRENCHES, Tappet

35	250	643	656	1132
2017	2714	2846	3256	3918
4003	4556	4600	4726	5611
6208	6491	6497		

Yoke Ends

See Yokes, Special

Yoke Pins

See Pins, Yoke

YOKES, Special

Dorman Star Washer Co., 219 E. Eighth St., Cincinnati, Ohio—*See adv. p. 102*

Es-M-Co Auto Products Corp., 31 34th St., Brooklyn, N. Y. (For Ford & Chevrolet cars) — *Illustration & warehouses, p. 70*

643	720	1626	1906	2619
3413	6370	6730		

ZINC (Plates, Slabs, Sheets and Strips)

1810	2044	2440	2695	3824

ZINCS, Battery

2440	3824

See Page 364 for Names of Companies Represented by Above Numbers

Manufacturers of Automotive Products

A Combined Alphabetical-Numerical List of Important Manufacturers Selling Automotive Products to the Trade. It Does Not Include Companies Who Sell Only to Other Manufacturers.

The name and address after the numbers here identify the companies listed by numbers anywhere in this book, as in the

CLASSIFIED BUYERS' GUIDE
TRADE NAME LIST

Also, arranged alphabetically, you can quickly find any company and its address.

Note: Advertisers are in bold type with page reference.

A

3—A & B Spring Mfg. Co., Tenth & Santa Fe Sts., Oklahoma City, Okla.
4—A. C. F. Motors Co., 30 Church St., New York, N. Y.
5—A-C Mfg. Co., 417 Sherman St., Pontiac, Ill.
6—AC Spark Plug Co., Flint, Mich.
8—Abbot-Downing Truck & Body Co., 80 S. Main St., Concord, N. H.
9—Abegg & Reinhold, 2533 E. 26th St., Los Angeles, Calif.
10—Abel & Bach Co., 1000 W. St. Paul Ave., Milwaukee, Wis.
11—Abrasive Co. (Div. of Simonds Saw & Steel Co.), Tacony & Fraley Sts., Philadelphia, Pa.
14—Accuralite Co., McCracken Rd., Muskegon, Mich.
15—Accurate Gear Div. Republic Gear Co., Fifth Floor, Greenawalt Bldg., Springfield, Ohio.
16—Accurate Parts Mfg. Co., 735 Central Ave., Cleveland, Ohio.
18—Acheson Graphite Corp., Buffalo Ave., Niagara Falls, N. Y.
20—Ackerman-Blaesser-Fezzey, Inc., 1258 Holden Ave., Detroit, Mich.
22—Acme Air Appliance Co., 254 Park Ave., Brooklyn, N. Y.
23—Acme Leather Belting Co., 88 Fairfax Rd., Rochester, N. Y.
24—Acme Machine Products Co., Willard St. & Hoyt Ave., Muncie, Ind.
26—Acme Mfg. Co., 1338 Clark St., Racine, Wis.
27—Acme Mfg. & Gasket Co., 3437 Market St., Philadelphia, Pa.
28—Acme Motor Truck Corp., Haynes St., Cadillac, Mich.
31—Acme Sales Co., 1783 E. 11th St., Cleveland, Ohio.
33—Acme White Lead & Color Works, 8250 St. Aubin Ave., Detroit, Mich.
35—Acorn Mfg. Co., 424 W. 19th St., Erie, Pa.
36—Adams-Barre Co., 1242 N. High St., Columbus, Ohio.
38—Adams & Elting Co., 1833 Seward St., Chicago, Ill.
39—Adams Grease Gun Corp., 239 Fourth Ave., New York, N. Y.
40—Adams Mfg. Co., 591 N. Chambers St., Galesburg, Ill.
41—Adell Mfg. Co., 61 E. River St., Orange, Mass.
42—Adjustable Bearing Co., 101-11 Transportation Bldg., Indianapolis, Ind.
43—Adjustable Clamp Co., 425 N. Ashland Ave., Chicago, Ill.
44—Adkins, Young & Allen Co., 32 S. Jefferson St., Chicago, Ill.
46—Adriance Machine Works, 80 Richards St., Brooklyn, N. Y.
47—Advance Felt & Cutting Co., 611-C W. Lake St., Chicago, Ill.
48—Advance Goggle Co., 4551 Diversey Ave., Chicago, Ill.
49—**Advance Packing & Supply Co., 806 W. Washington Blvd., Chicago, Ill. Adv. p. 87.**
50—Advance Products Corp., 69 S. 13th St., Minneapolis, Minn.
52—**Aetna Metal Products Co., 1824 Washington Ave., St. Louis, Mo. Adv. p. 97.**
53—Aetna Rubber Co., 132 Hanover Street, Boston, Mass.
56—Aff Machine Works, L. W., 231 Ninth St., San Francisco, Calif.
57—Aga Auto Lamp Co., 39 Oakland St., Amesbury, Mass.
58—Agner Simplex Co., 108 Dodge St., Burlington, Wis.
59—Ahlbell Battery Container Corp., 700 Market St., Waukegan, Ill.
60—Ahlberg Bearing Co., 317 E. 29th St., Chicago, Ill.
61—Ahrens-Fox Fire Engine Co., Colerain, Alfred & Cook Sts., Cincinnati, Ohio.
62—Aircraft Specialties, Inc., 1627 Brandywine St., Philadelphia, Pa.
66—Air-Maze Corp., 313 Caxton Bldg., Cleveland, Ohio.
67—Air Reduction Sales Co., Lincoln Bldg., 60 E. 42nd St., New York, N. Y.
69—Air-Tight Steel Tank Co., Mansion St. & B. & O. R. R., Pittsburgh, Pa.

70—Air Valve Spark Plug Co., 3331 Superior Ave., Cleveland, Ohio (Sole distributors, Animated Spark Plug Co., 128 N. Wells St., Room 302, Chicago, Ill.)
71—Ajax Auto Parts Co., 15th St. & C. & N. W. R. R., Racine, Wis.
75—Ajax Trunk & Sample Case Co., 418 W. 25th St., New York, N. Y.
76—Akron-Selle Co., High & Chestnut Sts., Akron, Ohio.
78—Akron Varnish Co., Firestone Parkway, Akron, Ohio.
81—Albany Hardware Specialty Mfg. Co., Albany, Wis.
82—Albaugh-Dover Mfg. Co., 2100 Marshall Blvd., Chicago, Ill.
83—Albertson & Co., 3100 Lowell Ave., Sioux City, Iowa.
84—Albion Metal Products Co., 310 Washington St., Albion, Mich.
85—Albright Co., S. S., 1300 U St., Sacramento, Calif.
86—Alemite Corp., 2650 N. Crawford Ave., Chicago, Ill.
87—Alemite Die-Casting & Mfg. Co., Woodstock, Ill.
89—Alert Sales Co., 712 N. 16th St., Philadelphia, Pa.
91—Alexander, A. D., Charlotte St., Fredericksburg, Va.
93—All-American Products, Inc., 215 E. Parson St., Galion, Ohio.
94—Allan Mfg. & Welding Co., 726 Washington St., Buffalo, N. Y.
95—Allbestos Corp., 21st St. & Godfrey Ave., Philadelphia, **Pa.**
96—Allen, E. W., Room 14, Auzerais Bldg., San Jose, Calif.
97—Allen Auto Specialty Co., 16 W. 61st St., New York, N. **Y.**
98—Allen-Bradley Co., 1326 S. Second St., Milwaukee, Wis.
100—Allen Electric & Equipment Co., 2101 N. Pitcher St., Kalamazoo, Mich.
101—Allengrade Co., 2413 N. Broad St., Philadelphia, Pa.
102—Allen Mfg. Co., 133 Sheldon St., Hartford, Conn.
103—Allen Mfg. Co., W. D., 566 W. Lake St., Chicago, Ill.
104—Allied Industrial Products Co., 17 W. Elizabeth St., Chicago, Ill.
107—Allis-Chalmers Mfg. Co., Milwaukee, Wis.
110—Allith-Prouty Co., 819 N. Bowman Ave., Danville, Ill.
112—Alloy Metal Wire Co., 13th & Pennsylvania Ave., Moores, Pa.
113—Alloy Steel Spring & Axle Co., Leroy & Horton Sts., Jackson, Mich.
114—All-Steel Equip Co., 100 John St., Aurora, Ill.
115—Alltex Products Corp., 265 Fourth Ave., New York, N. Y.
116—**Almetal Universal Joint Co., 1553 E. 55th St., Cleveland, Ohio. Adv. p. 81.**
116a—Almond Mfg. Co., T. R., Ashburnham, Mass.
118—Alto Mfg. Co., 1647 Wolfram St., Chicago, Ill.
120—Aluminum Co. of America, 2400 Oliver Bldg., Pittsburgh, **Pa.**
121—**Aluminum Industries, Inc., 2416 Beekman St., Cincinnati, Ohio. Adv. p. 10.**
124—Alvord-Polk Tool Co., 110 Gearhart St., Millersburg, Pa.
128—American Appliance Co. (Div. of American Signs Corp.), Willard & Cooley Sts., Kalamazoo, Mich.
130—American Asbestos Co., Stanbridge & Sterigere Sts., Norristown, Pa.
130a—American Austin Car Co., Butler, Pa.
131—American Automatic Devices Co., 500 S. Throop St., Chicago, Ill.
132—American Automobile Appliance Co., 2420 E. 14th St., Chattanooga, Tenn.
133—American Automotive Accessories Corp., Canton, Ill.
134—**American Auto Products Co., 219 Ascot Place, N. E., Washington, D. C. Adv. p. 93.**
135—American Blower Corp., 6000 Russell St., Detroit, Mich.
136—American Body Co., 5113 E. Grand Ave., Dallas, Tex.
137—American Brake Materials Corp., 4660 Merritt Ave., Detroit, Mich.
138—American Brush Corp., 1113 N. Franklin St., Chicago, Ill.
138a—American Cable Co., New York Central Bldg., 230 Park Ave., New York, N. Y.

MANUFACTURERS OF AUTOMOTIVE PRODUCTS—Continued

139—American Can Co., 230 Broadway, New York, N. Y.
141—American Car & Foundry Motors Co., 5718 Russell St., Detroit, Mich.
141a—American Cement Machine Co., Keokuk, Iowa.
142—American Chain Co., 929 Connecticut Ave., Bridgeport, Conn. Adv. p. 38.
143—American Chemical Paint Co., Brookside Ave. & Reading R. R., Ambler, Pa. Adv. p. 126.
146—American Cord & Webbing Co., 394 Broadway, New York, N. Y.
147—American Crayon Co., Sandusky, Ohio.
148—American Decalcomania Co., 4328 W. Fifth Ave., Chicago, Ill.
149—American Die & Tool Co., 401 N. Second St., Reading, Pa.
152—American Emery Wheel Works, Waterman, East River & Pitman Sts., Providence, R. I.
153—American Excelsior Corp., 1000 N. Halsted St., Chicago, Ill.
153a—American Flange & Manufacturing Co., 825 S. Kilpatrick Ave., Chicago, Ill.
154—American Flatlite Co., 712 Reading Rd., Cincinnati, Ohio.
156—American Forge & Machine Co., 1600 Barth Court, S. W., Canton, Ohio.
157—American Gas Furnace Co., Lafayette, Spring & Elizabeth Sts., Elizabeth, N. J.
160—American Hammered Piston Ring Co., Bush & Hamburg Sts., Baltimore, Md.
161—American Hard Rubber Co., Akron, Ohio.
163—American Injector Co., 1481 14th St., Detroit, Mich.
164—American Instrument Co., 774 Girard St., N. W., Washington, D. C.
165—American-LaFrance & Foamite Corp., 100 E. LaFrance St., Elmira, N. Y.
166—American Lava Corp., 1427 William St., Chattanooga, Tenn.
167—American Leather Mfg. Co., 258 New St., Newark, N. J.
169—American Machine Products Co., 207 Market St., Marshalltown, Iowa.
170—American Machine Works, 316 Sixth Ave., N., St. Cloud, Minn.
171—American Metal Hose Co., 67 Jewelry St., Waterbury, Conn. Adv. p. 100.
174—American Non-Gran Bronze Corp., Berwyn, Pa.
175—American Nut & Bolt Fastener Co., 2029 Doerr St., Pittsburgh, Pa.
176—American Oil Pump & Tank Co., Findlay & Dalton Sts., Cincinnati, Ohio.
177—American Paint Works, 424 Josephine St., New Orleans, La.
178—American Platinum Works, N. J. R. R. Ave. at Oliver St., Newark, N. J.
180—American Pulley Co., 4200 Wissahickon Ave., Philadelphia, Pa.
182—American Sales Book Co., Ltd., Fourth & Magee Sts., Elmira, N. Y.
182a—American Salpa Corp., 261 Fifth Ave., New York, N. Y.
184—American Scale Co., 210 Mfg. Exchange Bldg., Kansas City, Mo.
185—American Screw Co., 21 Stevens St., Providence, R. I.
186—American Shoe Machinery & Tool Co., 23rd & Dickson Sts., St. Louis, Mo.
188—American Sponge & Chamois Co., 23 Beekman St., New York, N. Y. (Importers.)
189—American Stamping Co., 81 Burchard St., Battle Creek, Mich.
190—American Steel & Wire Co., 208 S. LaSalle St., Chicago, Ill.
192—American Thermo-Ware Co., 16 Warren St., New York, N. Y.
194—American Truck & Body Co., Martinsville, Pa.
196—American Varnish Co., 1138 N. Branch St., Chicago, Ill.
197—American Viscosimeter Co., 110 E. 42nd St., New York, N. Y.
198—American Welding & Mfg. Co., Griswold St., Warren, Ohio.
200—Ames Co., B. C., Ames St., Waltham, Mass.
200a—Ampco Metal, Inc., 1350 Burnham St., Milwaukee, Wis.
201—Ampco Twist Drill Co., 811 Belden St., Jackson, Mich.
202—Anaconda Wire & Cable Co., 25 Broadway, New York, N. Y.
203—Anchor Electric Co., 7 N. Sixth Ave., Maywood, Ill.
204—Anchor Packing Co., 401 N. Broad St., Philadelphia, Pa.
205—Anchor Webbing Co., 300 Brook St., Pawtucket, R. I.
208—Anderson Co., 957 Garfield St., Gary, Ind.
209—Anderson Co., O. L., 1347 E. Fort St., Detroit, Mich.
210—Anderson Mfg. Co., 149 Sidney St., Cambridge, Mass.
211—Anderson Steam Vulcanizer Co., 1109 N. Hamilton Ave., Indianapolis, Ind.
212—Andrews & Co., 740 W. Superior Ave., Cleveland, Ohio.
213—Angle Steel Stool Co., Plainwell, Mich.
218—Annin & Co., 85 Fifth Ave., New York, N. Y.
219—Anshutz Co., 2183 Gratiot Ave., Detroit, Mich.
220—Anthony Co., Streator, Ill.
221—Anthony Co., 138 West Ave., Long Island City, N. Y.
222—Anti-Borax Compound Co., 1502 Wall St., Fort Wayne, Ind.
223—Anton-Ackerman Co., 130 Kansas Ave., Topeka, Kan.
224—Apco Mossberg Corp., Attleboro, Mass.
225—Apex Lamp & Mfg. Co., 2635 S. Wabash Ave., Chicago, Ill.
226—Aplus Products Co., 30 W. 61st St., New York, N. Y.
228—Apollo Magneto Corp., 79 Grand St., Kingston, N. Y.
229—Appleton Electric Co., 1701 Wellington Ave., Chicago, Ill.
231—Arbeka Webbing Co., N. Main & Bates Sts., Pawtucket, R. I.
233—Arcadia Truck Body Corp., 21 Murray St., Newark, N. Y.
234—Archibald Wheel Co., 140 West St., Lawrence, Mass.
235—Arco Battery & Plate Co., 209 E. Columbia Ave., Ft. Wayne, Ind.
236—Arco Co., 7301 Bessemer Ave., Cleveland, Ohio.
237—Arco Vacuum Corp., Div. of American Radiator Co., 40 W. 40th St., New York, N. Y.
240—Arizona Onyx Products Co., 114 E. Lincoln St., Phoenix, Ariz.
241—Armature Co., 7510 Stanton Ave., Cleveland, Ohio. Adv. p. 59.
243—Armiger Chemical Co., 2155 W. Austin Ave., Chicago, Ill.
244—Armitage & Co., John L. 245 Thomas St., Newark, N. J.
245—Armleder Truck Co., Eighth & Evans Sts., Cincinnati, Ohio.
246—Armour & Co., Curled Hair Div., 1355 W. 31st St., Chicago, Ill.

250—Armstrong Bros. Tool Co., 304 N. Francisco Ave., Chicago, Ill. Adv. p. 119.
251—Armstrong Cork Co., Cork Div., Lancaster, Pa.
252—Armstrong-Johnston Mfg. Co., 97 N. Washington Ave., Columbus, Ohio.
253—Armstrong Mfg. Co., 303 Knowlton St., Bridgeport, Conn.
254a—Aro Equipment Corp., Bryan, Ohio.
256—Arrow Head Steel Products Co., 1101 Stinson Blvd., Minneapolis, Minn.
258—Arrow Supply Co., 123 W. Maryland St., Indianapolis, Ind.
259—Artcraft Fabrics, Inc., 35 E. Eighth St., New York, N. Y.
261—Art Metal Works, Aronson Sq., Newark, N. J.
263—Arvey Corp., 6400 E. Nevada Ave., Detroit, Mich.
265—Asbestos & Allied Products Co., 19 W. 60th St., New York, N. Y.
265a—Asbestos Mfg. Co., Huntington, Ind.
267—Asbestos Textile Co., 369 Lexington Ave., New York, N. Y.
268—Ashco Corp., 1547 University Ave., St. Paul, Minn.
270—As-Ke Fuemer Co., 2921 Stevens Ave., Minneapolis, Minn.
272—Athol Machine & Foundry Co., 82 South St., Athol, Mass.
274—Atia Sales Corp., 206 Broadway, New York, N. Y.
275—Atkins & Co., E. C., 402 S. Illinois St., Indianapolis, Ind.
277—Atlantic Metal Hose Co., 360 W. 52nd St., New York, N. Y.
278—Atlantic-Pacific Mfg. Co., 124 Atlantic Ave., Brooklyn, N. Y.
279—Atlantic Stamping Co., 180 Ames St., Rochester, N. Y.
280—Atlantic Tubing Co., 1756 Cranston St., Providence, R. I.
281—Atlas Asbestos Co., North Wales, Pa.
284—Atlas Bolt & Screw Co., 1130 Ivanhoe Rd., Cleveland, Ohio.
285—Atlas Brass Foundry Co., 980 S. Park St., Columbus, Ohio.
286—Atlas Copper & Brass Mfg. Co., 2724-42 High St., Chicago, Ill. Adv. p. 117.
287—Atlas Foundry Co., 517 Lyons Ave., Irvington, N. J.
290—Atlas Press Co., 1840 N. Pitcher St., Kalamazoo, Mich.
291—Atlas Specialty Mfg. Co., 3255 Shields Ave., Chicago, Ill.
292—Atlas Tack Corp., 1079 Pleasant St., Fairhaven, Mass.
294—Atterbury Motor Car Co., Elmwood Ave. at Hertel, Buffalo, N. Y.
295—Attwood Brass Works, 745 Front St., Grand Rapids, Mich.
297—Atwood Vacuum Machine Co., 2500 N. Main St., Rockford, Ill.
298—Auburn Automobile Co., S. Main St., Auburn, Ind. Adv. p. 130.
299—Auburn Ball Bearing Co., 28 Industrial St., Rochester, N. Y.
300—Auburn Button Works, 48 Canoga St., Auburn, N. Y.
301—Audubon Wire Cloth Co., Nicholson Rd. & Atlantic Ave., Audubon, N. J.
304—Aurora Equipment Co., 422 Cleveland Ave., Aurora, Ill.
305a—Austin Co., J. H., 5427 Hecla Ave., Detroit, Mich.
307—Autoberth Co., 506 E. Michigan Ave., Lansing, Mich.
309—Autocar Co., Lancaster Ave., Ardmore, Pa.
310—Au-To Compressor Co., 233 S. Mulberry St., Wilmington, Ohio.
311—Auto Con-Den-So-Meter Corp., 800 N. Clark St., Chicago, Ill.
312—Auto-Diesel Piston Ring Co., 1440 E. 32nd St., Cleveland, Ohio.
315—Autographic Register Co., Tenth & Clinton Sts., Hoboken, N. J.
316—Auto-Kamp Trailer Co., 4014 Sheridan Ave., Saginaw, Mich.
319a—Automatic Door Corp., Owensboro, Ky.
319b—Automatic Drive & Transmission Co., 554 S. Broadway, Gloucester City, N. J.
320—Automatic Electric Heater Co., 1524 Race St., Philadelphia, Pa.
322—Automatic Safe Start Co., 313 Story Bldg., Los Angeles, Calif.
323—Automatic Screw Machine Products Co., 3415 W. 31st St., Chicago, Ill.
324—Auto-Matic Seat Cover Corp., 120 E. 16th St., New York, N. Y. Adv. p. 44.
325—Automatic Time Stamp Co., 139 Atlantic Ave., Boston, Mass.
330—Automotive Chemical Co., 38 17th St., Buffalo, N. Y.
331—Automotive Fan & Bearing Co., Wildwood & Fern Aves., Jackson, Mich.
332—Automotive Gear Works, Eighth & S. O Sts., Richmond, Ind.
334a—Automotive Lock Corp., Cunard Bldg., 25 Broadway, New York, N. Y.
336—Automotive Maintenance Machinery Co., 816 W. Washington Blvd., Chicago, Ill.
337—Automotive Manufacturers, Inc., 569 Broadway, New York, N. Y.
338—Automotives, Inc., 32 Euclid Ave., Newark, N. J.
339—Automotive Specialty Corp., 382 Jefferson St., Brooklyn, N. Y.
341—Automotive Thrust Bearing Corp., 2021 S. Michigan Ave., Chicago, Ill.
343—Auto Moulding & Mfg. Co., 1926 S. Wabash Ave., Chicago, Ill.
344—Autoprimer Corp., 603 E. Washington St., Indianapolis, Ind.
345—Autopulse Corp., 2821 Brooklyn Ave., Detroit, Mich.
347—Auto Radiator & Fender Co., 229 Dolphin St., Baltimore, Md.
349—Auto Renewal Equipment Co., 650 Gateway Bldg., Minneapolis, Minn.
350—Auto Roll-Out Corp., 1103 Grand St., Hoboken, N. J.
351—Autoscrew Co., 355 W. Broadway, New York, N. Y.
352—Auto Sheet Metal Works, 6106 Avalon Blvd., Los Angeles, Calif.
354—Auto Smock & Clamp Co., 25 Harrison St., Springfield, Mass.
356—Auto Specialties Mfg. Co., 557 Graves St., St. Joseph, Mich. Adv. p. 50.
357a—Auto-Tank Lock Co., 117 Bradman Bldg., Bluefield, W. Va.
360—Auto-Vehicle Parts Co., 1040 Saratoga St., Newport, Ky. Adv. pp. 34 & 35.
361—Autovent Fan & Blower Co., 1805 N. Kostner Ave., Chicago, Ill.
363—Available Truck Co., 2501 Elston Ave., Chicago, Ill.
364—Axelson Mfg. Co., Ltd., P. O. Box 337, Los Angeles, Calif.

B

501—B. & H. Mfg. Co., 2033 E. Tenth St., Indianapolis, Ind.
503a—B-L Electric Mfg. Co., 19th & Washington Aves., St. Louis, Mo.

MANUFACTURERS OF AUTOMOTIVE PRODUCTS—Continued

505—Babin, Luke B., Moss St., White Castle, La.
506—Bache & Co., Semon. 636 Greenwich St., New York, N. Y.
507—Backus, Jr., & Sons, A., 1533 W. Lafayette Blvd., Detroit, Mich.
508—Backus Novelty Co., 400 W. Water St., Smethport, Pa.
509—Bacon Felt Co., Winchester, Mass.
510—Bacon Vulcanizer Mfg. Co., 1267 67th St., Oakland, Calif.
515—**Badger Fire Extinguisher Co., 962 Park Square Bldg., Boston, Mass.**
518—Badger Tool & Mfg. Co., 134 S. Clinton St., Chicago, Ill.
520—Baer Bros., 438 W. 37th St., New York, N. Y.
521—Bailey Mfg. Co., 32 High St., Amesbury, Mass.
523—Baird Lock Co., 216 W. Ontario St., Chicago, Ill.
525—Baker-Hansen Mfg. Co., 1900 Park St., Alameda, Calif.
526—Baker Mfg. Co., 154 W. Water St., Kankakee, Ill.
527—Baker Mfg. Co., Springfield, Ill.
528a—Baker & Sons, Geo., 651 N. Montello St., Brockton, Mass.
529—Baldwin, Pierce, Hooper & Slauson Aves., Los Angeles, Calif.
530—Baldwin-Duckworth Chain Corp., 369 Plainfield St., Springfield, Mass.
531—Ball Chemical Co., Fulton Bldg., Pittsburgh, Pa.
532—Balloon Tire Mould Co., 3210 S. Grand Ave., Los Angeles, Calif.
533—Ballou, Walter T., 2232 S. Orange Drive, Los Angeles, Calif.
534—Baltimore Paint & Color Works, 148 S. Calverton Rd., Baltimore, Md.
535—Bantam Ball Bearing Co., 3702 W. Sample St., South Bend, Ind.
536—Barber Asphalt Co., 16th & Arch Sts., Philadelphia, Pa.
537—Barbour-Stockwell Co., 205 Broadway, Cambridge, Mass.
538—Barcalo Mfg. Co., 225 Louisiana St., Buffalo, N. Y.
539—Barclay Mfg. Co., 1013 S. Council St., Muncie, Ind.
541—Barcy-Nicholson Co., 2801 W. Fort St., Detroit, Mich.
542—Barkelew Electric Mfg. Co., 1208 Reynolds Ave., Middletown, Ohio.
544—Barker Machine & Foundry Co., Sixth & Cayuga Sts., Philadelphia, Pa.
545—Barnes Co., W. F. & John, 301 S. Water St., Rockford, Ill.
548—Barnes Tool Co., 152 Brewery St., New Haven, Conn.
549—Barnhardt Mfg. Co., Charlotte, N. C.
550—**Barnstead Still & Sterilizer Co.,** 40 Lanesville Terrace (Forest Hills), Boston, Mass.
551—Bartlett Co., Edwin E., 41 Crown St., Nashua, N. H.
553—Basca Mfg. Co., 1911 Martindale Ave., Indianapolis, Ind.
555—Bastian-Blessing Co., 240 E. Ontario St., Chicago, Ill.
556—Bastian Bros. Co., 1600 Clinton Ave., N., Rochester, N. Y.
558—Bates Wohlert Co., 700 E. Grand River Ave., Lansing, Mich.
559—Battery Equipment & Supply Co., 7524 Greenwood Ave., Chicago, Ill.
560—Battery Parts Co., 329 Penn Ave., Wilkinsburg, Pa.
561—Bauer & Black, 2500 S. Dearborn St., Chicago, Ill.
562—Baum's Castorine Co., 200 Mathew St., Rome, N. Y.
563—Baush Machine Tool Co., 156 Wason Ave., Springfield, Mass.
564—Bay City Foundry & Machine Co., 1613 Water St., Bay City, Mich.
568—Bay State Stamping Co., 380 Chandler St., Worcester, Mass.
569—Bay State Tap & Die Co., 75 Chauncy St., Mansfield, Mass.
570—Beach Air Brush Co., Willard C., Second & Warren Sts., Harrison, N. J.
575—Beall Tool Co., East Alton, Ill.
576—Beals & Selkirk Trunk Co., Seventh & Chestnut Sts., Wyandotte, Mich.
576a—Bean Mfg. Co., John, Burton & Rogers Equipment Div., 18 Hosmer St., Lansing. Mich.
577—**Bean Mfg. Co., John, 18 Hosmer St., Lansing, Mich. Adv. p. 31.**
578—Beardsley & Wolcott Mfg. Co., 1359 Thomaston Ave., Waterbury, Conn.
580—Bearings Industry Corp., 1834 Broadway, New York, N. Y. (Importers.)
581—**Bear Mfg. Co., 21st St. & Fifth Ave., Rock Island, Ill. Adv. p. 123.**
582—Beaver Mfg. Co., 625 N. Third St., Newark, N. J.
584—Beck-Frost Ohio Co., 1805 Clinton St., Toledo, Ohio.
586—Beckwith-Chandler Co., Delancey & Rutherford Sts., Newark, N. J.
587—Beckwith Machine Co., 553 N. Chestnut St., Ravenna, Ohio.
588—Becton, Dickinson & Co., Rutherford, N. J.
589—Beebe Bros., 3223 First Ave., S., Seattle, Wash.
590—Behrens Mfg. Co., H., Third & Grand Sts., Winona, Minn.
591—Behr-Manning Corp., Troy, N. Y.
591a—Belden Machine Co., Whalley & West Rock Aves., New Haven, Conn.
592—Belden Mfg. Co., 4647 W. Van Buren St., Chicago, Ill.
593—Bell Co., 407-11 N. Lincoln St., Chicago, Ill. Adv. p. 93.
595—Bellevue Mfg. Co., Ashford Ave., Bellevue, Ohio. Adv. p. 52.
597—Belmor Mfg. Co., 2300 Wabansia Ave., Chicago, Ill.
598—Belvidere Screw & Machine Co., 826 E. Madison St., Belvidere, Ill.
600—Beman Automatic Oil Can Co., Meadville, Pa.
602—Bemis Bro. Bag Co., 601 S. Fourth St., St. Louis, Mo.
603—Bemis & Call Co., 125 Main St., Springfield. Mass.
606—Bender Body Co., W. 62nd St. & Denison Ave., Cleveland, Ohio.
608—**Bendix Aviation Corp., 401 Bendix Drive, South Bend, Ind. Adv. Front Cover.**
609—**Bendix Brake Co., 401 Bendix Drive, South Bend, Ind. Adv. Front Cover.**
610—**Bendix-Cowdrey Brake Tester, Inc., South Bend, Ind. Adv. p. 107 & Front Cover.**
611—**Bendix Stromberg Carburetor Co., 701 Bendix Drive, South Bend, Ind. Adv. Front Cover.**
612—**Bendix-Westinghouse Automotive Air Brake Co., 5001 Centre Ave., Pittsburgh, Pa. Adv. Front Cover.**
613—Beneke Mfg. Co., 21st & Rockwell Sts., Chicago, Ill.
614—Benjamin Electric Mfg. Co., Northwest Highway & Seegar Rd., Des Plaines. Ill.
616—Benton Co., L. F., 300 Main St., Vergennes, Vt.
617—Benzer Corp., Myrtle & Cooper Aves., Brooklyn, N. Y.
618—Benz Spring Co., 89 N. Ninth St., Portland, Ore.
620—Berg Bros. Mfg. Co., 4520 W. North Ave., Chicago, Ill.
621—Berg Co., F. O., 318 Division St., Spokane, Wash.

622—**Berger Mfg. Co., Div. Republic Steel Corp., 1038 Belden Ave., N. E., Canton, Ohio. Adv. p. 105.**
623—Bergman Tool Mfg. Co., 1573 Niagara St., Buffalo, N. Y.
623a—**Berkley Mfg. Co., 16 W. 60th St., New York, N. Y.**
624—Berling Magneto Co., 129 Dearborn St., Buffalo, N. Y.
626—Bernz Co., Otto, 17 Ashland St., Newark, N. J.
627—Berry Bros., 211 Lieb St., Detroit, Mich.
629—Bethlehem Fabricators, Inc., W. Lehigh Ave., Bethlehem, Pa.
630—Bethlehem Steel Co., Bethlehem, Pa.
632—Betts Spring Co., 888 Folsom St., San Francisco, Calif.
632a—**Betz Motor Truck Co., 493 Lyman Ave., Hammond, Ind.**
633—Biax Flexible Shaft Co., 22-14 40th Ave., Long Island City, N. Y.
634—Bickett Rubber Products Corp., 600 First St., Watertown, Wis.
635—Bicknell Mfg. & Supply Co., 22 N. Academy St., Janesville, Wis.
636—Biddle Co., James G., 1211 Arch St., Philadelphia, Pa.
636a—Biederman Motors Co., 2100 Spring Grove Ave., Cincinnati, Ohio.
639—Biflex Products Co., Div. Houdaille-Hershey Corp., 2660 E. Grand Blvd., Detroit, Mich.
640—Biggs Boiler Works Co., 1007 Bank St., Akron, Ohio.
640a—Bigler Mfg. Co., 501 High St., Chippewa Falls, Wis.
641—**Biglow & Co., L. C., 250 W. 54th St., New York, N. Y. Adv. p. 129.**
641a—**Bijur Lubricating Corp., 22-08 43rd Ave., Long Island City, N. Y. Adv. p. 87.**
642—Billings-Chapin Co., 40th St. & N. Y. C. R. R., Cleveland, Ohio.
643—Billings & Spencer Co., 1 Laurel St., Hartford, Conn.
644—**Biltmore Mfg. Co., 1747 Central Ave., Cincinnati, Ohio. Adv. p. 40.**
645—Binghamton Flexible Shaft Co., 239 Water St., Binghamton, N. Y.
646—Binks Mfg. Co., 3114 Carroll Ave., Chicago, Ill.
647—Binswanger & Co., B., 835 N. Third St., Philadelphia, Pa.
649—Birch Mfg. Co., 1523 Sedgwick St., Chicago, Ill.
650—Birmingham Tank Co., Birmingham, Ala.
651—Bishop Mfg. Co., Robert, 157 W. Sixth St. (So. Boston), Boston, Mass.
652—Bishop Products Co., 7512 Carnegie Ave., Cleveland, Ohio.
653—Bishop Wire & Cable Corp., 420 E. 25th St., New York, N. Y.
655—Black & Decker Mfg. Co., Towson, Md.
656—**Blackhawk Mfg. Co., Dept. C., 120 N. Broadway, Milwaukee, Wis. Adv. p. 122.**
658—Blackmer Pump Co., 1809 Century Ave., Grand Rapids, Mich.
661—Blake Signal & Mfg. Co., 221 High St., Boston, Mass.
662—Blaw-Knox Co., Blawnox, Pa.
663—Blettner Co., Geo. H., 1841 W. Jackson Blvd., Chicago, Ill.
664—Bliss Co., E. W., 53rd St. & Second Ave., Brooklyn, N. Y.
665—Blitz Electric Co., 4344 Wentworth Ave., Chicago, Ill.
666—Bloch, Joseph, 51 Cliff St., New York, N. Y. (Importers.)
667—Bloch & Sons, Albert, 36 Walker St., New York, N. Y.
668—Blocksom & Co., Fifth & Canal Sts., Michigan City, Ind.
669—Blood-Bros. Machine Co., Allegan, Mich.
670—Blount Co., J. G., Woodland St., Everett, Mass.
671—Blue Co., W. F., 3540 N. Meridian St., Indianapolis, Ind.
677—Boardman Co., Maple & Hawk Sts., Oklahoma City, Okla.
678—Bock Machine Co., 3618 Colerain Ave., Cincinnati, Ohio.
679—Bodin Mfg. Co., Hanover Ave. & Dauphin St., Allentown, Pa.
681—Bog Mfg. Co., 2116 N. Menard Ave., Chicago, Ill.
682—Bohn Aluminum & Brass Corp., 2512 E. Grand Blvd., Detroit, Mich.
682a—**Boker & Co., H., 101 Duane St., New York, N. Y.**
684—Bond Electric Corp., 256 Cornelison Ave., Jersey City, N. J.
685—Bond Foundry & Machine Co., Manheim, Pa.
686—**Bonney Forge & Tool Works, Tilghman & Meadow Sts., Allentown, Pa.**
691—Boss Bolt & Nut Co., 3403 W. 47th St., Chicago, Ill.
692—Boston Leather Specialties, Inc., 210 Broadway, Everett, Mass.
693—Boston Woven Hose & Rubber Co., 29 Hampshire St., Cambridge, Mass.
694—Boullee Fraser Tanning Co., 52 Woolsey St., Irvington, N. J.
696—Bowen Products Corp., Auburn, N. Y.
697—Bower Roller Bearing Co., Hart & Goethe Aves., Detroit, Mich.
698—Bowes "Seal Fast" Corp., 228 N. Pine St., Indianapolis, Ind.
699—Bownes Bros., Frank, Chelsea, Mass.
700—Bowser & Co., S. F., 1314 E. Creighton Ave., Ft. Wayne, Ind.
701—Box Iron Works Co., Wm. A., 33rd & Blake Sts., Denver, Col.
701a—Boye & Emmes Machine Tool Co., Cincinnati, Ohio.
702—Boyer Chemical Laboratories, 2700 S. Wabash Ave., Chicago, Ill.
703—Boyer Fire Apparatus Co., Wheatland Ave., Logansport, Ind.
704—Boyle & Co., John, 112 Duane St., New York, N. Y.
704a—Boyle Mfg. Co., 5100 Santa Fe Ave., Los Angeles, Calif.
705—Boyle Valve Co., 5829 S. Ada St., Chicago, Ill.
706—Braden Steel & Winch Co., 3 N. Madison St., Tulsa, Okla.
707—Bradfield Motors, Inc., Otis Bldg., Chicago, Ill.
708—Bradley Motor Products Co., Union & Sycamore Sts., Fostoria, Ohio.
709—Bradney Machine Co., 70 Monhagen Ave., Middletown, N. Y.
710—**Bragg-Kliesrath Corp., 401 Bendix Drive, South Bend, Ind. Adv. p. 1 & Front Cover.**
712—Brake Synchrometer Co., 87 Lincoln St., Boston, Mass.
713—Brake Testing Equipment Corp., 1355 Van Ness Ave., San Francisco, Calif.
713a—Brandenburg Bros., 1112 S. Michigan Ave., Chicago, Ill.
714—Brandt-Warner Mfg. Co., Loucks Mill Rd., York, Pa.
717—Brawley Felt Co., T. R., 272 20th St., Brooklyn, N. Y.
718—Breeze Corporations, 24 S. Sixth St., Newark, N. J.
719—Breuer Electric Mfg. Co., 852 Blackhawk St., Chicago, Ill.
720—Brewer-Titchener Corp., 115 Pt. Watson St., Cortland, N. Y.
723—Bridgeport Brass Co., 774 E. Main St., Bridgeport, Conn.
724—Bridgeport Chain & Mfg. Co., 1200 Crescent Ave., Bridgeport, Conn.

MANUFACTURERS OF AUTOMOTIVE PRODUCTS—Continued

725—Bridgeport Coach Lace Co., 812 Wood Ave., Bridgeport, Conn.
726—Bridgeport Hardware Mfg. Corp., 461 Iranistan Ave., Bridgeport, Conn.
726a—Briggs Mfg. Co., 11631 Mack Ave., Detroit, Mich.
727—Briggs & Stratton Corp., 1047 13th St., Milwaukee, Wis.
728—Brightman Mfg. Co., Marion Rd., Columbus, Ohio.
729—Bright Star Battery Co., 15th St. & River Head, Hoboken, N. J.
730—Brilliant Mfg. Co., 1035 Ridge Ave., Philadelphia, Pa.
731—Brockway Motor Truck Corp., 106 Central Ave., Cortland, N. Y.
733—Brodie Co., R. N., 61st & Lowell Sts., Oakland, Calif.
734—Brookins Mfg. Co., 770 Hawthorne St., Dayton, Ohio. Adv. p. 117.
736—Brooklyn Metal Stamping Corp., 718 Atlantic Ave., Brooklyn, N. Y.
737—Brooks & Co., Clarence, 249 Chestnut St., Newark, N. J.
739—Brooks & Sons, M. S., Chester, Conn.
740—Brooks Tent & Awning Co., 1655 Arapahoe St., Denver, Col.
746—Brown & Green Ignition Sales Co., 245 W. 55th St., New York, N. Y.
747—Brown-Lipe-Chapin Co., Syracuse, N. Y.
748—Brown-Lipe Gear Co., Toledo, Ohio.
750—Brown Mfg. Co., John W., Marion Rd., Columbus, Ohio.
751—Brown Rubber Co., E. Union St., Lafayette, Ind.
752—Brown & Sharpe Mfg. Co., Promenade St., Providence, R. I.
753—Brown Sheet Iron & Steel Co., 964 Berry Ave., St. Paul, Minn.
756—Brubaker & Bros. Co., W. L., Millersburg, Pa.
759—Brunner Mfg. Co., 1800 Broad St., Utica, N. Y. Adv. p. 113.
760—Brunswick Engineering Co., 30 Cortlandt St., New Brunswick, N. J. Adv. p. 42.
763—Buckeye Belting & Supply Co., 1251 W. Third St., Cleveland, Ohio.
764—Buckeye Brass & Mfg. Co., 6410 Hawthorne Ave., Cleveland, Ohio.
765—Buckeye Jack Mfg. Co., Gaskill Rd., Alliance, Ohio.
766—Buckeye Reliner Producing Co., 653 N. Jackson St., Lima, Ohio.
767—Buckeye Twist Drill Co., W. Ely St., Alliance, Ohio.
768—Buckner Process Co., 86A Pleasant St., Worcester, Mass.
769—Buda Co., 154th St. & Commercial Ave., Harvey, Ill.
769a—Budd Mfg. Co., Edw. G., Hunting Park Ave. & 25th St., Philadelphia, Pa.
770—Budd Wheel Co., 12141 E. Charlevoix Ave., Detroit, Mich.
772—Buell Mfg. Co., 2975 Cottage Grove Ave., Chicago, Ill.
774—Buffalo Bolt Co., North Tonawanda, N. Y.
775—Buffalo Bronze Die Cast Corp., 100 Arthur St., Buffalo, N. Y.
777—Buffalo Fire Appliance Corp., 44 Central Ave., Buffalo, N. Y.
778—Buffalo Forge Co., 490 Broadway, Buffalo, N. Y.
779—Buffalo Gasoline Motor Co., 1280 Niagara St., Buffalo, N. Y.
780—Buffalo Meter Co., 2891 Main St., Buffalo, N. Y.
781—Buffalo Weaving & Belting Co., 215 Chandler St., Buffalo, N. Y.
782—Buffalo Wire Works Co., 431 Terrace, Buffalo, N. Y.
785—Buick Motor Co., Flint, Mich. Adv. p. 15.
786—Buko Oiler Mfg. Co., Clarkson, Neb.
788—Bull Grip, Inc., Chattanooga, Tenn.
789—Bumpers, Inc., 340 W. 70th St., New York, N. Y. Adv. p. 67.
790—Bunting Brass & Bronze Co., 715 Spencer St., Toledo, Ohio.
792—Burdett Oxygen Co. of Cleveland, 3300 Lakeside Ave., Cleveland, Ohio.
794—Burd Piston Ring Co., Tenth St. & 23rd Ave., Rockford, Ill.
798—Burgess Battery Co., 111 W. Monroe St., Chicago, Ill.
800—Burgess-Norton Mfg. Co., 517 Peyton St., Geneva, Ill. Adv. p. 187.
801—Burkhart Mfg. Co., F., 4900 N. Second St., St. Louis, Mo.
802—Burke Electric Co., 12th & Cranberry Sts., Erie, Pa.
803—Burke Machine Tool Co., 792 E. 12th St., Conneaut, Ohio.
806—Burlington Brass Works, Burlington, Wis.
808—Burrell Belting Co., 413 S. Hermitage Ave., Chicago, Ill.
809—Burr & Sons, John T., 429 Kent Ave., Brooklyn, N. Y.
810—Burton Auto Spring Corp., 2433 W. 48th St., Chicago, Ill.
811—Burton-Boston Brush Co., 122 Harvard St., Cambridge, Mass.
812—Burton Rubber Co., 5713 Euclid Ave., Cleveland, Ohio. ....
814—Bushey Co., J. S., 717 W. 11th St., Los Angeles, Calif.
816—Bussmann Mfg. Co., University St. at Jefferson Ave., St. Louis, Mo. Adv. p. 74.
817—Butler Mfg. Co., 7400 E. 13th St., Kansas City, Mo.
818—Butler Mfg. Co., 1810 E. 24th St., Cleveland, Ohio.
819—Butterfield & Co. (Div. of Union Twist Drill Co.), Derby Line, Vt.
819a—Buttonless Tire Cover Co., 1411 Fifth St., S. W., Canton, Ohio.
820—Buxbaum Co., 120 Elinor Ave., Akron, Ohio.

C

1000a—C & C Sales Corp., General Motors Bldg., Broadway at 57th St., New York, N. Y. (Importers.) Adv. p. 58.
1001—C & G Wheel Puller Co., Brooklyn Ave., Wellsville, N. Y. (Sole distributors, Raybestos Div. of Raybestos-Manhattan, Inc., Railroad Ave., Bridgeport, Conn.)
1002—C. H. C. Mfg. Co., 103 13th St., Portland, Ore.
1003—C & L Tire & Rubber Co., Foothill Blvd. & 105th Ave., Oakland, Calif.
1005—C-R Spark Plug Co., 555 Marietta St., Atlanta, Ga.
1006a—Cabot, Inc., Samuel, Polygon Products Div., 141 Milk St., Boston, Mass. (Sole distributors, Wilber & Williams Co., 31 St. James Ave., Boston, Mass.)
1007—Cactus Mfg. Co., 2700 San Fernando Rd., Los Angeles, Calif.
1008—Cadillac Motor Car Co., 2860 Clark Ave., Detroit, Mich. Adv. p. 24.
1009—Caldbeck Tool & Mfg. Co., 307 E. Third St., Des Moines, Iowa.
1012—California Motor Coach Co., 1346 Folsom St., San Francisco, Calif.
1014—California Steel Wheel Co. of Illinois, 3053 N. California Ave., Chicago, Ill. (Sole distributors, Fager 6-Wheel Attachment Co. of California, 3053 N. California Ave., Chicago. Ill.)
1016—Cambria Spring Co., 915 Santee St., Los Angeles, Calif.

1017—Cameron Electrical Mfg. Co., 205 Main St., Ansonia, Conn.
1019—Campbell Auto Works, 238 N. El Dorado St., Stockton, Calif.
1020—Campbell & Dann Mfg. Co., Tullahoma, Tenn.
1022—Campbell Paint & Varnish Co., 106 Gratiot St., St. Louis, Mo.
1023—Canedy-Otto Mfg. Co., Main & East End Ave., Chicago, Ill.
1025—Canton Foundry & Machine Co., Dime Savings Bank Bldg., Canton, Ohio.
1027—Capen Belting & Rubber Co., 1920 Washington Ave., St. Louis, Mo.
1027a—Capilizer Corp., 50 Church St., New York, N. Y.
1028—Carbex Chemical Co., West End, N. J.
1030—Carbo-Oxygen Co., Benedum-Trees Bldg., Pittsburgh, Pa.
1031—Carborundum Co., Buffalo Ave. near Portage Rd., Niagara Falls, N. Y.
1032—Cardinal Mfg. Co., 2005 Home Ave., Dayton, Ohio.
1033—Card Mfg. Co., S. W., Div. of Union Twist Drill Co., Rumford Ave., Mansfield, Mass.
1034—Carlisle & Finch Co., 229 E. Clinton Ave., Cincinnati, Ohio.
1035—Carlisle Mfg. Co., 243 W. 17th St., New York, N. Y.
1037—Carll's Sons, Chas. W., Cole & Linwood Sts., Trenton, N. J.
1041—Carpenter & Co., L. E., 444 Frelinghuysen Ave., Newark, N. J.
1045—Carr Co., F. S., 31 Beach St., Boston, Mass.
1045a—Carrier-York Corp., 1541 Sansom St., Philadelphia, Pa.
1046—Carroll-Jamieson Machine Tool Co., Davis Rd., Batavia, Ohio.
1047—Carter Carburetor Corp., 2838 N. Spring Ave., St. Louis, Mo.
1048—Carter Co., George R., 630 Lycaste Ave., Detroit, Mich.
1050—Carter Products Corp., 983 Front Ave., Cleveland, Ohio.
1052—Car-Van Steel Products Co., 1210 Fifth St., S. W., Canton, Ohio.
1053—Casco Products Corp., 1333 Railroad Ave., Bridgeport, Conn. Adv. p. 39.
1055—Cataract Auto Washer Co., 1269 Western Ave., Topeka, Kan.
1058—Cedar Rapids Engineering Co., 901 N. 17th St., Cedar Rapids, Iowa. Adv. p. 110.
1060—Celluloid Corp., 10 E. 40th St., New York, N. Y.
1063—Central Auto Ignition Co., 2230 S. Wood St., Chicago, Ill.
1064a—Central Iron & Steel Products Co., 440 Atlantic St., N. W., Warren, Ohio.
1066—Central Mfg. Co., 69 Clinton St., Newark, N. J.
1067—Central Stamping Co., 591 Ferry St., Newark, N. J.
1069—Central Steel & Wire Co., 4545 S. Western Blvd., Chicago, Ill.
1070—Century Hoist Mfg. Co., Canal & Myrtle Sts., Lock Haven, Pa.
1073—Century Motor Truck Co., Seneca St., Defiance, Ohio.
1075—Certain-Teed Products Corp., 100 E. 42nd St., New York, N. Y.
1076—Chadwick & Trefethen, 326 W. Madison St., Chicago, Ill.
1077—Chain Products Co., 3924 Cooper Ave., Cleveland, Ohio.
1079—Chalmers Chemical Co., 123 Chestnut St., Newark, N. J.
1081—Champion Auto Spring Co., 3141 Pine Blvd., St. Louis, Mo.
1082—Champion Blower & Forge Co., Harrisburg Ave. & Charlotte St., Lancaster Pa.
1083—Champion Brass Works, Kendallville, Ind.
1084—Champion DeArment Tool Co., S. Main St., Meadville, Pa.
1086—Champion Pneumatic Machinery Co., 8170 S. Chicago Ave., Chicago, Ill. Adv. p. 112.
1087—Champion Sheet Metal Co., 1 Squires St., Cortland, N. Y.
1088—Champion Spark Plug Co., Upton Ave., Toledo, Ohio. Adv. Back Cover.
1089—Champ Spring Co., 2109 Chouteau Ave., St. Louis, Mo.
1090—Chance Co., Allen & Wilson Sts., Centralia, Mo.
1091a—Chaney Mfg. Co., Springfield, Ohio.
1092—Chapin Co., Chas. E., 227 Fulton St., New York, N. Y. (Sole distributors, Automotive Specialty Corp., 382 Jefferson St., Brooklyn, N. Y.)
1095—Chase Brass & Copper Co., 236 Grand St., Waterbury, Conn.
1097—Chase Mfg. Co., 3216 Morgan St., St. Louis, Mo.
1099—Chaslyn Co., 4605 Ravenswood Ave., Chicago, Ill.
1104—Chattanooga Wheelbarrow Co., 1311 E. Main St., Chattanooga, Tenn.
1105—Checker Cab Mfg. Co., Kalamazoo, Mich.
1106—Chenango Equipment Mfg. Co., 37 Hale St., Norwich, N. Y.
1107—Cheney & Son, S., Manlius, N. Y.
1108—Chesterton Co., A. W., 64 India St., Boston, Mass
1109—Chevolair Motors, Inc., 410 W. Tenth St., Indianapolis, Ind.
1110—Chevrolet Motor Co., General Motors Bldg., Detroit, Mich.
1111—Chicago Belting Co., 113 N. Green St., Chicago, Ill.
1112—Chicago Boiler Co., 1965 Clybourn Ave., Chicago, Ill.
1113—Chicago Coil Spring Co., 3101 Carroll Ave., Chicago, Ill. Adv. p. 98.
1115—Chicago Eye Shield Co., 2300 Warren Ave., Chicago, Ill.
1117—Chicago Lock Co., 2024 W. Racine Ave., Chicago, Ill.
1118—Chicago Mfg. Co., 411 N. Trumbull Ave., Chicago, Ill.
1123—Chicago Pneumatic Tool Co., 6 E. 44th St., New York, N. Y.
1124—Chicago Rawhide Mfg. Co., 1281 Elston Ave., Chicago, Ill.
1126—Chicago Rivet & Machine Co., 1830 S. 54th Ave. (Cicero P. O.), Chicago, Ill. Adv. p. 92
1128—Chicago Screw Co., 1026 S. Homan Ave., Chicago, Ill.
1129—Chicago Steel Tank Co., 6400 W. 66th St., Chicago, Ill.
1130—Chicago Tool & Engineering Co., 8389 S. Chicago Ave., Chicago, Ill.
1132—Chicago Tool & Kit Mfg. Co., 429 W. Superior St., Chicago, Ill.
1133—Chicago Tubing & Braiding Co., 210 N. Clinton St., Chicago, Ill. Adv. p. 102.
1134—Chisholm-Moore Hoist Corp., Div. Columbus-McKinnon Chain Corp., Tonawanda, N. Y.
1135—Christen Products Co., 319 Orleans St., Detroit, Mich.
1137—Christie-Couse Corp., Taos, N. Mex.
1138—Chrysler Sales Corp., 341 Massachusetts Ave., Detroit, Mich.
1139—Cinch Mfg. Corp., 2335 W. Van Buren St., Chicago, Ill.
1141—Cincinnati Ball Crank Co., Cincinnati, Ohio.
1142—Cincinnati Car Corp., Winton Pl., Cincinnati, Ohio.
1143—Cincinnati Electrical Tool Co., 2699 Madison Rd., Cincinnati, Ohio.
1144—Cincinnati Grinders, Inc., 3058 South St. (Oakley), Cincinnati, Ohio.
1145—Cincinnati Lathe & Tool Co., 3207 Disney St. (Oakley), Cincinnati, Ohio.

MANUFACTURERS OF AUTOMOTIVE PRODUCTS—Continued

1146—Cincinnati Rubber Mfg. Co., Franklin Ave., Cincinnati, Ohio.
1147—Cincinnati Time Recorder Co., 1733 Central Ave., Cincinnati, Ohio.
1148—Cincinnati Tool Co., 1053 Waverly Ave., Cincinnati, Ohio.
1150—Cincinnati-Victor Co., 712 Reading Rd., Cincinnati, Ohio.
1151—Cities Service Oil Co. of Ohio, E. 46th & Prospect Sts., Cleveland, Ohio.
1152—City Auto Spring Works, Park Ave. & Preston St., Baltimore, Md.
1154—City Machine & Tool Works, E. Third & June Sts., Dayton, Ohio.
1156—Clarage Fan Co., North & Porter Sts., Kalamazoo, Mich.
1157—Clare Mfg. Co., Clare, Mich.
1158—Clark Bros. Bolt Co., Milldale, Conn.
1159—Clark-Cutler-McDermott Co., Fisher & Winter Sts., Franklin, Mass.
1160—Clark-Feather Mfg. Co., Fort Morgan, Col.
1161—Clark, Jr., Electric Co., James, 600 Bergman St., Louisville, Ky.
1162—Clark Mfg. Co., J. L., 519 High St., Oshkosh, Wis.
1163—Clarkspeed Truck Co., Pontiac, Mich.
1164—Clark Tructractor Co., Battle Creek, Mich.
1165—**Clawson & Bals, Inc., 4701 W. Lake St., Chicago, Ill. Adv. p. 95.**
1166—Claypool Machine Co., Claypool, Ind.
1168—Clayton & Lambert Mfg. Co., 11111 French Rd., Detroit, Mich.
1169—Clear Vision Pump Co., 822 E. Harry St., Wichita, Kan.
1170—Clements Mfg. Co., 601 Fulton St., Chicago, Ill.
1173—**Cleveland Cap Screw Co., 3004 E. 79th St., Cleveland, Ohio. Adv. p. 95.**
1174—**Cleveland Chain & Mfg. Co., Penn R. R. & Henry Rd., Cleveland, Ohio. Adv. p. 39.**
1177—Cleveland Metal Hose Co., 3708 E. 93rd St., Cleveland, Ohio.
1178—Cleveland National Machine Co., 1366 W. 70th St., Cleveland, Ohio.
1179—Cleveland Pneumatic Tool Co., 3734 E. 78th St., Cleveland, Ohio.
1180—Cleveland Shock Absorber Co., 3110 Payne Ave., Cleveland, Ohio.
1182—Cleveland Storage Battery Co., 1724 St. Clair Ave., Cleveland, Ohio.
1183—Cleveland Tanning Co., Dennison Ave. & Jennings Rd., Cleveland, Ohio.
1184—Cleveland Top & Specialty Co., 1929 E. 55th St., Cleveland, Ohio.
1185—Cleveland Twist Drill Co., 1242 E. 49th St., Cleveland, Ohio.
1186—Cleveland Varnish Co., 3111 E. 87th St., Cleveland, Ohio.
1187—Cleveland Welding Co., W. 117th St. & Berea Rd., Cleveland, Ohio.
1188—**Cleveland Worm & Gear Co., 3261 E. 80th St., Cleveland, Ohio. Adv. p. 79.**
1190—Clifford Mfg. Co., 564 E. First St., Boston, Mass.
1192—Clifton Mfg. Co., 323 Pleasant St., Waco, Texas.
1194—Clinton Motors Corp., Reading, Pa.
1195—Clipper Belt Lacer Co., 974 Front Ave., N. W., Grand Rapids, Mich.
1196—Clippinger Mfg. Co., A. B., 1100 S. Mill St., Kansas City, Kan.
1197—Clizbe Bros. Mfg. Co., 105 Place St., Plymouth, Ind.
1198—Clover Mfg. Co., 327 Main St., Norwalk, Conn.
1199—Cloyes Gear Works, 17214 Roseland Rd., N. E., Cleveland, Ohio.
1200—Cluff Cover Co., 549 W. 52nd St., New York, N. Y.
1201—Clum Mfg. Co., 601 National Ave., Milwaukee, Wis.
1202—Clydesdale Co., Amanda St., Clyde, Ohio.
1205—Coast Tire & Rubber Co., 50th Ave. & 12th St., Oakland, Calif.
1207—Codman & Shurtleff, 173 Massachusetts Ave., Boston, Mass.
1211—Cohutta Talc Co., Dalton, Ga.
1212—Coil Mfg. Co., 902 Maxwell Ave., Evansville, Ind.
1213—Cold Steam Corp., Charlottesville, Va. (Sole distributors, Fuelo Engineering Corp., Room 1932, 342 Madison Ave., New York, N. Y.)
1214—Cole Co., Henry, 54 Old Colony Ave., Boston (27), Mass. (Sole distributors, Do-Ray Lamp Co., 1458 S. Michigan Ave., Chicago, Ill.)
1216—Coleman Motors Corp., Littleton, Col.
1219—Coliseum Battery & Equipment Co., 1616 S. Wabash Ave., Chicago, Ill.
1222—Colonial Battery Co., 1014 S. Michigan Ave., Chicago, Ill.
1224—Colorado Gear Mfg. Co., 1361 S. Broadway, Denver, Col.
1225—Colorado Tent & Awning Co., 1636 Lawrence St., Denver, Col.
1226—Colpin Corp., Siloam Springs, Ark.
1227—Colt's Patent Fire Arms Mfg. Co., 17 Van Dyke Ave., Hartford, Conn.
1229—Columbia Engineering Co., 120 N. Main St., Columbia City, Ind.
1230—Columbia Mills, 225 Fifth Ave., New York, N. Y.
1232—**Columbian Vise & Mfg. Co., 9017 Bessemer Ave., Cleveland, Ohio. Adv. p. 122.**
1233—Columbus Auto Brass Co., 767 W. Fourth St., Columbus, Ohio.
1234—Columbus Bolt Works Co., 174 W. Chestnut St., Columbus, Ohio.
1235—Columbus Coated Fabrics Corp., Seventh & Grant Aves., Columbus, Ohio.
1237—**Columbus-McKinnon Chain Corp., Tonawanda, N. Y. Adv. p. 36.**
1240—Combination Rubber Mfg. Co., Mead St. & St. Joe's Ave., Trenton, N. J.
1242—Comet Electric Co., 1237 St. Paul St., Indianapolis, Ind.
1243—**Comfort Printing Specialty Co., 107 N. Eighth St., St. Louis, Mo. Adv. p. 108.**
1244—Commercial Acetylene Supply Co., 40 Rector St., New York, N. Y.
1245—Commercial Chemical Co., 212 Essex St., Boston, Mass.
1247—Commercial Mfg. Co., 817 Rees St., Chicago, Ill.
1249—Commonwealth Brass Corp., 5781 Commonwealth Ave., Detroit, Mich.
1250—Commonwealth Felt Co., 74 Summer St., Boston 9, Mass.

1253—Compton-Murrow Co., Citizens National Bank Bldg., Independence, Kan.
1253a—Conant & Donelson Co., Conway, Mass.
1254—Conco Crane & Engineering Works, Div. of H. D. Conkey & Co., Mendota, Ill.
1254a—Condon Motors, Inc., 223 W. Jackson Blvd., Chicago, Ill.
1255—Conneaut Packing Co., 353 Broad St., Conneaut, Ohio.
1257—Connecticut Telephone & Electric Corp., Tiffany Div., 70 Britannia St., Meriden, Conn.
1259—Conrad, Earl W., Warsaw, Ind.
1260—Consolidated Battery Co., 111 Colgate St., Buffalo, N. Y.
1261—Consolidated Brass Co., Summit Ave. & Wabash Ry., Detroit, Mich.
1262—Consolidated Car Heating Co., 413 N. Pearl St., Albany, N. Y.
1262a—Consolidated Foundries, California Steel Wheel Corp. Div., 8901 Railroad Ave., Oakland, Calif.
1263—Consolidated Packing & Supply Co., 21 Barclay St., New York, N. Y.
1265—**Consumers Paper Co., 6301 E. Lafayette Ave., Detroit, Mich. Adv. p. 56.**
1266—Contact Metals Co., 2502 S. Wabash Ave., Chicago, Ill.
1268—Continental Corp., 1601 S. Michigan Ave., Chicago, Ill.
1269—Continental Cushion Spring Co., 4925 S. Halsted St., Chicago, Ill.
1270—**Continental-Diamond Fibre Co., Newark, Del. Adv. p. 8.**
1271—Continental Felt Co., 890 Broadway, New York, N. Y.
1272—**Continental Motors Corp., 12801 E. Jefferson Ave., Detroit, Mich. Adv. p. 19.**
1273—**Continental Piston Ring Co., 276 Walnut St., Memphis, Tenn. Adv. p. 94.**
1274—**Continental Rubber Works, 1902 Liberty St., Erie, Pa. Adv. p. 64.**
1276—**Continental Tire Corp., Dept. C, 1805 Michigan Ave., Chicago, Ill. Adv. p. 82.**
1283—Cooper-Bessemer Corp., Mt. Vernon, Ohio.
1286—Cooper Corp., Findlay, Ohio.
1287—Cooper Mfg. Co., 411 S. First Ave., Marshalltown, Iowa.
1289—Copperweld Steel Co., 9th St., Glassport, Pa.
1290—Coranto, Incorporated, Old Forge, N. Y.
1291—Corbin Cabinet Lock Co., Div. American Hardware Corp., Park & Orchard Sts., New Britain, Conn.
1292—Corbin Screw Corp., 227 High St., New Britain, Conn.
1293—Corbitt Co., Henderson, N. C.
1294—Corcoran Mfg. Co., Section & Foraker Aves. (Norwood), Cincinnati, Ohio.
1295—Corduroy Tire Co., Grand Rapids, Mich.
1296—Cornell Iron Works, 3620 13th St., Long Island City, N. Y.
1297—Corning Glass Works, Corning, N. Y.
1299—Cornwell Quality Tools Co., Mogadore, Ohio.
1300—Correct Measure Co., Shields St., Rochester, Pa.
1303—Cosco Paint & Varnish Corp., 25 N. Portland Ave., Brooklyn, N. Y.
1304—Cotex Corp., 331 Oliver St., Newark, N. J.
1305—Cotta Transmission Corp., 2340 11th St., Rockford, Ill.
1307—Council Engineering Co., 1723 Third Ave., Moline, Ill.
1308—Covell Mfg. Co, Benton Harbor, Mich
1309—Cowles & Co., C., Water & Chestnut Sts., New Haven, Conn.
1310—Cox Products Corp., 2675 Pittsburgh Ave., Cleveland, Ohio.
1310a—Cragar Corp., Ltd., 940 N. Orange Drive, Hollywood, Cal.
1311—Cramer & Co., R. W., 69 Irving Place, New York, N. Y.
1314—Crane Packing Co., 1801 Belle Plain Ave., Chicago, Ill.
1316—Craveroiler Co. of America, 4523 Tacony St., Frankford, Philadelphia, Pa.
1318—Crawford Mfg. Co., Seventh & Wyandotte Sts., Kansas City, Mo.
1319—Crawford Mfg. Co., Second & Decatur Sts., Richmond, Va.
1321—Crescent Automotive Cable Co. (Crescent Braid, Inc.), 116 Elm St., Providence, R. I.
1322—Crescent Battery & Light Co., 916 Magazine St., New Orleans, La.
1323—Crescent Metal Works, Inc., 313 Chestnut St., Newark, N. J.
1324—Crescent Tool Co., 217 Harrison St., Jamestown, N. Y.
1326—Crittenden Mfg. Co., 33 Moreland St. (West Roxbury), Boston, Mass.
1327—Crone, F. G., 281 Ferry St., Buffalo, N. Y.
1328—Cross Engineering Co., 170 Dundoff St., Carbondale, Pa.
1330—Crown Motor Carriage Co., 2500 McPherson St., Los Angeles, Calif.
1331—Crown Spray Gun Mfg. Co., 1218 Venice Blvd., Los Angeles, Calif.
1333—Crump Co., Benj. T., 1314 E. Franklin St., Richmond, Va.
1334—Cuban-American Sponge Co., 317 Gravier St., New Orleans, La.
1339—Cunningham Mfg. Corp., 150 Lafayette St., New York, N. Y.
1340—Cunningham Sons & Co., James, 13 Canal St., Rochester, N. Y.
1341—**Cuno Engineering Corp., 80 S. Vine St., Meriden, Conn. Adv. p. 37.**
1342—Cunples Co., 401 S. Seventh St., St. Louis, Mo.
1342a—Curly-Head Steel Brush Co., 305 Norton St., Rochester, N. Y.
1343—Curfman Mfg. Co., F. L., 626 W. Second St., Maryville, Mo.
1344—Curry Co., J. W., 2615 Cummins St., Cincinnati, Ohio.
1345—**Curtis Pneumatic Machinery Co., 1927 Kienlen Ave., St. Louis, Mo. Adv. p. 111.**
1346—Cutting Co., Robert M., 401 N. Ogden Ave., Chicago, Ill.
1347—Cuyahoga Specialty Co. (Div. of Cuyahoga Spring Co.), 10252 Berea Rd., Cleveland, Ohio.

D

1499—D. & H. Mfg. Co., 18 W. Irvington Place, Denver, Col.
1500—D. & R. Auto Products Co., 23 Ninth Ave., Long Island City, N. Y.
1503—**Dall Motor Parts Co., P. O. Station D (Dept. CAM), Cleveland, Ohio. Adv. p. 187.**
1504—Dalton & Balch, Inc., 2333 Michigan Blvd., Chicago, Ill.
1505—Dalton Foundries, Inc., Warsaw, Ind.
1508—Damon Mfg. Co., 325 W. Ohio St., Chicago, Ill.
1510—Dangerlite Corp. of America, 300 Sugar Bldg., Denver, Col.
1513—Darcold Co., 179 Christopher St., New York, N. Y.

MANUFACTURERS OF AUTOMOTIVE PRODUCTS—Continued

1514—D'Arcy Spring Co., N. Pitcher St., Kalamazoo, Mich.
1517—Davenport Body Co., 1507 Rockingham Rd., Davenport, Iowa.
1518—Davis Brake Co., 2034 Fairmount Ave., Philadelphia, Pa.
1520—Davis, Kraus & Miller, 442 Jefferson Ave., E., Detroit, Mich.
1522—Davis & Son, 309 W. Third St., Winona, Minn.
1523—Davis Welding & Mfg. Co., 1110 Richmond St., Cincinnati, Ohio.
1524—Day & Co., James B., 1872 Clybourn Ave., Chicago, Ill.
1525—Day Mfg. Co., S. A., 1483 Niagara St., Buffalo, N. Y.
1526—Day-Nite, Inc., Waukesha, Wis.
1527—Dayton Air Compressor Co., 427 Valley St., Dayton, Ohio.
1528—Dayton Appliance Co., E. Monument Ave., Dayton, Ohio.
1530—Dayton Bronze Bearing Co., 303 Keowee St., Dayton, Ohio.
1532—Dayton Paper Novelty Co., 1126 E. Third St., Dayton, Ohio.
1533—Dayton Pump & Mg. Co., 500 N. Webster St., Dayton, Ohio.
1534—Dayton Rubber Mfg. Co., West Riverview Ave., Dayton, Ohio.
1535—Dayton Steel Foundry Co., Cor. Miami Chapel Rd. & B. & O. R. R., Dayton, Ohio.
1536—Dearborn Glass Co., 2500 W. 21st St., Chicago, Ill.
1537—Decker Co., Richard M., 3617 S. Ashland Ave., Chicago, Ill.
1540—Defiance Carriage & Body Co., Perry & Gorman Sts., Defiance, Ohio.
1541—Defiance Mfg. Co., Defiance, Ohio.
1542—Defiance Spark Plugs, Inc., 323 20th St., Toledo, Ohio.
1543—Defiance Welding Co., 513 Jackson St., Defiance, Ohio.
1545—De Laval Separator Co., 165 Broadway, New York, N. Y.
1547—Delco Appliance Corp., North East Div., 379 Lyell Ave., Rochester, N. Y.
1548—Delco Products Corp., 329 E. First St., Dayton, Ohio.
1548a—Delco-Remy Corp., Anderson, Ind.
1549—Dellinger, A. M., 723 N. Prince St., Lancaster, Pa.
1552—Delphos Bending Co., 901 S. Main St., Delphos, Ohio.
1553—Delta Electric Co., 33rd & Nebraska Sts., Marion, Ind.
1554—Delta File Works, 4837 James St., Philadelphia, Pa.
1555—De Luxe Metal Furniture Co., Struthers St., Warren, Pa.
1556—De Luxe Products Corp., 2001 Lake St., La Porte, Ind. Adv. p. 90.
1557—De Luxe Windshield Co., 1533 Franklin St., San Francisco, Calif.
1558a—De Martini Motor Truck Co., 435 Pacific St., San Francisco, Calif.
1559—Deming Co., Salem, Ohio.
1560—Denby Motor Truck Co., 2200 Diamond St., Philadelphia, Pa.
1560a—Denman Tire & Rubber Co., Warren, Ohio.
1561—Denning Mfg. Co., 1775 E. 87th St., Cleveland, Ohio.
1566—Desmond-Stephan Mfg. Co., 317 S. Walnut St., Urbana, Ohio.
1567—DeSoto Motor Corp., Div. Chrysler Sales Corp., Mt. Elliott & Lynch Rd., Detroit, Mich.
1568—Detroit Air Compressor Co., 89 E. Baltimore Ave., Detroit, Mich.
1569—Detroit Auto Piston Co., 1139 W. Baltimore Ave., Detroit, Mich.
1570—Detroit Belt Lacer Co., 3947 A St., Detroit, Mich.
1573—Detroit Cover Co., 3410 W. Fort St., Detroit, Mich.
1574—Detroit Gear & Machine Co., 670 E. Woodbridge St., Detroit, Mich.
1576—Detroit Metal Specialty Corp., 1651 Beard Ave., Detroit, Mich.
1580—Detroit Rubber Products, Inc., 2841 E. Grand Blvd., Detroit, Mich.
1582—Detroit Steel Products Co., 2250 E. Grand Blvd., Detriot, Mich.
1583—Detroit Tire Cover Co., 49 Selden Ave., Detroit, Mich.
1584—Detroit Trailer & Machine Co., 453 Beaufait Ave., Detroit, Mich.
1585—Dettra Flag Co., Oaks, Pa.
1586—De Vaux-Hall Motors Corp., Grand Rapid, Mich.
1587—DeVilbiss Co., 300 Phillips Ave., Toledo, Ohio.
1588—Devoe & Raynolds Co., 1 W. 47th St., New York, N. Y.
1589—Dexter Rubber Mfg. Co., 224 W. Main St., Goshen, N. Y.
1589a—Diamond Calk Horseshoe Co., 46th-47th Ave., W., & Grand, Duluth, Minn.
1589b—Diamond Drill Carbon Co., 53 Park Row, New York, N. Y.
1590—Diamond Machine Co., 9 Codding St., Providence, R. I.
1591—Diamond Rubber Co., 502 S. Main St., Akron, Ohio.
1592—Diamond Saw & Stamping Works, 347 Davey St., Buffalo, N. Y.
1593—Diamond T Motor Car Co., 4517 W. 26th St., Chicago, Ill.
1595—Dictograph Products Corp., 220 W. 42nd St., New York, N. Y.
1596—Diehl Mfg. Co., foot of Trumbull St., Elizabeth, N. J.
1597—Diener Mfg. Co., Geo. W., 400 Monticello Ave., Chicago, Ill.
1599—Dietz Co., R. E., 60 Laight St., New York, N. Y.
1602—Dill Mfg. Co., 686 E. 82nd St., Cleveland, Ohio. Adv. p. 43.
1603—Dilwood Mfg. Co., 215 Chestnut St. Newark, N. J.
1604—Disston & Sons, Henry (Tacony), Philadelphia, Pa.
1604a—Distillate Stove Co., 275 17th St., Chicago Heights, Ill.
1605—Dittmer Gear & Mfg. Corp., 193 Grand St., Lockport, N. Y.
1607—Divco-Detroit Corp., 2435 Merrick Ave., Detroit, Mich.
1608—Divine Bros. Co., 102 Whitesboro St., Utica, N. Y.
1609—Dixon Crucible Co., Joseph, Jersey City, N. J.
1609a—Dixon Motor Truck Co., 2501 Beale Ave., Altoona, Pa.
1611—Doane Motor Truck Co., 428 Third St., San Francisco, Calif.
1614—Dodge Brothers, Inc., Div. of Chrysler Corp., 7900 Jos. Campau Ave., Detroit, Mich.
1615—Doering Spark Plug Co., 136 Tichenor St., Newark, N. J.
1616—Doerr Brass, Bronze & Aluminum Co., C. J., 725 N. Delphos St., Kokomo, Ind. (Sole Distributors, Turner Mfg. Co., 404 W. Superior St., Kokomo, Ind.)
1618—Dole Valve Co., 1913-33 Carroll Ave., Chicago, Ill. Adv. p. 42.
1619—Dolphin Paint & Varnish Co., Champlain & Locust Sts., Toledo, Ohio.
1620—Donaldson Co., 666 Pelham St., St. Paul, Minn.
1623—Doran Lubricator Co., 150 Chestnut St., Providence, R. I.
1624—Do-Ray Lamp Co., 1458 S. Michigan Ave., Chicago, Ill.
1625—Dorbeck, R. V., Lenox & Woodgate Aves., West End, N. J.
1626—Dorman Star Washer Co., 219 E. Eighth St., Cincinnati, Ohio. Adv. p. 102.
1627—Dormeyer Mfg. Co., A. F., 2640 Greenview Ave., Chicago, Ill.
1628—Doublee Mfg. Corp., 10 Market St., Cold Spring, N. Y.
1629—Douglas Mfg. Co., H. A., Railroad St., Bronson, Mich.

1630—Douglas Truck Mfg. Co., 30th & Sprague Sts., Omaha, Neb.
1632—Dover Stamping & Mfg. Co., 385 Putnam Ave., Cambridge, Mass.
1633—Drake Lock-Nut Co., 2450 E. 75th St., Cleveland, Ohio.
1637—Dual Duty Co., Alma, Mich.
1639—Duby Co., J. F., 83 Southern Artery, Dorchester, Mass.
1640—Dudley Lock Corp., 26 N. Franklin St., Chicago, Ill.
1641—Duesenberg, Inc., 1511 W. Washington St., Indianapolis, Ind.
1642—Duff Engineering Co., Nebraska City, Neb.
1643—Duff-Norton Mfg. Co., Preble Ave., N. S., Pittsburgh, Pa.
1643a—Du-Gas Fire Extinguisher Corp., 11 W. 42nd St., New York, N. Y.
1644—Dumore Co., 16th & Junction Sts., Racine, Wis.
1646—Duncan Co., W. H., 70 Worth St., New York, N. Y.
1648—Dunham Co., C. A., 450 E. Ohio St., Chicago, Ill.
1649—Dunlop Tire & Rubber Co., Sheridan Drive, Buffalo, N. Y.
1650—Dunning & Boschert Press Co., 325 W. Water St., Syracuse, N. Y.
1651—Dunn Mfg. Co., 117 15th St., Clarinda, Iowa.
1653—Dunton Co., M. W., 670 Eddy St., Providence, R. I.
1654—Duoflex Piston Ring Co., 2000 S. 71st St., Philadelphia, Pa.
1655—Duplate Corp., 2130 Grant Bldg., Pittsburgh, Pa. (Sole distributors, Pittsburgh Plate Glass Co., Grant Bldg., Pittsburgh, Pa.)
1656—Duplex Accelerator Mfg. Co., 108 N. Center St., Marshalltown, Iowa.
1656a—Duplex Brake Engineering Co., 54 Garfield Ave., Trenton, N. J. Adv. p. 58.
1657—Duplex Truck Co., Hazel St., Lansing, Mich.
1658—Duplex Wrench Corp., Jamestown, N. Y.
1659—DuPont de Nemours & Co., E. I., Fairfield, Conn.
1660—DuPont de Nemours & Co., E. I., General Motors Bldg., Detroit, Mich.
1661—DuPont de Nemours & Co., E. I., Newburgh, N. Y.
1662—DuPont Motors, Inc., Springfield, Mass.
1663—DuPont Viscoloid Co., 626 Schuyler Ave., Arlington, N. J.
1664—Dural Rubber Corp., Maple Ave., Flemington, N. J.
1665—Durant Motor Co. of Mich., Lansing, Mich.
1666—Dura-Products Mfg. Co., 403 Tonner Court, Canton, Ohio.
1667—Durkee-Atwood Co., 40 Wilder St., Minneapolis, Minn. Adv. p. 63.
1668—Durlach Can & Iron Works, 234 Bridge St., Brooklyn, N. Y.
1669—Duro Metal Products Co., 2649 N. Kildare Ave., Chicago, Ill.
1670—Duroyd Gasket & Die Mfg. Co., 1828 Amsterdam Ave., New York, N. Y.
1671—Durston Gear Corp., 213 Maltbie St., Syracuse, N. Y.
1672—Durwyllan Co., 37 Kentucky Ave., Paterson, N. J.
1675—Dus-Pruf Auto Trunk Co., 414 W. Jefferson Ave., Detroit, Mich.

E

1800—E. A. Laboratories, Inc., 696 Myrtle Ave., Brooklyn, N. Y.
1801—E. M. G. Mfg. Co., Ethridge, Tenn.
1804—Eagle Electric Mfg. Co., 59 Hall St., Brooklyn, N. Y.
1805—Eagle Lock Co., 26 Warren St., New York, N. Y.
1806—Eagle Machine Co., 24 N. Noble St., Indianapolis, Ind.
1807—Eagle Mfg. Co., Wellsburg, W. Va.
1808—Eagle Motor Truck Corp., 6160 Bartmer Ave., St. Louis, Mo.
1809—Eagle-Ottawa Leather Co., Grand Haven, Mich.
1810—Eagle-Picher Lead Co., 134 N. La Salle St., Chicago, Ill.
1811—Eagle Truck Body & Mfg. Corp., 45 Columbus St., Auburn, N. Y.
1813—Eastern Machine Screw Corp., Truman & Barclay Sts., New Haven, Conn.
1815—Eastern Tube & Tool Co., 594 Johnson Ave., Brooklyn, N. Y.
1816—Eastman Kodak Co., Chemical Sales Dept., 343 State St., Rochester, N. Y.
1817—Eastman Mfg. Co., 1002 N. 11th St., Manitowoc, Wis.
1819—Eaton Products, Inc., E. 65th St. & Central Ave., Cleveland, Ohio.
1820—Eaton Metal Products, A. H., 13th & Willis Ave., Omaha, Neb.
1823—Eberhard Mfg. Co., 2734 Tennyson Rd., Cleveland, Ohio.
1824a—Eberly & Orris Mfg. Co., W. Allen St., Mechanicsburg, Pa.
1825—Ebinger Sanitary Mfg. Co., D. A., 401 W. Town St., Columbus, Ohio.
1827—Echlin & Echlin, Inc., 799 Golden Gate Ave., San Francisco, Calif.
1829—Eclat Rubber Co., 2009 Oakwood Drive., Cuyahoga Falls, Ohio.
1830—Eclipse Air Brush Co., 79 Orange St., Newark, N. J.
1831—Eclipse Fuel Engineering Co., 814 S. Main St., Rockford, Ill.
1832—Eclipse Machine Co., Div. of Bendix Aviation Corp., Dept. 5, Elmira, N. Y. Adv. p. 221.; also Front Cover.
1837—Economy Machine Products Co., 5214 Lawrence Ave., Chicago, Ill.
1838—Economy Products Corp., 2901 Indiana Ave., Chicago, Ill.
1840—Edde Mfg. Co., 102 E. Seeboth St., Milwaukee, Wis.
1841—Eddystone Steel Co., Ft. of Maddock St., Crum Lynne, Pa.
1842—Edelman & Co., E., 2332 Logan Blvd., Chicago, Ill.
1843—Edison Lamp Works of General Electric Co., Nela Park, Cleveland, Ohio.
1844—Edwards & Co., 140th & Exterior Sts., New York, N. Y.
1845—Edwards Mfg. Co., Fifth St. & Eggleston Ave., Cincinnati, Ohio.
1847—Efficiency Tool Corp., Morgan at Indiana Ave., Kokomo, Ind.
1849—Egry Register Co., 417 E. Monument Ave., Dayton, Ohio.
1850—Egyptian Lacquer Mfg. Co., 90 West St., New York, N. Y.
1851—Eisemann Magneto Corp., 60 E. 42nd St., New York, N. Y.
1853—Elcar Motor Co., 700 Beardsley Ave., Elkhart, Ind.
1854—Elco Tool & Screw Corp., Broadway at 13th, Rockford, Ill.
1855—Electra Mfg. Co., 2537 Madison St., Kansas City, Mo.
1856—Electric Arc Cutting & Welding Co., 152 Jelliff Ave., Newark, N. J.
1857—Electric Auto-Lite Co., Champlain & Chestnut Sts., Toledo, Ohio.
1860—Electric Heat Control Co., 5902 Carnegie Ave., Cleveland, Ohio.
1861—Electric Heating & Mfg. Co., Sixth Ave. North at Harrison St., Seattle, Wash.
1862—Electric Hose & Rubber Co., 12th & Dure Sts., Wilmington, Del.

MANUFACTURERS OF AUTOMOTIVE PRODUCTS—Continued

1864—Electric Materials Co., Clay & Washington Sts., North East, Pa.
1866—Electric Service Supplies Co., 17th & Cambria Sts., Philadelphia, Pa.
1867—Electric Sprayit Co., 1704 E. Colax Ave., South Bend, Ind.
1867a—Electric-Steam, Inc., Jackson, Mich.
1868—Electric Storage Battery Co., Allegheny Ave. & 19th St., Philadelphia, Pa.
1869—Electric Tachometer Corp., Broad & Spring Garden Sts., Philadelphia, Pa.
1870—Electric Wheel Co., Walton Heights, Quincy, Ill.
1871—Electrox Co., Ft. Bridge St., Peoria, Ill.
1872—Elgin Machine Works, 412 N. State St., Elgin, Ill.
1873—Elgin National Watch Co., Aircraft Instrument Div., Elgin, Ill.
1874—Elgin Sweeper Co., 5 Oak St., Elgin, Ill.
1875—Elgin Tool Works, 67 N. State St., Elgin, Ill.
1876—Elite Mfg. Co., 110 Ohio St., Ashland, Ohio.
1876a—Elkhart Motor Truck Co., 1730 S. Main St., Elkhart, Ind.
1877—Elliott Addressing Machine Co., Cambridge, Mass. Adv. p. 74.
1880—Elmes Engineering Works, Chas. F., 217 N. Morgan St., Chicago, Ill.
1881—Elwell-Parker Electric Co., 4250 St. Clair Ave., Cleveland, Ohio.
1883—Emerol Mfg. Co., 242 W. 69th St., New York, N. Y. Adv. p. 4.
1885—Emerson-Brantingham Corp., Preston & Tay Sts., Rockford, Ill.
1885a—Emerson Engineering Corp., Alexandria, Va.
1886—Emerson Mfg. Co., 161 Natoma St., San Francisco, Calif.
1887—Emmert Mfg. Co., W. Main St., Waynesboro, Pa.
1888—Empire Plow Co., Snow Plow Div., 3140 E. 65th St., Cleveland, Ohio.
1889—Emsco Asbestos Co., 206 S. Crawford St., Downey, Calif. Adv. p. 84.
1891—Endura Mfg. Corp., Quakertown, Pa.
1892—Englert Manufacturing Co., 2500 Jane St., Pittsburgh, Pa.
1893—Eno Rubber Corp., 110 E. 17th St., Los Angeles, Calif.
1894—Ensign Carburetor Co., 7019 S. Alameda St., Huntington Park, Calif.
1895a—Equipment Supply Co., 542 W. Washington Blvd., Chicago, Ill.
1896—Erdle Perforating Co., 171 York St., Rochester, N. Y.
1898—Erie Malleable Iron Co., Automotive Wheel Div., 12th & Cherry Sts., Erie, Pa.
1899—Erie Meter Systems, Inc., Pearl St. & Wagner Ave., Erie, Pa.
1904—Ermet Products Co., 2100 N. Caroline St., Indianapolis, Ind.
1905—Ero Mfg. Co., 2234 Ogden Ave., Chicago, Ill.
1906—Es-M-Co Auto Products Corp., 31 34th St., Brooklyn, N. Y. Adv. p. 70.
1907—EsoR Mfg. Co., 705 W. First St., Hastings, Neb.
1909—Essex Rubber Co., May & Beakes Sts., Trenton, N. J.
1910—Estwing Mfg. Co., Ninth St. & 19th Ave., Rockford, Ill.
1911—Etnyre & Co., E. D., First, Second & Jefferson Sts., Oregon, Ill.
1912—Ettco Tool Co., 594 Johnson Ave., Brooklyn, N. Y.
1917—Eureka Vacuum Cleaner Co., Hamilton & Dewey Aves., Detroit, Mich.
1918—Evans Flexible Reamer Corp., 3513 N. Lincoln Ave., Chicago, Ill.
1919—Evans Products Co., 3300 Union Trust Bldg., Detroit, Mich.
1920—Evans' Sons, John, 506 N. 13th St., Philadelphia, Pa.
1921—Evansville Tool Works, Ninth Ave. & Maryland St., Evansville, Ind.
1922—Everbright Mfg. Co., 724 Larkin St., San Francisco, Calif.
1923—Everhot Mfg. Co., Tenth Ave. & Seventh St., Maywood, Ill.
1926—Evr-Klean Seat Pad Co., 1511 N. 12th St., St. Louis, Mo.
1927—Excelsior Brass Works, 475 Tulpehocken St., Reading, Pa.
1928—Excelsior Trunk Co., 704 Delaware St., Kansas City, Mo.
1929—Excel Tool Co., 755 Union St., San Diego, Calif.
1930—Ezell Corp., Ltd., 1012 Financial Center Bldg., Oakland, Calif.

F

2000—F. A. B. Mfg. Co., 67th & Vallejo Sts., Oakland, Calif.
2003—F-K Auto Trunk Corp., 730 E. Washington St., Indianapolis, Ind.
2006—Fabric Products Corp., 11th & Fayette Sts., Indianapolis, Ind.
2007—Face-A-Lite Mfg. Co., 318 N. Lawler St., Mitchell, S. D.
2009—Factory Service Co., Sta. F, Milwaukee, Wis.
2010—Fafnir Bearing Co., New Britain, Conn. Adv. p. 167.
2011—Fageol Motors Co., 107th Ave. & Hollywood Blvd., Oakland, Calif.
2012—Fager 6-Wheel Attachment Co. of Calif., 2440 Irving Park Blvd., Chicago, Ill.
2013—Fahrig Bearing Metal Co., 623 N. Broad St., Elizabeth, N. J. (Sole distributors, Magnolia Metal Co., 75 West St., New York, N. Y.)
2014—Fairbanks, Morse & Co., 900 S. Wabash Ave., Chicago, Ill.
2015—Fairchild Deflector Corp., 2 W. 46th St., New York, N. Y.
2017—Fairmount Tool & Forging Co., 10611 Quincy Ave., Cleveland, Ohio.
2018—Faith Mfg. Co., 5920 N. Crawford Ave., Chicago, Ill.
2019—Falls Rubber Co., Main St., Cuyahoga Falls, Ohio.
2022—Fanner Mfg. Co., Brookside Park, Cleveland, Ohio.
2023—Fargo Motor Corp., Div. of Chrysler Corp., 341 Massachusetts Ave., Detroit, Mich.
2024—Faries Mfg. Co., 1036 E. Grand Ave., Decatur, Ill.
2025—Farm Tools, Inc., Hayes Pumps & Planter Div., Mansfield, Ohio.
2027—Farrell Mfg. Co., Joliet, Ill.
2029—Faultless Rubber Co., Ashland, Ohio.
2032—Fedders Mfg. Co., 57 Tonawanda St., Buffalo, N. Y.
2033—Federal Auto Products Co., 1601 S. Michigan Ave., Chicago, Ill.
2034—Federal Bearings Co., 17 Fairview Ave., Poughkeepsie, N. Y. Adv. p. 173.
2035—Federal Electric Co., 8700 S. State St., Chicago, Ill.
2036—Federal Leather Co., 681 Main St., Belleville, N. J.

2037—Federal Metal Hose Corp., 273 Military Rd., Buffalo, N. Y.
2038—Federal Metallic Packing Co., 29 Foundry St., Wakefield, Mass.
2039—Federal-Mogul Corp., 11031 Shoemaker Rd., Detroit, Mich. Adv. p. 189.
2040—Federal Motor Truck Co., 5780 Federal Ave., Detroit, Mich.
2041—Federal Press Co., 511 E. Division St., Elkhart, Ind.
2042—Federal Pressed Steel Corp., McGraw-Hill Bldg., 520 N. Michigan Ave., Chicago, Ill.
2044—Federated Metals Corp., Great Western Smelting & Refining Branch, 295 Madison Ave., New York, N. Y.
2046—Felters Company, 99 Bedford St., Boston, Mass.
2047—Felt Products Mfg. Co., 1510 Carroll Ave., Chicago, Ill. Adv. p. 75.
2049—Ferdinand & Co., L. W., 152 Kneeland St., Boston, Mass.
2051—Ferguson, D. E., Main St., Vernon, Mich.
2051a—Ferguson-Allan Co., Clinton St., Batavia, N. Y.
2052—Ferguson Mfg. Co., 105 Golf St., Maple Hill, New Britain, Conn.
2053—Fernald Mfg. Co., Dept. U, North East Pa.
2054—Ferodo and Asbestos, Inc., Extension of Codwise Ave., New Brunswick, N. J. Adv. p. 82.
2056—Ferry Cap & Set Screw Co., 2151 Scranton Rd., Cleveland, Ohio.
2058—Fey & Krause, Inc., 1616 S. Figueroa St., Los Angeles, Calif.
2059—Fiberloid Corp., Worcester St., Indian Orchard, Mass.
2064—Filmolens Sales Co., 1923 Ford Bldg., Detroit, Mich.
2065—Finch Road Light Corp., General Motors Bldg., New York, N. Y.
2068—Finnell System, Inc., Elkhart, Ind.
2070—Firestone Steel Products Co., S. Main St., Akron, Ohio.
2071—Firestone Tire & Rubber Co., S. Main St., Akron, Ohio.
2073—Fischer Co., J. A., 393 Seventh Ave., New York, N. Y.
2074—Fischer Spring Co., Chas., 240 Kent Ave., Brooklyn, N. Y.
2074b—Fisher Body Corp., General Motors Bldg., Detroit, Mich.
2075—Fiske Iron Works, J. W., 78 Park Place, New York, N. Y.
2076—Fisk Rubber Co., Chicopee Falls, Mass.
2079—Fitzgerald Mfg. Co., 691 Main St., Torrington, Conn. Adv. p. 76.
2080—Fitz Gibbon & Crisp, Inc., 467 Calhoun St., Trenton, N. J.
2084—Fleming Mfg. Co., 135 Stafford St., Worcester, Mass.
2085—Flexible Shafts, Inc., 443 State St., Binghamton, N. Y.
2087—Flexible Steel Lacing Co., 4607 Lexington St., Chicago, Ill.
2088—Flexlume Corp., 1878 Military Rd., Buffalo, N. Y.
2089—Flexo Mfg. Co., 1312 E. 12th St., Los Angeles, Calif.
2090—Florence Stove Co., 1011 Park Square Bldg., Boston, Mass.
2091—Florida Sponge & Chamois Co., 71 Gold St., New York, N. Y. (Importers.)
2092—Flower City Specialty Co., 250 Mill St., Rochester, N. Y. Adv. p. 17.
2094—Flexible Co., Haskell St., Loudonville, Ohio.
2095—Fogarty Mfg. Co., 800 E. Monument Ave., Dayton, Ohio.
2096—Follett Time Recording Co., 217 High St., Newark, N. J.
2101—Ford Chain Block Co., Second & Diamond Sts., Philadelphia, Pa.
2102—Ford Motor Co., 3674 Schaefer Rd. (Fordson), Detroit, Mich.
2103—Fore Electrical Mfg. Co., 5255 Wabada Ave., St. Louis, Mo.
2104—Foreman, W. D., 5353 S. State St., Chicago, Ill.
2106—Formica Insulation Co., 4655 Spring Grove Ave., Cincinnati, Ohio.
2107—Forsberg Mfg. Co., 125 Sea View Ave., Bridgeport, Conn.
2108—Forsyth Metal Goods Co., Elm St., East Aurora, N. Y.
2109—Fort Recovery Stirrup Co., Fort Recovery, Ohio.
2110—Fort Wayne Battery Mfg. Co., 230 E. Fourth St., Fort Wayne, Ind.
2112—Fosdick Machine Tool Co., Blue Rock & Apple Sts., Cincinnati, Ohio.
2113—Foster Johnson Reamer Co., 1136 W. Beardsley Ave., Elkhart, Ind.
2115—Fostoria Pressed Steel Corp., Dept. CM-1, N. Main St. Fostoria, Ohio. Adv. p. 71.
2116—Fostoria Screw Co., 1002 Blue Print Ave., Fostoria, Ohio. (Sole distributors, Toledo Steel Products Co., 3300 Summit St., Toledo, Ohio.)
2119—Four Wheel Drive Auto Co., Clintonville, Wis.
2120—Fox Automotive Products Corp., 4720 N. 18th St., Philadelphia, Pa.
2121—Fox Co., Fox Bldg., Cincinnati, Ohio.
2122—Fraim Lock Co., E. T., 237 Park Ave., Lancaster, Pa.
2123—France Mfg. Co., 10325 Berea Rd., Cleveland, Ohio.
2124—Francisco Auto Heater Co., Essex & Cleveland Aves., Columbus, Ohio. Adv. p. 46.
2128—Franklin Automobile Co., 101 W. Marcellus St., Syracuse, N. Y.
2129—Franklin Die-Casting Corp., Cor. Gifford & Magnolia Sts., Syracuse, N. Y.
2132—Freas Glass Works, Francis L., 140 E. Ninth Ave., Conshohocken, Pa.
2136—Freeman Motor Co., 1217 Beaufait Ave., Detroit, Mich.
2138—Fremont Automotive Products Co., Clauss Bldg., E. State St., Fremont, Ohio.
2139—Fremont Mfg. Co., Fremont, Ohio.
2141—French Battery Co., Madison, Wis.
2142—French & Co., Samuel H., 400 Callowhill St., Philadelphia, Pa.
2143—French & Hecht, Inc., Third & Farnam Sts., Davenport, Iowa.
2144—French Laboratories, L. S., 296 Broadway, New York, N. Y.
2145—Frew Machine Co., 126 W. Venango St., Philadelphia, Pa.
2146—Friedli Co., John T., 5311 Alaska St., Seattle, Wash.
2147—"Friend" Mfg. Co., East Ave., Gasport, N. Y.
2148—Froiland Chain & Mfg. Co., 430 St. James Ave., Springfield, Mass.
2151—Fruehauf Trailer Co., 10960 Harper Ave., Detroit, Mich.
2153—Fuhrman Trailer Co., 2006 Allen Ave., S. E., Canton, Ohio.
2154—Fuller Brush Co., 3580 Main St., Hartford, Conn.
2156—Fuller & Sons Mfg. Co., Div. of Unit Corp. of America, Bankers Bldg., Milwaukee, Wis.
2157—Fulton Bag & Cotton Mills, Atlanta, Ga.
2158—Fulton Co., 732 75th Ave., Milwaukee, Wis.
2159—Fulton Drop Forge Co., 19 W. Liberty St., Canal Fulton, Ohio.
2162—Fyrac Mfg. Co., 18th Ave. & Seventh St., Rockford, Ill.

MANUFACTURERS OF AUTOMOTIVE PRODUCTS—Continued

2164—Fyr-Fyter Co., 221 Crane St., Dayton, Ohio.

G

2300—G & G Specialty Mfg. Co., 9 W. 20th St., New York, N. Y.
2304—G & O Mfg. Co., 138 Winchester Ave., New Haven, Conn.
2305—Gabriel Co., 1407 E. 40th St., Cleveland, Ohio.
2306—Galef, J. L., 75 Chambers St., New York, N. Y.
2307—Galion Allsteel Body Co., Box 25, 500 S. Market St., Galion, Ohio.
2308—Gallivan, J. E., Rantoul, Ill.
2309—Gallmeyer & Livingston Co., 346 Straight Ave., Grand Rapids, Mich.
2311—Gammons-Holman Co., 395 Main St., Manchester, Conn.
2312—Ganz Bros., 11 Preston St., Ridgefield Park, N. J.
2313—Gardiner Metal Co., 1356 W. Lake St., Chicago, Ill.
2315—Gardner Motor Co., Main & Rutger Sts., St. Louis, Mo.
2317—Gardner Tap & Die Co., Marion, Ohio.
2319—Garland Trunk Co., Sixth & Cedar Sts., St. Paul, Minn.
2322—Gasket Shop, 129 Tenth St., San Francisco, Cal.
2324—Gates Rubber Co., 999 S. Broadway, Denver, Colo. Adv. p. 62.
2325—Gatke, Thos. L., 2143 Builders Bldg., Chicago, Ill.
2327—Gavitt Mfg. Co., Inc., Brookfield, Mass.
2328—Gaylord, Robert, 11th & Pestalozzi Sts., St. Louis, Mo.
2329—Gaylord Mfg. Co., 49 Park Ave., Rear, Paterson, N. J.
2331—Geier Co., P. A., 540 E. 105th St., Cleveland, Ohio.
2334—Gem Mfg. Co., 1229 Goebel St., N. S., Pittsburgh, Pa.
2335—Gem Striper Co., 15411 Ilene Ave., Detroit, Mich.
2336—General Abrasive Co., College Ave., Niagara Falls, N. Y.
2337—General Appliance Corp., 170 Otis St., San Francisco, Calif.
2338—General Asbestos & Rubber Div. of Raybestos-Manhattan, Inc., North Charleston, S. C.
2338a—General Automatic Lock Nut Corp., General Motors Bldg., New York, N. Y.
2339—General Body Mfg. Co., 2211 Campbell St., Kansas City, Mo.
2341—General Brass Co., 100 S. Campbell Ave., Detroit, Mich.
2341a—General Cable Corp., 420 Lexington Ave., New York, N. Y.
2342—General Dry Batteries, Inc., 13100 Athens Ave., W., Cleveland, Ohio.
2343—General Electric Co., Merchandising Dept., Bridgeport, Conn. Adv. p. 109.
2343a—General Electric Co., 1 River Rd., Schnectady, N. Y. Adv. p. 109.
2345—General Fireproofing Co., Youngstown, Ohio.
2346—General Grinder Corp., 240 N. Milwaukee St., Milwaukee, Wis.
2347—General Industries Co., Olive St., Elyria, Ohio.
2348—General Lead Batteries Co., 4 Lister Ave., Newark, N. J.
2349—General Leather Co., 420 Frelinghuysen Ave., Newark, N. J.
2350—General Mfg. Co., 4127 Forest Park Blvd., St. Louis, Mo.
2351—General Motors Truck Corp., Pontiac, Mich.
2355—General Tire & Rubber Co., E. Market St., Akron, Ohio.
2357—General Woodwork Corp., 1225 Budd St., Cincinnati, Ohio.
2358—Genesee Tack Co., 7 Norfolk Pl., Rochester, N. Y.
2359—Geneva Metal Wheel Co., 191 Factory Row, Geneva, Ohio.
2360—Georgia Webbing & Tape Co., 1325 12th St., Columbus, Ga.
2361—Gets Mfg. Co., Andrews, Ind.
2362—Geuder, Paeschke & Frey Co., 1401 W. St. Paul Ave., Milwaukee, Wis.
2364—Giant Grip Mfg. Co., 30 Osceola St., Oshkosh, Wis.
2365—Giant Tire & Rubber Co., Lima St. & Western Ave., Findlay, Ohio.
2366—Gibbs Battery Co., Corydon, Iowa.
2369—Gifford-Wood Co., 15 Hill St., Hudson, N. Y.
2370—Gilbert & Barker Mfg. Co., Church St. & B. & A. R. R., Springfield, Mass.
2372—Gilfillan Bros., 1815 Venice Blvd., Los Angeles, Calif.
2377—Gill & Sons Forge & Machine Works, P. H., 2 Lorraine St., Brooklyn, N. Y.
2378—Gilmer Co., L. H., Cottman & Keystone Sts., Philadelphia, Pa.
2379—Gilson Bolens Mfg. Co., Port Washington, Wis.
2383—Glade Mfg. Co., 1603 S. Michigan Blvd., Chicago, Ill.
2384—Gladiator Mfg. Co., 411 N. Indiana Ave., Auburn, Ind.
2387—Glenside Woolen Mills, Skaneateles Falls, N. Y.
2388—Glenzer Co., J. C., 6463 Epworth Blvd., Detroit, Mich.
2389—Glidden Co., W. Madison Ave. at Berea Rd., Cleveland, Ohio.
2389a—Glider Over-Drive Axle Co., 3400 Scotten Ave., Detroit, Mich.
2390—Globe Insulated Wire Co., 148 Old Colony Ave., Wollaston, Mass.
2391—Globe Machine & Mfg. Co., Albert Lea, Minn.
2392—Globe Machine & Stamping Co., 1212 W. 76th St., Cleveland, Ohio. Adv. p. 53.
2393—Globe Machinery & Supply Co., 205 W. Court Ave., Des Moines, Iowa.
2394—Globe Mfg. Co., 100 Aldrich St., Battle Creek, Mich.
2396—Globe Specialty Co., 1900 Southport Ave., Chicago, Ill.
2397—Globe Ticket Co., 112 N. 12th St., Philadelphia, Pa.
2398—Globe-Union Mfg. Co., 900 E. Keefe Ave., Milwaukee, Wis.
2401—Godward Gas Generator, Inc., 280 Broadway, New York, N. Y.
2402—Goerlich's, Inc., 1214 Norwood Ave., Toledo, Ohio.
2404—Golden Gate Brass Mfg. Co., 251 Second St., San Francisco, Calif.
2406—Golden State Truck Co., 1020 Folsom St., San Francisco, Calif.
2407—Golde-Patent Mfg. Co., Ypsilanti, Mich.
2408—Gold Metal Folding Furniture Co., 1700 Packard Ave., Racine, Wis.
2409—Good-All Electric, Inc., Ogallala, Neb.
2410—Goodell-Pratt Co., 57 Wells St., Greenfield, Mass.
2411—Goodrich-Lenhart Mfg. Co., Hamburg, Pa.
2412—Goodrich Rubber Co., B. F., S. Main St., Akron, Ohio.
2413—Good Roads Machinery Co., Kennett Square, Pa.
2415—Goodyear Sundries & Mechanical Co., 116 Chambers St., New York, N. Y.
2416—Goodyear Tire & Rubber Co., E. Market St., Akron, Ohio.
2418—Gordon Co., J. P., 272 N. Fourth St., Columbus, Ohio.
2419—Gordon Metals Corp., 627 E. Polk St., Milwaukee, Wis.
2420—Gordon Motor Crib Co., 8 Bridge St., New York, N. Y.
2421—Goshen Cushion & Body Co., N. Second St., Goshen, Ind.
2422—Goslin-Birmingham Mfg. Co., Box 631, Birmingham, Ala.

2423—Gotfredsen Truck Co., Rob't, 3601 Gratiot Ave., Detroit, Mich.
2425—Gould Storage Battery Corp., 1 Main St., Depew, N. Y.
2429—Graham Co., James, 293 Wooster St., New Haven, Conn.
2430—Graham-Paige Motors Corp., 8505 W. Warren Ave., Detroit, Mich.
2431—Gramm-Bernstein Corp., E. Wayne & Scott Sts., Lima, Ohio.
2433—Gramm Motors, Inc., Delphos, Ohio.
2436—Grant Auto Electric Co., 1425 12th Ave., Seattle, Wash.
2436a—Grant Engineering Corp., South & Lincoln Ave., E., Cranford, N. J.
2437—Grant Mfg. & Machine Co., 90 Silliman Ave., Bridgeport, Conn.
2438—Grant Storage Battery Co., 226 N. Second St., Minneapolis, Minn.
2439—Grapho-Metal Packing Co., 2232 Alvord St., Indianapolis, Ind.
2440—Grasselli Chemical Co., Guardian Bldg., Cleveland, Ohio.
2440a—Grasse Premier Truck Co., Sauk City, Wis.
2441—Graton & Knight Co., 356 Franklin St., Worcester, Mass.
2445—Gray Co., 120 S. 10th St., Minneapolis, Minn. Adv. p. 18.
2448—Greaves Machine Tool Co., Eastern Ave. & Hazen St., Cincinnati, Ohio.
2450—Greek-American Sponge Co., 158 N. Franklin St., Chicago, Ill.
2451—Green Co., 90 W. Broadway, New York, N. Y.
2453a—Greene Mfg. Co., 1028 Douglas Ave., Racine, Wis.
2454—Greene, Tweed & Co., 109 Duane St., New York, N. Y.
2456—Greenfield Tap & Die Corp., Sanderson St., Greenfield, Mass.
2461—Griffith-Hope Co., 57th Ave. & Mitchell St., West Allis, Wis.
2462—Grimes Brake Engineering Service, 617 E. Erie Blvd., Syracuse, N. Y.
2465—Grinnell Co., 260 W. Exchange St., Providence, R. I.
2467—Groetken Pump Co., 179 S. River St., Aurora, Ill.
2469a—Gross Mfg. Co., 2317 Ivor Ave., San Gabriel, Calif.
2472—Guaranteed Parts Co., 250 W. 54th St., New York, N. Y.
2474—Guibert Steel Co., Diamond Bank Bldg., Pittsburgh, Pa.
2475—Guide Lamp Corp., 25th St. & Belt Ry., Anderson, Ind.
2476—Guilder Engineering Co., Poughkeepsie, N. Y.
2477—Guild Mfg. Co., 354 N. Gay St., Baltimore, Md.
2478—Gunite Corp., 302 Peoples Ave., Rockford, Ill.
2479—Gurnard Mfg. Co., 97 Rantoul St., Beverly, Mass. (Sole distributors, McIlwaine, Inc., 16 Hudson St., New York, N. Y.)
2480—Gwilliam Co., 360 Furman St., Brooklyn, N. Y.
2482—Gyro Brush Co., 30 Orange St., Bloomfield, N. J.

H

2602—Haartz Co., J. C., 30 Lenox Street, New Haven, Conn.
2603—Haberer & Co., Gest & Summer Sts., Cincinnati, Ohio.
2604—Hackett Products Co., 407 Pine St., Providence, R. I. Adv. p. 40.
2607—Hagy & Son, Clayton L., 16th & Carpenter Sts., Philadelphia, Pa.
2608—Hagy Waste Works, J. Milton, 836 S. Swanson St., Philadelphia, Pa.
2612—Hale Fire Pump Co., 708 Spring Mill Ave., Conshohocken, Pa.
2614—Hall Curtain Corp., 1109 N. Lancaster Ave., Dallas, Tex.
2615—Hall Mfg. Co., 1600 Woodland Ave., Toledo, Ohio.
2616—Hall-Thompson Co., Hartford, Conn.
2617—Halstead Oil Co., Union Central Bldg., Cincinnati, Ohio.
2619—Hamerschlag, Arthur, 17 W. 60th St., New York, N. Y.
2620—Hamilton Autographic Register Co., 802 Symmes Ave., Hamilton, Ohio.
2621—Hamilton Caster & Mfg. Co., 1647 Dixie Highway, Hamilton, Ohio.
2622—Hamilton Co., 829 E. 15th St., Brooklyn, N. Y.
2623—Hamilton Glass Instrument Co., Alexander, Washington & Forrest Sts., Conshohocken, Pa.
2625—Hamilton-Wade Co., 52 Haverhill St., Brockton, Mass.
2626—Hammett, H. G., 466 Eighth St., Troy, N. Y.
2627—Hammett Mfg. Co., 13th & Oak Sts., Kansas City, Mo.
2628—Hampden Automotive Products, Inc., 21 Winter St., Springfield, Mass.
2630—Handy Cleaner Corp., 3925 W. Fort St., Detroit, Mich.
2631—Handy Governor Corp., 3921 W. Fort St., Detroit, Mich. Adv. p. 79.
2632—Handy & Harman, 57 William St., New York, N. Y.
2634—Handy Mfg. Co., 9 Library St., Grand Rapids, Mich.
2635—Handy Oiler Co., Danville, Ind.
2637—Hangliter Mfg. Co., 983 S. Raymond Ave., Pasadena, Calif.
2640—Hanlon & Wilson, 321 Pennwood Ave., Wilkinsburg, Pa. (Sole distributors, J. H. Spillman, Wilkinsburg, Pa.)
2641—Hansen Mfg. Co., 1786 E. 27th St., Cleveland, Ohio. Adv. p. 112.
2642—Hansen Mfg. Co., A. L., 5037 Ravenswood Ave., Chicago, Ill.
2643—Hanson Co., C. H., 303 W. Erie St., Chicago, Ill.
2646—Hardie Mfg. Co., Mechanic St., Hudson, Mich.
2647—Hardy Mfg. Co., Pendleton, Ind.
2648—Harley Soap Co., 2832 E. Pacific St., Philadelphia, Pa.
2649—Harnishfeger Corp., 4400 W. National Ave., Milwaukee, Wis.
2652—Harrington & King Perforating Co., 5655 Fillmore St., Chicago, Ill.
2653—Harrisburg Stanley Spring Works, Cameron & Calder Sts., Harrisburg, Pa.
2654—Harris Calorific Co., 2828 Washington Ave., Cleveland, Ohio.
2655—Harris & Co., Arthur, 212 N. Curtis St., Chicago, Ill.
2656—Harris Hdw. & Mfg. Co., D. P., 99 Chambers St., New York, N. Y.
2657—Harris Oil Co., A. W., 326 S. Water St., Providence, R. I.
2658—Harrison & Co., 487 Groveland St., Haverhill, Mass.
2659—Harrison Radiator Corp., Washburn & Walnut Sts., Lockport, N. Y.
2661—Harshaw Chemical Co., 1945 E. 97th St., Cleveland, Ohio.
2663—Hartford Machine Screw Co., 476 Capitol Ave., Hartford, Conn.
2664—Hartford Windshield Co., 1811 S. Hope St., Los Angeles, Calif.
2665—Hartshorn Co., Stewart, 250 Fifth Ave., New York, N. Y.
2665a—Hartung Co., Charles F., 740 E. 61st St., Los Angeles, Calif. (Sole distributors, Ohio Parts Co., Ohio Bldg., 2735 Colerain Ave., Cincinnati, Ohio.)
2667—Harvey Motor Truck Works, 155th St. & Commercial Ave., Harvey, Ill.

MANUFACTURERS OF AUTOMOTIVE PRODUCTS—Continued

2668—Harvey Spring & Forging Co., 17th St. & Murray Ave., Racine, Wis.
2669—Haskell Mfg. Co., Wm. H., 24 Commerce St., Pawtucket, R. I.
2670—Haskins Co., R. G., 4631 Fulton St., Chicago, Ill.
2671—Hassler Service Co., 426 Terrace Ave., Indianapolis, Ind.
2672—Hastings Mfg. Co., 375 E. Mill Street, Hastings, Mich.
2674—Hauck Mfg. Co., 126 Tenth St., Brooklyn, N. Y.
2675—Haughton Elevator & Machine Co., 671 Spencer St., Toledo, Ohio.
2676—Havana Mfg. Co., Havana, Ill.
2678—Hawkes & Co., T. G., 79 W. Market St., Corning, N. Y.
2679—Hawkeye Truck Co., 2700 Floyd Ave., Sioux City, Iowa.
2680—Haydon, A. & M., 304 N. 22nd St., Philadelphia, Pa.
2680a—Hayes Body Corp., Seventh & Muskegon Aves., Grand Rapids, Mich.
2681—Hayes Equipment Mfg. Co., 624 E. Gilbert St., Wichita, Kan.
2684—Haynes Stellite Co., Kokomo, Ind.
2686—Hazard Insulated Wire Works, Div. of Okonite Co., Wilkes-Barre, Pa.
2689—Heath & Milligan Mfg. Co., 1833 Seward St., Chicago, Ill.
2690—**Herbert Mfg. Co., Central St., Franklin, N. H. Adv. p. 91.**
2691—Hecht & Co., F., 10 Spruce St., New York, N. Y.
2693—Hedges Co., B. E., 303 W. Genesee St., Auburn, N. Y.
2694—Hedstrom Mfg. Co., 4647 Lake St., Chicago, Ill.
2695—Hegeler Zinc Co., Danville, Ill.
2697—Heil Co., 1142 Montana Ave., Milwaukee, Wis.
2699—Heintz & Co., James C., 3738 W. 143rd St., Cleveland, Ohio.
2700—Hein-Werner Motor Parts Corp., Waukesha, Wis.
2701—Heinze Electric Co., Lowell, Mass.
2702—Heiz & Heiz, Inc., 33 34th St., Brooklyn, N. Y.
2703—Heller Bros. Co., 865 Mt. Prospect Ave., Newark, N. J.
2705—Heller & Co., W. C., 1907 Wabash Ave., Montpelier, Ohio.
2707—Hempy-Cooper Mfg. Co., 418 Archibald St., Kansas City, Mo.
2707a—Henderson Bros., 311 N. Desplaines St., Chicago, Ill.
2708—Hendey Machine Co., 105 Summer St., Torrington, Conn.
2709—Hendrick Mfg. Co., 39 Dundaff St., Carbondale, Pa.
2710—Henney Motor Co., Chicago & Spring Sts., Freeport, Ill.
2711—Henry & Allen, 2 Wadsworth St., Auburn, N. Y.
2712—Henry & Wright Mfg. Co., 760 Windsor St., Hartford, Conn.
2714—Herbrand Co., Cor. Lake & Stone Sts., Fremont, Ohio.
2716—Hercules Motors Corp., Halliwell Ct., S. E., Canton, Ohio.
2717—Hercules Products Co., 113 State St., St. Joseph, Mich.
2718—Hercules Products, Inc., Morton Ave., Evansville, Ind.
2720—Herman Body Co., 4420 Clayton Ave., St. Louis, Mo.
2721—Herold Mfg. Co., 1104 W. Ninth St., Cleveland, Ohio.
2722—Herron-Zimmers Moulding Co., 3650 Beaufait St., Detroit, Mich.
2723—Hersee Co., F. C., 47 Bacon St., Watertown, Mass.
2724—Hertner Electric Co., 12690 Elmwood Ave., Cleveland, Ohio.
2728—Hettrick Mfg. Co., Summit & Magnolia Sts., Toledo, Ohio.
2731—Hewitt-Ludlow Auto Co., 75 Fremont St., San Francisco, Calif.
2732—Hewitt Metals Corp., 12th St. at Stanley Ave., Detroit, Mich.
2733—Hexcel Radiator Co., 277 E. Erie St., Milwaukee, Wis.
2734—Heywood-Wakefield Co., 174 Portland St., Boston, Mass.
2735—Hiawatha Sales Co., 1608 Pacific Ave., Atchison, Kan.
2740—Hicks Rubber Co., Waco, Tex.
2743—Highland Body Mfg. Co., 401 Elmwood Pl., Cincinnati, Ohio.
2744—Highway Trailer Co., 421 E. Fulton St., Edgerton, Wis.
2747—Hilliard Corp., 102 W. Fourth St., Elmira, N. Y.
2748—Hill Mfg. Co., Belmond, Iowa.
2750—Hillwood Mfg. Co., 21700 St. Clair Ave., Cleveland, Ohio.
2751—Hilo Varnish Corp., 1 Gerry St., Brooklyn, N. Y.
2756—Hindley Mfg. Co., 53 John St., Valley Falls, R. I.
2758—Hinson Mfg. Co., Westfield Ave. & Menges St., Waterloo, Iowa.
2760—Hi Pressure Sales Co., 1030 Golden Gate Ave., San Francisco, Calif.
2761—Hipwell Mfg. Co., 825 North Ave., Pittsburgh, Pa.
2763—Hirst-Roger Carpet Co., Allegheny & Kensington Aves., Philadelphia, Pa.
2764—Hisey-Wolf Machine Co., 2745 Colerain Ave., Cincinnati, Ohio.
2766—**Hobart Brothers, Box 51, Canal Locke Square, Troy, Ohio. Adv. p. 108.**
2767—Hobart Cabinet Co., 111 W. Water St., Troy, Ohio.
2768—Hobart Mfg. Co., Troy, Ohio.
2769—Hobart Metal Mfg. Co., 801 16th Ave., S. E., Minneapolis, Minn.
2772—Hobbs Mfg. Co., 609 N. Main St., Fort Worth, Tex.
2773—Hodes-Zink Mfg. Co., Fremont, Ohio.
2777—Hoffman Lion Mills Co., 542 W. Broadway, New York, N. Y.
2778—Hoggson & Pettis Mfg. Co., 141 Brewery St., New Haven, Conn.
2780—Holbrook Co., Hudson, N. Y.
2781—**Holfast Rubber Co., Lakewood Ave., Atlanta, Ga. Adv. p. 65.**
2782—Holland Mfg. Co., Central Ave. & Bank St., Baltimore, Md.
2783—Holley Carburetor Co., Vancouver Ave. & P. M. R. R., Detroit, Mich.
2784—Hollingshead Co., R. M., Ninth & Cooper Sts., Camden, N. J.
2785—Hollister-Whitney Co., 211 N. Second St., Quincy, Ill.
2786—Holmes Co., Ernest, 700 E. Main St., Chattanooga, Tenn.
2787—Holophane Co., 342 Madison Ave., New York, N. Y.
2792—Homestead Valve Mfg. Co. (Hypressure Jenny Div.), Coraopolis, Pa.
2793—Hones, Inc., Charles A., 122 S. Grand Ave., Baldwin, N. Y.
2794—Honeycutt-Harris Battery Corp., 411 Southwest Blvd., Kansas City, Mo.
2795—Honeycutt Mfg. Co., 18 E. 17th St., Kansas City, Mo.
2796—Honold Mfg. Co., 824 Pennsylvania Ave., Sheboygan, Wis.
2798—Hood Rubber Co., 98 Nichols Ave., Watertown, Mass.
2799—Hoof Co., John C., 162 N. Franklin St., Chicago, Ill.
2800—Hoopes Bro. & Darlington, Inc., West Chester, Pa. (Licensees.)
2801—Hoover Parts Co., 14154 Superior Rd., Cleveland, Ohio.
2802—Hoover Spring Co., 201 Franklin St., San Francisco, Calif.
2803—Hoover Steel Ball Co., Ann Arbor, Mich.
2807—Houde Engineering Corp., Div. Houdaille-Hershey Corp., 537-43 E. Delavan Ave., Buffalo, N. Y.
2808—Houghton & Co., E. F., 240 W. Somerset St., Philadelphia, Pa.

2809—Houze Convex Glass Co., L. J., Point Marion, Pa.
2812—Howard Foundries, Inc., 9500 W. Belmont Ave., Franklin Park, Ill.
2813—Howe Fire Apparatus Co., Anderson, Ind.
2814—Howe Scale Co., Rutland, Vt.
2817—Hoyt-Beardsley Mfg. Co., 506 Frances Bldg., Sioux City, Iowa.
2818—Hoyt Electrical Instrument Works, Penacook, N. H. (Sole distributors, Burton-Rogers Co., 755 Boylston St., Boston, Mass.)
2819—Hubbard Products Co., 201 W. North St., Kokomo, Ind.
2820—Hub Cap Co., 104 Oliver St., North Tonawanda, N. Y.
2821—Hub City Iron Works, 218 First Ave., S. W., Aberdeen, S. D.
2822—**Hubco Mfg. Co., 404 W. Conway St., Baltimore, Md. Adv. Mich. Adv. p. 104.**
2824—**Hudson Motor Car Co., 12601 E. Jefferson Ave., Detroit, Mich. Adv. p. 30.**
2825—Huetter Machine & Tool Co., 543 Kentucky Ave., Indianapolis, Ind.
2826—Huffman Mfg. Co., Davis & Gilbert Aves., Dayton, Ohio.
2827—Hug Co., Highland, Ill.
2829—Hughes-Keenan Co., Wayne & Newman Sts., Mansfield, Ohio.
2834—Humason Mfg. Co., Stafford Ave., Forestville, Conn.
2835—Hunt Automotive Equipment Co., Geo. L., 1017 Mound St., Davenport, Iowa.
2836—Hunt Battery Mfg. Co., 409 W. Okmulgee Ave., Muskogee, Okla.
2838—Hunter Pressed Steel Co., Lansdale, Pa.
2839—Hunter Saw & Machine Co., 57th & Butler Sts., Pittsburgh, Pa.
2840—Hunt-Helm-Ferris Co., Harvard, Ill.
2841—Hunt Mfg. Co., Geo. L., 1030 Wisconsin Ave., Boscobel, Wis.
2842—Hunt & Son, C. B., 636 McKinley Ave., Salem, Ohio.
2843—Hunt-Spiller Mfg. Corp., 383 Dorchester Ave., Boston, Mass.
2844—Hupp Motor Car Corp., 3501 E. Milwaukee Ave., Detroit, Mich.
2845—Hurd, E. P., 5822 Fisher Ave., Detroit, Mich.
2846—Husky Corporation, Lake Shore Rd., Kenosha, Wis.
2848—Hutto Engineering Co., 515 Lycaste Ave., Detroit, Mich.
2849—Hyatt Roller Bearing Co., Newark, N. J.
2850—Hyde Mfg. Co., Eastford Rd., Southbridge, Mass.
2851—**Hydraulic Brake Co., 2843 Grand Blvd., E., Detroit, Mich. Adv. Front Cover.**
2853—Hydraulic Pressed Bearing Co., Lincoln & Platt Sts., Niles, Mich.
2858—**Hygrade Products Co., 333 W. 52nd St., New York, N. Y. Adv. p. 86.**
2860—Hyman Co., S. E., Concord St., Fremont, Ohio.
2861—Hy-Power Mfg. Corp., Pearl St., Mt. Vernon, N. Y.
2862—Hyro Mfg. Co., 200 Varick St., New York, N. Y.

I

3000—**I. X. L. Glass Corp., 151 S. Waterman Ave., Detroit, Mich.** (Importers.)
3002—Ideal Clamp Mfg. Co., 200 Bradford St., Brooklyn, N. Y.
3003—Ideal Commutator Dresser Co., 1014 Park Ave., Sycamore, Ill.
3007—Ilg Electric Ventilating Co., 2850 N. Crawford Ave., Chicago, Ill.
3010—Illinois Iron & Bolt Co., Carpentersville, Ill.
3014—Illinois Stamping & Mfg. Co., 220 N. Jefferson St., Chicago, Ill.
3015—Imperial Bit & Snap Co., 14th & Clark Sts., Racine, Wis.
3016—**Imperial Brass Mfg. Co., 1225 W. Harrison St., Chicago, Ill. Adv. p. 126.**
3017—Imperial Electric Co., 64 Ira Ave., Akron, Ohio.
3017a—Imported Motors, Inc., 37 W. 65th St., New York, N. Y. (Importers.)
3018—Improved Gauge Mfg. Co., 105 Canal St., Syracuse, N. Y.
3021—Indestructible Wheel Co., 809 E. Walnut St., Lebanon, Ind.
3022—Indestructo Glass Corp., Farmingdale, L. I., N. Y.
3024—Indiana Body Co., Richmond, Ind.
3025—Indiana Lamp Corp., Div. Allied Products Corp., 20th St. & Milton Pike, Connersville, Ind.
3026—Indianapolis Brush & Broom Mfg. Co., 2260 Brush St., Indianapolis, Ind.
3027—Indianapolis Saddlery Co., 237 S. Meridian St., Indianapolis, Ind.
3028—Indiana Rubber & Insulated Wire Co., Jonesboro, Ind.
3029—Indiana Truck Corp., Indiana Park, Marion, Ind.
3030—Indian Refining Co., 1 Havoline St., Lawrenceville, Ill.
3031—India Tire & Rubber Co., Mogadore St., Akron, Ohio.
3032—Indicating Calipers Corp., 506 E. 19th St., New York, N. Y.
3033—Ingersoll-Rand Co., 11 Broadway, New York, N. Y.
3034—Ingraham Co., E., Bristol, Conn.
3035a—Inland Mfg. Co., 15 Coleman St., Dayton, Ohio.
3040—International Chain & Mfg. Co., York, Pa.
3041—International Chemical Co., 2628 N. Mascher St., Philadelphia, Pa.
3043—International Harvester Co., 606 S. Michigan Ave., Chicago, Ill.
3045—**International Metal Hose Co., 10109-15 Quincy Ave., Cleveland, Ohio. Adv. p. 99.**
3046—International Metal Polish Co., Quill St. & Belt R. R., Indianapolis, Ind.
3048—International Motor Co., 25 Broadway, New York, N. Y.
3048a—Internation Nutyp Tool Corp., W. First & Schuyler Sts., Oswego, N. Y. "Oswego."
3049—International Oxygen Co., 796 Frelinghuysen Ave., Newark, N. J.
3050—International Register Co., 15 S. Throop St., Chicago, Ill.
3051—International Screw Co., 2751 W. Kirby Ave., Detroit, Mich.
3054—International Steel & Iron Co., 1321 Edgar St., Evansville, Ind.
3056—International Time Recording Co., 270 Broadway, New York,
3060—Interstate Electric Co., 4339 Duncan Ave., St. Louis, Mo.
3062—Invincible Vacuum Cleaner Mfg. Co., 14th & Davis Sts., Dover, Ohio.
3064—Iron City Wiping Materials Co., Overhill & Reed Sts., Pittsburgh, Pa.

MANUFACTURERS OF AUTOMOTIVE PRODUCTS—Continued

3065—Irving Engineering Co., Seventh & Division Sts., Sioux City, Iowa.
3066—I-Sis Laboratories, Inc., Sunnyside Ave., Stamford, Conn.
3067—Iten Fibre Co., 5403 Bower Ave., Cleveland, Ohio.
3069—Izett Auto Body Co., 1448 Speer Blvd., Denver, Colo.

J

3101—Jacobs Mfg. Co., 2072 Park Rd., Hartford, Conn.
3102—Jadson Motor Valve Co., 8354 Wilcox Ave., Bell, Calif.
3103—Jaeger Watch Co., 304 E. 45th St., Allied Arts Bldg., New York, N. Y.
3104—Jambor Tool & Stamping Co., 1261 30th St., Milwaukee, Wis. Adv. p. 64.
3104a—Jamestown Metalsmiths, Inc. (Wrench Div.), 217 Hopkins Ave., Jamestown, N. Y.
3106—Jansen Machine Co., 741 21st St., Des Moines, Iowa.
3107—Jarecki Mfg. Co., 1305 W. 12th St., Erie, Pa.
3110—Jay Mfg. Co. of Illinois, 17 E. 24th St., Chicago, Ill. (Eastern territory.)
3111—Jeannette Glass Co., Jeannette, Pa.
3112—Jeavons Co., Clauss Bldg., 110 E. State St., Fremont, Ohio.
3113—Jefferis Co., R. W., 11th & Linden Sts., Camden, N. J.
3114—Jefferson Electric Co., 1508 S. Laflin St., Chicago, Ill. Adv. p. 75.
3115—Jefferson Glass Co., State St., Follansbee, W. Va.
3116—Jenkins Vulcan Spring Co., Eighth & N. G Sts., Richmond, Ind. Adv. p. 97.
3119—Jessop Co., S. T., 219 W. Chicago Ave., Chicago, Ill.
3120—Jewell Bros. Products Co., 549 Fulton St., Chicago, Ill.
3121—Jewell Electrical Instrument Co., 1650 W. Walnut St., Chicago, Ill. (Sole distributors, Battery Equipment & Supply Co., 7524 Greenwood Ave., Chicago, Ill.)
3122—Jewell Paint & Varnish Co., 345 N. Western Ave., Chicago, Ill.
3123—Jiffe Co., Ashburner & Hegerman Sts., Holmesburg, Philadelphia, Pa.
3127—Johns-Manville, 292 Madison Ave., New York, N. Y. Adv. p. 83.
3128—Johnson Belting Co., 423 E. 56th St., New York, N. Y.
3129—Johnson Bronze Co., S. Mill St., New Castle, Pa. Adv. p. 60.
3131—Johnson Gas Appliance Co., 520 E Ave., Cedar Rapids, Iowa.
3132—Johnson & Johnson, George St., New Brunswick, N. J.
3134—Johnson Mfg. Co., Geo. W., 209 W. 17th St., Kansas City, Mo.
3136—Johnson Piston Ring Co., 6010 Woodward Ave., Detroit, Mich.
3137a—Johnston Glass Co., Hartford City, Ind.
3138—Johnston & Jennings Co., 877 Addison Rd., Cleveland, Ohio.
3140—Jones, Mark W., 53rd St. & Lansdowne Ave., Philadelphia, Pa.
3141—Jones Clutch & Gear Co., Upper Sandusky, Ohio.
3143—Jones & Laughlin Steel Corp., Jones & Laughlin Bldg., Pittsburgh, Pa.
3146—Jones Spring Co., W. B., 809 Walnut St., Cincinnati, Ohio.
3147—Jordon Fabric Mfg. Co., 2920 McGee Trafficway, Kansas City, Mo.
3148—Jordon Motor Car Co., 1070 E. 152nd St., Cleveland, Ohio.
3149—Joyce-Cridland Co., 333 S. Linden Ave., Dayton, Ohio.
3150—Jubilee Mfg. Co., 1929 S. 20th St., Omaha, Neb.
3151—Judd & Leland Mfg. Co., Hibbard Ave., Clifton Springs, N. Y.
3155—Julian Pump & Mfg. Corp., Lakewood Rd. & Howard Ave., Jamestown, N. Y.
3156—Jungersen Dump Body Co., 1331 30th St., Milwaukee, Wis.
3158—Jupiter Spark Plug Co., 716 E. Pike St., Seattle, Wash.
3159—Justrite Mfg. Co., 2070 Southport Ave., Chicago, Ill.

K

3200—K-D Lamp Co., 108-18 W. Third St., Cincinnati, Ohio. Adv. p. 49.
3201—K-D Mfg. Co., 510 Plum St., Lancaster, Pa.
3202—K-E-M Mfg. Co., 245 West 55th St., New York, N. Y.
3203—K & G Mfg. Co., 1805 Sixth Ave., N., Birmingham, Ala.
3205—K-O Mfg. Corp., 603 American Bldg., Cincinnati, Ohio.
3207—K-W Ignition Corp., 1767 E. 27th St., Cleveland, Ohio.
3208—K & W Rubber Co., Delaware, Ohio.
3209—Kacena-Thaler Co., 2309 Indiana Ave., Chicago, Ill.
3210—Kahn Bros., 785 Humboldt St., Brooklyn, N. Y.
3211—Kalbfleisch Corp., 200 Fifth Ave., New York, N. Y.
3212—Kales Stamping Co., 1669 W. Lafayette Blvd., Detroit, Mich.
3213—Kane Mfg. Co., 734 Beacom Lane, Merion, Pa.
3220—Kant Slip Valve Lifter Co., Sidney, Ill.
3221—Kaplan Specialty Co., 31 Summer Ave., Newark, N. J.
3222—Kari-Keen Mfg. Co., Seventh & Division Sts., Sioux City, Iowa.
3227—Kautz & Co., Fred C., 2633 W. Lake St., Chicago, Ill.
3228—Kawneer Co., 931 Front St., Niles, Mich.
3230—Kay-Brunner Steel Products, Inc., 999 Meridian St., Alhambra, Calif.
3231—Kay & Ess Co., Leo & Kiser Sts., Dayton, Ohio.
3234—Keasbey & Mattison Co., Butler & Railroad Aves., Ambler, Pa.
3237—Keep Klean Cover Co., 11th and Tyler Sts., St. Louis, Mo.
3238—Keesee Mfg. Co., 723 W. Belgrave Ave., Huntington Park, Calif.
3239—Kehawke Mfg. Co., 825 Western Ave., Minneapolis, Minn.
3240—Kelley & Stewart Co., Water & Joiners Sts., South Brownsville, Pa.
3241—Kellogg Mfg. Co., 65 Humboldt St., Rochester, N. Y. Adv. p. 2.
3245—Kelly Foundry & Machine Works, 228 N. Town St., Mt. Gilead, Ohio.
3247—Kelly-Springfield Tire Co., General Motors Bldg., New York, N. Y.
3249—Kempsmith Mfg. Co., 45th Ave. & Rogers St., Milwaukee, Wis.
3250—Kennedy Car Liner & Bag Co., Shelbyville, Ind.
3251—Kennedy Mfg. Co., 501 N. Monroe St., Streator, Ill.
3252—Kennedy Mfg. Co., North Harrison St., Van Wert, Ohio.
3254—Kent Co., 108 Canal St., Rome, N. Y.

3256—Kent-Moore Organization, 3-158 General Motors Bldg., Detroit, Mich.
3258—Kentucky Wagon Mfg. Co., Third St. at Eastern Parkway, Louisville, Ky.
3259—Kenworth Motor Truck Corp., 1263 Mercer St., Seattle, Wash.
3260—Kenyon Co., C., First Ave & 57th St., Brooklyn, N. Y.
3262—Keratol Co., 348 Van Buren St., Newark, N. J.
3263—Kerlow Steel Flooring Co., 222 Culver Ave., Jersey City, N. J.
3264—Kerrihard Co., 401 W. Coolbaugh St., Red Oak, Iowa.
3265—Kester Solder Co., 4201 Wrightwood Ave., Chicago, Ill.
3266—Keystone Boiler & Foundry Co., Broad St., Landisville, Pa.
3267—Keystone Emery Mills, 1665 Church St., Philadelphia, Pa.
3268—Keystone Forging Co., Northumberland, Pa.
3270—Keystone Mfg. Co., 41 Chandler St., Buffalo, N. Y.
3271—Keystone Reamer & Tool Co., Millersburg, Pa.
3272—Keystone Sales Corp., 1826 Sixth St., Detroit, Mich.
3275—Kickhaefer Mfg. Co., 901 S. Second St., Milwaukee, Wis.
3276—Kidde & Co., Walter, 140 Cedar St., New York, N. Y.
3277—Kiernan & Co., W. C., 201 State St., Whitewater, Wis.
3278—Kilborn-Sauer Co., Post Road, Fairfield, Conn.
3279—Killark Electric Mfg. Co., 3940 Easton Ave., St. Louis, Mo. Adv. p. 76.
3280—Kimball Bros. Co., 1004 Ninth St., Council Bluffs, Iowa.
3282a—Kimble Electric Co., 2011 W. Hastings St., Chicago, Ill.
3283—Kingham Trailer Co., 235 Gaulbert Ave., Louisville, Ky.
3284—King Quality Products Co., 2320 Cooper St., St. Louis, Mo.
3285—King-Seeley Corp., 294 Second St., Ann Harbor, Mich. Adv. p. 45.
3287—Kingston Products Corp., 1400 N. Webster St., Kokomo, Ind.
3288—King-Zeitler Co., 315 N. Ada St., Chicago, Ill.
3289—Kinnear Mfg. Co., 718 Field Ave., Columbus, Ohio.
3290—Kinney Mfg. Co., 3529 Washington St., Jamaica Plain, Boston, Mass.
3291—Kinney Quick-Dim Co., 3529 Washington St., Jamaica Plain, Boston 30, Mass.
3292—Kinsman Co., H. W., Norwood, N. Y.
3293—Kirchberger & Co., M., 1425 37th St., Brooklyn, N. Y.
3294—Kirk & Blum Mfg. Co., 2858 Spring Grove Ave., Cincinnati, Ohio.
3296—Kirkman Engineering Corp., 1 Dominick St., New York, N. Y.
3297—Kirkpatrick, Inc., 122 Woodlawn Ave., Bywood Heights, Upper Darby, Pa.
3298—Kirk-Zwicker Co., 160 Second St., Cambridge, Mass.
3299—Kirstin Mfg. Co., Kirstin Bldg., Escanaba, Mich.
3300—Kissel Motor Car Co., 182 Kissel Ave., Hartford, Wis.
3303—Klaxon Co., Anderson, Ind.
3305—Kleenkar Fabric Equipment Co., 255 N. Water St., Milwaukee, Wis.
3307—Kleiber Motor Co., 1480 Folsom St., San Francisco, Calif.
3309—Klein Structural Steel Co., Bellevue, Ohio.
3310—Klemm Automotive Products Co., 1302 Halsted St., Chicago, Ill.
3311—Kliegl Bros. Universal Electric Stage Lighting Co., 321 W. 50th St., New York, N. Y.
3313—Knapp Electric, Inc., Div. P. R. Mallory & Co., 3029 E. Washington St., Indianapolis, Ind.
3316—Knapp-Monarch Co., 1413 Pine St., St. Louis, Mo.
3320—Knight & Thomas, 212 Summer St., Boston, Mass.
3321—Knopf, Paul, 3211 39th Ave., Long Island City, L. I., N. Y.
3323—Kodel Electric & Mfg. Co., 507 E. Pearl St., Cincinnati, Ohio.
3324—Koehler Rubber Co., 1369 W. Ninth St., Cleveland, Ohio.
3326—Koestlin Tool & Die Corp., 3601 Humboldt Ave., Detroit, Mich.
3327—Kokomo Rubber Co., 1016 S. Main St., Kokomo, Ind.
3327a—Kokomo Spring Co., Firmin & La Fountain Sts., Kokomo, Ind.
3328—Kolo Products Co., 320 Fifth Ave., New York, N. Y.
3329—Kool Kooshion Mfg. Co., 105 E. California Ave., Oklahoma City, Okla.
3330—Korect Air Meter Corp., 303 Grote St., Buffalo, N. Y. (Also sole distributors, Kellogg Mfg. Co., 65 Humboldt St., Rochester, N. Y.)
3331—Koscherak Siphon Bottle Works, 232 E. 42nd St., New York, N. Y.
3332—Koupet Auto Top Co., Reeb Station, Belleville, Ill.
3333—Kozak, Inc., 1 Park Place, Batavia, N. Y. Adv. p. 56.
3334—Kozekar, Inc., 910 13th Ave., S. E., Minneapolis, Minn.
3336—Kraeuter & Co., 583 18th Ave., Newark, N. J.
3337—Krahn Mfg. Co., 588 Clinton St., Milwaukee, Wis.
3340—Kratzer Carriage Co., 100 S. First St., Des Moines, Iowa.
3342—Kreamer, Inc., A., 307 Kent Ave., Brooklyn, N. Y.
3344—Kreiss Sign Co., 853 Washington St., Buffalo, N. Y.
3345—Krembs & Co., 669 W. Ohio St., Chicago, Ill.
3348—Krohn Differential Corp., 209 S. La Salle St., Chicago, Ill.
3349—Krone-Sebek Die Casting & Mfg. Co., 2935 W. 47th St., Chicago, Ill.
3349a—Kuller Electric Mfg. Co., 33-22 Northern Blvd., Long Island City, N. Y.
3350—Kund Cabinet Co., Bedford, Pa.
3352—Kurz-Kasch Co., Broadway & Morris Ave., Dayton, Ohio.
3355—Kysor Heater Co., Haynes St., Cadillac, Mich.

L

3401—L.M. Gear Co., 7203 Gratiot Ave., Detroit, Mich.
3402—L.M. & W. Mfg. Co., W. Gay St., West Chester, Pa.
3405—Laboratory Chemicals, Inc., 208 Amsterdam Ave., New York, N. Y.
3406—Lacer Corp., Ltd., 1224 E. Eighth St., Los Angeles, Calif.
3407—LaCrosse Tractor Co., LaCrosse, Wis.
3408—Ladew Co., Edward R., 29 Murray St., New York, N. Y.
3409—Lafayette Steel Products, Inc., Lafayette, Ind.
3409a—LaFrance-Republic Corp., 903 Michigan Ave., Alma, Mich.
3410—Laher Auto Spring Co., 26th & Magnolia Sts., Oakland, Calif.
3411—Laidlaw Co., 16 W. 60th St., New York, N. Y.
3413—Lakeview Drop Forge Co., Pittsburgh Ave., Erie, Pa.
3417—Lamb-Grays Harbor Co., Hoquiam, Wash.

MANUFACTURERS OF AUTOMOTIVE PRODUCTS—Continued

3418—Laminated Shim Co., 211 14th St., Long Island City, N. Y.
3420—Lamson & Sessions Co., 1971 W. 85th St., Cleveland, Ohio.
3421—Lancaster Lens Co., Lancaster, Ohio.
3422—Landers Corp., Buckingham & Blucher Sts., Toledo, Ohio.
3423—Landis Engineering & Mfg. Co., East Second St., Waynesboro, Pa.
3426—Lange Machine Works, Henry G., 150 N. May St., Chicago, Ill.
3429—Lansing Co., Lansing, Mich.
3431—Lapeer Trailer Corp., Fair St., Lapeer, Mich.
3433—La Plant-Choate Mfg. Co., Cedar Rapids, Iowa.
3436—Larrabee-Deyo Corp., Hillcrest, Binghamton, N. Y.
3437—Larson & Lunberg, 325 N. Main St., Kewanee, Ill.
3438—Larson Tool & Stamping Co., Olive St., Attleboro, Mass.
3439—LaSalle Machine Works, 3013 S. LaSalle St., Chicago, Ill.
3441—Lasco Corp., 2415 N. Howard St., Philadelphia, Pa.
3445—Lavietes Mfg. Co., Sta. A, New Haven, Conn.
3446—Lavo Co. of America, 300 N. Seventh St., Milwaukee Wis.
3447—Lawrence Leather Co., A. C., Peabody, Mass.
3448—Lawson Co., F. H., Evans & Whateley Sts., Cincinnati, Ohio.
3451—Leadox Battery Co., Neave & English Sts., Cincinnati, Ohio.
3452—Leak Micrometer Corp., 2926 Telegraph Ave., Berkeley, Calif.
3453—Leard Co., William, Fifth & 16th Sts., New Brighton, Pa.
3455—Leather Products Co., Front & Scott Sts., Covington, Ky.
3457—LeBlond Machine Tool Co., R. K., Madison & Edwards Rds., Cincinnati, Ohio.
3458—LeBlond-Schacht Truck Co., Eighth & Evans Sts., Cincinnati, Ohio.
3459—Lebzelter & Son Co., Philip, 241 N. Queen St., Lancaster, Pa.
3461—LeCount Tool Works, Wm. G., Merritt Place, South Norwalk, Conn.
3462—Leece-Neville Co., 5363 Hamilton Ave., Cleveland, Ohio.
3463—Lee Knight Lens Co., 210 East Ave., Rochester, N. Y.
3464—Lee-O-Lectric Mfg. Co., 1411 W. Front St., Monroe, Mich.
3465—Lees Co., John, 241 W. Georgia St., Indianapolis, Ind.
3466—Lees Mfg. Co., 320 Broadway, New York, N. Y.
3467—Lee & Son Co., K. O., 114 First Ave., N. E., Aberdeen, S. D.
3468—Lee's Tire Chain Industries, Inc., 308 E. Water St., Jefferson City, Mo.
3469—Lee Tire & Rubber Co. Conshohocken, Pa.
3472—Leland-Detroit Mfg. Co., 5680 12th St., Detroit, Mich.
3474—Lempco Products, Inc., Dunham Rd., Bedford, Ohio.
3477—Leonard Spark Plug Co., First Ave. & 21st St., N., St. Petersburg, Fla.
3478—Lepel High Frequency Laboratories, Inc., 39 W. 60th St., New York, N. Y.
3485—Levey, A. V. & B. W., 307 Canal St., New York, N. Y.
3488—Lewis-Shepard Co., 125 Walnut St., Watertown Station, Boston, Mass.
3489—Libbey-Owens-Ford Glass Co., Nicholas Bldg., Toledo, Ohio.
3492—Liberty Engineering Corp., 9 Elm Ave., Mt. Vernon, N. Y.
3493—Liberty Foundries Co., 23rd Ave. & Tenth St., Rockford, Ill.
3495—Lidseen, Inc., Gustave, 832 S. Central Ave., Chicago, Ill.
3497—Liggett Spring & Axle Co., Monongahela, Pa.
3498—Light Mfg. & Foundry Co., Queen St., Pottstown, Pa.
3500—Lima Sheet Metal Products Co., Lima, Ohio.
3502—Lincoln Brass Works, 2067 12th St., Detroit, Mich. Adv. p. 73.
3503—Lincoln Mfg. Co., Connersville, Ind.
3504—Lincoln Motor Co. Div. of Ford Motor Co., Detroit, Mich.
3505—Lincoln-Schlueter Machinery Co., 219 W. Grand Ave., Chicago, Ill.
3507—Linde Air Products Co., 30 E. 42nd St., New York, N. Y. Adv. p. 125.
3507a—Linderme Tube Co., 1291 E. 53rd St., Cleveland, Ohio.
3508—Lindsay, McMillan Co., 93 S. Water St., Milwaukee, Wis.
3509—Linendoll Corp., 228 N. La Salle St., Chicago, Ill.
3510—Link-Belt Co., Indianapolis, Ind. Adv. p. 70.
3511a—Linn Trailer Corp., 433 Chestnut St., Oneonta, N. Y.
3512—Lion Chain Company, 3124 W. 51st St., Chicago, Ill. Adv. p. 37.
3512a—Lipe, Inc., W. C., 208 S. Geddes St., Syracuse, N. Y.
3513—Lipman Pump Wks., 2310 11th St., Rockford, Ill.
3514—Lipschultz Bros., 155 E. Sixth St., St. Paul, Minn.
3515—Liquidometer Corp., Skillman Ave. at 37th St., Long Island City, N. Y.
3516—Liquid Veneer Corp., 822 Liquid Veneer Bldg., Buffalo, N. Y. Adv. p. 66.
3518—Lisle Mfg. Co., 813 E. Main St., Clarinda, Iowa,
3519—List Mfg. Co., E. J., Main & Adams Sts., Havana, Ill.
3521a—Little Giant Products, Inc., 1530 N. Adams St., Peoria, Ill.
3523—Livingston Co., 161 Day St., New Haven, Conn.
3526—Lloyd Mfg. Co., E. E., 416 N. Main St., Maryville, Mo.
3528—Lockport Cotton Batting Co., 304 Elmwood Ave., Lockport, N. Y.
3529—Locktite Patch Co., 4196 Bellevue Ave., Detroit, Mich.
3532—Lodge & Shipley Machine Tool Co., 3055 Colerain Ave., Cincinnati, Ohio.
3533—Logan Co., 201 E. Buchanan St., Louisville, Ky.
3534—Logan Gear Co., Westwood Ave., Toledo, Ohio.
3537—Loock & Co., R. J., 343-45 N. Gay St., Baltimore, Md. Adv. p. 51.
3539—Lorentzen, H. K., 155 Leonard St., New York, N. Y.
3540—Lorenz Trunk Works, Inc., 211 First Ave., N., Minneapolis, Minn.
3541—Lorraine Corp., Div. Van Sicklen Corp., Elgin, Ill.
3542—Los Angeles Rubber Stamp Co., 1500 S. Los Angeles St., Los Angeles, Calif.
3543—Los Angeles Spring & Forge Co., 1948 S. Los Angeles St., Los Angeles, Calif.
3543a—Losbough-Jordan Tool & Machine Co., Elkhart, Ind.
3544—Losee Motor Products Co., Hebron, Ill.
3545—Lothrop Co., Frank B., River St., South Acton, Mass.
3546—Louden Machinery Co., 1101 West Ave., Fairfield, Iowa.
3547—Louisville Electric Mfg. Co., 31st & Magazine Sts., Louisville, Ky.
3549—Lourie Mfg. Co., 565 Washington Blvd., Chicago, Ill.
3553—Lubrifac Corp., 47 Mt. Auburn St., Cambridge, Mass.
3554—Lubricating Devices Co., 2164 Sacramento St., Los Angeles, Calif.
3555—Lucas & Co., John, 322 Race St., Philadelphia, Pa.

3556—Luce Mfg. Co., 614 Delaware St., Kansas City, Mo.
3558—Luedinghaus-Espenschied Wagon Co., 1721 N. Broadway, St. Louis, Mo.
3559—Lufkin-Rule Co., Hess Ave., Saginaw, Mich.
3563a—Lunsford Mfg. Co., 2021 S. Michigan Ave., Chicago, Ill.
3564—Lupton's Sons Co., David, 5-130 General Motors Bldg., Detroit, Mich.
3566—Lux Clock Mfg. Co., 95 Johnson St., Waterbury, Conn. (Sole distributors, De Luxe Clock & Mfg. Co., 1107 Broadway, New York, N. Y.)
3567—Lycoming Mfg. Co., Olive St. & N. C. Ry., Williamsport, Pa.
3569—Lyon Cover Co., Div. of Houdaille-Hershey Corp., 2660 E. Grand Blvd., Detroit, Mich.
3570—Lyon Iron Works, Greene, N. Y.
3571—Lyon Metal Products, Inc., 2931 Montgomery St., Aurora, Ill. Adv. p. 106.
3573—Lyons Storage Battery Co., 355 Cortland St., Bellville, N. J.

M

3702—McAleer Mfg. Co., 7401 Lyndon Rd., Detroit, Mich.
3702a—McAllister Co., H. S., 549 W. Washington Blvd., Chicago, Ill.
3704—McCann's Sons, D. E., Portland, Me.
3705—McCarron Corp., W. E., 2639 Milwaukee Ave., Chicago, Ill.
3706—McClaren Rubber Co., W. Palmer St., Charlotte, N. C.
3708—McConnell Mfg. Co., 190 Emmet St., Newark, N. J.
3709—McCord Radiator & Mfg. Co., 2587 E. Grand Blvd., Detroit, Mich.
3710—McCreary Tire & Rubber Co., 15th & School Sts., Indiana, Pa.
3713—McDonald Mfg. Co., A. Y., 12th & Pine Sts., Dubuque, Iowa.
3714—McDougall-Butler Co., 24 Evans St., Buffalo, N. Y.
3715—McFarlane & Co., H., 322 S. Green St., Chicago, Ill.
3717—McGill Metal Co., Valparaiso, Ind.
3718—McGrew Machine Co., 2124 Y St., Lincoln, Neb.
3719—McHaig-Hatch, Inc., Ontario & Skillen Sts., Buffalo, N. Y.
3720—McKane-Lins Co., 209 E. Wisconsin Ave., Milwaukee, Wis.
3721—McKay Co., Union Trust Bldg., Pittsburgh, Pa. Adv. p. 33.
3724—McKinnon Dash Co., 252 Amherst St., Buffalo, N. Y.
3725—McLanathan & Son, F. W., Lawrence, Mass.
3727—McNutt, Inc., Wm. H., 83 Chambers St., New York, N. Y.
3728—McQuay-Norris Mfg. Co., Dept. H, Cooper & Southwest Aves., St. Louis, Mo. Adv. p. 88.
3730—McSavaney Co., 51 Walnut St., Springfield, Ohio.
3750—M. & H. Novelty Co., Dept. A, 1466 W. 28th St., Los Angeles, Calif.
3752a—Macbeth-Evans Glass Co., Charleroi, Pa.
3753—Maccar Truck Co., Gilligan St., Scranton, Pa.
3754—MacDonald Motors, Inc., Fifth & Harrison Sts., San Francisco, Calif.
3755—Machine Specialty Co., 1200 N. Main St., Ann Arbor, Mich. (Sole distributors, Precision Parts Co., Ann Arbor, Mich.)
3756b—MacLean-Fogg Lock Nut Co., 2649 N. Kildare Ave., Chicago, Ill.
3759—Maginnis, Inc., Earl A., 121 W. 35th St., Los Angeles, Calif.
3760—Magnavox Co., 4250 Horton St., Oakland, Calif.
3762—Magnolia Metal Co., 75 West St., New York, N. Y.
3764—Maine Steel Products Co., South Portland, Me.
3764a—Majestic Co., 330 Erie St., Huntington, Ind.
3765—Majestic Metal Specialties, Inc., 342 W. 14th St., New York, N. Y.
3765a—Malco Div. of Trico Products Corp., 817 Washington St., Buffalo, N. Y.
3766—Malis Supply Co., 421 Arch St., Philadelphia, Pa.
3767—Malleable Iron Fittings Co., Branford, Conn.
3768—Mallory Electric Corp., Woodruff & Wakeman Sts., Toledo, Ohio.
3769—Mall Tool Co., 7740 S. Chicago Ave., Chicago, Ill.
3771—Manhattan Insulated Wire Co., 17-23 W. 60th St., New York, N. Y. Adv. p. 65.
3772—Manhattan Mirror Works, 46 Wooster St., New York, N. Y.
3774—Manley Mfg. Co., 929 Connecticut Ave., Bridgeport, Conn.
3775—Mann Mfg. Co., Dwight Way at Ninth St., Berkeley, Calif.
3776—Mansfield, J. F., 15 Maiden Lane, New York, N. Y.
3777—Mansfield Lock Washer Co., 9771 French Road, Detroit, Mich.
3778—Mansfield Tire & Rubber Co., Newman St., Mansfield, Ohio.
3779—Manufacturers' Auto Equipment Co., 995 E. Green St., Pasadena, Calif.
3780—Manufacturer's Belt Hook Co., 1315-21 W. Congress St., Chicago, Ill. Adv. p. 94.
3781—Manufacturers Brush Co., 12601 Elmwood Ave., Cleveland, Ohio.
3782—Manufacturers Surplus Outlet Co., 542 S. Dearborn St., Chicago, Ill. Adv. p. 66.
3782b—Manufacturing Equipment & Engineering Co., Framingham, Mass.
3783—Marathon Electric Mfg. Co., 31 Island St., Wausau, Wis.
3787—Marion Basket Co., 100 Marion St., Marion, Ind.
3790—Marko Storage Battery Co., 100 Varick Ave., Brooklyn, N. Y.
3792—Marmon Motor Car Co., 1101 W. Morris St., Indianapolis, Ind.
3793—Marnall Steel Products, Inc., 501 Fifth Ave., New York, N.Y.
3794—Marquette Mfg. Co., 218 S. Wabasha St., St. Paul, Minn.
3795—Marschke Grinder Div. of Black & Decker Mfg. Co., 1815 Madison Ave., Indianapolis, Ind.
3797—Marshall Asbestos Corp., Green Island, Troy, N. Y.
3798—Marshall Electric Co., McNaughton & Myrtle Sts., Elkhart, Ind.
3800—Marshalltown Mfg. Co., Marshalltown, Iowa.
3801—Martin-Parry Corp., W. Market St., York, Pa.
3802—Martin Rocking Fifth Wheel & Trailer Co., Westfield, Mass.
3802a—Martin & Stoner Co., 2326 S. Michigan Ave., Chicago, Ill. Adv. p. 80.
3803—Marvel Carbureter Co., 2300 St. John St., Flint, Mich. Adv. p. 68.
3805—Marvel Products Co., 4227 Lorain Ave., Cleveland, Ohio.
3806—Marvin Mfg. Co., W. B., 600 Miami St., Urbana, Ohio.
3809—Maryland Motor & Mfg. Co., 1915 Maryland Ave., Baltimore, Md.
3811—Masland & Sons, C. H., Carlisle, Pa. (Sole distributors, W. & J. Sloane, 577 Fifth Ave., New York, N. Y.)

MANUFACTURERS OF AUTOMOTIVE PRODUCTS—Continued

3814—Massasoit Mfg. Co., 136 Pocasset St., Fall River, Mass.
3815—Master Electric Co., Linden & Master Aves., Dayton, Ohio.
3816—Master Lock Co., 926 W. Juneau Ave., Milwaukee, Wis.
3817—Master Products Corp., 1340 Howard St., San Francisco, Calif. (Sole distributors Brake-Rite Co., 1340 Howard St., San Francisco, Calif.)
3818—Master Products Corp., 332 Broadway, Denver, Colo.
3818a—Master Tool Mfg. Co., 1609 Broadway, St. Louis, Mo.
3819—Matchless Electric Co., 564 W. Randolph St., Chicago, Ill.
3820—Mathes Co., G., 3100 N. Broadway, St. Louis, Mo.
3822—Matthews & Co., Jas. H., 2630 Forbes Field, Pittsburgh, Pa.
3823—Matthews Corp., W. N., 3722 Forest Park Blvd., St. Louis, Mo.
3824—Matthiessen & Hegeler Zinc Co., LaSalle, Ill.
3825—Maxwell Automotive Engineering Co., 44 Binford St., Boston, Mass. Adv. p. 115.
3828a—Mayer Co., Geo. J., 36 S. Meridian St., Indianapolis, Ind.
3829—Mayer Mfg. Corp., 1436 W. Randolph St., Chicago, Ill.
3830—Mayhew Steel Products, Shelburne Falls, Mass.
3831—Mayo Co., Spring Lane, Portsmouth, Ohio.
3832—May Trailers, Inc., Shreveport, La.
3833—Mead-Morrison Mfg. Co., 446 Prescott St., East Boston, Mass.
3836—Mears-Kane-Ofeldt, Inc., 1907 E. Hagert St., Philadelphia, Pa.
3838—Mechanics Universal Joint Co., 19th Ave. & Ninth St., Rockford, Ill.
3840—Medart Mfg. Co., Fred, Potomac & De Kalb Sts., St. Louis, Mo.
3841—Medina Rubber Co., Medina, Ohio.
3842—Meili-Blumberg Co., 1615 Wisconsin Ave., New Holstein, Wis.
3842a—Meisel Press Mfg. Co., 944 Dorchester Ave., Boston 25, Mass.
3843—Mercedes Benz Co., 247 Park Ave., New York, N. Y.
3844—Mercer Rubber Co., Hamilton Square, N. J.
3845—Mercury Mfg. Co., 4118 S. Halsted St., Chicago, Ill.
3846—Merit Equipment Corp., 6616 Morgan Ave., Cleveland, Ohio.
3848—Merz Engineering Co., 937 N. Capitol Ave., Indianapolis, Ind.
3849—Mesinger Mfg. Co., H. & F. 432 Austin Pl., New York, N. Y.
3850—Mesker & Co., Geo. L., First & Ingle Sts., Evansville, Ind.
3853—Metal Hose & Tubing Co., 233 Tillary St., Brooklyn, N. Y.
3854—Metallite Corp., 20 N. High St., Akron, Ohio (Sole distributors, Springulators, 614 Second National Bldg., Akron, Ohio.)
3855—Metal Products Co., 406 S. W. Ninth St., Des Moines, Iowa.
3856—Metal Specialties Mfg. Co., 3200 Carroll Ave., Chicago, Ill.
3857—Metal Stamping Co., 14th St. & Boulevard, Long Island City, N. Y.
3858—Metal Stamping & Mfg. Co., 16816 Waterloo Rd., Cleveland, Ohio.
3859—Metalweld, Inc., 26th St. & Hunting Park Ave., Philadelphia, Pa.
3860—Meteor Motor Car Co., South Ave., Piqua, Ohio.
3861—Metropolitan Body Co., 430 Grand St., Bridgeport, Conn.
3862—Metropolitan Camp Goods Co., 105 Marble St., Athol, Mass.
3865—Meyer Automatic Door, Inc., Milford, Ill.
3868—Meyercord Co., 120 S. La Salle St., Chicago, Ill.
3868a—Meyer Thread Works, John C., 1495 Middlesex St., Lowell, Mass.
3869—Meyer & Wenthe, 30 S. Jefferson St., Chicago, Ill.
3870—Michaels & Mourre, 514 W. 53rd St., New York, N. Y.
3872—Michiana Products Corp., Sheet Steel Products Div., Michigan City, Ind.
3873—Michigan Engine Valve Co., 437 W. Columbia St., Detroit, Mich.
3873a—Michigan Malleable Iron Co., 7740 Gould St., Detroit, Mich.
3874—Michigan Metal Products Co., 21st St. & M. C. R. R., Battle Creek, Mich.
3877—Michigan Tool Co., 147 Jos. Campau Ave., Detroit, Mich.
3879—Micromatic Hone Corp., 7401 Dubois St., Detroit, Mich.
3882—Midland Specialties Co., 536 W. 25th St., Chicago, Ill.
3883—Mid-States Gummed Paper Co., 2433 Damen Ave., Chicago, Ill.
3885—Mid-West Glass Co., 2235 Buck St., Cincinnati, Ohio.
3887—Mielke Mfg. & Sales Co., New Hampton, Iowa.
3890—Miho Co., 717 Sycamore St., Cincinnati, Ohio. (Sole distributors, Ohio Parts Co., Ohio Bldg., 2735 Colerain Ave., Cincinnati, Ohio.)
3891—Milburn Co., Alexander, 1416 W. Baltimore St., Baltimore, Md.
3891a—Miley Co., L. J., 1462 S. Michigan Ave., Chicago, Ill.
3892—Milhander Rubber Co., 2109 S. San Pedro St., Los Angeles, Calif.
3893—Miller Mfg. Co., 7 Water St., Boston, Mass.
3894—Miller, Chas. E. (Anderson Rubber Works), 1400 S. Meridian St., Anderson, Ind.
3895—Miller Auto Bed & Mfg. Co., 4001 E. Tenth St., Oakland, Calif.
3897—Miller & Co., Clyde L., 1544 Cahuenga Ave., Los Angeles, Calif.
3899—Miller Co., J. Walter, 411 E. Chestnut St., Lancaster, Pa.
3901—Miller, Inc., Harry A., 6233 S. Gramercy Place, Los Angeles, Calif.
3902—Miller-Way Corp., Monmouth, Ill.
3903—Miller Rubber Co. of N. Y., 1347 S. High St., Akron, Ohio.
3904—Millersburg Reamer & Tool Co., Millersburg, Pa.
3905—Millers Falls Co., Greenfield, Mass.
3907a—Miller Tool & Mfg. Co., 1725 16th St., Detroit, Mich.
3908—Miller Wagon Co., Calmar, Iowa.
3910—Milwaukee Air Power Pump Co., 8 Keefe Ave., Milwaukee, Wis.
3911—Milwaukee Bearings Co., Massachusetts & Steel Sts., Indianapolis, Ind. (Sole distributors, King Quality Products Co., Massachusetts & Steel Sts., Indianapolis, Ind.)
3912—Milwaukee Brush Mfg. Co., 2212 N. 30th St., Milwaukee, Wis.
3913—Milwaukee Cylinder Grinding Co., Humboldt & Concordia Aves., Milwaukee, Wis.
3914—Milwaukee Forge & Machine Co., 1532 E. Oklahoma Ave., Milwaukee, Wis.

3914a—Milwaukee Gear Co., 3002 N. Third St., Milwaukee, Wis.
3915—Milwaukee Motor Products, Inc., 2206 N. 30th St., Milwaukee, Wis.
3916—Milwaukee Tack Co., 3118 W. Pabst Ave., Milwaukee, Wis.
3917—Milwaukee Tank Works, 728 E. Nash St., Milwaukee, Wis.
3918—Milwaukee Tool & Forge Co., Ninth & Marion Sts. (South Milwaukee), Milwaukee, Wis.
3921—Minnesota Mining & Mfg. Co., 791 Forest St., St. Paul, Minn.
3922—Mirro-Like Mfg. Co., Queens Blvd. & Buckley St., Long Island City, N. Y.
3925—Mitchell-Rand Mfg. Co., 18 Vesey St., New York, N. Y.
3926—Mitchell Specialty Co., Shelmire & Edmund Sts. (Holmesburg), Philadelphia, Pa.
3928a—Modern Engineering Co., 3411 Pine Blvd., St. Louis, Mo.
3929—Modine Mfg. Co., 17th St. & Racine Ave., Racine, Wis.
3930—Moebes & Hoffman Mfg. Co., Vallejo, Calif.
3932—Mohawk Carpet Mills, Amsterdam, N. Y.
3934—Mohawk Rubber Co., 1235 Second St., Akron, Ohio.
3937—Moline Mfg. Corp., 2430 Third Ave., Moline, Ill.
3938—Moller Motor Car Co., M. P., Pope Ave., Hagerstown, Md.
3942—Mona Motor Oil Co., 12th Ave. & Sixth St., Council Bluffs, Iowa.
3943—Monarch Bumper Mfg. Co., 1622 Euclid Ave., E., Detroit, Mich.
3944—Monarch Cap Screw & Mfg. Co., 3446 E. 65th St., Cleveland, Ohio.
3946—Monarch Governor Co., 1847 W. Bethune Ave., Detroit, Mich.
3948—Monarch Insulated Wire Corp., 250 W. 54th St., New York, N. Y.
3949—Monarch Rubber Co., Hartville, Ohio.
3950—Monarch Tool & Machinery Co., 4450 Fifth Ave., Chicago, Ill.
3951—Monark Battery Co., 125 N. Peoria St., Chicago, Ill.
3954—Monmouth Products Co., 882 E. 72nd St., Cleveland, Ohio. Adv. p. 72.
3955—Monocraft Products Co., 137 Fifth Ave., New York, N. Y.
3956—Monogram Lens Corp., 11-236 General Motors Bldg., Detroit, Mich.
3958—Monroe Auto Equipment Co., 1411 E. First St., Monroe, Mich.
3959—Monroe Paper Products Co., Monroe, Mich.
3962—Montpelier Mfg. Co., Montpelier, Ohio.
3965—Moore Body Co., Schiller & Division Sts., Reading, Pa.
3966—Moore Co., H. L., Cochranton, Pa.
3967—Morand Cushion Wheel Co., 800 S. May St. Chicago, Ill.
3968—Moreland Motor Truck Co., E. San Fernando Rd., Burbank, Calif.
3974—Morris Co., George W., 427 Lake Ave., Racine, Wis.
3975—Morris Co., J. Leslie, 924 Venice Blvd., Los Angeles, Calif.
3978—Morrison & Co., L. E., 27 W. Washington St., Indianapolis, Ind.
3979—Morrison Jack Co., 108 E. Patterson St., Alliance, Ohio.
3982—Morse Chain Co. (Div. Borg-Warner Corp.), Ithaca, N. Y. Adv. p. 203.
3983—Morse Co., L. E., 205 N. Hyde Park Ave., Scranton, Pa.
3985—Morse Mfg. Co., 402 S. Franklin St., Syracuse, N. Y.
3986—Morse Twist Drill & Machine Co., 163 Pleasant St., New Bedford, Mass. Adv. p. 118.
3986a—Morton & Brett, 811 E. 23rd St., Indianapolis, Ind.
3987—Morton Mfg. Co., Broadway & Hoyt St., Muskegon Heights, Mich.
3988—Moss & Co., Henry, 113 53rd St., Brooklyn, N. Y.
3989—Moss Tool Mfg. Co., Wichita, Kan.
3992—Moto Meter Gauge & Equipment Corp., Toledo, Ohio. Adv. p. 60.
3993—Motor-Bed Mfg. Co., 616 S. Michigan Ave., Chicago, Ill.
3995—Motor City Filling Pad Co., 4739 Woodward Ave., Detroit, Mich.
3996—Motor City Spring Co., 1821 Trombly Ave., Detroit, Mich.
3998—Motor Improvements, Inc., 385 Frelinghuysen Ave., Newark, N. J.
3999—Motor Industries Co., La Crosse, Wis.
4000—Motor Products Manufacturing Corp., 2652 Lacy St., Los Angeles, Calif.
4002—Motor Suit Mfg. Co., 816 Central St., Kansas City, Mo. Adv. p. 119.
4004—Motor Transit Co., 220 E. Market St., Los Angeles, Calif.
4005—Motor Wheel Corp., Lansing, Mich. Adv. p. 103.
4007—Motor X Ray Co., 228 N. LaSalle St., Chicago, Ill.
4009—Mountain Chemical Co., 1025 13th St., Denver, Colo.
4010—Muehlhausen Spring Co., Logansport, Ind.
4011—Mueller Brass Co., 1925 Lapeer Ave., Port Huron, Mich.
4012—Mueller Electric Co., 1583 E. 31st St., Cleveland, Ohio.
4014—Mulconroy Co., 54th & Jefferson Sts., Philadelphia, Pa.
4016—Mullins Body & Tank Co., 2081 S. 56th St., Milwaukee, Wis.
4017—Mullins Mfg. Corp., 605 S. Ellsworth St., Salem, Ohio.
4018—Multibestos Co., 235 Harvey St., Cambridge B, Mass. Adv. p. 255.
4019—Multispark Ignition Co., 713 W. Eighth St., Los Angeles, Calif.
4019a—Mummert-Dixon Co., Philadelphia & Gay Sts., Hanover, Pa.
4020—Muncie Gear Co., 405 N. Vine St., Muncie, Ind.
4020a—Muncie Products Div. (General Motors Corp.), 1220 W. Eighth St., Muncie, Ind.
4021—Mundet & Son, L., 65 S. 11th St., Brooklyn, N. Y.
4022—Mundo Products, Inc., 229 E. 42nd St., New York, N. Y.
4025—Muntz Chemical Co., 171 Main St., Greenville, Pa.
4027—Murphy Co., Walter M., 55 N. Vernon Ave., Pasadena, Calif.
4027a—Murray Corp. of America, 1424 Aberle St., Detroit, Mich.
4028—Murray Rubber Co., N. Clinton Ave. Trenton, N. J.
4029—Musgrave Mfg. Co., Pittsburg, Kan.
4030—Muskegon Motor Specialties Co., Seventh & Larch Sts., Muskegon, Mich.
4031—Muskogee Iron Works, Automotive Div., Frankfort & Spaulding Sts., Muskogee, Okla.
4034—Muther Mfg. Co., 44 Binford St., Boston, Mass. Adv. p. 115.
4036—Myers & Bros Co., F. E., 10 Orange St., Ashland, Ohio.
4037—Myers Mfg. Co., Chas. A., 2915 Detroit Ave., Cleveland, Ohio.

MANUFACTURERS OF AUTOMOTIVE PRODUCTS—Continued

N

4201—Nabors Co., W. C., Mansfield, La.
4202—Nacco Mfg. Co., 1482 Clara Ave., St. Louis, Mo.
4203—Naceskid Service Chain Co., Third & Schenck Sts., Trenton, N. J.
4205—Napier Saw Works, 22 Cottage St., Middletown, N. Y.
4207—Nash Motors Co., Edward & Parks Sts., Kenosha, Wis.
4209—Nassau Sponge Co., 124 W. Kinzie St., Chicago, Ill.
4211—National Acme Co., 170 E. 131st St., Cleveland, Ohio.
4214—National Alloys Co., 2118 Woodbridge St., E., Detroit, Mich.
4215—National Aluminum Co., 1912 Frederick St., Racine, Wis.
4218—National Automotive Fibres, Inc., Railroad Ave. & Kennedy St., Oakland, Calif.
4220—National Auto Top & Mfg. Co., 3900 Moneta Ave., Los Angeles, Calif.
4221—National Battery Co., 1704 Roblyn Ave., St. Paul, Minn.
4222—National Brake & Electric Co., Belleview Pl. & River, Milwaukee, Wis.
4222a—National Bronze & Aluminum Foundry Co., E. 88th St. & Laisy Ave., Cleveland, Ohio.
4223—National Carbon Co., 30 E. 42nd St., New York, N. Y.
4224—National Cash Register Co., Main & K Sts., Dayton, Ohio.
4225—National Chemical & Mfg. Co., 3617 Wall St., Chicago, Ill.
4227—National Colortype Co., Lafayette & Grandview Aves., Bellevue, Ky.
4228—National Copper & Smelting Co., 1862 E. 123rd St., Cleveland, Ohio.
4230—National Electric Corp., 216 High St., Newark, N. J.
4233a—National-Erie Co. (Williams Foundry & Machine Div.), Erie, Pa.
4235—National Grinding Wheel Co., Erie Ave. & Walck Rd., North Tonawanda, N. Y.
4236—National-Harris Wire Co., 221 Verona Ave., Newark, N. J.
4237—National Lamp Works of General Electric Co., Nela Park, Cleveland, Ohio.
4238—National Lead Co., 111 Broadway, New York, N. Y.
4239—National Lock Co., 18th Ave. & Seventh St., Rockford, Ill.
4240—National Lock Washer Co., 40 Hermon St., Newark, N. J.
4241—National Machine & Tool Co., 801 S. Water St., Jackson, Mich. Adv. p. 120.
4242—National-Marshall Spring Corp., Div. of Nachman Spring-Filled Corp., Front Ave. & Wealthy St., Grand Rapids, Mich.
4243—National Motor Bearing Co., 460 Natoma St., San Francisco, Calif.
4244—National Motors Mfg. Co., 464 Coit St., Irvington, N. J.
4245—National Oxygen Co., 29 S. La Salle St., Chicago, Ill.
4246—National Recording Pump Co., Kiser St. & Pennsylvania Ave., Dayton, Ohio.
4248—National Rivet & Mfg. Co., Waupen, Wis.
4249—National Rubber Machinery Co., Akron Rubber Mold Plant, 917 Sweitzer Ave., Akron, Ohio.
4250—National Rubber Machinery Co., DeMattia Div., Wellington St. & Getty Ave., Clifton, N. J.
4252—National Sanding Machine Co., 4353 Avondale Ave., Chicago, Ill.
4253—National Scale Corp., 9 Montgomery St., Chicopee Falls, Mass.
4254—National Screw & Mfg. Co., 2440 E. 75th St., Cleveland, Ohio.
4255—National Sewing Machine Co., State & Meadow Sts., Belvidere, Ill.
4258—National-Standard Co., Eighth & Howard Sts., Niles, Mich. (Sole distributors, John Bean Mfg. Co., 18 Hosmer St., Lansing, Mich.)
4259—National Steel Products Co., 1611 Crystal Ave., Kansas City, Mo. Adv. p. 130.
4260—National Store Specialty Co., Bareville, Pa.
4261—National Tool Co., W. 112th St. & Madison Ave., Cleveland, Ohio.
4262—National Trunk Corp., Hamilton & Railroad Sts., Racine, Wis.
4263—National Twist Drill & Tool Co., 6522 Brush St., Detroit, Mich.
4264—National Umbrella Frame Co., Penn St. & Belfield Ave., Philadelphia, Pa. Adv. p. 104.
4265—National Used Car Market Report, Inc., 1315 S. Michigan Ave., Chicago, Ill. Adv. p. 128.
4266—National Vulcanized Fibre Co., Maryland Ave. & Beech St., Wilmington, Del.
4266a—Naylor Bros., 2 N. Water St., Peekskill, N. Y.
4269—Nedco Co., 50 South Ave., Natick, Mass.
4270—Needham, Claude C., 146 W. 17th St., Los Angeles, Calif.
4271—Neider Co., F. A., Seminary Ave., Augusta, Ky.
4273—Nelson Iron Works, Inc., N. P., Bloomfield Ave., Passaic, N. J.
4273a—Nelson-LeMoon Truck Co., 849 N. Kedzie Ave., Chicago, Ill.
4275—Ness Bros. Mfg. Co., Broad & Philadelphia Sts., York, Pa.
4277—Nestler Rubber Fusing Co., 245 W. 55th St., New York, N. Y.
4279a—Neveroil Bearing Co., 29 Foundry St., Wakefield, Mass.
4280—Never Rust Mfg. Co., 1771 E. 18th St., Brooklyn, N. Y.
4282—New Albany Machine Mfg. Co., E. Tenth & Water Sts., New Albany, Ind.
4284—New Britain Machine Co., 140 Chestnut St., New Britain, Conn.
4285—New Comer Trailer Mfg. Co., 1119 Santa Fe Ave., Los Angeles, Calif.
4286—New Departure Mfg. Co., 269 N. Main St., Bristol, Conn. Adv. p. 165.
4287—New Doty Mfg. Co., 302 N. Main St., Janesville, Wis.
4288—New England Auto Products Corp., Pottstown, Pa.
4288a—New England Box Co., 173 Main St., Greenfield, Mass.
4288b—New England Pressed Steel Co., Washington Ave., Natick, Mass.
4290—New England Truck Co., 80 Lunenburg St., Fitchburg, Mass.
4292—New Haven Clock Co. (Automatic Clock Div.), 133 Hamilton St., New Haven, Conn.
4296—Newman Mfg. Co., Norwood Sta., Cincinnati, Ohio.
4297—New Process Gear Co., 500 Plum St., Syracuse, N. Y. Adv. p. 237.
4299—Newton Corp., E. C., 635 W. Ave. 26, Los Angeles, Calif.

4299a—Newtype Connector Corp., Canadian Pacific Bldg., 342 Madison Ave., New York, N. Y.
4300—New Ulm Mfg. Co., New Ulm, Minn. (Sole distributors, Truth Tool Co., 711 S. Front St., Mankato, Minn.)
4301—New Way Spray Gun Co., 5713 Euclid Ave., Cleveland, Ohio.
4302—New York Belting & Packing Co., 91 Chambers St., New York, N. Y.
4303—New York Blower Co., 3155 Shields Ave., Chicago, Ill.
4304—New York Coil Co., Mont Clare, Pa.
4305—New York Rubber Corp. (Airubber Dept.), Beacon, N. Y.
4306—Ney Mfg. Co., 1006 High Ave., S. W., Canton, Ohio.
4308—Niagara Fabric Mfg. Co., 47 Greene St., New York, N. Y.
4309—Niagara Machine & Tool Works, 683 Northland Ave., Buffalo, N. Y.
4310—Niagara Motor Corp., 219 Niagara Blvd., Dunkirk, N. Y.
4311—Niagara Searchlight Co., 800 Ferry Ave., Niagara Falls, N. Y.
4312—Nice Ball Bearing Co., 30th St. & Nicetown Lane, Philadelphia, Pa.
4313—Nice Co., Eugene E., 268 S. Second St., Philadelphia, Pa.
4314—Nicholson File Co., 23 Acorn St., Providence, R. I.
4315—Nichol-Straight Foundry Co., 3174 Archer Ave., Chicago, Ill.
4316—Niehaus & Co., Jos., 341 W. Fourth St., Cincinnati, Ohio. (Importers.)
4317—Niehoff & Co., C. E., 230 W. Superior St., Chicago, Ill. Adv. p. 63.
4319—Nikolas & Co., G. J., 1227 Van Buren St., Chicago, Ill.
4320—Niles Steel Tank Co., Niles, Mich.
4321—Nil Melior, Inc., 100 W. 56th St., New York, N. Y. (Importers.)
4323—Nixon Gear & Machine Co., 200 Oxford St., Syracuse, N. Y.
4324—Nixon Nitration Works, Nixon, N. J.
4325—Noble Motor Truck Corp., Kendallville, Ind.
4326—Noblitt-Sparks Industries, Inc., Ninth Floor, Spink Bldg., 603 E. Washington St., Indianapolis, Ind. Adv. p. 27.
4327—Noera Mfg. Co., 230 Grand Ave., Waterbury, Conn.
4328—Noisom Auto-Compass, Inc., 321 Michigan St., South Bend, Ind.
4332—Norbom Engineering Co., Darby, Pa. (Sole distributors, Eagle Machine Co., 24 N. Noble St., Indianapolis, Ind.)
4335—Norma-Hoffmann Bearings Corp., Stamford, Conn. Adv. p. 169.
4337—North American Smelting Co., 900 W. Thompson St., Philadelphia, Pa.
4338—North Bros. Mfg. Co., American St. & Lehigh Ave., Philadelphia, Pa.
4340—North East Appliance Corp., 379 Lyell Ave., Rochester, N. Y.
4342—Northern Rubber Co., Akron, Ohio.
4343—North Ridge Brush Co., Henney Bldg., Freeport, Ill. (Sole distributors, Jean Caro Products Co., Freeport, Ill.)
4346—North Wales Machine Co., Elm Ave. & Center St., North Wales, Pa.
4347—Northwestern Chemical Co., 785 State St., Marietta, Ohio.
4348a—Northwestern Machine & Tool Co., 314 Third Ave., South Minneapolis, Minn.
4349—Northwestern Mfg. Co., 1300 S. First St., Milwaukee, Wis.
4350—North Western Steel Products Co., 4545 W. Homer St., Chicago, Ill.
4351—Norton Co., 1 New Bond St., Worcester, Mass.
4352—Norton Electrical Instrument Inc., 81 Hilliard St., Manchester, Conn.
4352a—Norton Lamp Mfg. Co., 217 W. Illinois St., Chicago, Ill.
4353—Norwalk Auto Parts Co., 4 S. Foster Ave., Norwalk, Ohio.
4354—Norwalk Tire & Rubber Co., Belden Hill Ave., Norwalk, Conn.
4358—Novelty Trimming Works, 18 E. 16th St., New York, N. Y.
4360—Nu-Cord Tire & Rubber Co., Penn, Pa.
4362—Nurre Companies, Bloomington, Ind.

O

4500—O. B. Electric Truck, Inc., 101 Jane St., New York, N. Y.
4501—O. K. Machine Co., Fairfield Ave. & Poplar St., Ft. Wayne, Ind.
4503—Oakes Products Corp., Div. Houdaille-Hershey Corp., South Chicago, Ill.
4504—Oakite Products, Inc., 22 Thames St., New York, N. Y.
4505—Oakland Motor Car Co., 240 Oakland Ave., Pontiac, Mich.
4506—Oberdorfer Brass Co., M. L., 140 Thompson Rd., East Syracuse, N. Y.
4507—O'Brien Mfg. Co., Joseph F., 47 W. 63rd St., New York, N. Y.
4508—O'Brien Varnish Co., Johnson & Washington Sts., South Bend, Ind.
4514—Oesterlein Machine Co., 3301 Colerain Ave., Cincinnati, Ohio.
4515—Ohio Art Co., Bryan, Ohio.
4517—Ohio Carbon Co., 12508 Berea Rd., Cleveland, Ohio.
4518—Ohio Electric Mfg. Co., 5900 Maurice Ave., Cleveland, Ohio.
4519—Ohio Grease Co., Loudonville, Ohio.
4520—Ohio Hammered Piston Ring Co., 2401 Superior Ave., N. W., Cleveland, Ohio. Adv. p. 88.
4522—Ohio Nut & Bolt Co., 600 Front St., Berea, Ohio.
4523—Ohio Parts Co., Ohio Bldg., 2735 Colerain Ave., Cincinnati, Ohio.
4524—Ohio Piston Co., 5339 St. Clair Ave., Cleveland, Ohio.
4525—Ohio Rubber Co., Willoughby, Ohio.
4527—Ohio Valley Oxygen Co., 934 Kenyon Ave., Cincinnati, Ohio.
4528—Ohmer Fare Register Co., Bolender & Big Four R. R., Dayton, Ohio.
4529—Ohmlac Paint & Refining Co., 140 S. Dearborn St., Chicago, Ill.
4530—Oildraulic Lift Co., 2105 Sterick Bldg., Memphis, Tenn. (Sole distributors, Marquette Mfg. Co., 218 S. Wabasha St., St. Paul, Minn.)
4531—Oil Jack Co., 129 Glenridge Ave., Montclair, N. J.
4533—Okonite Co., 501 Fifth Ave., New York, N. Y.
4534—Oldberg Mfg. Co., Detroit, Mich. (Sole distributors, Associated Parts, Inc., Norwood at Hoag, Toledo, Ohio.)
4535—Olds Motor Works, Olds Ave., Lansing, Mich.
4536—Oliver Iron & Steel Corp., 1001 Muriel St., Pittsburgh, Pa.

MANUFACTURERS OF AUTOMOTIVE PRODUCTS—Continued

4537—Oliver Machinery Co., 1032 Coldbrook St., **Grand Rapids,** Mich.
4538—Omaha Folding Machine Co., 2009 Cuming St., Omaha, Neb.
4540—Omaha Steel Works, 48th & Leavenworth Sts., Omaha, Neb.
4541—Omaha Welding Co., 15th & Jackson Sts., Omaha, Neb.
4542—Onondaga Textile Mills, Inc., Cor. Smith & Trumbull Sts., New London, Conn.
4543—**Opco Co.,** 1894 Niagara St., **Buffalo, N. Y. Adv. p. 52.**
4544—Orange Roller Bearing Co., 557 Main St., Orange, N. J.
4546—Orem Motor Protector Co., 2827 Calvert St., Baltimore, Md.
4547—Orr's Machine & Mfg. Co., Sixth & Alabama Sts., Okmulgee, Okla.
4549—Osborne & Co., C. S., Jersey & Second Sts., Harrison, N. J.
4550—Osporn Mfg. Co., 5401 Hamilton Ave., N. E., Cleveland, Ohio.
4551—Oshkosh Auto Specialties Co., 809 Ninth St., Oshkosh, Wis.
4552—Oskosh Motor Truck, Inc., 23rd & Oregon Sts., Oshkosh, Wis.
4555—Ottemiller Co., Wm. H., Pattison St. & M. & P. R. R., York, Pa.
4556—Otter Mfg. Co., 596 Broadway, New York, N. Y.
4557—Otwell Co., 17005 Fullerton St., Detroit, Mich.
4558—Out West Mfg. Co., 1180 Kalamath St., Denver, Colo.
4559—Overhead Door Corp., Hartford City, Ind.
4560—Overman Cushion Tire Co., 250 W. 54th St., New York, N. Y.
4561—Owen-Dyneto Corp., 1920 Park St., Syracuse, N. Y.
Oxweld Acetylene Co.—See Linde Air Products Co.

P

4600—P & C Hand Forged Tool Co., Portland, Ore.
4601—P & D Mfg. Co., 38-02-10 22nd St., Long Island City, N. Y.
4603—Paasche Airbrush Co., 1909 Diversey Parkway, Chicago, Ill.
4604—Pacific Ball Bearing Co., 415 W. Pico St., Los Angeles, Calif.
4605—Pacific Metal Bearing Co., Div. of Federal-Mogul Co., 1710 Howard St., San Francisco, Calif.
4607—Pacific States Felt & Mfg. Co., 843 Howard St., San Francisco, Calif.
4610—Packard Electric Co., Warren, Ohio.
4611—Packard Motor Car Co., 1580 E. Grand Blvd., Detroit, Mich.
4612—Paddock Cork Co., 1209 DeKalb Ave., Brooklyn, N. Y.
4613—Paf Mfg. Co., Greenville, Ill.
4613a—Paine & Williams Co., 4614 Prospect Ave., Cleveland, Ohio.
4614—Palm Bros. Decalcomania Co., South Norwood, Cincinnati, Ohio.
4615—Palmen Mfg. Co., Akron, Ohio.
4616—Palmer Asbestos & Rubber Corp., 2741 Clybourn Ave., Chicago, Ill.
4617—Pal-Weld Mfg. Co., First Ave., South & Lander Sts., Seattle, Wash.
4618—Pantasote Company, 250 Park Ave., New York, N. Y.
4619—Panyard Piston Ring Co., Getty St., Muskegon, Mich.
4620—Paragon Mfg. Co., Austin & Murray Sts., Newark, N. J.
4621—Paragon Mfg. Co., Hickory, N. C.
4622a—Park Chemical Co., Military & Vancouver Aves., Detroit, Mich.
4624—**Parker Co., Chas.,** 48 Elm St., Meriden Conn. **Adv. p. 120.**
4625—Parker-Kalon Corp., 200 Varick St., New York, N. Y.
4626—Parker, Stearns & Co., 286 Sheffield Ave., Brooklyn, N. Y.
4627—Parker Truck Co., 606 Linus St., Milwaukee, Wis.
4629—Parker Wheel Co., 7700 Stanton Ave., Cleveland, Ohio.
4630—Parker White-Metal & Machine Co., 23rd St. & Pennsylvania Ave., Erie, Pa.
4631—Parkin, Inc., 4712 Chester Ave., Cleveland, Ohio.
4632—Park Metalware Company, Thorn Ave., & B. R. & P. Tracks, Orchard Park, N. Y.
4634—Partridge, E. O., 2047 W. Lake St., Chicago, Ill.
4636—Paschall Oxygen Co., 73rd & Woodland Ave., Philadelphia, Pa.
4637—Patchetts & Carstensen, Inc., Newman, Calif.
4639—Pathfinder Accessories Corp., Div. Gluntz Brass Foundry Co., 10803 Harvard Ave., Cleveland, Ohio.
4640—Patriot Mfg. Co., Havelock, Neb.
4642—Paul & Co., J. C., 930 Roscoe St., Chicago, Ill.
4643—**Peck Spring Co.,** 68 Broad St., **Plainville, Conn. Adv. p. 55.**
4644—**Peck, Stow & Wilcox Co., 217-313 Center St., Southington, Conn. Adv. p. 124.**
4647—Peerless Chain Co., Front & Walnut Sts., Winona, Minn. (Sole distributors, Peerless Sales Corp., Front & Walnut Sts., Winona, Minn.)
4648—Peerless Cushion Wheel Co., 455 Seventh Ave., New York, N. Y.
4649—Peerless Machine Co., 1615 Racine St., Racine, Wis.
4650—Peerless Motor Car Corp., Quincy Ave. & E. 93rd St., Cleveland, Ohio.
4651—Peerless Novelty Co., First & Fulton Sts., Grand Haven, Mich.
4651b—Pekin Foundry & Mfg. Co., 228 Sabella St., Pekin, Ill.
4652—Penberthy Injector Co., 1242 Holden Ave., Detroit, Mich.
4653—Penn Brass & Copper Co., 1120 W. 18th St., Erie, Pa.
4654—Penn Metal Co., Oregon Ave. & Swanson St., Philadelphia, Pa.
4655—Penn Rivet Corp., Third & Huntingdon Sts., Philadelphia, Pa.
4656—Pennsylvania Flexible Metallic Tubing Co., 72nd St. & Powers Lane, Philadelphia, Pa.
4657—Pennsylvania Gear & Machine Co., E. Tioga, Weikel & Janney Sts., Philadelphia, Pa.
4658—Pennsylvania Pump & Compressor Co., Easton, Pa.
4659—Pennsylvania Rubber Co. of America, Jeannette, Pa.
4661—Peoria Overhead Washer Co., 115 S. Jefferson St., Peoria, Ill.
4662—Pep Mfg. Company, 33 W. 42d St., New York, N. Y.
4662a—Pequot Wire Cloth Co., 142 Water St., South Norwalk, Conn.
4663—Perfect Circle Co., Hagerstown, Ind.
4663a—Perfect Fit Mfg. Co., E. Sixth & Madison Sts., Portland, Ore.
4665—Perfection Gear Co., 213 N. Morgan St., Chicago, Ill.
4666—Perfection Mfg. Co., 2701 N. Leffingwell Ave., St. Louis, Mo.
4668—Perfection Steel Body Co., Perfection Bldg., Galion, Ohio.
4669—Perfex Corporation, 415 W Oklahoma Place, Milwaukee, Wis.
4670—Perfex Electric Co., 124 Southard Ave., Toledo, Ohio.
4672—Perlick Brass Co., R., 1125 N. Ninth St., Milwaukee, Wis.

4673—Permatex Co., Sheepshead Bay, N. Y.
4676—Perrot Mfg. Co., Beaver Falls, Pa.
4677—Persons-Majestic Mfg. Co., 54 Commercial St., Worcester, Mass.
4678—Peters Engineering Co., 3452 Ludlow St., Philadelphia, Pa. (Sole distributors, General Metals Co., 419 Wesley Bldg., 17th & Arch Sts., Philadelphia, Pa.)
4680—Peterson Spring Co., 1660 Beard Ave., Detroit, Mich.
4681—Peters & Russell, Inc., Fifth Floor Shuey Bldg., Cor. Center & Jefferson Sts., Springfield, Ohio.
4682—Petry Co., N. A., 328 N. Randolph St., Philadelphia, Pa.
4686—Pharis Tire & Rubber Co., Newark, Ohio.
4687—Phenix Mfg. Co., 026 Center St., Milwaukee, Wis.
4688—Pheoll Mfg. Co., 5700 W. Roosevelt Rd., Chicago, Ill.
4689—Philadelphia Solder Co., 2910 N. 16th St., Philadelphia, Pa.
4690—Philadelphia Storage Battery Co., Ontario & C Sts., Philadelphia, Pa.
4691—Phillips & Co., H., 904 Evans St., Cincinnati, Ohio.
4692—Phinney-Walker Co., 216 W. 14th St., New York, N. Y.
4693—Phister Mfg. Co., 903 Broadway, Cincinnati. Ohio.
4694—Phoenix Hardware Mfg. Co., 49 Illinois St., Buffalo, N. Y.
4695—Phoenix Lock Works, 321 Third Ave., Newark, N. J.
4696—Phoenix Paint & Varnish Co., 124 Market St., Philadelphia, Pa.
4697—Phoenix Specialty Mfg. Co., 155 Wooster St., New York, N. Y.
4698—Phoenix Tent & Awning Co., 226 W. Adams St., Phoenix, Ariz.
4700—Phosphor Bronze Smelting Co., 2200 Washington Ave., Philadelphia, Pa.
4701—Pickard Co., H. M., Avoca, N. Y.
4702—Pick Mfg. Co., West Bend, Wis.
4704—Pierce-Arrow Motor Car Co., 1695 Elmwood Ave., Buffalo, N. Y.
4705—Pierce Governor Co., 1605 Ohio Ave., Anderson, Ind.
4706—Pierce Renewable Fuses, Inc., 77 E. Swan St., Buffalo, N. Y.
4707—Pierce-Roberts Rubber Co., Heath & Brian Aves., Trenton, N. J.
4708—Pier Equipment Mfg. Co., North Shore Drive, Benton Harbor, Mich.
4709—Pilley Packing & Fuse Brush Mfg. Co., 606 S. Third St., St. Louis, Mo. (Sole distributors, United States Electrical Tool Co., 2483 W. Sixth St., Cincinnati, Ohio.)
4711—Pimbley Paint & Glass Co., 213 S. Sixth St., St. Joseph, Mo.
4712—**Pines Winterfront Co., 1125 N. Cicero Ave., Chicago, Ill. Adv. p. 54.**
4713—Pioneer Air Compressor Co., 243 Canal St., New York, N. Y.
4716—Pioneer Rubber Mills, 345 Sacramento St., San Francisco, Calif.
4718—Pirsch & Sons Co., Peter, 1308 35th St., Kenosha, Wis.
4719—**Piston Ring Co., Sanford & Keating Sts., Muskegon, Mich. Adv. p. 14.**
4720—Pittsburgh Auto Spring Co., 5900 Center Ave., Pittsburgh, Pa.
4721—Pittsburgh Plate Glass Co., Grant Bldg., Pittsburgh, Pa.
4721a—Pittsburgh Plate Glass Co. (Brush Div.), Baltimore, Md.
4722—Pittsburgh Plate Glass Co. (Paint & Varnish Div.), 213 Pittsburgh Ave., Milwaukee, Wis.
4723—Pittsburgh Taximeter Co., 530 Duquesne Way, Pittsburgh, Pa.
4725—Plant Co., 322 First Ave., Minneapolis, Minn.
4726—Plomb Tool Co., 2209 Sante Fe Ave., Los Angeles, Calif.
4729—Plummer Spray Equipment Corp., 206 W. Front St., Napoleon, Ohio.
4731—Plymouth Mfg. Co., 2155 Walnut St., Chicago, Ill.
4732—Plymouth Motor Corp. (Div. of Chrysler Corp.), 10060 Mt. Elliott Ave., Detroit, Mich.
4733—Plymouth Rubber Co., Revere St., Canton, Mass.
4734—Pocono Rubber Cloth Co., 1851 E. State St., Trenton, N. J.
4735—Pollak Tool & Stamping Co., Joseph, 81 Freeport St., Boston, Mass.
4736—Polson Rubber Co., Garrettsville, Ohio.
4738—Popper-Addison Co., 118 E. Court St., Cincinnati, Ohio. (Importers.)
4741—Portable Tool Co., Monroeton, Pa.
4743—Porter, Inc., H. K., 17 Ashland St., Everett, Mass.
4744—Porter Mirror & Glass Co., Fort Smith, Ark.
4745—Porter Safety Seal Co., 267 N. California Ave., Chicago, Ill.
4746—Positive Lock Washer Co., 181 Miller St., Newark, N. J.
4747—Potter Mfg. Co., Jackson, Mich.
4748—Potts, Robert, 1509 Wood St., Philadelphia, Pa.
4749—Powell Co., Wm., 2525 Spring Grove Ave., Cincinnati, Ohio.
4750—**Powell Muffler Co., 316 Catherine St., Utica, N. Y. Adv. p. 86.**
4751—Powell Pressed Steel Co., Hubbard, Ohio.
4752—Powell Rubber Bushing Co., Utica, N. Y.
4753—Power Door Corp., 5201 W. 65th St., Chicago, Ill.
4754—Power-Dyne Mfg. Co., 136 W. 22nd St., New York, N. Y.
4755—Pratt Chuck Co., Frankfort, N. Y.
4756—Pratt & Lambert, Inc., 79 Tonawanda St., Buffalo, N. Y.
4757—Pratt Mfg. Co., Wm. E., Joliet, Ill.
4758—Pratt & Whitney Co., 436 Capitol Ave., Hartford, Conn.
4760—Precision Electric Tool & Mfg. Co., 98 Union St., Worcester, Mass.
4761—Precision Grinding Wheel Co. (Holmesburg), Philadelphia, Pa.
4762—Precision Machine Co., 7127 Beach Drive, Seattle, Wash.
4763—Premax Products, Inc., 235 Tenth St., Niagara Falls, N. Y.
4764—Premier Electric Co., 3800 Ravenswood Ave., Chicago, Ill.
4764a—Premier Metal Etching Co., 2103 44th Ave., Long Island City, N. Y.
4765—Premier Vacuum Cleaner Co., 1734 Ivanhoe Rd., Cleveland, Ohio.
4766—Prentiss Vise Co., 110 Lafayette St., New York, N. Y.
Prest-O-Lite Co.—See Linde Air Products Co.
4771—Prest-O-Lite Storage Battery Corp., Indianapolis, Ind. (Sole distributors, Prest-O-Lite Storage Battery Sales Corp., Indianapolis, Ind.)
4773—Price Battery Corp., Melvale, Schiller & Allen Sts., Philadelphia, Pa.
4775—Price-Hollister Co., Rockford, Ill.
4777—Procunier Safety Chuck Co., 18 S. Clinton St., Chicago, Ill.
4779—Production Machine Tool Co., 629 E. Pearl St., Cincinnati, Ohio.

MANUFACTURERS OF AUTOMOTIVE PRODUCTS—Continued

4782—Progressive Brass Mfg. Co., 1711 Cherry St., Kansas City, Mo.
4784—Progress Mfg. Co., Arthur, Ill.
4785—Proof Machine & Brass Foundry Co., 936 E. 72nd St., Cleveland, Ohio.
4786—Protectahood Corp., 4 Osborne St., Auburn, N. Y.
4787—Protection Products Co., 729 Milwaukee Ave., Chicago, Ill.
4791—Protex-A-Motor Mfg. Co., Penn Ave., Exeter Borough, Pittston, Pa.
4792—Protex Chain Co., Waynesboro, Pa.
4794—Protex Glass Co., 220 Fifth Ave., New York, N. Y.
4798—Pueblo Tent & Awning Co., First St. & Sante Fe Ave., Pueblo, Colo.
4799—Pugh Printing Co., A. H., 400 Pike St., Cincinnati, Ohio.
4800—Purcell & Co., F. C., 2847 Grand River Ave., Detroit, Mich.
4801—Purfex Mfg. Co., 712 N. 16th St., Philadelphia, Pa.
4801a—Puritan Compressed Gas Corp., 2012 Grand Ave., Kansas City, Mo.
4802—Puritan Soap Co., 500 Exchange St., Rochester, N. Y.
4803—Purox Division, Oxweld Acetylene Co., 2101 Blake St., Denver, Colo.
4804—Pye & Co., Robert E., 60 McLean Ave., Yonkers, N. Y.
4806—Pyrene Mfg. Co., 560 Belmont Ave., Newark, N. J.

Q

5000—Quaker City Iron Works, Tioga & Richmond Sts., Philadelphia, Pa.
5001—Quaker Oil Products Corp., Conshohocken, Pa.
5002—Quality Tools Corp., New Wilmington, Pa.
5002a—Quantiproducts Machine Corp., 341 39th St., Brooklyn, N. Y.
5003—Queen Quality Luggage Corp., 327 W. Fayette St., Syracuse, N. Y. (Sole distributors, Bi-Sell Corp., 327 W. Fayette St., Syracuse, N. Y.)
5004—Quincy Compressor Co., 217 Main St., Quincy, Ill.

R

5025—RBF Ball Bearings Co., 27 W. 60th St., New York, N. Y. (Importers.)
5026—R.I.V. Co., 1775 Broadway, New York, N. Y. (Importers.)
5029—Racine Tool & Machine Co., 1750 State St., Racine, Wis.
5030—Racine Universal Motor Co., 1637 Gould St., Racine, Wis.
5031—Radel Leather Mfg. Co., Wilson & Hyatt Aves., Newark, N. J.
5032—Radiator Engineering Co., Factories Bldg., Toledo, Ohio.
5033—Rahn-Larmon Co., 2941 Spring Grove Ave., Cincinnati, Ohio.
5034—Raike & Co., Damon, 1417 W. Jackson Blvd., Chicago, Ill. (Importers.)
5035—Rainey-Pettler Mfg. Co., 339 W. Spring St., Titusville, Pa.
5036—Rajah Co., Locust Ave. & Nelson St., Bloomfield, N. J. Adv. p. 100.
5038—Ramsdell Mfg. Co., 6536 Carnegie Ave., Cleveland, Ohio.
5039—Ramsey Accessories Mfg. Corp., 3693 Forest Park Blvd., St. Louis, Mo.
5040—Ramsey Chain Co., Albany, N. Y.
5040a—Ramsey-Martin Corp., 315 City Bank Bldg., Kansas City, Mo.
5041—Randall Co., 5000 Spring Grove Ave., Cincinnati, Ohio.
5042—Rand, McNally & Co., 536 S. Clark St., Chicago, Ill.
5043—Ransom Mfg. Co., 320 Eighth St., Oshkosh, Wis.
5044—Ransom & Randolph Co., Superior & Chestnut Sts., Toledo, Ohio.
5044a—Raser Tanning Co., Evans St., Ashtabula, Ohio.
5045—Rauch & Co., F. A., 410 S. Market St., Chicago, Ill.
5046—Rawhide Products Co., Michigan Ave., Kenilworth, N. J.
5047—Rawle Co., M., 210 West 65th St., New York, N. Y. (Importers.)
5048—Rawson & Evans Co., 710 W. Washington Blvd., Chicago, Ill.
5049—Raybestos Div. of Raybestos-Manhattan, Inc., Railroad Ave., Bridgeport, Conn. Adv. p. 253.
5050—Ray Day Piston Corp., Walton & W. Warren Sts., Detroit, Mich.
5051—Raymond Mfg. Co., 226 S. Center St., Corry, Pa.
5052—Reach Textile Co., A. L., 6 W. 20th St., New York, N. Y.
5053—Read & Co., A. P., 568 W. Washington St., Chicago, Ill.
5055—Reading Rubber Mfg. Co., Reading, Mass. (Sole distributors, L. C. Chase & Co., 89 Franklin St., Boston, Mass.)
5056—Reading Screw Co., Main & Gay Sts., Norristown, Pa.
5058—Ready Tool Co., 550 Iranistan Ave., Bridgeport, Conn.
5059—Reda Mfg. Co., 4 Birnie Ave., Springfield, Mass.
5061—Red Ball Motor Truck Corp., Frankfort, Ind.
5062—Red Bar Battery Co., Bacon & Bainbridge Sts., Dayton, Ohio.
5064—Red Head Mfg. Co., 1983 E. 57th St., Cleveland, Ohio.
5065—Red-Line Reamer Co., Millersburg, Pa.
5066—Redmond Co., A. G., 1109 Stewart Ave., Flint, Mich.
5068—Reed Mfg. Co., W. Eighth St. & E. P. Crossing, Erie, Pa.
5069—Reed & Prince Mfg. Co., Duncan Ave., Worcester, Mass.
5071—Reedy Auto-Truck & Trailer Co., Xanthus & Frisco Tracks, Tulsa, Okla.
5072—Reese Padlock Company, 128 Sherman St., Lancaster, Pa.
5075—Reeve Hold Ever Products, Inc., 253 Chadwick Ave., Newark, N. J.
5076—Reeves, W. G., Stockbridge, Mich.
5079—Reflex Spark Plug Co., 10804 Berea Rd., Cleveland, Ohio.
5081—Rehberger & Son, Arthur, 316 Ferry St., Newark, N. J.
5082—Reichard Mfg. Co., F. H., Bangor, Pa.
5083—Reiff & Nestor Co., Lykens, Pa.
5083a—Reiland & Bree Truck Mfg. Co., Northbrook, Ill.
5084—Reilly Co., John, 40 Ave. C, Newark, N. J.
5085—Relay Motors Corp., Lima, Ohio.
5091—Reliable Stove Co., Div. of American Stove Co., 1825 E. 40th St., Cleveland, Ohio.
5092—Reliance Battery Products Co., 2211 S. Eighth St., Council Bluffs, Iowa.
5093—Reliance Mfg. Co., Massillon, Ohio.
5094—Reliance Specialty Co., Holyoke Water Co. Bldg., Rear Cabot St., Holyoke, Mass.
5095—Reliance Trailer & Truck Co., 2765 16th St., San Francisco, Calif.

5096—Remington-Keystone Mfg. Co., 400 Chester Rd., Ridley Park, Pa.
5098—Renu Hetepruf Co., Holland, Mich. Adv. p. 23.
5099—Reo Motor Car Co., 1331 S. Washington Ave., Lansing, Mich. Adv. p. 16.
5100—Repcal Brass Mfg. Co., 2109 E. 27th St., Los Angeles, Calif.
5101—Republic Gear Co., 3171 Bellevue Ave., Detroit, Mich.
5102—Republic Rubber Co., Youngstown, Ohio.
5103—Reschke Machine Works, 908 N. Washington Ave., Wichita, Kan.
5103a—Resistcor Engineering Corp., Tulsa, Okla.
5104—Revere Copper & Brass, Inc., Rome, N. Y.
5105—Rex Accessories Co., 415 Lake Ave., Racine, Wis.
5106—Rex Metal Products Co., 365 First Ave., New York, N. Y. Adv. p. 114.
5108—Reynolds Aluminum Co., New Washington, Ohio.
5110—Reynolds & Reynolds Co., Washington & Dudley Sts., Dayton, Ohio.
5111—Reynolds Spring Co., S. Water St., Jackson, Mich.
5112—Rhamstine, J. Thos., 500 E. Woodbridge St., Detroit, Mich.
5112a—Rheem Mfg. Co., 4535 Horton St., Emeryville, Calif.
5113—Rhoads & Sons, J. E., 35 N. Sixth St., Philadelphia, Pa.
5114—Rhode Island Tool Co., 148 W. River St., Providence, R. I.
5115—Rhodes & Co., James H., 153 W. Austin Ave., Chicago, Ill.
5115a—Rhopac Products Co., 925 Wrightwood Ave., Chicago, Ill.
5116—Rice & Co., Chas. W., Union City, Ind.
5117—Richards Machinery Co., 3423 W. Vliet St., Milwaukee, Wis.
5117a—Richardson Co., Lockland, Ohio.
5118—Richards-Wilcox Mfg. Co., Third St. & C. B. & Q. R. R. Tracks, Aurora, Ill.
5120—Richman Chemical Products Co., 2738 W. Van Buren St., Chicago, Ill.
5122—Richmond Engineering Co., 935 Brook Ave., Richmond, Va.
5123—Richmond Hammered Ring Co., Souderton, Pa.
5125—Richmond Mica Corp., 323 S. Ninth St., Richmond, Va.
5126—Richmond Pressed Metal Works, 506 Maury St., Richmond, Va.
5129—Ridgely Trimmer Co., Kenton St., Springfield, Ohio.
5130—Riebe Ball Bearing Co. of N. J., 250 W. 54th St., New York, N. Y.
5131—Rieker Instrument Co., 1919 Fairmount Ave., Philadelphia, Pa.
5132—Riess Mfg. Co., 315 S. Union St., Kokomo, Ind.
5133—Right-Way Brake Tester Co., 110 N. Water St., Watertown, Wis.
5133a—Rightway Corp., 228 N. LaSalle St., Chicago, Ill.
5134—Rinck-McIlwaine, Inc., 16 Hudson St., New York, N. Y.
5135—Ringleader Mfg. Co., 1033 N. E St., Richmond, Ind.
5136—Rinshed-Mason Co., 5135 Milford St., Detroit, Mich.
5137—Rippner Bros. Mfg. Co., 2125 Superior Ave., Cleveland, Ohio.
5139—Riverside Mfg. Co., Moultrie, Ga.
5140—Rix Co., 500 Fourth St., San Francisco, Calif.
5141—Roamer Consolidated Corp., 410 E. South St., Kalamazoo, Mich.
5142—Robbins & Myers, Inc., Lagonda Ave., Springfield, Ohio.
5142a—Roberts Brass Mfg. Co., 5435 W. Fort St., Detroit, Mich.
5144—Robertson Products Co., Theo. B., 700 W. Division St., Chicago, Ill.
5147—Robinson Co., G. H., 1455 S. Michigan Ave., Chicago, Ill.
5148—Robinson Co., M. W., 28 Warren St., New York, N. Y.
5149—Robinson Fire Apparatus Mfg. Co., 4250 N. 20th St., St. Louis, Mo.
5154—Rochester Mfg. Co., Rockwood St. (Brighton), Rochester, N. Y.
5155—Rochester Tool & Gauge Co., 45 Halsted St., Rochester, N. Y.
5156—Rockford Bolt Co., 230 Mill St., Rockford, Ill.
5157—Rockford Machine Tool Co., 2400 Kishwaukee St., Rockford, Ill.
5159—Rock Island Mfg. Co., 4140 Fullerton Ave., Chicago, Ill.
5162—Rodenhausen's Excelsior Wagon Works, Ninth & Jefferson Sts., Philadelphia, Pa.
5163—Roebling's Sons Co., John A., 640 S. Broad St., Trenton, N. J.
5164—Rogers Brothers Corp., Albion, Pa.
5165—Rogers Products Co., 198 Pacific Ave., Jersey City, N. J. Adv. p. 110.
5166—Roland & Koch, 220 Sotello St., Los Angeles, Calif.
5167—Roller Bearing Co. of America, Whitehead Rd., Trenton, N. J. Adv. p. 175.
5168—Rolls-Royce of America, Inc., Page Blvd., Springfield, Mass.
5170—Rollway Bearing Co., 541 Seymour St., Syracuse, N. Y. Adv. p. 185.
5171—Rome Brass & Copper Co., Div. Revere Copper & Brass, Inc., Bouck St., Rome, N. Y.
5172—Rome-Turney Radiator Co., 300 S. James St., Rome, N. Y.
5173—Romort Mfg. Co., Oakfield, Wis.
5174—Ronan Co., T. J., 17 Atlantic Ave., Brooklyn, N. Y.
5175—Roper Corp., Geo. D., 707 S. Main St., Rockford, Ill.
5176—Rose Mfg. Co., 37th & Filbert Sts., Philadelphia, Pa.
5178—Rose Mfg. Co., Frank, Second St. & Kansas Ave., Hastings, Neb.
5179—Rosen & Co., A. W., 418 E. 106th St., New York, N. Y.
5180—Roser & Son, Herman, Glastonbury, Conn.
5181—Rosier-Howard Co., 14 W. First St., Hutchinson, Kan.
5182—Rossendale-Reddaway Co., 30 Euclid Ave., Newark, N. J.
5183—Ross Gear & Tool Co., 800 Heath St., Lafayette, Ind.
5185—Rostand Mfg. Co., R. R. Ave., Milford, Conn.
5185a—Rotary Lift Co., 1055 Kentucky St., Memphis, Tenn.
5187—Rotary Snow Plow Co., 1615 Polk St., N. E., Minneapolis, Minn.
5188—Rotawasher Corp., 203 St. Clair Ave., E., Cleveland, Ohio.
5190—Roth Bros. & Co., 1400 W. Adams St., Chicago, Ill.
5191—Roth Mfg. Co., G. A., 810 W. First St., Hastings, Neb.
5192—Rottler Boring Bar Co., 1515 Eighth Ave., N., Seattle, Wash.
5193—Round & Son, D., Penna. R. R. & Henry Rd., Cleveland, Ohio.
5195—Rowe Mfg. Co., 18th & Hampshire Sts., San Francisco, Calif.
5196—Rowland, Inc., William & Harvey, Lewis & Tacony Sts., Philadelphia, Pa.
5197—Royal Brass Mfg. Co., 1420 E. 43rd St., Cleveland, Ohio.
5198—Royal Glass Works Corp., Fourth & Haywood Sts., Long Island City, L. I., N. Y.

MANUFACTURERS OF AUTOMOTIVE PRODUCTS—Continued

5199—Royal Piston Ring Co., Bath, N. Y.
5200—Royal Textile Co., 18 Kingston St., Boston, Mass.
5201—Royersford Foundry & Machine Co., Royersford, Pa.
5202—Royersford Spring Bed Co., First Ave. & Main St., Royersford, Pa.
5206a—Rubin Trimming Works, 54 W. 21st St., New York, N. Y.
5207—Rub-Tex Products Co., 20th & Olney Sts., Indianapolis, Ind.
5209—Ruckstell Distributing Co., 739 E. 140th St., Cleveland, Ohio.
5210—Rupert Diecasting & Stamping Co., 1404 Agnes Ave., Kansas City, Mo.
5212—Rush & Co., W. S., 1815 N. Broadway, Los Angeles, Calif.
5213—**Russell, Burdsall & Ward Bolt & Nut Co., Port Chester, N. Y. Adv. p. 61.**
5214—Russell Mfg. Co., Middletown, Conn.
5214a—Russell Mfg. Co., Carpenters Lane, Greenfield, Mass.
5215—Russell & Stoll Co., 53 Rose St., New York, N. Y.
5216—Rusticide Co., 416 Frankfort Ave., Cleveland, Ohio.
5217—Ruth Glass Co., Tenth Ave. & Hallowell St., Conshohocken, Pa.
5218—Ryco, Inc., 417 23rd St., Oakland, Calif.
5219—Ryerson & Haynes, Inc., 2307 E. Ganson St., Jackson, Mich.

S

5400—S. B. R. Specialty Co., 17 Princeton St., East Orange, N. J.
5401—**SKF Industries, Inc., 40 E. 34th St., New York, N. Y.** (Supervising: Hess-Bright Mfg. Co., Skayef Ball Bearing Co., Atlas Ball Co.) Adv. p. 171.
5402—S & M Lamp C., 118 W. 36th St., Los Angeles, Calif.
5402a—S. P. A. Truck Corp., South Bend, Ind.
5403—**S-W-S Co., 15 Wilder St., Minneapolis, Minn.**
5405—Saf-De-Lite Corp., Connersville, Ind.
5406—Safetee Glass Co., 905 N. Broad St., Philadelphia, Pa.
5407—Safety Fire Extinguisher Co., 293 Seventh Ave., New York, N. Y.
5408—Safety Lift Co., 16 Beaver St., New York, N. Y.
5409a—Saginaw Stamping & Tool Co., Saginaw, Mich.
5410—Saintclair Products Co., 17 Sherman Ave., East Newark, N. J.
5411—St. Louis Car Co., 8000 N. Broadway, St. Louis, Mo.
5413—St. Louis Rubber Cement Co., 3952 W. Pine Blvd., St. Louis, Mo.
5414—**St. Louis Spring Co., 3129-39 Washington Ave., St. Louis, Mo. Adv. p. 96.**
5415—St. Louis Tag Co., 217 Locust St., St. Louis, Mo. Adv. p .114.
5416—St. Louis Tool & Mfg. Co., 3300 N. Broadway, St. Louis, Mo.
5417—St. Marys Wheel & Spoke Co., St. Marys, Ohio.
5418—St. Paul Hydraulic Hoist Co., 292 Walnut St., St. Paul, Minn.
5419—St. Paul Welding & Mfg. Co., 168 W. Third St., St. Paul, Minn.
5420—St. Pierre Chain Corp., Frank St., Worcester, Mass.
5421—Saks Mfg. Co., 14 W. Lake St., Chicago, Ill.
5424—Sampson Tool Co., 916 State St., East St. Louis, Ill.
5425—Samson Products Co., 663 N. Broad St., Philadelphia, Pa.
5426—Samson Tire & Rubber Corp., 5725 Telegraph Rd., Los Angeles, Calif.
5428—San Antonio Body Co., 823 Roosevelt Ave., San Antonio, Tex.
5430—Sanderson-Cyclone Drill Co., Orrville, Ohio.
5430a—Sandoz-Vuille, Inc., 701 Stephenson Bldg., Detroit, Mich.
5433—Sanford Mills, Sanford, Me.
5434—Sanford Motor Truck Co., 107 St. Marks Ave., Syracuse, N. Y.
5435—Sapolin Co., 229 E. 42nd St., New York, N. Y.
5438—Sasgen Derrick Co., 3101 Grand Ave., Chicago, Ill. (Sole distributors, Automotive Maintenance Machinery Co., 810 W. Washington Blvd., Chicago, Ill.)
5440—Sav-Oil Ring Mfg. Co., 1718 S. Hill St., Los Angeles, Calif.
5441—Sawyer-Weber Tool Mfg. Co., 4148 Whiteside Ave., Los Angeles, Calif.
5442—Sayers & Scoville Co., Gest & Summer Sts., Cincinnati, Ohio.
5443—Saylor Electric & Mfg. Co., 1014 Lynn St., Detroit, Mich.
5444—Scaife & Sons Co., Wm. B., First National Bank Bldg., Pittsburgh, Pa.
5445—Scandinavia Belting Co., 248 Central Ave., Newark, N. J.
5446—Schaefer Co., Gustav, 4180 Lorain Ave., Cleveland, Ohio.
5448—Schaefer Tent & Awning Co., 1421 Larimer St., Denver, Colo.
5449—Schaffer, M., 597 St. Anns Ave., New York, N. Y.
5451—Schartow Iron Products Co., Sattley Bldg., Racine, Wis.
5452—Schauer Machine Co., 905 Broadway, Cincinnati, Ohio.
5453—Schellenbach-Hunt Tool Co., 116 Opera Pl., Cincinnati, Ohio.
5456—Schmelz Mfg. Co., 290 Fremont St., San Francisco, Calif.
5457—Schmidt Corp., Charles D., 276 Canal St., New York, N. Y.
5458a—**Schoedinger, F. O., 322-58 Mt. Vernon Ave., Columbus, Ohio. Adv. p. 48.**
5459—Schoelkopf Mfg. Co., 210 E. Washington Ave., Madison, Wis.
5460—Schoellkopf Co., 814 Jackson St., Dallas, Tex.
5461—Schoettle Co., Edwin J., 533 N. 11th St., Philadelphia, Pa.
5462—Scholler Mfg. Co., 147 Leslie St., Buffalo, N. Y.
5465—**Schrader's Son, A., 470 Vanderbilt Ave., Brooklyn, N. Y. Adv. p. 29.**
5468—Schroeder & Tremayne, Inc., 500 N. Commercial St., St. Louis, Mo.
5471—Schultz & Hirsch Co., 1300 Fulton St., Chicago, Ill.
5472—Schultz & Son, A. L., 1675 Elston Ave., Chicago, Ill.
5476—**Schwarze Electric Co., Grace, Church & Payne Sts., Adrian, Mich. Adv. p. 47.**
5477—Schwarzenbach Huber Co., 470 Fourth Ave., New York, N. Y.
5478—Schweig & Son, George E., 2829 N. Broad St., Philadelphia, Pa. (Importers.)
5479—Scientific Heater Co., 1406 Builders Exchange Bldg., Cleveland, Ohio.
5480—**Scintilla Magneto Co., Div. of Bendix Aviation Corp., Sherman Ave., Sidney, N. Y. Adv. Front Cover.**
5481—Scott & Ewing Co., 238 Cherry St., Bluffton, Ohio.
5485—Scully Steel & Iron Co., 2364 S. Ashland Ave., Chicago, Ill.
5486—Seagrave Co., S. High St., Columbus, Ohio.

5486a—Seamon Body Corp., 3880 N. Richards St., Milwaukee, Wis.
5489—Sease-Crowell Co., 57 S. Cameron St., Harrisburg, Pa. (Sole distributors, Engineering Equipment Sales Co., 800 N. Delaware Ave., Philadelphia, Pa.)
5490—Sebastian Lathe Co., Third & Philadelphia Sts., Cincinnati, Ohio.
5493—Sedgwick Machine Works, 150 W. 15th St., New York, N. Y.
5494a—Segal Lock & Hardware Co., 12 Warren St., New York, N. Y.
5495—Seiberling Rubber Co., Akron, Ohio.
5496—Seiss Mfg. Co., 3839 Alexis Ave., Toledo, Ohio.
5497—Sek-Reliance Corp., 211 Madison Ave., Covington, Ky.
5498—Selden-Hahn Motor Truck Corp., Allentown, Pa.
5502—Seneca Falls Machine Co., 314 Fall St., Seneca Falls, N. Y.
5503—Seneca Wire & Mfg. Co., Vine St., Fostoria, Ohio.
5504—Service Caster & Truck Co., 519 N. Albion St., Albion, Mich.
5505—Service Equipment Co., 8459 Dearborn Ave., Southgate, Calif.
5508—Service Recorder Co., 454 Hanna Bldg., Cleveland, Ohio.
5509—**Service Spring Co., 735 St. Paul St., Indianapolis, Ind. Adv. p. 98.**
5510—**Service Station Equipment Co., Conshohocken, Pa. Adv. p. 121.**
5510a—Service Steel Co., 1431 Franklin St., Detroit, Mich.
5511—Servwell Sales Corp., 1749 N. Winchester Ave., Chicago, Ill.
5513—Sevison Magneto Engineering Co., 397 Phillips Ave., Toledo, Ohio.
5514—Sewall Paint & Varnish Co., 1009 W. Eighth St., Kansas City, Mo.
5515—Seward Trunk & Bag Co., High St., Petersburg, Va.
5519—Shakeproof Lock Washer Co., 2501 N. Keeler Ave., Chicago, Ill.
5520—Shaler Co., 728 Fourth St., Waupun, Wis.
5522—Shank Sign Co., E. A., 25 W. 43rd St., New York, N. Y.
5524—Sharpe Mfg. Co., 1356 S. Flower St., Los Angeles, Calif.
5525—Sharples Specialty Co., 2300 Westmoreland St., Philadelphia, Pa.
5526—Sharpsville Boiler Works Co., Sharpsville, Pa.
5529—Shawver Co., 21 W. Pleasant St., Springfield, Ohio.
5531—Sheldon Machine Co., 3253 Cottage Grove Ave., Chicago, Ill.
5532—Shelton Tack Co., Shelton, Conn.
5533—Shelton Tubular Rivet Co., Shelton, Conn.
5534—**Shepard & Moore, Inc., Advance Bldg., Cleveland, Ohio. Adv. p. 47.**
5535—Shepard Niles Crane & Hoist Corp., Montour Falls, N. Y.
5536—Shepard-Thomason Co., 506 W. Pico St., Los Angeles, Calif.
5538—Sherman-Klove Co., 3535 W. 47th St., Chicago, Ill.
5539—Sherman Mfg. Co., H. B., 22 Barney St., Battle Creek, Mich.
5541—**Sherwin-Williams Co., Dept. 733, 101 Prospect Ave., N. W., Cleveland, Ohio. Adv. p. 21.**
5542—Sherwood Brass Works, 6631 E. Jefferson Ave., Detroit, Mich.
5543—Sherwood Co., A. S., 258 W. 54th St., New York, N. Y.
5544—Shirley Webbing Mills, Rex Cole Bldg., Fourth Ave. at 21st St., New York, N. Y.
5545—**Shoemaker Automotive Equipment Co., Henney Bldg., Freeport, Ill. Adv. p. 106.**
5547—Shop of Siebert, 614 Southard Ave., Toledo, Ohio.
5549—Shur-Gloss Mfg. Co., 3555 W. Grand Ave., Chicago, Ill.
5550—**Shurhit Products, Inc., Waukegan, Ill. Adv. p. 80.**
5552—Shwayder Trunk Mfg. Co., 1050 S. Broadway, Denver, Colo.
5553—Sibley Machine Co., 206 E. Tutt St., South Bend, Ind.
5554—Sickles Co., J. B., 2100 Washington Ave., St. Louis, Mo.
5555—Sidney Elevator Mfg. Co., Miami & Shelby Sts., Sidney, Ohio.
5556—**Signal Mfg. Co., 587 Washington St., Lynn, Mass. Adv. p. 45.**
5557—Silent Hoist Winch & Crane Co., 762 Henry St., Brooklyn, N. Y.
5559—Siltop Mfg. Co., 1241 N. Vine St., Los Angeles, Calif.
5560—**Silver King Hydraulic Jack Co., 5604 Cedar Ave., Cleveland, Ohio. Adv. p. 49.**
5562—Simmen Hydraulic Jack Corp., 44 Clay St., Newark, N. J.
5563—**Simmons Mfg. Co., 3405-11 Perkins Ave., Cleveland, Ohio. Adv. p. 62.**
5565—Simonds Saw & Steel Co., 470 Main St., Fitchburg, Mass.
5565a—Simonds Worden White Co., Dayton, Ohio.
5566—Simoniz Co., 2101 Indiana Ave., Chicago, Ill.
5567—Simonsen Iron Works, Sioux Rapids, Iowa.
5568—Simons Paint Spray Brush Co., 1106 Maryland Ave., Dayton, Ohio.
5570—Simplex Body & Mfg. Co., Conneautville, Pa.
5571—Simplex Mfg. Co., 12 Franklin St., Auburn, N. Y.
5572—Simplex Paper Corp., Adrian, Mich.
5573—Simplex Piston Ring Co. of America, 1966 E. 66th St., Cleveland, Ohio.
5575—**Simplex Time Recorder Co., 50 Time Ave., Gardner, Mass. Adv. p. 127.**
5576—Simplex Universal Joint, Inc., 149 North Ave., Plainfield, N. J.
5577—Simplex Wire & Cable Co., 201 Devonshire St., Boston, Mass.
5578—Simplicity Mfg. Co., 70 Spring St., Port Washington, Wis.
5580—Singer Machine Works, Joe, 2116 S. Los Angeles St., Los Angeles, Calif.
5581—Sinko Tool & Mfg. Co., 351 N. Crawford Ave., Chicago, Ill.
5584—Sistersville Tank & Boiler Works, Sistersville, W. Va.
5585—Six Wheels, Inc., 1223 Santa Fe Ave., Los Angeles, Calif.
5588—Skilsaw, Inc., 1801 Bernice Ave., Chicago, Ill.
5589—Skinner Motors, Inc., 2231 Dalzelle St., Detroit, Mich.
5589a—Sky Specialties Corp., 3651 Hart Ave., Chicago, Ill.
5592—Slaymaker Electric Welding Co., 686 W. Grand Blvd., Detroit, Mich.
5593—Slaymaker Lock Co., West End Ave. & First St., Lancaster, Pa.
5595—Sloane Mfg. Co., W. & J., Trenton, N. J. (Sole distributors, W. & J. Sloane, 575 Fifth Ave., New York, N. Y.)
5596—Slocomb Co., J. T., 35 Oxford St., Providence, R. I.
5597—Sly Co., W. W., 4700 Train Ave., Cleveland, Ohio.
5598—Smith Belting Co., Manning J., Tenth St. & Allegheny Ave., Philadelphia, Pa.
5599—Smith & Co., F. P., Sharon Hill, Pa.

MANUFACTURERS OF AUTOMOTIVE PRODUCTS—Continued

5600—Smith Co., Harrison, 711 N. Broadway, Oklahoma City, Okla.
5601—Smith Glass Co., L. E., Mount Pleasant, Pa.
5602—Smith & Hemenway (Div. Crescent Tool Co.), 217 Harrison St., Jamestown, N. Y.
5604—Smith Mfg. Co., F. A., 183 N. Water St., Rochester, N. Y.
5604a—Smith Products Co., 1239 W. Third St., Cleveland, Ohio.
5605—Smith-Schifflin Co., 149 Church St., New York, N. Y.
5607—Smith Stamping Co., Peter, 10501 Haggerty Ave., Detroit, Mich.
5608—Smith Welding Equipment Corp., 2633 Fourth St., S. E., Minneapolis, Minn.
5609—Smith Wood-Products, Inc., 1900 Armour Rd., North Kansas City, Mo.
5610—Smooth-On Mfg. Co., 572 Communipaw Ave., Jersey City, N. J.
5611—Snap-On Tools, Inc., Kenosha, Wis. (Sole distributors, Motor Tool Specialty Co., 2025 S. Michigan Ave., Chicago, Ill.)
5612—Snider Industries, Inc., A. G., 227 S. Meridian St., Indianapolis, Ind.
5613—Snellex Mfg. Co., 304 Franklin St., Rochester, N. Y.
5616—Snow Flyer Co., New Holstein, Wis.
5617—Snyder & Son, M. L., 116 N. Third St., Philadelphia, Pa.
5619—So-Lo-Jack Co., Attleboro, Mass.
5624—Sommer & Maca Glass Machinery Corp., 3600 S. Oakley Ave., Chicago, Ill.
5625—Sonneborn Sons, L., 114 Fifth Ave., New York, N. Y.
5626—Sorenson Mfg. Co., 17 W. 60th St., New York, N. Y.
5627—Soss Mfg. Co., 647 E. First Ave., Roselle, N. J.
5628—South Atlantic Waste Co., N. Brevard St., Charlotte, N. C.
5629—South Bend Lathe Works, 373 E. Madison St., South Bend, Ind. Adv. p. 124.
5633—Southern Friction Fabric Co., Charlotte, N. C.
5635—Southern Iron & Equipment Co., Hemphill Ave. & Southern Ry., Atlanta, Ga.
5636—Southern Oxygen Co., Alexandria Rd., South Washington, Va.
5637—Southern Weaving Co., Greenville, S. C.
5639—Southwest Onyx & Marble Co., Foot of Crosby St., San Diego, Calif.
5640—Southwest Pump Co., First & Center Sts., Bonham, Tex.
5641—Sparks-Withington Co., Jackson, Mich. Adv. p. 48.
5647—Speednut Wrench Corp., 846 State-Lake Bldg., Chicago, Ill.
5648—Speedwell Bearings, Inc., 1834 Broadway, New York, N. Y.
5649—Speidel Elevator Corp., W. Buttonwood & Gordon Sts., Reading, Pa.
5650—Spence-Bergen Motor Co., 524 Crawford St., Middletown, Ohio. (Sole distributors, Simplicity Mfg. Co., 70 Spring St., Port Washington, Wis.)
5651—Spencer Mfg. Co., Main St., Spencer, Ohio. Adv. p. 96.
5652—Spencer-Smith Machine Co., Howell, Mich.
5653—Spicer Mfg. Corp., 4100 Bennett Rd., Toledo, Ohio.
5654—Spiro Mfg. Co., C., Spiro Bldg., Dobbs Ferry, N. Y.
5654a—Split Coach Motor Corp., Philadelphia & Broad Sts., York, Pa.
5655—Splitdorf Electrical Co., 392 High St., Newark, N. J.
5656—Spraco, Inc., 114 Central St., Somerville, Mass.
5657—Spraker Mfg. Co., 1440 E. 19th St., Indianapolis, Ind.
5658—Springboro Mfg. Co., Beaver St., Springboro, Pa.
5662—Springfield Machine Tool Co., 631 W. Southern Ave., Springfield, Ohio.
5663—Springfield Mfg. Co., 317 Mt. Grove St., Bridgeport, Conn.
5664—Springfield Mfg. Co., Bechtle Ave. & Columbia St., Springfield, Ohio. Adv. p. 78.
5665—Springfield Wagon & Trailer Co., Springfield, Mo.
5665a—Springfield Wheel Puller Co., 510 Hubert Ave., Springfield, Ohio.
5667—Stafford, Inc., S. S., 603 Washington St., New York, N. Y.
5668—Staley Co., Earl B., 915 Eleventh Ave., Seattle, Wash.
5670—Standard Arm Rest Co., 40 Clifford St., Providence, R. I.
5671—Standard Battery Mfg. Co., 1103 N. Main St., Fort Worth, Tex.
5672—Standard Belt Co., 617 Broadway, Chelsea, Mass.
5674—Standard Brass Works, 1810 W. St. Paul Ave., Milwaukee, Wis.
5676—Standard Electrical Tool Co., 1938 W. Eighth St., Cincinnati, Ohio.
5677—Standard Electric Co., 115 San Pedro Ave., San Antonio, Tex.
5679—Standard Flag & Mfg. Co., 716 Chestnut St., Philadelphia, Pa.
5681—Standard Heel & Counter Co., 1024 N. 11th St., St. Louis, Mo.
5683—Standard Machinery Co., 1475 Elmwood Ave., Auburn, N. J.
5684—Standard Mfg. & Sales Corp., 701 La Fayette Ave., Lebanon, Ind.
5685—Standard Mirror Co., 147 Harrison St., Buffalo, N. Y.
5687—Standard Motor Products, Inc., 10 46th Ave., Long Island City, N. Y.
5688—Standard Motor Truck Co., 1111 Bellevue Ave., Detroit, Mich.
5690—Standard Pressed Steel Co., Jenkintown, Pa.
5691—Standard Register Co., Albany & Campbell Sts., Dayton, Ohio.
5692—Standard Safety Corp., 1425 W. Pico St., Los Angeles, Calif.
5694—Standard Sheet Metal Works, 3295 N. 30th St., Milwaukee, Wis.
5695a—Standard Steel & Bearings, Inc., Woodford Ave., Plainville, Conn. (Sole distributors, M-R-C Bearings Service Co., 402 Chandler St., Jamestown, N. Y.)
5696—Standard Steel Specialty Co., Beaver Falls, Pa.
5697—Standard Steel Stamping Co., W. Louisiana Ave. & D. & R. G. W. Tracks, Denver, Colo.
5699—Standard Textile Products Co., 320 Broadway, New York, N. Y.
5700—Standard Tool Co., 6900 Central Ave., Cleveland, Ohio.
5701—Standard Trailer Co., 162 Grant St., Cambridge Springs, Pa.
5702—Standard Tube & Mfg. Co., 2435 Scotten Ave., Detroit, Mich.
5703—Standard Underground Cable Co., Perth Amboy, N. J.
5704—Standard Varnish Works, 443 Fourth Ave., New York, N. Y.
5705—Standard Waste Mfg. Co., 2306 N. American St., Philadelphia, Pa.
5706—Stanley Baggage Co., Stanley, Wis.

5707—Stanley Co., John T., 642 W. 30th St., New York, N. Y.
5708—Stanley Electric Tool Co., 111 Elm St., New Britain, Conn.
5709—Stanley Rule & Level Plant, 111 Elm St., New Britain, Conn.
5710—Stant Machine Co., 1620 Columbia St., Connersville, Ind.
5711—Stanton, Inc., Edwin L., 3954 Whiteside Ave., Los Angeles, Calif.
5713—Star Carriage Co., 91 Stacy St., Seattle, Wash.
5715—Stark Metal Works, 4058 Flora Blvd., St. Louis, Mo.
5718—Star Products, Inc., 15105 Darwin Ave., Cleveland, Ohio.
5719—Starrett Co., L. S., 165 Crescent St., Athol, Mass.
5720—Star Specialty Mfg. Co., 2034 Daily News Bldg., Chicago, Ill.
5721a—Star Tool Co., 119 N. Fourth St., Minneapolis, Minn.
5722—Statite Rubber Products Co., 1909 Glenway Ave., Covington, Ky.
5723—Staude Mfg. Co., E. G., 2675 University Ave., St. Paul, Minn.
5725—Steel Blanking Co., 504 E. Market St., Sandusky, Ohio.
5726—Steel or Bronze Piston Ring Corp., 564 S. Meridian St., Indianapolis, Ind.
5727—Steelcote Mfg. Co., 3418 Gratiot Ave., St. Louis, Mo.
5728—Steel Equipment Corp., Avenel, N. J.
5730—Steel Sales Corp., 129 S. Jefferson St., Chicago, Ill.
5731—Steel and Tubes, Inc., 224 E. 131st St., Cleveland, Ohio.
5733—Steiner Electric Corp., 590 Northern Blvd., Long Island City, N. Y.
5736—Step-N-Drive Div. of Divco-Detroit Corp., 2435 Merrick Ave., Detroit, Mich.
5739—Sterling Cable & Carbon Corp., 5005 Euclid Ave., Cleveland, Ohio.
5740—Sterling Clock Co., Div. of Western Clock Co., La Salle, Ill. Adv. p. 41.
5741—Sterling Electric Motors, Inc., Telegraph Rd. & Atlantic Blvd., Los Angeles, Calif.
5742—Sterling Engine Co., 1252 Niagara St., Buffalo, N. Y.
5744—Sterling Grinding Wheel Co., Tiffin, Ohio.
5747—Sterling Motor Truck Co., 45th Ave. & Rogers St. (West Allis), Milwaukee, Wis.
5748—Sterling Products Corp., 2916 N. Market St., St. Louis, Mo.
5749—Sterling Siren Fire Alarm Co., 53 Allen St., Rochester, N. Y.
5750—Sterling Varnish Co., Beaver Rd., Haysville, Pa.
5751—Stern-Brown, Inc., 257 W. 17th St., New York, N. Y.
5753—Stevens Walden, Inc., 475 Shrewsbury St., Worcester, Mass.
5757—Stewart Iron Works Co., 727 Stewart Block, Cincinnati, Ohio.
5758—Stewart Mfg. Co., William E., 14th & Elm Sts., Flint, Mich.
5759—Stewart Mfg. Corp., F. W., 512 W. Huron St., Chicago, Ill.
5760—Stewart Motor Corp., Dept. 16, 93 Dewey Ave., Buffalo, N. Y. Adv. p. 28.
5761—Stewart-Warner Corp., 1826 Diversey Parkway, Chicago, Ill.
5763—Stiles-Herman Mfg. Co., 3617 S. Grand Blvd., St. Louis, Mo.
5764—Stimmel Winch & Machine Works, 518 W. 37th St., New York, N. Y.
5765—Stimson Co., Edwin B., 70 Franklin Ave., Brooklyn, N. Y.
5766—Stiner Piston Ring, Inc., 533 Larned St., Detroit, Mich.
5767—Stitt Ignition Co., 86 E. First Ave., Columbus, Ohio.
5771—Stokes Machine Co., F. J., 5836 Tabor Rd. (Olney), Philadelphia, Pa.
5772—Stokes Mfg. Co., A. H., W. Main & Ann Arbor R. R., Owosso, Mich.
5773—Stoll Mfg. Co., 3227 Larimer St., Denver, Colo.
5774—Storm-King Electric Corp., Dry Harbor Rd. & L. I. R. R., Glendale, L. I., N. Y.
5775—Storm Mfg. Co., 406 Sixth Ave., S., Minneapolis, Minn.
5777—Stortz & Son, John, 210 Vine St., Philadelphia, Pa.
5778—Stoughton Co. (Motor Truck Div.), Stoughton, Wis.
5779a—Stover Mfg. & Engine Co., Swartz Automotive Div., Freeport, Ill.
5781—Stowe, Jr., Geo. M., 73 Forest Ave., Buffalo, N. Y.
5782—Stow Flexible Shaft Co., 3623 Brandywine St., Philadelphia, Pa.
5783—Stow Mfg. Co., 445 State St., Binghamton, N. Y.
5784—Strand & Co., N. A., 5001 N. Lincoln St., Chicago, Ill.
5785—Straus-Frank Co., 301 S. Flores St., San Antonio, Tex.
5786—Strom Bearings Co., 4535 Palmer St., Chicago, Ill. (Sole distributors, M-R-C Bearings Service Co., 402 Chandler St., Jamestown, N. Y.)
5787a—Stromberg Motoscope Corp., 1143 Diversey Parkway, Chicago, Ill.
5788—Strom Steel Ball Co., 360 N. Michigan Ave., Chicago, Ill.
5789—Strong, Carlisle & Hammond Co., 1392 W. Third St., Cleveland, Ohio.
5791—Studebaker Corp., Main & Bronson Sts., South Bend, Ind.
5792—Stunkard Bros., Cor. Church & Meridian Sts., Brazil, Ind.
5794—Sturges Mfg. Co., 2030 Sunset Ave., Utica, N. Y.
5795—Sturtevant Co., B. F., 15 Damon St. (Hyde Park), Boston, Mass.
5796—Stutz Motor Car Co. of America, Inc., Tenth St. & Capitol Ave., Indianapolis, Ind.
5797—Summers Equipment Co., 214 Lippincott Ave., Ardmore, Pa.
5800—Sunstrand Machine Tool Co., 2410 11th St., Rockford, Ill.
5801—Sunnen Products Co., 7900 Manchester St., St. Louis, Mo. Adv. p. 26.
5803—Superior Auto Fabrics Co., 2911 Indiana Ave., Chicago, Ill.
5805—Superior Body Corp., Branson & 18th Sts., Marion, Ind.
5807—Superior Insulating Tape Co., 3100 Lambkin Ave., St. Louis, Mo.
5808—Superior Machine & Engineering Co., 1930 Ferry Park, Detroit, Mich.
5809—Superior Machine Tool Co., E. Defenbaugh St., Kokomo, Ind.
5811—Superior Oxy-Acetylene Machine Co., 1102 E. High St., Hamilton, Ohio.
5812—Superior Piston Ring Co., 6423 Epworth Blvd., Detroit, Mich. Adv. p. 90.
5813—Superior Rebound Control, Inc., 2905 60th St., Kenosha, Wis.
5814—Superior Running Board Mfg. Co., 111 E. 12th St., New York, N. Y.
5815—Superior Screw & Bolt Mfg. Co., E. 93rd St. & Aetna Rd., Cleveland, Ohio.
5816—Superior Seal & Stamp Co., 1401 Vermont Ave., Detroit, Mich.
5817—Superior Spring Winding Tool Co., 2218 N. Third St., Milwaukee, Wis.
5819—Supreme Auto Trunk & Luggage Co., 653 Broadway, New York, N. Y.

MANUFACTURERS OF AUTOMOTIVE PRODUCTS—Continued

5821—Surface Combustion Corp., 2375 Dorr St., Toledo, Ohio.
5822—Surtin Safety Signal Co., 870 Market St., San Francisco, Calif.
5828—Swedish Crucible Steel Co., Butler Ave. & G. T. R. R., Detroit, Mich.
5831—Swing-Spout Measure Co., 3700 Mines Ave., Los Angeles, Calif.
5832—Swivel Joint & Shaft Co., Plymouth, Ind.
5833—Syntron Co., 400 N. Lexington Ave., Pittsburgh, Pa.
5834—Syracuse Gauge Mfg. Corp., 212 Bear St., Syracuse, N. Y. Adv. p. 44.

T

6100—T & A Mfg. Co., 916 University Ave., St. Paul, Minn.
6101—T-Grip Chain Co., 13th & Grace Sts., Omaha, Neb.
6102—Tabor Mfg. Co., 6225 Tacony St., Philadelphia, Pa.
6103—Tacony File & Hardware Co., 2438 N. Orianna St., Philadelphia, Pa.
6104—Taft-Peirce Mfg. Co., 32 Mechanic Ave., Woonsocke., R. I.
6106—Tapered Roller Bearing Co., 250 W. 54th St., New York, N. Y.
6107—Taylor Battery Supply Co., John, 2706 McGee Trafficway, Kansas City, Mo.
6108—Taylor Bros. Mfg. Corp., Elkhart, Ind.
6109—Taylor Instrument Companies, 95 Ames St., Rochester, N. Y.
6110—Taylor Machine Co., 1917 E. 61st St., Cleveland, Ohio.
6112—Taylor Mfg. Co., James L., 108 Parker Ave., Poughkeepsie, N. Y.
6113—Taylor Products & Mfg. Co., 26 W. Naghten St., Columbus, Ohio.
6114—Taylor Trunk Works, C. A., 678 N. Halsted St., Chicago, Ill.
6117—Teleoptic Corp., Terminal Bldg., Racine, Wis.
6118—Temco Electric Motor Co., 504 Sugar St., Leipsic, Ohio.
6119—Temme Spring Corp., 65 E. 28th St., Chicago, Ill.
6121—Temple Malleable Iron & Steel Corp., Temple, Pa.
6122—Templeton, Kenly & Co., 1026 S. Central Ave., Chicago, Ill.
6123—Tennessee Glove Co., Tullahoma, Tenn.
6124—Terrell's Equipment Co., Hall & Hilton Sts., Grand Rapids, Mich.
6125—Testrite Instrument Co., 57 E. 11th St., New York, N. Y.
6126—Texas Body & Trailer Co., 4516 Harrisburg Rd., Houston, Tex.
6127—Texas Co., 17 Battery Pl., New York, N. Y.
6128—Textileather Corp., Stickney Ave. & Dayton St., Toledo, Ohio.
6129—Thermoid Rubber Co., Whitehead Rd., Trenton, N. J. Adv. p. 85.
6129a—Theurer Wagon Works, Inc., 601 W. 56th St., New York, N. Y.
6130—Thiem Mfg. Co., 121 Fifth Ave., S., Minneapolis, Minn.
6131—Thoma Glass, Inc., 406 Depot St., Fairfield, Iowa.
6132—Thomas Clock Co., Seth, 19 W. 44th St., New York, N. Y.
6133—Thomas-Griffith Corp., Perkins & Kilgore Sts., Muncie, Ind.
6133a—Thomas Heater Co., Thomas, W. Va.
6134—Thomas Mfg. Co., W. H., 412 W. Sixth St., Spencer, Iowa.
6135—Thomas Stationery Mfg. Co., Springfield, Ohio.
6136—Thompson Co., Robert, 1015 S. Grand Ave., Los Angeles, Calif.
6139—Thompson-Neaylon Mfg. Co., 3545 S. Morgan St., Chicago, Ill.
6140—Thompson-Owens Corp., York & Wheeling Sts., Toledo, Ohio.
6141—Thompson Products, Inc., 2196 Clarkwood Rd., Cleveland, Ohio. Adv. p. 89.
6142—Thompson & Son Co., Henry G., 277 Chapel St., New Haven, Conn.
6143—Thompson Specialties, Inc., Chandler St., Springfield, Mass.
6144—Thomson Mfg. Co., 1706 Main St., Peoria, Ill.
6144a—Thomson Mfg. Co., Judson L., Sawyer Rd., Waltham, Mass.
6145—Thomson Mfg. Co., S. H., Fourth & St. Clair Sts., Dayton, Ohio.
6146a—Threadwell Tool Co., 16 Arch St., Greenfield, Mass.
9150—Thurman Mfg. Co., 2729 Oak St., Kansas City, Mo.
6151—Tiffany Aluminum Products Co., 19th & Branch Sts., St. Louis, Mo.
6153—Tilden, Inc., S. G., 3036 Northern Blvd., Long Island City, N. Y. (Sole distributors, Raybestos Div. of Raybestos-Manhattan, Inc., Railroad Ave., Bridgeport, Conn.)
6156—Timing Gear Corp., 2801 Fulton St., Chicago, Ill.
6157—Timken-Detroit Axle Co., 400 Clarke Ave., Detroit, Mich.
6159—Timken Roller Bearing Service & Sales Co., 19th St. & Dueber Ave. S. W., Canton, Ohio. Adv. p. 57.
6159a—Timesaver Products Co., 31 S. Desplaines St., Chicago, Ill.
6160—Tingley-Reliance Rubber Corp., Ross St. & St. George Ave., Rahway, N. J.
6161—Tio-Ma Products Corp., 5100 Sweeney Ave., Cleveland, Ohio.
6162—Titchener & Co., E. H., 136 Walnut St., Binghamton, N. Y.
6163—Titeflex Metal Hose Co., 500 Frelinghuysen Ave., Newark, N. J.
6165—Tokheim Oil Tank & Pump Co., 1618 Wabash Ave., Fort Wayne, Ind.
6165a—Toledo Alloyed Castings Co., Hamilton & Division Sts., Toledo, Ohio.
6166—Toledo Pipe Threading Machine Co., 1445 Summit Ave., Toledo, Ohio.
6166a—Toledo Pressed Steel Co., Phillips Ave. at Detroit, Toledo, Ohio.
6167—Toledo Scale Co., Monroe & Albion Sts., Toledo, Ohio.
6168—Toledo Standard Commutator Co., 2242 Smead Ave., Toledo, Ohio.
6169—Toledo Steel Products Co., 3300 Summit St., Toledo, Ohio.
6170—Toledo Timer Co., 3118 Monroe St., Toledo, Ohio.
6171—Tolman Mfg. Co., 19 W. Third St. (South Boston), Boston, Mass.
6174—Tonneau Shield Co., 518 W. 57th St., New York, N. Y.
6176—Torchweld Equipment Co., 224 N. Carpenter St., Chicago, Ill.
6177—Torrington Co., 56 Field St., Torrington, Conn.
6178—Tot Industries of Detroit, 2270 First National Bank Bldg., Detroit, Mich. Adv. p. 46.
6179—Tower Co., A. J., 24 Simmons St., Boston, Mass.
6180—Tower Mfg. Co., Madison, Ind.
6182—Trailmobile Co., 31st & Robertson Sts., Cincinnati, Ohio.
6183—Trainor National Spring Co., Newcastle, Ind.

6184—Trane Co., 205 Cameron Ave., La Crosse, Wis.
6185—Trautner Mfg. Co., 916 University Ave., St. Paul, Minn.
6187—Trenton Auto Radiator Works, 626 Brunswick Ave., Trenton, N. J.
6188—Triangle Auto Spring Co., Dubois, Pa.
6189a—Trico Fuse Mfg. Co., Tenth St. & McKinley Ave., Milwaukee, Wis.
6190—Trico Products Corp., 817 Washington St., Buffalo, N. Y. Adv. p. 55.
6191—Trimont Mfg. Co., 55 Amory St. (Roxbury), Boston, Mass.
6192—Trindl Corp., Aurora & Hankes Aves., Aurora, Ill.
6193—Triple-A-Specialty Co., 2101 Walnut St., Chicago, Ill.
6194—Triplex Safety Glass Co. of North America, Clifton, N. J.
6195—Triplex Screw Co., 5300 Grant Ave., Cleveland, Ohio.
6196—Trippe Mfg. Co., 1731 Belmont Ave., Chicago, Ill.
6197—Tripp Products, Inc., 450 E. Woodbridge St., Detroit, Mich.
6197a—Trojan Auto Products Co., 1018 S. Los Angeles St., Los Angeles, Cal.
6198—Tropic-Aire, Inc., 36 11th Ave., N. E., Minneapolis, Minn. Adv. p. 50.
6200—Troy Sunshade Co., Troy, Ohio.
6203a—Trucktor Corp., 156 Wilson Ave., Newark, N. J.
6205—Trump Bros. Rubber Co., 1857 E. Market St., Akron, Ohio.
6206—Truscon Laboratories, Caniff & G. T. R. R., Detroit, Mich.
6207—Truscon Steel Co., Albert St., Youngstown, Ohio.
6208—Truth Tool Co., 711 S. Front St., Mankato, Minn. Adv. p. 128.
6209—Tsungani Piston Co., 625 E. 11th St., Tacoma, Wash.
6210—Tube Manifold Corp., 30 Letchworth St., Buffalo, N. Y.
6211—Tubular Rivet & Stud Co., 87 Lincoln St., Boston, Mass. Adv. p. 91.
6212—Tucker, W. W. & C. F., 618 Capitol Ave., Hartford, Conn.
6213—Tucker-Gilmore Mfg. Co., 1414 Del Paso Blvd., North Sacramento, Calif.
6214—Tuck Mfg. Co., 74 Ames St., Brockton, Mass.
6214a—Tuckwell, William S., 20 High St., Merrimacport, Mass.
6216—Tung-Sol Lamp Works, 95 Eighth Ave., Newark, N. J.
6216a—Turley Gear & Machine Co., 1505 N. Tenth St., St. Louis, Mo.
6217—Turner Brass Works, Sycamore, Ill.
6218—Turner Mfg. Co., 404 W. Superior St., Kokomo, Ind.
6221—Turner Warner Screw Co., 13th Ave. & Jasper St., North Kansas City, Mo.
6222—Tuthill Spring Co., 760 W. Polk St., Chicago, Ill.
6223—Twentieth Century Brass Works, 2601 E. Hennepin Ave., Minneapolis, Minn.
6224—Twentieth Century Mfg. Co., Midlothian, Tex.
6225—Twin Coach Co., Kent, Ohio.
6228—Tyler Sales Fixtures Co., Peck & Columbia Sts., Muskegon Heights, Mich.

U

6300—USL Battery Corp., Niagara Falls, N. Y.
6301—Una Welding & Bonding Co., 1615 Collamer Ave., Cleveland, Ohio.
6303—Uniform Hood Lace Co., Indianapolis, Ind.
6304—Union Asbestos & Rubber Co., 1821 S. 54th Ave., Cicero, Ill.
Union Carbide & Carbon Corp.—See Linde Air Products Co.
Union Carbide Sales Co.—See Linde Air Products Co.
6306—Union Chest & Cabinet Corp., 17 Hand St., Rochester, N. Y.
6307—Union Forging Co., 500 North St., Union, N. Y.
6308—Union Metal Mfg. Co., 1432 Maple Ave., N. E., Canton, Ohio.
6309—Union Screw & Mfg. Co., 207 S. Main St., Pittsburgh, Pa.
6310—Union Steel Products Co., 612 Berrien St., Albion, Mich.
6311—Union Tool Company, E. River St., Orange, Mass.
6312—Union Twist Drill Co., Athol, Mass.
6313—Unique Printed Products Co., 2224 N. 13th St., Terre Haute, Ind. Adv. p. 127.
6314—United Air Cleaner Corp., 9705 Cottage Grove Ave., Chicago, Ill.
6314a—United American Bosch Corp., 3664 Main St., Springfield Mass. Adv. p. 69.
6315—United American Metals Corp., 200 Diamond St., Brooklyn, N. Y.
6316—United Autographic Register Co., 5000 S. California Ave., Chicago, Ill.
6318—United-Carr Fastener Corp., 31 Ames St., Cambridge, Mass. Adv. p. 72.
6319—United Electrical Mfg. Co., Logan St., Adrian, Mich.
6320—United Engine & Machine Co., 310 Preda St. (San Leandro), Oakland, Calif.
6321—United Hardware & Tool Corp., 50 Howard St., New York, N. Y.
6322—United Metal Hose Co., 724 Garrison Ave., New York, N. Y.
6323a—United Screw & Bolt Corp., 3590 W. 58th St., Cleveland, Ohio.
6324—United States Air Compressor Co., 5320 Harvard Ave., Cleveland, Ohio.
6324a—U.-S. Armature Corp., 1315 S. Wabash Ave., Chicago, Ill.
6325—United States Asbestos Div. of Raybestos-Manhattan, Inc., Manheim, Pa. Adv. p. 81.
6326—U. S. Auto Lamp Co., 509 W. 56th St., New York, N. Y.
6328—U. S. Axle Co., Water St., Pottstown, Pa. Adv. p. 59.
6329—U. S. Body & Forging Co., 135 Tonawanda St., Buffalo, N. Y.
United States Chain & Forging Co.—See McKay Co.
6331—U. S. Electrical Mfg. Co., 200 E. Slauson Ave., Los Angeles, Calif.
6332—United States Electrical Tool Co., Dept. T, 2483 W. Sixth St., Cincinnati, Ohio. Adv. p. 25.
6333—United States Electric Appliance Corp., 338 Broadway, Denver, Colo.
6336—United States Gauge Co., 44 Beaver St., New York, N. Y.
6337—United States Glass Co., Ninth & Bingham Sts., Pittsburgh, Pa.
6338—U. S. Hammered Piston Ring Co., E. Railway & Kentucky Aves., Paterson, N. J.
6339a—United States Machine Tool Co., 1950 W. Sixth St., Cincinnati, Ohio.
6340—U. S. Mica Mfg. Co., 1521 Circle Ave., Forest Park, Ill.
6343—U. S. Reamer & Tool Corp., 3191 Casitas Ave., Los Angeles, Calif.
6344—United States Rubber Co., 1790 Broadway, New York, N. Y.; also Detroit, Mich. Adv. p. 84.

MANUFACTURERS OF AUTOMOTIVE PRODUCTS—Continued

6344a—U. S. Rubber Specialty Co., 159 Hamilton Ave., Trenton, N. J.
6345—United States Sand Paper Co., 1560 Memorial Ave., Williamsport, Pa.
6346—U. S. Seat Cover Co., Kankakee, Ill.
6347—United States Spring & Bumper Co., 1120 S. Los Angeles St., Los Angeles, Calif.
6350—United Vacuum Appliance Corp., Columbia Ave., Connersville, Ind.
6351—United Wheel & Rim Co., 1351 Niles Ave., Warren, Ohio.
6352—Unity Lap Robe Mfg. Co., 49 E. 21st St., New York, N. Y.
6353—Unity Mfg. Co., 2909 Indiana Ave., Chicago, Ill.
6354—Universal Armature Corp., 87 Broadway, Cambridge, Mass.
6355—Universal Battery Co., 3410 S. La Salle St., Chicago, Ill.
6356—Universal Bearing Metals Corp., 258 State St., Rochester, N. Y.
6358—Universal Circular Gauge Co., 1014 Howard St., San Francisco, Calif.
6361—Universal Endless Belt Co., College St., North Vernon, Ind.
6362—Universal Gear Shift Corp., 150 Munson St., New Haven, Conn.
6364—Universal Industrial Corp., 787 Main St., Hackensack, N. J.
6370—Universal Steel Products Co., 177 Stillman St., San Francisco, Calif.
6374—Utica Drop Forge & Tool Co., 2409 Whitesboro St., Utica, N. Y.
6375—**Utility-Strate Mfg. Co., 105 Glasgow Ave., Fort Wayne, Ind. Adv. p. 118.**
6376—Utility Supply Co., E. 12th St., Clintonville, Wis.
6377—Utility Trailer Mfg. Co., P. O. Box 1407, Arcade Sta., Los Angeles, Calif.

V

6452—Vacuum Oil Co., 122 E. 42nd St., New York, N. Y.
6453—Valentine & Co., 386 Fourth Ave., New York, N. Y.
6454—Valley Electric Corp., 4221 Forest Park Blvd., St. Louis, Mo.
6456—Van Cleef Bros., Woodlawn Ave., 77th to 78th St., Chicago, Ill.
6458—Vanderman Mfg. Co., Mansfield Ave., Willimantic, Conn.
6458a—Van Doorn Co., 319 N. Third St., Quincy, Ill.
6459—Van Dorn Electric Tool Co., Towson, Md.
6460—Van Dorn Iron Works Co., 2685 E. 79th St., Cleveland, Ohio.
6461—Van Norman Machine Tool Co., 160 Wilbraham Ave., Springfield, Mass.
6463—Van Schaack & Sons, Peter, 310 W. Washington St., Chicago, Ill.
6464—Van Sicklen Corp., Bluff City Blvd., at Raymond St., Elgin, Ill.
6465—Van Tine, C. C., 325 Keeler St., Bartlesville, Okla.
6466—Van Wheel Corp., 218 Liberty St., Oneida, N. Y.
6469—Vatco Mfg. Co., 19 Deerfield St., Boston, Mass.
6470—Vaughan & Bushnell Mfg. Co., 2114 Carroll Ave., Chicago, Ill.
6471—Vedoe-Peterson Co., 22 Fayette St., Norfolk Downs, Mass.
6472—**Veeder-Root, Inc., 22 Sargeant St., Hartford, Conn. Adv. p. 54.**
6475—**Vellumoid Co., 54 Rockdale St., Worcester, Mass. Adv. p. 78.**
6476—Vesta Battery Corp., 6501 W. 65th St., Chicago, Ill.
6477—Vesuvius Graphite Corp., 168 N. May St., Chicago, Ill.
6478—Vickers Mfg. Co., M. & T. Bldg., Buffalo, N. Y.
6480—**Victor Mfg. & Gasket Co., 5750 Roosevelt Rd., Chicago, Ill. Adv. p. 77.**
6482—Victor Piston Pin Co., 115 N. Noble St., Indianapolis, Ind.
6483—Victor Products Corp., 2635 Belmont Ave., Chicago, Ill.
6484—Victor Rubber Co., Springfield, Ohio.
6485—Victor Saw Works, Middletown, N. Y.
6487—Victor Welding Equipment Co., 844 Folsom St., San Francisco, Calif.
6489—Village Blacksmith Folks, Watertown, Wis.
6491—Vim Tool Co., 515 N. Seventh St., Minneapolis, Minn.
6492—Vincent Steel Process Company, 2434 Bellevue Ave., Detroit, Mich.
6493—Visco-Meter Corp., 315 Grote St., Buffalo, N. Y.
6495—Vitek Mfg. Co., 2606 St. Marys Ave., Omaha, Neb.
6497—Vlchek Tool Co., 3018 E. 87th St., Cleveland, Ohio.
6498—Vogt Mfg. Corp., 100 Fernwood Ave., Rochester, N. Y.
6500—Volker & Co., William, Third & Main Sts., Kansas City, Mo.
6502—Vortox Mfg. Co., 121 S. Alexander Ave., Claremont, Calif.
6503—Vosbikian Bros. & Co., 180 W. Oxford St., Philadelphia, Pa.
6505—Vulcan Varnish Co., 1108 W. Main St., Louisville, Ky.
6506—Vulcan Wheels, Inc., Ave. L & Thornton St., Newark, N. J.

W

6551—Wadell Engineering Co., 354 Mulberry St., Newark, N. J.
6553—Wagner Electric Corp., 6400 Plymouth Ave., St. Louis, Mo.
6554—Wagner Mfg. Co., Cedar Falls, Iowa.
6556—Wahl Trunk Co., 600 Randall St., Eau Claire, Wis.
6557—Wakefield All-Steel Wrench Co., 89 Exchange St., Worcester, Mass.
6559—Wald Mfg. Co., Maysville, Ky.
6559a—Waldron Corp., John, Box 75, New Brunswick, N. J.
6560—Walker Mfg. Co., Michigan & Hamilton Sts., Racine, Wis.
6561—Walker Products Co., 3767 Moneta Ave., Los Angeles, Calif.
6561a—Walker-Turner Co., South Ave. & Berckman St., Plainfield, N. J.
6562—Walker Vehicle Co., 101 W. 87th St., Chicago, Ill.
6563—Wallace Co., Hugh, 2616 E. Grand Blvd., Detroit, Mich.
6565—Wallace Supplies Mfg. Co., 1310 Diversey Parkway, Chicago, Ill.
6566—Wall Mfg. Supply Co., P., 3126 Preble Ave., N. S., Pittsburgh, Pa.
6567—Walsh Press and Die Co., 4709 W. Kinzie St., Chicago, Ill.
6568—Walter Machine & Screw Co., 500 Bellevue Ave., Detroit, Mich.
6569—Walter Motor Truck Co., Queens Blvd. & 37th St., Long Island City, N. Y.
6570—Waltham Watch Co., Waltham, Mass.
6571—Wappat, Inc. (Div. of Simonds Saw & Steel Co.), 7522 Meade St., Pittsburgh, Pa.
6572—Ward-LaFrance Truck Corp., Elmira, N. Y.
6573—Ward Leonard Electric Co., South St., Mt. Vernon, N. Y.

6574—Ward Motor Vehicle Co., 718 S. Fulton Ave., Mt. Vernon, N. Y.
6574a—Ward Williams Co., 1069 Main St., Buffalo, N. Y. (Sole distributors, Baker Motz Co., 1069 Main St., Buffalo, N. Y.)
6575—Warford Corp., 44 Whitehall St., New York, N. Y.
6576—Warner Elevator Mfg. Co., 2613 Spring Grove Ave., Cincinnati, Ohio.
6577—**Warner Gear Co., Clerk and Penn Sts., Muncie, Ind. Adv. p. 20.**
6580—Warner-Patterson Co., 920 S. Michigan Ave., Chicago, Ill.
6581—Warren Mfg. Co., J. D., 208 W. Washington St., Chicago, Ill.
6582—Warren Tool & Forge Co., 418 Griswold St., Warren, Ohio.
6584—**Warshawsky & Co., 1915-35 S. State St., Chicago, Ill. Adv. p. 68.**
6586—Washburn Co. (Wire Goods Division), 28 Union St., Worcester, Mass.
6586a—Washburn Mfg. Co., Kokomo, Ind.
6589—Waterbury Steel Ball Co., Poughkeepsie, N. Y.
6590—Waterloo Bodies, Inc., Waterloo, N. Y.
6592—Waterous Co., 80 E. Fillmore Ave., St. Paul, Minn.
6593—Watervliet Tool Co., 1031 Broadway, Albany, N. Y.
6596—Watson Company, John Warren, Bridge St. & P. R. R., Philadelphia, Pa.
6597—Watts Morehouse Mfg. Corp., 2322 E. Michigan Ave., Jackson, Mich.
6599—Waukesha Motor Co., 960 St. Paul Ave., Waukesha, Wis.
6601—Wausau Iron Works, Wausau, Wis. (Sole distributors, Hi-Way Service Corp., Wisconsin Ave. & 38th St., Milwaukee, Wis.)
6602—Wausau Motor Parts Co., 125 W. Washington St., Wausau, Wis.
6604—Wayne Company, Tecumseh & Cochran Sts., Fort Wayne, Ind.
6605—Wayne Tool Mfg. Co., 274 N. Franklin St., Waynesboro, Pa.
6608—Weatherhead Co., 632 Frankfort Ave., N. W., Cleveland, Ohio.
6609—**Weatherproof Body Corp., 480 Shiawassee St., Corunna, Mich. Adv. p. 32.**
6610—Weaver Brothers Co., 416 Lawrence Ave., Adrian, Mich.
6611—Weaver Mfg. Co., 2177 S. Ninth St., Springfield, Ill.
6612—Weber Auto Accessory Co., 210 Sylvan Ave., Newark, N. J.
6615—Wedler-Shuford Co., 1116 S. Grand Blvd., St. Louis, Mo.
6616—Weidenhoff, Inc., Joseph, 4358 W. Roosevelt Rd., Chicago, Ill.
6618—Weikert, Wm. P., McKnightstown, Pa.
6619—Weil-Ransom Co., 816 Fulton St., Chicago, Ill.
6621—Welded Products Mfg. Co., 2203 Kirkwood Ave., Cudahy, Wis.
6622—Weldit Acetylene Co., 638 Bagley Ave., Detroit, Mich.
6625—**Wel-Ever Piston Ring Co., Speilbusch Ave., near Jackson, Toledo, Ohio. Adv. p. 92.**
6626—Welker-Hoops Mfg. Co., 193 William St., Middletown, Conn.
6627—Wellman Bronze & Aluminum Co., 6017 Superior Ave., Cleveland, Ohio.
6628—Wellman Co., S. K., 1381 E. 49th St., Cleveland, Ohio.
6629—Wellman Engineering Co., 7000 Central Ave., Cleveland, Ohio.
6629a—Wells & Co., A. H., 563 Watertown Ave., Waterbury, Conn.
6630—Wells Mfg. Co., Box 613, Greenfield, Mass.
6631—Wells Mfg. Co., 114 S. Brooke St., Fond du Lac, Wis.
6632—Wellston Mfg. Co., 200 W. Second St., Wellston, Ohio.
6634—Welworth Automotive Corp., Bush Terminal Bldg., Brooklyn, N. Y.
6637—Wensley Metal Products Co., 1445 Osage St., Denver, Colo.
6638—Wentworth & Irwin, 327 Oregon St., Portland, Ore.
6639—Wenzel Tent & Duck Co., H., 1035 Paul St., St. Louis, Mo.
6640—Wertsch Co., Wm., 24 Page St., San Francisco, Calif.
6642—Wesbar Corp., West Bend, Wis.
6642a—West Bend Aluminum Co., West Bend, Wis.
6643—Westcott Chuck Co., 316 E. Walnut St., Oneida, N. Y.
6643a—Western Aluminum Foundries, 760 23rd Ave., Oakland, Calif.
6644—Western Automatic Machine Screw Co., Elyria, Ohio.
6646—Western Cable & Light Co., Baldwin, Wis.
6647—Western Chain Products Co., 1807 Belmont Ave., Chicago, Ill.
6648—Western Clock Co., La Salle, Ill.
6649—Western "Dri-Kure" Vulcanizer Mfg. Co., 908 W. Pico St., Los Angeles, Calif.
6651—Western Felt Works, 4031 Ogden Ave., Chicago, Ill.
6652—Western Gear Co., Morgan at Lake St., Chicago, Ill.
6653—Western Gear Works, 417 Ninth Ave., S., Seattle, Wash.
6654—Western Iron & Foundry Co., 702 E. Second St., Wichita, Kan.
6656—Western Oil Pump & Tank Co., 2437 Kosciusko St., St. Louis, Mo.
6657—Western Rawhide & Belting Co., 1230 N. Tenth St., Milwaukee, Wis.
6658—Western Screw-Products Co., Main & St. George Sts., St. Louis, Mo.
6659—Western Shade Cloth Co., 22nd & Jefferson Sts., Chicago, Ill.
6660—Western Tool & Mfg. Co., E. Pleasant St., Springfield, Ohio.
6662—Western Wire Products Co., 324 S. Third St., St. Louis, Mo.
6663—Westinghouse Air Brake Co. (Wilmerding), Pittsburgh, Pa.
6664—Westinghouse Electric & Mfg. Co., East Pittsburgh, Pa.
6665—Westinghouse Lamp Co., 150 Broadway, New York, N. Y.
6667—Weston Electrical Instrument Corp., 614 Frelinghuysen Ave., Newark, N. J.
6668—Westport Mfg. Co., Westport, Mass.
6670—West Steel Casting Co., 805 E. 70th St., Cleveland, Ohio.
6671—West Tire Setter Co., 255 Mill St., Rochester, N. Y.
6671a—Westwood Lumber & Veneer Co., 1717 W. Pershing Rd., Chicago, Ill.
6672—Wetzig Mfg. Co., 2600 Fletcher St., Chicago, Ill.
6673—Weymouth Art Leather Co., East Weymouth, Mass.
6674—Whalen-Noxon Lamp Corp., 241 W. Adams St., Syracuse, N. Y.
6675—Wheeler Mfg. Co., 4673 Alger St., Los Angeles, Calif.
6676—Wheeler-Schebler Carburetor Co., Sanders St. & Barth Ave., Indianapolis, Ind.
6677—Wheel Parts & Mfg. Co., 1840 S. Michigan Ave., Chicago, Ill.
6678—Whitaker Battery Supply Co., 1301 Burlington Ave., North Kansas City, Mo.
6679—Whitaker Mfg. Co., 409 S. Green St., Chicago, Ill.
6681—White, J. M., 1116 Olive St., Philadelphia, Pa.

MANUFACTURERS OF AUTOMOTIVE PRODUCTS—Continued

6683—White Co., O. C., 17 Herman St., Worcester, Mass.
6684—White Dental Mfg. Co., S. S. (Industrial Div.), 152 W. 42nd St., New York, N. Y.
6685—Whitehead & Kales Co., River Rouge Pl., Detroit, Mich.
6686—Whitehouse Mfg. Co., 42 Elm St., Newark, N. J.
6689—White Machine Works, 740 Wisconsin St., Eau Claire, Wis.
6691—White Motor Co., 842 E. 79th St., Cleveland, Ohio.
6694—Whiting-Adams Co., 690 Harrison Ave., Boston, Mass.
6695—Whiting Corp., 157th & Lathrop Sts., Harvey, Ill.
6696—Whiting Leather & Belting Co., 504 Jackson Ave., Long Island City, N. Y.
6697—Whitman & Barnes, Inc., 2108 W. Fort St., Detroit, Mich.
6699—Whitney Mfg. Co., 237 Hamilton St., Hartford, Conn. Adv. p. 201.
6701—Whitney Metal Tool Co., 110 Forbes St., Rockford, Ill.
6702—Whiton Machine Co., 190 Howard St., New London, Conn.
6703—Whittelsey Mfg. Co., Howard & Spruce Sts., Bridgeport, Conn.
6704—Whittemore Stamping Co., R. L. S., 31 N. Foster St., Worcester, Mass.
6705—Wichita Falls Motors Co., Wichita Falls, Tex.
6710—Wiese & Co., Wm., 234 W. 56th St., New York, N. Y.
6711—Wiesenmeyer, C. F., 419 E. Washington St., Springfield, Ill.
6717—Wilcox-Rich Corp., 9771 French Rd., Detroit, Mich. Adv. p. 101.
6717a—Wilde Drop Forge & Tool Co., 2936 Fairmount Ave., Kansas City, Mo.
6719—Wilder Co., M. B., 2012 Farnam St., Omaha, Neb.
6723—Wilkening Mfg. Co., 71st St. & Kingsessing Ave., Philadelphia, Pa.
6725—Wilkens Mfg. Corp., 50 Orawaupum St., White Plains, N. Y.
6725a—Willard Rubber Co., 2320 Newton Ave., San Diego Calif. (Sole distributor, Siltop Mfg. Co., 1241 N. Vine St., Los Angeles, Calif.).
6726—Willard Storage Battery Co., 246 E. 131st St., Cleveland, Ohio.
6727—Willgood Mfg. Co., Washington, Pa.
6728—Williams Bros. Co., 3077 Jasper St., Philadelphia, Pa.
6729—Williams & Co., C. K., 640 N. 13th St., Easton, Pa.
6730—Williams & Co., J. H., 75 Spring St., New York, N. Y.
6731—Williams & Miller Gin Co., Elk City, Okla.
6733—Williams Products Co., H. E., 100 S. Main St., Carthage, Mo. Adv. p. 32.
6734—Williams & Sons, I. B., 9 Orchard St., Dover, N. H.
6735—Williams Valve Co., D. T., Spring Grove Ave. & Township St., Cincinnati, Ohio.
6737—Willits Mfg. Co., 7805 Atlantic Ave., Atlantic City, N. J. (Sole distributors, P. & D. Mfg. Co., 38-02-10 22nd St., Long Island City, N. Y.)
6738—Will Motors Corp., C. H., 60 11th Ave., N. E., Minneapolis, Minn.
6741—Willson Products, Inc., Second & Washington Sts., Reading, Pa.
6741a—Willys-Morrow Co., S. Main St., Elmira, N. Y. Sole Licensees (Sole distributors Thompson Products, Inc., 2196 Clarkwood Rd., Cleveland, Ohio.)
6742—Willys-Overland, Inc., Walcott Blvd., Toledo, Ohio. Adv. p. 22.
6744—Wilmington Fibre Specialty Co., Wilmington, Del.
6745—Wilson, K. R., 10 Lock St., Buffalo, N. Y.
6746—Wilson-Imperial Co., 115 Chestnut St., Newark, N. J.
6747—Wilson Rubber Co., 1216 Garfield Ave., Canton, Ohio.
6748—Wilson Truck Mfg. Co., Henderson, Iowa.
6750—Winchester Repeating Arms Co., 275 Winchester Ave., New Haven, Conn.
6752—Windsor Corp., 4400 N. Main St., St. Louis, Mo.
6753—Winfield Carburetor Co., 3053 Treadwell St., Los Angeles, Calif.
6754—Wing Mfg. Co., L. J., 154 W. 14th St., New York, N. Y.
6755—Winter Brothers Co., Kendrick St., Wrentham, Mass.
6756—Winterhoff Tool & Machine Co., 112 S. Elkhart Ave., Elkhart, Ind.
6757—Winter Stamping Co., 221 W. Washington St., Goshen, Ind.
6758—Wisconsin Machinery & Mfg. Co., 52nd St. & Beloit Rd., West Allis, Wis.

6759—Wisconsin Motor Co., 44th Ave. & Burnham St., Milwaukee, Wis.
6760—Witherbee Storage Battery Co., 75 Columbus Ave., New York, N. Y.
6763—Wittek Mfg. Co., 4305-9 W. 24th Pl., Chicago, Ill. Adv. p. 279.
6765—Witt-Will Co., 52 N St., N. E., Washington, D. C.
6766—Wodack Electric Tool Corp., 4627 W. Huron St., Chicago, Ill.
6767—Wold Air Brush Mfg. Co., 2173 N. California Ave., Chicago, Ill.
6772—Wolverine Tube Co., 1411 Central Ave., Detroit, Mich.
6773—Wonder-Mist Polish Co., 130 Essex St., Melrose, Mass.
6773a—Woodall Industries, Inc., 7567 Six Mile Road, Detroit, Mich.
6774—Woodall Tool Co. 75 N. 18th St., Holland, Mich.
6776—Wood Co., W. A., 373 Atlantic Ave., Boston, Mass.
6778—Woodhouse Chain Works, Third & Schenck Sts., Trenton, N. J.
6779—Wood Hydraulic Hoist & Body Co., 7958 Riopelle St., Detroit, Mich.
6780—Woodison Co., E. J., 7415 St. Aubin St., Detroit, Mich.
6783—Woodruff & Sons Co., Walter W., Mt. Carmel, Conn.
6785—Woodward Mfg. Corp., Austin, Tex.
6787—Woodworth Specialties Co., 121-25 Montgomery St., Binghamton, N. Y. Adv. p. 36.
6789—Woolsey Paint & Color Co., C. A., 500 Grand St., Jersey City, N. J.
6790—Woolwine Metal Products Co., Atlantic Blvd. & Riverside Drive, Los Angeles, Calif.
6791—Wooster Brush Co., Wooster, Ohio.
6792—Worcester Brush & Scraper Co., 38 Austin St., Worcester, Mass.
6793—Worcester Gear Works, 18 Grafton St., Worcester, Mass.
6794—Worcester Taper Pin Co., 47 Lagrange St., Worcester, Mass.
6795—World Bestos Corp., 52 Courtland St., Paterson, N. J.
6795a—World Motor Co., 3289 Spring Grove Ave., Cincinnati, Ohio.
6796—Woven Steel Hose & Rubber Co., Dale St., Trenton, N. J.
6797a—Wright & Corson Co., Post Rd., Milford, Conn.
6797b—Wright Cover Mfg. Co., 1411 S. Michigan Ave., Chicago, Ill.
6798—Wright Machine Co., Owensboro, Ky.
6799—Wright Mfg. Co., 929 Connecticut Ave., Bridgeport, Conn.
6801—Wright Textile Co., Jasper & Orleans Sts., Philadelphia, Pa.
6803—Wubco Battery Co., Swissvale, Pa.

Y

6806—Yale Mfg. Co., 49 Amsterdam Ave., New York, N. Y.
6808—Yale & Towne Mfg. Co., Chrysler Bldg., New York, N. Y.
6810—Yankee Metal Products Corp., 460 W. 34th St., New York, N. Y.
6811—Yellow Jack-it Mfg. Co., 211 N. Green St., Chicago, Ill.
6812—Yerdon, Wm., Main & Centre Sts., Fort Plain, N. Y.
6814—Yoder-Morris Co., 5500 Walworth Ave., Cleveland, Ohio.
6814a—York Corrugating Co., Adams St. & W. Md. R. R., York, Pa.
6815—York Hoover Body Corp., York, Pa.
6816—York Tack & Nail Works, York, Pa.
6817—Yost Mfg. Co., S. Main St., Meadville, Pa.
6818—Yost Superior Co., Center & Jefferson Sts., Springfield, Ohio.
6819—Young Radiator Co., 709 Mead St., Racine, Wis.
6819a—Youngstown Steel Car Corp., Hunter St., Niles, Ohio.

Z

6820—Zagora Machine & Parts Co., J., 1225 S. Mint St., Charlotte, N. C.
6821—Zamboni & Sons, C., 301 N. Cedar St., Owatonna, Minn.
6822a—Zenite Metal Co., 201 N. West St., Indianapolis, Ind.
6822b—Zeller Lacquer Mfg. Co., 20 E. 49th St., New York, N. Y.
6823—Zenith-Detroit Corp., Foot of Hart Ave., Detroit, Mich.
6825—Zim Mfg. Co., 3037 Carroll Ave., Chicago, Ill.
6827—Zip Abrasive Co., Washington & Center Sts., Cleveland, Ohio.
6830—Zoerman-Clark Mfg. Co., 219 W. Huron St., Chicago, Ill.
6832—Zyle Ware Corp., 181 Eighth St., Long Island City, N. Y.

TRADE NAMES

HOW TO USE THIS LIST

When the Trade Name is known, and the name and address of the manufacturer are wanted—

1. Find the Trade Name in its alphabetical order in this list. Note its Number.

2. Turn to numerical list of all manufacturers starting page 364. Find your number in its proper place—alongside it will be the name and address of manufacturer you want.

3. Where two or more products of different manufacturers bear the same Trade Name, the product is listed after each trade name to help identification.

4. If trade name does not appear here, look for the same name in the complete numerical list of all manufacturers, arranged alphabetically also, starting on page 364.

A-A 93
AAA 275
A.B.C. (cabs)....1196
ABC (brushes)... 138
A-B-Z 265
A-C 107
A-C-F 141
A.C.F.-Hall-Scott 4
ADL 41
A.E.S. 4317
A-1 338
APW 178
A-S-E 114
A.T.B. 341
A-Y-A 44
Aabs 4300
Abesco 667
Acadia 6651
Acco 142, 3774
Accuratime 4030
Ace (bat. parts).. 161
Ace (brake
  lining) 5214
Ace (brushes) ..3002
Ace (jigs) 3140
Ace (pumps).... 723
Ace-Aero 6131
Ace-Ite 161
Acme (cur. cut-
  outs) 5626
Acme (washers,
  stor. tanks) ..2051a
Acorn (belting).. 763
Acorn (pump con.)5753
Adamant (bearing
  metals) 3762
Adamant (decalco-
  manias) 4614
Ad-Awning 1651
Adco (differen-
  tials) 149
Adco (compounds) 44
Adco (piston ring
  compressing
  tools) 131
Ad-el-ite (l a c -
  quers, paint re-
  movers) 38
Adequate 3426
Adheso 5612
Adpasco 49
Advance 3781
Ad-Vr-Ti-Zr ... 208
Aeraloy 6165a
Aermore 2158
Aetna 3727
Aff Peerless 56
Agasote 4618
Agrippa 6730
Airace 2394
Airco 67
Airco-Davis-Bour-
  nonville ... 67
Airco-National ... 67
Air-Dor 3874

Airdraulic 4530
Air-Flate 277
Air Furnace 2843
Air Lec 5459
Airo 3208
Airspring 2838
Airubber 4305
Ajax (chisels)... 726
Ajax (curtain fast-
  eners) 3857
Akbar 3289
Akro Blak ... 78
Akron-
  Williams ...4233a
Akros 78
Alabestos 1263
Alaskan 2350
Alcoa 120
Alcoa Albron.... 120
Alco 166
Alemite-Electro-
  gun 86
Alert 165
Alfatan 1183
Alfite 165
Alfoam 165
Allen Portometer. 100
Allen Portostat... 100
Alligator 2087
All-In-One (elec.
  condensers) ...4317
All-In-One (vul-
  canizers) 3894
Allova 4002
All-Service 3426
All Steel
  (Trunks) 4747
Allsteel (bodies,
  hoists) 2307
Alltraffic 1672
All Weather
  (tires) 2416
Allweather (fire
  ext.) 165
All-Weld 3870
Almanc 94
Aloxite 1031
Alpha 4626
Alpo 124
Alten 3138
Alternarc 1856
Alumino 131
Aluminox 152
Alundum 4351
Alupak 2047
Alustrium 1588
Always Ready
  (jacks) 5562
Always Ready
  (wrenches) ...6730
Always Reliable . 626
Amalie 5625
Ambesco 130
Ambler Autobes-
  tos 3234
Amco (access.,
  tools) 35

Amco (wings)... 163
American (air or
  water stations,
  wrenches) 4741
American (belt-
  ing) 3128
American (files,
  rasps) 4314
American (metal
  hose, tubing).. 171
American Auster.6174
American-Beauty .1648
American Bosch.6314a
American Brake-
  bloks 137
American-La-
  France 3409a
Ames 2701
Aminco 164
Ammco 336
Amo 337
Am-Pe-Co 169
Anchor 3027
Anco 208
Anderson-Ajax .. 210
Androck 6586
Angelus 644
Ankorite 204
Anti-Theft 357a
Any-Lite 5823
Apex (piston
  rings) 6144
Arapahoe 740
Arcade 4314
Arco 5617
Arco Wand 237
Arcus 4292
Argyll 1272
Arico 160
Ariel 4292
Aristocrat (radia-
  tor caps).....2018
Aristocrat (fire-
  ext.) 5617
Aristocrat (license
  frames & hold-
  ers) 2129
Aristocrat (instru-
  ment board
  panels) 1651
Aristocrat (mono-
  grams) 3955
Arkay 3350
Armorcoid 244
Armorcote 244
Armorite 244
Armorlac 244
Armstrong 250
Ar-Nu 241
Arrow 5617
Arrow Head
  (shafts) 2104
Arrowhead (un-
  dercoats) 1186
Art Relief.......3868
Arvin 4326
Asbesgraphite ..2325

Asbestex 267
Asbestopak 2047
Asco 2735
Ashco 2694
Atlas 5401
Atsco 69
Attach-O-Wipe .. 131
Auburn 298
Aurora (drilling
  mch.) 4514
Aurora (heaters) 2108
Australian 621
Auto 4292
Autocrat (bush-
  ings) 6315
Autocrat (gog-
  gles) 192
Autocrat (tires) ..3706
Autofan 331
Autoglass 5624
Auto Knits......1184
Auto-Lite 1857
Autoloc 5593
Autom 343
Automatch 2033
Automatic 324
Auto Niblick ...2694
Auto-Pep 6113
Autoreelite 229
Autorobe 5515
Autosan 1227
Autoscreen 307
Aut-O-Sek 5497
Autoshade 6733
Auto Start 6331
Auto-Tour 1157
Auto-Vac 1842
Au-Ve-Co 360
Au-Ve-Colite ... 360
Avee 196
Avenue Brand ..6797b
Avery 3913
Avigo 1873
Awebco 205
Ayanbee 1842
Aztec 267

B 2418
BA 3921
B/B 620
B/C 586
B & C 603
B-K 710
B.K.F. 5130
B.M.S. 736
B-N 800
B & R (bat. rep.
  tools) 576a
B & R (paints) ..2144
B-P 2116
Babco 570
Babcock 165
Babinmoss 505
Bagnall 5813
Bair 356
Bakatax 528a
Balcrank 1141
Ball & Ball 4652

Banner Blue ...3891a
Barlow 3709
Barrett 1643
Basco 727
Bat 5105
Batrometer 1842
Bayonne 704
Beacon-Lite ... 573
Bear (gages) ... 581
Bear (emergency
  cans) 6790
Bear Brand 1827
Bearium 6356
Beco 760
Bedrock 6696
Beckspar 78
Beech 3986
Bee Hive 3978
Bee-Jay 2623
Bel-den 591a
Bell's 593
Bendix 1832
Benford 2053
Bengal 3422
Benlock 5214
Bennett (oil cups,
  covers) 568
Bennett (pumps,
  tanks) 5510
Bennett Eco 5510
Bennett Shotwell.5510
Berloy 622
Berryloid 627
Besco 559
Bestallic 49
Bestex 267
Best-O-Seal 5425
Bethlehem 5655
Better 4270
Better Built (bear-
  ings) 764
Better Built (cush-
  ions).........2421
Bevoyl 5123
Bexco 78
Bi-Focal 6216
Big Boss 3155
Big Boy (gear
  pullers, tire
  pumps) 1505
Big Boy (auto
  transmissions).. 733
Big Chief 3540
Bijur 641a
Billmont 1132
Bilt-Well 714
Birmingham ...2422
Birtank 650
Black Bear 5031
Black Bird 3151
Black Diamond .1653
Black Hawk (brake
  lining) 5633
Blackstone 3469
Blake 4766
Blake's 2454

Blind Man 5116
Block, Jr. 6825
Blue-Bird
  (pumps) 2700
Blue Bird (tire
  chain & storage
  battery tools,
  shears & snips) 623
Blue Box 1344
Blue Boy..1134, 1237
Blue Edge (brake
  lining) 6796
Blue Edge (gas-
  kets) 6480
Blue Label 4362
Blue Point 5611
Blue Print......2116
Blue Ribbon ...3046
Blu-Wite 6216
Bodyfill 2017
Bolens 2379
Bo-Peep 1543
Borolon 11
Bosch 6314a
Boss (bodies)...141a
Boss (clocks)....1842
Boufra 694
Bowden 2480
Bowen 2711
Bowes 1179
Boxco 701
Boyce Moto-Meter 3992
Boyco 704a
Brake Friction...5182
Brake-ite 3817
Branford 3767
Brasbestos 2038
Braz-Cast 222
Break-Not 1842
Breeze Filter 84
Breeze Flexmet . 718
Bright 6582
Brite-Lite 4230
Broadway 4692
Brookins 78
Brown (reflectors) 3759
Brown (tire rep.
  mch.) 532
Brownie
  (mattresses) ..3862
Brownie (spring
  oilers) 754
Brude 2809
Brunner 759
Buckeye 3420
Budd-Michelin . 770
Buffalo 1649
Buick 785
Bull Dog (dress-
  ing) 3030
Bull Dog (mats,
  hose, tape) ... 693
Bull Dog (parts,
  access.) 3104
Bull Dog (web
  straps) 5182
Bull Dog (vises).4766

TRADE NAMES—Continued

Bull Dog
(wrenches) ...6730
Bulldog (brake
lining) 5214
Bull-Pup 726
Burd-Ox 792
Burmaline 808
Burt 81
Buss 816
Button-On 338
Buxco 820
Buzzer 2793

C-A 42
C & B........1165
C.C.C. 1099
C F 1034
CG 639
C & H 760
C & J 1046
C J B 60
C-M 1134
C.O.T. 6160
C.O.T. Gum Gum 6160
CP 1123
C & S 1207
C & T 1076
C-T-K 1132
CV 686
Cadet 6642a
Cadillac 1008
California 1262a
Camel Hitch ...1018
Campbell (cotter
pins) 142
Campbell (shutters
tire covers) ..3027
Campbell (tire
chains) 3040
Canco 139
Cantilever 6108
Capillary 5671
Capitol 3026
Captor 5671
Carbic (calcium
carbide) 3507
Carbic (welding
mch.) 4565
Carbolite (calcium
carbide) 3507
Carbolite (grinding
wheels) 152
Carbonite 2336
Carbon-No 70
Carbonox 4347
Carbo-Solve ... 86
Cardinal 2074
Carrcohyde 1045
Carrocerk 2047
Car-Testometer .3857
Cartridge 6750
Casco 1053
Castorol 1108
Catseye 1233
Cavalier 2412
Ceewell 131
Cel-O-Finish .. 38
Celoron 1270
Century 6223
Certified (gasoline
& oil storage
tanks & sys-
tems) 753
Certified (storage
battery separa-
tors) 1904
Cesco 1115
Chaco 1090
Challenge (belts,
lining, straps) .5598
Challenge (lug-
gage carriers) .1905
Challenge (oil
dispensers) ...6586
Chamo (felt chan-
nels) 3426
Chamo (artificial
or imitation
leather) 1045
Chamoline 6463
Champion (bat-
teries) 1892
Champion
(casters) 2621

Champion (wash-
ers, sprayers,
compressors) ..1086
Champion (spark
plugs) 1088
Champion
(pumps) 3151
Champion (tools) .6660
Champion (tool
boxes) 6108
Champion (trailers,
winches) 4031
Champion
(trunks) 2319
Chanson 3010
Chartreuse 2809
Chase Drednaut..5055
Chase
Leatherwove ..5433
Chase Velmo ...5433
Cheat Proof ...3310
Check All 4619
Chemo 4025
Cheney 4766
Chicago (automo-
biles) 1346
Chicago (rivets,
clamps, lathes) .1126
Chicago King ...4757
Chicago-Quality .1113
Childs 165
Chroline 1183
Cig-Out 1557
Cinch Flush Type .1139
Cincinnati 678
Circle Ess 5759
Clarion 163
Clarkat 1164
Claw 1237
Clearsite 131
Clearview 2132
Clear-Vision .. 131
Cleco 1179
Cleflex 1177
Cle-Forge 1185
Cletan 1183
Cleveco 1186
Cleveland (gears) 1188
Cleveland
(screws) 1173
Cleveweld 1187
Climax 6586
Clinch-Core ...5041
Clipper 1591
Close Down 2722
Cocheco 6734
Coes 603
Cole 5092
Colonial 2396
Colossus 5115
Columbia 1334
Columbian 1232
Columbus 2360
Colvin 2454
Combine 3128
Comet 4303
Comfoot 5592
Comfy (back rests) 4308
Comfy (step
plates) 6218
Commerce 5085
Common-Sense
(ventilators, win-
dow reg.) 20
Commonsense
(tool kits) 6679
Conaphore 1297
Concord 8
Con-Den-So-Meter 311
Connersville ...6350
Conqueror 31
Consol 1262
Consolco 1263
Continental 1272
Conventional ...4242
Copperhead 2158
Cord 298
Correct Measure..1300
Correct-O-Meter .1300
Cortland 720
Courtesy 1648
Cowdrey 610
Craftsman 3340

Crescent (bearing
scrapers,
wrenches) 1324
Crescent (burners)3293
Crescent (solder).4337
Crescent (valves) 4749
Crescentart 1323
Crestoloy 1324
Critchley 1076
Crouse 1169
Crown 723
Crystal Bay ...3921
Crystolon 4351
Cub 3512
Cuno 1341
Curtex 1344
Curtis 1345
Curvex 4758
Custom-Bilt ...2058
Cutrite 3921
Cyclone (blocks,
hoist) 1134
Cyclone (pumps).3151
Cyclone (washers) 4036
Cyclone(wrenches)6208
Cyclone-WSM ...5430
Cy-Lent 6156
Cylolator 3998

D & B 1504
D-D 1589
D.L.M.F. 3498
Daco 1568
Dagmar 3938
Daisy (horns) ..1800
Daisy (pumps) ..5178
Daleway 5182
Dall 1503
Dandee 2773
Dan-D-Karrier ..3409
Dandy 5191
Daraike 5034
Darsie 3759
Davisbilt 1523
Day-Elder 4244
Dayton 5565a
Dead Easy 2394
Dean 316
Decktex 6128
Defiance 1073
Delco 3508
De Luxe (air or
water sta.) ...3774
De Luxe (assist
cords, nets) ..4358
De Luxe (auxil-
iary seats) ...2734
De Luxe (broad-
cloth) 3411
De Luxe (hub
caps) 2820
De Luxe (lamps)3278
De Luxe (pistons)1556
De Luxe (tents) .4798
De Luxe (tires) .3469
De Luxe (tire cov-
ers) 2418
De Luxe (vanity
cases) 4764
Deoxidine 143
Deoxylyte 143
Dependable (enam-
els, dressing) ..2689
Dependable (parts,
access.) 5697
Detco 1573
Diamo-Carbo ...1566
Diamond (ball re-
tainers) 4312
Diamond (fibre
parts) 1270
Diamond (taps,
dies) 1033
Diamond Diachrome 122
Diamond E 1904
Diamond K 3720
Diamond T 1270
Diamond U 5505
Dill 1602
Dim-Brite 6218
Dimeret 3539
Director 3855
Disteel 4005
Distillator 5589
Diverter Pole ...1865

Dolfinite 1619
Dolly 2333
Domestic 3254
Dominator 5115a
Dominion 1513
Dorman 1626
Dot 6318
Double Diamond .. 332
Double Eagle ...2416
Double Service ..3526
Double Slot 4719
Dover 2824
Dragon 1892
Drainoil 4719
Dreadnaught
(furnaces) 6566
Dreadnaught (tire
chains, locks,
tow ropes) 1237
Dreadnaught
(trunks) 4701
Drednaut 356
Dri-Kure 6649
Dropfo 2159
Dualarc 1856
Duby-Manley ...138a
Ducksbak 3537
Duckworth 530
Duco 1660
Du Lux 1660
Duncombe 5040a
Dundee 4533
Duo-Adjuster .. 720
Duodraulic 1548
Du-O-Tan 6696
Duotrol 4681
Duo-Wear 1174
Duplex (air clean-
ers) 1620
Duplex (buckets).4798
Duplex (glass
grinding mch.).3426
Duplex (hat hold-
ers) 2092
Duplex (tire car-
riers) 6197
Duplex Brake-
Aid 1656a
Durabestos 6325
Durabrite 1648
Duracos 6325
Duraflex 4028
Dural 5514
Duraplastic ...6325
Durasote 4618
Durex 2348
Durkee-Atwood ..1667
Durmalite 640a
Durobal 6832
Duro-Bilt 4701
Duro-Gloss 2602
Durwood 1667
Dusie-Durable ..1674
Dusie-Howe 1674
Dutch Boy 4238
Dutch Brand ...6456
Dynamo (belting) 763
Dynamo (timers).2795
Dyneto 4561

EAM 3759
E.B. 3925
E.C. 2802
E.C.V. 2802
EE 1628
E W C 1870
E-Z (back rests).1838
E-Z (creepers)..6554
E-Z (wire strip-
ping tools)...3003
E.Z. (wrenches).5103
E.Z. Grip 808
E.Z. In 1905
E-Z-On 2722
Eagle (belts) ..5214
Eagle (clamps) .6783
Eagle (files,
rasps) 4314
Eagle (leather) .5084
Eagle (tents) ..6639
Ear 1233
Easy 4787
Easy-Back 4787
Easy-On (covers).2418
Easyon (chains).6787

Eaton-Lite 1819
Eclipse 2350
Eco 5510
Economic 2621
Economy (glass
mch.) 3426
Economy (wash-
ers) 2702
Economy-
Ex-Ray 4007
Eez-Zee 3349
Egyptian 6679
Ekla 1829
Elastic 1273
Elbon 1591
Elcaro 2092
Electric Doorman.4753
Electrolock 3926
Electrolon 11
Elephant (bush-
ings, bearing
metal) 4700
Elephant (steel
wool) 5129
Elliott's 3015
Elvo 2027
Elysee 3938
Embassy 4692
Em-C-Lac 1882
Emco 1892
Empire (clocks) .4692
Empire (hammers)2454
Empire (nuts,
bolts, screws) .5213
Empress 696
Emsco 1889
Equipto 304
Erco 1842
Erie 4692
Esco (back rests).1838
Esco (brushes) .1895a
Eskimo 6319
Es-M-Co 1906
Essex 2824
Ettco 1815
Evalast 506
Everbright Pontop 1659
Everdry 693
Eveready (flash-
lights, lamp
bulbs) 4223
Eveready
(switches) ...5556
Eveready Colum-
bia 4223
Eveready Prestone4223
Ever-Easy 3996
Everflo 5135
Everlasting 6566
Ever Ready (tire
patches) 2773
Everready (jacks,
lubricators) ..5165
Ever-Rite 3800
Ever Safe 5082
Everstay 4541
Ever Step 5199
Everstick 2044
Every-Day 5199
Excelsior 5664
Exide 1868
Expedite 4756
Ez-Chain-On ...4791
Ezell 713
Ezy-Out 1185

F-J 2113
F-S (locks) 5593
F & S
(bearings) ...1000a
F W D.........2119
Fabco 2000
Fabrikoid 1661
Fabroil 2343a
Fafnir 2010
Fageol 141
Fairfield 1659
Falls 2019
Fanco 4271
Faraday 1866
Fargo 4732
Fasthold 3925
Faultless 3855
Favorite 1033

Fay-O-Rite 726
Feather 1160
Federal 2034
Federalite 2038
Federal-Mogul ..2039
Felpak 2047
Fel-Pro 2047
Fender-Fix 3509
Fender Spat ... 338
Fend-R-Guide ..2053
Fenix 4698
Fercrome 3102
Ferdico 2049
Ferodo 2054
Ferropac 6480
Fex 4540
Fiberlac 2059
Fidelity 2608
Fifth Avenue ... 338
Fireball 4227
Fire-Gun 165
Fisher ......,..5688
Fit-All ...2039, 3418
Fits-All 3016
Fitz-Rite 2079
Fitzwell 4308
Flampruf Silva-
plate 2144
Flash (priming
fluids) 2616
Flash (radiator
caps) 2053
Flash-A-Lite ...3926
Flatlite 154
Flexite 1603
Flexo (oiling cans)1632
Flexo (piston
rings) 6625
Flex-Tan 6734
Flintstone 3408
Floafome 2350
Flosol 143
Flushkleen 4009
Fluxine 3345
Foamite 165
Fobafimi 801
Foldaway 6733
Fontaine 194
Forford 3891a
Forge-Steel ...3268
Fosco 5458a
Fostoria (fenders,
tools, luggage
carriers) 2115
Fostoria (trunk
racks) 708
4 in 1 6672
Four-Way 6218
Francisco 2124
Freeztector ...3018
Fren-Lac 2142
Fron Toms 2628
Fronty 1109
Frothex 3320
Fry 1032
Fyber-Weld 1115
Fyre-Freez 3276
Fyr Fly 6145

G-B (batteries,
parts) 2366
G-E 2343
G.E. Mazda 4237
G-H 4665
G.L. 3495
G.M. 3925
G-P (automo-
biles) 2440a
G-P (reamers) ..2113
GP (elec. parts).2472
G T D 2456
G.W.W. 6748
Gabriel-Anderson-
Ajax 2305
Gacor Stop-It ..2337
Garco 2338
Garcobestos ...2338
Garford 5085
Gargoyle 6452
Garrett 4779
Gas-Co-Lator ... 86
Gas-Lube 5625
Gas-O-Meter ...1842

TRADE NAMES—Continued

TRADE NAMES—Continued

TRADE NAMES—Continued

ASSOCIATIONS—Automotive

Including National and Sectional Trade Associations and Certain National Associations of the Manufacturers in Which the Trade Has an Interest

---

NATIONAL ASSOCIATIONS

AUTOMOTIVE ENGINE RE-BUILDERS ASSOCIATION

Headquarters—1 Broadway, New York City, N. Y.
Secretary—Robert C. McWane.

AUTOMOTIVE JOBBERS ASSOCIATION

Headquarters—304 Arcade Bldg., 616 S. Michigan Ave., Chicago, Ill.
Executive Secretary—Walter N. Drew.

INDUSTRIAL ALCOHOL INSTITUTE, INC.

An Association of Industrial Alcohol Producers

Headquarters—420 Lexington Ave., New York, N. Y.
President—S. S. Neuman.
Executive Secretary — Dr. Lewis H. Marks.
Treasurer—R. H. Grimm.

MOTOR TRUCK ASSOCIATION OF AMERICA, INC. (M. T. A.)

Headquarters—1440 Broadway, New York, N. Y.

Object: This Association is a rallying ground for owners and all others interested in any form of self-propelled or mechanically propelled commercial vehicles, aiming to promote conditions favorable to their efficient and economical operation.

Officers

President—I. A. Hungerford.
First Vice-President—Hermann Irion.
Second Vice-President—Roderick Stephens.
Third Vice-President—H. E. De Lisser.
Secretary—Lyman Da F. Brandon.
Treasurer—A. G. Baumgartner.
General Manager—Theodore D. Pratt.
Directors—D. C. Fenner, E. E. La Schum, Emanuel Lascaris, Herman J. Harms, J. B. Dolan, Henry V. Middleworth, Henry K. Jaburg, C. Brettel, Wm. Murray, Wm. T. Bostwick, J. D. Bradley, E. A. Buchmann, L. E. Buswell, D. A. Glover, John H. Jacobs, John F. Kreisa, W. H. Moore, P. V. V. Tobin, E. P. McDowell, John B. Rosenquest, William J. Sommers, Jos. Husson, E. John Ducan, A. L. Pfeiffer.

MOTOR VEHICLE CONFERENCE COMMITTEE

Secretary—366 Madison Ave. at 46th St., New York, N. Y.

Object: To develop and promulgate, through the medium of its state sub-committees, and through educational work carried on by means of pamphlets and correspondence, sound and equitable principles which should underlie state motor vehicle legislation.

The national organizations represented on the committee are as follows:
American Automobile Association.
Motor & Equipment Association.
National Association of Motor Bus Operators.
National Automobile Chamber of Commerce.
National Automobile Dealers Association.
Rubber Manufacturers Association.

Officers

Chairman of the Committee—D. C. Fenner.
Secretary—R. S. Armstrong.

MOTOR AND EQUIPMENT ASSOCIATION (M. & E. A.)

Headquarters—Chicago, Daily News Bldg., 400 W. Madison St.; New York, 250 W. 57th St.

Officers

President—E. T. Satchell, Motor Accessories Co.
Vice-President, Div. A—David Beecroft, Bendix Aviation Corp.
Vice-President, Div. B—C. C. Secrist, Victor Gasket & Mfg. Co.
Vice-President, Div. C—C. F. Wright, Ballou & Wright.
Secretary—H. J. Lange, Marquette Mfg. Co.
Treasurer—C. H. Burr, SKF Industries, Inc.
Headquarters Staff—E. T. Satchell, Acting Executive Head; A. H. Eichholtz, Ass't to Prest.; B. W. Ruark, Sales Development Manager; J. A. Laansma, Director of Publicity; A. H. Fagan, Manager, Credit Dept.

Div. A—Manufacturers selling for original equipment; producers of raw materials and manufacturers of machinery and tools sold to manufacturers.

Div. B—Manufacturers who distribute through wholesale channels only; or manufacturers who distribute through wholesale channels and sell also for original equipment.

Div. C—Wholesale distributors.

Directors—C. P. Brewster, K-D Mfg. Co., Lancaster, Pa.; F. G. Wacker, Automotive Maintenance Machinery Co., Chicago, Ill.; Lothair Teetor, Perfect Circle Co., Hagerstown, Ind.; A. V. Hall, Sherwood Hall Co., Grand Rapids, Mich.; F. H. Floyd, Ward-Dossett-Floyd Co., Waco, Tex.; W. R. Crow, Crow-Burlingame Co., Little Rock, Ark.; J. M. McComb, Crucible Steel Co. of America, New York, N. Y.; G. T. Brunner, Brunner Mfg. Co., Utica, N. Y.; F. S. Durham, Bonney Forge & Tool Works, Allentown, Pa.; G. H. Niekamp, Beck & Corbitt Co., St. Louis, Mo.; C. C. Carlton, Motor Vehicle Corp., Lansing, Mich.; J. C. Ferguson, Eclipse Machine Co., Elmira, N. Y.

Sales Development Committee:
W. S. Isherwood, Chairman (AC Spark Plug Co., Flint, Mich.)

Committee on Distribution:
Geo. L. Brunner, **Chairman for Manufacturers** (Brunner Mfg. Co., Utica, N. Y.)
Geo. H. Niekamp, **Chairman for Jobbers** (Beck & Corbitt, St. Louis, Mo.)

Committee on Retail Service Facilities
Victor C. Allen, **Chairman** (Automotive Maintenance Machinery Co., Chicago, Ill.)

Safety and Traffic Committee:
A. V. Hall, **Chairman** (Sherwood-Hall, Ltd., Grand Rapids, Mich.)

Advisory Committee:
N. H. Boynton, **Chairman** (National Lamp Works, Cleveland, Ohio).

Finance Committee:
J. M. McComb, **Chairman** (Crucible Steel Co., New York, N. Y.)

Credit Committee:
M. Moynihan, **Chairman** (Gemmer Mfg. Co., Detroit, Mich.)

New York Show Annual Banquet Committee:
M. B. Ericson, **Chairman** (Houdaille-Hershey Corp., Chicago, Ill.)

NATIONAL ASSOCIATION OF AUTOMOBILE SHOW AND ASSOCIATION MANAGERS

Headquarters—Chestnut & 56th Sts., Philadelphia, Pa.

Membership made up of automobile show managers and secretaries of city automobile dealer associations.

Officers

President—Robert E. Lee, St. Louis, Mo.
Vice-President—Herbert Buckman.
Secretary-Treasurer—Leon F. Banigan, Motor World Wholesale.

NATIONAL ASSOCIATION OF TAXICAB OWNERS

Headquarters—500 N. Dearborn St., Chicago, Ill.

Object: To afford our members a medium of cooperation. To collect and disseminate information that promotes the economical conduct of the taxicab business. To establish and maintain cordial relations with the public. To strive for safety on the highways.

Officers

President—W. W. Cloud.
Vice-President—Lewis A. Robertson.
Secretary—J. G. Williams.
Treasurer—Russell Reel.

NATIONAL AUTOMOBILE CHAMBER OF COMMERCE (N. A. C. C.)

Headquarters — Marlin-Rockwell Bldg., Madison Ave. & 46th St., New York, N. Y.

ASSOCIATIONS—Automotive—Continued

Officers

President—Alvan Macauley (Packard).
Vice - President — Alfred H. Swayne (G.M.C.).
Vice-President, Passenger Car Div.—A. R. Erskine (Studebaker).
Vice-President, Motor Truck Div.—A. J. Brosseau (Mack).
Secretary—C. W. Nash (Nash Motors Co.).
Treasurer—H. H. Rice (General Motors).
Directors—A. J. Brosseau (Mack); Roy D. Chapin (Hudson); Walter P. Chrysler (Chrysler); A. R. Erskine (Studebaker); Robert C. Graham (Graham-Paige); Charles D. Hastings (Hupp); F. J. Haynes (Franklin); Alvan Macauley (Packard); C. W. Nash (Nash); William E. Metzger (Federal); Alfred P. Sloan, Jr. (General Motors); Alfred H. Swayne (General Motors); E. L. Cord (Auburn); Robert W. Woodruff (White); L. A. Miller (Willys-Overland).
General Manager—Alfred Reeves.

NATIONAL AUTOMOBILE DEALERS ASSOCIATION (N. A. D. A.)

Headquarters— Room 1210 Mather Tower, 75 E. Wacker Drive, Chicago, Ill.

Officers

President—Frank J. Edwards, Grand Ave. at 36th St., Milwaukee, Wis.
First Vice-President—Geo. D. Wray, 320 Market St., Shreveport, La.
Second Vice-President—Floris Nagelvoort, 1201 E. Madison St., Seattle, Wash.
Treasurer—F. W. A. Vesper, 4003 La Clede Ave., St. Louis, Mo.
Directors—Clarence Fisher, Newark, N. J.; Geo. Hoeveler, Pittsburgh, Pa.; J. W. Tarbill, Cincinnati, Ohio; Chas. E. Gambill, Chicago, Ill.; Frank A. Winerich, San Antonio, Tex.; Russell P. Taber, Hartford, Conn.; E. C. Bull, Buffalo, N. Y.; Stanley J. Horner, Washington, D. C.; G. G. G. Peckham, Cleveland, Ohio; J. L. Garrity, Minneapolis, Minn.; J. A. Peverill, Des Moines, Ia.; Chester N. Weaver, San Francisco, Cal.; Tom Botterill, Denver, Col.; John E. Smith, Atlanta, Ga.; L. D. Frint, Milwaukee, Wis.; J. T. Stewart, Omaha, Neb.; Homer C. Lathrop, Indianapolis, Ind.; P. H. Greer, Los Angeles, Cal.; C. B. Warren, New York, N. Y.; John A. Butler, Kansas City, Mo.
Executive Committee—Frank J. Edwards, Milwaukee, Ex-officio chairman; C. B. Warren, New York; C. E. Gambill, Chicago; John A. Butler, Kansas City; F. W. A. Vesper, St. Louis; G. G. G. Peckham, Cleveland; C. A. Vane, Chicago.
Headquarters Staff—C. A. Vane, General Manager; G. H. Ford, Asst. General Manager; Edward Payton, Accounting Supervisor; W. B. Spaulding, General Counsel; G. W. Derr, Field Representative.

Washington (D. C.) Staff—Pyke Johnson, Highways Representative; Walter B. Guy, Taxation Counsel.

NATIONAL AUTOMOTIVE PARTS ASSOCIATION

Headquarters—Suite 513, 120 Madison Ave., Detroit, Mich.
President—W. W. Martin.
Vice-President—A. F. Baxter.
Vice-President and General Manager—Henry Lansdale.
Secretary and Treasurer—J. E. Aff.
Directors—J. E. Aff, A. F. Baxter, F. E. Brittain, C. C. Colyear, Henry Eagle, Henry Lansdale, W. W. Martin, H. G. Root, R. W. Boozer.

NATIONAL STANDARD PARTS ASSOCIATION

Headquarters—1304 Eaton Tower, Detroit, Mich.
Object: Promotion and stabilizing of the replacement parts industry.

Officers

President—C. M. Burgess, Burgess-Dall Corp.
Executive Vice-President—E. P. Chalfant.
Vice-President—Verne Olson, Automotive Service Co.
Secretary—Orville B. Gault.
Merchandising Service Director—T. O. Duggan.
Director of Publicity—H. J. Moore.
Manufacturers' Division Directors:
H. Reisser, Link-Belt Co., Indianapolis, Ind.; W. G. Hancock, McCord Radiator & Mfg. Co., Detroit, Mich.; S. F. Dupree, Jr., Almetal Universal Joint Co., Cleveland, Ohio; H. J. Lange, Marquette Mfg. Co., St. Paul, Minn.; R. B. Davis, Raybestos-Manhattan, Inc., Bridgeport, Conn.; T. L. Ford, American Hammered Piston Ring Co., Baltimore, Md.
These six directors and the following make up the manufacturers' divisional committee: John Dages, Chairman, Republic Gear Co., Detroit, Mich.; Geo. L. Briggs, Wilkening Mfg. Co., Philadelphia, Pa.; and F. J. Glennon, Aluminum Industries, Inc., Cincinnati, Ohio.
Jobbers' Division Directors:
J. P. Muller, Fort Worth Wheel and Rim Co., Fort Worth, Tex.; O. M. Anderson, Northern Automotive Supply Co., Bay City, Mich.; L. N. Diedrich, L. N. Diedrich Automotive Parts, Ventura, Calif.; I. Gordon, Gordon Motor Parts, Inc., Rochester, N. Y.; T. C. Olson, Thomas C. Olson Co., Madison, Wis.; J. C. Rogers, Automobile Piston Co., Atlanta, Ga.
These six directors and the following make up the jobbers' divisional committee: H. N. Nigg, Chairman, Piston Service Co., Inc., Detroit, Mich.; L. H. Phelps, Phelps-Roberts Corp., Washington, D. C., and W. T. Mills Auto Parts Co., St. Louis, Mo.
Canadian Member of the Board—T. H. Peacock.

NATIONAL TIRE DEALERS ASSOCIATION (N.T.D.A.)

Headquarters—100 N. La Salle St., Chicago, Ill.

Officers

President—Martin J. Barry.
First Vice-President—A. L. Glick.
Second Vice-President—H. A. Ruhnke.
Secretary-Manager—Norval P. Trimborn.
Treasurer—Geo. J. Erlinger.
Directors—L. A. Brown, Frank Casazza, Geo. E. DeWald, Abe Goldstein, Keely Grice, S. B. Harper, Max Katz, Jos. H. Walsh, J. B. Williams, Hoyt Wood.

NATIONAL WHEEL & RIM ASSOCIATION

Headquarters—63 E. Lake St., Chicago, Ill.
President—W. D. Smith.
First Vice-President—John F. Creamer.
Second Vice-President—H. Milt Young.
Executive Secretary—George Fritz.
Treasurer—A. I. Carney.

SOCIETY OF AUTOMOTIVE ENGINEERS, INC. (S.A.E.)

Headquarters—Engineering Societies Bldg., 29 W. 39th St., New York, N. Y.
Officers and Members of the Council
President—Vincent Bendix.
Vice-President—Dr. G. W. Lewis (representing Aircraft Engineering).
Vice-President—Arthur Nutt (representing Aircraft-Engine Engineering).
Vice-President—W. F. Joachim (representing Diesel Engine Engineering).
Vice-President—L. R. Beickendale (representing Motor Truck and Motor Coach Engineering).
Vice-President—E. S. Marks (representing Passenger Car Engineering).
Vice-President—C. B. Parsons (representing Passenger-Car-Body Engineering).
Vice-President—A. K. Brumbaugh (representing Production Engineering).
Vice-President—F. K. Glynn (representing Transportation and Maintenance Engineering).
Councilors—F. S. Dusenberg, Norman G. Shidle, C. E. Tilston, Ralph R. Teetor, L. C. Hill, A. W. S. Herrington.
Treasurer—C. W. Spicer.
Past-President—E. P. Warner.
Past-President—W. R. Strickland.
Secretary and Gen. Mgr.—John A. C. Warner.
Assistant Gen. Mgr.—C. B. Veal.
Manager Research Dept.—C. B. Veal.
Asst. to the Gen. Mgr.—C. B. Whittelsey, Jr.
Manager Standards Dept.—R. S. Burnett.
Manager Sections Dept.—A. J. Underwood.

STATE AND SECTIONAL ASSOCIATIONS

Alabama—Alabama Automotive Trades Ass'n. Sec., Grace Riviere Scott, Box 777, Montgomery, Ala.
Arizona — Arizona Automobile Dealers Ass'n. Sec., C. P. Stephens, 817 N. Central Ave., Phoenix, Ariz.
Connecticut—Motor Truck Ass'n of Conn., Inc. Sec., Myles W. Illingworth, 410 Asylum St., Hartford, Conn.
Delaware—Delaware Automobile Ass'n., Executive Sec., Lennaeus L. Hoopes, 11th & West Sts., Wilmington.
Illinois—Illinois Automotive Trade Ass'n.

Mgr., C. W. Coons, 212 Lehmann Bldg., Peoria, Ill.
Iowa—Iowa Automotive Merchants Ass'n. Sec., Walter Ferrell, 309 Masonic Temple Bldg., Des Moines, Iowa.
Kentucky—Kentucky Automotive Trade Ass'n. Sec., Garland Lea, 419 Finzer St., Louisville, Ky.
Louisiana—Automotive Trades Ass'n of Louisiana. Sec., Clem G. Hearsey, 721 St. Charles St., New Orleans, La.
Maine—Maine Automobile Ass'n, 212 Middle St., Portland, Me.

Maryland—Automobile Trade Assn. of Maryland. Gen. Mgr., John E. Raine, 1200 St. Paul St., Baltimore, Md.
Massachusetts — Massachusetts Auto Dealers & Garage Ass'n. Mgr., Day Baker, 126 Massachusetts Ave., Boston, Mass.
Michigan—Michigan Automotive Trade Ass'n. Mgr., W. D. Edenburn, 5-218 General Motors Bldg., Detroit, Mich.
Minnesota — Minnesota Motor Trades Ass'n. Sec., Arnon N. Benson, 317 Plymouth Bldg., Minneapolis, Minn.
Montana—Montana Motor Trades Assn. Sec., R. C. Bricker, Great Falls, Mont.

New Hampshire—New Hampshire Truck Owners' Ass'n. Sec., Robert E. Thomas, Eagle Hotel, Concord, N. H. New Hampshire Automobile Dealers' Ass'n. Sec., Robert E. Thomas, Eagle Hotel, Concord, N. H.

New Jersey—New Jersey Automotive Trade Ass'n. Sec., Raymond Beck, 292 Main St., Hackensack, N. J.

New Mexico—New Mexico Automobile Dealers' Ass'n, Inc. Sec., Thos. S. Miur, Santa Fe.

New York—Empire State Automobile Merchants Ass'n. Gen. Mgr., L. G. Stapley, 184 State St., Albany, N. Y.

North Carolina—North Carolina Automotive Trades Ass'n. Sec., Coleman W. Roberts, Greensboro, N. C.

North Dakota—North Dakota Motor Trades Ass'n. Sec. and Treas., E. V. Bailey, P. O. Box 411, Bismarck, N. D.

Ohio—Ohio Council National Automobile Dealers' Ass'n. Sec., J. H. Cummings, 175 S. High St., Columbus, Ohio.

Oregon—Oregon Automotive Trade Ass'n. Sec., Jas. H. Cassell, 9 Myler Bldg., Portland, Ore.

Pennsylvania—Pennsylvania Automotive Ass'n. Mgr., Claude S. Klugh, 208 Walnut St., Harrisburg, Pa.

Rhode Island—Rhode Island Automobile Dealers Ass'n. Sec., Ralph P. Lord, 1609 New Industrial Trust Bldg., Providence, R. I.

South Dakota—Automobile Trades Ass'n of S. D. Sec., H. M. Whisman, Huron, S. D.

Texas—Texas Automotive Dealers Ass'n. P. O. Box 926, San Antonio, Tex. Sec., M. H. Doody.

Utah—Utah State Automobile Ass'n. Mgr. W. D. Rishel, Hotel Utah, Salt Lake City, Utah.

Virginia—Virginia Automotive Trades Ass'n. Prest., J. A. Kline, 111 N. Fifth St., Richmond, Va.

Washington — Automotive Maintenance Ass'n. Sec., Ed. Westfield, 1424 11th Ave., Seattle, Wash.

West Virginia—West Virginia State Dealers' Ass'n. Sec., W. T. Slicer, 217 Broad St., Charleston, W. Va.

Wisconsin—Wisconsin Automotive Trades Ass'n. Ass't. Mgr., L. Milan, 413 Brumder Bldg., Milwaukee, Wis.

For Contents of Book
See Page 5